July 8–11, 2018
Singapore

I0027519

Association for
Computing Machinery

Advancing Computing as a Science & Profession

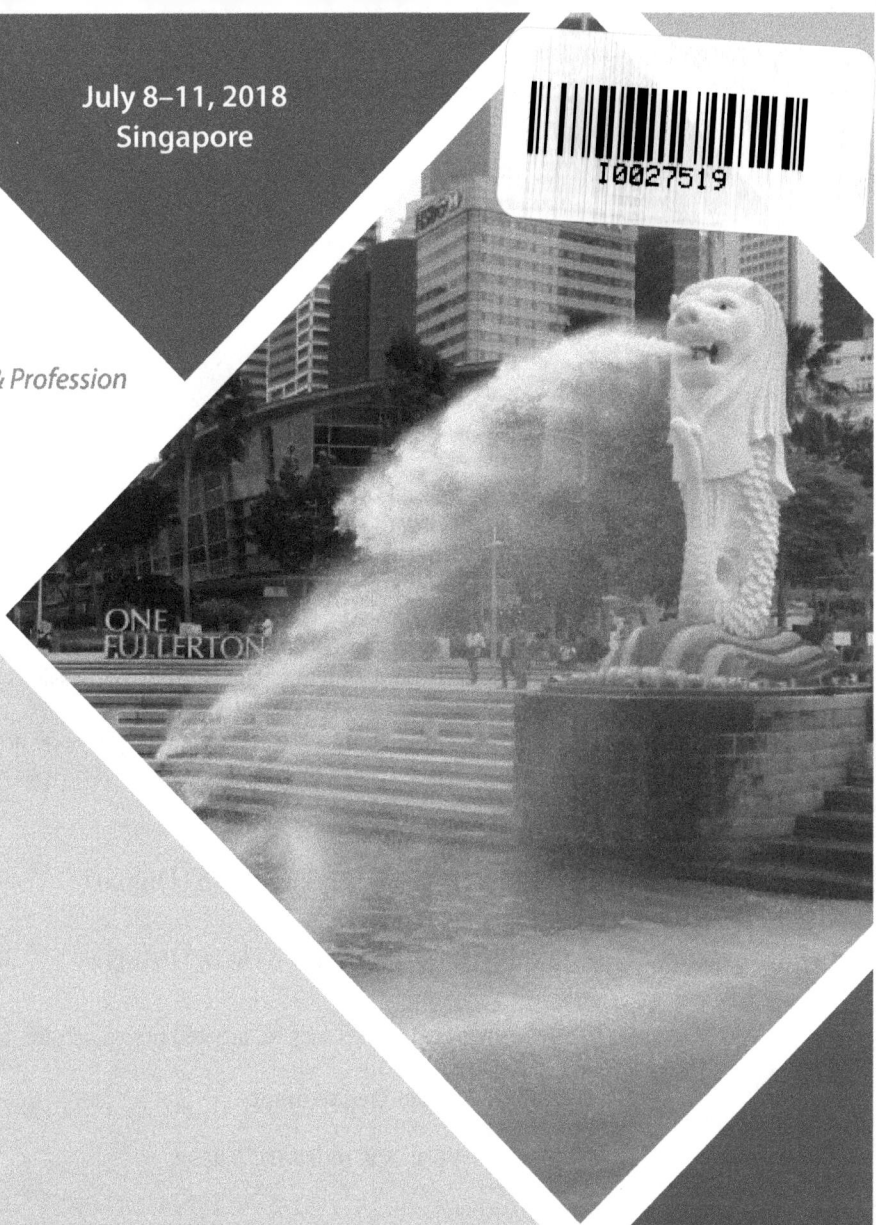

UMAP'18

Proceedings of the 26th Conference on
User Modeling, Adaptation and Personalization

Sponsored by:
ACM SIGCHI & ACM SIGWEB

General Chairs:
Tanja Mitrovic (University of Canterbury, New Zealand)
Jie Zhang (Nanyang Technological University, Singapore)

Program Chairs:
Li Chen (Hong Kong Baptist University, China)
David Chin (University of Hawaii, USA)

Association for
Computing Machinery

Advancing Computing as a Science & Profession

The Association for Computing Machinery
2 Penn Plaza, Suite 701
New York, New York 10121-0701

ISBN: 978-1-4503-5784-5 (Digital)

ISBN: 978-1-4503-6166-8 (Print)

Additional copies may be ordered prepaid from:

ACM Order Department
PO Box 30777
New York, NY 10087-0777, USA

Phone: 1-800-342-6626 (USA and Canada)
+1-212-626-0500 (Global)
Fax: +1-212-944-1318
E-mail: acmhelp@acm.org
Hours of Operation: 8:30 am – 4:30 pm ET

UMAP 2018 Chairs' Welcome

It is our great pleasure to welcome you to the *26th ACM International Conference on User modeling, Adaptation and personalization – UMAP 2018.* UMAP is the premier international conference for researchers and practitioners working on systems that adapt to individual users or to groups of users. UMAP is the successor of the biennial User Modeling (UM) and Adaptive Hypermedia and Adaptive Web-based Systems (AH) conferences that were merged in 2009. It has traditionally been organized under the auspices of User Modeling Inc. Since 2016, UMAP is an ACM conference, sponsored by ACM SIGCHI and SIGWEB.

UMAP 2018 is a very special conference, as this is the very first time UMAP will be located in Asia! We hope to meet many like-minded researchers from Singapore and other Asian countries. The conference spans a wide scope of topics related to user modeling, adaptation, and personalization. UMAP 2018 is focused on bringing together cutting-edge research from user interaction and modeling, adaptive technologies, and delivery platforms. It includes high-quality peer-reviewed papers featuring substantive new research in one of five research tracks, each chaired by leaders in the field:

- Adaptive Hypermedia and the Semantic Web (track chairs Peter Brusilovsky and Geert-Jan Houben)

- Intelligent User interfaces (track chairs Shlomo Berkovsky and Markus Schedl)

- Personalized Recommender Systems (track chairs Dietmar Jannach and Markus Zanker)

- Personalized Social Web (track chairs Cecile Paris and Julita Vassileva)

- Technology-Enhanced Adaptive Learning (track chairs Olga Santos and Carla Limongelli)

The call for papers attracted 137 submissions from 33 different countries on all continents except Antarctica: Argentina, Australia, Austria, Belgium, Brazil, Canada, China, Cyprus, Denmark, Finland, France, Germany, India, Indonesia, Ireland, Israel, Italy, Japan, Netherlands, New Zealand, Nigeria, Norway, Pakistan, Philippines, Portugal, Saudi Arabia, Singapore, South Korea, Spain, Sweden, Switzerland, United Kingdom, and the United States The international program committee consisted of 131 reviewers. Each submission received at least 3 reviews. After the initial reviews were submitted, the designated track chairs (TCs) facilitated discussion amongst reviewers in order to resolve differences and correct misunderstandings. The TCs then provided a recommendation to the Program Chairs. The final decisions were based on these recommendations, meta-reviews, and reviewer scores.

Review and acceptance statistics are as follows:

UMAP Venue	Reviewed	Accepted	Acceptance rate
Full Papers	93	26	28%
Short Papers	44	10	23%
Full + Short Papers	137	36	26%

Moreover, 10 papers were accepted as extended abstracts, and 13 were included in Late Breaking Results track (LBR). We thank Hui Fang and Pasquale Lops, LBR and Demo Chairs, for their efforts on selecting addition papers submitted to this track. As a result, there are 3 Demos, 3 Theory, Opinion and Reflection papers, and 20 Late Breaking Results papers presented in the

UMAP poster sessions, which collectively showcase the wide spectrum of novel ideas and latest results in user modeling, adaptation and personalization.

We also encourage attendees to attend the keynote presentations; these valuable and insightful talks guide us to a better understanding of the future.

- *Running Recommendations: Personalisation Opportunities for Health and Fitness,* Barry Smith (University College Dublin, Ireland)

- *Robots that Listen to People's Hearts: the Role of Emotions in the Communication between Humans and Social Robots,* Ana Paiva (University of Lisbon, Portugal)

- *Interpreting User Input Intention in Natural Human Computer Interaction,* Yuanchun Shi (Tsinghua University, China)

We would also like to thank Vania Dimitrova and Pearl Pu, who organized the Doctoral Consortium. There were eight doctoral papers selected for oral presentations, and four poster presentations.

Marko Tkalcic and Marco de Gemmis invited proposals for workshops and tutorials. After reviewing, four workshops and three tutorials were selected. Our gratitude goes to the workshop and tutorial organizers.

The four workshops were:

- *HAAPIE: Human Aspects in Adaptive and Personalized Interactive Environments,* by Panagiotis Germanakos (SAP SE & University of Cyprus, CY), Styliani Kleanthous (University of Cyprus, CY), George Samaras (University of Cyprus, CY), Vania Dimitrova (University of Leeds, UK), Ben Steichen (California State Polytechnic University Pomona, US), Alicja Piotrkowicz (University of Leeds, UK)

- *IUadaptMe: Intelligent User-Adapted Interfaces: Design and Multi-Modal Evaluation,* by Ilknur Celik (Cyprus International University, CY), Ilaria Torre (University of Genoa, IT), Frosina Koceva (University of Genoa, IT), Christine Bauer (Johannes Kepler University Linz, AT), Eva Zangerle (University of Innsbruck, AT), Bart P. Knijnenburg (Clemson University, US)

- *HUM: Holistic User Modeling,* by Cataldo Musto (University of Bari, IT), Amon Rapp (University of Torino, IT), Federica Cena (University of Torino, IT), Frank Hopfgartner (University of Sheffield, UK), Judy Kay (University of Sydney, AU), Giovanni Semeraro (University of Bari, IT)

- *FairUMAP: Fairness in User Modeling, Adaptation and Personalization,* by Bamshad Mobasher (DePaul University, US), Robin Burke (DePaul University, US), Michael Ekstrand (Boise State University, US), Bettina Berendt (KU Leuven, BE)

The three tutorials were:

- *Group Recommender Systems,* by Judith Masthoff (University of Aberdeen, UK) and Amra Delic (Research Division of E-Commerce at TU Wien, AT)

- *Sequence-aware Recommender Systems,* by Massimo Quadrana (Pandora Media, IT), Paolo Cremonesi (Politecnico di Milano, IT), and Dietmar Jannach (Alpen-Adria-Universitat Klagenfurt, AT)

- *Personalisation and Privacy issues in the Age of Exposure,* by Esma Aimeur (University of Montreal, CA)

We also thank our Student Support Chairs, Yue Xu and Yong Zheng, for obtaining funds from our supporters to enable doctoral students to attend the conference and present their research; thank Publicity Chairs, Nilufar Baghaei, Mi Zhang and Guibing Guo, for spreading the news about UMAP 2018; thank Proceeding Chairs, Neil Yorke-Smith and Kirsten Smith, for helping publish the main and adjunct proceedings in ACM; thank Yang Li in charge of finances; thank Jason Zhao who attracted sponsors and supporters for UMAP 2018; thank Local Arrangement Chairs, Zhu Sun and Zehong Hu, for taking care of UMAP 2018 participants so ably; and thank Jie Yang for the wonderful website.

Putting together *UMAP 2018* was a team effort. We first thank the authors for providing the content of the program. We are grateful to the program committee, who worked very hard in reviewing papers and providing feedback for authors. Finally, we thank the Nanyang Technological University for hosting the conference, ACM SIGCHI and SIGWEB, and our generous supporters, Singapore Tourism Board, USA National Science Foundation, Springer, Microsoft Research, and Yixue Education.

We hope that you will find this program interesting and thought-provoking and that the conference will provide you with a valuable opportunity to share ideas with other researchers and practitioners from institutions around the world.

General Chairs

Jie Zhang, *Nanyang Technological University, Singapore*

Tanja Mitrovic, *University of Canterbury, New Zealand*

Programme Chairs

David Chin, *University of Hawaii, USA*

Li Chen, *Hong Kong Baptist University, China*

Table of Contents

Session: Technology-Enhanced Adaptive Learning II

Session Chair: Olga C. Santos *(aDeNu Research Group - UNED)*

Session: Personalized Social Web I

Session Chair: Marco de Gemmis *(University of Bari Aldo Moro)*

Keynote Address II

Session Chair: Tanja Mitrovic *(University of Canterbury)*

Session: Personalized Recommender Systems III

Session Chair: Cataldo Musto *(University of Bari Aldo Moro)*

Session: Adaptive Hypermedia and the Semantic Web

Session Chair: Judith Masthoff *(University of Aberdeen)*

Doctoral Consortium II

Session Chairs: Shlomo Berkovsky *(CSIRO)* & Vania Dimitrova *(University of Leeds)*

Extended Abstracts

Tutorials

UMAP 2018 Conference Organization

General Chairs: Tanja Mitrovic *(University of Canterbury, New Zealand)*
Jie Zhang *(Nanyang Technological University, Singapore)*

Program Chairs: Li Chen *(Hong Kong Baptist University, China)*
David Chin *(University of Hawaii, USA)*

Track Chairs: **Personalized Recommender Systems**
Dietmar Jannach *(Technical University of Dortmund, Germany)*
Markus Zanker *(Free University of Bolzano-Bozen, Italy)*

Adaptive Hypermedia and the Semantic Web
Peter Brusilovsky *(University of Pittsburgh, USA)*
Geert-Jan Houben *(Delft Univeristy of Technology, The Netherlands)*

Intelligent User Interfaces
Shlomo Berkovsky *(CSIRO, Australia)*
Markus Schedl *(Johannes Kepler University Linz, Austria)*

Technology-Enhanced Adaptive Learning
Carla Limongelli *(Roma Tre University, Italy)*
Olga Santos *(National Distance Education University, Spain)*

Personalized Social Web
Cecile Paris *(CSIRO, Australia)*
Julita Vassileva *(University of Saskatchewan, Canada)*

Late-Breaking Result and Demo Chairs: Hui Fang *(Shanghai University of Finance and Economics, China)*
Pasquale Lops *(University of Bari Aldo Moro, Italy)*

Doctoral Consortium Chairs: Vania Dimitrova *(University of Leeds, UK)*
Pearl Pu *(EPFL, Switzerland)*

Workshop and Tutorials Chairs: Marco de Gemmis *(University of Bari Aldo Moro, Italy)*
Marko Tkalcic *(Free University of Bolzano, Italy)*

Student Support Chairs: Yue Xu *(Queensland University of Technology, Australia)*
Yong Zheng *(Illinois Institute of Technology, USA)*

Publicity Chairs: Nilufar Baghaei *(Unitec, Auckland, New Zealand)*
Guibing Guo *(Northeastern University China)*
Mi Zhang *(Fudan University, China)*

Proceedings Chairs: Kirsten A. Smith *(University of Southampton, UK)*
Neil Yorke-Smith *(Delft University of Technology, Netherlands)*

Finance Chair: Yang Liu *(Nanyang Technological University, Singapore)*

Sponsorship Chair: Jason Zhao *(Douban, China)*

Web Master: Jie Yang *(Delft University of Technology, Netherlands)*

Local Arrangements Chairs: Zehong Hu *(Nanyang Technological University, Singapore)*
Zhu Sun *(Nanyang Technological University, Singapore)*

Program Committee: Kenro Aihara *(National Institute of Informatics)*
Esma Aimeur *(University of Montreal)*
Liliana Ardissono *(University of Torino)*
Sören Auer *(University of Hannover)*
Ryan Baker *(Columbia University)*
Shenghua Bao *(IBM)*
Joeran Beel *(Trinity College Dublin)*
Alejandro Bellogin *(Universidad Autonoma de Madrid)*
Maria Bielikova *(Slovak University of Technology in Bratislava)*
Ludovico Boratto *(Eurecat)*
Alessandro Bozzon *(Delft University of Technology)*
Paul Brna *(University of Leeds)*
Robin Burke *(DePaul University)*
Iván Cantador *(Universidad Autónoma de Madrid)*
Sylvain Castagnos *(LORIA)*
Federica Cena *(University of Torino)*
Eva Cerezo *(Universidad de Zaragoza)*
Cristina Conati *(The University of British Columbia)*
Owen Conlan *(Trinity College Dublin)*
Evandro Costa *(Federal University of Alagoas)*
Paolo Cremonesi *(Politecnico di Milano)*
Alexandra Cristea *(University of Warwick*
Florian Daniel *(Politecnico di Milano)*
Berardina Nadja De Carolis *(University of Bari)*
Marco De Gemmis *(University of Bari)*
Pasquale De Meo *(Università degli Studi di Messina)*
Michel Desmarais *(Ecole Polytechnique de Montreal)*
Ernesto Diaz-Aviles *(Libre AI)*
Yannis Dimitriadis *(University of Valladolid)*
Vania Dimitrova *(University of Leeds)*
Peter Dolog *(Aalborg University)*
Tommaso Di Noia *(Politecnico di Bari)*
Sidney D'Mello *(University of Colorado Boulder)*
Benedict Du Boulay *(University of Sussex)*
Michael Ekstrand *(Boise State University)*
Mehdi Elahi *(Free University of Bozen-Bolzano)*
Alexander Felfernig *(Graz University of Technology)*
Bruce Ferwerda *(Jönköping University)*
Flavius Frasincar *(Erasmus University Rotterdam)*
Ujwal Gadiraju *(L3S Research Center)*
Fabio Gasparetti *(ROMA TRE University)*
Jonathan Gemmell *(DePaul University)*

Program Committee (continued):

Cristina Gena *(University of Torino)*
Panagiotis Germanakos *(SAP SE & University of Cyprus)*
Fabientestpc Gouyontestpc *(JHS)*
Ido Guy *(eBay Research)*
Alan Hanjalic *(Delft University of Technology)*
Max Harper *(University of Minnesota)*
Eelco Herder *(Radboud University)*
Balázs Hidasi *(Gravity R&D)*
Sharon Hsiao *(Arizona State University)*
Xiao Hu *(The University of Hong Kong)*
Bogdan Ionescu *(University Politehnica of Bucharest)*
Seiji Isotani *(University of São Paulo)*
W. Lewis Johnson *(Alelo Inc.)*
Michael Jugovac *(TU Dortmund)*
Styliani Kleanthous *(University of Cyprus)*
Peter Knees *(Vienna University of Technology)*
Alfred Kobsa *(University of California, Irvine)*
Joseph Konstan *(University of Minnesota)*
Irena Koprinska *(The University of Sydney)*
Antonio Krueger *(DFKI)*
Tsvi Kuflik *(The University of Haifa)*
Bob Kummerfeld *(The University of Sydney)*
Neal Lathia *(Skyscanner)*
Edith Law *(University of Waterloo)*
Séamus Lawless *(Trinity College Dublin)*
James Lester *(North Carolina State University)*
Tobias Ley *(Tallinn University)*
Pasquale Lops *(University of Bari)*
Bernd Ludwig *(University Regensburg)*
Brian Mac Namee *(University College Dublin)*
George Magoulas *(Birkbeck College)*
Estefania Martin *(Universidad Rey Juan Carlos)*
Roberto Martinez-Maldonado *(University of Technology, Sydney)*
Judith Masthoff *(University of Aberdeen)*
Gordon McCalla *(University of Saskatchewan)*
Alessandro Micarelli *(Roma Tre University)*
Tanja Mitrovic *(University of Canterbury, Christchurch)*
Riichiro Mizoguchi *(Japan Advanced Institute of Science and Technology)*
Bamshad Mobasher *(DePaul University)*
Osnat Mokryn *(University of Haifa)*
Inge Molenaar *(Radboud Universiteit Nijmegen)*
Pablo Moreno-Ger *(Universidad Internacional de La Rioja)*
Kasia Muldner *(Carleton University)*
Cataldo Musto *(University of Bari)*
Julia Neidhardt *(Vienna University of Technology)*

Program Committee (continued):

Wolfgang Nejdl *(L3S and University of Hannover)*
Roger Nkambou *(Université du Québec À Montréal)*
Ingrid Nunes *(Universidade Federal do Rio Grande do Sul)*
Xavier Ochoa *(Escuela Superior Politécnica del Litoral)*
Michael O'Mahony *(University College Dublin)*
Georgios Paliouras *(Institute of Informatics & Telecommunications, NCSR "Demokritos")*
Alexandros Paramythis *(Contexity AG)*
Denis Parra *(Pontificia Universidad Catolica de Chile)*
Mykola Pechenizkiy *(Eindhoven University of Technology)*
Johanna Pirker *(Graz University of Technology)*
Luiz Pizzato *(Commonwealth Bank of Australia)*
Amon Rapp *(University of Torinom)*
Francesco Ricci *(Free University of Bozen-Bolzano)*
Ma. Mercedes T. Rodrigo *(Ateneo de Manila University)*
Cristobal Romero *(University of Cordoba)*
Laurens Rook *(Delft University of Technology)*
Domenico Rosaci *(University Mediterranea of Reggio Calabria)*
Alan Said *(University of Skövde)*
George Samaras *(University of Cyprus)*
Giuseppe Sansonetti *(Roma Tre University)*
Filippo Sciarrone *(Roma Tre University)*
Giovanni Semeraro *(University of Bari)*
Shilad Sen *(Macalester College)*
Elena Simperl *(University of Southampton)*
Barry Smyth *(University College Dublin)*
Sergey Sosnovsky *(Utrecht University)*
Ben Steichen *(California State Polytechnic University, Pomona)*
Sebastian Stober *(University of Potsdam)*
Panagiotis Symeonidis *(Free University of Bolzano)*
Andrea Tagarelli *(University of Calabria)*
Marco Temperini *(Sapienza University of Rome)*
Nava Tintarev *(Delft University of Technology)*
Marko Tkalcic *(Free University of Bolzano)*
Ilaria Torre *(University of Geno)*
Christoph Trattner *(MODUL University Vienna)*
Katrien Verbert *(Katholieke Universiteit Leuven)*
Ji-Rong Wen *(Renmin University of China)*
Fridolin Wild *(Oxford Brookes University)*
Martijn Willemsen *(Eindhoven University of Technology)*
Chang Xu *(CSIRO)*
Kun Yu *(CSIRO)*
Massimo Zancanaro *(FBK-cit)*
Yong Zheng *(Illinois Institute of Technology)*
Ingrid Zukerman *(Monash University)*

UMAP 2018 Sponsors & Supporters

Sponsors:

 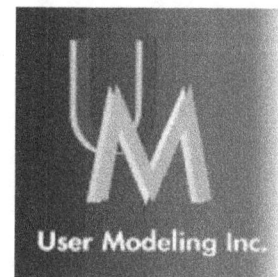

Running Recommendations:
Personalisation Opportunities for Health and Fitness
Extended Abstract

Barry Smyth
Insight Centre for Data Analytics
School of Computer Science
University College Dublin
Dublin, Ireland
barry.smyth@ucd.ie

ABSTRACT

The history of user modelling, personalisation and recommender systems is, in large part, a web-tale: a story of sites and services learning about users, in order to provide more tailored online experiences. The rapid rise of mobile computing, combined with wearable sensors, has begun to shift the potential for personalisation, from the virtual world of the web, to the physical world in which we live, work, and play.

In our increasingly digitized world almost everything we do creates a record that is stored somewhere, whether we are purchasing a book, calling a friend, or watching a movie. But in the connected world of the *internet of things* (IoT) this no longer limited to our online activities: whether we are exercising in the park, shopping for groceries, or even falling asleep, data continues to be created and captured by a variety of apps and service providers. All of this introduces exciting new application opportunities for user modelling, personalisation, and recommendation, by providing new types of data, and new reasons to harness these data in a host of novel contexts. Of course it also amplifies some critical challenges, especially when it comes to personal data and privacy.

This keynote will consider some of these challenges and opportunities, with a particular emphasis on health and exercise. One example of a open opportunity is embodied in the many and varied ways that people are using data-driven apps to track and share their exercise. This is just the beginning of a new generation of intelligent assistants capable of harnessing personalisation technologies to better support users as they strive to get the most from their exercise, and help them to live healthier more active lifestyles. As a concrete case-study this keynote will draw on recent work to support recreational runners as they train for, plan, and run marathon races.

Marathon running is a popular mass-participation sport that attracts millions of runners, from all walks of life, to our city streets. Running a marathon is hard, but completing the 42.2km course on race-day is just the final stage after months of long, hard training. While a variety of apps exist to support runners — e.g. Strava,

RunKeeper, MapMyRun, to name just a few — most focus on helping users to track and share their activities, but stop short when it comes to more proactivitely supporting runners as they train and compete. For example, the opportunity exists to automatically create more personalised training programmes that better suit a runner's lifestyle, fitness goals, and ability; plans that can automaticaly adapt to a user's evolving preferences and changing fitness levels. And, as race day approaches, runners can benefit from improved performance predictors, which not only suggest a challenging but achievable finish-time, but that also provide runners with a pacing-plan to help them achieve this time on the day. As the saying goes, few plans survive first contact with the enemy, and marathon pacing plans are no different. Hence runners also require improved in-race feedback and a plan that automatically adjusts to the conditions on the day.

These are just a few examples that harness ideas from user modelling, personalisation, and recommender systems, but apply them in an exercise context, rather than more conventional online settings. At the same time, the features of physical exercise, and the complex lives of users, introduce a range of new challenges to be solved by our community. As a result there is much that the user modelling and personalisation community can bring to the world of personal fitness and performance, but there is also much that the personal fitness community can bring to user modelling and personalisation research. Perhaps together, these communities have the potential to help address some of society's most significant challenges by helping people to live happier, healthier, more active lives.

CCS CONCEPTS

• **Information systems** → **Personalization**; *Data analytics*;

KEYWORDS

Recommender systems, sports analytics

ACM Reference Format:
Barry Smyth. 2018. Running Recommendations: Personalisation Opportunities for Health and Fitness : Extended Abstract. In *UMAP '18: 26th Conference on User Modeling, Adaptation and Personalization, July 8–11, 2018, Singapore, Singapore*. ACM, New York, NY, USA, 1 page. https://doi.org/10.1145/3209219.3209269

Energy Saving Recommendations and User Location Modeling in Commercial Buildings

Peter Wei
Columbia University
wei.peter@columbia.edu

Stephen Xia
Columbia University
stephen.xia@columbia.edu

Xiaofan Jiang
Columbia University
jiang@ee.columbia.edu

ABSTRACT

Commercial buildings consume a large portion of the total electricity in the United States. One method for energy saving in commercial buildings targets inefficiencies of unoccupied spaces by relaxing the setpoint temperature. However, energy savings are severely limited when occupants are assumed to be "immovable objects"; instead, by encouraging occupant participation in the optimization, a much greater amount of energy savings can be achieved. In this work, we build on this idea and introduce energy saving recommendations based on occupant location. We introduce two types of energy saving recommendations based on location: move recommendations, which recommends the occupant to move from one space to another, and shift schedule recommendations, which recommends the occupant to arrive or depart a set amount of time earlier or later. To investigate the effects of the energy saving recommendations, we introduced a tightly coupled system composing of a simulator and a recommender system. Simulations in our building testbed revealed that energy saving recommendations coupled with occupancy-based HVAC energy management saves 25% more energy than occupancy-based HVAC energy management alone.

CCS CONCEPTS

• **Information systems** → **Recommender systems**; • **Human-centered computing** → **Ubiquitous and mobile computing**; • **Computer systems organization** → *Real-time systems*; • **Spatial-temporal systems** → Location based services;

KEYWORDS

Recommender systems; building optimization; reinforcement learning; user modeling

ACM Reference Format:
Peter Wei, Stephen Xia, and Xiaofan Jiang. 2018. Energy Saving Recommendations and User Location Modeling in Commercial Buildings. In *UMAP'18: 26th Conference on User Modeling, Adaptation and Personalization, July 8-11, 2018, Singapore.* ACM, New York, NY, USA, 9 pages. https://doi.org/10.1145/3209219.3209244

1 INTRODUCTION

Buildings consume a large portion of the total electricity in the United States. In residential homes, products such as Nest smart thermostats have emerged in recent years to help people reduce their daily energy consumption; however, people spend a significant portion of their active moments during the day inside commercial buildings such as office spaces. There exists a great opportunity for us to consciously modify our behaviors to reduce energy usage when at work and inside offices spaces.

While buildings are becoming smarter with increasing numbers of energy monitoring endpoints, the effect of an occupant's *personal actions* on the *overall energy consumption of the building* is still unknown. As a result, any energy inefficiencies in commercial buildings are often unnoticed since public resources and appliances are shared across multiple occupants. In comparison to homes where families pay their own energy bills, occupants in offices are not liable for energy usage on their behalf, and therefore have little incentive to save energy.

One popular research topic towards energy savings in commercial buildings is occupancy-based heating and air conditioning energy management [1, 3, 6–8, 10]. These works take advantage of unoccupied spaces by reducing the service requirements; for example, lowering the setpoint temperature of a room by 1.5 degrees can reduce the energy consumption of the space significantly. The percentage of energy saved ranges between 10 − 40% of the total energy, according to these studies.

However, there are substantial limitations to the occupancy-based HVAC management methods. By assuming that occupants are immovable, occupancy-based HVAC management is only able to optimize energy **given human occupancy constraints**. Spaces with high potential energy savings cannot be optimized if the space is occupied, even if only by one person. By encouraging occupant participation through recommendations, the potential energy savings of these spaces can be realized.

In this work, we introduce human concepts such as user models and recommender systems to the traditionally non-human field of building energy optimization. Building on the ideas of occupancy-based energy management and recommender systems, we propose a system for generating *personalized energy saving recommendations* for encouraging occupants to reduce energy consumption. Our system is composed of two integrated subsystems: an energy consumption simulator and a recommender system. The simulator incorporates models of the building based on EnergyPlus simulations, as well as user models based on collected historical location data over a four month period, to simulate energy consumption. The recommender system utilizes the simulated energy consumption to learn personalized recommendations.

We present the following contributions:

- We extend traditional space-level energy models to incorporate effects of varying levels of occupancy to improve building level energy simulations.
- We generate novel, personalized, energy saving recommendations through building simulation, reinforcement learning, and occupant location models.
- We demonstrate a 25% improvement in energy savings using energy saving recommendations over traditional occupancy-based energy management.

2 BACKGROUND

This work draws primarily from two drastically different sets of research areas: building energy optimization and location-based recommender systems. We focus on the intersection of these research areas towards a recommender system capable of significantly reducing a **building's energy consumption** with the aid of **user location models**.

2.1 Building Energy Optimization

Recently, building energy optimization has become a popular topic in commercial buildings. Energy monitoring is a critical research topic towards optimization, allowing building managers to identify inefficient energy consuming resources. Occupancy-based energy optimization utilizes energy monitoring, as well as occupancy sensing, to optimize inefficient energy consuming resources.

Energy monitoring in commercial buildings often includes monitoring of miscellaneous electric loads (MELs), lighting, and HVAC (heating, ventilation and air conditioning). In MELs monitoring, plug-load meters, both wired [11] and wireless [12, 14], have been used to monitor plug-loads directly. Lighting and HVAC in commercial buildings can be monitored directly by connecting to the building management system (BMS) through protocols such as BACNet, LonTalk, and Modbus [2].

Occupancy-based energy management largely focuses on optimizing HVAC systems in empty spaces. Different research studies [1, 3, 6–8, 10] have found potential energy savings between 10 − 40% by relaxing the setpoint temperatures of the HVAC systems by 1.5 degrees. These studies optimize HVAC usage based on the schedules of the people within the building. The general idea behind these approaches is that we can relax setpoint temperatures of the HVAC systems when periods of vacancies are detected. This approach has limitations, however. In many situations, a large space is occupied by a single occupant; even though a significant amount of energy is used to service the space, no optimization is possible with this method due to the constraint of occupancy. By encouraging mobility of these occupants through recommendations, occupancy-based energy management of these spaces becomes possible.

In this work, we use the building energy monitoring and occupancy sensing subsystems developed in [22] to collect occupant location data. This data is used to explore how providing the **right type** of recommendation to the **right occupant** at the **right time** can substantially reduce the overall energy consumption, while having minimal impact on the occupant's comfort. The building energy

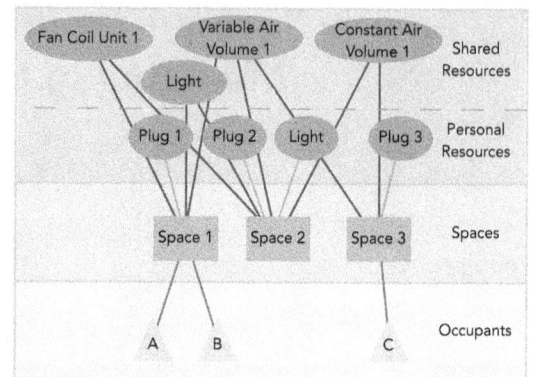

Figure 1: Tripartite graph representation of the building-occupant model, taken from [22].

monitoring subsystem consists of a software interface through BACNet to monitor HVAC and wind sensing nodes for HVAC resources not connected to BACNet, light sensing nodes to sense lighting, and electric plugmeters to sense electrical consumption. For occupancy sensing, we deployed 41 Bluetooth beacons throughout the deployment testbed, and implemented Bluetooth localization on Android and iOS mobile applications.

2.2 Location-Based Recommender Systems

Recommender systems have become an important part of daily life, with companies such as Netflix and Amazon learning about user preferences and recommending items that are relevant to the user. Recently, a variant of recommender systems has emerged, called **location-based recommender systems**. Location-based recommender systems recommend suggestions (e.g. places to eat and visit) based on the current and past locations as well as the personal preferences of the user [4]. Generally, these methods match user preferences with features that characterize a location [17], or analyze the similarity between multiple locations to recommend suggestions [23] [16]. Additionally, location-based recommender systems often make use of collaborative filtering, using the data collected from existing users to recommend suggestions to similar or new users [24] [18].

In context of building energy optimization, this work aims to model how suggesting changes in human behavior through recommendations (e.g. move from one room to another, or come in 15 minutes earlier) can be used to achieve a reduction of total energy consumption in commercial buildings.

3 CHALLENGES

To create a recommender system that generates **personalized**, **actionable**, and **energy saving** recommendations, three challenges must be addressed: what types of recommendations are effective in saving energy, how much energy can a recommendation save, and how to personalize these recommendations.

3.1 Recommendations

The ultimate goal of the recommender system is to influence user behavior to reduce energy consumption within the building. To determine potential recommendations, we borrow the building-occupant representation developed in a previous work [22] which utilizes a tripartite graph data structure as shown in Figure 1. The graph is separated into three partitioned layers consisting of the energy consuming resources (HVAC, lighting, electric loads), spaces, and occupants. This representation emphasizes the relationship between spaces and occupants, which is critical in our recommendation definitions.

In this representation, there are two events that cause changes in the total energy consumption: energy resource consumption changes and occupant location changes. This work focuses on the latter; occupant location changes are common in commercial buildings. Occupant location changes have two characteristics that affect energy consumption: spatial and temporal. Spatially, a location change can occur between any two spaces, including outside of the commercial building. Temporally, a location change can occur at any time during the day. We leverage these characteristics in our recommendation definitions.

We define two types of energy saving recommendations:

- Recommend an occupant to **move** to a different space.
- Recommend an occupant to **change schedule** for entering and exiting the commercial building.

Illustrations of example scenarios when each recommendation saves energy are shown in Figures 2a and 2b. In Figure 2a, occupant A is given a recommendation to move from Lab Space 1 to Lab Space 2. The energy service decreases significantly in Lab Space 1 and increases in Lab Space 2; however, there is an overall reduction in energy consumption. In Figure 2b, occupant A arrives in Lab Space 1 at 8:15, thus increasing the energy consumption of Lab 1 at 8:15. The next week, occupant A receives a recommendation to arrive **30 minutes later**, when occupant B arrives in Lab Space 1. The increase in energy requirement of Lab A occurs 30 minutes later, thus saving energy. There may be other types of recommendations that can help reduce energy consumption, but we defer those recommendations to future work.

3.2 Building Response

The second challenge is to determine how much energy a recommendation saves. There are many factors that influence the energy consumption of a space, including: outside temperature, internal thermal load (such as appliances, or people), adjacent room air temperature, and the thermal setpoint. To model all of these factors requires complex models and computational resources. In this work, we focus on two important factors: outside temperature and occupancy. We run simulations using a standard building simulation program to generate approximate models for each space; these simulations are discussed in Section 4.1.

The Northwest Corner Building at Columbia University does not provide an interface for programmatically changing the setpoint of a room as in [1]; this prevents us from directly studying the effects of the recommendations on the building energy consumption. However, we are able to monitor the energy consuming resources through BACNet. We utilize the monitored energy data, along with the building models developed in Section 4.1 to produce more accurate simulations.

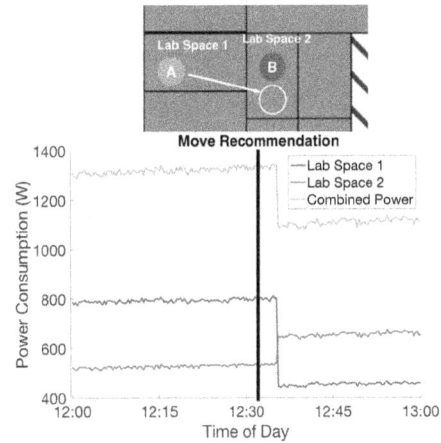

(a) Example of energy consumption savings from a move recommendation. Occupant A receives and accepts a move recommendation at 12:30.

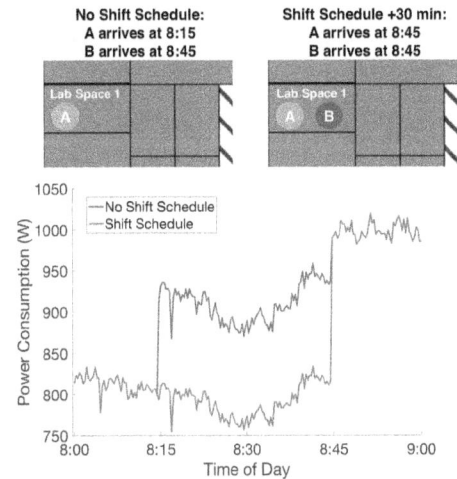

(b) Example of energy consumption savings from a shift schedule recommendation.

Figure 2: Example scenarios of energy savings for a move recommendation and a shift schedule recommendation.

3.3 Personalization

The final challenge that arises is the personalization of the recommendations. A recommender system that gives recommendations unlikely to be accepted by a certain occupant may quickly lose the attention of the occupant. To illustrate the challenge in personalizing recommendations, we present two realistic scenarios.

In our first example, occupant A spends the majority of time alone in Laboratory A. Office Space B consumes less energy than Laboratory A; thus, if occupant A moves to Office Space B, energy service can be reduced in Laboratory A. However, occupant A does not spend time in Office Space B, and would not accept a recommendation to move. A recommender system without knowledge of **occupant behavior** may require a significant amount of feedback

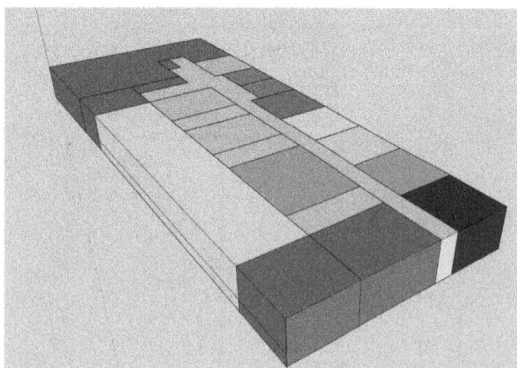

(a) Model of the 10th floor laboratories in the Northwest Corner Building at Columbia University. Different colors indicate different thermal zones.

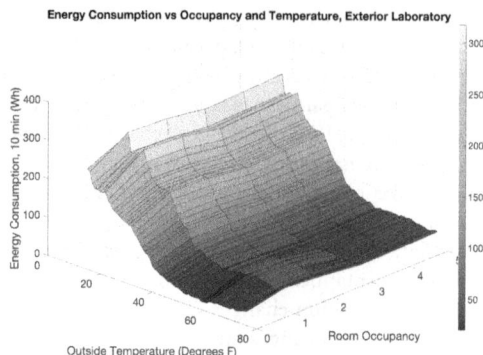

(b) Energy Consumption vs Occupancy and Temperature of an exterior laboratory.

Figure 3: Space level modeling using EnergyPlus.

Occupant	Office 1	Laboratory 1	Laboratory 2	Work Space 1	Public Space 1	Avg Change Location Time
Professor 1	87%	5%	0%	0%	5%	1.5 hr
Student 1	2%	25%	12%	51%	6%	1.0 hr
Student 2	1%	74%	6%	8%	6%	1.25 hr
Student 3	1%	3%	21%	70%	5%	1.0 hr

Table 1: Occupant location preferences and average location change times extracted from historical location data.

to learn these behaviors, which is an undesirable characteristic in a real deployment.

The second example concerns occupant A who is the first to arrive at work at 8 am on Monday. After 30 minutes, other occupants arrive and join occupant A. A naive recommender system may recommend occupant A to shift schedule 30 minutes later on Tuesday; however, occupant A may have a meeting every Tuesday at 7:30 am that cannot be skipped. Again, without knowledge of occupant behavior, the recommender system will require significant amounts of feedback from the occupants.

These examples demonstrate the importance of a user model. In both examples, the recommendations can be altered based on past location behavior to be more relevant to the occupant. Human behavior is incredibly complex, but certain features can be extracted from historical location data to better inform recommendations.

4 SYSTEM DESIGN

4.1 EnergyPlus

Although we do not have access to HVAC or lighting actuation in the Northwest Corner Building (NWC), modeling the behavior of NWC as if it were a smart building through simulation is possible. For simulating HVAC, we use EnergyPlus [5], an open source software program for simulating energy consumption of user defined space models. A model of the testbed was constructed in SketchUp as shown in Figure 3a, and EnergyPlus was used to simulate HVAC requirements in each room.

In order to account for different types of weather conditions, we simulated the service requirements of each space over a year of

weather data in New York City. Further, we simulated the effects of occupancy in each space for the various weather conditions. Similar to [1], we relax the setpoint requirement by 1.5 degrees when the space is unoccupied. A multivariate energy curve was generated for each space. An example for an exterior space is shown in Figure 3b.

In Figure 3b, there is a noticeable change in energy consumption between an unoccupied space and an occupied space over the entire range of outdoor temperatures. This is due to the relaxation of the setpoint by 1.5 degrees. Note that the thermal load from the occupants contributes to the heating requirements of the space, which accounts for the decrease in HVAC energy consumption for higher occupancies.

4.2 User Location Model

Both types of recommendation relate to different features of an occupant's historical location history. The move recommendation is closely tied to the location preferences of an occupant, and the shift schedule recommendation is closely tied to the arrival and departure times of an occupant. These features are extracted from collected historical location data, and used to construct the user's location model.

4.2.1 Data Collection. To construct the user model for each occupant, we sought to discover patterns through historical location data. As both types of recommendation rely on the occupancy of each space, location data of each occupant reveals information about the recommendations an occupant is more likely to accept. Four months of location data were collected from 20 occupants using the ePrints system [22]. Location data was collected every

Occupant	Day of Week	Arrival Time μ	Arrival Time σ	Departure Time μ	Departure Time σ
Professor 1	Monday	12:00	15 m	17:00	15 m
	Tuesday	13:45	15 m	17:30	15 m
	Wednesday	12:45	15 m	20:00	60 m
	Thursday	14:00	30 m	16:15	60 m
	Friday	8:30	15 m	17:00	15 m
Student 1	Monday	10:30	45 m	21:15	30 m
	Tuesday	11:45	30 m	21:00	90 m
	Wednesday	11:30	60 m	20:30	90 m
	Thursday	11:30	90 m	21:00	90 m
	Friday	11:30	90 m	20:15	60 m
Student 2	Monday	11:45	30 m	21:30	90 m
	Tuesday	11:30	60 m	20:30	30 m
	Wednesday	11:45	90 m	21:30	90 m
	Thursday	12:15	90 m	20:00	60 m
	Friday	11:45	60 m	19:30	90 m

Table 2: Arrival Time and Departure Time Gaussian model parameters for three example occupants.

minute, and includes arrival and departure times to the testbed building. This location data is used to build the user model as well as inform the occupant survey discussed in the next section.

4.2.2 Location Preferences. The likelihood for an occupant to accept a move recommendation depends highly on the source and destination spaces. A commercial building is divided into many different spaces; if an occupant historically does not spend any time in a certain space, a move recommendation to that space is unlikely to be accepted.

Using the historical data, occupant "location preferences" were extracted. The location preferences consist of the distribution of time over the spaces for an occupants. A few examples are shown in Table 1. From the data, we observed that occupants tend to spend a constant proportionate amount of time in certain spaces, even across different days and different times of day. For the few occupants whose time spent in certain spaces varies throughout the day, a separate model of location preferences is generated for each part of the day (morning, early afternoon, late afternoon).

Another important feature is the average time an occupant spends in a certain location. After a move recommendation is given and completed, the occupant can change location at any time, thus ending the energy savings of the recommendation. This feature gives an estimate for how long the benefit of a recommendation persists. In simulation, this feature aids in the estimation of the recommendation's energy savings.

4.2.3 Arrival and Departure Time. The arrival and departure time of an occupant varies depending on multiple factors. In order to create an approximate model, we utilized the historical location data collected in Section 4.2.1 and extracted the arrival and departure times of each occupant over the four month study.

Though different occupants have differing arrival and departure patterns, there exist underlying similarities. Firstly, arrival and departure times vary depending on the day of the week; this observation was sensible, as people often had different schedules for each day of the week. Secondly, arrival and departure times for a specific day of the week (e.g. Monday) can often be approximated by a Gaussian distribution, as shown in Figure 4.

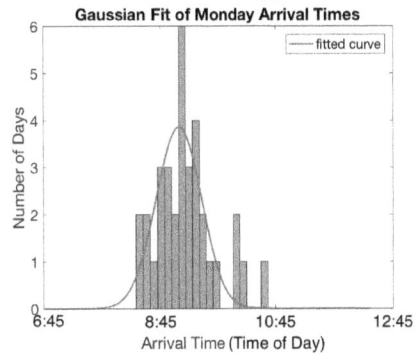

Figure 4: Gaussian fit of the arrival times of one occupant on Mondays.

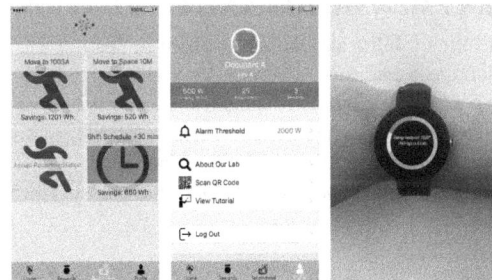

Figure 5: From left to right: iOS recommendations tab, iOS settings tab, Android Wear application.

With these observations, we modeled each occupant's arrival times and departure times separately for each day of the week according to a Gaussian distribution. In the simulations discussed in Section 5.1, these Gaussian distributions are sampled to simulate the arrival and departure times of an occupant. The Gaussian model parameters of three example occupants are shown in Table 2.

4.2.4 Occupant Survey. Using the occupant location preferences and arrival and departure times, move recommendations and shift schedule recommendations can be formulated. However, a difficult question arises: how likely is an occupant to accept one of these recommendations? Many factors influence an occupant's decision, such as: time of day, how "busy" the occupant is, the recommendation's destination space, or the recommended shift in schedule. Empirically deriving this data by sending recommendations to the occupants would require a long deployment, as well as significant investment from the occupants. Thus, to obtain an informed estimate, we directly ask the occupants about the likelihood of accepting certain move recommendations between these spaces.

We conducted a focus group survey to gauge how likely an occupant is to accept different recommendations. Six occupants participated in the survey. In the survey, we present recommendations as we would in a real deployment, and asked the occupants how likely they are to accept different types of recommendations. We present the recommendations through an iOS mobile application, built off of the ePrints application [22]. A screenshot of the recommendations tab is shown in the left screenshot of Figure 5.

As the number of possible move recommendations can be large, we reduced the number of questions by considering occupant location preference. Using occupant location preferences such as in Table 1, we can partition spaces into spaces frequently visited and infrequently visited. We use these categories in forming the recommendation survey questions. A summary of the questions and the recommendations they pertain to are shown in Table 3.

The reason for collecting this data via survey is to overcome the "cold start" problem of many recommender systems. While sending these recommendations in a real deployment may eventually converge to a better estimate of the true acceptance likelihood, this method would require a **significant** amount of time and occupant effort. A survey, on the other hand, provides an informed estimate that can be gathered with little effort from the occupant.

5 IMPLEMENTATION AND EVALUATION

Based on the building simulator described in Section 4.1, recommendation types described in Section 3.1, and user model described in Section 4.2, we implemented a tightly coupled system as shown in Figure 6. The system has two subsystems: the energy simulator, and the recommender system. Monitored energy data is discretized into 15 minute time steps, and each phase of the system runs at each time step.

5.1 Energy Simulation

The energy simulation uses the space energy models, occupant locations, and the energy monitoring inputs to determine the current energy consumption of the building testbed. The simulator also takes as input the occupant location models, and the space level energy models. The simulator can change the location of occupants in the building and observe the change in energy consumption, which enables testing of the effects of different recommendations. A diagram of the simulator is shown in Figure 7.

At each timestep, the simulator sends to the recommender system a reward, and the current power state of the building. For a set of spaces, S, the HVAC energy consumption of a single space, $s_i \in S$ with occupancy p_i, is defined as:

$$H(s_i, p_i, t, T) = H(s_i, t)\beta(s_i, p_i, T)$$

where $H(s_i, t)$ is the monitored energy consumption of a room at time t. $\beta(s_i, p_i, T)$ is the HVAC discount factor of a space s_i with occupancy p_i and outside temperature T, derived from the model generated in Section 4.1. The lighting energy consumption of space s_i is defined as a function

$$L(s_i, p_i) = \begin{cases} 0 & \text{if } p_i == 0 \\ L(s_i) & \text{if } p_i > 0 \end{cases}$$

The algorithm for computing the total power of all spaces is shown in Algorithm 1.

Algorithm 1: Testbed Power Computation

1: **procedure** TESTBEDPOWER(S, P, β, H, L, T)
2:     $testbedPower \leftarrow 0$
3:     **for** $s_i \in S$ **do**
4:         $H(s_i, p_i, t, T) \leftarrow H(s_i, t)\beta(s_i, p_i, T)$
5:         $L(s_i, p_i) \leftarrow L(s_i)\mathbb{1}_{(p_i==0)}$
6:         $testbedPower \leftarrow testbedPower + H(s_i, p_i, t, T) + L(s_i, p_i)$
7:     **end for**
8: **end procedure**

5.2 Learning Energy Saving Recommendations

The output of the energy simulator is fed into the recommender system as a reward and a building state, as shown in Figure 6. In order to learn the potential energy savings of the recommendations, the recommender system utilizes Q-learning. A Q-Table is maintained for each move and shift schedule recommendation, as these recommendations are independent (they are not given at the same time). The value iteration update for learning the Q-Table is shown in Equation 1. This update is used for learning both move recommendations, and shift schedule recommendations.

5.2.1 Move Recommendation Learning. There are two parts to learning the move recommendations: contextual prefiltering and the value iteration update. During the training phase, a random occupant is selected. Initially, all recommendations **except** the move recommendations related to the occupant and the occupant's current space are prefiltered. Based on the occupant's location preferences, a different space is selected, using an ϵ-greedy method. With an occupant, source and destination spaces selected, the recommendation is fully defined.

Once the recommendation has been given and either completed or not, the energy simulator provides the recommender system with a reward, r. This reward represents the power reduction due to the move recommendation. As the benefit of the recommendation is not limited strictly to the current power reduction, the discount factor γ is set to a low, but non-zero, value in order to reward high energy saving future states.

$$Q(s_t, a_t) \leftarrow (1 - \alpha_t)Q(s_t, a_t) + \alpha_t(r_t + \gamma \max_a Q(s_{t+1}, a)) \quad (1)$$

5.2.2 Shift Schedule Learning. The value iteration update is also implemented for shift schedule learning. To learn the shift schedule

Recommendation Type	Recommendation	Accept %
Move Recommendation	Move from Frequent to Frequent	62%
Move Recommendation	Move from Frequent to Infrequent	3%
Move Recommendation	Move from Infrequent to Frequent	83%
Shift Schedule	Shift Schedule Later	15%
Shift Schedule	Shift Schedule Earlier	75%

Table 3: Example survey questions and responses for each type of recommendation.

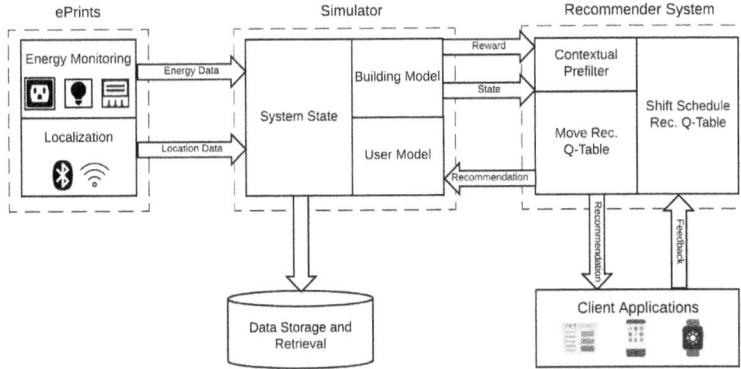

Figure 6: Architecture diagram of the complete system.

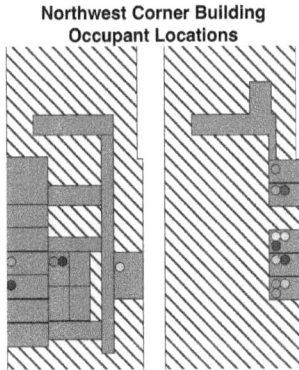

Figure 7: Screenshot of the simulator. Colored dots indicate simulated locations of the occupants.

recommendations, a random occupant is selected each day to shift their schedule. The schedule can be shifted 15, 30, or 60 minutes either earlier or later. The longer the shift in schedule, the larger the effect on energy saving; for example, a shift of 60 minutes later potentially postpones the normal HVAC operation of a space more than a shift of 30 minutes can.

Thus, the reward for the shift schedule is generated by the energy simulator at the end of the day. Two simulations are generated: one that assumes a shift in schedule, and the other which does not. The simulations are run in parallel, and the difference in energy consumption throughout the day is passed to the recommender system as a reward. The future states $Q(s_{t+1}, a)$ are not required for learning the potential energy savings of shift schedule recommendations, so γ is set to 0.

5.3 Energy Savings

In this section, we evaluate the energy saving potential of the learned recommendations. In the following studies, the evaluation was performed using four weeks of monitored energy data and location data from two floors in the Northwest Corner Building. Move recommendations were given every 15 minutes to an occupant, and shift schedule recommendations were given to occupants before the beginning of the day.

5.3.1 Move Recommendation. To evaluate the learning of the move recommendations, we simulated giving move recommendations, and measured the energy saved. The move recommendations are sorted by energy saved and shown in Figure 8. A small percentage of the move recommendations lead to increases in building energy consumption; this is due to variations in the energy and location data in the test days. However, most of the recommendations lead to a reduction in the total energy consumption.

5.3.2 Shift Schedule. To evaluate the shift schedule recommendations, we simulated shift schedule recommendations for −15, −30, −60, +15, +30, and +60 minutes. The simulated recommendations were compared to the ground truth monitored data. Because occupants' schedules often change between days of the week, each day of the week was simulated individually and averaged. Figure 9 shows the average simulated energy consumption savings of an occupant. This example occupant often arrives earlier than other occupants; thus, the higher energy savings for shifting schedule later is reasonable. Additionally, the energy savings for each shift schedule recommendation change depending on the day of the week. The variations in energy savings throughout the week demonstrate the importance of generating different arrival/departure models for each day for an occupant.

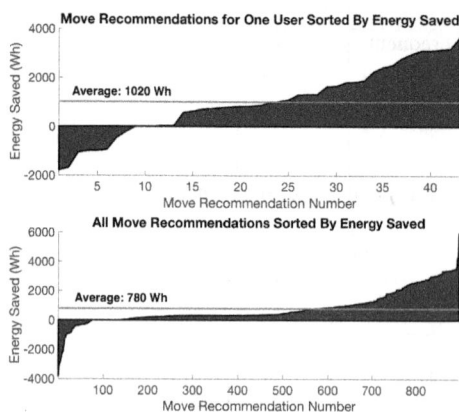

Figure 8: Sorted move recommendations by saved energy consumption for one occupant and all occupants.

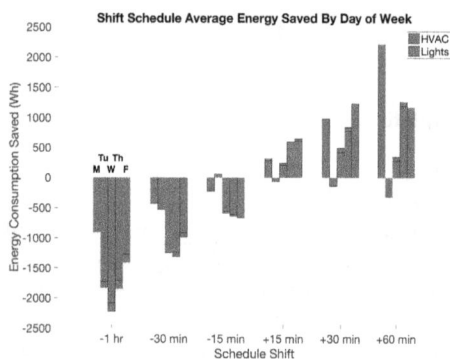

Figure 9: Simulated energy savings for different shift schedule recommendations for an occupant. Each group consists of the five days of the week, with Monday as the leftmost bar, and Friday as the rightmost bar.

5.3.3 Total Energy Saved. Figure 10 shows the simulated energy savings for five days and the average over the four weeks of test data. The "no recommendations" bars show the simulated energy savings by only relaxing the setpoint temperature, with no recommendations given. The "realistic recommendations" bars utilize the responses from the occupant survey in Section 4.2.4 to determine how often recommendations are accepted. The "all recommendations" curve demonstrates the maximum energy savings if all occupants took every energy saving recommendation.

Using the occupant responses, the recommendations led to 25% more energy saved than relaxing setpoint temperature alone **in commonly occupied spaces**. Though the optimal energy savings (shown by the "all recommendations" bars) can save up to 50% more energy than without recommendations, only a fraction of the recommendations need to be accepted in order to see substantial energy savings.

6 FUTURE WORK

The largest point of uncertainty in this recommender system is: how likely is an occupant to accept a recommendation? In this

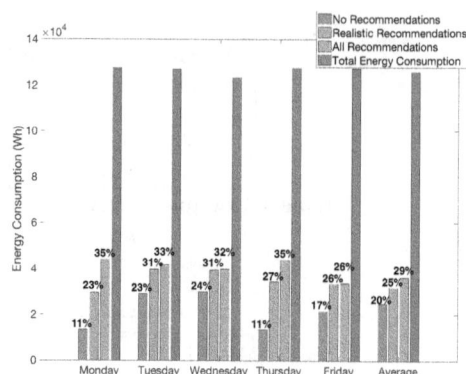

Figure 10: Move recommendation energy savings for five test days and average over two weeks.

work, a survey was used to gauge an occupant's *attitude* towards a type of recommendation. However, a variety of literature exists showing the "intention gap" between attitudes and intention; works such as [9, 13, 15], cover various models and case studies used to demonstrate the gap between environmental awareness and behavior. The "intention gap" also appears in recommender systems of other applications such as sustainable food consumption and physical exercise [20, 21]. In recommender systems for energy saving, this intention gap can be seen between an occupant's attitude towards a recommendation and an occupant's intention (likelihood) to accept a recommendation. Towards this end, a study on a physical deployment with real occupants, along with considerations of existing literature on the intention gap, is a crucial next step.

Further, we sought to personalize recommendations by tailoring to each individual occupant. In [19], the authors show that tailoring recommendations by reducing perceived and actual effort led to positive user experiences. Additional parameters can be included to increase personalization of location recommendations, such as available work facilities, whether the occupant can be productive in the new work space, and convenience.

7 CONCLUSION

In this work, we introduce a novel idea: applying human modeling and recommendations to the traditionally non-human building energy consumption optimization problem. We introduced two new energy saving recommendations based on location: move recommendations, which recommends the occupant to move from one space to another, and shift schedule recommendations, which recommends the occupant to arrive or depart a set amount of time earlier or later. To investigate the effects of the energy saving recommendations, we introduced a tightly coupled system composing of a simulator and a recommender system. The simulator utilized building models, based on simulations from EnergyPlus, and user location models, extracted from collected historical location data, to generate simulations of the building energy consumption. The simulations were given to the recommender system to learn recommendations. The simulations revealed that in our testbed, energy saving recommendations along with occupancy-based HVAC energy management saves 25% more energy consumption than occupancy-based HVAC energy management alone.

REFERENCES

[1] Yuvraj Agarwal, Bharathan Balaji, Rajesh Gupta, Jacob Lyles, Michael Wei, and Thomas Weng. 2010. Occupancy-driven energy management for smart building automation. In *Proceedings of the 2nd ACM workshop on embedded sensing systems for energy-efficiency in building*. ACM, 1–6.

[2] Bharathan Balaji, Hidetoshi Teraoka, Rajesh Gupta, and Yuvraj Agarwal. 2013. ZonePAC: Zonal Power Estimation and Control via HVAC Metering and Occupant Feedback. In *Proceedings of the 5th ACM Workshop on Embedded Systems For Energy-Efficient Buildings*. ACM, 1–8.

[3] Bharathan Balaji, Jian Xu, Anthony Nwokafor, Rajesh Gupta, and Yuvraj Agarwal. 2013. Sentinel: occupancy based HVAC actuation using existing WiFi infrastructure within commercial buildings. In *Proceedings of the 11th ACM Conference on Embedded Networked Sensor Systems*. ACM, 17.

[4] Jie Bao and Yu Zheng. 2017. *Location-Based Recommendation Systems*. Springer International Publishing, Cham, 1145–1153. https://doi.org/10.1007/978-3-319-17885-1_1580

[5] Drury B Crawley, Linda K Lawrie, Frederick C Winkelmann, Walter F Buhl, Y Joe Huang, Curtis O Pedersen, Richard K Strand, Richard J Liesen, Daniel E Fisher, Michael J Witte, et al. 2001. EnergyPlus: creating a new-generation building energy simulation program. *Energy and buildings* 33, 4 (2001), 319–331.

[6] Varick L Erickson, Miguel Á Carreira-Perpiñán, and Alberto E Cerpa. 2011. OBSERVE: Occupancy-based system for efficient reduction of HVAC energy. In *Information Processing in Sensor Networks (IPSN), 2011 10th International Conference on*. IEEE, 258–269.

[7] Varick L Erickson and Alberto E Cerpa. 2010. Occupancy based demand response HVAC control strategy. In *Proceedings of the 2nd ACM Workshop on Embedded Sensing Systems for Energy-Efficiency in Building*. ACM, 7–12.

[8] Varick L Erickson, Yiqing Lin, Ankur Kamthe, Rohini Brahme, Amit Surana, Alberto E Cerpa, Michael D Sohn, and Satish Narayanan. 2009. Energy efficient building environment control strategies using real-time occupancy measurements. In *Proceedings of the First ACM Workshop on Embedded Sensing Systems for Energy-Efficiency in Buildings*. ACM, 19–24.

[9] David Gadenne, Bishnu Sharma, Don Kerr, and Tim Smith. 2011. The influence of consumers' environmental beliefs and attitudes on energy saving behaviours. *Energy policy* 39, 12 (2011), 7684–7694.

[10] Tyler Hoyt, Edward Arens, and Hui Zhang. 2015. Extending air temperature setpoints: Simulated energy savings and design considerations for new and retrofit buildings. *Building and Environment* 88 (2015), 89–96.

[11] P3 International. 2017. Energy Saving Solutions, Solar Devices and More. http://www.p3international.com/. (2017).

[12] Xiaofan Jiang, Stephen Dawson-Haggerty, Prabal Dutta, and David Culler. 2009. Design and Implementation of a High-fidelity AC Metering Network. In *Proceedings of the 2009 International Conference on Information Processing in Sensor Networks*. ACM, 253–264.

[13] Anja Kollmuss and Julian Agyeman. 2002. Mind the gap: why do people act environmentally and what are the barriers to pro-environmental behavior? *Environmental education research* 8, 3 (2002), 239–260.

[14] Joshua Lifton, Mark Feldmeier, Yasuhiro Ono, Cameron Lewis, and Joseph A. Paradiso. 2007. A Platform for Ubiquitous Sensor Deployment in Occupational and Domestic Environments. In *Proceedings of the 6th International Conference on Information Processing in Sensor Networks*. ACM, 119–127.

[15] Ritsuko Ozaki. 2011. Adopting sustainable innovation: what makes consumers sign up to green electricity? *Business strategy and the environment* 20, 1 (2011), 1–17.

[16] Lawrence Page, Sergey Brin, Rajeev Motwani, and Terry Winograd. 1999. *The PageRank Citation Ranking: Bringing Order to the Web*. Technical Report 1999-66. Stanford InfoLab. http://ilpubs.stanford.edu:8090/422/ Previous number = SIDL-WP-1999-0120.

[17] Moon-Hee Park, Jin-Hyuk Hong, and Sung-Bae Cho. 2007. Location-based recommendation system using bayesian userâĂŹs preference model in mobile devices. In *International Conference on Ubiquitous Intelligence and Computing*. Springer, 1130–1139.

[18] J. Ben Schafer, Dan Frankowski, Jon Herlocker, and Shilad Sen. 2007. *Collaborative Filtering Recommender Systems*. Springer Berlin Heidelberg, Berlin, Heidelberg, 291–324. https://doi.org/10.1007/978-3-540-72079-9_9

[19] Alain Starke, Martijn Willemsen, and Chris Snijders. 2017. Effective user interface designs to increase energy-efficient behavior in a Rasch-based energy recommender system. In *Proceedings of the Eleventh ACM Conference on Recommender Systems*. ACM, 65–73.

[20] Iris Vermeir and Wim Verbeke. 2006. Sustainable food consumption: Exploring the consumer âĂIJattitude–behavioral intentionâĂI gap. *Journal of Agricultural and Environmental ethics* 19, 2 (2006), 169–194.

[21] Weiquan Wang and Izak Benbasat. 2007. Recommendation agents for electronic commerce: Effects of explanation facilities on trusting beliefs. *Journal of Management Information Systems* 23, 4 (2007), 217–246.

[22] Peter Wei, Xiaoqi Chen, Jordan Vega, Stephen Xia, Rishikanth Chandrasekaran, and Xiaofan Jiang. 2017. Adaptive and Personalized Energy Saving Suggestions for Occupants in Smart Buildings. In *Proceedings of the 4th ACM International Conference on Systems for Energy-Efficient Built Environments*. ACM.

[23] Yu Zheng, Lizhu Zhang, Xing Xie, and Wei-Ying Ma. 2009. Mining Interesting Locations and Travel Sequences from GPS Trajectories. In *Proceedings of the 18th International Conference on World Wide Web (WWW '09)*. ACM, New York, NY, USA, 791–800. https://doi.org/10.1145/1526709.1526816

[24] Yunhong Zhou, Dennis Wilkinson, Robert Schreiber, and Rong Pan. 2008. Large-Scale Parallel Collaborative Filtering for the Netflix Prize. In *Algorithmic Aspects in Information and Management*, Rudolf Fleischer and Jinhui Xu (Eds.). Springer Berlin Heidelberg, Berlin, Heidelberg, 337–348.

PACELA: A Neural Framework for User Visitation in Location-based Social Networks

Thanh-Nam Doan
School of Information Systems
Singapore Management University
tndoan.2012@smu.edu.sg

Ee-Peng Lim
School of Information Systems
Singapore Management University
eplim@smu.edu.sg

ABSTRACT

Check-in prediction using location-based social network data is an important research problem for both academia and industry since an accurate check-in predictive model is useful to many applications, e.g. urban planning, venue recommendation, route suggestion, and context-aware advertising. Intuitively, when considering venues to visit, users may rely on their past observed visit histories as well as some latent attributes associated with the venues. In this paper, we therefore propose a check-in prediction model based on a neural framework called **Preference and Context Embeddings with Latent Attributes (PACELA)**. PACELA learns the embeddings space for the user and venue data as well as the latent attributes of both users and venues. More specifically, we use a probabilistic matrix factorization-based technique to infer the latent attributes specific to users and locations in location-based social networks (LBSNs), considering the user visitation decisions that could be affected by area attraction, neighborhood competition, and social homophily. PACELA also includes a deep learning neural network to combine both embedding and latent features to predict if a user performs check-in on a location. Our experiments on three different real world datasets show that PACELA yields the best check-in prediction accuracy against several baseline methods.

KEYWORDS

Neural Network, Check-in Prediction, Location-based social networks, User visitation

ACM Reference Format:
Thanh-Nam Doan and Ee-Peng Lim. 2018. PACELA: A Neural Framework for User Visitation in Location-based Social Networks. In *UMAP '18: 26th Conference on User Modeling, Adaptation and Personalization, July 8–11, 2018, Singapore, Singapore.* ACM, New York, NY, USA, 9 pages. https://doi.org/10.1145/3209219.3209231

1 INTRODUCTION

Motivation. The wide adoption of smart phones and wearable devices in recent years has offered an ideal platform for growing location based social networking (LBSN) applications. In these applications, users publish their visits to different venues as check-ins

which are in turn shared with the users' online friends. Foursquare, one the most popular LBSN applications, is used by 50 millions users each month and it covers more than 65 million venues around the world. These users have so far generated more than 8 billion check-ins worldwide [1]. By analyzing these check-in data, one can derive useful insights for urban planning [29, 32, 33], business recommendation [22, 23, 39], and other applications [1, 9]. Along with the rise of LBSNs, check-in prediction becomes an important problem that attracts interest from both academia and industry. Check-in prediction refers to the prediction of missing or future check-ins of a user based on her observed LBSN data. Once check-ins are predicted, they can be used for predicting the user movement and visits to venues.

While there are already much research on check-in prediction, it remains to be a challenging problem. First of all, the set of candidate venues for check-in prediction is usually very large. It is therefore difficult for any check-in prediction methods to return high accuracy results. Secondly, the sparsity of check-in data among some users and venues is a major cold start issue that check-in prediction has to overcome. Compared to the typical movie recommendation problem, the density of check-in data in LBSNs is much lower. For instance, the density of check-in data (e.g., in Foursquare or Yelp) is about 0.1% while movie rating data (e.g., Netflix) enjoys a much higher density of 1.2% [37]. Furthermore, check-in is represented as a binary value between a user and venue pair. Movie ratings are assigned rating values (e.g., from 1 to 5) and are thus more fine-grained. Thirdly, user visitation can be attributed to multiple factors and the interaction of these factors is not well studied. For example, *distance effect* states that users frequently visit venues nearby their homes rather than venues further away.

The recent breakthroughs in deep learning, on the other hand, have brought about a plethora of new unsupervised and supervised learning techniques. Word embedding and deep neural networks are the respective examples. These techniques, despite their higher computation costs, are shown to yield high accuracy in prediction tasks. Given the check-in prediction challenges, it is therefore interesting to explore a deep learning or neural framework to generate better prediction results at the same time incorporating both embedding and the latent attribute features behind the various factors relevant to check-in behavior.

Research Objectives. In this paper, we propose a neural framework to leverage on both embedding and latent attributes of users and venues to more accurately predict check-in venues for LBSN users. To the best of knowledge, this is the first attempt to adopt such an approach. We use a matrix factorization based method to learn latent attributes of users and venues from LBSN data. These

---

[1] https://foursquare.com/about - Retrieved in August 2017

latent attributes include user topical interests, venue topical interests, and other attributes relevant to the modeling of *area attraction*, *neighborhood competition* and *social homophily* factors in check-in behavior.

The research steps carried out in this paper are as follows. We first crawl the check-in data from the selected LBSN platforms to construct datasets for our research. We then have to carry out two sub-steps: (a) learning latent attribute features of users and venues by modeling the area attraction, neighborhood competition, and social homophily effects in check-in behavior, and (b) integrating these latent attribute features with other embedding features of users and venue into a deep neural network for training and test. The former involves matrix factorization and the outcomes are the latent attributes of users and venues. The latter step develops a neural network that combines these latent features with embedding of users and venues to enhance the predictive power. Finally, the accuracy and robustness of our proposed framework known as PACELA are evaluated in the check-in prediction task using our real world datasets. Our experiments also evaluate our PACELA predictive model under different parameter settings.

Our results and findings of this research are as follows:

- With real world LBSN datasets collected for three urban cities, we conduct an empirical analysis of the gathered check-in data and demonstrate the existence of neighborhood competition, area attraction factors. Furthermore, the effect of social homophily is also illustrated in our empirical analysis.
- We propose a matrix factorization-based model to capture the check-in behavior of users incorporating area attraction and neighborhood competition as well as *social homophily*.
- We propose a neural model named *PACELA* to integrate the latent features of users and venues derived above to enhanced the check-in prediction performance.
- The performance of **PACELA** model is evaluated on real world datasets so as to demonstrate its superior accuracy and robustness. In our experiments, we compare **PACELA** model with other baselines in check-in prediction task. We show that **PACELA** model outperforms the baselines. The parameters and behaviors of **PACELA** model are also carefully examined in our experiments.

Paper Outline. The remainder of the paper is organized as follows. Section 2 covers the literature review of previous works related to our research. Section 3 describes the datasets constructed for this research. Section 4 describes and formalizes PACELA model. Section 5 presents the experiment results on real datasets. Lastly, Section 6 concludes the paper and suggests some future works.

2 RELATED WORKS

In this section, we give an overview of related works. We divide these works into those that focus on modeling location or venue factors which affect check-in behavior of users in LBSNs, and those that adopt neural frameworks to model user movement in LBSNs.

Modeling of Latent Location and Venue Factors. The visitation of users to different venues and locations occurs under the influence of multiple factors [5, 9, 16, 21]. Some of these factors are associated with users. Examples are users' topical interests, e.g.,

music, sports, etc.. There are also factors associated with venues or locations. For example, an location area may be attractive making it popular to be visited. There is also competition from neighbors a location has to face before gaining visits. In the following, we will only focus on surveying research works on *area attraction*, *neighborhood competition* and *social homophily* effects.

The *area attraction* factor is based on the hypothesis that venues within some specific spatial areas tend to gain visitation from users. There are various possible reasons that could explain these popular areas. Easy accessibility by public transport, wide selection of shops/restaurants, high-density population, popular POIs in the area are among the possible reasons. Previous works [6, 13, 17, 28, 38] focused on ranking areas by attractiveness derived from LBSN data. However, without considering user's preference, the application of these works is limited to only area ranking.

The *neighborhood competition* factor refers to venues competing with their neighbors to attract users' visitation. Liu *et. al.* [24] defined the popularity of each venue as its competitiveness score. The authors assumed that the probability of observing a check-in by user u on venue v is proportional to inverse of distance between u and v, popularity of venue v, and the interest of u on v. To model the interest between users and venues, the authors adopted *Latent Dirichlet Allocation* model [2] and *Bayesian Non-negative Matrix Factorization* [31] to model latent factors of users and venues. In [7], PageRank model has been adopted to measure the competitiveness of venues by deriving transition probabilities between venues. Doan *et. al.* [9] provides the first neighborhood competition evidence via real datasets. Moreover, they proposed a probabilistic model to combine neighborhood competition with distance effect and area attraction. They showed that using these effects could improve the performance of check-in prediction task and home prediction task.

Social homophily refers to users who are connected to each other tend to share more common visited venues. This factor has been widely used in LBSNs to predict users' check-in behavior [14, 21, 30]. The work in [8] derived features based on social homophily to predict the number of check-ins by a user on venues. Cheng *et. al.* [4] modeled social homophily using a regularizer to penalize the difference between users and their friends. Cho *et. al.* [5] extended their periodic mobility model by considering the influence of users' friends. Their results concluded that using *social homophily* could more accurately predict users' movement behavior.

Neural Network Framework. With the recent advances in GPU-based hardware, deep learning and availability of big data with ground truth labels, several *neural frameworks* have been proposed for prediction problems in LBSNs. These frameworks include both unsupervised techniques such as embeddings and supervised techniques such as multilayer perceptrons. Check-in prediction task is a sub problem of user-item adoption so we can adopt neural network framework [15, 34, 36] to model the adoption but the accuracy could be low. POI2Vec [11] is an extension of Word2vec embedding model that considers geographical influence in the future visitor prediction problem. Their model wants to conver the case that a user is more likely to visit nearby locations in the near future. POI2Vec however does not consider the neighbor competition factor in the prediction. C-WARP [25] and Geo-Teaser [40] are two other embedding-based methods to model the temporal sequential of users' visitation based on pairwise venue ranking.

The two works nevertheless ignore the venue and location factors. Wang *et. al.* [35] incorporated visual embedding features of user-generated images to enhance the accuracy of point-of-interest prediction. Yang *et. al.* [37] proposed a neural framework call PACE that combines collaborative filtering and semi-supervised learning for point-of-interest recommendation task. Our work is built upon this neural framework but with extensions to handle user and venue latent attributes, as well as new loss functions to learn the user and venue embeddings.

3 DATASETS

In our research, we gathered the Foursquare check-in data of users and venues from two cities, Singapore and Jakarta. Both are major cities in Southeast Asia with more than 5M population. The two cities also have relatively many active Foursquare users performing check-ins. For more extensive evaluation, we also include the publicly available Gowalla dataset covering users and venues from New York City [5]. The statistics of the three datasets are shown in Table 1.

SG Dataset. This dataset consists of 1.11 millions check-ins by 55,891 Singapore Foursquare users on 75,346 venues from August 15, 2012 to June 3, 2013 (see Table 1). The users and venues are determined to be located in Singapore based on their profile locations and venue location coordinates respectively. This dataset is the largest among the three by number of venues, number of users and check-ins. Nevertheless, this dataset is also very sparse. On average, each user performs check-ins to less than 10 venues, out of 75K+ venues. Each venue also receives check-ins from about 7 users, out of 55K users. The same sparsity can be observed in the other two datasets.

JK Dataset. Similarly, we crawled another Foursquare dataset for the users and venues in Jakarta from July 2014 to May 2015. There are 119,618 check-ins performed by 14,974 users on 38,183 venues. **JK** dataset is the smallest among the three datasets.

NYC Dataset. To test our model in other LBSN platform, we use the public dataset of Gowalla from February 2009 to October 2010. Since we only focus on venues within city, we select check-ins of venues from New York City.

Table 1: Dataset Statistics

Dataset	# users	# venues	# check-ins	# user-venue pairs with > 0 check-ins
SG	55,891	75,346	1.11M	541,588
JK	14,974	38,183	119,618	81,188
NYC	7,092	21,287	138,067	102,906

Since these datasets have been empirically analyzed for area attraction, neighborhood competition and social homophily effects in our previous works [9, 10], we do not repeat the analysis in this paper.

4 PREFERENCE AND CONTEXT EMBEDDINGS WITH LATENT ATTRIBUTES

In this section, we propose a framework called Preference And Context Embeddings with Latent Attributes (PACELA).

The input of PACELA framework consists of: (a) users and their social connections; (b) venues with locations; and (c) check-ins

performed by users on venues. We use N and M to denote the total number of users and venues respectively. In this paper, we denote the context of a user i as $\mathbf{u}_i$ and $\mathbf{u}_i$ is derived from the set of users who have social connections with user i. We also denote the context of a venue j as $\mathbf{v}_j$ and $\mathbf{v}_j$ is derived from the set of venues that are nearby. The set of check-ins is denoted by C which consists of a set of tuples $\{(u_i, v_j)\}$ such that user i has performed check-in on venue j. From C, we can define a check-in variable y_{ij} such that $y_{ij} = 1$ if $(u_i, v_j) \in C$, and $y_{ij} = 0$ otherwise.

As shown in Figure 1, this framework consists of four components, namely, the two *network embedding* components for learning user context and venue context, a *latent attribute modeling* component for learning user and venue attributes, and a *neural network* component for predicting check-ins between users and venues. By instantiating these components with an appropriate model, we can realize different methods of check-in prediction.

The figure shows that the network embedding component for user context essentially takes the user social network data and learns an embedding space. Users will be mapped into a common space such that users with similar context will be close to one another in this space. Similarly, the network embedding component for venue context learns an embedding space using the venue proximity network. This way, venues with similar spatial neighbors will be close to one another in the embedding space.

The latent attribute modeling component takes all check-in history data of users as well as the users' social networks and venues' proximity networks to learn the latent attributes of users and venues respectively.

Finally, we have the neural network component introducing for each user a user embedding vector, and each venue a venue embedding vector. These embedding vectors will be merged with the corresponding latent feature vector. The reason is that there are some interesting features which are hard to formalize using deep learning but easy using an explicit latent attribute modeling techniques. The new merged feature vector is given as an input to the neural network component to predict user context, venue context and user-item check-in.

In the following, we will introduce a specific model instantiation using the framework.

4.1 Model Description

Network Embedding Components. We use DeepWalk, a well known network embedding model, to learn the embeddings of user context and venue context [27]. DeepWalk uses random walk to establish the local information of each node in the network and learns the distributed representation vector of the node. In this paper, users form a social network and venues form a venue proximity network. We set the dimension of representative vector of a user or venue to 64 by default. The representative vectors of all users can then be represented by a $N \times 64$ matrix X_u. To retrieve the representative vector of user i, we can compute $X_u^T u_i$ where u_i is represented as a one-hot vector. Similarly, for venue, we can define another embedding matrix X_v whose size is $M \times 64$ and retrieve the representative vector of venue j by $X_v^T v_j$. For the ease of reading, we denote the representative vectors of context of user i and venue j as $\mathbf{u}_i$ and $\mathbf{v}_j$ respectively.

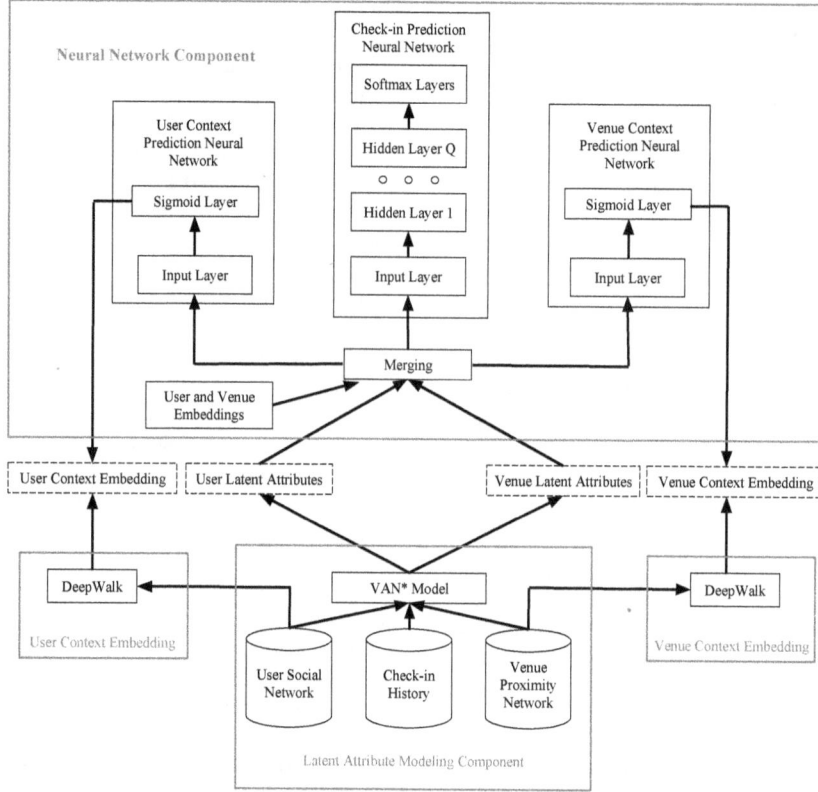

Figure 1: Neural Architecture of PACELA model.

Neural Network Component. We use a single layer neural network in PACELA to return predictions of user context of user i, and another similar neural network for venue context of venue j. A multi-layer neural network is used to predict check-in of i on j. The predicted variables are denoted as $\hat{u}_i$, $\hat{v}_j$, and $\hat{y}_{ij}$ respectively.

These predictions are generated by the softmax layer of the three neural networks. We first describe the prediction of check-in variable y_{ij} using a multi-layer neural network $\mathcal{H}$.

$$\hat{y}_{ij} = h(E_u^T u_i, E_v^T v_j | \Theta_e, \Theta_h, u_i', v_j') \quad (1)$$

where Θ_e denotes the parameters of the embedding layer while Θ_h represents the parameter of preference prediction layer. Moreover, the latent attributes of i and j are denoted as u_i' and v_j' respectively. We will elaborate the derivation of u_i' and v_j' in latent attribute modeling (see Section 4.2).

As shown in Figure 1, $\mathcal{H}$ has Q layers. The input layer consists of the embedding vectors of user i and venue j and their latent attributes u_i' and v_j'. Hence, we denote the input layer by $x_{ij} = [E_u^T u_i; u_i'; E_v^T v_j; v_j']$. We will describe the modeling of latent attributes u_i' and v_j' in Section 4.2.

x_{ij} is then fed into the first hidden layer of $\mathcal{H}$ which has full connectivity between input layer and the first hidden layer, as well as full connectivity between two hidden layers. The q-th hidden

layer of $\mathcal{H}$ denoted as h^q is defined as a non-linear function of its previous hidden layer h^{q-1}. Formally, we have:

$$h^q(x) = ReLU(W^q h^{q-1}(x) + b^q) \quad (2)$$

where W^q and b^q are the parameters of the q-th layer of $\mathcal{H}$ while $h^0(x_{ij}) = x_{ij} = [E_u^T u_i; u_i'; E_v^T v_j; v_j']$. We choose the rectified linear unit $ReLU(x) = max(0, x)$ as the non-linear function.

After Q layers of computation, the prediction of check-in variable, $\hat{y}_{ij}$, can be expressed as:

$$\begin{aligned}
\hat{y}_{ij} &= h_{pred}(h^Q(\cdots h^1(h^0([E_u^T u_i; u_i'; E_v^T v_j; v_j'])) \cdots)) \\
&= h_{pred}(H^Q([E_u^T u_i; u_i'; E_v^T v_j; v_j']))
\end{aligned} \quad (3)$$

where h_{pred} is a softmax involving logistic regression with Sigmoid function. It turns the output of $H^Q([E_u^T u_i; u_i'; E_v^T v_j; v_j'])$ from a vector form to a prediction value between 0 and 1. In other words, we have the formula:

$$\hat{y}_{ij} = S(H^Q([E_u^T u_i; u_i'; E_v^T v_j; v_j'])^T w_y) \quad (4)$$

where the Sigmoid function is defined as $S(x) = 1/(1 + e^{-x})$ and w_y is the parameter vector of the softmax layer.

The multi-layer neural network has two configuration parameters, Q (number of hidden layers) and R (capacity). The capacity is the size of the last hidden layer Q, i.e., h^Q. The size of each hidden layer (except the last one) is assigned to be twice the size of the next hidden layer. Hence, for a multi-layer neural network with $Q = 4$ and $R = 2$, the size of layer q of the network is $h^q = R^{Q-q+1} = 2^{4-2+1} = 8$. Recall the h^0 refers to the input layer and its size is determined by the embedding vectors and latent attributes.

A single layer perceptron network is used to predict the context of user i. Again, we concatenate the embedding vector of user i with his latent attribute vector u_i'. Formally, the context prediction vector of user i is generated by

$$\hat{u}_i = S([E_u^T u_i; u_i'] | \phi_{u_i}) = S([E_u^T u_i; u_i']^T \phi_{u_i}) \quad (5)$$

where $S(\cdot)$ is the sigmoid function that applies to each element of the given vector and ϕ_{u_i} is the parameter of the densely connected neural network for user i. Recall that $E_u^T u_i$ is the embedding vector of user u_i.

Similarly, we also have a single layer perceptron to predict the context of venue j as follows.

$$\hat{v}_j = S([E_v^T v_j; v_j'] | \psi_{v_j}) = S([E_v^T v_j; v_j']^T \psi_{v_j}) \quad (6)$$

where ψ_{v_j} is the network parameter of venue j.

Loss functions (Neural Network). The above three neural networks are jointly trained by optimizing the sum of three loss functions as follows

$$\mathcal{J} = \mathcal{J}_Y + \lambda_1 \mathcal{J}_{C_U} + \lambda_2 \mathcal{J}_{C_V} \quad (7)$$

where $\mathcal{J}_Y$ denotes the loss of predicting check-in between users and venues, while $\mathcal{J}_{C_U}$ and $\mathcal{J}_{C_V}$ denote the losses of user and venue context predictions respectively. The two values λ_1 and λ_2 are the regularization to control the trade-off among the three losses.

Specifically, $\mathcal{J}_Y$ is the log-loss function which is a special case of cross entropy for softmax input. Formally, it is defined by:

$$\begin{aligned}\mathcal{J}_Y &= \log p(\mathcal{L}|\Theta_e, \Theta_h) \\ &= - \sum_{(u_i,v_j)\in\mathcal{L}^+} \log \hat{y}_{ij} - \sum_{(u_i,v_j)\in\mathcal{L}^-} \log(1 - \hat{y}_{ij}) \\ &= - \sum_{(u_i,v_j)\in\mathcal{L}} y_{ij} \log \hat{y}_{ij} + (1 - y_{ij})\log(1 - \hat{y}_{ij})\end{aligned} \quad (8)$$

In the above equation, $\mathcal{L}$ represents the collection of labeled check-in pairs of users and venues. $\mathcal{L}$ consists of two subsets $\mathcal{L}^+$ ($\mathcal{L}^+ \subseteq C$) and $\mathcal{L}^-$ ($\mathcal{L}^- \cap C = \emptyset$) corresponding to positive and negative labeled pairs respectively. Θ_e and Θ_h are the parameters used to predict the preference of users and venues. y_{ij} and $\hat{y}_{ij}$ are the actual and prediction of preference of user i and venue j.

The loss functions of user context prediction and venue context prediction, $\mathcal{J}_{C_U}$ and $\mathcal{J}_{C_V}$ are defined by mean square errors:

$$\mathcal{J}_{C_U} = \sum_{u_i} MSE(\hat{u}_i, \mathbf{u}_i) = \sum_{u_i} \|\hat{u}_i - \mathbf{u}_i\|^2 \quad (9)$$

where $\hat{u}_i$ is the predicted context vector of user i and $\mathbf{u}_i$ is the actual context vector of user i. We would like to minimize the difference between the two vectors.

$$\mathcal{J}_{C_V} = \sum_{v_j} MSE(\hat{v}_j, \mathbf{v}_j) = \sum_{v_j} \|\hat{v}_j - \mathbf{v}_j\|^2 \quad (10)$$

where $\hat{v}_j$ is the predicted context vector of venue j and $\mathbf{v}_j$ is the actual context vector of venue j.

Model Learning. To learn the parameters Θ_e and Θ_h of the neural network component, we use the optimization technique SGD (stochastic gradient descent) with mini-batch ADAM [18]. The algorithm is the iterative process containing two steps. First of all, we sample the batch of labeled pairs of users and venues from $\mathcal{L}$. Secondly, we optimize the loss functions $\mathcal{J}_Y$, $\mathcal{J}_{C_U}$ and $\mathcal{J}_{C_V}$. We repeat the steps until the loss function converges.

4.2 Learning of User and Venue Latent Attributes

We adapt a latent attribute model for check-in data from our earlier work [9] to the PACELA framework. The goal is to model check-in behavior incorporating *area attraction, neighborhood competition,* and *social homphily* effects and to learn the latent attributes of users and venues that account to these effects in addition to the general preference of users. Unlike [9], the latent attribute model defined here does not assume any knowledge of users' home locations. This new model is called VAN* to distinguish it from the earlier VAN model defined in [9].

In VAN*, we model each user i (or venue j) as a vector of latent features U_i (or V_j). To determine if user i has a preference to check into venue j, we compute the value of $U_i^T V_j$. A large $U_i^T V_j$ implies that user i is likely to perform check-in on venue j. We use w_{iv} to denote the number of check-ins by user i performing on venue j.

To model area attraction, we divide a city into mutually exclusive square grid cells of width s. We use a_j to denote the square or *area* which contains j. The area a_j has an attraction value denoted by σ_j. A large σ_j suggests that a_j is attractive, and small σ_j otherwise.

The VAN* model makes the following assumptions about how each check-in between a user i and a venue j is generated:

- First of all, user i chooses an area to perform a check-in based on a combination of area attractiveness σ_j and i's preference on the venues $v \in a_j$.
- User i finally selects a venue j to check in when j wins over all neighboring venues of j.

The neighbors of a venue j, denoted as $N(v_j)$, are venues within a_j and the areas adjacent to a_j are denoted by $A(a_j)$. That is, $N(v_j) = \{v|v \in a_j\} \cup \{v|v \in a_k, a_k \in A(a_j)\} \setminus \{v\}$. We consider the venues in $A(a_j)$ as neighbors because we want to include venues in a larger nearby areas as potential competitors of j for check-ins. The attraction of area a to user i is defined by $\sum_{j' \in a} U_i^T V_{j'}$.

Every check-in of user i to venue j follows a two-step process. Firstly, user i must select the area a_j. Secondly, the venue j in area a_j must win over all other neighboring venues in $N(v_j)$ to gain a check-in from user i.

- User i selects the area a_j based on $\sigma_{a_j}^i$. Hence, we assigning this event a probability which is proportional to $\sigma_{a_j}^i$.
- To model the winning of venue j over all its neighbors, we refer to the preference of user i. We assume that if the latent similarity between user i and venue j is higher than that of user i and the neighbors of venue j, the probability that user i visits venue j (denoted as $p_i(v_j > v_k)$) is higher than the one between user i and venue k, $k \in N(v_j)$. We therefore map the value of $U_i^T V_j - U_i^T V_k$ to the interval $[0, 1]$ so as to model $p_i(v_j > v_k)$. When $p_i(v_j > v_k) > 0.5$, user i is

more likely to make check-in on venue j than the neighbor k. We define $p_i(v_j > v_k) = S(U_i^T V_j - U_i^T V_k)$ where $S(\cdot)$ is a Sigmoid function.

Formalization of VAN* Model: We now formally define the VAN* model. Firstly, the probability p_{ij} of a check-in from user i to venue j is defined by the following formula:

$$p_{ij} = p(i \rightarrow a_j) \prod_{k \in N(v_j)} p_i(v_j > v_k) \tag{11}$$

Equation 11 says that p_{ij} has two components, $p(i \rightarrow a_j)$ denoting the probability of user i selecting area a_j, and $p_i(v_j > v_k)$ representing the probability that i prefers to perform check-in on venue j over its neighbor k. Recall that U_i and V_j denote the latent feature vectors of user i and venue j respectively. We thus define $p(i \rightarrow a_j)$ as

$$p(i \rightarrow a_j) = \sum_{j' \in a_j} p(v_{j'}|i) = \sigma_{a_j}^i = \sum_{j' \in a_j} U_i^T V_{j'} \tag{12}$$

The second component of Equation 11 is defined as:

$$p_i(v_j > v_k) = S(U_i^T V_j - U_i^T V_k) \tag{13}$$

By substituting the components in Equation 11, we have:

$$
\begin{aligned}
p_{ij} &= \left(\sum_{j' \in a_j} p(v_{j'}|u_i) \right) \prod_{k \in N(v_j)} p_i(v_j > v_k) \\
&= \left(\sum_{j' \in a_j} U_i^T V_{j'} \right) \prod_{k \in N(v_j)} S(U_i^T V_j - U_i^T V_k)
\end{aligned}
\tag{14}
$$

Next, we define the log-likelihood $\mathcal{L}(C)$ of a set of check-ins C from users of U on venues of V to be as follows:

$$\mathcal{L}(C) = \sum_{(i,j) \in C} w_{ij} \log p_{ij} = L_1(C) + L_2(C) \tag{15}$$

where

$$
\begin{aligned}
L_1(C) &= \sum_{(i,j) \in C} w_{ij} \log \left(\sum_{j' \in a_j} U_i^T V_{j'} \right) \\
L_2(C) &= \sum_{(i,j) \in C} w_{ij} \sum_{k \in N(v_j)} \log S(U_i^T V_j - U_i^T V_k)
\end{aligned}
\tag{16}
$$

To learn the latent features of users and venues in VAN* model, we maximize the log-likelihood defined in Equation 15. Formally, we have the optimization problem as below:

$$\{U_i^*, V_j^*\}_{i \in U, j \in V} = \arg \max_{i \in U, j \in V} (\mathcal{L}(C) - \lambda(C)) \tag{17}$$

where $\lambda(C)$ is the regularization term that prevent overfitting [12]. In our model, we use L-2 norm for $\lambda(C)$ since it can be solved easily [12] and it is widely applied in matrix factorization method [19, 20, 26]. Formally, $\lambda(C)$ is defined as

$$\lambda(C) = \lambda_u \sum_i \|U_i\|_2^2 + \lambda_v \sum_j \|V_j\|_2^2 \tag{18}$$

where λ_u and λ_v are the regularization parameters for the latent features of users and venues respectively.

Incorporating social homophily: We model social homophily by adding a social regularizer $\lambda_f \sum_{(i,i') \in F} \|U_i - U_{i'}\|^2$ to Equation 18. In other words, if two users i and i' have social connection between them, their latent feature vectors U_i and $U_{i'}$ are expected to be similar. λ_f is the parameter which is used to control the importance of social homophily effect.

To learn the latent features of users and venues through VAN* model, we employ stochastic gradient descent algorithms (SGD) [3] which is widely adopted in matrix factorization based models [4, 10, 26].

5 EXPERIMENT

In this section, we describe our experiments on three real world datasets to evaluate our proposed model against relevant baselines. Furthermore, other intensive experiments are also conducted to illustrate the robustness of our model.

5.1 Check-in Prediction Task

In this experiment, we evaluate the performance of our model in check-in prediction task. We use three datasets **SG**, **JK** and **NYC**. For each dataset, we sort the check-ins by created time and divide them into the training and testing sets. For the purpose of check-in prediction, we consider the first check-in a user performs on a venue and ignore the subsequent the same user checks into the same venue. The user-venue pairs of these check-ins form the positive data instances. The first 80% of these check-ins forms the training set and the latter 20% forms the testing. We then need to select user-venue pairs for the negative data instances. To keep the positive and negative data instances balanced, we randomly select equal number of user-venue pairs without any check-ins as the negative data instances.

To infer the vector of user/venue context, we apply DeepWalk [27]. The dimension of embedding space of each user or venue is 64 (the default setting). The context graph of users is the social network among them. Specifically, user a connects to user b if a follows b in three datasets. To construct the graph of venues, we assume that venue a and venue b are connected if the physical distance between them is not larger than 100 meter.

Accuracy Measures. To measure the accuracy of prediction results, we use accuracy and F1-score defined by:

$$Accuracy = \frac{\# \text{ of Test Instances with Correct Predictions}}{\# \text{ of Test Instances}}$$

$$F1 = \frac{2 \times Precision \cdot Recall}{Precision + Recall}$$

where

$$Precision = \frac{\# \text{ of Correctly Predicted Check-In Test Instances}}{\# \text{ of Predicted Check-In Test Instances}}$$

$$Recall = \frac{\# \text{ of Correctly Predicted Check-In Test Instances}}{\# \text{ of Check-In Test Instances}}$$

Methods. We evaluate two variants of PACELA method. Other than the full method PACELA, we introduce a variant method PACELA$_v$ that includes only the latent attributes of venues only. We also include the following baseline methods:

- VAN: It is the first model studied neighborhood competition and area attraction [9]. In this model, we use CDF function to model the competition among venues in one area and

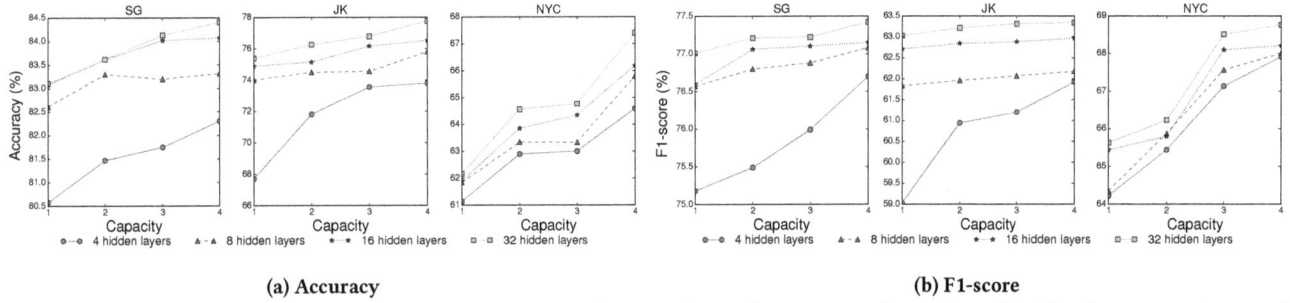

(a) Accuracy

(b) F1-score

Figure 2: The prediction performance of PACELA with different values of capacity and number of hidden layers in SG, JK and NYC datasets.

Table 2: Check-in prediction performance of PACELA and baselines. We boldface the best performance in each dataset.

	Accuracy			F1 score		
	SG	JK	NYC	SG	JK	NYC
VAN	60.74%	59.93%	55.8%	58.59%	56.66%	58.51%
VAN*	75.92%	67.92%	62.12%	68.27%	57.25%	62.45%
PACE	79.3%	66.28%	62.32%	70.84%	57.7%	65.7%
PACELA$_v$	80.1%	70.53%	62%	71.91%	60.49%	66.55%
PACELA	**82.3%**	**72.81%**	**64.59%**	**73.7%**	**61.93%**	**67.92%**

the size of area is 0.1 degree. The parameters are selected since they generated the best prediction performance [9]. The home location of users are required as input for this model so we estimate the home location of each user by his/her center of the mass of check-ined locations.

- VAN*: It is the matrix factorization model to derive the latent attributes of users and venues. To use VAN* for check-in prediction, we learn the matrices U and V from the training data. Unlike the training check-in data used in PACELA, PACELA$_v$ and PACE, we train VAN* to learn the actual check-in counts by users on venues. We then use $U_i^T V_j$ to predict for a user-venue pair (i, j). We predict a check-in for the pair if $U_i^T V_j \geq TH$ where TH is a threshold that has been set to 1, as it is the natural threshold to separate the positive from negative instances in our training data. The latent dimension size is set to 10.

- PACE: PACE method has been proposed in [37] to predict POI visitations. The method learns embedding vectors of users and venues to predict user context, venue context and check-in data in a neural network framework. As PACELA can be seen as an extension of PACE, we include it for comparison. The multi-layer neural network model of PACE requires two configuration parameters, R capacity and Q number of hidden layers. They are set to 4 and 4 respectively which are similar to PACELA.

Parameter Settings: The default configuration parameters of PACE, PACELA$_v$, and PACELA are capacity R and number of hidden layers Q with default values 4 and 4 respectively. We keep the size of user/venue embedding vector size to 10. The number of latent feature of users and venues in latent attribute modeling is set to 10. For VAN*, we set the area size to 0.1, and $\lambda_u = \lambda_v = \lambda_f = 0.01$ since this setting gives the best performance when we use the VAN* for check-in prediction task. In model training, we set the batch size as 1024, and learning rate as 0.0001.

Results. Table 2 provides the accuracy and F1-score of different methods. From the table, we observe that PACELA method outperforms all other methods across the three datasets. For instance, in the **SG** dataset, PACELA has improved 3.7% in accuracy and 4% in F1-score compared with PACE, a state-of-the-art method. We also observe the inclusion of venue latent features also enhances the accuracy of PACE. The PACELA$_v$ method using latent venue features outperforms PACE. This results show that the full PACELA method benefits from latent features from both users and venues.

5.2 Parameter Study Experiment

We next evaluate the impact of two configuration parameters R and Q to PACELA method. Recall R is the capacity which is the length of last output layer of the network while Q is the number of hidden layers. Figures 2a and 2b show the accuracy and F1-score of PACELA method respectively for different R and Q settings and for the three datasets **SG**, **JK** and **NYC**. In the experiment, we vary R between 1 to 4, and Q between 4 to 32. We seek to determine the performance impact of parameter settings to the methods. The remaining parameters are assigned their default values.

First of all, we observe that higher accuracy can be achieved by PACELA with larger Q values. The improvement however reduces as Q increases to 32. Setting the capacity R higher is also shown to improve accuracy and F1 scores. This can be due to the use of larger neural networks for prediction.

5.3 Effectiveness of Latent Attributes of Users and Venues

To gain a deeper understanding of the contribution of user and venue latent attributes, we compare the prediction loss of PACE and PACELA methods through epochs. The faster the convergence of prediction loss, the better the method is.

Experiment Setup. The parameters are set to default values as mention in Section 5.1. The number of epochs in this experiment is 100. The three methods that we include in this experiment study are PACE, PACELA$_v$ and PACELA methods.

Experiment Results. Figure 4 shows the results of the experiment on **SG**, **JK** and **NYC** datasets. As shown in the figure, we observe that.

- When the number of epochs increases, the prediction loss generally decreases. After a certain threshold, the losses become stable and converge to a fixed point.

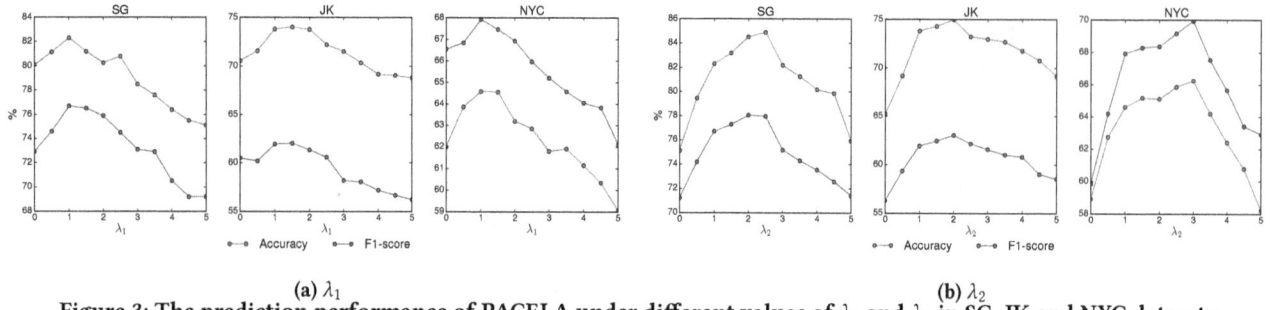

(a) λ_1 **(b)** λ_2

Figure 3: The prediction performance of PACELA under different values of λ_1 and λ_2 in SG, JK and NYC datasets.

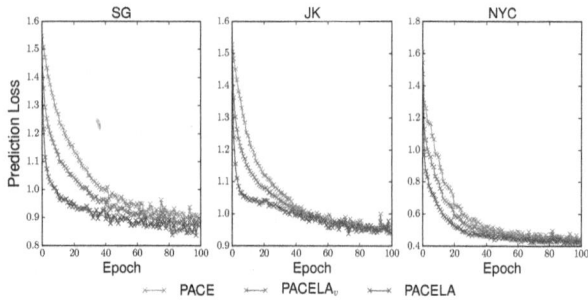

Figure 4: The prediction loss of training process in SG, JK and NYC datasets.

- The three methods seem to converge to the same stable point in the three datasets. The difference is that the stable points of **SG** and **NYC** datasets are lower than the ones of **JK** dataset. It could be explained by the fact that **JK** is sparser than **SG** and **NYC**. A deep learning method needs huge data to achieve the better training loss.

- Finally, the PACELA method extended from PACE by latent attributes of users and venues converges faster than the original model. For instance, at the epoch 10, PACELA method reaches the stable point in the **SG** dataset. The phenomenon clearly happens in the three datasets. It is a clear suggestion that the latent features are useful to enhance the performance of PACELA method.

5.4 Tuning Regularization

In this experiment, we tune the values of λ_1 and λ_2 in Equation 7 to further understand the importance of user and venue context to the PACELA model. Recall that λ_1 and λ_2 control the contribution of user context and venue context respectively to the objective function. Setting λ_1 or λ_2 to 0 means that the contribution of user context or venue context is omitted from PACELA method, while increasing λ_1 or λ_2 makes the impact of user or venue context larger to PACELA model, respectively.

Setup: We first set $\lambda_1 = 1$ and vary λ_2 from 0 to 5 with step size as 0.5 to evaluate the accuracy of check-in prediction for the PACELA method. Secondly, we repeat the experiment with λ_2 is set to 1 and λ_1 varied between 0 and 5 with step size 0.5. For other parameters, default values are used (see Section 5.1).

Result: Figures 3a and 3b illustrate the performance of the PACELA method. Our findings include:

- Using user context or venue context actually improves the accuracy of PACELA. Nevertheless, if we increase the importance of the context too much, it could harm the prediction accuracy. From both figures, we observe that if $\lambda_1 = 0$ or $\lambda_2 = 0$, PACELA yields its lowest accuracy performance. Positive λ_1 or λ_2 values give us prediction accuracy but the improvement declines as these parameters increase. For instance, increasing λ_2 from 0 to 3 improves the accuracy and F1-score of PACELA in **NYC** dataset, but when λ_2 is greater than 3, the prediction accuracy of PACELA deteriorates.

- Venue context helps to improve PACELA more than user context. Specifically, from the two figures, we observe that the peak performance of PACELA occurs when $\lambda_2 \in [2, 3]$ but $\lambda_1 \in [1, 2]$. The reason for the phenomenon is that we have more information about venues than about users. For example, the number of venues is three times larger than that of users in the **NYC** dataset.

6 CONCLUSION

In this paper, we have proposed a model to extract the latent features of users and venues in LBSN. Then, we use the learned latent features to enhance the check-in prediction performance of neural network model called *PACELA*. Through extensive experiments, we show that *PACELA* improves the check-in prediction performance and its performance is robust under different parameter settings.

There are some limitations in our model. Firstly, the temporal information plays a significant role to the decision of users but it is not covered in *PACELA*. Secondly, we simplify the movement behaviors of users by inspecting *area attraction*, *neighborhood competition* and *social homophily* but other features such as *distance effect* also contribute to the behavior. Thirdly, we want to extend *PACELA* to automatically learn the latent attributes of users and venues. Hence, these limitations will be handled in our future works to improve *PACELA* model further.

7 ACKNOWLEDGEMENT

This research is supported by the National Research Foundation, Prime Ministers Office, Singapore under its International Research Centres in Singapore Funding Initiative.

REFERENCES

[1] Lars Backstrom, Eric Sun, and Cameron Marlow. 2010. Find me if you can: improving geographical prediction with social and spatial proximity. In *WWW*.

[2] David M. Blei, Andrew Y. Ng, and Michael I. Jordan. 2003. Latent Dirichlet Allocation. *JMLR* 3 (March 2003).

[3] Stephen Boyd and Lieven Vandenberghe. 2004. *Convex Optimization*. Cambridge University Press, New York, NY, USA.

[4] Chen Cheng, Haiqin Yang, Irwin King, and Michael R Lyu. 2012. Fused Matrix Factorization with Geographical and Social Influence in Location-Based Social Networks.. In *AAAI*, Vol. 12.

[5] Eunjoon Cho, Seth A. Myers, and Jure Leskovec. 2011. Friendship and Mobility: User Movement in Location-based Social Networks. In *KDD*.

[6] Richard L Church and Alan T Murray. 2009. *Business site selection, location analysis, and GIS*. Wiley Online Library.

[7] Thanh-Nam Doan, Freddy Chong Tat Chua, and Ee-Peng Lim. 2015. Mining Business Competitiveness from User Visitation Data. In *SBP*.

[8] Thanh-Nam Doan, Freddy Chong Tat Chua, and Ee-Peng Lim. 2015. On Neighborhood Effects in Location-based Social Networks. In *WI-IAT*.

[9] Thanh-Nam Doan and Ee-Peng Lim. 2016. Attractiveness versus Competition: Towards an Unified Model for User Visitation. In *CIKM*.

[10] Thanh-Nam Doan and Ee-Peng Lim. 2017. Modeling Check-In Behavior with Geographical Neighborhood Influence of Venues. In *ADMA*.

[11] Shanshan Feng, Gao Cong, Bo An, and Yeow Meng Chee. 2017. POI2Vec: Geographical Latent Representation for Predicting Future Visitors.. In *AAAI*. 102–108.

[12] Jerome Friedman, Trevor Hastie, and Robert Tibshirani. 2001. *The elements of statistical learning*. Vol. 1. Springer series in statistics New York.

[13] Yanjie Fu, Hui Xiong, Yong Ge, Yu Zheng, Zijun Yao, and Zhi-Hua Zhou. 2016. Modeling of Geographic Dependencies for Real Estate Ranking. *ACM Transaction on Knowledge Discovery from Data (TKDD)* 11, 1 (Aug. 2016).

[14] Huiji Gao, Jiliang Tang, and Huan Liu. 2012. gSCorr: modeling geo-social correlations for new check-ins on location-based social networks. In *CIKM*.

[15] Xiangnan He, Lizi Liao, Hanwang Zhang, Liqiang Nie, Xia Hu, and Tat-Seng Chua. 2017. Neural collaborative filtering. In *Proceedings of the 26th International Conference on World Wide Web*. International World Wide Web Conferences Steering Committee, 173–182.

[16] D. L Huff. 1963. A Probabilistic Analysis of Shopping Center Trade Areas. *Land Economics* (1963), 81–90.

[17] Dmytro Karamshuk, Anastasios Noulas, Salvatore Scellato, Vincenzo Nicosia, and Cecilia Mascolo. 2013. Geo-spotting: mining online location-based services for optimal retail store placement. In *The 19th ACM SIGKDD International Conference on Knowledge Discovery and Data Mining (SIGKDD)*. 793–801.

[18] Diederik P. Kingma and Jimmy Ba. 2014. Adam: A Method for Stochastic Optimization. *CoRR* abs/1412.6980 (2014). arXiv:1412.6980 http://arxiv.org/abs/1412.6980

[19] Yehuda Koren, Robert Bell, Chris Volinsky, et al. 2009. Matrix factorization techniques for recommender systems. *Computer* 42, 8 (2009), 30–37.

[20] Daniel D Lee and H Sebastian Seung. 2001. Algorithms for non-negative matrix factorization. In *14th Advances in Neural Information Processing Systems (NIPS)*. 556–562.

[21] Rui Li, Shengjie Wang, Hongbo Deng, Rui Wang, and Kevin Chen-Chuan Chang. 2012. Towards social user profiling: unified and discriminative influence model for inferring home locations. In *KDD*.

[22] Jovian Lin, Richard Oentaryo, Ee-Peng Lim, Casey Vu, Adrian Vu, and Agus Kwee. 2016. Where is the Goldmine?: Finding Promising Business Locations through Facebook Data Analytics. In *The 27th ACM Conference on Hypertext and Social Media (HT)*. ACM, 93–102.

[23] Jovian Lin, Richard J Oentaryo, Ee-Peng Lim, Casey Vu, Adrian Vu, Agus T Kwee, and Philips K Prasetyo. 2016. A business zone recommender system based on Facebook and urban planning data. In *European Conference on Information Retrieval*. Springer, 641–647.

[24] Bin Liu, Yanjie Fu, Zijun Yao, and Hui Xiong. 2013. Learning Geographical Preferences for Point-of-interest Recommendation. In *KDD*.

[25] Xin Liu, Yong Liu, and Xiaoli Li. 2016. Exploring the Context of Locations for Personalized Location Recommendations.. In *IJCAI*. 1188–1194.

[26] Andriy Mnih and Ruslan Salakhutdinov. 2007. Probabilistic matrix factorization. In *NIPS*.

[27] Bryan Perozzi, Rami Al-Rfou, and Steven Skiena. 2014. DeepWalk: Online Learning of Social Representations. In *Proceedings of the 20th ACM SIGKDD International Conference on Knowledge Discovery and Data Mining (KDD '14)*. ACM, New York, NY, USA, 701–710.

[28] X. Quan, L. Wenyin, W. Dou, H. Xiong, and Y. Ge. 2012. Link Graph Analysis for Business Site Selection. *IEEE Computer* 45, 3 (March 2012), 64–69.

[29] Daniele Quercia and Diego Saez. 2014. Mining urban deprivation from foursquare: Implicit crowdsourcing of city land use. *IEEE Pervasive Computing* 13, 2 (2014), 30–36.

[30] Salvatore Scellato, Anastasios Noulas, and Cecilia Mascolo. 2011. Exploiting Place Features in Link Prediction on Location-based Social Networks. In *KDD*.

[31] Mikkel N Schmidt, Ole Winther, and Lars Kai Hansen. 2009. Bayesian non-negative matrix factorization. In *Independent Component Analysis and Signal Separation*. Springer, 540–547.

[32] Rodrigo Smarzaro, Tiago França Melo de Lima, and Clodoveu Augusto Davis Jr. 2017. Quality of Urban Life Index From Location-Based Social Networks Data: A Case Study in Belo Horizonte, Brazil. In *Volunteered Geographic Information and the Future of Geospatial Data*. IGI Global, 185–207.

[33] Rodrigo Smarzaro, Tiago França de Melo Lima, and Clodoveu A Davis Jr. 2017. Could Data from Location-Based Social Networks Be Used to Support Urban Planning?. In *The 26th International Conference on World Wide Web (WWW)*.

[34] Hao Wang, Naiyan Wang, and Dit-Yan Yeung. 2015. Collaborative deep learning for recommender systems. In *Proceedings of the 21th ACM SIGKDD International Conference on Knowledge Discovery and Data Mining*. ACM, 1235–1244.

[35] Suhang Wang, Yilin Wang, Jiliang Tang, Kai Shu, Suhas Ranganath, and Huan Liu. 2017. What your images reveal: Exploiting visual contents for point-of-interest recommendation. In *Proceedings of the 26th International Conference on World Wide Web*. International World Wide Web Conferences Steering Committee, 391–400.

[36] Jian Wei, Jianhua He, Kai Chen, Yi Zhou, and Zuoyin Tang. 2017. Collaborative filtering and deep learning based recommendation system for cold start items. *Expert Systems with Applications* 69 (2017), 29–39.

[37] Carl Yang, Lanxiao Bai, Chao Zhang, Quan Yuan, and Jiawei Han. 2017. Bridging Collaborative Filtering and Semi-Supervised Learning: A Neural Approach for POI Recommendation. In *Proceedings of the 23rd ACM SIGKDD International Conference on Knowledge Discovery and Data Mining (KDD '17)*. ACM, New York, NY, USA, 1245–1254. https://doi.org/10.1145/3097983.3098094

[38] Zhiyong Yu, Daqing Zhang, and Dingqi Yang. 2013. Where is the largest market: Ranking areas by popularity from location based social networks. In *Ubiquitous Intelligence and Computing, 2013 IEEE 10th International Conference on and 10th International Conference on Autonomic and Trusted Computing (UIC/ATC)*. 157–162.

[39] Shenglin Zhao, Irwin King, Michael R. Lyu, Jia Zeng, and Mingxuan Yuan. 2017. Mining Business Opportunities from Location-based Social Networks. In *The 40th International ACM SIGIR Conference on Research and Development in Information Retrieval (SIGIR)*. 1037–1040.

[40] Shenglin Zhao, Tong Zhao, Irwin King, and Michael R Lyu. 2017. Geo-teaser: Geo-temporal sequential embedding rank for point-of-interest recommendation. In *Proceedings of the 26th international conference on world wide web companion*. International World Wide Web Conferences Steering Committee, 153–162.

ReEL: Review aware Explanation of Location Recommendation

Ramesh Baral, XiaoLong Zhu, S. S. Iyengar, Tao Li
School of Computing and Information Sciences
Florida International University
Miami, FL, 33199, USA
rbara012@fiu.edu,xzhu009@fiu.edu,(iyengar,taoli)@cs.fiu.edu

ABSTRACT

The Location-Based Social Networks (LBSN) (e.g., Facebook, etc.) have many attributes (e.g., ratings, reviews, etc.) that play a crucial role for the Point-of-Interest (POI) recommendations. Unlike ratings, the reviews can help users to elaborate their consumption experience in terms of relevant factors of interest (aspects). Though some of the existing systems have exploited user reviews, most of them are less transparent and non-interpretable (as they conceal the reason behind recommendation). These reasons have motivated us towards explainable and interpretable recommendation. To the best of our knowledge, only few of the researchers have exploited user reviews to incorporate the sentiment and opinions on different aspects for personalized and explainable POI recommendation.

This paper proposes a model termed as **ReEL** (Review aware Explanation of Location Recommendation) which models the review-aspect correlation by exploiting deep neural network, formulates user-aspect bipartite relation as a bipartite graph, and models the explainable recommendation by using dense subgraph extraction and ranking-based techniques. The major contributions of this paper are: (i) it models users and POIs using the aspects posted on user reviews, and it provisions incorporation of multiple contexts (e.g., categorical, spatial, etc.) in POI recommendation, (ii) it formulates preference of users' on aspects as a bipartite relation, represents it as a location-aspect bipartite graph, and models the explainable recommendation with the notion of ordered dense subgraph extraction using bipartite cores, shingles, and ranking-based techniques, and (iii) it extensively evaluates the proposed models using three real-world datasets and demonstrates an improvement of 5.8% to 29.5% on F-score metric, when compared to the relevant studies.

KEYWORDS

Explainable Recommendation; Social Networks; Information Retrieval

ACM Reference Format:
Ramesh Baral, XiaoLong Zhu, S. S. Iyengar, Tao Li. 2018. ReEL: Review aware Explanation of Location Recommendation. In *Proceedings of 26th Conference on User Modeling, Adaptation and Personalization (UMAP '18)*. ACM, New York, NY, USA, 10 pages. https://doi.org/10.1145/3209219.3209237

1 INTRODUCTION

Most of the existing e-commerce systems (e.g., Amazon.com, etc.) have been facilitating users to share their consumption experience via ratings and reviews. The LBSNs have also been a useful platform to share consumption experiences on different factors of interest (e.g., price, service, accessibility, product quality, etc.). For instance, the review text *"The breakfast was awesome but the front-desk service was really bad"* implies a positive experience of the reviewer towards "breakfast" and opposite for "front-desk". The words "breakfast" and "front-desk" are known as **aspect terms** and their equivalent categories "Food" and "Service" are known as **aspects**. Such experiences from a real customer have been crucial in the purchase decision for potential customers, and product improvement for manufacturers.

Despite the usefulness, reading time and uniform interpretability of reviews have been a major concern. It would have been easier if one can summarize and explain the opinions on key aspects, for instance, (i) *place A has a good rating for food*, (ii) *place B is renowned for cleanliness*, etc. Though a dedicated community has been focusing on the extraction of such aspects and opinions [12, 45, 47], the recommendation domain can also use such aspect-based summarization to enhance and explain the generated recommendation.

The exploitation of different factors of LBSN for an efficient recommendation has been quite popular in the last decade [51, 55]. Most of the studies have focused on non-text attributes, such as categorical, temporal, spatial, and social [1–3, 48, 49] but have been less transparent and less interpretable (i.e. the factors used for recommendation are hidden from end users). Contrary to that, some of the studies [17, 18, 35, 36, 40, 41, 43, 57] have already claimed the user persuasiveness due to explainability in real-world systems. The similarity-based approaches [4, 23] have proposed user-based neighbor style (e.g., *"users with similar interest have purchased the following items..."*) explanations. The item-based neighbor style (e.g., *"items similar to you viewed or purchased in the past..."*), influence style (how the users' input have influenced the generation of recommendation), and keyword-style (items that have similar description content to purchase history) can be other variants of explanations.

To the best of our knowledge, only few studies have focused on review-aware explainable recommendation. There are many factors that make this problem challenging and interesting. The aspect extraction from ambiguous and noisy text, organizing the numerous aspect terms into relevant categories (e.g., food, service, etc.), and personalization of recommendation are some of the main challenges. The aspect-based personalized explanation is challenging as it needs to handle the sentiments of each aspects, and also the individual user preferences and item features to get relevant explanation.

The ease of adaptation of arbitrary continuous and categorical attributes in a scalable manner makes the Convolutional Neural Networks (CNN) a good candidate for classification problems (e.g., [13, 25]). This also makes them ideal for a supervised review-aspect classification problem. We formulate the problem of review and aspect correlation using CNNs. This simplifies the process of mapping the user sentiments to the *(POI, aspect)* tuples and modeling the users' aspect preferences as the aspect-POI bipartite relation. We represent such a bipartite relation using a bipartite graph, extract users' ordered aspect preferences using dense subgraph extraction and ranking-based methods, and generate an explainable POI recommendation. The core contributions of this paper are: (i) it models users and POIs using the aspects extracted from reviews and different contexts (e.g., categorical, spatial, etc.), (ii) it formulates the user preferences as an ordered aspect-POI bipartite relation, represents it as a bipartite graph, and proposes bipartite core, shingles, and ranking-based methods to generate personalized and explainable POI recommendation, and (iii) it evaluates the proposed model using three real-world datasets. As an important by-product, our model can implicitly identify the user communities and categorize them by their preferred aspects. It can also identify the implicit POI groups that are known for a set of aspects.

2 RELATED RESEARCH

The problem of aspect extraction from review text has been quite popular [8, 28, 52] for various problems (e.g., rating prediction [31], aspect-sentiment summarization [24, 34, 42], recommendation [30, 53], etc.). To the best of our knowledge, exploitation of aspects for explainable POI recommendation has been less explored. We present the relevant studies in following two categories:

Aspect-based approaches: Yang et al. [50] exploited sentiment lexicon (e.g., SentiWordNet)-based approach and defined user preferences based on tips, check-ins, and social relations but did not fully exploit user preferences at aspect level. Wang et al. [46] exploited multi-modal (i.e. text, image, etc.) topics-based POI semantic similarity but ignored aspect level preference modeling and recommendation explanation. Covington et al. [14] exploited different factors, such as users' activity history, demographics, etc., but did not incorporate opinions from user comments and also did not focus on recommendation for each aspect. Guo et al. [19] represented users, POIs, aspects, and geo-social relations with a graph and ranked the nodes to define the POI recommendations. Some of the studies [15] used the features extracted from user reviews to build user and item profiles and generated the recommendation. Zhang et al. [53] used the aspect opinions, social, and geographical attributes to generate the recommendation. Chen et al. [9] used aspect-based user preferences in their recommendation. Recently, Zheng et al. [58] adapted [13] to exploit user reviews and mapped user and item feature vectors into same space to estimate user-item rating. Our model has following advantages than [58]: (i) it uses sentiment polarity of reviews at sentence level rather than the whole review text, (ii) it learns to classify each review sentence into aspects and models users and places using these aspects and embedding of additional contexts (e.g., POI category, check-in time, etc.),

and (iii) it efficiently exploits a bipartite core extraction, shingles extraction, and ranking-based methods to extract densely connected aspects and relevant POIs for an explainable recommendation.

Explanation-based approaches: Chen et al. [11] personalized ranking based tensor factorization model and used phrase-level sentiment analysis across multiple categories. They extracted aspect-sentiment pairs from review text and used Bayesian Personalized Ranking [38] to rank the features from user reviews. Finally, feature wise preference of a user was derived using the user-item-feature cube and rank of the feature obtained earlier. Zhang et al. [56] used matrix factorization to estimate the missing values and a recommendation was made by matching the most favorite features of a user and properties of items. They used simple text templates to generate a feature-based explanation of positive and negative recommendations. However, incorporation of additional features (e.g., POI category) was not explored. Lawlor et al. [27] exploited sentiment-based approach to explain why a place might(not) be interesting to a user. For each aspect, they compared the recommended place to the alternatives and provided explanation (e.g., better (worse) than 90% (20%) of alternatives for *room quality* (*price*), etc.). However, they relied on frequency of aspects of POIs and users to get such relation and incorporation of additional features remained unexplored. He et al. [21] exploited tri-partite modeling of user-item-aspect tuples and used graph-based ranking to find the most relevant aspects of a user that match with relevant aspects of places. The common relevant aspects were used in the explanation. Li et al. [10] proposed an explanation interface to explain the tradeoff properties within a set of recommendations, in terms of their static specifications and feature sentiments. However, their interface requires users to explicitly provide their preference on different aspects.

We have found that only few of the existing studies have fused few additional attributes (e.g., social), whereas most of them had no provision for them. Most of the studies were tightly coupled to aspects and their sentiments, and analyzed influence of all aspects together. The influence of aspects among each other can have adverse impact on recommendation quality, for e.g., a place that is good in "Price" aspect might be opposite in "Service" aspect. A user who just cares about "Price" aspect might ignore some "Service" related problems in that place. So we need to minimize the influence of aspects among each other. This is crucial for aspect-based recommendation systems, and to the best of our knowledge, this direction is less explored and is still a viable research problem. We attempt to fill this gap by exploiting bipartite graph and dense subgraph extraction techniques. For a user, the most dense subgraph represents the set of most preferred aspects and places popular for those aspects. The dense subgraph extraction is followed by disconnecting the edges within the dense subgraph which ensures less interference from the aspects already discovered in previous dense subgraphs. This claim is also supported by our evaluation where one of our model **ReEL-Core** performs better than our another model **ReEL-Rank** (see Sec. 4.1, Sec. 4.3, and Sec. 5 for detail).

3 METHODOLOGY

The overview of proposed system is illustrated in Figure 1. The core components of the proposed system are as follows:

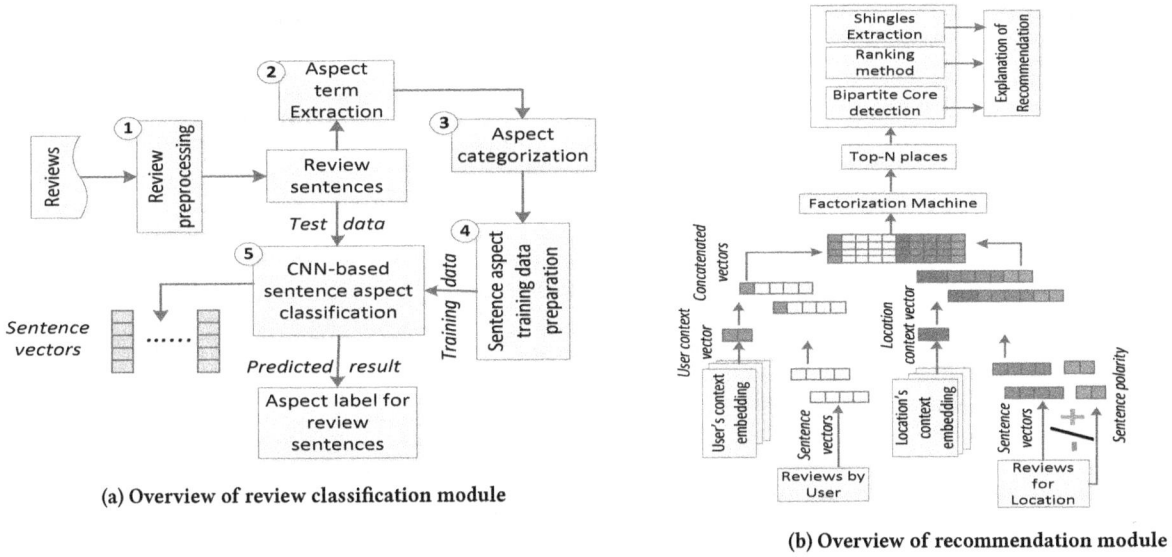

(a) Overview of review classification module

(b) Overview of recommendation module

Figure 1: High level overview of system architecture

(1) **Review preprocessing**: The review texts are splitted into individual sentences and the stop words are removed.

(2) **Aspect term extraction**: The pre-processed review sentences are fed to the aspect extraction module to extract aspect terms. A simple two-step process is applied. First, we filter out nouns and noun phrases using some experimentally set frequency threshold. Most of the reviews focus on a set of topics, hence this approach can capture such topics [33]. Second, we use a rule-based approach [54] that adopts the dependency parsing [29] to capture the aspect terms missed in the previous step.

(3) **Aspect-categorization**: As there can be numerous aspect terms, we narrow down them to few well-known aspects (see Table 2b) for easy computation. The aspect terms and their synsets from WordNet [16] are used to assign the best matching aspect. We select top 3 synsets to handle ambiguity of aspect terms and to capture the relevant aspect.

(4) **Sentence-aspect training data preparation**: As the aspect extraction and labeling is not the core focus of this paper, we rely on supervised sentence-aspect classification concept. The review text (after aspect term extraction) is labeled by the aspect that has closest match to its aspect terms. The distance between aspect terms and the aspects (and their synonyms) from the WordNet [16] are used to assign the closest possible label. As we assign top 3 matching synsets, a single aspect term can have three matching aspects. The sentences with multiple aspect terms get multiple label. This labeled data is used to train the CNN-based sentence-aspect classifier. The performance of this module is defined in the evaluation section (see Section 5).

(5) **CNN-based sentence-aspect classifier**: The review-aspect correlation module is a multi-class classifier (see Figure 1a) that classifies a review sentence into relevant aspects. Inspired from [25], we use a CNN-based classifier to label each review sentence. The network consists of a convolution, an activation function, a max-pooling, a dense layer, and a softmax layer (see [25] for detail). The input to this classifier is word embedding of review sentences. We use Word2Vec [32] to map every word to a uniform size vector in a latent feature space. The outcome of the classifier is a bipartite relation between review and the aspects.

For every user, the classifier gives a set of sentence feature vectors (later known as *user feature vectors*) that are embedding of her preferred aspects. Similarly, for every POI, the sentence feature vectors (later known as *POI feature vectors*) are embeddings of the aspects specified in its reviews. As every user tends to mention some opinion on preferred aspects in her reviews and every place is mentioned about the aspects it was reviewed for, such vectors incorporate the aspects relevant to users and POIs. As a POI can be positively or negatively reviewed for an aspect, we extract the sentiments of each review sentence by using the trigrams around the aspect terms. The embeddings of the sentiment term [32] is concatenated to the POI feature vector. As each POI can get multiple reviews on same aspect, the POI feature vector is normalized on feature vectors of each aspect. This review-aspect bipartite relation is then used to define the POI-aspect tuples and user-aspect tuples. Such a bipartite relation can be exploited to model user preferences via ordered aspect-POI relation using bipartite graph and dense subgraphs of such graph (see Sec. 4.1, and Sec. 4.3 for details). The POI-aspect pair is supplemented with the aggregated sentiment extracted from all the review sentences.

(6) **Recommendation generation**: This variant of proposed model is termed as **D**eep **A**spect-based **P**OI recommender (**DAP**). Besides the review text, we also incorporate additional context (e.g., categorical, spatial, etc.) into the feature vector of the POIs obtained from the classifier.

We formulate the recommendation problem as a matrix, whose rows represent a user, POI, and elements of different contexts. For each row, the check-in flag of a user to a POI is treated as the target. For instance, if a user u_i has feature vector as $\langle ue_1, ue_2, ..., ue_m \rangle$, a place l_j has its sentiment concatenated feature vector as $\langle le_1, le_2, ..., le_n \rangle$, and the user u_i has visited the place l_j, then a row in the design matrix is obtained simply by concatenating the user feature vector, POI feature vector, and context vectors, and is defined as: $\overrightarrow{u_i, l_j, f_k} = \langle u_i e_1, u_i e_2, ..., u_i e_m, l_j e_1, l_j e_2, ..., l_j e_n, f_k e_1, f_k e_2, ... f_k e_o, 1 \rangle$, where $u_i e_a$, $l_j e_a$, and $f_k e_a$ are the ath item (a real-valued number) of the feature vector of user (u_i), place (l_j), and context (f_k). The last element 1 represents the check-in flag for user-place-context tuple in the training data and represents the score to be estimated on test data. For a user u, the context vector is concatenation of temporal, spatial, categorical, and social vectors: $\langle v_{t_1}, v_{t_2}, v_{t_3} \rangle$, $\langle v_{dist_1}, v_{dist_2}, v_{dist_3} \rangle$, $\langle v_{cat_1}, v_{cat_2}, ..., v_{cat_k} \rangle$, and $\langle v_{soc} \rangle$. v_{cat_1} is the multiplication of embedding vector of category cat_1 and the factor $r_{cat_1} = (\sum_{l.cat=cat_1} V_u(l))/(\sum_{l' \in u_L} V_u(l))$ (i.e. the ratio of total check-ins made to places with category cat_1 to that of all check-ins). $v_{dist_1} = (\sum_{dist(l) \leq \epsilon_1} V_u(l))/(\sum_{l' \in u_L} V_u(l'))$ is ratio of total check-ins on places within a threshold distance ϵ_1 (from users' home, work place or most frequently checked-in place) to that of all check-ins (we consider $\epsilon_1 \leq 1, 1 < \epsilon_2 \leq 5, \epsilon_3 > 5$ as three distance thresholds (in K.M.)). $v_{soc} = (\sum_{l \in u_{f_L}} V_u(l))/(\sum_{l' \in u_L} V_u(l'))$ is the ratio of total check-ins made on places visited due to social influence to that of all check-ins. v_{t_1} is the ratio of total check-ins made in time t_1 (we use three values for time - morning, afternoon, and others (night and evening)). The POI context vector consists of category, time, and distance vectors.

A factorization machine [37] is exploited to estimate the value of the check-in flag for every user-place-context tuple. As the factorization machine has the ability to deal with additional features, a user-place pair can have multiple rows but just one row for each user-place-context tuple. So, the prediction is already personalized for the user-place-context tuple. The top-N scorers from factorization machine are further filtered out using the preferred aspects of user (determined by the frequency of aspects mentioned on her reviews) and are recommended to the users. The high-level overview of the recommendation module is illustrated in Figure 1b.

(7) Explanation of recommendation: After getting the place-aspect bipartite relation from CNN-based classifier, we represent the user-aspect preference as a bipartite graph and generate the recommendation explanation by extracting the most dense subgraphs from this bipartite graph. We propose three different methods- a bipartite core extraction, shingles extraction, and ranking-based methods for explanation generation (see Sec. 4 for detail).

3.1 Factorization Machine

The Factorization Machine [37] formulates the prediction problem as a design matrix $X \in \mathbb{R}^{n \times p}$. The ith row $\vec{x}_i \in \mathbb{R}^p$ of the design matrix defines a case with p real-valued variables. The main goal is to predict the target variable $\hat{y}(\vec{x})$ using Eqn. 1. The proposed recommendation module is formulated as a sparse matrix. The rows of the matrix are generated by concatenating the embeddings of a user feature vector, POI feature vector, and context vector. We consider the check-in flag as the target variable for each row. The proposed model is operated with the following objective function:

$$\hat{y}(\vec{x}) = w_0 + \sum_{i=1}^{n} w_i x_i + \sum_{i=1}^{n} \sum_{j=i+1}^{n} < \vec{v}_i, \vec{v}_j > x_i x_j, \quad (1)$$

where w_0 is the global bias of all user-POI-context tuples, $\vec{x}$ is a concatenation of user feature vector, POI feature vector, and context vector, n is the size of input variables, $< \vec{v}_i, \vec{v}_j > = \sum_{f=1}^{k} v_{i,f} . v_{j,f}$, and k is the dimensionality of factorization. The Factorization Machine can learn latent factors for all the variables, and can also allow the interactions between all pairs of variables. This makes them an ideal candidate to model complex relationships in the data.

4 EXPLANATION OF RECOMMENDATION

The POI-aspect bipartite relation derived from Sec. 3 is represented as a bipartite graph and the ordered preference of user on aspect categories is extracted and used for explanation.

4.1 Bipartite Core Extraction (ReEL-Core)

A k-core of a graph is a maximal connected subgraph whose every vertex is connected to at least k other vertices. The k-core analysis is popular for community detection, dense subgraph extraction, and in dynamic graphs. Our method for bipartite core detection is inspired from [26] where each node is assigned two scores - hub score and authority score, which are defined in terms of the outgoing and incoming edges respectively. The hub score (h_i) of a node is proportional to the sum of authority scores of the nodes it links to. The authority score (a_i) of a node is proportional to the sum of hub scores of the nodes it is linked from. Given the initial authority and hub scores of all the nodes, the scores are iteratively updated until the graph converges. For a given user, we consider all the recommended places as the seed nodes and connect them to the aspect nodes for which they have overall positive sentiments (i.e. (no. of positive opinions)> (no. of negative opinions)). This filters out the negatively reviewed places and gives us a bipartite graph as shown in Fig 2a (left graph).

We calculate the eigenvectors of the adjacency matrix of the graph to identify the primary eigenpair (largest eigenvalue). The eigenvalue is used as a measure of the density of links in the graph. The iterative algorithm gives the largest eigenvalue (primary eigenpair). The primary eigenpair corresponds to the primary bipartite core (most prevalent set of POI-aspect pairs) and non-primary eigenpairs correspond to the secondary bipartite cores (less prevalent set of POI-aspect pairs). The most dense subgraph (e.g., the right subgraph in Figure 2a with nodes AC_1, P_1, P_2, and P_3) is extracted as the primary bipartite core. After finding the primary core, the edges relevant to this core are removed and the process is repeated

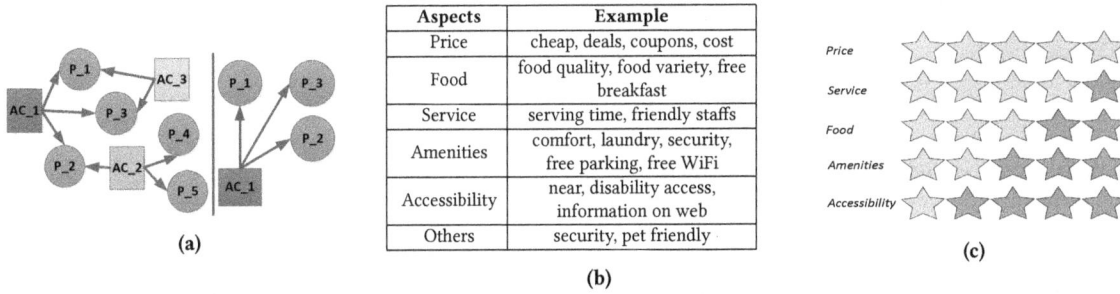

Aspects	Example
Price	cheap, deals, coupons, cost
Food	food quality, food variety, free breakfast
Service	serving time, friendly staffs
Amenities	comfort, laundry, security, free parking, free WiFi
Accessibility	near, disability access, information on web
Others	security, pet friendly

(a)   (b)   (c)

Figure 2: (a) Place Aspect Graph (AC_k = aspect k, P_i = places) (Left subgraph is a bipartite graph and the right one is a primary bipartite core), (b) Aspects, and (c) Aspect score to star ratings for a POI

on residual graph to get the next prevalent bipartite cores. Removal of edges from the primary core will still leave the nodes relevant to other aspect nodes that belong to other bipartite cores. The bipartite cores are used in the order (primary, secondary, etc.) and the aspects in bipartite cores are used to explain the recommendation.

Explanation generation: A bipartite core consists of densely connected nodes and resembles the set of place nodes which are mostly known for the relevant aspect nodes. For a user, we generate the POI-aspect relations from the ordered bipartite cores as:
Aspect 1: $POI_1, POI_2, ..., POI_i$
Aspect 2: $POI_i, POI_j, ..., POI_{j+k}$
.....
Aspect k: $POI_1, POI_i, ..., POI_j$,
where each row gives the aspect from the ordered bipartite core and the relevant set of POIs that are popular for that aspect. We also generate the score of each POI_i on each aspect as:
Aspect 1: $Score_{i,1}$
Aspect 2: $Score_{i,2}$
.....
Aspect k: $Score_{i,k}$,
where $Score_{l,a}$ represents the score of POI_l by the aspect a for all users, and is defined as: $Score_{l,a} = \sum_{i=1}^{k} \frac{1}{i} * |core_{l,a,i}|$, where the term $|core_{l,a,i}|$ represents the number of times the POI_l was in i^{th} bipartite core for the aspect a on all users, and k represents the ordered number of bipartite cores used (e.g., k=1 is for primary bipartite core, k=2 for secondary core, and so on). The scores computed are interpolated to the 5-star rating scheme (see Figure 2c). As an example, the review text "*Tasty free hot breakfast and friendly staffs*", implies that the reviewer cares about the **"Price"** and **"Service"** aspects, and a primary bipartite core for this user should contain these aspects and relevant places. Given the place "Hyatt Regency" and "The Setai Miami Beach" have overall positive opinions for the "Price" aspect, they are included in the primary bipartite core (i.e. related to "Price") and the explanation is generated graphically as shown in Figure 2c and is supplemented with text as:
Recommended Place: Hyatt Regency, The Setai Miami Beach, ...;
Explanation: Popular for Price.

4.2 Dense subgraph extraction (ReEL-Dense)

This model exploits the weight of user-aspect and place-aspect relation to incorporate the extent of user preferences on aspects and the popularity information of a place through the aspects.

Figure 3a shows a basic representation of the network and extraction of dense subgraphs. The POI-aspect edge is weighted by the normalized measure of frequency of overall positive opinions on the aspect for the POI. The user-aspect edge is weighted by the normalized measure of number of times the user reviewed on the aspect. We exploit the random extraction of connected components from the network and proceed with the components having high similarity score. If γ is a random permutation applied on the homogeneous sets A and B (e.g., set A has only user nodes and set B has only aspect nodes), then their similarity score is defined as:

$$Sim^{\gamma}(A, B) = \frac{f(A, B)}{f(A) + f(B)} \quad (2)$$

where $f(A, B) = \sum_{\substack{a \in A, b \in B \\ (a,b) \in E}} W_{a,b}$, where $W_{a,b}$ is the weight of edge (a,b) that is normalized to all the edges outgoing from node a, $f(A) = \sum_{(a,i) \in E} W_{a,i}$ is the sum of normalized weights of all edges outgoing from node a, and $f(B) = \sum_{(i,b) \in E} W_{i,b}$ is the sum of normalized weights of all edges incidence on node b. We assume that absence of POI-aspect edge indicates that the place is not known for that aspect (e.g., the aspect is irrelevant). We can use the min-wise independent permutations [6, 7] technique to avoid exploitation on each and every permutation to find the sets with high similarity score. We use some predefined number of permutations (c=10) and do not focus on the min-wise independence of permutations. Algorithm 1

Algorithm 1 ShingleFinder(G = (V,E), c, s, k)

1: //G is the input graph, V is the set of vertices, and E is the set of edges, c is the number of permutations, s is the length of each set, k is the number of shingles to be extracted
2: initialize L as an empty list
3: **for** each place node **do**
4:     **for** j = 1 to c **do**
5:         get a set of s aspect nodes
6:         find aggregated similarity for the place and aspect nodes in this set using Eqn. 2
7:         store this set and its score in L
8: return k sets with high similarity score (*these sets are called shingles*) from L

---

defines shingles extraction process from a bipartite graph. For each POI, we apply Algorithm 1 to find the set of aspect nodes linked to it and extract the k shingles for it. For each shingle, we find the list of all POI nodes that contain it. These are the POIs that are mostly reviewed for the aspect nodes contained in the shingle (see Figure 3a). As shingles can contain overlapping set of aspects, it can represent the POIs and user preferences of overlapping aspects as well. The shingles of a user node represent the set of aspects that adhere to her preferences (the preference can be ordered based on the similarity score of a user node to the shingles). As our goal is to cluster (user, POI) tuples, we need to find the sets of user and POI nodes that share sufficiently large number of shingles. Each shingle contains the associated aspects which relates users and POIs. We can easily find the top n_u users and top n_l POIs whose similarity score is high for this shingle. The overall process can be achieved in polynomial time [6, 7] and is dependent on the number of nodes in the graph, number of shingles to use, and the size of a shingle. The normalized similarity score between a POI_l and an aspect (a) from all shingles is defined as:

$$Score(l, a) = \frac{1}{|Sh|} \sum_{a \in Sh} \frac{1}{k} sim^Y(l, Sh), \qquad (3)$$

where Sh is the set of ordered shingles that contain aspect a, and k is the similarity-based order of the relevant shingle. This score is interpolated to the 5-star rating scheme similar to ReEL-Core.

Finding the subsets of aspects with highest similarity score not only facilitates explanation of recommendation but also provisions clustering of users who have similar preferences on aspects (even in absence of explicit social links) and generating a group recommendation. It can also be used to generate preference wise recommendation (e.g., for the set of users $\{u_1, u_2, u_5\}$ the set of aspects {"food", "service"} might be interesting, for the set of users $\{u_1, u_2, u_3\}$ the set of aspects {"food", "price"} might be interesting, etc.). This can also facilitate the clustering of POIs that are preferred for similar aspects (e.g., the set of hotels that are popular for "Service").

4.3 Ranking Method (ReEL-Rank)

This model uses the frequency of usage of an aspect to a place. The places recommended to a user and the places' relevant aspects are used as graph nodes. The weight of a place-aspect edge indicates the overall positive opinions on the place for the aspect. A ranking function is then defined as:

$$Rank(i) = \frac{1-d}{N} + d * \sum_{(j, i) \in E} \frac{Rank(j) * W_{j,i}}{O_j}, \qquad (4)$$

where Rank(i) is the rank of a node i, d (=0.85) is the damping factor, N is number of nodes in the graph, E is set of edges in the graph, $W_{j,i}$ is weight of the edge (j, i), and O_j is number of outgoing links from node j. The ranks are iteratively updated till the graph is converged. The highest ranking aspect node and its highest ranking neighbors give the places that are noted for this aspect. Similarly, other higher ranking aspect nodes and their neighbors are accessed to get the other place-aspect pairs. For a given aspect, the neighbor nodes are sorted based on their rank before the explanation is generated. An explanation of the following form is generated: (i) *Food*: Places ordered by rank: Place 1, Place 2, ...(ii) *Service*: Places ordered by rank: Place 4, Place 5, ..., etc. The rank of a place on an aspect is aggregated from all the users to get the star rating score.

---
1 https://www.yelp.com/dataset_challenge   2 Wang et al. [44]   3 http://insideairbnb.com/get-the-data.html
4 explicitly missing ratings, neutral, and zero ratings are not shown

Attributes	Yelp[1]	TripAdvisor[2]	AirBnB[3]
Reviews	2,225,213	246,399	570,654
Users	552,339	148,480	472,701
Places	77,079	1,850	26,734
Words	302,979,760	43,273,874	54,878,077
Sentences	18,972,604	2,167,783	284,1004
Avgerage Sentences/review	8.53	8.79	4.98
Avgerage Words/review	136.15	175.62	96.16
Avgerage Reviews/user	4.03	1.66	1.20
Avgerage Reviews/place	28.87	133.18	21.34
4, 5 stars[4]	591,618 and 900,940	78,404 and 104,442	479,842
1, 2 stars	260,492 and 190,048	15,152 and 20,040	5,766

Table 1: Statistics of the datasets

5 EVALUATION

We defined four models: (i) **DAP** - the model that used a deep network and factorization machine for recommendations and has no provision for explanation, (ii) **ReEL-Core** - the model that used bipartite core, (iii) **ReEL-Dense** - the model that used dense subgraph extraction, and (iv) **ReEL-Rank** - the model that used a ranking approach for explanation generation. We also evaluated the Aspect extraction, Aspect categorization, Sentence-aspect classification modules in terms of accuracy.

(1) Aspect extraction: We used the SemEval 2014 Task 4: Aspect Based Sentiment Analysis Annotation dataset as the benchmark data and were able to get an accuracy of 70.04%.

(2) Aspect categorization: We got an accuracy of 67.12% with the SemEval 2014 Task 4: Aspect Based Sentiment Analysis Annotation dataset.

(3) Sentence-aspect classification: We used 100, 150, and 200 epochs with 32 and 64 batches. With 200 epochs and 64 batches, we got 69.01% accuracy on Yelp dataset.

We compared the performance of our proposed models with the following models: (1) UCF [22] uses the user-based collaborative filtering technique, (2) ICF [39] uses item-based collaborative filtering, (3) PPR [20] uses personalized page ranking, (4) Guo et al. [19] uses aspect-aware POI recommendation, (5) ORec [53] uses opinion-based POI recommendation, (6) *Word-embedding approach*: In this approach, the review sentences from a user and the one for an item are mapped to a latent space using the word embedding [32]. For a user, the K-nearest neighbors in the space were considered as the top-K recommendations, (7) *Latent Dirichlet Allocation approach* [5]: In this model, we extract the topics relevant to a user and the topics relevant to places. The user-place tuples with most common topics are used for the recommendation, and (8) *DeepConn* [58]: This is the CNN-based model which uses the review embeddings but ignores the other contextual embedding and the polarity of reviews.

5.1 Dataset

We used three real-world datasets to evaluate the proposed models. Table 1 shows that in all three datasets, most of the users tend to give high (positive) ratings to the places. The top-10 terms of different aspects are illustrated in Table 3b.

Experimental settings We used a 5-fold cross validation to evaluate the models. The frequency thresholds for noun and noun

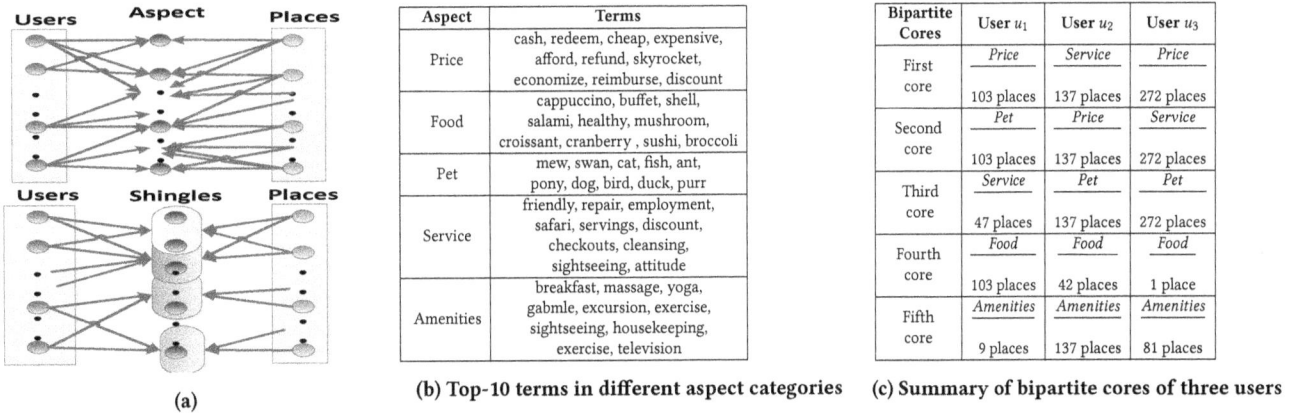

Aspect	Terms
Price	cash, redeem, cheap, expensive, afford, refund, skyrocket, economize, reimburse, discount
Food	cappuccino, buffet, shell, salami, healthy, mushroom, croissant, cranberry , sushi, broccoli
Pet	mew, swan, cat, fish, ant, pony, dog, bird, duck, purr
Service	friendly, repair, employment, safari, servings, discount, checkouts, cleansing, sightseeing, attitude
Amenities	breakfast, massage, yoga, gabmle, excursion, exercise, sightseeing, housekeeping, exercise, television

(b) Top-10 terms in different aspect categories

Bipartite Cores	User u_1	User u_2	User u_3
First core	*Price* 103 places	*Service* 137 places	*Price* 272 places
Second core	*Pet* 103 places	*Price* 137 places	*Service* 272 places
Third core	*Service* 47 places	*Pet* 137 places	*Pet* 272 places
Fourth core	*Food* 103 places	*Food* 42 places	*Food* 1 place
Fifth core	*Amenities* 9 places	*Amenities* 137 places	*Amenities* 81 places

(c) Summary of bipartite cores of three users

Figure 3: (a) Shingles extraction (shown without edge weights), (b) Top-terms in different categories, (c) bipartite cores

Models	Precision	Recall	F-Score
Yelp Data			
UCF [22]	0.23000	0.56800	0.32741
ICF [39]	0.20100	0.51000	0.28835
PPR [20]	0.23640	0.57000	0.33420
Guo et al. [19]	0.52000	0.77420	0.62213
ORec [53]	0.50030	0.61000	0.54973
LDA [5]	0.50160	0.48280	0.49200
Embedding [30]	0.50020	0.71250	0.58780
DeepConn [58]	0.50510	0.79350	0.61720
DAP	0.61550	0.89630	0.72980
ReEL-Core	**0.71680**	**0.89960**	**0.79780***
ReEL-Rank	0.67740	0.88420	0.76710
ReEL-Dense	0.67310	0.87940	0.76250
TripAdvisor Data			
UCF [22]	0.30000	0.55700	0.38996
ICF [39]	0.25000	0.52000	0.33766
PPR [20]	0.35000	0.58000	0.43656
Guo et al. [19]	0.55000	0.77430	0.64315
ORec [53]	0.51000	0.65130	0.57205
LDA [5]	0.50000	0.79680	0.61440
Embedding [30]	0.57110	0.79710	0.66540
DeepConn [58]	0.56340	**0.87810**	0.68640
DAP	0.61310	0.79880	0.69370
ReEL-Core	**0.63880**	0.83410	**0.72350***
ReEL-Rank	0.63660	0.81120	0.71330
ReEL-Dense	0.62540	0.79980	0.70190
AirBnB Data			
UCF [22]	0.23200	0.56500	0.32893
ICF [39]	0.20200	0.50000	0.28775
PPR [20]	0.24700	0.56000	0.34280
Guo et al. [19]	0.54000	0.76100	0.63173
ORec [53]	0.52700	0.60200	0.56201
LDA [5]	0.50000	0.59480	0.54330
Embedding [30]	0.61640	0.62430	0.62030
DeepConn [58]	0.60010	0.68320	0.63890
DAP	0.59720	0.78450	0.67810
ReEL-Core	**0.62160**	**0.81830**	**0.70650***
ReEL-Rank	0.61610	0.80730	0.69880
ReEL-Dense	0.60770	0.79700	0.68960

(a) Performance of different models(* $\Rightarrow$ statistically significant at 95% confidence interval)

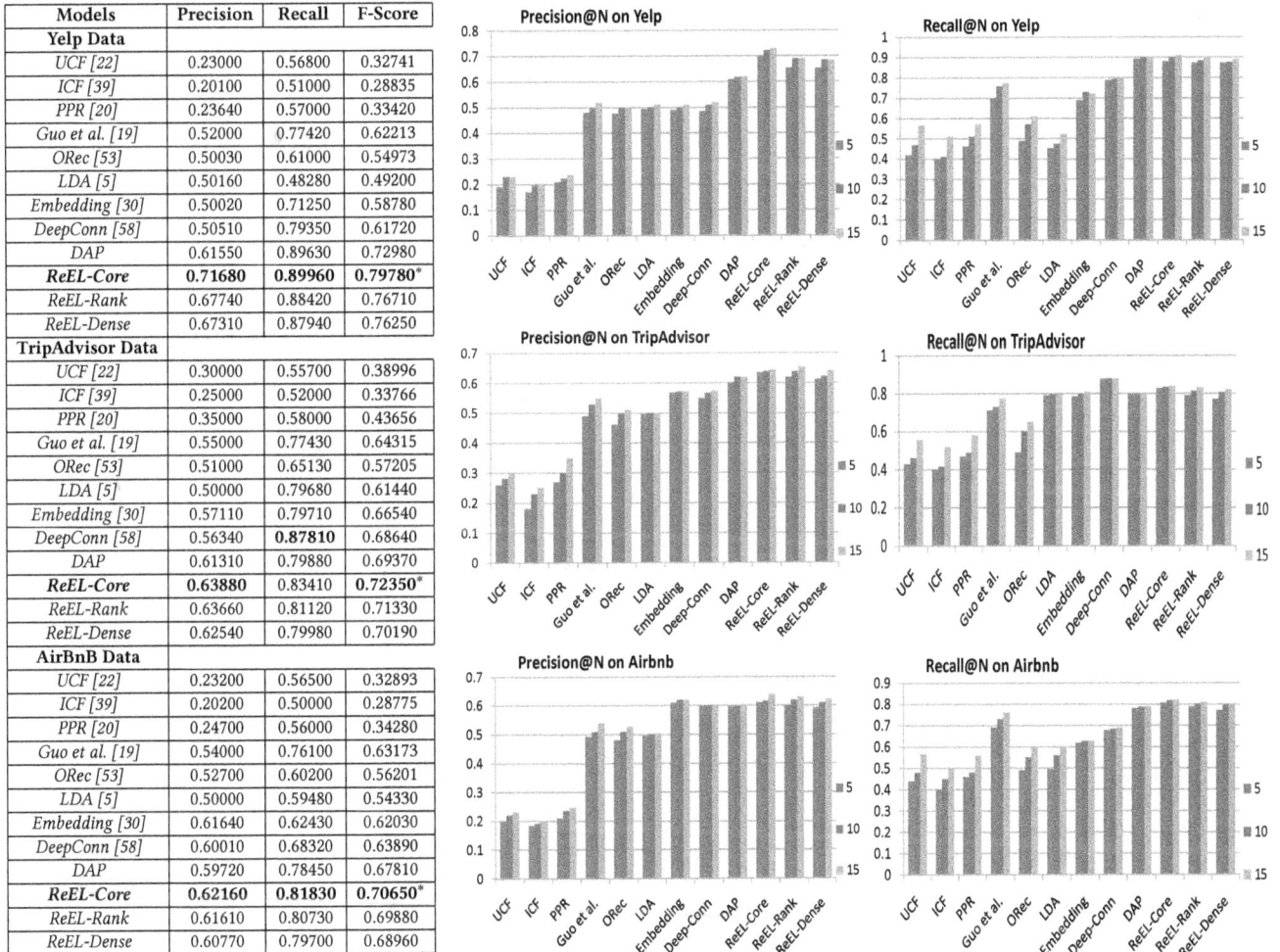

(b) Precision@N and Recall@N of different models

Figure 4: (a) Average performance of different models (b) Precision@N and Recall@N of different models

phrase extraction were set to 100, 250, and 500. Our experimental analysis show better results with 100. The CNN used 128 filters, 64 batches, 200 epochs, and embedding vectors of size 384. We used an Ubuntu 14.04.5 LTS, 32 GB RAM, a Quadcore Intel(R) Core(TM) i7-3820 CPU @ 3.60 GHz machine. We used the same configuration with Tesla K20c 6 GB GPU to evaluate neural network-based models.

5.2 Experimental Results and Discussion

We used the reviews of users and places with at least five reviews. We used a 5-fold cross validation and the precision (p), recall (r), and f-score (2*p*r/(p+r)) metrics for evaluation. We considered the top @5, @10, @15, and @20 recommended items for the evaluation. The evaluation of different models is shown in Table 4a. The Precision@N and Recall@N of different models is shown in Figure 4b.

The results show that the ICF performed least, UCF and PPR performed on par, model from Guo et al. [19] performed better than ORec [53], LDA [5], and Embedding [30] models. Among the ones without explanation, **DAP** performed best on the Yelp dataset. Though it outperformed in other two datasets as well, the difference was not significant. This implies that for larger datasets, the performance of the proposed model is outstanding. This is common with DNNs which need a reasonably large training data for better performance. The recall of DeepConn [58] was higher than that of **DAP** in the TripAdvisor dataset but its precision was lower. This might be because of the sentence-level sentiment which was exploited in DAP but not in DeepConn [58].

Unlike **DAP**, which provided a single list of recommendations and selected top@N POIs from the list, the **ReEL-Core** and **ReEL-Rank** produced individual lists for each aspect, and outperformed **DAP** because they categorized recommendations into different aspect categories which led to the re-ordering of the items into small recommendation lists. This re-ordering can help increase the number of true positives and decrease the false positives, as the least preferred items might move to the later part of the recommended lists and the more preferred ones move to the front part of the lists. The **ReEL-Core** outperformed **ReEL-Rank** and **ReEL-Dense**. One reason is due to the repeated bipartite core extraction by **ReEL-Core** where the nodes got re-ranked for every bipartite core but the **ReEL-Rank** only ranked all the nodes just once. After having the ordered set of places within each aspect, having an explanation of type similar to [27] (i.e. place A is better than 80% of places for "Food", etc.) can be achieved by counting the number of places behind the target place in the recommended list.

5.3 Evaluation of Explainability

For a place p, the aspect popularity of an aspect a can be defined in terms of the number of positive and negative mentions:

$$AspectPopularity(p_a) = \sum_{sentence \in Review_p} (| positive | a- | negative | a). \quad (5)$$

To check the presence of correct aspects in the explanation, we ordered the aspects of every place based on the aspect popularity score. We used a trigram across the extracted aspects to identify the sentiment polarity of the aspects. The relevant aspects were ordered by the aspect popularity score. So, a place can be represented by the set of aspects ordered by the popularity: $p_a = \{a_1, a_2, .., a_n\}$. For every explanation, we took the aspects for which a place was recommended. The aspects were ordered based on the order of cores (primary, secondary, etc.). This gave us another set of aspects for

every place. The performance of explainability was then measured in terms of Levenshtein distance between the lists. The average Levenshtein distance across all places was observed to be 20%.

5.4 Impact of Explanation- A Case Study

We analyzed the role of **ReEL-Core**, using the top-5 bipartite cores (see Table 3c) extracted for three users - "7iigQ2XM-V0ciwmCIdrIBA", "7Mg6r6g7RUwQH_Bllrd-wQ", and "9HDElil2309UajBgtYcD4w", hereafter called as u_1 and u_2, and u_3 respectively. We can see that the ordered preferences of user u_1 are "Price", "Pet", "Service", "Food", and "Amenities". This implies the highest preference of u_1 on "Price", regardless of the order of POIs recommended.

For user u_1, the POI "NK3S3U6TQtysH_-eqT3bBQ" was the second highly recommended place by regular recommender. With the **ReEL-Core**, it is categorized into "Others" bipartite core - *the sixth core*. If the user really cares about other cores (i.e. related to other aspect categories) then having it in sixth core is better than having it in front list. The least recommended POI "p9Bl3BxPltz2WnIxJLnBvw" by simple recommender is now categorized as the least popular item for the primary bipartite core (i.e. related to "Price"), and three other secondary cores (i.e. related to "Service", "Pet", and "Food"). Many POIs ranked in the later part of the list by the simple recommenders are found within top-20 of the different bipartite cores. Have this user used the simple recommendation, and considered only the top-20 recommendations, then these items would have been missed. A sample explanation for user u_1 is the ordered set of places taken from the ordered bipartite cores:

Recommendation: (1) Place 1, Place 2,...; **Explanation**: Popular for Price. (2) Place 3, Place 4,...; **Explanation**: Popular for Service.

Similarly, the place "v4iA8kusUrB19y2QNOiUbw" that was most recommended item for user u_2 by the simple recommender is categorized to sixth bipartite core (i.e. "Others"). The place "HxP-pZSY6Q1eARuiahhra6A" that did not fit in top-20 of simple recommender is found in the sixth position of first three bipartite cores. The location "mh1le9QGMrZLohAjfheJJg" which was the second least recommended by simple recommender is categorized as the second least preferred item for the first five bipartite core (i.e. "Service", "Price", "Pet", "Food", and "Amenities"). A similar analysis observed for 500 other users is skipped due to space constraint.

6 CONCLUSION AND FUTURE WORK

We formulated user-aspect bipartite relation as a bipartite graph and exploited bipartite-core, shingles, and ranking-based techniques to predict the ordered aspect preferences of users for explainable recommendation. The proposed models supplemented with explanations outperformed the ones without explanation, and gained significant improvement (e.g., 5.8% to 29.5% from DeepConn [58], and 11.1% to 27.4% from Guo et al. [19]) on F-score over relevant studies. In future, we would like to exploit different aspect extraction techniques, cluster the users based on their preference order on aspect categories, and generate group recommendations.

ACKNOWLEDGEMENT

This research is partially supported by US Army Research Lab under the grant number W911NF-12-R-0012.

REFERENCES

[1] Ramesh Baral and Tao Li. 2016. MAPS: A multi aspect personalized poi recommender system. In *Proceedings of the 10th ACM Conference on Recommender Systems*. ACM, 281–284.

[2] Ramesh Baral and Tao Li. 2017. Exploiting the roles of aspects in personalized POI recommender systems. *Data Mining and Knowledge Discovery* (2017), 1–24.

[3] Ramesh Baral, Dingding Wang, Tao Li, and Shu-Ching Chen. 2016. Geotecs: exploiting geographical, temporal, categorical and social aspects for personalized poi recommendation. In *Information Reuse and Integration (IRI), 2016 IEEE 17th International Conference on*. IEEE, 94–101.

[4] Mustafa Bilgic and Raymond J Mooney. 2005. Explaining recommendations: Satisfaction vs. promotion. In *Beyond Personalization Workshop, IUI*, Vol. 5. 153.

[5] David M Blei, Andrew Y Ng, and Michael I Jordan. 2003. Latent dirichlet allocation. *Journal of machine Learning research* 3, Jan (2003), 993–1022.

[6] Andrei Z Broder, Moses Charikar, Alan M Frieze, and Michael Mitzenmacher. 2000. Min-wise independent permutations. *J. Comput. System Sci.* 60, 3 (2000), 630–659.

[7] Andrei Z Broder, Steven C Glassman, Mark S Manasse, and Geoffrey Zweig. 1997. Syntactic clustering of the web. *Computer Networks and ISDN Systems* 29, 8-13 (1997), 1157–1166.

[8] Annalina Caputo, Pierpaolo Basile, Marco de Gemmis, Pasquale Lops, Giovanni Semeraro, and Gaetano Rossiello. 2017. SABRE: A Sentiment Aspect-Based Retrieval Engine. In *Information Filtering and Retrieval*. Springer, 63–78.

[9] Guanliang Chen and Li Chen. 2015. Augmenting service recommender systems by incorporating contextual opinions from user reviews. *User Modeling and User-Adapted Interaction* 25, 3 (2015), 295–329.

[10] Li Chen and Feng Wang. 2017. Explaining recommendations based on feature sentiments in product reviews. In *Proceedings of the 22nd International Conference on Intelligent User Interfaces*. ACM, 17–28.

[11] Xu Chen, Zheng Qin, Yongfeng Zhang, and Tao Xu. 2016. Learning to rank features for recommendation over multiple categories. In *Proceedings of the 39th International ACM SIGIR conference on Research and Development in Information Retrieval*. ACM, 305–314.

[12] Jiajun Cheng, Shenglin Zhao, Jiani Zhang, Irwin King, Xin Zhang, and Hui Wang. 2017. Aspect-level Sentiment Classification with HEAT (HiErarchical ATtention) Network. In *Proceedings of the 2017 ACM on Conference on Information and Knowledge Management*. ACM, 97–106.

[13] Ronan Collobert, Jason Weston, Léon Bottou, Michael Karlen, Koray Kavukcuoglu, and Pavel Kuksa. 2011. Natural language processing (almost) from scratch. *Journal of Machine Learning Research* 12, Aug (2011), 2493–2537.

[14] Paul Covington, Jay Adams, and Emre Sargin. 2016. Deep neural networks for youtube recommendations. In *Proceedings of the 10th ACM Conference on Recommender Systems*. ACM, 191–198.

[15] Ruihai Dong and Barry Smyth. 2017. User-based Opinion-based Recommendation. In *Proceedings of the 26th International Joint Conference on Artificial Intelligence*. AAAI Press, 4821–4825.

[16] Christiane Fellbaum. 1998. *WordNet*. Wiley Online Library.

[17] Fatih Gedikli, Mouzhi Ge, and Dietmar Jannach. 2011. Understanding recommendations by reading the clouds. In *International Conference on Electronic Commerce and Web Technologies*. Springer, 196–208.

[18] Fatih Gedikli, Dietmar Jannach, and Mouzhi Ge. 2014. How should I explain? A comparison of different explanation types for recommender systems. *International Journal of Human-Computer Studies* 72, 4 (2014), 367–382.

[19] Qing Guo, Zhu Sun, Jie Zhang, Qi Chen, and Yin-Leng Theng. 2017. Aspect-aware Point-of-Interest Recommendation with Geo-Social Influence. In *Adjunct Publication of the 25th Conference on User Modeling, Adaptation and Personalization*. ACM, 17–22.

[20] Taher H Haveliwala. 2002. Topic-sensitive pagerank. In *Proceedings of the 11th international conference on World Wide Web*. ACM, 517–526.

[21] Xiangnan He, Tao Chen, Min-Yen Kan, and Xiao Chen. 2015. Trirank: Review-aware explainable recommendation by modeling aspects. In *Proceedings of the 24th ACM International on Conference on Information and Knowledge Management*. ACM, 1661–1670.

[22] Jonathan L Herlocker, Joseph A Konstan, Al Borchers, and John Riedl. 1999. An algorithmic framework for performing collaborative filtering. In *Proceedings of the 22nd annual international ACM SIGIR conference on Research and development in information retrieval*. ACM, 230–237.

[23] Jonathan L Herlocker, Joseph A Konstan, and John Riedl. 2000. Explaining collaborative filtering recommendations. In *Proceedings of the 2000 ACM conference on Computer supported cooperative work*. ACM, 241–250.

[24] Yohan Jo and Alice H Oh. 2011. Aspect and sentiment unification model for online review analysis. In *Proceedings of the fourth ACM international conference on Web search and data mining*. ACM, 815–824.

[25] Yoon Kim. 2014. Convolutional neural networks for sentence classification. *arXiv preprint arXiv:1408.5882* (2014).

[26] Jon M Kleinberg. 1999. Authoritative sources in a hyperlinked environment. *Journal of the ACM (JACM)* 46, 5 (1999), 604–632.

[27] Aonghus Lawlor, Khalil Muhammad, Rachael Rafter, and Barry Smyth. 2015. Opinionated explanations for recommendation systems. In *Research and Development in Intelligent Systems XXXII*. Springer, 331–344.

[28] Shoushan Li, Rongyang Wang, and Guodong Zhou. 2012. Opinion target extraction using a shallow semantic parsing framework. In *Proceedings of the Twenty-Sixth AAAI Conference on Artificial Intelligence*. AAAI Press, 1671–1677.

[29] Christopher D Manning, Mihai Surdeanu, John Bauer, Jenny Rose Finkel, Steven Bethard, and David McClosky. 2014. The stanford corenlp natural language processing toolkit.. In *ACL (System Demonstrations)*. 55–60.

[30] Jarana Manotumruksa, Craig Macdonald, and Iadh Ounis. 2016. Modelling user preferences using word embeddings for context-aware venue recommendation. *arXiv preprint arXiv:1606.07828* (2016).

[31] Julian McAuley and Jure Leskovec. 2013. Hidden factors and hidden topics: understanding rating dimensions with review text. In *Proceedings of the 7th ACM conference on Recommender systems*. ACM, 165–172.

[32] Tomas Mikolov, Ilya Sutskever, Kai Chen, Greg S Corrado, and Jeff Dean. 2013. Distributed representations of words and phrases and their compositionality. In *Advances in neural information processing systems*. 3111–3119.

[33] Samaneh Moghaddam and Martin Ester. 2010. Opinion digger: an unsupervised opinion miner from unstructured product reviews. In *Proceedings of the 19th ACM international conference on Information and knowledge management*. ACM, 1825–1828.

[34] Samaneh Moghaddam and Martin Ester. 2011. ILDA: interdependent LDA model for learning latent aspects and their ratings from online product reviews. In *Proceedings of the 34th international ACM SIGIR conference on Research and development in Information Retrieval*. ACM, 665–674.

[35] Khalil Ibrahim Muhammad, Aonghus Lawlor, and Barry Smyth. 2016. A live-user study of opinionated explanations for recommender systems. In *Proceedings of the 21st International Conference on Intelligent User Interfaces*. ACM, 256–260.

[36] Cataldo Musto, Fedelucio Narducci, Pasquale Lops, Marco De Gemmis, and Giovanni Semeraro. 2016. Explod: A framework for explaining recommendations based on the linked open data cloud. In *Proceedings of the 10th ACM Conference on Recommender Systems*. ACM, 151–154.

[37] Steffen Rendle. 2012. Factorization machines with libfm. *ACM Transactions on Intelligent Systems and Technology (TIST)* 3, 3 (2012), 57.

[38] Steffen Rendle, Christoph Freudenthaler, Zeno Gantner, and Lars Schmidt-Thieme. 2009. BPR: Bayesian personalized ranking from implicit feedback. In *Proceedings of the twenty-fifth conference on uncertainty in artificial intelligence*. AUAI Press, 452–461.

[39] Badrul Sarwar, George Karypis, Joseph Konstan, and John Riedl. 2001. Item-based collaborative filtering recommendation algorithms. In *Proceedings of the 10th international conference on World Wide Web*. ACM, 285–295.

[40] Panagiotis Symeonidis, Alexandros Nanopoulos, and Yannis Manolopoulos. 2008. Providing justifications in recommender systems. *IEEE Transactions on Systems, Man, and Cybernetics-Part A: Systems and Humans* 38, 6 (2008), 1262–1272.

[41] Nava Tintarev and Judith Masthoff. 2012. Evaluating the effectiveness of explanations for recommender systems. *User Modeling and User-Adapted Interaction* 22, 4 (2012), 399–439.

[42] Ivan Titov and Ryan T McDonald. 2008. A Joint Model of Text and Aspect Ratings for Sentiment Summarization.. In *ACL*, Vol. 8. Citeseer, 308–316.

[43] Jesse Vig, Shilad Sen, and John Riedl. 2009. Tagsplanations: explaining recommendations using tags. In *Proceedings of the 14th international conference on Intelligent user interfaces*. ACM, 47–56.

[44] Hongning Wang, Yue Lu, and ChengXiang Zhai. 2011. Latent aspect rating analysis without aspect keyword supervision. In *Proceedings of the 17th ACM SIGKDD international conference on Knowledge discovery and data mining*. ACM, 618–626.

[45] Wenya Wang, Sinno Jialin Pan, Daniel Dahlmeier, and Xiaokui Xiao. 2017. Coupled Multi-Layer Attentions for Co-Extraction of Aspect and Opinion Terms.. In *AAAI*. 3316–3322.

[46] Xiangyu Wang, Yi-Liang Zhao, Liqiang Nie, Yue Gao, Weizhi Nie, Zheng-Jun Zha, and Tat-Seng Chua. 2015. Semantic-based location recommendation with multimodal venue semantics. *IEEE Transactions on Multimedia* 17, 3 (2015), 409–419.

[47] Yequan Wang, Minlie Huang, Li Zhao, and others. 2016. Attention-based lstm for aspect-level sentiment classification. In *Proceedings of the 2016 Conference on Empirical Methods in Natural Language Processing*. 606–615.

[48] Bin Xia, Tao Li, Qianmu Li, and Hong Zhang. 2018. Noise-tolerance matrix completion for location recommendation. *Data Mining and Knowledge Discovery* 32, 1 (2018), 1–24.

[49] Bin Xia, Zhen Ni, Tao Li, Qianmu Li, and Qifeng Zhou. 2017. Vrer: context-based venue recommendation using embedded space ranking SVM in location-based social network. *Expert Systems with Applications* 83 (2017), 18–29.

[50] Dingqi Yang, Daqing Zhang, Zhiyong Yu, and Zhu Wang. 2013. A sentiment-enhanced personalized location recommendation system. In *Proceedings of the 24th ACM Conference on Hypertext and Social Media*. ACM, 119–128.

[51] Quan Yuan, Gao Cong, Zongyang Ma, Aixin Sun, and Nadia Magnenat Thalmann. 2013. Time-aware point-of-interest recommendation. In *Proceedings of the 36th international ACM SIGIR conference on Research and development in information

retrieval. ACM, 363–372.

[52] Zhongwu Zhai, Bing Liu, Hua Xu, and Peifa Jia. 2011. Clustering product features for opinion mining. In *Proceedings of the fourth ACM international conference on Web search and data mining.* ACM, 347–354.

[53] Jia-Dong Zhang, Chi-Yin Chow, and Yu Zheng. 2015. ORec: An opinion-based point-of-interest recommendation framework. In *Proceedings of the 24th ACM International on Conference on Information and Knowledge Management.* ACM, 1641–1650.

[54] Lei Zhang and Bing Liu. 2014. Aspect and entity extraction for opinion mining. In *Data mining and knowledge discovery for big data.* Springer, 1–40.

[55] Wei Zhang, Quan Yuan, Jiawei Han, and Jianyong Wang. 2016. Collaborative Multi-Level Embedding Learning from Reviews for Rating Prediction.. In *IJCAI.*

2986–2992.

[56] Yongfeng Zhang, Guokun Lai, Min Zhang, Yi Zhang, Yiqun Liu, and Shaoping Ma. 2014. Explicit factor models for explainable recommendation based on phrase-level sentiment analysis. In *Proceedings of the 37th international ACM SIGIR conference on Research & development in information retrieval.* ACM, 83–92.

[57] Kaiqi Zhao, Gao Cong, Quan Yuan, and Kenny Q Zhu. 2015. SAR: A sentiment-aspect-region model for user preference analysis in geo-tagged reviews. In *Data Engineering (ICDE), 2015 IEEE 31st International Conference on.* IEEE, 675–686.

[58] Lei Zheng, Vahid Noroozi, and Philip S Yu. 2017. Joint Deep Modeling of Users and Items Using Reviews for Recommendation. In *Proceedings of the Tenth ACM International Conference on Web Search and Data Mining.* ACM, 425–434.

A Framework for Interaction-driven User Modeling of Mobile News Reading Behaviour

Marios Constantinides
Dept. of Computer Science, University College London
London, United Kingdom
m.constantinides@cs.ucl.ac.uk

John Dowell
Dept. of Computer Science, University College London
London, United Kingdom
j.dowell@cs.ucl.ac.uk

ABSTRACT

The news you read is, of course, a highly individual choice and one for which substantial and successful news recommendation techniques have been developed. But as well as *what* news you read, the *way* you choose and read that news is also known to be highly individual. We propose a framework for extending the user profile of news readers with features of these interactions. The extensions are dynamic through monitoring an individual's reading and browsing activity. They include factors learned from the user's interaction log and also factors inferred from category level definitions contained in the framework. We report a study in which users' interaction logs with a news app are used to generate user profiles that are verified with self-reported questionnaire data about reading habits. We discuss the implications of our user modeling approach in news personalisation for both recommendation and user interface personalisation for news apps.

CCS CONCEPTS

• **Human-centered computing** → *HCI theory, concepts and models*; • **Computing methodologies** → *Machine learning*;

KEYWORDS

User Modeling; Personalisation; News Reading Behaviour;

ACM Reference Format:
Marios Constantinides and John Dowell. 2018. A Framework for Interaction-driven User Modeling of Mobile News Reading Behaviour. In *UMAP '18: 26th Conference on User Modeling, Adaptation and Personalization, July 8–11, 2018, Singapore, Singapore*. ACM, New York, NY, USA, 9 pages. https://doi.org/10.1145/3209219.3209229

1 INTRODUCTION

Smartphones and tablets might well be the epitome of personal computing but their personalisation has some distinct

limits. Personalisation occurs in the services users access, for example, news services can learn about a user's news interests and make recommendations of stories they might want to read. Personalisation also occurs in the customisations and adaptations made by users, for example, news apps give users choices in the display of preferred topics and in how content will be displayed (e.g., the optional interactive story carousel feature in the BBC news app), but with the risk that users might never customize the interface themselves [32]. Mobile platforms in general do not learn about the user from their use of the device nor do they attempt to adapt to the user's habits and preferences. In user interface research, adaptation has been a longstanding interest [7], although the desirability of adaptivity ('automatic adaptation') in user interfaces has been sometimes questioned [15, 35] and contrasted with the consistency and predictability of generic but customisable interfaces. A common focus for research on user interface adaptivity has been the re-ordering of frequently visited items within menu systems to quicken visual search and selection. This work has been able to provide clear evidence of the value of adaptivity for users and their preference for it [18, 19].

In the domain of news reading, a rich and relevant domain in which to explore adaptivity in user interfaces, progress in personalising the choice of news content has not been matched by progress in personalising the way that content is accessed and read. News apps such as Flipboard, BuzzFeed, Feedly, News360, Pulse, web-based news portals such Google News and Yahoo News, and research prototypes (WebClipping2 [9], Buzzer [34], SmartMedia [24], LumiNews [29], PEN [20], Focal [21]) frequently do adapt to users' individual news interests through content recommendation services and many allow user customization of news feeds [4]. But their user interfaces do not adapt to how individual users characteristically select and read the news, as opposed to what news they are interested in reading. For example, the frequency and time spent reading news will vary considerably between people, as will their patterns of navigating news headlines and reading articles. This means that different users would likely be better served by different interfaces, for example, a user who likes to review all the headlines before choosing an article to read would be best served by a summary presentation of all headlines and a way of marking them as a reading list of articles. It might be expected that news app interfaces would benefit from personalization to the same extent as the news content they provide access to. Moreover, the growing number of news apps available on Google's and

Apple's marketplaces and the plethora of news portals respond to demand for news consumption, but also create the need for that access to be adaptive and personalised which is yet an open question for news services.

In this paper we argue that news service personalisation needs to extend beyond news content recommendation to adapting the user interface to reflect the user's interaction and news consumption habits. We propose a framework that illustrates a user model acquisition by extending user profiles of news readers with features of their interaction habits and preferences. Our approach utilises both data-driven acquisition and prior knowledge from category definitions of news reader types that are contained in the framework. Unlike previous attempts in modeling news reading behaviour, our method includes dynamic monitoring of a user's reading activity including how she browses news headlines and how many scrolls she uses to read a story. We demonstrate our framework in a study in which interaction logs from 47 users were used to generate user profiles. We build a user profile consisting of six factors that reflect the user's news reading interaction behaviour and we explore different methods for the acquisition including inferences, transformation functions and a supervised learning method. We discuss the implications of our user modeling approach in news personalised systems and suggest initial ideas that could be used to drive user interface personalisation in news services.

This paper makes two contributions to user modeling and user interface personalisation. First, it proposes a framework for extending the user profiles for news readers by incorporating facts about their reading habits and preferences, extending beyond their profile of news content interests. Second, it examines alternative approaches to the acquisition of this extended user profile and discusses how it can be exploited in a personalised news app.

2 RELATED WORK

2.1 The News Domain

A relevant and rich domain for investigating personalisation and developing personalised systems is digital news reading. Reading the news has been transformed by digital news gateways and mobile platforms. Prominent news providers including CNN, BBC, Guardian and others are now giving increased priority to their digital news services. The proliferation and recent technological advancements of smartphones, in conjunction with their indispensable roles in peoples everyday lives, have established smartphones as a prominent channel for news consumption [12]. Recent reports [11, 27] place news as the second most popular activity on smartphones after accessing social media, yet provision of a personalised service in this domain is under developed.

News reading is a highly individual activity with marked differences in peoples' preferences for news content, but also in the way they browse, choose and read news stories. Grzeschik et al. [23] reported individual differences in reading activity, which were influenced strongly by the nature of the text than by the reading devices. A distinctive 'screen-based' mode

of reading the news is apparent [31] characterised by 'more time spent on browsing and scanning, keyword spotting, one-time reading, non-linear reading, and reading more selectively, while less time is spent on in-depth reading, and concentrated reading'. Evidently, the nature of today's smartphones that are able to deliver news anywhere and anytime encourages this new reading behaviour.

2.2 Adaptive Presentation and Navigation

A cornerstone of our work is the adaptive hypermedia area. Brusilovsky [5] defines an adaptive hypermedia system as one that "builds a model of the goals, preferences and knowledge of each individual user, and uses this model throughout the interaction with the user, in order to adapt to the needs of that user". Two techniques often utilised by adaptive systems are adaptive presentation and navigation support. The former consists of text and multimedia adaptation, whereas the latter includes hiding, sorting, annotation, direct guidance, and hypertext map adaptation. Although adaptive hypermedia research flourished along with the explosion of the Web, these ideas continue to have applicability. In the news domain, content adaptation has been explored for years and researchers have proposed successful recommendation engines to adapt news content. News services are now able to help people find news of interest [4] and get fresh content that is relevant to them and to their current context, even while the future of mobile news is still taking shape. The plethora of news apps on marketplaces already provide personalised experience to mobile news readers, but we believe that the personalised news access needs to broaden its scope to further include not only what content users access but also how they access and interact with that content.

2.3 Modeling User's Behaviour

User profiles often contain user's related information such as user's interests, knowledge, background and skills, goals, tasks [6]. User interests can be anything from a specific web page to a hobby-related topic, classified either as short-term or long-term interest. For example, a user attends an opera once a year (short-term) or a user's favorite music genre is jazz (long-term). Modeling users' news interests has been demonstrated in various research prototypes. The NewsDude [3] learns user's interests in daily news by classifying recent events as short-term interests and general news preferences as long-term. Another system [24] utilised articles views and preview time, clicks on news categories and information from Facebook and Twitter as implicit signals of a user's interest in particular articles. Further, Carreira et al. [9] utilised total reading time, total number of the article's lines, number of lines read by the user and an approximation of the user's average line reading time to classify news articles. User's knowledge and skills mainly capture domain related information (e.g. experts, intermediate, novices). User's background may include work experience, profession or education, among others. For example, an adaptive healthcare information system [10] delivers personalised information based on user's

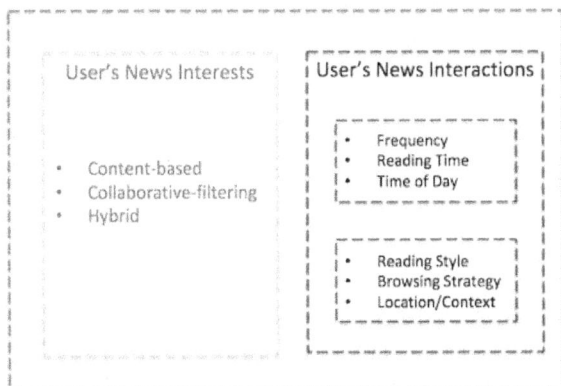

Figure 1: A conceptual diagram of a user profile for personalised news access. (left) A user profile that consists of user's news interests (e.g. article preference) (right) A user profile that consists of user's news reading interactions (e.g. reading style)

literacy and medical background. Finally, user's goals and tasks represent the user's objective or simply what the user aims to achieve in the system, which may vary across application domains.

The modeling mechanism is considered indispensable for any adaptive system. Adaptive systems often rely on effective user models wherein "unobservable information about a user is inferred from observable information from that user" [16]. Unobservable information may include any user's related information, as previously explained. Observable information is collected either explicitly through direct user intervention and/or implicitly through monitoring user activity [22, 38]; the latter being often preferred by users. User models vary in the methods used for inferring unobservable information from the observable. A large body of research has focused on modeling users directly from their actions with specific user interface elements, clickstream behaviour [39], usage patterns [14] and others, often without any prior knowledge about users. More sophisticated methods of user modelling involve supervised learning techniques for inferring preferences from interaction data [4, 26] specifically on desktop environments but also in the mobile environment in relation to search engines [2], web page navigation [9], and using function usage histories to refine menu displays [17]. A less widely used paradigm has focused on the use of stereotypes [28, 36]. In this approach, an individual user is associated with a class of users and facts about the class are then attributed to the individual. This stereotype based approach has been applied to user modelling in natural dialogues [8], accessible systems for users with disabilities [37], and digital guides for museum visitors [30]. In our user modeling approach to news reading, we propose to extend the user profile with facts about an individual user's habits and preferences relating to how they access and read the news. This extended user profile would enable tailored adaptive presentation and navigation

support in news apps that extends beyond news content recommendation.

3 FRAMEWORK

A domain-specific user profile for personalised news access will contain facts about a user's news interests (i.e. what news content they prefer to read) and facts about their news reading interaction patterns (i.e. how they access and interact with that content) (Figure 1). While many successful techniques for news recommendation (i.e. content-based, collaborative filtering or hybrid) have been developed, techniques for modelling users news reading interaction patterns have not been developed. By incorporating user modeling of news reading interaction patterns as part of their personalisation engines, as well as the news content, news services would be able to adapt the user interface to the individual user.

Our prior research work [13] has identified three news reader types, namely as 'Trackers', 'Reviewers', and 'Dippers', discriminated by interaction factors arising in the users news reading interaction behaviour. The framework characterizes the hierarchical relationship of these abstracted factors with data that can be captured from logging the user's interactions. Building on our previous work, we propose a hierarchical framework that would enable the analysis of mobile-sensing data in order to build a user profile.

Our user modeling approach aims to build a user profile that consists of the six factors that reflect a user's news reading interaction behaviour. As might be seen, the factors of Frequency, Reading Time and Time of Day can be directly computed from users usage with the news app without the need of a learning process. For example, one can track the sessions of opening/closing the app and compute whether a user is a frequent news reader or not. However, the factors of reading style, browsing strategy and location/context are more high-level behaviours and more complicated constructs to determine. We explain in Section 4 the different approaches in inferring, computing and learning these factors. The factors are defined as follows:

- *Frequency*: How often users read the news(many times a day, once a day or occasionally)
- *Reading Time*: The daily time spent on reading the news(0-5 minutes, 5-10 minutes, or 10+ minutes)
- *Time of Day*: The period in the day when the user usually reads the news (morning, afternoon or evening)
- *Reading Style*: How people read a selected news article (i.e. detailed reading, skimming or scanning)
- *Browsing Strategy*: How people browse headlines and select news stories (i.e. scan headlines in a particular section, navigate through all sections)
- *Location/Context*: Where people read the news (at home, at work, public)

The framework characterises the raw interaction data collected from users' interactions with a news app (Figure 3) and the layers of abstraction over those data that constitute the user model, achieved by both bottom up and top down processes. A similar layered hierarchical framework has been

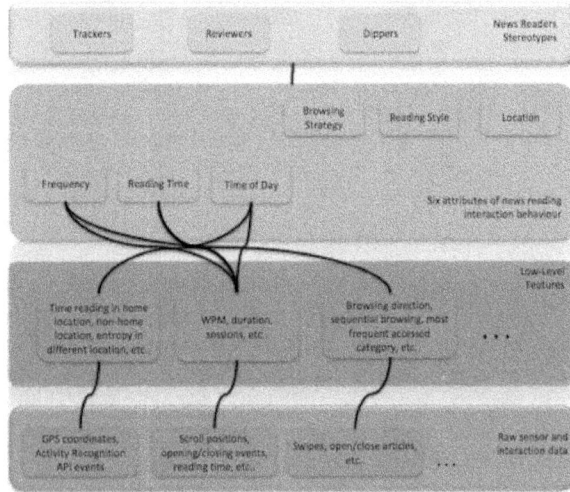

Figure 2: Mobile-sensing framework for analysing news reading behaviour

proposed by Mohr [33] to support the monitoring of the mental health of at-risk people from their low level interactions with their mobile phones. The framework is fundamental in our approach, as it enriches low-level interactions with high-level constructs of news reading behaviour.

The framework consists of four layers (Figure 2). Layer 1 consists of low-level values related with sensors data and news reading interactions (e.g. GPS coordinates, scroll positions). Layer 2 defines functions for extraction and aggregation of raw data into low-level features. By doing so, we extract meaningful information from the raw data (e.g. daily reading sessions, swipes directions). Layer 3 defines transformation functions of low-level features into the six factors of news reading interaction behaviour. Layer 4 integrates a News Reader Typology into the framework [13]. The framework defines the layers in relation to users' patterns of news consumption rather than the news content they consume.

3.1 Layer 1: Raw interaction data

Layer 1 defines the raw sensor data and low-level news reading interaction data collected using our prototype news app. The app logged different interactions made while reading articles, browsing to choose articles and context related data through the devices sensors. For example, a number of low-level events related with scroll positions that can determine how the user read an article, the trajectory of swipes and navigation behaviour for choosing articles to read. The app also utilised location services of the device as well as the Google's Activity Recognition API that allowed us to capture whether the phone was still or moving while reading.

3.2 Layer 2: Low-level features

Layer 2 of the hierarchical framework adds information to the low-level behaviourial and sensor data. It defines functions for extraction and aggregation of raw data into low-level

features. For example, the different articles read on a day are aggregated into a low-level feature of number of daily articles read. The feature engineering is structured around three categories of features; the Reading, the Navigation and the Context related features.

The low-level features were chosen with the aim of revealing all aspects of news reading behaviour according with the six factors. All the features were aggregated on a daily level as well as intra-daily features were computed, dividing a day into three periods (Morning: 4-11 TW1, Afternoon: 12-19 TW2 and Evening: 20-3 TW3). A Boolean value was also extracted that indicates whether a date falls into weekend or not. Combining all features (including the Boolean value of isWeekend), a set of 103 features was extracted.

3.2.1 Reading Features. Reading features refer to data related with how users perform the reading task. We computed unique reading sessions, number of unique articles read, articles that were read more than once, reading duration, number of articles that scroll was used, number of articles that were read in whole (computed using scroll reached the end of the window), spikes in reading that could be an indication whether they followed a constant reading fast scroll up and down vs. constant ascending scrolling, and words per minute in terms of how much of the article exposed to the user divided by how much time required to read it (min, max, mean, median and std were computed for these features). For all reading features we computed one value for their overall daily behaviour as well as three more values for the intra-daily behaviour, which resulted in 30 reading features.

3.2.2 Navigation Features. Navigation features refer to data related with how users navigated and chose news stories to read. We computed unique navigation sessions, total news categories browsed, number of news categories that all headlines were browsed (we use number of swipes of direction in order to find whether a user browsed all headlines of a particular category), number of non-sequential and sequential navigation (i.e. the trajectory of user's browsing across categories - e.g. a. [1, 3, 7, 2, 4]→non-sequential or b. [1, 4, 8 or 9, 7, 2]→sequential numbers indicate the category id), number of swipes left, number of swipes right, total number of swipes, time spent in browsing headlines, most frequent news story reached across categories. The final navigation features set including the overall daily and intra-daily values resulting in 40 features.

3.2.3 Context Features. Context features refer to data related mainly with users' location while they were accessing the news. We treated location as sensitive user's data, thus we further preprocessed all location related data. All locations were obfuscated with unique identifiers (UUID) and a new identifier was generated if two locations were more than 10m away. By doing so, we ensure that users' location data will not be exposed to the researcher who performed the analysis. Further, data preprocessing consisted of determining a possible Home location for each individual. To compute the home location, we took the two most frequently appearing identifiers in TW1 and TW3 (in this case 5am-9am for TW1 and 10pm-4am for TW3) for each user session, under the assumption that people are more likely to be at their homes during those time intervals. Then, the most frequent identifier of the two was marked as home and subsequently all of a user's entries were marked as home or non-home locations.

The context features list consisted of unique context sessions, time reading at home and non-home location daily, ratio of time reading at home over non-home location, total movements while reading, entropy at non- home location (as a measure of the temporal dispersion of locations), entropy of different locations visited while reading throughout the day. Again, the final context features list including daily and intra-daily values resulted in 32 features.

3.3 Layer 3: High-level six factors

Having introduced the mechanisms to transform the raw sensor data and users' interactions into low-level features, Layer 3 defines functions that can transform the low-level features into the six factors that describe news reading behaviour. As previously explained the factors of Frequency, Reading Time and Time of Day can be directly computed from low-level features, whereas the factors of Reading Style, Browsing Strategy and Location/Context are more complicated but we defined transformation functions for this set of factors, as one of the approaches we examined make use of them.

3.3.1 Transformation Functions to compute Frequency, Reading Time and Time of Day. 'Frequency': We aggregate the number of reading sessions on a daily basis to determine the frequency of reading. For example, if two or more reading sessions appear on the log of one particular day then we mark it as 'many times a day'.

'Reading Time': We compute the average daily reading time low-level feature and accordingly we mark it as 0-5 minutes, 5- 10 minutes or 10+ minutes.

'Time of Day': We compute the time spent in reading in the three time windows (TW1, TW2, TW3) and we assign accordingly the output as 'Morning', 'Afternoon', and 'Evening' using the highest value among the three time windows.

3.3.2 Transformation Functions to compute Browsing Strategy, Reading Style and Location/Context. These factors involve interpretations of behavior and therefore cannot be computed simply by aggregation over low-level features. The functions we created to compute these factors inevitably make several assumptions and simplifications. Here we summarise those functions. A comparison of the algorithms performance with both inferences from the canonical News Reader Typology and with a supervised learning method is described in Section (4.2.6) and the results summarized in Table 2.

'Reading Style': We estimate the user's pace of reading in words per minute (wpm) from approximating how much text of the article was exposed by the user's scrolling actions and the period during which the article was opened. Different reading styles are associated with different speeds of reading:

detailed reading as speeds up to 230 wpm; scan reading as speeds over 700 wpm, and; skim reading as speeds in between.

'Browsing Strategy': We use low-level features such as the number of different categories of headlines browsed and the number of times headlines were browsed in a day as well as the total number of headlines categories browsed. We compute two ratios: (a) categories in which all headlines were browsed over different sessions which indicates whether a user has a preferred category, and (b) unique categories browsed over unique navigation sessions which indicates whether a user accesses most of the categories available. Given the nine news categories present in the news app we set a threshold for particular category browsing as 1 and for browsing through all categories as 6. Given the two ratios and the thresholds then a rule-based algorithm produces three possible outputs (a) 'both', meaning that the user on different occasions either only reads articles in a selected category or categories, and at other times chooses to view articles in all categories, (b) 'particular', meaning that the user navigates only in particular categories, and (c) 'all', meaning that the user navigates most of the cases through all categories.

'Location': A rule-based algorithm is used to determine whether the user is reading the news at home or in a non-home location. A location where the user spends more time than any other specific location is designated as home. The inference is modified by the time at which the news is read making the assumption that most people are at work in the second time window. We use entropy of location to describe the variability in different locations, meaning that if the user has a high entropy they are more likely to be in a public setting, while low entropy indicates a work environment.

3.4 Layer 4: News Reader Types

Integration of the News Reader Typology from our previous work [13]. It is used by one of the approaches we take to building the user profile through making inferences about the high-level behaviourial factors as an alternative to computing them directly from the low-level features.

4 BUILDING A USER PROFILE

The framework characterises the abstraction of an extended user profile from a user's interactions with a news reading app. The extended user profile consists of a set of interaction factors that are particular to an individual user. We now report a study which demonstrates the application of the framework to generate user profiles for people reading the news with a news app. The study involved users using a news app created for the purpose and capable of reporting data about the users interactive behaviours such as swipes, scrolls and taps.

4.1 Data Collection with Habito News

Habito News (Figure 3) is a news app we developed to explore news reading interactions [13]. It mimics the BBC news app in terms of the organisation and presentation of headlines and the layout of news stories; live news is fed from the BBC

Figure 3: Our prototype news app, Habito News. (a) Login page (b) Built-in consent form (c) Survey related with the six factors (d) News headlines menu (e) News article presentation

news API and presents the news in row of thumbnails (nine news categories and nine news articles in each category). The app was implemented on the Android platform, deployed through the Google Play store and installed by 47 users on their own smartphones. Apart from delivering news stories, the app is capable of logging the low-level data explained in Layer 1 of the framework.

4.1.1 Participants. Mainly recruited through university and social-network posts, but also as the app was listed on Google Play it was practically accessible to everyone. Participants who were recruited through university entered a draw for a £50 Amazon voucher, whereas anyone else who directly downloaded the app did not receive any compensation for their participation. The inclusion criteria consisted of (a) participants own an Android device with OS greater than 4.3 and (b) use Habito News as the their primary news reading application for a period of 2-weeks. To ensure that participants used our app as their primary source, we logged the apps running in the background (while our was open), but also applying filters for the News&Magazines category to ensure privacy, as we did not want to obtain any other information about users running apps.

4.1.2 Procedure. Upon download, users signed up with Habito News. Before providing any data, users had to agree to a built-in consent form disclosing the type of data that was being monitored as well as providing information related with the setup of the study. The registration process consisted of two steps with data gathered using explicit methods through a built-in form and a questionnaire. Participants provided demographic information such as their age, gender and date of birth through a built-in form. They also answered six questions about their news reading behaviour. We use this source of information to validate the models that predict the high-level behaviourial constructs of news reading

interaction behaviour. The six questions along with the potential responses (users chose one answer for each question) are (Figure 3(c)):

(1) How often do you read news on your mobile device? [a. Many times b. Once c. Occasionally]
(2) How much time a day do you spend reading news on your mobile device? [a. 0-5 min b. 5-10 min c. 10+ min]
(3) How do you look for stories of interest? [a. All b. Particular c. Both]
(4) How do you read a news story? [a. Detailed b. Skimming c. Scanning]
(5) Where do you often read news? [a. Home b. Work c. Public Transport]
(6) What time of the day do you usually read news? [a. Morning b. Afternoon c.Evening]

4.2 Modeling the six factors

The interaction factors of Frequency, Reading Time and Time of Day were computed directly from the low-level features using the transformation functions provided in layer 2 of the framework. To model the interaction factors of Reading Style, Browsing Strategy and Location/Context we explored three approaches, (a) inferences from the News Reader Typology, (b) using the transformation functions and (c) supervised machine learning method.

4.2.1 Ground-truth information. To evaluate the approaches we used participants' answers to the questions they were asked at initial registration about their news reading habits and preferences. Specifically, their answers to the three questions about how they browsed headlines, how they read articles and where they read the news were used as the ground truth against which the different approaches would be assessed. Table 1 shows the distribution of the answers for each question related with the three factors. We set the baseline model for each factor as the majority class in their distribution. For example, the factor of Reading Style has a distribution of detailed reading 27.3%, skimming 31.3% and scanning 41.4%; baseline model is set to the 'scanning class' distribution. A similar approach was followed for the other factors. Therefore, we expect our models to outperform the baseline models.

4.2.2 Preparing the datasets for the analysis. A common problem when dealing with mobile-sensing data is missing values. Although Habito News was designed in such a way as to minimise this problem, our dataset suffered from missing values. For example, it prompted the user to enable location services in order not to miss context related values. At the same time, however, nothing could have been done for the other two categories of data as we did not want to intervene and force people to read under given instructions but rather allow them to read on their own pace. Therefore, there are cases in our dataset where values for some categories are missing (e.g. navigation is missing due to the user read a few articles without performing any browsing). Such cases were dropped from the final dataset used for the analysis. Further data pruning was carried out in order to eliminate users with one-day usage (Figure 4). In particular the 47 users initial dataset reduced down to 33 users. We treated this set of users as outliers as their behaviour could have added noise to the data due to these users have downloaded the app and then after a day's usage opted-out. Therefore, the final dataset consisted of 198 daily datapoints and a 103 features space.

4.2.3 Inferences from the News Reader Typology. Given the computed factors of the Frequency, Reading Time and Time of Day, we derived the other three factors from the typology based on the characteristics of the stereotypical profiles. To derive Reading Style we used frequency and reading time, we used frequency for Browsing Strategy and we used frequency and time of day for Location/Context. For example, the typology defines skimming as the reading style of a news reader type who reads the news many times a day. It defines 'looking for particular section' as a browsing strategy of a news reader who reads the news occasionally. Similar definitions are provided in the original News Reader Typology, which can be retrieved in [13]. Table 2 shows the accuracy in inferring the three behavioural factors.

4.2.4 Using the transformation functions. The second approach we explored, made use of the transformation functions that are defined in layer 2 of the framework to compute the factors of reading style, browsing strategy and location/context. It is important to mention the assumptions and heuristics that were used to create those functions. For example, we used words per minute as an indication of the pace while reading, which in turn was used to distinguish detailed reading from skimming and from scanning. At first glance it may seem straightforward, but the factor of reading style might be more complicated and depend on other variables than simply on words per minute.

4.2.5 Performance of rule-based approaches. We used a Cosine Similarity function in which we transformed the output of the derived (4.2.3) and computed (4.2.4) behavioural

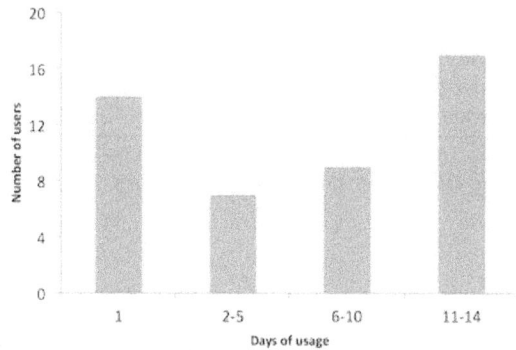

Figure 4: Habito News usage for the 2-week trial

Factor	Values	Distribution
Reading Style	detailed	27.28%
	skimming	31.30%
	scanning	41.42%
Browsing Strategy	particular	28.79%
	all	49.49%
	both	21.72%
Location/Context	home	80.81%
	public	19.19%

Table 1: Distribution of the ground truth information for each factor

factors into binary vectors and compared them with binary vectors of the ground truth, i.e. the survey data. Table 2 shows the accuracy in computing the three behavioural factors. The accuracies were below the baseline models except for the reading style that was computed using the function provided by the framework. For the location/context factor both algorithms completely failed. A possible explanation might be that these behavioural factors depend on different variables that the rule-based approaches failed to capture, thus we examine a learning method in the next section.

4.2.6 Supervised learning method. Given that the results produced by the rule-based approaches did not outperform the baseline models for each factor, in the third approach we examined the use of a supervised machine learning method with the low-level feaures set as input, allowing the algorithm to learn and detect any hidden structure and associations between the low-level features and the high-level factors. We trained three Random Forest (RF) classifiers, one for each individual factor. The choice of RF was reinforced by the fairly small dataset used to train the algorithm, as it is recognised for its accuracy and its ability to deal with small sample sizes. We tuned each individual RF classifier with 500 estimators (trees) and due to the imbalanced datasets we used a balanced class weight mode that automatically adjusts the weights inversely proportional to the classes distributions.

Factor	Inferences	Functions	RF
Reading Style	36.36%	52.02%	60.00%
Browsing Strategy	42.42%	24.74%	54.73%
Location/Context	45.95%	36.86%	82.10%

Table 2: Accuracies of inferring, computing and learning the three behavioural factors

To avoid overfitting of the algorithms, we ran a k-fold (k=10) validation by leaving one instance out. Table 2 shows the performance in learning the three behavioural factors.

The learning method produced better results compared to the rule-based approaches, as all three learnt behavioural factors exceeded the baseline values. The browsing strategy improved by 12.31%, reading style by 23.64% and location/context compared to the inferences approach. Further, the browsing strategy improved by 29.99%, reading style by 7.98% and location/context by 45.24% compared to the accuracies observed using the transformation functions.

Another important insight that can be drawn from the learning method is the features importance, which can be used to inform the heuristics and the design/refinement of the transformation functions or lead to better understanding of the behavioural factors. For example, the current transformation function of reading style (4.2.4) uses an approximation of the speed of reading in wpm. Among the 10 most predictive features of the reading style classifier were the different statistics for wpm (max, min, median, std) and daily reading time, which currently the function makes use of, but also navigation related features (e.g. number of swipes, categories browsed) that the heuristics did not to consider.

5 DISCUSSION

In this paper we present a framework for extending user profiles of news readers with attributes of their interaction habits and preferences. Our framework characterises the process of analysing news reading interaction patterns. We demonstrate it with a corpus of interactions logs obtained from a prototype news app in order to build a user profile consisting of six factors. We directly compute the factors of frequency, reading time and time of day from the low-level features, and we explore three approaches for the factors of reading style, browsing strategy and location/context including inferences, computation using heuristics and learning methods.

The rule-based approaches did not yield good performances but the learning method was able to learn and predict the high-level behavioural factors. The learning method outperformed the baseline models for each factor and improved significantly the accuracies of predicting these factors compared to the rule-based approaches. The results suggest that our method is feasible in principle and with further training and tuning of the algorithms it can be deployable. Our framework has the potential to enrich existing news personalised services, as it captures another aspect of news reading

behaviour that reflects users' interaction habits and preferences. The six factors of the extended news reader profile could be matched with preferences for different user interface elements or interactions in order to generate personalised compositional user interfaces. that would aim to enhance user's news reading experience. For example, a user who tracks and follows the news throughout the day could be given access to features such as tagged previously-read articles or stories with updates, as opposed to a casual news reader who is more likely not to benefit from these features. Likewise, a user who likes to read an article underneath a top headline while commuting at work would be better served by a different user interface and interaction than the user who reads the very same article at home. These examples illustrate the application of our user modeling framework in which the six factors of the news reader profile reflect the user interface choice in a personalised news app.

Finally, it is important to highlight some of the limitations of the current work and discuss future directions of this research. First, the relatively small sample size used is of an immediate future work as it might yield better algorithms' performances. Second, the ground truth used to train the models obtained through self-reported questionnaires. Despite the fact that it is a standard technique, it relies on peoples' ability to accurately assess themselves, which can be considered as a limitation. This could be explained by the fact that "humans do not remember experiences in a consistent and linear way, but rather recall events selectively and with various biases" [1, 25]. Alternatively, we could observe users' interaction behaviour in a laboratory setting with video recordings in order to obtain the ground truth information. However, doing so implies that we lose ecological validity of our results, thus we aimed to investigate it in a field study to explore as much as possible users' natural behaviour while reading the news. Further future directions include the generalisation of our framework in order to provide generic methods that can translate news interaction patterns from different news apps and providers other than the BBC. This would enable the integration of our framework in different news layout organisations and interactions, and thus it would enable the generation of extended news reader profiles for news consumption despite the different news apps layouts.

6 CONCLUSIONS

We have shown how the framework for extending news user profiles can be deployed. The study with Habito news was able to collect the data required by the framework and the user model then transformed these data by three alternative methods into a user profile. The consistency with the user profile values provided by the users themselves in questionnaires shows that the learning methods are viable.

ACKNOWLEDGMENTS

The authors would like to thank the anonymous referees for their valuable comments and helpful suggestions. The work is supported by EPSRC under Grant No.:EP/J50225X/1.

REFERENCES

[1] Lorraine G Allan. 1979. The perception of time. *Perception & Psychophysics* 26, 5 (1979), 340–354.

[2] Enrico Bertini, Andrea Calì, Tiziana Catarci, Silvia Gabrielli, and Stephen Kimani. 2005. Interaction-based adaptation for small screen devices. In *International Conference on User Modeling.* Springer, 277–281.

[3] Daniel Billsus and Michael J Pazzani. 1999. A hybrid user model for news story classification. In *UM99 User Modeling.* Springer, 99–108.

[4] Daniel Billsus and Michael J Pazzani. 2000. User modeling for adaptive news access. *User modeling and user-adapted interaction* 10, 2-3 (2000), 147–180.

[5] Peter Brusilovsky. 1996. Methods and techniques of adaptive hypermedia. *User modeling and user-adapted interaction* 6, 2-3 (1996), 87–129.

[6] Peter Brusilovsky and Eva Millán. 2007. User models for adaptive hypermedia and adaptive educational systems. In *The adaptive web.* Springer, 3–53.

[7] Andrea Bunt, Cristina Conati, and Joanna McGrenere. 2004. What role can adaptive support play in an adaptable system?. In *Proceedings of the 9th international conference on Intelligent user interfaces.* ACM, 117–124.

[8] Sandra Carberry, JG Carbonell, DN Chin, R Cohen, J Fain Lehman, TW Finin, A Jameson, M Jones, R Kass, A Kobsa, et al. 2012. *User models in dialog systems.* Springer Science & Business Media.

[9] Ricardo Carreira, Jaime M Crato, Daniel Gonçalves, and Joaquim A Jorge. 2004. Evaluating adaptive user profiles for news classification. In *Proceedings of the 9th international conference on Intelligent user interfaces.* ACM, 206–212.

[10] Alison Cawsey, Floriana Grasso, and Cécile Paris. 2007. Adaptive information for consumers of healthcare. In *The adaptive web.* Springer, 465–484.

[11] Pew Research Centre. 2012. Future of Mobile News. (2012). http://www.journalism.org/2012/10/01/future-mobile-news/

[12] Michael Chan. 2015. Examining the influences of news use patterns, motivations, and age cohort on mobile news use: The case of Hong Kong. *Mobile Media & Communication* 3, 2 (2015), 179–195.

[13] Marios Constantinides, John Dowell, David Johnson, and Sylvain Malacria. 2015. Exploring mobile news reading interactions for news app personalisation. In *Proceedings of the 17th International Conference on Human-Computer Interaction with Mobile Devices and Services.* ACM, 457–462.

[14] Himel Dev and Zhicheng Liu. 2017. Identifying Frequent User Tasks from Application Logs. In *Proceedings of the 22nd International Conference on Intelligent User Interfaces.* ACM, 263–273.

[15] Leah Findlater and Joanna McGrenere. 2004. A comparison of static, adaptive, and adaptable menus. In *Proceedings of the SIGCHI conference on Human factors in computing systems.* ACM, 89–96.

[16] Enrique Frias-Martinez, G Magoulas, S Chen, and R Macredie. 2005. Modeling human behavior in user-adaptive systems: Recent advances using soft computing techniques. *Expert Systems with Applications* 29, 2 (2005), 320–329.

[17] Yusuke Fukazawa, Mirai Hara, Masashi Onogi, and Hidetoshi Ueno. 2009. Automatic mobile menu customization based on user operation history. In *Proceedings of the 11th International Conference on Human-Computer Interaction with Mobile Devices and Services.* ACM, 50.

[18] Krzysztof Z Gajos, Mary Czerwinski, Desney S Tan, and Daniel S Weld. 2006. Exploring the design space for adaptive graphical user interfaces. In *Proceedings of the working conference on Advanced visual interfaces.* ACM, 201–208.

[19] Krzysztof Z Gajos, Katherine Everitt, Desney S Tan, Mary Czerwinski, and Daniel S Weld. 2008. Predictability and accuracy in adaptive user interfaces. In *Proceedings of the SIGCHI Conference on Human Factors in Computing Systems.* ACM, 1271–1274.

[20] Florent Garcin and Boi Faltings. 2013. Pen recsys: A personalized news recommender systems framework. In *Proceedings of the 2013 International News Recommender Systems Workshop and Challenge.* ACM, 3–9.

[21] Florent Garcin, Frederik Galle, and Boi Faltings. 2014. Focal: A personalized mobile news reader. In *Proceedings of the 8th ACM Conference on Recommender systems.* ACM, 369–370.

[22] Susan Gauch, Mirco Speretta, Aravind Chandramouli, and Alessandro Micarelli. 2007. User profiles for personalized information access. In *The adaptive web.* Springer, 54–89.

[23] Kathrin Grzeschik, Yevgeniya Kruppa, Diana Marti, and Paul Donner. 2011. Reading in 2110–Reading behavior and reading devices: A case study. *The Electronic Library* 29, 3 (2011), 288–302.

[24] Jon Atle Gulla, Arne Dag Fidjestøl, Xiaomeng Su, and Humberto Nicolás Castejón Martínez. 2014. Implicit User Profiling in News Recommender Systems.. In *WEBIST (1).* 185–192.

[25] H Wayne Hogan. 1978. A theoretical reconciliation of competing views of time perception. *The American Journal of Psychology* (1978), 417–428.

[26] Eric Horvitz, Jack Breese, David Heckerman, David Hovel, and Koos Rommelse. 1998. The Lumiere project: Bayesian user modeling for inferring the goals and needs of software users. In *Proceedings of the Fourteenth conference on Uncertainty in artificial intelligence.* Morgan Kaufmann Publishers Inc., 256–265.

[27] Reuters Institute. 2014. Reuters Institute Digital News Report. (2014). http://reutersinstitute.politics.ox.ac.uk/sites/default/files/research/files/Reuters%2520Institute%2520Digital%2520News%2520Report%25202014.pdf

[28] Anthony Jameson. 2009. Adaptive interfaces and agents. *Human-Computer Interaction: Design Issues, Solutions, and Applications* 105 (2009), 105–130.

[29] Gabriella Kazai, Iskander Yusof, and Daoud Clarke. 2016. Personalised news and blog recommendations based on user location, Facebook and twitter user profiling. In *Proceedings of the 39th International ACM SIGIR conference on Research and Development in Information Retrieval.* ACM, 1129–1132.

[30] Tsvi Kuflik, Zvi Boger, and Massimo Zancanaro. 2012. Analysis and prediction of museum visitors? behavioral pattern types. In *Ubiquitous Display Environments.* Springer, 161–176.

[31] Ziming Liu. 2005. Reading behavior in the digital environment: Changes in reading behavior over the past ten years. *Journal of documentation* 61, 6 (2005), 700–712.

[32] Wendy E Mackay. 1991. Triggers and barriers to customizing software. In *Proceedings of the SIGCHI conference on Human factors in computing systems.* ACM, 153–160.

[33] David C Mohr, Mi Zhang, and Stephen M Schueller. 2017. Personal sensing: understanding mental health using ubiquitous sensors and machine learning. *Annual review of clinical psychology* 13 (2017), 23–47.

[34] Owen Phelan, Kevin McCarthy, and Barry Smyth. 2009. Using twitter to recommend real-time topical news. In *Proceedings of the third ACM conference on Recommender systems.* ACM, 385–388.

[35] Ben Shneiderman. 1997. Direct manipulation for comprehensible, predictable and controllable user interfaces. In *Proceedings of the 2nd international conference on Intelligent user interfaces.* ACM, 33–39.

[36] Kerry-Louise Skillen, Liming Chen, Chris D Nugent, Mark P Donnelly, William Burns, and Ivar Solheim. 2012. Ontological user profile modeling for context-aware application personalization. In *International conference on ubiquitous computing and ambient intelligence.* Springer, 261–268.

[37] Constantine Stephanidis, Alex Paramythis, Michael Sfyrakis, A Stergiou, Napoleon Maou, A Leventis, George Paparoulis, and Charalampos Karagiannidis. 1998. Adaptable and adaptive user interfaces for disabled users in the AVANTI project. In *International Conference on Intelligence in Services and Networks.* Springer, 153–166.

[38] Jaime Teevan, Susan T Dumais, and Eric Horvitz. 2010. Potential for personalization. *ACM Transactions on Computer-Human Interaction (TOCHI)* 17, 1 (2010), 4.

[39] Gang Wang, Xinyi Zhang, Shiliang Tang, Haitao Zheng, and Ben Y Zhao. 2016. Unsupervised clickstream clustering for user behavior analysis. In *Proceedings of the 2016 CHI Conference on Human Factors in Computing Systems.* ACM, 225–236.

Improving Learning & Reducing Time: A Constrained Action-Based Reinforcement Learning Approach

Shitian Shen, Markel Sanz Ausin, Behrooz Mostafavi, Min Chi
Department of Computer Science
North Carolina State University
Raleigh, NC
<sshen,msanzau,bzmostaf,mchi>@ncsu.edu

ABSTRACT

Constrained action-based decision-making is one of the most challenging decision-making problems. It refers to a scenario where an agent takes action in an environment not only to maximize the expected cumulative reward but where it is subject to certain action-based constraints; for example, an upper limit on the total number of certain actions being carried out. In this work, we construct a general data-driven framework called Constrained Action-based Partially Observable Markov Decision Process (CAPOMDP) to induce effective pedagogical policies. Specifically, we induce two types of policies: $CAPOMDP_{LG}$ using learning gain as reward with the goal of improving students' learning performance, and $CAPOMDP_{Time}$ using time as reward for reducing students' time on task. The effectiveness of $CAPOMDP_{LG}$ is compared against a random yet reasonable policy and the effectiveness of $CAPOMDP_{Time}$ is compared against both a Deep Reinforcement Learning induced policy and a random policy. Empirical results show that there is an Aptitude-Treatment Interaction effect: students are split into High vs. Low based on their incoming competence; while no significant difference is found among the High incoming competence groups, for the Low groups, students following $CAPOMDP_{Time}$ indeed spent significantly less time than those using the two baseline policies and students following $CAPOMDP_{LG}$ significantly outperform their peers on both learning gain and learning efficiency.

KEYWORDS

Constrained Reinforcement Learning, POMDP, Intelligent Tutoring System

ACM Reference Format:
Shitian Shen, Markel Sanz Ausin, Behrooz Mostafavi, Min Chi. 2018. Improving Learning & Reducing Time: A Constrained Action-Based Reinforcement Learning Approach. In *UMAP '18: 26th Conference on User Modeling, Adaptation and Personalization, July 8–11, 2018, Singapore, Singapore.* ACM, New York, NY, USA, 9 pages. https://doi.org/10.1145/3209219.3209232

1 INTRODUCTION

Intelligent Tutoring Systems (ITSs), as one type of highly interactive e-learning environment, have been widely used in the educational domain. ITSs generally provide step-by-step adaptive support and contextualized feedback to individual learners at run-time [13, 25]. Specifically, ITSs often apply the *pedagogical strategies* to decide which action to take (e.g. give a hint, show an example) in the face of alternatives at each time step with the purpose of improving student learning. Reinforcement Learning (RL) is one of the most promising data-driven approaches to induce an effective pedagogical strategy (policy) in ITSs. Most of prior research [6, 12, 22] apply the RL approaches in *unconstrained* contexts, where the agent selects actions given a situation to maximize expected cumulative reward. Specifically, the agent chooses actions at each step based on the current state alone, regardless of prior decisions.

In this work, we mainly focus on inducing pedagogical strategy in a *constrained action-based* RL (CARL) scenario, which involves the additional action-based constraints such as a maximum number of times that an agent may take a specific action. For example, in American football, when the referee makes a call against a team the coaches can challenge it but they can only do so 3 times per game. And if the challenge is rejected, they not only lose an opportunity but they may face an additional penalty. Similarly in law, when prosecutors decide to charge someone with a crime, they are committed to proving it under the relevant law and they have limited options to add or modify the charges later on. In both scenarios, the early decisions impose special constraints on the future actions. In other words, the available actions for an agent at any given situation are governed not only by the current state but also by prior decisions. Therefore, when deciding the next action, the agent should take the constraints into account.

Prior research on *constrained* RL has focused on inducing the optimal policy subject to constraints such as *safety* and *risk avoidance*. Systems that physically interact with humans, for example, need to satisfy the basic safety parameters or engage in risk avoidance [1]. Similarly, robots that seek to reach a target position as quickly as possible should also avoid dangerous places (say a crater) that might render them irretrievable [15]. Prior researchers [2, 9, 10, 21] who have sought to address such *constrained* scenarios have typically specified an additional *cost* function which has a similar format to the reward and then imposing constraints on the values of the cost functions. However, such constraints are different from the action-based constraints on which our work is focused. So far as we know, no prior work has directly sought to address the action-based constraints in an interactive e-learning environment.

In order to solve the CARL problem, we propose a general framework called Constrained Action-based Partially-observable Markov Decision Processes (CAPOMDP). In particular, we apply this framework to transform CARL problems into normal RL problems by leveraging factored state representations to incorporate constraints into the state space itself (see Sec. 4.1). The CARL scenario we investigated is an ITS called Deep Thought (DT) [18], which contains the action-based constraints and one type of tutorial decision: whether to provide students with a *Worked Example (WE)* or to ask them to engage in *Problem Solving (PS)*. When providing a WE, DT presents an expert solution to a problem step by step so that the student sees both the answer and the solution procedure. During PS, students are required to complete the problem with tutor's support. In DT, the action-based constraints are: the last problem on each level must be done in PS, and prior to reaching that problem the students must complete at least one PS and one WE.

In applying CAPOMDP to DT, we explore two types of reward functions: learning gain and time. For the former, the goal is to maximize learning gain, while the goal for the latter is to reduce the amount of time spent on completing the entire tutor. Prior research use either learning gain or time but *not both*. In this work, we apply CAPOMDP to induce two pedagogical policies using learning gain and time as reward respectively, and then evaluate them through two empirical experiments. In Experiment 1 (Exp1), we compare the CAPOMDP policies induced by learning gain against a policy where the system *randomly* decides whether to present the next problem as WE or as PS. Because both PS and WE are always considered to be *reasonable* educational interventions in our learning context, we refer to such policy as a *random yet reasonable* policy or *random* in the following. In Experiment 2 (Exp2), we compare the CAPOMDP policies induced by time against a Deep Q-Network (DQN) induced policy and a random policy.

Our empirical results suggest that there is an Aptitude-Treatment Interaction (ATI) effect [8]. Specifically, we find that students with high incoming competence are less sensitive to the induced policies in that they achieve a similar learning performance regardless of policies employed whereas students with low incoming competence are more sensitive in that their learning is highly dependant on the effectiveness of the policies. Furthermore, Exp1 shows that CAPOMDP using learning gains as reward significantly outperforms the random policy in both learning gain and learning efficiency, and Exp2 shows that CAPOMDP using time as reward helps low incoming competence students spend significantly less time than the two baseline policies. The post-hoc comparison suggests that CAPOMDP using learning gains as reward also beats the DQN induced policy in terms of learning efficiency.

2 RELATED WORK

2.1 Applying RL into Educational Domain

MDP Framework. Both *learning gain* (LG) and *time* were explored as the reward functions in prior work in applying MDP to ITSs. For LG, Chi et al. [6] applied a model-based RL method with LG as reward to induce pedagogical policies for improving the effectiveness of an ITS that teaches students college physics. However, they found that the RL policy did not outperform the random policy. Similarly, Shen et al. [24] designed the immediate and delayed rewards based

on learning gain and implemented a model-based MDP framework on a rule-based ITS for deductive logic. They found that the RL policies were more effective than random baseline for a particular type of learners. In addition, Rowe et al. [23] investigated an MDP framework with normalized LG (NLG) as reward for tutorial planning in a game-based learning system. They found that students in the induced planner condition had significantly different behavior patterns from the controlled group but no significant difference was found between the two groups on the post-test.

When using *time* as reward function, Iglesias et al. [12] applied online Q-learning to generate a policy in an ITS that teaches students database design, with the purpose of providing students with direct navigation support through the system's content and minimizing the time spent in the teaching process. Similarly, Beck et al. [3] investigated temporal difference learning to induce pedagogical policies that would minimize the time that students take to complete each problem in an ITS that teaches arithmetic to grade school students. For both works, they found that the policy group spent significantly less time than the non-policy peers.

POMDP Framework. Mandel et al. [16] applied POMDP using *LG* as reward to induce policies in an educational game for teaching students concepts related to refraction. Their results showed that the induced POMDP policies outperformed both random and expert-designed policies in both simulated and empirical evaluations. Similarly, Clement et al. [7] constructed a student model to track students' individual mastery of knowledge components, and treated the mastery as hidden state and LG as reward in POMDP for inducing instructional policies. Their results showed that the POMDP policies outperformed the theory-based policies in terms of students' knowledge levels on task.

Different from the above POMDP applications, Rafferty et al. [22] applied the POMDP framework using *time* as reward in the domain of alphabet arithmetic. They interpreted the hidden states of POMDP as the students' latent knowledge related to concept learning. Their empirical study showed that the POMDP policies significantly outperformed the random policy in terms of time in that the former spent significantly less time than the latter.

Deep RL Framework. Wang et al.[26] applied a deep RL framework for personalizing interactive narratives in an educational game. They designed the rewards based on NLG and found that in simulation studies the students with the Deep RL policy achieved a higher NLG score than with the linear RL agent. Furthermore, Narasimhan et al. [20] implemented a DQN approach in a text-based strategy game, where the state is represented by a Long Short-Term Memory (LSTM) network, and the Q value is approximated by a multi-layered neural network, and the reward is designed based on the performance of game quest. Using simulations, they found that the deep RL policy significantly outperformed the random policy in terms of quest completion.

In summary, much of the prior work on applying RL in ITSs used either LG or time as reward but not both. Furthermore, compared with MDP and POMDP, relatively little research has been done on applying Deep RL to the field of ITS nor has it directly empirically compared Deep RL with other RL frameworks. Last but not least, none of the prior research has investigated the impact of different reward functions on RL frameworks by considering the action-based constraints in interactive learning environments.

2.2 Aptitude Treatment Interaction (ATI) Effect

Prior research in instructional strategies [8] assert that for any type of instructional interventions, an ATI effect is often exhibited, which claims that the instructional interventions are more or less effective for the learners depending on their abilities or aptitudes. Chi & VanLehn [5] investigated the ATI effect in the domain of probability and physics and their results showed that the high incoming competence students can learn regardless of instructional interventions, while for students with low incoming competence, those who follow the effective instructional interventions learned significantly more than those following less effective interventions. In our prior work, it is consistently shown that for pedagogical decisions on WE vs. PS, certain learners are always less sensitive in that their learning is not affected, while others are more sensitive to variations in different policies. For example, Shen et al. [24] trained students in an ITS for logic proofs, then divided students into the Fast and Slow groups based on time, and found that the Slow groups are more sensitive to the pedagogical strategies while the Fast groups are less sensitive.

3 BACKGROUND

3.1 Problem Statement

In the original RL scenarios, the agent selects the optimal action at any given situation to maximize the expected cumulative reward (ECR), which is represented as formula (1). In prior work in solving the classic constrained RL scenarios, the constrained MDP [2] or the constrained POMDP [15] frameworks generally search for the optimal policy that maximizes ECR while staying below the upper *bound* of the expected cumulative *cost (ECC)*, which involves defining a *cost function* for each pair of state and action.

By contrast, in the *constrained action-based RL* (CARL) scenarios described here, the agent chooses an action from a set of alternatives to both maximize its expected cumulative reward while obeying the action-based constraints. For example, the constraints in our application limit the total number of times that PS and WE can be selected at a given level. Therefore, rather than defining a cost function for each pair of state and action as the classic constrained RL scenarios, we formalize CARL problems as:

$$\max_{\pi} E_{\pi} \left[\sum_{t=0}^{L} \gamma^t R(s_t, a_t) \right] \tag{1}$$

$$\text{s.t. } 0 < C_{\pi}(a) = \left[\sum_{t=0}^{L} \mathbb{I}(a_t^{\pi} = a) \right] < \widehat{c_a}, \forall a \in A \tag{2}$$

where formula (2) is the action-based constraint. More specifically, A is the set of all possible actions and L is the length of a trajectory; $\widehat{c_a}$ and 0 denote the upper and lower bounds on the number of times that action a can be selected; a_t^{π} indicates that action a is selected by policy π at time step t, and $\mathbb{I}(\cdot)$ is the indicator function in that it would return 1 if the expression in $(\cdot)$ is true and 0 otherwise. $C_{\pi}(a)$ represents the cost function (2) for the action-based constraints and only depends on the actions. For our application, if the action-based constraint is active at time t, then state s_t is treated as a terminal state, where the agent cannot take any more actions.

3.2 POMDP Framework

POMDP is defined as a tuple: $\langle$ S, O, A, R, P_s, P_o, $Prior$, B $\rangle$. S represents the set of hidden states $\{S_1, S_2..., S_K\}$ with the set size K; O is the set of observations with a wide range of features; A and R denote the set of actions and the reward function respectively. P_s denotes the hidden state transition probability: $P_s(s', s, a) = Pr(s'|s, a)$, and P_o is the emission probability: $P_o(o, s, a) = Pr(o|s, a)$. $Prior$ denotes the prior probability distribution of hidden states. In addition, B denotes the belief state space, where each element $b_t(s) = Pr(s|o_{1:t}, a_{1:t})$ is the probability distribution of the hidden state s at each time step t after executing the action sequence $a_{1:t}$ and obtaining the observation sequence $o_{1:t}$. Specifically, we can estimate $b_t(s)$ as:

$$b_t(s) = \frac{1}{Z} \sum_{s'} b_{t-1}(s') P_s(s', s, a_t) P_o(o_t, s, a_t) \tag{3}$$

Where Z is the normalization value. The belief state at the first step is calculated by multiplying $Prior$ with the emission probability P_o. In our work, we utilize Input-Output Hidden Markov Models (IOHMM) [4] to translate the observations into belief states. In this context the input and output denote the action and observation. More specifically, the belief state at each time step is calculated by following formula (3) via the forward-backward IOHMM algorithm.

4 CONSTRAINED ACTION-BASED POMDP

As an extension of the POMDP framework, CAPOMDP modifies the state representation and the reward function to incorporate action-based constraints, shown in the following sections.

4.1 Factored State Representation

The factored state representation is constructed by concatenating the belief state with a constrained state. Specifically, the belief state is defined in the POMDP framework. The constrained state at time step t is defined as $[c_1^t, c_2^t, ..., c_{|A|}^t]$, where each element is a constrained feature which counts the total number of times that the action was chosen up to the present time point. If an action a is selected at a particular time step, the value of the corresponding constrained feature c_a is incremented by 1. Thus, we can estimate c_a^t efficiently as:

$$c_a^t = \begin{cases} c_a^{t-1} + 1 & a^t = a \\ c_a^{t-1} & \text{else} \end{cases} \tag{4}$$

Consequently, the factored state at time t is represented as $S^t = \left[b_1^t, b_2^t, ..., b_K^t, c_1^t, c_2^t, ..., c_{|A|}^t \right]$. In other words, the factored state contains two independent components: the belief state and the constrained state. The former is used to model the learning process, while the latter only tracks the status of the actions and whether the selection of the action triggers the constraints. Therefore, the factored state transition can be decomposed into separate estimates of the transition for the belief state component via function (3) and the transition for the constrained state component via function (4).

Furthermore, we designate a factored state as *safe* if all of the elements in its constrained state component satisfy the constraint function (2). *Error* states are defined as any state where one or more elements of its constrained state component violate function (2).

Error states are treated as one type of terminal state since they are disallowed in the system, while safe states permit actions to be taken which can transit to other states.

4.2 Reward Function

Since the basic ITS prohibits any appearance of an error state, we need to assign a strong negative reward for any transition from a safe state to an error state and treat error states as terminal states. We still retain the original reward for transitions between safe states in the training corpus since these transitions impose no additional cost. Therefore we define the new constrained reward function as:

$$R_c(s_t, a_t) = \begin{cases} R(s_t, a_t) & s_t \in S_{safe}, s_{t+1} \in S_{safe} \\ -\widehat{c} & s_t \in S_{safe}, s_{t+1} \in S_{error} \end{cases} \quad (5)$$

Where $-\widehat{c}$ indicates a strong negative value. $R_c(s_t, a_t)$ represents the reward function with constraints, and $R(s_t, a_t)$ denotes the real reward in the training corpus. However, our training corpus does not contain error states because the original system has hard-coded rules to avoid them. Thus, we are required to manually add transitions from the safe states to error states with strong negative rewards in training dataset as shown in formula (5).

4.3 CAPOMDP Policy Induction

We implement Least Squares Policy Iteration (LSPI) [14] on the factor state of CAPOMDP to induce the optimal policy, which consists of two steps: *policy evaluation* and *policy improvement*.

In the *policy evaluation* step, we approximate the Q-function $Q(s, a)$, the expected reward of taking action a at state s, using a linear model generalized as:

$$Q(s, a) = \sum_{i=0}^{|S|*|A|} w_i \phi_i(s, a) \quad (6)$$

Where $\phi_i(s, a)$ indicates the basic element in state s associated with the action a, and s is a factored state representation in CAPOMDP framework (see Sec 4.1). $|S|$ and $|A|$ denote the size of the state set and action set respectively. w_i is the parameter of the linear model and it also involves a constant item (when $i = 0$). Additionally, we have that the Q-function follows the Bellman equation:

$$Q^\pi = R + \gamma P \Pi_\pi Q^\pi \quad (7)$$

By integrating equation (6) and (7), Least Square Temporal Difference Q learning approach [14] estimates the parameter w as:

$$\begin{cases} w = H^{-1}f \\ H = \sum_{(s,a,s') \in D} \phi(s,a)[\phi(s,a) - \gamma\phi(s', \pi(s'))]^T \\ f = \sum_{(s,a,s') \in D} \phi(s,a)R(s,a) \end{cases} \quad (8)$$

Where D is the training corpus, and $\pi(s')$ denotes the action selected by current policy π given a state s'. H and f can be estimated from the training corpus.

In the *policy improvement* step, w is updated through the gradient decent approach toward to minimize the loss function, then LSPI checks whether w converges. If w does not converge, it goes back to the policy estimation step; otherwise, it terminates.

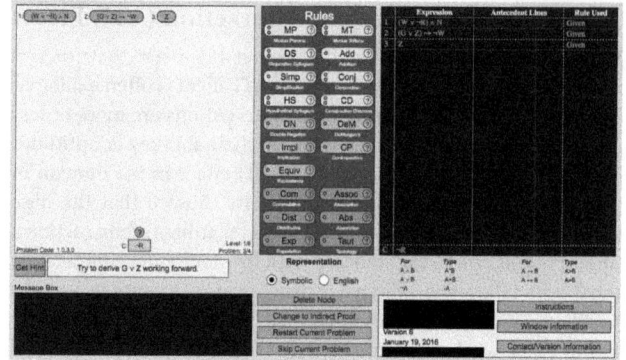

Figure 1: Interface of PS in ITS

5 EXPERIMENT SETUP

5.1 Intelligent Tutoring System: Deep Thought

Deep Thought (DT) is a data-driven ITS used in the undergraduate-level Discrete Mathematics (DM) course at North Carolina State University (NCSU). DT [19] provides students with a graph-based representation of logic proofs which allows students to solve problems by adding rule applications (represented as nodes). The system automatically verifies proofs and provides immediate feedback on logical errors. Every problem in DT can be presented in the form of either Worked Example (WE) or Problem Solving (PS). In WE, students are given a detailed example showing the expert solution for the problem or were shown the best step to take given their current solution state. In PS (shown in Figure 1), by contrast, students are tasked with solving the same problem using the ITS or completing an individual problem-solving step. By focusing on the pedagogical decisions of choosing WE vs. PS, which would allow us to strictly control the content to be *equivalent* for all students. In addition to the problems, DT has two hard-coded *action-based constraints* that are required by the class instructors: the last problem on each level must be done as PS, and prior to reaching that problem the students must complete at least one PS and one WE.

Procedure. The problems in DT are organized into seven strictly ordered levels and in each level students are required to complete 3–4 problems. In the **pre-test** (level 1), all participants receive the same set of PS problems and students performance at this level is used to measure their incoming competence. In the following five **training levels** 2–6, before the students proceed to a new problem, the system followed the corresponding RL-induced or random policies to decide whether to present it as PS or WE. The last question on each level is a PS without DT's help and thus functioned as a mini-test for evaluating students' knowledge of the concepts of that level. In the **post-test** (level 7), all participants also receive the same set of PS problems and their performance at this level is evaluated as the post-test score. In addition, we defined the **Normalized Learning Gain (NLG)** as:

$$NLG = \begin{cases} \frac{post-pre}{100-pre} & post >= pre \\ \frac{post-pre}{pre} & post < pre \end{cases} \quad (9)$$

Therefore, we evaluate students performance based on 1) pre- and post-test scores, 2) NLG, 3) time and 4) **Learning Efficiency** (LE ∝

NLG/Time). In the following, it is important to note that due to class constraints the pre- and post-tests covered different concepts and were collected at different times: the pre-test occurred in a single session before the policies were employed, while the post-test scores were collected at the end of later levels. Therefore the two scores cannot be directly aligned.

5.2 Training Corpus

The training corpus for RL policy induction was collected from training 570 students in DT in the Fall 2014, 15, and 16 semesters of a Discrete Mathematics course. In these semesters, DT was programmed to make random decisions when selecting PS and WE. Note that, when collecting our original training data, DT had already implemented the action-based constraints requested by the class instructors. The average number of solved problems in the form of both PS and WE is 24.1 (SD=2.59). Furthermore, DT recorded the observation as a set of 133 state features, including 59 discrete and 74 continuous features, for representing the students' behaviors and learning environment. DT calculated the level score based on the last problem in each of training levels 2–6. For simplicity reasons, the range of level scores is normalized to [0, 100].

When inducing RL policies using learning gain as reward, we calculated the difference between the student's current and prior level scores. If students quit the tutor during the training, we assigned a strong negative reward of -300 on the last problem he/she attempted. When inducing RL policies using time as reward, we used the *negative* log of time as the reward for inducing the policy: that is, when training on DT, the less time a student spent on completing the entire training portion, the better. There is a significant correlation between the *negative* log of times and student post-test scores: $cor = 0.19$, $p = .006$.

5.3 Deep RL Policy

We apply the Deep Q-Network (DQN) algorithm, proposed by Mnih et al. [17], to construct a strong baseline policy. DQN uses a neural network to map state features to Q-values $Q(s, a)$ for each action. The neural network consists of three LSTM layers [11] with 1000 units each, followed by a fully connected layer with 2 output units, one for each action. We trained the network using the DQN algorithm on the training corpus until convergence of the loss function. When implementing the neural network in the ITS, the action selected for each student was the action with the highest Q-value, between $Q(s, PS)$ and $Q(s, WE)$.

5.4 Policy Execution

Due to the hard-coded constraints, whenever DT makes a tutorial decision, the baseline policy execution process will first check whether the selected action violates the hard-coded action-based constraints shown in Figure 2 (a). If the action is valid then it will be carried out; otherwise, DT uses hard-coded rules to choose an alternative that satisfies the constraints. By contrast, the CAPOMDP policy execution is shown in Figure 2 (b). Since the action-based constraints are already incorporated into the policy, we expect that the induced CAPOMDP policy will be fully carried out and that the hard-coded rules will not be violated.

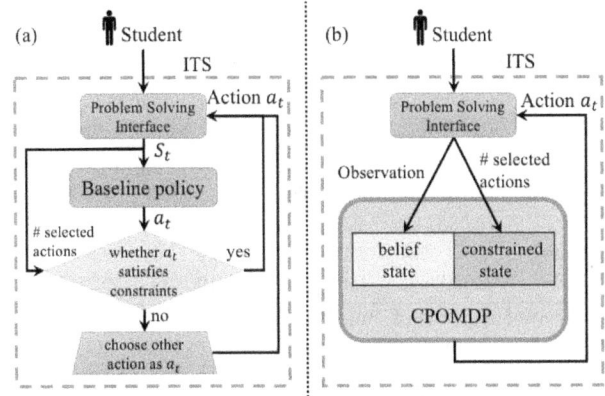

Figure 2: (a) Baseline policy execution with action-based constraints; (b) the CAPOMDP policy execution

5.5 Study Overview

In this work, we investigate two primary research questions: 1) whether using learning gain or time as reward makes the CAPOMDP framework induce a more effective pedagogical strategy; and 2) Can the CAPOMDP framework outperform the Deep Q-learning approach? We conducted two empirical experiments, involving the following four policies:

1. $CAPOMDP_{LG}$: CAPOMDP with learning gain as reward;
2. $CAPOMDP_{Time}$: CAPOMDP with time as reward;
3. DQN_{LG}: Deep Q-Network with learning gain as reward;
4. **Random**: Random yet reasonable decision (baseline).

Exp1 implements and compares the $CAPOMDP_{LG}$ and Random policies, and Exp2 applies the four policies including: $CAPOMDP_{LG}$, $CAPOMDP_{Time}$, DQN_{LG} and Random. However, due to administration errors, very few students were randomly assigned to $CAPOMDP_{LG}$ and thus we will mainly focus on comparing the effectiveness of $CAPOMDP_{Time}$, DQN_{LG} and Random in Exp2. Since all students are drawn from the same target population, we combine two $CAPOMDP_{LG}$ groups in Exp1 and Exp2 and also integrate the two Random groups in Exp1 and Exp2, and then conduct a post-hoc comparison across two experiments. In order to measure the Aptitude-Treatment Interaction effect, we defined High and Low groups based on students incoming competence, the pre-test score. More specifically, we did a single median split of pre-test scores for all groups in both experiments since all students experienced an identical procedure. As shown in the following sections, this split reasonably reflects the incoming competence of the students.

6 EXPERIMENT 1 (EXP1)

6.1 Participants & Conditions

77 students enrolled in the DM course at NCSU in the Fall 2017 and were randomly assigned into two conditions: $CAPOMDP_{LG}$ ($N = 40$) and Random ($N = 37$). They were further divided into the High and Low groups using the median split on the pre-test scores as described above. Thus, we have: $CAPOMDP_{LG}$-*High* ($N = 25$),

Table 1: Students' learning performance in Experiment 1

Measure	High		Low	
	$CAPOMDP_{LG}$	Random	$CAPOMDP_{LG}$	Random
Pre-test	63.37(15.44)	66.02(15.01)	19.71(11.98)	14.87(11.15)
Post-test	54.36(20.34)	59.27(23.56)	57.13(16.77)	38.98(17.63)
NLG	-0.08(0.41)	-0.03(0.51)	**0.46(0.19)**	0.23(0.34)
Time	2.40(1.08)	3.15(1.49)	3.24(1.36)	3.83(1.37)
LE	0.02(0.64)	-0.01(0.67)	**0.49(0.31)**	0.21(0.28)

Note: Mean and SD of Time is in hours.

$CAPOMDP_{LG}$-Low ($N = 15$), Random-High ($N = 20$) and Random-Low ($N = 17$). While more students were assigned to $CAPOMDP_{LG}$-High, a χ^2 test shows no significant difference in the distribution of High vs.Low between conditions: $\chi^2(2, N = 77) = 1.5, p = 0.22$.

6.2 Results

Table 1 presents the mean and SD for students' corresponding learning performance and time in Exp1. One-way ANOVA tests show that no significant difference is found on the pre-test score either between the two conditions, or between $CAPOMDP_{LG}$-High and Random-High, or between $CAPOMDP_{LG}$-Low and Random-Low. As expected, the High groups ($M = 64.44, SD = 15.14$) score significantly higher than the Low groups ($M = 16.95, SD = 11.59$): $F(1, 75) = 231.2, p < .000$ on the pre-test score.

Post-Test: A two-way ANCOVA test using policy {$CAPOMDP_{LG}$, Random} and incoming competence {High, Low} as factors and the pre-test scores as covariate shows that there is a significant interaction effect on their post-test scores: $F(1, 72) = 5.78, p = .018$. A one-way ANCOVA shows that no significant difference is found either between $CAPOMDP_{LG}$ and Random, or between the High and Low groups. Additionally, one-way ANCOVA tests on policy using pre-test as covariate show that while there is no significant difference between the two High groups, a significant difference was found between the two Low groups: $CAPOMDP_{LG}$-Low achieves a significantly higher post-test score than Random-Low: $F(1, 32) = 8.65, p = .006$ (see Table 1).

NLG: Similarly, a two-way ANOVA test using policy and incoming competence as factors and the pre-test score as covariate yields a significant interaction effect on NLG: $F(1, 72) = 4.27, p = .018$. One-way ANOVAs shows that while there is no significant difference between $CAPOMDP_{LG}$ and Random, there is a significant between High and Low: $F(1, 75) = 4.16, p = .045$. The Low groups ($M = 0.33, SD = 0.30$) achieve a significantly higher NLG than the High groups ($M = -0.06, SD = 0.44$). Furthermore, while there is no significant difference between $CAPOMDP_{LG}$-High and Random-High, a one-way ANCOVA on policy using pre-test as covariate shows that $CAPOMDP_{LG}$-Low scores significantly higher NLG than Random-Low: $F(1, 33) = 5.46, p = .025$ (see Table 1).

Time: A two-way ANOVA test using condition and incoming competence as factors shows no significant interaction effect on total time that students spend in the tutor. One-way ANOVA tests show that there is no significant difference between $CAPOMDP_{LG}$ and Random, but the Low groups ($M = 3.57, SD = 1.28$) spend significantly more time than the High groups ($M = 2.70, SD = 1.30$):

$F(1, 75) = 8.84, p = .004$. No significant difference is found either between the two High groups or between the two Low groups.

Learning Efficiency (LE): A two-way ANOVA test using policy and incoming competence as factors shows no significant interaction effect on LE, and a one-way ANOVA test also shows no significant difference between $CAPOMDP_{LG}$ and Random, but a significant difference is found between High and Low groups in that the Low groups ($M = 0.33, SD = 0.32$) score significantly higher than the High groups ($M = 0.005, SD = 0.64$): $F(1, 75) = 7.20, p = .009$. Despite this, while no significant difference is found between $CAPOMDP_{LG}$-High and Random-High, a one-way ANOVA test shows that $CAPOMDP_{LG}$-Low scores significantly higher LE than Random-Low: $F(1, 33) = 7.77, p = .009$.

6.3 Discussion

To summarize, we find the significant difference between the High and the Low groups: the latter has significantly higher NLG, spends significantly longer time on DT, and achieves significantly higher LE than the High groups. More importantly, Exp1 exhibits an ATI effect: while no significant difference is found between the two High groups, significant differences are found between the two Low groups on post-test score, NLG and LE. In short, for the High incoming competence students it seems that both their learning performance and time on task is not impacted by the induced pedagogical strategies; for the low incoming competence students, however, by using LG as reward our CAPOMDP framework significantly benefits them more than the baseline Random policy on post-test, NLG and LE.

7 EXPERIMENT 2 (EXP2)

7.1 Participants & Conditions

139 students enrolled in the DM course at NCSU in Spring 2018 were randomly assigned into four conditions: $CAPOMDP_{LG}$ ($N = 12$), $CAPOMDP_{Time}$ ($N = 52$), DQN_{LG} ($N = 34$) and Random ($N = 41$). Due to administration errors, only 12 students were assigned to $CAPOMDP_{LG}$ and thus it is excluded in the following analysis. Similar to Exp1, students in Exp2 were divided into the High and Low groups using median split on the pre-test scores. Combining condition and incoming competence, we have a total of six groups: $CAPOMDP_{Time}$-High ($N = 34$), $CAPOMDP_{Time}$-Low ($N = 18$), DQN_{LG}-High ($N = 21$), DQN_{LG}-Low ($N = 13$), Random-High ($N = 26$) and Random-Low ($N = 15$). While it seems that High vs. Low is imbalanced, a χ^2 test shows no significant difference in the distribution of High vs. Low among the three conditions: $\chi^2(2, N = 139) = 0.12, p = 0.94$.

7.2 Results

Table 2 presents the mean (and SD) of students' corresponding learning performance and time in Exp2. A one-way ANOVA test shows no significant difference among the three conditions on their pre-test. As expected, the High groups ($M = 62.26, SD = 16.59$) score significantly higher pre-test than the Low groups ($M = 21.55, SD = 9.08$): $F(1, 137) = 240.6, p < .000$. Finally, no significant difference is found either among the three High groups or among the three Low groups.

Table 2: Students' learning performance in Experiment 2

Measure	High			Low		
	$CAPOMDP_{Time}$	DQN_{LG}	Random	$CAPOMDP_{Time}$	DQN_{LG}	Random
Pre-test	63.33(15.36)	63.72(15.45)	63.88(15.35)	23.26(9.07)	19.09(9.57)	21.63(8.79)
Post-test	55.99(22.01)	57.47(23.81)	64.46(19.11)	52.51(19.01)	45.65(21.84)	50.22(19.02)
NLG	-0.06(0.44)	-0.02(0.44)	0.08(0.42)	**0.37(0.26)**	0.27(0.39)	0.33(0.32)
Time	3.12(1.66)	3.13(1.58)	2.34(0.92)	**3.00(1.08)**	4.15(1.20)	3.88(1.38)
LE	0.04(0.55)	0.16(0.64)	0.13(0.58)	**0.39(0.34)**	0.21(0.27)	0.28(0.23)

Note: Mean and SD of Time is in hours; LE denotes the learning efficiency.

Post-test & NLG: Using policy {$CAPOMDP_{Time}$, DQN_{LG}, Random} and incoming competence {High, Low} as factors and the pre-test score as covariate, a two-way ANCOVA test shows there is no significant interaction effect on either their post-test scores or NLG. Additionally, one-way ANCOVA tests show that there is no significant difference either among conditions, or among the High groups, or among the Low groups on both post-test and NLG. Finally, while no significant difference is found between High and Low on post-test, the Low groups ($M = 0.31$, $SD = 0.29$) achieve significantly higher NLG than the High groups ($M = .08$, $SD = 0.55$): $F(1, 137) = 20.52, p < .000$. Therefore, much to our surprise, while DQN_{LG} is induced using learning gain as reward, it did not outperform Random; additionally, while $CAPOMDP_{Time}$ is induced using time as reward, it seems that it does not hurt students' learning performance as we are originally concerned about.

Time: To investigate whether $CAPOMDP_{Time}$ would indeed reduce student training time as expected, a two-way ANOVA test using condition and incoming competence as factors yields significant interaction effect on time: $F(2, 121) = 4.15, p = .018$. While one-way ANOVA tests show there is no significant difference among conditions, there is a significant difference between High and Low groups in that the Low groups ($M = 3.61$, $SD = 1.29$) spent significantly more time than the High groups ($M = 2.87$, $SD = 1.47$): $F(1, 125) = 8.10, p = .005$. More importantly, one-way ANOVA tests show that while there is no significant difference among the three High groups, there is a significant difference among the Low groups: $F(2, 43) = 3.90, p = .027$. Specifically, pairwise t-tests show that $CAPOMDP_{Time}$-Low spent significantly less time than either Random-Low or DQN_{LG}-Low: $p = .045$ and $p = .013$ respectively, and no significant difference was found between the latter two.

Learning Efficiency (LE): A two-way ANOVA test using condition and incoming competence as factors shows no significant interaction effect on LE. One-way ANOVAs indicate that there is no significant difference among the three conditions, but there is significant difference between High and Low in that the Low groups ($M = 3.61$, $SD = 1.29$) achieve significant higher LE than the High groups ($M = 0.10$, $SD = 0.57$): $F(1, 125) = 5.11, p = .025$. Although one-way ANOVA tests show that no significant difference is found among the High groups or among the Low groups, pairwise t-tests indicate that $CAPOMDP_{Time}$-Low scores marginally significantly higher LE than DQN_{LG}-Low ($p = .085$) (see Table 2).

7.3 Discussion

To summarize, in Exp2 we mainly focus on evaluating the effectiveness of CAPOMDP using time as reward against DQN using LG as reward and random group. Similar to Exp1, students are split into High vs. Low based on their pretest scores and the same patterns are found between the High and the Low groups: the latter had a significantly higher NLG, spent significantly longer time on DT, and achieved a significantly higher LE than their High peers. More importantly, while Exp1 exhibits an ATI effect on learning performance (post-test score, NLG and LE), Exp2 exhibits an ATI effect on time: while no significant difference is found among the three High groups, significant difference is found among the three Low groups in that students following $CAPOMDP_{Time}$ spent significantly less time than either DQN_{LG} or Random. In short, Exp2 shows that for the high incoming competence students, it seems that both their learning performance and time on task is not impacted by the induced pedagogical strategies; for the low incoming competence students, CAPOMDP using time as reward seemingly did not hurt their learning performance (post-test and NLG) and they indeed spent significantly less time than their peers under DQN_{LG} and Random. Much to our surprise, DQN_{LG} performs closely to Random. One of the possible reasons is that action-based constraints restrict the effectiveness of the DQN_{LG} policy. The DQN_{LG} and Random policies are only carried out 50.8% ($SD = 14.3\%$) and 51.1% ($SD = 11.3\%$) of the time respectively, while both the $CAPOMDP_{LG}$ and $CAPOMDP_{Time}$ policies can be fully followed.

8 POST-HOC COMPARISONS

In both Exp1 and Exp2, students were drawn from the same target population and all of them were enrolled in the experiments with the same method but in different semesters. By assigning students to each condition randomly, it provides the most rigorous test of our hypotheses. In this section, we conduct a post-hoc comparison across the two experiments in the hope that this wider view will shed some light on our main results. Especially while $CAPOMDP_{LG}$ outperformed Random in Exp1, it is not sure whether the same results would hold for Exp2 because we only have a small number of students assigned to $CAPOMDP_{LG}$ due to administration errors. Therefore, we want to combine the two Random groups into a single Random group and the two $CAPOMDP_{LG}$ into a single $CAPOMDP_{LG}$, and then compare their performance.

Additionally, one-way ANOVA tests show that while there is no significant difference between two Random groups in Exp1

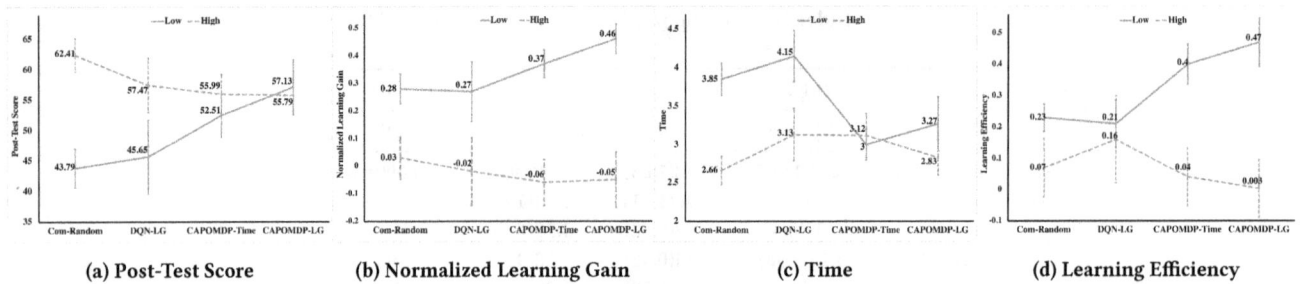

| (a) Post-Test Score | (b) Normalized Learning Gain | (c) Time | (d) Learning Efficiency |

Figure 3: Students' learning performance across Experiment 1 and 2

and Exp2 on pre-test: $F(1, 76) = 2.76, p = 0.1$, NLG: $F(1, 76) = 0.43, p = 0.52$, and LE: $F(1, 76) = 0.46, p = 0.49$, there is a significant difference on time: $F(1, 76) = 4.08, p = .046$ in that Random in Exp1 ($M = 3.51, SD = 1.34$) spent significantly more time than Random in Exp2 ($M = 2.90, SD = 1.32$), and there is a significant difference on post-test: $F(1, 76) = 5.10, p = .027$ in that Random in Exp2 ($M = 59.25, SD = 20.08$) scored a significantly higher post-test than Random in Exp1 ($M = 48.31, SD = 22.71$). In short, Random in Exp2 performed better in post-test and spent less time than Random in Exp1. Therefore, by combining the two Random groups, we get a stronger baseline condition than Random in Exp1 alone.

We combine the two Random groups into a single Random group referred as *Com-Random* ($N = 78$) and the two *CAPOMDP$_{LG}$* groups in Exp1 and Exp2 into a single *CAPOMDP$_{LG}$* group ($N = 52$). Therefore, we have a total of four groups as described in section 5.5. One-way ANOVA tests show no significant difference among the four conditions on the pre-test score.

All students were further divided into High and Low using the same median split described above. Combining policy and incoming competence, we have a total of eight groups: *Random-High* ($N = 43$), *Random-Low* ($N = 35$), *CAPOMDP$_{LG}$-High* ($N = 34$), *CAPOMDP$_{LG}$-Low* ($N = 18$), *CAPOMDP$_{Time}$-High* ($N = 34$), *CAPOMDP$_{Time}$-Low* ($N = 18$), *DQN$_{LG}$-High* ($N = 21$), *DQN$_{LG}$-Low* ($N = 13$). A χ^2 test shows no significant difference in the distribution of High vs. Low among four policy groups: $\chi^2(3, N = 216) = 0.12, p = 0.57$.

Pre-test: As expected, the High groups ($M = 63.85, SD = 15.11$) score significantly higher than the Low groups ($M = 19.68, SD = 10.26$): $F(1, 214) = 554, p < .000$ on pre-test. Except that, one-way ANOVA tests show that there is no significant difference either among *CAPOMDP$_{LG}$*, *CAPOMDP$_{Time}$*, *DQN$_{LG}$* and *Com-Random*, or among the four High groups, or among the four Low groups.

Post-test: Figure 3a presents the post-test scores of High vs. Low across the four policies. A two-way ANCOVA test using policy and incoming competence as factors and the pre-test score as covariate, yields no significant interaction effect on their post-test scores. Additionally, a two-way ANOVA test using policy and incoming competence as factors shows a significant interaction effect on their post-test scores: $F(3, 208) = 2.81, p = .041$. Although one-way ANOVA tests show there is no significant difference among the High groups, there is a marginally significant difference among the Low groups: $F(3, 80) = 2.29, p = .084$. Pairwise t-tests show that *CAPOMDP$_{LG}$-Low* scores the significantly higher post-test than *Random-Low*: ($p = .018$).

NLG: A two-way ANOVA test, using condition and incoming competence as factors yields no significant interaction effect on NLG. Additionally, a one-way ANOVA shows no significant difference among the four High groups, but a significant difference among the Low groups: $F(3, 80) = 3.57, p = .017$. Pairwise t-tests show that *CAPOMDP$_{LG}$-Low* scores a significantly higher NLG than *Com-Random-Low*: $p = .043$ and a marginally significant higher NLG than *DQN$_{LG}$-Low*: $p = .094$, shown in Figure 3b.

Time: A two-way ANOVA test using policy and incoming competence as factors shows a marginally significant interaction effect on time: $F(3, 208) = 2.50, p = .060$. Moreover, one-way ANOVA tests show that there is no significant difference among the four High groups, but there is a significant difference among the Low groups: $F(3, 80) = 3.19, p = .027$. Specifically, pairwise t-tests show that *CAPOMDP$_{Time}$-Low* spends significantly less time than both *Com-Random-Low* and *DQN$_{LG}$-Low*: $p = .020$ and $p = .012$ respectively; *CAPOMDP$_{LG}$-Low* spends marginally significantly less time than *DQN$_{LG}$-Low*: $p = .053$, shown in Figure 3c.

Learning Efficiency (LE): A two-way ANOVA test using policy and incoming competence as factors shows no significant interaction effect on LE. Additionally, while one-way ANOVA tests indicate that there is no significant difference among the High groups, a significant difference is found among the Low groups: $F(3, 80) = 3.57, p = .018$. Specifically, pairwise t-tests indicate that *CAPOMDP$_{LG}$-Low* scores significantly higher than both *Com-Random-Low* and *DQN$_{LG}$-Low*: $p = .007$ and $p = .016$ respectively; *CAPOMDP$_{Time}$-Low* achieves a marginally significantly higher LE than *Com-Random-Low* and *DQN$_{LG}$-Low*: $p = .065$ and $p = .083$ respectively, shown in Figure 3d.

9 CONCLUSION

We propose the CAPOMDP framework to deal with the action-based constraints in Deep Thought and explored CAPOMDP using both learning gain (LG) and time as rewards. Empirical results show that for the low incoming competence students, the *CAPOMDP$_{LG}$* policy significantly outperforms the baseline random policy in terms of post-test score, NLG, and learning efficiency; the *CAPOMDP$_{Time}$* policy significantly outperforms both *DQN$_{LG}$* and Random policies in terms of time. It seems that CAPOMDP indeed fulfills its promise for the low incoming students' learning in that it can improve their learning when using LG as reward and reduce their time on task when using time as reward. However, for the high incoming students, both their learning performance and time are not impacted by either policies using LG as reward or those using time as reward.

Much to our surprise, DQN_{LG} performs close to Random. One of the possible reasons is that action-based constraints restrict the effectiveness of the DQN_{LG} policy. The DQN_{LG} and *Random* policies are only carried out 50.8% ($SD = 14.3\%$) and 51.1% ($SD = 11.3\%$) of the time respectively, while both the $CAPOMDP_{LG}$ and $CAPOMDP_{Time}$ policies can be fully followed. In future work, we will integrate the Deep Q-Network framework with the action-based constraints in our ITS. Moreover, we will induce the policy which can significantly improve LG as well as reduce the time, considering the learning gain and time as the objective simultaneously.

Acknowledgements. This research was supported by the National Science Foundation under Grant No.: 1726550, 1651909, and 1432156.

REFERENCES

[1] Joshua Achiam, David Held, Aviv Tamar, and Pieter Abbeel. 2017. Constrained policy optimization. *arXiv preprint arXiv:1705.10528* (2017).

[2] Eitan Altman. 1999. *Constrained Markov decision processes*. Vol. 7. CRC Press.

[3] Joseph Beck, Beverly Park Woolf, and Carole R Beal. 2000. ADVISOR: A machine learning architecture for intelligent tutor construction. *AAAI/IAAI* 2000, 552-557 (2000), 1–1.

[4] Yoshua Bengio and Paolo Frasconi. 1995. An input output HMM architecture. In *Advances in neural information processing systems*. 427–434.

[5] Min Chi and Kurt VanLehn. 2010. Meta-cognitive strategy instruction in intelligent tutoring systems: how, when, and why. *Journal of Educational Technology & Society* 13, 1 (2010), 25.

[6] Min Chi, Kurt VanLehn, Diane Litman, and Pamela Jordan. 2011. Empirically evaluating the application of reinforcement learning to the induction of effective and adaptive pedagogical strategies. *User Modeling and User-Adapted Interaction* 21, 1-2 (2011), 137–180.

[7] Benjamin Clement, Pierre-Yves Oudeyer, and Manuel Lopes. 2016. A Comparison of Automatic Teaching Strategies for Heterogeneous Student Populations. In *EDM 16-9th International Conference on Educational Data Mining.*

[8] Lee J Cronbach and Richard E Snow. 1977. *Aptitudes and instructional methods: A handbook for research on interactions*. Irvington.

[9] Dmitri Dolgov and Edmund Durfee. 2005. Stationary deterministic policies for constrained MDPs with multiple rewards, costs, and discount factors. *Ann Arbor* 1001 (2005), 48109.

[10] Javier Garcia and Fernando Fernández. 2012. Safe exploration of state and action spaces in reinforcement learning. *Journal of Artificial Intelligence Research* 45 (2012), 515–564.

[11] Sepp Hochreiter and Jürgen Schmidhuber. 1997. Long short-term memory. *Neural computation* 9, 8 (1997), 1735–1780.

[12] Ana Iglesias, Paloma Martínez, Ricardo Aler, and Fernando Fernández. 2009. Reinforcement learning of pedagogical policies in adaptive and intelligent educational systems. *Knowledge-Based Systems* 22, 4 (2009), 266–270. https://doi.org/DOI: 10.1016/j.knosys.2009.01.007 Artificial Intelligence (AI) in Blended Learning - (AI) in Blended Learning.

[13] Kenneth R Koedinger, John R Anderson, William H Hadley, and Mary A Mark. 1997. Intelligent tutoring goes to school in the big city. (1997).

[14] Michail G Lagoudakis and Ronald Parr. 2003. Least-squares policy iteration. *Journal of machine learning research* 4, Dec (2003), 1107–1149.

[15] Jongmin Lee, Youngsoo Jang, Pascal Poupart, and Kee-Eung Kim. 2017. Constrained Bayesian Reinforcement Learning via Approximate Linear Programming. In *Proceedings of the Twenty-Sixth International Joint Conference on Artificial Intelligence.*

[16] Travis Mandel, Yun-En Liu, Sergey Levine, Emma Brunskill, and Zoran Popovic. 2014. Offline policy evaluation across representations with applications to educational games. In *Proceedings of the 2014 international conference on Autonomous agents and multi-agent systems*. 1077–1084.

[17] Volodymyr Mnih, Koray Kavukcuoglu, David Silver, Andrei A Rusu, Joel Veness, Marc G Bellemare, Alex Graves, Martin Riedmiller, Andreas K Fidjeland, Georg Ostrovski, et al. 2015. Human-level control through deep reinforcement learning. *Nature* 518, 7540 (2015), 529.

[18] Behrooz Mostafavi and Tiffany Barnes. 2017. Evolution of an intelligent deductive logic tutor using data-driven elements. *International Journal of Artificial Intelligence in Education* 27, 1 (2017), 5–36.

[19] Behrooz Mostafavi, Zhongxiu Liu, and Tiffany Barnes. 2015. Data-Driven Proficiency Profiling. *International Educational Data Mining Society* (2015).

[20] Karthik Narasimhan, Tejas Kulkarni, and Regina Barzilay. 2015. Language understanding for text-based games using deep reinforcement learning. *arXiv preprint arXiv:1506.08941* (2015).

[21] Pascal Poupart, Aarti Malhotra, Pei Pei, Kee-Eung Kim, Bongseok Goh, and Michael Bowling. 2015. Approximate Linear Programming for Constrained Partially Observable Markov Decision Processes.. In *AAAI*. 3342–3348.

[22] Anna N Rafferty, Emma Brunskill, Thomas L Griffiths, and Patrick Shafto. 2016. Faster teaching via pomdp planning. *Cognitive science* 40, 6 (2016), 1290–1332.

[23] Jonathan P Rowe and James C Lester. 2015. Improving student problem solving in narrative-centered learning environments: A modular reinforcement learning framework. In *International Conference on Artificial Intelligence in Education*. Springer, 419–428.

[24] Shitian Shen and Min Chi. 2016. Reinforcement Learning: the Sooner the Better, or the Later the Better?. In *Proceedings of the 2016 Conference on User Modeling Adaptation and Personalization*. ACM, 37–44.

[25] Kurt Vanlehn. 2006. The behavior of tutoring systems. *International journal of artificial intelligence in education* 16, 3 (2006), 227–265.

[26] Pengcheng Wang, Jonathan Rowe, Wookhee Min, Bradford Mott, and James Lester. 2017. Interactive narrative personalization with deep reinforcement learning. In *Proceedings of the Twenty-Sixth International Joint Conference on Artificial Intelligence.*

A Fine-Grained Open Learner Model for an Introductory Programming Course

Jordan Barria-Pineda
School of Computing and
Information, University of Pittsburgh
Pittsburgh, PA, USA
jab464@pitt.edu

Julio Guerra-Hollstein
Instituto de Informática, Universidad
Austral de Chile
Valdivia, Chile
jguerra@inf.uach.cl

Peter Brusilovsky
School of Computing and
Information, University of Pittsburgh
Pittsburgh, PA, USA
peterb@pitt.edu

ABSTRACT

Guiding students to the learning activities that are most appropriate for their current level of knowledge is one of the goals that adaptive educational systems tried to achieve during the last decades. Recently, several attempts have been made to use Open Learner Models (OLM) as a tool for achieving this goal. While the original goal of OLM is to help students reflect about their own learning process, extending OLM with navigation support functionality enables students to take immediate actions towards improving their knowledge. In this work, we attempted to extend the navigation support functionality of OLM by developing a fine-grained OLM that offers student knowledge visualization on both topic and concept levels. The fine-grained OLM enables students to directly explore connections between their knowledge and available learning activities, making an informed decision about their next learning steps. To assess the impact of the new type of OLM, we evaluated several versions of it in a classroom study, while also comparing it with data from our earlier studies that featured a coarse-grained OLM. Our results suggest that the fine-grained OLM considerably impacts student choice of learning activities, making student learning more efficient. We also found that the specific design features of fine-grained OLM could affect students' confidence and persistence while selecting and attempting the learning activities.

CCS CONCEPTS

• **Human-centered computing** → **Information visualization**; **User models**; • **Social and professional topics** → **Computer science education**; • **Applied computing** → **Interactive learning environments**;

KEYWORDS

Open Learner Models; Information Visualization; Computer Science Education; Self-Regulated Learning

ACM Reference Format:
Jordan Barria-Pineda, Julio Guerra-Hollstein, and Peter Brusilovsky. 2018. A Fine-Grained Open Learner Model for an Introductory Programming Course. In *UMAP '18: 26th Conference on User Modeling, Adaptation and Personalization, July 8–11, 2018, Singapore, Singapore*. ACM, New York, NY, USA, 9 pages. https://doi.org/10.1145/3209219.3209242

1 INTRODUCTION

When students work with an adaptive educational system, one of the main processes that takes place behind the scenes is the inference of their current state of knowledge. For achieving this, a learner model is maintained and updated by observing student behavior in the system (e.g. actions made, problems solved, examples explored, etc.). In most cases, learner modeling is based on a predefined structured representation of the study domain (e.g. a set of fundamental knowledge components - KCs) and connections between learning activities and KCs. Historically, these underlying models are kept hidden from learners. However, the proponents of Open Learner Models (OLM) argue that making learner models visible opens a new communication channel between the student and the learning system and brings some valuable benefits. A number of studies with OLMs confirmed their ability to prompt students' reflection and raise their awareness about their current state of knowledge, leading students to a better understanding of their learning process, feeling more responsible for it and planning it in a better way [6].

In our past work, we attempted to extend traditional awareness-oriented OLM with other features such as adaptive navigation support [1] and social comparison features [2]. In these works, we focused on topic-level learner models [24], which use coarse-grained *topics* as KCs. Each topic represents a broad course study unit that can integrate several atomic *concepts*, e.g. the topic of *Arithmetic Operators* can cover several concepts such as addition, multiplication, modulus, and exponentiation, among others. We demonstrated that topic-level OLMs could guide students to the most appropriate topics, increase their engagement with the system, and improve their learning outcomes. We also demonstrated that topic-level modeling could be successfully extended with social comparison [11]. Including information of how other peers are progressing increases the perceived value of OLM for students as well as their motivation to work [2, 15].

While coarse-grained OLMs offered a range of benefits, their navigation support power is limited. Topic-level knowledge tracking and social comparison could efficiently guide students to the most appropriate topics to work on, but it is not sufficient to provide guidance on selecting the most appropriate learning activity. Indeed, from the perspective of topic-level modeling, all learning activities belonging to the same topic are indistinguishable with respect to learning opportunity. While some of these activities could be more beneficial for the student at a given time, this could be only observed with a finer grain (concept-level) modeling. We hypothesized that offering fine-grained OLM on the level of concepts could provide better navigation support for students in selecting the most relevant learning activities. To assess this hypothesis, we designed and implemented a concept-level extension for our topic-level OLM interface Mastery Grids [2]. The new OLM (which we call *Rich-OLM*) combines topic-based progress visualization with concept-level knowledge visualization for knowledge monitoring and activity selection, which are critical components of self-regulated learning.

This paper presents the details of our two-level Rich-OLM and reports the results of its evaluation in a semester-long classroom study with a cohort of university students taking an introductory object-oriented programming course. The study compared several design options that we considered important for fine-grained OLM. To assess the overall impact of the Rich-OLM, we also used data from an earlier version of the same course, which used a topic-level OLM interface. Our work attempted to answer the following research questions:

(1) Does adding a fine-grained OLM to a topic-level OLM affect students' content navigation and learning outcomes?
(2) How can the demonstrated positive influence of the social OLMs be affected by the addition of a fine-grained OLM?
(3) Given complex connections between learning activities and fine-grained OLM concepts, what is the best way to summarize this information for students?

2 RELATED WORK

Open Learner Models have been implemented in multiple learning domains (e.g. programming, second language, science, math, etc.) and with different levels of complexity and interactivity [6]. In the context of this study, most relevant is the work on the presentation and understandability of OLM. It has been recognized that an OLM has to be designed to be understandable and interpretable in order to provide the intended instructional support [3, 18]. While some studies have found that simple indicators like *skill meters* are preferred by students [9], other studies support more complex representations (such as concept maps [21]) as tools to represent and refine assessment claims about learners' knowledge [25]. In [3] experienced OLM users indicated a preference for having both simple and more complex OLM visualizations available.

A number of researchers proposed offering multiple OLM views, from simple to detailed to structured, giving options that satisfy different students' preferences [5, 7, 9, 20]. More recent work addressed the issue of complexity and interpretability by extending the OLM with more elaborate features such as indicators of effort, progress, or working style [23]. A study of a wide variety of visualizations from different systems [4] found that students expected structured visualizations such as visualizations of prerequisites or a Hierarchical Tree (from [20]) to best support the task of identifying what to work on next. However, it was unclear whether students might prefer these representations over other structured views such as concept maps.

3 RICH-OLM DESIGN FOR MASTERY GRIDS

Rich-OLM presented in this paper was designed as an extension of Mastery Grids [13, 19], is an intelligent interface that provides access to different kinds of practice content for an introductory programming course. Mastery Grids combines a topic-level OLM with social comparison features offering both personalized and social navigation support to help students in selecting most appropriate content. It has been shown that this tool has positive effects on both student engagement and efficiency [2, 13].

Mastery Grids visualizes course structure as a grid of cells where the horizontal dimension represents the chronological progression of topics in the course and the color density of each cell represented the current level of knowledge of the topic: the darker the color is, the higher is the knowledge. The upper (green) row of cells shown in Figure 1 represents learner's own knowledge of each topic (i.e, topic-level OLM). The lower (blue) row represents the progress of a selected group of peers (e.g. the whole class or a subgroup of students). The middle (green-blue) row makes social comparison easier - it is shown in green for topics where student knowledge are higher than group average and in blue otherwise. Note that the social comparison part could be switch off leaving only the top OLM row. The topic knowledge is calculated by analyzing student or group progress with various activities belonging to each topic. The activities belonging to a topic could be accessed by clicking on the topic cell and moving to the activity section, where all the learning content associated with that topic are displayed (lower half in Figure 1).

The Rich-OLM extends the topic-level OLM interface with a concept-level OLM component visualized as a bar chart underneath the topic grid (Figure 2). Each bar represents a programming concept, such as *modulus operator*. The height and the color density of each concept bar indicates the estimated level of knowledge of the user (in green) or of the group (in blue): the longer and darker the bar, the higher the level of estimated knowledge. Similarly to the topic level, the social comparison component could be switched on and off. When enabled, it allows students to compare themselves with their peers on the concept level for the price of making the visualization more complex. This visualization approach was designed and refined through a sequence of user studies reported in [14]. In particular, these studies revealed that students value the fine-grained information and prefer a simple visualization approach for depicting a fine-grained OLM such as a bar chart. An important feature of navigation-oriented OLM is the ability to explore the knowledge space and its connection with learning activities. As shown in Figure 1, the original Mastery Grids enabled students to explore connections between topics and activities. With its richer knowledge space, the Rich-OLM was designed to enable a much broader set of exploration opportunities:

(1) *Exploring topic-concept relationships*: When students *mouse over* a cell that represents a course topic, the interface focuses on concepts covered by the selected topic (see Figure 3). Students can check their estimated current knowledge of the related concepts and map their observed strengths or weaknesses in a specific topic to their finer-grained knowledge of specific concepts. When social comparison is enabled, they can easily compare their knowledge of topic concepts with the peer group.

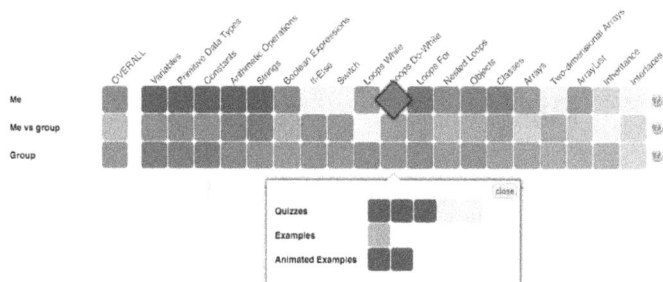

Figure 1: Coarse-grained OLM (topic level) in Mastery Grids for Java programming

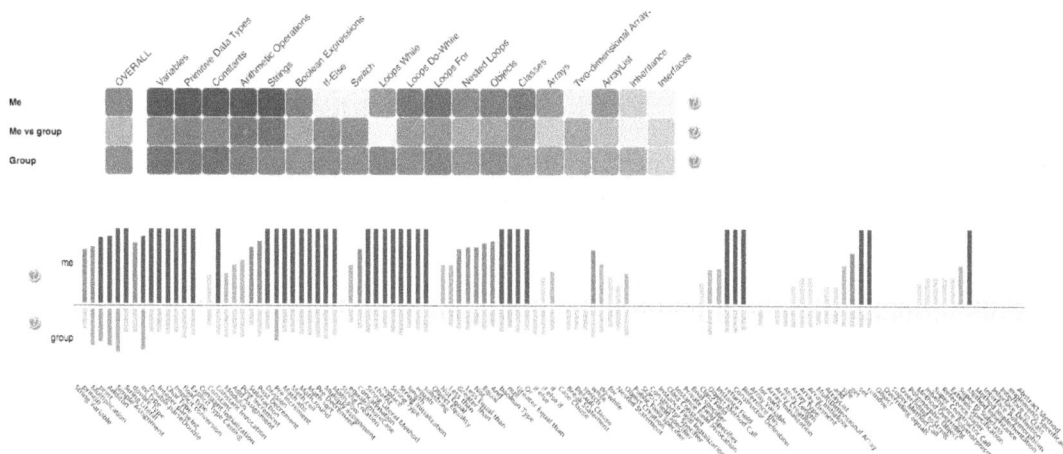

Figure 2: Rich-OLM interface with enabled social comparison. The top part of the figure shows the topic-based (coarse-grained) OLM, and the bottom part shows a long bar-chart representing the concept space (fine-grained) OLM.

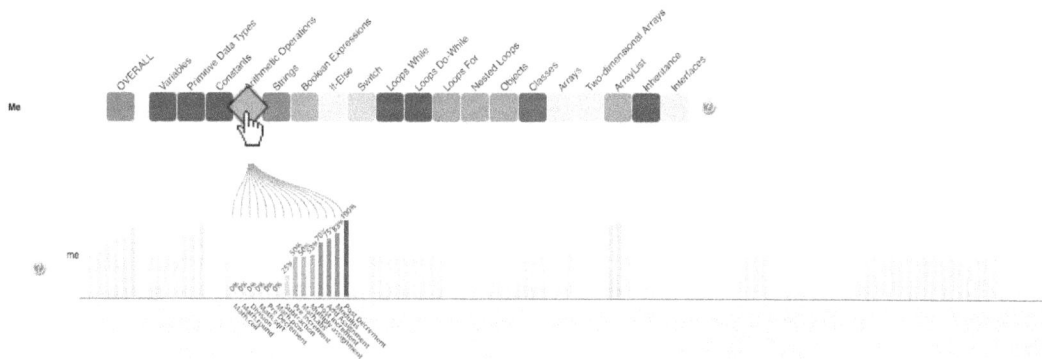

Figure 3: Rich-OLM interface without social comparison. When *mousing over* a topic, related concepts are highlighted and connected to the pointed topic.

(2) *Exploring the activity-concept relationship*: When *clicking* on a topic, the set of associated learning activities (examples, problems, animations) is opened. Here the concept-level knowledge visualization can be used to examine concepts covered by each activity. When the student mouses over an activity cell, the concepts that can be practiced by performing this activity are highlighted in the bar chart (see Figures 4 and 5). Note that when working within a topic, the core concepts of the current topic are always shown.

As a result, student can see to which extent each activity can contribute to mastering the current topic, to bridge the gaps in their knowledge, or to connect to KCs in other topics. This visualization offers students a kind of "x-ray vision" to select most appropriate activities to practice.

(3) *Visualizing a learning opportunity indicator for each activity*: One of our research goals was exploring how to summarize the complex information presented in the fine-grained OLM in a form

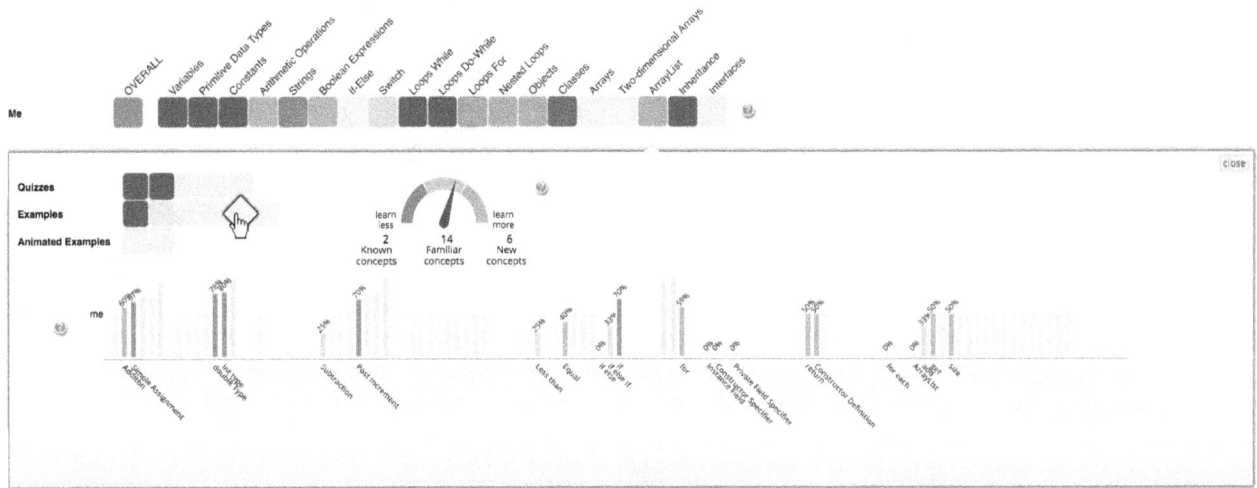

Figure 4: Activity selection support in Rich-OLM interface with an *impact learning gauge*. When the learner mouses over an activity cell the concepts related to the pointed activity are highlighted.

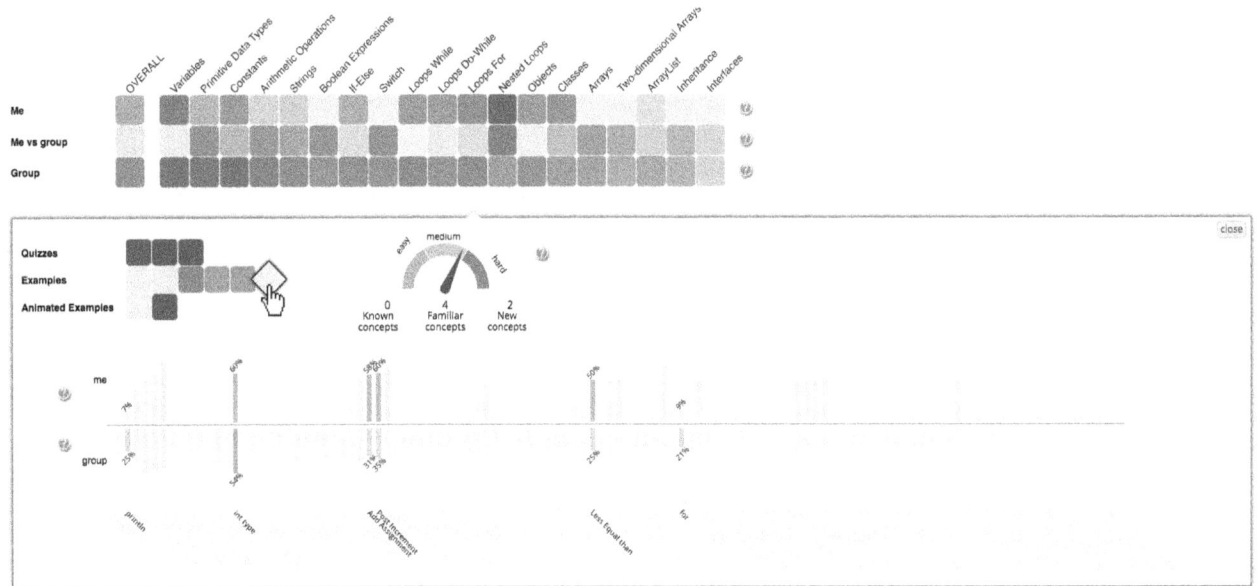

Figure 5: Activity selection support in social Rich-OLM interface with a *difficulty learning gauge*. When the learner mouses over an activity cell the individual and group concepts related to the pointed activity are highlighted.

of a single indicator that might help students to select the right learning activity. The need for such an indicator has been expressed by the students in the Rich-OLM formative design studies [14]. To support this need we decided to visualize a *learning opportunity* score for each content item, which is calculated using the current level of student knowledge of the concepts practiced by the activity. The score balances the presence of the KCs that are already known, partially known, and not known to the learner based on predefined thresholds (see Equation 1). In order to visualize this *learning opportunity* score, we designed a widget that represents a gauge (we called the *learning gauge*), which is placed next to the set of content items (see Figures 4 and 5). Gauges have been repeatedly used in

critical interfaces such as cars and cockpit panels because of its ability to deliver a straightforward message [16], and have also been used successfully in learning analytics visualizations [8, 10, 12, 17]. When a student mouses over one of the activity cells, the needle of the *learning gauge* moves to display the *learning opportunity* score for the activity (from 0 at the left to 1 at the right).

$$learning\ opportunity = \frac{0.5 * KCs_{familiar} + KCs_{new}}{KCs_{known} + KCs_{familiar} + KCs_{new}}$$

$$(1)$$

According to the Equation 1, the larger is the number of unknown concepts related to an activity, the higher is the learning opportunity. It means that it is more likely that the student will learn more after a successful work with the activity (positive case), but at the same time, it is also more likely that the student will fail given their lack of knowledge of the related concepts (negative case). Given this dual nature of the *learning opportunity*, we decided to test two variations of the message shown next to the *learning gauge* in order to explore how the focus on opportunity vs. difficulty affects student navigational behavior. The first version of the gauge shows a *difficulty* message, conveying how difficult is a specific content for the student given his or her knowledge inferred by the system (Figure 5). The second variation shows an *impact on learning* message in terms of how much the student will learn after attempting a learning activity (Figure 4). Visually, both gauges (learning and difficulty) present the same number. The only difference is the interpretation of this number shown by the text labels of the extremes and the order of the color zones (red-orange-green from left to right for *impact on learning* gauge, and the opposite order of colors for the *difficulty* gauge).

4 CLASSROOM STUDY DESIGN

To assess the impact of our Rich-OLM design on student navigation and learning, we performed a semester-long study in an introductory object-oriented programming course (*Java*-based) taught at the University of Pittsburgh in the Fall term of 2016. The course was divided into two sections, *IS17Fall20161* and *IS17Fall20162* taught by different instructors, but having the same syllabus, readings and assessments. In both sections, Rich-OLM was used as the interface to access a collection of three types of non-mandatory practice content: examples, animated examples and parameterized problems. To engage students in working with the non-mandatory content, 3 extra-points for course final score (out of 100) were offered to those who solved correctly at least 10 problems (out of 100+ available problems in the system). Learners that surpassed this activity threshold (have solved more than 10 problems in the system) were considered as "active students" in our analysis.

We designed the study to assess two factors in the design of the Rich-OLM: i) the *social* factor, i.e., the presence or absence of social comparison features and ii) the *message* factor associated to the *learning gauge*, i.e., the **difficulty** or the **impact** message. Due to practical reasons, the treatment related to *social* factor was not randomly assigned among the cohort of students: the *IS17Fall20161* group was assigned with a social Rich-OLM, while the *IS17Fall20162* group was assigned with an individual Rich-OLM. The difficulty vs. impact message was assigned randomly for each student in the course regardless the section that they belonged. The study lasted 12 weeks in total (from mid-September to mid-December).

To compare the Rich-OLM design as a whole with a simpler topic-based interface, we used data from the earlier section of the same course taught in the Fall of 2015. Pedagogically, both classes (2015 and 2016) were comparable, they had the same instructors, syllabus, readings, and assessments. However, the practice system offered for 2015 class used the original topic-level Mastery Grids as shown in Figure 1. Similarly to 2016, the 2015 class had two groups with one assigned to a social version of Mastery Grids and another to the Mastery Grids interface without social comparison.

5 RESULTS
5.1 Student Cohorts and Learning Gain

The Fall 2015 class selected as the baseline for comparison had in total 40 active students and the Fall 2016 classroom study had a total of 38 active students. All students took a pretest in the beginning of the course and posttest in the end in order to be able to measure their learning gain during the course. The pretest score of students in 2015 was significantly higher than the pretest of students in 2016 ($U=573$, $p<.01$, *Diff. medians*=.096). This means that students in 2015 came with higher previous knowledge that students that used the Rich-OLM. We found, however, no significant differences between 2015 and 2016 in posttest or normalized learning gain calculated as NLG = ((*posttest - pretest*)/(*max_pretest_score - pretest*)).

5.2 Student Behavior

To compare student behavior with different OLMs, we computed several metrics related to the use of OLM and access of learning content (Table 1). We distinguished three levels of navigational behavior : (1) *explorations - mouseovers* (not present in 2015) which allow students to pre-examine concept-level knowledge for candidate topics and activities before opening a topic or an activity; (2) *accesses* - clicks on topics or activities to *open* it and receive more information before deciding to proceed further (i.e., attempt an activity); (3) *learning actions* - real work with opened learning activities. Note that an exploration might not result in opening as well as an opening might not lead to the decision to engage with the opened content. To avoid counting unintended *mouseovers*, we considered only "reliable" *mouseovers* that were at least 2 sec. long.

As the data shows, all kinds of Rich-OLM *mouseovers* were used by students quite extensively. Overall, the proportion of time spent by students in the OLM interface (i.e. exploring and navigating the interface) was significantly larger for Rich-OLM ($U=420$, $p<0.01$, *Diff. medians*=8%). This could be considered as an indication that the extended exploration opportunities were appreciated by students. At the same time the number of problem attempts ($U=512$, $p<.05$, *Diff. medians*=24.5) and the number of solved problems ($U=486.5$, $p<.01$, *Diff. medians*=27) were significantly smaller for Rich-OLM.

Overall, the number of attempted activities was the most visible difference between student behavior in 2015 and 2016. Students working with Rich-OLM accessed and attempted fewer learning activities within each type. We know, however, that there was no difference between years in learning gain or posttest. In other words, starting with a significantly lower level of knowledge and using fewer activities, the students working with Rich-OLM interface were able to achieve the same learning outcomes as the 2015 class working with topic-level OLM. This may indicate that Rich-OLM enabled students in 2016 to work more efficiently. To explore this idea further, we computed two metrics:

(1) *Problem effectiveness*: This indicator illustrates to which degree each of the correctly solved problems contributed to an increase of students learning gain. It is calculated by dividing the normalized learning gain by the total number of distinct problems that were solved correctly by the student. The analysis revealed that students

Metric	2015			2016		
	Mean	Sd	Median	Mean	Sd	Median
Learning indicators						
Pretest	.342	.227	.286	.207	.166	.190
Posttest	.769	.168	.786	.770	.201	.786
Norm. Learn. Gain	.637	.232	.627	.714	.241	.757
General activity						
Sessions	10.93	8.34	8	10	8.66	8
Prop. of time spent on MG	31.34	8.94	29.74	39.43	12.04	37.73
Exploration & Accesses						
Topic *mouseovers*	-	-	-	56.11	34.33	53.5
Activity *mouseovers*	-	-	-	35.58	32.94	22.5
Concept *mouseovers*	-	-	-	38.32	39.06	25
Topic clicks	53.03	82.64	37.5	50.26	51.85	38.5
Activity clicks	191.4	133.8	153	131.2	80.52	115.5
Learning actions						
Problems attempted	83.75	49.98	74	57.82	30.4	49.5
Examples attempted	60.73	48.43	66.5	41.95	39.13	28.5
Anim. examples attempted	22.95	21.81	16	16.71	15.56	12
Distinct problems solved	62.53	23.06	67.5	46.68	24.12	40.5

Table 1: Student behavior summary

Metric	Explorers			Non-Explorers			Sign. test
	Mean	Sd	Median	Mean	Sd	Median	
Pretest	.22	.2	.16	.19	.13	.19	not sign.
Norm. learn. gain	.81	.19	.89	.62	.26	.6	$U=96$ *
Sessions	6.11	3.53	5	13.89	10.47	10	$U=81.5$ **
Time per session	2242.1	1837	1894.2	767.06	613.82	767.1	$U=86$ **
Prop. of time spent on MG	.4	.11	.41	.38	.37	.33	not sign.
Learn. efficiency	.32	.57	.38	-.077	.37	-.13	$t=-2.834$ **

Table 2: Explorers vs Non-Explorers (* $p<.05$, ** $p<.01$)

in 2016 achieved significantly higher problem effectiveness ($U=426$, $p<.01$, *Median 2015*=.0096, *Median 2016*=.015), i.e., with a fewer problems solved correctly, the students who selected their problems using the Rich-OLM achieved the same level of learning gain as the students selecting their problems through the topic-level OLM.
(2) *Learning efficiency*: This metric is inspired by Instructional Effectiveness [22], which reflects how mental efforts in the context of an learning task translate into a certain level of performance. Learning efficiency uses the total time a student spent on problems as a measure of mental effort and the number of distinct problems solved correctly as an indicator of performance. Negative numbers reflect low efficiency on the learning task and high positive numbers reflect a high efficiency on performing the task. Given that the learning efficiency can be influenced by the student's previous knowledge level, we performed a two-way ANCOVA analysis by using the pretest score as covariate variable and *year* and *social* as factors (we used *social* because in both years the OLM had social and individual versions). The results show that the learning efficiency of students was marginally higher in 2016 ($F=3.576$, $p=.063$, partial $\eta^2=.047$, *Mean 2015*=.0, *Mean 2016*=.127).

Both indicators suggested that students in 2016 were, indeed, more efficient. Given the significant increase of the proportion of their time spent in the interface, we could hypothesize that it was the use of Rich-OLM that made the students more efficient. To make a more reliable connection between student efficiency and their work with OLM, we divided the 2016 students into two groups: *explorers* and *non-explorers*. We normalized the total number of the three types of interactive actions with the Rich-OLM per student, and we averaged them in order to get an *exploration score* to represent each learner. We ranked students according to their exploration score and split them in two groups by the median. Students in the lower half formed the group of *non-explorers* and students in the upper half were considered as *explorers*. We analyzed the differences between these two groups by using many of the metrics we have used above. We summarize this analysis in Table 2. While we found no significant differences between pretest scores of *explorers* and *non-explorers*, we observed that *explorers* obtained

significantly higher learning gain than *non-explorers*. Moreover, the *explorers* exhibited significantly higher *learning efficiency* scores than non-explorers (see Table 2 for detailed statistics). This data offers a stronger connection between student work with OLM and the increase of their knowledge and efficiency.

To better understand differences between *explorers* and *non-explorers*, we examined session-level performance for students in both groups and we found that students that interacted more with the Rich-OLM had a different pattern of work with the system. They performed significantly fewer sessions in the system that *non-explorer* students. However, their sessions were significantly longer than sessions of *non-explorer* students (See Table 2 for details).

5.3 Characteristics of Attempted Problems

One possible explanation for the increased efficiency of learning with Rich-OLM could be an increase of complexity of the selected problems enabled by its content exploration interface. If students target more complex problems they might gain more new knowledge per problem and avoid over-practicing the already mastered knowledge. To assess this hypothesis, we examined whether different interfaces option (coarse-grained, Rich-OLM, presence of social features, *learning gauge* messages) affected the complexity of selected and solved problems.

As a measure of problem complexity, we used the number of different concepts associated with the problems (i.e. the more concepts the student practices while working with an activity, the more complex it is). To characterize the distribution of the problem complexity attempted by a student we compute two measures, $Q1_{KCs}$ and $Q3_{KCs}$. We got these measures in the following way. For each student, we sorted all the attempted problems by the number of concepts associated (each problem has between 3 and 65 concepts), thus easier activities performed are first in the list. Then $Q1_{KCs}$ and $Q3_{KCs}$ correspond to the number of concepts in the 1st quartile (median of the lower half) and 3rd quartile (median of the upper half) of the list (see Figure 6). These measures allow us to see different patterns in the distribution of complexity focusing separately on the easier and harder subsets of problems. We used these measures as the dependent variables in the following analyses.

5.3.1 Between-years differences. By using the data from both studies (2015-2016), we built linear regression models for $Q1_{KCs}$ and $Q3_{KCs}$. We used 6 independent variables in the regression model: (*pretest*), presence of Rich-OLM represented by the dummy variable *year* (only 2016 groups had Rich-OLM), presence of social comparison features (dummy variable *social*), as well as the interactions *pretest*year*, *pretest*social*, and *year*social*. We used SPSS software and a backward stepwise approach, i.e., the model is first built by adding all the independent variables and subsequent

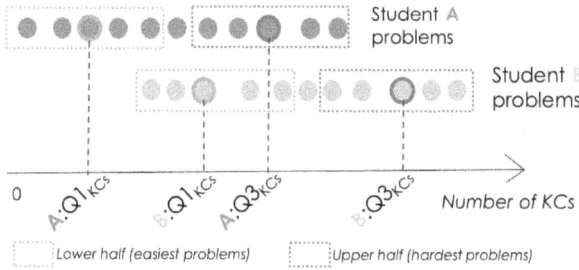

Figure 6: Procedure for determining the complexity of easiest and hardest problems attempted by each student

Outcome	Adj. R^2	social	pretest * year	pretest * social	year * social
$Q1_{KCs}$	.139	-3.01 *	6.79 *	5.89 *	4.14 **
$Q3_{KCs}$	.052	-	15.97 .	-	6.34 *

(a) Across years 2015-2016

Outcome	Adj. R^2	pretest * social	pretest * message
$Q1_{KCs}$	.247	12.810 **	7.369 *
$Q3_{KCs}$	.167	28.604 *	13.258 .

(b) 2016

Table 3: Regression models for number of KCs of easier ($Q1_{KCs}$) and harder ($Q3_{KCs}$) attempted problems (. p<.1, * p<.05, ** p<.01, *** p<.001)

models are built removing variables one by one. Results of both models are shown in table 3a where coefficients of the significant variables are reported, as well as the models' adjusted R^2.

The regression model for $Q1_{KCs}$ (Table 3a) shows that the students with higher pretest who had access to Rich-OLM (*pretest * year*) were able to significantly rise the complexity of the easier half of attempted problems (from 8.8 concepts on average in 2015 to 11.15 concepts in 2016). The analysis of the social factor shows a more complex influence. Taken as a whole, the access to a social OLM was associated with a decrease of complexity of the easier half of problems (*social*). However, the presence of the Rich-OLM encouraged all students to increase significantly the complexity of the easier half of problems (*year * social*). Moreover, students with higher pretest who have access to social comparison attempted more complex problems in both years (*pretest * social*).

The regression model for the hardest half of attempted problems ($Q3_{KCs}$ in Table 3a) shows similar trends. The Rich-OLM encouraged students with higher pretest (*pretest * year*, p=.055) to increase the complexity of the upper half of problems (from 19.4 concepts on average in 2015 to 22.8 concepts in 2016). All students who had access to the social version of Rich-OLM also significantly increased the complexity of the harder half of attempted problems (*year * social*). However, given the low value of R^2 in this model we need to take these results with caution. In summary, both innovations, concept-level OLM and social comparison enabled students to focus on more complex problems, however, in some cases only students with better prior knowledge were able to leverage the presence of these innovations.

5.3.2 2016 study differences. Using the same approach, we built linear regression models for $Q1_{KCs}$ and $Q3_{KCs}$ using 2016 class

data. We used 6 independent variables in the regression model: *pretest*, access to the social comparison (*social*), access to *impact* or *difficulty* message in the *learning gauge* (0 or 1 value of dummy variable *message*), as well as the interactions *pretest*social*, *pretest*message*, and *social*message*. Table 3b reports coefficients of the significant variables as well as adjusted R^2 for both models. The results indicate that the presence of *difficulty learning gauge* or social comparison in Rich-OLM could lead to a significant increase of complexity for both easier and harder half of problems, however, only students with higher pretest were able to take advantage of these visual features.

5.4 Problem-Solving Persistence

The results presented above indicated that Rich-OLM features caused a significant shift to more complex problem providing one possible explanations for the increase of learning efficiency in Rich-OLM. To assess whether this shift was a result of an *an informed decision* enabled by Rich-OLM, we calculated a series of indicators for student confidence about their choice, i.e, the perception that they are *solving the right problem*. We hypothesized that if a student thinks that a problem is appropriate to solve given their (and peers) current knowledge level, she will be more persistent, i.e., more likely to keep attempting to solve a problem after initial failure. For reflecting this, we defined a measure called "probability of keep trying" (*prob_keep_trying*) that reflects the proportion of cases where a student kept trying to solve a problem until succeeding. In the same context, we also calculated the mean number of attempts that students made on problems that were not solved correctly in a particular trial (*attempts_fail*). Finally, we calculated a navigational indicator named "ratio of overhead problems" (*ratio_overhead*), which represents the proportion of problems that were attempted but left without being solved correctly.

5.4.1 Between-years differences. To examine 2015-2016 differences, we calculated regression models for each of the three persistence metrics following the approach described in section 5.3.1. We used *pretest, year, social,* and their interactions as predictor variables. Results of the three models are shown in Table 4a, which reports coefficients of the significant variables as well as the models' adjusted R^2. We found that students working with Rich-OLM were significantly more persistent in their problem solving making a significantly higher mean number of attempts for problems where they failed (*Median attempts_fail 2015*=1.25, *Median attempts_fail 2016*=1.55). Students with higher prior knowledge were generally more persistent as shown by a significantly lower ration of overhead problems. Note that some results shown in Table 4a should be interpreted with caution due to low R^2.

5.4.2 2016 study differences. To examine the effects of different OLM setups in 2016 study, we built three regression models by following the approach described in section 5.3.2 and using each of the persistence metrics as outcome variable. Table 4b shows the adjusted R^2 and the significant predictor variables. The data clearly shows three factors that positively affect persistence leading to significantly higher probability to keep trying and lower ratio of overhead problems. First, the starting level of knowledge (*pretest*) is a

Outcome	Adj. R^2	pretest	year	year $*$ social
attempts_fail	.071	-	.333 *	-
prob_keep_trying	.041	.167 **	-	
ratio_overhead	.088	-.149 **		-.041 .

(a) Across years 2015-2016

Outcome	Adj. R^2	pretest	social	message
prob_keep_trying	.335	.468 **	.167 **	.191 **
ratio_overhead	.252	-.228 **	-.066 *	-.073 **

(b) 2016

Table 4: Regression models for persistence metrics (. p<.1, * p<.05, ** p<.01, *** p<.001)

strong predictor of persistence, i.e., stronger students are more confident about their choices across the interface conditions. Second, the students that received the difficulty message were significantly more persistent than those receiving the impact message, (*Median prob_keep_trying difficulty*=90.24% , *Median prob_keep_trying impact*=67.38%), and which also resulted in a lower number of problems that were never completed (*Median ratio_overhead difficulty*=3.32%, *Median ratio_overhead impact*=13.15%). One explanation is that the difficulty message warned the students in advance that the problem might be difficult, so they were less discouraged by the failure. Alternatively, the message focused on the learning impact encouraged them to explore other opportunities when they failed rather than keep trying. Third, we found that the social comparison in Rich-OLM (*social*) is also a significant persistence booster: the probability of keep trying was significantly higher for students who could see the performance of their peers (*Median prob_keep_trying social*=80% , *Median prob_keep_trying individual*=64.15%).

Summing up the results above, we can state that the students who accessed a Rich-OLM exhibited in general a higher persistent profile indicating that their shift to more complex problems was likely a result of an informed decision enabled by Rich-OLM. Within Rich-OLM, we found that the difficulty message as well as social comparison positively affected persistence. Students with higher prior knowledge were generally more persistent (i.e., more confident about their choice) across all conditions.

6 CONCLUSIONS

This paper presented a design of a Rich-OLM that integrated a coarse-grained and a fine-grained OLM in a hope to better support students in selecting learning activities to practice. To assess the value of Rich-OLM as well as to compare several design alternatives (see research questions above), we performed a semester-long classroom study. Answering the first research question about the overall impact of Rich-OLM, the study demonstrated that the information presented by the fine-grained OLM affected both learning outcomes and content navigation. Students who accessed practice content using Rich-OLM worked more efficiently as shown by several parameters. Further analysis associated the increase of learning efficiency with the increased exploration of OLM and learning content supported by Rich-OLM. The study also indicated that the observed increase of learning efficiency was caused by a shift to more complex learning activities in Rich-OLM group, which enabled students to move towards the course learning goal

with larger steps. In turn, the increased problem-solving persistence exhibited by the Rich-OLM group hinted that the increased complexity of selected problems was a result of informed decision enabled by Rich-OLM. In addition, several measures demonstrated that learners with higher levels of previous knowledge were better in leveraging the functionality provided by Rich-OLM exhibiting a stronger shift to more complex learning activities and higher persistence to complete them.

Answering the second research question, the study indicated that social information could further increase the impact of fine-grained OLM on problem selection. Students who worked with social version of Rich-OLM focused on more difficult problems in general (higher values on $Q1_{KCs}$ and $Q3_{KCs}$) and exhibited higher level of persistence when attempting to solve them.

A less expected result was a strong impact of the type of message used by the "learning gauge" to report the complexity of each learning activity. The message focused on *difficulty* of examined activities caused a significantly higher shift to more complex problems and higher persistence to complete them than the message focused on *learning impact*. These result also demonstrated that even a simple ad-hoc way of calculating learning opportunity score could significantly affect students problem selection and performance.

7 LIMITATIONS AND FUTURE WORK

One of the limitations of this study was the lack of fully randomized assignment of treatments in 2016. Only the message factor was randomly assigned across groups. In addition, a relatively small size of groups engaged in the study might prevented us from detecting significant differences in some study variables. Given this situation, replicating this study in larger classes with fully randomized conditions is our first priority on the way to generalize these results.

In addition, we have not examined how individual differences (e.g. personality traits, achievement goals, etc.) influence student work with Rich-OLM. Further analysis is required to find most suitable OLM design for unique personal characteristic of each student. In the same context, it would be valuable to explore the value of user-controllable Rich-OLM, which offers various features of Rich-OLM (concept-level model, social comparison, *learning gauge*, etc.) as optional enabling the students to select most suitable combination of features themselves. System or user-driven controllability might improve positive effects of Rich-OLM for a wider range of students, given the existent trade-off between adding more visual information and the complexity of understanding the visualization, which is different for each individual learner given their own cognitive capacity.

Finally, this study assumes that some logged interactions with the interface, as *mouseovers* or clicks, are a reliable proxy of Rich-OLM exploration by the students. For more accurate conclusions, however, a study augmented with eye-tracking will be necessary. Using eye-tracking, we will be able to examine student work with the Rich-OLM more reliably. While these experiments have to be performed in the controlled lab context lacking the ecological validity of the work presented in this paper, it is critical for better understanding of student work with Rich-OLM.

REFERENCES

[1] Peter Brusilovsky. 2007. *Adaptive navigation support*. Lecture Notes in Computer Science, Vol. 4321. Springer-Verlag, Berlin Heidelberg New York, 263–290.

[2] Peter Brusilovsky, Sibel Somyürek, Julio Guerra, Roya Hosseini, Vladimir Zadorozhny, and Paula Durlach. 2016. Open Social Student Modeling for Personalized Learning. *IEEE Transactions on Emerging Topics in Computing* 4, 3 (2016), 450–461.

[3] Susan Bull. 2012. Preferred features of open learner models for university students. In *International Conference on Intelligent Tutoring Systems*. Springer, 411–421.

[4] Susan Bull, Peter Brusilovsky, Rafael Araujo, and Julio Guerra. 2016. Individual and Peer Comparison Open Learner Model Visualisations to Identify What to Work On Next. In *24th Conference on User Modeling, Adaptation and Personalization*. http://ceur-ws.org/Vol-1618/LBR4.pdf

[5] Susan Bull, Inderdip Gakhal, Daniel Grundy, Matthew Johnson, Andrew Mabbott, and Jing Xu. 2010. Preferences in multiple-view open learner models. In *European Conference on Technology Enhanced Learning*. Springer, 476–481.

[6] Susan Bull and Judy Kay. 2010. Open learner models. In *Advances in intelligent tutoring systems*. Springer, 301–322.

[7] Ricardo Conejo, Monica Trella, Ivan Cruces, and Rafael Garcia. 2011. INGRID: A web service tool for hierarchical open learner model visualization. In *International Conference on User Modeling, Adaptation, and Personalization*. Springer, 406–409.

[8] Luis de la Fuente Valentín and Daniel Burgos Solans. 2014. Am I doing well? A4Learning as a self-awareness tool to integrate in Learning Management Systems. *Campus Virtuales* 3, 1 (2014), 32–40.

[9] Dandi Duan, Antonija Mitrovic, and Neville Churcher. 2010. Evaluating the effectiveness of multiple open student models in EER-Tutor. (2010). https://ir.canterbury.ac.nz/handle/10092/5052

[10] Mohammad Hassan Falakmasir, I-Han Hsiao, Luca Mazzola, Nancy Grant, and Peter Brusilovsky. 2012. The impact of social performance visualization on students. In *ICALT 2012, IEEE 12th International Conference on Advanced Learning Technologies*. 565–569.

[11] Leon Festinger. 1954. A Theory of Social Comparison Processes. *Human Relations* 7, 2 (1954), 117–140.

[12] Giovanni Fulantelli, Davide Taibi, and Marco Arrigo. 2013. A semantic approach to mobile learning analytics. In *Proceedings of the First International Conference on Technological Ecosystem for Enhancing Multiculturality*. ACM, 287–292.

[13] Julio Guerra, Roya Hosseini, Sibel Somyürek, and Peter Brusilovsky. 2016. An Intelligent Interface for Learning Content: Combining an Open Learner Model and Social Comparison to Support Self-Regulated Learning and Engagement. In *Proceedings of the 21st International Conference on Intelligent User Interfaces (IUI '16)*. ACM, 152–163.

[14] Julio Guerra-Hollstein, Jordan Barria-Pineda, Christian D. Schunn, Susan Bull, and Peter Brusilovsky. 2017. Fine-Grained Open Learner Models: Complexity Versus Support. In *Proceedings of the 25th Conference on User Modeling, Adaptation and Personalization (UMAP '17)*. ACM, New York, NY, USA, 41–49.

[15] I. Han Hsiao, Fedor Bakalov, Peter Brusilovsky, and Birgitta König-Ries. 2013. Progressor: social navigation support through open social student modeling. *New Review of Hypermedia and Multimedia* 19, 2 (2013), 112–131.

[16] Edwin Hutchins. 1995. How a cockpit remembers its speeds. *Cognitive science* 19, 3 (1995), 265–288.

[17] Imran Khan and Abelardo Pardo. 2016. Data2U: scalable real time student feedback in active learning environments. In *Proceedings of the Sixth International Conference on Learning Analytics & Knowledge*. ACM, 249–253.

[18] Check Yee Law, John Grundy, Andrew Cain, and Rajesh Vasa. 2015. A preliminary study of open learner model representation formats to support formative assessment. In *Computer Software and Applications Conference (COMPSAC), 2015 IEEE 39th Annual*, Vol. 2. IEEE, 887–892.

[19] Tomasz D Loboda, Julio Guerra, Roya Hosseini, and Peter Brusilovsky. 2014. Mastery Grids: An Open Source Social Educational Progress Visualization. In *Open Learning and Teaching in Educational Communities*. Springer, 235–248.

[20] Andrew Mabbott and Susan Bull. 2006. Student preferences for editing, persuading, and negotiating the open learner model. In *International Conference on Intelligent Tutoring Systems*. Springer, 481–490.

[21] Adrian Maries and Amruth Kumar. 2008. The effect of student model on learning. In *ICALT'08. Eighth IEEE International Conference on Advanced Learning Technologies*. IEEE, 877–881.

[22] Fred G. W. C. Paas and Jeroen J. G. Van Merriënboer. 1993. The Efficiency of Instructional Conditions: An Approach to Combine Mental Effort and Performance Measures. *Human Factors* 35, 4 (1993), 737–743.

[23] Kyparisia A Papanikolaou. 2015. Constructing interpretative views of learners' interaction behavior in an open learner model. *IEEE Transactions on Learning Technologies* 8, 2 (2015), 201–214.

[24] Sergey Sosnovsky and Peter Brusilovsky. 2015. Evaluation of Topic-based Adaptation and Student Modeling in QuizGuide. *User Modeling and User-Adapted Interaction* 25, 4 (2015), 371–424.

[25] Diego Zapata-Rivera, Eric Hansen, Valerie J Shute, Jody S Underwood, and Malcolm Bauer. 2007. Evidence-based approach to interacting with open student models. *International Journal of Artificial Intelligence in Education* 17, 3 (2007), 273–303.

Gaze-Enhanced Student Modeling for Game-based Learning

Andrew Emerson
Department of Computer Science
North Carolina State University
ajemerso@ncsu.edu

Robert Sawyer
Department of Computer Science
North Carolina State University
rssawyer@ncsu.edu

Roger Azevedo
Department of Psychology
North Carolina State University
razeved@ncsu.edu

James Lester
Department of Computer Science
North Carolina State University
lester@ncsu.edu

ABSTRACT

Recent advances in eye-tracking technologies have introduced the opportunity to incorporate gaze into student modeling. Creating student models that leverage gaze information holds significant promise for game-based learning environments. This paper introduces a gaze-enhanced student modeling framework that incorporates student eye tracking to dynamically predict students' performance in a game-based learning environment for microbiology education, CRYSTAL ISLAND. The gaze-enhanced student modeling framework was investigated in a study comparing a gaze-enhanced student model with a baseline student model that does not utilize student eye-tracking. Results of a study conducted with 65 college students interacting with the CRYSTAL ISLAND game-based learning environment indicate that the gaze-enhanced student model significantly outperforms the baseline model in dynamically predicting student problem-solving performance. The findings suggest that incorporating gaze into student modeling can contribute to a new generation of student models for game-based learning environments.

KEYWORDS

Student modeling; Gaze; Game-based learning

ACM Reference format:

Andrew Emerson, Robert Sawyer, Roger Azevedo, and James Lester. 2018. Gaze-Enhanced Student Modeling for Game-based Learning. In *Proceedings of the Twenty-Sixth ACM Conference on User Modeling, Adaptation and Personalization, Singapore, Singapore, July 2018*, (UMAP'18), 10 pages. https://doi.org/10.1145/3209219.3209238.

1 INTRODUCTION

Student modeling plays a central role in user-adaptive environments for learning [12]. Student models offer an explicit

representation of a learning environment's representation of student characteristics. Student modeling techniques have been devised to infer a broad range of student characteristics, including student knowledge [3, 9, 25, 35], plans and goals [1, 25, 30-32], and affective states [4, 7, 17, 40, 43, 46]. Despite these advances, with only a few notable exceptions [11, 21, 28, 45], limited work has investigated the potential of leveraging information about student gaze to improve the accuracy of student modeling.

Gaze offers a potentially rich source of information about student learning. Temporal patterns in eye movements, such as variations in fixations and saccades, may indicate the attentional foci of student interactions with a learning environment. Recent work such as the investigation of how gaze may signal the presence of cognitive processes [37] suggests that gaze can inform student modeling. While emerging work has begun to examine how learning can be inferred from gaze data [6, 24, 34] and how to infer mind wandering from gaze data [29], there has been limited investigation of how gaze can enhance student modeling to improve predictive accuracy for student problem-solving performance during learning interactions.

Game-based learning environments offer a promising context for investigating gaze-enhanced student modeling. Over the past decade game-based learning environments have emerged as a vehicle for creating engaging learning experiences through game mechanics [5, 14, 18, 27, 39, 47]. Immersive game-based learning environments, such as the CRYSTAL ISLAND learning environment for microbiology education [39], feature rich story worlds, an expansive cast of characters, and a large set of digital artifacts that students interact with during learning episodes. Because immersive game-based learning environments feature 3D worlds that students navigate during problem solving, these environments may elicit fine-grained gaze behaviors that provide significant diagnostic value for student modeling, while providing a manifestation of intent-related cognitive processes [19, 33, 44].

This paper reports on an investigation of gaze-enhanced student modeling for game-based learning. With the goal of creating student models augmented with gaze data to improve the predictive accuracy of student models, in a study with 65 students we evaluate two student modeling approaches: a gaze-enhanced student model that leverages gaze data collected from a version of CRYSTAL ISLAND that was instrumented with eye-tracking, and a baseline student model that does not use gaze data. We compare both with respect to their predictive accuracy on student problem-

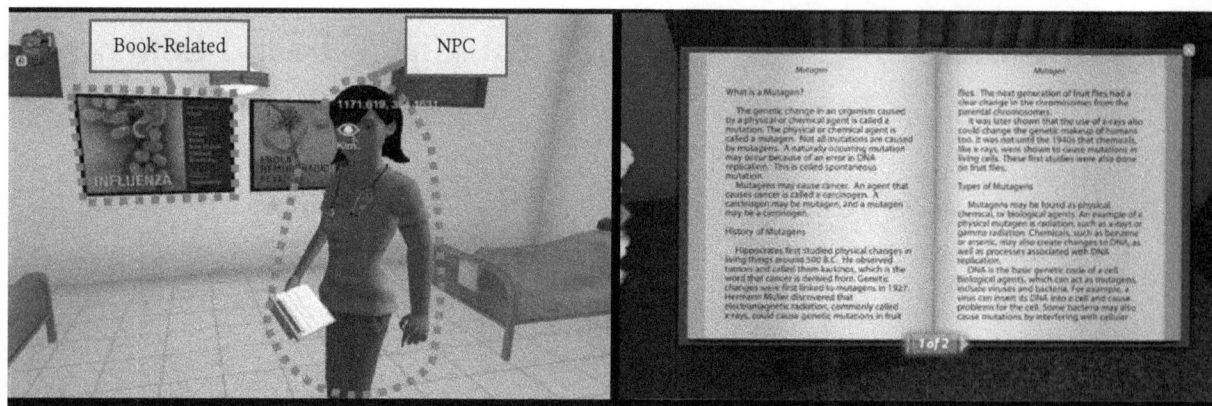

Figure 1. The CRYSTAL ISLAND learning environment with gaze entity categories (left) and book related content (right).

solving performance during the game-based problem-solving episodes. In developing student models that can dynamically predict problem-solving performance, we investigate the capability of gaze-enhanced student models to predict student problem-solving effectiveness and efficiency throughout learning interactions, depicting the fruitfulness of the learning experience.

2 RELATED WORK

Gaze holds considerable promise for guiding user-adaptive interactions. Because movements of the human eye may indicate attention, engagement, and motivation [2, 13, 36], they may signal cognitive states such as foci of attention [10] as well as mind wandering, and thus offer significant potential for designing "attention-adaptive" learning environments [19-21, 28, 29]. Gaze may also be used to recognize off-task behavior and disengagement. For example, Mills et al. used reading patterns to predict a severe form of disengagement, quitting [30]. Gaze may also be able to play an important role in user-adaptive systems that consider learners' metacognitive processes [11, 22, 23, 27, 42] and assess or predict learning [6, 24]. While we only explore gaze, prior work has explored affect and gameplay interactions for this problem [3, 17, 42, 43, 45].

Gaze has successfully been applied to student goal recognition in game-based learning environments [33]. Deep learning, and more specifically sequence-based recurrent neural networks using eye-tracking features, has emerged as a powerful student modeling technique for goal recognition. This line of investigation has shown that using multimodal data, including eye tracking, can yield high predictive accuracy for student goal recognition.

Building on these developments, the work reported here explores how gaze data can be used to improve student modeling. By exploiting gaze transition data streams-in contrast to saccade patterns previously explored, which offer a potentially complementary source of gaze information-for improving student modeling, we explore how gaze-enhanced student models can improve the accuracy of dynamically predicting student problem-solving effectiveness and student problem-solving efficiency. This work can inform future research that builds internal student models and use gaze as an indicator of cognitive states.

3 GAME-BASED LEARNING ENVIRONMENT TESTBED

To investigate gaze-enhanced student modeling, we conducted a study with college students interacting with the CRYSTAL ISLAND game-based learning environment for microbiology education [39] (Figure 1). When students interact with CRYSTAL ISLAND, they embark on a mission to solve a mysterious illness outbreak by collecting evidence and testing hypotheses. Students first arrive at the central research camp and travel to buildings such as the infirmary, dining hall, virtual laboratory, and living quarters. At each location, students interact with non-player characters (NPCs). Students speak with a variety of NPCs to collect evidence and obtain guidance. Two of the NPCs are domain experts in bacteria and viruses, allowing the students to gather information through dialogue. Students can read text resources distributed throughout the island including books, articles, and posters, which they use to learn about the potential diseases causing the outbreak. All student actions including navigation, dialogue, and text resource interactions are recorded in log files.

4 METHODS AND DATA

To evaluate the potential contribution of gaze information to student modeling, we compare two approaches. First, we instrumented CRYSTAL ISLAND with eye-tracking and introduced a real-time gaze-driven entity tracker (described in Section 4.4) to monitor the in-game objects of students' focus on a moment-to-moment basis. We then created a gaze-enhanced student model that uses student gaze data stream information together with students' goal orientation [15], gameplay time, and prior knowledge (as assessed with a pre-test) to predict student problem-solving performance. Second, we created a baseline student model that uses all information in the gaze-enhanced student model but does not have access to any gaze information. We compared the performance of the two student models on predictions of student problem-solving effectiveness and student problem-solving efficiency.

4.1 Participants and Experimental Set-Up

During the study, 65 college students interacted with the CRYSTAL ISLAND game-based learning environment in a controlled setting. Three students were removed because they were missing key pieces of data, which resulted in 62 students ($M = 20.0$ years old, $SD = 1.57$). In this group, 42 subjects (68%) were female. Each of the students played CRYSTAL ISLAND until successfully solving the mystery, with game times ranging from a minimum of 39.7 minutes to a maximum of 170.3 minutes ($M = 81.3$, $SD = 22.8$). Before playing the game, each student completed the 12-question Achievement Goal Questionnaire to measure their goal orientation [16]. The students also took a pre-test preceding their interaction with CRYSTAL ISLAND to assess their prior knowledge and a post-test following gameplay.

4.2 Goal Orientation

Because gameplay in CRYSTAL ISLAND features goal-oriented problem-solving activities, we used students' goal orientation to inform the student model. To measure goal orientation, prior to gameplay each student was asked to complete the Achievement Goal Questionnaire (AGQ) to measure their goal orientation [16], which is represented with a 2x2 matrix (Table 1).

A student may exhibit traits from all four categories. Each competency is scored on a scale of 1 to 5. The self-reported measure includes four subscales with averages for Mastery-Approach ($M = 3.98$, $SD = 0.53$), Mastery-Avoidance ($M = 3.42$, $SD = 0.83$), Performance-Approach ($M = 3.47$, $SD = 0.80$), and Performance-Avoidance ($M = 3.43$, $SD = 0.85$). We standardize each of these categories to a unit normal distribution to allow comparison among the four subscales of the AGQ.

Table 1. 2x2 Framework for goal orientation construct.

		Definition	
		Mastery	*Performance*
Valence	*Approach (towards success)*	Mastery-Approach Goal	Performance-Approach Goal
	Avoidance (of failure)	Mastery-Avoidance Goal	Performance-Avoidance Goal

4.3 Problem-Solving Performance

We designed the gaze-enhanced student model and baseline student model to predict real-time student problem-solving performance. Rather than designing student models to predict end-of-session metrics such as post-test scores, we sought to devise models that dynamically predict student in-game problem-solving performance as this family of models could yield actionable information to inform the user-adaptive tailoring of gameplay and scaffolding. To measure students' in-game problem-solving performance in CRYSTAL ISLAND, the actions they take, and the timing of those actions are used to compute their problem-solving performance scores at a given moment.

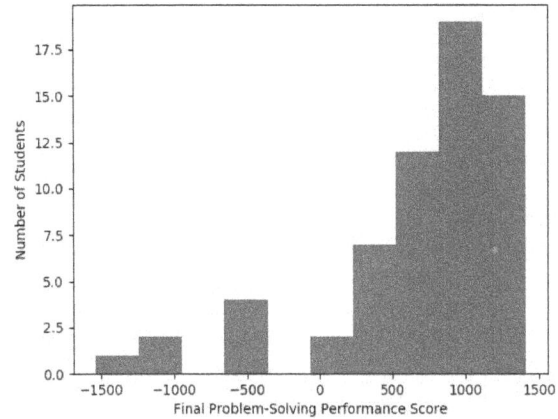

Figure 2. Problem-solving performance distribution.

Performance scores increase or decrease as students make progress (or fail to make progress) in solving the science mystery. The game-based problem-solving performance metric is parameterized on action types and elapsed time (Table 2). For example, a correct solution of the CRYSTAL ISLAND science mystery yields (+500) points, whereas scans of incorrect objects are penalized up to 35 points if the student is also scanning for the wrong contaminant. As such, there is usually an increase in the

Table 2. Student game-based problem-solving performance metric.

Action	Points (pts)
Overall Mystery Solution	
Correct Solution	500 pts
Solution Efficiency	(7500 / elapsed mins) pts
Incorrect Solution Attempt	-100 pts
In-game Quiz Questions	
First Attempt Correct	25 pts
Second Attempt Correct	10 pts
Second Attempt Incorrect	-10 pts
Object Contaminant Testing	
Correct Object and Correct Contaminant	200 pts
Incorrect Object and Correct Contaminant	15 pts
Correct Object and Incorrect Contaminant	-15 pts
Incorrect Object and Incorrect Contaminant	-35 pts
Character Interactions	
Talk to Kim	(25 / elapsed mins) pts
Talk to Teresa	(50 / elapsed mins) pts
Talk to Ford	(125 / elapsed mins) pts
Talk to Robert	(125 / elapsed mins) pts
Talk to Quentin	(125 / elapsed mins) pts
Total Maximum Points	**1665 pts**

score at the conclusion of gameplay if the student correctly solves the mystery. The metric thereby provides a real-time assessment of two facets of student problem solving: problem-solving effectiveness and problem-solving efficiency. It should also be noted that while the problem-solving performance measure was developed to assess student problem solving, it has also been used as a factor in measuring in-game student engagement with the problem-solving scenario [39].

In this student gameplay data, the final problem-solving scores have a mean of 679.9 and standard deviation of 608.80. We note that the score can be a negative value; the minimum score achieved was a -1542.73, and the maximum score was 1413.17.

Figure 2 displays a histogram of the problem-solving performance scores. Previous work has shown problem-solving performance to be significantly correlated with learning [38] and a marginally significant correlation between problem-solving performance and normalized learning gain was observed in this study ($r(60) = 0.271$ $p = 0.033$).

4.4 Eye Tracking and Gaze-based Entity Tracking

To provide eye gaze data stream information to the gaze-enhanced student model, students' gaze was tracked during gameplay using the SMI RED 250 eye tracker, which was mounted on a desktop (Figure 3). As students interacted with CRYSTAL ISLAND, the system pinpointed the coordinates on the screen at each timestamp where the student was gazing to log gaze data. Eye movements were tracked at 120 Hz, and following established conventions [38], a "fixation" is operationalized as engaging in a sustained gaze for a minimal threshold of 250 milliseconds.

The gaze-enhanced student model utilizes a gaze-driven entity tracking system that we have incorporated into the CRYSTAL ISLAND game-based learning environment. The gaze-driven entity tracker automatically detects which in-game objects the student is fixating on by analyzing the angle and gaze point on the screen by using ray casting to detect the intersection with specific in-game objects. It operates in real-time to generate a gaze data stream from synchronized sequences of data representing each

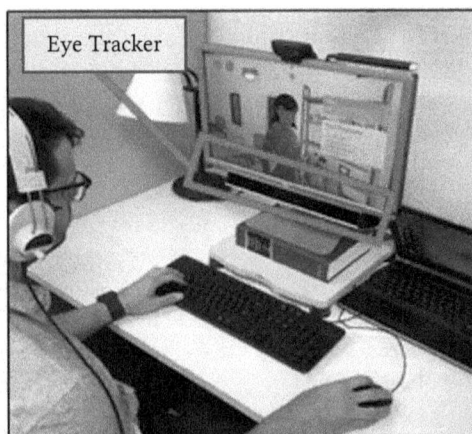

Figure 3. Gaze-instrumented CRYSTAL ISLAND **environment.**

fixation event, the in-game object that is the subject of the fixation, and the duration of the fixation. The gaze-enhanced student model uses these three elements to compute proportions for multiple categories of gaze objects, and it uses the fixation duration to compute total fixation time per student.

5 RESULTS

We compared the predictive accuracies of the gaze-enhanced student model with the baseline student model to explore the potential additive value of gaze. The gaze-enhanced student model used gaze data in addition to students' goal orientation, gameplay time, and prior knowledge, while the baseline model had access to the same information sources as the gaze-enhanced student model except for gaze. The gaze-enhanced student model used 15 features (9 gaze proportions and 6 baseline features), while the baseline model only had access to the 6 baseline features: 4 goal-orientation subscales, pre-test score, and gameplay duration.

We conducted two sets of evaluations to compare the performance of the two student models. To begin, we compare the baseline model and gaze-enhanced model using data generated from full gameplay sessions (Baseline Full-Gameplay Model and Gaze-Enhanced Full-Gameplay Model). We then compare the baseline model and gaze-enhanced model on interval-based models that make dynamic predictions throughout gameplay from incrementally available data (Baseline Interval-Based Model and Gaze-Enhanced Interval-Based Model). In these comparisons, we evaluate the dynamic predictive capabilities of these models by using incrementally available cumulative gameplay to predict the problem-solving performance after discrete time intervals. Specifically, we investigate the use of percentage gameplay versus constant time-elapsed intervals.

The evaluation uses two machine learning frameworks for student modeling: an L2-regularized linear regression model (Ridge Regression) and an ensemble partitioning method (Random Forests). We compare the use of Ridge Regression and Random Forests for each feature set and each gameplay accumulation setup. Ridge Regression provides a simple, interpretable, and regularized method for predicting a continuous outcome from continuous variables. Random Forests are better suited to avoid overfitting due to their ensemble nature, which is a concern when presented with relatively small datasets. These models were chosen because of their ability to prevent overfitting. To evaluate each model, we use leave-one-out cross-validation (LOOCV). In this context, we are leaving one student out of each iteration to create the test set. When examining each model's performance, we evaluate the model test set R^2. We also examine the mean absolute error (MAE) for each model. R^2 is a way to determine the model's relative fit, and it provides a quantified evaluation of explained variance (using held-out data) versus total variance in the data. MAE is advantageous with respect to interpretability because it determines the average error of the model predictions.

5.1 Baseline Full-Gameplay Models

Baseline models include 6 features. Out of these, 5 are known beforehand (4 AGQ values, pretest score). The remaining value is the total time the student spent playing the game. This can be an important factor in predicting problem-solving performance because depending on students' pre-test score and goal orientation, a longer game time could indicate a lack of self-regulatory skills, spending a disproportionate amount of time acquiring knowledge, or using less efficient learning strategies. For Ridge Regression, we set up and evaluate the models by standardizing the input features and reporting the most significant features using the standard error of coefficients to calculate the t-statistic under the null hypothesis that the coefficient is equal to zero. We also report both the R^2 and MAE.

In addition to using Ridge Regression (RR), we also use a Random Forest (RF), where we use MAE as the criterion for deciding the quality split. We report leave one out cross validation R^2 and MAE for this model as well. The "feature importance" of each feature is also presented for each RF model. This accounts for the sum of the decision tree splits that include the given feature in proportion to the number of students that it splits. Baseline student model results are shown in Tables 3, 4, and 5.

Table 3. Overall baseline model LOOCV accuracy results.

	R^2	MAE
Baseline RR	0.225	372.248
Baseline RF	0.140	409.517

Table 4. Baseline Ridge Regression model.

Feature	Coefficient (B)	STD Error (B)	β	p-value
Constant	391.165	621.592	3.88e-16	1.0
Mastery-Approach	232.162	139.094	0.146	0.885
Performance-Approach	-101.717	126.289	-0.141	0.890
Mastery-Avoidance	110.104	86.213	0.139	0.891
Performance-Avoidance	73.270	116.963	0.0834	0.935
Game Time	-24.757	1.001	-0.5839	0.564
Pre-Test Score	25.624	25.599	0.0614	0.952

Ridge Regression was conducted on the baseline data to determine significant attributes. The model coefficients are significantly different from a null model, $F(6,55) = 15.221$ ($p < 0.001$) with an R^2 of 0.398 and an adjusted R^2 of 0.332.

We note that we are able to achieve an R^2 of 0.225 for the Ridge Regression model with the baseline feature set. With this performance, it is clear that the most significant feature is gameplay duration (Game Time). There are two plausible explanations for this result. A longer gameplay duration could indicate there is a lack of understanding of the game content or

less efficient problem-solving strategies, which would negatively affect their problem-solving performance. Alternatively, the student may be exploring the environment or performing other off-task behaviors unrelated to solving the science mystery.

Table 5. Random Forest results for baseline feature set.

Feature	Feature Importance
Mastery-Approach	0.0828
Performance-Approach	0.0928
Mastery-Avoidance	0.136
Performance-Avoidance	0.0828
Game Time	0.422
Pre-Test Score	0.184

5.2 Gaze-Enhanced Full-Gameplay Models

Next, we investigated gaze-enhanced student models that extend the baseline models with gaze data streams. We augmented the baseline model with category-based gaze patterns representing the sequence of categories of in-game objects that were the focus of students' fixations. Specifically, gaze-enhanced student models use gaze pertaining to in-game objects in the following categories: non-player characters (NPCs), Travel/Game Items, Food-Related, Lab-Related, Diagnosis-Related, Book-Related, Concept-Matrix-Related, Miscellaneous, and Fixations-per-second. "Book Related" refers to the material that the students read throughout the game in order to gather information; "Concept-Matrix-Related" refers to the in-game testing the students complete after reading scientific content; "Travel/Game Items" refers to objects within the game that are related to transitioning between locations; "Lab Related", "Diagnosis Related", and "Food Related" are objects within the game that are relevant to solving the mystery (e.g., pieces of evidence towards a hypothesis, equipment to test hypotheses). "Miscellaneous" in this context encompasses game-related objects that are not associated with game content, such as the heads-up display, settings menu, and achievement panel. The "Fixations per second" feature quantifies the student's general fixation pattern. These categories were chosen to group specific game world objects identified by the gaze-driven entity tracker into higher-level game-based learning objects.

Table 6. Overall gaze-enhanced model LOOCV accuracy.

	R^2	MAE
Gaze RR	0.361	343.051
Gaze RF	0.453	326.968
PCA RR	0.212	373.339
PCA RF	0.389	330.102

We perform dimensionality reduction on these features to determine a transformed, reduced set of features that helps remove subjective bias of the categories, noise from a high dimensionality relative to the size of the data, and multicollinearity among the features. We used principal component analysis (PCA) with 5 components and then used these new orthogonal features in Ridge Regression and Random Forest gaze-enhanced student models for comparison. Tables 6, 7, and 8, display the results from the overall gaze-enhanced models and the PCA reduced models.

As performed previously, Ridge Regression was performed on the gaze-enhanced data to determine if there were significant attributes. The model coefficients are significantly different from a null model, $F(15,46) = 9.096$ ($p < 0.001$) with an R^2 of 0.662 and an adjusted R^2 of 0.553.

Table 7. Gaze-enhanced Ridge Regression model.

Feature	Coefficient (B)	STD Error (B)	β	p-value
Constant	337.381	1.86e4	4.44e-16	1.0
NPCs	-101.452	2.19e4	-0.206	0.858
Travel/Game Items	-274.562	1.87e4	-0.0937	0.968
Food-Related	9.996	1.97e4	0.0795	0.942
Lab-Related	-394.812	1.87e4	-0.341	0.839
Diagnosis-Related	-137.246	1.87e4	-0.203	0.872
Miscellaneous	170.129	2.00e4	-0.0853	0.956
Book-Related	839.123	1.86e4	0.135	0.955
Concept-Matrix-Related	216.927	1.84e4	0.0933	0.947
Fixations/Second	-36.119	6.96e2	-0.0299	0.976
Mastery-Approach	221.771	1.49e2	0.120	0.906
Performance-Approach	-92.090	1.34e2	-0.0384	0.970
Mastery-Avoidance	87.125	9.84e1	0.0271	0.979
Performance-Avoidance	76.264	1.29e2	-7.82e-3	0.994
Game Time	-24.790	1.00	-0.598	0.556
Pre-Test Score	26.564	2.70e1	0.152	0.880

The gaze-enhanced full-gameplay models were the best performing models. With respect to contribution to problem-solving performance prediction, we note that "Lab Related," "Diagnosis Related," and "Book Related" are of interest. The RF regressor model found these to be strong elements in predicting student performance according to feature importance. The RR model also found these to be important features (although not significant), as well as "Travel/Game Items." The negative impact

of "Lab Related" fixations could be due to the fact that students are awarded points based on whether their testing is correct. Thus, the longer a student spends fixated on testing equipment in-game, could indicate they are performing additional, incorrect tests.

The negative impact of fixation proportion of "Lab Related" is reinforced by the fact the Ridge Regression model found a negative coefficient, while the Random Forest Regressor found this feature to be the most important feature. "Book Related" fixations are important since book material within the environment is a primary source of how the student acquires content learning. Perhaps the longer students are fixating on these content items, the more relevant scientific information they acquire, which might enable them to solve the science mystery more efficiently. The negative impact of "Travel/Game Items" on problem-solving performance could indicate that a student performed more off-task behavior, as travel and game-related objects have little relevance to solving the mystery.

Table 8. Random Forest results for gaze-enhanced models.

Feature	Feature Importance
NPCs	0.0278
Travel/Game Items	0.0409
Food Related	0.0144
Lab Related	0.207
Diagnosis Related	0.124
Miscellaneous	0.110
Book Related	0.120
Concept Matrix Related	0.0232
Fixations/Sec	0.0367
Mastery-Approach	0.0268
Performance-Approach	0.0262
Mastery-Avoidance	0.0161
Performance-Avoidance	0.00927
Game Time	0.125
Pre-Test Score	0.0935

Another explanation could be that the students have reached an impasse with respect to understanding the content, and they could be navigating widely to try out many different ideas. Previous work has shown that large amounts of time spent in irrelevant locations in the game may indicate off-task behavior, as there are no relevant materials in these locations [41]. Another interesting result is the fact that the duration of "Game Time" is considered to be a strong predictor of problem-solving performance. This could be attributed to the fact that students who are spending longer times in the environment are either (1) not fully engaged in the game and take longer to complete it or (2) do not fully grasp the material as quickly as other students and must devote more time to gain this level of understanding. It is also worth noting that problem-solving performance considers efficiency, which is based on game duration.

Another interesting result from the Ridge Regression model evaluation is the fact that "Mastery-Approach" is weighted so highly. This poses an important question. Are students who exhibit this goal orientation potentially better performers in this type of environment? While difficult to determine, we note that each of the other goal orientation categories were weighted much lower in magnitude. Mastery-Approach students might strive to comprehend the material in its entirety and not leave the learning environment without gaining a firm understanding of these materials. In CRYSTAL ISLAND, an example of this phenomenon would be a student striving to understand a particular disease or microbiology concept at a deep level.

5.3 Interval-Based Models

The evaluations of Full-Gameplay student models shed light on the additive diagnostic value of gaze for problem-solving performance in *toto*, and we are particularly interested in investigating the additive diagnostic value of gaze for student models that are to operate dynamically and only have access to gaze data and gameplay data that have been produced before the current moment in the gameplay. A user-adaptive learning environment could exploit such models at runtime to make in-game adaptations dynamically. The objective of informing runtime adaptations motivates the exploration of interval-based student models that predict students' problem-solving performance in a cumulative fashion. We seek to design student models that can accurately predict students' problem-solving performance scores in cumulative intervals using the same feature sets as the non-interval-based (i.e., Full-Gameplay) models.

The baseline feature set containing goal orientation values are static throughout gameplay since these are calculated from a pre-game survey. However, the gaze features will be dynamic throughout gameplay. For example, if an interval of the gameplay contains predominantly "Book Related" objects, this proportion will be very high relative to the other gaze attributes for this period. Table 9 shows that the gaze-enhanced models showed a predictive accuracy improvement of 62.3% over the baseline based on R^2 using the RF model.

We can distinguish two alternative approaches to interval-based models. First, a percentage of total time played up to each point (i.e., 10%, 20%, ... 100%) could be adopted, or second, a constant-time approach (i.e., 1 minute, 2 minutes, ... total minutes played) could be used. We chose the constant-time approach as it supports the use of a more standard time period for each student. If we chose the percentage-based approach, then each student would likely have very different amounts of gameplay in each segment. It should be noted that using a constant time approach also presents the challenge of having a different number of time segments per student, which we address below. A constant time approach is more realistic for real-time prediction, and the results shown below in Table 9 use 1-minute intervals. Thus, predictions were made each minute during the student's gameplay, using all student actions and gaze behavior up to the current prediction.

The best performing models for using the cumulative interval-based gameplay models were the gaze-enhanced models. The Random Forest regressors performed well, but we note that as expected the general performance of these models was not as high as the Full-Game models. This could be because students generally proceed through different phases in the CRYSTAL ISLAND

game. For example, the tutorial will feature different objects than latter parts of the game, thus creating a difference in gaze proportions between intervals. Early predictions may therefore be more inaccurate than later gameplay predictions, and because of the dynamic nature of student problem-solving in game-based learning, the models will improve over time as they observe additional gameplay for each student.

Table 9. Summary results for interval-based models.

	R^2	MAE
Gaze RR	0.00599	202.613
Gaze RF	0.227	161.617

5.4 Convergence of Interval-Based Models

A desirable characteristic of dynamic models is continual improvement as they observe more gameplay. As a student progresses through the game, this would manifest as the student model achieving increases in predictive accuracy, which could enable user-adaptive learning environment to better adapt to the student's needs as indicated by changes to predicted problem-solving scores. Below, in Figure 4, we can see that the best models from the cumulative interval-based gameplay evaluation improve as they observe additional gameplay.

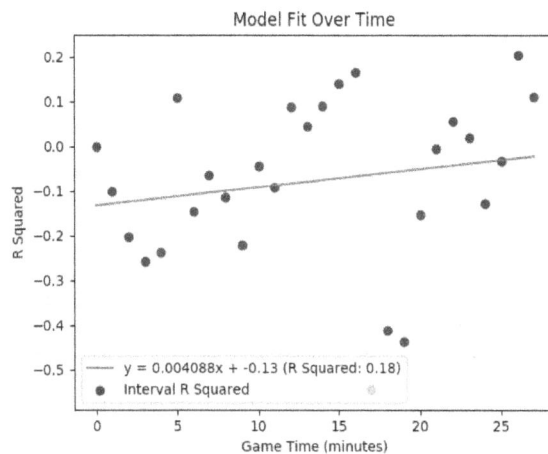

Figure 4. Random Forest model accuracy over time.

It should be noted that for purposes of evaluation, we use the predictions up to the time of the shortest student gameplay to guarantee that we have a prediction value for each student. As we can see, the R^2 value starts off very unstable, and then appears to approach a positive, improving value. We believe the reason for the less accurate early fit is that much of the time early in the game is unrelated to problem-solving performance, e.g., becoming familiar with the environment.

In addition, there are different stages of the game for which different types of objects may be present. Thus, significant features the model finds may not be present at certain early stages of the game. After an initial period, the model fit improves continually, suggesting that the model is useful in predicting student problem-solving performance over time as it observes more student gameplay and gaze behavior.

6 DISCUSSION

The results of this evaluation demonstrate that gaze-enhanced student models achieve higher predictive accuracy on student problem-solving performance than baseline student models. After evaluating the baseline student models on the entire gameplay data for each student, we find that we significantly improve these models by augmenting them with student gaze patterns. Specifically, the gaze-enhanced student models use gaze proportions with respect to categories of objects within the game. Notably, the strongest predictor categories of objects within the game were "Book Related," "Lab Related," and "Diagnosis Related" materials. "Travel/Game Items" were also informative, which could be due to off-task behavior [41]. For "Book Related" objects, this could be generalized to learning science content within the game. Many game-based learning environments feature learning content in one form or another, and CRYSTAL ISLAND uses books, articles, and posters (reading material) to convey relevant microbiology and science content to students. If students are fixated upon these types of objects for a larger proportion of time, it could indicate that they are spending additional time using sophisticated cognitive strategies (e.g., making inferences) to understand material deeply, or it could mean that they are trying to absorb a large amount of science related material using a combination of accurate metacognitive monitoring and cognitive strategies. Either way, it would seem "Book Related" material has a positive effect on their problem-solving performance. Examining more fine-grained gaze information for this category, e.g., saccades while reading, offers a promising direction for future work, as it has been shown that various patterns in reading can affect performance and learning [45].

For "Lab Related" and "Diagnosis Related" objects, we note that these can be generalized to be a form of applying scientific reasoning processes associated with generating hypotheses, collecting relevant evidence, and confirming or contradicting hypotheses through testing evidence. In terms of this specific learning environment, a higher proportion of time could indicate that a student is spending more time testing items they believe are related to solving the mysterious outbreak. At a high level, this would appear to have a positive effect on one's performance. However, there are ways a student could "game the system" by exhibiting "guess-and-check" problem-solving behavior to simply test every single item to determine the correct answer, without learning the material or engaging in scientific reasoning [39]. Thus, the prediction model seems to be able to identify students pursuing a "guess-and-check" strategy.

It is possible that students who spend more time testing items are not grasping concepts as well (e.g., differences between viruses and bacteria) and are perhaps testing irrelevant evidence. In fact, it would be logical for a student who efficiently determines the solution to the science mystery to have a very low proportion of their time fixating upon these test related objects, since they would use the test related areas of the environment less after confirming their hypothesis. This is perhaps related to self-regulated learning in that students who employ certain strategies may have a particular learner profile [8].

The fixation object categories were chosen to create generalizable, common categories that are broadly applicable. Data-driven methods of aggregating specific fixation items into higher-level categories, such as sparse autoencoders, should be explored to increase the generalizability of fixation models to other game-based learning environments. To address the concern of generalizability, dimensionality reduction (PCA) was used to calculate the components that maximize the total variance of the data. We chose 5 components, and the performance of the PCA components within the same prediction models outperformed the baseline. However, because a side effect of dimensionality reduction is losing interpretability of the original features, more interpretable aggregation techniques should be investigated.

7 CONCLUSION

With rapid improvements in eye-tracking technologies, incorporating gaze data streams into student modeling offers considerable promise for creating more robust student models, which in turn can yield user-adaptive learning environments that are more effective and engaging. To explore the potential of gaze for student modeling, we created gaze-enhanced student models that use student gaze fixation transitions to predict student problem-solving performance in a game-based learning environment. We conducted a comparative evaluation of the predictive accuracy of the gaze-enhanced student models relative to baseline models and found that the gaze-enhanced student models significantly outperformed baseline student models that did not have access to gaze data streams. The results also demonstrate that gaze-enhanced student models more accurately predict student problem-solving performance in both static contexts (when full-session gameplay data is made available) and in dynamic contexts (when predictions must be made incrementally in an interval-based fashion).

Gaze-based student modeling can inform dynamic user-adaptations, and it will be important to investigate this in future work. Two additional lines of investigation that are also promising are to explore sequence-based models that directly represent the temporal dimension of fixations, and multimodal student models that further extend gaze-enhanced models with additional modalities such as affect and posture to yield even higher predictive accuracies and support more effective user-adaptation.

Acknowledgements

We would like to thank our group's collaborators at the Center for Educational Informatics and the SMART Lab at North Carolina State University. This study was supported by funding from the Social Sciences and Humanities Research Council of Canada. Any opinions, findings, and conclusions or recommendations expressed in this material are those of the author(s) and do not necessarily reflect the views of the Social Sciences and Humanities Research Council of Canada.

REFERENCES

[1]   Alvarez, N., Sanchez-Ruiz, A., Cavazza, M., Shigematsu, M. and Prendinger, H. 2015. Narrative Balance Management in an Intelligent Biosafety Training Application for Improving User Performance. *International Journal of Artificial Intelligence in Education*. 25, 1, 35–59.

[2]   Baker, R. 2007. Modeling and Understanding Students' Off-Task Behavior in Intelligent Tutoring Systems. *Proceedings of the SIGCHI Conference on Human Factors in Computing Systems.*, 1059.

[3]   Baker, R., Corbett, A. and Aleven, V. 2008. More Accurate Student Modeling through Contextual Estimation of Slip and Guess Probabilities in Bayesian Knowledge Tracing. *Intelligent Tutoring Systems.*, 406–415.

[4]   Baker, R., K. D'Mello, S., Mercedes T. Rodrigo, M. and Graesser, A. 2010. Better to be Frustrated than Bored: The Incidence, Persistence, and Impact of Learners' Cognitive Affective States during Interactions with three Different Computer-Based Learning Environments. *International Journal of Human-Computer Studies*. 68, 4, 223–241.

[5]   Bergey, B., Ketelhut, D.J., Liang, S., Natarajan, U. and Karakus, M. 2015. Scientific Inquiry Self-Efficacy and Computer Game Self-Efficacy as Predictors and Outcomes of Middle School Boys' and Girls' Performance in a Science Assessment in a Virtual Environment. *Journal of Science Education and Technology*. 24, 5, 696–708.

[6]   Bondareva, D., Conati, C., Feyzi-Behnagh, R., Harley, J.M., Azevedo, R. and Bouchet, F. 2013. Inferring Learning from Gaze Data during Interaction with an Environment to Support Self-Regulated Learning. *Proceedings of the 16th International Conference on Artificial Intelligence in Education*. 229–238.

[7]   Botelho, A., Baker, R. and Heffernan, N. 2017. Improving Sensor-Free Affect Detection Using Deep Learning. *Proceedings of the International Conference on Artificial Intelligence in Education*. 40–51.

[8]   Bouchet, F., Harley, J.M., Trevors, G. and Azevedo, R. 2013. Clustering and Profiling Students According to their Interactions with an Intelligent Tutoring System Fostering Self-Regulated Learning. *Journal of Educational Data Mining*. 5, 1, 104–146.

[9]   Conati, C., Gertner, A. and VanLehn, K. 2002. Using Bayesian Networks to Manage Uncertainty in Student Modeling. *User Modeling and User-Adapted Interaction*. 12, 4, 371–417.

[10] Conati, C., Jaques, N. and Muir, M. 2013. Understanding attention to adaptive hints in educational games: an eye-tracking study. *International Journal of Artificial Intelligence in Education*. 23, 1–4, 136–161.

[11] Conati, C. and Merten, C. 2007. Eye-Tracking for User Modeling in Exploratory Learning Environments: an Empirical Evaluation. *Knowledge-Based Systems*. 20, 6, 557–574.

[12] Desmarais, M. and Baker, R. 2012. A Review of Recent Advances in Learner and Skill Modeling in Intelligent Learning Environments. *User Modeling and User-Adapted Interaction*. 22, 1, 9–38.

[13] Deubel, H. and Schneider, W. 1996. Saccade Target Selection and Object Recognition: Evidence for a Common Attentional Mechanism. *Vision Research*. 36, 12, 1827–1837.

[14] Easterday, M., Aleven, V., Scheines, R. and Carver, S. 2017. Using Tutors to Improve Educational Games: A Cognitive Game for Policy Argument. *Journal of the Learning Sciences*. 26, 2, 226–256.

[15] Elliot, A. and McGregor, H. 2001. A 2 × 2 achievement goal framework. *Journal of Personality and Social Psychology*. 80, 3, 501–519.

[16] Elliot, A.J. and Murayama, K. 2008. On the Measurement of Achievement Goals: Critique, Illustration, and Application. *Journal of Educational Psychology*. 100, 3, 613–628.

[17] Grafsgaard, J., Wiggins, J., Boyer, K., Wiebe, E. and Lester, J. 2014. Predicting Learning and Affect from Multimodal Data Streams in Task-Oriented Tutorial Dialogue. *Proceedings of the 7th International Conference on Educational Data Mining.*, 122–129.

[18] Habgood, J. and Ainsworth, S. 2011. Motivating Children to Learn Effectively: Exploring the Value of Intrinsic Integration in Educational Games. *The Journal of the Learning Sciences*. 20, 2, 169–206.

[19] Huang, C.-M., Andrist, S., Sauppé, A. and Mutlu, B. 2015. Using gaze patterns to predict task intent in collaboration. *Frontiers in Psychology*. 6, 1–12.

[20] Hutt, S., Hardey, J., Bixler, R., Stewart, A., Risko, E. and D'Mello, S. 2017. Gaze-based Detection of Mind Wandering during Lecture Viewing. *10th International Conference on Educational Data Mining.* , 226–231.

[21] Hutt, S., Mills, C., Bosch, N., Krasich, K., Brockmole, J. and D'Mello, S. 2017. Out of the Fr-"Eye"-ing Pan. *Proceedings of the 25th Conference on User Modeling, Adaptation and Personalization*. 94–103.

[22] Hutt, S., Mills, C., White, S., Donnelly, P. and D 'Mello, S. 2016. The Eyes Have It: Gaze-based Detection of Mind Wandering during Learning with an Intelligent Tutoring System. *Proceedings of the 9th International Conference on Educational Data Mining. International Educational Data Mining Society*. 86–93.

[23] Jaques, N., Conati, C., Harley, J. and Azevedo, R. 2014. Predicting Affect from Gaze Data During Interaction with an Intelligent Tutoring System. *Intelligent Tutoring Systems*. 29–38.

[24] Kardan, S. and Conati, C. 2012. Exploring Gaze Data for Determining User Learning with an Interactive Simulation. *Proceedings of 20th International Conference on User Modeling, Adaptation, and Personalization*. 126–138.

[25] Khajah, M., V. Lindsey, R. and Mozer, M. 2016. How deep is knowledge tracing? *Proceedings of the Ninth International Conference on Educational Data Mining*. 94–101.

[26] Lee, S.J., Liu, Y. and Popovi, Z. 2014. Learning Individual Behavior in an Educational Game: A Data-Driven Approach. *Proceedings of the 7th International Conference on Educational Data Mining*. 114–121.

[27] M. McLaren, B., M. Adams, D., Mayer, R. and Forlizzi, J. 2017. A Computer-Based Game that Promotes Mathematics Learning More than a Conventional Approach. *International Journal of Game-Based Learning*. 7, 1, 36–56.

[28]   Merten, C. and Conati, C. 2006. Eye-Tracking to Model and Adapt to User Meta-cognition in Intelligent Learning Environments. *Proceedings of the 11th International Conference on Intelligent User Interfaces*. 39.

[29]   Mills, C., Bixler, R., Wang, X. and D'Mello, S. 2016. Automatic Gaze-Based Detection of Mind Wandering during Narrative Film Comprehension. *Proceedings of the 9th International Conference on Educational Data Mining*. 30–37.

[30]   Mills, C., Bosch, N., Graesser, A. and D'Mello, S. 2014. To Quit or Not to Quit: Predicting Future Behavioral Disengagement from Reading Patterns. *Proceedings of the 12th International Conference on Intelligent Tutoring Systems*. 19–28.

[31]   Min, W., Ha, E.Y., Rowe, J., Mott, B. and Lester, J. 2014. Deep Learning-Based Goal Recognition in Open-Ended Digital Games. *Proceedings of the Tenth Annual Conference on Artificial Intelligence and Interactive Digital Entertainment*. 37–43.

[32]   Min, W., Mott, B., Rowe, J., Liu, B. and Lester, J. 2016. Player Goal Recognition in Open-World Digital Games with Long Short-Term Memory Networks. *Proceedings of the Twenty-Fifth International Joint Conference on Artificial Intelligence*. 2590–2596.

[33]   Min, W., Mott, B., Rowe, J., Taylor, R., Wiebe, E., Boyer, K. and Lester, J. 2017. Multimodal Goal Recognition in Open-World Digital Games. *Proceedings of the Thirteenth Annual AAAI Conference on Artificial Intelligence and Interactive Digital Entertainment*. 80–86.

[34]   Peterson, J., Pardos, Z., Rau, M., Swigart, A., Gerber, C. and McKinsey, J. 2015. Understanding Student Success in Chemistry Using Gaze Tracking and Pupillometry. *Proceedings of the 17th International Conference on Artificial Intelligence in Education*. 883.

[35]   Piech, C., Spencer, J., Huang, J., Ganguli, S., Sahami, M., Guibas, L. and Sohl-Dickstein, J. 2015. Deep Knowledge Tracing. *Advances in Neural Information Processing Systems*. 505–513.

[36]   Randall, J., Oswald, F. and Beier, M. 2014. Mind-Wandering, Cognition, and Performance: A Theory-Driven Meta-Analysis of Attention Regulation. *Psychological Bulletin*. 140, 6, 1411–1431.

[37]   Raptis, G., Katsini, C., Belk, M., Fidas, C., Samaras, G. and Avouris, N. 2017. Using Eye Gaze Data and Visual Activities to Infer Human Cognitive Styles: Method and Feasibility Studies. *Proceedings of the 25th Conference on User Modeling, Adaptation and Personalization*. 164–173.

[38]   Rayner, K. 1998. Eye Movements in Reading and Information Processing: 20 Years of Research. *Psychological Bulletin*. 124, 3, 372–422.

[39]   Rowe, J., Shores, L., Mott, B. and Lester, J. 2011. Integrating Learning, problem Solving, and Engagement in Narrative-Centered Learning Environments. *International Journal of Artificial Intelligence in Education*. 21, 1–2, 115–133.

[40]   Sabourin, J. and Lester, J. 2014. Affect and Engagement in Game-Based Learning Environments. *IEEE Transactions on Affective Computing*. 5, 1, 45–56.

[41]   Sabourin, J., Rowe, J., Mott, B. and Lester, J. 2011. When Off-Task is On-Task: The Affective Role of Off-Task Behavior in Narrative-Centered Learning Environments. *Proceedings of the Fifteenth International Conference on Artificial Intelligence in Education.*, 534–536.

[42]   Sabourin, J.L. and Lester, J.C. 2014. Affect and Engagement in Game-Based Learning Environments. *IEEE Transactions on Affective Computing*. 5, 1, 45–56.

[43]   Sawyer, R., Smith, A., Rowe, J., Azevedo, R. and Lester, J. 2017. Enhancing Student Models in Game-based Learning with Facial Expression Recognition. *Proceedings of the 25th Conference on User Modeling, Adaptation and Personalization*, 1–10.

[44]   Slanzi, G., Balazs, J.A. and Velásquez, J.D. 2017. Combining eye tracking, pupil dilation and EEG analysis for predicting web users click intention. *Information Fusion*. 35, 51–57.

[45]   Taub, M., Mudrick, N., Azevedo, R., Millar, G., Rowe, J. and Lester, J. 2017. Using multi-channel data with multi-level modeling to assess in-game performance during gameplay with CRYSTAL ISLAND. *Computers in Human Behavior*. 76, 641–655.

[46]   Vail, A., Grafsgaard, J., Boyer, K.E., Wiebe, E. and Lester, J. 2016. Gender Differences in Facial Expressions of Affect During Learning. *Proceedings of the Twenty-Fourth Conference on User Modeling, Adaptation, and Personalization*. 65–73.

[47]   Wiburg, K., Chamberlin, B., Valdez, A., Trujillo, K. and Stanford, T. 2016. Impact of Math Snacks Games on Students' Conceptual Understanding. *Journal of Computers in Mathematics and Science Teaching*. 35, 2, 173–193.

Co-embeddings for Student Modeling in Virtual Learning Environments

Milagro Teruel
Universidad Nacional de Córdoba
Córdoba, Argentina
mteruel@unc.edu.ar

Laura Alonso Alemany
Universidad Nacional de Córdoba
Córdoba, Argentina
lauraalonsoalemany@unc.edu.ar

ABSTRACT

We present a neural architecture to model student behavior in virtual educational environments using purely unsupervised information. A crucial part of this architecture is the optimization of a joint embedding function to represent both students and course elements into a single shared space. This joint representation is more adequate than disjoint representations because it elicits insights on the relations between students and contents. Moreover, the model is trained only with interactions of the student with online learning platforms, without requiring any additional manual labeling by experts.

We obtain state-of-the-art results using this approach in two types of task: first, dropout prediction in online courses (MOOCs), and second Knowledge Tracing in Intelligent Tutoring Systems (ITS). We explore how the deep architecture is flexible enough to capture variables related to different phenomena, such as engagement or skill mastery.

CCS CONCEPTS

• **Computing methodologies** → **Neural networks**; **Learning latent representations**; • **Applied computing** → *Interactive learning environments*; *E-learning*;

KEYWORDS

Deep Representation Learning, Student Modeling, Educational Data Mining, Dropout Prediction, Knowledge Tracing

ACM Reference Format:
Milagro Teruel and Laura Alonso Alemany. 2018. Co-embeddings for Student Modeling in Virtual Learning Environments. In *UMAP '18: 26th Conference on User Modeling, Adaptation and Personalization, July 8–11, 2018, Singapore, Singapore*. ACM, New York, NY, USA, 8 pages. https://doi.org/10.1145/3209219.3209227

1 INTRODUCTION

Educational Data Mining (EDM) is a complex area, with hidden, unknown causes governing the behavior of students and the success or failure of courses. In this context, Student Modeling, a specialized area of user modeling, has been growing steadily in the past decade. The increased development of Massive Open Online Courses (MOOCs) and the new availability of Intelligent Tutoring Systems (ITS) allow researchers to gather large amounts of data. A clear example is the Carnegie Mellon University DataShop [1], that acts as a dataset repository and also provides standard learning analytics tools. These large datasets facilitate the application of machine learning and data science approaches, for example to address tasks like dropout prediction and prevention, or personalization to improve learning.

However, various factors are hindering advances in this area. First, the scarcity of manually labeled datasets freely available for research, which are costly to develop and to anonymize. Secondly, it is hard to obtain adequate abstractions, because the available datasets are composed of low-level logs generated by learning platforms. In this paper we try to address both these problems by applying unsupervised methods for representation learning. These methods can be applied to datasets without manual labels, and they provide generalizations over the low-level data that may be useful to attain human-level abstractions. These abstractions, although not directly interpretable, can be used in visualization, personalization, or to support decision-making in general.

Educational content has such a diversity that it becomes problematic to discover patterns and systematize it in a uniform manner. Different courses will have a completely different set of lessons and exercises, can be designed for other levels of engagement and work load, the units can be independent or highly correlated, among others.

Diversity is even more acute when we compare data from MOOCs with data from ITSs, where the learning environment and the organization of materials is quite different. For example, the content used by ITSs are selected and labeled with meta-information necessary for the recommendations produced by the system, which involves expert human annotation. The static format of MOOCs makes them less expensive to create and usually do not include such detailed meta-information.

We expect a general method based on deep architectures will be flexible enough to deal with different kinds of data and still preserve basic properties. In addition, neural networks have been proved to generalize well without the need of additional meta-information, as the models construct their own representations (embeddings) only from access traces.

---
[1]https://pslcdatashop.web.cmu.edu/about/

Therefore, to tackle the challenge of modeling students with low-level unlabeled data, we propose not only to model student actions but also course elements using neural embeddings. Embeddings will provide an abstraction and aggregation layer over the low-level data, which can then be used by domain experts to interpret student behavior. As neural models do not require an intensive effort of the experts to previously annotate the data, we can encompass unlabeled content developed with less resources.

Along with the modeling of students and course content through embeddings, we explore the impact of joint representations where both embeddings are in the same latent space. A shared space allows us to explicitly model properties of the relations between students and content, rather than letting the model infer them. Through a modification in the recurrent architecture, we can inject in the model with knowledge of the phenomena it is trying to discover, which can have a significant impact in tasks with few examples available.

In summary, the main contribution of this paper as the proposal to model student interactions with a **joint embedding of course elements and students**, using a recurrent neural architecture. We describe the general model and how to adapt it to solve two tasks: dropout prediction in MOOCs using the KDDCup 2015 competition dataset, and knowledge tracing in ITSs using the ASSISTments 2009-2010 dataset.

We compare the performance of the system with an architecture without embeddings and with disjoint embeddings. We include the state of the art and an upper bound of performance provided by a manually labeled dataset. Results show that, besides providing a conceptually more adequate representation of students and contents, embeddings provide an improvement in performance, and that co-embeddings perform at least as well as disjoint embeddings, and outperform them in some contexts, like smaller courses.

We also asses the impact of pretrained embeddings for course elements obtained with the word2vec unsupervised algorithm, using them as a starting point to train the final model. Results show that the pretraining improves performance only in some courses with few examples.

2 RELEVANT WORK

Representation of students and course elements has been usually carried out by explicitly incorporating expert domain knowledge into the data. For example, Bayesian Knowledge Tracing (BKT) [1], one of the most used methods for knowledge tracing, requires each exercise to be labeled with a set of skills. This type of annotated information is not usually available, for example in the case of MOOCs. The underlying representations for such approaches are strongly based on the manually added information, and as a consequence they can suffer from a theoretical bias. This implies that the main variation factors are set by the domain expert and not discovered by the model.

However, in recent years there has been an increase in unsupervised approaches to modeling students and course elements. These approaches are more flexible than supervised ones because they serve as general methods to obtain representations from any dataset. In other words, they are not based on aspects of specific courses or platforms that have to be adapted later, or that acquire

different relevance in a different context. For example, Performance Factor Analysis (PFA), [8] and SPARse Factor Analysis (SPARFA) [5], show that factor analysis has a positive impact in knowledge tracing, discovering or refining the skills associated to each exercise. These works use a form of embedding based on variable correlation to discover a useful underlying representation of phenomena.

Deep learning architectures have also proven to be very helpful in discovering latent causes from observable phenomena. The multiple layers in a deep architecture build a number of internal representations of the input data, optimized for a certain prediction task. These internal representations, when the model is applied to tasks like dropout prediction, are liable to capture underlying causes like the diversity in student background and interests. In this context, we can train a model only to obtain these internal representations, called embeddings, which will then be used to represent examples for a different task. The task used to train embeddings is called a *pretext task*. When the model trained to obtain such embeddings is a neural network, we call them *neural embeddings*.

Neural models, and in particular deep neural models, have shown to be very effective for a wide range of problems, also for EDM. Deep Knowledge Tracing (DKT) [10] is a method that proposes to model student knowledge using the hidden state of a recurrent neural network. The pretext task for the model is to predict if the student will be able to solve the next exercise presented by a tutoring system. In contrast with BKT, it does not depend on manually assigned skills. Furthermore, it can be used to automatically detect relations between exercises and cluster them. The work of [13] models students also using RNNs trained to predict the next action to be performed by the student. This approach does not require exercises to be graded, as is often the case in MOOCs.

In addition to representing student state with neural embeddings, our proposal is to embed course elements in the same space. This implies learning a joint representation for both students and course contents. Co-embeddings have been successfully used before in MOOC environments [11]. In this study, the authors propose an embedded representations of students in a "latent skill space" that can be interpreted as the knowledge level of the student on each skill. Along with them, they find embeddings for course elements in the same skill space. The pretext task used to obtain these embeddings was performance prediction. Our approach differs from [11] in the use of a neural architecture to obtain the embeddings, and in the pretext task selected for optimization.

Modeling students and course elements in the same space is convenient in two aspects. On the one hand, it allows us to model better the relations between them using distances in the shared space. On the other hand, it opens the door for possible joint visualization and interpretation, leading to better insights on the causes of a certain phenomenon, for example dropout. A study of 2017 [7] shows how visualizations of student states can be interpreted and contribute to the work of course designers.

Dropout prediction is a task that differs from Knowledge Tracing in several aspects. One of the most important ones is the lack of a consensus about the definition of dropout. For example, some lines of work focus on the prediction of student behavior at the end of the course, while others seek to prevent dropout and focus on the prediction of actions in the near future [14]. It is also worth noticing that the factors involved in dropout prediction are not throughly understood. In [4] an analysis is done on the difference of background and expectations from students, which leads to diverse levels of engagement. We expect a deep learning model can capture this type of variability, represent it with an adequate level of abstraction, and help course creators understand it.

Some neural approaches have been applied to dropout prediction, for example [2], who reports an increase in performance compared to Markov models, logistic regressions and support vector machines. However, instead of using the full sequence of interactions, the data is aggregated in weekly periods.

3 NEURAL CO-EMBEDDINGS FOR STUDENT STATES AND COURSE ELEMENTS

As presented in previous sections, our aim is to obtain a representation of students and course elements that highlights the major factors involved in the human learning experience. To do that, we learn how to project students and course elements to a shared space, bringing forth their most indicative aspects and the relations between them. In this section we describe the concrete computational architecture to obtain the neural co-embeddings that represent students and course elements.

Our goal is to find the embedding functions φ_E and φ_S that project course elements and students from their representation in log data into a shared space, respectively. In the shared space each course element is represented as a vector. Students, on the other hand, are continuously changing as they progress through the course. As a result, they are represented as a sequence of vectors, corresponding to a given point of time. Individual vectors represent the state of the student after each interaction with a course element.

To find this shared space and the functions embedding students and course elements in this space, we propose a recurrent neural architecture to optimize φ_S and φ_E, shown in Figure 1. The base of this architecture is a Recurrent Neural Network (RNN), which is designed to selectively *remember* some aspect of previously seen input. The network is trained with some identifier (ids) of the course elements seen by students and possibly the outcome of the interaction. The output of the network will depend on the pretext taks used for the optimization. The difference between the output and the true labels is used to calculate the loss of the model over all examples, which is minimized using the BackPropagation Through Time algorithm (BPPT), until the model converges.

3.1 Integrating embeddings in the RNN architecture

A basic RNN structure has tree layers: input, hidden state and output. What characterizes a RNN is that the new hidden state h_t is calculated using the information from the input layer x_t and from the previous hidden state h_{t-1}, where t represents the position of the interaction in the sequence. Following, the output o_t is calculated as a transformation of the hidden state h_t.

The specific update equations for a basic RNN are the following:

$$y^{(t)} = \sigma(W^{(hy)}h^{(t)} + b^{(y)})$$

$$h_t = tanh(W^{(xh)}x^{(t)} + W^{(hh)}h^{(t-1)} + b^{(h)}) \qquad (1)$$

Inspired by [10], we will interpret the hidden state after t interactions (h_t) of the RNN classifier as the embedding of the student at

Figure 1: RNN architecture with co-embeddings.

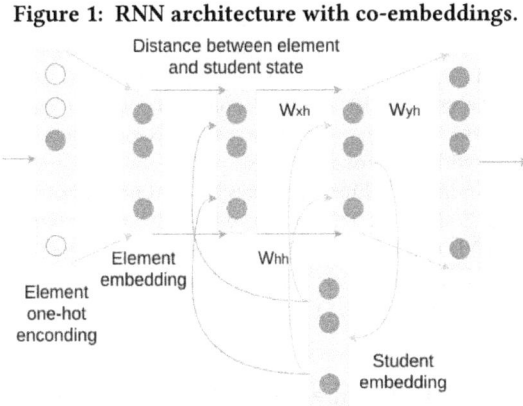

time $T + 1$. Once trained, the network has learned which information from the input is useful to keep during time, and a codification of such input is recorded in the hidden state. This hidden state is our function φ_S that encodes the student states.

To integrate the embedding of course elements φ_E into the RNN classifier, we add a new embedding layer between the input layer and the recurrent layer. An embedding layer is nothing more than a matrix that works as a look-up table, where the column j is the embedding of the element with index j.

At this point we have an architecture that projects students and course elements to a space, but we haven't ensured yet that this space is shared. In other words, the dimensions of this space do not necessarily have the same meaning for students and for course elements. To ensure that both embeddings are indeed in the same space, we will calculate the new hidden state as a combination of the previous state and a *point-wise function between the student current embedding and the embedding of the course element* in the current interaction. An illustration of these architecture is depicted in Figure 1

The relation between the course element embedding and the student embedding will have different impacts depending on the pretext task. For example, in KT, the dimensions of the latent space are interpreted as the mastery level of the student in a given skill. Then, the course element embedding can be seen as a prerequisite vector, as in [11]. If students are close enough to the course element, then they will get the major possible gain of interacting with the course element. If they are too far, then the lesson content will be either too easy or too hard.

The point-wise aspect of the function is also important, as we want to distinguish the influence of each dimension in the resulting state. This is an important distinction between our model and [11], which uses only the length of projection of the student embedding over the lesson embedding. As a result, our approach does not compensate a small value on a dimension (seen as skill level) with a large value in other one, but preserves the relation between student and course element for every dimension.

After introducing these changes, Equation 1 is rewritten as:

$$h_t = tanh(W^{(xh)}\delta(\varphi_E(x^{(t)}), h^{(t-1)}) + W^{(hh)}h^{(t-1)} + b^{(h)})$$

where δ is the pointwise function measure. We propose several δ functions, some examples are: $\delta(x, y) = (x - y)^2$, $\delta(x, y) = |(x - y)|$ and $\delta(x, y) = norm(x - y, 0, std)$ (all operations are pointwise). In the last function, *norm* refers to the probability of the vector following a normal distribution centered in 0 and with standard deviation *std*. The value of *std* is originally fixed, but it can be also optimized with the network.

More sophisticated networks can be used instead of a vanilla RNN, like Long Short Term Memory (LSTM) or Gated Recurrent Unit (GRU) networks. Their variation is not in the layers but in the neurons, so they can be trained to produce co-embeddings as long as the input vector to the recurrent layer is modified with the δ function.

3.2 Neural co-embeddings for Knowledge Tracing

For the task of KT, the RNN network will be used to produce one output for each element of the sequence, in a configuration known as *sequence labeling*. Just as in DKT, our model estimates the probability of success for every exercise, given all the previous interactions of the student. In consequence, the model's output layer has one neuron for each possible exercise. However, only the probability for the exercise that the student actually faced on the next time step is used to optimize the classifier, as we do not know what the performance could have been in other exercises. The output layer does not have a softmax activation, but rather a sigmoid one to normalize each individual neuron.

The loss function selected is the mean binary cross entropy or log loss between the model prediction and the true label over all examples. The loss for a student is sum of the cross entropy for all the interactions in the sequence. If we define the exercise index in the interaction at time t as e_t, the loss for a student is:

$$loss = \sum_t log(y_{t,e_t})o_t + log(1 - y_{t,e_t})(1 - o_t) \quad (2)$$

The representation of the input data is also modified with respect to the base model. This task provides two values for each interaction: the id of the exercise and if the student solves it successfully on the first attempt. To model both aspects, we use the sum of two embeddings for each exercise: one that corresponds to the base exercise, and one for the successful outcome of the interaction. If the student does not solve the exercise in the first try, only the base embedding is used.

3.3 Neural co-embeddings for dropout prediction

Neural embeddings and co-embeddings can be useful as well for less defined tasks like dropout prediction. In this case, we do not expect them to model skill mastery or knowledge, but mainly other variables, like engagement.

It is important to note that, from a classification point of view, this task is very different from KT. For every sequence, a single output is expected instead of one for each time step. This scenario is usually called sequence classification. As a result, the vanishing gradient problem associated with RNNs can be more problematic: we need to propagate a very weak signal of error up to the very first interaction of the sequence, which can be many steps away from the training label.

There are two possible configurations in a neural network to predict a binary variable like dropout: to output only the probability of the positive layer, or to output the probability of both classes as a multilabel classification task. This affects the size of the output layer, as one neuron is needed per output class. The loss function is in both cases the average of the cross entropy.

3.4 Pre-trained embeddings

A possible variation in this model is to initialize the embedding layer with pre-trained course element embeddings, obtained with an unsupervised method.

Pre-trained embeddings have the advantage of including information about the order in which students access course elements, using algorithms specialized for this kind of task. Indeed, methods like word2vec [6] and GloVe [9] have been shown to adequately model the underlying distribution of sequences of events with incomplete samples. These models seem to capture latent causes, like word semantics in language modeling. We expect pre-trained models will capture aspects of the datasets pertinent to the relation between course elements independently of their impact in the pre-text task. In [7], the author modeled student sequences using only word2vec and analyzed the usefulness of visualizations from those embeddings, rated by course creators. Results show that high-level organization of the course content was captured by the embeddings, and they even clustered successful and unsuccessful students.

Additionally, these embeddings have the possibility to be optimized or fine-tuned along with the optimization of the model for the pretext task. If we do not allow fine-tuning, the impact of the pre-trained embeddings on the student embedding will be higher. Another important advantage is that pre-trained embeddings, as an unsupervised method, can also be trained with instances from the same domain but without labels for the pretext task.

4 EXPERIMENTAL SETTING

4.1 Datasets

The KDDCup 2015 competition [2] proposed predicting the dropout of students in MOOCs. The data was provided by XuetangX, a Chinese MOOC learning platform initiated by Tsinghua University, a partner of EdX.

Although the information is no longer available in the competition website, this dataset was, to our knowledge, one of the few freely available big datasets of detailed logging in a MOOC environment. The data provided logs of events like access to video content, resolution of a problem, etc., for 39 different courses. Events are timestamped and identified with the corresponding student and course.

For the competition the dropout event was defined as the absence of student activity in the ten days following the end of the course. With this definition, 79% of the students in this dataset (19072) are labeled as dropouts. The distribution of dropouts is similar across courses and it ranges between 70% and 90%.

---

[2]https://biendata.com/competition/kddcup2015/

One model was optimized for each course. We have found that courses with different numbers of students have very different results, therefore we decided to distinguish results in three different segments of courses: 5 big courses with more than 6000 training students, 9 medium courses with between 5000 and 2000 students and 24 small courses with less than 2000 students.

On the other hand, we explored the performance of our approach in the Knowledge Tracing task using the ASSISTments 2009-2010 dataset, described in [3]. This dataset is a typical example of the data generated by an ITS system. It also has other desirable properties: it contains a fairly big amount of student interactions, nearly 350000, and the class imbalance is not pronounced, with 65% of positive labels. Furthermore, it is a reference dataset for the field of EDM, as it has been used for experimentation by several works.

As noted by Xiong et al. [15], the interactions between a student and an exercise labeled with multiple skills are stored duplicating the row for the interaction and labeling each of them with a different skill. This leads to duplicated data and can affect the test performance of any classifier if there is leaked information between the training and testing dataset. Following [15], we represent exercises with multiple skills with a new skill that serves as the merge of the original ones.

To reduce the noise of the dataset, the interactions involving exercises that appear less than 5 times in total were deleted. It is a common technique, used for example by word2vec, as no meaningful embedding can be trained from such a small amount of instances.

For all experiments, the entire student sequences of actions in both datasets were divided in three portions, training (70%), testing (20%) and validation (10%). The performances reported are obtained by applying the trained model over the testing dataset, after the best hyperparameters have been chosen using the validation dataset.

4.2 Variations in classifiers and learned representations

The neural architectures we tested are all based on RNNs. The simplest one (**LSTM**) has a single layer of LSTM cells. The input for this model is the one-hot encoding representations of the course element id. The output of the recurrent layer is connected to a dropout layer, and later to a regular dense layer with sigmoid activation and L2 regularization. The output layer is composed of two neurons with softmax activation, one for each class.

The second model (**E-LSTM**) has the same structure as the LSTM model, but the input layer is replaced by an embedding layer. Since students and course elements are not forced to share the same space, we call this approach *disjoint embeddings*. It is followed by a dropout layer using the same ratio as the one after the recurrent layer.

As mentioned before, the embedding for the KT task is composed of two parts. There is a base embedding for each exercise. Later, another embedding is added if the student has successfully solved the input exercise. In dropout prediction, one embedding is created for the merged module id and event id of the element seen by the student. We experimented using only the module id, with consistently worse results.

The final model (**CoE-LSTM**) is the one described in section 3, implementing the proposed co-embeddings. It has the same dropout layers as the E-LSTM.

For the two embedded models, we also explored the use of pre-trained embeddings, as developed in 3.4. To obtain the embedding we used the training sequences as input to the word2vec SkipGram algorithm. The parameters used are: window size of 5 events, minimum frequency of 5 events, an alpha initial learning rate of 0.01 and a negative sampling of 5 examples. Both settings with and without fine-tuning are explored.

The hyperparamenters of the networks optimized included embedding size (20, 50, 100 and 200), hidden layer size (20, 50, 100 and 200), number of events in the sequence used (20, 50, 100, 200 and 300) and dropout ratio (0, 0.2, 0.3 and 0.5). The optimizer used is the Adam implementation of Tensorflow with a learning rate of 0.001. Other configurations were also tested: RNN and GRU cells; bidirectional networks; RMSEProp, SGD, Adagrad and Adaboost optimizers; and higher and lower learning rates. Results for these other parameters are not reported as the performance decreased.

In the case of dropout prediction, we report the results of the model with the better AUC score for each course.

4.3 Optimization

The algorithm used to optimize a recurrent neural architecture is called Back Propagation Through Time (BPTT). However, propagating the gradients over very long sequences of time can be a prolonged process, producing vanishing gradients for the upper most steps. LSTM networks are designed to avoid vanishing gradients, but in practice they also have a limited propagation point. A technique used to overcome this problem is truncating the gradients after certain amount of steps, leading to a Truncated BPTT (TBPTT).

In dropout prediction, TBPTT decreased the performance significantly. As a result, for this task we used only the last portion of the sequences to train the model.

4.4 Metrics

To assess performance of different approaches, we measure the difference between the predicted probability of dropout or success and what is actually found in the dataset. Note that the prediction is probabilistic, while the true label value is binary. The metrics used are the Area Under the ROC Curve (AUC), the reference metric in the KDDCup, the Root Mean Square Error (RSME) and the coefficient of determination R2. The R2 score [12] estimates the proximity of the performance of the classifier to a random classifier.

5 RESULTS

5.1 Dropout prediction

In table 1 we present the results for AUC, RMSE and R2 for the best performing models for dropout prediction. In general, we can see the three metrics increase with the use of embeddings, and raise even more with joint representations. This supports our initial hypothesis that co-embeddings capture the underlying causes of dropout better than other representations.

It is worth noticing that the winner team at KDDCup 2016 reached an AUC of 0.91 with an ensemble model. Those results

Table 1: Model performance for dropout prediction

Model	AUC	RMSE	R2
LSTM	0.831	0.333	0.331
E-LSTM	0.842	0.327	0.356
CoE-LSTM	0.852	0.322	0.368

were obtained with the official test dataset, to which we don't have access. In addition to that, the winning solution used all the information available, while we only use the identifier of each course element, in order to evaluate the models in a scenario of minimal information. In this work, we have not focused in performance, hyperparameter tuning or ensemble of different models, but in assessing the impact of embeddings with simpler models, and also assessing the utility of different kinds of embeddings.

Figure 2: AUC for dropout prediction, grouped by course size

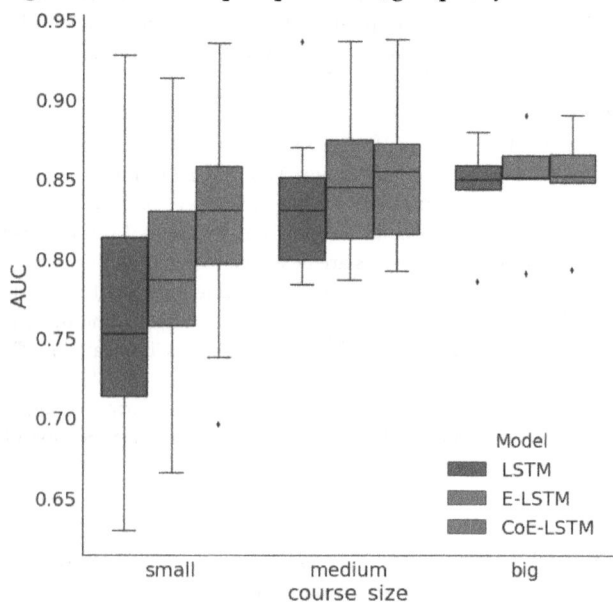

When we disaggregate courses by size, we can see that co-embeddings perform much better in smaller courses, even if the general performance in such courses is worse than for bigger courses. In Figure 2 we can see that for the biggest courses all classifiers perform indistinguishably, with small variations, hence the smaller spread of the boxplot. However, for smaller courses, where data is more scarce and performance is worse, co-embeddings seem to provide useful generalizations over the low-level data. It is noteworthy that, while co-embeddings do not seem to impact positively on the performance on bigger courses, they do not impact negatively either.

Exploring the differences in performance for different courses we found another factor of correlation. The proportion of students that dropped out, i.e. the class imbalance, impacts on the difficulty of the task. The less examples in one of the classes, the harder it is to learn the differences with the majority class. In figure 3 we plot

the AUC values for each type of model in each course, according to the dropout rate in the test dataset. The lines represent regression models fitted to the data. They helps us to see that, in average, CoE-LSTM models have a greater impact on the performance over courses with more class imbalance.

For this task, embedding sizes of 50 and 20 are more successful. The number of steps used in training varies from 50 to 300, and they are inversely proportional to the size of the recurrent layer.

Figure 3: AUC for dropout prediction, in relation with the course no-dropout rate

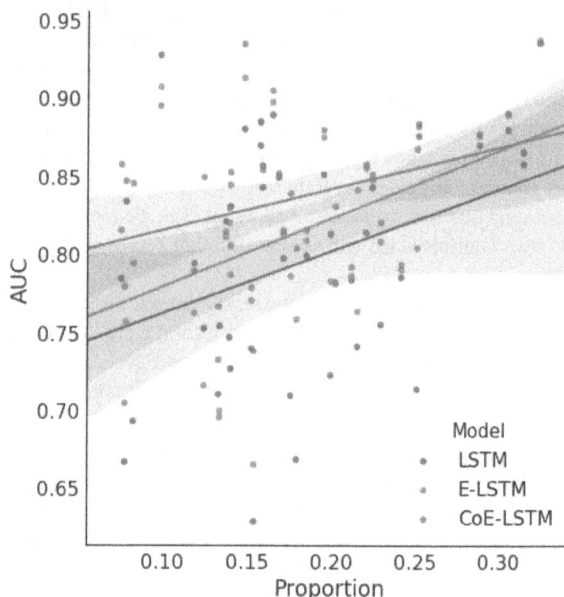

5.2 Knowledge Tracing

In table 2 we present the model performances for the Knowledge Tracing task. To facilitate comparison with the state of the art, we display the results reported by Xiong et al. [15] for the same dataset, marked with an asterisk. However, it must be noted that these results are not directly comparable because they don't use the same dataset for testing. In particular, the whole set of problems is used, instead of filtering less common problems as we do.

Table 2: Model performance for knowledge tracing

Model	Identifier	AUC	RMSE	R2
DKT*	Skill ID	0.75		
LSTM	Skill ID	0.746	0.432	0.176
LSTM	Problem ID	0.721	0.462	0.069
E-LSTM	Problem ID	0.740	0.443	0.131
CoE-LSTM	Problem ID	0.741	0.448	0.130

The wording in Xiong et al. [15] seems to indicate the method is using DKT with the skill ID. Indeed, when we use our LSTM with skill IDs (second row in the table), we obtain a comparable

Figure 4: Impact of pre-training embeddings for dropout prediction, grouped by model type and course size, reporting AUC.

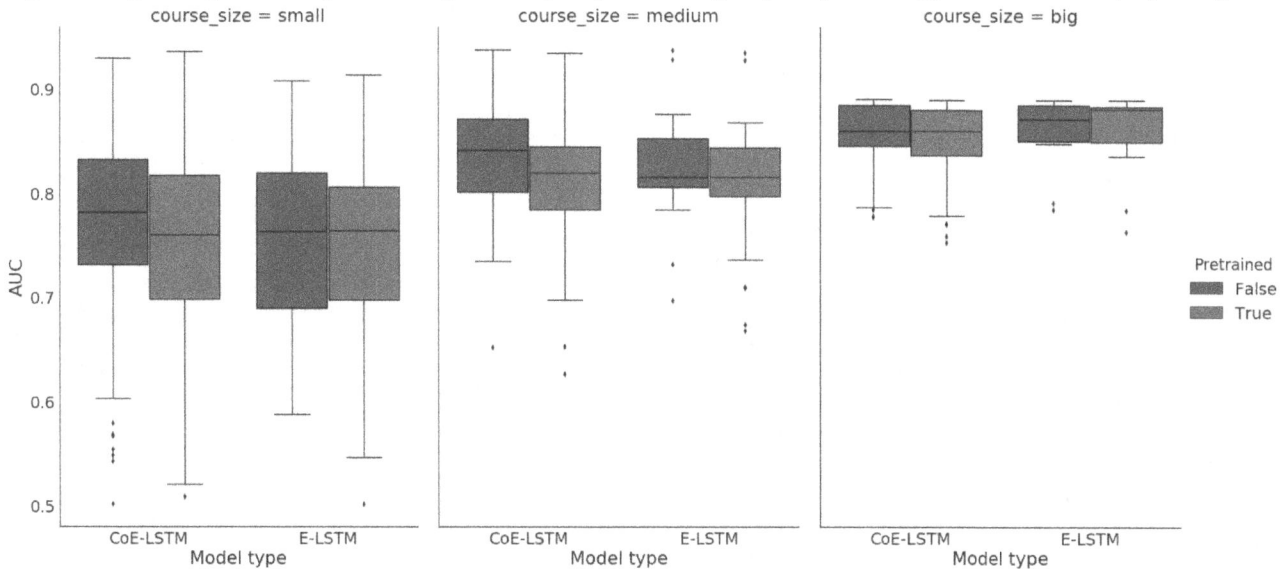

performance. However, the original intention of Piech et al. [10] was to avoid using this manually added information, treating the problem with unsupervised information only, using the problem ID as input.

The performance of the LSTM classifier with skill IDs is presented as an upper bound of performance, a point of comparison of the model in the optimal case: when labeled information is present. We can see that using only unsupervised information (the problem ID), the performance of the embedded methods is comparable to the performance using manually labeled information (skill IDs). Results indicates that, with this setting, embedded models have a positive impact with respect to the basic LSTM network. The joint representation obtains slightly better results than the disjoint representation, but further exploration needs to be carried out to discover the causes for these differences in performance.

The selection of the δ function had a great impact on the co-embedding performance. The best results where obtained with $\delta(x, y) = tanh(x - y)$, and the absolute value of the difference displayed good results as well. Other possibilities, like a sigmoid or square function lowered the AUC up to 4 points below the results shown. Such impact suggest that this function is vital to model the relations between student state and course elements correctly. In the case of dropout prediction, the results are highly dependent on the course and not so drastically variable. In general the the square function and the normal function with a fixed 0.5 standard deviation were the best performing ones.

For the sake of reproducibility, it is worth reporting that the best hyperparameter configuration for KT is an embedding size of 50, a maximum number of steps in the TBPTT of 50, between 200 and 500 training epochs and a dropout rate of 0.3. This contrasts with results reported in previous work, where they use a recurrent layer size of 200 neurons. Note that embeddings for this task are the same

size as embeddings for the task of dropout prediction, even if the dataset for each course was smaller.

5.3 Impact of pre-trained embeddings

Finally, we have compared the performance of embeddings trained together with the whole model, and embeddings pre-trained as explained in Section 3.4.

In Figure 4 we present the AUC scores of *all* experiments conducted with the KDDCup 2015 dataset, to compare the general performance of embedded methods with and without a pre-training step. We see that pre-trained embeddings are just as sensitive to course size as models without pre-training. Indeed, for bigger courses the performance is better, regardless of pre-training. In contrast, for medium and smaller courses, we can see that CoE-LSTM models perform slightly better without pre-training, while E-LSTM models are not remarkably affected by the use of pre-trained embeddings. Our strongest hypothesis to explain this difference is that co-embeddings are able to capture relevant information of the dataset more adequately than a pre-training step. This seems to advocate for a superiority of co-embeddings over disjoint embeddings, because the latter perform indistinguishably from pre-trained embeddings, thus they seem to be capturing roughly the same information, and they are both surpassed by co-embeddings.

For the case of Knowledge Tracing, the use of pre-trained embeddings had a smaller impact. Some δ functions performed better with pre-trained embeddings and others without, but the results varied in less than 0.01 points. One consistent result across all experiments is the improvement for fine-tuning the pre-trained embeddings while learning the pretext task.

The differences in the impact of pre-trained embeddings between dropout prediction and knowledge tracing may be due to the difference in the classification task, as described in Section 3.3. Dropout prediction is a sequence labeling task, while knowledge tracing predicts an output for each item in the sequence. The information needed to detect dropout is encoded in the entire sequence, not in the properties of the individual course elements. Methods like word2vec are not intended to characterize elements with respect to the entire sequence but rather in relation with their surrounding elements. It is coherent then that injecting that kind information does not help, and even hinders performance.

6 CONCLUSIONS

We have proposed a purely unsupervised approach to model student behavior in learning platforms with joint embeddings of course elements and students. The joint embeddings are obtained with a recurrent neural architecture is modified to directly model the relation between both types of embeddings, using knowledge of the task to be solved. We have evaluated and compared the architecture in two different tasks: dropout prediction and knowledge tracing.

Results indicate that co-embeddings are able to capture the latent causes involved in dropout, outperforming disjoint and not-embedded representations. This improvement in performance increases in courses with less students, and courses with higher dropout rate.

For the knowledge tracing task, results indicate that embedded representations reach state-of-the-art performance, even without labeled information used in previous work, like manual annotation of skills. For this task, disjoint representations do not outperform joint ones (co-embeddings), but the difference in performance is only within 0.001 point of AUC. However, we expect that joint embeddings will add value to other applications in Learning Analytics, like visualizations or other interpretation tools.

Indeed, this work has shown promising results from performance point of view, but there is still work to do on the effectiveness of the joint representation for interpretation of human learning. We are currently exploring this line of research through visualization techniques and recommendation of content (personalization).

Future work will include the application of these methods to other datasets from ITS and MOOC platforms to further evaluate how different configurations affect the obtained embeddings.

Another interesting line of future work is to further analyze the impact of pre-trained and possibly fine-tuned embeddings, with special attention to cases that suffer from data sparseness. The diversity of results obtained for different courses in the KDDCup dataset indicate there is a potential for the inclusion of this unsupervised information when the number of examples is limited.

REFERENCES

[1] Albert T. Corbett and John R. Anderson. 1994. Knowledge tracing: Modeling the acquisition of procedural knowledge. *User Modeling and User-Adapted Interaction* 4, 4 (1994), 253–278. https://doi.org/10.1007/BF01099821

[2] Mi Fei and Dit-Yan Yeung. 2015. Temporal models for predicting student dropout in massive open online courses. In *Data Mining Workshop (ICDMW), 2015 IEEE International Conference on Data Mining*. IEEE, 256–263.

[3] Mingyu Feng, Neil Heffernan, and Kenneth Koedinger. 2009. Addressing the Assessment Challenge with an Online System That Tutors As It Assesses. *User Modeling and User-Adapted Interaction* 19, 3 (Aug. 2009), 243–266. https://doi.org/10.1007/s11257-009-9063-7

[4] René F Kizilcec, Chris Piech, and Emily Schneider. 2013. Deconstructing disengagement: analyzing learner subpopulations in massive open online courses. In *Proceedings of the third international conference on learning analytics and knowledge*. ACM, 170–179.

[5] Andrew S. Lan, Andrew E. Waters, Christoph Studer, and Richard G. Baraniuk. 2014. Sparse Factor Analysis for Learning and Content Analytics. *J. Mach. Learn. Res.* 15, 1 (Jan. 2014), 1959–2008. http://dl.acm.org/citation.cfm?id=2627435.2670314

[6] Tomas Mikolov, Ilya Sutskever, Kai Chen, Greg Corrado, and Jeffrey Dean. 2013. Distributed Representations of Words and Phrases and Their Compositionality. In *Proceedings of the 26th International Conference on Neural Information Processing Systems - Volume 2 (NIPS'13)*. Curran Associates Inc., USA, 3111–3119. http://dl.acm.org/citation.cfm?id=2999792.2999959

[7] Zachary A. Pardos and Lev Horodyskyj. 2017. Analysis of Student Behaviour in Habitable Worlds Using Continuous Representation Visualization. *CoRR* abs/1710.06654 (2017). arXiv:1710.06654 http://arxiv.org/abs/1710.06654

[8] Philip I. Pavlik, Hao Cen, and Kenneth R. Koedinger. 2009. Performance Factors Analysis –A New Alternative to Knowledge Tracing. In *Proceedings of the 2009 Conference on Artificial Intelligence in Education: Building Learning Systems That Care: From Knowledge Representation to Affective Modelling*. IOS Press, Amsterdam, The Netherlands, The Netherlands, 531–538. http://dl.acm.org/citation.cfm?id=1659450.1659529

[9] Jeffrey Pennington, Richard Socher, and Christopher D. Manning. 2014. GloVe: Global Vectors for Word Representation. In *Empirical Methods in Natural Language Processing (EMNLP)*. 1532–1543. http://www.aclweb.org/anthology/D14-1162

[10] Chris Piech, Jonathan Bassen, Jonathan Huang, Surya Ganguli, Mehran Sahami, Leonidas Guibas, and Jascha Sohl-Dickstein. 2015. Deep Knowledge Tracing. In *Proceedings of the 28th International Conference on Neural Information Processing Systems (NIPS'15)*. MIT Press, Cambridge, MA, USA, 505–513. http://dl.acm.org/citation.cfm?id=2969239.2969296

[11] Siddharth Reddy, Igor Labutov, and Thorsten Joachims. 2016. Learning Student and Content Embeddings for Personalized Lesson Sequence Recommendation. In *Proceedings of the Third (2016) ACM Conference on Learning @ Scale (L@S '16)*. ACM, New York, NY, USA, 93–96. https://doi.org/10.1145/2876034.2893375

[12] R.G.D. Steel and J.H. Torrie. 1960. *Principles and procedures of statistics: with special reference to the biological sciences*. McGraw-Hill. https://books.google.com.ar/books?id=o6FpAAAAMAAJ

[13] Steven Tang, Joshua C. Peterson, and Zachary A. Pardos. 2016. Deep Neural Networks and How They Apply to Sequential Education Data. In *Proceedings of the Third (2016) ACM Conference on Learning @ Scale (L@S '16)*. ACM, New York, NY, USA, 321–324. https://doi.org/10.1145/2876034.2893444

[14] Jacob Whitehill, Kiran Mohan, Daniel Seaton, Yigal Rosen, and Dustin Tingley. 2017. MOOC Dropout Prediction: How to Measure Accuracy?. In *Proceedings of the Fourth (2017) ACM Conference on Learning @ Scale (L@S '17)*. ACM, New York, NY, USA, 161–164. https://doi.org/10.1145/3051457.3053974

[15] Xiaolu Xiong, Siyuan Zhao, Eric G Van Inwegen, and Joseph E Beck. 2016. Going deeper with deep knowledge tracing. In *Proceedings of the 9th International Conference on Educational Data Mining (EDM 2016)*. 545–550.

Intent-aware Item-based Collaborative Filtering for Personalised Diversification

Jacek Wasilewski
Insight Centre for Data Analytics
University College Dublin
Dublin, Ireland
jacek.wasilewski@insight-centre.org

Neil Hurley
Insight Centre for Data Analytics
University College Dublin
Dublin, Ireland
neil.hurley@insight-centre.org

ABSTRACT

Diversity has been identified as one of the key dimensions of recommendation utility that should be considered besides the overall accuracy of the system. A common diversification approach is to rerank results produced by a baseline recommendation engine according to a diversification criterion. The intent-aware framework is one of the frameworks that has been proposed for recommendations diversification. It assumes existence of a set of aspects associated with items, which also represent user intentions, and the framework promotes diversity across the aspects to address user expectations more accurately.

In this paper we consider item-based collaborative filtering and suggest that the traditional view of item similarity is lacking a user perspective. We argue that user preferences towards different aspects should be reflected in recommendations produced by the system. We incorporate the intent-aware framework into the item-based recommendation algorithm by injecting personalised intent-aware covariance into the item similarity measure, and explore the impact of such change on the performance of the algorithm. Our experiments show that the proposed method improves both accuracy and diversity of recommendations, offering better accuracy/diversity tradeoff than existing solutions.

ACM Reference Format:
Jacek Wasilewski and Neil Hurley. 2018. Intent-aware Item-based Collaborative Filtering for Personalised Diversification. In *UMAP '18: 26th Conference on User Modeling, Adaptation and Personalization, July 8–11, 2018, Singapore, Singapore.* ACM, New York, NY, USA, 9 pages. https://doi.org/10.1145/3209219.3209234

1 INTRODUCTION

The goal of recommender systems is to help to address the choice overload problem by filtering a large set of possible selections into a much smaller set of recommended items. User interactions, as explicit or implicit evidence of user needs, involve a great deal of uncertainty. Engaging and holding a user's interest is a complex matter. Simply identifying relevant items, without taking into account the user's context, can lead to accurate recommendations when measured directly against user's past preferences, but may not

meet current need of the user. For example, considering a movies streaming application, without any context it is hard to predict if at the time of a visit the user would like to see a comedy or rather a thriller, given the user has expressed an interest in these in the past. Recommendation diversification addresses this issue, by widening the range of possible item types recommended to the user, hoping that something will attract the user's attention. From this viewpoint, diversity can be treated as a strategy to favour practical accuracy in matching true user needs in an uncertain environment.

Different diversification frameworks have been proposed to define and enhance diversity. One of them, the intent-aware diversification framework has been proposed to deal with the ambiguity of users' intents. It attempts to ensure that all relevant interests are represented in the recommendations. It is a probabilistic framework based on the aspect model, which assumes the existence of aspects through which users' intents can be expressed, and by which items can be described. Given an aspect model, methods such as xQuAD [16] rerank baseline recommendations such that a user's propensity towards different aspects is reflected in the final recommendations, and multiple aspects are covered to maximise the likelihood of matching the user's current need. While post-filtering diversification approaches are confirmed to be successful in diversity enhancement, their performance depends on the quality of the baseline recommendations. Rerankers will not succeed in their task if the baseline recommendations are homogeneous in terms of aspects.

In this paper we suggest that instead of generating recommendations first and reranking them such that they cover more aspects and reflect better the user's taste, we propose to combine information about relevance, user intentions and item-aspect associations to produce richer recommendations in one step. In order to achieve that, we introduce personalised item similarity based on the intent-aware personalised covariance proposed in [26], which drives the item-based nearest-neighbour collaborative filtering algorithm. Item neighbourhoods based on such personalised similarity happen to be much more richer and diverse when compared to the state-of-the-art methods, making the final recommendations of better utility as well. Produced recommendations are not only more diverse over aspects, but also of a higher accuracy than the item-based algorithm, and they offer better accuracy/diversity tradeoffs than existing diversification methods.

The rest of the paper is structured as follows. In section 2 we discuss popular variations of the neighbourhood-based recommenders, how additional sources of information can be incorporated to improve accuracy, and how utilities other than accuracy can be addressed. Section 3 contains a brief description of the item-based collaborative filtering algorithm for ranking and points out limitations of commonly used similarity functions. In section 4 we first introduce the intent-aware framework, later describe how intent-aware personalised covariance can be used as a measure of item similarity, and finally, we propose the intent-aware version of item-based collaborative filtering. Description and analysis of our experiments can be found in section 5. We conclude with a summary in section 6.

2 BACKGROUND

The task of a recommender system is simple: helping users in browsing huge catalogues of items by serving items of relevance, based on past user-item interactions, such as ratings given by a user to an item. Historically, given such input, recommender systems were trying to predict ratings of unobserved interactions in order to find the most relevant items, while now the ranking task—returning a list of items ordered by relevance—seems to be more related to real recommendation scenarios [7].

Neighbourhood-based collaborative filtering methods (kNN) are simple, yet still powerful (and one of the most popular) solutions proposed to address the recommendation task. They rely on the similarity assumption that similar profiles (in terms of past interactions) make good candidates of items to be recommended to users. There are two types of kNN algorithms, user-based and item-based, which differ in the type of input data used by similarity functions, and type of neighbourhood used to form final recommendations. Here we are interested in the item-based kNN algorithm which utilises neighbourhoods oriented around items. The performance of neighbourhood-based methods depends heavily on the characteristics of the similarity function used in the process of neighbourhood creation [9]. Over the years, a number of variations have been proposed to improve accuracy and reduce prediction error, or promote other utilities of recommendations, such as diversity. Some of the popular choices for similarity functions [8, 9, 17] are Cosine Vector similarity between item vectors of ratings given to them by users, Pearson Correlation similarity which removes differences in means and variances of items, and Adjusted Cosine similarity which is a modification of the Pearson Correlation similarity where user-mean-centred ratings are used. While these different similarity functions offer different performance, depending on the application, they all focus on improving the accuracy of recommendations, solely using ratings information.

In [13] it is suggested that the emphasis that has been put on the user similarity (in case of the user-based kNN) may be overstated and additional factors should be taken into consideration. They proposed that trustworthiness of users should be an important consideration. This indeed led to improved performance on the rating prediction task.

While the item-based kNN method is understood to be more stable, efficient and justifiable, especially in cases where there are many more users than items, recommender systems using this approach will tend to recommend highly similar items to those previously appreciated by the users. This may lead to safer recommendations, however less surprising or broadening of user awareness of different types of items [9].

In [20], Smyth et al. propose to retrieve k diverse neighbours instead of retrieving the k most similar neighbours. Most similar item profiles in item neighbourhoods tend to be very similar to each other, therefore the recommendation space may be limited if left as is. Selecting a diverse set of most similar items leads to better utilisation of the item space and a more diverse final recommendation. With the same motivation, in [27] a neighbour diversification-based kNN algorithm has been proposed, extending the user-based kNN approach, where a diverse set of users is used instead of the most similar ones to the target user. In this case, a set of users is diverse if they have few items in common. Another user-based diversification algorithm has been proposed in [29] where users are associated with interests and a diverse set of users consist of users that have different interests.

A different approach has been proposed in [15] where using k furthest neighbours is suggested instead of k nearest neighbours. In this technique, the final recommendations are based on what is disliked by the least similar users to the target user. As a result, recommendations tend to be more diverse if compared to the original algorithm, with a tolerable loss in accuracy.

In the literature, two lines of research can be identified for diversity enhancement, these being post-filtering and novel solutions enhancing the utility of interest. Most of the approaches discussed above fall into the former group. State-of-the-art diversification methods, such as MMR [4], IA-Select [1], xQuAD [16] are examples of the post-filtering approach. Their advantage is that they can be applied on any candidate recommendation lists. These are examples of a greedy optimisation scheme that selects a subset from a candidate set by balancing accuracy of recommendations with other utilities—originally diversity but also extended to improve unexpectedness, serendipity and other types of novelty. In [29] it is argued that the performance of post-filtering optimisation techniques is limited by the quality of the input candidate items generated by the baseline recommendation system engine. If the candidate set is not diverse enough, the best subset selected by a post-filtering algorithm will not be diverse enough as well.

In [25], an extension of matrix factorisation techniques has been proposed to produce recommendations that are both relevant and diverse. This has been done through regularisation of the learning objective, similarly to regularisers that have been used in machine learning models to prevent overfitting. This method, however, had troubles in producing recommendations of better accuracy/diversity tradeoff when compared with the current state-of-the-art, like the MMR post-filtering algorithm.

3 ITEM-BASED COLLABORATIVE FILTERING

The recommendation task can be formulated as defining a scoring function $s : \mathcal{U} \times \mathcal{I} \rightarrow \mathbb{R}$ for pairs of users $u \in \mathcal{U}$ and items $i \in \mathcal{I}$ so that, for each user, a ranked list of items $\mathcal{R}_u \subset \mathcal{I}$ (or simply $\mathcal{R}$ if the user context is clear) is defined by sorting items by decreasing score order, and keeping the top-N items. The scoring function of a recommender algorithm is based on previous interactions between users and items.

3.1 Item-based kNN

Given a similarity function $\mathrm{sim}(i, j)$ which estimates how much two items are alike, we define the neighbourhood $N^k(j)$ of item j such that $|N^k(j)| \leq k$ and items in the neighbourhood $N^k(j)$ are the most similar items to j according to the function $\mathrm{sim}(i, j)$. Then, the item-based (IB) kNN recommender for the top-N [2, 7] can be defined according to the following formula:

$$s(u, i) = \sum_{j \in I_u} \mathbb{1}_{i \in N^k(j)} \cdot \text{sim}(i, j) \cdot r_{uj} \qquad (1)$$

where indicator function $\mathbb{1}_{i \in N^k(j)}$ filters out items if they do not belong to the neighbourhood $N^k(j)$, r_{uj} denotes the rating that user u gave in the past to the item j which works as a relevance weighting, and I_u is the set of items that user u interacted with in the past. Top-N items with highest scores s form the final recommendation list.

Equation (1) shows that the utility of the recommendation generated by the item-based kNN algorithm depends strongly on the similarity, used both to weight items in the neighbourhoods, and also to select those neighbourhoods, which are made of top-k items according to the same similarity function $\text{sim}(i, j)$.

In our study we use the cosine similarity as a baseline function to represent the similarity between items. Using the rating feedback given by users, similarity between two items can be defined as:

$$\text{sim}(i, j) = \frac{\sum_{u \in \mathcal{U}} r_{ui} r_{uj}}{\sqrt{\sum_{u \in \mathcal{U}} r_{ui}^2} \sqrt{\sum_{u \in \mathcal{U}} r_{uj}^2}}$$

The above assigns a high similarity value if ratings for items i and j are aligned.

3.2 Analysis of item neighbourhoods

The quality of neighbourhoods impacts the quality of recommendations. We investigate the items forming item neighbourhoods based on the cosine similarity to judge their quality. We define neighbourhood's quality through the neighbourhood novelty, richness and diversity. We conduct this analysis on the MovieLens 1M dataset (the dataset's description can be found in section 5.1). We consider the neighbourhoods of $k = 10$ most similar movies to the target movie, according to the cosine similarity. Each movie in the dataset is enriched with genre information, which we lean our analysis on.

Interactions-based similarity functions build item neighbourhoods by aggregating items that are liked together. It is a common belief that neighbourhoods of alike items in terms of interactions also tend to represent the same genre, as people who liked e.g. drama movies highly likely also watched other drama movies. While this is logical, it introduces choice limitations as only certain item types— the most similar ones— are promoted to be recommended from. As this is not a desired situation, we would like to understand how many of the items in the neighbourhoods represent the same genre as the target item. We looked at the neighbourhoods of all items in the dataset and we found that on average 8 out of 10 movies in each of the neighbourhoods have a common genre with the target movie. This suggests that neighbourhoods are of low novelty.

Instead of simply counting how many items are representing the same item type, it is possible to quantify how consistent a neighbourhood is in terms of all genres, by measuring its *richness*. We define richness as a number of different genres found among movies in the neighbourhood (this is similar to S-recall metric defined in section 5.2 however we simply count genres). On average, neighbourhoods cover 5 genres out of 18 available in the dataset. As comparison, we looked at user profiles in the dataset and we

measured the richness of movies that users have interacted with. The average user profile shows interactions with movies covering 15 genres all together. If we constrain the interactions to those that users have rated positively (at least with a rating of 4), and ignore single occurrences of genres, the average user has shown an interest in 11 genres. We can see that interactions-based neighbourhoods do not trace these interests well. It tells us that to find the most suitable movies for a target movie we take a narrow perspective, limited in terms of genres.

We have found that items in the neighbourhoods are similar to the target item and cover only few genres. The quality of the neighbourhood is not only defined by how items are similar to the target item but also how items in the neighbourhood relate to each other. To assess that, we measure the intra-neighbourhood dissimilarity in terms of genres—genre-based distance between each two items in the neighbourhood is calculated and averaged over all pairs (this follows the EILD metric which is described in section 5.2). Similarly as with other properties, neighbourhoods present low genre diversity—approximately 0.37 (on 0-1 scale). This stresses even stronger that neighbourhoods are generally homogeneous, and promoting similar movies.

This analysis has looked at the different properties that item neighbourhoods can be assessed on. General conclusions are that items in neighbourhood are similar to target items, represent only a fraction of genres and are of low diversity. As neighbourhoods are driving the item-based collaborative filtering, these characteristics may propagate to final recommendations, leading to less appealing or engaging recommendations. The neighbourhoods (based on the cosine similarity in this case) not only aggregate items representing the same genre as the target, but also they assume that perception of the similarity is independent from the user. We believe that a personal perspective on items should be taken into account in similarity calculations. The individual perception of similarity and diversity has been studied by cognitivists. Studies, like [19], looked into this problem by considering how thematically related and unrelated concepts differ in perception. They demonstrated the necessity of an individualised model for perceived similarity and suggested that models of similarity should be tuned to individual variability. If we were to apply the above into the neighbourhood creation process, items should not only be selected based on the interactions-based similarity but also on user's taste profile.

4 INTENT-AWARE RECOMMENDATIONS

In this section we first introduce the intent-aware framework that typically has been used for diversification. We explain the intent-aware personalised covariance of two items upon which we build the intent-aware item-based kNN algorithm.

4.1 Intent-aware Framework

The intent-aware diversification framework, proposed in [16] and extended in [23], has been used in information retrieval to mitigate the uncertainty of user queries. If a search engine is queried with "jaguar", without any additional context, it is uncertain whether the results are expected to be related to the animal or the car manufacturer. In information retrieval, if multiple aspects are related to a search query (like the animal and the car manufacturer), without explicit information about the query's intent, the intent-aware diversification framework ensures a good spread of explicit aspects among the relevant items in the result list, hoping that at least one will satisfy user's needs.

In the recommender systems setting, Vargas et al. [22] introduced the notion of user intent as an analogue of query intent. User intents are described in terms of a probability distribution over a set of aspects based on the interests previously expressed through interactions with items.

The intent-aware framework assumes the existence of a predefined set of aspects (latent or explicit), $\mathcal{A}$, over which the aspect model [11] is formed. It is composed of two components: user's intents in terms of a probability $p(a|u)$, such that $\sum_{a \in \mathcal{A}} p(a|u) = 1$, which can be seen as the user's taste profile, and the probability $p(\text{rel}_i | a, u)$ which holds the information about relevance of item i if we know the user u is interested in aspect a. Combining the probabilities of the aspect model entails a recommendation relevance model:

$$p(\text{rel}_i | u) = \sum_{a \in \mathcal{A}} p(a|u) p(\text{rel}_i | a, u)$$

In the relevance model, $p(\text{rel}_i | u)$ models the binary relevance of an item i to a given user u. An item is classed as either relevant or not relevant and it is possible that many items may be simultaneously relevant to the user. We also assume that relevance is independent, given the aspect, so that:

$$p(\text{rel}_i \wedge \text{rel}_j | u) = \sum_{a \in \mathcal{A}} p(a|u) p(\text{rel}_i | a, u) p(\text{rel}_j | a, u)$$

4.2 Intent-aware Personalised Covariance

The portfolio diversification framework proposed by Markowitz [12] has been used in the financial context to maximise the expected return on investment, while minimising the risk as measured by the variance of the return. Diversification across negatively correlated assets allows the risk to be hedged, and more stable returns. This idea has been adapted to the context of information retrieval and recommender systems [24] where, similarly as in the financial domain, recommender systems seek to maximise a recommendation's return—user satisfaction with the recommended items—while the variance of the relevance (i.e. the risk) is minimised.

In order for the framework to work, accurate estimates of item relevance and covariance of relevance are required. These can be estimated using historical ratings or item-aspect associations, as suggested in [24], however these are global estimates, independent of the user's preferences. An intent-aware item relevance covariance has been proposed in [26] which incorporates items' relevances, aspect relationships between items, and user preferences towards aspects. Using the conditional independence of relevance, the user-dependent covariance can be derived from the aspect model as:

$$\text{cov}_{\text{IA}}(\text{rel}_i, \text{rel}_j, u) = \sum_a p(a|u) p(\text{rel}_i | a, u) p(\text{rel}_j | a, u)$$
$$- \sum_a p(a|u) p(\text{rel}_i | a, u) \sum_a p(a|u) p(\text{rel}_j | a, u)$$

for $i \neq j$, and

$$\text{cov}_{\text{IA}}(\text{rel}_i, \text{rel}_i, u) = \sum_a p(a|u) p(\text{rel}_i | a, u)(1 - \sum_a p(a|u) p(\text{rel}_i | a, u)) .$$

As the personalised covariance is based on more than one source of information, the interpretation differs from the standard one. Positive value of $\text{cov}_{\text{IA}}(.)$ indicates that both items i and j are relevant on aspects important to the user, and items share these aspects. Negative values of covariance occur when two items are still highly relevant to the aspects liked by the user, but items do not share these aspects. The value of 0 is observed when at least one item is not relevant to the aspect the user is interested in.

The above shows that if $\text{cov}_{\text{IA}}(.)$ was used to promote items, relevant items with aspects exactly like the target item's would be preferred, resulting in low novelty and diversity. In our application it makes more sense to promote items with a negative covariance, as these items still would be relevant, but representing totally different aspects and this is the analogue of risk minimisation in portfolio optimisation.

4.3 Intent-aware Item-based kNN

Similarly as in [13, 20], the intent-aware covariance can be combined with different components of the IB algorithm, namely the neighbourhood selection and the weighting. We explore these possibilities by using the intent-aware weighting to form neighbourhoods and/or weight the items returned from the neighbourhoods.

4.3.1 Intent-aware Weighting.
The simplest way to incorporate intent-aware relationships between items into the recommendation process is to replace the pure similarity function with a weighting based on the intent-aware covariance, $w_{\text{IA}}(i, j, u)$. We define the weighting as a product of intent-aware covariance and the similarity value:

$$w_{\text{IA}}(i, j, u) = (-\text{cov}_{\text{IA}}(\text{rel}_i, \text{rel}_j, u)) \cdot \text{sim}(i, j) \qquad (2)$$

Negative covariance is used as we would like to promote items of different aspects. We chose a multiplicative combination of intent-aware covariance and similarity, over addition, arithmetic, harmonic or geometric mean, or pure intent-aware covariance as it performed best in our preliminary experiments.

Using the $w_{\text{IA}}(i, j, u)$, we reformulate Equation (1) into:

$$s(u, i) = \sum_{j \in I_u} \mathbb{1}_{i \in N_{\text{IA}}^k(j)} w_{\text{IA}}(i, j, u) \cdot r_{uj} \qquad (3)$$

where $N_{\text{IA}}^k(j)$ is the neighbourhood of j—a set of k items most similar to j according to $w_{\text{IA}}(i, j, u)$.

4.3.2 Intent-aware Bounding.
Intent-aware weighting requires calculation of $w_{\text{IA}}(i, j, u)$ for all item pairs in order to build the neighbourhoods. To reduce complexity, similarly to [20], a bounded version of $N_{\text{IA}}^k(j)$ neighbourhoods can be used. We build the bounded neighbourhood $B_{\text{IA}}^{bk}(j)$ of item j by selecting the bk (multiple b of k) most similar items to j from the original neighbourhood $N^{bk}(j)$, which are later reordered by $w_{\text{IA}}(i, j, u)$. The top k items form the bounded neighbourhood $B_{\text{IA}}^{bk}(j)$ which are selected instead of $N^k(j)$. The modified recommendation formula is then:

$$s(u, i) = \sum_{j \in I_u} \mathbb{1}_{i \in B_{\text{IA}}^{bk}(j)} \text{sim}(i, j) \cdot r_{uj} \qquad (4)$$

Note that the original similarity weighting is used to aggregate items coming from the neighbourhood, not the intent-aware one. The difference then, between the original IB and the above approach is that here we force the neighbourhood to return items that are similar in terms of ratings, relevant to the user, but representing different aspects.

Because we are no longer examining all of the pairs of items to form a neighbourhood, we may miss an item with a marginally higher intent-aware weight value then the best bk items retrieved from $N^{bk}(j)$. However the likelihood of this happening decreases with the item similarity $sim(i, j)$ so that for suitable values of b it becomes unlikely.

4.3.3 Combining Intent-aware Weighting and Bounding.
Both of the proposed schemes can be combined into one, such that neighbourhoods of relevant and different items are first found, which later are re-weighted to form final recommendations. Equation (5) shows both approaches used in combination:

$$s(u, i) = \sum_{j \in \mathcal{I}_u} \mathbb{1}_{i \in B_{\text{IA}}^{bk}(j)} w_{\text{IA}}(i, j, u) \cdot r_{uj} \qquad (5)$$

4.4 Aspect Model Estimation

Covariance $\text{cov}_{\text{IA}}(\text{rel}_i, \text{rel}_j, u)$ depends on the existence of an aspect model. Following [26], we build the aspect model using a source of good quality covariance estimation, in this case based on past recommendations which form scores $s(u, i)$.

To transform scores into probabilities, the Platt scaling [14] is applied. Given a threshold τ, we create class labels $\text{rel}(i, u) = 1$ if $r_{ui} \geq \tau$, and $\text{rel}(i, u) = 0$ otherwise. We generate a sample of scores $s(i|u)$ for a set of randomly chosen user-item pairs, and choose a class label $\text{rated}(i, u) = 1$ if (u, i) pair is in our training set, and $\text{rated}(i, u) = 0$ otherwise. The relevance function $g(.)$ is inferred using logistic regression as a combination of relevance of a (u, i) pair given that it has been rated by the user $(l(s))$, and the probability that a user-item pair is rated $(r(s))$, given score s:

$$g(s) = p(\text{rel} | \text{rated}, s) p(\text{rated} | s) + p(\text{rel} | \neg\text{rated}, s) p(\neg\text{rated} | s)$$
$$= l(s) r(s) + \text{relb}(1 - r(s))$$

where relb is a background (prior) relevance score for unrated user-item pairs, which we take relb = 0.

To estimate components of the aspect model we consider the combination of aspect coverage and learned relevance function, following [5, 21, 22]. Given the function $g(s)$ and items rated by users, $\mathcal{I}_u$, we can estimate components of the aspect model as:

$$p(a|u) = \frac{|\{i \in \mathcal{I}_u : a \in \mathcal{A}_i\}|}{\sum_{a' \in \mathcal{A}} |\{i \in \mathcal{I}_u : a' \in \mathcal{A}_i\}|}$$

$$p(\text{rel}_i | a, u) = \frac{2^{\mathbb{1}_{a \in \mathcal{A}_i} \frac{g(s(u,i))}{g(s^*(u,a))}} - 1}{2}$$

where $s^*(u, a)$ is the max score that any item with aspect a obtained for the user u. Probabilities $p(a|u)$ are based purely on the items in the user's profile, and $p(\text{rel}_i | a, u)$ are based on item-aspect associations, the relevance function $g(s)$ and scores s.

5 EVALUATION

5.1 Datasets

To show the effectiveness of our approach, we perform our evaluation on three datasets: MovieLens 1M, MovieLens 20M [10] and Netflix [3].

The biggest MovieLens dataset, MovieLens 20M (ML-20M), consists of about 20M ratings on scale from 0.5 to 5, with a step-size of 0.5, from 138K users on 28K movies collected thought the https://movielens.org application. Movies are enriched by 20 genres, however interactions for items without any genre information have been removed from the dataset. All users had rated at least 20 items. We also use the smaller MovieLens dataset, MovieLens 1M (ML-1M), which contains 1M ratings given by 6K users who joined the application in 2000. It holds 1M ratings on 3.7K movies, enriched by 18 genres. Ratings are made on a 5-star scale.

The full Netflix dataset consists of 100M ratings from 1 to 5, from 480K users on 18K movies. Using IMDb, 28 movie genres have been identified and associated with the movies in the dataset, such that 9K movies have at least one associated genre. Similarly as before, ratings for movies without genres have been removed.

The datasets have been split into 5 folds, where in each turn 1 fold becomes the test set, and the rest form the training set. Results of this 5-fold cross-validation are averaged over all runs. For the MovieLens 20M and Netflix datasets, evaluation is performed on a randomly sampled 10K users.

5.2 Metrics

In our experiments, to measure the effectiveness of the ranked recommendation list we use two common metrics: Precision and nDCG. In order to calculate these, we set the relevance threshold as rating 4, meaning we consider items with rating at least 4 to be relevant. Same threshold has been used in the relevance-aware measures of diversity.

A large number of metrics have been proposed to measure diversity. A good review can be found in [21]. For the investigation of the tradeoff of the relevance and diversity, we utilise a number of metrics: S-recall, DNG, α-nDCG, ERR-IA and EILD. Except for the S-recall, we use relevance-aware versions of metrics, following [22]. For EILD we report also the relevance-unaware version. Also, we apply a logarithmic discount to items in the ranked list, making items higher in the list more impactful. Below we briefly summarise each of the considered diversity metrics:

- Subtopic Recall (S-recall) [28] is a simple metric which measures how well the recommendations cover the aspect space:

$$\text{S-recall}(\mathcal{R}) = \frac{|\cup_{i \in \mathcal{R}} \mathcal{A}_i|}{|\mathcal{A}|}$$

- DNG, proposed in [18], measures how early new aspects are introduced to a ranked list:

$$\text{DNG}(\mathcal{R}) = \sum_{k=1}^{|\mathcal{R}|} \frac{1}{\log_2(k+1)} \text{rel}(i_k|u) G(k)$$

where $G(k)$ is the number of new aspects at rank k at which a relevant item appears; i_k denotes the item at rank k.

- Intra-List Diversity (ILD) [22, 30, 31] measures the average pairwise distance of the items in a recommendation set:

$$\text{ILD}(\mathcal{R}) = \frac{1}{|\mathcal{R}|(|\mathcal{R}| - 1)} \sum_{i, j \in \mathcal{R}} \text{dist}(i, j)$$

where $\text{dist}(i, j)$ is a distance function based on item features. We use the Expected Intra-List Diversity (EILD) which is a rank and relevance-aware version of the ILD metric.

- Aspect-aware version of the nDCG metric has been proposed in [6], the α-nDCG metric. It can be defined as:

$$\alpha\text{-nDCG}(\mathcal{R}) = \frac{\alpha\text{-DCG}(\mathcal{R})}{\alpha\text{-IDCG}(\mathcal{R})}$$

in which

$$\alpha\text{-DCG}(\mathcal{R}) = \sum_{i \in \mathcal{R}} \frac{1}{\log_2(k_i + 1)} \sum_{a \in \mathcal{A}} \text{rel}(i|u, a)$$
$$\prod_{j \in \mathcal{R}:k_j < k_i} (1 - \alpha \, \text{rel}(j|u, a))$$

where k_i denotes the position of item i in the ranked list, and $\text{rel}(i|u, a) = \mathbb{1}_{a \in \mathcal{A}_i} \text{rel}(i|u)$. $\alpha\text{-IDCG}(\mathcal{R})$ denotes the highest possible value of $\alpha\text{-DCG}(\mathcal{R})$ representing the case when the recommendations is made of ideally diversified relevant items. α is a constant set to control the penalty for the redundancy of the recommended items - in our experiment we use $\alpha = 0.5$ for moderate penalty.

- In [1], Agrawal et al. proposed an intent-aware generalisation of some standard metrics to account for aspects, for instance ERR-IA [6], the intent-aware expected reciprocal rank, which is similar to α-nDCG but it takes personal preferences towards aspects into account, different rank discount and it is not normalised:

$$\text{ERR-IA}(\mathcal{R}) = \sum_{a \in \mathcal{A}} p(a|u) \sum_{i \in \mathcal{R}} \frac{1}{k_i} p(\text{rel}\,|i, u, a)$$
$$\prod_{j \in \mathcal{R}:k_j < k_i} (1 - p(\text{rel}\,|j, u, a))$$

5.3 Setup

In this paper we are interested to assess whether using intent-aware item similarity to drive the item-based collaborative filtering has advantages over the original algorithm and other diversification approaches. For the considered solutions, we generate ranked lists of top $N = 10$ recommendations. As we do not aim to find the best parameters for the dataset used in evaluation, we set the $k = 10$ for both methods for fair comparison. To distinguish different versions we refer to the original item-based algorithm as IB, IB version using intent-aware weighting as IA-IB$_w$, IB version using intent-aware bounding as IA-IB$_b$, and version following both as IA-IB$_{wb}$. Both IA-IB$_b$ and IA-IB$_{wb}$ depend on an additional parameter b. We explore its impact by setting it to $b = \{1, 2, 5, 10, 20\}$.

We compare the diversification performance of the proposed methods with the state-of-the-art methods: xQuAD [16] and MMR [4] reranking applied on the IB baseline, and neighbourhood diversification as in [20]—DivIB. For the reranking methods, we generate a set C of 50 candidate items for each user, then we iteratively construct the reranked list, $\mathcal{S}$, by greedily selecting at each iteration the item i that satisfies:

$$i^* = \arg\max_{i \in C \setminus \mathcal{S}} (1 - \lambda)s(u, i) + \lambda \, \text{div}(i, \mathcal{S}),$$

and updating $\mathcal{S} \leftarrow \mathcal{S} \cup \{i^*\}$. The two terms in this expression represent the item quality component and the item diversity component, and are mixed together using a tradeoff controlling parameter $0 \leq \lambda \leq 1$. Both components are first standardised before mixing.

Depending on the reranking method used, we consider $\text{div}(i, \mathcal{S})$ of one of the following forms:

$$\text{div}_{\text{xQuAD}}(i, \mathcal{S}) = \sum_{a \in \mathcal{A}} p(a|u)p(\text{rel}_i\,|u, a) \prod_{j \in \mathcal{S}} (1 - p(\text{rel}_j\,|u, a))$$
$$\text{div}_{\text{MMR}}(i, \mathcal{S}) = \max_{j \in \mathcal{S}} \text{dist}(i, j)$$

The $\text{dist}(i, j)$ function depicts a distance between two items, i and j, in the item features space. For the DivIB method, we perform greedy neighbourhood diversification in a similar fashion to the MMR algorithm. We construct the neighbourhood $N_{\text{div}}^{bk}(j)$ by iteratively selecting from the top bk candidates produced by the baseline neighbourhood, items with the highest weight:

$$q(i, j) = (1 - \lambda) \sim(i, j) + \lambda \frac{\sum_{i \in N_{\text{div}}^{bk}(j)} \text{dist}(i, j)}{|N_{\text{div}}^{bk}(j)|}$$

until $|N_{\text{div}}^{bk}(j)| = k$. Additionally, weight $q(i, j)$ is used instead of the similarity function in Equation (1). For DivIB, the parameter b has been set to $b = 2$, as greater values resulted in huge performance drop.

5.4 Results and Analysis

5.4.1 Analysis of item neighbourhoods.

Similarly as in section 3.2, we performed an analysis of the intent-aware personalised neighbourhoods. We compare the neighbourhoods based on pure cosine-based similarity with neighbourhoods used in DivIB and IA-IB methods. As the item neighbourhoods in the IA-IB methods are user-dependent, unlike cosine-based neighbourhoods which are user-independent, we need to project the neighbourhoods for a fair comparison. For each item in our dataset, we select a set of $m = 100$ random users. For each item-user pair we assess the quality of the intent-aware neighbourhood, and we average the results over users to obtain an item quality score.

Analysis of cosine-based neighbourhoods showed a low neighbourhood novelty—8 items out of 10 sharing a genre with the target item. Neighbourhood diversification, DivIB, improves the novelty, however not significantly—after diversification, 7 items out of 10 share a genre. On the other hand, the intent-aware neighbourhood reduced the number of similar items (based on genres) to only 2, showing that neighbourhoods now are rather made of items that are different to the target items but as the later analysis shows, still relevant to the user.

Not only more items in the intent-aware neighbourhoods represent different aspect than the target items but also more aspects are covered. The richness of the neighbourhoods has risen significantly from 5 to almost 10 aspects appearing in the neighbourhoods. Although the neighbourhood diversification method has also improved aspects coverage, it does not perform as well as the intent-aware method—between 6 and 7 aspects can be seen in the results, but leading to a deterioration in accuracy.

Finally, the intra-neighbourhood diversity expresses how on average items in the neighbourhoods differ from each other. We showed that cosine-based neighbourhoods are characterised as of low diversity meaning items are really similar to each other in terms of genres. Neighbourhoods in DivIB have been shown an increase in diversity, from 0.37 to 0.45. However more notable improvements could be achieved with greater values of λ, the advantages

		Precision	nDCG	α-nDCG	ERR-IA	S-recall	DNG	EILD	EILD (rel)
ML-1M	IB	0.2425	0.2450	0.2885	0.1826	0.5292	1.6129	0.6399	0.1499
	+ xQuAD (λ = 0.7)	0.2278	0.2295	△0.3058	▲0.1964	▲0.6651	△1.7631	△0.7189	△0.1530
	+ MMR (λ = 0.5)	0.2296	0.2348	0.2827	0.1786	△0.6246	1.6306	▲0.7688	△0.1625
	DivIB (λ = 0.1)	0.2342	0.2361	△0.2918	0.1731	△0.5925	△1.6420	△0.7021	△0.1535
	IA-IB$_w$	△0.2561	△0.2570	▲0.3521	△0.1876	△0.6295	△1.9428	△0.6960	△0.1691
	IA-IB$_b$ (b = 20)	△0.2525	△0.2491	△0.3372	0.1775	△0.6468	△1.8632	△0.7065	△0.1675
	IA-IB$_{wb}$ (b = 20)	▲0.2584	▲0.2595	△0.3510	△0.1901	△0.6381	▲1.9557	△0.6977	▲0.1714
ML-20M	IB	0.1941	0.2230	0.2643	0.1343	0.5703	1.4626	0.6536	0.1219
	+ xQuAD (λ = 1.0)	0.1821	0.2073	△0.2857	▲0.1593	▲0.7164	△1.7227	△0.7005	0.1182
	+ MMR (λ = 0.5)	0.1899	0.2200	0.2614	0.1322	△0.6586	△1.4912	▲0.7786	△0.1355
	DivIB (λ = 0.1)	0.1875	0.2149	0.2537	0.1199	△0.6175	1.3704	△0.7209	△0.1257
	IA-IB$_b$ (b = 20)	△0.2186	△0.2435	△0.3102	△0.1360	△0.6797	△1.7468	△0.7194	△0.1460
	IA-IB$_{wb}$ (b = 20)	▲0.2233	▲0.2572	▲0.3289	△0.1520	△0.6743	▲1.9187	△0.7060	▲0.1489
Netflix	IB	0.2254	0.2195	0.2310	0.1390	0.3718	1.4485	0.6688	0.1458
	+ xQuAD (λ = 0.7)	0.2183	0.2092	△0.2520	▲0.1592	△0.4530	△1.6391	△0.7143	△0.1476
	+ MMR (λ = 0.5)	0.2179	0.2122	0.2246	0.1361	△0.4281	△1.4615	▲0.7921	△0.1616
	DivIB (λ = 0.1)	0.2111	0.2021	0.2162	0.1192	△0.4179	1.3250	△0.7557	△0.1479
	IA-IB$_b$ (b = 20)	△0.2466	△0.2369	△0.2906	△0.1441	▲0.4688	△1.8357	△0.7175	△0.1661
	IA-IB$_{wb}$ (b = 20)	▲0.2542	▲0.2482	▲0.3073	△0.1567	△0.4649	▲1.9799	△0.7070	▲0.1709

Table 1: Accuracy and diversity performance results obtained on three dataset. For each dataset and metric, improvements over the baseline are denoted with △, best results are underlined and denoted with ▲. All differences with respect to the IB are statistically significant (Wilcoxon $p < 0.05$), except when in italics. Presented λ values represent settings with the best performance on *ERR-IA* (for xQuAD) and *EILD (rel)* (for MMR and DivIB), b parameter for IA-IB has been selected such that best α-nDCG is obtained. Parameters are reported in parentheses.

would be diminish by the loss in accuracy of the DivIB. The personalised neighbourhoods show a much higher performance on the intra-neighbourhood diversity measure—it doubles the DivIB's neighbourhoods average diversity by reaching an a diversity value of 0.9.

All of the above show superiority of the intent-aware neighbourhoods over simple cosine-based neighbourhoods or diversified ones. We expect that seeing these improved properties leads to improvements of final recommendations produced by the item-based algorithm.

5.4.2 Accuracy analysis.
Table 1 presents the results obtained of the proposed methods, together with the results of the state-of-the-art for item-based collaborative filtering, neighbourhood diversification and reranking approaches for diversity and personalised diversity. Results of our experiments on all analysed datasets show that IA-IB methods outperform the original IB algorithm in terms of precision and nDCG. We could expect that from the IA-IB methods, the weighted IA-IB (IA-IB$_w$) would be the best performing as it analyses utility of all item pairs to create the neighbourhoods, however the weighted-bounded IA-IB performs slight better. Due to the computational complexity of the weighted IA-IB we only run it on the ML-1M dataset.

It is commonly said that diversification by its nature results in deterioration in accuracy as a cost of introducing diversity. The results of the IA-IB methods show that by introducing diversity the

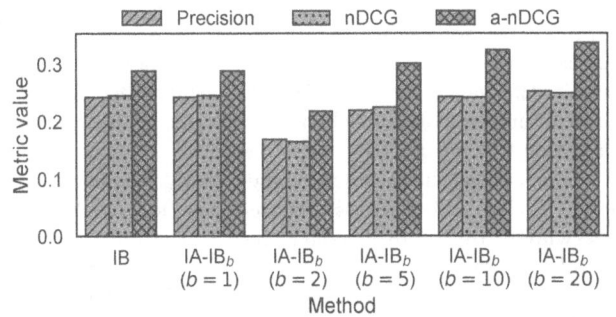

Figure 1: Comparison of the IA-IB$_b$ method and the original IB algorithm, on ML-1M dataset. Similar characteristics can be seen on the two other datasets.

accuracy got improved as well, suggesting that user's needs have been addressed more accurately.

5.4.3 Impact of bounding.
The weighted IA-IB method requires the computation of covariance of all item pairs in order to build the intent-aware neighbourhoods. This may be an impractical task, but also unnecessary as our definition of weighting depends both on the similarity and intent-aware covariance. In such case, if items are not similar to each other in terms of ratings, the likelihood of them being relevant according

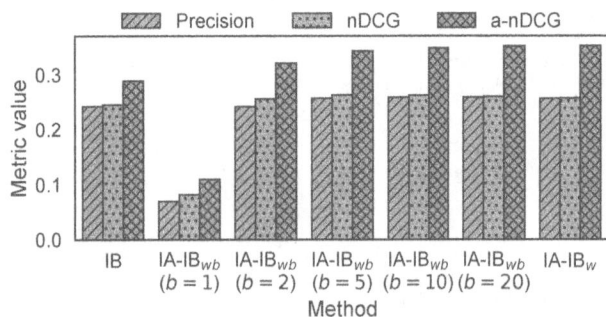

Figure 2: Comparison of the IA-IB$_w$, IA-IB$_{wb}$ and the original IB algorithm, on ML-1M dataset. Similar characteristics can be seen on the two other datasets.

to the intent-aware covariance is low. This means that instead of analysing the covariance of all item pairs, it is enough to calculate the covariance of top bk candidate items. However it is important to understand the impact of such bounding.

Figure 1 compares the original IB algorithm with the bounded version of the IA-IB where the number of candidate items from which the final neighbourhoods are create, varies from 10 to 200 (bk, for $k = 10$ and $b = 1, 2, 5, 10, 20$). As the $b = 1$ is equal to the original IB, the performance on three analysed metrics is exactly the same. We can see that if more items are considered, the performance drops at first, at $b = 2$. This can be explained by the fact that top candidate items tend to be similar in terms of genres thus it is hard for the intent-aware covariance to find good matches. However, for $b = 10$ performance matches the IB, and for $b = 20$ it exceeds the performance of IB. It is worth to remind that here the method uses intent-aware covariance only in the neighbourhood creation process, and not in item weighting. This is done by the weighted-bounded IA-IB.

Figure 2 shows the performance of the IA-IB$_{wb}$ method for different b values, as before it is compared with the IB method, but also with the IA-IB$_w$. IA-IB$_w$ can be seen as the IA-IB$_{wb}$ method with $b = \infty$. Differently than before, for $b = 1$ the performance of the methods is not the same as the IB but it drops significantly. While neighbourhoods are made of the same items as the original IB, the intent-aware weighting diminishes their usefulness. When more candidate items are available, the performance on all metrics visibly is improved. As the b parameter increase, all considered metrics improve—α-nDCG most significantly. Also, we can notice that performance of IA-IB$_{wb}$ tends to IA-IB$_w$ when b increases, thus good results can be obtained without the computation of similarity for all item pairs.

5.4.4 Diversity analysis.
Finally, we compare the diversity performance of proposed methods with related state-of-the-art diversification techniques. The IA-IB methods show general improvements on all diversity metrics over the IB, and offer the best accuracy/diversity tradeoffs. It is worth noting that IA-IB methods do not directly optimise for any of the metrics, improvements come from the nature of the proposed method.

α-nDCG and ERR-IA are measures of diversity which favour recommendations in which many aspects are represented and not over-represented. IA-IB methods perform particularly well on the α-nDCG, showing over 20% improvement over the baseline. While xQuAD method is known for offering good performance on that metric, it does not outperform IA-IB. However, it does perform the best on ERR-IA and S-recall (with an exception on the Netflix dataset). This is expected as the xQuAD explicitly optimises the ERR-IA objective, however the difference between xQuAD and IA-IB$_{wb}$ is relatively small. Similarly with the S-recall, xQuAD obtains the highest performance, however IA-IB produces better accuracy/S-recall tradeoff.

While S-recall measures the coverage of aspects in the recommendations, DNG measures how early new aspects are introduced in the list. All analysed methods show improvements in this matter when compared to the baseline however the best performance is obtained by the IA-IB$_{wb}$.

EILD and relevance-aware EILD are simpler measures of diversity in comparison to α-nDCG or ERR-IA. They measure dissimilarity between items in the recommendation, ignoring redundancy or personal preferences. While it is expected that the MMR offers best performance on the EILD, due to improvements in accuracy, the IA-IB methods obtain the best performance on the relevance-aware version of EILD. However IA-IB does not offer performance on EILD close to the one obtained by MMR, it is still a positive improvement compared to the baseline, comparable to the DivIB method.

The neighbourhood diversification method, DivIB, which we directly compare our solution against, does not show comparable results on metrics other than EILD. The diversification level of the DivIB, expressed through the λ parameter, is mild, however higher diversity level leads to significant loss in accuracy.

6 CONCLUSIONS

In this paper, we tackled the problem of intent-aware recommendations. We showed that item neighbourhoods used by the item-based collaborative filtering are homogeneous, of little novelty and diversity, which impacts the recommendations produced by the item-based algorithm. We proposed a novel approach, combining the item-based scheme with the intent-aware framework through the intent-aware personalised covariance which has been used to measure items similarity. Our experiments showed that neighbourhoods based on such similarity are richer, much more novel and diverse, impacting positively the recommendations. In comparison to the existing diversification approaches, the proposed methods offer superior accuracy/diversity tradeoff.

Many of the existing recommender systems utilise the item similarity component. As brining the user factor into the item similarity component has shown improvements in terms of diversity and accuracy of recommendations, the future work will explore new areas where the personalised item similarity could be applied, and how it is perceived by users in user studies.

ACKNOWLEDGMENTS

This project has been funded by Science Foundation Ireland under Grant No. SFI/12/RC/2289.

REFERENCES

[1] R. Agrawal, S. Gollapudi, A. Halverson, and S. Ieong. 2009. Diversifying Search Results. In *Proceedings of the Second ACM International Conference on Web Search and Data Mining (WSDM '09)*. ACM, New York, NY, USA, 5–14. https://doi.org/10.1145/1498759.1498766

[2] F. Aiolli. 2013. Efficient Top-n Recommendation for Very Large Scale Binary Rated Datasets. In *Proceedings of the 7th ACM Conference on Recommender Systems (RecSys '13)*. ACM, New York, NY, USA, 273–280. https://doi.org/10.1145/2507157.2507189

[3] J. Bennett and S. Lanning. 2007. The Netflix Prize. In *In KDD Cup and Workshop in conjunction with KDD*.

[4] J. Carbonell and J. Goldstein. 1998. The Use of MMR, Diversity-based Reranking for Reordering Documents and Producing Summaries. In *Proceedings of the 21st Annual International ACM SIGIR Conference on Research and Development in Information Retrieval (SIGIR '98)*. ACM, New York, NY, USA, 335–336. https://doi.org/10.1145/290941.291025

[5] O. Chapelle, D. Metlzer, Y. Zhang, and P. Grinspan. 2009. Expected Reciprocal Rank for Graded Relevance. In *Proceedings of the 18th ACM Conference on Information and Knowledge Management (CIKM '09)*. ACM, New York, NY, USA, 621–630. https://doi.org/10.1145/1645953.1646033

[6] C. L. A. Clarke, M. Kolla, G. V. Cormack, O. Vechtomova, Z. Ashkan, S. Büttcher, and I. MacKinnon. 2008. Novelty and Diversity in Information Retrieval Evaluation. In *Proceedings of the 31st Annual International ACM SIGIR Conference on Research and Development in Information Retrieval (SIGIR '08)*. ACM, New York, NY, USA, 659–666. https://doi.org/10.1145/1390334.1390446

[7] P. Cremonesi, Y. Koren, and R. Turrin. 2010. Performance of Recommender Algorithms on Top-n Recommendation Tasks. In *Proceedings of the Fourth ACM Conference on Recommender Systems (RecSys '10)*. ACM, New York, NY, USA, 39–46. https://doi.org/10.1145/1864708.1864721

[8] M. Deshpande and G. Karypis. 2004. Item-based top-N Recommendation Algorithms. *ACM Trans. Inf. Syst.* 22, 1 (Jan. 2004), 143–177. https://doi.org/10.1145/963770.963776

[9] C. Desrosiers and G. Karypis. 2011. *A Comprehensive Survey of Neighborhood-based Recommendation Methods*. Springer US, Boston, MA, 107–144. https://doi.org/10.1007/978-0-387-85820-3_4

[10] F. M. Harper and J. A. Konstan. 2015. The MovieLens Datasets: History and Context. *ACM Trans. Interact. Intell. Syst.* 5, 4, Article 19 (Dec. 2015), 19 pages. https://doi.org/10.1145/2827872

[11] T. Hofmann. 2004. Latent Semantic Models for Collaborative Filtering. *ACM Trans. Inf. Syst.* 22, 1 (Jan. 2004), 89–115. https://doi.org/10.1145/963770.963774

[12] H. Markowitz. 1952. Portfolio Selection. *The Journal of Finance* 7, 1 (1952), 77–91. http://www.jstor.org/stable/2975974

[13] J. O'Donovan and B. Smyth. 2005. Trust in Recommender Systems. In *Proceedings of the 10th International Conference on Intelligent User Interfaces (IUI '05)*. ACM, New York, NY, USA, 167–174. https://doi.org/10.1145/1040830.1040870

[14] J. Platt. 2000. Probabilistic outputs for support vector machines and comparison to regularized likelihood methods. In *Advances in Large Margin Classifiers*.

[15] A. Said, B. J. Jain, B. Kille, and S. Albayrak. 2012. Increasing Diversity Through Furthest Neighbor-Based Recommendation. In *Proceedings of the WSDM'12 Workshop on Diversity in Document Retrieval (DDR'12)*.

[16] R. L. T. Santos, C. Macdonald, and I. Ounis. 2012. On the role of novelty for search result diversification. *Information Retrieval* 15, 5 (01 Oct 2012), 478–502. https://doi.org/10.1007/s10791-011-9180-x

[17] B. Sarwar, G. Karypis, J. Konstan, and J. Riedl. 2001. Item-based Collaborative Filtering Recommendation Algorithms. In *Proceedings of the 10th International Conference on World Wide Web (WWW '01)*. ACM, New York, NY, USA, 285–295. https://doi.org/10.1145/371920.372071

[18] Y. Shi, X. Zhao, J. Wang, M. Larson, and A. Hanjalic. 2012. Adaptive Diversification of Recommendation Results via Latent Factor Portfolio. In *Proceedings of the 35th International ACM SIGIR Conference on Research and Development in Information Retrieval (SIGIR '12)*. ACM, New York, NY, USA, 175–184. https://doi.org/10.1145/2348283.2348310

[19] S. Simmons and Zachary Estes. 2008. Individual differences in the perception of similarity and difference. *Cognition* 108, 3 (21 Aug 2008), 781–795. https://doi.org/10.1016/j.cognition.2008.07.003

[20] B. Smyth and P. McClave. 2001. Similarity vs. Diversity. In *Proceedings of the 4th International Conference on Case-Based Reasoning: Case-Based Reasoning Research and Development (ICCBR '01)*. Springer-Verlag, London, UK, UK, 347–361. http://dl.acm.org/citation.cfm?id=646268.758890

[21] S. Vargas. 2015. *Novelty and Diversity Evaluation and Enhancement in Recommender Systems*. Ph.D. Dissertation. Universidad Autónoma de Madrid.

[22] S. Vargas, P. Castells, and D. Vallet. 2011. Intent-oriented Diversity in Recommender Systems. In *Proceedings of the 34th International ACM SIGIR Conference on Research and Development in Information Retrieval (SIGIR '11)*. ACM, New York, NY, USA, 1211–1212. https://doi.org/10.1145/2009916.2010124

[23] S. Vargas, P. Castells, and D. Vallet. 2012. Explicit Relevance Models in Intent-oriented Information Retrieval Diversification. In *Proceedings of the 35th International ACM SIGIR Conference on Research and Development in Information Retrieval (SIGIR '12)*. ACM, New York, NY, USA, 75–84. https://doi.org/10.1145/2348283.2348297

[24] J. Wang. 2009. Mean-Variance analysis: A new document ranking theory in information retrieval. *Lecture Notes in Computer Science (including subseries Lecture Notes in Artificial Intelligence and Lecture Notes in Bioinformatics)* 5478 LNCS (2009), 4–16. https://doi.org/10.1007/978-3-642-00958-7_4

[25] J. Wasilewski and N. Hurley. 2016. Incorporating Diversity in a Learning to Rank Recommender System. In *Proceedings of the Twenty-Ninth International Florida Artificial Intelligence Research Society Conference, FLAIRS 2016, Key Largo, Florida, May 16-18, 2016*. 572–578. http://www.aaai.org/ocs/index.php/FLAIRS/FLAIRS16/paper/view/12944

[26] J. Wasilewski and N. Hurley. 2017. Personalised Diversification Using Intent-Aware Portfolio. In *Adjunct Publication of the 25th Conference on User Modeling, Adaptation and Personalization (UMAP '17)*. ACM, New York, NY, USA, 71–76. https://doi.org/10.1145/3099023.3099067

[27] C. Yang, C. C. Ai, and R. F. Li. 2013. Neighbor Diversification-Based Collaborative Filtering for Improving Recommendation Lists. In *2013 IEEE 10th International Conference on High Performance Computing and Communications 2013 IEEE International Conference on Embedded and Ubiquitous Computing*. 1658–1664. https://doi.org/10.1109/HPCC.and.EUC.2013.234

[28] C. X. Zhai, W. W. Cohen, and J. Lafferty. 2003. Beyond Independent Relevance: Methods and Evaluation Metrics for Subtopic Retrieval. In *Proceedings of the 26th Annual International ACM SIGIR Conference on Research and Development in Informaion Retrieval (SIGIR '03)*. ACM, New York, NY, USA, 10–17. https://doi.org/10.1145/860435.860440

[29] F. Zhang. 2009. Improving recommendation lists through neighbor diversification. In *2009 IEEE International Conference on Intelligent Computing and Intelligent Systems*, Vol. 3. 222–225. https://doi.org/10.1109/ICICISYS.2009.5358201

[30] M. Zhang and N. Hurley. 2008. Avoiding Monotony: Improving the Diversity of Recommendation Lists. In *Proceedings of the 2008 ACM Conference on Recommender Systems (RecSys '08)*. ACM, New York, NY, USA, 123–130. https://doi.org/10.1145/1454008.1454030

[31] C. Ziegler, S. M. McNee, J. A. Konstan, and G. Lausen. 2005. Improving Recommendation Lists Through Topic Diversification. In *Proceedings of the 14th International Conference on World Wide Web (WWW '05)*. ACM, New York, NY, USA, 22–32. https://doi.org/10.1145/1060745.1060754

Collaborative Filtering with Behavioral Models

Dušan Sovilj
University of Toronto
Toronto, Ontario
dusans@mie.utoronto.ca

Scott Sanner
University of Toronto
Toronto, Ontario
ssanner@mie.utoronto.ca

Harold Soh
National University of Singapore
Singapore, Singapore
harold@comp.nus.edu.sg

Hanze Li
University of Toronto
Toronto, Ontario
litos.li@mail.utoronto.ca

ABSTRACT

Collaborative filtering (CF) has made it possible to build personalized recommendation models leveraging the collective data of large user groups, albeit with prescribed models that cannot easily leverage the existence of known behavioral models in particular settings. In this paper, we facilitate the combination of CF with existing behavioral models by introducing Bayesian Behavioral Collaborative Filtering (BBCF). BBCF works by embedding arbitrary (black-box) probabilistic models of human behavior in a latent variable Bayesian framework capable of collectively leveraging behavioral models trained on all users for personalized recommendation. There are three key advantages of BBCF compared to traditional CF and non-CF methods: (1) BBCF can leverage highly specialized behavioral models for specific CF use cases that may outperform existing generic models used in standard CF, (2) the behavioral models used in BBCF may offer enhanced intepretability and explainability compared to generic CF methods, and (3) compared to non-CF methods that would train a behavioral model per specific user and thus may suffer when individual user data is limited, BBCF leverages the data of all users thus enabling strong performance across the data availability spectrum including the near cold-start case. Experimentally, we compare BBCF to individual and global behavioral models as well as CF techniques; our evaluation domains span sequential and non-sequential tasks with a range of behavioral models for individual users, tasks, or goal-oriented behavior. Our results demonstrate that BBCF is competitive if not better than existing methods while still offering the interpretability and explainability benefits intrinsic to many behavioral models.

CCS CONCEPTS

• **Computing methodologies** → **Learning in probabilistic graphical models**; **Mixture models**; **Learning latent representations**;

UMAP'18, July 8–11, 2018, Singapore, Singapore
© 2018 Association for Computing Machinery.
ACM ISBN 978-1-4503-5589-6/18/07...$15.00
https://doi.org/10.1145/3209219.3209235

KEYWORDS

collaborative filtering; behavioral modeling; bayesian model averaging

ACM Reference Format:
Dušan Sovilj, Scott Sanner, Harold Soh, and Hanze Li. 2018. Collaborative Filtering with Behavioral Models. In *UMAP '18: 26th Conference on User Modeling, Adaptation and Personalization, July 8–11, 2018, Singapore, Singapore.* ACM, New York, NY, USA, 9 pages. https://doi.org/10.1145/3209219.3209235

1 INTRODUCTION

Collaborative filtering (CF) methods [8] for personalized recommendation leverage data from multiple users, under the basic assumption that some users share similar behavior (preferences, actions) and thus one's behavior may be predicted by leveraging observations of others' behaviors. CF methods have become popular in recent years due to their performance and success in various competitions (e.g., the Netflix Challenge). Typical CF methods can be split into two basic variants [4]: (a) memory-based methods (e.g, k-Nearest Neighbor methods [20]) that use similarity functions between users or items to produce predictions, and (b) model-based methods (e.g., matrix/tensor factorizers [19] or deep learning methods [12, 21]) that apply machine-learning techniques to learn latent factors that best describe the observed data.

While highly successful, one caveat of existing personalized CF recommenders is that they prescribe their own models of behavior using generic machine learning methodologies such as nearest neighbors or latent embeddings inherent to matrix/tensor and deep models. However, in this paper, we ask how one can start with an individual application-specific behavioral model germane to a particular recommendation setting and leverage this behavioral model in a more general CF framework? The answer we provide comes in the form of Bayesian Behavioral Collaborative Filtering (BBCF), which works by embedding arbitrary (black-box) probabilistic models of human behavior in a latent variable Bayesian graphical model framework. Through principles of Bayesian inference, BBCF learns to recommend for a given user by leveraging a vote of the prediction of each behavioral model weighted according to the posterior probability that it could have generated the user's observed behavioral history. Critically for the behavioral modeling foundations of BBCF, users may explore a large space with very few overlapping preferences or actions, yet evidence of common behavioral patterns may still suggest strong similarity for recommendation purposes.

BBCF provides three key advantages compared to traditional CF and non-CF methods: (1) BBCF can leverage highly specialized behavioral models for specific use cases that may outperform existing application-independent models used in standard CF; (2) the behavioral models used in BBCF may offer enhanced intepretability and explainability compared to generic CF methods (i.e., a recommendation is now a weighted combination of these behavioral models); and (3) compared to non-CF methods that would train a behavioral model per specific user and thus may suffer when individual user data is limited, BBCF leverages the data of all users thus enabling strong performance across the data availability spectrum including the near cold-start case.

We evaluate BBCF on a range of datasets covering collaborative content-based movie tagging, adaptive user interface behavior prediction, navigation choice recommendation, and educational tutoring, where we demonstrate broad applicability of our method. Experimentally, we compare BBCF to individual and global behavioral models as well as CF techniques; our evaluation domains span both sequential and non-sequential tasks with a range of behavioral models for individual users, tasks, or goal-oriented behavior. Our overall results demonstrate that BBCF is competitive if not better than existing state-of-the-art methods. In short, BBCF provides a highly general collaborative filtering methodology for building personalized recommender systems from known behavioral models while enjoying the interpretability and explainability benefits of these underlying behavioral models.

2 RELATED WORK

We are not the first to suggest collaborative filtering through inferred behavioral similarity, however we strictly generalize the range of applicability of existing frameworks. An early proposal for leveraging behavioral similarity in collaborative filtering was provided by Personality Diagnosis (PD) [17], but it focused only on simple Gaussian rating vectors. In this work, we generalize this approach to arbitrary graphical user models and do not require common item sets or pre-agreed rating or label meanings. More recently, the robotics and controls communities have focused on leveraging multi-user data in intent-aware navigation, gesture, and other goal-oriented human action prediction models [2, 3, 5, 18]. This work did not identify connections nor applications to collaborative filtering nor compare to such methods as we do in this paper; further we will show that one can instantiate our framework for this specific goal-oriented setting as we demonstrate empirically on the Taxi trajectory prediction task, but our framework is strictly more general and intended for a broader range of CF applications.

3 BAYESIAN BEHAVIORAL COLLABORATIVE FILTERING

3.1 General Framework

In this section, we provide a probabilistic derivation of Bayesian Behavioral Collaborative Filtering (BBCF), where we assume the existence of a known class of pretrained behavioral models. These behavioral models, in principle, capture a broad range of models aimed at tackling a variety of user-oriented data, including but not limited to individual user behaviors, task-defined behaviors, and goal-driven behaviors.

We begin with a general modeling framework for BBCF, then provide a variant for the special case of temporal data. Graphical models for both formulations of BBCF are given in Figure 1.

Let $b \in B$ be a specific behavior label drawn from a discrete set B. Given the data generated by b denoted as $\mathcal{D}_b = \{(x_i, y_i)\}_{i=1}^{|\mathcal{D}_b|}$, an individualized behavioral model M_b can be trained with $\mathcal{D}_b$ to predict y_i given x_i. Specifically, we assume that training the model results in a learned parameter vector θ_b and that the model produces predictive distributions $p(y|x, M_b) = p(y|x, \theta_b)$.

Now, assume we have a collection of behavioral models $\mathcal{M} = \{M_b\}_{b=1}^{|B|}$. Each behavioral model M_b is trained independently and has associated parameters θ_b obtained using $\mathcal{D}_b$. Similar to the framework in [6, 14], we assume we have some historical data $\mathcal{D}_r$ for a user (with unknown behavior) for whom we wish to make a future prediction. We define a data-dependent weight vector $\mathbf{w}(\mathcal{D}_r) = [w_b(\mathcal{D}_r)]_{b=1}^{|B|} \in \mathcal{W}$, where $\sum_b w_b(\mathcal{D}_r) = 1$, and our prediction,

$$y_*(x_*; \mathcal{D}_r) = \sum_{b=1}^{|B|} w_b(\mathcal{D}_r) y_b(x_*), \tag{1}$$

which is a convex combination of individual behavioral model predictions $y_b(x_*)$.

But what form should the weights $\mathbf{w}$ take[1]? Under the assumption that a "sufficiently good" model exists in $\mathcal{M}$, we argue that $\mathbf{w}$ is a one-hot binary vector. To elaborate, when r's model is in this collection, $M_r \in \mathcal{M}$, under typical losses (e.g., squared loss) and consistent estimators, the asymptotically optimal weight is a one-hot binary vector with 1 at the index of r. In the non-limiting case, we make the basic assumption underlying collaborative filtering methods: that users are not completely distinct and share similar behaviors. Specifically, we assume that there exists another model $M_a \in \mathcal{M}$ with θ_a sufficiently close to θ_r^*, making it a good proxy for the true model.

In both cases, there is one "correct" model responsible for generating the observed data and thus, we limit $\mathcal{W}$ to the space of one-hot binary vectors $\mathcal{W} = \{\mathbf{w} \in \{0, 1\}^{|B|} : \sum_t w_b = 1\}$ and place a categorical distribution over $\mathbf{w}$.

Here, the distribution over the averaged prediction $y_*(x)$ is

$$p(y_*|x, \mathbf{w}, \mathcal{D}_r, \mathcal{M}) = \sum_{b=1}^{|B|} w_b(\mathcal{D}_r) p(y_*|x, M_b), \tag{2}$$

which we can recognize as a finite mixture model with $\mathbf{w}$ acting as the latent "membership" variable; $w_b(\mathcal{D}_r)$ selects the appropriate model M_b given the observed data $\mathcal{D}_r$. Marginalizing (2) over the probability of $\mathbf{w} = [w_b]$ yields:

$$p(y_*|x, \mathcal{D}_r, \mathcal{M}) = \sum_{b=1}^{|B|} p(w_b = 1|\mathcal{D}_r) p(y_*|x, M_b)$$

$$= \sum_{b=1}^{|B|} p(M_b|\mathcal{D}_r) p(y_*|x, M_b) \tag{3}$$

---

[1]We omit denoting $\mathbf{w}$'s dependence on $\mathcal{D}_r$ to simplify the exposition.

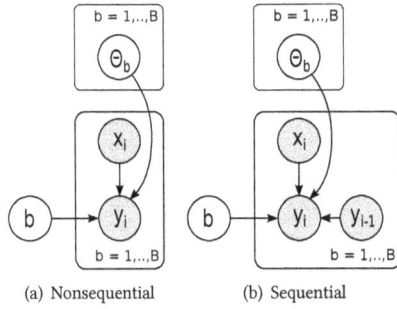

(a) Nonsequential   (b) Sequential

Figure 1: Graphical representations for the individual behavior-centric data. For both cases we have B underlying behavioral patterns each parameterized by specific instantiations θ_b. (a) The general BBCF model where behavioral context x_i in conjunction with behavioral model b generates observed behavior y_i. (b) The special case of BBCF for Markovian temporal models where the behavioral context x_i, previous observed behavior y_{i-1}, and behavioral model b generates current observed behavior y_i.

since $p(w_b = 1|\mathcal{D}_r) = p(M_b|\mathcal{D}_r)$, and

$$p(M_b|\mathcal{D}_r) = p(\mathcal{D}_r|M_b)p(M_b)/p(\mathcal{D}_r)$$

$$= \frac{\prod_i p(y_i|x_i, M_b)p(M_b)}{\sum_{b'} \prod_i p(y_i|x_i, M_{b'})p(M_{b'})}. \qquad (4)$$

Equation (3) with (4) can be identified as Bayesian Model Averaging (BMA) applied over a collection of behavioral models.

3.2 General BBCF

As an example of Figure 1(a) for the general case of BBCF, we assume data originates from a group of users, where each behavioral model b is defined per user and produces tag y_i given item context x_i. Given a new user, we want to find other users with similar tagging styles. Here, we see that a distribution over latent tagging behavior model b would be inferred for the new user based on their tagging history and the tagging predictions of each model b for new context x_i would be averaged according to this distribution to produce tag prediction y_i.

3.3 Sequential BBCF

In the special case of temporal or sequential data provided in Figure 1(b), we again assume data originates from many users, where each behavioral model b is defined per user (or task or goal, as appropriate) and produces observed behavior y_i given context x_i and previous observed behavior y_{i-1}. Note that context x_i can be empty. To make this concrete, we consider two examples from our experiments. For an adaptive user interface model, we define a behavior b per user task where interface context x_i, previous action y_{i-1}, and task b combine to predict the next interface action y_i. For navigation recommendation, we define a behavior b per navigation goal where driving context x_i, goal b, and previous location y_{i-1} combine to predict the next recommended location y_i.

4 BASELINE MODELS

4.1 Generative Models

We first cover two generative probabilistic models for non-sequential and sequential data respectively that can be incorporated as behavioral models for use in BBCF. In conjunction with application-specific feature representations, these models represent two of many possible probabilistic behavioral models for use in BBCF.

4.1.1 Naïve Bayes. For non-sequential data where samples x_i are feature vectors containing features x_{ij}, we can use the Naïve Bayes as our baseline behavioral model used to predict $P(y_i|x_i) \propto P(y_i) \prod_j P(x_{ij}|y_i, b)$ for each behavior b.

4.1.2 (Hidden) Markov model. A common approach to time series modeling for a sequence of observations is to assume that y_i is generated not only from the current behavior b and context x_i, but also from y_{i-1} generated in the immediately preceding time step. The modeling of such Markov Models requires the estimation of a stationary distribution $P(y_i|y_{i-1}, b, x_i) = P(y_{i-1}|y_{i-2}, b, x_{i-1}), \forall i$. When x_i and y_i are finite discrete random variables, $P(y_i|y_{i-1}, b, x_i)$ may be defined in terms of a well-known transition matrix T_{b, x_i} : $y_{i-1} \times y_i \rightarrow [0, 1]$.

A Hidden Markov Model (HMM) assumes additional structure wherein the Markovian transition structure is not directly over the observable y_i, but instead over a latent state variable z_i that generates y_i. The HMM requires a transition model over latent state $P(z_i|z_{i-1}, b, x_i)$ along with an additional observation model $P(y_i|z_i)$ representing a generalization of the provided sequential Markov model.

4.2 Recommendation Baselines

In addition to the previous generative models for BBCF, we also provide standard baselines for recommendation that will be compared to in this paper.

4.2.1 Nearest neighbors. k nearest-neighbor methods (kNN) represent one of the most common types of recommender system [1]. For the extension of kNN methods to sequential data, we transform sequences into frequency counts between adjacent pairs of states; for a problem with N states, each sequence is therefore transformed into an $N \times N$ count matrix (or N^2 length vector).

We use two standard distance functions to match observable behavior: cosine and Euclidean distance. Given the k nearest neighbors, we predict or recommend y_i as the majority vote among the y_i predicted by the neighbors with ties broken randomly. The number of neighbors k is chosen via cross-validation with $k \in \{1, \ldots, 10\}$.

4.2.2 LSTM Recurrent Neural Network. Specifically for sequential data, Long-Short Term Memory (LSTM) [13] based neural networks have gained recent popularity as a strong baseline recommendation model [12]. Our models use a single layer of LSTM cells with training data composed of sequences of prespecified length. The network learns to predict the next state by producing the probabilities for all states (via softmax layer). Hyperparameters of the model (learning rate, number of neurons in LSTM cell, batch size during training phase, dropout rate) are obtained via 3-fold cross validation on available data. Once the hyperparameter values are selected, the final training phase runs for a maximum of 50 epochs

Table 1: Summary of sequential data sets

	#samples		seq. length		
Data	train	test	min	max	avg
synthetic	13500	1500	13	50	32.0
Taxi	64881	7209	2	48	10.3
UI	89	8	43	572	185.8
KT-SK1	141	15	17	115	36.6
KT-SK2	168	29	16	195	68.4
KT-SK3	116	12	17	96	38.8
KT-SK4	505	56	7	213	50.8

with an early stopping criterion defined on a separate validation set to prevent overfitting.

5 EXPERIMENTAL DOMAINS

To test the proposed BBCF method against commonly used approaches, we use four data sets: one synthetic, three sequential real-world data sets, and one collaborative tagging data set. Table 1 summarizes all sequential data sets.

5.1 Synthetic Sequential Prediction

The rationale for synthetic data construction is to vary the degree of separation between different behaviors to observe how this affects BBCF and other recommenders. Synthetic data is constructed by first specifying several transition models/matrices T^k by hand and the uniform transition matrix T^U. We introduce a separation level λ to indicate distinction between the individual models T^k and the uniform model T^U as $\bar{T}^k = \lambda T^k + (1-\lambda)T^U$. With $\lambda = 1$ all transition matrices are intact and sufficiently different, while $\lambda = 0$ squashes all transitions to a single uniform model. Varying λ provides some intermediate level between two extremes. For each λ, we generate up to N samples for each task T^k ending with a total of $K * N$ samples. We have chosen $K = 3$ tasks, each containing 4 states and sampled 5000 points for each task ending with 15k data sequences in total. The lengths of sequences varied between 5 and 50.

5.2 Taxi Navigation Recommendation

This data set was provided as part of a competition affiliated with ECML/PKDD in 2015 entitled *The Taxi Service Trip Time* competition [16], but we are interested in recommending the next position given a particular prior travel path of a taxi.

The trajectories of taxi cars are monitored via GPS from the initial state to their goal state and the locations are given in (longitude, latitude) pairs over a period of time. In order to simplify calculations, all sequences have been converted to fall within a grid of prespecified size.

Unusually long sequences have been removed prior to removing self-transitions since they heavily dominate the data. For our experiments, we chose first 100k samples of the training data file, and a grid map of size 20×20, giving us roughly 70k samples.

5.3 Adaptive User Interface Recommendation

The third sequential data set is constructed from logs of an experiment involving an adaptive user interface (UI). The participants

were asked to perform two tasks involving communication network (of users and emails) while the logger recorded their actions. The two tasks were set up as follows: (1) identify the source user who issued a *malicious* email, and (2) label as many nodes that satisfy certain conditions. More details about the interface itself are given in [15]. There are total of 14 actions possible within the interface and the problem is predicting the next action the user will perform.

The number of available samples in this domain is very low due to the limited number of human participants observed in this dataset. For task (1) there are 76 available samples and 13 samples for task (2). For our experiments we use 4 samples from each task to form the test set.

5.4 Assistments Tutoring Prediction

Knowledge Tracing (KT) models are designed to capture the student learning process by inferring latent knowledge states and future student performance. In this domain, Bayesian knowledge tracing (BKT) remains one of the most applied models due to its relative performance and interpretability. One downside of the standard BKT method is the need to train per-user (individual) models when the interaction data is limited [7]. On the other hand, pooling all available data in order to train a single (global) model ignores the fact that each student's learning characteristics can vary substantially and that individualized models provide better accuracy [22].

Here, we use Assistments dataset [9] that we further categorize into four skill sets: Charts & Graphs, Probability & Statistics, Angles and Fractions, where each skill set consists of several conceptually related skills. For each skill, we observe a sequence of binary problem outcomes indicating whether the student answered each problem correctly. The summary statistics given in Table 1 involve *pooling* all users together across their assignments for each chosen skill set.

5.5 MovieLens Collaborative Tagging

Collaborative tagging (CT) systems (e.g., MovieLens, Flickr) allow users to "tag" content (e.g., movies, documents, photos) with keywords, thus providing socially-procured metadata for exploration, search and retrieval [10]. Often, CT systems provide assistance to users in the form of recommended tags that can be suggested based on tagging history and resource content.

We evaluate the non-sequential aspect of our method on the MovieLens dataset [11], which contains approximately 580k tags applied by 247k users across 34k movies. Similar to prior studies (e.g., [19]), we work with a 10-core dataset (movies with at least 10 tags, with users that have tagged at least 10 movies), leaving 46k tagging events by 1198 users on 1597 movies using 198 tags. To generate movie content features, we transformed movie synopses obtained from the IMDB database into normalized 5000-word count histograms $\mathbf{x}_j \in \mathbb{R}^{5000}$.

6 EXPERIMENTAL RESULTS

In our experiments[2], we aim to evaluate the performance of BBCF under a wide variety of behavioral models on real datasets: one

---

[2]Code is available at https://github.com/dusansovilj/umap18_bbcf

non-sequential classification behavior model (MovieLens Collaborative Tagging), and on the sequential side, one *user-based* behavioral model (Assistments Tutoring Prediction), one *goal-oriented* behavioral model (Taxi Navigation Recommendation), and one *task-oriented* behavioral model (Adaptive User Interface Recommendation). We include an additional sequential behavioral model (Synthetic) to explore how BBCF and other baseline systems perform as the similarity between different behaviors varies from complete behavioral overlap to complete independence (since this can be directly modulated for synthetic data).

For baseline methods, we use (Hidden) Markov model, nearest-neighbor and Long-Short Term Memory (LSTM) neural nets in the case of sequential data, and the Naïve Bayes classifier for feature-based data. We omit the nearest-neighbor and neural network based models for the non-sequential collaborative tagging case as both require a common set of items between different users to be tagged, which does not hold in our experiments (i.e., our objective is to learn tagging behavior conditioned on document content, not to recommend specific tags for specific documents).

First, we aim to address two important questions regarding our approach for both non-sequential and temporal data:

1. How does BBCF compare to non-collaborative filtering baselines using per-user trained **individual** behavioral models and a single **global** behavioral model that pools all data?
2. How does BBCF compare to standard recommendation baselines?

Outcomes from these first two questions served as guidelines for the next set of questions targeting the sequential domains only:

3. How well does each method perform in a variable task separation scenario?
4. How does the number of samples impact overall performance?
5. How does the performance change as prediction horizon increases?

6.1 Baseline comparisons

6.1.1 Non-sequential (tagging) case. In this experiment, we combine individualized content-based tag recommenders using the BBCF framework. Our base user content-based classifier is a generative model, where given resource j with content $\mathbf{x}_j$ and user-tag parameters $\theta_u = \{\theta_{u,i}\}_{i \in I}$, the probability that tag $i \in I$ is applied by user u is given by,

$$p(y_{i,u,j}|\mathbf{x}_j, \theta_u) = \frac{1}{Z}p(\mathbf{x}_j|y_{i,u,j}, \theta_{u,i})p(y_{i,u,j})$$
$$= \frac{1}{Z}\prod_k^K p(x_{j,k}|y_{i,u,j}, \theta_{u,i})p(y_{i,u,j}) \quad (5)$$

where $y_{i,u,j} \in \{0,1\}$, $Z = \sum_{i,j} p(\mathbf{x}_j|y_{i,u,j}, \theta_{u,i})p(y_{i,u,j})$ is the normalization factor, and we have assumed that the K content features factorize given the tag (Naïve Bayes assumption). To obtain a recommendation, we marginalize over the parameters (obtained by training each user model separately),

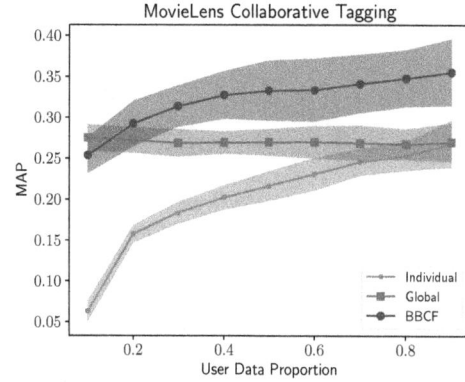

Figure 2: Mean Average Precision (MAP) for the three approaches: global, individual and BBCF framework on MovieLens data. Global model is trained on *full* data, while individual models are trained per user data set $\mathcal{D}_r$.

$$p(y_{i,v,j}|\mathbf{x}_j, \{\theta_u\}_u) = \sum_u p(y_{i,u,j}|\mathbf{x}_j, \theta_u)p(\theta_u|\mathcal{D}_v) \quad (6)$$

where $\mathcal{D}_u = \{(\mathbf{x}_j, \hat{a}_{i,u,j})_{l=1}^L\}$ is a set of observed tags by the user u. The user model posterior given a likelihood function $\ell(\cdot)$ is

$$p(\theta_u|\mathcal{D}_v) = \frac{1}{Z}\prod_l^L \sum_{y_{i,v,j}} \ell(\hat{a}_{i,v,j}|y_{i,v,j})p(y_{i,v,j}|\mathbf{x}_j, \theta_u)p(\theta_u). \quad (7)$$

In the following, we used a Bernoulli likelihood,

$$\ell(\hat{y}_{i,v,j}|y_{i,u,j}, \beta) = \begin{cases} \beta & \text{if } \hat{y}_{i,v,j} = y_{i,v,j} \\ 1 - \beta & \text{otherwise} \end{cases} \quad (8)$$

with observation noise parameter $\beta = 0.3$, and multinomial likelihoods for $p(y_{i,u,j}|\mathbf{x}_j, \theta_u)$.

We conducted 10-fold cross-validation where 80% of the users were used for training the models and the remaining 20% for testing. Model performance was measured using mean average precision (MAP):

$$\text{MAP} = \frac{1}{L}\sum_{l=1}^L \sum_{r=1}^R \text{Prec}(r)\Delta\text{Recall}(r) \quad (9)$$

where r is the cut-off rank, R is the number of recommended tags, $\text{Prec}(r)$ is the precision at the cut-off r, and $\Delta\text{Recall}(r)$ is the change in recall. For each test user, we measured the MAP for different proportions of user data to evaluate performance under varying test data volume conditions.

Figure 2 illustrates the MAP scores achieved by the three models as varying proportions of user tags from 10-90% were revealed. The global model was largely unaffected by the additional tags (MAP scores ~ 0.27) since the newly observed tags consisted small proportions of the overall data. As expected, the MAP scores increased as more tags were revealed for both the individual (0.06-0.27) and BBCF (0.25-0.35) models. The BBCF model clearly outperformed

Table 2: Accuracy of prediction (with 95% confidence intervals in brackets) across four skill categories in Assistments data.

method	KT-SK1	KT-SK2	KT-SK3	KT-SK4
BBCF	79.30 (1.82)	**72.71** (1.19)	69.06 (1.63)	78.15 (0.66)
HMM global	78.24 (1.37)	67.44 (0.81)	66.42 (1.62)	74.37 (0.48)
HMM individual	74.37 (2.22)	66.95 (1.55)	63.82 (2.44)	74.83 (0.72)
NN(cos) global	70.40 (1.79)	57.26 (1.88)	55.38 (1.94)	65.92 (1.39)
NN(cos) individual	63.26 (1.52)	55.06 (0.76)	50.44 (1.33)	65.45 (0.70)
NN(euc) global	70.12 (2.40)	57.26 (1.88)	57.41 (1.51)	67.62 (1.31)
NN(euc) individual	63.26 (1.52)	55.06 (0.76)	50.44 (1.33)	65.45 (0.70)
LSTM global	**88.32** (3.09)	70.32 (4.13)	**78.52** (5.11)	79.24 (1.28)
LSTM individual	87.88 (3.75)	69.05 (4.73)	56.76 (8.29)	**79.52** (4.07)

the individual model at all proportions, indicating that movie tagging behaviors were not entirely distinct between users. Although not directly observed here, it is expected that the individual model would eventually "catch up" to BBCF as more data is provided.

6.1.2 Sequential cases. For the initial testing case, we use Assistments Tutoring data where we performed 10-fold cross validation with the following scheme: 80% of the users were used to train individualized models and testing was performed on the remaining 20% of the users. At each test iteration, the models were used to predict the attempted problem outcome, and after each sequence, the test user's model was updated with the observations. To enhance performance in the global model setting, the global model was re-trained with the newly observed test sequence included in the training set since it is computationally viable to incrementally retrain a single global model.

Table 2 shows the performance across four extracted skill sets. The outcome heavily depends on the specific skill category, with some being easier to predict than others. Overall, the LSTM provides the best results (both in global and individualized aspects), while our BBCF method is close to LSTM performance in two cases (KT-SK2 and KT-SK3). Compared to other baselines, BBCF is able to surpass both the Markov model and nearest-neighbor methods. Another gain over LSTMs is reduced variance as tuning LSTM hyperparameters is noisy and depends on the quality of available training data. BBCF also supports explainability and interpretability regarding how students are similar to each other via their learning behavior provided as their posterior model weights over $b \in B$.

Given that individualized models are slightly inferior to their global counterparts for both MovieLens and Assistments data, we resort to testing only single global model for the rest of the experiments. In addition to accuracy, we also measure performance in terms of Hit Rate at 2 (HR@2), that is, among the two highest rated predictions, is there one that is correct. The results are obtained via 10-fold cross-validation procedure.

Table 3 shows the performance of all methods on the remaining sequential data sets with results averaged across complete test sequences. Overall, the proposed BBCF outperforms the other methods and in some cases by quite a margin (Synthetic and Taxi data) which can be attributed to incorporating historical (and behavioral) information into the approach. In the case of synthetic data, we see that if "exact" models are in the pool of behavioral models B, BBCF can easily identify the underlying pattern and provide substantially better results than other methods. On the other hand, results on

Table 3: Performance measurements (with 95% confidence intervals in brackets) across three data sets tested over complete sequences. HR@1 is the same as accuracy.

Data	method	HR@1	HR@2
Synthetic	BBCF	**84.10** (4.85)	**96.15** (1.49)
	HMM	43.93 (10.72)	67.09 (3.53)
	NN(cos)	36.64 (3.72)	37.72 (2.18)
	NN(euc)	36.71 (3.68)	37.80 (2.15)
	LSTM	39.01 (1.71)	70.70 (4.48)
Taxi	BBCF	**64.80** (0.03)	**85.01** (0.20)
	HMM	44.37 (0.02)	72.62 (0.24)
	NN(cos)	28.45 (0.03)	45.26 (0.24)
	NN(euc)	28.74 (0.04)	44.65 (0.36)
	LSTM	47.84 (0.05)	68.98 (0.71)
User Interface	BBCF	52.13 (0.06)	70.59 (0.71)
	HMM	46.60 (0.02)	64.80 (0.72)
	NN(cos)	20.01 (0.13)	20.01 (0.13)
	NN(euc)	36.37 (0.03)	36.37 (0.03)
	LSTM	**54.22** (0.08)	**74.38** (1.00)

Adaptive User Interface indicate low numbers of samples lead to similar predictions for Markov and BBCF , while the superior performance of neural nets might signify that the tasks in this context are not easily separated and behavioral patterns are more similar than for the Taxi domain, which has considerably more goal states.

In both sequential and non-sequential domains, we are able to increase our prediction accuracy when compared to the baseline model (for both individualized and global modeling approaches) and still provide comparable performance to the more advanced (but less intepretable and explainable) models. Stronger behavioral generative models may also further reduce the gap.

6.2 Varying conditions for sequential data

For this set of experiments, we measure both accuracy and hit rate at 2 and report average performance and confidence intervals via 10-fold cross-validation.

For the Markov model, all trajectories are taken into account to compute the transition matrix of probabilities T. In order to make all transitions possible from a particular state s to all its adjacent states (given the constraints in the domain), a small Laplace smoothing prior of 0.1 is added to frequency counts. For BBCF , a Markov model is the individual model, where M_b is constructed on sequences

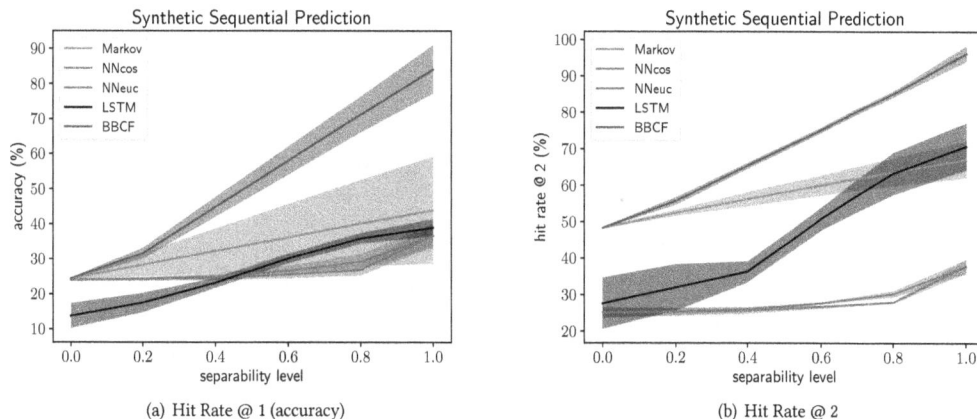

(a) Hit Rate @ 1 (accuracy)   (b) Hit Rate @ 2

Figure 3: Performance (and 95% confidence intervals) of methods under varying levels of separability between three tasks.

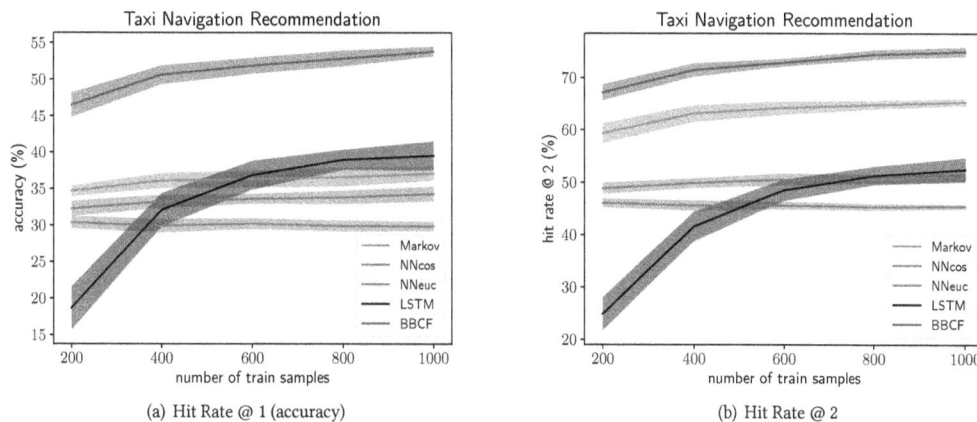

(a) Hit Rate @ 1 (accuracy)   (b) Hit Rate @ 2

Figure 4: Performance (and 95% confidence intervals) of methods under varying number of samples on the Taxi data.

belonging to behavioral pattern b. For kNN, we use only the first neighbor (selected via cross-validation for all data sets) and we also take partial trajectories into account, that is, we introduce new samples that are shorter versions of original data. In this way, we ensure that sequences of similar lengths are used for matching neighbors.

6.2.1 Varying task separability. First, we wish to assess how well we are able to distinguish between different behavioral patterns associated with specific underlying tasks. We use the Synthetic data where we can easily control the level of separation between tasks by construction. Figure 3 shows the accuracy of all tested methods under different separability values. When the tasks are indistinguishable, all methods have very similar outcomes which is quite close to a random guess (given the domain with 4 states), but as the separation increases, BBCF is able to detect more precisely which tasks y_* is responsible for the given trace x_*. In this setting, we are able to heavily outperform the more complex deep learning based LSTM baseline since BBCF's behavioral models are very accurate

as the separability level increases and BBCF can easily identify the correct behavioral model for a user with high probability.

6.2.2 Varying number of data samples. In order to assess how fast BBCF can learn to recommend accurately, we vary the number of available training samples. For this experiment, we use the Taxi Navigation data set, but limit the domain to the 50 most frequently visited destinations and ensure that all goals are equally represented during the training phase. Figure 4 showcases the outcome for all methods. We see that BBCF is able to outperform other methods even in the low-sample scenario and the performance increases with more available data. The Markov model and NN do not benefit greatly from more data and either remain constant (NN) or slightly improve (Markov), partially because all necessary information is already present in the reduced case. The LSTM model greatly benefits from increased training data, but the performance is still far inferior to BBCF. In this goal-oriented scenario where users do not necessarily traverse similar paths and where there are only a few overlapping points, BBCF is able to extract the *intended behavior* for

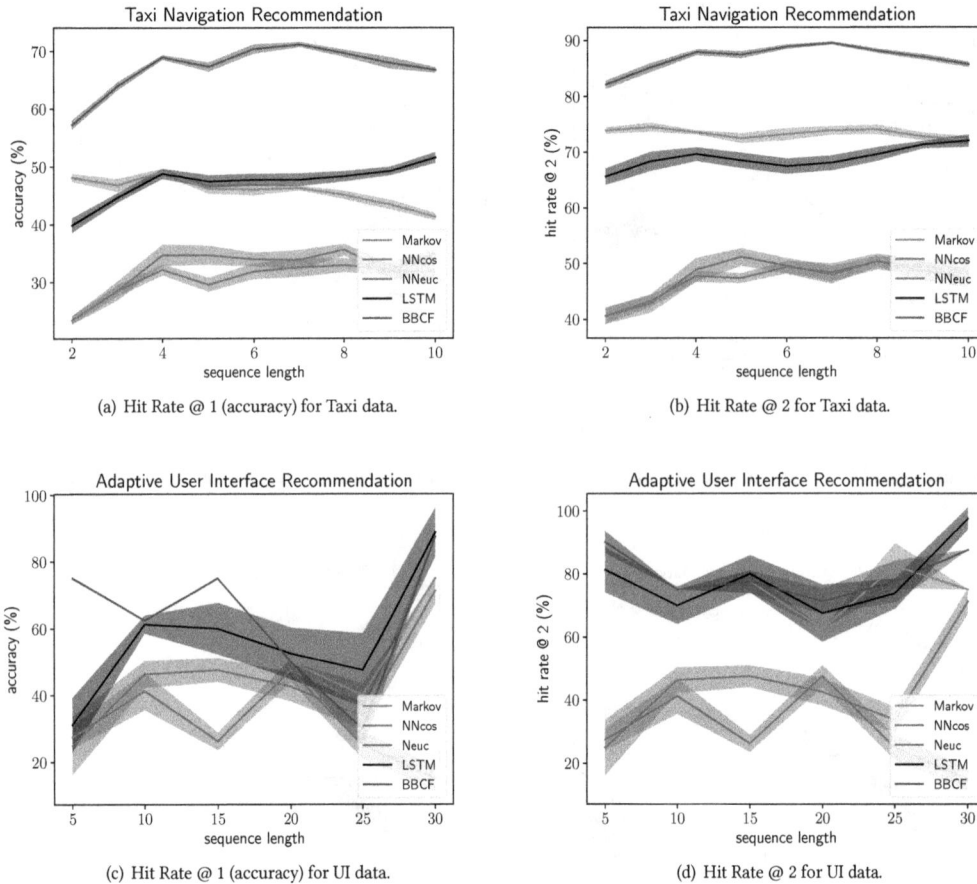

(a) Hit Rate @ 1 (accuracy) for Taxi data.

(b) Hit Rate @ 2 for Taxi data.

(c) Hit Rate @ 1 (accuracy) for UI data.

(d) Hit Rate @ 2 for UI data.

Figure 5: Performance (with 95% confidence intervals) of methods on sequential data given specific sequence length.

new taxi customers by leveraging all encountered behaviors, while the LSTM appears unable to infer such goal-oriented behavior.

6.2.3 Varying prediction horizon. In our final experiment, Figure 5 shows recommendation performance with respect to test sequence length for the Taxi Navigation and Adaptive User Interface domains. We see that BBCF is increasingly able to model the correct posterior weighting over goal states with increasing sequence length on the Taxi data. This holds for several steps as we predict the general or initial direction for new traces. However, the performance (of all methods) drops slightly the longer the sequences become. The reason is that reaching the *exact* destination of a long test sequence may not be feasible since outlying destinations prevalent in longer sequences might not be present in the training data. Regardless, BBCF dominates all other methods.

The number of test cases for the Adaptive User Interface domain is considerably low (only 8) per segment so the variance is high for nearest-neighbor and LSTM, while Markov and BBCF perform comparably up to sequence length 20 then diverge. This divergence indicates that initial data traces up to length 20 (the average sequence length is 180) follow the same pattern and only beyond this point can BBCF identify a clear behavioral task separation.

7   CONCLUSION

We proposed the novel BBCF approach to collaborative filtering of behavioral models for personalized recommendation and prediction. This approach led to a convenient and efficient Bayesian model averaging solution for leveraging existing application-specific behavioral models. The BBCF framework is quite general as evidenced by its application to non-sequential collaborative tagging as well as sequential tasks with user-level, goal-oriented, and task-oriented behavioral models. Our results demonstrate that BBCF is competitive if not better than existing recommenders including deep learning models under a large variety of conditions (task separation, horizon length, and amount of data) while still offering the interpretability and explainability benefits intrinsic to many behavioral models.

ACKNOWLEDGMENTS

The authors would like to thank Cong Shi for his help developing the initial codebase for some of the experiments. This work was partially supported by a NUS Office of the Deputy President (Research and Technology) Startup Grant.

REFERENCES

[1] Robert M. Bell and Yehuda Koren. 2007. Scalable Collaborative Filtering with Jointly Derived Neighborhood Interpolation Weights. In *ICDM*. IEEE Computer Society, 43–52.

[2] Graeme Best and Robert Fitch. 2015. Bayesian intention inference for trajectory prediction with an unknown goal destination. In *2015 IEEE/RSJ International Conference on Intelligent Robots and Systems, IROS 2015, Hamburg, Germany, September 28 - October 2, 2015.* 5817–5823. https://doi.org/10.1109/IROS.2015.7354203

[3] Graeme Best, Wolfram Martens, and Robert Fitch. 2017. Path Planning With Spatiotemporal Optimal Stopping for Stochastic Mission Monitoring. *IEEE Trans. Robotics* 33, 3 (2017), 629–646. https://doi.org/10.1109/TRO.2017.2653196

[4] John S Breese, David Heckerman, and Carl Kadie. 1998. Empirical analysis of predictive algorithms for collaborative filtering. In *Proceedings of the Fourteenth conference on Uncertainty in artificial intelligence.* Morgan Kaufmann Publishers Inc., 43–52.

[5] Herbert Buchner, Karim Helwani, Bashar I. Ahmad, and Simon J. Godsill. 2017. Efficient adaptive filtering in compressive domains for sparse systems and relation to transform-domain adaptive filtering. In *2017 IEEE International Conference on Acoustics, Speech and Signal Processing, ICASSP 2017, New Orleans, LA, USA, March 5-9, 2017.* 3859–3863. https://doi.org/10.1109/ICASSP.2017.7952879

[6] Bertrand Clarke. 2003. Comparing Bayes Model Averaging and Stacking When Model Approximation Error Cannot Be Ignored. *Journal of Machine Learning Research* 4 (2003), 683–712. https://doi.org/10.1162/153244304773936090

[7] Albert T. Corbett and John R. Anderson. 1994. Knowledge tracing: Modeling the acquisition of procedural knowledge. In *User Modelling and User-Adapted Interaction*, Vol. 4. 253–278. https://doi.org/10.1007/BF01099821

[8] Michael D. Ekstrand, John T. Riedl, and Joseph A. Konstan. 2007. Collaborative Filtering Recommender Systems. *Foundations and Trends in Human-Computer Interaction* 4321, 1 (2007), 291–324. https://doi.org/10.1504/IJEB.2004.004560 arXiv:ISSN 0018-9162

[9] Mingyu Feng, Neil T Heffernan, and Kenneth R Koedinger. 2006. Addressing the testing challenge with a web-based e-assessment system that tutors as it assesses. *Proceedings of the 15th international conference on World Wide Web - WWW '06* (2006), 307. https://doi.org/10.1145/1135777.1135825

[10] George W. Furnas, Caterina Fake, Luis von Ahn, Joshua Schachter, Scott Golder, Kevin Fox, Marc Davis, Cameron Marlow, and Mor Naaman. 2006. Why Do Tagging Systems Work?. In *CHI '06 Extended Abstracts on Human Factors in Computing Systems (CHI EA '06).* ACM, New York, NY, USA, 36–39. https://doi.org/10.1145/1125451.1125462

[11] F. Maxwell Harper and Joseph A. Konstan. 2015. The MovieLens Datasets: History and Context. *ACM Trans. Interact. Intell. Syst.* 5, 4, Article 19 (Dec. 2015), 19 pages.

https://doi.org/10.1145/2827872

[12] Balázs Hidasi, Alexandros Karatzoglou, Linas Baltrunas, and Domonkos Tikk. 2015. Session-based Recommendations with Recurrent Neural Networks. *CoRR* abs/1511.06939 (2015).

[13] Sepp Hochreiter and Jürgen Schmidhuber. 1997. Long Short-Term Memory. *Neural Comput.* 9, 8 (Nov. 1997), 1735–1780. https://doi.org/10.1162/neco.1997.9.8.1735

[14] A. Juditsky and A. Nemirovski. 2000. Functional aggregation for nonparametric regression. *Annals of Statistics* 28, 3 (2000), 681–712. https://doi.org/10.1214/aos/1015951994

[15] Sean W Kortschot, Dusan Sovilj, Harold Soh, Greg A Jamieson, Scott Sanner, Chelsea Carrasco, Scott Ralph, and Scott Langevin. 2017. An open source adaptive user interface for network monitoring. In *Systems, Man, and Cybernetics (SMC), 2017 IEEE International Conference on.* IEEE, 1535–1539.

[16] Luis Moreira-Matias, Joao Gama, Michel Ferreira, Joao Mendes-Moreira, and Luis Damas. 2013. Predicting taxi–passenger demand using streaming data. *IEEE Transactions on Intelligent Transportation Systems* 14, 3 (2013), 1393–1402.

[17] D M Pennock, E Horvitz, S Lawrence, and C L Giles. 2000. Collaborative filtering by personality diagnosis: A hybrid memory-and model-based approach. *Proceedings of the 16th Conference on Uncertainty in Artificial Intelligence* 64, 10 (2000), 473–480. http://citeseerx.ist.psu.edu/viewdoc/download?doi=10.1.1.38.6498{&}rep=rep1{&}type=pdf

[18] Eike Rehder and Horst Kloeden. 2015. Goal-Directed Pedestrian Prediction. *2015 IEEE International Conference on Computer Vision Workshop (ICCVW)* 00 (2015), 139–147. https://doi.org/doi.ieeecomputersociety.org/10.1109/ICCVW.2015.28

[19] Steffen Rendle and Lars Schmidt-Thieme. 2010. Pairwise interaction tensor factorization for personalized tag recommendation. *Proceedings of the third ACM international conference on Web search and data mining (WSDM '10)* (2010), 81–90. https://doi.org/10.1145/1718487.1718498

[20] Paul Resnick, Neophytos Iacovou, Mitesh Suchak, Peter Bergstrom, and John Riedl. 1994. GroupLens: an open architecture for collaborative filtering of netnews. In *Proceedings of the 1994 ACM conference on Computer supported cooperative work.* ACM, 175–186.

[21] S. Sedhain, A. Menon, S. Sanner, and L. Xie. 2015. AutoRec: Autoencoders Meet Collaborative Filtering. In *Proceedings of the 24th International Conference on the World Wide Web (WWW-15).* Florence, Italy.

[22] Michael V. Yudelson, Kenneth R. Koedinger, and Geoffrey J. Gordon. 2013. Individualized bayesian knowledge tracing models. *Lecture Notes in Computer Science (including subseries Lecture Notes in Artificial Intelligence and Lecture Notes in Bioinformatics)* 7926 LNAI (2013), 171–180. https://doi.org/10.1007/978-3-642-39112-5-18

Controlling Spotify Recommendations: Effects of Personal Characteristics on Music Recommender User Interfaces

Martijn Millecamp*
Department of Computer Science, KU Leuven
Leuven, Belgium
martijn.millecamp@cs.kuleuven.be

Nyi Nyi Htun*
Department of Computer Science, KU Leuven
Leuven, Belgium
nyinyi.htun@cs.kuleuven.be

Yucheng Jin
Department of Computer Science, KU Leuven
Leuven, Belgium
yucheng.jin@cs.kuleuven.be

Katrien Verbert
Department of Computer Science, KU Leuven
Leuven, Belgium
katrien.verbert@cs.kuleuven.be

ABSTRACT

The "black box" nature of today's recommender systems raises a number of challenges for users, including a lack of trust and limited user control. Providing more user control is interesting to enable end-users to help steer the recommendation process with additional input and feedback. However, different users may have different preferences with regard to such control. To the best of our knowledge, no research has investigated the effect of personal characteristics on visual control techniques in the music recommendation domain. In this paper, we present results of a user study on the web using two different visualisation techniques (a radar chart and sliders) that allows users to control Spotify recommendations. A within-subject design with *Latin Square* counterbalancing measures was used for the study. Results indicate that the radar chart helped the participants discover a significantly higher number of new songs compared to the sliders. We also found that users' experience with Spotify had an influence on their interaction with different musical attributes. The participants who used Spotify frequently and users with a high individual musical sophistication interacted with the attributes significantly more with the radar chart compared to the sliders. Individual musical sophistication also had a significant impact on their interaction with the interaction techniques. The participants with high musical sophistication interacted significantly more with the radar chart in comparison to the sliders. Based on the feedback from our participants, we provide design suggestions to further improve user control in music recommendation.

---

*These authors contributed equally to this work.

UMAP'18, July 8–11, 2018, Singapore
© 2018 Association for Computing Machinery.
ACM ISBN 978-1-4503-5589-6/18/07... $15.00
https://doi.org/10.1145/3209219.3209223

CCS CONCEPTS

• **Information systems → Personalization**; **Personalization**; **Recommender systems**; • **Human-centered computing →** *Visualization design and evaluation methods*;

KEYWORDS

recommender system; Spotify; recommender user interface; personal characteristics

ACM Reference Format:
Martijn Millecamp, Nyi Nyi Htun, Yucheng Jin, and Katrien Verbert. 2018. Controlling Spotify Recommendations: Effects of Personal Characteristics on Music Recommender User Interfaces. In *Proceedings of 26th Conference on User Modeling, Adaptation and Personalization (UMAP'18)*. ACM, New York, NY, USA, 9 pages. https://doi.org/10.1145/3209219.3209223

1 INTRODUCTION

Many services that are available on the Web today utilise recommender algorithms to suggest personalised contents to their users. Amazon.com, Spotify, YouTube and Netflix are well-known examples of such services. With the help of recommender algorithms and abundant data, many of these services can provide users with highly relevant items leading to improved user satisfaction and content discovery.

All recommender systems, at their basic form, rely on user behaviour by recording activities of users who interact with a service or system, or by simply asking users for their preference. While much of previous research has focused on developing and evaluating recommender algorithms, recommender systems still face a number of challenges. One such a challenge is known as the lack of "transparency" [34], meaning that existing recommender systems do not provide users with any insight into the logic of recommendations. To many users, this "black box" behaviour raises the issue of not understanding why they are receiving certain recommendations, which in turn could lead to trust issues [21]. To solve the "transparency" issue, giving users control over the recommendation process may help, as previous research has shown that the relation between satisfaction and user control is affected by the knowledge level of users [27] and their interests [22].

O'Donovan et al. [30] also argued that many recommender systems are opaque to users and that users need more control to tailor recommendations to their current moods and influences. To address this issue, O'Donovan et al. [30] designed PeerChooser to provide users with a visual explanation of the recommendation process and the opportunity to manipulate input weightings to steer the recommendations. SmallWorld, designed by Gretarsson et al. [19], is similar to PeerChooser in that it allows users to manipulate the recommendation process with additional visualisation techniques. These authors [19, 30] focused on movie and social media domains respectively. Jin et al. [24] investigated the effect of user control on cognitive load and acceptance of recommendations in the music domain and found that a higher level of control produced the best recommendations, while requiring the highest cognitive load. To the best of our knowledge, no research has been conducted to understand the effect of personal characteristics on the perception of visual interaction techniques in the music domain. Therefore, in this paper, we attempt to address the following research questions:

RQ1: In what way do personal characteristics influence *perception* of the visual control techniques in music recommendation?

RQ2: In what way do personal characteristics influence *interaction* with the visual control techniques in music recommendation?

RQ3: Which visual control technique(s) is/are better suited for users to manipulate music recommendation?

RQ4: How can we design an interface to allow better user control for music recommendation?

The remainder of the paper is organised as follows: in Section 2, we discuss background work on interactive recommender systems, as well as existing work on different personal characteristics that may influence the utility of such systems. In Section 3, we describe our experimental design, including the interface, study procedure, and evaluation metrics. In Section 4, we present the results of the study. In Section 5, findings and their implications are discussed based on the evaluation results. Finally, in Section 6, we conclude the paper by highlighting our contributions and by discussing possible future work.

2 BACKGROUND

2.1 Interactive Recommender Systems

Interactive recommender systems have been researched to some extent by the research community over the past two decades. For example, PeerChooser [30] and SmallWorlds [19] are two approaches that focus on interaction with collaborative filtering recommender engines to users. Both systems allow users to interact with representations of relations between items and other users to support transparency and user control. PeerChooser uses a graph-based visualisation to represent these relationships. SmallWorlds allows users to explore the relationships between recommended items and similar friends in multiple layers of similarity.

In addition, a number of visualisations have been developed to interact with hybrid recommender systems. TasteWeights [4] is a system that allows users to control the impact of different algorithms as well as different input data sources on the recommendation results, eliciting preference data and relevance feedback from users at runtime in order to adapt recommendations. This idea can be traced back to the work of Schafer et al. [33] on meta-recommendation systems, where users are provided with personalised control over the generation of recommendations by altering the importance of

specific factors on a scale from 1 to 5. Similarly, SetFusion [31] is a more recent example that allows users to fine-tune weights of a hybrid recommender system, using a Venn diagram [36] to visualise relationships between recommendations. MoodPlay [2] is a hybrid music recommender system that integrates different techniques in an interactive interface supporting explanation and control of affective data. The system allows the user to explore a music collection through latent affective dimensions, thereby improving acceptance and understanding of recommendations. MyMovieMixer [29] is an interactive movie recommender that integrates different recommender techniques with interactive faceted filtering methods, called "blended recommending". The approach allows users to interact with a set of filter facets representing criteria that can serve as input for different recommendation methods, including collaborative and content-based filtering.

Our previous work [11] is focused on various factors that affect acceptance of recommendations, such as user satisfaction, trust and sense of control. Specifically, based on the analysis of research on interactive recommender systems, we derived a framework proposing five important attributes for trust-aware and interactive recommender systems, namely: transparency, controllability, justification, diversity and context. We also investigated how information visualisation can improve user understanding of the rationale behind recommendations in order to increase their perceived relevance and meaning and to support exploration and user involvement in the recommendation process. To this end, we performed a study using TalkExplorer [38], an interactive visualisation tool developed for attendees of academic conferences based on a Cluster Map [17]. We combined different user-generated data sources in the study, but rather than automatically merging these data as it is done in hybrid recommender systems, end-users were allowed to select which users or tags should be considered. In addition, users could select different recommendation techniques that are represented as agents, similar to Ekstrand et al.'s [15] idea of enabling users to switch between recommenders. While the results of user studies indicated an increase in recommendation effectiveness when using the visualisation as opposed to a ranked list representation, we found that non-technical users did not receive the same benefits from the visualisation as technical users because they only interacted in a limit way with the visualization [37]. In this paper, we are researching the use of two different representations to interact with recommender systems: a radar chart and sliders. The overall objective is to gain insight into the utility of more advanced versus simpler visualisations for interacting with recommender systems and the interplay of these representations with different personal characteristics.

2.2 Personal Characteristics

The influence of personal characteristics on the performance of users has been researched elaborately. In this existing body of research, the influence of a variety of personal characteristics has been investigated. Because of this variety, we will use the classification of Aykin et al. [3] to describe the different personal characteristics.

2.2.1 Level of experience. One of the most commonly researched personal characteristics is expertise or experience [1, 3, 9, 13, 14, 23, 35, 42]. Depending on the domain of the research, experience is expressed in different ways. For example, in the user interface domain, experience can be seen as the experience with computers [42] or the visualisation expertise [9, 13]. In our research, we measured *level of experience* using metrics such as musical sophistication, the number of hours participants listen to Spotify, and tech-savviness. Musical sophistication was measured by 10 seven-point Likert scale questions based on the Goldsmiths Musical Sophistication Index (Gold-MSI)[1]. As for tech-savviness, participants were asked to rate themselves between *confident, not confident* and *somewhere in-between* when it comes to trying new technology.

2.2.2 Demographic characteristics. Demographic characteristics have also been researched extensively [3, 8, 10, 14, 16, 28]. Some research only takes into account basic demographic characteristics such as age, sex and gender [3, 14, 28]. Other research goes deeper and investigates personal interests, goals, background, country, education level, marriage status, (sector of) job, income and first language [8, 10, 16, 42]. In our research we only asked for age and gender.

2.2.3 Personality traits. In previous research, it has been shown that personality traits can have an impact on the performance and preference of a user [3]. Aykin et al. [3] list seven different personality traits: Jungian personality type, field dependence/independence, locus of control, imagery, spatial ability, type A/B personality and ambiguity tolerance. Brusilovsky and Millán [8] researched more in depth cognitive and learning styles. Other research investigated colour characteristics such as colour perception, colour memory, colour ranking [14] and psychographic or psychological characteristics (e.g. sensitivity, disabilities, emotion, etc.) [28]. There are a number of other user-related characteristics that are influencing perception and performance of the user [3]. One popular category of personal characteristics not mentioned above is cognitive skill [1, 8, 9, 13, 14, 35]. Especially working memory is a popular metric that is commonly measured as a cognitive skill. Working memory can be categorised into visual and verbal working memory. As we were comparing visualisation techniques in this paper, we measured visual working memory of participants using a block-tapping test which is based on Corsi block-tapping [26].

3 EXPERIMENTAL DESIGN

The following sub-sections present a detailed description of the experimental design deployed in the study.

3.1 Participants

Participants were recruited from personal contacts, Reddit, research groups and university contacts for the study. A total of 80 people participated, of which 40 were removed as they did not finish the study. Out of the remaining 40 participants, 10 were female and 30 were male. Twenty-three participants belonged to the age group of 15-24, 15 to the group of 25-34 and two to the group of 35-44. We also asked the participants to report their confidence with trying new technology. Twenty-nine out of 40 participants reported that they were confident with trying new technology, while one participant reported to feel not confident and 10 participants reported that they were somewhere in-between. Regarding Spotify usage,

8 out of 40 participants reported that they used Spotify between 1 and 5 hours per week, 10 between 6 and 10 hours per week, 11 between 11 and 15 hours per week, 2 between 16 and 20 hours per week and 9 more than 21 hours per week. For visual working memory, the participants were divided into two group at the 50th percentile. Both low and high visual working memory groups had 20 participants each. Similarly for music sophistication, the participants were divided into two groups at the 50th percentile. The high music sophistication group had 18 participants and the low music sophistication group 22 participants.

3.2 Implementation

In our earlier work, we analysed existing interactive recommender systems in detail [11] and found different visualisation techniques that have been used to support user control as a basis to improve recommendations or to explore the recommendation space. Among these techniques, we found that sliders and graphs with draggable and droppable elements are the most popular. Sliders are often visualised as a stack on top of each other [4, 31]. Many visualisations support to drag data points presented in a circular layout, either closer to the center (more similar) or, vice versa, closer to the outer region (less similar) [12, 25, 39–41]. In addition, nodes in a graph can often be dragged to similarly indicate the level of similarity with other items [7, 19, 30]. Because of the common use of sliders and draggable elements, we also adopted these elements, but in two different modalities: sliders and a radar chart, both with draggable elements. As shown in Figure 1, the two visual control techniques were implemented into two separate interfaces. Both interfaces were designed using a 3-column format similar to previous music recommender systems [4, 5, 24, 31]. The column on the left side enables users to select artists from the list of top artists they listen to. These artists are used as input for generating recommendations. The visualisation in the second column represents different parameters that can be used to adjust recommendations. Users can for instance increase the weight of parameters such as danceability and energy. The third column represents the generated recommendations. As explained above, two different visualisations were implemented to enable users to adjust parameters weights: sliders and a more advanced, potentially more appealing, radar chart.

As an experimental platform, we chose Spotify because it is one of the largest on-line music providers and offers a free API[2]. The Spotify API allows to generate recommendations based on up to five favourite artists. In addition, the API also allows modification of 14 musical attributes[3] in order to describe musical preference. We selected five out of 14 available musical attributes based on [18], where the authors found that different song genres can be represented by only three categories: arousal, valence and depth. According to the authors, *arousal* represents intensity and energy in music, *valence* the spectrum of emotions in music, and *depth* the intellect and sophistication in music. In line with these three categories, the five music attributes we selected were: energy, danceability, valence, instrumentalness and acousticness.

---

[1] https://www.gold.ac.uk/music-mind-brain/gold-msi/

[2] https://developer.spotify.com/web-api/get-recommendations
[3] https://developer.spotify.com/web-api/get-recommendations/#tablepress-220

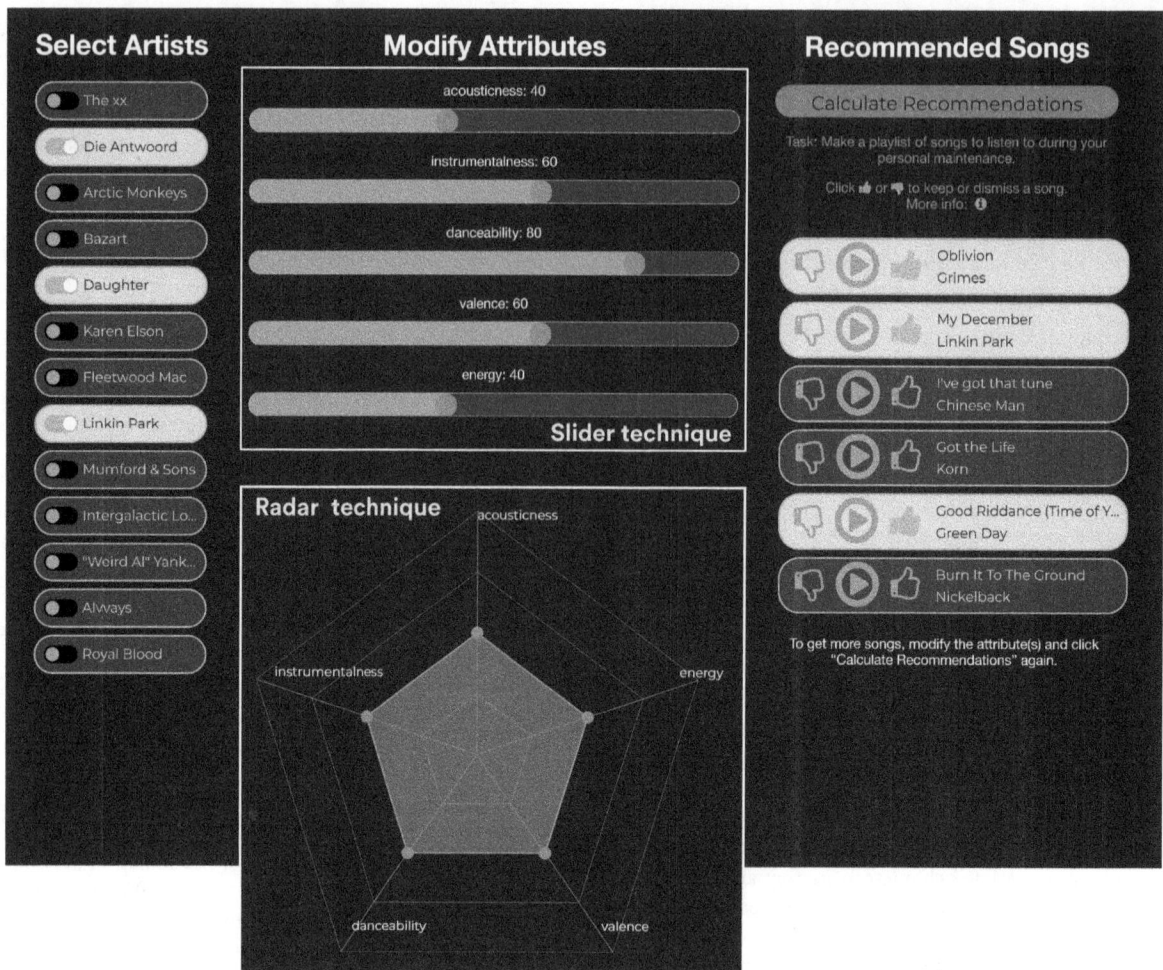

Figure 1: Interface variations used in the study.

As in the Spotify application, we presented each recommended song by its title and artist. Album art and album name were not displayed in order to have a clean and manageable layout. The Spotify API provides a way to play a preview of up to 30 seconds for each recommended song (complete songs are inaccessible). We attached this feature with a play button in our interfaces which allowed users to listen to a preview of the recommended songs. Similar to the Spotify radio feature, we used "Thumb up" and "Thumb down" buttons to allow users to like or dislike the recommended songs. Disliking a song dismisses the song from the list, whereas liking a song keeps it in the list.

3.3 Study Procedure

As soon as the study URL was loaded, participants were presented with detailed information about the study and a consent form. After they agreed to participate in the study, a new page was presented where they had to authorise their Spotify account to be accessible by the study. Following the authorisation, a new page with demographic questions was presented to collect individual participants' personal characteristics which include age, gender, music sophistication, visual working memory, tech-savviness, Spotify usage, familiarity with recommender systems and attitude towards recommender systems.

Once the demographic questions were completed, the participants were shown detailed instructions and a task requesting them to make a playlist of nine songs to listen to when travelling (e.g. for commuting). This task was chosen for the study because travelling and personal maintenance are the two most common activities associated with listening to music [20]. Next, the participants completed the task by selecting their favourite artists, manipulating the musical attributes and selecting nine songs from the recommendations. The participants were then presented with a number of evaluation questions which included a set of questions from the ResQue user-centric recommender systems evaluation framework [32] and open-ended questions (see Section 3.4.1 for details).

Next, the participants were displayed a different task and instructions which requested them to make a playlist of nine songs to listen to during their personal maintenance. Similar to the steps for the first task, the participants completed the second task and answered another set of evaluation questions. The participants were then asked to complete a set of open-ended exit questions (see Section 4.2 for details).

To counteract any fatigue effect during the study, the order in which the interfaces were presented was rotated using a *Latin Square* counterbalancing measure.

3.4 Evaluation Metrics

3.4.1 Recommender System Evaluation Questions. To evaluate the interfaces, a set of modified ResQue questions [32] and open-ended questions were used. A total of 13 ResQue questions were selected and made minor modifications to fit our evaluation requirements. These questions are as follow:

- The songs recommended to me are of various kinds (Q1).
- The songs recommended to me are similar to each other (Q2).
- This recommender system helped me discover new songs (Q3).
- I haven't heard of some songs in the list before (Q4).
- This recommender system helped me find ideal songs (Q5).
- Using this recommender system to find what I like was easy (Q6).
- This recommender system gave me good suggestions (Q7).
- Overall, I am satisfied with this recommender system (Q8).
- I am convinced of the songs recommended to me (Q9).
- This recommender system made me more confident about my selection/decision (Q10).
- I will use this recommender system again (Q11).
- I will tell my friends about this recommender system (Q12).
- I will keep the songs recommended so that I can listen again (Q13).

The questions were in the form of 7-point Likert scales and the answers ranged from 1 (strongly disagree) to 7 (strongly agree). Following the ResQue questions, a number of open-ended questions were also administered to capture feedback from the participants about the most and the least useful parts of each interface.

3.4.2 Interaction Log. Both interfaces recorded a log of the participants interactions with different components. Specifically, the log captured:

- The number of times the musical attributes were changed (*attribute*).
- The number of times any given musical attribute was changed (*nbAttribute*, e.g. nbEnergy for the energy attribute)
- The number of times the "Calculate Recommendations" button was clicked (*calculate*).
- The number of times the dislike button was clicked (*disliked*).
- The number of times the like button was clicked. (*liked*)
- The total number of clicks on all components of the interface throughout a session. (*interactions*)

This log was then used to understand the impact of participants' personal characteristics on their interactions with the interfaces.

3.4.3 Exit Questions. In the exit questions, the participants were first presented with all of the 14 musical attributes, as well as their definitions, that are supported by the Spotify API. They were then asked to rate each of these musical attributes on a scale of 1 (least likely) to 7 (most likely) to indicate how likely they will use it

Table 1: Result of Wilcoxon signed rank tests showing significant differences between the two interfaces without personal characteristics. M = mean, SD = standard deviation

	Z	p	Radar Chart			Slider		
			M	Median	SD	M	Median	SD
Q3	-2.623	0.009	4.72	5	1.8	4.2	5	1.7
liked	-2.073	0.038	11.2	9.5	4.6	9.975	9	3.5
nbEnergy	-2.032	0.042	5.475	4	4.5	4.275	2	5.8

in order to control music recommendations. This allowed us to understand if there may be other potentially useful attributes than those we used in our current interfaces. Finally, the participants were asked to suggest any other visual techniques that they think may be helpful for them to better control the recommendation process.

4 RESULTS

A normality test was initially performed on data using the Shapiro-Wilk test. To compare the differences between the two interfaces, we used t-tests for normally distributed data and Wilcoxon signed rank tests for non-normally distributed data. Independent variables were the interfaces whereas dependent variables were questionnaire scores and log data. Details of the statistical analysis results are presented in Section 4.1. Responses for open-ended questions were analysed using Thematic Analysis [6] and the results are presented in Section 4.2.

4.1 User Perception and Log Analysis

4.1.1 Comparisons without Personal Characteristics. To understand an overall difference between the two interfaces, comparisons were firstly performed between the interfaces without taking personal characteristics into account. Results showed that the two interfaces yielded significantly different outcomes in terms of interactions and perceived discovery of new songs. As shown in Table 1, the radar chart interface had a significantly higher score than the slider interface (Z = -2.623, p = 0.009) in terms of perceived discovery of new songs (Q3). Looking at Figure 2, it was found that the scores between all of the 13 questions were similar. Participants rated the highest for Q4 (I haven't heard of some songs in the list before). Having the ability to control musical attributes may have allowed the participants to discover the songs which may otherwise have been ignored by either themselves or the system.

In addition, the participants used the like button significantly higher in the radar chart interface (Z = -2.073, p = 0.038). Since the participants were required to choose exactly nine songs in each interface, it appears that they refined their list as more favourite songs appeared through the session which led to using the like button more frequently in the radar chart interface. Interestingly, it was also found that the energy attribute was more frequently used in the radar chart interface (Z = -2.032 p = 0.042). Although the attributes are in the same order, we suspect that this different behaviour could be due to the way the participants are looking to the two interfaces. Further studies should be performed to investigate this.

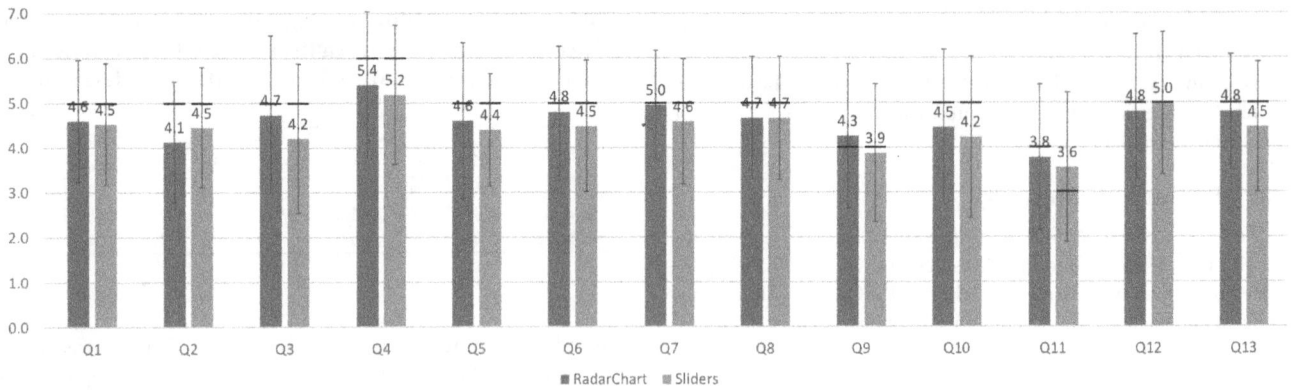

Figure 2: Results of the ResQue questions between the two interfaces without personal characteristics. Values above the columns = mean

4.1.2 Comparisons by Personal Characteristics. To analyse the effect of personal characteristics, the participants were divided based on each category of their personal characteristics (e.g. male, female, high music sophistication, low music sophistication, etc.). According to the analysis results, certain characteristics such as age, gender, familiarity with recommender systems, and attitude towards recommender systems had no significant impact on usage and perception between the two interfaces. In the following paragraphs, results of other characteristics that had significant impact on usage and perception between the two interfaces are presented.

Tech-savviness: Tech-savviness was divided into three categories by individuals who are 1) *confident*, 2) *not confident*, and 3) *somewhere in-between*. Only the participants in the category of *somewhere in-between* indicated that they found more ideal songs (Q5) with the radar chart interface than with the sliders interface (Z = -2.032, p = 0.042, see Table 3). For the participants in the *confident* and *not confident* categories, however, neither of the interfaces was significantly better at finding ideal songs than the other.

Spotify Usage: Interestingly, the participants who use Spotify more than 21 hours a week interacted with the musical attributes significantly higher within the radar chart interface (Z = -2.08, p = 0.038, see Table 3). In addition to this, for the participants in the same category, we found that the instrumentalness attribute was used significantly more with the radar chart interface (Z = -2.27, p = 0.023, see Table 3). It appears that experience with Spotify may play a role when it comes to interaction with the musical attributes for certain visual techniques.

Musical Sophistication (MS): Based on their musical sophistication, the participants were divided into high and low MS categories. Interestingly, those with a high MS had significantly higher overall interactions with the radar chart interface (Z = -2.2, p = 0.028, see Table 3). In addition, for the radar chart interface the same group of participants had significantly higher interactions with the acousticness attribute (t(17) = 2.114, p = 0.05, see Table 2) and the "Calculate Recommendations" buttons (Z = -2.078, p = 0.038, see Table 3). On the contrary, the participants with a low MS had significantly higher interactions within the sliders interface with the acousticness attribute (t(21) = -2.46, p = 0.015, see Table 2) and the "Calculate Recommendations" buttons (Z = -2.138, p = 0.033, see

Table 2: Result of t-tests showing significant differences between the two interfaces based on personal characteristics. M = mean, SD = standard deviation

Personal Characteristics	Category	Metrics	t	df	p	Radar Chart M	Radar Chart SD	Slider M	Slider SD
MS	low	nbAcousticness	-2.46	21	0.015	3.86	3.47	5.81	8.89
	high	nbAcousticness	2.114	17	0.05	4.83	4.72	2.89	2.40
VWM	low	nbAcousticness	-2.238	19	0.037	3.25	2.98	4.9	5.74

Table 3). This suggests that an individual's musical sophistication may also greatly impact on interaction with the musical attributes for certain visual techniques.

Visual Working Memory (VWM): To test the visual working memory of individual participants, we used a test based on the Corsi block-tapping test [26]. Just as musical sophistication, we divided the participants into low and high VWM categories. Again, we found that the participants with a high VWM had significantly higher interactions with the danceability attribute within the radar chart interface (Z = -2.71, p = 0.007, see Table 3). Meanwhile, the participants with a low VWM had significantly higher interactions with the acousticness attribute within the sliders interface (t(19) = -2.238, p = 0.037, see Table 2).

4.2 Design Feedback

A thematic analysis [6] of the responses for the open-ended questions resulted in three main themes: track-attribute visualisation, relevance feedback and usability. We present these themes in detail in the following sub-sections.

4.2.1 Track-Attribute Visualisation. Four participants reported that a visualisation of the relationship between recommended tracks and selected attributes may be helpful for better understanding of the recommended tracks. For example, one participant explained that "one way to gain intuitive understanding would be to have an option to scroll through a 2d space of different features such as valence vs mode, and be able to see some of my most played tracks there." (P3). Another participant explained that "It would be great to visualise the timeline of the playlist. For example if I was creating a 2-hour long playlist it would be great to see the length of each track

Table 3: Results of Wilcoxon signed rank tests showing significant differences between the two interfaces based on personal characteristics. M = mean, SD = standard deviation

Personal Characteristics	Category	Metrics	Z	p	Radar Chart			Sliders		
					M	Median	SD	M	Median	SD
Tech-savviness	somewhere in-between	Q5	-2.032	0.042	5.5	6	0.97	4.4	5	1.34
Spotify usage	21+	attributes	-2.08	0.038	11.6	11	6.44	6.89	7	2.67
	21+	nbInstrumentalness	-2.27	0.023	4.2	4	1.86	2	2	1.41
MS	Low	calculate	-2.138	0.033	6.18	4	4.75	8.91	6	9.00
	High	calculate	-2.078	0.038	7.33	6	6.2	4.33	3	3.86
	High	interactions	-2.2	0.028	104.8	101.5	62.77	74.55	69	37.63
VWM	High	nbDanceability	-2.71	0.007	5.75	4	5.70	2.7	2	2.08

and the BPM associated with each song so you can better create a playlist for an extended period of time for a workout session, party or during work." (P14). We believe that users can benefit greatly from having a visual representation of the recommended songs. By looking at the relationship between the recommended songs and the attributes, they may better understand why particular songs are being recommended. At the same time, this visualisation technique itself should allow users to explore further and refine the list. In addition, we believe that by showing the songs from their playlists on this track-attribute visualisation, users can better understand their music taste and information about their favourite songs.

4.2.2 Relevance feedback. While musical attributes are a great way to describe one's preference, some might find them difficult to utilise. Therefore, one participant suggested to "Let me 'dial' [the songs I liked] to influence the future song recommendations. It requires less intimacy with the musical traits and seems less subjective? I mean, people dance to different things." (P13). We believe that when their desired musical attributes are unknown, it may be easier for users to express their preference as "show me more songs like this". The recommended songs in this case should display their relationship with the input song in the musical attribute spectrum so that users can easily understand why particular songs are being recommended.

4.2.3 Usability. The majority of the participants expressed positiveness towards having the ability to steer the recommendations. Three participants reported that they preferred the sliders and 10 reported that they preferred the radar chart. Those who preferred the radar chart also mentioned that it offers a better overview of the current settings. Therefore, while the ability to steer recommendations was seen as a good aspect, many participants preferred the radar chart.

Finally, five of the participants reported that they could not easily understand which musical attribute had an impact on a particular song in the recommended list. Therefore, one participant explained, "...it was difficult to say which aspect I should change to get better recommendations." (P4). This is similar to the findings presented in Section 4.2.1, confirming that visualisation of track-attribute relationship will be greatly beneficial for users.

5 DISCUSSION

In the context of our first research question (RQ1): "In what way do personal characteristics influence perception of the visual control techniques in music recommendation?", we found that tech-saviness of an individual had an influence on the outcomes between the two visual control techniques. The participants who expressed themselves as somewhere in-between on the tech-savviness scale also indicated that they found more ideal songs with the radar chart interface than with the sliders interface. However, those who expressed themselves as either confident or not confident at trying new technology had no different responses between the two interfaces. Overall, personal characteristics do not seem to play much role on perception of the visual control techniques in music recommendation. In the future, it may be interesting to explore the outcomes of other visual control techniques.

In the context of our second research question (RQ2): "In what way do personal characteristics influence interaction with the visual control techniques in music recommendation?", we found that Spotify usage, music sophistication and visual working memory had an influence on the outcomes between the two visual control techniques. The participants with a high Spotify usage interacted with the musical attributes significantly more with the radar chart interface. In addition, the participants with a high musical sophistication had significantly higher overall interactions with the radar chart interface than with the sliders. Similarly, the participants with a high visual working memory had significantly higher interactions with the danceability attribute within the radar chart interface. Overall, the radar chart encouraged more interactions with the interface itself and musical attributes for those who had a high Spotify usage, musical sophistication and visual working memory.

In the context of our third research question (RQ3): "Which visual control technique(s) is/are better suited for users to manipulate music recommendation?", we found that the radar chart interface scored higher at discovering new songs. In addition, 10 of the participants reported that they preferred the radar chart as it is better at displaying an overview of the attribute settings. Meanwhile, only three participants reported that they preferred the sliders. Different personal characteristics did not have considerable impact on the outcomes between the two techniques.

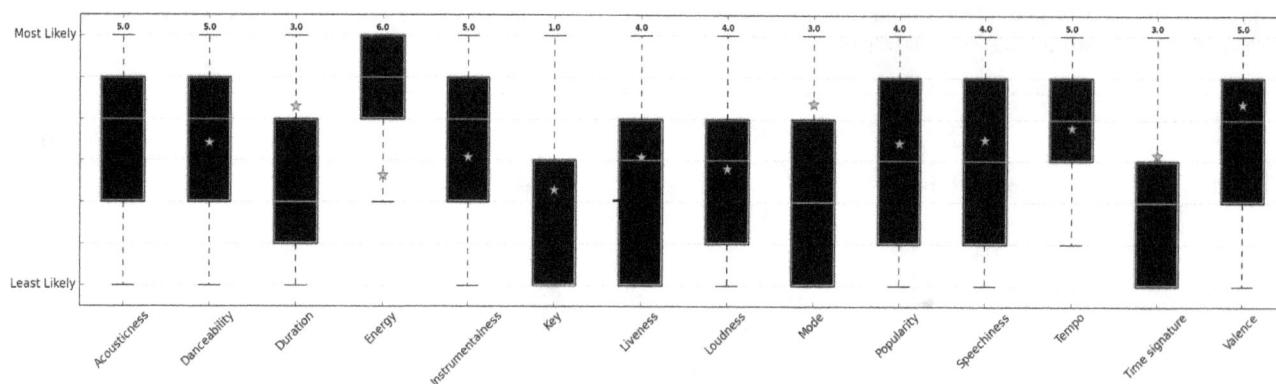

Figure 3: Evaluation of the 14 Spotify musical attributes based on how likely they will be used by participants. The star indicates the mean. The value above and the green line inside each box represent the median.

As shown in Figure 3, amongst the 14 available musical attributes of Spotify, the majority of the participants preferred the energy attribute the most, followed by acousticness, danceability, instrumentalness, tempo and valence. Therefore, these six attributes: energy, acousticness, danceability, instrumentalness, tempo and valence should be considered when implementing a visual control technique.

In the context of our fourth research question (RQ4): "How can we design an interface to allow better user control for music recommendation?", we found a number of design considerations. The first consideration should be given to visualise the relationship between recommended tracks and musical attributes. Such a visualisation can help users understand why particular songs are being recommended to them. In addition, this visualisation technique itself should allow users to explore further songs and keep refining their list. In addition, to help users better understand their music taste and information about their favourite songs, we believe that the songs from their playlist could also be associated within this visualisation.

The second but equally important consideration is that the interface should not only support controlling musical attributes but also a way for users to express their preference by selecting a song. In the latter, the interface should also be able to visualise the relationship between the recommended songs and the input song using the musical attribute spectrum so that users can easily understand why particular songs are being recommended.

6 CONCLUSION

In this paper, we presented an online evaluation of two different visual control techniques for steering the music recommendations process: sliders and a radar chart. The two techniques were implemented into two separate music recommender interfaces. The Spotify API was employed in order to generate recommendations. The visual control techniques allowed users to manipulate five musical attributes used to produce recommendations by Spotify. A within-subject design with *Latin Square* counterbalancing measures was used in the study. A number of evaluation questions including ResQue [32] and open-ended questions were administered. Results showed that the radar chart helped the participants to discover a

significantly higher number of new songs compared to the sliders. In addition, a number of participants reported that they preferred the radar chart over the sliders as it provides an overview of the musical attribute settings. Next, we found that personal characteristics did not play much role on the perception towards the visual control techniques. Interestingly, the radar chart encouraged more interactions with the interface and musical attributes for those who had a high Spotify usage, musical sophistication and visual working memory. When implementing a visual control technique for music recommender systems, considerations should be given to these particular music attributes: energy, acousticness, danceability, instrumentalness, tempo and valence. In addition, based on the feedback from our participants, we found that visualisation of the relationship between recommended tracks and musical attribute can be greatly beneficial for users. Also, when their desired musical attributes are unknown, it may be easier for users to express their preference by indicating a song. Recommender systems must be able to take such an input and display recommendations together with a visualisation of the relationship between the input song and the recommended songs using the musical attributes. In summary, our findings presented in this paper provide an important contribution for personalised music recommender systems. Future work should focus on implementing a new generation of music recommender systems that provide users with comprehensive visual techniques and input methods to steer the recommendation process. We plan to extend this study with different visualisation techniques and further investigate users' reasoning and decision-making process when steering music recommendations.

7 ACKNOWLEDGEMENTS

Part of this research has been supported by the Research Foundation Flanders (FWO, grant agreement no. G0C9515N) and the KU Leuven Research Council (grant agreement C24/16/017).

REFERENCES

[1] Azzah Al-Maskari and Mark Sanderson. 2011. The effect of user characteristics on search effectiveness in information retrieval. *Information Processing & Management* 47, 5 (2011), 719–729.

[2] Ivana Andjelkovic, Denis Parra, and John O'Donovan. 2016. Moodplay: Interactive Mood-based Music Discovery and Recommendation. In *Proceedings of the 2016 Conference on User Modeling Adaptation and Personalization*. ACM, 275–279.

[3] Nuray M Aykin and Turgut Aykin. 1991. Individual differences in human-computer interaction. *Computers & industrial engineering* 20, 3 (1991), 373–379.

[4] Svetlin Bostandjiev, John O'Donovan, and Tobias Höllerer. 2012. TasteWeights: a visual interactive hybrid recommender system. In *Proc. RecSys'12*. ACM, 35–42.

[5] Svetlin Bostandjiev, John O'Donovan, and Tobias Höllerer. 2013. LinkedVis: exploring social and semantic career recommendations. In *Proceedings of the 2013 international conference on Intelligent user interfaces*. ACM, 107–116.

[6] Virginia Braun and Victoria Clarke. 2006. Using thematic analysis in psychology. *Qualitative research in psychology* 3, 2 (2006), 77–101.

[7] Simon Bruns, André Calero Valdez, Christoph Greven, Martina Ziefle, and Ulrik Schroeder. 2015. What should i read next? a personalized visual publication recommender system. In *International Conference on Human Interface and the Management of Information*. Springer, 89–100.

[8] Peter Brusilovsky and Eva Millán. 2007. User models for adaptive hypermedia and adaptive educational systems. In *The adaptive web*. Springer, 3–53.

[9] Giuseppe Carenini, Cristina Conati, Enamul Hoque, Ben Steichen, Dereck Toker, and James Enns. 2014. Highlighting interventions and user differences: informing adaptive information visualization support. In *Proceedings of the 32nd annual ACM conference on Human factors in computing systems*. ACM, 1835–1844.

[10] Zohreh Dehghani Champiri, Seyed Reza Shahamiri, and Siti Salwah Binti Salim. 2015. A systematic review of scholar context-aware recommender systems. *Expert Systems with Applications* 42, 3 (2015), 1743–1758.

[11] He Chen, Denis Parra, and Katrien Verbert. 2016. Interactive recommender systems: a survey of the state of the art and future research challenges and opportunities. *Expert Systems with Applications* 56 (2016), 9–27.

[12] Yu Chen and Pearl Pu. 2013. Cofeel: Using emotions to enhance social interaction in group recommender systems. In *Alpine Rendez-Vous (ARV) 2013 Workshop on Tools and Technology for Emotion-Awareness in Computer Mediated Collaboration and Learning*.

[13] Cristina Conati, Giuseppe Carenini, Enamul Hoque, Ben Steichen, and Dereck Toker. 2014. Evaluating the impact of user characteristics and different layouts on an interactive visualization for decision making. In *Computer Graphics Forum*, Vol. 33. Wiley Online Library, 371–380.

[14] Gitta O Domik and Bernd Gutkauf. 1994. User modeling for adaptive visualization systems. In *Visualization, 1994., Visualization'94, Proceedings., IEEE Conference on*. IEEE, 217–223.

[15] Michael D Ekstrand, Daniel Kluver, F Maxwell Harper, and Joseph A Konstan. 2015. Letting Users Choose Recommender Algorithms: An Experimental Study. In *Proceedings of the 9th ACM Conference on Recommender Systems (RecSys '15)*. ACM, New York, NY, USA, 11–18. https://doi.org/10.1145/2792838.2800195

[16] Susan Gauch, Mirco Speretta, Aravind Chandramouli, and Alessandro Micarelli. 2007. User profiles for personalized information access. In *The adaptive web*. Springer, 54–89.

[17] Vladimir Geroimenko and Chaomei Chen. 2006. *Visualizing the semantic web: XML-based internet and information visualization*. Springer, London.

[18] David M Greenberg, Michal Kosinski, David J Stillwell, Brian L Monteiro, Daniel J Levitin, and Peter J Rentfrow. 2016. The Song Is You: Preferences for Musical Attribute Dimensions Reflect Personality. *Social Psychological and Personality Science* 7, 6 (2016), 597–605. https://doi.org/10.1177/1948550616641473

[19] Brynjar Gretarsson, John O'Donovan, Svetlin Bostandjiev, Christopher Hall, and Tobias Höllerer. 2010. Smallworlds: visualizing social recommendations. In *Computer Graphics Forum*, Vol. 29. Wiley Online Library, 833–842.

[20] Ruth Herbert. 2013. *Everyday music listening: Absorption, dissociation and trancing*. Ashgate Publishing, Ltd.

[21] Jonathan L Herlocker, Joseph A Konstan, and John Riedl. 2000. Explaining collaborative filtering recommendations. In *Proceedings of the 2000 ACM conference on Computer supported cooperative work*. ACM, 241–250.

[22] Yoshinori Hijikata, Yuki Kai, and Shogo Nishida. 2012. The Relation Between User Intervention and User Satisfaction for Information Recommendation. In *Proceedings of the 27th Annual ACM Symposium on Applied Computing (SAC '12)*. ACM, New York, NY, USA, 2002–2007. https://doi.org/10.1145/2245276.2232109

[23] Satoru Inoue, Hisae Aoyama, and Keiichi Nakata. 2011. Cognitive analysis for knowledge modeling in air traffic control work. In *International Conference on Human-Computer Interaction*. Springer, 341–350.

[24] Yucheng Jin, Bruno Cardoso, and Katrien Verbert. 2017. How do different levels of user control affect cognitive load and acceptance of recommendations?. In *Proceedings of the 4th Joint Workshop on Interfaces and Human Decision Making for Recommender Systems co-located with ACM Conference on Recommender Systems (RecSys 2017)*. CEUR-WS, 35–42.

[25] Antti Kangasrääsiö, Dorota Glowacka, and Samuel Kaski. 2015. Improving controllability and predictability of interactive recommendation interfaces for exploratory search. In *Proceedings of the 20th international conference on intelligent user interfaces*. ACM, 247–251.

[26] Roy PC Kessels, Martine JE Van Zandvoort, Albert Postma, L Jaap Kappelle, and Edward HF De Haan. 2000. The Corsi block-tapping task: standardization and normative data. *Applied neuropsychology* 7, 4 (2000), 252–258.

[27] Bart P Knijnenburg, Niels J M Reijmer, and Martijn C Willemsen. 2011. Each to His Own: How Different Users Call for Different Interaction Methods in Recommender Systems. In *Proceedings of the Fifth ACM Conference on Recommender Systems (RecSys '11)*. ACM, New York, NY, USA, 141–148. https://doi.org/10.1145/2043932.2043960

[28] Zacharias Lekkas, Nikos Tsianos, Panagiotis Germanakos, Constantinos Mourlas, and George Samaras. 2011. The effects of personality type in user-centered appraisal systems. In *International Conference on Human-Computer Interaction*. Springer, 388–396.

[29] Benedikt Loepp, Katja Herrmanny, and Jürgen Ziegler. 2015. Blended recommending: Integrating interactive information filtering and algorithmic recommender techniques. In *Proceedings of the 33rd Annual ACM Conference on Human Factors in Computing Systems*. ACM, 975–984.

[30] John O'Donovan, Barry Smyth, Brynjar Gretarsson, Svetlin Bostandjiev, and Tobias Höllerer. 2008. PeerChooser: visual interactive recommendation. In *Proceedings of the SIGCHI Conference on Human Factors in Computing Systems*. ACM, 1085–1088.

[31] Denis Parra and Peter Brusilovsky. 2015. User-controllable personalization: A case study with SetFusion. *International Journal of Human-Computer Studies* 78 (2015), 43–67.

[32] Pearl Pu, Li Chen, and Rong Hu. 2011. A user-centric evaluation framework for recommender systems. In *Proc. RecSys'11*. ACM, 157–164.

[33] James Schaffer, Tobias Höllerer, and John O'Donovan. 2015. Hypothetical Recommendation: A Study of Interactive Profile Manipulation Behavior for Recommender Systems.. In *FLAIRS Conference*. 507–512.

[34] Rashmi Sinha and Kirsten Swearingen. 2002. The role of transparency in recommender systems. In *CHI'02 extended abstracts on Human factors in computing systems*. ACM, 830–831.

[35] Dereck Toker, Cristina Conati, Giuseppe Carenini, and Mona Haraty. 2012. Towards adaptive information visualization: on the influence of user characteristics. In *International Conference on User Modeling, Adaptation, and Personalization*. Springer, 274–285.

[36] John Venn. 1880. I. On the diagrammatic and mechanical representation of propositions and reasonings. *The London, Edinburgh, and Dublin Philosophical Magazine and Journal of Science* 10, 59 (1880), 1–18.

[37] Katrien Verbert, Denis Parra, and Peter Brusilovsky. 2016. Agents Vs. Users: Visual Recommendation of Research Talks with Multiple Dimension of Relevance. *ACM Transactions on Interactive Intelligent Systems (TiiS)* 6, 2 (2016), 11.

[38] Katrien Verbert, Denis Parra, Peter Brusilovsky, and Erik Duval. 2013. Visualizing recommendations to support exploration, transparency and controllability. In *Proceedings of the 2013 international conference on Intelligent user interfaces*. ACM, 351–362.

[39] Jesse Vig, Shilad Sen, and John Riedl. 2009. Tagsplanations: explaining recommendations using tags. In *Proceedings of the 14th international conference on Intelligent user interfaces*. ACM, 47–56.

[40] Michail Vlachos and Daniel Svonava. 2012. Graph embeddings for movie visualization and recommendation. In *First International Workshop on Recommendation Technologies for Lifestyle Change (LIFESTYLE 2012)*. 56.

[41] David Wong, Siamak Faridani, Ephrat Bitton, Björn Hartmann, and Ken Goldberg. 2011. The diversity donut: enabling participant control over the diversity of recommended responses. In *CHI'11 Extended Abstracts on Human Factors in Computing Systems*. ACM, 1471–1476.

[42] Xiangmin Zhang and Mark Chignell. 2001. Assessment of the effects of user characteristics on mental models of information retrieval systems. *Journal of the Association for Information Science and Technology* 52, 6 (2001), 445–459.

Incorporating Constraints into Matrix Factorization for Clothes Package Recommendation

Agung Toto Wibowo*
Computing Science / Informatics Engineering
University of Aberdeen / Telkom University
wibowo.agung@abdn.ac.uk /
agungtoto@telkomuniversity.ac.id

Advaith Siddharthan
Knowledge Media Institute
The Open University
advaith.siddharthan@open.ac.uk

Judith Masthoff
Computing Science
University of Aberdeen
j.masthoff@abdn.ac.uk

Chenghua Lin
Computing Science
University of Aberdeen
chenghua.lin@abdn.ac.uk

ABSTRACT

Recommender systems have been widely applied in the literature to suggest individual items to users. In this paper, we consider the harder problem of package recommendation, where items are recommended together as a package. We focus on the clothing domain, where a package recommendation involves a combination of a "top" (e.g. a shirt) and a "bottom" (e.g. a pair of trousers). The novelty in this work is that we combined matrix factorisation methods for collaborative filtering with hand-crafted and learnt fashion constraints on combining item features such as colour, formality and patterns. Finally, to better understand where the algorithms are underperforming, we conducted focus groups, which lead to deeper insights into how to use constraints to improve package recommendation in this domain.

CCS CONCEPTS

• **Information systems** → **Recommender systems**;

KEYWORDS

Constraints; Package Recommendation; Matrix Factorization; Clothes Domain

ACM Reference Format:
Agung Toto Wibowo, Advaith Siddharthan, Judith Masthoff, and Chenghua Lin. 2018. Incorporating Constraints into Matrix Factorization for Clothes Package Recommendation. In *UMAP '18: 26th Conference on User Modeling, Adaptation and Personalization, July 8–11, 2018, Singapore, Singapore*. ACM, New York, NY, USA, 9 pages. https://doi.org/10.1145/3209219.3209228

*Computing Science PhD Student at University of Aberdeen, UK. Lecturer at Telkom University, Indonesia, (agungtoto@telkomunivesity.ac.id)

1 INTRODUCTION

Research in recommender systems (RS) has been influenced by e-commerce websites (e.g., Amazon and Netflix) that produce recommendations for their users by exploiting implicit and explicit user interaction data from their systems [9]. For instance, implicit feedback may be gleaned from browsing or buying behaviors of a user, whereas explicit feedback might be gathered each time a user provides a rating for or comments about an item. These interactions together with users' personal data and items' descriptions are valuable input for recommender system approaches such as collaborative filtering [4, 14], content based filtering [9], and hybrid methods [16].

Most research on generating recommendations focuses on predicting ratings by a user for individual items. However, there are many cases where recommendations as a package better serve users' need. For example, a collection of music tracks as a play list [2], a collection of plants to support a particular animal species [17], a set of travel destinations as a tour package [5, 8], or in the clothing domain, a combination of a top (e.g. a shirt) and a bottom (e.g. trousers) [18].

One approach to package recommendations involves optimization. For example, in a travel planning task, a user (or group) can be recommended a package of places of interest (POI) that are within budget; i.e., which satisfy expressed constraints on budget or time [19, 20]. Travel recommender systems also need to be able to handle constraints, e.g. "no more than 3 museums" or "travel distance is less than 10 km" and provide alternatives for restaurants, transportation and hotels [1].

A second approach to package recommendations involves search. In the clothes domain, there are some package recommendation approaches based on image features [7, 13]. These approaches collect images (each image containing both a top and a bottom) from fashion websites [13] or fashion magazines [7] to create a package reference database. Using image processing techniques, they automatically separate the top and the bottom. Miura et al. [13] extracted image features (such as a RGB histogram and scale invariant features transform [SIFT] [10] values) for both tops and bottoms. To provide package recommendations, they required the user to provide a query (top or bottom) image. This image was then compared with packages in the reference database, and the closest package reference returned as a recommendation. Similar to Miura's work, Iwata et al. [7] extracted visual features (such as colour, texture and SIFT as a bag-of-features, and derived a topic model over these using Latent Dirichlet Allocation (LDA). When a user provided a query image (top/bottom), Iwata et al. recommended the other part by searching the topic model in their package reference database. Search can also take account of user context. Shen et al. [15] developed a clothes package recommendation system based on user context. First, they stored clothing items and combinations of items in a user wardrobe database. They also annotated its contents using English words. To generate recommendations, their system asked the user about their goals ("destinations" and "want to look like") and mapped them to possible characteristics of clothes in the user wardrobe.

More recently, we suggested a collaborative filtering approach to package recommendations in the clothing domain using matrix factorization (MF) [18]. We showed that the user-package ratings matrix is too sparce to successfully apply MF methods. Instead, we applied matrix factorization separately to user-top and user-bottom rating matrices and predicted a package rating by combining the predicted ratings for the top and bottom using either the minimum function or the harmonic means. This was the first collaborative approach to package recommendation, but had clear shortcomings in that it did not take into account fashion constraints that exist between the choice of a top and a bottom. For example, patterns and colors might clash between top and bottom, and they might not even be suitable for the same season. The work presented in [18] did not handle these scenarios.

In this paper, we propose a novel approach to package recommendation in the clothes domain that combines collaborative filtering on user-item matrices with constraints on the items within a package. To incorporate item constraints, we (a) enriched the dataset described in [18] by adding item attributes such as dress code, color and patterns through an annotation process; (b) constructed matrices of constraints (first hand-crafted and later through machine learning) on tops and bottoms within a package; and (c) proposed means to incorporate these constraints within matrix factorization to provide package recommendations.

The remainder of this paper is organized as follows. Section 2 defines the package recommendation task and the notation used, describes how the dataset was generated and enhanced, and formulates several matrix factorization approaches for package recommendation. Section 3 describes our motivations for using constraints, formulates how the handcrafted constraints were incorporated into matrix factorization for package recommendation, and describes how a supervised learning algorithm J48 [6] was used to learn constraints automatically. Section 4 details our experimental settings and Section 5 reports our experiment results. Section 6 describes the motivation, participants, materials, procedures, and findings of our focus group discussion to gain a deeper insight into how to improve cloths package recommendation. Finally, Section 7 provides a discussion and suggests directions for future work.

2 PACKAGE RECOMMENDATIONS

Consider a set of clothes $I^a = \{i_1^t, i_2^t, \ldots, i_o^t, i_1^b, i_2^b, \ldots, i_p^b\}$, consisting of two disjoint complementary sets: a set of o top items

$I^t = \{i_1^t, i_2^t, \ldots, i_o^t\}$ and a set of p bottom items $I^b = \{i_1^b, i_2^b, \ldots, i_p^b\}$, where $I^t \cup I^b = I^a$; $o + p = n$. Each item in I^a is associated with a set of q attributes $f^{1 \cdots q}$, each of which takes one from a finite set of values, $\{f_{1 \ldots r_1}^1, f_{1 \ldots r_2}^2, \ldots, f_{1 \ldots r_q}^q\}$.

Further, some of these items and their combinations (a package) have received ratings from one or more of m possible users $U = \{u_1, u_2, \ldots, u_m\}$. The individual ratings are denoted as a triple $(u, i, r_{u,i})$, where $u \in U$, $i \in I^a$ and $r_{u,i}$ is the rating given by user u to item i. Package ratings are denoted as a quadruple $(u, i^t, i^b, r_{u,(i^t, i^b)})$, where $u \in U$, $i^t \in I^t$, $i^b \in I^b$, and $r_{u,(i^t, i^b)}$ is the rating provided by user u to the package (i^t, i^b).

Our task is then to identify the best top-N package recommendations, based on both user–item and user–package ratings, and on the item features.

2.1 Dataset

In this paper, we extend the package recommendations dataset for the clothes domain [18]. This dataset contains 12,000 individual ratings and 6,000 package ratings from 200 users. The items consist of 1,400 "tops" and 600 "bottoms" extracted from Amazon product data [11, 12]. The dataset is publicly available and can be downloaded from a GitHub repository[1].

We further annotate all individual items by adding color, pattern and formality attributes. We use twelve different colors (black, gray, white, red, green, blue, yellow, orange, purple, brown, pink and other), seven different patterns (clean, text, checker, stripes, pattern, floral and picture) and four different formalities (casual, sport/outdoor, work and formal). Figure 1 shows examples of dress codes and patterns used in our dataset.

2.2 MF For Package Recommendations

Our starting point is previous work on MF for package recommendations [18]. There are two types of ratings matrices used in that study:

CAT category ratings, where we use separate matrices for user–top ratings V^t and user–bottom ratings V^b

ALL all ratings, where we use a single matrix for user–item ratings V^a.

There were four high performing solutions in [18], labeled MF-MIN-ALL, MF-MIN-CAT, MF-MUL-ALL, and MF-MUL-CAT. To understand these labels, each consists of three parts separated by a dash ("-") sign. The first part ("MF") describes that the solution is based on matrix factorization. The second part ("MIN" or "MUL") describes the use of minimum or multiplicative (harmonic mean) operations over individual rating predictions for top and bottom to generate a package rating prediction. The last part ("CAT" or "ALL") describes the use of separate matrices for top and bottom categories or a single matrix with all items, as described above.

The focus of this work is to combine these purely collaborative predictions with constraints pertaining to item features.

---

[1]https://github.com/atwRecsys/PackageRecDataset

| (a) Casual | (b) Sport/Outdoor | (c) Work | (d) Formal | (e) Clean Pattern | (f) Checker Pattern |

| (g) Text Pattern | (h) Picture Pattern | (i) Floral Pattern | (j) Stripes Pattern | (k) Pattern Pattern |

Figure 1: Example of Images with Different Formality and Pattern Attributes

3 INCORPORATING CONSTRAINTS INTO MF

As discussed in Section 2.1, we enhanced our dataset by adding three attributes (color, pattern, and formality). In this section, we describe two methods (hand-crafted and automated) to determine the appropriateness of different combinations of tops and bottoms.

3.1 Hand Crafted Constraints

The annotation process as mentioned in Section 2.1 added color, pattern and formality attributes to each item in our dataset. Therefore, for each package rating we obtained information such as user (u), top item (i^t), bottom item (i^b), package rating $(u, i^t, i^b, r_{i^t, i^b})$, top color (cl^{i^t}), top pattern (pt^{i^t}), top formality (fm^{i^t}), bottom color (cl^{i^b}), bottom pattern (pt^{i^b}) and bottom formality (fm^{i^b}).

3.1.1 Appropriateness Constraints Matrices. In order to identify the appropriateness of clothes combinations, we collected rules from fashion websites (i.e. Telegraph Fashion[2], AskMen[3], Looksgud[4], Effortless Gent[5], Gurl[6], Quora[7]). We collected statements pertaining to our attributes, and represented these as appropriateness matrices for each attribute. For example a statement of *"The best colors to wear together are shades that are complimentary of each other. ... These include red and green, violet and yellow and blue and orange."* gives a clues that combination of red and green, or violet and yellow, or blue and orange works together.

For each attribute we experimented with three different matrices that we will refer to as: stick, carrot, and stick–carrot. We use the stick matrix to decrease the rating prediction when the top

and bottom are identified as a non-appropriate combination, but if the combination is appropriate we do not give a reward. On the other hand, we use the carrot matrix to increase the rating prediction when the top and bottom are identified as an appropriate combination, but if the combination is not appropriate we do not give a penalty. When using the stick–carrot matrix, we apply either a reward or penalty to a combination depending on whether it is appropriate or not.

Table 1 shows example matrices for color, pattern and formality attributes. We provide an example each for carrot, stick and carrot–stick. A statement "White shirts go with everything", resulted in the values in the entire row for white tops having the value 1. Another statement "Keep red and pink separate" would have resulted in a value of -1 in the stick and carrot–stick matrices (not shown) for two cells: pink top and red bottom and vice versa.

3.1.2 Incorporating Color Constraint. To incorporate the color constraint into matrix factorization for package recommendations we follow Equation (1):

$$\hat{r}_{u_x, (i^t_y, i^b_z)} = f(u_x, (i^t_y, i^b_z)) + A^{cl}_{cl^{i^t}, cl^{i^b}} * \rho^{cl} \qquad (1)$$

where $f(u_x, (i^t_y, i^b_z))$ is the MF prediction for the package (using one of the algorithms MF-MUL-ALL, MF-MIN-ALL, MF-MIN-CAT, MF-MUL-CAT reported in [18]); $A^{cl}_{cl^{i^t}, cl^{i^b}}$ is the prediction from the color appropriateness matrix for the top color (cl^{i^t}) and the bottom color (cl^{i^b}). Meanwhile, ρ^{cl} is the weight assigned to the color constraint prediction.

3.1.3 Pattern Constraint. Likewise, to incorporate pattern constraints into matrix factorization for package recommendations we follow Equation (2):

$$\hat{r}_{u_x, (i^t_y, i^b_z)} = f(u_x, (i^t_y, i^b_z)) + A^{pt}_{pt^{i^t}, pt^{i^b}} * \rho^{pt} \qquad (2)$$

[2]http://www.telegraph.co.uk/fashion/

[3]https://uk.askmen.com/style/

[4]https://www.looksgud.in/

[5]https://effortlessgent.com/

[6]http://www.gurl.com/

[7]https://www.quora.com/What-are-some-good-rules-of-thumb-for-women-when-putting-an-outfit-together

Table 1: Color appropriateness matrices (*A*), (a) Carrot appropriateness matrix for color, (b) Stick appropriateness matrix for pattern, and (c) Stick-Carrot appropriateness matrix for formality.

Carrot		cl^{i^b}											
		Black	Gray	White	Red	Green	Blue	Yellow	Orange	Purple	Brown	Pink	Others
													?
	Black	1	1	1	1	1	1	1	1	1	1	1	1
	Gray	1	1	1	1	1	0	1	1	0	0	1	0
	White	1	1	1	1	1	1	1	1	1	1	1	1
	Red	1	0	1	1	1	0	0	1	0	0	0	0
	Green	1	0	0	1	1	1	1	0	0	0	1	0
cl^{i^t}	Blue	1	0	0	0	1	1	0	1	1	0	0	0
	Yellow	1	0	1	0	1	0	1	0	1	0	0	0
	Orange	1	0	1	1	0	1	0	1	0	0	0	0
	Purple	1	0	0	1	0	1	1	0	1	0	0	0
	Brown	1	0	0	0	0	0	0	0	0	1	0	0
	Pink	1	0	1	0	1	0	0	0	0	0	1	0
	Others	?	1	0	0	0	0	0	0	0	0	0	1

(a)

Stick		pt^{i^b}						
		Clean	Text	Checker	Stripes	Pattern	Floral	Picture
	Clean	0	0	0	0	0	0	0
	Text	0	-1	-1	0	-1	-1	-1
	Checker	0	-1	-1	0	-1	-1	-1
pt^{i^t}	Stripes	0	0	0	0	0	0	0
	Pattern	0	-1	-1	0	-1	-1	-1
	Floral	0	-1	-1	0	-1	-1	-1
	Picture	0	-1	-1	0	-1	-1	-1

(b)

Stick-Carrot		fm^{i^b}			
		Casual	Sport/Outdoor	Work	Formal
	Casual	1	1	1	-1
fm^{i^t}	Sport/Outdoor	1	1	-1	-1
	Work	-1	-1	1	1
	Formal	-1	-1	1	1

(c)

where $A^{pt}_{pt^{i^t},pt^{i^b}}$ is the prediction from the pattern appropriateness matrix and ρ^{pt} is the weight assigned to the pattern constraint prediction.

3.1.4 Formality Constraint. Likewise, to incorporate the formality constraint into matrix factorization for package recommendations we follow Equation (3):

$$\hat{r}_{u_x,(i_y^t,i_z^b)} = f(u_x,(i_y^t,i_z^b)) + A^{fm}_{fm^{i^t},fm^{i^b}} * \rho^{fm} \qquad (3)$$

where $A^{fm}_{fm^{i^t},fm^{i^b}}$ is the prediction from the formality matrix and ρ^{fm} is weight assigned to the formality constraint prediction.

3.1.5 Incorporating Multiple Constraints. In Equation (1), (2) and (3), the color, pattern and formality constraints are only incorporated individually. We also experiment with combining two or three constraints together by using Equation (4).

$$\hat{r}_{u_x,(i_y^t,i_z^b)} = f(u_x,(i_y^t,i_z^b)) + A^{cl}_{cl^{i^t},cl^{i^b}} * \rho^{cl}$$
$$+ A^{pt}_{pt^{i^t},pt^{i^b}} * \rho^{pt} + A^{fm}_{fm^{i^t},fm^{i^b}} * \rho^{fm} \qquad (4)$$

For instance, the combination of color and pattern is achieved by setting the formality appropriateness weight (ρ^{fm}) to 0.

3.2 Automatically Learned Constraints

As an alternative to hand-crafting attribute constraints from fashion literature, we also explored the option of learning constraints from the dataset.

In this scenario, we consider each package rating $(u, i^t, i^b, r_{i^t,i^b})$ in the training set, and:

(1) discard the user u;
(2) represent the top and bottom by their attributes (top color cl^{i^t}, pattern pt^{i^t} and formality fm^{i^t}; bottom color cl^{i^b}, pattern pt^{i^b} and formality fm^{i^b});
(3) convert the package rating r_{i^t,i^b} into a binary label "good" (rating of 4–5) or "bad" (rating of 1–3); and

Then we train the J48 classifier [6] over this converted training set to classify packages as good (1) or bad (0). To obtain a rating prediction, we take the strength of the prediction of the classifier $pred(i_y^t,i_z^b)$, whose value ranges from 0 (bad) to 1 (good), and normalize this by the following Equation 5.

$$g_{(i_y^t,i_z^b)} = min + (max - min) \times pred(i_y^t,i_z^b) \qquad (5)$$

where *min* and *max* are the minimum and maximum rating values (in our dataset, 1 and 5).

3.2.1 Incorporating Decision Trees with MF. To get ranking predictions, we combine the MF-MUL-CAT prediction with the J48 prediction as follows:

$$\hat{r}_{u_x,(i_y^t,i_z^b)} = f(u_x,(i_y^t,i_z^b)) * pred(i_y^t,i_z^b) \qquad (6)$$

where the $f(u_x,(i_y^t,i_z^b))$ is the rating prediction produced by the matrix factorization adaptation, and the $pred(i_y^t,i_z^b)$ is the strength of the predictions produced by the decision tree/J48 classifier (see Equation (5)).

4 EXPERIMENTAL SETTINGS

4.1 Evaluation Metric

In this paper we evaluate based on a top-N package recommendation scenario, where we evaluate the quality of the top N recommendations we make for different users. This is a more realistic evaluation that those based on average rating prediction accuracy using metrics, e.g. root mean squared error (RMSE), which give undue importance to items that are not being recommended. There are several metrics that can be used to determine top-N performance, e.g. Normalised Discounted Cumulative Gain (NDCG), recall@N, precission@N, etc. In this paper, we adopt recall@N as described by Cremenosi et.al [3], as its assumptions are a good fit for package recommendations. We will say more about this after describing the method.

The recall@N metric is calculated as follows: First, from the testing set we collect all the packages (i^t, i^b) rated 5 by each user u into a set T. Second, for each package contained in T:

(1) We select 99 random packages and assume that the user u will not like these packages as much;
(2) We predict the ratings given by user u for the test package (i^t, i^b), which has a known score of 5, and for the 99 additional packages, which are assumed to be rated lower;
(3) We form a ranked list by ordering all 100 packages according to the rating predictions. Let p denote the rank of the test package (i^t, i^b) within the list.
(4) We form a top-N recommendation list by picking the N top ranked packages from the list. If $p \leq N$ we have a *hit*, otherwise we have a *miss*. Chances of a hit increase with an increase in the N value and are guaranteed at $N = 100$.

Average Recall@N performance is then defined by Equation 7:

$$recall(N) = \frac{\#hit}{|T|} \qquad (7)$$

4.2 Crossvalidation Method

We apply a 4-fold crossvalidation methodology. This is done by randomly splitting the individual ratings into four parts, and then rotating and using three parts as the training set and one for testing. Following [18], in each fold we used only 25% of package ratings $r_{u,(i^t,i^b)}$ as the training set, and the remaining 75% package ratings $r_{u,(i^t,i^b)}$ as the test set.

4.3 Experimental Settings

Wibowo et.al [18] cast package recommendation as a rating predictions task. In their work they used RMSE as a performance metric. Since in this paper we use the top-N package recommendation as scenario, to get a fair comparison we first reran those algorithms (MF-MIN-ALL, MF-MIN-CAT, MF-MUL-ALL, and MF-MUL-CAT) and report the top-N package performance. In this paper, we will use these algorithms as baselines.

To obtain a better understanding on how our adaptations produce improvements, we report the recall@10 performance over a combination of each constraint with the best baseline performance from above:

(1) We report a combination of the best solution (from our baselines) with each constraint attributes (color, pattern and formality) as described in Section 3.1.2. We report results for the best performing value of the weights ρ=0.8.
(2) We report combinations of constraints which produced an improvement using the scenario as explained in Section 3.1.5.
(3) We report using the decision tree algorithm (Section 3.2).
(4) We report the combination of the decision tree algorithm with the best performing MF baseline.

5 RESULTS

5.1 MF For Package Recommendation Baseline

Table 2 shows the average recall@10 on the testing set for different algorithms described in [18]. The green cell in this table shows the best recall@10 from purely collaborative approaches. In this section we will use this algorithm MF-MUL-CAT as our baseline and incorporate constraints as described in Section 3.1 into MF-MUL-CAT for comparison.

Table 2: Average Recall@10 Performance of the baseline.

Scenario	recall@10
MF-MIN-ALL	0.1220
MF-MIN-CAT	0.1147
MF-MUL-ALL	0.1253
MF-MUL-CAT	0.1293

5.2 Incorporating Handcrafted Constraints Individually

Table 3 shows the average recall@10 for combining MF-MUL-CAT with handcrafted rules. The column "Attribute" denotes one of our attributes (color, pattern, and formality) as mentioned in Section 2.1. The column "Type" denotes one of our constraint matrix types (Carrot, Stick, and Stick–Carrot) in each attribute as mentioned in Section 3.1.

Table 3: Average Recall@10 Performance for MF with Handcrafted Constraints

Scenario	Attribute	Type	recall@10
MF-MUL-CAT			0.1293
MF-MUL-CAT	Color	Carrot	0.1296
MF-MUL-CAT	Color	Stick	0.1391
MF-MUL-CAT	Color	Stick–Carrot	0.1332
MF-MUL-CAT	Pattern	Carrot	0.1260
MF-MUL-CAT	Pattern	Stick	0.1364
MF-MUL-CAT	Pattern	Stick–Carrot	0.1245
MF-MUL-CAT	Formality	Carrot	0.1532
MF-MUL-CAT	Formality	Stick	0.1461
MF-MUL-CAT	Formality	Stick–Carrot	0.1522

As we can see from Table 3, all but two of our adaptations outperform the MT-MUL-CAT baseline (the yellow cell in the recall@10 column). The green cells in Table 3 represent the best combinations for each attribute, and we can see that incorporating constraints for each of our attribute types improves performance compared to a purely collaborative approach, with constraints on formality providing the biggest gain.

5.3 Incorporating Combinations of Handcrafted Constraints

Table 4 shows the average recall@10 for different combinations of handcrafted rules. The first four rows in Table 4 summarise our best recall@10 for each attribute in Table 3. The remaining four rows report combinations of those attributes following the formula in Section 3.1.5.

Table 4: Average Recall@10 Performance for MF with combinations of handcrafted constraints

Scenario	Attribute	App. Type	recall@10
MF-MUL-CAT			0.1293
MF-MUL-CAT	Color	Stick	0.1391
MF-MUL-CAT	Pattern	Stick	0.1364
MF-MUL-CAT	Formality	Carrot	0.1532
MF-MUL-CAT	Comb. of Color and Pattern		0.1398
MF-MUL-CAT	Comb. of Color and Formality		0.1548
MF-MUL-CAT	Comb. of Pattern and Formality		0.1488
MF-MUL-CAT	Comb. of All Attributes		0.1604

As we can see from Table 4, all of our adaptations outperform the MF-MUL-CAT baseline. The best performance comes from incorporating all three attributes (the green cell with a recall@10 value of 0.1604).

5.4 Decision Tree Performance

Table 5 shows the average recall@10 using the decision tree (J48). The column "Upsampling" shows the factor used for upsampling the minority class of good packages (defined as those for which $r_{u,(i^t,i^b)} = 4, 5$) in our traning set. We used upsampling to handle the imbalanced data, where the number of bad versus good packages ratio is 5:1 [18]. The first two rows show the recall@10 for MF-MUL-CAT and also the best combination of MF-MUL-CAT with handcrafted constraints, summarized from previous tables. The next three rows report results using only the learned constraints, i.e. with no collaborative element. As expected these are worse than the results of collaborative filtering, highlighting that user preferences play a key role in this domain. The last three rows report results for the combination of J48 predictions with the baseline MF approach. While there is an improvement over the baseline, the automatically learned constraints do not perform as well as the manually curated ones.

Table 5: Average Recall@N Performance using Automatically Learned Constraints

Scenario	Upsampling	recall@10
MF-MUL-CAT		0.1293
MF-MUL-CAT (All Attributes)		0.1604
J48	2	0.0990
J48	3	0.1016
J48	4	0.0981
J48 * MF-MUL-CAT	2	0.1439
J48 * MF-MUL-CAT	3	0.1509
J48 * MF-MUL-CAT	4	0.1477

To summarize, we have reported several results for package recommendations by combining matrix factorization predictions with constraints about which attributes can go well together and

which ones can clash. To better understand our results and also gain insights as to how to improve the system for the future, we conducted focus groups on package recommendations, described next.

6 FOCUS GROUPS ON CLOTHES COMBINATION ASPECTS

The aim of our focus groups (FGs) was to gain a better understanding of what aspects affect whether clothes are good to combine together. We were interested in people's arguments and preferences for combining a "top" (e.g. a shirt or t-shirt) and "bottom" (e.g. trousers, shorts, skirts). We were also interested in the clothing features that result in a positive, negative or neutral judgment on a particular clothing combination. This study leads to a deeper insight into how to improve package recommendation in the clothes domain, such as what constraints may be better to use and how to use them.

6.1 Participants

Eight FGs were held with 3-5 participants per group. 30 participants were recruited (14 female and 16 male) using convenience sampling from the University of Aberdeen. They came from 11 different countries. All were over 18; further demographic data was not collected.

6.2 Materials

We ran our FGs in two scenarios. In the first scenario, we showed the FGs some images of "top" and "bottom" clothes and their ratings by an anonymous user. We selected the clothes at random, and varied the number of clothes shown to the participants (see Table 6). We also showed 3 combinations of tops and bottoms to the participants. In the second scenario, we showed the FGs 15 combinations, selected at random.

For our anonymous users, we randomly selected 4 male and 4 female users from our previous dataset[8]. To make the discussion easier, we provided pseudonames in each scenario: Alice, Barbara, Carol, and Deborah as female pseudonames, and Andy, Bob, Charles, and David as male pseudonames.

Table 6: Frequency Distribution of Individual Preferences Samples Involved in FGD

Pseudoname	Gender	#Tops at Rating					#Bottoms at Rating				
		1	2	3	4	5	1	2	3	4	5
Alice	Female	2	2	2	2	4	3	1	0	4	4
Andy	Male	2	2	1	2	3	0	0	1	2	4
Barbara	Female	0	1	3	4	3	1	4	1	1	2
Bob	Male	1	3	3	4	2	1	3	2	2	4
Carol	Female	1	1	3	3	3	3	3	2	3	3
Charles	Male	4	1	2	2	2	2	1	2	1	1
Deborah	Female	3	2	3	3	4	2	2	2	2	1
David	Male	3	0	3	3	3	3	1	2	1	3

---

[8]https://github.com/atwRecsys/PackageRecDataset

6.3 Procedure

Participants were told the purpose of the FG was to understand what aspects affect whether clothes are good to combine together. Next, the FGs were run using the following steps:

Step 1. The FG was given the user preferences, e.g with pseudoname is "Alice", and asked to discuss whether "Alice" will like/dislike each combination from the 3 given pairs. The FG was also asked to identify why "Alice" will like/dislike the particular combination.

Step 2. With the first scenario still visible, 15 combinations were provided for "Alice" and the FG was asked to select the 3 combinations that "Alice" might like the best. We also asked them to identify what makes these the best combinations for "Alice".

Step 3. Participants were invited to share any other thoughts they had related to clothes combination aspects.

Step 4. Step 1-3 were repeated for another user with different gender.

FGs were audio recorded, and a thematic analysis was conducted based on these recordings.

6.4 Results

Even though we conducted our discussion using two scenarios, we do not distinguish our findings into two separate tables because both scenarios are intended to provide insights into what aspects affect whether clothes are good to combine together.

Table 7 summarizes the finding on clothes combination aspects. This table contains 9 columns, with the first column indicating aspects mentioned by the FGs. The other columns represent the FGs. Each FG is named by taking the first letter from the pseudonames discussed in it and adding the FG sequence number. Therefore, column "C5" represents FG number 5 which discussed users "Carol" and "Charles". The user pseudonames are listed in Table 6. The check-mark (✓) indicates that a particular aspect was mentioned in the FG discussion.

In Table 7, we group the aspects findings into two different sets: combination aspects and individual preferences. Even though there are similar aspects that appear in both sets, participants tended to use them in different situations. For example, in statement "*agree on combinations six [..] six is the formal shirt and the formal trousers*" the formality aspect is more about the combination rather than individual preferences. In contrast, a statement such as "*He doesn't quite like the more formal shirt [..]. So in all I wouldn't say yes or no to this shirt*" is more about individual preferences.

6.4.1 Combination Aspects.
From the FGs, we identified some combination aspects that affect whether clothes are good to combine together. As mentioned in Table 7, there are 9 of these:

(1) Formality agreement (all FGs). Participants conveyed that a clothes combination must satisfy the dress code formality agreement. They also identified formal, semi-formal/work, casual, and sport as types of formality.

(2) Use high ratings (all FGs). Participants argued that people tend to use clothes from the items they love when creating a clothes combination. The set of loved items can also be expanded to include items of similar type and color.

Table 7: Clothes Combination Aspects Discussed in the Study

Aspects		A1	A2	B3	B4	C5	C6	D7	D8
Combination Aspects									
Formality agreement		✓	✓	✓	✓	✓	✓	✓	✓
Use the high rating		✓	✓	✓	✓	✓	✓	✓	✓
Color compatibility		✓	✓		✓	✓	✓	✓	✓
Brightness composition			✓	✓	✓	✓		✓	✓
Eliminate the low rating		✓	✓	✓			✓		✓
Motif harmony					✓	✓		✓	✓
Length of the dress			✓		✓				
Functional agreement			✓		✓				
Seasonal agreement								✓	
Individual Preferences									
Color	Favorite color	✓	✓	✓	✓	✓	✓	✓	✓
	Color brightness		✓	✓	✓	✓	✓	✓	✓
Style	Sleeve length	✓	✓	✓	✓	✓	✓	✓	✓
	Bottom length	✓	✓	✓	✓	✓	✓	✓	✓
	Cutting shapes	✓	✓	✓	✓	✓	✓	✓	✓
	Shirt type	✓	✓	✓	✓	✓	✓		
	Loose style			✓	✓	✓		✓	✓
	Collar			✓	✓		✓		✓
	Body exposure		✓			✓	✓		
	Formality		✓		✓	✓			
Patterns		✓	✓		✓	✓	✓	✓	✓
User personality		✓			✓	✓			✓
Fabric			✓		✓	✓			
Cloth details					✓			✓	

(3) Color compatibility (7 FGs). Participants argued that a good combination should have good color compatibility. A combination from gradation colors was considered as a good combination. They also mentioned some conflicts caused by colors when clothes are combined together.

(4) Brightness composition (6 FGs). Most participants who considered the brightness composition aspect said that the composition of bright and dark or bright and neutral for clothes works well together.

(5) Eliminate low ratings (5 FGs). This aspect was strongly expressed when the FGs were asked to find 3 out of 15 as the best combinations. They easily discarded combinations which contained lowly rated items. They felt that the combination was ruined when it contained any disliked item.

(6) Motif harmony (4 FGs). Some participants expressed that it will be better for a combination to have patterns only in one part of clothing. The pattern can be in the top or the bottom as long as the other part is plain.

(7) Length of dress (2 FGs). Participants noted that there are some dresses that do not need a bottom.

(8) Functional agreement (2 FGs). Some participants argued that we can classify clothes into some functional categories e.g go to beach. Some clothes combinations are better when they are in the same category.

(9) Seasonal agreement (1 FG). Participants argued that a winter jacket and summer pants did not work together.

6.4.2 Individual Preferences. The individual preferences described the reason why a user like/dislike a particular item. These individual preferences might affected user judgment to the whole combinations. As shown in Table 7, there are 14 matters involved in individual preferences, which can be grouped into categories.

Color.

- *Favorite color* (all FGs). Participants argued that some users tend to select clothes based on their favorite color. These colors were identified from the samples provided with ratings 4 and 5
- *Color brightness* (7 FGs). Participants argued that some users tend to select clothes with similar brightness (e.g. neutral, calm, dark, bright). Here, we distinguish the favorite color from the color brightness since in the discussion there were participants who believed that the user did not have any objection to bright blue and dark blue.

Style. Participants discussed many different aspects of style, far more than just the distinction between formal and informal that we had been making.

- Sleeve length (all FGs). Respondents argued that some users tends to choose clothes with a particular length of sleeve.
- Bottom length (all FGs). Participants argued that some users tends to choose a bottom with a particular length (e.g. capri jeans, sort jeans).
- Cutting shapes (all FGs). Participants argued that some users tend to choose bottoms with a particular cutting shape e.g. bell bottom, boot cut, slim fit (tight), baggy pants.
- Shirt type (6 FGs). Participants argued that some users have preferences for the shirt type (e.g. polo, T-shirt, long T-shirt, shirt, formal shirt, hoodie).
- Loose style (5 FGs). Participants described the loose style as clothes which are extra wide at the bottom, and they believed that these aspects influence user preferences. They added that a loose cloth style provides freedom to a person wearing it.
- Collar (4 FGs). Participants argued that some users tend to wear/avoid clothes with or without collar.
- Formality (3 FGs). Participants argued that some users tends to choose individual items based on formality. Even though formality agreement was discussed by all FGs, the formality aspect in individual preferences was not discussed by all. Participants argued that some users would like to select different formality to wear to different occasions.
- Body exposure (3 FGs). Participants argued that some users prefer to wear/avoid clothes which expose some part of their body.

Patterns (7 FGs). Participants argued that some users love to wear clothes with patterns (e.g. checker) either on top or bottom.

User personality (5 FGs). Participants argued that a user's personality (e.g. mature, easy going) affects the selection of individual items. A mature user prefers to select a particular type of clothes.

Fabric (3 FGs). Participants argued that some users did not have any objection to clothes with thick fabric (e.g jeans), or thin/loose fabric (e.g cotton, silk, or satin).

Cloth details (2 FGs). Participants argued that some users prefer to wear/avoid clothes with tiny details on them (e.g. gold buttons on a black shirt).

7 DISCUSSION AND FUTURE WORK

We have presented a novel approach to package recommendations by incorporating constraints on the item attributes into a matrix factorization based collaborative filtering algorithm. Our results show that modeling constraints, either through manual curation from external resources, or through automated acquisition from within the dataset, is an important step in the cloths domain.

To gain further insights into package recommendation in this domain, we conducted focus groups that revealed two types of considerations: combination aspects and individual preferences. The combination aspects reflect the reasons why a user might like or dislike a combination of clothes, while the individual preferences identify item features that are relevant for modeling whether a user will like or dislike a top or a bottom individually. The focus group validated several aspects of our algorithm, for instance, the importance of considering colors, formalities, and patterns, and our choice of minimum and harmonic mean operations for combining individual ratings for tops and bottoms.

The focus groups also identified several other features that affect user preferences, for example, the brightness, lengths, cuts and looseness of outfits, as well as the fabric. We do not explicitly model these features in our algorithm and instead rely on matrix factorization to identify latent item and user features from the training data.

Our work can immediately be extended in three ways: (a) by investigating different weighting mechanisms for combining constraints and also incorporating constraints within the update process of matrix factorization, (b) by incorporating our focus group findings which suggest explicit item and user attributes to consider for recommending individual items, and (c) by incorporating our focus group findings to expand the number of item features modeled for the purpose of constraining potential combinations of clothes.

In future work we also propose to extend our model to handle other types of constraints, for instance, budget, and to allow for packages with a larger number of items. In this context, we would also like to investigate the package recommendation challenge in other domains, for example food or travel.

ACKNOWLEDGMENTS

We would like to thank Lembaga Pengelola Dana Pendidikan (LPDP), Departemen Keuangan Indonesia for awarding a scholarship to support the studies of the lead author. We would also like to thank the participants in our focus groups who communicated precious feedback during our discussions.

REFERENCES

[1] Sihem Amer-Yahia, Francesco Bonchi, Carlos Castillo, Esteban Feuerstein, Isabel Mendez-Diaz, and Paula Zabala. 2014. Composite retrieval of diverse and complementary bundles. *IEEE Transactions on Knowledge and Data Engineering* 26, 11 (2014), 2662–2675.

[2] Da Cao, Liqiang Nie, Xiangnan He, Xiaochi Wei, Shunzhi Zhu, and Tat-Seng Chua. 2017. Embedding Factorization Models for Jointly Recommending Items and User Generated Lists. In *Proceedings of the 40th International ACM SIGIR Conference on Research and Development in Information Retrieval.* ACM, 585–594.

[3] Paolo Cremonesi, Yehuda Koren, and Roberto Turrin. 2010. Performance of recommender algorithms on top-n recommendation tasks. In *Proceedings of the fourth ACM conference on Recommender systems.* ACM, 39–46.

[4] Michael D Ekstrand, John T Riedl, and Joseph A Konstan. 2011. Collaborative filtering recommender systems. *Foundations and Trends in Human-Computer Interaction* 4, 2 (2011), 81–173.

[5] A Felfernig, S Gordea, D Jannach, E Teppan, and M Zanker. 2007. A short survey of recommendation technologies in travel and tourism. *OEGAI journal* 25, 7 (2007), 17–22.

[6] Mark Hall, Eibe Frank, Geoffrey Holmes, Bernhard Pfahringer, Peter Reutemann, and Ian H Witten. 2009. The WEKA data mining software: an update. *ACM SIGKDD explorations newsletter* 11, 1 (2009), 10–18.

[7] Tomoharu Iwata, Shinji Wanatabe, and Hiroshi Sawada. 2011. Fashion coordinates recommender system using photographs from fashion magazines. In *IJCAI,* Vol. 22. Citeseer, 2262.

[8] Qi Liu, Enhong Chen, Hui Xiong, Yong Ge, Zhongmou Li, and Xiang Wu. 2014. A cocktail approach for travel package recommendation. *IEEE Transactions on Knowledge and Data Engineering* 26, 2 (2014), 278–293.

[9] Pasquale Lops, Marco Gemmis, and Giovanni Semeraro. 2011. Recommender Systems Handbook. Content-based Recommender Systems: State of the Art and Trends (2011), 73–105. http://dx.doi.org/10.1007/978-0-387-85820-3_3

[10] David G Lowe. 1999. Object recognition from local scale-invariant features. In *Computer vision, 1999. The proceedings of the seventh IEEE international conference on,* Vol. 2. Ieee, 1150–1157.

[11] Julian McAuley, Rahul Pandey, and Jure Leskovec. 2015. Inferring networks of substitutable and complementary products. In *Proceedings of the 21th ACM SIGKDD International Conference on Knowledge Discovery and Data Mining.* ACM, 785–794.

[12] Julian McAuley, Christopher Targett, Qinfeng Shi, and Anton Van Den Hengel. 2015. Image-based recommendations on styles and substitutes. In *Proceedings of the 38th International ACM SIGIR Conference on Research and Development in Information Retrieval.* ACM, 43–52.

[13] Shinya Miura, Toshihiko Yamasaki, and Kiyoharu Aizawa. 2013. SNAPPER: fashion coordinate image retrieval system. In *Signal-Image Technology & Internet-Based Systems (SITIS), 2013 International Conference on.* IEEE, 784–789.

[14] X. Ning, C. Desrosiers, and G. Karypis. 2015. *A comprehensive survey of neighborhood-based recommendation methods.* 37–76.

[15] Edward Shen, Henry Lieberman, and Francis Lam. 2007. What am I gonna wear?: scenario-oriented recommendation. In *Proceedings of the 12th international conference on Intelligent user interfaces.* ACM, 365–368.

[16] Xiaoyuan Su and Taghi M Khoshgoftaar. 2009. A survey of collaborative filtering techniques. *Advances in artificial intelligence* 2009 (2009), 4.

[17] A. T. Wibowo, A. Siddharthan, H. Anderson, A. Robinson, Nirwan Sharma, H. Bostock, A. Salisbury, R. Comont, and R. V. D. Wal. 2017. Bumblebee Friendly Planting Recommendations with Citizen Science Data. In *Proceedings of the RecSys 2017 Workshop on Recommender Systems for Citizens co-located with 11th ACM Conference on Recommender Systems (RecSys 2017), Como, Italy, August 31, 2017.*

[18] A. T. Wibowo, A. Siddharthan, C. Lin, and J. Masthoff. 2017. Matrix Factorization for Package Recommendations. In *Proceedings of the RecSys 2017 Workshop on Recommendation in Complex Scenarios co-located with 11th ACM Conference on Recommender Systems (RecSys 2017), Como, Italy, August 31, 2017.* 23–28. http://ceur-ws.org/Vol-1892/paper5.pdf

[19] Min Xie, Laks VS Lakshmanan, and Peter T Wood. 2010. Breaking out of the box of recommendations: from items to packages. In *Proceedings of the fourth ACM conference on Recommender systems.* ACM, 151–158.

[20] Min Xie, Laks VS Lakshmanan, and Peter T Wood. 2011. Comprec-trip: A composite recommendation system for travel planning. In *Data Engineering (ICDE), 2011 IEEE 27th International Conference on.* IEEE, 1352–1355.

How to Use Social Relationships in Group Recommenders: Empirical Evidence

Amra Delic
TU Wien
Research Division of E-Commerce
Vienna, Austria
amra.delic@tuwien.ac.at

Judith Masthoff
University of Aberdeen
Department of Computing Science
Aberdeen, Scotland, U.K.
j.masthoff@abdn.ac.uk

Julia Neidhardt
TU Wien
Research Division of E-Commerce
Vienna, Austria
julia.neidhardt@tuwien.ac.at

Hannes Werthner
TU Wien
Research Division of E-Commerce
Vienna, Austria
hannes.werthner@tuwien.ac.at

ABSTRACT

In this paper we present the results of a user study focusing on social relationships within small groups. The goal is to better understand how to incorporate the information about social relationships in group recommendation models. Our analysis, conducted on a data set of 150 participants in 41 groups deciding on a travel destination to visit together, brings out some intriguing outcomes. We demonstrate that social centrality is hardly an indicator of the social influence in the decision-making process of *"equality matching"* types of groups. However, socially central group members and socially close groups are significantly happier with group decisions than those who are loosely related. Moreover, in this paper we show that social relationships are indicators of other concepts relevant in group settings, therefore in group recommender systems as well.

CCS CONCEPTS

• **Information systems** → *Recommender systems*; • **Human-centered computing** → *User models*; *User studies*; *Social network analysis*;

KEYWORDS

User modeling; Group recommender systems; Social relationships; Social network analysis

ACM Reference Format:
Amra Delic, Judith Masthoff, Julia Neidhardt, and Hannes Werthner. 2018. How to Use Social Relationships in Group Recommenders: Empirical Evidence. In *UMAP '18: 26th Conference on User Modeling, Adaptation and Personalization, July 8–11, 2018, Singapore, Singapore.* ACM, New York, NY, USA, 9 pages. https://doi.org/10.1145/3209219.3209226

1 INTRODUCTION

Recommender systems help their users to find content of interest, for instance, by supporting them in handling the existing information overload on the Web [31]. These systems are employed in various domains, suggesting different types of items, such as books, movies, music, restaurants, food, travel destinations, points of interest or even people. Often, items being recommended are actually experienced by groups rather than individual users. Therefore, group recommender systems (GRSs) are becoming more and more the focus of research. A detailed survey of the state-of-the-art of GRSs is provided by Masthoff [21].

Current research is primarily focusing on how group members' individual preferences should be aggregated into a group preference model. In [17], Jameson summarized three aggregation approaches: 1) aggregation of the generated individual recommendations; 2) aggregation of individual ratings; and 3) creation of a group preference model. Beside the aggregation approach, the most commonly used aggregation strategies, i.e., methods to aggregate individuals' ratings, or recommendations into a group model are overwhelmingly motivated by the Social Choice Theory. However, Arrow's theorem clearly states that there is no aggregation strategy that outperforms all the other strategies in all the situations. The research in GRSs has shown the same [9].

Thus, the aggregation of preferences and decision-making in a group setting cannot be considered as a function of individuals' preferences only, but also a function of inter-subjects' relations [9]. Moreover, group decisions are often not rational, they cannot always be deduced from group members' individual preferences, and they are not always a result of a majority opinion [12]. Especially, individual satisfaction with the group choice is strongly related with personality and group behavioral attitudes (i.e., Thomas-Kilmann Conflict Resolution Styles [19]) [9, 10]. Therefore, building GRSs requires a better understanding of group dynamics and other concepts that play an important role in group decision-making processes and outcomes. In this paper, we focus on a specific, and yet crucial concept, namely social relationships within groups, and we will explore the role of those relationships for the outcomes of the group decision-making process.

There has been an increasing interest in studying social relationships in groups and teams as it has proven to lead to relevant insights. Various studies have identified a positive impact of social relationships on collaboration and performance in a number of domains, e.g., academic output and interdisciplinary work [16, 20, 34], viability and dynamics of virtual teams in organizations [4, 23], success in sports and e-sports [11, 26, 29] as well as satisfaction and perception of students [3].

Following this line of research, we aim to introduce a stronger focus on social relationships also within the area of GRSs since it can help to enrich our understanding of group dynamics and decision-making outcomes. Therefore, the main contributions of this paper are as follows:

- Providing evidence on whether or not the intra-group social relationships, for "equality matching" types of groups (i.e., all group members are considered as equal), should be used in group preference models;
- Establishing a connection between the intra-group social relationships, and 1) the level of group identification, as well as, 2) the perceived group similarity in terms of preferences;
- Showing how the intra-group social relationships can be used to predict group members' satisfaction with the final group choice.

The rest of the paper is organized as follows: in Section 2 we give an overview of the related work, and we introduce our hypotheses. In Section 3 the methodological approach of the study is illustrated, and analysis variables are defined. In Section 4 the results are presented, and Section 5 comprises the discussion of these results. Finally, in Section 6 we provide conclusions of the current analysis, and outline the future work.

2 RELATED WORK AND HYPOTHESES

Substantial research has been done in GRSs to identify sources of influence in groups, and accordingly adjust the group preference model. Masthoff and Gatt [22], e.g., analyzed emotional contagion and conformity; Ali and Kim [1] defined a group preference model based on the members' activity in the system (i.e., the more item-ratings a group member provided the higher the assigned weight); Berkovsky and Freyne [6] introduced three role-based models similar to the previous one, making a difference by introducing a group context (i.e., the role of a member within a family).

However, relatively few studies have focused on social relationships in GRSs. Quijano-Sanchez et al. [30] used group members' personality and social trust between the pairs of members to address influence in groups. It was demonstrated that the hit-rate for two items in the top-three items list was significantly improved when accounting for both personality and social trust. However, a group model including only social trust performed worse than the baseline approach. In Alina and Schiaffino [2], the authors used three social "factors" to account for the social influence in a group model, i.e., 1) Social trust between pairs of members (as reported by the group members); 2) Social similarity between the pairs of members (i.e., shared interests, extracted from a social network - Facebook); and 3) Social centrality of each group member (extracted from a social network - Facebook). The task that was given to groups was to rate a set of items, which was later used to evaluate the proposed

approach. The authors showed that the best results were obtained when the group model included all three social "factors". Moreover, even when separately used, the improvement of recommendation accuracy was evident, where social trust outperformed social centrality and social centrality outperformed social similarity. Finally, in Gartrell et al.[13], three "group descriptors" were used to determine the best preference aggregation approach for a given group, 1) Social descriptor (i.e., frequency of contact and type of relationship); 2) Expertise descriptor (i.e., the number of item-ratings the group members provided for the preselected set of items); and 3) The dissimilarity descriptor (i.e., average pairwise dissimilarity of group members' item-ratings). The authors concluded that the best aggregation strategy for a) Couples (i.e., groups with strong social relationships) was the most pleasure strategy; b) For acquaintances (i.e., groups with medium strength social relationships) was the average strategy; while c) For new acquaintances (i.e., groups with weak or no social relationships), was the least misery strategy.

In our analysis, we focus on social relationships, specifically, closeness of the group in terms of social relationships, as the characteristic of a group, and social centrality as the characteristic of group members, and their impact on the group decision-making outcomes. However, in our study, the social relationships of group members are explicitly obtained with a questionnaire, therefore, we believe a more accurate representation of within group relations is captured. Our approach is guided by one of the key concepts of social network theory, i.e., the identification of prominent actors in a social network. Therefore, based on the characterization of "prominent actor" in a social network: "the one who is the object of extensive ties, focusing solely on the actor as a recipient" [35], we derive the following two hypotheses:

Hypothesis I: Socially central members of the group are perceived as more influential in the group decision-making process.

Hypothesis II: Socially central members of the group have their individual preferences closer to the final group choice.

Another concept shown to be relevant in GRSs research, due to its significant correlation with choice satisfaction (i.e., individuals' satisfaction with the group choice as the outcome of the group decision-making process), is the concept of group identity [7]. Group / social identity is defined as the "individuals' self-concept derived from their knowledge of their membership to a social group together with the value and emotional significance attached to that membership" [32]. Therefore, an important question is whether or not we can capture group identity with the help of social relationships. To this end, and based on the definition of group identity we derive the following hypotheses:

Hypothesis III-A: Socially central members of the group report higher group identity.

Hypothesis III-B: Participants belonging to socially close groups report higher group identity.

In [5], the authors showed that, beside group identity, also group similarity is significantly related with choice satisfaction. On the one hand, the principle of "homophily", indicates that "people's personal networks are homogeneous with regard to many sociodemographic, behavioral, and intra-personal characteristics" [24]. On the other hand, social influence indicates that change in opinions, attitudes, behaviors of an individual occurs as a result of the tendency to match opinions, attitudes and behaviors of those from the social environment [33]. So, it is natural to assume that closely related groups perceive and have higher group similarity. Therefore, we derive the following hypotheses:

Hypothesis IV-A: Socially central members of the group perceive their groups as more similar with respect to preferences.

Hypothesis IV-B: Participants belonging to socially close groups perceive their groups as more similar with respect to preferences.

Hypothesis IV-C: Participants belonging to socially close groups have higher preference similarity.

Consequently, we assume that those in closely related groups report higher choice satisfaction, and therefore, the last hypotheses are as follows:

Hypothesis V-A: Socially central members of the group report higher choice satisfaction.

Hypothesis V-B: Participants belonging to socially close groups report higher choice satisfaction.

3 METHODOLOGY

3.1 Data collection and data description

The study was initiated in a cooperation with the International Federation for Information Technologies in Travel and Tourism (IFITT) and several universities in Europe. The first implementation of the study took place in 2015 and 2016, with the methodology described in detail in [8]. The new study implementation presented here was enriched with additional aspects of group behavior that are explained in detail in this section.

The data collection process was conducted as a part of regular lectures at TU Wien and University of Sarajevo, and it followed a three-phases structure: 1) a pre-questionnaire phase, 2) group meetings / discussions phase, and 3) a post-questionnaire phase. Prior to the first study phase, the participants were asked to form groups of maximum five members of their choice. Here, we describe data aspects relevant for the analysis presented in this paper.

The pre-questionnaire tapped into participants' individual preferences, and the social relationships within the formed groups.

The *preferences* section requested ten-point ratings (i.e., from 1 - *"Don't like the destination at all"*, to 10 - *"Absolutely like the destination"*) for ten pre-selected European destinations. The destinations were chosen to match ten types of vacation, i.e., 1) Beach & relaxing (Porquerolles, France), 2) Culture, architecture & museums (Riga, Latvia), 3) Nightlife & parties (Budapest, Hungary), 4) Shopping (Serravalle Scrivia, Italy), 5) Great food & meeting local people (Girona, Spain), 6) Lakes & mountains (Lake Bled, Slovenia), 7) Extreme sports & thrill-seeking (Interlaken, Switzerland), 8) Eco-tourism (Snaefellsnes, Island), 9) Exploration of the scenic wild regions (Portree, Scotland), and 10) Archaeological sites (Segovia, Spain), which were identified based on literature review [14, 15, 25, 27, 36]. The goal of having well defined types of destinations in the choice set was an attempt to increase the diversity and conflict of preferences in groups.

The *social relationships* section contained three questions, for which participants provided answers for each fellow members of their group:

(1) Duration of the relationship (on a five-point scale: 1 - *"For less than six months"*; 2 - *"For more than six months, but less than a year"*; 3 - *"For more than a year, but less than three*

years"; 4 - *"For more than three years, but less than five years"*; 5 - *"For more than five years"*);

(2) Frequency of the contact (on a five-point scale: 1 - *"Very infrequently"*; 2 - *"Somewhat infrequently"*; 3 - *"About average"*; 4 - *"Somewhat frequently"*; 5 - *"Very frequently"*);

(3) Emotional proximity (on a ten-point scale: from 1 - *"not emotionally close at all"*; to 10 - *"very emotionally close"*).

In the second phase, the groups were given a realistic travel scenario, and asked as a group to choose one destination (from the set of destinations introduced previously in the pre-questionnaire) that they as a group would like to visit together, and a second one in case the first one becomes unavailable.

In the post-questionnaire, participants were asked for:

- Group choice, i.e., the first and the second destination selected by the group;
- Participants' individual satisfaction with the group choice, evaluated with four statements, e.g., *"I like the destination that we have chosen."*, *"The chosen destination fits my preference."*, etc. (further referred as the choice satisfaction, abbreviation *CHOICE_SAT*);
- Participants' individual group identification, evaluated with four statements, e.g., *"I see myself as a member of this group."*, *"I am glad to be a member of this group."*, etc. (further referred as the group identity, abbreviation *GROUP_IDENT*);
- Participants' individual perception of preferences similarity within the group, evaluated with two statements, i.e., *"I considered myself similar to the other members in my group in terms of our preferences."*, and *"I considered the other members in my group to be similar to each other in terms of their preference"* (further referred to as the perceived group similarity, abbreviation *GROUP_SIM*);
- Participants' individual perception of influence that the fellow group members had on their acceptance of the final group choice, evaluated with one statement, i.e., *"To what extent did each of your group members influence your acceptance of the final group choice?"*, and a five-point scale: 1 - *"No influence at all"*, to 5 - *"Strongly influenced"*.

For the statements related to the choice satisfaction, group identity, and group similarity, the participants were asked to provide their level of agreement on a five-point Likert scale, from 1 - *"Strongly disagree"*, to 5 - *"Strongly agree"*.

The collected data consisted of 150 (i.e, 38% from TU Wien and 62% from University of Sarajevo; 75 male, 75 female) participants in 41 groups of two (6 groups), three (8), four (21) and five (6) group members. The minimum, maximum and mean age of the participants were respectively, 19, 48 and 24.51, with the standard deviation of 4.096. The ratings of the ten destinations were mostly positive, with more than 60% scoring seven or higher, and only around 10% scoring three or lower (see Figure 1). The vast majority of participants reported a high choice satisfaction (the mean reported value was 4.5), strong group identity (mean of 4.1) and moderate perceived group similarity (mean of 3.8), see Table 1.

3.2 Networks' construction

Based on the social relationships data of the pre-questionnaire a *social network* was built for each group. Since the participants

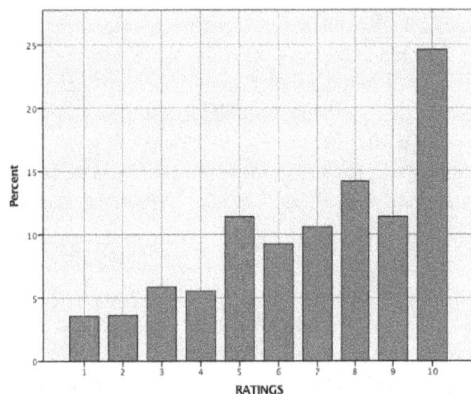

Figure 1: Ratings distribution

Table 1: Decision-process outputs

Variable	MIN	MAX	Mean	Std. Dev
Choice satisfaction	2.50	5.00	4.51	.51
Group identity	2.25	5.00	4.10	.65
Group similarity	1.00	5.00	3.77	.76

provided answers for each fellow group member, and two members might have reported different levels of social closeness to each other, the networks are directed. Moreover, each edge between two members is weighted according to the average value of the answers provided for the three questions. An illustrated example of a group social network is shown in Figure 2a. Each node represents a group member, the nodes are sized (and numbered) according to their In-Degree Centrality (see subsection 3.3), and the edges are thickened according to the weight assigned to them.

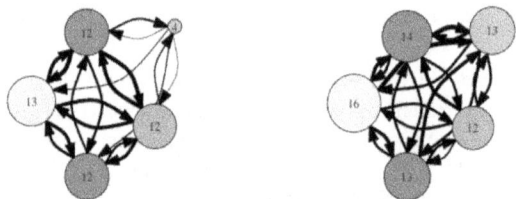

(a) Social network   (b) Influence network

Figure 2: Example of one group

Based on perceived influence section from the post-questionnaire another network was constructed for each group, which we will refer to as the *perceived influence network*. Again, participants were asked about the level of influence that each fellow group member exerted on them, and of course, two members might have reported different levels of influence between each other, therefore the network is directed. Moreover, the edges between members are weighted according to the reported level of influence. For the same group as before, the perceived influence network is illustrated in Figure 2b. Each node represents a group member, the nodes are sized according to their Out-Degree Centrality (see Subsection 3.3),

and the edges are thickened according to the weight assigned to them.

3.3 Variable definitions

In the next step, we define different types of variables for testing our hypotheses.

Network variables. From the social networks and the perceived influence networks of the groups, basic weighted network measurements were calculated. Therefore, two levels were considered, i.e., the individual level, capturing each group member separately, and the group level, capturing the group as a whole. In Table 2 the resulting network variables for the two networks are listed, and in the following text we explain them in more details.

Table 2: Network variables

Variable	Definition
INDEGREE	Normalized In-Degree Centrality score from the social network
INDEGREE_CENTRAL	$\begin{cases} 1, & INDEGREE > median(INDEGREE) \\ 0, & \text{otherwise} \end{cases}$
OUTDEGREE	Normalized Out-Degree Centrality score from the social network
DEGREE	Normalized Degree Centrality score from the social network
DEGREE_CENTRAL	$\begin{cases} 1, & DEGREE > median(DEGREE) \\ 0, & \text{otherwise} \end{cases}$
PAGE_RANK	Page-Rank Centrality score from the social network
CLOSENESS	Degree score for the group as a whole from the social network
CLOSE_GR	$\begin{cases} 1, & CLOSENESS > median(CLOSENESS) \\ 0, & \text{otherwise} \end{cases}$
INFL	Normalized Out-Degree Centrality score from the perceived influence network
INFLUENTIAL	$\begin{cases} 1, & INFL > median(INFL) \\ 0, & \text{otherwise} \end{cases}$

The *In-Degree Centrality* of a group member measures a member's prestige in the group. It indicates how a member is perceived by her fellow group members and what status that member has in the group. The In-Degree Centrality is calculated as the sum of the weights of all in-links, i.e., the edges directed to that node.

The *Out-Degree Centrality* of a group member measures how a member perceives others in the group, in the sense of how close she feels to them. The Out-Degree Centrality is calculated as the sum of the weights of all out-links, i.e., the edges from that node directed to others.

The *Degree Centrality* of a group member in a directed graph is the combination of the In-Degree and Out-Degree, and represents the overall status of a member in the group (i.e., how she feels about the group, and how the group feels about her). The Degree Centrality is therefore calculated as the sum of In-Degree and Out-Degree scores.

The *Page-Rank Centrality* is another measure of a member's prestige in the group. The Page-Rank Centrality score of a node is not only determined by its number and weights of in-links but also by the Page-Rank Centrality scores of all nodes pointing at it [28]. Thus, it extends the concept of In-Degree centrality by also taking the prestige of the connections into account, i.e., a node can have a high prestige either because it has many in-links, or because nodes with a high prestige themselves are pointing at it, or both.

Clearly, the centrality measure scores that a group member can achieve depends on the group size (i.e., the larger the group, the more edges there will be in the network). Therefore, to be able to compare members belonging to groups of different sizes, the centrality scores were normalized accordingly (i.e., the centrality scores were divided by $n - 1$ where n is the size of the group).

Furthermore, in order to capture the social closeness of the group as a whole, we define a *Closeness* score at the group level as the mean value of the weighted edges in the network.

Distance variables. From the members' individual preferences and the group choices, metrics were calculated to capture how much the individual preferences differed from the group choice.

Distance$_1$ for a group member measures the distance between the member's individual preferences and the first group choice. It is calculated using the Kendall-tau distance between the first group choice and the rank of that destination in the group members' individual preference list:

$$\underset{mem_n \in G_q}{DISTANCE_1} = rank_{mem_n}(first\_choice_{G_q}) - 1$$

Where G_q is a group, mem_n a member of the group, and $rank_{mem_n}(first\_choice_{G_q})$ is the rank position in the list of mem_n of the first choice of G_q.

Similarly, *Distance$_2$* for a group member measures the distance between the member's individual preferences and the second group choice, in the same way as the previous measure:

$$\underset{mem_n \in G_q}{DISTANCE_2} = rank_{mem_n}(second\_choice_{G_q}) - 1$$

Where $rank_{mem_n}(second\_choice_{G_q})$ is the rank position in the list of mem_n of the second choice of G_q.

One more variable was introduced that captures whether or not the preferences of a group member were close to the group choice or not. Those whose preferences were close we call *Winners* of the decision-making process.

To summarize, the set of variables that capture differences between group members' individual and group preferences is given in Table 3.

Table 3: Difference variables

Variable	Definition
$DISTANCE_1$	Distance of member's preference to first group choice
$DISTANCE_2$	Distance of member's preference to second group choice
$WINNER$	$\begin{cases} 1, & DISTANCE_1 < median(DISTANCE_1) \\ 0, & \text{otherwise} \end{cases}$

Diversity variables. Finally, to capture the diversity / similarity of the group with respect to explicit preferences (i.e., the ratings of the

ten destinations), two measures were introduced, 1) *Group Euclidean Similarity* (*EUCL_SIM*), and 2) *Group Top-Choices Diversity* (*#TOP*). The Group Euclidean Similarity captures the similarity of the group over the whole choice-set (i.e., the ten destinations). In the first step the average value of the group members' pairwise Euclidean distances between destinations ratings is calculated:

$$EUCL\_DIST_{G_q} = \frac{2}{n(n-1)} * \sum_{j=1}^{n-1} \sum_{i=j+1}^{n} \underset{mem_j, mem_i \in G_q}{Euclidean} (mem_j, mem_i)$$

In the second step, $EUCL\_DIST_{G_q}$ is transformed into the similarity measure *EUCL_SIM*, and in further analysis used as such.

$$EUCL\_SIM = max(EUCL\_DIST_{G_q}) - EUCL\_DIST_{G_q}$$

The Group Top-Choice Diversity captures the diversity of the group over the group members' individual top choices (not the whole choice-set). The measure simply counts the number of different top choices that occur in the group. Since the number of different top choices in the group largely depends on the size of the group, the measure is normalized according to the group size:

$$\#TOP = \frac{|\{TopChoice(mem_i)\}|}{n}, i = 1..n \wedge n = GroupSize$$

To summarize, the set of variables that capture similarity / diversity of the group in terms of preferences is given in Table 4.

Table 4: Diversity variables

Variable	Definition
$EUCL\_SIM$	Group Euclidean Similarity
$EUCL\_SIMILAR$	$\begin{cases} 1, & EUCL\_SIM > median(EUCL\_SIM) \\ 0, & \text{otherwise} \end{cases}$
$\#TOP$	Group Top-Choice Diversity
$\#TOP\_DIVERSE$	$\begin{cases} 1, & \#TOP > median(\#TOP) \\ 0, & \text{otherwise} \end{cases}$

To test our hypotheses non-parametric tests were used, i.e., Independent-Samples Median Test, and Kruskal-Wallis Test. The choice was made based on the results of Kolmogorov-Smirnov and Shapiro-Wilk normality tests of our variables.

4 RESULTS

For the sake of clarity, Table 5 shows which set of variables were used to test which hypotheses.

Hypothesis I: **Are socially central members perceived as more influential?** Independent samples tests showed no significant difference in perceived influence between socially central and non-central members of the group. However, a significant and positive correlation was found between social centrality (i.e., the In-Degree Centrality) and perceived influence ($r = .307^{***}$, $p < .001$). This provides some support for Hypothesis I.

As our hypothesis is partially supported by the significant correlation, we decided to further analyze the issue. Clearly, groups that are diverse with respect to their preferences might need actors

Table 5: Hypotheses and variables

Variables	Hypothesis								
	I	II	III-A	III-B	IV-A	IV-B	IV-C	V-A	V-B
INDEGREE	✓								
INDEGREE_CENTRAL	✓	✓	✓					✓	
INFL	✓								
EUCL_SIMILAR	✓	✓					✓		
#TOP_DIVERSE	✓	✓					✓		
PAGE_RANK		✓							
DISTANCE$_1$		✓							
DISTANCE$_2$		✓							
INFLUENTIAL		✓							
DEGREE_CENTRAL					✓				
GROUP_IDENT			✓	✓					
CLOSENESS									✓
CLOSE_GR				✓		✓	✓		✓
GROUP_SIM					✓	✓			
OUTDEGREE								✓	
CHOICE_SAT								✓	✓
WINNER								✓	

with stronger influence to come up with the final group choice. Therefore, the same hypothesis was tested for the set of groups who do not have similar preferences as captured with the Group Euclidean Similarity (i.e., $EUCL\_SIMILAR = 0$), and for groups who have diverse preferences as captured with the Group Top-Choices Diversity (i.e., $\#TOP\_DIVERSE = 1$).

No significant differences were found for groups who do not have similar preferences as captured by the Group Euclidean Similarity. However, the Independent-Samples Median Test ($p = .028$) showed that socially central members of diverse groups as captured with the Group Top-Choices Diversity are perceived as significantly more influential, see Figure 3.

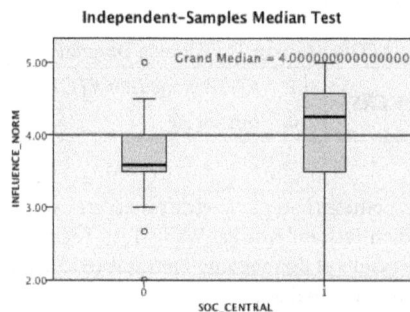

Figure 3: Differences in distribution of perceived influence for socially central and non-central members of diverse groups

Hypothesis II: Do socially central members get their way more? Independent samples tests showed no evidence that socially central group members have their individual preferences closer to the first or the second group choice (i.e., their ranking of the first and second group choice is not higher than of those who are not socially central). However, a significant and positive, but low correlation was found between the Page-Rank Centrality and group members' distance to the second group choice ($r = .163^*, p < .05$).

As for the previous hypothesis, again we were interested if socially central members of the diverse groups would have their individual preferences closer to the final group choice. Even though, we did confirm that socially central members of diverse groups are perceived as significantly more influential, the independent samples tests did not show any difference for the distance between their individual preferences and the final choices of the group. However, the correlation between the Page-Rank Centrality and group members' distance to the second group choice was emphasized ($r = .374^*, p < .05$) for diverse groups as captured with the Group Top-Choices Diversity (i.e., $\#TOP\_DIVERSE = 1$).

Additionally, we also tested whether or not those who were perceived as influential had their preferences closer to the first group choice. The Kruskal-Wallis Test showed that influential group members, as they were perceived, did not have their preferences closer to the first group choice, but their preferences were significantly closer to the second group choice ($p = .007$), see Figure 4.

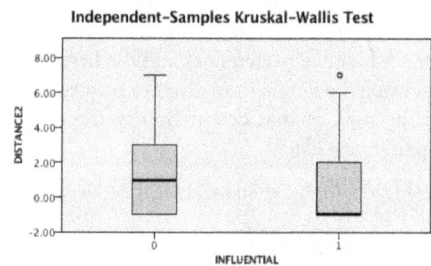

Figure 4: Differences in distribution of members' distance to the second group choice for influential and non-influential group members

Hypothesis III-A: Do socially central members identify stronger with their groups?
The Kruskal-Wallis Test showed that socially central group members do report significantly higher group identity ($p = .001$), see Figure 5.

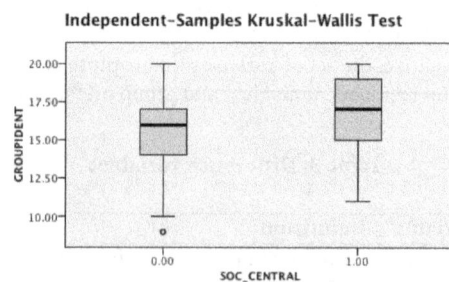

Figure 5: Differences in distribution of the group identity for the socially central and non-central group members

Hypothesis III-B: Do members from socially close groups identify stronger with their groups? The Kruskal-Wallis Test again showed that members from socially close groups do report significantly higher group identity ($p = .000$), see Figure 6.

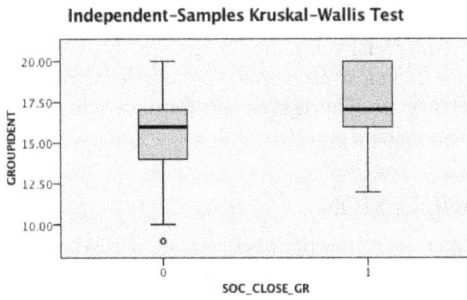

Figure 6: Differences in distribution of the group identity for the socially close and non-close groups

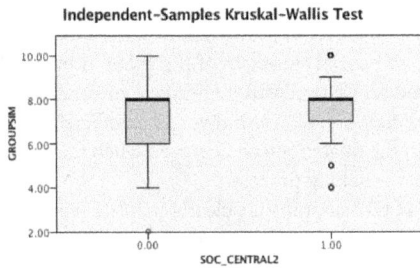

Figure 7: Perceived similarity distribution differences for socially central and non-central members of the group

Hypothesis IV-A: Do socially central group members perceive their groups as more similar? The Kruskal-Wallis Test showed that socially central group members (i.e., the Degree Centrality) do perceive their group similarity significantly differently than socially non-central group members ($p = 0.008$), see Figure 7.

Hypothesis IV-B: Do members from socially close groups perceive their groups as more similar? Group members belonging to the socially close groups do perceive their groups as significantly more similar ($p = .019$), see Figure 8.

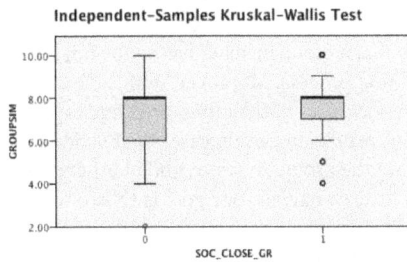

Figure 8: Perceived similarity distribution differences for socially close and non-close groups

Hypothesis IV-C: Do members from socially close groups have more similar preferences? Independent samples tests showed no significant difference of preferences similarity as captured with the Group Euclidean Similarity between socially close and non-close groups. However, the Independent-Samples Median Test ($p = .006$)

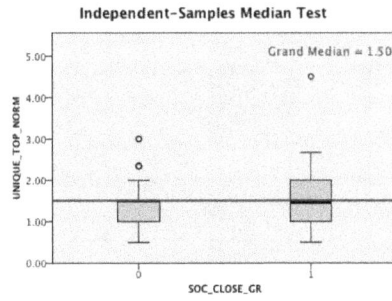

Figure 9: Differences in distribution of group preference diversity for socially close and non-close groups

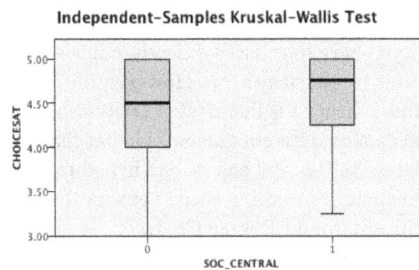

Figure 10: Choice satisfaction distribution differences for socially central and non-central members of the group

showed significant difference in distribution of the preferences diversity as captured with the Group Top-Choices Diversity for socially close and non-close groups, see Figure 9. Moreover, a significant and positive correlation between the social closeness of the group and the similarity of group preferences as captured with the Group Euclidean Similarity measure was found ($r = .210 * *$, $p < .01$). Therefore, the more socially close a group is the more likely it is that the preferences of group members are similar.

Hypothesis V-A: Are socially central group members more satisfied? The Kruskal-Wallis Test showed that socially central group members are significantly more satisfied ($p = 0.034$), see Figure 10. The test ($p = .032$) also showed that this was true even for those group members who *"lost"* in the decision-making process according to their individual preferences distance from the first group choice (i.e., $WINNER = 0$), see Figure 11.

Interestingly, a significant positive correlation was also found between the social network Out-Degree Centrality (not only the In-Degree Centrality) and the choice satisfaction ($r = .335^{**}, p < .01$).

Hypothesis V-B: Are members from socially close groups more satisfied? Independent samples tests showed no significant difference of the choice satisfaction for members from socially close and non-close groups. However, a significant and positive correlation was found between social closeness of the group and the mean choice satisfaction of the group ($r = .287^{**}, p < .01$). Meaning, the stronger the social relationships of the group members are, the higher the choice satisfaction of the group as a whole will be.

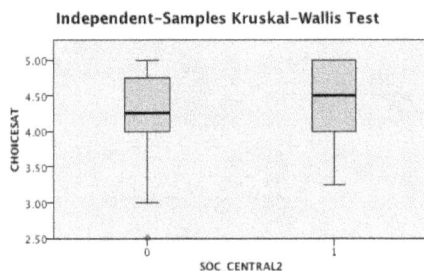

Figure 11: Choice satisfaction distribution differences for socially central and non-central *"losers"*

5 DISCUSSION

Numerous different directions and theories in the area of social network analysis have introduced different implications of the network structures for social systems. However, the common thread that unites these theories is that a set of relationships among a set of actors will explain different outcomes better than individual or group attributes [3]. Our first and second hypotheses were derived from the elementary concepts of social network theory. Social centrality, specifically the In-Degree Centrality is, by its definition, the measure of a subject's prominence or prestige in the network. Moreover, the motivation can also be found in GRSs research, even though in a low number of studies [2, 13]. Our results indicate that socially central group members are perceived as significantly more influential, especially in groups that are diverse in terms of group members' preferences. Nevertheless, socially central group members, even though perceived as more influential, did not have their way more often, i.e., their individual preferences were not closer to the group preferences. This was partially true only for the second group choice.

Obviously this was not expected, and it raises a question about the meaning of social relationships and social centrality in such intra-group social networks. In a group decision-making process, a group member can behold various types of roles [12], either a *"task role - performs behaviors that promote completion of tasks"* (e.g., leader, expert, organizer) or a *"relationship role - performs behaviors that improve the nature and quality of interpersonal relations among members,"* (e.g., coordinator, supporter, energizer). Therefore, socially central group members, could have been perceived as more influential due to their role in the decision-making process, e.g., an organizer, a coordinator, or a supporter, but in essence their individual preferences were not closer to the group preferences.

This brings us to the second part of our analysis (Hypotheses III to V), where the focus is more profound, i.e., the meaning of the social relationships for other group related concepts that, as research showed [5, 7, 12], are of great importance for GRSs as well. The results indicate that social relationships, as captured with the pre-questionnaire, are a useful measure of the group identity level that members feel about each other. Moreover, even though the participants were asked about group similarity only in terms of their travel preferences, we observed that social closeness of the group is strongly related with the perceived similarity as such. In addition, we also show that socially close groups truly have their preferences more similar than non-close groups. This result, is in-line with the

theory of *"homophily"*, and social influence. Finally, we provide evidence that social centrality, in terms of both In-Degree and Out-Degree Centrality plays an important role for group members' choice satisfaction. This is even true for those who have *"lost"* in the decision-making process.

6 CONCLUSION

In this paper the connections between social relationships, social centrality and different outcomes of the group decision-making process (i.e., group choice, choice satisfaction, group identity, and perceived group similarity of preferences) are analyzed. We show that socially central members of the group are perceived as more influential in the group decision-making process, but they do not get their way more often. Moreover, social relationships can be used to grasp the level of group identity that members feel about each other, and social closeness of the group is even related with the perceived group similarity in terms of preferences. Finally, we demonstrate that socially central group members are significantly happier with the final group choice, even when they are the *"losers"* in the decision-making process.

In terms of GRSs our results clearly indicate how important it is to include social relationships in group preference models. Indeed, we did not provide evidence that social centrality should be used, for instance, to generate weights assigned to group members in the group preference model. Nevertheless, choice satisfaction is one of the crucial outputs of the group decision-making process, and it should be addressed in a GRS as such. To this end, it is clear that social relationships can be used to predict individual group members' choice satisfaction as well as the overall group satisfaction. In this way, social centrality and social closeness can be used as a measure of group members' resilience to dissatisfaction. For example, we can define a constraint interval in which the distance between individuals' preferences and the group recommendation should reside, based on group members' social centrality and social closeness of the whole groups.

In our future work, we plan to further investigate other types of networks that occur in small groups, and their usability in GRSs. For instance, in [18] the authors have shown a strong relationship between centrality in the socio-cognitive network of the group and the influence that a group member has on the final outcomes of the decision-making process. Moreover, in this paper we introduced two diversity measures of the group preferences, and as we could observe in our results, in certain cases the Euclidean measure was able to capture the group diversity, and in others the Top-choices measure. In future analysis, our goal is to explore how different preference diversity measures can be used in GRSs. For example, whether or not we can use some diversity measure, or a combination of diversity measures, to choose a specific preference aggregation strategy for the group at hand. Clearly, all the different aspects, together with the results about intra-group social relationships, add up to designing more effective GRSs.

The scope of our study lies in the travel and tourism domain. Moreover, the type of groups that we investigated is the *"equality matching"* type. Also, the data we used had no sparsity. Thus, more investigations are needed to see if the results can be generalized to other domains, other group types, and data sets with more sparsity.

REFERENCES

[1] I. Ali and S. W. Kim. 2015. Group recommendations: approaches and evaluation. In *Proceedings of the 9th International Conference on Ubiquitous Information Management and Communication*. ACM, 105.

[2] I. Alina Christensen and S. Schiaffino. 2014. Social influence in group recommender systems. *Online Information Review* 38, 4 (2014), 524–542.

[3] T. T. Baldwin, M. D. Bedell, and J. L. Johnson. 1997. The social fabric of a team-based MBA program: Network effects on student satisfaction and performance. *Academy of management journal* 40, 6 (1997), 1369–1397.

[4] P. Balkundi and D. A. Harrison. 2006. Ties, leaders, and time in teams: Strong inference about network structureâĂŹs effects on team viability and performance. *Academy of Management Journal* 49, 1 (2006), 49–68.

[5] L. Baltrunas, T. Makcinskas, and F. Ricci. 2010. Group recommendations with rank aggregation and collaborative filtering. In *Proceedings of the fourth ACM conference on Recommender systems, RecSys'10*. Barcelona, Spain, 119–126.

[6] S. Berkovsky and J. Freyne. 2010. Group-based recipe recommendations: analysis of data aggreagation strategies. In *Proceedings of the 4th ACM conference on Recommender systems*. 111–118.

[7] A. Delic and J. Neidhardt. 2017. A Comprehensive Approach to Group Recommendations in the Travel and Tourism Domain. In *Adjunct Publication of the 25th Conference on User Modeling, Adaptation and Personalization*. ACM, 11–16.

[8] A. Delic, J. Neidhardt, T. N. Nguyen, and F. Ricci. 2018. An observational user study for group recommender systems in the tourism domain. *Information Technology & Tourism* (19 Feb 2018).

[9] A. Delic, J. Neidhardt, T. N. Nguyen, F. Ricci, L. Rook, H. Werthner, and M. Zanker. 2016. Observing Group Decision Making Processes. In *Proceedings of the tenth ACM conference on Recommender systems, RecSys'16*.

[10] A. Delic, J. Neidhardt, L. Rook, H. Werthner, and M. Zanker. 2017. Researching Individual Satisfaction with Group Decisions in Tourism: Experimental Evidence. In *Information and Communication Technologies in Tourism 2017*. Springer, 73–85.

[11] J. Duch, J. S. Waitzman, and journal=PloS one volume=5 number=6 pages=e10937 year=2010 publisher=Public Library of Science Amaral, L. A. N. [n. d.]. Quantifying the performance of individual players in a team activity. ([n. d.]).

[12] D.R. Forsyth. 2014. *Group Dynamics* (6th ed.). Wadsworth Cengage Learning.

[13] M. Gartrell, X. Xing, Q. Lv, A. Beach, R. Han, S. Mishra, and K. Seada. 2010. Enhancing group recommendation by incorporating social relationship interactions. In *Proceedings of the 16th ACM international conference on Supporting group work*. ACM, 97–106.

[14] H. Gibson and A. Yiannakis. 2002. Tourist roles: Needs and the lifecourse. *Annals of tourism research* 29(2) (2002), 358–383.

[15] U. Gretzel, N. Mitsche, Y.-H. Hwang, and D. R. Fesenmaier. 2004. Tell me who you are and I will tell you where to go: Use of travel personalities in destination recommendation systems. *Information Technology & Tourism* 7, 1 (2004), 3–12.

[16] R. Guimera, B. Uzzi, J. Spiro, and L. A. N. Amaral. 2005. Team assembly mechanisms determine collaboration network structure and team performance. *Science* 308, 5722 (2005), 697–702.

[17] A. Jameson. 2004. More than the sum of its members: challenges for group recommender systems. In *Proceedings of the working conference on Advanced visual interfaces*. 48–54.

[18] T. Kameda, Y. Ohtsubo, and M. Takezawa. 1997. Centrality in sociocognitive networks and social influence: An illustration in a group decision-making context. *Journal of personality and social psychology* 73, 2 (1997), 296.

[19] R H Kilmann and K W Thomas. 1977. Developing a forced-choice measure of conflict-handling behavior: The" MODE" instrument. *Educational and psychological measurement* 37, 2 (1977), 309–325.

[20] A. Lungeanu, Y. Huang, and N. S. Contractor. 2014. Understanding the assembly of interdisciplinary teams and its impact on performance. *Journal of informetrics* 8, 1 (2014), 59–70.

[21] J. Masthoff. 2015. Group recommender systems: aggregation, satisfaction and group attributes. In *Recommender Systems Handbook* (2nd ed.), F. Ricci, L. Rokach, and B. Shapira (Eds.). Springer, 743–776.

[22] J. Masthoff and A. Gatt. 2006. In pursuit of satisfaction and the prevention of embarrassment: affective state in group recommender systems. In *User Modeling and User-Adapted Interaction*, Vol. 16. Springer, 281–319.

[23] M. L. Maznevski and K. M. Chudoba. 2000. Bridging space over time: Global virtual team dynamics and effectiveness. *Organization science* 11, 5 (2000), 473–492.

[24] M. McPherson, L. Smith-Lovin, and J. M. Cook. 2001. Birds of a feather: Homophily in social networks. *Annual review of sociology* 27, 1 (2001), 415–444.

[25] G. Moscardo, A. M. Morrison, P. L. Pearce, C.-T. Lang, and J. T. O'Leary. 1996. Understanding vacation destination choice through travel motivation and activities. *Journal of Vacation Marketing* 2, 2 (1996), 109–122.

[26] J. Neidhardt, Y. Huang, and N. Contractor. 2015. Team vs. team: Success factors in a multiplayer online battle arena game. In *Academy of Management Proceedings*, Vol. 1. Academy of Management, 18725.

[27] J. Neidhardt, R. Schuster, L. Seyfang, and H. Werthner. 2014. Eliciting the users' unknown preferences. In *Proceedings of the 8th ACM Conference on Recommender systems*. ACM, 2645767, 309–312. https://doi.org/10.1145/2645710.2645767

[28] L. Page, S. Brin, R. Motwani, and T. Winograd. 1999. *The PageRank citation ranking: Bringing order to the web*. Technical Report. Stanford InfoLab.

[29] N. Pobiedina, J. Neidhardt, M. d. C. Calatrava Moreno, and H. Werthner. 2013. Ranking factors of team success. In *Proceedings of the 22nd International Conference on World Wide Web (WWW '13 Companion)*. ACM, 1185–1194.

[30] L. Quijano-Sanchez, J. A. Recio-Garcia, B. Diaz-Agudo, and G. Jimenez-Diaz. 2013. Social factors in group recommender systems. *ACM Transactions on Intelligent Systems and Technology (TIST)* 4, 1 (2013), 8.

[31] F. Ricci, L. Rokach, and B. Shapira. 2015. *Recommender Systems Handbook* (2nd ed.). Springer US, Boston, MA, Chapter Recommender Systems: Introduction and Challenges, 1–34. https://doi.org/10.1007/978-1-4899-7637-6

[32] H. Tajfel. 2010. *Social identity and intergroup relations*. Cambridge University Press.

[33] J. C. Turner. 1991. *Social influence*. Thomson Brooks/Cole Publishing Co.

[34] B. Uzzi, S. Mukherjee, M. Stringer, and B. Jones. 2013. Atypical combinations and scientific impact. *Science* 342, 6157 (2013), 468–472.

[35] S. Wasserman and K. Faust. 1994. *Social network analysis: Methods and applications*. Vol. 8. Cambridge university press.

[36] A. Yiannakis and H. Gibson. 1992. Roles tourists play. *Annals of tourism Research* 19, 2 (1992), 287–303.

Modeling Learners' Cognitive and Affective States to Scaffold SRL in Open-Ended Learning Environments

Anabil Munshi
Institute for Software
Integrated Systems
Vanderbilt University
Nashville, TN, USA
anabil.munshi@vanderbilt.edu

Ramkumar Rajendran
Institute for Software
Integrated Systems
Vanderbilt University
Nashville, TN, USA
ramkumar.rajendran@vanderbilt.edu

Jaclyn Ocumpaugh
Penn Center for Learning Analytics
University of Pennsylvania
Philadelphia, PA, USA
jlocumpaugh@gmail.com

Gautam Biswas
Institute for Software
Integrated Systems
Vanderbilt University
Nashville, TN, USA
gautam.biswas@vanderbilt.edu

Ryan S. Baker
University of Pennsylvania
Philadelphia, PA, USA
ryanshaunbaker@gmail.com

Luc Paquette
University of Illinois at
Urbana-Champaign
Champaign, IL, USA
lpaq@illinois.edu

ABSTRACT

The relationship between learners' cognitive and affective states has become a topic of increased interest, especially because it is an important component of self-regulated learning (SRL) processes. This paper studies sixth grade students' SRL processes as they work in Betty's Brain, an agent-based open-ended learning environment (OELE). In this environment, students learn science topics by building causal models. Our analyses combine observational data on student affect with log files of students' interactions within the OELE. Preliminary analyses show that two relatively infrequent affective states, boredom and delight, show especially marked differences among high and low performing students. Further analysis shows that many of these differences occur after receiving feedback from the virtual agents in the Betty's Brain environment. We discuss the implications of these differences and how they can be used to construct adaptive personalized scaffolds.

ACM Reference format:
A. Munshi, R. Rajendran, J. Ocumpaugh, G. Biswas, R. S. Baker, and L. Paquette. 2018. Modeling Learners' Cognitive and Affective States to Scaffold SRL in Open-Ended Learning Environments. In *Proceedings of ACM UMAP conference, Singapore, July 2018 (UMAP'18), 8 pages.* https://doi.org/10.1145/3209219.3209241

KEYWORDS

Cognitive and affective states, self-regulated learning, open-ended learning environments, affect recognition, adaptive scaffolding

1 INTRODUCTION

Researchers have highlighted the importance of modeling and scaffolding students' self-regulated learning (SRL) processes to improve their learning effectiveness in computer-based learning environments. SRL theories focus on how the regulation of cognitive, metacognitive, affective and motivational processes relate to student learning [1, 23, 28, 30-34]. SRL has been studied in a wide variety of contexts, including those where students are learning complex science phenomena [26]. Analyzing the interactions between students' cognitive and affective processes in open-ended learning environments (OELEs) can help us tailor these environments to provide personalized adaptive scaffolds [2] that make the learning more effective and engaging.

OELEs provide users with complex learning goals and a set of tools that support knowledge acquisition, solution construction, and solution checking [5]. Learners have choices in the way they use these tools to accomplish their learning and problem-solving goals. While these environments encourage exploration, strategic thinking, and developing monitoring skills, the open-ended nature of OELEs can make the process of tracking and interpreting learners' strategic and regulatory behaviors a challenging task. At the same time, it is essential to understand learners' behaviors to provide them with appropriate feedback when they encounter difficulties in achieving their learning goals in these environments.

This paper examines students' cognitive and affective states as they work with Betty's Brain [16], an OELE where students learn about scientific phenomena by building causal maps of complex science topics. From our classroom studies, we derive empirical evidence of how students' cognition and affect interplay is influenced by their learning activities and interactions with the agents in the learning environment. These findings provide us with information on how students' regulatory skills unfold in OELEs, allowing us to consider how adaptive scaffolding can be appropriately deployed to better support learning and performance.

2 BACKGROUND

Self-regulated learning (SRL) models seek to explain the recursive nature of students' behavioral, cognitive and metacognitive processes in learning [29-30], emphasizing the roles of self and external feedback on the regulation of these processes. Later versions of Winne's model of SRL [29], which has been empirically supported by several studies (cf., review in [11]), include affective states. Several other SRL researchers [10, 23, 32] also point to affect as an important component of SRL.

The role of affect in SRL presents unique modeling challenges, as do the techniques typically employed to study them [20]. For example, retrospective self-reports rely on the accuracy of student memory [6]. Coarse-grained log-file measures that trace students' activities during the learning task do not accurately reflect affective processes, though more fine-grained detectors [e.g. 3] may be more relevant. Reflection methods that use self-assessment to help students plan and understand their actions (e.g., learning diaries) often annoy students because they interrupt learning activities.

The relationship between cognition and affect has been studied broadly [4, 24], but also specifically within academic contexts, where epistemic emotions like boredom, confusion, delight and frustration are the focus [21]. Several researchers have modeled affect dynamics among learners [e.g., 19], showing links that complement predictions from other theories of learning. For example, the observed link from frustration to boredom (where the learner shifts from an activating emotion to a deactivating one) matches the forced-effort theory of boredom [15].

Research also suggests that in demanding achievement settings, learners' effort and achievement are determined by their perceived task difficulty and ability beliefs [27]. Bridging the gap between task demand and learner capabilities can increase self-efficacy and reduce negative affective experiences like boredom [22]. This calls for adaptive scaffolding to help deal with task complexity and regulate affect by providing support based on cognitive and affective experiences in specific task contexts.

To design such scaffolds, it helps to understand how learners' cognitive and affective behaviors interact with their performance on different tasks within the learning environment. This study combines log file analysis with field observations to study the links between learners cognitive and affective states as they perform different activities in the Betty's Brain environment [5, 13].

3 BETTY'S BRAIN

3.1 Learning-by-Teaching in Betty's Brain

Betty's Brain uses a learning-by-teaching paradigm to help middle school students develop cognitive and metacognitive processes as they build causal models of scientific processes to teach Betty, a virtual agent [13]. Students have access to a number of learning

resources including an online hypermedia science book that covers domain content, and a "teacher's guide" that provides suggestions on how to teach Betty by constructing and reasoning with causal maps. Learners can also seek help from the mentor agent, Mr. Davis, who tracks students' activities and performance (i.e., how well Betty is doing), and provides information on effective teaching and map debugging strategies.

Students can further probe Betty's understanding by asking her to explain her answers to questions they formulate, or by asking her to take quizzes administered by Mr. Davis that evaluate the current state of the map. Through this feedback, students can assess Betty's learning, (which reflects their own knowledge of the science concepts and processes), and then perform relevant activities to improve Betty's and their own knowledge.

3.2 Conversations with the Teachable and Mentor Agents

Students' interactions with the mentor agent, Mr. Davis, can be initiated by either Mr. Davis or the student. These conversations can be further classified as: (1) *Progress reports*, where Mr. Davis periodically provides feedback (e.g., praise if the student is doing well i.e., the map score is increasing, or suggestions on how the student could improve their performance e.g., by reading specific pages in the resources); and (2) *Post-Quiz Hints*, where Mr. Davis analyzes the quiz results and provides hints to help the student improve their causal map. Such hints may be direct (e.g., *"You are missing a link from precipitation to condensation. You may add it to your map."*) or indirect (e.g., *"You should go and read the page on Droughts and Water Cycle."*).

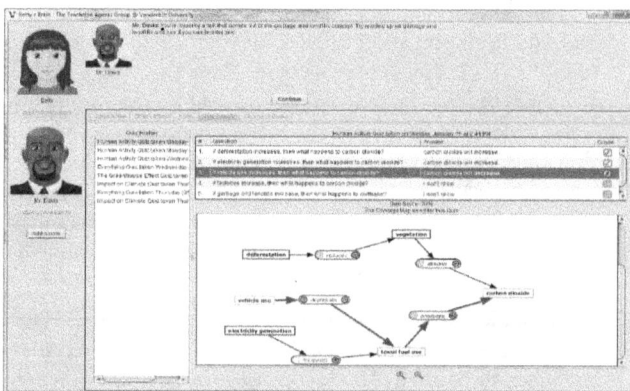

Figure 1: Mr. Davis giving the student a hint after student makes Betty take a quiz in Betty's Brain.

In addition, Betty may provide "encouragement" prompts. When the student is performing well, she praises the student for being a good teacher. Periodically, Betty also asks the student *"How are you feeling?"* Depending on the student's response, she may encourage additional effort, (e.g., If student's response is *"I am feeling bored"*, Betty says *"I know you can teach me. Keep at it!"*).

4 METHODS

Our study included 93 sixth-grade students from four science classes in an urban public school in Nashville, TN, USA. The study was conducted over seven days. It included a pre-test on day 1, training on the system on day 2, working on Betty's Brain to model the human causes and effects of climate change on days 3-6, and a post-test on day 7. The map that the students were expected to construct to teach Betty include a total of 25 causal links. The paper-based pre- and post-tests were identical and tested students' knowledge on the science domain concepts and understanding of causal relations using a combination of multiple-choice (MC) and short-answer (SA) questions. Students could receive maximum scores of 7 points for the former and 9 points for the later, for a total maximum score of 16.

4.1 Affect Data

We analyse students' logged actions (as described in Table 1) and their observed affective states while they work with Betty's Brain. Data on affective states were collected using the Baker Rodrigo Ocumpaugh Monitoring Protocol (BROMP; [18]). In this protocol, trained observers (inter-rater reliability: *Cohen's kappa* > 0.6) code students individually, in a pre-determined order using a momentary time sampling technique. Observers make holistic judgments, recording both affective states (i.e. *bored, confused, delight, engaged concentration, frustrated, other*) and behavioral categories (i.e. *on-task, off-task, on-task conversation, other*). Observers are trained to record the first thing they see, but have up to 20 seconds to make a decision, after which they are supposed to mark the observation as "other." (For the purposes of this study, only affective categories are considered.)

Observations are recorded using an Android app [17], which enforces the protocol and synchronizes with an internet time server allowing each observation to be aligned with log files of student activities within the system. The app also helps to speed the recording process. In this study, an expert coder (the 3rd author) trained a second observer during the first two days. (None of the trainee's data was used from this period.) After the trainee was certified, each observer coded independently. A total of 4233 affect observations was generated across the 2 classes over 4 days.

4.2 Learning Outcomes

This study considers both system internal learning measures (the final map score) and system external summative learning measures (pre- and post-test scores). The former was calculated as the difference between the number of correct and incorrect causal relations on each student's concept map at the end of the study. The latter were used to generate a normalized learning gain score (This normalized learning gain, calculated as $\frac{Post-Pre}{Max-Pre}$, accounted for the effect of pre-test score on post-test score).

For our analyses, we divided students ($n = 93$) into "Hi" (*high performers*) and "Lo" (*low performers*) based on the median value of their final map scores ($median = 11$). Students with a map score greater than 11 were labeled "Hi" ($n = 47$) and those with a map score less than 10 were labeled "Lo" ($n = 42$). Data for students

at the median value ($n = 4$) was discarded to maintain the distinction between the two groups. There was a 16.5-point difference between the average Hi group ($mean = 19.5, sd = 9.4$), and Lo group ($mean = 3, sd = 9.5$) map scores. The difference in the normalized learning gains score was also substantial, with a mean of 0.36 ($sd = 0.27$) for students in the Hi group and 0.17 ($sd = 0.27$) for students in the Lo group.

4.3 Action Log Files

Students' cognitive activities in Betty's Brain were logged and classified into five primary action categories based on the Betty's Brain task model [14]. As shown in Table 1, they are: *Read, Edit, Assess, Note* and *Conv (Conversation)*.

The combination of these actions illustrates the coordination of students' learning and problem-solving activities with corresponding skills and cognitive processes.

Table 1: Cognitive Activities in Betty's Brain

Primary Action	Description
Read	Learner reads resource pages or teacher's guide (*information acquisition*)
Edit	Learner edits the concept map to teach Betty (*solution construction*)
Assess	Learner has Betty answer a causal question or take a quiz to evaluate the state of the map (*solution assessment*)
Note	Learner takes/edits notes used to track acquired information
Conv	Learner converses with one of the agents (Betty or Mr. Davis)

These cognitive activities (primary student actions) serve as the primary unit of analyses, but more specific actions (e.g., requesting/receiving certain kinds of hints, moving elements on the map, looking at quiz results, etc.), are also considered.

4.4 Analyses

We conducted several analyses. We studied performance by computing the significance of students' normalized pre-to-post learning gains. We also computed correlations between student map scores and their normalized learning gains to establish the relationship between students' performance in the system and their overall learnings.

Next, we compared the time spent by the Hi and Lo students on each of the 5 primary activities in the Betty's Brain system. To compare the differences in the affective states between the two groups, we computed the relative number of times each of the affective states were recorded for each group and determined how the observed affective states were distributed across each of the 5 primary actions for the Hi versus Lo groups.

Finally, we used the system log files to study situations where Hi and Lo students showed marked differences in delight and boredom to understand the interactions between students' cognitive and affective states. We then compared students' performance after observations of four affective states (boredom, delight, confusion and frustration) to see how each affective state was associated with developments in student performance and learning.

5 RESULTS

5.1 Pre-Post Learning Gains and Performance in Betty's Brain

Learners' pre-test scores, post-tests scores and learning gains for multiple choice (MC) and short answer (SA) questions are reported in Table 2. A one-way ANOVA across all students indicates significant gains from pre- to post-test ($p < 0.00001$) with medium to large effect sizes. We also calculated the Pearson correlation coefficient between learning gains and learners' final map scores in Betty's Brain. The results show a moderate ($r = 0.2$) but statistically significant ($p < 0.05$, $t = 1.95$) correlation between learners' map scores and learning gains, indicating that the OELE provided moderate support to students' learning of the science content. (Some of the learning may be attributed to just reading the science resources).

Table 2: Pre-to-post learning gains - all students ($n = 93$)

Question Type	Pre-test score mean (sd)	Post-test score mean (sd)	Normalized Learning Gains $\frac{Post - Pre}{Max - Pre}$ mean (sd)	1-way ANOVA F-ratio (p-value)	Effect Size Cohen's d
MC (Max=7)	4.08 (1.42)	5.48 (1.31)	0.45 (0.52)	45.11 (< 0.0001)	1.02
SA (Max=9)	2.28 (1.79)	3.5 (2.29)	0.16 (0.31)	15.24 (< 0.00015)	0.59
Overall (Max=16)	6.35 (2.93)	8.98 (3.25)	0.26 (0.28)	30.64 (< 0.0001)	0.85

5.2 Distribution of Cognitive Activities

Students' cognitive activities were categorized into five primary actions based on the Betty's Brain task model [11]. Overall, each Hi performer showed a higher count of actions (437 more actions on an average) than Lo performers. We inferred the relative time spent doing each primary action from system logs. Our analysis (Table 3) shows minimal differences in the percentage of total time duration for each primary action across Hi and Lo performers. However, students in the Hi group spent a significantly higher percentage of their total time doing *Assess* actions *(such as evaluating the map)* compared to Lo groups (data tested for normality using Shapiro-Wilk test, 1-way ANOVA $p < 0.05$, corrected post-hoc using Benjamini-Hochberg procedure). This finding, that self-initiated assessment appears to be significantly higher for Hi performers, may relate to psychological memory research by Karpicke et al. [12], who demonstrate that repeated testing is more

effective than repeated studying for a later recall of learning content.

Table 3: Percentage of total duration spent in each primary action (Hi vs Lo)

Category	Read %	Edit %	**Assess %**	Note %	Conv %
Hi (n=47)	26.6	48.4	**12.3**	1.4	11.3
Lo (n=42)	29.6	49.5	**6.5**	2.8	11.6

5.3 Observations of Affective States

We analyzed the data collected on students' affective states by performance (Hi vs Lo). The total observations (for both Hi and Lo groups) for each affective state were 91 cases of *boredom*, 238 cases of *confusion*, 118 cases of *delight*, 3506 cases of *engaged concentration*, 207 cases of *frustration* and 73 cases of *other*. Table 4 presents the proportion of each affective state as a percentage of total affect observations for each group. Significant differences between high and low performers were observed for two affective states: (1) Delight was significantly higher for the Hi group; and (2) boredom was significantly higher for the Lo group ($p = 0.05$ for both delight and boredom, adjusted post-hoc for Type 1 error rate using Benjamini-Hochberg procedure).

Table 4: Affective states as percentage of total affect observations (Hi vs Lo)

Category	**Boredom %**	Confusion %	**Delight %**	Engaged %	Frustration %
Hi (n=47)	**0.83**	5.59	**3.39**	84.71	5.48
Lo (n=42)	**4.31**	5.91	**1.97**	83.63	4.18

5.4 Distribution of Observed Affective States Across Primary Actions

We next analyze how affective states are distributed across the five primary actions (Read, Edit, Assess, Note and Conversation) for the high versus low performers, to understand if these differences are more prominent in certain action contexts. We focus our attention specifically on the *boredom* and *delight* scenarios (since these two affective states showed significant differences between Hi and Lo groups). The results are presented in Table 5.

Table 5: Distribution of affective states across the 5 primary actions (Hi vs Lo)

Values denote affect instances observed during each action

Action	Category	Boredom	Confusion	Delight	Engagement	Frustration
Read	Hi	7	27	10	329	26
	Lo	10	23	4	200	11
Edit	Hi	6	52	20	888	42
	Lo	24	33	15	618	27
Assess	Hi	2	33	25	345	31
	Lo	6	14	3	156	11
Note	Hi	1	1	2	33	2
	Lo	1	3	3	35	2
Conv	Hi	5	29	29	553	38
	Lo	29	23	7	342	17

Looking at *boredom* and *delight*, we observe 5 cases (*shaded in Table 5*) where large differences were observed between Hi and Lo groups for a specific action. Boredom was substantially more likely among Lo learners during Edit actions (24 vs. 6 instances) and Conversation actions (29 vs. 5 instances). Conversely, delight was substantially more common for the Hi group than for the Lo group during Read actions (10 vs. 4 instances) Assess actions (25 vs. 3 instances), and Conversation actions (29 vs. 7 instances).

5.5 Temporal Relations between Students' Cognition and Affect States

To better understand the interactions between affective states and cognitive activities, we considered more specific actions rather than just the five primary ones discussed above. We examined the temporal ordering of these actions, to determine the common antecedents, if any, to boredom and delight. The results of this case-by-case analysis are presented in Table 6, which shows differences between the Hi and Low groups.

Table 6: Temporal antecedents for substantial differences in boredom and delight

Case 1: Instances of Boredom during Conv		
Antecedent	Hi (n=5)	Lo (n=29)
Post-quiz *indirect* hint	0	5
Agent progress report (bad)	1	8
Agent response to query	2	4
Long MapView or Read	2	11
Off-task	0	1

Case 2: Instances of Boredom during Edit		
Antecedent	Hi (n=6)	Lo (n=24)
Hint→MapView	0	7
Long period of MapView & MapElementsMove	4	8
Agent progress report (bad)	1	3
Read multipletimes→MapView	1	1
ConceptEdit multiple times	0	1
QuizProvenWrong→MapView	0	3
Query agent → MapView	0	1

Case 3: Instances of Delight during Assess		
Antecedent	Hi (n=25)	Lo (n=3)
Quiz results correct	23	2
Quiz explanations correct	2	1

Case 4: Instances of Delight during Conv		
Antecedent	Hi (n=29)	Lo (n=7)
Post-quiz hint	6	2
Encouragement prompt	1	1
Agent progress report (good)	5	1
Agent response to query	2	0
MapView/Read→Quiz	14	1
Off-task	1	2

Case 5: Instances of Delight during Read		
Antecedent	Hi (n=10)	Lo (n=4)
MapView → Read guide	1	1
Hint → Read	4	1
Off-task	1	2
Agent progress report (good)→Read	2	0
MapEdit→Read	2	0

As shown in Table 6, several of the shaded antecedents seem to trigger major differences in the number of instances observed in Hi (*high performers*) versus Lo (*low performers*). Therefore, we study these cases in greater detail below.

1. Case 1 - *Boredom during Conversation*: Several antecedents of boredom observed during agent conversations are noted in Table 6. Again, we explore the ones showing large Hi vs Lo differences below:

(i) Post-quiz *indirect* hint: Lo students were bored in 5 instances after receiving *indirect* post-quiz hints from the mentor agent. No such instances of boredom were observed in Hi students. In Scenario 2, we found that Hi students showed more delight instances compared to Lo students when they got post-quiz hints from the mentor. In contrast, the Lo students showed higher instances of boredom (*Hi students show none*) after receiving *indirect* hints, implying these students did not find the hints to be useful, or they could not use them to overcome their difficulties.

(ii) Bad progress report by agent: A second instance, of large differences between Hi and Lo students, is when the mentor agent informs them that they are not making sufficient progress toward completing their map. This occurs more for low performers, and lack of progress results in boredom for these students. This is a situation, where we have to rethink the type of feedback provided by the mentor agent, and it may differ for Lo versus Hi performers.

(iii) Long MapView or Read→ *boredom*, Conv: In this case boredom started with a previous action i.e., long periods of reading the resources or viewing the causal map. This boredom was still present when the conversation action occurred. For high performers, there were two such instances (both due to long reads), and for low performers there were 11 such instances (4 due to long reads and 7 due to long map views). This result also suggests that scaffolds should be designed to help low-performing students regulate their affect with more helpful hints, especially when they spend too much time on a resource page or just viewing the causal map without making changes.

2. Case 2 - *Boredom during Edit actions*: The three notable antecedents of boredom in this case are summarized below:

(i) Hint → MapView is an antecedent of boredom during map edit. This case is only seen among Lo performers, with 7 instances in Lo performers. The student received a hint from the mentor agent and then started looking at the causal map, and then got bored. This result appears to follow from [19] in that the gap between task difficulty and learner ability leads to boredom. Scaffolding Lo students in such a situation can ensure that they are able to utilize the mentor's hint effectively and do not get disengaged from the task at hand.

(ii) Long period of viewing map or moving map elements (no read, quiz or link-edit): These are several instances (4 for Hi and 8 for Lo) where long periods of viewing the map and moving map elements on the screen (idle period with no quiz taking or reading or link editing in between) were followed by an observed bored state. This implies that it may be important to detect unproductive phases and to provide adequate scaffolds to help the students become more productive.

(iii) QuizProvenWrong→MapView: Students got bored when viewing their causal map following a quiz result that was graded as incorrect. This is more frequent for Lo, most likely because Lo students generally have worse quiz results, and not much of an idea of how to fix the errors in their map.

3. Case 3 - *Delight during Assess*. For both Hi and Lo learners, there are only two antecedents to delight during Assess actions: (i) when they looked at their quiz results and found that all the answers were correct; and (ii) when the causal explanations to quiz answers were correct. The first antecedent shows large differences between Hi and Lo groups. It is not surprising that the count of such instances was much higher for Hi group, since they were more successful in their map building efforts and hence obtained higher quiz scores.

4. Case 4 - *Delight during Conversation*. The antecedents of delight during conversation, as observed from the action logs, can be subdivided into different cases. Of these, the cases where large differences are noted between instances observed in Hi and Lo groups are discussed below:

(i) Post-quiz hint: this is the situation when the mentor agent gave a post-quiz hint. These hints may be *direct* or *indirect* (*discussed in Section 3.2*).

It was found that Hi students got delighted more often after receiving hints from the mentor agent. (We later observe, in Scenario 3, that Lo students show higher instances of boredom following *indirect* hints.)

(ii) Good progress report by agent: Delight also occurs when the mentor agent analyzes the state of the students' maps and praises their progress toward generating the correct map from the last

time the mentor performed this check. Unsurprisingly, these situations occur more often for the Hi group

(iii) MapView or Read→Quiz: In this situation, the student starts showing delight much before they have even begun a conversation with an agent. In all instances of this type, the student is delighted when they follow up a map view or read action by taking a quiz action i.e., looking at the map or reading resource pages and then asking Betty to take a quiz. This delight continues through the conversation with her, presumably because the student does well in the quiz. In other words, students had figured out how to improve their map, and this resulted in delight. The delight continued through the quiz taking action. This case occurred 14 times for the Hi performers and only once for the Lo performers.

5. Case 5 - *Delight during Read*: 5 antecedents were identified from student logs for the scenario where student got delighted during reading a resource or the teacher's guide page in Betty's Brain. Hint → Read is the only case where a large difference between Hi and Lo instances was observed.

Hint → Read: This is when students got delighted upon reading resource pages after the mentor agent gave a hint. Hi students have more instances of this type, possibly since they were better able to connect the hint to causal relations discussed in resource pages that the hint mentioned. This finding, along with the Hint→MapView antecedent of boredom discussed in Scenario 4, give us a very fine-grained insight into student cognition and affect, and call for the design of scaffolds to regulate cognitive and affective states in these situations.

Tracing the temporal activity sequences in the log files that occurred around affect events that were recorded by researchers using the BROMP protocol provides us with insights on the interactions between students' activities, performance, and affect. Also, one of the most important findings in this section is that an incongruity between the students' capabilities and the feedback provided to them by the agents in the Betty's Brain environment leads to unproductive affect states. This happens disproportionately for low performers, who are the ones likely to need the most encouragement and hints that help them get back to more productive behaviors. We discuss this further in the discussion section.

5.6 Performance Consequents of Affective States

Finally, we explore the immediate influence of affective experiences on student performance in Betty's Brain by comparing how Hi and Lo students edit their causal model in the 3 min interval after each affect occurs. Specifically, we compare the number of *effective* (correct) and *ineffective* (incorrect) link edits in the causal model. We chose a 3 min interval for this purpose since two consecutive affect observations for a given student had a mean duration of 3 min.

Link edit effectiveness, the measure of performance used here, is determined by comparing the current state of the student map after each causal link edit with an expert map embedded in the system that is hidden from the student's view.

The results of this analysis, given in Table 7, show how boredom is associated with poorer future performance among both Hi and Lo students. After experiencing delight, Hi students make 48% more effective than ineffective link edits. But Lo students appear to make more mistakes in map building after getting delighted and show 70% more ineffective than effective link edits, possibly due to careless errors from over-confidence [7, 25]. It appears that Hi students can regulate their frustration more productively than Lo students, as they do 22% more effective edits than ineffective edits after frustration. But frustration is associated with poorer performance for Lo students who show 32% more ineffective than effective links. As for confusion, it appears to be productive for both, it is more so for Hi students. This finding is supported by prior research on the positive influence of confusion on learning [8]. The precedence of confusion to positive performance would also harmonize with empirical studies around the co-evolution framework, which predict and find cognitive conflicts to make people accommodate their shared knowledge representations in social web environments [13].

Table 7: Comparing student performance in Hi vs Lo after each affective state

	Preceding Affect	Effective Links		Ineffective Links		Effective – Ineffective Links
		N	%	N	%	
HI	Confusion	244	61%	156	39%	22%
	Frustration	258	56%	201	44%	12%
	Delight	130	66%	67	34%	32%
	Boredom	40	42%	55	58%	-16%
LO	Confusion	144	57%	107	43%	15%
	Frustration	52	40%	77	60%	-19%
	Delight	9	23%	31	78%	-55%
	Boredom	74	45%	90	55%	-10%

6 DISCUSSION AND FUTURE WORK

In this paper, we analyzed cognitive and affective experiences of sixth grade students modeling a complex science topic in the Betty's Brain OELE. Our analyses demonstrate that a combined study of students' activities in an open-ended learning environment, their resulting learning performance and their recorded affective states can allow for a systematic and detailed investigation of the interactions between cognitive and affective processes, both important components of their self-regulated learning behaviors, within different task contexts in the OELE.

We found that learners' cognitive and affective states within an agent-based OELE are contextualized by their interactions with the environment as well as their performance within the system. Our initial results revealed significant differences in the levels of *delight* and *boredom* between high and low performers. So, we

identified five specific task contexts in which these affect differences were most pronounced. Then we determined the cognitive processes, which were temporal antecedents to these contextualized affect cases in high versus low performers. However, our findings on temporal relationships between cognition and affect states do not claim any possible affect-cognition causality.

One particularly fascinating finding from our temporal analyses is how the virtual "mentor" agent's feedback (*in the form of hints or reports of progress*) appeared to lead to different cognitive and affective experiences in high versus low performers. The different learner reactions to feedback recalls previous research on learner's beliefs about the nature of learning [9].

These findings suggest that it may be valuable to scaffold students, especially low performers, based on their cognitive and affective interactions in specific learning situations to help regulate their SRL processes and create a more productive learning experience. The findings in this paper show the value of aligning affect with students' performance and their actions, and then developing the ability to track them online, so that personalized hints and positive encouragements can be provided to help students get back to productive learning behaviors.

A primary limitation of this work was that students' affect was recorded at discrete intervals, therefore, it was not possible to track transitions and evolution of their affective states in a fully fine-grained manner. On the other hand, recording of students' activities in context, and their performance over time, though discrete and recorded as events in log files, was available in a more complete form.

In future, to enable better alignment between affect, learning activities and performance, we plan to develop and deploy affect detectors that will be capable of recording students' affective states at finer-grained intervals. Once this is established we hope to develop temporal models of the interactions between learning activity and behaviors, affective states and performance, their transitions, and their evolutions over time. This will provide a better framework for developing rich learner models of SRL processes, which, in turn, will lead to richer frameworks for scaffolding and feedback in OELEs.

ACKNOWLEDGMENTS
This research was supported by NSF ECR Award #1561676.

REFERENCES
[1] R Azevedo, R Behnagh, M Duffy, J Harley and G Trevors. 2012. Metacognition and self-regulated learning in student-centered leaning environments, *Theoretical foundations of student-centered learning* 171-197.

[2] Roger Azevedo and Allyson Hadwin. 2005. Scaffolding Self-Regulated Learning and Metacognition—Implications for the Design of Computer-Based Scaffolds. *Instructional Science*, Vol 33. 367-379. 10.1007/s11251-005-1272-9.

[3] Ryan Baker and Jaclyn Ocumpaugh. 2015. Interaction-Based Affect Detection in Educational Software. *In the Oxford Handbook of Affective Computing*: Oxford University Press.

[4] L F Barrett. 2009. Variety is the spice of life: a psychological construction approach to understanding variability in emotion. *Cognition & Emotion*, Vol 23(7), 1284-1306.

[5] Gautam Biswas, James R Segedy and Kritya Bunchongchit. 2016. From Design to Implementation to Practice a Learning by Teaching System: Betty's Brain. *Int J Artif Intell Educ*, Vol 26: 350. https://doi.org/10.1007/s40593-015-0057-9

[6] M Boekaerts, M and L Corno. 2005. Self-regulation in the classroom: A perspective on assessment and intervention. *Applied Psychology*, Vol 54(2), 199–231

[7] K Clements. 1982. Careless errors made by sixth-grade children on written mathematical tasks. *Journal for Research in Mathematics Education*, Vol 13, 136–144.

[8] S D'Mello, B Lehman, B, R Pekrun and A Graesser. 2014. Confusion can be beneficial for learning. *Learning and Instruction*, Vol 29: 153-170.

[9] C S Dweck. 2002. Messages that motivate: How praise molds students' beliefs, motivation, and performance (In surprising ways*). In J. Aronson (Ed.), Improving academic achievement*. New York: Academic Press.

[10] A Efklides. 2011. Interactions of metacognition with motivation and affect in self-regulated learning: the MASRL model. *Educ. Psychol.* Vol 46, 6–25. doi: 10.1080/00461520.2011.538645

[11] Jeffrey Alan Greene and Roger Azevedo. 2007. A Theoretical Review of Winne and Hadwin's Model of Self-Regulated Learning: New Perspectives and Directions. *Review of Educational Research* Vol 77, Issue 3, 334 – 372.

[12] Jeffrey D Karpicke and Henry L Roedinger. 2008. The Critical Importance of Retrieval for Learning. *Science,* Vol 319, 5865, 966-968.

[13] Joachim Kimmerle, Ulrike Cress, Christoph Held and Johannes Moskaliuk. 2010. Social software and knowledge building: supporting co-evolution of individual and collective knowledge. *Proceedings of the 9th International Conference of the Learning Sciences*, Vol 1, 9-16.

[14] John Kinnebrew, James R Segedy and Gautam Biswas. 2017. Integrating model-driven and data-driven techniques for analyzing learning behaviors in open-ended learning environments. *IEEE Trans. Learn. Technol.* doi: 10.1109/TLT.2015.2513387

[15] Reed W Larson and Maryse H Richards. 1991. Boredom in the Middle School Years: Blaming Schools versus Blaming Students. *American Journal of Education*, Vol 99, 4, 418-443.

[16] K Leelawong and G Biswas. 2008. Designing learning by teaching agents: The Betty's Brain system. *International Journal of Artificial Intelligence in Education*, Vol 18(3), 181–208. IOS Press.

[17] Jaclyn Ocumpaugh, Ryan Shaun Joazeiro de Baker, Ma Mercedes T Rodrigo, Aatish Salvi, Martin Van Velsen, Ani Aghababyan and Taylor Martin. 2015. HART: the human affect recording tool. *SIGDOC 2015.*

[18] J Ocumpaugh, R S Baker and M M T Rodrigo. 2015. Baker Rodrigo Ocumpaugh Monitoring Protocol (BROMP) 2.0 technical and training manual. *Technical Report. New York, NY: Teachers College, Columbia University. Manila, Philippines: Ateneo Laboratory for the Learning Sciences.*

[19] J Ocumpaugh et al. 2017. Affect Dynamics in Military Trainees Using vMedic: From Engaged Concentration to Boredom to Confusion. In: *André E., Baker R., Hu X., Rodrigo M., du Boulay B. (eds) Artificial Intelligence in Education. AIED 2017. Lecture Notes in Computer Science*, Vol 10331. Springer

[20] Ernesto Panadero, Julia Klug and Sanna Järvelä. 2015. Third wave of measurement in the self-regulated learning field: when measurement and intervention come hand in hand. *Scandinavian Journal of Educational Research*, DOI: 10.1080/00313831.2015.1066436

[21] R Pekrun. 2010. Academic emotions. In *T. Urdan (Ed.), APA educational psychology handbook*, Vol. 2. Washington, DC: American Psychological Association

[22] R Pekrun. 2006. *Educ Psychol Rev.* 18: 315. https://doi.org/10.1007/s10648-006-9029-9

[23] P R Pintrich. 2000. The role of goal orientation in self-regulated learning. In Handbook of Self-Regulation, eds M. Boekaerts, P. R. Pintrich, and M. Zeidner (San Diego, CA: Academic Press), 452–502.

[24] Russell, J. (2003). Core affect and the psychological construction of emotion. Psychological Review, 110, 145e172.

[25] M O Z San Pedro, R S J Baker and M M T Rodrigo. 2014. *Int J Artif Intell Educ*, Vol 24, 189. https://doi.org/10.1007/s40593-014-0015-y

[26] G Schraw, K J Crippen and K Hartley. 2006. Promoting self-regulation in science education: Metacognition as part of a broader perspective on learning. *Research in science education*, Vol 36(1-2), 111-139.

[27] Allan Wigfield, Jacquelynne S Eccles. 2000. Expectancy–Value Theory of Achievement Motivation. *Contemporary Educational Psychology*, Vol 25, 1, 68-81, ISSN 0361-476X, https://doi.org/10.1006/ceps.1999.1015

[28] P H Winne. 2001. Self-regulated learning viewed from models of information processing. In Self-Regulated Learning and Academic Achievement, eds B. J. Zimmerman and D. H. Schunk (New York, NY: Lawrence Erlbaum Associates), 153–190.

[29] P H Winne. 2011. A cognitive and metacognitive analysis of self-regulated learning. In *Handbook of Self-Regulation of Learning and Performance*, eds B. J. Zimmerman and D. H. Schunk (New York, NY: Routledge), 15–32.

[30] P H Winne, A F Hadwin. 1998. Studying as self-regulated engagement in learning. In *Metacognition in Educational Theory and Practice*, eds D. Hacker, J. Dunlosky, and A. Graesser (Hillsdale, NJ: Erlbaum), 277–304.

[31] P H Winne and A F Hadwin. 2008. The weave of motivation and self-regulated learning. In *Motivation and Self-Regulated Learning: Theory, Research and Applications*, eds D. H. Schunk and B. J. Zimmerman (New York, NY: Lawrence Erlbaum Associates), 297–314.

[32] B J Zimmerman. 2000. Attaining self-regulation: a social cognitive perspective. In *Handbook of Self-Regulation*, eds M. Boekaerts, P. R. Pintrich, and M. Zeidner (San Diego, CA: Academic Press), 13–40. doi: 10.1016/b978-012109890-2/50031-7

[33] Barry J Zimmerman. 2008. Investigating Self-Regulation and Motivation: Historical Background, Methodological Developments, and Future Prospects. *American Educational Research Journal*, Vol 45, 1, 166 - 183.

[34] B J Zimmerman, D H Schunk. 2011. *Handbook of Self-Regulation of Learning and Performance.* New York, NY: Routledge.

Exploring Adaptive Strategies for Providing Learning Activities

Xingliang Chen
Intelligent Computer Tutoring Group
University of Canterbury
Christchurch, New Zealand
xingliang.chen@pg.canterbury.ac.nz

Antonija Mitrovic
Intelligent Computer Tutoring Group
University of Canterbury
Christchurch, New Zealand
tanja.mitrovic@canterbury.ac.nz

Moffat Mathews
Intelligent Computer Tutoring Group
University of Canterbury
Christchurch, New Zealand
moffat.mathews@canterbury.ac.nz

ABSTRACT

Research shows that Worked Examples (WE) and Erroneous Examples (ErrEx) provide learning benefits, particularly when presented alternatively with problems to solve. We previously proposed an adaptive strategy for selecting WE, ErrEx, and Problem Solving (PS) adaptively based on the student's problem-solving score and found that the adaptive strategy was beneficial for students in comparison to learning from a fixed sequence of alternating WE/PS pairs and ErrEx/PS pairs [1]. Students who received learning activities adaptively achieved the same learning outcomes as their peers in a fixed condition, but with fewer learning activities [2]. In this paper, we investigate a different adaptive strategy, which provides WEs and ErrExs to novices, and ErrEx and PS to advanced students. We found that the original adaptive strategy [2] is more effective than the new adaptive strategy. Furthermore, both novices and advanced students who learned with the original adaptive strategy demonstrated better performance on the post-test.[1]

CCS CONCEPTS

• **Applied computing** → **Education** → Computer-assisted instruction;

KEYWORDS

Worked Examples; Erroneous Examples; Problem Solving; Adaptive Learning; Adaptive Strategy; SQL-Tutor; Intelligent Tutoring System

ACM Reference format:

X. Chen, A. Mitrovic, and M. Mathews. 2018. SIG Proceedings Paper in word Format. In *Proceedings of ACM UMAP conference, Singapore, July 2018 (UMAP'2018)*, x pages.
DOI: 10.1145/3209219.3209221

1 INTRODUCTION

Worked examples (WEs), which consist of a problem statement with its solution and additional explanations, reduce the cognitive load on students' working memory, thus allowing the student to learn faster and solve more complex problems [3]. Numerous studies have shown the benefits of learning from WEs, e.g. [4-7]. WEs are more beneficial for novices [5], but PS was shown to be superior to WEs for advanced students who have sufficient knowledge to learn from practice without much feedback or support [8]. The effects of PS only, WE only, WE/PS pairs (WE-PS) and PS/WE pairs (PS-WE) have also been studied on novices [6]. The WE and WE-PS conditions resulted in significantly higher learning effectiveness in comparison to the PS and PS-WE conditions, and PS-WE pairs did not lead to better learning than PS only. However, van Gog [7] later claimed that the WE-PS and PS-WE conditions were not comparable, because the examples and problems should be identical within and across pairs. As the consequence, she employed an example-problem sequence (EP condition) and a problem-example sequence (PE condition) for learning in the Leap Frog game. The students learned significantly more in the EP condition than in the PE condition. Additionally, students' prior knowledge was an important factor when providing instructional assistance.

Compared with unsupported problem solving, many studies also show the benefits of learning from WE and PS in Intelligent Tutoring Systems (ITSs) [9-12]. ITSs provide adaptive feedback, hints, or other types of help to students in order to support their learning. Schwonke et al. [10] and Schwonke et al. [11] conducted two studies, which compared tutored problem solving with alternating worked examples and tutored problem solving. The first study showed that there was no significant difference in the effectiveness of the two conditions, but learning was more efficient when students studied with example-enriched tutor. The results of the second study also revealed a learning time advantage for WEs. McLaren and Isotani [9] investigated the effects of WE only, PS only, and alternating example/problem pairs in Stoichiometry Tutor. The results showed that there was no difference in learning gain for those three conditions, but WEs resulted in shorter learning times. Contrary to that, Shareghi Najar and Mitrovic [12] compared a condition receiving alternating example and problem pairs (AEP) to problem solving only (PO) and worked example only (EO) in SQL-Tutor, a constraint-based tutor for teaching database querying in SQL.

The results indicated that both the advanced students and novices learned more from the AEP condition which presented isomorphic pairs of WE and PS to students. The results also showed that the AEP condition outperformed the PO condition in conceptual acquisition.

Several recent studies focused on erroneous examples (ErrExs), which require students to find and fix errors in solutions. Erroneous examples may help students to become better at evaluating problem solutions. Siegler and Chen [13] compared correct and erroneous examples for mathematical equality problems. Their results show that students who studied both types of examples had better learning outcomes than those who studied only correct examples. Große and Renkl [14] examined learning outcomes in the domain of mathematical probability when students explained both correct and erroneous examples. Their studies show the learning benefit of ErrEx for students with a high level of prior knowledge. Additionally, novices did significantly better when errors were highlighted, but there was no benefit for advanced students. Durkin and Rittle-Johnson [15] compared correct examples with correct and erroneous examples of decimal problems. They found that studying from both types of examples resulted in higher declarative and procedural knowledge compared with correct examples only.

The studies on ErrEx discussed above were paper based; there have also been a few studies on the benefits of learning from ErrEx in ITSs [16, 17, 18]. Tsovaltzi et al. [16] conducted three studies with students of different ages to investigate the effect of studying erroneous examples of fractions in an ITS. The results showed that 6th graders who studied ErrEx with interactive help improved metacognitive skills in comparison with students who worked with problem solving and ErrEx with no help. In addition, erroneous examples with interactive help improved 9th and 10th grade students' problem-solving skills and conceptual knowledge. Another study [17] with the computer-based Algebra I Cognitive Tutor found that learners who studied the correct and incorrect examples significantly improved their scores on the post-test compared with learners who only received correct examples. Furthermore, they also found that the ErrEx condition and the combined correct and erroneous examples condition were beneficial for improving conceptual understanding of algebra, but not for improving procedural knowledge. Our previous study [18] compared a fixed sequence of alternating WE/PS pairs and ErrEx/PS pairs in SQL-Tutor to a condition who only had WE/PS pairs. The results showed students who studied with erroneous examples showed better performance on problem solving than students who did not receive any ErrExs. Additionally, explaining and correcting erroneous examples led to better learning outcomes on debugging and problem-solving skills.

In spite of many studies that investigated the effectiveness of various kinds of learning activities, there is no agreement on what kind of learning activities are best to support learners with varying levels of prior knowledge. In previous work, we reported on a study [1] that compared learning from a fixed WE/PS and ErrEx/PS pairs (WPEP) to an adaptive strategy which adaptively selected learning activities (WE, ErrEx, or PS) for students based on their performance on problem solving. The results indicated that students who studied with the adaptive strategy significantly improved their post-test scores on conceptual, procedural, and debugging questions. Both novices and advanced students who received learning activities adaptively achieved the same learning outcomes as their peers in the fixed condition, but with fewer learning activities [2]. Furthermore, we found no difference between novices and advanced students on how many learning activities they received in the adaptive condition.

However, despite many studies that investigated the effectiveness of various kinds of learning activities, there is no agreement on what kind of learning activities best support learners with varying levels of prior knowledge. Prior studies show that worked examples are more beneficial for students with a low prior level of knowledge (i.e., novices) [5, 6, 19, 20]. For high prior knowledge learners (i.e., advanced students), worked examples lose their effectiveness or may even become less effective for learning than practicing with problem solving [8, 21]. Erroneous examples have so far been shown to be particularly beneficial to students with some prior knowledge [14, 16]. Based on those findings, we developed a new adaptive strategy that takes into account the student's previous knowledge: for novices, the new strategy selects easier learning activities (i.e. WE or ErrEx, based on the student's performance), while for advanced students the next learning activity could be an ErrEx, or a problem to be solved. In this paper, we compare the previously studied adaptive strategy [1, 2] to the new adaptive strategy. We hypothesized that the new adaptive strategy would be superior to the original one (Hypothesis 1). We also expected that novices would learn more conceptual and debugging knowledge (Hypothesis 2a), and advanced students would learn more procedural and debugging knowledge (2b) with the new adaptive strategy.

2 SQL-Tutor

The study was conducted in the context of SQL-Tutor [22], a constraint-based ITS for teaching the Structured Query Language (SQL). We modified SQL-Tutor by developing three modes to correspond to WE, ErrEx, and PS. The problem-solving mode is shown in Fig. 1. Students can access the database schema using the left pane. The database schema provides information about tables, their attributes, and the data stored in the database. The middle pane provides the problem-solving environment. The right pane presents the feedback. The WE mode (Fig. 2) presents the problem with its solution and explanation in the center pane. A student can confirm that s/he has read the example by clicking the Continue button. Fig. 3 presents a screenshot of the ErrEx mode. A problem with an incorrect solution is provided in the center pane. The student's task is to analyze and correct the errors. In the situation shown in Fig. 3, the student has identified the WHERE clause as being incorrect and is defining the new version of it.

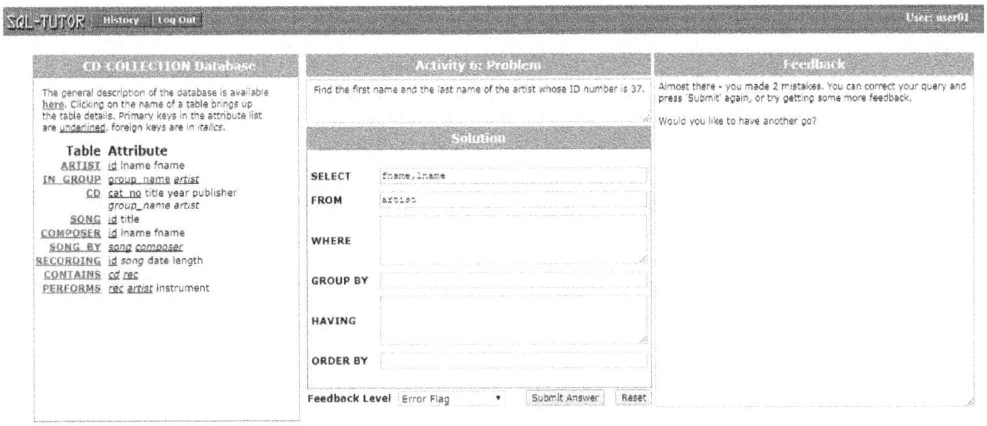

Figure 1: Problem Solving Mode.

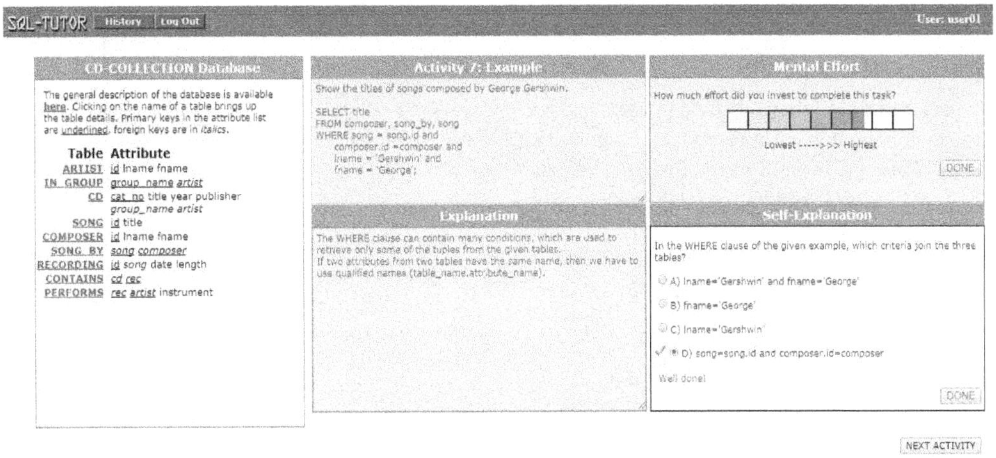

Figure 2: Worked Example Mode.

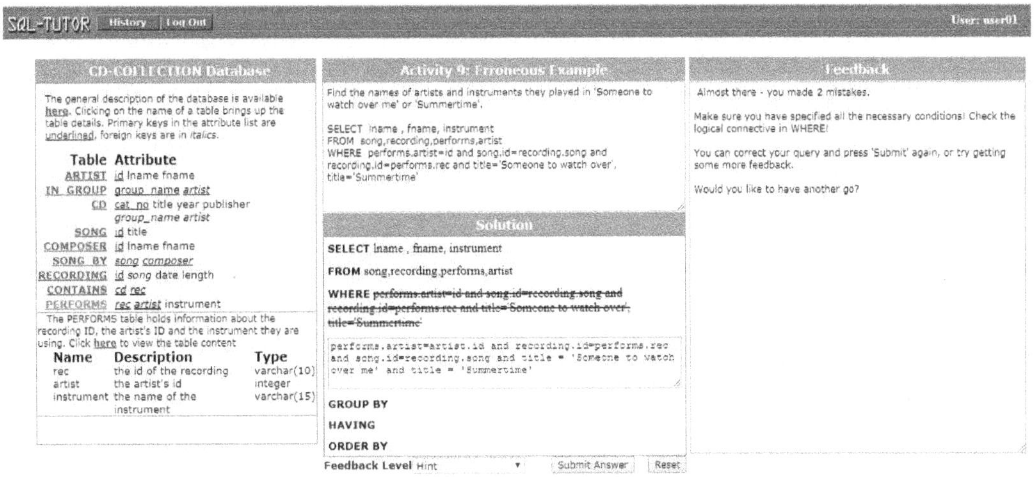

Figure 3: Erroneous Example Mode.

Previous research has shown the importance of Self-Explanation (SE) for learning [23-25]. Providing SE prompts is a common approach to encourage students to self-explain. Similar to our previous work [18], we provided students with SE prompts after examples and problems. Previous studies found that problem solving assisted students to learn more procedural knowledge than conceptual knowledge, whereas examples help improve conceptual knowledge than procedural knowledge [11]. Consequently, different types of SE are required to scaffold examples and problems [12]. A Conceptual-focused SE (C-SE) prompt supports students to self-explain relevant domain concepts after problem solving, and a Procedural-focused SE (P-SE) prompt supports students to self-explain solution procedure after WEs (illustrated in Fig. 2). In the case of ErrEx, the student is required to analyze the solution and fix the errors. Erroneous examples involve problem-solving steps and the properties of WEs. Therefore, we provided P-SE and C-SE prompts alternatively after erroneous examples

3 METHOD

The study was performed in the scheduled labs for an introductory database course at the University of Canterbury, with the 2016 and 2017 classes. In both years, the students had learned about SQL in the lectures, and had one lab session prior to the study. The procedure was the same in 2016 and 2017, with the only difference being the adaptive strategy used. In 2016, there were 22 volunteers who completed the study. In 2017, we had a new set of volunteers from the same course. Twenty of them completed all phases of the study.

Fig. 4 illustrates the design of the study. The study started and ended with the online pre-/post-tests. The tests had 11 questions each, of similar complexity. Questions 1 to 6 measured conceptual knowledge and were multi-choice or true-false questions (with the maximum of 6 marks). Three questions focused on procedural knowledge; question 7 was a multi-choice question (1 mark), question 8 was a true-false question (1 mark), while question 9 required the student to write a query for a given problem (4 marks). The last two questions presented incorrect solutions to two problems and required students to correct them, thus measuring debugging knowledge (6 marks). The maximum mark on tests was 18.

After the pre-test, the participants worked on 20 tasks, organized into ten isomorphic pairs and sorted by increasing complexity. Each task can be presented in the following forms: a problem to be solved, a WE, or as an erroneous example with one or two errors. The first component of each pair is a preparation task, while the second component is a problem to be solved. We used adaptive strategies to decide how to present the preparation task for all pairs of tasks except the very first one.

The first preparation task was different from the other pairs, because the student models were empty. For that reason, we used the pre-test score to determine whether the first preparation tasks should be a problem, a WE, or an ErrEx. If the conceptual score on the pre-test was lower than the procedural and debugging scores, the first preparation task was presented as the worked example. If the student's procedural score was lower

than the other two scores, s/he received a problem as the first task. If the lowest score was on debugging questions, the first task was presented as an ErrEx.

Online Pre-Test		
SQL-Tutor	10 isomorphic pairs (preparation task, problem) Each problem followed by a C-SE prompt; Each example followed by a P-SE prompt	
Pair 1	Lowest conceptual score: WE; Lowest procedural score: PS; Lowest debugging score: ErrEx	
Pairs 2-10	**Strategy 1: (2016)** **1st task**: WE, 1- or 2-errors ErrEx, problem, or skip **2nd task**: problem	**Strategy 2: (2017)** **1st task**: *Novices*. WE, 1- or 2-error ErrEx; *Advanced*: 1- or 2-errors ErrEx, PS or skip **2nd task**: problem
Online Post-Test		

Figure 4: Study Design.

Strategy 1 uses Cognitive Efficiency (CE) to decide what the preparation task should be. It also allowed the preparation task to be skipped, if the student's problem-solving performance on the previous problem was high. The details of Strategy 1 are presented in [2]. CE is computed as the quotient between the problem-solving score (on the most recent problem) and the (self-reported) mental effort score, as originally proposed in [26]. Both scores had the same range, 0 (lowest) to 9 (highest). The participants were asked to report the effort after each task they completed (as in Figure 2). If CE is higher than 1, that illustrated very high problem-solving performance, and the preparation task is skipped. CE below 1 and greater than 0.75 shows a relatively good performance on the previous problem, and the preparation task is a problem to be solved. A student receives a 2-error or 1-error ErrEx before next problem if CE is between 0.75 and 0.25. A WE is provided to a student if his/her CE is below 0.25.

Strategy 2 is similar to Strategy1, with only difference being what kind of learning activities should be given to novices and advanced students. The participants were labelled as novices if their pre-test score was less than the Split score (S), defined in Equation 1. M represents the median pre-test score (67%) from 2016, while X_k represents the pre-test score of student k. Please note that the value of S changes dynamically, as students complete the pre-test. For novices, Strategy 2 selects between WEs or ErrExs. For advanced students, the preparation task could be skipped, or they get a problem or (1-error or 2-error) ErrEx.

$$S = (M + \sum_{k=0}^{n} X_k/n)/2 \qquad (1)$$

4 RESULTS

4.1 Is there a Difference between the Two Adaptive Strategies on Learning Outcomes?

Strategy 1 was designed to select learning activities (a WE, a 1-error or 2-error ErrEx, or a problem) for a student based on his/her performance on problem solving [2]. Strategy 2 also selects learning activities adaptively, but it uses two factors: the performance on problem solving and the prior level of knowledge. We hypothesized that Strategy 2 would be superior to Strategy 1.

We used the Mann-Whitney U test to analyze the differences between the two conditions (Table 1). We compared the incoming knowledge (i.e. the pre-test scores) of the participants from the two groups, in order to identify whether they were comparable. There were no significant differences between the two conditions on overall pre-test scores, as well as on the scores for conceptual, procedural, and debugging questions. The 42 participants from the 2016 and 2017 classes had the same level of background knowledge.

Table 1: Basic statistics for the two conditions (* denotes significance at the .05 level)

	Strategy 1 (22)	Strategy 2 (20)	U
Pre-Test	62.84 (14.85)	63.5 (12.42)	
Post-Test	88.47 (9.24)	82.49 (9.07)	
Learning gain	0.67 (0.27)	0.51 (0.25)	135.5*
Conceptual knowledge gain	0.88 (0.21)	0.69 (0.37)	

There was a marginally significant difference on the post-test scores (U = 145, p = .058) between the Strategy 1 condition and Strategy 2 condition. The normalized learning gain for the Strategy 1 condition was significantly higher to the other condition. There were no significant differences between the two conditions on conceptual, procedural, and debugging scores on the post test. The conceptual knowledge gain of the Strategy 1 condition was marginally significantly higher than the Strategy 2 condition (U = 153, p = .057).

On average, the Strategy 1 condition had fewer learning activities than the Strategy 2 condition; this condition also received significantly more problems and fewer ErrExs (Table 2). There was a marginally significant difference on the number of WEs received by the two conditions (U = 152, p = .055). It is interesting that the students in the Strategy 1 condition learned significantly more than their peers even though they had fewer learning activities. However, the reported mental effort was significantly higher in the Strategy 1 condition. On average, the participants spent 85 minutes interacting with the learning tasks. There was no significant difference on the total interaction time between the two conditions.

The participants received C-SE prompts after problems, P-SE prompts after WEs, and alternatively received C-SE and P-SE prompts after ErrExs. SE success rate of the Strategy 1 condition is significantly higher than that of the Strategy 2 condition.

Table 2: Students Performance (** and *** denote significance at the .01 and .001 levels)

	Strategy 1 (22)	Strategy 2 (20)	U
Number of learning activities	14.5 (2.16)	18.1 (3.21)	83.5***
Problems	11.5 (1.47)	10.5 (0.95)	118**
ErrExs	1.45 (1.22)	6.8 (3.58)	62.5***
WEs	1.55 (1.63)	0.8 (0.77)	
Mental Effort	5.28 (1.24)	4.26 (1.09)	140*
SE Success Rate	0.93 (0.08)	0.77 (0.2)	116**

4.2 Are Learning Outcomes Different for Students with Low or High Prior Knowledge?

An additional analysis was conducted to determine whether the two strategies had different outcomes for novices and advanced students. We classified the 2016 students based on a median split on pre-test score (67%) into novices and advanced students. In 2017, as soon as a student submitted the pre-test, SQL-Tutor classified him/her immediately as a novice or advanced (see Section 3).

Table 3: Post-test scores (in %) for Novices and Advanced (Adv.) students

		Strategy 1	Strategy 2	U
Novices	Pre-test	51.57 (12.53)	53.62 (8.84)	
	Post-test	85.73 (10.15)	78.4 (9.82)	
	Post-test Conceptual	85.73 (10.15)	78.4 (9.82)	
	Learning gain	0.69 (0.24)	0.53 (0.24)	
Adv.	Pre-test	74.12 (5.13)	73.38 (5.53)	
	Post-test	91.21 (7.72)	86.59 (6.33)	
	Post-test Conceptual	100 (0)	88.33 (13.72)	27.5**
	Conceptual knowledge gain	1 (0)	0.68 (0.41)	27.5**
	Learning gain	0.66 (0.30)	0.49 (0.27)	

The Mann-Whitney U test revealed no significant differences between the two conditions for novices on any measures reported in Table 3. There were no significant differences for advanced students form the two conditions on the pre/post-test scores and normalized learning gain. Advanced students in Strategy 1 had a significantly higher conceptual knowledge gain compared to their peers in the Strategy 2 condition. This suggests that both conditions were beneficial for low prior knowledge students, but Strategy 1 was superior to Strategy 2 for advanced students.

Table 4: Performance of Novice Students

	Strategy 1 (11)	Strategy 2 (10)	U
Total learning activities	14.46 (2.34)	20 (0)	110***
Problems	11.45 (1.57)	10 (0)	20**
ErrExs	1.55 (1.44)	9 (0.82)	110***
WEs	1.45 (1.44)	1 (0.82)	ns
Mental Effort	5.2 (1.33)	4.62 (0.92)	ns
SE Success Rate	0.89 (0.05)	0.71 (0.19)	24.5*

Students in the Strategy 1 condition and advanced students in the Strategy 2 condition skipped preparation tasks when they performed well on previous problems. We found several significant differences between novices from the two conditions: novices from Strategy 1 on average completed significantly fewer learning activities overall, fewer ErrExs, but more problems and ErrExs (Table 4). Furthermore, novices in the Strategy 1 condition had a significantly higher SE success rate than their peers in the other condition.

Table 5: Performance of Advanced Students

	Strategy 1 (11)	Strategy 2 (10)	U
Total learning activities	14.55 (2.07)	16.2 (3.71)	ns
Problems	11.55 (1.44)	11 (1.16)	ns
ErrExs	1.36 (1.03)	4.6 (3.95)	ns
WEs	1.64 (1.86)	0.6 (0.7)	29.5*
Mental Effort	5.37 (1.2)	3.9 (1.17)	23*
SE Success Rate	0.96 (0.08)	0.83 (0.2)	27.5*

Advanced students in the Strategy 1 condition received significantly more WEs than the advanced students in the Strategy 2 (Table 5). There was also a significant difference for the SE success rate and mental effort. Therefore, the WEs in addition to ErrExs and PS is necessary for improving learners' conceptual knowledge [17-18], even for advanced students. There were no significant differences between the two conditions on the post-test of procedural and debugging scores for either novices or advanced students. These findings reject our Hypotheses 2a and 2b.

5 CONCLUSIONS AND DISCUSSION

Previous studies showed that worked examples are more beneficial for novices [6, 12], while the effect of erroneous examples is more pronounced for advanced students [14]. In our previous study [18], the addition of ErrExs improved learning on top of WEs and PS. Additionally, both novices and advanced students improved their problem-solving skills while explaining and correcting erroneous examples. We later designed an adaptive strategy (Strategy 1), which selects learning activities based on students' performance on the problems [1]. We found

that students in the adaptive condition significantly improved their post-test scores on conceptual, procedural and debugging questions. We also investigated the effect of Strategy 1 for students who started with different levels of background knowledge. We found that both novices and advanced students learning with Strategy 1 achieved the same learning outcomes as their peers in a fixed condition, but with fewer learning activities. We also surprisingly found that there was no significant difference on the number of learning activities between novices and advanced students. In this paper, we compared Strategy 1 to a new strategy (Strategy 2), which restricted the types of activities novices and advanced students could do. Strategy 2 adaptively provided WE or ErrEx to novices, and ErrEx or PS to advanced students.

Students in the Strategy 1 condition had a significantly higher learning gain, and marginally significantly higher post-test scores and conceptual knowledge gains. Our results also indicate that students in the Strategy 1 condition received significantly fewer learning activities than students in the Strategy 2 condition. Particularly, Strategy 1 condition students experienced significantly more problems and fewer erroneous examples. However, they still had significantly higher SE success rates and learning gains. In general, this suggests that the Strategy 1 is more effective than the Strategy 2 in selecting learning activities, thus our Hypothesis 1 is rejected.

There were no significant differences on the post-test scores (overall and the components) between novices from the two conditions, although Strategy 1 resulted in fewer learning activities and a higher mental effort scores. Advanced students did not show significant differences in post-test scores and learning gains between the two conditions. However, advanced students in the Strategy 1 condition had significantly higher conceptual knowledge gains and post-test scores of conceptual questions in comparison to the Strategy 2 condition. This suggests that both novices and advanced students showed better performance when learning with Strategy 1 compared with Strategy 2.

Although the present results still suggest that the Strategy 1 is a better learning strategy in SQL-Tutor, an important practical issue concerns the proper balance of worked examples, problem solving, and erroneous examples. In the present study, students who experienced fewer WEs and ErrExs achieved similar learning outcomes to their peers who received a lot of worked examples or erroneous examples. We expected that, like Große and Renkl [14], advanced students would benefit more from erroneous examples than novices. However, it seems that advanced students did not receive many erroneous examples in either condition.

Our adaptive strategy selects the learning activities for students based on their cognitive efficiency score on previous problems. The performance is computed from the student's score on the first submission on a problem. However, students may ask for feedback by submitting an empty solution as the first submission. Therefore, in future work, the performance scores can be calculated more precisely by adding the timing element as well as the feedback element or other elements that may affect students' learning during the problem solving. Furthermore, the erroneous examples in our study were designed by the instructors; that is, the erroneous examples were fixed, not adaptive. In SQL-Tutor, there is a set of related constraints for each clause of the SELECT statement. The system analyzes each attempt the student submitted, and records which constraints were satisfied or violated. The system estimates the students' knowledge of the clauses by aggregating the information about satisfied and violated constraints related to the clauses. Therefore, it is also interesting to investigate the adaptive erroneous examples that are based on students' gradually increased knowledge.

REFERENCES

[1] Chen, X., Mitrovic, A., & Mathews, M. (2017a). Does Adaptive Provision of Learning Activities Improve Learning in SQL-Tutor? In E. André, R. Baker, X. Hu, M. M. T. Rodrigo, & B. du Boulay (Eds.), *Proc. 18th International Conference on Artificial Intelligence in Education* (pp. 476-479). Wuhan, China: Springer.

[2] Chen, X., Mitrovic, A., & Mathews, M. (2017b). How Much Learning Support Should be Provided to Novices and Advanced Students? In M. Chang, N. S. Chen, R. Huang, Kinshuk, D. G. Sampson, & R. Vasiu (Eds.), *Proc. IEEE 17th International Conference on Advanced Learning Technologies* (pp. 39-43). Timisoara, Romania: IEEE Computer Society.

[3] Sweller, J., Van Merrienboer, J. J., & Paas, F. G. (1998). Cognitive architecture and instructional design. *Educational psychology review*, 10(3), 251-296.

[4] Atkinson, R. K., Derry, S. J., Renkl, A., & Wortham, D. (2000). Learning from examples: Instructional principles from the worked examples research. *Review of Educational Research*, 70(2), 181-214.

[5] Kirschner, P. A., Sweller, J., & Clark, R. E. (2006). Why minimal guidance during instruction does not work: An analysis of the failure of constructivist, discovery, problem-based, experiential, and inquiry-based teaching. *Educational Psychologist*, 41(2), 75-86

[6] van Gog, T., Kester, L., & Paas, F. (2011). Effects of worked examples, example-problem, and problem-example pairs on novices' learning. *Contemporary Educational Psychology*, 36(3), 212-218

[7] van Gog, T. (2011). Effects of identical example–problem and problem-example pairs on learning. *Computers & Education*, 57(2), 1775-1779

[8] Kalyuga, S., Chandler, P., Tuovinen, J., & Sweller, J. (2001). When problem solving is superior to studying worked examples. *Journal of Educational Psychology*, 93(3), 579-588.

[9] McLaren, B. M., & Isotani, S. (2011). When is it best to learn with all worked examples? In G. Biswas, S. Bull, J. Kay, & A. Mitrovic (Eds.), *Proc. 15th International Conference on Artificial Intelligence in Education* (pp. 222-229). Auckland, New Zealand: Springer.

[10] Schwonke, R., Wittwer, J., Aleven, V., Salden, R., Krieg, C., & Renkl, A. (2007). Can tutored problem solving benefit from faded worked-out examples. In S. Vosniadou, D. Kayser, & A. Protopapas (Eds.), *Proc. 2nd European Cognitive Science Conference* (pp. 59-64). Greece: Erlbaum.

[11] Schwonke, R., Renkl, A., Krieg, C., Wittwer, J., Aleven, V., & Salden, R. (2009). The worked-example effect: Not an artefact of lousy control conditions. *Computers in Human Behavior*, 25(2), 258-266

[12] Shareghi Najar, A. & Mitrovic, A. (2014) Examples and tutored problems: is alternating examples and problems the best instructional strategy? *Research and Practice in Technology-Enhanced Learning*, 9(3), 439-459.

[13] Siegler, R. S. & Chen, Z. (2008). Differentiation and integration: Guiding principles for analyzing cognitive change. *Developmental Science*, 11(4), 433-448.

[14] Große, C. S., & Renkl, A. (2007). Finding and fixing errors in worked examples: Can this foster learning outcomes? *Learning and instruction*, 17(6), 612-634.

[15] Durkin, K., & Rittle-Johnson, B. (2012). The effectiveness of using incorrect examples to support learning about decimal magnitude. *Learning and Instruction*, 22(3), 206-214.

[16] Tsovaltzi, D., McLaren, B. M., Melis, E., & Meyer, A.-K. (2012). Erroneous examples: effects on learning fractions in a web-based setting. *International Journal of Technology Enhanced Learning*, 4(3-4), 191-230.

[17] Booth, J. L., Lange, K. E., Koedinger, K. R., & Newton, K. J. (2013). Using example problems to improve student learning in algebra: Differentiating between correct and incorrect examples. *Learning and Instruction*, 25, 24-34.

[18] Chen, X., Mitrovic, A., & Mathews, M. (2016). Do Erroneous Examples Improve Learning in Addition to Problem Solving and Worked Examples? In A. Micarelli, J. Stamper, & K. Panourgia (Eds.), *Proc. 13th International Conference on Intelligent Tutoring Systems* (pp. 13-22). Zagreb, Croatia: Springer.

[19] Atkinson, R. K., Derry, S. J., Renkl, A., & Wortham, D. (2000). Learning from examples: Instructional principles from the worked examples research. *Review of Educational Research*, 70(2), 181-214.

[20] McLaren, B. M., Lim, S. J., & Koedinger, K. R. (2008). When and how often should worked examples be given to students? New results and a summary of the current state of research. In B. C. Love, K. McRae, & V. M. Sloutsky (Eds.), *Proc. 30th Annual Conference of the Cognitive Science Society* (pp. 2176-2181). Austin, TX: Cognitive Science Society.

[21] Kalyuga, S., Chandler, P., & Sweller, J. (1998). Levels of expertise and instructional design. *Human Factors*, 40(1), 1-17.

[22] Mitrovic, A. (2003). An intelligent SQL tutor on the web. *Artificial Intelligence in Education*, 13, 173-197.

[23] Chi, M. T., Leeuw, N., Chiu, M. H., & LaVancher, C. (1994). Eliciting self-explanations improves understanding. *Cognitive Science*, 18(3), 439-477.

[24] Kim, R. S., Weitz, R., Heffernan, N. T., & Krach, N. (2009). Tutored problem solving vs. "pure" worked examples. In N. Taatgen & H. van Rijn (Eds.), *Proc. 31st Annual Conference of the Cognitive Science Society* (pp. 3121-3126). Austin, TX: Cognitive Science Society.

[25] Weerasinghe, A., & Mitrovic, A. (2006). Studying human tutors to facilitate self-explanation. In M. Ikeda, K. Ashlay, & T.-W. Chan (Eds.), *Proc. 8th International Conference on Intelligent Tutoring Systems* (pp. 713-715). Jhongli, Taiwan: Springer.

[26] Kalyuga, S., & Sweller, J. (2005). Rapid dynamic assessment of expertise to improve the efficiency of adaptive e-learning. *Educational Technology Research and Development*, 53(3), 83-93.

Scaffolding for an OLM for Long-Term Physical Activity Goals

Lie Ming Tang
University Of Sydney
Darlington, NSW, Australia
ltan8012@uni.sydney.edu.au

Judy Kay
University Of Sydney
Darlington, NSW, Australia
judy.kay@sydney.edu.au

ABSTRACT

An important role of open learner models (OLMs) is to support *self-reflection*. We explore how to do this for an OLM based on fine-grained long term physical activity tracker data that many people are accumulating. We aim to tackle two well-documented challenges that people face, in making effective use of an OLM for reflection. 1. We created a tutorial to scaffold *sense-making* needed to understand the meaning of the OLM. 2. We integrated an interface scaffold to help users *consider key questions* for effective reflection. We report the results of a qualitative think-aloud lab study with 21 participants viewing their own long term OLM. To evaluate the *tutorial scaffolding*, we split participants into an experimental group, who did a tutorial before exploring the OLM and a control group which explored the interface without the tutorial. To evaluate the *reflection scaffolding*, all participants first explored the interface as they wished. We then provided *goal prompts* to scaffold reflection. Our study revealed that, under lab conditions, the tutorial scaffolding was not needed – all participants in both groups could readily understand the OLM. However, we found that several of the goal prompts were important to help participants consider key questions for effective reflection. Our key contribution is insights into the *design of scaffolding for reflection in a life-long learning context* of gaining insights and setting goals for physical activity.

CCS CONCEPTS

• **Human-centered computing** → **User studies**; **Walkthrough evaluations**; **Interaction design**; *User models*;

KEYWORDS

OLM, Scaffolding, User Interface, Long Term Physical Activity Data

ACM Reference Format:
Lie Ming Tang and Judy Kay. 2018. Scaffolding for an OLM for Long-Term Physical Activity Goals. In *UMAP '18: 26th Conference on User Modeling, Adaptation and Personalization, July 8–11, 2018, Singapore, Singapore*. ACM, New York, NY, USA, Article 4, 10 pages. https://doi.org/10.1145/3209219.3209220

1 INTRODUCTION

There is a growing body of work that aims to create Open Learner Models (OLMs) to support meta-cognition [10, 17, 28, 38, 51]. Much OLM research has been in the context of formal education. However, this important role of user models is also important in *life-long* and *life-wide* learning. In particular, one key role of an OLM is to support *self-reflection* [5, 11, 13, 16, 17]. This is especially important for achieving very long term goals, such as achieving and maintaining healthy levels of physical activity [6, 32, 39]. OLMs can play several important roles, including support users' curiosity about their data, allowing for playfulness in tracking style [44], learner trust [1] and several broader important meta-cognitive activities [12, 13, 18, 25].

Our work aims to take insights from OLM research into the area of *personal informatics*, where emerging sensor technologies enable people to collect considerable personal data. We focus on the goal to harness data from worn sensors about physical activity. Such sensors are becoming ubiquitous with the emergence of dedicated devices such as the Fitbit [1] as well as through ambient tracking via non-dedicated devices such as smartphones [2] [3]. Our work takes an OLM perspective, first to transform long term physical activity data into a user model, then to create an OLM interface, called *iStuckWithIt*, to support self-reflection on the user model.

In this paper, we consider two research questions about the scaffolding for self-reflection using *iStuckWithIt*:

- Do users need a scaffolding introductory tutorial to self-reflect using *iStuckWithIt*?
- Do users benefit from a reflection scaffold to systematically self-reflect on core long term goals represented in the OLM?

To explore this, we conducted a lab study where 21 existing long term physical activity trackers were asked to use *iStuckWithIt* [53], with 2 additional scaffolding elements: *tutorial* introduction and *goal prompts* for reflection. The tutorial scaffolding asks users to review the data of 2 hypothetical users, with data that highlights critical features of the dashboard. The goal prompt scaffolding is a side panel (pop-up) that asks users to answer 5 questions about their goals and their behaviour including whether they are achieving their goal, whether they should change their goal and to consider differences between when they are at work and not at work, weekend and weekdays or on holidays. These questions prompt users to considering their goal setting as well as how environmental and temporal factors that are known to affect physical activity, as documented in health literature [14].

The next section reviews related work followed by the study design and results. We conclude with a discussion of the findings and lessons learned for future designs.

---

[1]fitbit.com
[2]https://www.apple.com/au/ios/health/
[3]https://support.apple.com/en-au/HT203037

2 BACKGROUND

This section positions our work in relation to three bodies of previous research. First, we build on OLM research, where a user model is made available to the user to support goals such as self-reflection. Then we introduce the largely independent work on personal informatics, including an overview of the design of the basic *iStuckWithIt* interface. The third key strand is on meta-cognitive scaffolding for OLMs. We then introduce the main *iStuckWithIt* interface and explain the goals of our work in terms of the new contributions we aim to achieve.

Open Learner Modelling has a long history, beginning with the recognition that a user model (also called student or learner model) could be made available to the user [9, 31]. An OLM could serve several roles, including the learner interacting to negotiate or argue about the user model [9], supporting user control over their personal data [31] and for metacognitive processes of self-reflection, self-monitoring and planning [11, 13, 17]. There has been considerable research on the ways to present learner models, comparing various forms [13, 29]. There is also a body of studies that have demonstrated their effectiveness for learning in formal educational contexts [17, 38, 41, 42].

While OLM research has been largely concerned with formal educational settings, emerging sensor and mobile technologies have led to Personal Informatics research [34] and the similar Quantified Self movement in the broader community[4]. These communities also aim to create useful representations of users, available in interfaces that have similar goals to OLMs. This community has demonstrated that, while people see the potential value of such data for self-reflection, current tools fail to support this well [15, 27, 35, 45, 47, 53]. Indeed, there is a growing body of evidence that points to a lack of perceived usefulness of long term tracker data [26, 45, 46]. In personal informatics, the user models need to be designed to represent aspects of user's goals, linking the available sensor data to those goals. A key problem in creating the model, and associated OLM interfaces, relates to problems in the accuracy of the data due to incompleteness. For example, a worn activity tracker only gives reliable data when the user wears it and this should be considered in reasoning about the user's activity level and modelling their goal achievement. Incomplete data compromises the usefulness of tracking. People can lose confidence when they are confronted with gaps or incorrect reports due to gaps [8, 45]. Failure to account for, or recognise, incomplete data can mean that people consider the data not to be useful which has been reported in recent years [19, 26, 30, 33, 45, 48, 54]. A similar problem has been identified for OLMs for formal learning, with the need to represent the uncertainty in the model [2, 21].

While the ideal OLM interface would be readily understood by the user, in practice this may be difficult to achieve. Even with a quite simple skillometer, consisting of just seven bars [37], there were challenges in both understanding the model and the meaning of the components display as well as in reflection. Self-evaluation is especially important for achieving the very long term goals, such as achieving and maintaining healthy levels of physical activity [6, 32, 39]. OLMs can play several important roles, including supporting users' curiosity about their data, allowing for playfulness in tracking

---

[4]http://quantifiedself.com/

---

style [44], facilitating learner trust [1] and several other important meta-cognitive activities [12, 13, 18, 25].

This work explores the role of scaffolding for the *iStuckWithIt* interface. The design of this interface and the nature of insights people made when using it have been previously reported [53]. We now briefly introduce that version of the interface, as shown at the left of Figure 1. Broadly, the design is based on a calendar visualisation. The labels A-H illustrate key features. A marks the drop-down menu to select the class of goal the user wants to see; those in the study are steps per day, count of active minutes per day and distance walked per day. The main interface is marked B for a period when the user has data about their activity levels (with all cells either white or shades of blue) and C when there was a period with no data because the user did not wear their tracker in that period (grey cells). The figure shows the interface configured for a goal target of 10,000 steps a day and only cells exceeding this are bright blue. The configuration in the figure sets a 50%, or 5,000 step threshold for the lighter blue and then white indicates days that have data (>= 1 step) but less than 5,000 steps. The bars marked with D were designed to help the user take account of the impact of their actual wearing behaviour on the results shows. The bars show the average number of hours per day the user wore the tracker in each week. When this is low, as in the case of weeks nearest the D, the results are based on just the limited data that is available. In the figure, the user has clicked on the cell near E to see more details for that day. The upper middle is the configuration section, labeled F. This enables the user to change the thresholds for the goals. The right part of the figure, G, is the reflection scaffolding that is the focus of this paper. H enables the user to alter the display from goal oriented, as in this figure, to a gradient.

In summary, there has been considerable research in OLMs, especially in formal educational settings. There is a growing body of work in personal informatics and broader community interest in Quantified Self. Both have identified a key challenge for effective use of personal data – although they have not used the term, OLM, they highlight the need for scaffolding to help people make sense of complex collections of personal data, user models, so as to support their self-reflection. Our work tackles this problem. This paper goes beyond our previous report of *iStuckWithIt*'s design [53] as we now describe the study of the two forms of scaffolding we explored for the *iStuckWithIt* OLM interface: the tutorial scaffolding to introduce the interface and the reflection scaffolding.

3 STUDY DESIGN

Our two research questions were:

- RQ1: Tutorial scaffold: Do users need a scaffolding introductory tutorial to self-reflect using *iStuckWithIt*?
- RQ2: Goal prompts scaffold: Do users benefit from a reflection scaffold to systematically self-reflect on core long term goals represented in the OLM?

This section first describes the overall design of the study and then the detailed design for each research question.

We recruited 21 long term Fitbit users, people who had collected at least 6 months of personal physical activity data. We then conducted a between-subjects lab study in terms of the first research question. This study session had the following stages

(1) Nine participants (9) worked through the scaffolding tutorial, described below.

(2) All participants were asked to explore the main interface in *iStuckWithIt*. We asked them to *think-aloud* [43], explaining what they saw, understood and their insights.

(3) We then asked all participants to consider the reflective questions, labeled (G) in Figure 1.

(4) Finally, we interviewed them on their experiences of viewing their own data and what insights they learned.

In the next two sub-sections, we present the motivation and design of the tutorial and goal prompt scaffolding. We also explain the study design to evaluate each of them.

3.1 RQ1: Tutorial Scaffolding

While some long term physical activity trackers do use their tracker over the long term, most fail to make use of their own long term data [26, 45, 53]. This means that our study design should account for the likelihood that the *iStuckWithIt* interface would provide the first opportunity for participants to see their own *long term* goal performance for physical activity, in terms of steps, active minutes and distance. We anticipated that participants would benefit from a tutorial that introduced them to *iStuckWithIt*.

To evaluate this, we prepared a tutorial, based on a set of exercises to explore the *iStuckWithIt* OLM for two hypothetical users, Alice and Alex. These provided carefully designed datasets which highlighted key aspects that the interface was intended to enable people to understand about their own long term physical activity model. We asked 9 of our participants to complete this prior to seeing *iStuckWithIt* with their own data. The steps in this tutorial were:

(1) Participants were told that Alex and Alice's each had a goal of "at least 30 very active minutes per day".

(2) Participants were asked to consider whether Alice achieved her goal or not.

(3) They then did this for Alex.

(4) In each case, the experimenter allowed the participant to explore the OLM, thinking aloud to explain how they interpreted it.

(5) At the end, if participants had failed to see and understand key features, the experimenter explained them.

Figure 2 shows the data for Alice who started using her Fitbit in August 2015. Key features are:

(1) The first month of tracking had quite high tracker use - few grey cells;

(2) In mid-September, there is a 2-week gap in tracking - all grey cells;

(3) After this, there are many grey cells, reflecting days Alice did not wear her tracker, especially on weekends.

(4) Consistently higher wear time in August and September and then consistently lower hourly wear-time after September.

(5) Scaffold users to reflect or speculate on the *potential causes* for this change from Aug/Sept to afterwards.

Figure 1 shows Alex's data which highlights the following:

(1) Low physical activity levels during weekend compared with weekdays.

(2) Large gaps of several months (blocks of grey cells) between wearing activity tracker.

(3) Overall inconsistent hourly wear-time and some periods with low wear-time.

We recorded observations and participant comments in their think-aloud exploration of the interface. If, after some exploration, the participant did not notice key aspects, they were prompted about them. We also recorded whether the user commented on how missing data could have affected accuracy of the step counts as well as comments around wearing behaviour of Alice and Alex.

The aim of the tutorial scaffolding study is two-fold. First, we wanted to discover which features of the long term physical activity tracker data are easily understood and which are not. We also wanted to see the impact of the tutorial, to learn whether participants who had the extra learning scaffolding were better able to make sense of their own data than those who did not do the tutorial.

3.2 RQ2: Goal prompts scaffolding

After participants had finished exploring the main *iStuckWithIt* interface with their own data, we asked them to open the goal prompt scaffolding, labelled G at the right of Figure 1. This was designed around two core forms of reflection:

(1) Reflect on *goal achievement* and consider reviewing the *goal setting* – the first two questions, marked +.

(2) Reflect on *factors affecting goal achievement* – the last 3 prompts, also marked with +, about weekend (versus weekdays), holidays and work versus non-work.

The benefits of scaffolding or support for self-regulation skills such as self-monitoring, goals and goal setting are well documented [3, 4]. Also, previous work [49, 50] using goal setting as a strategy to promote health and physical activity behaviour change has demonstrated the potential of this approach. The first category of our questions aims to remind users to reflect on their goals and goal setting. The second category of questions called for the participant to consider factors that are known to be important for people's physical activity levels. Health studies have consistently indicated differences between activity levels on weekends versus weekdays [7, 24, 52]. Moreover, previous studies have shown that by helping users consider such questions can support reflection on activity tracker data [22]. Therefore, our scaffolding design was based on literature indicating the benefits of reminding users to consider the context of their activity levels and behaviour is likely to be useful.

In addition to our prompt questions, we did consider others. For example, studies of existing users of physical activity trackers have reported that such users are quite interested in peaks and lows [26, 36]. On the matter of influencing people to change tracking behaviour, Epstein et al. [23] found potential value in using visualisations for encouraging users to return after a long gap in tracker use. While these are potentially useful, we did not include them as our focus was of studying whether people could make sense of their data at the OLM interface and reflect on important features associated with learning about their own long-term goal achievement.

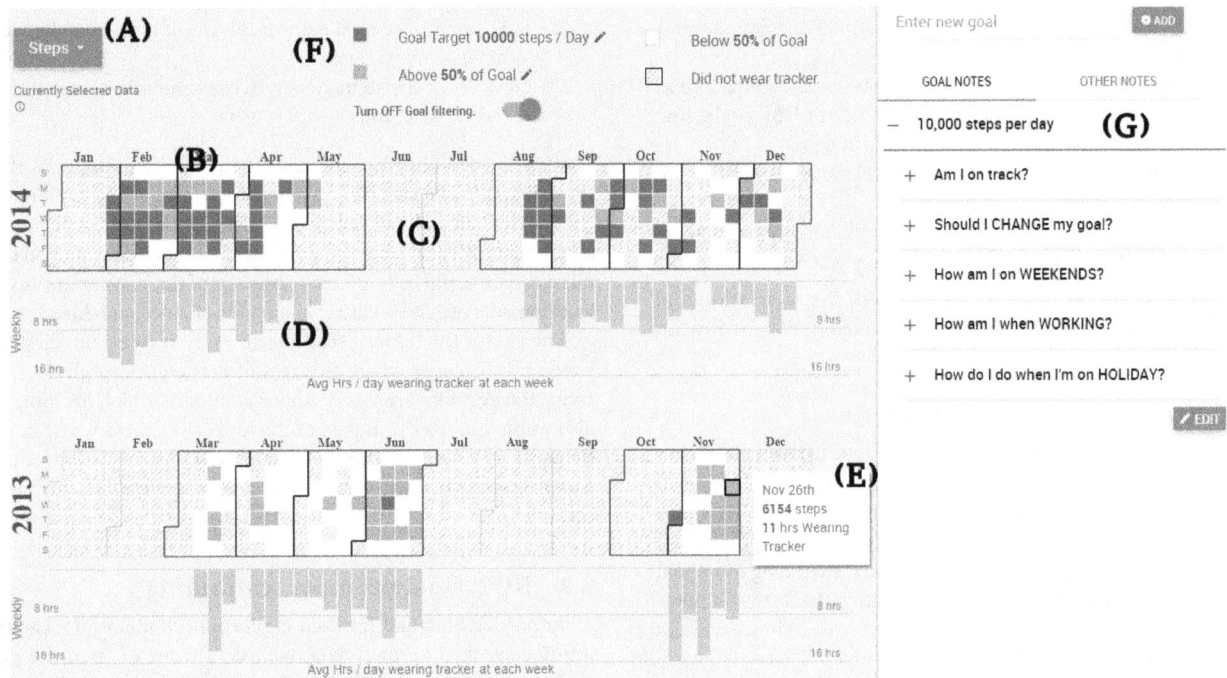

Figure 1: OLM to support reflection on achievement of long term physical activity goals. (A): Drop down menu to select between datasets (i.e., steps, active minutes, distance). (B): Calendar visualisation, with colour showing activity level on each day – dark blue means 10,000+ steps, light blue >5,000 but <10,000 steps, white has >0 but <5,000 steps. (C): Grey striped cells are days with no data. (D): Bar graph showing average wear-time in hours per day for each week. (E): Pop-up showing additional details of a particular day / cell. (F): Configuration – to adjust the thresholds for colouring of the cells. (G): Goal prompt scaffolding questions.

Figure 2: Data for hypothetical user Alice where she started using data in August until Dec. Her daily wear-time declined after September especially on weekends and wear-time is also lower but consistent.

4   RESULTS

In this section, we first introduce the participants of our study then we discuss the results around the two research questions.

4.1   Participants

Table 1 presents details of our participants, ordered by gender in Col. 2, then by scaffolding condition Col. 3. This shows 9 participants

did tutorial (Y) and 12 did not (N). In terms of background, many participants were highly educated and several worked or studied in IT, shown in Col. 5 and Col. 6. This group may have higher literacy and skills levels in data analysis than a more general population. This is similar to participants in other qualitative studies of existing long term personal trackers [26]. There were more male participants (14) than female (7). Our participants ages are spread across the age groups shown in Col. 4 with 25-34 being the largest group at 6, the lowest 18-24 (3) and 4 participants in the others. Our demographic is similar, in terms of age and gender, to the population of personal activity tracker users and wearable technology adopters [20]. The duration of tracker use varied from 6 to 38 months shown in Col. 7 (average: 23 months).

Col. 8 shows the %-age of days with at least 1 step. This varied widely (min: 15%, max: 100%, average: 68%, std: 30%). Col. 9 is the wear-time (number of hours per day users with >= 1 step recorded). Our participants generally had high wear-time (min: 9 hours, max: 20, average: 15, std: 3) and Col. 10 shows the standard deviation (min: 2, max: 6, average: 4, std: 1). Col. 9 and Col. 10 show that while overall wear-time is high there is large variation both between and within individuals.

Overall, our participants had very wide differences in consistency of days with tracking – the %-age of days with any data. For example, 6 participants (P8, P9, P10, P14, P15 and P20) had 100% of

Table 1: Participant profiles grouped by gender. Col. 1 participant identifier. Col. 2 gender. Col. 3 whether participant is in the tutorial scaffolding condition. Col. 4 to Col. 6 participant age, occupation and education. Col. 7 duration in months of tracking data (first to last day with data). Col. 8 %-age of days with at least 1 step Col. 7). Col. 9 and Col. 10 the median and standard deviation of wear-time (number of hours per day with at least 1 step). The last 4 rows are summary statistics over all participants (average, standard deviation, min and max) of Col. 8, Col. 9 and Col. 10. N=21

1	2	3	4	5	6	7	8	9	10
P#	M/F	Tut	Age	Occupation	Education	Dur	Daily	Hours (med)	Hours (std)
P1	F	N	25 - 34	Part-time	U-Grad	7	86%	13	6
P2	F	N	25 - 34	Property Admin	U-Grad	9	96%	17	5
P3	F	N	45 - 54	Manager	P-Grad	38	39%	14	3
P4	F	N	35 - 44	IT Support	P-Grad	8	88%	16	4
P5	F	Y	55 - 64	Academic	Prof	15	15%	14	6
P6	F	Y	25 - 34	IT Developer	U-Grad	27	62%	9	4
P7	F	Y	45 - 54	Academic	P-Grad	37	32%	13	4
P8	M	N	55 - 64	IT Developer	U-Grad	6	100%	16	3
P9	M	N	55 - 64	Retired Military	U-Grad	13	100%	17	5
P10	M	N	45 - 54	Dir of IT	P-Grad	21	100%	18	2
P11	M	N	35 - 44	Engineer	Prof	23	60%	16	4
P12	M	N	18 - 24	Student	U-Grad	27	31%	13	4
P13	M	N	25 - 34	Researcher	P-Grad	29	70%	13	3
P14	M	N	35 - 44	Self Employed	U-Grad	36	100%	20	4
P15	M	N	45 - 54	Manager	U-Grad	38	100%	17	2
P16	M	Y	25 - 34	Student	P-Grad	18	29%	N/A	N/A
P17	M	Y	25 - 34	Student	P-Grad	18	38%	11	5
P18	M	Y	18 - 24	Student	Highschool	22	44%	13	3
P19	M	Y	55 - 64	Professor	P-Grad	26	41%	12	4
P20	M	Y	18 - 24	Student	P-Grad	27	100%	18	3
P21	M	Y	35 - 44	Professor	P-Grad	29	91%	13	4
Summary Stats						Avg	68%	15	4
						Std	30%	3	1
						Min	15%	9	2
						Max	100%	20	6

Table 2: Table showing whether users identified each of the notable items as part of their tutorial scaffolding. Row. 1 participant ID. Row. 2 %-age of days with at least 1 step. Row. 3 median hours per day with >1 step. Row. 4 to Row. 6 3 notable items in the Alice tutorial. Row. 7 to Row. 9 notable items in the Alex tutorial Row. 10 notable items identified by each participant as %-age of all 6 such items. N=9.

		P20	P21	P6	P18	P19	P17	P7	P16	P5	
1	Participant ID	P20	P21	P6	P18	P19	P17	P7	P16	P5	
2	Daily Adherence %	100	91	62	44	41	38	32	29	15	
3	Wear-time (median hours / day)	18	13	9	13	12	11	13	N/A	14	
4	**Alice:** Lower daily adherence after September, during 2 weeks gap during September to October especially on weekends.	x	x	x	x	x	x	x	x	x	100%
5	Lower wear-time after September.	x	x	x		x			x		56%
6	Reflect or speculate on the causes for this change from Aug/Sept to afterwards.	x	x	x	x	x	x	x	x	x	100%
7	**Alex:** Low physical activity levels during weekend versus weekdays.	x		x					x		33%
8	Large gaps between wearing activity tracker.	x	x	x	x	x	x	x	x	x	100%
9	Inconsistent and lower wear-time.		x						x		22%
10	Items identified (%)	83%	83%	83%	50%	67%	50%	50%	83%	67%	

4.2 RQ1: Tutorial Scaffolding

Table 2 shows which notable item each participant identified for hypothetical users, Alice from Row. 4 to Row. 6 and Alex, from Row. 7 to Row. 9 during the tutorial scaffolding condition. All participants identified at least 50% of these but none could identify all items.

Our participants readily identified whole day wearing patterns, distinguishing days with any data (appearing as white or light or dark blue cells) against days with no data (grey cells). In the Alice condition, all participants observed that she had more missing days after September (Row. 4) and all commented or speculated on the causes for this (Row. 6). For example, P20 commented on Alice's gap in data during September, *"Stopped wearing in September, October returned, maybe had gone on holiday"*. In the Alex condition, all participants commented on the large gaps between periods of more consistent tracking over the 2 year period (Row. 8). They also commented on Alex being more consistent in wearing his tracker on more days in the second year.

The notion of the wear-time in terms of *number of hours with any data in a day*, was harder for our participants to discover. Row. 5 shows that 4 participants (44%) did not comment on the low wear-time for Alice after September. Moreover, only 2 participants (22%) noticed the drop in Alice's wear-time (Row. 5) as well as the inconsistent wear-time across different months and years in Alex's data (Row. 9). P16 commented when viewing Alice's data, *"I see she is not always using her tracker, especially in the last few months. Only 4 - 5 hours per day"* and when viewing Alex's data *"He used to wear the tracker more longer than recently"*. P21 when viewing Alice's data, *"Towards the end, not only was [Alice] less active but also wearing it for shorter periods"*. When viewing Alex's data, he commented, *"Alex is also more consistently wearing the tracker in the second year."*.

days with data - meaning they wore their tracker every day in the period from the first day to the last in the dataset. These participants also averaged higher wear-time within each day, recording between 16 and 20 hours per day.

In contrast, the 6 participants with lowest consistency in wearing the tracker had between 15% and 39% of days that had any data (P6, P10, P2, P17, P20 and P18) and their median wear-time was 9 to 16 hours per day. Since in medical research 10 hours of wear-time is considered sufficient for meaningful data [40], even those who averaged 9 hours (P6) may have acceptable data quality. Interestingly, these 2 groups of users had similar wear-time variation indicated by the standard deviation (i.e., variation in the number of hours per day with at least 1 step) between averaging 4 hours for lower daily adherence users and 3 for highly daily adherent users.

These participant statistics indicate that while there are large variations in the *number of days with data* (%-age of days with at least 1 step) all participants had high wear-time.

Interestingly, most participants (3 of 4) who commented or reflected on wear-time also commented on their own wear-time when viewing their own data during the think-aloud. (The outlier is P16 the sole participant who did not have wear-time data).

Notably, several participants in the *control condition* – who did *not* do the tutorial scaffolding, also commented on wear-time in their own data. For example, P12 commented on how the hours of wear (wear-time) may affect his activity levels, *"If I wear my tracker longer, it will track more of my activity. I take off my tracker when I get home. So maybe I should just leave my tracker on myself at home as well to get more steps, little steps I do walking around home"*. P4 was surprised at the number of hours she wore her tracker, *"I was surprised I was wearing it for 19 hours"*. When investigating a day that had very low steps as well as hours of wear, P5 commented, *"I thought I wore it for longer that day, it could be that I bumped it and turned it off. I think it happens sometimes when I bump it"*.

Row. 7 indicates that only 3 participants (33%) noticed the substantially lower steps and lower days with any data on weekends. One of the three who did, P7 reflected on the differences between Alice and Alex, commenting, *"Alex didn't wear it on weekends, which I didn't notice on Alice"*.

Row. 2 and Row. 3 of Table 2 shows each participant's own daily %-age of days with data (Daily Adherence) and wear-time against the number of notable items in each tutorial scenario. This shows the completeness of their own data, so we can see this against the notable items they identified. For example, P6 had the lowest median wear-time (9 hours per day) and P5 had the lowest daily adherence (with just 15% of days with data). During the scaffolding tutorial, we found several cases where users related their own experiences and thinking when viewing these 2 hypothetical user's data. For example, P5 explained their low, 15% of days with data, was due to significant medical conditions, and commented *"Sometimes she doesn't wear her tracker, so she's like me"*. P17 who had 38% daily adherence commented, *"I can see Alex is achieving his goal. But as time passes, he started to drop in his wear. In the beginning, I think he is more motivated, like myself as well."*. When looking at Alice's data, P17 commented, *"I think people forget to wear or perhaps it doesn't match the fashion"*. Interestingly, when he explored his own long term data, after the tutorial, he explained that he stopped wearing his Fitbit tracker because his did a sport that required a wrist based apparel that prevented him from wearing his Fitbit. His earlier speculation on the reason for Alice's missing days could be due to fashion concerns, is similar to this reasoning. P21 commented, *"I can see there are some days where Alex forgot to wear it or forgot to track properly – maybe she was on holiday or something"*. When analysing his own long term tracker data, P21 who has relatively high daily adherence (91%) commented on the days he did not wear the tracker due to holidays and work travels. P18 who has daily adherence of 44% also commented on the motivational effect of adherence and missing data, *"She was very consistent but she stopped. I think it's discouraging to have so much missing data."*.

This section summarised results for the first research question which explored whether the tutorial scaffold was needed and useful. Comparing the participants' understanding of their own *iStuckWithIt* OLM, we observed that participants in both the tutorial and control conditions could understand the main features in terms of *days the goals* were met and how to interpret the display of days

Table 3: Summary of participant insights triggered by scaffolding of the goal prompt questions. Col. 1 the participant ID. Col. 3 daily adherence (%-age of days with >1 step). Col. 4 wear-time (median hours of wear per day with >1 step). Col. 5 to Col. 8 the 4 types of insights associated with the goal prompt questions. N=21

1	2	3	4	5	6	7	8
PID	Tutorial	Daily	Hours (med)	Wkend Vs Wkdays	Work Vs Non Work	Holiday	Change Goals
P20	Y	100	18			Y	Y
P21	Y	91	13	Y		Y	Y
P6	Y	62	9				
P18	Y	44	13				
P19	Y	41	12				
P17	Y	38	11				
P7	Y	32	13	Y		Y	
P16	Y	29	N/A	Y			
P5	Y	15	14	Y			Y
P4	-	88	16	Y			
P15	-	100	17				
P10	-	100	18				
P8	-	100	16				
P9	-	100	17			Y	Y
P14	-	100	20	Y	Y		Y
P2	-	96	17				
P1	-	86	12	Y			
P13	-	70	13	Y	Y		
P11	-	60	16				
P3	-	39	14				
P12	-	31	13				
			Total	38% (8)	10% (2)	19% (4)	24% (5)
			Total	38%	10%	19%	24%

with any data. Both groups also performed similarly on wear-time (median hours of wear per day with >1 step), with most people tending to miss this aspect and similar levels of awareness of it between the conditions. Overall, both conditions performed similarly.

4.3 RQ2: Goal Prompts

We now consider the results for the scaffolding for reflection. While the tutorial was done only be the 9 participants in the tutorial group, all participants then used the interface to explore their own data. When they had finishing doing this, the experimenter asked them to open the scaffolding section of the interface to consider the questions intended to help them consider and reflect on key features. Table 3 summarises the new insights that participants gained in this scaffolded reflection phase. Col. 5 to Col. 7of the table show where the goal prompt enabled a participant to gain new insights **in addition** to those the experimenter recorded them as making already.

When asked about weekend versus weekdays, 8 participants (38%) identified new insights – shown in Col. 5. For example, P4 commented, *"I'm not doing very well on weekends"*. Interestingly, this was only true more recently in the last year because she was more active during weekends and weekdays in the previous year in her data. P14 was confident during the think-aloud and pre-interview that he was more active on weekend than weekdays. *"More physically active during weekends because I go hiking or something"*. However, his actual data contradicts this belief and during the think-aloud session, he did not seem to identify this. When prompted by the goal prompt panel questions, he considered this more closely and commented, *"When I see on your website, there is a lot of white [referring to weekends]. I wonder why that is"*. During post interview, when asked if he found anything surprising, he commented, *"I thought I was hitting my step goals more than I was on the weekends, it was definitely an eye opener"*. P21 commenting on doing better on weekends, *"I'm actually overshooting my goal, quite consistently"*. P7 commented on the differences between Saturday and Sundays, *"good on Saturday but not on Sundays"*.

Our participants were generally aware of their work versus non-work periods and most made observations about this during the think-aloud session when they reflected on their own data. The goal prompt questions helped 2 participants find something new, shown in Col. 6. P14 commented that he is not doing as well during work times, *"I seem to have a little more difficulty especially when I'm in the car a lot"*. P13 commented, *"Doing well when going to the office, not so well when working from home. More recently working during the week has been less good"*. During the post interview, when asked whether he learned something new, he commented, *"Going through the Goal prompts, it got me to think about things like looking at weekends versus during the week – it definitely got me thinking about different ways to divide up my time"*. This question did not apply to 2 participants (P9,P1) because they did not work or study. For example, P9 commented, *"doesn't matter because weekend and weekdays are pretty much the same to me, I'm retired"*.

During the main think-aloud exploration of *iStuckWithIt*, most participants reflected on the effect of holidays – this was triggered by visible trends in their own goal achievement. The goal prompt question (Col. 7) helped 4 participants (19%) find more. For example, P21 went back to the *iStuckWithIt* display, reviewing holiday periods more closely and commented, *"I'm mixed on holidays, there are some holidays where I do walking, there are holidays where I was in [location] , ... , wasn't wearing it back there, I was wearing it sometimes but not much"*. P7 reflected on their broad wearing patterns, daily and hourly, during holidays, *"generally I forget to wear it, and I don't take it often and I fear losing it, and I don't want to take all the charging cables"*. Others focused on goal achievement consistency, for example, P9 commented, *"I walked on Christmas day. I walked on New Year's Day – so I'm quite consistent"*.

While most participants reflected upon both their activity levels and wearing behaviour in the main session exploring *iStuckWithIt*, the goal prompt questions helped 4 participants (19%) to consider changing their goal targets. For example, P21 commented, *"I guess I should lower it to something more realistic to achieve that the 10K steps per day. Maybe if I change to 8K"*. P14, after realising that he was less active on weekends commented, *"I want to make sure I hit my step goals more on the weekends, walking a little bit more"*. P9 commented, *"I should change my goal because I'm exceeding it too easily."*. Notably, P4 was confused by the wording of the prompt and failed to see the usefulness of this question. She commented, *"I don't understand why this question is here, I compare myself to myself, it doesn't matter to me"*.

Not all participants considered the goal prompts useful. For example, P16 commented, *"I think the ideas of these questions are interesting but these ones are not as useful for me. I prefer it gives me advice or record what I did"*. P16 also suggested that a prompt about how he achieved a goal each day might be useful in helping him remember. *"I think if each day when I achieve the goal, I get a question about how I achieved the goal, I think that could be useful. It might be useful if it can help me remember how I achieved the goal"*. P21 commented, *"I'm not sure how I would use it, I don't have so many goals that I have to write them down"*. He went on to suggest that these types of prompts might be better integrated into the regular weekly email that that Fitbit currently sends – he suggest this should also highlight notable items, like peaks and ask for reflection on those days then. *"I would like to be prompted as part of the weekly email if there was something interesting e.g., 28K steps days, to note things like I went hiking into the note. It would be nice to have it integrated with my weekly email to complement what I currently see"*.

To summarize, the goal prompt helped 10 participants (48%) gain new insights and 7 of these participants gained two or more insights. Broadly, our results indicate that the goal prompt scaffolding for reflection is valuable.

5 DISCUSSION

To understand our long term OLM, and reflect on their long term behaviour and its implications, users needed to *make sense of their long term data*. Our interface transforms that data into an OLM which highlight two key aspects. It shows a person's *apparent goal achievement*, in terms of how they did compared with their target for steps per day, active minutes or distance. However, to related this to the actual activity level, they also need to appreciate the *implications of their wearing behaviour*. This determines the completeness and meaningfulness of their data. The tutorial scaffold was intended to both support this and to enable us to study how readily people could learn about these aspects with all tutorial condition participants doing this in the context of two sets of carefully designed data, for the hypothetical users Alice and Alex. This section first considers what we learnt from the study of the tutorial scaffolding. We then discuss what our findings reveal about goal prompt scaffolding. Finally, we discuss lessons learned and insights for designing future OLMs for this class of lifelong, life-wide learning for an important aspect of health.

No tutorial is needed to understand daily goal achievement trends (RQ1)

Our study results show that all participants, in either the tutorial or control group found it easy to see that blocks of missing data (grey cells) meant there was no data and that other cells indicated whether they met their goal. In the tutorial condition, participants could do this without assistance for the case of both Alice and Alex. They then went on to make a similar interpretation of their own data. The control condition participants also found this aspect of the interface intuitive and a good basis for reflection about the reasons they met their goals, commenting on aspects like holidays, injury and motivation. So, the tutorial was not needed for this case.

The tutorial did not make a difference in helping people understand wear-time (RQ1)

We observed that a minority of participants could *discover this* from the carefully crafted data for Alice and Alex. Only 56% of participants noted the low wear-time for Alice in the later months of tracking. Even fewer speculated or commented on its meaning. Moreover, only 2 participants noticed inconsistent wear-time for Alex over the long term. Our design of the tutorial was based on providing very clear cases that should have made this concept easier to discover. For the participants who did not work this out, the experimenter explained it to them. Our observations of participants studying their own data indicate that both the tutorial and control condition participants performed similarly on this aspect. So, the tutorial was not helpful for this case and further, many participants found it difficult to appreciate the concept of wear-time. This is unfortunate since it is critical to take account of the number of hours with data to judge whether there is enough data to conclude about whether they have met their goal. There appear to be two main ways to tackle this problem. First, we may need to help people appreciate the importance of taking account of wear-time, particularly the number of hours of wear in a day. Second, the interface should make this clearer than it currently does.

Can scaffolding support insights? (RQ2)

We designed *iStuckWithIt* to present and overview model of people's goal achievement for levels of physical activity. The goal prompt scaffolding was designed to help users reflect on questions that they may not have considered when reviewing their own data. Our study showed that even for our population of existing long term physical activity trackers who are highly educated and familiar with technology, the goal prompt scaffolding could help many of them reflect on important aspects that they had not considered. Our results showed that while *iStuckWithIt* design was useful in supporting reflection on its own, the goal prompt scaffold helped many to consider and discover insights they missed.

Adherence scaffolding design: lessons learned

In this section, we discuss lessons learned and opportunities for future user interfaces that aims to support daily adherence and wear-time for reflecting on long term physical activity data.

First, our results suggest that a more adaptive or personalised approach is needed to teach about wear-time. This should take account of the user's actual wear-time. For people who had high wear-time (e.g., 15 hours or more per day) and consistent wear (near 100% of days have >0 steps), there is no need to consider wear-time when interpreting the interface's goal achievement display. In this case, future interfaces could highlight just the low wear-time days. The configuration interface could be enhanced to define suitable thresholds for this. Then the interface could filter the display to show only days that meet the threshold. For those who do *not* have high wear-time, further work is needed. However, since our long term physical activity tracker participants had high wear-time we have limited information for this type of user.

The goal prompt scaffolding findings demonstrate the insights gained by half our participants, by considering salient aspects. This is also an opportunity for personalisation, so that the cases that deserve attention are provided as prompts. This is particularly likely to be valuable for real world use, rather than our laboratory study. It will be important in ensuring users can readily tackle the challenge of reflection, when confronted for the first time with an unfamiliar OLM interface for their long term performance on physical activity. Opportunities for scaffolding include highlighting aspects known to be important, such as weekend versus weekdays, asking users to consider their performance and behaviour across different environments (e.g., work versus non-work). Our findings show that there is a need to personalise such prompts based on the individual's behaviour. Prompts or questions that do not apply to the participants or do not fit the user's circumstances (e.g., work situation) or goals should not be shown.

Finally, it may be useful to send goal prompts or reflective questions via regular email messages to capture contextual and qualitative information about days of interest (e.g., what did they do or how they achieved a peak day or goal-met day). Participant comments suggest they believe capturing such data may help them remember to consider and reflect on goal prompt questions.

5.1 Limitations

Our study was restricted to existing FitBit users. As FitBits had been widely available for many years [5], this allowed us to recruit participants who has already collected long term data. Also, our study is a lab study of the scaffolding designs. This may limit generalisability of our findings for wider populations of activity trackers in authentic settings. Moreover, since the iStuckWithIt user interface and study was designed for long term data, the usefulness of our scaffolding design on short term data was not examined. Our work paves the way for longer term field studies. Further work is still needed on scaffolding designs that help people understand the impact of data incompleteness in short term physical activity tracker data.

6 CONCLUSION

In this study, we explored how to help people reflect on their long term physical activity goal achievement. We extended previous work by exploring two forms of scaffolding (tutorial, goal prompt) and reported on a lab study of 21 existing long term physical activity tracker's experiences. The tutorial scaffolding results reveal that missing or incompleteness in data on a day-to-day basis (daily adherence) is intuitive and well understood. However, for wear-time (hours of wear per day), it may be more appropriate to provide prompts and alerts based on automatic detection of features such as low wear-time on certain days, weeks or highlighting inconsistencies over time. In addition, our prompt scaffolding (reflective questionnaire) proved effective support for reflection, resulting in new insights. We go beyond previous OLM work, particularly in the focus on a lifelong, life-wide learning goal associated with long term physical activity goal achievement. Our findings provide design insights about these two scaffolding approaches apply, with recommendations on future work and potential roles for reflection scaffolding and its personalisation.

---

[5] http://www.wareable.com/fitbit/fitness-tracker-sales-2015-fitbit-1169

REFERENCES

[1] Norasnita Ahmad and Susan Bull. 2009. Learner Trust in Learner Model Externalisations.. In *AIED*. 617–619.

[2] Lamiya Al-Shanfari, Carrie Demmans Epp, and Susan Bull. 2016. Uncertainty in Open Learner Models: Visualising Inconsistencies in the Underlying Data.. In *LAL@ LAK*. 23–30.

[3] Roger Azevedo and Jennifer G Cromley. 2004. Does training on self-regulated learning facilitate students' learning with hypermedia? *Journal of educational psychology* 96, 3 (2004), 523.

[4] Albert Bandura. 2005. The growing centrality of self-regulation in health promotion and disease prevention. *The european health psychologist* 1 (2005), 11–12.

[5] Albert Bandura. 2005. The Primacy of Self-Regulation in Health Promotion. *Applied Psychology* 54, 2 (apr 2005), 245–254.

[6] Debjanee Barua, Judy Kay, Bob Kummerfeld, and Cécile Paris. 2014. Modelling long term goals. In *International Conference on User Modeling, Adaptation, and Personalization*. Springer, 1–12.

[7] Timothy K. Behrens and Mary K. Dinger. 2005. Ambulatory Physical Activity Patterns of College Students. *American Journal of Health Education* 36, 4 (2005), 221–227.

[8] F Bentley, K Tollmar, and P Stephenson. 2013. Health Mashups: Presenting Statistical Patterns between Wellbeing Data and Context in Natural Language to Promote Behavior Change. *Tochi* 20, 5 (2013), 1–27.

[9] Susan Bull, Paul Brna, and Helen Pain. 1995. Extending the scope of the student model. *User Modeling and User-Adapted Interaction* 5, 1 (1995), 45–65.

[10] Susan Bull, Blandine Ginon, Clelia Boscolo, and Matthew Johnson. 2016. Introduction of Learning Visualisations and Metacognitive Support in a Persuadable Open Learner Model. In *Proceedings of the Sixth International Conference on Learning Analytics & Knowledge (LAK '16)*. ACM, New York, NY, USA, 30–39. https://doi.org/10.1145/2883851.2883853

[11] Susan Bull and Judy Kay. 2010. Open learner models. In *Advances in intelligent tutoring systems*. Springer, 301–322.

[12] Susan Bull and Judy Kay. 2013. Open learner models as drivers for metacognitive processes. In *International handbook of metacognition and learning technologies*. Springer, 349–365.

[13] Susan Bull and Judy Kay. 2016. SMILI: a framework for interfaces to learning data in open learner models, learning analytics and related fields. *International Journal of Artificial Intelligence in Education* 26, 1 (2016), 293–331.

[14] Lisa Cadmus-Bertram, Bess H Marcus, Ruth E Patterson, Barbara A Parker, and Brittany L Morey. 2015. Use of the Fitbit to Measure Adherence to a Physical Activity Intervention Among Overweight or Obese, Postmenopausal Women: Self-Monitoring Trajectory During 16 Weeks. *JMIR mHealth and uHealth* 3, 4 (2015), e96.

[15] Eun Kyoung Choe, Bongshin Lee, Haining Zhu, Nathalie Henry Riche, and Dominikus Baur. 2017. Understanding Self-Reflection: How People Reflect on Personal Data through Visual Data Exploration. In *Proceedings of the 11th EAI International Conference on Pervasive Computing Technologies for Healthcare (PervasiveHealthâĂŹ17)*. ACM, New York, NY, USA, Vol. 10.

[16] Edward L Deci and Richard M Ryan. 2000. The" what" and" why" of goal pursuits: Human needs and the self-determination of behavior. *Psychological inquiry* 11, 4 (2000), 227–268.

[17] Michel C Desmarais and Ryan S Baker. 2012. A review of recent advances in learner and skill modeling in intelligent learning environments. *User Modeling and User-Adapted Interaction* 22, 1-2 (2012), 9–38.

[18] Melissa C Duffy and Roger Azevedo. 2015. Motivation matters: Interactions between achievement goals and agent scaffolding for self-regulated learning within an intelligent tutoring system. *Computers in Human Behavior* 52 (2015), 338–348.

[19] Chris Elsden, David S Kirk, and Abigail C Durrant. 2015. A Quantified Past: Toward Design for Remembering With Personal Informatics. *Human–Computer Interaction* (2015), 1–40.

[20] Endeavour. 2014. Inside wearables part 2, How the Science of Behavior Change Offers the Secret to Long-Term Engagement. *https://blog.endeavour.partners/inside-wearable-how-the-science-of-human-behavior-change-offers-the-secret-to-long-term-engagement-a15b3c7d4cf3* Jan (2014). https://doi.org/wp-content/uploads/2015/11/2014-Inside-Wearables-Part-2-July-2014.pdf

[21] Carrie Demmans Epp and Susan Bull. 2015. Uncertainty representation in visualizations of learning analytics for learners: current approaches and opportunities. *IEEE Transactions on Learning Technologies* 8, 3 (2015), 242–260.

[22] Daniel Epstein, Felicia Cordeiro, Elizabeth Bales, James Fogarty, and Sean Munson. 2014. Taming data complexity in lifelogs: exploring visual cuts of personal informatics data. In *Proceedings of the 2014 conference on Designing interactive systems*. ACM, 667–676.

[23] Daniel A Epstein, Jennifer H Kang, Laura R Pina, James Fogarty, and Sean A Munson. 2016. Reconsidering the device in the drawer: lapses as a design opportunity in personal informatics. In *Proceedings of the 2016 ACM International Joint Conference on Pervasive and Ubiquitous Computing*. ACM, 829–840.

[24] Stuart J Fairclough, Lynne M Boddy, Kelly a Mackintosh, Alexandra Valencia-Peris, and Elena Ramirez-Rico. 2014. Weekday and weekend sedentary time and physical activity in differentially active children. *Journal of Science and Medicine in Sport* In Press (2014). https://doi.org/10.1016/j.jsams.2014.06.005

[25] Reza Feyzi-Behnagh, Roger Azevedo, Elizabeth Legowski, Kayse Reitmeyer, Eugene Tseytlin, and Rebecca S Crowley. 2014. Metacognitive scaffolds improve self-judgments of accuracy in a medical intelligent tutoring system. *Instructional science* 42, 2 (2014), 159–181.

[26] Thomas Fritz, Elaine M Huang, Gail C Murphy, and Thomas Zimmermann. 2014. Persuasive technology in the real world: a study of long-term use of activity sensing devices for fitness. In *Proceedings of the SIGCHI Conference on Human Factors in Computing Systems*. ACM, 487–496.

[27] Rúben Gouveia, Evangelos Karapanos, and Marc Hassenzahl. 2015. How do we engage with activity trackers?: a longitudinal study of Habito. In *Proceedings of the 2015 ACM International Joint Conference on Pervasive and Ubiquitous Computing*. ACM, 1305–1316.

[28] Julio Guerra. 2016. Open Social Learner Models for Self-Regulated Learning and Learning Motivation. In *Proceedings of the 2016 Conference on User Modeling Adaptation and Personalization*. ACM, 329–332.

[29] Julio Guerra-Hollstein, Jordan Barria-Pineda, Christian D Schunn, Susan Bull, and Peter Brusilovsky. 2017. Fine-Grained Open Learner Models: Complexity Versus Support. In *Proceedings of the 25th Conference on User Modeling, Adaptation and Personalization*. ACM, 41–49.

[30] Daniel Harrison, Paul Marshall, Nadia Bianchi-Berthouze, and Jon Bird. 2015. Activity tracking: barriers, workarounds and customisation. In *Proceedings of the 2015 ACM International Joint Conference on Pervasive and Ubiquitous Computing*. ACM, 617–621.

[31] Judy Kay. 1994. The um toolkit for cooperative user modelling. *User Modeling and User-Adapted Interaction* 4, 3 (1994), 149–196.

[32] Judy Kay. 2016. Enabling people to harness and control EDM for lifelong, life-wide learning.. In *EDM*. 10–20.

[33] Amanda Lazar, Christian Koehler, Joshua Tanenbaum, and David H Nguyen. 2015. Why we use and abandon smart devices. In *Proceedings of the 2015 ACM International Joint Conference on Pervasive and Ubiquitous Computing*. ACM, 635–646.

[34] Ian Li, Anind Dey, and Jodi Forlizzi. 2010. A stage-based model of personal informatics systems. In *Proceedings of the SIGCHI Conference on Human Factors in Computing Systems*. ACM, 557–566.

[35] Ian Li, Anind K Dey, and Jodi Forlizzi. 2011. Understanding my data, myself: supporting self-reflection with ubicomp technologies. In *Proceedings of the 13th international conference on Ubiquitous computing (UbiComp '11)*. ACM, New York, NY, USA, 405–414.

[36] Ian Li, Anind K. Dey, and Jodi Forlizzi. 2012. Using context to reveal factors that affect physical activity. *ACM Transactions on Computer-Human Interaction* 19, 1 (2012), 1–21.

[37] Yanjin Long and Vincent Aleven. 2011. StudentsâĂŹ understanding of their student model. In *International Conference on Artificial Intelligence in Education*. Springer, 179–186.

[38] Yanjin Long and Vincent Aleven. 2013. Supporting studentsâĂŹ self-regulated learning with an open learner model in a linear equation tutor. In *Artificial intelligence in education*. Springer, 219–228.

[39] Alessandro Marcengo, Amon Rapp, Federica Cena, and Marina Geymonat. 2016. The Falsified Self: Complexities in Personal Data Collection. *UAHCI 2016* 9737 (2016), 351–358. https://doi.org/10.1007/978-3-319-40250-5

[40] Jairo H. Migueles, Cristina Cadenas-Sanchez, Ulf Ekelund, Christine Delisle Nystr??m, Jose Mora-Gonzalez, Marie L??f, Idoia Labayen, Jonatan R. Ruiz, and Francisco B. Ortega. 2017. Accelerometer Data Collection and Processing Criteria to Assess Physical Activity and Other Outcomes: A Systematic Review and Practical Considerations. *Sports Medicine* (2017), 1–25. https://doi.org/10.1007/s40279-017-0716-0

[41] Antonija Mitrovic and Brent Martin. 2002. Evaluating the effects of open student models on learning. In *International Conference on Adaptive Hypermedia and Adaptive Web-Based Systems*. Springer, 296–305.

[42] Antonija Mitrovic and Brent Martin. 2007. Evaluating the effect of open student models on self-assessment. *International Journal of Artificial Intelligence in Education* 17, 2 (2007), 121–144.

[43] Jakob Nielsen. 1994. *Usability engineering*. Elsevier.

[44] Amon Rapp and Federica Cena. 2016. Personal Informatics for Everyday Life: How Users without Prior Self-Tracking Experience Engage with Personal Data. *International Journal of Human-Computer Studies* (2016).

[45] Amon Rapp and Federica Cena. 2016. Personal Informatics for Everyday Life: How Users without Prior Self-Tracking Experience Engage with Personal Data. *International Journal of Human-Computer Studies* 94 (2016), 1–17.

[46] John Rooksby, Mattias Rost, Alistair Morrison, and Matthew Chalmers Chalmers. 2014. Personal tracking as lived informatics. In *Proceedings of the 32nd annual ACM conference on Human factors in computing systems*. ACM, 1163–1172.

[47] Brenda Rooney, Kathy Smalley, Jennifer Larson, and Sarah Havens. 2003. Is knowing enough? Increasing physical activity by wearing a pedometer. *WMJ-MADISON-* 102, 4 (2003), 31–36.

[48] Patrick C Shih, Kyungsik Han, Erika Shehan Poole, Mary Beth Rosson, and John M Carroll. 2015. Use and adoption challenges of wearable activity trackers. *iConference 2015 Proceedings* (2015).

[49] Mical Kay Shilts, Marcel Horowitz, and Marilyn S Townsend. 2004. Goal setting as a strategy for dietary and physical activity behavior change: a review of the literature. *American journal of health promotion : AJHP* 19, 2 (2004), 81–93. https://doi.org/10.4278/0890-1171-19.2.81

[50] V J Strecher, G H Seijts, G J Kok, G P Latham, R Glasgow, B DeVellis, R M Meertens, and D W Bulger. 1995. Goal setting as a strategy for health behavior change. *Health education quarterly* 22, 2 (1995), 190–200. https://doi.org/10.1177/109019819502200207

[51] Bernardo Tabuenca, Marco Kalz, Hendrik Drachsler, and Marcus Specht. 2015. Time will tell: The role of mobile learning analytics in self-regulated learning.

Computers & Education 89 (2015), 53–74.

[52] Lie Ming Tang, Margot Day, Lina Engelen, Philip Poronnik, Adrian Bauman, and Judy Kay. 2016. Daily & Hourly Adherence: Towards Understanding Activity Tracker Accuracy. In *Proceedings of the 2016 CHI Conference Extended Abstracts on Human Factors in Computing Systems*. ACM, 3211–3218.

[53] Lie Ming Tang and Judy Kay. 2017. Harnessing Long Term Physical Activity Data: How Long-term Trackers Use Data and How an Adherence-based Interface Supports New Insights. *Proc. ACM Interact. Mob. Wearable Ubiquitous Technol.* 1, 2 (jun 2017), 26:1—-26:28. https://doi.org/10.1145/3090091

[54] Rayoung Yang, Eunice Shin, Mark W Newman, and Mark S Ackerman. 2015. When fitness trackers don't 'fit': end-user difficulties in the assessment of personal tracking device accuracy. In *Proceedings of the 2015 ACM International Joint Conference on Pervasive and Ubiquitous Computing*. ACM, 623–634.

Predicting Users' Personality from Instagram Pictures: Using Visual and/or Content Features?

Bruce Ferwerda
Department of Computer Science and Informatics
School of Engineering
Jönköping University
Jönköping, Sweden
bruce.ferwerda@ju.se

Marko Tkalcic
Department of Computer Science
Free University of Bozen-Bolzano
Bozen-Bolzano, Italy
marko.tkalcic@unibz.it

ABSTRACT

Instagram is a popular social networking application that allows users to express themselves through the uploaded content and the different filters they can apply. In this study we look at personality prediction from Instagram picture features. We explore two different features that can be extracted from pictures: 1) visual features (e.g., hue, valence, saturation), and 2) content features (i.e., the content of the pictures). To collect data, we conducted an online survey where we asked participants to fill in a personality questionnaire and grant us access to their Instagram account through the Instagram API. We gathered 54,962 pictures of 193 Instagram users. With our results we show that visual and content features can be used to predict personality from and perform in general equally well. Combining the two however does not result in an increased predictive power. Seemingly, they are not adding more value than they already consist of independently.

CCS CONCEPTS

• **Information systems** → *Recommender systems*; • **Human-centered computing** → *User models*; *User studies*;

KEYWORDS

Personality, Instagram, picture content, social media

ACM Reference Format:
Bruce Ferwerda and Marko Tkalcic. 2018. Predicting Users' Personality from Instagram Pictures: Using Visual and/or Content Features?. In *UMAP '18: 26th Conference on User Modeling, Adaptation and Personalization, July 8–11, 2018, Singapore, Singapore*, Jennifer B. Sartor, Theo D'Hondt, and Wolfgang De Meuter (Eds.). ACM, New York, NY, USA, Article 4, 5 pages. https://doi.org/10.1145/3209219.3209248

1 INTRODUCTION

Personality is considered a stable construct to capture individual characteristics to explain behavioral differences with [27]. These personality-based individual differences has shown to be a useful

factor to rely personalization strategies on. Hu and Pu [19] showed that personality-based systems are more effective in increasing users' loyalty towards the system and decreasing cognitive effort compared to systems without personality information. In addition, the domain independent nature of personality allows it being incorporated across domains [1]. Hence, once personality is known of a user, it can be incorporated into different platforms.

Given the usefulness of personality traits to personalize experiences in systems, research has started to give attention to map the relations between personality and behaviors (e.g., health [18, 32], education [3, 26], movies [4], music [6–9, 14, 15, 33], marketing [28]). Although there is an increased interest in identifying the relationships between personality and behaviors, the question remains on how to obtain users' personality for incorporation. A common approach is to use self-report measurements: a questionnaire is being used in order to assess the user's personality. However, questionnaires are time consuming and intrusive; it interrupts the flow between the user and the system.

To overcome the intrusiveness of using questionnairs to measure users' personality traits, several researchers have made an attempt to predict personality from the digital footprint that users leave behind. The usefulness of social networking sites (SNSs) as an external information source to predict personalities from becomes especially apparent through the increased interconnectedness of systems. Through single sign-on (SSO) buttons users are given the opportunity to easily register and login to the system with their SNS account. Besides providing convenience to users, it also allows access to information that can be exploited for personality acquisition and thereby circumvent the usage of questionnaires.

SNSs such as Facebook, Twitter, and Instagram consist of an abundance of additional information that can be used to infer personality traits from: Golbeck, Robles, and Turner [17] looked at Facebook profiles to make a personality predictor, and Quercia et al. [29] used Twitter messages to indicate personalities of users. In this work we focus specifically on personality predictions from Instagram pictures. Instagram is a popular mobile photo-sharing application with currently over 800 million users. [1] With the use of picture filters, Instagram allows its users to create and express a distinct personal style by adjusting and manipulating the appearance of the content they want to share. Previous work of Ferwerda et al. [12, 16] on predicting personality traits from Instagram pictures extracted the visual features of Instagram pictures and showed that these properties consist of personality information of users. A few

---

[1] https://instagram.com/press/ (accessed: 08/12/2017)

other works showed that personality can be predicted from pictures. However they mainly focus on content features instead of the visual features. For example, Celli et al. [2] analyzed compositions of Facebook profile pictures (e.g., facial close-ups, facial expressions, alone or with others) for personality prediction.

The contributions of this work to personality research comes in two fold: 1) we extend prior research by Ferwerda et al. [12, 16] by exploring the predictive value of personality in the content features of Instagram pictures, and 2) we explore whether combining visual features with content features improves personality prediction of Instagram users.

2 RELATED WORK

There is an increasing body of work that looks at how to implicitly acquire personality traits of users. Since all kind of information can relate to personality traits, even information that is not directly relevant for a specific purpose may still contain information that is useful for the extraction of personality (e.g., Facebook [11], Twitter [29, 31], and Instagram [10, 12, 13, 25]). The increased connectedness between SNSs and applications through SSO buttons provide an abundance of information that can be exploited to implicitly acquire personality traits of users. Except for basic information, SSOs often gain access to other parts of the user's profile as well [5].

Quercia et al. [29] looked at Twitter profiles and were able to predict users' personality traits by using their number of followers, following, and listed counts. With these three characteristics they were able to predict personality scores with a root-mean-square error 0.88 on a [1,5] scale. Similar work has been done by Golbeck, Robles, and Turner [17] on Facebook profiles. They looked at the sentiment of posted content and were able to create a reliable personality predictor with that information. More comprehensive work on the prediction of personality and other user characteristics using Facebook likes was done by Kosinski, Stillwell and Graepel [24].

Besides posted content on SNSs, the features of pictures has shown to consist of personality information as well. Work of Ferwerda, Schedl, and Tkalcic [12, 16] on Instagram pictures, showed that the way filters are applied to create a certain distinctiveness can be used to predict personality traits of the poster. Others (e.g., [2, 30]) have focused on the content of pictures. They showed that compositions of Facebook profile pictures consist of indicators of users' personality. This makes us believe that the content of Instagram pictures may consist of useful information as well about the poster's personality. Additionally, Skowron et al. [31] showed by combining linguistic and picture features they were able to improve predictions with 10-20% in each trait. Hence, besides exploring the content features of pictures for personality information, we further explore combining the content and visual features of pictures as well.

3 METHOD

To investigate the relationship between personality traits and picture features, we asked participants to fill in the 44-item BFI personality questionnaire (5-point Likert scale; Disagree strongly - Agree strongly [21]). The questionnaire includes questions that aggregate into the five basic personality traits of the FFM: openness, conscientiousness, extraversion, agreeableness, and neuroticism.

Additionally, we asked participants to grant us access to their Instagram account through the Instagram API [2] to crawl their pictures.

We recruited 193 participants through Amazon Mechanical Turk, a popular recruitment tool for user-experiments [23]. Participation was restricted to those located in the United States, and also to those with a very good reputation ($\geq$95% HIT approval rate and $\geq$1000 HITs approved) [3] to avoid careless contributions. Several control questions were used to filter out fake and careless entries. Pictures of each participant were crawled after the study. This resulted in a total of 54,962 pictures. The Mahalanobis distance was calculated to further identify outliers. This left us with 134 completed and valid responses. Age (18-64, median 31) and gender (60 male, 74 female) information indicated an adequate distribution. From hereon, we define the term "picture-collection" as all the Instagram pictures of a single user.

3.1 Visual Features

For each picture in a picture-collection that was crawled, we extracted several features. The extracted features are discussed below. Most of the features are color-based, some are content-based. For color-based features we use the color space that is most closely related to the human visual system, i.e., the Hue-Saturation-Value (HSV) color space [34].

3.1.1 Brightness. For each picture, we calculated the average brightness and variance across all the pixels in the picture. Pictures that have a high average brightness tend to be bright, obviously. These features represent how light/dark a picture is and how much contrast there is in the picture, respectively. Pictures that have a high variance tend to have both dark and light areas, whereas pictures with a low variance tend to be equally bright across the picture. Furthermore, we divided the brightness axis into three equal intervals and counted the share of pixels that fall into each of these intervals (low/mid/high brightness). Pictures that have a high value in the *low brightness* feature tend to be darker, those that have a high value in the *mid brightness* feature tend to have mostly neither dark nor bright areas, while those pictures that have a high value in the *high brightness* feature tend to have lots of bright areas.

3.1.2 Saturation. We calculated the average saturation and the variance for each picture. Pictures with low average saturation tend to be bleak, colorless, while pictures with high saturation have more vivid colors. Pictures with a high saturation variance tend to have both bleak and vivid colors. Here we also divided the saturation axis into three equal intervals and calculated the share of pixels that fall into each interval (low/mid/high saturation). pictures that have a high value in the *low saturation* tend to have more bleak colors, those with a high value in the *mid saturation* feature tend to have neither bleak nor vivid colors while those pictures that have a high value in the *high saturation* feature tend to have vivid colors across most of the picture area.

3.1.3 Pleasure-Arousal-Dominance (PAD). As the filters on Instagram intend to create a certain expression, we adopted the PAD model of Valdez and Merhabian [35]. They created general rules of

---

[2]https://www.instagram.com/developer/
[3]HITs (Human Intelligence Tasks) represent the assignments a user has participated in on Amazon Mechanical Turk prior to this study.

the expression of pleasure, arousal, and dominance in a picture as a combination of brightness and saturation levels:

(1) Pleasure = .69 Brightness + .22 Saturation

(2) Arousal = -.31 Brightness + .60 Saturation

(3) Dominance = -.76 Brightness + .32 Saturation

3.1.4 Hue-related features. We extracted features that represented the prevalent hues in pictures. We chose features that represent various aspects of the hues. For each of the basic colors (red, green, blue, yellow, orange, and violet) we counted the share of pixels that fall into each color. As the discrete color clustering of the hue dimension is nonlinear and subjective, we divided the hue into 10 equal intervals and calculated the share of pixels for each interval. However, these intervals are hard to describe with subjective color descriptions. Furthermore, we calculated the share of pixels that fall into cold (violet, blue, green) and warm (yellow, red, orange) colors.

3.2 Content Features

To analyze the content of the pictures, we used the Google Vision API. [4] The Google Vision API uses a deep neural network to analyze the pictures and assign tags ("description") with a confidence level ("score": $r\epsilon[0,1]$) to classify the content. For each picture in a picture-collection a JSON file was returned with tags and the confidence level (example given in Listing 1).

```
1  [{
2        "score": 0.8734813,
3        "mid": "/m/06__v",
4        "description": "snowboard"
5  }, {
6        "score": 0.8640924,
7        "mid": "/m/01fklc",
8        "description": "pink"
9  }, {
10       "score": 0.81754106,
11       "mid": "/m/0bpn3c2",
12       "description": "skateboarding
                  equipment and supplies"
13 }, {
14       "score": 0.8131781,
15       "mid": "/m/06_fw",
16       "description": "skateboard"
17 }, {
18       "score": 0.7329241,
19       "mid": "/m/05y5lj",
20       "description": "sports equipment"
21 }, {
22       "score": 0.64866644,
23       "mid": "/m/02nnq5",
24       "description": "longboard"
25 }]
```

Listing 1: Example JSON file returned by the Google Vision API for one picture

[4]https://cloud.google.com/vision/

Using the Google Vision API, we were able to retrieve 4090 unique labels from the Instagram pictures. In order to create an initial clustering of the labels, we used a k-means clustering method that is applied to the vectors that represent the terms in the joint vector space. The vectors were generated with the doc2vec approach using a set of embeddings that are pre-trained on the English Wikipedia [5]. Using this method we collated the labels into 400 clusters. [6] After that, the output of the k-means was manually checked and the clusters were further (manually) collated into similar categories. This resulted into 17 categories representing:

(1) Architecture	(10) Foods
(2) Body parts	(11) Sports
(3) Clothing	(12) Vehicles
(4) Music instruments	(13) Electronics
(5) Art	(14) Babies
(6) Performances	(15) Leisure
(7) Botanical	(16) Jewelry
(8) Cartoons	(17) Weapons
(9) Animals	

For each participant, we accumulated the number of category occurrences in their Instagram picture-collection. Since the number of Instagram pictures in each picture-collection is different, we normalized the number of category occurrences to represent a range of $r\epsilon[0,1]$. This to be able to compare users with differences in the total amount of pictures.

In addition to the Google Vision API, we counted the number of faces and the number of people in each picture. We used the standard Viola-Jones algorithm [36]. A manual inspection of the Viola-Jones face detector results revealed some false positives (e.g., a portrait within the picture) and false negatives (e.g., some rotated and tilted faces). However, in general the users who tended to take pictures of people (e.g., selfies) had a higher number of average number of faces/people per picture than those users who tended to take mostly still photographs.

4 PERSONALITY PREDICTION MODELS

We trained our predictive model with several classifiers in Weka, with a 10-fold cross-validation with 10 iterations. For each classifier we used, we report the root-mean-square error (RMSE) in Table 1, to indicate the root mean square difference between predicted and observed values. The RMSE of each personality trait relates to the [1,5] score scale (see Table 1).

A ZeroR classifier was used to create a baseline model. Three different classifiers were used and compared against the baseline model: M5' rules, random forest, and radial basis function network (RBF network). Each classifier was applied to the visual properties, content properties, and a combination of the two picture features (i.e., visual+content features).

We first started to train our predictive model with the M5' rules [37]. This is a classifier that has shown to be an effective classifier in

[5]https://github.com/jhlau/doc2vec

[6]The k-means clustering method allows for setting a parameter for the number of clusters to be forced. Different number of clusters were tried out. Setting the k-means to automatically define 400 clusters resulted in clusters with least errors in clustering the labels.

Pers. Trait	Classifier	RMSE		
		Visual Prop.	Content Prop.	Comb. Prop.
O	ZeroR	0.7619	0.7619	0.7619
	M5'Rules	0.7741	**0.7222**	0.7676
	Random Forest	**0.7318**	**0.7142**	**0.7513**
	RBF Network	**0.7231**	**0.7133**	**0.7141**
C	ZeroR	0.7201	0.7201	0.7201
	M5'Rules	**0.6277**	**0.6074**	0.7409
	Random Forest	**0.6542**	**0.6317**	**0.6546**
	RBF Network	**0.6175**	**0.6375**	**0.6275**
E	ZeroR	1.0539	1.0539	1.0539
	M5'Rules	**1.028**	0.9525	0.9961
	Random Forest	1.0622	1.0418	1.0592
	RBF Network	**0.9918**	**0.9777**	**0.9836**
A	ZeroR	0.6483	0.6483	0.6483
	M5'Rules	**0.6405**	**0.575**	**0.6177**
	Random Forest	**0.6025**	**0.5826**	**0.6201**
	RBF Network	**0.5971**	**0.6207**	**0.6108**
N	ZeroR	1.0122	1.0122	1.0122
	M5'Rules	**0.7907**	**0.8711**	**0.8766**
	Random Forest	**0.8819**	**0.8141**	**0.8923**
	RBF Network	**0.894**	**0.8978**	**0.8931**

Table 1: Different prediction models for each personality trait using only the visual properties, content properties, and a combination of both. ZeroR classifier represents the baseline. The boldfaced numbers indicate an out performance of the baseline. Root-mean-square error (RMSE) is reported ($r \in [1,5]$) to indicate prediction performance of the personality traits: (O)penness, (C)onscientiousness, (E)xtraversion, (A)greeableness, (N)euroticism.

Since both the visual as well as the content features showed to be reliable predictors of personality traits, we also explored personality prediction by combining the two. However, combining visual and content features does not result in an improvement of the personality prediction. Instead, the RMSE values adjust towards the average of the visual and content features. Hence, although the visual and content features are good predictors on their own, they do not complement each other much.

Table 2 displays a comparison with prior research that use similar approaches to predict personality from SNS data. Compared to prior work of Ferwerda et al. [16] and Quercia et al. [29] we are able to outperform predictions in some traits. Whereas, visual and content properties do not complement each other in our study, Skowron et al. [31] found features that were able to improve prediction when being combined. Nevertheless, across all studies we found similar patterns and comparable results whereas most difficult traits to predict are consistently extraversion and neuroticism.

Pers. traits	RMSE			
	Comb. Prop.	[16]	[31]	[29]
O	0.71	0.68	0.51	0.69
C	0.62	0.66	0.67	0.73
E	0.98	0.90	0.71	0.96
A	0.61	0.69	0.50	0.78
N	0.89	0.95	0.73	0.97

Table 2: Comparison of personality prediction compared to prior work of Ferwerda et al. [16], Skowron et al. [31], and Quercia et al. [29]. Root-mean-square error (RMSE) is reported ($r \in [1,5]$) to indicate prediction performance of the personality traits: (O)penness, (C)onscientiousness, (E)xtraversion, (A)greeableness, (N)euroticism.

previous work of Quercia et al. [29] on personality prediction from Twitter data. The M5' rules outperform the baseline model in predicting most of the personality traits (except for the openness trait using the visual features).

To further explore possible improvements by other classifiers, we tried out the random forests classifier. Random forests are known to have a reasonable performance when the features consist of high amounts of noise [20]. Compared to the M5' rules, the random forest classifier show slight improvements on half of the personality traits: openness to experience, agreeableness, and neuroticism (for the latter prediction only improved based on content features). For the other half of the personality traits M5' rules outperforms the random forest classifier.

As the M5' rules and random forest classifiers failed to outperform the baseline in all personality traits, we used the RBF network classifier. The RBF network is a neural network that has shown to work well on smaller datasets [22]. Applying the RBF network classifier we were able to gain an prediction improvement on all personality traits using the visual as well as the content features.

5 CONCLUSION

We explored the predictive value of different kind of features that can be extracted from pictures. Prior work of Ferwerda et al. [16] already showed that the visual features of Instagram consist of useful information to predict personality from. However, they did not explore other features that can be extracted from the pictures (i.e., content features). In this work we show that the visual features as well as the content features consist of information for personality prediction that attain similar results.

Although prior work [31] showed to be able to improve their personality predictor by combining information from SNSs, we were not able to achieve that. The visual and content features show to be good predictors on their own, but they do not seem to provide added value to each other when being combined. When combining the two features into one predictor, our results show that the RMSE adjust towards the average instead of showing an improvement. Hence, when personality prediction from Instagram picture is ought to be done, a focus on either visual features or content features will suffice to create a personality prediction model.

REFERENCES

[1] Iván Cantador, Ignacio Fernández-Tobías, and Alejandro Bellogín. 2013. Relating personality types with user preferences in multiple entertainment domains. In *CEUR Workshop Proceedings*. Shlomo Berkovsky.

[2] Fabio Celli, Elia Bruni, and Bruno Lepri. 2014. Automatic personality and interaction style recognition from facebook profile pictures. In *Proceedings of the 22nd ACM international conference on Multimedia*. ACM, 1101–1104.

[3] Guanliang Chen, Dan Davis, Claudia Hauff, and Geert-Jan Houben. 2016. On the impact of personality in massive open online learning. In *Proceedings of the 2016 conference on user modeling adaptation and personalization*. ACM, 121–130.

[4] Li Chen, Wen Wu, and Liang He. 2013. How personality influences users' needs for recommendation diversity?. In *CHI'13 Extended Abstracts on Human Factors in Computing Systems*. ACM, 829–834.

[5] Pern Hui Chia, Yusuke Yamamoto, and N Asokan. 2012. Is this app safe?: a large scale study on application permissions and risk signals. In *Proceedings of the 21st international conference on World Wide Web*. ACM, 311–320.

[6] Bruce Ferwerda, Mark Graus, Andreu Vall, Marko Tkalcic, and Markus Schedl. 2016. The influence of users' personality traits on satisfaction and attractiveness of diversified recommendation lists. In *4 th Workshop on Emotions and Personality in Personalized Systems (EMPIRE) 2016*. 43.

[7] Bruce Ferwerda and Markus Schedl. 2014. Enhancing Music Recommender Systems with Personality Information and Emotional States: A Proposal.. In *UMAP Workshops*.

[8] Bruce Ferwerda and Markus Schedl. 2016. Personality-Based User Modeling for Music Recommender Systems. In *Joint European Conference on Machine Learning and Knowledge Discovery in Databases*. Springer, 254–257.

[9] Bruce Ferwerda, Markus Schedl, and Marko Tkalcic. 2015. Personality & Emotional States: Understanding Users' Music Listening Needs.. In *UMAP Workshops*.

[10] Bruce Ferwerda, Markus Schedl, and Marko Tkalcic. 2015. Predicting personality traits with instagram pictures. In *Proceedings of the 3rd Workshop on Emotions and Personality in Personalized Systems 2015*. ACM, 7–10.

[11] Bruce Ferwerda, Markus Schedl, and Marko Tkalcic. 2016. Personality traits and the relationship with (non-) disclosure behavior on facebook. In *Proceedings of the 25th International Conference Companion on World Wide Web*. International World Wide Web Conferences Steering Committee, 565–568.

[12] Bruce Ferwerda, Markus Schedl, and Marko Tkalcic. 2016. Using instagram picture features to predict users' personality. In *International Conference on Multimedia Modeling*. Springer, 850–861.

[13] Bruce Ferwerda and Marko Tkalcic. 2018. You Are What You Post: What the Content of Instagram Pictures Tells About Users' Personality. In *The 23rd International on Intelligent User Interfaces*.

[14] Bruce Ferwerda, Marko Tkalcic, and Markus Schedl. 2017. Personality Traits and Music Genre Preferences: How Music Taste Varies Over Age Groups. In *Proceedings of the 1st Workshop on Temporal Reasoning in Recommender Systems (RecTemp) at the 11th ACM Conference on Recommender Systems, Como, August 31, 2017*.

[15] Bruce Ferwerda, Marko Tkalcic, and Markus Schedl. 2017. Personality Traits and Music Genres: What Do People Prefer to Listen To?. In *Proceedings of the 25th Conference on User Modeling, Adaptation and Personalization*. ACM, 285–288.

[16] Bruce Ferwerda, Emily Yang, Markus Schedl, and Marko Tkalcic. 2015. Personality traits predict music taxonomy preferences. In *Proceedings of the 33rd Annual ACM Conference Extended Abstracts on Human Factors in Computing Systems*. ACM, 2241–2246.

[17] Jennifer Golbeck, Cristina Robles, and Karen Turner. 2011. Predicting personality with social media. In *CHI'11 extended abstracts on human factors in computing systems*. ACM, 253–262.

[18] Sajanee Halko and Julie A Kientz. 2010. Personality and persuasive technology: an exploratory study on health-promoting mobile applications. In *International Conference on Persuasive Technology*. Springer, 150–161.

[19] Rong Hu and Pearl Pu. 2011. Enhancing collaborative filtering systems with personality information. In *Proceedings of the fifth ACM conference on Recommender systems*. ACM, 197–204.

[20] Elizabeth M Humston, Joshua D Knowles, Andrew McShea, and Robert E Synovec. 2010. Quantitative assessment of moisture damage for cacao bean quality using two-dimensional gas chromatography combined with time-of-flight mass spectrometry and chemometrics. *Journal of Chromatography A* 1217, 12 (2010), 1963–1970.

[21] Oliver P John and Sanjay Srivastava. 1999. The Big Five trait taxonomy: History, measurement, and theoretical perspectives. *Handbook of personality: Theory and research* 2, 1999 (1999), 102–138.

[22] Lav R Khot, Suranjan Panigrahi, Curt Doetkott, Young Chang, Jacob Glower, Jayendra Amamcharla, Catherine Logue, and Julie Sherwood. 2012. Evaluation of technique to overcome small dataset problems during neural-network based contamination classification of packaged beef using integrated olfactory sensor system. *LWT-Food Science and Technology* (2012).

[23] Aniket Kittur, Ed H Chi, and Bongwon Suh. 2008. Crowdsourcing user studies with Mechanical Turk. In *Proceedings of the SIGCHI conference on human factors in computing systems*. ACM, 453–456.

[24] Michal Kosinski, David Stillwell, and Thore Graepel. 2013. Private traits and attributes are predictable from digital records of human behavior. *Proceedings of the National Academy of Sciences of the United States of America* 110, 15 (mar 2013), 5802–5. https://doi.org/10.1073/pnas.1218772110

[25] Alixe Lay and Bruce Ferwerda. 2018. Predicting Usersâ ĂŹ Personality Based on Their âĂŸLikedâĂŹImages on Instagram. In *The 23rd International on Intelligent User Interfaces*.

[26] Michael J Lee and Bruce Ferwerda. 2017. Personalizing online educational tools. In *Proceedings of the 2017 ACM Workshop on Theory-Informed User Modeling for Tailoring and Personalizing Interfaces*. ACM, 27–30.

[27] Gerald Matthews, Ian J Deary, and Martha C Whiteman. 2003. *Personality traits*. Cambridge University Press.

[28] S C Matz, M Kosinski, G Nave, and D J Stillwell. 2017. Psychological targeting as an effective approach to digital mass persuasion. *Proceedings of the National Academy of Sciences* 114, 48 (nov 2017), 12714–12719. https://doi.org/10.1073/pnas.1710966114

[29] Daniele Quercia, Michal Kosinski, David Stillwell, and Jon Crowcroft. 2011. Our Twitter profiles, our selves: Predicting personality with Twitter. In *IEEE Third Conference on Social Computing*. 180–185.

[30] Cristina Segalin, Fabio Celli, Luca Polonio, Michal Kosinski, David Stillwell, Nicu Sebe, Marco Cristani, and Bruno Lepri. 2017. What your Facebook Profile Picture Reveals about your Personality. In *Proceedings of the 2017 ACM on Multimedia Conference, MM 2017, Mountain View, CA, USA, October 23-27, 2017*. 460–468. https://doi.org/10.1145/3123266.3123331

[31] Marcin Skowron, Marko Tkalčič, Bruce Ferwerda, and Markus Schedl. 2016. Fusing social media cues: personality prediction from twitter and instagram. In *Proceedings of the 25th international conference companion on world wide web*. International World Wide Web Conferences Steering Committee, 107–108.

[32] Kirsten A Smith, Matt Dennis, and Judith Masthoff. 2016. Personalizing reminders to personality for melanoma self-checking. In *Proceedings of the 2016 Conference on User Modeling Adaptation and Personalization*. ACM, 85–93.

[33] Marko Tkalčič, Bruce Ferwerda, David Hauger, and Markus Schedl. 2015. Personality correlates for digital concert program notes. In *International Conference on User Modeling, Adaptation, and Personalization*. Springer, 364–369.

[34] Marko Tkalcic and Jurij Tasic. 2003. Colour spaces: perceptual, historical and applicational background. *IEEE EUROCON. Computer as a Tool* (2003), 304–308. https://doi.org/10.1109/EURCON.2003.1248032

[35] Patricia Valdez and Albert Mehrabian. 1994. Effects of color on emotions. *Journal of Experimental Psychology: General* 123, 4 (1994), 394.

[36] Paul Viola and Michael J. Jones. 2004. Robust Real-Time Face Detection. *International Journal of Computer Vision* 57, 2 (May 2004), 137–154. https://doi.org/10.1023/B:VISI.0000013087.49260.fb

[37] Ian H Witten and Eibe Frank. 2005. *Data Mining: Practical machine learning tools and techniques*. Morgan Kaufmann.

Eudaimonic Modeling of Moviegoers

Marko Tkalčič
Faculty of Computer Science
Free University of Bozen-Bolzano
Bozen-Bolzano, Italy
marko.tkalcic@unibz.it

Bruce Ferwerda
Department of Computer Science and Informatics
School of Engineering
Jönköping University
Jönköping, Sweden
bruce.ferwerda@ju.se

ABSTRACT

One of the important aspects of movie-making is to trigger emotional responses in viewers. These emotional experiences can be divided into hedonic and eudaimonic. While the former are characterized as plain enjoyment, the latter deal with getting greater insight, self-reflection or contemplation. So far, modeling of user preferences about movies and personalization algorithms have largely ignored the eudaimonic aspect of the consumption of movies. In this paper we fill this gap by exploring what are the relationship between (i) eudaimonic and hedonic characteristics of movies, (ii) users' preferences and (iii) users' personality. Our results show that eudaimonic user profiling effectively divides users into pleasure-seekers and meaning-seekers.

CCS CONCEPTS

• **Human-centered computing** → *User models*; *User studies*;

KEYWORDS

eudaimonia, movie preferences, user model

ACM Reference Format:
Marko Tkalčič and Bruce Ferwerda. 2018. Eudaimonic Modeling of Moviegoers. In *UMAP '18: 26th Conference on User Modeling, Adaptation and Personalization, July 8–11, 2018, Singapore, Singapore.* ACM, New York, NY, USA, 5 pages. https://doi.org/10.1145/3209219.3209249

1 INTRODUCTION

Recent research on user feedback in personalized systems, such as recommender systems, is focusing on how much a user *likes* an item. For example, in Facebook, users can rate a post using the *like* button. However, a single like or rating on a numeric scale does not capture the whole experience. Furthermore, the experience of consumption of an item (listening to a song, watching a movie) does not have only hedonic qualities (fun, enjoyment, relaxation) but also eudaimonic qualities, which are related to meaning and purpose [8].

A general research direction related to eudaimonic qualities of experience of content consumption we are pursuing is to use eudaimonia for personalization. The assumption is that users differ in their need for eudaimonic experiences, i.e. some people prefer to just have fun, while other people may prefer to spend their time contemplating meaning and purpose. Similarly, content differs in the experience quality they induce. For example, the movies *The Hangover* and *La vita e' bella* are both comedies. But while the former is a shallow comedy with a series of simple jokes the latter deals with deeper issues, such as the holocaust.

In order to devise personalization approaches using eudaimonia there are a lot of steps to make, since it is an unexplored area. We foresee the following steps need to be taken: (i) unobtrusive inference of eudaimonic and hedonic user preferences, (ii) automatic labeling of movies' eudaimonic and hedonic qualities, and (iii) a personalized recommender system that takes advantage of eudaimonic and hedonic features. We aim at kicking-off the research path in this direction with the results reported here. The contributions of this paper are: (i) a characterization of users in terms of eudaimonic and hedonic preferences (Sect. 4.1), (ii) a characterization of movies in terms of their eudaimonic and hedonic qualities (Sect. 4.2) and (iii) a correlation analysis between users' reported eudaimonic and hedonic preferences and their reported personalities (Sect. 4.3).

2 RELATED WORK

There is substantial disjoint work in the domains of (i) conceptualizing eudaimonic and hedonic experiences for entertainment and (ii) work covering the relationships between personality and user preferences.

In positive psychology, happiness is often described through two opposite concepts: hedonism and eudaimonism [1]: *the hedonic view equates happiness with pleasure, comfort, and enjoyment, whereas the eudaimonic view equates happiness with the human ability to pursue complex goals which are meaningful to the individual and society.* Oliver and Raney [9] have carried out research to identify whether there are distinct eudaimonic and hedonic motivations for consuming entertainment. Through a series of studies they devised an instrument for measuring the eudaimonic and hedonic qualities of entertainment experiences. They showed that *in addition to viewing movies for purposes of fun and pleasure, individuals also turn to entertainment for purposes of greater insight and meaningfulness.* Wirth et al. [13] further extended Oliver's work by analyzing what are the hedonic and eudaimonic qualities of movies with good and bad endings and found significant differences.

Personality traits account for our individual differences. Among several models of personality the most widely used is the Five

Factor Model (FFM), which contains the following factors: openness, conscientiousness, extraversion, agreeableness and neuroticism [7]. Several works has shown that personality is related to user preferences for entertainment content, such as music [3, 10, 12] and movies [5].

Little work has been done on relating personality and eudaimonic experiences. One of these is a study using functional magnetic resonance to identify neural pathways linking personality traits and eudaimonic well-being [6].

With this work we aim at bringing together the disjoint work of user modeling, with the intent of personalizing movie recommendations, and eudaimonic characterization of entertainment experiences. We do this by profiling users in terms of eudaimonic and hedonic preferences, characterizing movies in terms of their eudaimonic and hedonic qualities and correlating users' reported eudaimonic and hedonic preferences and their reported personalities.

3 EXPERIMENT

In order to perform the analysis we performed a user study to acquire data. We let the subjects choose movies from a pool of popular movies. For the hypothetical context of choosing a movie to watch alone on a Saturday evening, each subject had to choose the most appropriate movie (the *liked* movie) and the least appropriate movie (the *disliked* movie). The subjects were then asked to describe, for each of the two movies, their viewing experience in terms of hedonic and eudaimonic experience using an adaptation of the scale developed by [9]. After answering the movie-related questions, the subjects filled in the ten-items personality questionnaire (TIPI).

Table 1: Excerpt of movie titles used in the experiment. The eudaimonic and hedonic qualities are our subjective assessments before the data acquisition took place.

Title	Eudaimonic	Hedonic
Manchester by the sea	Y	N
Bad Moms	N	Y
Mad Max: Fury Road	N	Y
The Shawshank Redemption	Y	N
Inside Out	Y	Y

The pool of movies has been hand-picked by the authors by choosing the most popular movies from the years 2015, 2016, 2017, and a subset of all-time most popular movies. This maximized the probability that the subjects had watched at least a couple of movies. We choose to limit the subjects to a limited pool of movies instead of giving them freedom to choose their own movies to assess in order to increase the chance of having overlapping movie evaluations. We manually balanced the pool of movies in such a way that it contained a roughly equal amount of movies that contained eudaimonic qualities (e.g., *Manchester by the sea*) and not (e.g,. *Bad Moms*) according to our judgment. We used the IMDB most popular movies list as the source[1]. Some titles of the movies are listed in Tab. 1. In total we had 36 movies.

[1]the movies were retrieved from the source http://www.imdb.com/search/title?year= 2016&title_type=feature& and sorted by popularity

In order to assess the true hedonic and eudaimonic qualities of the movie watching experience we adapted the instrument proposed by [9]. For each movie, chosen as *liked*, the subjects had to answer the following eudaimonic-related questions on an agreement scale from 1 (I totally disagree) to 7 (I totally agree):

- I liked the movie because it challenged my way of seeing the world.
- I liked the movie because it made me more reflective.
- I liked the movie because it focused on meaningful human conditions.
- I liked the movie because it made me think.
- I liked the movie because it was about people's search for greater understanding in life.
- I liked the movie because it conveyed a profound message.

and on the following hedonic-related questions on the same scale:

- I liked the movie because I had fun watching it.
- I liked the movie because it made me laugh.
- I liked the movie because it was entertaining.
- I liked the movie because it was happy and positive.

The single eudaimonic and hedonic qualities for each liked movie-user pair were calculated by averaging the scores of the individual questions.

For the disliked movies, we inverted the questions above into the form *I did not like the movie because it did/was not ....* Similarly, we aggregated these scores into single eudaimonic and hedonic scores for each disliked movie-user pair. We also checked the internal consistency using Cronbach's alpha, which yielded $\alpha = 0.890$ for eudaimonia and $\alpha = 0.733$ for hedonia.

We further used the TIPI instrument to measure personality [4] in terms of the five factors openness, conscientiousness, extraversion, agreeableness and neuroticism. We used the [1, 5] scale.

We ran the study through Amazon Mechanical Turk. After removing subjects who did not pass a control question and removing outliers using the Mahalanobis distance we had the answers of 84 subjects ($M = 34.2$ years, $SD = 9.5$ years, 29 females).

4 RESULTS

4.1 Eudaimonic and Hedonic Characteristics of Users

The data we collected shows an interesting pattern. In the case of liked movies, the users liked movies with high hedonic quality, which was expected. Figure 1 shows the histograms for individual questions, which exhibit skewness towards high values. However, when it comes to the eudaimonic qualities of liked movies, several factors of eudaimonia (first, second and third question) exhibit a tendency to divide in two clusters : some users liked movies with high eudaimonic qualities (scores > 3) while some users liked movies with low eudaimonic qualities (scores < 3), which is reflected in the bimodal shape of three histograms in Fig. 2. This interesting shape of the eudaimonic histogram indicates that the users can be clustered into *pleasure-seekers* (high hedonic and low eudaimonic quality) and *meaning-seekers* (high hedonic and high eudaimonic quality).

We further performed a k-means clustering over all the hedonic and eudaimonic variables, not only on individual ones. The clustering outcome shows two clusters of users, which are separated by a line in the hedonic-eudaimonic scores space, which can be seen in Fig. 3.

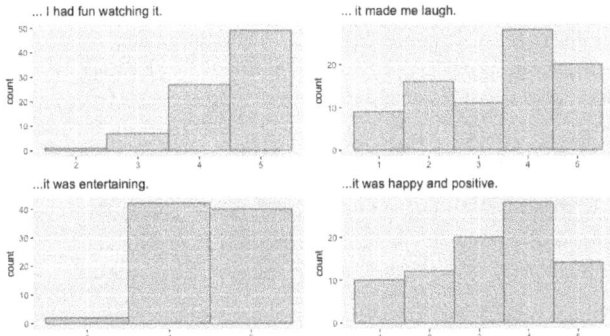

Figure 1: Distribution of hedonic qualities of liked movies. The variables reported in this figure are the agreements with the statements *I liked this movie because ... I had fun watching it* (top-left), *...it made me laugh* (top-right), *...it was entertaining* (bottom-left) and *...it was happy and positive* (bottom-right) .

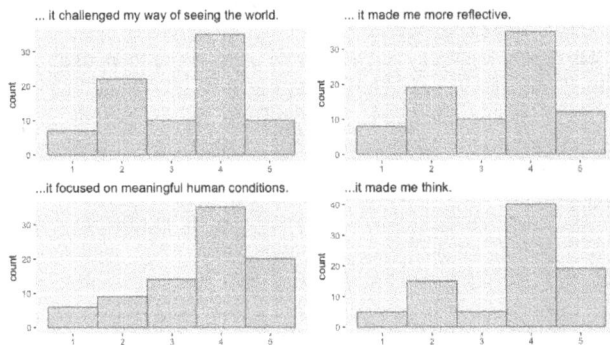

Figure 2: Distribution of eudaimonic qualities of liked movies. The variables reported in this figure are the agreements with the statements *I liked this movie because ... it challenged my way of seeing the world* (top-left), *...it made me more reflective* (top-right), *...it focused on meaningful human conditions* (bottom-left) and *...it made me think* (bottom-right) .

4.2 Eudaimonic and Hedonic Characteristics of Movies

Here we cluster the movies, used in our study, into three clusters: (a) movies with predominantly eudaimonic quality, (b) movies with equal eudaimonic and hedonic qualities, and (c) movies with predominantly hedonic quality. In order to cluster the movies we perform the Wilcoxon rank sum test in order to test the hypothesis

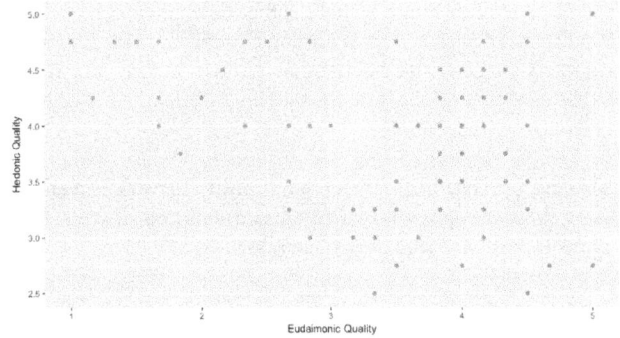

Figure 3: Two clusters of users (blue:pleasure-seekers and red:meaning-seekers) were identified using k-means over all eudaimonic and hedonic variables.

of the mean reported hedonic and eudaimonic quality being equal. Examples from all three clusters are reported in Tab. 2.

Table 2: Examples from clusters of movies. The movies in the upper part of the table (eudaimonic movies) are movies that have a stronger eudaimonic quality, the middle part (mixed movies) shows movies that are equally hedonic and eudaimonic and the lower part (hedonic movies) shows movies with a stronger hedonic quality

Eudaimonic movies	Eudaimonic Score	Hedonic Score
Hacksaw Ridge	3.47	2.30
Fifty Shades of Gray	3.62	2.37
The Godfather	4.25	2.56
Mixed movies	Eudaimonic Score	Hedonic Score
Forrest Gump	3.89	3.54
The Revenant	3.50	3.25
Bad Moms	3.25	3.11
The Martian	3.81	3.92
Hedonic movies	Eudaimonic Score	Hedonic Score
Deadpool	2.52	4.00
Mad Max: Fury Road	2.87	3.95

Beside the movies reported in Tab. 2, we observed strong differences in mean eudaimonic and hedonic qualities in some other movies, such as *12 Angry Men*, and *The Shawshank Redemption* (higher eudaimonic quality) and *Jurassic World* and *Baby Driver* (higher hedonic quality). However, due to too little data at our disposal, the differences of means were not significant at $\alpha = 0.05$.

4.3 Personality Correlates with Eudaimonic and Hedonic Preferences

We further analyze the relationships between user personality, and preferences for hedonic and eudaimonic content.

In our experiment, each subject picked a movie she liked and another she disliked. The correlations between personality factors in terms of the Five Factor Model end the chosen movie characteristics in terms of eudaimonic and hedonic preferences are presented separately for liked and disliked movies (Tab. 3). The personality factors were on the scale [1, 5] whereas the eudaimonic and hedonic values are on the scale [1, 7].

Table 3: Correlations between personality factors and eudaimonic/hedonic qualities of liked and disliked movies. The values in bold are significant correlations at 0.05

personality	liked		disliked	
	eud	hed	eud	hed
openness	0.09	**-0.29**	**0.27**	0.19
conscientiousness	-0.19	0.13	0.14	0
extraversion	0.12	-0.03	0.09	-0.05
agreeableness	0.12	0.06	**-0.25**	-0.09
neuroticism	**0.23**	-0.02	-0.21	0.04

The data shows that there are significant correlations between openness, agreeableness, and neuroticism on one side and eudaimonic and hedonic qualities on the other side.

The questions for the eudaimonic/hedonic quality of the movies they liked (as reported in Sect 3) could be summarized as *I like the movie because it has eudaimonic quality* (the liked-eud column in Tab 3) and *I like the movie because it has hedonic quality* (the liked-hed column in Tab 3). Hence, the positive correlation between neuroticism and liked-hed means that subjects who score high on neuroticism liked movies with high eudaimonic quality whereas those with low neuroticism liked movies with low eudaimonic quality. A similar pattern is observed for openness, but as a negative correlation to hedonic quality. In fact, subjects who scored high on openness liked movies with low hedonic quality whereas subjects with low openness liked movies with high hedonic qualities.

The questions for the eudaimonic/hedonic quality of the movies they disliked could be summarized as *I did not like the movie because it did not have eudaimonic quality* (the disliked-eud column in Tab 3) and *I did not like the movie because it did not have hedonic quality* (the disliked-hed column in Tab 3). Hence, the positive correlation between openness and disliked-eud indicates that people who scored high on openness did not like movies that did not contain eudaimonic quality. An opposite effect can be observed for people who score high on agreeableness. Agreeable people make it clear that the lack of eudaimonic quality is not the reason they don't like a movie, whereas non-agreeable people dislike movies because of the lack of eudaimonic content.

5 LIMITATIONS AND FUTURE WORK

Our study shows promising reults and we plan to carry on with research. The main limitations of our study are:

- small number of subjects
- intrusive assessment of user preferences through questionnaires
- intrusive assessment of the movies' qualities

While the first limitation can be addressed simply by extending the study to a larger sample, the other two require additional work.

The assessment of user preferences through questionnaires, such as the one used in this study, is too intrusive and cumbersome. Based on our prior work on inference of personality from social media [2, 11] we plan to adopt a similar approach to infer the propensity of user for eudaimonic and hedonic content from social media. We plan to train a model that takes as input features extracted from social media activity and make a prediction of the propensity of each user for eudaimonic and hedonic entertainment.

Similarly, inferring the quality of movies through extensive questionnaires is not feasible for a personalized system of large scale. Based on the work of Wirth et al. [13] we conjecture that movie content contains information pertaining to eudaimonic and hedonic qualities. In order to devise an automatic method we plan to train a predictive model that takes as input movies' subtitles and infers their eudaimonic and hedonic qualities. Feature engineering will be done using Natural Language Processing techniques.

6 CONCLUSION

In this short paper we present the outcomes of a preliminary study on the influence of eudaimonic and hedonic qualities of movies on user preferences.

The results of our study show that the variance in user preferences (in terms of eudaimonic and hedonic qualities) is reflected also in personality. A correlational analysis showed that people who score high on openness and neuroticism tend to prefer movies with more eudaimonic than hedonic qualities. Similarly, people high in openness dislike a movie if it does not contain eudaimonic qualities. The opposite effect was found for agreeableness.

Furthermore, we lay out a research plan for the following steps, which include: (i) unobtrusive inference of user preferences in terms of eudaimonic and hedonic qualities from social media, (ii) robust automatic inference of movie quality from subtitles and (iii) prediction of movie preference in the form of a recommender system.

REFERENCES

[1] Antonella Delle Fave, Fausto Massimini, and Marta Bassi. 2011. *Hedonism and Eudaimonism in Positive Psychology*. Springer Netherlands, Dordrecht, 3–18. https://doi.org/10.1007/978-90-481-9876-4_1

[2] Bruce Ferwerda, Markus Schedl, and Marko Tkalcic. 2015. Predicting Personality Traits with Instagram Pictures. In *Proceedings of the 3rd Workshop on Emotions and Personality in Personalized Systems 2015 - EMPIRE '15*, Marko Tkalčič, Berardina De Carolis, Marco de Gemmis, Ante Odić, and Andrej Košir (Eds.). ACM Press, New York, New York, USA, 7–10. https://doi.org/10.1145/2809643.2809644

[3] Bruce Ferwerda, Marko Tkalcic, and Markus Schedl. 2017. Personality Traits and Music Genres. In *Proceedings of the 25th Conference on User Modeling, Adaptation and Personalization - UMAP '17*. ACM Press, New York, New York, USA, 285–288. https://doi.org/10.1145/3079628.3079693

[4] Samuel D Gosling, Peter J Rentfrow, and William B Swann. 2003. A very brief measure of the Big-Five personality domains. *Journal of Research in Personality* 37, 6 (dec 2003), 504–528. https://doi.org/10.1016/S0092-6566(03)00046-1

[5] Raghav Pavan Karumur, Tien T. Nguyen, and Joseph A. Konstan. 2016. Exploring the Value of Personality in Predicting Rating Behaviors. In *Proceedings of the 10th ACM Conference on Recommender Systems - RecSys '16*. ACM Press, New York, New York, USA, 139–142. https://doi.org/10.1145/2959100.2959140

[6] Feng Kong, Ling Liu, Xu Wang, Siyuan Hu, Yiying Song, and Jia Liu. 2015. Different neural pathways linking personality traits and eudaimonic well-being: a resting-state functional magnetic resonance imaging study. *Cognitive, Affective, & Behavioral Neuroscience* 15, 2 (01 Jun 2015), 299–309. https://doi.org/10.3758/s13415-014-0328-1

[7] Robert R McCrae and Oliver P John. 1992. An Introduction to the Five-Factor Model and its Applications. *Journal of Personality* 60, 2 (1992), p175 – 215.

[8] Elisa D. Mekler and Kasper Hornbæk. 2016. Momentary Pleasure or Lasting Meaning?: Distinguishing Eudaimonic and Hedonic User Experiences. *Proceedings of the 2016 CHI Conference on Human Factors in Computing Systems - CHI '16* (2016), 4509–4520. https://doi.org/10.1145/2858036.2858225

[9] Mary Beth Oliver and Arthur A. Raney. 2011. Entertainment as Pleasurable and Meaningful: Identifying Hedonic and Eudaimonic Motivations for Entertainment Consumption. *Journal of Communication* 61, 5 (2011), 984–1004. https://doi.org/10.1111/j.1460-2466.2011.01585.x

[10] Peter J. Rentfrow and Samuel D. Gosling. 2003. The do re mi's of everyday life: The structure and personality correlates of music preferences. *Journal of Personality and Social Psychology* 84, 6 (2003), 1236–1256. https://doi.org/10.1037/0022-3514.84.6.1236

[11] Marcin Skowron, Marko Tkalčič, Bruce Ferwerda, and Markus Schedl. 2016. Fusing Social Media Cues. In *Proceedings of the 25th International Conference Companion on World Wide Web - WWW '16 Companion*. ACM Press, New York, New York, USA, 107–108. https://doi.org/10.1145/2872518.2889368

[12] Marko Tkalčič, Bruce Ferwerda, David Hauger, and Markus Schedl. 2015. Personality Correlates for Digital Concert Program Notes. In *UMAP 2015, Lecture Notes On Computer Science 9146*. Vol. 9146. 364–369. https://doi.org/10.1007/978-3-319-20267-9_32

[13] Werner Wirth, Matthias Hofer, and Holger Schramm. 2012. Beyond Pleasure: Exploring the Eudaimonic Entertainment Experience. *Human Communication Research* 38, 4 (2012), 406–428. https://doi.org/10.1111/j.1468-2958.2012.01434.x

Orient Me! – Important Event Identification in an Enterprise Activity Stream

Naama Zwerdling
IBM Research AI
Haifa, Israel
naamaz@il.ibm.com

Inbal Ronen
IBM Research AI
Haifa, Israel
inbal@il.ibm.com

Lior Leiba
IBM Research AI
Haifa, Israel
leiba@il.ibm.com

Maya Barnea
IBM Research AI
Haifa, Israel
mayab@il.ibm.com

ABSTRACT

Social media [1] platforms such as blogs, wikis and file sharing have become very popular in enterprises. Despite their effectiveness in increasing collaboration in the organization, employees are overloaded with information originating from these many sources and find it hard to orient themselves in the stream of events occurring in their organizational news feed. In this paper we identify what makes an event in an organizational social media platform important to employees. Once important factors of an event to an employee are identified, the stream of events can be personalized and prioritized based on those and thus reduce the overload and assist in work efficiency. Through interviews and two extensive user surveys, the first hypothetical and the second empirical, we identified which factors of an event make it important and compare results from the hypothetical and empirical surveys.

ACM Reference format:

N. Zwerdling, I. Ronen, S. L. Leiba, M. Barnea. 2018. Orient Me! – Important Event Identification in an Enterprise Activity Stream. In *UMAP'18, July 8–11, 2018, Singapore July 8–11, 2018, Singapore*, ACM, NY, NY, 4 pages. https://doi.org/10.1145/3209219.3209247

1 INTRODUCTION

Information overload has become a severe problem in our everyday life, particularly in the workplace. Employees are flooded with information from various sources, such as emails, chats, enterprise social networks and specific business applications. This information varies in its importance and relevance to the user. While for some pieces of information users will want to be notified immediately, others can be read later, and yet others are simply noise that should be filtered out. This variance highlights the need to identify the personalized importance of an information piece to employees – helping them

to cope with this information overload and identifying where to invest their time and effort.

Many of these applications – such as micro blogs, file sharing and forums - are collaborative or social in nature and generate many content items such as blog posts, wiki pages and files. People can comment on and like those. Creation and updates on these items are often published as events on an organizational activity stream which employees can follow. The variety of social applications creates a very heterogeneous set of events causing additional load. A combination of the events' features can determine the importance of the event, e.g., the person who created the event (actor), its content and the community in which it was created. In the organizational context, the actor of the event could be a manager, executive or peer of the employee. The content can be a blog post or a wiki page the employee created or interacted with before. It can occur in a community the employee is active in or owns. To assess the importance of an event to a specific user the user's interests need to be modeled: Which people, content items and topics are of interest to the user? Based on such a user profile, an event can be scored according to its various personalized features. In a live system these features can be learned based on the user's interactions with the system which serves as implicit feedback. However, for an initial configuration, and for overcoming the cold start problem, general preferences of users need to be configured.

In this paper we present two wide user surveys investigating the importance of an activity stream event in the enterprise. Our results enable a deep view into what features employees believe are important. This is an initial study before implementing a solution for scoring activity stream items. It could be used to define the initial personalized configuration of an activity stream scoring algorithm in the enterprise social networking environment.

Most research work analyzing what makes a social event interesting and engaging for a user has been conducted over 'consumer' non-enterprise social networks. Facebook's algorithm EdgeRank [1,7] considers thousands of different signals. Its main factors are the author of the post, how other people engaged with this post, the type of post (e.g., status update, video etc.) and the post's recency. Twitter, the leading microblogging service, is selecting tweets the user would like to be aware of. Its algorithm is mostly based on the accounts the user interacted with most, tweets the users engaged with, and more [1,15]. Several studies on Twitter's data suggested extending the Twitter personalization model by taking into account topical context [4,8] and others focused on personalized

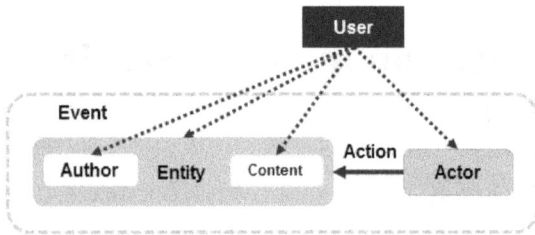

Figure 1 Entity Model

tweet ranking and recommendation [5,9]. LinkedIn is another prominent example of a heterogeneous professional social network which personalizes its feed by ranking activities according to their relevance to the user. In [3] Agarwal et al from LinkedIn showed a feed ranking model that considered activity freshness, feed diversity, and viewer-actor connection relationships while in [2] they focused on personalization modeling and scoring based on signals like the affinity of a viewer to interact with an activity type, with an actor and the three-way interactions among viewer, actor and the activity type. Hong et al. [12] ranked the LinkedIn feed by using a probabilistic latent factor model that combined information retrieval and collaborative filtering techniques.

The literature on enterprise social streams is rather sparse. Guy et al.[10] compared the use of people, terms, and entities in a user's profile for personalizing an enterprise activity stream. They showed that building the user's profile based on data from the stream itself is effective for the personalization task. This approach differs from ours in the kind of events users rated. We asked users to rate a randomized unscored set of items, whereas in [10] users rated already scored items; in addition, [10] used only public activity stream data while we used the users' private stream. In [11] Guy et al. compared the effectiveness of an entity-based user profile to a stream-based user profile for activity stream item scoring. Lunze et al. [14] ran a small experiment with 9 users over the Communote enterprise social stream and found that analyzing an item's text is essential for identifying important items.

2 RESEARCH SETTING

2.1 IBM Connections

We conducted our research on our company's internal social networking environment which is a deployment of IBM Connections ("Connections") [13]. Connections includes a wide and diverse set of social applications including user organizational profiles, microblogs, blogs, wikis, file sharing, communities and more. All applications enable commenting on and liking their entries. Employees can choose to follow any entity, community or person. A Community is a container of these application which is organized around a theme or a team. The user's homepage of Connections exposes an activity stream of all events on entities followed by this user or when the user was explicitly mentioned. Users can also choose to receive a digest email of events. For both options, events are ordered by recency.

2.2 Events

An event in the activity stream, represents any creation or update of an entity in Connections. As depicted in Figure 1 an event consists of several components. An *entity* can be either a content item such as a wiki page or blog entry, a container such as a blog or wiki, a community or a person. Each entity has an *author* which is the person who created the entity, such as the author of a blog entry or wiki page. An entity usually also has *content*. The *actor* is the person who performed an action on the entity such as creating it (in which case author and actor will be the same), updating it, liking it or commenting on it.

The user of Connections can be related to each of these parts through different relationships. For example, to the actor or author through organizational chart, collaboration or following. To the entity, through authorship, following or previous interactions such as commenting and liking.

To illustrate, consider an event such as "John commented on Sue's message in the XXX community". When mapping to Figure 1 the actor would be John, the entity is the Sue's message and the author - Sue. The message also has content. The user is the person who is following John for example. Users can be related to the event not only because of following John, but also because of other additional reasons such as that they are active in the community this entry was written in or because they have commented on it in the past.

Our aim in this paper was to find out which of these relationships were more significant to make an event important to a user.

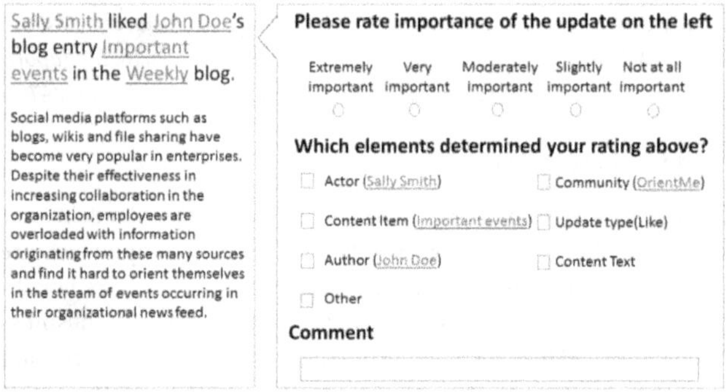

Figure 2 Empirical Survey Sample Question

2.3 User Studies

In our research we conducted three kinds of studies, consisting of interviews, a hypothetical user survey and an empirical user survey.

2.3.1 Interviews: To get a first idea of what employees felt made an event important we interviewed 5 employees and asked them to look at their homepage and identify which events were important and why. Based on these interviews we formulated the hypothetical user survey.

2.3.2 Hypothetical User Survey: In this user survey we identified the theoretical factors the user perceives as significant for determining the importance of an event. Participants were asked to rate on a 5-point Likert scale to what extend actor, author, entity, content or action type determined the importance of an event in general and then more detailed questions about features of each of those. For example, to what extend an event was important if the author was a manager, peer, employee, collaborator, someone they followed, etc. We sent the survey to 1155 active Connections users out of which we received responses from 286 (25%). Respondents originated from 31 countries across all organizations with 20% managers.

2.3.3 Empirical User Survey: In this survey we identified the actual factors which made an event important. For each participant we extracted the latest 100 events from their private activity stream and selected a sample of 20 events covering a maximum diversity of features we wanted to examine, such as action type, entity type, relationship type of the user to the actor, entity author and community. Figure 2 depicts a sample question (right part) on an event (left part) in the survey. Participants were asked to rate the importance of an event and which of the factors determined their rating.

We sent out the survey to additional different 2450 active Connections users and received at least one rating from 369. All in all, we received about 5K rated events.

3 RESULTS

In this section we explore the global factors determining the importance of an event (actor, entity, author and community) and then drill down into each factor to conduct a deeper analysis. We also compare results from our hypothetical to the empirical survey.

3.1 Global Factors

In the hypothetical user survey, we asked participants: "To what extent does each of the following factors determine the importance of an event?" Participants marked their rating on a Likert scale of 1-5 from "Not important" to "Extremely important" respectively.

Table 1: **To what extent does each of the following factors determine the importance of an event?**

Factor	% Important	OLR value
Topic	82.37**	0.03
Entity	78.75**	0.48
Actor	77.42**	0.63
Author	62.04*	0.73
Community	54.68	0.76
Action type	52.16	0.22

Table 1 presents in the second column the percentage of users who chose level of importance 4 or 5 for each feature. Throughout all tables, we refer to "important" as these two ratings. Wilcoxon paired test showed that topic, entity and the actor were significantly more important than all the other factors (p<0.01). Author was significantly more important than community and action type.

We analyzed the results of the empirical survey using ordered logistic regression (OLR) which is shown in the third column of Table 1. The OLR value represents the impact of each factor on the event's rating. All values except topic were significant (p<0.01).

It is interesting to note that in the hypothetical survey users claimed that the most important factor was the topic's content. However, for real events, it turned out that topic was the least important factor. The action type was ranked lower in both surveys. In real events, the most important factors were community, author and actor. We continue investigating these factors in depth in the next sections.

3.2 Person Factors

As shown in section 3.1, two of the key global factors were the person who performed the action (actor) and the person who wrote the entity's content (author). In our hypothetical survey we asked users: "To what extent is an event important if the person who did the event is: ..." The results are described in Table 2.

Table 2: **To what extent is an event important if the person who did the event is:**

Factor	% Important
Your first line manager****	79.18
Your second line manager****	78.36
Your Direct report***	73.89
Your third line manager**	72.66
Your team member**	69.66
Your peer**	67.16
An executive*	56.49
Someone whose content you read*	52.08
Someone you follow*	50.38
Someone you interacted or collaborated with*	49.43
From your organization	42.32
Network contact	41.44
Someone with the same job role	40.16
From your country	22.31

Table 3: **OLR of the influence of each type of actor**

Actor	OLR value
Your third line manager	1.37*
Your second line manager	1.15*
Your peer	0.84*
Your Direct report	0.73
Someone you interacted or collaborated with	0.71*
Your first line manager	0.64*
Network contact	0.34*
Someone you follow	0.10

As can be expected in an organizational setting, an event from users' organizational chart is scored higher than an event from other people they interacted with. In particular, events triggered by management were considered more important. The closer the manager to the user, the more important the event of the manager. Managers were followed by team members and peers. The asterisks (*) next to each actor type indicate significance over other actor types, e.g., first line manager is not significantly more important than second line manager, but both are significantly more important than the direct reports. We calculated significance using Wilcoxon paired test with p<0.01. We observed similar results when comparing the empirical survey, described in Table 3, to the hypothetical survey. For each real event the user ranked, we extracted the relationship of the user to the actor. Based on the relationship we analyzed the results using OLR. All results are statistically significant apart from Follow and Direct report (only managers have reports). When shown real events, management was still ranked with high importance. However, third and second line managers got a higher rank than first line managers. Peers also got higher importance than first line managers. Followed people and network contacts got low ranks in both surveys. Due to social conventions employees seldom un-fried or unfollow another employee. These weak relationships might explain this low rank.

We compared the distribution of the events' importance ratings between two populations of users: managers and regular employees (non-managers). In the hypothetical survey we used t-test and in the empirical survey Wilcoxon test. In both surveys managers considered actors from their management significantly higher than non-managers. In the hypothetical survey we found actors acting as second and third line managers as well as executives getting higher importance from the population of managers. In the empirical survey we noticed that the first line managers got significantly higher ratings from managers than from non-managers. We can deduce that managers recognize the importance of management's actions higher than non-managers.

Table 4 shows the results when inspecting the importance of the author's relationship to the user. Again, people from the user's organizational chart were assigned a higher importance rating. However, for the author feature, peers and even people the user interacted with were significantly more important than managers. We can conclude from author and actor analysis that our users considered highly the *actions* of their management but were more interested in their peers' *content*. Thus, users liked to stay up to date with their manager's actions: what they liked, their status updates, who they mentioned, etc. However, they were interested in the content of their peers for their work: the content of their wiki pages, their blogs and comments etc.

Table 4: OLR of the influence of each type of author

Author	OLR value
Your peer	1.10*
Your third line manager	0.74
Your first line manager	0.70
Someone you interacted or collaborated with	0.66*
Your second line manager	0.46
Network contact	0.38*
Your Direct report	0.11
Someone you follow	0.08

Table 5: To what extent is an event important if its content is something:

Factor	% important
You created ***	89.05
Created in a community you own**	76.58
You commented on**	72.53
You follow*	59.26
You liked*	51.85
Created in a community you follow	33.58
Popular (got many likes or comments)	30.88
You viewed	26.22
Just created by someone else	13.81

3.3 Entity and Community Factors

In the empirical survey the most important factor determining the importance of an event was its community and in the hypothetical survey the second most important factor was the entity. We now drill more deeply into these two factors. Table 5 shows the level of importance depending on the user's relationship to the entity. We can see correlation between the effort invested by the user on the entity or the time the user spent to create the entity's content and the importance of the event. For example, liking a blog the user wrote was more important than liking a blog the user only commented on.

In the empirical survey we extracted the user's relationship to the event's entity for each event the user ranked. We performed an ordered logistic regression to analyze the influence of the user's relationship to the entity on the rating of the event. The results of the empirical survey were consistent with the hypothetical survey. Table 6 shows that authoring an entity, e.g., creating content which is a more time-consuming action was most important, followed by contributing to the entity such as through editing a wiki or commenting. Liking and following which are one click actions and take very little time to commit got the lowest influence.

Table 6 also shows the influence of the users' relationship to the community on the event's score. Contributing content to the community was the most important factor, however without significance. This aligns with our entity results correlating effort of creation to importance rating. Owing a community does not necessarily demand more effort.

Table 6: OLR of the influence of the user's relationship to the entity and the community

OLR value	Entity	Community
Author /Community Owner	0.87*	1.13*
Contributor	0.74*	1.92
Liker	0.63*	1.62*
Follower	0.31	-0.27*

4 CONCLUSIONS AND FUTURE WORK

In this paper we identified globally important factors of events to users of an organizational social activity stream. Each factor is personalized based on the user profile of people and entities related to the user. Over time, a live system should learn individual preferences of each user as those will certainly vary. But for an activity stream event scoring system to work relatively well from the start, initial cold start parameters need to be set for each user.

We found that different organizational populations have different preferences. In particular, we identified significant differences between managers and non-managers. Similarly, preferences regarding the author of events in the organizational setting varied. Users preferred content *created* by their peers and events *initiated* by their managers. Moreover, users viewed events on content they created or made substantial contributions to as more important.

As we saw in this work, a hypothetical survey does not necessarily represent users' actual preferences. For example, users stated that the content of an event was most important whereas in reality other factors turned out to be more significant. As future work we plan to analyze the content of event items for deeper analysis of this point.

5 REFERENCES

[1]   About your Twitter timeline: https://support.twitter.com/articles/164083

[2]   Deepak Agarwal, Bee-Chung Chen, Rupesh Gupta, Joshua Hartman, Qi He, Anand Iyer, Sumanth Kolar, Yiming Ma, Pannagadatta Shivaswamy, Ajit Singh, and Liang Zhang. 2014. Activity ranking in LinkedIn feed. *In Proceedings of the 20th ACM SIGKDD international conference on Knowledge discovery and data mining (KDD '14)*. ACM, New York, NY, USA, 1603-1612. DOI: https://doi.org/10.1145/2623330.2623362

[3]   Deepak Agarwal, Bee-Chung Chen, Qi He, Zhenhao Hua, Guy Lebanon, Yiming Ma, Pannagadatta Shivaswamy, Hsiao-Ping Tseng, Jaewon Yang, and Liang Zhang. 2015. Personalizing LinkedIn Feed. *In Proceedings of the 21th ACM SIGKDD International Conference on Knowledge Discovery and Data Mining (KDD '15)*. ACM, New York, NY, USA, 1651-1660. DOI: https://doi.org/10.1145/2783258.2788614

[4]   Michael S. Bernstein, Bongwon Suh, Lichan Hong, Jilin Chen, Sanjay Kairam, and Ed H. Chi. 2010. Eddi: interactive topic-based browsing of social status streams. *In Proceedings of the 23nd annual ACM symposium on User interface software and technology (UIST '10)*. ACM, New York, NY, USA, 303-312. DOI: https://doi.org/10.1145/1866029.1866077

[5]   Kailong Chen, Tianqi Chen, Guoqing Zheng, Ou Jin, Enpeng Yao, and Yong Yu. 2012. Collaborative personalized tweet recommendation. *In Proceedings of the 35th international ACM SIGIR conference on Research*

and development in information retrieval (SIGIR '12). ACM, New York, NY, USA, 661-670. DOI: https://doi.org/10.1145/2348283.2348372

[6]   EdgeRank: http://edgerank.net/. Retrieved April 2018.

[7]   Edgerank: A Guide to the Facebook News Feed Algorithm: http://sproutsocial.com/insights/facebook-news-feed-algorithm-guide/. Retrieved April 2018.

[8]   Sandra Garcia Esparza, Michael P. O'Mahony, and Barry Smyth. 2013. CatStream: categorising tweets for user profiling and stream filtering. *In Proceedings of the 2013 international conference on Intelligent user interfaces (IUI '13)*. ACM, New York, NY, USA, 25-36. DOI: https://doi.org/10.1145/2449396.2449402

[9]   Wei Feng and Jianyong Wang. 2013. Retweet or not?: personalized tweet re-ranking. *In Proceedings of the sixth ACM international conference on Web search and data mining (WSDM '13)*. ACM, New York, NY, USA, 577-586. DOI=http://dx.doi.org/10.1145/2433396.2433470

[10] Ido Guy, Roy Levin, Tal Daniel, and Ella Bolshinsky. 2015. Islands in the Stream: A Study of Item Recommendation within an Enterprise Social Stream. *In Proceedings of the 38th International ACM SIGIR Conference on Research and Development in Information Retrieval (SIGIR '15)*. ACM, New York, NY, USA, 665-674. DOI: http://dx.doi.org/10.1145/2766462.2767746

[11] Ido Guy, Inbal Ronen, and Ariel Raviv. 2011. Personalized activity streams: sifting through the "river of news". *In Proceedings of the fifth ACM conference on Recommender systems (RecSys '11)*. ACM, New York, NY, USA, 181-188. DOI=http://dx.doi.org/10.1145/2043932.2043966

[12] Liangjie Hong, Ron Bekkerman, Joseph Adler, and Brian D. Davison. 2012. Learning to rank social update streams. *In Proceedings of the 35th international ACM SIGIR conference on Research and development in information retrieval (SIGIR '12)*. ACM, New York, NY, USA, 651-660. DOI: https://doi.org/10.1145/2348283.2348371

[13] IBM Connections: https://www.ibm.com/us-en/marketplace/ibm-connections. Retrieved April 2018.

[14] Lunze, Torsten, Philipp Katz, Dirk Röhrborn, and Alexander Schill. 2013. Stream-based recommendation for enterprise social media streams. *In International Conference on Business Information Systems*, pp. 175-186. Springer, Berlin, Heidelberg,

[15] Twitter's Algorithmic Timeline Is Working: https://www.buzzfeed.com/alexkantrowitz/twitters-algorithmic-timeline-is-working?utm_term=.jxqr1WY7n#.ig30RXG5V. Retrieved April 2018.

Robots that Listen to People's Hearts: The Role of Emotions in the Communication between Humans and Social Robots

Ana Paiva

INESC-ID & Instituto Superior Técnico, Universidade de Lisboa

Lisbon, Portugal 2744-016

ana.paiva@inesc-id.pt

ABSTRACT

As robots begin to integrate our world and invade our streets and homes, they must act as autonomous and intelligent beings. However, so far, they are deprived of our responsive and emotional capacities, lacking awareness of the social world we live in. In the future, robots should be able to take into account these distinctive dimensions of human social interactions to be able to act appropriately within such social contexts. To do this, they must adapt and embody the essence of social and emotional intelligence. ⊠is not only includes the ability to recognise human emotions and social interactions but also understand them, deliberate them and act accordingly.

Lately, significant research has been carried out in an att⊠empt to fi⊠nd ways to build social and emotional robots that are able to perceive the user's emotions, adapt to them, and react appropriately.

This talk will therefore provide an overview of the area of emotions in social interactions established between humans and social robots. In this analysis, I will use scenarios from educational and entertainment robotics, outline the process of building emotional social robots and finally proceed to interpret the effect that such capabilities have on user's interactions, learning, motivation, relationship and trust.

I believe that by studying and engineering emotional and social interactions "for" and "with" robots, we have the opportunity tobuild a new generation of natural, engaging, effective and, most importantly, "humane" AI.

CCS Concepts

Human-centered computing ~ Interactive systems and tools

ACM Reference Format

Ana Paiva. 2018. Robots that Listen to People's Hearts: The Role of Emotions in the Communication between Humans and Social Robots. *In Proceedings of 26th Conference on User Modeling, Adaptation and Personalization (UMAP'18),* July 8–11, 2018, Singapore. ACM, NY, NY, 1 page. DOI: https://doi.org/10.1145/3209219.3209268

BIOGRAPHY

Ana Paiva is a Full Professor in the Department of Computer Engineering at Instituto Superior Tecnico (IST) from the University of Lisbon and is also the Coordinator of GAIPS, the "Intelligent Agents and Synthetic Characters Group" at INESC-ID (see http://gaips.inesc-id.pt). Her group investigates the creation of complex systems using an agent-based approach, with a special focus on social agents. Prof. Paiva's main research focuses on the problems and techniques for creating social agents that can simulate human-like behaviours, be transparent, natural and eventually, give the illusion of life. Over the years she has addressed this problem by engineering agents that exhibit specific social capabilities, including emotions, personality, culture, non-verbal behaviour, empathy, collaboration, and others. Her main contributions in the area of social agents have been in the field of embodied conversational agents, multi-agent systems, affective computing and social robotics.

2 ACKNOWLEDGEMENTS

The work reported in this talk was supported by national funds through Fundação para a Ciência e a Tecnologia (FCT), with reference UID/CEC/50021/2013, through the project AMIGOS (PTDC/EEISII/7174/2014).

Easy to Please: Separating User Experience from Choice Satisfaction

James Schaffer
US Army Research Laboratory
Playa Vista, California
james.a.schaffer20.civ@mail.mil

John O'Donovan
University of California Santa Barbara
Santa Barbara, California
jod@cs.ucsb.edu

Tobias Höllerer
University of California Santa Barbara
Santa Barbara, California
holl@cs.ucsb.edu

ABSTRACT

Recommender systems are evaluated based on both their ability to create a satisfying user experience and their ability to help a user make better choices. Despite this, quantitative evidence from previous research in recommender systems indicate very high correlations between user experience attitudes and choice satisfaction. This might imply invalidity in the measurement methodologies of these constructs, whereas they may not be measuring what researchers think they are measuring. To remedy this, we present a new methodology for the measurement of choice satisfaction. Part of our approach is to measure a user's "ease of satisfaction," or that user's natural propensity to be satisfied, which is measured using three different approaches. An (N=526) observational study is conducted wherein users browse a movie catalog. A factor analysis is done to assess the discriminant validity of our proposed choice satisfaction apparatus from user experience. A statistical analysis suggests that accounting for ease-of-satisfaction allows for a model of choice satisfaction that is not only discriminant, but independent, from user experience. This enables researchers to more objectively identify recommender system factors that lead users to good choices.

CCS CONCEPTS

• **Human-centered computing** → *User models*; *HCI design and evaluation methods*; • **Information systems** → *Personalization*;

KEYWORDS

Choice satisfaction, user experience, construct validity, recommender systems, user models, evaluation

ACM Reference Format:
James Schaffer, John O'Donovan, and Tobias Höllerer. 2018. Easy to Please: Separating User Experience from Choice Satisfaction. In *UMAP '18: 26th Conference on User Modeling, Adaptation and Personalization, July 8–11, 2018, Singapore, Singapore*. ACM, New York, NY, USA, 9 pages. https://doi.org/10.1145/3209219.3209222

1 INTRODUCTION

One end goal of recommender systems is to assist in the decision-making process by assessing which items are relevant to a user. In order to evaluate a recommender's ability to satisfy this goal, recent research has moved towards quantifying both a user's choice satisfaction (CS) and user experience (UX) [21][28][29]. Based on common definitions of UX (subjective satisfaction with a recommender interface) and CS (a user's subjective satisfaction with a particular choice), these constructs should not be strongly correlated, but yet, this has been demonstrated [3][22]. A contributing issue is that CS and UX are measured in a subjective way due to difficulty in obtaining the ground truth. Factor analysis [35] has been used as a way to assess the validity of these self-reported metrics [22][28]. The UX/CS measurement process consists of exposing a user to recommendations and then obtaining the user's agreement (on a 1-7 Likert scale) with multiple question items that represent CS. Moreover, while some definitions of UX include only a "good-bad" scale (a single feeling) [13], quantification of subjectivity in recommender systems has moved to using multiple "sub-constructs" of attitudes, which are phrased as "user beliefs" [28] or "subjective system aspects" [21]. In this work, we will refer to these sub-constructs as UX attitudes.

Researchers should be concerned both about the use of self-reported UX/CS and the validity of fine-grained UX attitudes, for three reasons. First, although self-reported metrics may have predictive power, the content of the questions presented may not reflect what is actually measured. For example, the Dunning-Kruger test of self-reported expertise is more likely to indicate a test subject's *incompetence* rather than competence [8]. For this reason, it is important to rationalize what observable behavior or outcomes correlate with a proposed factor. Since we can infer high correlation between UX/CS from the work of Knijnenburg et al. [22], this may lead us to believe that self-assessed UX and CS may be affected by other situational or personal characteristics. For instance, users could simply be feeling good "in the moment" due to a sleek interface, which may incidentally lead researchers to believe they are making good decisions through inflated CS. Second, discriminant validity [9][16] appears to be an issue, since it has not been assessed in studies of recommender systems UX. This is more troublesome in light of large inter-attitude β coefficients reported in [22] (and to some extent, [28]). Finally, the predictive validity of many UX sub-constructs appears to be weak. This is because predicting attitudes with attitudes is not useful, especially when the effort required to collect these attitudes is equal. If behaviors can be predicted adequately using a single UX attitude, only that attitude need be measured.

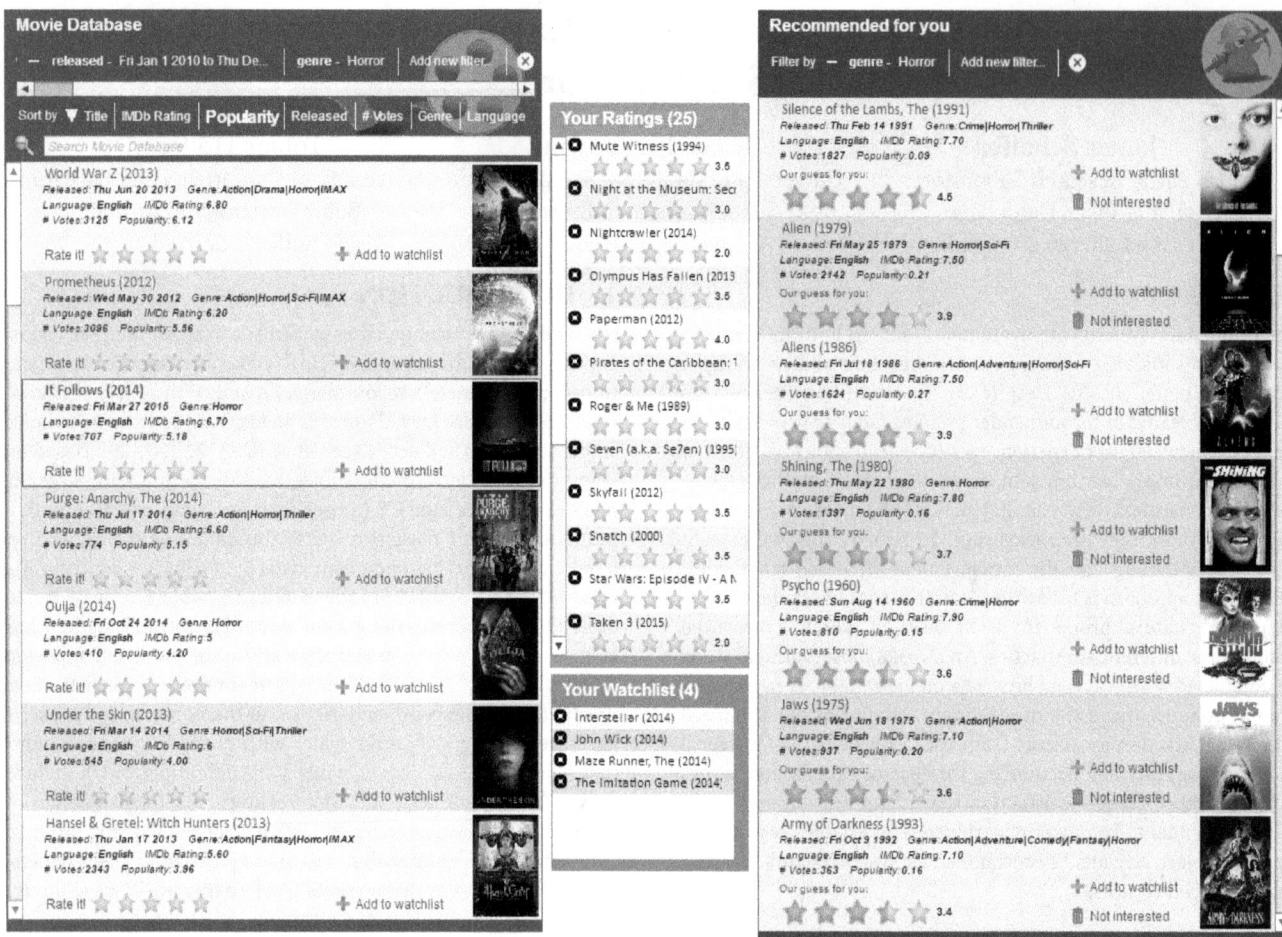

Figure 1: A screenshot of "Movie Miner," a faux movie discovery interface, which was used in the study.

This research is principally concerned with the statistical validity of CS measurement in recommender evaluation. A first step toward this is to measure CS in such a way that it is independent, or at least discriminant, from UX. We hypothesized that a person's "ease-of-satisfaction" is a contributor to the large correlations previously observed between UX and CS. Moreover, we suspect that past methodologies for measuring CS may have lead to low discriminant validity with UX attitudes, due to restrictive study designs. To address this, we conducted a user study (N=526) wherein users freely interacted with a recommendation interface to make a movie selection. CS and UX were measured. The proposed method for measuring CS accounts for baseline satisfaction, which is measured on a random selection of movies. Likert-scale questions are used, but feedback is taken for each individually selected movie and then parceled together. We also test whether users can self-assess their own ease-of-satisfaction as an easier-to-measure stand-in for baseline satisfaction. Finally, we examined the correlation between a user's average item rating and baseline satisfaction. In summary, our research questions are:

(1) What is the statistical validity of the recommender systems approach to modeling attitudes and UX?

(2) Can CS be measured in a way that makes it discriminant from UX?

(3) How can a user's personal ease-of-satisfaction be measured and does it predict both UX and CS?

2 RELATED WORK

Here we give a brief overview of methods for measuring CS in the psychology of consumer behavior, how to establish statistical validity, and details of UX and CS in recommender systems evaluation.

2.1 Measurement of CS

CS is studied in the psychology of consumer behavior (recent works include [7][20][37]). Satisfaction can be elicited, for instance, through user feedback on a Likert scale and studies often use longitudinal measures, since a person's initial estimate of their satisfaction with a particular product is suspect. CS can also be thought of as "projected" satisfaction - a feeling about a decision that was made today, but the consequences of which will not accrue until the future, at which point the product would be thoroughly evaluated. A valid concern is whether or not users can even accurately self-report their own CS at the time of choosing – an issue that is further confounded by recent research in the psychology of happiness, which indicates people may overestimate both past and future levels of happiness [38]. Additionally, people have a "sticky happiness baseline" [10], that is, positive or negative events can temporarily disturb a person's reported happiness level but it will always bounce back. This might imply that CS measurements taken before and after the moment of evaluation might be inflated and that baseline happiness might need to be accounted for. An ideal approach might be to measure the baseline state of a particular person before a stimulus is applied and then compare that with a measurement of CS that is taken longitudinally at the time of choice evaluation (in the case of movie selection, this could be just after the movie was viewed).

Establishing the statistical validity of a CS measurement in recommender systems is a difficult research challenge. First, predictive validity would need to be established. Since CS can be thought of as an attitude, the Theory of Reasoned Action [32] would suggest that this attitude would need to accurately predict behavior. For example, users self-reporting that they are completely satisfied with a choice in a movie should later rate that movie highly, or at least reflect that watching the movie was a good use of their time. Second, recommender interfaces can be affective [34] and features such as explanations can inflate a user's satisfaction [33]. For instance, a user could become frustrated with a system during interaction but still end up discovering a high quality item. The CS measurement thus should be statistically discriminant from any measurement of UX and ideally their measurements would be independent.

This research draws inspiration from the above observations and herein we model a user's ease-of-satisfaction to improve the measurement model for CS. A comparison of the effectiveness of longitudinal and immediate measurements of CS is left for future work.

2.2 Recommender Systems Evaluation

In recommender systems, CS and UX first explicitly converge in Knijnenburg et al. [22], which contains descriptions of multiple studies of UX in recommender systems. Here, CS is measured on three occasions in aggregate (and once for a single item) and an introduction to the fine-grained UX attitudes is given, such as perceived recommendation quality, perceived system effectiveness, and perceived recommendation variety. Other attitudes such as understandability and perceived control are given in [21]. The definition of UX in this work seems to stem from Hassenzahl [13], who defined UX as a single "good-bad" feeling about an interface. Knijnenburg et al. instead proposes an evaluation framework which uses multiple attitudinal and perceptual measurements, but one limitation is that the work does not provide statistically-grounded justification for its modeling choices. Discriminant validity is lost between reliable (Cronbach's $\alpha > 0.8$ [6]) constructs when inter-construct correlations reach 0.7. For instance, in [22], high correlations (> 0.7) can be inferred between perceived system effectiveness and CS (study 1), between CS, perceived recommendation quality, perceived system effectiveness, and perceived effort (study 2), between perceived recommendation quality and perceived system effectiveness (study

3), and between perceived recommendation variety, perceived recommendation quality, and perceived system effectiveness (study 4). Moreover, although the UX attitudes appear to correlate with interaction behavior in this work, the attitudes are never used to measure longitudinal CS.

An alternative perspective on UX and CS is given in Pu et al. [28]. Different UX attitudes are proposed, e.g., transparency, confidence/trust, and adequacy to explain use intentions and purchase intention (which are also self-reported). Purchase intention reasonably represents self-reported CS ("I would buy the items recommended, given the opportunity"). An issue with this work is that, while discriminant validity appears slightly better, internal reliability of several proposed constructs would be considered statistically questionable or unacceptable by standards of Cronbach's α [6] (additionally, some constructs are indicated by fewer than 3 items, which makes the construct unidentifiable). This means that correlations of 0.5 or higher might indicate poor discriminant validity (due to attenuation), for instance, between interface adequacy and perceived ease of use, between trust/confidence and purchase intention, and between perceived control and overall satisfaction.

2.3 Other Concepts of UX

Other attempts have been made to quantify and validate UX. We have previously mentioned Hassenzahl's work [13][14], which views UX as a single scale (which would imply a single construct). Two highly cited books on UX [1][25] take a different approach by defining UX and usability to be essentially the same and propose measuring UX through metrics like task completion time. While this might indeed be useful, we agree more with Hassenzahl, Knijnenburg, and Pu that UX is an attitude of a user, not behavioral symptoms of that attitude, or the competence of the user. Next, a general purpose UX apparatus was proposed in [26]. Predictive validity is established in this work through a measure of task time, but this work has shortcomings that are similar to recommender systems UX (internal reliability is reported but discriminant validity is not assessed, high correlations between constructs might be inferred from their similar correlations with the task time metric).

Our background research lead us to conclude that the methodology for measuring UX and CS in recommender systems is still in question. Here, we re-open the issue of how to measure UX and CS in recommender systems research. In a previous study we discovered that users could not provide discriminant answers when asked about understandability, system satisfaction, and perceived persuasion [24] when exposed to recommendation interfaces. Now, we conduct a more expansive user study with a more realistic, open task design and evaluate a new method for measuring CS. We re-evaluate several UX attitudes (understandability, perceived effectiveness, perceived control, and trust/confidence) and directly assess their discriminant validity. The goal for this work is identify reliable **and** discriminant constructs for UX and CS.

3 SYSTEM DESIGN

This section describes the design of the interface in more detail. In designing the system for this study, we kept the following three goals in mind: a) to make the system as familiar to modern web users as possible, b) to make the system as similar to currently deployed recommender systems as possible, and c) to ensure that the study can be completed without forcing the users to accept recommendations from the system, so adherence can be measured. The use of novelty in any design aspect was minimized so that results would have more impact on current practice.

Participants were presented with a user interface called *Movie Miner* (Figure 1). The interface was closely modeled after modern movie "browsers" (such as IMDb or Movielens) that typically have recommender functionality. On the left side, the system featured basic search, sort, and filter for the entire movie dataset. The right side of the interface provided a ranked list of recommendations derived from collaborative filtering, which interactively updated as rating data was provided.

The "Movielens 20M" dataset was used for this experimental task. The Movielens dataset has been widely studied in recommender systems research [27][18][12]. Due to update speed limitations of collaborative filtering, the dataset was randomly sampled for 4 million ratings, rather than the full 20 million.

3.1 Generating Recommendations

A traditional user-user collaborative filtering approach was chosen for the system. Details for this can be found in Resnick et al. [31]. Collaborative filtering was chosen due to the fact that it is well understood in the recommender systems community and it achieves extremely high performance on dense datasets such as MovieLens [23]. The results from this study should generalize reasonably well to other collaborative-filtering based techniques, such as matrix factorization and neighborhood models. We made two minor modifications to the default algorithm based on test results from our benchmark dataset: Herlocker damping and rating normalization[1].

3.2 User Interface Design

The interface provided the following functionality: mousing over a movie would pop up a panel that contained the movie poster, metadata information, and a plot synopsis of the movie (taken from IMDb); for any movie, users could click anywhere on the star bar to provide a rating for that movie, and they could click the green "Add to watchlist" button to save the movie in their watchlist (CS was measured on their chosen movies at the end of the task). Clicking the title of any movie would take a user to the IMDb page where a trailer could be watched (this was also available during the CS feedback stage).

3.2.1 Browser Side. On the left (browser) side of this interface, users had three primary modes of interaction which were modeled after the most typical features found on movie browsing websites:

(1) **SEARCH**: Typing a keyword or phrase into the keyword matching box at the top of the list returned all movies that matched the keyword. Matches were not personalized in any way (a simple text matching algorithm was used).

(2) **SORT**: Clicking a metadata parameter (e.g. Title, IMDb Rating, Release Date) at the top of the list re-sorted the movies according to that parameter. Users could also change the sort direction.

(3) **FILTER**: Clicking "Add New Filter" at the top of the list brought up a small popup dialog that prompted the user for a min, max, or set coverage value of a metadata parameter. Users could add as many filters as they wanted and re-edit or delete them at any time.

3.2.2 Recommendation Side. The recommendation side operated identically to the browser side, except that the list was always sorted by the collaborative filtering prediction and the user could not override this behavior.

4 EXPERIMENT DESIGN

An observational study was conducted where participants interacted with the Movie Miner interface to find a set of movies to watch in the future. Participant behavior was not restricted and the entire setup was designed to match typical online sessions as closely as possible.

Participants were recruited on Amazon Mechanical Turk (AMT). AMT is a web service that gives tools to researchers who require large numbers of participants and are capable of collecting data for their experiment in an online setting. AMT has been studied extensively for validity, notably Buhrmester [4] has found that the quality of data collected from AMT is comparable to what would be collected from laboratory experiments [15]. Furthermore, since clickstream data can be collected, satisficing is easy to detect.

A list of all measurements taken in the study are given in Table 1. All of these items were taken on a Likert scale, except for when ratings were elicited, where a 5-star rating bar was used. Cronbach's alpha [6], a measurement of internal reliability, is reported. For this number, values above 0.8 are considered good fit, while values below 0.6 are considered unacceptable.

In this section, we first give a brief overview of the participant's experience with the study materials. Then, we discuss the measurements shown in Table 1 in detail. Finally, we detail the analysis strategy and hypotheses.

4.1 Procedure

Participants made their way through four phases: the pre-study, the ratings phase, the watchlist phase, and the post-study. The pre-study and post-study were designed using Qualtrics[2]. In the "ratings" phase, participants accessed Movie Miner and were shown only the blue *Movie Database* list and the ratings box (refer back to Figure 1). We asked participants to find and rate *at least* 10 movies that they believed would best represent their tastes, but many participants rated more than the minimum. In the "watchlist phase," participants were shown the brown *Recommended for You* list and the watchlist box. Instructions appeared in a popup window and were also shown at the top of the screen when the popup was closed. Participants were told to freely use whichever tool they preferred to find some new movies to watch. They could add movies to their watchlist with the green button that appeared on each individual movie (regardless of the list that it appeared in). We asked them not to add any movies that they had already seen, required them to add at least 5 movies (limited to 7 maximum), and we required them to spend at least 12 minutes interacting with the

---

[1]Our approach was nearly identical to: http://grouplens.org/blog/similarity-functions-for-user-user-collaborative-filtering/

[2]https://www.qualtrics.com/

interface. A twelve minute session in which 5-7 items are selected was deemed sufficient time to select quality items, given that people only browse Netflix for 60-90 seconds to find a single item before giving up [11].

4.2 Measurement Model

We considered two new approaches to quantifying CS: 1) a simple approach that uses ease-of-satisfaction as a statistical control for CS (the EoS control approach), and 2) a more complicated method that builds a change-score model between ease-of-satisfaction and CS (the two-wave approach).

Three ease-of-satisfaction measurements were considered. The first is baseline satisfaction (BS), which was measured shortly after the pre-study by getting participant feedback on movies that were chosen from the database at random. Ten random movies were shown, one at a time, and the responses were averaged together. Next, participants were asked to self-report their own ease-of-satisfaction (SREoS) during the pre-study. Finally, we also considered the user's average item rating as a form of ease-of-satisfaction. It is important to note that the first metric is the only one that can be used for the two-wave approach while remaining statistically valid - this is because the measurement of CS and BS is identical.

CS and UX were measured after the participant had made their selection. For CS, the recommender interface was removed and the questions items were shown for each item chosen by the participant. Note that the question items are phrased in terms of the recommendations, not the interface. This is to help the participant distinguish between the browsing tools and the features of the recommender system. The UX attitudes were collected during the post-study using random-order questionnaires.

To assess predictive validity of CS and UX, we measured three behavioral variables: interaction with the browser tool, interaction with the recommendation tool, and adherence to recommendations. The interaction variables were measured as the total number of times that a user clicked within one of the two tools available, whether it was for inspecting a particular movie, rating a particular movie, or adding a movie to the watchlist. Adherence to recommendations was taken as the ratio of items in the final watchlist that originated from the recommendation side of the interface. This measurement was only possible since we didn't "force" participants to accept recommendations (the browser tool could be used to complete the entire study, if desired). It can be argued that adherence is one of the most important behavioral variables for recommendation research, since it represents behavioral evidence of a user's acceptance of recommendations, rather than a self-reported attitude. Adherence is typically not measured in recommender systems, which we believe is due to a lack of open methodologies, but it has been studied before in expert systems research [2].

4.3 Evaluation Strategy and Hypotheses

Here we describe the methodology for answering the research questions outlined in the introduction.

First, we evaluate the statistical validity of the following user attitudes: understandability, perceived system effectiveness, perceived control, and self-reported trust. Convergent validity of these constructs has already been demonstrated [22][28] and it is reproduced

here. Therefore, we focus on discriminant and predictive validity. Discriminant validity is assessed using the Campbell and Fiske test [5], that is, checking that the correlation between constructs is < 0.85 while correcting for attenuation:

$$\frac{r_{xy}}{\sqrt{r_{xx} \cdot r_{yy}}} \quad (1)$$

where r_{xy} is the correlation between construct x and y and r_{xx} is the Cronbach's reliability of construct x. Predictive validity is tested by checking for the significance of regression coefficients when predicting interaction, adherence, and CS. Predictive power is tested through SEM. This leads us to the following hypotheses:

- H_1: Understandability is discriminant from perceived effectiveness, perceived control, and self-reported trust.
- H_2: Perceived effectiveness is discriminant from understandability, perceived control, and self-reported trust.
- H_3: Perceived control is discriminant from understandability, perceived effectiveness, perceived control, and self-reported trust.
- H_4: Self-reported trust is discriminant from understandability, perceived effectiveness, perceived control, and self-reported trust.
- H_5: UX predicts increased or decreased interaction behavior.
- H_6: UX predicts increased or decreased adherence.

Second, we test whether or not the BS and CS metrics are discriminant. Discriminant validity with BS provides additional evidence that the EoS control approach would be valid (it should not be expected that choosing random movies out of the database would satisfy anyone). More importantly, this test is the first step in assessing whether or not the SREoS factor is a valid replacement for BS. The BS construct and the CS construct should also be discriminant from UX for the EoS control approach to be valid. Discriminant validity is again assessed with Equation 1. Thus:

- H_7: CS is discriminant from UX.
- H_8: BS is discriminant from CS.

Third, we test whether a user's ease-of-satisfaction is a factor in UX and CS. That is, we want to know if ease-of-satisfaction is a personal factor that affects *all* attitudes in recommender systems research, even CS. If this were true, we would expect to see significant regression estimates between the ease-of-satisfaction metric and all other attitudes, including CS. For these tests, we use BS, since it is likely the most objective metric of the user's ease-of-satisfaction. This leads to the following hypotheses:

- H_9: BS predicts increased understandability, p. effectiveness, p. control, and trust.
- H_{10}: BS predicts increased CS.

Next, we can use a Raykov change score model [30] to assess the validity of the two-wave approach. A Raykov change model is essentially a repeated-measures ANOVA for factor analysis. However, researchers may not want to require participants to answer multiple questions when assessing CS. Therefore, we can also test a simple two-wave growth curve model [36] using representative question items from baseline and CS. That is,

- H_{11}: UX is discriminant from changes in CS.

Factor	Item Description	R^2	Est.
SREoS *ALPHA* : 0.92	[r1] I think I will trust the movie recommendations given in this task.	0.81	1.17
	[r2] I think I will be satisfied with the movie recommendations given in this task.	0.83	1.18
	[r3] I think the movie recommendations in this task will be accurate.	0.75	1.15
UX/Understand. *ALPHA* : 0.61	[u1] How understandable were the recommendations?	0.538	1.174
	[u1] Movie Miner succeeded at justifying its recommendations.	0.756	1.482
	[u1] The recommendations seemed to be completely random.	0.427	-1.227
UX/Effectiveness *ALPHA* : 0.91	[e1] I preferred these recommendations over past recommendations.	0.643	1.406
	[e2] How accurate do you think the recommendations were?	0.781	1.494
	[e3] How satisfied were you with the recommendations?	0.852	1.602
	[e4] To what degree did the recommendations help you find movies for your watchlist?	0.653	1.387
UX/Control *ALPHA* : 0.86	[c1] How much control do you feel you had over which movies were recommended?	0.666	1.293
	[c2] To what degree do you think you positively improved recommendations?	0.638	1.238
	[c3] I could get Movie Miner to show the recommendations I wanted.	0.706	1.436
UX/Trust *ALPHA* : 0.93	[t1] I trust the recommendations.	0.861	1.573
	[t2] I feel like I could rely on Movie Miner's recommendations in the future.	0.845	1.640
	[t3] I would advise a friend to use the recommender.	0.723	1.575
UX, *ALPHA* : 0.93	All Understandability, Effectiveness, Control, and Trust items (similar R^2 and Est.)		
Choice Sat. (CS) *ALPHA* : 0.93	[cs1] How excited are you to watch <movie>?	0.78	0.66
	[cs2] How satisfied were you with your choice in <movie>?	0.89	0.70
	[cs3] How much do you think you will enjoy <movie>?	0.92	0.67
	[cs4] What rating do you think you will end up giving to <movie>?	0.57	0.34
Baseline Sat. (BS) *ALPHA* : 0.97	[bs1] How excited would you be to watch <movie>?	0.91	0.66
	[bs2] Would you be satisfied with choosing <movie>?	0.964	0.70
	[bs3] How much do you think you would enjoy <movie>?	0.955	0.67
	[bs4] What rating do you think you would end up giving to <movie>?	0.756	0.34

Table 1: Factors determined by participant responses to subjective questions. R^2 reports the fit of the item to the factor. Est. is the estimated loading of the item to the factor. Items that were removed due to poor fit are not shown. *ALPHA* indicates the Cronbach's alpha.

To test whether the two-wave approach would be advantageous over the EoS control approach, we can compare the correlations observed between UX and CS in each model.

Fourth, we assess whether or not the SREoS metric can stand in for BS, so it can be used as a stand-in for the EoS control method, which would help researchers save time. This is done again through Equation 1. Additionally, we can also check the model fit metrics, specifically, Bayesian information criterion (BIC) [19]. Next, we want to know whether or not BS can be implicitly teased out from a user's rating profile. This can be done just by testing the R^2 of the user's average profile rating when used as an indicator variable of BS. This leads to:

- H_{12}: SREoS and BS are discriminant.
- H_{13}: Replacing BS with SREoS results in $2 \ln B_{ij} > 10$.
- H_{14}: A user's average profile rating has an R^2 of > 0.5 when used as an indicator variable of BS.

Correlation ($\leftrightarrow$)	Corr.	Att. Corr.	D?
Understandability $\leftrightarrow$ Effectiveness	0.977	1.311	N
Understandability $\leftrightarrow$ Control	0.960	1.325	N
Understandability $\leftrightarrow$ Trust	0.954	1.267	N
Effectiveness $\leftrightarrow$ Control	0.953	1.077	N
Effectiveness $\leftrightarrow$ Trust	0.985	1.070	N
Trust $\leftrightarrow$ Control	0.953	1.066	N
UX $\leftrightarrow$ CS	0.391	0.420	Y
UX $\leftrightarrow$ Change in CS	0.060	0.065	Y
BS $\leftrightarrow$ CS	0.243	0.256	Y
BS $\leftrightarrow$ SREoS	0.223	0.236	Y

Table 2: Correlations and attenuated correlations between UX attitudes. The attenuated correlation cutoff for (D)iscriminant validity is 0.85, resulting in (Y)es/(N)o.

5 RESULTS

We collected more than 526 samples of participant data using AMT. Participants were paid $1.50 and spent between 25 and 60 minutes doing the study. Participants were between 18 and 71 years of age and were 45% male. Participant data was checked carefully for satisficing and violating records were removed, resulting in the 526 complete records. Factor analysis was used to test the internal reliability and convergent validity of the factors shown in Table 1, which all resulted in good internal reliability, except for understandability ($\alpha = 0.61$), which was questionable. Grouping the UX attitudes into one factor also resulted in excellent reliability ($\alpha = 0.93$).

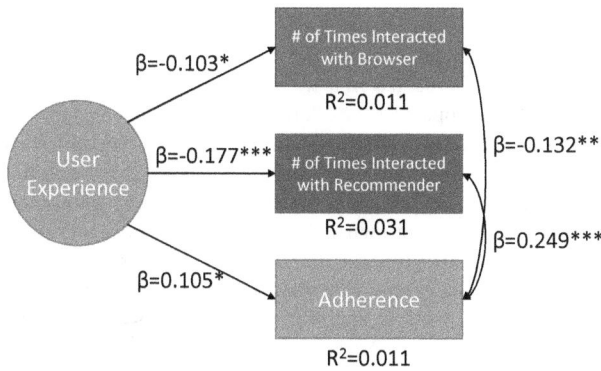

Figure 2: A visual of an SEM that predicts behavior based on the combined UX attitudes. Model fit metrics: $N = 526$ with 102 free parameters, $RMSEA = 0.054$ ($CI : [0.046, 0.062]$), $TLI = 0.972$, $CFI = 0.977$ over null baseline model, $\chi^2(102) = 257.515$.

5.1 Discriminant Validity

Table 2 indicates discriminant validity between constructs. Discriminant validity was tested by first correcting for attenuation (Equation 1) and then examining correlations between the factors. All UX attitudes were found to not be discriminant from each other, thus we reject H_{1-4}. Next, the UX attitudes were grouped into a single factor to avoid multi-collinearity when assessing predictive validity. An SEM was built (Figure 2)wherein the regression coefficients of browser interaction, recommender interaction, and adherence were determined. Minor, but significant, coefficients were found for each behavior, leading us to accept H_5 and H_6.

Next, we assess the discriminant validity of the BS and CS constructs. Table 2 shows that UX is discriminant from CS, with an attenuated correlation of 0.420. BS is also discriminant from CS, with an attenuated correlation of 0.256. Thus we accept H_7 and H_8.

5.2 Ease-of-Satisfaction: Baseline

Here we assess the predictive validity of the first ease-of-satisfaction metric: BS. An SEM was built (Figure 3) where BS was used as a predictor of the UX attitudes and CS. Regression coefficients of BS for the UX attitudes all achieved a significance of $p < 0.001$. The significance of the BS regression coefficient for CS was found to be $p < 0.01$. Additionally, an alternate SEM was tested where the UX attitudes were combined into a single construct. This again lead to significant coefficients for BS for UX and CS ($p < 0.001$). It should be noted that when controlling for BS, the correlation between CS and UX becomes 0.323, down from 0.391, increasing their discriminant validity. This leads us to accept H_9 and H_{10}.

Next, we assess the validity of using a growth curve model to measure change in CS (the two-wave method). This models the difference between CS and BS, rather than just the magnitude of CS. First, a Raykov change model is built (Figure 4), where BS is used as wave 1 and CS is used as wave 2. Variances of the change variables are not modeled, thus they are fixed (shown by a 0 in the figure). All pairs of items and the latent constructs are correlated. Then, to test UX as a predictor of change in CS, it is correlated with the wave 1 construct and the correlation coefficient is checked for the

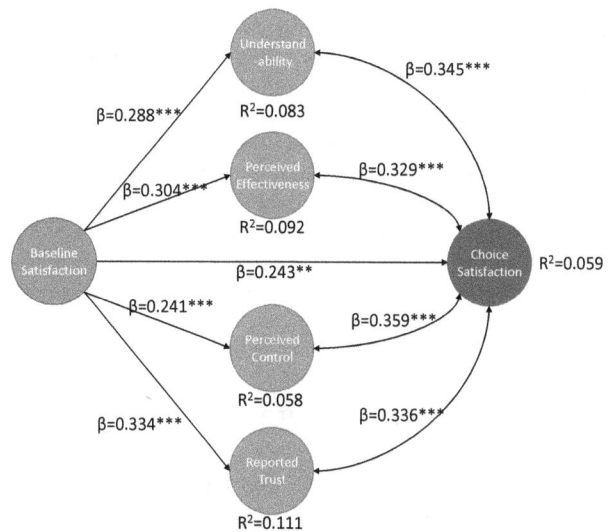

Figure 3: A visual of an SEM that shows the role of BS on UX attitudes. Model fit metrics: $N = 526$ with 180 free parameters, $RMSEA = 0.062$ ($CI : [0.056, 0.068]$), $TLI = 0.971$, $CFI = 0.965$ over null baseline model, $\chi^2(174) = 527.717$.

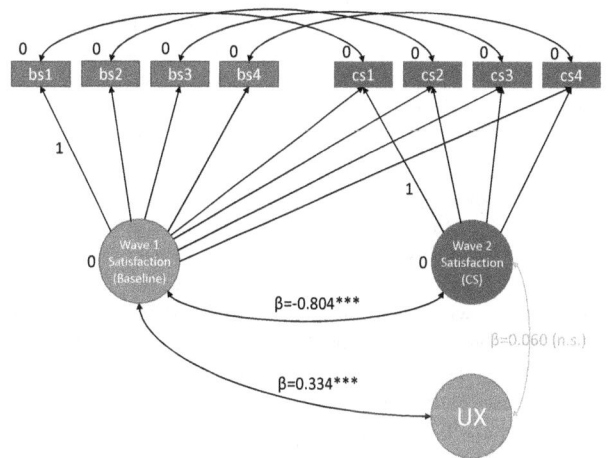

Figure 4: A Raykov change model using two waves: BS (first) and CS (second). UX does not predict a change in satisfaction. Items for satisfaction are shown in this figure to demonstrate how item loadings were configured. Overall fit metrics are typically not reported for growth curve models.

wave 2 construct. The coefficient was found to be non-signficant ($p = 0.240$, $\beta = 0.060$), so we accept H_{11}. This model indicates that the change in CS over the baseline is independent of the UX attitudes that were reported by participants.

5.3 Ease-of-Satisfaction: Stand-ins

Finally, we assess stand-ins for the BS metric. First, self-reported ease-of-satisfaction and BS were found to be discriminant with an attenuated correlation of 0.236 (see Table 2). Thus H_{12} is rejected. Second, the BIC score (a measure of model fit, lower is better) in

Figure 3 was 26156.811. To test H_{13}, we swapped BS with self-reported ease-of-satisfaction (the rest of the model remained the same), which changed the BIC score to 27133.771. To check for significant differences, we evaluate $2 \ln B_{ij} = 20.41 - 20.33 = 0.08 < 10$ [19], so we reject H_{13} (indicating the two models are roughly equivalent). Since it was found that BS and SREoS are discriminant, we tested a model where both measures were used to predict UX attitudes and CS. Although the resulting model had lower BIC, improvements were observed in RMSEA, CFI, and TLI, as well as the R^2 for each UX attitude and CS. Third, the average profile rating of each user (which was collected in this study) was loaded onto BS. The R^2 for the user's average rating was 0.007, so we reject H_{14}.

6   DISCUSSION OF RESULTS

1. What is the statistical validity of the recommender systems approach to modeling attitudes and UX? In this experiment, there was no statistical evidence in favor of the multi-attitude approach described by Pu et al. [28] and Knijnenburg et al. [22]. Inter-construct correlations far exceeded the 0.85 cutoff for discriminant validity. Moreover, consider that the *less* correlation there is between each construct, the more efficient each construct becomes as a measurement (discriminant constructs are more likely to have better combined predictive power) – 0.85 is just a recommended cutoff. The results in this experiment indicate it is unlikely that *good* discriminant validity could be reached using a nuanced attitudinal approach. The reason for this might be that users simply do not, at least without attentional direction, form complex mental models of recommendation interfaces. Next, assessing the predictive validity of UX might be supported by the Theory of Reasoned Action [32], however, previous work has shown little evidence to suggest that modeling UX attitudes leads to the ability to predict adherence to recommendations or good decisions, only other user attitudes and interaction behavior. Here, the regression coefficient when predicting adherence was significant but minor ($\beta = 0.105$), which does not create a particularly strong case for predictive validity. Still, more interaction correlated with a slightly worsened UX, which in turn correlates with a slightly worsened CS. This result reinforces research results in consumer product selection, where it is known that more deliberation results in lower CS [7][37].

Although no evidence was found here that nuanced UX attitudes are discriminant, this does not close the book on them. There are some methodological differences between this work and [22]/[28] that could explain the differences. First, question phrasing was slightly different. Second, not all attitudes measured in the other studies were measured here. Finally, this study used a more open, realistic methodology where users undertook a typical movie selection task. While focusing on this task, users may not have paid much attention to scrutinizing the particular features of the system. This is in contrast with [22]/[28], which were more restrictive and had large differences between experiment treatments.

Our current recommendation is for recommender systems practitioners to allocate only a few questions towards assessing the UX attitudes that were trialed here. This is also supported by our previous study [24]. This suggestion implies a return to the single scale, "good-bad" feeling espoused by Hassenzahl [13]. Substantially more research is needed to determine if UX is a consistent predictor of behavior or if users are like to form detailed mental models of recommender systems.

2. Can CS be modeled in a way that makes it discriminant from UX? Our apparatus for CS, regardless of modeling approach, achieved discriminant validity from UX, with an attenuated correlation of 0.420. Although this is quite auspicious, this result may be dependent on the particular design that we chose for this study (users freely made their own selections). In algorithm experiments where users are asked to rate items which are pre-selected by the recommender, we cannot say whether or not the construct will again be discriminant. Despite this, it would be ideal if the correlation between CS and UX was very nearly zero, since a person's feeling about a particular movie should not be affected by the information tool that was used to discover that movie. Our analysis suggests that if BS is measured, researchers can create a two-wave model of CS that we have demonstrated to be independent of UX. While our method does require substantial feedback for each item (and collection of the baseline), we believe the construct could be represented by a single question "How much do you think you will enjoy <movie>?" due to an R^2 value of 0.92. In this case, a repeated measures ANOVA could be used instead of a growth curve model, which would simplify analysis.

3. How can a user's personal ease-of-satisfaction be measured and does it predict both UX and CS? Although self-reported ease-of-satisfaction is not a valid replacement for measuring BS, it had the same effect on statistical conclusions in the model given in Figure 3. If the two-wave method (Figure 4) is not possible, self-reported ease-of-satisfaction could be used as a controlling variable so that the portion of CS variance explained by UX is minimized. Unfortunately, a user's average rating cannot stand in for either of these metrics, so ease-of-satisfaction cannot be inferred just by examining a user's rating profile.

One limitation of this work is that, outside of user experiments, recommendation practitioners may find it difficult to set up a scenario where the ease-of-satisfaction method is practical or useful. However, this research also clearly demonstrates that positive feelings felt by users during a user interface evaluation may easily confuse any practitioner's tests of good decision making. Having happy users does not necessarily mean having a useful and effective information system. Still, more research is needed on the validity of CS measurement, specifically, how it correlates with longitudinal satisfaction with selected items.

7   CONCLUSION

In summary, we investigated ways to account for a user's ease-of-satisfaction when measuring choice satisfaction in studies of recommendation. Our statistical analysis lead us to the conclusion that a two-wave approach to choice satisfaction would be ideal for identifying factors that lead users to good decisions, since changes in choice satisfaction appear to be independent from user experience. We have also identified a shortcut to controlling for ease-of-satisfaction by asking users to perform a self-assessment. The methodology proposed here has the potential to help future researchers identify factors in recommender systems that lead users to satisfying choices.

REFERENCES

[1] William Albert and Thomas Tullis. 2013. *Measuring the user experience: collecting, analyzing, and presenting usability metrics.* Newnes.

[2] Vicky Arnold, Nicole Clark, Philip A Collier, Stewart A Leech, and Steve G Sutton. 2006. The differential use and effect of knowledge-based system explanations in novice and expert judgment decisions. *Mis Quarterly* (2006), 79–97.

[3] Dirk Bollen, Bart P Knijnenburg, Martijn C Willemsen, and Mark Graus. 2010. Understanding choice overload in recommender systems. In *Proceedings of the fourth ACM conference on Recommender systems.* ACM, 63–70.

[4] Michael Buhrmester, Tracy Kwang, and Samuel D Gosling. 2011. Amazon's Mechanical Turk a new source of inexpensive, yet high-quality, data? *Perspectives on psychological science* 6, 1 (2011), 3–5.

[5] Donald T Campbell and Donald W Fiske. 1959. Convergent and discriminant validation by the multitrait-multimethod matrix. *Psychological bulletin* 56, 2 (1959), 81.

[6] Lee J Cronbach, Peter Schönemann, and Douglas McKie. 1965. Alpha coefficients for stratified-parallel tests. *Educational and Psychological Measurement* 25, 2 (1965), 291–312.

[7] Ap Dijksterhuis and Zeger Van Olden. 2006. On the benefits of thinking unconsciously: Unconscious thought can increase post-choice satisfaction. *Journal of Experimental Social Psychology* 42, 5 (2006), 627–631.

[8] David Dunning. 2011. The Dunning–Kruger effect: On being ignorant of one's own ignorance. In *Advances in experimental social psychology.* Vol. 44. Elsevier, 247–296.

[9] Claes Fornell and David F Larcker. 1981. Evaluating structural equation models with unobservable variables and measurement error. *Journal of marketing research* (1981), 39–50.

[10] Daniel Gilbert. 2009. *Stumbling on happiness.* Vintage Canada.

[11] Carlos A Gomez-Uribe and Neil Hunt. 2016. The Netflix recommender system: Algorithms, business value, and innovation. *ACM Transactions on Management Information Systems (TMIS)* 6, 4 (2016), 13.

[12] F Maxwell Harper and Joseph A Konstan. 2016. The movielens datasets: History and context. *ACM Transactions on Interactive Intelligent Systems (TiiS)* 5, 4 (2016), 19.

[13] Marc Hassenzahl. 2008. User experience (UX): towards an experiential perspective on product quality. In *Proceedings of the 20th Conference on l'Interaction Homme-Machine.* ACM, 11–15.

[14] Marc Hassenzahl and Noam Tractinsky. 2006. User experience-a research agenda. *Behaviour & information technology* 25, 2 (2006), 91–97.

[15] David J Hauser and Norbert Schwarz. 2015. Attentive Turkers: MTurk participants perform better on online attention checks than do subject pool participants. *Behavior research methods* (2015), 1–8.

[16] Jörg Henseler, Christian M Ringle, and Marko Sarstedt. 2015. A new criterion for assessing discriminant validity in variance-based structural equation modeling. *Journal of the academy of marketing science* 43, 1 (2015), 115–135.

[17] Jonathan L Herlocker, Joseph A Konstan, Al Borchers, and John Riedl. 1999. An algorithmic framework for performing collaborative filtering. In *Proceedings of the 22nd annual international ACM SIGIR conference on Research and development in information retrieval.* ACM, 230–237.

[18] Jason J Jung. 2012. Attribute selection-based recommendation framework for short-head user group: An empirical study by MovieLens and IMDB. *Expert Systems with Applications* 39, 4 (2012), 4049–4054.

[19] Robert E Kass and Adrian E Raftery. 1995. Bayes factors. *Journal of the american statistical association* 90, 430 (1995), 773–795.

[20] Sunghan Kim, M Karl Healey, David Goldstein, Lynn Hasher, and Ursula J Wiprzycka. 2008. Age differences in choice satisfaction: A positivity effect in decision making. *Psychology and aging* 23, 1 (2008), 33.

[21] Bart P Knijnenburg, Svetlin Bostandjiev, John O'Donovan, and Alfred Kobsa. 2012. Inspectability and control in social recommenders. In *Proceedings of the sixth ACM conference on Recommender systems.* ACM, 43–50.

[22] Bart P Knijnenburg, Martijn C Willemsen, Zeno Gantner, Hakan Soncu, and Chris Newell. 2012. Explaining the user experience of recommender systems. *User Modeling and User-Adapted Interaction* 22, 4-5 (2012), 441–504.

[23] Yehuda Koren and Robert Bell. 2015. Advances in collaborative filtering. In *Recommender systems handbook.* Springer, 77–118.

[24] Pigi Kouki, James Schaffer, Jay Pujara, John O'Donovan, and Lise Getoor. 2017. User Preferences for Hybrid Explanations. In *Proceedings of the Eleventh ACM Conference on Recommender Systems.* ACM, 84–88.

[25] Mike Kuniavsky. 2003. *Observing the user experience: a practitioner's guide to user research.* Elsevier.

[26] Bettina Laugwitz, Theo Held, and Martin Schrepp. 2008. Construction and evaluation of a user experience questionnaire. In *Symposium of the Austrian HCI and Usability Engineering Group.* Springer, 63–76.

[27] Bradley N Miller, Istvan Albert, Shyong K Lam, Joseph A Konstan, and John Riedl. 2003. MovieLens unplugged: experiences with an occasionally connected recommender system. In *Proceedings of the 8th international conference on Intelligent user interfaces.* ACM, 263–266.

[28] Pearl Pu, Li Chen, and Rong Hu. 2011. A user-centric evaluation framework for recommender systems. In *Proceedings of the fifth ACM conference on Recommender systems.* ACM, 157–164.

[29] Pearl Pu, Li Chen, and Rong Hu. 2012. Evaluating recommender systems from the userâĂŹs perspective: survey of the state of the art. *User Modeling and User-Adapted Interaction* 22, 4-5 (2012), 317–355.

[30] Tenko Raykov. 1992. Structural models for studying correlates and predictors of change. *Australian Journal of Psychology* 44, 2 (1992), 101–112.

[31] Paul Resnick, Neophytos Iacovou, Mitesh Suchak, Peter Bergstrom, and John Riedl. 1994. GroupLens: An Open Architecture for Collaborative Filtering of Netnews. In *Proceedings of ACM CSCW'94 Conference on Computer-Supported Cooperative Work.* 175–186. http://www.acm.org/pubs/articles/proceedings/cscw/192844/p175-resnick/p175-resnick.pdf

[32] Michael J Ryan and Edward H Bonfield. 1975. The Fishbein extended model and consumer behavior. *Journal of Consumer Research* 2, 2 (1975), 118–136.

[33] Nava Tintarev and Judith Masthoff. 2007. A survey of explanations in recommender systems. In *Data Engineering Workshop, 2007 IEEE 23rd International Conference on.* IEEE, 801–810.

[34] Marko Tkalcic, Andrej Kosir, and Jurij Tasic. 2011. Affective recommender systems: the role of emotions in recommender systems. In *Proc. The RecSys 2011 Workshop on Human Decision Making in Recommender Systems.* Citeseer, 9–13.

[35] Jodie B Ullman and Peter M Bentler. 2003. *Structural equation modeling.* Wiley Online Library.

[36] Dietrich Von Rosen. 1991. The growth curve model: a review. *Communications in Statistics-Theory and Methods* 20, 9 (1991), 2791–2822.

[37] Timothy D Wilson, Douglas J Lisle, Jonathan W Schooler, Sara D Hodges, Kristen J Klaaren, and Suzanne J LaFleur. 1993. Introspecting about reasons can reduce post-choice satisfaction. *Personality and Social Psychology Bulletin* 19, 3 (1993), 331–339.

[38] Timothy D Wilson, Jay Meyers, and Daniel T Gilbert. 2003. âĂIJHow happy was I, anyway?âĂİ A retrospective impact bias. *Social Cognition* 21, 6 (2003), 421–446.

Explanations that are Intrinsic to Recommendations

Arpit Rana
Insight Centre for Data Analytics
University College Cork, Ireland
arpit.rana@insight-centre.org

Derek Bridge
Insight Centre for Data Analytics
University College Cork, Ireland
derek.bridge@insight-centre.org

ABSTRACT

Explanations can give credibility to recommendations and help users to make better choices. In current recommender systems, explanation is a step that comes after recommendation. In this paper, we describe an approach that turns recommender systems on their head. In our approach, which we call *Recommendation-by-Explanation (r-by-e)*, the system constructs a reason, or explanation, for recommending each candidate item; then it recommends those candidate items that have the best explanations. By unifying recommendation and explanation, *r-by-e* finds relevant recommendations with explanations that have a high degree of fidelity.

We present the results of an offline experiment using a movie recommendation dataset. We show that *r-by-e* achieves higher precision than a comparable recommender, while both produce recommendations with roughly equal levels of diversity and serendipity.

We also present the results of deploying a web-based system through which we have conducted two user trials. In one trial, we evaluate recommendation quality. Participants in this trial found *r-by-e*'s recommendations to be more diverse, serendipitous and relevant than those of the competitor system. In another trial, we evaluate explanation quality. We used a re-rating task: users rated recommendations initially in the case where they were given only the explanation and not the identity of the movie, and then re-rated in the case where they were given information about the recommended movie. We found a stronger correlation between the pairs of ratings in the case of *r-by-e*. This suggests that *r-by-e*'s explanations allow users to make more accurate judgments about the quality of recommended items.

CCS CONCEPTS

• **Information systems** → **Recommender systems**; • **Human-centered computing** → **User studies**;

KEYWORDS

Explanation; Recommendation; User Trial

ACM Reference Format:
Arpit Rana and Derek Bridge. 2018. Explanations that are Intrinsic to Recommendations. In *UMAP '18: 26th Conference on User Modeling, Adaptation and Personalization, July 8–11, 2018, Singapore, Singapore*. ACM, New York, NY, USA, 9 pages. https://doi.org/10.1145/3209219.3209230

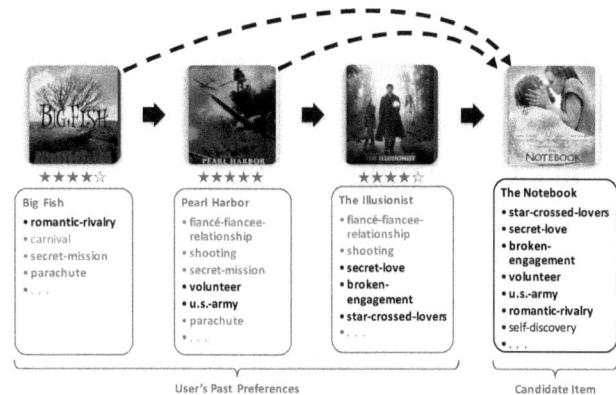

Figure 1: An Explanation Chain.

1 INTRODUCTION

Recommender systems provide explanations to help the user understand the rationale for a recommendation and to help her make a decision [1]. Conventionally, computing recommendations and generating corresponding explanations are two separate, sequential processes. This separation is one cause of low fidelity between the explanations and the operation of the recommender.

In this paper, we present Recommendation-by-Explanation *r-by-e*, in which explanation is intrinsic to recommendation. In *r-by-e*, the system constructs a reason, or explanation, for recommending each candidate item; then it recommends those candidates that have the best explanations. *r-by-e*'s explanations take the form of what we call *Explanation Chains*. Figure 1 shows an example of an Explanation Chain in the movie domain. The rightmost item (in this case, *The Notebook*) is the candidate for recommendation to the user, and will typically not already be in the user's profile. The other items (*Big Fish*, *Pearl Harbour* and *The Illusionist*) form the chain. They are drawn from positively-rated items in the user's profile and are intended to support recommendation of the candidate item. Pairs of successive items in a chain satisfy a local constraint in the form of a similarity threshold; additionally, each item in the chain satisfies a global constraint in the form of a threshold on the level of coverage it contributes towards features of the candidate item. For example, *Big Fish* has the keywords: secret-mission and parachute in common with *Pearl Harbour*, as well as the keyword romantic-rivalry in common with *The Notebook*.

We believe that *r-by-e* has the following characteristics:

- *Unified approach:* It is a unified approach that combines the processes of computing recommendations and generating corresponding explanations.

- *Fidelity:* By unifying recommendation and explanation, there is a guaranteed level of fidelity between explanations and the operation of the recommender.
- *Diversity and serendipity:* The approach uses hyperparameters whose values can be adjusted to loosen or tighten constraints between items in the chain and thus increase or decrease the diversity and serendipity of the recommendations.

We introduced *r-by-e* and the concept of Explanation Chains in [16]. In this paper, our contributions are: we present the algorithms in detail; we present more comprehensive results for an offline experiment; and we present previously-unpublished user trials.

2 RELATED WORK

Explanations of recommendations vary in many ways. They may vary in their goals: they may be intended to help the user make a better decision (effectiveness), change the user's behaviour (persuasion), make a system more correctable (scrutability), and so on [20]. In our work, we are interested in effectiveness, which is why one of our user trials is a re-ranking task.

Explanations of recommendations often relate the recommended item to the user through *intermediary entities*, which may be other users, other items, or features [1, 21]:

- user-based explanations say that an item is being recommended because users who are similar to the active user liked it, e.g. in [8], the explanation is a histogram of the active user's neighbours' ratings of the item;
- item-based explanations say that the item is being recommended because the user liked similar items, e.g. [3, 11];
- feature-based explanations say that the recommended item has features that the user likes, where the features might be, e.g., attribute-value pairs [19], linked data [14], item content [2], user-generated tags [7, 21], or features and opinions mined from user reviews [4, 5].

However, in the case of item-based explanations, we often want to show why the items in the explanation are similar to the recommended item, and this is typically done by showing the features that they have in common. Since these item-based explanations combine items and features, they have also been designated as 'hybrid' explanations [15]. Explanation Chains are of this kind: they are item-based but they expose item relationships through features.

More generally, the explanations of systems in Artificial Intelligence are categorized as white-box explanations and black-box (or model-agnostic) explanations. White-box explanations are built from traces of the system's reasoning. For example, if we have a recommender that makes recommendations by finding items liked by the active user's nearest neighbours, then a histogram of the neighbours' ratings [8] is a white-box explanation. By contrast, black-box explanations have no knowledge of how the system produced its decision. The explanations are post-hoc rationalizations. For example, the LIME system explains classification decisions by interrogating the classifier to obtain a dataset from which LIME builds a distinct explanation model [17]. Some black-box explanations even resort to using data that was not used by the decision-making system. In [18], for example, recommendations are made by matrix factorization on a ratings matrix but the recommendations are explained using

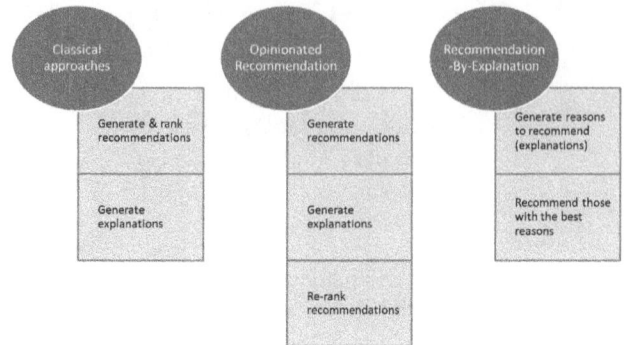

Figure 2: Ways of computing recommendation explanations.

topic models that are mined from textual data associated with the items but not used by the recommender. By contrast, Explanation Chains are white-box explanations.

This raises the issue of fidelity [10] (also called objective transparency [7]): the extent to which the explanation reveals the logic of the underlying recommender. In an experiment with a music recommender, Kulesza et al. found that the more that explanations were both sound and complete with respect to the recommender, the greater the users' trust in the recommender and the better their understanding [10]. Arguably, black-box systems cannot achieve fidelity. (The LIME system[17], which is model-agnostic, claims to achieve 'local fidelity', but this is not the same concept.) Recommendation-by-Explanation seeks to achieve quite high fidelity since, in *r-by-e*, explanation is intrinsic to recommendation.

Finally, it seems obvious that a recommender should first produce its recommendations and then seek to build explanations for them. This is the classic approach depicted leftmost in Figure 2. All of the systems that we have cited so far work in this way. A new approach, Opinionated Recommendation, shown in the middle of Figure 2, modifies this a little [12, 13]: the system finds some recommendations, it generates explanations for the recommendations, it scores the explanations, and it re-ranks the recommendations based on their explanation scores before showing them to the user. Recommendation-by-Explanation is shown rightmost in Figure 2: it finds explanations for the candidates and recommends the candidates that have the best explanations.

3 RECOMMENDATION-BY-EXPLANATION

Recommendation by Explanation (*r-by-e*) is a novel approach that unifies recommendation and explanation: it computes recommendations by generating and ranking corresponding personalized explanations in the form of Explanation Chains. Here we explain in detail how *r-by-e* constructs the chains for candidate items and select the *n* that it will recommend.

3.1 *r-by-e* top-*n* recommendation

Let $\mathbb{I}$ be the set of all items. *r-by-e* works in a scenario of implicit ratings, where the user's profile $P \subseteq \mathbb{I}$ is the set of items that she likes. *r-by-e* will recommend up to *n* items from a set of candidate items, $I \subseteq \mathbb{I}$. Candidates I can be defined in whatever way is suited

---

Algorithm 1 *r-by-e* top-*n* recommendation.

Input: *n*, number of recommendations
    I, set of candidate items
    P, user's profile
    θ, similarity threshold
    ϵ, marginal gain threshold
Output: L^*, ranked list of top-*n* Explanation Chains.

1: **function** RECOMMEND($n, I, P, \theta, \epsilon$)
2:     $L \leftarrow [\ ]$
3:     **for each** $i \in I$ **do**
4:         $C \leftarrow$ GENERATECHAIN(i, P, θ, ϵ)
5:         **if** $|C| > 0$ **then**
6:             append $\langle C, i \rangle$ onto L
7:     **return** SELECTCHAINS(L, n)

---

to the task in hand. Typically, for example, they will be items not already in *P*. But they could be further constrained by contextual factors such as time or location, e.g. recently-released movies, TV shows to be broadcast in the next few hours, or restaurants in the vicinity of the user. Another way to obtain candidates is to take the top-*n'* recommendations of another recommender system ($n' >> n$); in this case, *r-by-e* will filter and re-rank the other system's recommendations. In our experiments later in this paper, we define *I* to be items that are not in the user's profile but which do have at least a certain degree of similarity to the user's profile, $I = \left\{ i \in I \setminus P \mid \text{sim}(f_i, f_p) > \theta, \exists p \in P \right\}$. Here f_i and f_p denote the features of items *i* and *p*, and we define sim as Jaccard similarity.

For each candidate item, *r-by-e* generates an Explanation Chain and then it selects the top *n* of those chains to recommend to the user; see Algorithm 1.

3.2 Explanation chain generation

Given a candidate item, *r-by-e* works backwards to construct a chain: starting with the candidate item, it finds predecessors, greedily selects one, finds its predecessors, selects one; and so on; see Algorithm 2. The predecessors of an item are all its neighbours in the item-item similarity graph that satisfy four conditions: (a) they are members of the user's profile *P*; (b) they are not already in this chain; (c) their similarity to the subsequent item in the chain exceeds a similarity threshold θ; and (d) their reward (see below) exceeds a marginal gain threshold ϵ. When there are no further predecessors, the chain is complete.

At each step, the predecessor that gets selected is the one with the highest *reward*. The reward $rwd(p, i, C)$ of adding predecessor *p* to partial chain *C* that explains candidate item *i* is given by:

$$rwd(p, i, C) = \frac{\left| (f_p \setminus \text{covered}(i, C)) \cap f_i \right|}{|f_i|} + \frac{\left| (f_p \setminus \text{covered}(i, C)) \cap f_i \right|}{\left| f_p \right|} \tag{1}$$

Here again f_i and f_p denote the features of items *i* and *j*. covered(i, C) is the set of features of candidate *i* that are already covered by members of the chain *C*, i.e. covered(i, C) = $\bigcup_{j \in C} f_j \cap f_i$. Then the first term in the definition of $rwd(p, i, C)$ measures *p*'s coverage of those features of *i* that are not yet covered by the chain. The second term in the definition measures the same but with respect to the size

---

Algorithm 2 Explanation Chain generation.

Input: *i*, a candidate item
    P, user's-profile
    θ, similarity threshold
    ϵ, marginal gain threshold
Output: *C*, an Explanation Chain *C* for candidate *i*.

1: **function** GENERATECHAIN(i, P, θ, ϵ)
2:     $C \leftarrow [\ ]$
3:     $sum\_rwds = 0$
4:     $j \leftarrow i$
5:     **while** True **do**
6:         $J \leftarrow \{ p \in P \setminus C \mid \text{sim}(f_j, f_p) > \theta \wedge \text{rwd}(p, i, C) > \epsilon \}$
7:         **if** $|J| = 0$ **then**
8:             **return** *C*
9:         $j = \arg\max_{p \in J} \text{rwd}(p, i, C)$
10:        append *j* onto *C*
11:        $sum\_rwds = sum\_rwds + \text{rwd}(j, i, C)$

Algorithm 3 Chain selection.

Input: *L*, list of Explanation Chains for different candidate items
    n, number of recommendations
Output: L^*, ranked list of top-*n* Explanation Chains.

1: **function** SELECTCHAINS(L, n)
2:     **if** $|L| \leq n$ **then**
3:         sort *L* using *score*
4:         **return** *L*
5:     $L^* \leftarrow [\ ]$
6:     **while** $|L^*| < n$ **do**
7:         $\langle C, i \rangle^* = \arg\max_{\langle C, i \rangle \in L} \text{score}(\langle C, i \rangle, L^*)$
8:         append $\langle C, i \rangle^*$ onto L^*
9:         remove $\langle C, i \rangle^*$ from *L*
10:     **return** L^*

---

of f_j rather than the size of f_i and therefore assures *j*'s fitness to explain the candidate by penalizing items that have high coverage simply by virtue of having more features.

3.3 Chain selection

After constructing a chain *C* for each candidate item *i*, we must select the top-*n* chains so that we can recommend *n* items to the user, along with their explanations. This is done iteratively based on a chain's total coverage of the candidate item's features and the chain's dissimilarity to other chains already included in the top-*n*; see Algorithm 3.

Specifically, we score $\langle C, i \rangle$ relative to a list of all the items that appear in already-selected chains L^* using the following:

$$\text{score}(\langle C, i \rangle, L^*) = \frac{sum\_rwds}{|C| + 1} + \frac{\left| C \setminus \bigcup_{j \in L^*} j \right|}{|C| + 1} \tag{2}$$

Here, the first term is the sum of the rewards of the items in the chain divided by its length plus 1 (so as to include candidate item *i*). It gives higher scores to chains that do a better job of covering the features of their candidate item. The second term gives higher

---

Table 1: Results of the Offline Experiment. All of the *r-by-e* results are statistically significant with respect to *CB-|C|* (Wilcoxon signed rank test with $p < 0.05$) except the one shown in italics.

Recommender	θ & ϵ optimized for	Precision	$Div_{keywords}$	Div_{genres}	Surprise	Novelty	Coverage	% of explanations of size 2–4
r-by-e	Precision	0.1089	0.9352	0.7631	0.7834	0.3771	0.1358	0.2868
CB-|C|		0.0701	0.9091	0.7272	0.8135	0.4179	0.1509	0.2719
r-by-e	$Div_{keywords}$	0.0370	0.9760	0.8177	0.8886	*0.5404*	0.6014	0.3156
CB-|C|		0.0087	0.9736	0.7834	0.9370	0.5365	0.8700	0.6534
r-by-e	% of explanations	0.0677	0.9626	0.8007	0.8635	0.4756	0.3541	0.7598
CB-|C|	of size 2–4	0.0097	0.9711	0.7820	0.9336	0.5119	0.8976	0.7506

scores to a chain if its members are not also members of already-selected chains and hence encourages the final recommendation list to cover as many items in the user's profile as possible. (Note that the second term is about coverage of *items* that appear in already-selected chains, not their features.) We have found this term to have the effect of diversifying the recommendation list.

4 OFFLINE EXPERIMENT

We ran an offline experiment to evaluate *r-by-e*'s performance. We compare it with a content-based recommender, which works as follows. Given candidate item i, it finds the items in P whose similarity to i exceeds θ; it takes the k of these neighbours with highest similarity; it scores the candidate by taking a similarity-weighted average of their ratings. It recommends the n candidates with highest scores.

The main difference between the two recommenders is that the content-based recommender relies on similarity relationships between members of P and the candidate item, whereas *r-by-e*, by requiring consecutive members of chains to be similar to each other, additionally takes into account similarity relationships between members of P themselves. We wanted this experiment to reveal the effect of this difference. So we otherwise tried to ensure that the two systems were as similar as possible. They both use the same item features (keywords, see below), and they both use the same similarity measure (Jaccard). For the content-based system, we chose to set k in a dynamic fashion, as follows. If, for candidate item i, *r-by-e* generates a chain of length $|C|$, then the content-based system uses $k = |C|$ when it scores that candidate item. It follows that k is set dynamically: different candidates may have different values for k. We designate this system *CB-|C|*, using a name that emphasizes that dynamically $k = |C|$.

Although in this paper we only report results that compare *r-by-e* with *CB-|C|*, in [16], we have also compared with a more conventional content-based system with a fixed value for k (set at 7 by a hyperparameter optimization process). The results in that paper show that *CB-|C|* and *CB-7* have quite similar performance.

4.1 Experiment settings

We used the hetrec2011-movielens-2k dataset[1] augmented by keywords from IMDb[2]. The dataset comprises 2113 users, 5992 movies,

80639 keywords, and over half a million ratings. On average, each movie has 107 keywords (ranging from 2 to 626) and has non-zero similarity with 77% of the other movies.

In *r-by-e*, user profiles simply contain items the user likes. We treated ratings of 4 and 5 as 'likes', so user u's profile is given by $\{i \mid r_{u,i} \geq 4\}$. We split each user's ratings into training, validation and test sets in the ratio $60 : 20 : 20$, repeated five times.

On the test sets, for $n = 10$, we measured precision, diversity, surprise, novelty and coverage using definitions of these measures given in Section 7 of [9]. In the case of diversity, we use the measure that [9] denotes by $obj_{diversity}$, which is the average all-pairs distance between items in the recommendation list. For distance, we use the complement of Jaccard similarity, and we measure it both using all keywords (designated $Div_{keywords}$) and using just genres (designated Div_{genres}). In the case of surprise, we use the measure that [9] denotes by $obj_{cont}^{surprise}$, which is based on minimum distances between recommended items and the user's profile.

We also suspect that users will find an explanation to be easily intelligible only if it is fairly small (chains or sets of neighbours of size 2–4 items), so we recorded the percentage of explanations that were of this size.

We experimented with five different values of each of the similarity threshold (θ) and the marginal gain threshold (ϵ): [0.03, 0.06, 0.09, 0.12, 0.15], giving 25 configurations of *r-by-e*. When choosing the best configuration, there is an issue about what to optimize. It makes sense, for example, to choose the configuration that optimizes precision on the validation sets. But it could be interesting to choose configurations that optimize other criteria. Therefore, we also show results in the case where we choose the configuration that optimizes for diversity on the validation set, and in the case where we choose the configuration that maximizes the percentage of explanations of size 2–4.

4.2 Experiment results

Table 1 summarizes the results. For the most part differences in the results for *r-by-e* and *CB-|C|* are small but, since standard deviations are low, in all but one case they are statistically significant. In two cases, differences are larger: *r-by-e* has better precision and *CB-|C|* has better catalogue coverage. It is noteworthy that *r-by-e* can produce more accurate recommendations without sacrificing diversity and surprise.

---

[1]https://grouplens.org/datasets/hetrec-2011/
[2]http://www.imdb.com

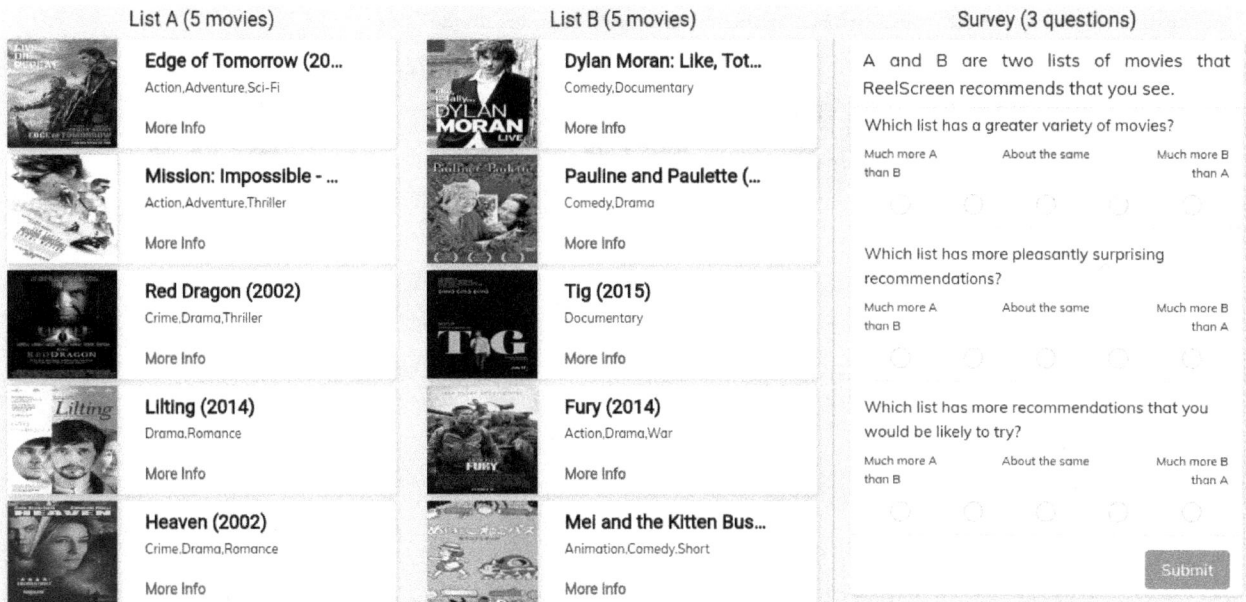

Figure 3: A screenshot showing top-5 recommendations from the two recommenders and survey questions.

5 USER TRIALS

We also built a web-based system in order to conduct user trials, again comparing *r-by-e* with *CB-|C|* using the hyperparameter values (θ and ϵ) that optimized the percentage of explanations of size 2–4. *r-by-e* is, above all, a recommender and so we designed one trial to measure recommendation quality as well as a trial to measure explanation quality. In total, 190 people attempted the trials. The majority of them were undergraduate and postgraduate students recruited online from universities in India and Ireland. To increase the chances of user familiarity with the movies, the web-based recommenders use only movies released between the years 2000 and 2016 inclusive: 3668 of the 5992 movies in the dataset used in the offline experiment.

Each participant begins by creating a user profile containing at least 30 movies. The instructions were that the movies should be the ones the user likes. The user interface offers both a scrollable grid of movies and a search box to enable her to find these movies.

We assigned half the participants to the recommendation trial and the other half to the explanation trial. Of the 190, only 115 completed all parts of the trial to which they were assigned.

5.1 Recommendation trial

5.1.1 Experiment settings. The recommendation trial is a within-subjects trial: users see two lists of recommendations, one list from *r-by-e* and the other from *CB-|C|* and they answer questions that compare the quality of the two lists [6]; see Figure 3. Lists have length 5 and are sorted in decreasing order of recommender scores.

Before displaying the recommendations, we ensured that the two lists contained different movies. Each movie that was common to both lists was removed and the next best recommendations from the top-10 were added to the end of the lists. (If it was not possible

Table 2: Results of the Recommendation Trial.

User's opinion	Diversity	Serendipity	Satisfaction
Much more *r-by-e*	14	15	28
More *r-by-e*	14	11	13
About the same	14	23	8
More *CB-|C|*	11	10	7
Much more *CB-|C|*	13	7	10

to create two different lists of length 5 from the top-10 recommendations, the user's responses to the survey were discarded. We did this to avoid skewing responses about the diversity of recommendations: shorter lists are less likely to be diverse.)

For half the users, the list on the left ('List A') came from *r-by-e* and the list on the right ('List B') from *CB-|C|*; for the other half of the users, List A was from *CB-|C|* and List B from *r-by-e*.

Participants were required to answer three questions:

- Diversity: Which list has a greater variety of movies?
- Serendipity: Which list has more pleasantly surprising recommendations?
- Satisfaction: Which list has more recommendations that you would be likely to try?

Their answers were on a 5-point: Much more List A than List B; More List A than List B; About the Same; More List B than List A; and Much more List B than List A.

5.1.2 Experiment results. Sixty-six participants completed this trial. Table 2 summarizes their responses.

- *Diversity question:* 42.4% of participants found *r-by-e* recommendations to be much more or more diverse than *CB-|C|* recommendations, 21.2% found the recommendation lists to

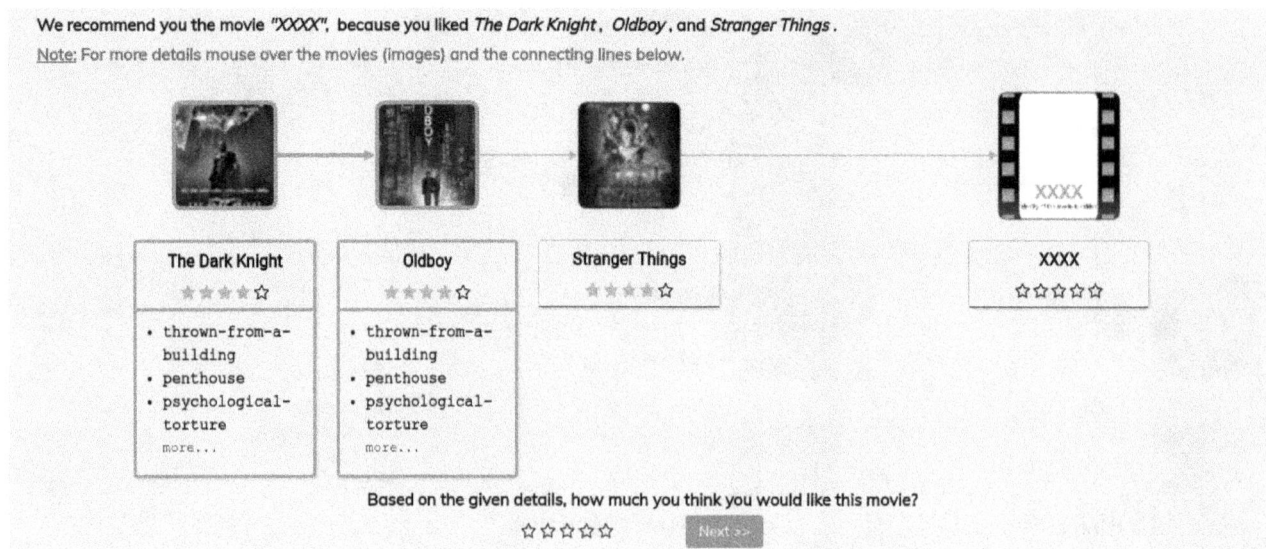

Figure 4: A screenshot of an Explanation Chain. The user has moused over the arrow that connects the first two movies, which causes the system to bring up boxes of keywords that these two movies have in common.

be equally diverse, leaving 36.4% finding CB-$|C|$ to be much more or more diverse.

- *Serendipity question:* 39.4% of participants found r-by-e recommendations to be much more or more pleasantly surprising, 34.8% found the recommendation lists to be equally surprising, leaving 25.8% finding CB-$|C|$ to be much more or more surprising.

- *Satisfaction question:* 62.1% of participants found r-by-e recommendations to be ones they would be much more or more likely to try, 12.1% found the recommendations to be equally worthy of trying, leaving 25.8% finding CB-$|C|$ to be much more or more worth trying.

On all criteria r-by-e produced the better recommendation lists. However, only in the case of the satisfaction question was this statistically significant. (We used two-tailed proportion tests with significance level $p_0 = 0.05$. The null hypothesis was that those preferring r-by-e was equal to those preferring CB-$|C|$, i.e., ignoring those who thought the two lists were about the same.)

5.2 Explanation Trial

Users who were directed to this trial participated in a re-rating task. Re-rating tasks are an established method of evaluating explanation quality when the goal of the explanation is effectiveness: helping users make better decisions [1, 7]. A user is initially asked to rate a recommendation in the case where she is given only the explanation and not the identity of the movie. This is called the *explanation-rating*. The user is asked later to re-rate the recommended item in the case where she is given information about the item, including its identity. This is called the *actual-rating*. An effective explanation is one where the explanation-rating is close to the actual-rating: the explanation allowed the user to predict how much she would like the item. Effective explanations will be ones for which (a) μ_d (the mean difference between explanation-ratings and corresponding

actual-ratings) is close to zero; (b) σ_d (their standard deviation) is small; and (c) r (their Pearson correlation) is highest.

5.2.1 Experiment settings. In our Explanation Trial, we used r-by-e to generate the top-n recommendations for the user, $n = 5$. Each of these, of course, came with an explanation in the form of Explanation Chain, C. For the *same* movies, we then generated the explanations that the CB-$|C|$ system would have produced had it made these recommendations: the $k = |C|$ most similar movies in the user's profile. If the set of movies in r-by-e's chain and CB-$|C|$'s neighbours were identical, we replaced the recommendation by the next best recommendation from r-by-e's top-10 recommendations. (In contrast to the Recommendation Trial, in this trial, where we were not able to make 5 recommendations from the top-10, we did not discard the user's responses: we are comparing the effectiveness of pairs of corresponding explanations not, for example, the diversity of lists of recommendations.)

For n recommendations, we have $2n$ explanations to show to the user: two of each kind. We show them to the user in a random order and with the identity of the recommended movie redacted (shown as "XXXX"). Explanation Chains were displayed in the fashion shown in Figures 4 and 5: arrows connect a movie to its successor in the chain. CB-$|C|$'s explanations (sets of neighbours, rather than chains) were displayed in the fashion shown in Figure 6: arrows connect each movie to the recommended movie. In both cases, the user can mouse over parts of the explanation, which causes the system to display keywords that movies have in common (see the captions of the Figures). A maximum of three keywords is displayed in any box, and they are selected by their *tf-idf* scores.

As can be seen at the foot of Figures 4, 5 and 6, we asked the user to supply an explanation-rating (1-5 stars): how much they thought they might like the movie based only on the explanation.

We recommend you the movie *"XXXX"*, because you liked *The Dark Knight*, *Oldboy*, and *Stranger Things*.

Note: For more details mouse over the movies (images) and the connecting lines below.

The Dark Knight	Oldboy	Stranger Things		XXXX
★★★★☆	★★★★☆	★★★★☆		☆☆☆☆☆
	• hit-with-a-hammer • framed-for-murder • diary more...			• hit-with-a-hammer • framed-for-murder • diary more...

Based on the given details, how much you think you would like this movie?

☆ ☆ ☆ ☆ ☆   Next >>

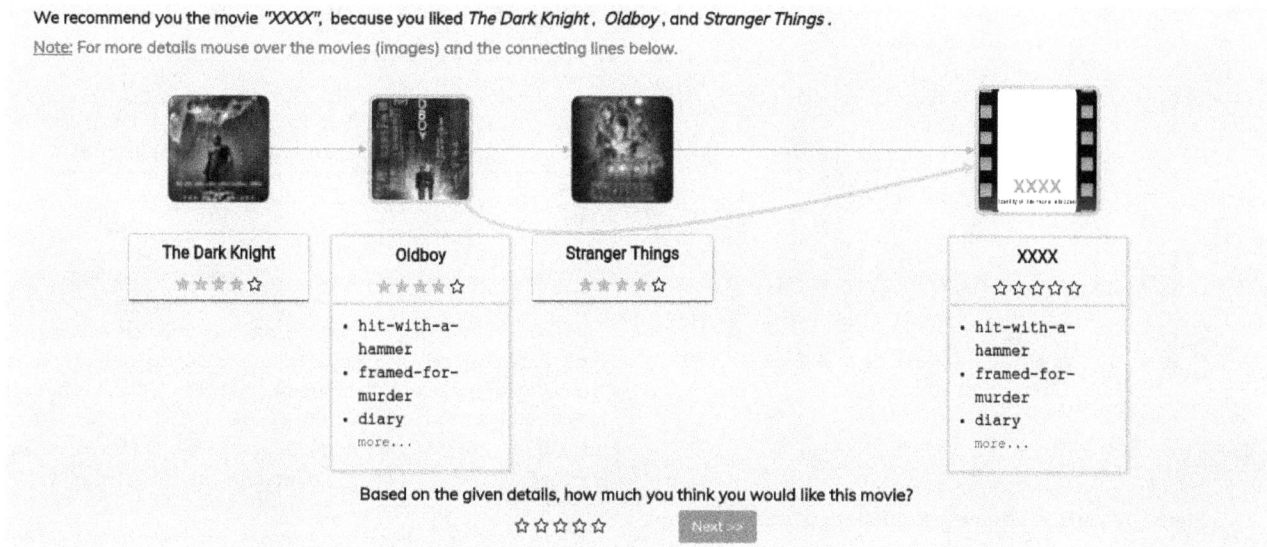

Figure 5: A screenshot of an Explanation Chain. The user has moused over the icon for the second movie, which causes the system to display an arrow between that movie and the recommended movie and to bring up boxes of keywords that these two movies have in common.

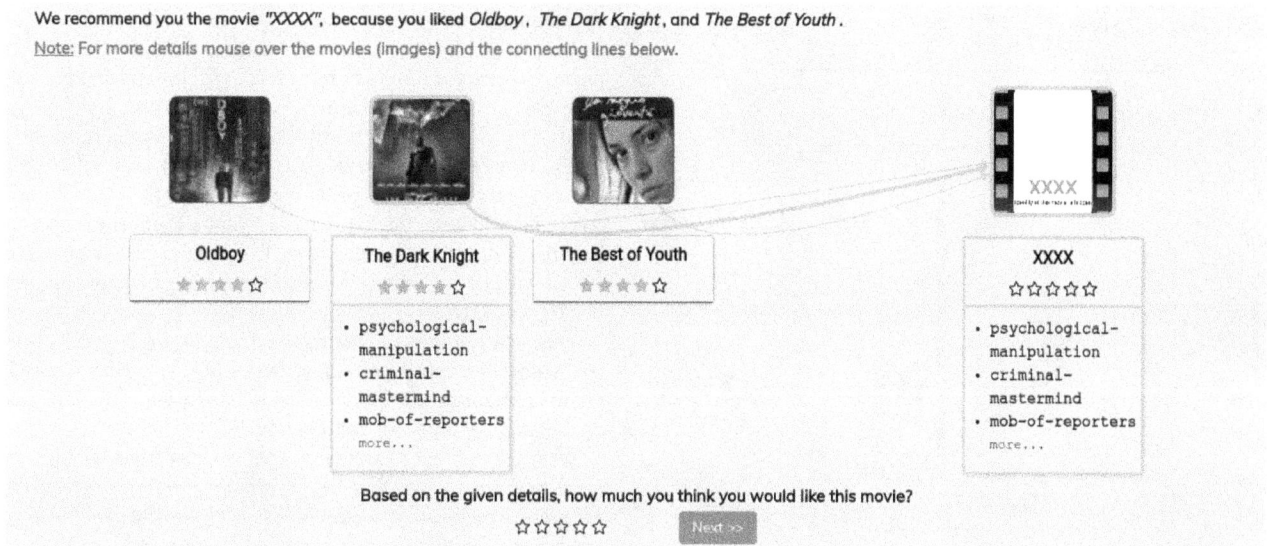

We recommend you the movie *"XXXX"*, because you liked *Oldboy*, *The Dark Knight*, and *The Best of Youth*.

Note: For more details mouse over the movies (images) and the connecting lines below.

Oldboy	The Dark Knight	The Best of Youth		XXXX
★★★★☆	★★★★☆	★★★★☆		☆☆☆☆☆
	• psychological-manipulation • criminal-mastermind • mob-of-reporters more...			• psychological-manipulation • criminal-mastermind • mob-of-reporters more...

Based on the given details, how much you think you would like this movie?

☆ ☆ ☆ ☆ ☆   Next >>

Figure 6: A screenshot of a *CB-|C|* explanation. The user has moused over the icon for the second movie, which causes the system to increase the width of the arrow between that movie and the recommended movie and to bring up boxes of keywords that these two movies have in common.

After the user has given these $2n$ ratings, the system then shows her in a random order each of the n recommended movies again. This time, the identity of the movie is not redacted but no explanation is shown. Instead, we show genre, plot synopsis, main cast members, directors, writers, duration, and release date. Again we ask the user for a rating (the so-called actual-rating) to indicate how much she thinks she will like the movie.

Note that, although the user has rated the same movie three times, nothing in the on-screen instructions makes this apparent.

5.2.2 Experiment results. Forty-nine participants completed this trial: it is quite onerous and more participants abandoned it partway through than did for the other trial. In total, we obtained 597 ratings, this being three ratings for 199 recommended movies. (As

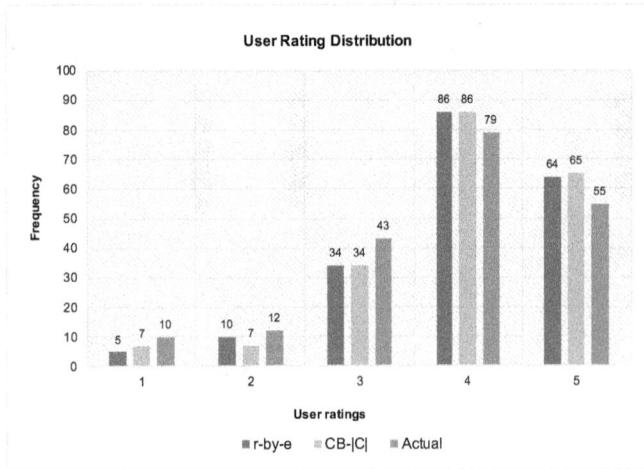

Figure 7: Ratings from the Explanation Trial.

Table 3: Ratings from the Explanation Trial.

Rating type	μ	σ	r
Actual	3.7889	1.0711	–
r-by-e	3.9749	0.9610	0.4855
CB-|C|	3.9799	0.9794	0.2367

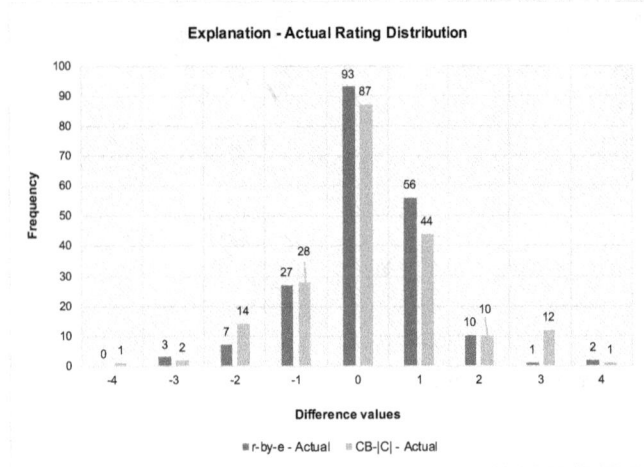

Figure 8: Differences in ratings from the Explanation Trial.

we mentioned above, we did not always have 5 recommendations per user, e.g. where explanations contained identical movies).

Figure 7 shows the distribution of the users' ratings; Table 3 gives summary statistics. We can see that users mostly think they will like the movies that the system recommends, both when they see explanations only and when they see movie identity. For the differences between explanation-ratings and actual-ratings, Figure 8 shows the distribution of values and Table 4 gives summary statistics. The mean difference between r-by-e ratings and actual

Table 4: Differences in ratings from the Explanation Trial.

Explanation type	μ_d	σ_d	95% Conf. Int.
r-by-e	0.1859	1.0350	(0.0412, 0.3306)
CB-|C|	0.1910	1.2688	(0.0136, 0.3683)

ratings is 0.1859; for CB-\|C\|, it is 0.1910. Hence, both kinds of explanations cause users to overestimate their actual-ratings. Using a two-tailed paired t-test ($p_0 = 0.05$), we observed that in this study, i) the difference between r-by-e-ratings and actual-ratings are statistically different; ii) the differences between CB-\|C\|ratings and actual-ratings are also statistically significant; and iii) r-by-e-ratings and CB-\|C\|-ratings are not statistically different. In terms of μ_d and σ_d, then, neither kind of explanation is better than the other. But there is still the question of correlation with the actual-ratings.

Table 3 shows r, the Pearson correlation between explanation-ratings and actual-ratings. We see that r-by-e-ratings are better correlated with actual-ratings. We calculated the probability of getting this correlation due to chance to be 0 in both cases.

6 CONCLUSIONS

Recommendation-by-Explanation (r-by-e) unifies recommendation and explanation. It computes explanations first and then recommends the items with the best explanations. Its explanations take the form of Explanation Chains, which are sequences of items from the user's profile. There are local relationships between consecutive items in the chain: they have some similarity to each other. There are also global relationships between items in the chain and the recommended item: the items are chosen in an effort to cover the features of the recommended item. The items to be recommended are selected based both on this feature coverage relationship and the degree of coverage of item's in the user's profile.

This paper presents experiments to evaluate r-by-e. An offline trial shows the approach to have better precision than a closely-related content-based recommender, while remaining competitive on measures of diversity and serendipity.

We use a web-based system to conduct user trials. The Recommendation Trial shows that r-by-e produces recommendations that are more diverse and serendipitous than those of a content-based recommender (although not statistically significantly so) and with statistically significantly higher levels of satisfaction. The Explanation Trial is a re-rating task for measuring explanation effectiveness. Users rate an item given only an explanation (with its identity hidden) and later re-rate when given the identity without the explanation. The correlation between these pairs of ratings is much greater in the case of r-by-e explanations.

ACKNOWLEDGMENTS

We thank Kapil Bhagchandani & Arpit Jain for help with web design. This paper emanates from research supported by a grant from Science Foundation Ireland (SFI) under Grant Number SFI/12/RC/2289 which is co-funded under the European Regional Development Fund.

REFERENCES

[1] Mustafa Bilgic and Raymond J Mooney. 2005. Explaining recommendations: Satisfaction vs. promotion. In *Beyond Personalization Workshop, IUI*, Vol. 5. 153.

[2] Roi Blanco, Diego Ceccarelli, Claudio Lucchese, Raffaele Perego, and Fabrizio Silvestri. 2012. You should read this! let me explain you why: explaining news recommendations to users. In *Proceedings of the 21st ACM international conference on Information and knowledge management*. ACM, 1995–1999.

[3] Derek Bridge and Kevin Dunleavy. 2014. If you liked Herlocker et al.âĂŹs explanations paper, then you might like this paper too. In *Joint Workshop on Interfaces and Human Decision Making in Recommender Systems*. 22.

[4] Shuo Chang, F Maxwell Harper, and Loren Gilbert Terveen. 2016. Crowd-based personalized natural language explanations for recommendations. In *Proceedings of the 10th ACM Conference on Recommender Systems*. ACM, 175–182.

[5] Li Chen and Feng Wang. 2017. Explaining Recommendations Based on Feature Sentiments in Product Reviews. In *Proceedings of the 22nd International Conference on Intelligent User Interfaces*. 17–28.

[6] Michael D Ekstrand, F Maxwell Harper, Martijn C Willemsen, and Joseph A Konstan. 2014. User perception of differences in recommender algorithms. In *Proceedings of the 8th ACM Conference on Recommender systems*. ACM, 161–168.

[7] Fatih Gedikli, Dietmar Jannach, and Mouzhi Ge. 2014. How should I explain? A comparison of different explanation types for recommender systems. *International Journal of Human-Computer Studies* 72, 4 (2014), 367–382.

[8] Jonathan L Herlocker, Joseph A Konstan, and John Riedl. 2000. Explaining collaborative filtering recommendations. In *Proceedings of the 2000 ACM conference on Computer supported cooperative work*. ACM, 241–250.

[9] Marius Kaminskas and Derek Bridge. 2016. Diversity, Serendipity, Novelty, and Coverage: A Survey and Empirical Analysis of Beyond-Accuracy Objectives in Recommender Systems. *ACM Transactions on Interactive Intelligent Systems* 7, 1 (December 2016), 2:1–2:42.

[10] Todd Kulesza, Simone Stumpf, Margaret Burnett, Sherry Yang, Irwin Kwan, and Weng-Keen Wong. 2013. Too much, too little, or just right? Ways explanations impact end users' mental models. In *Visual Languages and Human-Centric Computing (VL/HCC), 2013 IEEE Symposium on*. IEEE, 3–10.

[11] Greg Linden, Brent Smith, and Jeremy York. 2003. Amazon. com recommendations: Item-to-item collaborative filtering. *IEEE Internet computing* 7, 1 (2003), 76–80.

[12] Khalil Muhammad, Aonghus Lawlor, Rachael Rafter, and Barry Smyth. 2015. Great explanations: Opinionated explanations for recommendations. In *International Conference on Case-Based Reasoning*. Springer, 244–258.

[13] Khalil Muhammad, Aonghus Lawlor, and Barry Smyth. 2016. On the Use of Opinionated Explanations to Rank and Justify Recommendations. In *Proceedings of the FLAIRS Conference*. 554–559.

[14] Cataldo Musto, Fedelucio Narducci, Pasquale Lops, Marco De Gemmis, and Giovanni Semeraro. 2016. ExpLOD: A Framework for Explaining Recommendations Based on the Linked Open Data Cloud. In *Proceedings of the 10th ACM Conference on Recommender Systems*. 151–154.

[15] Alexis Papadimitriou, Panagiotis Symeonidis, and Yannis Manolopoulos. 2012. A generalized taxonomy of explanations styles for traditional and social recommender systems. *Data Mining and Knowledge Discovery* 24, 3 (2012), 555–583.

[16] Arpit Rana and Derek Bridge. 2017. Explanation Chains: Recommendations by Explanation. In *Procs. of the Poster Track of the 11th ACM Conference on Recommender Systems*, Domonkos Tikk and Pearl Pu (Eds.). CEUR Workshop Proceedings, vol-1905.

[17] Marco Túlio Ribeiro, Sameer Singh, and Carlos Guestrin. 2016. "Why Should I Trust You?": Explaining the Predictions of Any Classifier. *CoRR* abs/1602.04938 (2016).

[18] Marco Rossetti, Fabio Stella, and Markus Zanker. 2013. Towards explaining latent factors with topic models in collaborative recommender systems. In *Database and Expert Systems Applications (DEXA), 2013 24th International Workshop on*. IEEE, 162–167.

[19] Christian Scheel, Angel Castellanos, Thebin Lee, and Ernesto William De Luca. 2012. The reason why: A survey of explanations for recommender systems. In *International Workshop on Adaptive Multimedia Retrieval*. Springer, 67–84.

[20] Nava Tintarev and Judith Masthoff. 2007. A survey of explanations in recommender systems. In *Data Engineering Workshop, 2007 IEEE 23rd International Conference on*. IEEE, 801–810.

[21] Jesse Vig, Shilad Sen, and John Riedl. 2009. Tagsplanations: explaining recommendations using tags. In *Proceedings of the 14th international conference on Intelligent user interfaces*. ACM, 47–56.

Multi-Modal Adversarial Autoencoders for Recommendations of Citations and Subject Labels

Lukas Galke
Kiel University
Germany
lga@informatik.uni-kiel.de

Florian Mai
Kiel University
Germany
stu96542@informatik.uni-kiel.de

Iacopo Vagliano
ZBW – Leibniz Information Centre for Economics
Kiel, Germany
I.Vagliano@zbw.eu

Ansgar Scherp
Kiel University
Germany
asc@informatik.uni-kiel.de

ABSTRACT

We present multi-modal adversarial autoencoders for recommendation and evaluate them on two different tasks: citation recommendation and subject label recommendation. We analyze the effects of adversarial regularization, sparsity, and different input modalities. By conducting 408 experiments, we show that adversarial regularization consistently improves the performance of autoencoders for recommendation. We demonstrate, however, that the two tasks differ in the semantics of item co-occurrence in the sense that item co-occurrence resembles relatedness in case of citations, yet implies diversity in case of subject labels. Our results reveal that supplying the partial item set as input is only helpful, when item co-occurrence resembles relatedness. When facing a new recommendation task it is therefore crucial to consider the semantics of item co-occurrence for the choice of an appropriate model.

CCS CONCEPTS

• **Information systems** → **Recommender systems**; • **Computing methodologies** → **Neural networks**; *Learning from implicit feedback*;

KEYWORDS

recommender systems; neural networks; adversarial autoencoders; multi-modal; sparsity

ACM Reference Format:
Lukas Galke, Florian Mai, Iacopo Vagliano, and Ansgar Scherp. 2018. Multi-Modal Adversarial Autoencoders for Recommendations of Citations and Subject Labels. In *UMAP '18: 26th Conference on User Modeling, Adaptation and Personalization, July 8–11, 2018, Singapore, Singapore*. ACM, New York, NY, USA, 9 pages. https://doi.org/10.1145/3209219.3209236

1 INTRODUCTION

Recent advances in autoencoders on images have shown that adversarial regularization can improve the performance of autoencoders [24]. The so-called adversarial autoencoders [24] are not only trained to reconstruct the input, but also to match the code with a selected prior distribution. We hypothesize that the thereby imposed smoothness on the code aids autoencoders in reconstructing highly sparse item vectors for recommendation. The rationale is that smoothness is one of the criteria for good representations that disentangle the explanatory factors of variation [4]. In this paper, we analyze whether adversarial autoencoders can be applied to highly sparse recommendation tasks. We evaluate the effect of adversarial regularization with respect to the degree of sparsity and different input modalities on two exemplary tasks: citation and subject label recommendation.

Citation Recommendation More and more publishers decide to contribute to the Initiative for Open Citations[1], which aims to make citation metadata publicly available. This motivates us to consider the following scenario as a recommendation task. When writing a new paper, it is essential that the authors reference other publications which are key in the respective field of study or relevant to the paper being written. Failing to do so can be rated negatively by reviewers in a peer-reviewing process. However, due to increasing volume of scientific literature, even some critical paper are sometimes overlooked. Hence, in this paper we study the problem of recommending publications to consider as citation candidates, given that the authors have already selected some other references and assuming that the paper is close to completion, i. e., information such as the title (or a tentative title) of the paper is available.

Subject Indexing Apart from citation data, also subject labels, or tags, are publicly available for numerous domains, such as MeSH[2] for medicine or EconBiz[3] for economics. Subject indexing is a common task in scientific libraries to make documents accessible for search. New documents are annotated with a set of subjects by professional subject indexers. Fully-automated multi-label classification approaches to subject

---

[1]https://i4oc.org
[2]https://www.nlm.nih.gov/mesh/
[3]https://www.econbiz.de/

indexing are promising [29], even when merely the metadata of the publications is used [9]. Professional subject indexers, however, typically use the result of these approaches only as recommendations, so that the human-level quality can still be guaranteed. This circumstance motivates us to build a subject label recommender system that explicitly takes the partial list of already assigned subjects into account.

To unify these two scenarios, we take either the citations or the assigned subjects as implicit feedback for a considered recommendation task. In the former case, citations are known to resemble credit assignment [41], whereas in the latter case the subject labels are selected by respective professionals such that their relevance to the paper is guaranteed by human supervision.

Traditionally, the recommendation problem is modeled as the prediction of missing ratings in a $U \times I$ matrix with set of users U and set of items I (matrix completion). In our case, following McNee et al. [25], we view research papers themselves as users over their authors or the responsible subject indexers. The rationale is that one author may be involved in multiple papers of different domains but that all authors for a given paper should receive the same recommendations. Analogously, a given paper should receive the same recommendations for candidate subjects, independently of the current subject indexer in charge of annotating it.

We have transferred the approach of Makhzani et al. [24], which was applied to images, and extended it to our problem of a general recommendation task. By developing a novel interpretation of the adversarial autoencoder, we show how it can be applied to recommendation tasks and how multiple input modalities can be incorporated. We make use of this capability in our experiments by considering besides the ratings also additional metadata, namely the documents' title, as content-based features. We performed 408 experiments for our two recommendation tasks to study how adversarial autoencoders perform while exploiting titles along with the partial list of citations or the already assigned subjects, respectively. For a close investigation of the adversarial autoencoders' performance, we not only consider the adversarial autoencoder as a whole but also individually assess its components.

We further evaluate to which degree these models are robust to sparsity in the dataset. When conducting citation or research paper recommendation, it is not desirable that only already frequently cited papers get recommended and less frequently cited papers are ignored. Common pruning strategies comprise removing rarely cited documents and documents that cite too few other works [2]. This pruning step affects the number of considered items, and thus, the degree of sparsity. To gain a better understanding of how the pruning threshold affects the models' performance, we conduct experiments, in which the pruning threshold is a controlled variable.

Our results show that the partial list of items is more important for the citation recommendation task than it is for the subject labeling task. This is interesting because an inspection of the semantics of item co-occurrence may help researchers or practitioners to tackle new recommendation tasks, specifically to decide whether to supply the partial list of items as input. For citation recommendation, item co-occurrence implied relatedness, i. e., it is of high relevance which other works have been cited so far. For subject labels, in contrast, co-occurrence implies diversity: similar subjects

are rarely used together for annotation of a single document. Thus, the title is more relevant than the already assigned subjects. All of the evaluated methods appeared similarly sensitive to data sparsity despite the differences in the number of parameters.

Due to the use of the titles, the adversarial autoencoders yields competitive performance to the baselines. On the subject label recommendation task, they outperform the baselines. A closer look at the individual components of the adversarial autoencoder revealed that the sole MLP decoder achieved better performance than the whole model on the subject labelling task, while its performance fell behind the whole model on the citation recommendation task.

In summary, our contributions are the following:

- We present an adaption of adversarial autoencoders as a novel approach for multi-modal recommendation tasks on scientific documents.
- We analyze this new method along with all of its components on citation and subject label recommendation tasks while varying the input modalities. We gain valuable insights on the interactions between input modalities and the task: when item co-occurrence resembles relatedness, multi-modal variants are preferable, otherwise solely content-based variants may be more suitable.
- We evaluate the autoencoder models in realistic scenarios, as we split the datasets on the time axis and consider different thresholds for pruning by minimum item occurrence. This is especially important for the citations task because only already existing papers can be cited and it is desirable that also less cited papers are recommended.

The remainder of this paper is organized as follows. In Section 2, we review previous work on citation and tag recommendation as well as recommendation approaches from the deep learning field. After formally stating the problem in Section 3, we introduce the employed models in Section 4, describe the citation and subject recommendation experiments in Section 5. We discuss the results in Section 6, before we conclude.

2 RELATED WORK

Research paper and subject label recommendation. An extensive survey [2] shows that research paper recommendation is a well-known topic. In this context, BibTip [11] and bX [5] are well-known recommender systems, which operate on the basis of citations harvested by CiteSeer [12]. Docear is a more recent research paper recommender system, which takes user profiles into account [3]. For citation recommendation specifically, Huang et al. distinguish between recommendations based on a partial list of references and recommendations based on the content of a manuscript [17]. While the former is suited for finding matching citations for a given statement during writing, the latter strives to identify missing citations on the broader, document level. Citation recommendation recently focuses on context-sensitive applications, in which concrete sentences are mapped to, preferably relevant, citations [2, 8, 17]. Instead, we revisit the reference list completion problem and we do not take into account the context of the citation, as the full text of a papers is rarely available in large-scale metadata sources. In 1973, Small started the field of co-citation analysis [37]. Co-citation analysis assumes that two papers are more related to each other, the more they are co-cited. Following that idea, Caragea et al. relied on singular value decomposition as a more efficient and extendable approach [6]. We recognize the need for new methods that are not only based on item co-occurrence but also take supplementary metadata into account for these partial list completion problems.

Subject label recommendation is similar to tag recommendation, as in both cases the goal is to suggest a descriptive label for some content. Sen et al. propose algorithms that predict users' preferences for items based on their inferred preferences for tags [35]. Montañés et al. exploit probabilistic regression for collaborative tag recommendation [27], while Krestel et al. relied on Latent Dirichlet allocation [23]. Similarly, Sigurbjörnsson and van Zwol propose a tag recommender for Flickr to support the user in the photo annotation task [36], whereas Posch et al. predict hashtag categories on Twitter [32]. Dellschaft and Staab measure the influence of tag recommender systems on the indexing quality in collaborative tagging systems [7]. These works, however, focus on tags for social media, while we consider subject labels from a standardized thesaurus for scientific documents.

Recommendation and Link Prediction based on Deep Learning. Multiple recommender systems based on deep learning have been proposed. Wang et al. used deep learning for collaborative filtering [40]. Another recent collaborative-filtering approach explicitly takes side information into account for autoencoders [1]. We include a similar model in our comparison, as it is one component of the adversarial autoencoder. Additional techniques employ recurrent neural networks to provide session-based recommendations [33] or combine knowledge graphs with deep learning [30, 34]. To the best of our knowledge, only two approaches makes use of deep learning techniques for citation recommendation. However, both of them focus on context-sensitive scenarios [8, 18].

Citation networks are also considered in many studies on link prediction. By making use of the network structure, dedicated architectures learn representations of its nodes. One of the most prominent approaches is DeepWalk [31], together with its extension Node2vec [16]. These methods perform a random walk over the graph and feed the generated sequence into skip-gram negative sampling methods [26]. Kipf and Welling recently proposed Graph Auto-Encoders [21] and Graph Convolutional Networks [20]. However, all of these graph-based approaches assume that all nodes (research papers) are known during training. Hence, they are unable to deal with unknown nodes (new, unseen citing documents) at test time. Instead, we focus on a more realistic application scenario, where we need to predict citations for a paper which is being written and thus yet unknown. To simulate such practical settings, we ensure that all documents of the test set are unknown to the system during training. Such a scenario is challenging as it corresponds to a cold-start situation.

3 PROBLEM STATEMENT

In the following, we provide a formal problem statement for the considered recommender task. The documents can be considered users in a traditional recommendation scenario, while the items are either cited documents or subject labels, respectively.

Given a set of m documents $\mathbb{D}$ and a set of n items $\mathbb{I}$, the typical recommendation task is to model the spanned space, $\mathbb{D} \times \mathbb{I}$. We

Table 1: Notation

Symbol	Description
$\mathbb{D}$	Set of m documents
$\mathbb{I}$	Set of n items
$X \in \{0,1\}^{m \times n}$	Sparse ratings matrix
$S \in \mathbb{R}^{m \times d}$	Supplementary document information
x, s	Row vectors of X or S, respectively
$[x; s]$	Concatenation of vectors x and s
$\bowtie$	Natural join (on document identifiers)
I	Identity matrix

model the ratings as a sparse matrix $X \in \{0,1\}^{m \times n}$, in which X_{jk} indicates implicit feedback from document j to item k. To simulate a real-world scenario, we split the documents $\mathbb{D}$ into m_{train} documents for training $\mathbb{D}_{\text{train}}$ and m_{test} documents for evaluation $\mathbb{D}_{\text{test}}$, such that $\mathbb{D}_{\text{train}} \cap \mathbb{D}_{\text{test}} = \emptyset$. More precisely, we conduct this split into training and test documents based on the publication year. All documents that were published before a certain year are used as training, and the remaining documents as test data. This leads to an experimental setup that is close to a real-world application. More details will be provided in Section 5.1. All models are supplied with the complete ratings of the users $X_{\text{train}} = \mathbb{D}_{\text{train}} \bowtie X$ along with the supplementary information $S_{\text{train}} = \mathbb{D}_{\text{train}} \bowtie S$ for training. In the present work, we use the title of the documents as supplementary information. Still, in theory, more sources of supplementary information may be considered. The test set $X_{\text{test}}, S_{\text{test}}$ is obtained analogously.

For evaluation, we remove randomly selected items in X_{test} by setting one non-zero entry in each row to zero. We denote the hereby created test set by $\tilde{X}_{\text{test}}$. The model ought to predict values $X_{\text{pred}} \in [0,1]^{m_{\text{test}} \times n}$, given the test set $\tilde{X}_{\text{test}}$ along with the title information S_{test}. Finally, we compare the predicted ratings X_{pred} with the true ratings X_{test} via ranking metrics. The goal is that those items, that were omitted in $\tilde{X}_{\text{test}}$, are highly ranked in X_{pred}.

In both scenarios, i. e., citation recommendation and subject label recommendation, we regard documents and items as a bipartite graph (see Figure 1). Considering citations, this point of view may be counter-intuitive since a scientific document is typically both a citing paper and a cited paper. Still, the out-degree of typical citation network datasets is so high that we cannot expect to have metadata for all cited papers available. For instance, the PubMed citation dataset we use for our experiments offers metadata of 224,092 documents that cite 2,896,764 distinct other documents. Therefore it is reasonable to rely only on the metadata of the citing documents itself as basis for recommendations.

4 MODELS

In the following, we describe the employed models. We start with two baselines based on item co-occurrence. Subsequently, we briefly introduce the multi-layer perceptron as a building block for the two autoencoder variants. We show how title information can be incorporated in undercomplete and adversarial autoencoders. We provide information on hyperparameters in the final paragraph of this section.

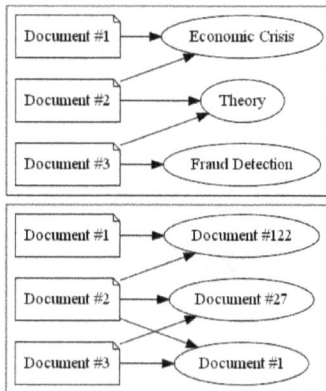

Figure 1: Exemplary bipartite graphs of documents annotated with subject labels (top) and citation relationships between documents (bottom). It becomes apparent how the two recommendation tasks share a similar structure.

Item Co-Occurrence. As a non-parametric yet strong baseline we consider the co-citation score [37] that is purely based on item co-occurrence. The rationale is that two papers, which have been cited more often together in the past, are more likely to be cited together in the future than papers that were less often cited together. Given training data X_{train}, we compute the full item co-occurrence matrix $C = X_{\text{train}}^T \cdot X_{\text{train}} \in \mathbb{R}^{n \times n}$. At prediction time, we obtain the scores by aggregating the co-occurrence values via matrix multiplication $X_{\text{test}} \cdot C$. On the diagonal of C, the (squared) occurrence count of each item is retained to model the prior probability.

Singular Value Decomposition. Singular value decomposition (SVD) is an approach that factorizes the co-occurrence matrix of items $X^T \cdot X$. Caragea et al. showed that SVD can be successfully used for citation recommendation [6]. We therefore include SVD in our comparison and extend it by the capability of incorporating title information, which has already been proposed as future work by Caragea et al. [6]. We concatenate the textual features as TF-IDF weighted bag-of-words with the items and perform singular value decomposition on the resulting matrix. To obtain predictions, we only use those indices of the reconstructed matrix that are associated with items.

Multi-Layer Perceptron. A multi-layer perceptron (MLP) is a fully-connected feed-forward neural network with one or multiple hidden layers. The output is computed by consecutive applications of $h^{(i)} = f(h^{(i-1)} \cdot W^{(i)} + b^{(i)})$ with f being a nonlinear activation function. In the description of the following models, we abbreviate a two hidden-layer perceptron module by MLP-2. This MLP-2 module is not only used as a building block for subsequent architectures, but also as a full model that only operates on the documents' titles. In this case, we optimize binary cross-entropy $\text{BCE}(x, \text{MLP-2}(s))$, where the titles s are used as input and citations or subject labels x as target outputs. We chose to operate on an TF-IDF weighted embedded bag-of-words representation [10] for a fair comparison with the autoencoder variants, which are described below.

Undercomplete Autoencoders. The general concept of an autoencoder (AE) involves two components: the encoder enc and the decoder dec. The encoder transforms the input into a hidden representation (the code) $z = \text{enc}(x)$. Then the decoder reconstructs the input from the code $r = \text{dec}(z)$. The two components are jointly trained to minimize the loss function $\text{BCE}(x, r)$. To avoid learning to merely copy the input x to the output r, autoencoders need to be regularized. The most common way to regularize autoencoders is by imposing a lower dimensionality on the code (undercomplete). In short, autoencoders are trained to capture the most important explanatory factors of variation for reconstruction [4].

For both the encoder and the decoder we chose an MLP-2 module, such that the model function becomes $r = \text{MLP-2}_{\text{dec}}(\text{MLP-2}_{\text{enc}}(x))$. When the documents' title is available, we supply it as additional input to the decoder $r = \text{MLP-2}_{\text{dec}}([\text{MLP-2}_{\text{enc}}(x); s])$. We embed the textual features into a lower dimensional space by using pre-trained word embeddings [26]. The rationale here is that the rather low code dimension is not overwhelmed by the high amount of vocabulary terms. For a fair comparison of the models, also the MLP described above is supplied the same text representation as input. More precisely, we employ a TF-IDF weighted bag of embedded words representation which has proven to be useful for information retrieval [10]. The usage of title information in an undercomplete autoencoder is comparable to the approach by Barbieri et al. [1]. A minor difference is that we supply the side information (titles) only to the decoder, yet use two hidden layers for both the encoder and the decoder to enable a fair comparison to the adversarial variant, which is described below.

Adversarial Autoencoders. We extend the work of Makhzani et al. on adversarial autoencoders (AAE) [24], who combine generative adversarial networks [14] with autoencoders. The autoencoder component reconstructs the sparse item vectors, while the discriminator distinguishes between the generated codes and samples from a selected prior distribution (see Figure 2). Hence, the distribution of the latent code is shaped to match the prior distribution. We hypothesize that the latent representations learned by distinguishing the code from a smooth prior lead to a model that is more robust to sparse input vectors than undercomplete autoencoders. The rationale is that smoothness is a main criterion for good representations that disentangle the explanatory factors of variation [4].

Formally, we first compute $h = \text{MLP-2}_{\text{enc}}(x)$ and $r = \text{MLP-2}_{\text{dec}}(h)$ and then update the parameters of the encoder and the decoder with respect to binary cross-entropy $\text{BCE}(x, r)$. Hence, in the regularization phase, we draw samples $z \sim \mathcal{N}(0, I)$ from independent Gaussian distributions matching the size of h. The parameters of the discriminator $\text{MLP-2}_{\text{disc}}$ are then updated, to minimize $\log \text{MLP-2}_{\text{disc}}(z) + \log(1 - \text{MLP-2}_{\text{disc}}(h))$ [14]. Finally, the parameters of the encoder are updated to maximize $\log \text{MLP-2}_{\text{disc}}(h)$, such that the encoder is trained to fool the discriminator. As a result, the encoder is jointly optimized for matching the prior distribution and for reconstruction of the input [24].

To incorporate the documents' title, we once again concatenate on the code level. This scenario corresponds to the supervised case from the original work of Makhzani et al. on images, in which the purpose was to separate the style from the class. All information that cannot be reconstructed from the class is drawn from the style (the code) [24]. We adapt this interpretation by supplying title information as additional input to the decoder. Hence, the model is optimized to exploit the title information when it is helpful for reconstruction but also take the partial item set into account. At prediction time, we perform one reconstruction step by applying one encoding and one decoding step.

Hyperparameters. The hyperparameters are selected by conducting pre-experiments on the citation recommendation dataset by considering only items that appear 50 or more times in the whole corpus. We chose this scenario because this aggressive pruning results in numbers of distinct items and documents that are similar to the ones of the subject label recommendation dataset. Considering the MLP-modules, we conducted a grid search with hidden layer sizes between 50 and 1,000, initial learning rates between 0.01 and 0.00005, activation functions Tanh, ReLU [28], SELU [22] along with dropout [38] (or alpha-dropout in case of SELUs) probabilities between .1 and .5 and as optimization algorithms stochastic gradient descent and Adam [19]. For the autoencoder-based models, we considered code sizes between 10 and 500, but only if the size was smaller than the hidden layer sizes of the MLP modules. In case of adversarial autoencoders, we experimented with Gaussian, Bernoulli, and Multinomial prior distributions, and with linear, sigmoid, and softmax activation on the code layer, respectively.

While we do not exclude that a certain set of hyperparameters may perform better in a specific scenario, we select the following, most robust, hyperparameters: hidden layer sizes of 100 with ReLU [28] nonlinearities and drop probabilities of .2 after each hidden layer. The optimization is carried out by Adam [19] with initial learning rate 0.001. The two autoencoder variants use a code size of 50. We further select a Gaussian prior distribution for the adversarial autoencoder. For SVD, we consecutively increased the number of singular values up to 1,000. Using higher amounts of singular values decreased the performance. We keep this set of hyperparameters fixed across all models and across all subsequent experiments to ensure a reliable comparison of the models' quality.

5 EXPERIMENTS

To evaluate adversarial autoencoders for recommendation tasks on scientific documents, we conduct a citation recommendation experiment as presented in Section 5.1 and a subject label recommendation experiment as presented in Section 5.2. Adversarial autoencoders are not only evaluated against the two baselines (item co-occurrence and SVD), but also against its own components: undercomplete autoencoders and multi-layer perceptrons.

5.1 Citation Recommendation

In this section, we describe our experimental setup which is designed to resemble a real-world application of missing citation recommendation.

Dataset. The CITREC[4] PubMed citation dataset [13] consists of 7,546,982 citations. The dataset comprises 224,092 distinct citing documents published between 1928 and 2011 and 2,896,764 distinct cited documents. The documents are cited between 1 and 3,247 times with a median of 1 and a mean of 2.61 (SD: 6.71). The citing

---

[4]https://www.isg.uni-konstanz.de/projects/citrec/

Table 2: Dataset characteristics with respect to pruning thresholds on minimum item occurrence for the PubMed citation recommendation task.

pruning	cited documents	citations	documents	density
15	35,664	1,173,568	136,911	0.000240
20	20,270	878,359	121,374	0.000357
25	12,881	692,037	105,170	0.000511
30	8,906	568,563	96,980	0.000658
35	6,469	478,693	87,498	0.000846
40	4,939	413,746	79,830	0.001049
45	3,904	363,870	73,200	0.001273
50	3,185	324,693	67,703	0.001506
55	2,643	292,791	62,647	0.001768

documents hold on average 33.68 (SD: 27.49) citations to other documents (minimum: 1, maximum 2,242) with a median of 29.

Split on Time Axis. To simulate a real-world citation prediction setting, we split the data on the time axis of the citing documents. This resembles the natural constraint that publications cannot cite other publications that do not exist yet. Given a specific publication year T, we ensure that the training set D_{train} consists of all documents that were published earlier than year T and use the remaining documents as test data D_{test}. Figure 3 shows the distribution of documents over the years along with the split into training and test set. We select the year 2011 for evaluation to obtain a 90:10 ratio between training and test documents.

Preprocessing and Dataset Pruning as Controlled Variable. For preprocessing the datasets, we conduct the following three steps:

(1) Build a vocabulary on the training set with items that received implicit feedback more than α times.
(2) Filter both the training and test set and retain only items from the vocabulary.
(3) Remove documents that are assigned to fewer than two of the vocabulary items.

The pruning threshold α is crucial since it affects both the number of considered items as well as the number of documents. Thus, we identify α as a controllable parameter and evaluate the models' performance with respect to different values for α. Table 2 shows the dataset characteristics with respect to the pruning threshold.

Evaluation Metric. For evaluation, certain items were omitted on purpose in the test set. For each document, the models ought to predict the omitted item as good as possible. Thus, we choose mean reciprocal rank as our evaluation metric. We are given a set of predictions X_{pred} for the test set $\tilde{X}_{test}$. Hence for each row, we compute the reciprocal rank of the missing element from $x_{test} - \tilde{x}_{test}$. The reciprocal rank corresponds to one divided by the position of the omitted item in the sorted list of predictions x_{pred}. We then average over all documents of the test set to obtain the mean reciprocal rank. To alleviate random effects of model initialization, training data shuffling, and selecting the elements to omit, we conduct three runs for each of the experiments. To allow a fair comparison, the

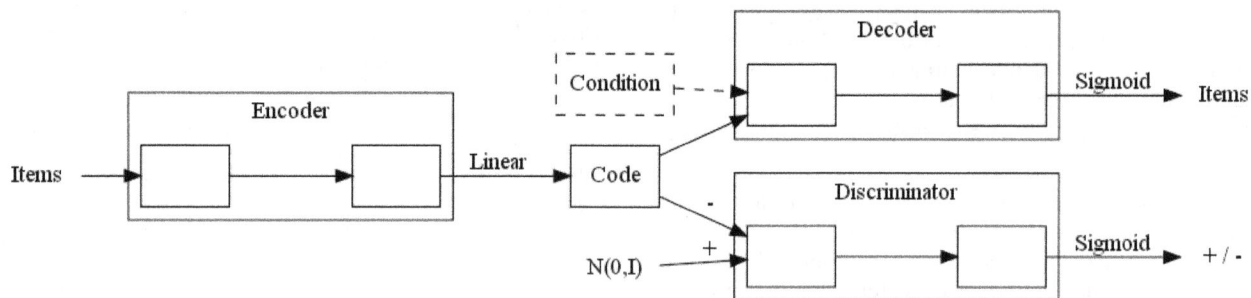

Figure 2: Adversarial autoencoder for item-based recommendations. Each edge resembles a parametrized mapping $f(Wx + b)$ with activation function f and parameters W, b. When not labeled differently, the activation function is rectified linear followed by dropout.

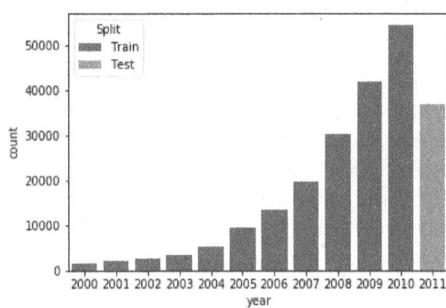

Figure 3: Count of documents by publication year starting with 2000 along with the split in training and test set for the PubMed citation dataset.

Table 3: Dataset characteristics with respect to pruning thresholds on minimum item occurrence for the EconBiz subject label recommendation task.

pruning	labels	assigned labels	documents	density
1	4,568	323,670	61,104	0.001160
2	4,103	323,060	61,090	0.001289
3	3,760	322,199	61,060	0.001403
4	3,497	321,213	61,039	0.001505
5	3,259	320,048	60,983	0.001610
10	2,597	314,738	60,778	0.001994
15	2,192	309,101	60,524	0.002330
20	1,924	303,693	60,272	0.002619

4,669 assigned labels are a subset of the controlled vocabulary Standardthesaurus Wirtschaft[5]. The number of documents to which a label is assigned ranges between 1 and 13,925 with mean 69 (SD: 316) and median 14. The label annotations of a document ranges between 1 and 23 with mean 5.24 (SD: 1.83) and median 5 labels.

Evaluation. The preprocessing steps and evaluation procedure for the subject label recommendation task is the same as in Section 5.1. We also conduct the split between training set and test set on the time axis (see Figure 5). This is challenging because label annotations suffer from concept drift over time [39]. We use the years 2012 and 2013 as test documents to obtain a train-test ratio similar to the scenario in Section 5.1. The dataset characteristics affected by dataset pruning are given in Table 3.

removed items in the test set remain the same for all models during one run with a fixed pruning parameter.

Results. Figure 4 shows the results for the models with respect to the pruning parameter that controls the number of considered items as well as the sparsity (see Table 2). We observe a trend that a more aggressive pruning threshold leads to higher scores among all models. When no title information is given, the item co-occurrence approach consistently yields the highest scores. When title information is available, adversarial autoencoders become competitive to the item co-occurrence approach and yield higher scores than all of their components.

5.2 Subject Label Recommendation

On the basis of our experience in multi-label classification [9, 15], we now consider a subject label recommendation task, which is close to how professional subject indexers work.

Dataset. The EconBiz dataset provided by ZBW — Leibniz Information Centre for Economics consists of 61,619 documents with label annotations from professional subject indexers [9, 15]. The

Results. Figure 6 shows the results for the models with respect to the pruning parameter that controls the number of considered items and therefore also the sparsity (see Table 3). When no title information is available, the adversarial autoencoder is competitive to the item co-occurrence approach. When title information is given, the adversarial autoencoder yields considerably higher scores than all models operating without this information. The sole decoder part (an MLP-2 module) of the adversarial autoencoder yields, however, consistently higher scores than the model as a whole.

---

[5]http://zbw.eu/stw/version/latest/about

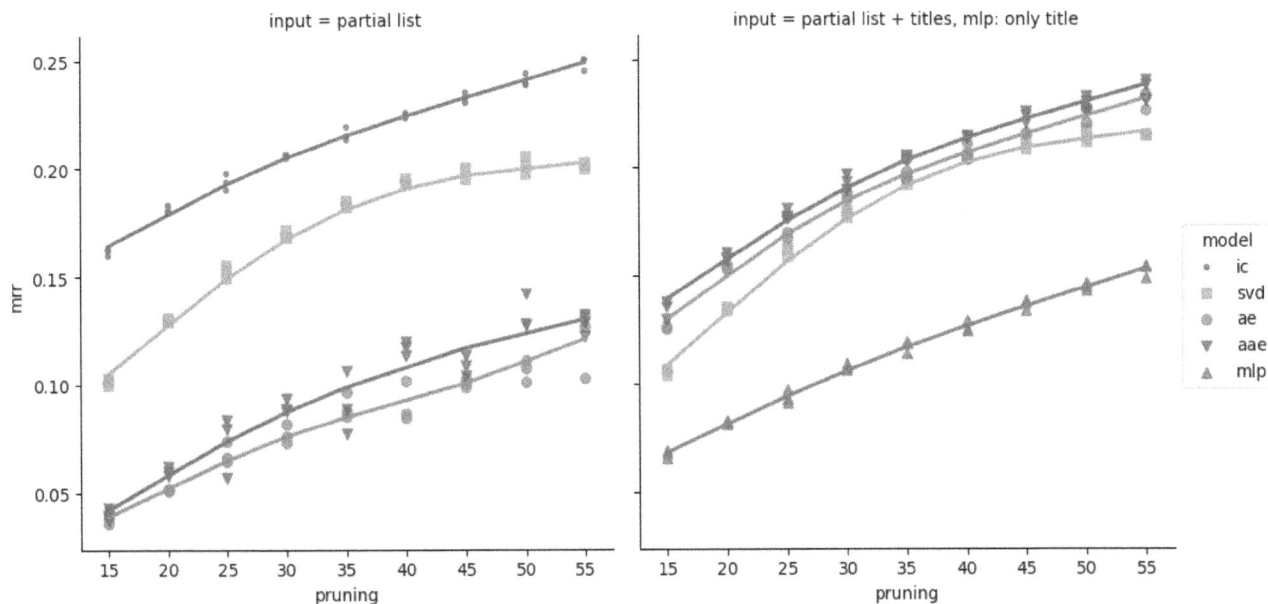

Figure 4: Mean reciprocal rank of missing citation on the test set with varying minimum item occurence (pruning) thresholds. Left: Only the partial list of items is given. Right: The partial list of items along with the document title is given, except for the MLP, which can only make use of the title.

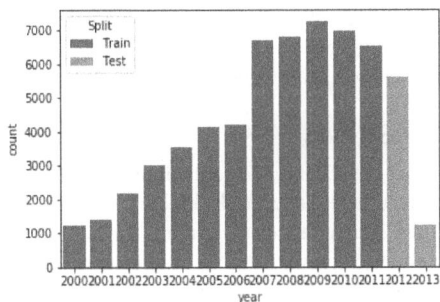

Figure 5: Count of documents by publication year starting with 2000 along with the split in training and test set for the Economics subject label dataset.

6 DISCUSSION

We have evaluated adversarial autoencoders for two different recommendation tasks on scientific documents with varying input modalities and varying numbers of considered items. Our results reveal relationships between the type of recommendation task and the input modalities. On the citation task, the partial list of citations is relevant to recommend potentially missing citations. For the subject label recommendation task, however, using solely the decoder on the title information yields even better performance than the whole model. Thus, our experiments show in which cases adversarial autoencoders are beneficial. On the citation recommendation task the title information enables adversarial autoencoders to become competitive to the strong baseline from co-citation analysis. The

effect of the adversarial regularization component is marginal, yet leads to a consistent improvement over traditional, undercomplete autoencoders. By imposing different thresholds on minimum item occurrence, we varied the number of considered items and thus, the degree of sparsity. We observe that all considered models are similarly affected by the increased difficulty caused by higher numbers of considered items, despite the high amount of parameters.

Even though it is not surprising that co-citation count is highly relevant for citation recommendation [37], we have shown that adversarial autoencoders have a conceptual benefit: they offer the capability of exploiting additional information along with the partial list of citations. From the perspective of the model, it is of high importance to learn about the prior distribution of the data, which explains the strength of the item co-occurrence baseline. Autoencoders retain this benefit and may learn to put appropriate weights in the bias parameters if it is helpful for the overall objective. We envision that further types of information, such as the authors and publication year may further increase the overall performance.

Compared to item co-occurrence or singular value decomposition, all neural network approaches have a large number of learnable parameters as well as hyperparameters that require tuning. To assess the quality of the model itself, we used a fixed set of hyperparameters across all experiments and conducted multiple runs of the same experimental setup to alleviate random effects in initialization and shuffling.

On the subject recommendation task, we observed that the MLP decoder alone yields higher mean reciprocal rank scores than the adversarial autoencoder. Thus, already assigned subjects are less informative for a subject recommendation task than the titles are. This can be explained by a specific guideline for subject indexers

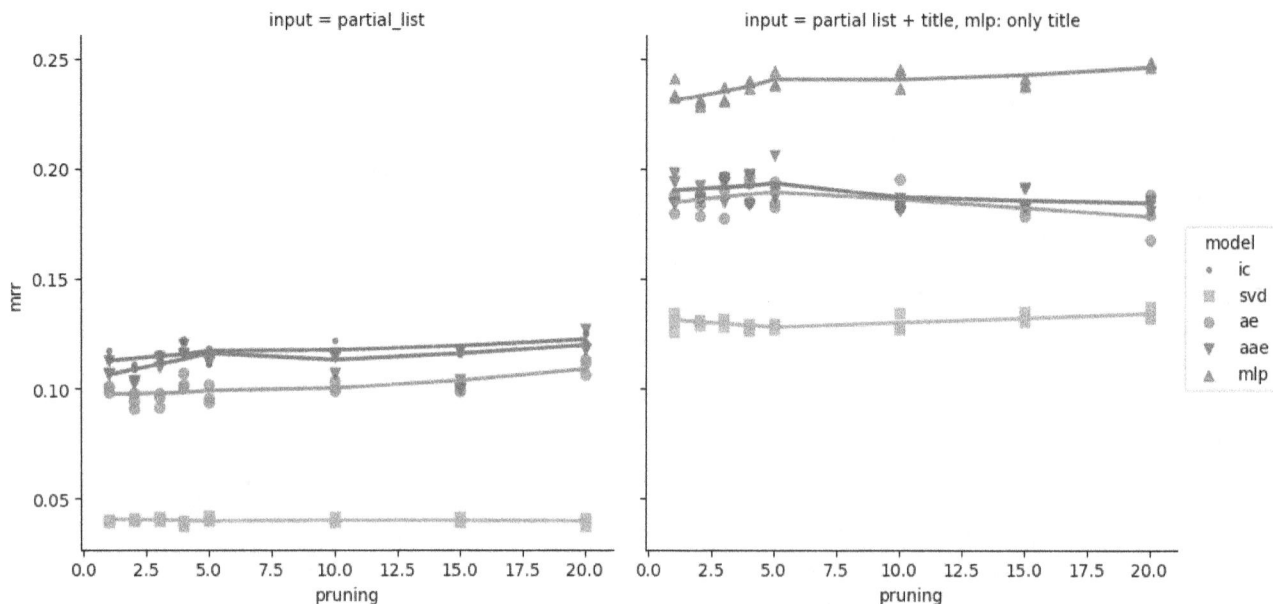

Figure 6: Mean reciprocal rank of missing subject label on the test set with varying minimum item occurence thresholds. Left: Only the partial list of items is given. Right: The partial list of items along with the document title is given, except for the MLP, which can only make use of the title.

working on the specific EconBiz dataset that we used for our experiments: when two or more subjects with a common ancestor in the hierarchical thesaurus of subjects match, it is preferred to assign the ancestor instead of the child subjects [15]. Thus, two subjects that are semantically related because they share a common ancestor are, because of the guideline, unlikely to co-occur in the annotations of a single document.

We conducted 408 experiments over two different recommendation tasks with different input modalities and varying degrees of sparsity. While it is a limitation that we only use one dataset per task, this enabled us to investigate the interactions across tasks, input modalities and the effect of sparsity. As a result, we can state that, on the one hand, there are tasks in which co-occurrence implies relatedness. On the other hand, there are recommendation tasks, in which co-occurrence of items rather implies diversity.

In the present work, we used one prototypical task for each of these two types of recommendations, i. e., citations, where it is known that co-citation reflects relatedness of the cited resources [2, 37], and subject labels, where the guidelines of subject indexers suggest that semantically related subjects are less likely to co-occur. We have carefully investigated the interaction between the semantics of item co-occurrence and supplying the partial list of items as input for a recommender system.

For practical recommender systems, the present work offers evidence that the aforementioned semantics of item co-occurrence is relevant for the decision, whether the partial list of items should be supplied to a recommendation model as input. We have shown that also on recommendation tasks, adversarial autoencoders consistently outperform their traditional, undercomplete counterpart and how additional information can be incorporated in such models.

Our results show that both models with no learnable parameters and models with a high amount of learnable parameters are equally sensitive to the number of considered items, which we controlled by pruning the datasets with respect to minimum item occurrence.

7 CONCLUSION

We conclude that the different semantic interpretation of item co-occurrence in recommendation tasks highly affects the preferable input modalities. When item co-occurrence resembles relatedness such as in citations, supplying the list of already cited documents is beneficial for the overall performance. For subject recommendations, we observe that co-occurring subjects does not imply that these subjects are semantically similar. Rather, the document's subject needs to be described by multiple, diverse subject annotations. In such cases, we have shown that a single multi-layer perceptron component that operates only on the documents' titles is stronger than the whole adversarial autoencoder. We have shown that adversarial autoencoders consistently outperform undercomplete autoencoders, and that their capability of incorporating multiple input modalities offers a conceptual benefit.

Reproducibility. The source code for reproducing our experiments is openly available on GitHub[6].

ACKNOWLEDGMENTS

This work was supported by the German Research Foundation under project number 311018540 (Linked Open Citation Database) as well as by the EU H2020 project MOVING (contract no 693092).

---

[6]https://github.com/lgalke/aae-recommender

REFERENCES

[1] Julio Barbieri, Leandro G. M. Alvim, Filipe Braida, and Geraldo Zimbrão. 2017. Autoencoders and recommender systems: COFILS approach. *Expert Syst. Appl.* 89 (2017), 81–90.

[2] Joeran Beel, Bela Gipp, Stefan Langer, and Corinna Breitinger. 2016. paper recommender systems: a literature survey. *International Journal on Digital Libraries* 17, 4 (2016), 305–338.

[3] Jöran Beel, Stefan Langer, Bela Gipp, and Andreas Nürnberger. 2014. The Architecture and Datasets of Docear's Research Paper Recommender System. *D-Lib Magazine* 20, 11/12 (2014).

[4] Yoshua Bengio, Aaron C. Courville, and Pascal Vincent. 2012. Unsupervised Feature Learning and Deep Learning: A Review and New Perspectives. *CoRR* abs/1206.5538 (2012).

[5] Johan Bollen and Herbert Van de Sompel. 2006. An architecture for the aggregation and analysis of scholarly usage data. In *JCDL*. ACM, 298–307.

[6] Cornelia Caragea, Adrian Silvescu, Prasenjit Mitra, and C. Lee Giles. 2013. Can't see the forest for the trees?: a citation recommendation system. In *JCDL*. ACM, 111–114.

[7] Klaas Dellschaft and Steffen Staab. 2012. Measuring the influence of tag recommenders on the indexing quality in tagging systems. In *HT*. ACM, 73–82.

[8] Travis Ebesu and Yi Fang. 2017. Neural Citation Network for Context-Aware Citation Recommendation. In *SIGIR*. ACM, 1093–1096.

[9] Lukas Galke, Florian Mai, Alan Schelten, Dennis Brunsch, and Ansgar Scherp. 2017. Using Titles vs. Full-text as Source for Automated Semantic Document Annotation. In *K-CAP*. ACM, 20:1–20:4.

[10] Lukas Galke, Ahmed Saleh, and Ansgar Scherp. 2017. Word Embeddings for Practical Information Retrieval. In *GI-Jahrestagung (LNI)*, Vol. P-275. GI, 2155–2167.

[11] Andreas Geyer-Schulz, Michael Hahsler, and Maximilian Jahn. 2002. Recommendations for virtual universities from observed user behavior. In *Classification, Automation, and New Media*. Springer, 273–280.

[12] C. Lee Giles, Kurt D. Bollacker, and Steve Lawrence. 1998. CiteSeer: An Automatic Citation Indexing System. In *ACM DL*. ACM, 89–98.

[13] Bela Gipp, Norman Meuschke, and Mario Lipinski. 2015. CITREC: An Evaluation Framework for Citation-Based Similarity Measures based on TREC Genomics and PubMed Central. In *Proceedings of the iConference 2015*. Newport Beach, California. http://ischools.org/the-iconference/

[14] Ian J. Goodfellow, Jean Pouget-Abadie, Mehdi Mirza, Bing Xu, David Warde-Farley, Sherjil Ozair, Aaron C. Courville, and Yoshua Bengio. 2014. Generative Adversarial Nets. In *NIPS*. 2672–2680.

[15] Gregor Große-Bölting, Chifumi Nishioka, and Ansgar Scherp. 2015. A Comparison of Different Strategies for Automated Semantic Document Annotation. In *K-CAP*. ACM, 8:1–8:8.

[16] Aditya Grover and Jure Leskovec. 2016. node2vec: Scalable Feature Learning for Networks. In *KDD*. ACM, 855–864.

[17] Wenyi Huang, Saurabh Kataria, Cornelia Caragea, Prasenjit Mitra, C. Lee Giles, and Lior Rokach. 2012. Recommending citations: translating papers into references. In *CIKM*. ACM, 1910–1914.

[18] Wenyi Huang, Zhaohui Wu, Liang Chen, Prasenjit Mitra, and C. Lee Giles. 2015. A Neural Probabilistic Model for Context Based Citation Recommendation. In *AAAI*. AAAI Press, 2404–2410.

[19] Diederik P. Kingma and Jimmy Ba. 2014. Adam: A Method for Stochastic Optimization. *CoRR* abs/1412.6980 (2014).

[20] Thomas N. Kipf and Max Welling. 2016. Semi-Supervised Classification with Graph Convolutional Networks. *CoRR* abs/1609.02907 (2016).

[21] Thomas N. Kipf and Max Welling. 2016. Variational Graph Auto-Encoders. *CoRR* abs/1611.07308 (2016). http://arxiv.org/abs/1611.07308

[22] Günter Klambauer, Thomas Unterthiner, Andreas Mayr, and Sepp Hochreiter. 2017. Self-Normalizing Neural Networks. In *NIPS*. 972–981.

[23] Ralf Krestel, Peter Fankhauser, and Wolfgang Nejdl. 2009. Latent dirichlet allocation for tag recommendation. In *RecSys*. ACM, 61–68.

[24] Alireza Makhzani, Jonathon Shlens, Navdeep Jaitly, and Ian J. Goodfellow. 2015. Adversarial Autoencoders. *CoRR* abs/1511.05644 (2015).

[25] Sean M. McNee, Istvan Albert, Dan Cosley, Prateep Gopalkrishnan, Shyong K. Lam, Al Mamunur Rashid, Joseph A. Konstan, and John Riedl. 2002. On the recommending of citations for research papers. In *CSCW*. ACM, 116–125.

[26] Tomas Mikolov, Ilya Sutskever, Kai Chen, Gregory S. Corrado, and Jeffrey Dean. 2013. Distributed Representations of Words and Phrases and their Compositionality. In *NIPS*. 3111–3119.

[27] Elena Montañés, José Ramón Quevedo, Irene Díaz, and José Ranilla. 2009. Collaborative Tag Recommendation System based on Logistic Regression. In *DC@PKDD/ECML (CEUR Workshop Proceedings)*, Vol. 497. CEUR-WS.org.

[28] Vinod Nair and Geoffrey E. Hinton. 2010. Rectified Linear Units Improve Restricted Boltzmann Machines. In *ICML*. Omnipress, 807–814.

[29] Jinseok Nam, Eneldo Loza Mencía, Hyunwoo J. Kim, and Johannes Fürnkranz. 2017. Maximizing Subset Accuracy with Recurrent Neural Networks in Multi-label Classification. In *NIPS*. 5419–5429.

[30] Enrico Palumbo, Giuseppe Rizzo, and Raphaël Troncy. 2017. entity2rec: Learning User-Item Relatedness from Knowledge Graphs for Top-N Item Recommendation. In *RecSys*. ACM, 32–36.

[31] Bryan Perozzi, Rami Al-Rfou, and Steven Skiena. 2014. DeepWalk: online learning of social representations. In *KDD*. ACM, 701–710.

[32] Lisa Posch, Claudia Wagner, Philipp Singer, and Markus Strohmaier. 2013. Meaning as collective use: predicting semantic hashtag categories on twitter. In *WWW (Companion Volume)*. International World Wide Web Conferences Steering Committee / ACM, 621–628.

[33] Massimo Quadrana, Alexandros Karatzoglou, Balázs Hidasi, and Paolo Cremonesi. 2017. Personalizing Session-based Recommendations with Hierarchical Recurrent Neural Networks. In *RecSys*. ACM, 130–137.

[34] Jessica Rosati, Petar Ristoski, Tommaso Di Noia, Renato De Leone, and Heiko Paulheim. 2016. RDF Graph Embeddings for Content-based Recommender Systems. In *CBRecSys@RecSys (CEUR Workshop Proceedings)*, Vol. 1673. CEUR-WS.org, 23–30.

[35] Shilad Sen, Jesse Vig, and John Riedl. 2009. Tagommenders: connecting users to items through tags. In *WWW*. ACM, 671–680.

[36] Börkur Sigurbjörnsson and Roelof van Zwol. 2008. Flickr tag recommendation based on collective knowledge. In *WWW*. ACM, 327–336.

[37] Henry Small. 1973. Co-citation in the scientific literature: A new measure of the relationship between two documents. *JASIS* 24, 4 (1973), 265–269.

[38] Nitish Srivastava, Geoffrey E. Hinton, Alex Krizhevsky, Ilya Sutskever, and Ruslan Salakhutdinov. 2014. Dropout: a simple way to prevent neural networks from overfitting. *Journal of Machine Learning Research* 15, 1 (2014), 1929–1958.

[39] Martin Toepfer and Christin Seifert. 2017. Descriptor-Invariant Fusion Architectures for Automatic Subject Indexing. In *JCDL*. IEEE Computer Society, 31–40.

[40] Hao Wang, Naiyan Wang, and Dit-Yan Yeung. 2015. Collaborative Deep Learning for Recommender Systems. In *KDD*. ACM, 1235–1244.

[41] Paulus Franciscus Wouters et al. 1999. *The citation culture*. Ph.D. Dissertation. Universiteit van Amsterdam. https://pure.uva.nl/ws/files/3164315/8231_13.pdf

A Hybrid Recommendation Approach for Open Research Datasets

Anusuriya Devaraju
CSIRO Mineral Resources
Kensington, Western Australia, 6151
anusuriya.devaraju@csiro.au

Shlomo Berkovsky
CSIRO Data61
Eveleigh, New South Wales, 2015
shlomo.berkovsky@csiro.au

ABSTRACT

Open data initiatives and policies have triggered a dramatic increase in the volume of available research data. This, in turn, has brought to the fore the challenge of helping users to discover relevant datasets. Research data repositories support data search primarily through keyword search and faceted navigation. However, these mechanisms may suit users, who are familiar with the structure and terminology of the repository. This raises the problem of personalized dataset recommendations for users unfamiliar with the repository or not able to clearly articulate their information needs. To this end, we present and evaluate in this paper a recommendation approach applied to a new task — recommending research datasets. Our approach hybridizes content-based similarity with item-to-item co-occurrence, tuned to a feature weighting model obtained through a survey involving real users. We applied the approach in the context of a live research data repository and evaluated it in a user study. The obtained user judgments reveal the ability of the proposed approach to accurately quantify the relevance of datasets and they constitute an important step towards developing a practical dataset recommender.

CCS CONCEPTS

•**Information systems** → **Content ranking; Collaborative filtering; Similarity measures; Recommender systems;** •**Applied computing** → **Digital libraries and archives;**

KEYWORDS

Recommender system; content-based filtering; item-to-item similarity; open research data; user judgment; digital library.

ACM Reference format:
Anusuriya Devaraju and Shlomo Berkovsky. 2018. A Hybrid Recommendation Approach for Open Research Datasets . In *Proceedings of 26th Conference on User Modeling, Adaptation and Personalization, Singapore, Singapore, July 8–11, 2018 (UMAP '18),* 5 pages.
DOI: 10.1145/3209219.3209250

1 INTRODUCTION

The Open Science paradigm has led to rapid proliferation of open research data on the Web [18]. Examples of research data include observations, measurements, model outputs, statistics and survey outcomes. Various discipline-specific and common repositories have been established to simplify dissemination of research data. For example, the Registry of Research Data Repository[1] has recorded more than 2000 repositories from various disciplines, and the DataCite portal[2] currently provides access to more than 3.8 millions research datasets.

A number of recent studies [4, 6, 8, 12, 23] have revealed that the current data repositories lack effective data discovery solutions that accurately deliver relevant datasets. Currently, users may find datasets-of-interest in the repositories through keyword search and faceted navigation. These mechanisms may be appropriate for users performing known-item searches, e.g., search by author, title or Digital Object Identifier (DOI), or users, who are familiar with the nature and structure of the repository. However, when users are unable to clearly articulate their needs, seek for datasets in an unfamiliar domain or merely address their ephemeral needs, such search mechanisms may be inadequate [24]. Also, since the search primarily relies on a data description (metadata), top-ranked search results may belong to the same collection and fall short in uncovering novel datasets. These challenges reflect the emergent need for a data discovery solution that complements the search functionality and can deliver personalized dataset recommendations to users.

In this paper, we set out to develop a recommendation approach for open research datasets. Although our approach leverages established recommendation methods, it applies them to a new problem of dataset recommendations. The proposed approach identifies datasets of relevance using a hybrid similarity function that incorporates properties of datasets, e.g., metadata features, as well as their usage patterns, e.g., search/download co-occurrence. The approach is underpinned by a data-driven weighting model derived empirically in a user study involving 151 users of the Data Access Portal (DAP) repository deployed by CSIRO [5]. The recommendation approach is evaluated in another user study that considers more than 1,000 explicit relevance judgments provided by 113 DAP users. The results of the study demonstrate that our approach is capable of accurately predicting the relevance scores of datasets that align with the user judgments. Hence, this is an important step towards practical deployment of recommendation technologies in research data repositories.

In summary, the main contributions of this work are two-fold. First, we propose a new recommendation approach that hybridizes established recommendation techniques to address a *new problem of open research dataset discovery*. Second, we apply the proposed approach in the context of a live dataset repository and *evaluate its accuracy in a user study* that involves dataset creators and consumers alike.

---

[1]http://www.re3data.org/
[2]https://search.datacite.org/

2 RELATED WORK

Recommender systems have been recognized as an important feature in the design of scientific digital libraries [2, 19]. However, existing work has primarily focused on recommendable items like publications [7], scholars [25] and citations [10]. Previous studies have also indicated that these method may be insufficient for research dataset discovery purposes, as users may have different requirements and employ a range of strategies searching for datasets compared to publication-related discovery [8, 12–14, 20, 22]. For example, the representation of datasets is more complex than that of publications [20, 22], serendipity and diversity are important considerations in dataset discovery [1, 8], and users also appreciate more the novelty of recommendations [12].

To the best of our knowledge, little work has focused on research dataset recommendations. A notable exception to this is the work of Singhal *et al.* on context-based search for research datasets [21]. There, the authors employed content-based similarity based on three features – topic, abstract, and author – in order to identify datasets of interest. Catania *et al.* demonstrated a prototype recommendation approach for spatial data based on the topological similarities of spatial objects [3]. Although their work is applicable to the problem of discovering spatial datasets by considering fine-grained geometrical information, such an approach may be less practical if applied to datasets in open data repositories, as these usually contain only coarse spatial information like bounding boxes and points.

3 DATASET RECOMMENDATION

Our approach combines content-based similarity [16] with item-to-item co-occurrence [15]. The former quantifies the similarity of datasets by comparing their metadata, e.g., keywords and fields of research, while the latter considers their statistical co-occurrence, e.g., downloads by the same users.

3.1 Data Sources

We distinguish between two types of information associated with open research datasets. The first is the metadata of the datasets, as specified by data creators or providers (see Figure 1). The metadata is usually represented using standard schemas, such as Dublin Core[3], DataCite Metadata Schema[4] and Registry Interchange Format - Collections and Services[5]. The second contains the observable user interactions with datasets and the repository. For example, past searches and dataset downloads may be extracted from the repository logs and these reveal commonalities or behavioral patterns of the users. Typically, this information is more abundant than metadata and can be used for dataset recommendations.

Based on the metadata of the DAP repository and the available repository logs, we identified 10 features to be exploited by the proposed recommendation approach: *title, description, keywords, activity, research fields, creators, contributors, spatial, search* and *download*. A brief explanation of these features is provided in Table 1. Note that the first eight features belong to metadata, while the last two are derived from user interaction logs.

[3]http://dublincore.org/documents/dces/
[4]https://schema.datacite.org/
[5]http://www.ands.org.au/online-services/rif-cs-schema

Figure 1: An example of a research dataset and its metadata.

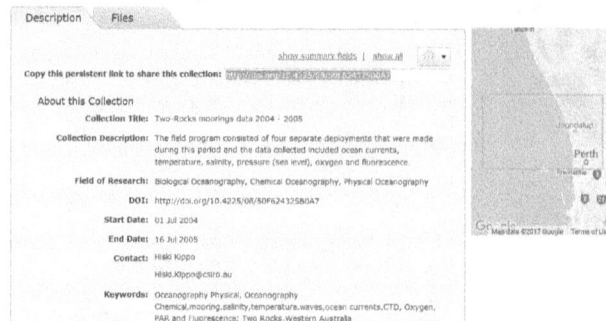

Table 1: Features, descriptions and weights.

Feature	Description	Score	ω_i
title	Name of the dataset	4.106	0.123
description	Textual description of the data	3.887	0.116
keywords	User-specified tags	3.815	0.114
activity	Data provenance: related project, methods, experiments, instruments	3.311	0.099
research fields	Research classification areas	2.669	0.080
creators	Users who created the dataset	2.868	0.086
contributors	Users who contributed to the dataset	2.589	0.077
spatial	Spatial location of the data collected, e.g., point or bounding box	3.523	0.105
download	Downloading-related server logs	N/A	0.100
search	Search-related server logs	N/A	0.100

3.2 Feature-Based Similarity

The proposed dataset recommendation task considers the following use case. We assume that a DAP repository user is examining a target dataset d, e.g., sample dataset shown in Figure 1, and would like to be recommended a list of n related datasets $(d_1, d_2, ..., d_n)$. This is similar to the familiar *"users who buy this product are also interested in"* recommendation paradigm, deployed by eCommerce sites. Note that this list of recommended datasets should be ranked according to their relevance to d, quantified using a similarity function $overall\_sim(d, d_k)$, such that d_1 is the most similar and d_n is the least similar dataset.

We compute the similarity of the datasets using a linearly weighted hybridization of two methods. **Content-based** (CB) similarity component determines similar datasets based on the eight metadata features: *title, description, keywords, activity, research fields, creators, contributors* and *spatial*. For the textual features *title, description, keywords* and *activity*, we conduct standard text pre-processing steps, such as stop-word removal, tokenization and stemming, and then use the TF-IDF term weighting and Cosine Similarity to compute the similarity score for each feature [17].

For the categorial *research fields, creators* and *contributors* features, we apply the Jaccard similarity coefficient to compute feature-specific similarity scores. The *spatial* information of research datasets is expressed as a point or bounding box. We transform the spatial information into a standardized geographic coordinate system, compute the centroids of the bounding boxes and then apply the Euclidean distance to compute the spatial distance between datasets. We also normalize the obtained distance matrix and convert it into the similarity matrix.

We also use **item-to-item** (I2I) dataset co-occurrence similarity. This is based on the frequency of joint downloads by DAP users extracted from the *download logs* feature. The underlying idea is that the more two datasets are downloaded jointly by users, the more likely they are to be similar. From the DAP download logs, we extract the associations between datasets and users based on the observed download activity. Then, we represent each dataset as a vector expressing the number of downloads by every user and compute the download-based dataset-to-dataset similarity by applying Cosine Similarity to the two vectors.

To compute similarity using the *search logs* feature, we uncover the relations between datasets and search terms from the DAP logs. To this end, we are able to track which datasets were examined by users from the results[6] returned by DAP in response to search queries. The underlying assumption here is that two datasets are related if they are examined by users after launching similar queries. Hence, we extract the relations between the queries and examined datasets and then compute the search-based dataset-to-dataset similarity by applying Cosine Similarity to the vectors representing the queries.

3.3 Relevance Ranking

In order to compute the overall dataset-to-dataset similarity score $overall\_sim(d, d_k)$, we combine the 10 individual feature-based similarity scores in a linear manner. More formally, the overall similarity of datasets d and d_k is computed by

$$overall\_sim(d, d_k) = \sum_i (\omega_i \cdot sim_i (d, d_k)), \qquad (1)$$

where ω_i refers to the weight associated with a feature i and $sim_i(d, d_k)$ is the similarity of d and d_k with respect to i.

The features specified in Section 3.2 may have different levels of importance for discovering relevant datasets. We use a heuristic weighting model that assigns 0.8 of the weight to the CB similarity score computed using the metadata features and the remaining 0.2 to the I2I co-occurrence similarity. This is in line with the previously used heuristic weights assigned in [11].

Individual weights associated with the eight metadata features were determined empirically through a user study involving the users of DAP [5]. The users were shown all the features and asked to rate on a 5-Likert scale the perceived importance of the features. 151 users provided their ratings and the average scores of the metadata features are shown in Table 1. The survey reveals that *title, description* and *keywords* are deemed to be the more important features scoring closely to 4, whereas *creators, contributors* and *resarch fields* are less important. The obtained importance scores informed the weights of the features, ω_i, which are listed in the right column

---

[6]We disregard the search mechanism of DAP and treat is a "deterministic black box".

Figure 2: **Average similarity of 1000 most similar datasets.**

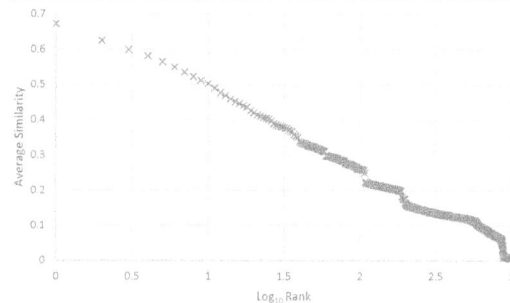

in Table 1. The weights of the metadata features were normalized, such that $\sum_i \omega_i = 0.8$, as per our heuristic assignment. The weights of the interaction-based *search logs* and *download logs* features were uniformly split to $\omega_i = 0.1$ each.

Finally, we compile the recommendation lists and include there the datasets with the highest similarity $overall\_sim(d, d_i)$. More precisely, we compute offline the dataset-to-dataset similarity matrix and consider n most similar entries of a target dataset d to be the recommended datasets of relevance.

4 EVALUATION

This section presents the experimental setting and the results obtained in our user study.

4.1 Experimental Setting

DAP is a data repository deployed by CSIRO, which provides access to datasets published by researchers across various disciplines. In this study, we used 1877 datasets published between 2011 and 2017. We retrieved their metadata and extracted the search and download logs of DAP . After cleansing, the search logs contain 58K unique queries submitted by 13.5K users between 2012 and 2014. The download logs contain more than 10K dataset downloads performed by 6.5K users between 2012 and 2016.

For each of the 1877 datasets in the evaluation, we applied the similarity function given in Equation 1 to compute the similarity scores of all the other datasets in DAP and selected 1000 most relevant datasets. The average $overall\_sim(d, d_k)$ at rank $k \in [1, 1000]$ computed across all the datasets is shown in Figure 2. As can be seen, the similarity scores exhibit a power law distribution. Only the top 10 datasets have $overall\_sim(d, d_k) > 0.5$, whereas datasets ranked 40 and on all have $overall\_sim(d, d_k) < 0.35$.

DAP datasets are published through predefined data descriptors, which leads to consistent nomenclature of the datasets. Hence, it is difficult to accurately establish the ground truth relevance of datasets and evaluate either predictive (MAE, RMSE, etc), classification (precision, recall, etc), or ranking (NDCG, MRR, etc) accuracy metrics [9]. Due to this, we assessed the ability of our approach to predict the relevance of the recommended datasets in a user study involving real DAP users.

We invited a selection of active DAP users to trial a new dataset recommendation feature. For each of the 1877 datasets, we computed offline the list of 1000 most relevant datasets, selected five

Figure 3: Distribution of relevance judgments.

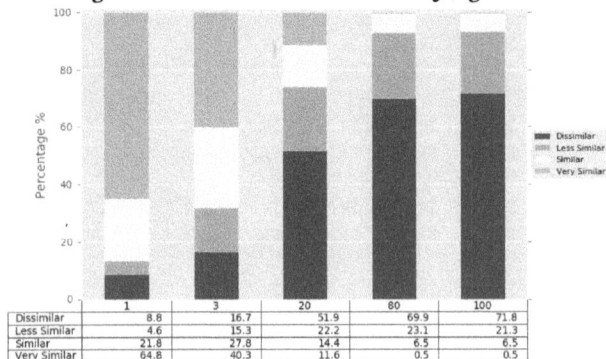

	1	3	20	80	100
Dissimilar	8.8	16.7	51.9	69.9	71.8
Less Similar	4.6	15.3	22.2	23.1	21.3
Similar	21.8	27.8	14.4	6.5	6.5
Very Similar	64.8	40.3	11.6	0.5	0.5

datasets at fixed[7] ranks $k = 1, 3, 20, 80, 100$ and showed these to users as "similar datasets". The users were asked to rate the relevance of the five recommended datasets on a 4-Likert scale ranging from 'very similar' to 'dissimilar'. The datasets were displayed in a random order to avoid selection bias, were visualized in the same way and included DAP links allowing users to inspect them. Users could also include free-text feedback justifying their ratings.

4.2 Results

113 DAP users participate in the second study and evaluated 216 target datasets, i.e., five "similar datasets" for each, such that, in total, we obtained 1080 explicit relevance judgments. Figure 2 illustrates the distribution of the relevance judgements assigned by the users. The five bars represent the distributions of user judgments at ranks 1, 3, 20, 80, and 100, respectively.

Overall, more than 86% of the datasets at rank 1 were judged to be either 'relevant' or 'highly relevant'. Notably, less than 9% of the datasets at this rank were rated as 'dissimilar'. This shows that the proposed approach in most cases can accurately predict the relevance of the top-ranked dataset. Inspecting the free-text feedback provided by the users, we discovered that they rated these datasets as relevant due to a range of reasons: target dataset and the recommended dataset were thematically related, were generated by the same project or using a similar method, formed a series of measurements or were just derived one from another.

For example, one user wrote: "[The target dataset] was an input to [the recommended dataset]. I consider this to be very similar or strongly related". Another user commented: "[The target dataset] and [the recommended dataset] are soil property predictions for the project. They have different attributes, but are similar because users usually look for a suite of soil attributes covering the same area".

Similarly, out of all the datasets at rank 3, more than 68% were judged as 'relevant' or 'highly relevant' and less than 17% were rated as 'dissimilar'. Although positive sentiment toward datasets at rank 3 still dominates, the number of negative judgments is almost twice larger than for datasets at rank 1. This observation shows that the proposed approach is sensitive enough to differentiate even

between datasets at ranks as high as 1 and 3, and this is evident in the users' relevance judgments.

The situation is different, however, at ranks 20, 80 and 100, where, respectively, close to 74%, 93% and 93% of the obtained judgements rated the recommended datasets as either 'dissimilar' or 'less similar'. In fact, results obtained for ranks 80 and 100 were very close and at both ranks only 7% of the datasets were judged to be 'relevant' or 'highly relevant'. This aligns with the similarity distribution observed in Figure 2, as both the ranks are located at the tail of the distribution. Although the results at rank 20 were slightly better than at 80 and 100, only 26% of the datasets at this rank were rated as 'relevant' or 'highly relevant'. This shows that the users perceive the moderately-ranked datasets to be mostly irrelevant for the recommendation purposes.

Interestingly, only one dataset at rank 80 was rated as 'very similar' and this happened to be collected by the same project as the target dataset. Also among the datasets at rank 100, only one dataset was rated as 'very similar'. The user who positively evaluated this dataset commented: "[The recommended dataset] contains the sea temperatures measured on a vessel as it steams underway. [The target dataset] is also a sea temperature dataset taken by a vessel. Because both datasets have the same measured parameter with the same temporal and spatial attributes, I classified them as similar, albeit [the recommended dataset] has many other parameters. Someone searching for sea temperature data could use that data from [the recommended dataset]".

5 CONCLUSIONS AND FUTURE WORK

The proliferation of open research datasets may aggravate the discovery of datasets-of-interest by users. In order to address this growing issue, we have turned in this paper to the problem of recommending datasets. We developed a recommendation approach that identifies relevant datasets by leveraging a hybrid similarity metric, which incorporates content-based metadata features and observable usage patterns. Notably, the linear weighting model deployed by our approach was derived in a user study involving the users of a real DAP open dataset repository.

We evaluated the proposed approach in another user study that is reported in this paper. The results of the latter verified the ability of the proposed approach to accurately predict the relevance of datasets, which we consider to be an important contribution to the challenge of recommending research datasets. The obtained relevance judgements of DAP users indicate that the datasets recommended at ranks 1 and 3 were mainly deemed as relevant, whereas those at ranks 20, 80 and 100 were clearly irrelevant.

The study addresses a novel recommendation problem, and its results may serve as baseline for future research in this direction. In particular, we will measure the performance of three methods, i.e., content-based, co-occurrence and hybrid proposed in the paper. We intend to compare the performance of our approach with established content-based recommenders from other domains, deployed for dataset recommendations. We will then conduct a large-scale live evaluation of the recommender and assess its uptake by the DAP users.

---

[7]These ranks were picked based on the distribution of the average similarity scores (see Figure 2) and represent different relevance levels. Specifically, dataset at ranks 1 and 3 have $overall\_sim(d, d_k) > 0.6$ and are expected to be relevant, whereas those at ranks 80 and 100 have $overall\_sim(d, d_k) < 0.3$ and should be irrelevant.

REFERENCES

[1] Azin Ashkan, Branislav Kveton, Shlomo Berkovsky, and Zheng Wen. 2015. Optimal Greedy Diversity for Recommendation. In *Proceedings of the Twenty-Fourth International Joint Conference on Artificial Intelligence, IJCAI 2015, Buenos Aires, Argentina, July 25-31, 2015*. 1742–1748. http://ijcai.org/Abstract/15/248

[2] Joeran Beel, Bela Gipp, Stefan Langer, and Corinna Breitinger. 2016. Research-paper recommender systems: a literature survey. *International Journal on Digital Libraries* 17, 4 (2016), 305–338. https://doi.org/10.1007/s00799-015-0156-0

[3] Barbara Catania, Maria Teresa Pinto, Paola Podestà, and Davide Pomerano. 2011. *A Recommendation Technique for Spatial Data*. Springer Berlin Heidelberg, Berlin, Heidelberg, 200–213. https://doi.org/10.1007/978-3-642-23737-9_15

[4] Miriam L. E. Steiner Davis, Carol Tenopir, Suzie Allard, and Michael T. Frame. 2014. Facilitating Access to Biodiversity Information: A Survey of Users' Needs and Practices. *Environmental Management* 53, 3 (01 Mar 2014), 690–701. https://doi.org/10.1007/s00267-014-0229-7

[5] Anusuriya Devaraju and Shlomo Berkovsky. 2017. Do Users Matter? The Contribution of User-Driven Feature Weights to Open Dataset Recommendations. In *Proceedings of the Poster Track of the 11th ACM Conference on Recommender Systems (RecSys 2017), Como, Italy, August 28, 2017*. http://ceur-ws.org/Vol-1905/recsys2017_poster16.pdf

[6] Ixchel M. Faniel, Adam Kriesberg, and Elizabeth Yakel. 2016. Social scientists' satisfaction with data reuse. *Journal of the Association for Information Science and Technology* 67, 6 (2016), 1404–1416. https://doi.org/10.1002/asi.23480

[7] C. Lee Giles, Kurt D. Bollacker, and Steve Lawrence. 1998. CiteSeer: An Automatic Citation Indexing System. In *Proceedings of the Third ACM Conference on Digital Libraries (DL '98)*. ACM, New York, NY, USA, 89–98. https://doi.org/10.1145/276675.276685

[8] Kathleen Gregory, Paul T. Groth, Helena Cousijn, Andrea Scharnhorst, and Sally Wyatt. 2017. Searching Data: A Review of Observational Data Retrieval Practices. *CoRR* abs/1707.06937 (2017). http://arxiv.org/abs/1707.06937

[9] Asela Gunawardana and Guy Shani. 2015. Evaluating Recommender Systems. In *Recommender Systems Handbook*. 265–308. https://doi.org/10.1007/978-1-4899-7637-6_8

[10] Qi He, Jian Pei, Daniel Kifer, Prasenjit Mitra, and Lee Giles. 2010. Context-aware Citation Recommendation. In *Proceedings of the 19th International Conference on World Wide Web (WWW '10)*. ACM, New York, NY, USA, 421–430. https://doi.org/10.1145/1772690.1772734

[11] Pijitra Jomsri, Siripun Sanguansintukul, and Worasit Choochaiwattana. 2011. CiteRank: combination similarity and static ranking with research paper searching. *International Journal of Internet Technology and Secured Transactions* 3, 2 (2011), 161–177. http://www.inderscienceonline.com/doi/abs/10.1504/IJITST.2011.039776

[12] Dagmar Kern and Brigitte Mathiak. 2015. *Are there any differences in data set retrieval compared to well-known literature retrieval?* Springer International Publishing, Cham, 197–208. https://doi.org/10.1007/978-3-319-24592-8_15

[13] Sven R. Kunze and Sören Auer. 2013. Dataset Retrieval. In *2013 IEEE Seventh International Conference on Semantic Computing, Irvine, CA, USA, September 16-18, 2013*. 1–8. https://doi.org/10.1109/ICSC.2013.12

[14] Branislav Kveton and Shlomo Berkovsky. 2016. Minimal Interaction Content Discovery in Recommender Systems. *TiiS* 6, 2 (2016), 15:1–15:25. https://doi.org/10.1145/2845090

[15] Loet Leydesdorff and Liwen Vaughan. 2006. Co-occurrence Matrices and Their Applications in Information Science: Extending ACA to the Web Environment. *J. Am. Soc. Inf. Sci. Technol.* 57, 12 (Oct. 2006), 1616–1628. https://doi.org/10.1002/asi.v57:12

[16] Pasquale Lops, Marco de Gemmis, and Giovanni Semeraro. 2011. *Content-based Recommender Systems: State of the Art and Trends*. Springer US, Boston, MA, 73–105. https://doi.org/10.1007/978-0-387-85820-3_3

[17] Christopher D. Manning, Prabhakar Raghavan, and Hinrich Schütze. 2008. *Introduction to Information Retrieval*. Cambridge University Press, New York, NY, USA. https://nlp.stanford.edu/IR-book/html/htmledition/contents-1.html

[18] Jennifer C Molloy. 2011. The Open Knowledge Foundation: open data means better science. *PLoS biology* 9, 12 (Dec. 2011), e1001195. https://doi.org/10.1371/journal.pbio.1001195

[19] D. De Nart and C. Tasso. 2014. A Personalized Concept-driven Recommender System for Scientific Libraries. *Procedia Computer Science* 38 (2014), 84 – 91. https://doi.org/10.1016/j.procs.2014.10.015 10th Italian Research Conference on Digital Libraries, IRCDL 2014.

[20] S. L. Pallickara, S. Pallickara, M. Zupanski, and S. Sullivan. 2010. Efficient Metadata Generation to Enable Interactive Data Discovery over Large-Scale Scientific Data Collections. In *2010 IEEE Second International Conference on Cloud Computing Technology and Science*. 573–580. https://doi.org/10.1109/CloudCom.2010.99

[21] A. Singhal, R. Kasturi, and J. Srivastava. 2014. DataGopher: Context-based search for research datasets. In *Proceedings of the 2014 IEEE 15th International Conference on Information Reuse and Integration (IEEE IRI 2014)*. 749–756. https://doi.org/10.1109/IRI.2014.7051964

[22] Maximilian Stempfhuber and Benjamin Zapilko. 2009. Integrated Retrieval of Research Data and Publications in Digital Libraries. In *Rethinking Electronic Publishing: Innovation in Communication Paradigms and Technologies - Proceedings of the 13th International Conference on Electronic Publishing*, Susanna Mornati and Turid Hedlund (Eds.). 613–620. http://elpub.scix.net/cgi-bin/works/Show?144_elpub2009

[23] Christine Stohn. 2015. *How Do Users Search and Discover? Findings from Ex Libris User Research*. Technical Report. Ex Libris. http://www.exlibrisgroup.com/files/Products/Primo/HowDoUsersSearchandDiscover.pdf

[24] Ryen W. White and Resa A. Roth. 2009. *Exploratory Search: Beyond the Query-Response Paradigm*. Morgan & Claypool Publishers. http://dx.doi.org/10.2200/S00174ED1V01Y200901ICR003

[25] A. Yang, J. Li, Y. Tang, J. Wang, and Y. Zhao. 2012. The similar scholar recommendation in Schol@t. In *Proceedings of the 2012 IEEE 16th International Conference on Computer Supported Cooperative Work in Design (CSCWD)*. 666–670. https://doi.org/10.1109/CSCWD.2012.6221889

Are You Reaching Your Audience? Exploring Item Exposure over Consumer Segments in Recommender Systems

Jacek Wasilewski
Insight Centre for Data Analytics
University College Dublin
Dublin, Ireland
jacek.wasilewski@insight-centre.org

Neil Hurley
Insight Centre for Data Analytics
University College Dublin
Dublin, Ireland
neil.hurley@insight-centre.org

ABSTRACT

Many state-of-the-art recommender systems are known to suffer from popularity bias, which means that they have a tendency to recommend items that are already popular, making those items even more popular. This results in the item catalogue being not fully utilised, which is far from ideal from the business' perspective. Issues of item exposure are actually more complex than simply overexposure of popular items. In this paper we look at the exposure of individual items to different groups of consumers, the item's *audience*, and address the question of whether recommender systems reach each item's potential audience. Thus, we go beyond state-of-the-art analyses that have simply addressed the extent to which items are recommended, regardless of whether they are reaching their target audience. We conduct an empirical study on the MovieLens 20M dataset showing that recommender systems do not fully utilise items' audiences, and existing sales diversity optimisers do not improve their exposure.

ACM Reference Format:
Jacek Wasilewski and Neil Hurley. 2018. Are You Reaching Your Audience? Exploring Item Exposure over Consumer Segments in Recommender Systems. In *UMAP '18: 26th Conference on User Modeling, Adaptation and Personalization, July 8–11, 2018, Singapore, Singapore*. ACM, New York, NY, USA, 5 pages. https://doi.org/10.1145/3209219.3209246

1 INTRODUCTION

Recommender systems have become ubiquitous in the interfaces to product catalogues provided by on-line retailers. From the user's perspective, recommender algorithms are used to filter a large set of possible selections into a much smaller set of items that the user is likely to be interested in. However, engaging and holding a user's interest is a complex matter and simply identifying relevant items might not be enough to satisfy a user. On the other hand, from the business point of view, as important as users receiving engaging recommendations, is the utilisation of products in the catalogue.

It has been shown [5] that on-line systems suffer from the *long tail effect*, where a few items (the "head") are responsible for the most of the interactions, while the rest (the "long tail") are much

less known. Many of the state-of-the-art collaborative filtering recommender engines worsen the situation and promote already popular items, making both users and business suffer—only few items are engaged in sales and users are offered popular items of little surprise. Promoting the long tail items in recommendations offers benefits to both sides. It helps users to discover new items, which corresponds to the goal of a recommender system and, from the business side, it exposes the full product catalogue, increasing the chance of long-tail sales.

Viewed from the business perspective, recommender systems are marketing tools that identify which customers a product in the catalogue should be promoted to. Each item has its audience to which the item ideally should be exposed and making sure that items are exposed to the right users is an important step towards increasing sales. As one illustration, consider as an example the movie, *The Shining*, a well-known and acclaimed movie. Users may have watched it for various reasons, e.g. because it was directed by Stanley Kubrick, or because Jack Nicholson was the leading actor, or because it is based on a Stephen King novel, or because it is a horror, or just because it is a popular movie. Marketeers should ideally identify all these user interests and make sure the movie is exposed to users with similar interests in future, so that, if one of the movie's main attractions is the writer of the novel on which it is based, it is exposed to people who showed an interest in King's other novels.

Automating this item perspective in a top-N recommender system is not straight-forward. As each interaction is the recommendation of N relevant items to a single user, the system can directly control the user-perspective. In contrast, item exposure is built through a sequence of separate interactions with different users. Ensuring that an item is recommended to a relevant user, does not necessarily imply that this item's set of recommendations are properly spread across its full potential audience.

In this paper we tackle the problem of *item exposure* over consumer segments to understand who consumes items and if potential consumers are reached by recommendations. While there have been many studies of long-tail sales promotion, this work differs from previous studies and evaluation techniques in that it considers not only the number of times items are exposed but also to whom it is exposed, not treating all users the same. The main goal of this paper is to explore : a) whether items have specialised audiences, b) whether item audiences are fully targeted by recommender systems, and c) whether state-of-the-art sales diversity re-rankers improve exposure to audiences.

2 BACKGROUND

Improving user satisfaction and optimising business performance are two of the main goals that recommender systems are tasked with. While analysing different aspects of user satisfaction has drawn more attention in the research community, the business-oriented perspective on how recommender systems perform is equally important.

"Selling less of more"[5, 6], a concept formulated by Anderson suggests that the full catalogue of items should be utilised rather than having sales concentrated around a few heavily consumed items. Recommending less obvious items can potentially optimise both the user and business goals; the business promotes less popular but still relevant items, resulting in a richer user experience.

A number of researchers have looked at the problem of catalogue utilisation in recommender systems. Adomavicius and Kwon [3, 4] proposed a measure called *Aggregate Diversity*, defined as the total number of items that a system recommends to a given set of users. It measures the extent to which the item catalogue is exposed to the users of the system and can also be understood as a measure of item coverage. Following the "selling less of more" idea, systems with high Aggregate Diveristy are preferred. It has been shown, however, that classic collaborative filtering algorithms do not expose the full catalogue to the users. In fact they are biased towards recommending items coming from the so-called, *short head*—items that account for a significant portion of interaction with users—as opposed to the rest, the *long tail*. Celma and Herrera [7, 8] showed that the topology of the item similarity network could be the reason for poor discovery and low catalogue utilisation.

Another notion of item performance was presented by Fleder and Hosanagar in [10, 15], where sales diversity was measured through the sales concentration defined by the *Gini Index*. As opposed to the Aggregate Diversity, this metric does not only check whether items have been consumed, but how evenly/unevenly consumption is distributed across items. A similar measure of distributional inequality is the *Shannon Entropy* [15, 16] which is 0 if only one item is utilised by a system, and $\log |I|$ if all items are recommended equally often. The Gini Index and Shannon Entropy measure pure distributional dispersion of item consumption or recommendation but do not account for prior item popularity. They cannot therefore be used to examine whether a recommender system reinforces or reduces prior concentration of popularity. Adamopoulos and Tuzhilin [1, 2] proposed popularity reinforcement measures to assess whether recommender systems follow prior popularity of items.

Several methods to promote sales diversity have been proposed [3, 4, 14, 17, 18, 20]. A simple approach is to promote items that are more likely to be unknown by a user, through expected popularity complement (EPC), defined as item novelty:

$$nov(i) = 1 - \frac{|\mathcal{U}_i|}{|\mathcal{U}|}$$

where $|\mathcal{U}_i|$ is item popularity and $|\mathcal{U}|$ is the total number of users. Recommendations can be re-scored by a linear combination of scores $s(u, i)$ provided by the recommendations and item novelty:

$$s^*(u, i) = (1 - \lambda)s(u, i) + \lambda nov(i)$$

λ is used to control the balance between relevance and novelty.

In all of the above, item exposure is measured by counting the number of times items are being consumed, i.e. item popularity.

This assumes that all users consuming an item are alike and does not distinguish between users. In marketing, it is quite common to split the user-base into consumer segments in order to examine how each segment perceives an item of interest. Prior work leaves open the question of how items are exposed to different segments of people, and what is the impact of recommender systems on exposure across segments.

3 ITEM EXPOSURE OVER CONSUMER SEGMENTS

Recommender systems have to deal with the long tail of items that are rarely recommended. This includes niche items that are rarely liked, but also includes items that have not yet succeeded in penetrating the market. The interaction matrix may contain few entries associated with such items because users are not aware of their utility. Increasing their exposure may result in them eventually cascading through the marketplace and their popularity increasing. To identify and promote these items, we argue it is not enough to ask *how many* users have rated each item in the past, but also *which users* have rated the items, which define its *item exposure*.

By looking at the set of users who consumed and rated an item in the past, the item's user profile $\mathcal{U}_i$, it is possible to model exposure of the item to different user types. Similarly, the set of users to whom the item is recommended, $\mathcal{R}_i$, can be analysed to reveal the extent to which a recommendation algorithm follows the exposure of the item. For that, a notion of user types is required.

As it is commonplace for marketeers to model their customer-base through customer segmentation, we find it useful to measure the exposure in terms of the spread across different consumer segments, where a segment represents a common taste. Given a partition of the taste space C into k consumer segments, we define *item exposure* of a set of consumers S as a function of the probability distribution P over consumer segments, where probability $P(c)$ describes the consumers' preference towards segment c, and $\sum_{c \in C} P(c) = 1$. To measure the item exposure, we find it useful to compare the distribution P against a baseline distribution Q, which we consider to be one of ideal exposure. Then, a useful measure of the exposure of P, is its distance from the ideal distribution. We can measure the distance in terms of the Kullback-Leibler (KL) divergence:

$$D_{\mathrm{KL}}(P||Q) = \sum_{c \in C} P(c) \log_2 \frac{P(c)}{Q(c)}$$

which can be seen as the relative entropy of P with respect to Q. It is easier, however, to interpret another divergence, based on KL, the Jensen-Shannon (JS) divergence, as it is symmetric, always finite and bounded between 0 and 1 if $\log_2$ is used in D_{KL}:

$$D_{\mathrm{JS}}(P||Q) = \frac{1}{2}D_{\mathrm{KL}}(P||M) + \frac{1}{2}D_{\mathrm{KL}}(Q||M)$$

where $M = \frac{1}{2}(P + Q)$. The square root of D_{JS} is a distance metric (JSD).

In our context, the JSD is useful to analyse whether a distribution over consumer segments to which item is recommended, matches the ideal distribution of consumer segments for the item, or how far the item is from the ideal distribution. This requires a notion of ideal distribution. It can be built upon past user-item interactions. It can be assumed that if enough interactions are recorded for an item, we obtain an accurate estimate of the ideal distribution, and the item has a developed profile of consumer segments. Then, if recommendations are compared to such a profile, a large JSD value indicate that these recommendations were made differently to the ideal item customer profile.

4 EVALUATION

4.1 Dataset

We analyse item exposure on the MovieLens 20M dataset [11] which contains user ratings on movies. The dataset consists of 20M ratings on 5-star scale given by 138K users on 27K movies. All users have rated at least 20 movies. No demographic information is included. As we do not evaluate the recommendation performance against a hold-out sample, the full dataset is used in our analysis.

4.2 User Segmentation

To measure item exposure, a partition into consumer segments is required. Geographic, demographic or behavioural information is commonly used by marketeers to segment consumers. As the dataset consists only of interactions between users and items, the only source for segmentation is behavioural information inferred from the interactions.

In [19], consumers are partitioned into segments picked by the X-means clustering algorithm, which is an extension of the k-means algorithm. Clustering is run on user feature vectors coming from a matrix factorisation. Each of the resulting segments represents a common taste. This approach assumes that tastes are exclusive and users belong only to one segment. Other disadvantage of this approach is its hard reproducibility as X-means clustering is highly dependent on initialisation conditions.

A more natural assumption is that users have multiple interests, with different preferences towards them. Considering the movie domain, a user might be interested in e.g. comedy and drama movies, but may prefer dramas more. Such interests might be more complex and abstract than just genres, and we think more generally of user interests as abstractions of general user behaviours. In [12], Hofmann proposed a statistical modelling technique that decomposes user preferences through latent class variables. This method has been successfully used in the recommendation task to predict the likelihood of an item being chosen by a user, according to the aspect model:

$$p(i|u) = \sum_{a \in \mathcal{A}} p(i|a)p(a|u)$$

where $\mathcal{A}$ is a set of latent aspects representing tastes/user communities, $p(i|a)$ is the probability of picking item i if aspect a has been chosen, and $p(a|u)$ holds the user preference towards the aspect. Hofmann showed that the above model can also be used for mining overlapping user communities, where aspect a represents a community and $p(a|u)$ represents a user's association to the community. For each item i, its exposure over consumer segments can be expressed as the exposure of the user group to whom it is relevant, $\mathcal{U}_i$:

$$P(c) = p(a|u \in \mathcal{U}_i) = \sum_{u \in \mathcal{U}_i} p(a|u)p(u|\mathcal{U}_i)$$

where $p(u|\mathcal{U}_i)$ is the relative frequency of obtaining interactions from user u. This can be proportional to the size of user's profile, or uniform, $\frac{1}{|\mathcal{U}_i|}$, which we adopt here. Taking this distribution as the item's ideal audience, we can compare it against the audience

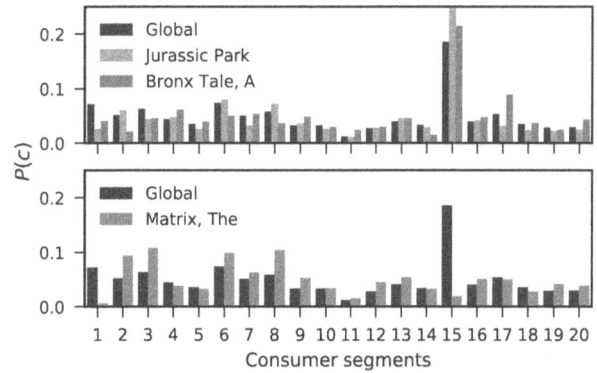

Figure 1: Exposure over consumer segments. Global exposure is compared with sample movies, showing similar (top) exposure to the global, and different (bottom).

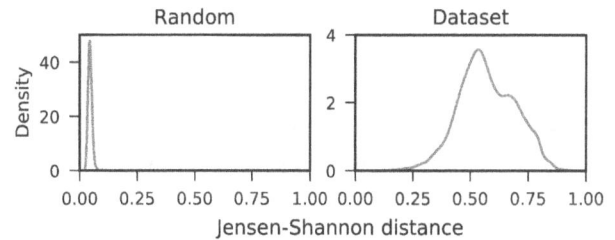

Figure 2: Distribution of JSD for random recommendations and the dataset, with the global distribution taken as the reference.

targeted by the recommender algorithm, which can be computed by using $\mathcal{R}_i$ instead of $\mathcal{U}_i$ above.

4.3 Experiment Setup

We analyse item exposure of recommendations produced by three well-known collaborative filtering algorithms: item- (IB; 10 neighbours) and user-based (UB; 100 neighbours) neighbourhood methods [9] and matrix factorisation (MF; 50 factors) [13]. We simulate the process of consuming recommendations by recommending 10 items to each user from which a random one is selected. Selected item is added to the training set and the whole process it repeated 100 times. Selected items form the $\mathcal{R}_i$ sets which are used to analyse the items' exposure in recommendations. The process is repeated with EPC re-ranker applied (as described in Sec. 2) to see if improving sales diversity improves performance in terms of item exposure over consumer segments. Re-ranker is set up with $\lambda = 0.5$ to give equal importance to relevance and novelty. The RankSys framework (http://ranksys.org) has been used to generate recommendations, and train the aspect model used in the user segmentation.

To mitigate the problem of measuring exposure of items without developed profiles over consumer segments, or without enough recommendations to observe exposure, we ignore items that have been consumed less than 100 times. Also, when comparing exposures produced by original and re-ranked recommendations, in order to perform paired statistical test, we focus on common items.

(a) Reference exposure: global.

(b) Reference exposure: dataset.

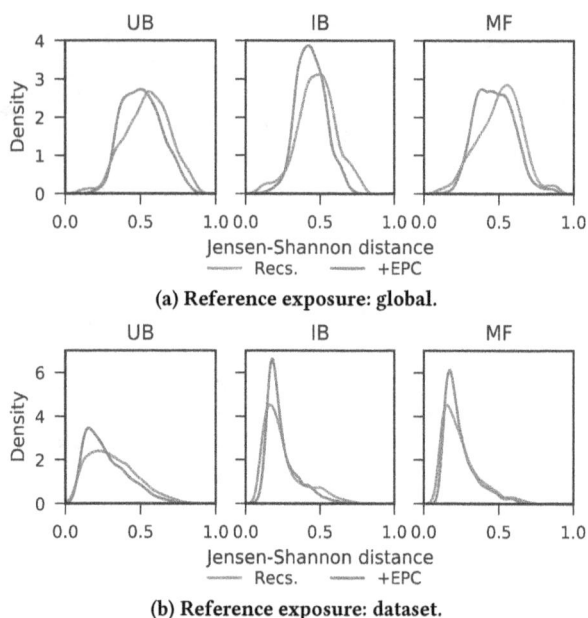

Figure 3: Distribution of JSD for recommendations coming from UB, IB and MF, using different reference exposures.

4.4 Results

In Fig. 1 global exposure over consumer segments is plotted, which can be seen as a hypothetical item that is exposed to all users of the system. An item that is randomly exposed to users, without a specific audience, would follow the global distribution. This is confirmed in Fig. 2 where items exposed by a random recommender follow the global, which is reflected in very low JSD values. It can also be seen that items recorded in the dataset are far from the random, suggesting that they have their own, specialised audiences.

The exposure of three sample items, *Jurassic Park*, *A Bronx Tale* and *The Matrix*, is shown in Fig. 1. First two are in the top closest items to the global, with JSD of 0.15 and 0.3 for the third one. If we compare all three items, we see that they all do not match perfectly the global, however first two follow it to some extend. For *The Matrix* movie, more significant differences can be observed – two major segments, 1 and 15, have been diminished, and exposure moved to other segments, e.g. 2, 3, 6 and 8.

A correlation between item popularity and JS distance to global has been observed: more popular items are generally closer to the global. This is expected if whilst increasing popularity items are exposed to users at random. However there are plenty of interesting examples where this is not the case, e.g. *A Bronx Tale* has similar characteristic as popular *Jurassic Park* while being 10 times less popular (exposed to only 3% of users), and *The Matrix* being exposed to 40% and still having a specific audience, different than the global.

If recommendation systems were unaware of items' audiences, exposure would be following the global distribution of users across segments. Distribution over items' JSD values showed in Fig. 3a suggests that state-of-the-art recommenders (blue lines) expose differently then the global exposure, thus they learn non-random item preferences towards consumer segments. Averages of JSDs

for UB, IB and MF are in range of 0.5-0.55 which shows a strong disagreements with the global.

Knowing that items have specific audiences and that recommender systems are not exposing items to users at random, we wonder if recommendations follow exposures seen in past interactions. From Fig. 3b we can read that recommendations are closer to exposures built upon past interactions than the global, however they still do not follow them perfectly and for many items the exposure is greatly different – averages of JSDs of approx. 0.25-0.3.

If we compare recommendations against each other we can observe that that exposures coming from IB and MF are concentrated closer to 0 than those from UB. We suspect that this comes from the way how the UB works – UB finds best items based on target user's neighbours which most likely share consumer segment associations. If an item is recommended to the similar neighbourhoods, this might interfere the expected exposure of that item by overexposing some consumer segments and making the exposure distant from the expected one.

As items' exposures do not ideally follow past seen in the dataset, we wonder if promoting less popular items (using the EPC greedy re-ranker) would improve not only utilisation of the catalogue but also exposure over consumer segments. Fig. 3a shows that EPC moved items towards the global exposure, which suggests adding random exposure. Wilcoxon signed-rank test of log differences in JSD showed statistically significant changes, with $\alpha = 0.05$. The average improvement is approx. 0.04.

Similarly, we compared exposures against the past interactions – small changes can be seen in Fig. 3b, with largest on the UB recommendations. For the UB, re-rankers moved the recommendations closer to the dataset exposure significantly (according to the statistical test) by 0.05 on average. The average change for IB and MF is approx. 0.01 and not statistically significant. It is interesting that re-rankers only change exposure for recommendations coming from the UB. As we suspect items in UB to be overexposed to some segments, EPC re-ranker by introducing randomness might be reducing the bias effect and making the exposures a bit closer to those based on past interactions. However, even if exposures of all items were reduced by 0.05, they still would be greatly different than the expected ones, suggesting that existing methods do not improve exposure over consumer segments.

5 CONCLUSIONS

In this paper we proposed to evaluate the exposure of items to different user types, instead of measuring just items coverage. Such analysis helps us understand how each user type perceive an item, and if recommender systems expose items to correct users. Our empirical analysis of the MovieLens dataset and state-of-the-art recommendation techniques showed that movies indeed have specific audiences however these are not targeted and reached by the recommendations. We also showed that sales diversity optimisation does not help much in reaching the expected audiences. Further work could focus on methods of improving item exposure over consumer segments in recommendations.

ACKNOWLEDGMENTS

This project has been funded by Science Foundation Ireland under Grant No. SFI/12/RC/2289.

REFERENCES

[1] P. Adamopoulos and A. Tuzhilin. 2014. On Over-specialization and Concentration Bias of Recommendations: Probabilistic Neighborhood Selection in Collaborative Filtering Systems. In *Proceedings of the 8th ACM Conference on Recommender Systems (RecSys '14)*. ACM, New York, NY, USA, 153–160. https://doi.org/10.1145/2645710.2645752

[2] P. Adamopoulos, A. Tuzhilin, and P. Mountanos. 2015. Measuring the concentration reinforcement bias of recommender systems. *CEUR Workshop Proc.* 1441 (2015).

[3] G. Adomavicius and Y. Kwon. 2011. *Maximizing aggregate recommendation diversity: A graph-theoretic approach.* Vol. 816. CEUR-WS, 3–10.

[4] G. Adomavicius and Y. Kwon. 2012. Improving Aggregate Recommendation Diversity Using Ranking-Based Techniques. *IEEE Trans. on Knowl. and Data Eng.* 24, 5 (May 2012), 896–911. https://doi.org/10.1109/TKDE.2011.15

[5] C. Anderson. 2006. *The Long Tail: Why the Future of Business Is Selling Less of More.* Hyperion.

[6] E. Brynjolfsson, Y. U. Hu, and M. D. Smith. 2006. From Niches to Riches: Anatomy of the Long Tail. *MIT SLOAN MANAGEMENT REVIEW* 47, 4 (2006), 67–71.

[7] O. Celma. 2010. *The Long Tail in Recommender Systems.* Springer Berlin Heidelberg, Berlin, Heidelberg, 87–107. https://doi.org/10.1007/978-3-642-13287-2_4

[8] O. Celma and P. Herrera. 2008. A New Approach to Evaluating Novel Recommendations. In *Proceedings of the 2008 ACM Conference on Recommender Systems (RecSys '08)*. ACM, New York, NY, USA, 179–186. https://doi.org/10.1145/1454008.1454038

[9] C. Desrosiers and G. Karypis. 2011. *A Comprehensive Survey of Neighborhood-based Recommendation Methods.* Springer US, Boston, MA, 107–144. https://doi.org/10.1007/978-0-387-85820-3_4

[10] D. Fleder and K. Hosanagar. 2009. Blockbuster Culture's Next Rise or Fall: The Impact of Recommender Systems on Sales Diversity. *Manage. Sci.* 55, 5 (May 2009), 697–712. https://doi.org/10.1287/mnsc.1080.0974

[11] F. M. Harper and J. A. Konstan. 2015. The MovieLens Datasets: History and Context. *ACM Trans. Interact. Intell. Syst.* 5, 4, Article 19 (Dec. 2015), 19 pages. https://doi.org/10.1145/2827872

[12] T. Hofmann. 2004. Latent semantic models for collaborative filtering. *ACM Trans. Inf. Syst. (ACM TOIS)* 22, 1 (2004), 89–115. https://doi.org/10.1145/963770.963774

[13] Y. Hu, Y. Koren, and C. Volinsky. 2008. Collaborative Filtering for Implicit Feedback Datasets. (2008). https://doi.org/10.1109/ICDM.2008.22

[14] K. Niemann and M. Wolpers. 2013. A New Collaborative Filtering Approach for Increasing the Aggregate Diversity of Recommender Systems. In *Proceedings of the 19th ACM SIGKDD International Conference on Knowledge Discovery and Data Mining (KDD '13)*. ACM, New York, NY, USA, 955–963. https://doi.org/10.1145/2487575.2487656

[15] G. Shani and A. Gunawardana. 2011. *Evaluating Recommendation Systems.* Springer US, Boston, MA, 257–297. https://doi.org/10.1007/978-0-387-85820-3_8

[16] Z. Szlavik, W. J. Kowalczyk, and M. C. Schut. 2011. *Diversity measurement of recommender systems under different user choice models.*

[17] S. Vargas and P. Castells. 2011. Rank and relevance in novelty and diversity metrics for recommender systems. *Proc. fifth ACM Conf. Recomm. Syst. - RecSys '11* (2011), 109. https://doi.org/10.1145/2043932.2043955

[18] S. Vargas and P. Castells. 2014. Improving Sales Diversity by Recommending Users to Items. In *Proceedings of the 8th ACM Conference on Recommender Systems (RecSys '14)*. ACM, New York, NY, USA, 145–152. https://doi.org/10.1145/2645710.2645744

[19] J. Wasilewski and N. Hurley. 2017. How Diverse Is Your Audience? Exploring Consumer Diversity in Recommender Systems. *RecSys 2017 Poster Proceedings* (2017).

[20] T. Zhou, Z. Kuscsik, J. Liu, M. Medo, J. R. Wakeling, and Y. Zhang. 2010. Solving the apparent diversity-accuracy dilemma of recommender systems. *Proceedings of the National Academy of Sciences* 107, 10 (2010), 4511–4515. https://doi.org/10.1073/pnas.1000488107

Perceived Persuasive Effect of Behavior Model Design in Fitness Apps

Kiemute Oyibo
University of Saskatchewan
S7N 5C9, Saskatoon, Canada
kiemute.oyibo@usask.ca

Ifeoma Adaji
University of Saskatchewan
S7N 5C9, Saskatoon, Canada
ifeoma.adaji@usask.ca

Rita Orji
Dalhousie University
B3H 4R2, Halifax, Canada
rita.orji@dal.ca

Babatunde Olabenjo
University of Saskatchewan
S7N 5C9, Saskatoon, Canada
b.olabenjo@usask.ca

Mahsa Azizi
University of Saskatchewan
S7N 5C9, Saskatoon, Canada
maa790@mail.usask.ca

Julita Vassileva
University of Saskatchewan
S7N 5C9, Saskatoon, Canada
jiv@cs.usask.ca

ABSTRACT

Behavior modeling has become a very important behavior change technique employed in most fitness apps. However, its effect as a persuasive strategy on users has not been well investigated. Consequently, we conducted an empirical study among 669 participants to uncover: (1) how the *perceived persuasiveness* of behavior model design influences three social cognitive theory (SCT) determinants of behavior: *self-efficacy, self-regulation and outcome expectation*; and (2) the moderating effect of gender-based personalization. We based our study on user evaluation of prototypes of behavior models performing push-up and squat exercise behaviors as a case study. Our results show that, overall, the *perceived persuasiveness* of behavior models significantly influences all of the three SCT factors. The effect of *persuasiveness* on *self-regulation* (β = 0.42, p < 0.001) and *outcome expectation* (β = 0.41, p < 0.001) is stronger than on *self-efficacy* (β = 0.13, p < 0.05). Moreover, the behavior model design has a stronger effect on females' *self-efficacy* and males' *outcome expectation* if personalized to their gender. We discuss the implication of our findings.

KEYWORDS

persuasive technology; self-efficacy; self-regulation; outcome expectation; SCT; behavior model; persuasiveness; personalization

ACM Reference format:

K. Oyibo, I. Adaji, R. Orji, B. Olabenjo, M. Azizi, and J. Vassileva. 2018. Perceived Persuasive Effect of Behavior Model Design in Fitness Apps. In *Proceedings of ACM UMAP conference, Singapore, July 2018 (UMAP'18), 10 pages. https://doi.org/10.1145/3209219.3209240*

1 INTRODUCTION

Behavior modeling has become a trending persuasive strategy employed in most fitness apps to motivate behavior change. In behavior modeling, "*an expert shows [a] person how to correctly perform a behavior, for example, in class or on video*" (p. 382) [1]. The use of this behavior change technique in the physical activity domain has become important given that some people do not possess the proper knowledge or have access to the right information to carry out the target behavior. Moreover, performing a given exercise the wrong way can result in body injury. These factors, coupled with the ever-growing awareness to being active through regular exercise, continue to drive the use of behavior modeling in the fitness domain. In a systematic review, Conroy et al. [10] found that behavior modeling (in the form of instructions and demonstrations) is the most commonly used behavior change technique in fitness apps on the market.

However, there are limited studies in the literature, which have evaluated the effectiveness of behavior modeling as a persuasive strategy. To bridge this gap and advance research in human-computer interaction (HCI), we conducted an empirical study (n = 669) to investigate the *perceived persuasiveness* of behavior model design using the SCT as an analytical framework and Push-up and Squat bodyweight exercises as a case study. We chose the SCT as the theoretic framework for our study because: (1) it is one of the most applied behavioral theories for promoting physical activity in the health domain [14]; and (2) all human actions stem from cognition and motivation [15]. Specifically, we chose to investigate the effect of the *perceived persuasiveness* of behavior model design on *self-efficacy, self-regulation* and *outcome expectation* because they are among the three most investigated constructs in the SCT literature. Moreover, we based our study on Push-Up and Squat exercise-types because they are among the most commonly modeled exercise behaviors in fitness apps.

Bodyweight exercise—the use of one's weight as a tool for resistance training—has become very popular among fitness professionals around the world. For example, in the annual global survey in 2015, 2016 and 2017 on fitness trends, Thompson [28] found that bodyweight training topped the chart by emerging in the first and second positions. Moreover, Smartphone exercise apps made the top global fitness trends in 2016 [27] and 2017 [28]. As a result, this makes it pertinent for researchers to investigate the effectiveness of using mobile apps to model behavior change.

The results of our investigation show that the *perceived persuasiveness* of behavior model design has the capacity to influence the SCT factors of behavior change. Overall, *persuasiveness* significantly influences *self-regulation* (β = 0.42, p < 0.001), *outcome expectation* (β = 0.41, p < 0.001) and *self-efficacy* (β = 0.13, p < 0.001). Specifically, our results show that, with respect to *self-efficacy* and *outcome expectation*, personalized behavior models are more likely to be effective for female and male users, respectively.

2 BACKGROUND AND RELATED WORK

In this section, we provide an overview on behavior modeling, social cognitive determinants of behavior and related work.

2.1 Background

Behavior modeling is a behavior change technique, which is used to motivate behavior change. According to Bandura [5], as cited in [25], people are more likely to attempt changing their lifestyle if they are taught how or shown ways to change their existing habits. Behavior modeling is predicated on the Social Learning Theory (SLT) in general and observational learning in particular. The SLT holds that individuals can learn new behaviors by observing and imitating the behaviors of others [6]. Over time, the SLT evolved into the SCT. The SCT focuses on how the behaviors of individuals are influenced by their experiences, the actions of others and the environment in which they live [26]. Specifically, the SCT states that people acquire new ideas and knowledge of new practices from their immediate environment through the observation of the actions of other people and their consequences [25]. Thus, the SCT holds that personal factors, environmental factors and the behavior itself reciprocally influence one another to shape human behavior [7].

The SCT comprises a number of cognitive factors, which are determinants of behavior (see Table 1). In the context of observational learning, social cognitive factors (such as *self-efficacy, self-regulation, outcome expectation*, etc.) determine whether the new ideas and practices learned by individuals will be eventually adopted and imitated [25]. Among the SCT constructs, *self-efficacy*, which refers to the belief in one's ability to perform a given behavior, has been found to be the strongest determinant of behavior [14]. Besides, *self-regulation* and *outcome expectation* have also been found to be important determinants of behavior. Self-regulation has to do with the ability of people to regulate themselves towards achieving a behavior. There are various forms of *self-regulation*, which include planning, goal-setting, monitoring and tracking of one's progress. Finally, outcome expectation has to do with the notion that people will take a certain course of action if they believe it will lead to a beneficial outcome, while they will avoid it if they believe it will result in an unfavorable outcome. *Outcome expectation* can be physical, social or self-evaluative. Physical outcomes relate to physiological, biological or material gains. Social outcomes relate to social approval or recognition. Finally, self-evaluative outcomes have to do with the feelings

about oneself after engaging in a behavior [31]. Research shows that behavior modeling, aka vicarious modeling, has the capacity to impact SCT factors such as *self-efficacy, outcome expectation*, etc. [25]. (Note: all of these constructs are based on user perception. However, for brevity, the word "perceived" will, sometimes, be dropped out of their names as shown in Table 1.)

Table 1: Study's constructs and definition [2, 3]

Construct	Definition
Self-Efficacy	Self-efficacy is the belief that one has the capability to perform a given behavior. It is regarded as the strongest (proximal) determinant of behavior.
Self-Regulation	It is the ability of individuals to reguate their behavior through planning, self-monitoring and goal-setting.
Outcome Expectation	Outcome expectation is the belief that engaging in a given behavior will result in certain outcomes, positive or negative.
Persuasiveness	It is the capacity of persuasive systems to influence or motivate users to change their behavior in the positive direction.

2.2 Related Work

Very few studies have been carried out in the context of behavior modeling and its impact on SCT factors in the physical activity domain. In the context of health research, we were only able to find one study by Sheeshka et al. [25] on the influence of *social modeling* and *media* on SCT factors. Sheeshka [25] conducted an empirical study on using SCT to explain the intentions to practice healthy eating behavior. They found that *social modeling* of behaviors by friends and family members directly influences *outcome expectation* (aka *outcome expectancy*) and indirectly influences *self-efficacy* through *outcome expectation*. They also found that *media* (newspaper, magazine and TV) significantly influences *outcome expectation* and *self-efficacy*.

However, Sheeshka et al.'s [25] *social modeling* and *media* constructs do not entail behavior modeling on a computerized media. They are specifically based on friends/family and traditional media in the context of healthy eating. Fogg [12] and Oinas-Kukkonen and Harjumaa [16] have also looked at behavior modeling (aka simulation [30]) as a persuasive strategy. However, their works are not based on investigating the relationship between *perceived persuasiveness* and the SCT factors in the exercise domain. Our study differs from theirs in that we are examining how the *perceived persuasiveness* of behavior models, employed in today's fitness apps as a persuasive strategy, influences the primary SCT factors, which mediate behavior change.

3 METHOD

In this section, we present our research question, measurement instruments and the demographics of participants in our survey.

3.1 Research Objective

The aim of our study is to investigate the effectiveness of behavior models by answering the following research questions:

1. Are fitness apps' behavior models effective in motivating behavior change?
2. What is the relationship between the *persuasiveness* of behavior model design and the SCT determinants of behavior change?
3. Which of the SCT factors does the *persuasiveness* of behavior model design influence the most?
4. Does gender-based personalization moderate the relationships between the *persuasiveness* of behavior model design and the SCT factors?

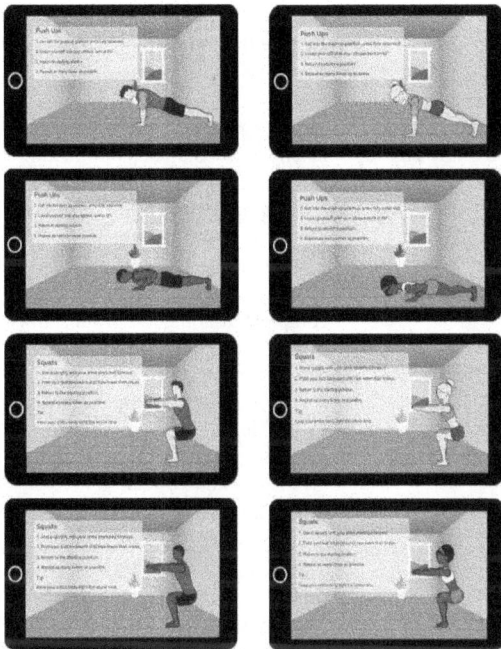

Figure 1: Behavior models demonstrating how to carry out different types of bodyweight exercise (push-up and squat)

3.2 Research Design

To answer our research questions, we implemented a hypothetical fitness app, which we called *"Homex App,"* aimed at motivating behavior change on the home front. The app features eight versions of exercise behavior models, which demonstrate to the user how to correctly perform a given bodyweight exercise. In designing the behavior models, we considered gender, race and user's exercise-type preference. This resulted in eight versions of the behavior models as shown in Figure 1. (However, in this paper, we are only focusing on the moderating effect of the gender of the model and the gender of the observer.) To contextualize our study, we provided participants at the beginning of the questionnaire with a brief description of our hypothetical fitness app aimed at promoting physical activity. Thereafter, we presented them with

questions on the *perceived persuasiveness* of behavior model design and the SCT determinants of behavior change. This study builds on our prior studies on SCT model of physical activity [17] and using persuasive technology, such as social influence [18–21], to promote engagement in physical activity.

3.3 Research Hypotheses

Based on theories and empirical findings in the extant literature, we formulated a number of hypotheses. We based our first three hypotheses on the SCT triad of reciprocal determinism, which states that personal factors, environmental factors and the behavior itself interact with one another to shape the behaviors of individuals. The triad is shown in Figure 2. The environmental factors comprise social influence (e.g., friends and family) and information systems (e.g., fitness app). The personal factors include cognitive factors such as *self-efficacy, self-regulation* and *outcome expectation*. Finally, the user behavioral factors include adoption or usage of a system and performance of the target behavior. The focus of our study is on the relationship between the personal factors and the environmental factors. Specifically, we are interested in the influence of a persuasive system on the three social cognitive factors. For example, Sheeshka [25] found that *social modeling*, in the context of healthy eating, significantly influences *outcome expectation* (directly) and *self-efficacy* (indirectly). Therefore, in the context of exercise behavior modeling in fitness apps, we hypothesize that the *persuasiveness* of the behavior models will significantly influence *outcome expectation* and *self-efficacy*. These hypotheses, represented in Figure 3, are formally stated as follows:

> H1: The *perceived persuasiveness* of behavior model design will significantly influence the *self-efficacy* belief of the user.

> H2: The *perceived persuasiveness* of behavior model design will significantly influence the *self-regulation* belief of the user.

Given that in the SCT model, as found in previous study [2], *self-efficacy* and *outcome expectation* significantly influences *self-regulation*, by extension, we hypothesize that:

> H3: The *perceived persuasiveness* of behavior model design will significantly influence the *outcome expectation* of the user.

Moreover, given that prior research has found that persuasive strategies will be more effective if personalized to the user, we hypothesize, in the context of behavior modeling, as follows:

> H4: The influence of *perceived persuasiveness* on *self-efficacy* will be stronger when the genders of the behavior model and the observer are the same than when they are different.

> H5: The influence of *perceived persuasiveness* on *self-regulation* will be stronger when the genders of the behavior model and the observer are the same than when they are different.

> H6: The influence of *perceived persuasiveness* on *outcome expectation* will be stronger when the genders of the behavior model and the observer are the same than when they are different.

Finally, given the paucity of research on the current topic, we used exploratory approach to uncover the SCT factor(s) on which *perceived persuasiveness* has the strongest or weakest effect.

3.4 Measurement Instruments

In the online survey, we presented in a randomized fashion one of the behavior models shown in Figure 1 to each participant and requested him or her to respond to questions on *persuasiveness* and SCT determinants of behavior change. The respective questions in the SCT-construct and persuasiveness scales are shown in Table 2 together with the ranges of the respective scales.

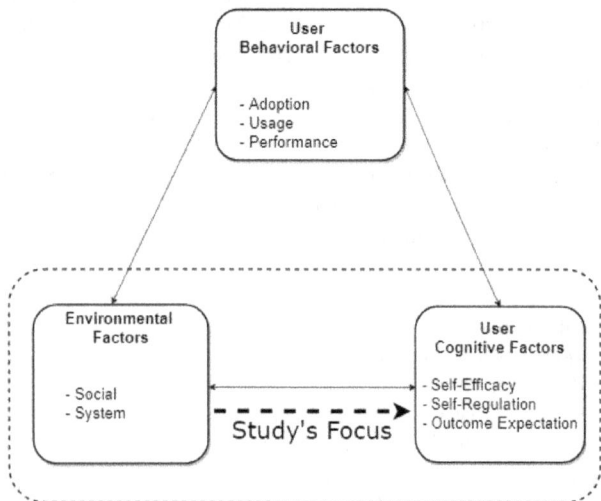

Figure 2: SCT's reciprocal determinism (adapted from [8])

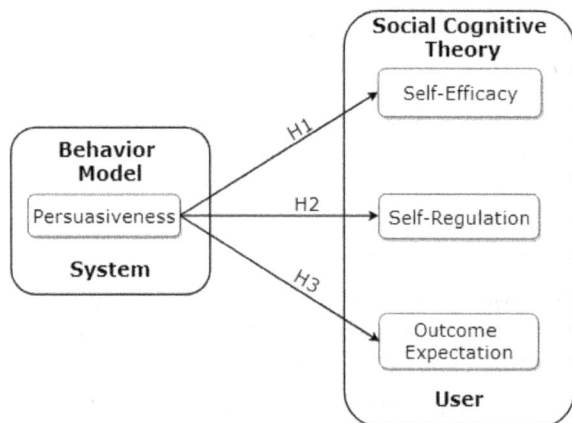

Figure 3: Research model based on the unidirectional environmental determinism shown in Figure 2 [7]

3.5 Participants

The Behavioral Research Ethics Board of the first authors' university approved the survey. Thereafter, it was posted on Amazon Mechanical Turk to recruit participants in North America (our target audience). Each participant was compensated with $0.6 in appreciation of his or her time. A total of 673 participants took part in the study. Upon cleaning, 669 were left for data analysis. Table

3 shows participants' demographics. Both gender groups are almost balanced: females (48.9%) and males (51.1%).

4 RESULT

In this section, we present our results, which include the measurement models and structural models at the global and subgroup levels, and a brief analysis of the results. Our SEM analysis was carried out using the partial least square path modeling ("plspm") package in R programming language [23].

Table 2: Study's constructs and indicators [2, 3]

Criterion	Overall Question and Items
Persuasiveness [11] [1 – Strongly Disagree to 7 – Strongly Agree]	Assume the Homex App works as described at the beginning of the survey and seen in the previous video. Please answer the following general questions about yourself and regarding the app. 1) The app would influence me. 2) The app would be convincing. 3) The app would be personally relevant for me. 4) The app would make me reconsider my physical activity habits.
Self-Efficacy [24] [0 – Not Confident to 100 - Confident]	How confident are you that you can complete at home the proposed weekly number of push-ups (entered previously) for the next 3 months. (1) Even when you have worries and problems? (2) Even if you feel depressed? (3) Even when you feel tense? (4) Even when you are tired? (5) Even when you are busy?
Outcome Expectation [29] [1 – Strongly Disagree to 5 – Strongly Agree]	The [name of exercise] will... (1) Improve my ability to perform daily activities. (2) Improve my overall body functioning. (3) Strengthen my bones. (4) Increase my muscle strength. (5) Improve the functioning of my cardiovascular system. (6) Improve my social standing. (7) Make me more at ease with people. (8) Increase my acceptance by others.
Self-Regulation [22] [1 – Strongly Disagree to 5 – Strongly Agree]	To achieve my proposed weekly average number of push-ups.... (1) I will set a goal. (2) I will develop a series of steps to reach my weekly goal. (3) I will keep track of my progress in meeting my goal. (4) I will endeavor to achieve the set goal for myself. (5) I will make goal public by telling others about it.

222

Table 3: Demographics of participants (n = 669)

Criterion	Breakdown [(Female, male) = (327, 342)]
Age	18-24 (56, 70); 25-34 (139, 157); 35-34 (79, 76); 45-54 (38, 22); 54+ (15, 17)
Education	Technical/Trade School (47, 39); High School (66, 70); BSc (154, 162); MSc (42, 54); PhD (9, 6); Others (9, 11)
Country	Canada (104, 110); United States (194, 184); Others (26, 51)
Years on the Internet	0-3 (2, 2); 4-6 (18, 13); 7-9 (20, 40); 10+ (287, 287)

4.1 Measurement Models

Prior to analyzing our structural equation models (SEMs), we evaluated the required criteria for analyzing SEM models. They include indicator reliability, internal consistency reliability, convergent validity and discriminant validity of the constructs in our respective measurement models. We provide the result of the evaluation of each of the criteria. ***Indicator Reliability:*** All the indicators in the measurement models had an outer loading greater than 0.7, except for two items in *outcome expectation* and one item in *self-regulation*. Item 5 ("*I will make goal public by telling others about it*") in *self-regulation*, which loading was less than 0.5, was dropped from the respective models. However, items 3 and 4 in *outcome expectation* (see Table 2), which loading was greater than 0.6, were retained for the sake of content validity [13]. ***Internal Consistency Reliability:*** This criterion for each construct was evaluated using the composite reliability criterion (DG.rho), which was greater than 0.7. ***Convergent Validity:*** This criterion for each construct was evaluated using the Average Variance Extracted, which was greater than 0.5. ***Discriminant Validity:*** It was evaluated using the crossloading measure. Our result showed that no indicator loaded higher on any other construct than the one it actually measured.

4.2 Structural Models

In this paper, we are interested in understanding the *perceived persuasiveness* of behavior model designs and the gender-based tailoring on the user. Thus, we began our SEM analysis by building the global model for the general population. Secondly, we built a personalized subgroup path models based on the gender of the performer and observer of the behavior model and compared them to the non-personalized subgroup path models.

4.3 Global model

Figure 4 shows the global model for the general population. The model is characterized by path coefficients (β's) and coefficients of determination (R^2's). β captures the strength of the relationship between two constructs, while R^2 indicates the amount of variance of a given SCT construct explained by *persuasiveness*. In the global model, *persuasiveness* has the strongest effect on *self-regulation* ($\beta = 0.42$, p < 0.001) and *outcome expectation* ($\beta = 0.41$, p <

0.001) and the weakest effect on *self-efficacy* ($\beta = 0.13$, p < 0.01). Thus, *persuasiveness* explains more variance of *self-regulation* and *outcome expectation* ($R^2 = 17\%$) than of *self-efficacy* ($R^2 = 0.02\%$).

4.4 Gender-based Personalized Submodels

To uncover, how gender of the behavior model affects the relationships between *persuasiveness* and the SCT factors, we built two pairs of subgroup models based on the personalization and non-personalization of the behavior models to each gender of observers. The submodels are based on the following subgroups:

1. *Males* observing *male* behavior models (MM)
2. *Males* observing *female* behavior models (MF)
3. *Females* observing *female* behavior models (FF)
4. *Females* observing *male* behavior models (FM)

Figure 5 shows the respective models for the various subgroups enumerated above. The y-axis represents the gender of the observer, while the x-axis represents the gender of the behavior model. Thus, the submodels in the first and fourth quadrants represent two female groups of observers' evaluation of male and female behavior models, respectively. Similarly, the submodels in the second and third quadrants represent two male groups of observers' evaluation of the male and female behavior models, respectively. In the four submodels, we find that the influence of the *persuasiveness* of the behavior models on *self-regulation* and *outcome expectation* is significant at p < 0.001, irrespective of the gender of the behavior model and/or observer. The path coefficients range from 0.31 to 0.53. Based on Chin's guideline [9], for a path coefficient to be considered relevant, it should be equal to or greater than 0.2. Thus, overall, irrespective of the gender of the behavior model and/or the gender of the observer, the behavior model design has a significant effect on users' *outcome expectations* and *self-regulation* beliefs. However, the relationship between *persuasiveness* and *self-efficacy* is only significant for female observers of female behavior models ($\beta = 0.32$, p < 0.001).

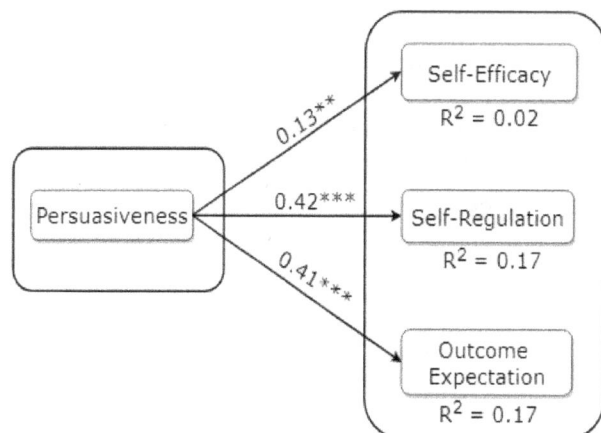

Figure 4: Global model showing the influence of behavior models' persuasiveness on SCT determinants of behavior

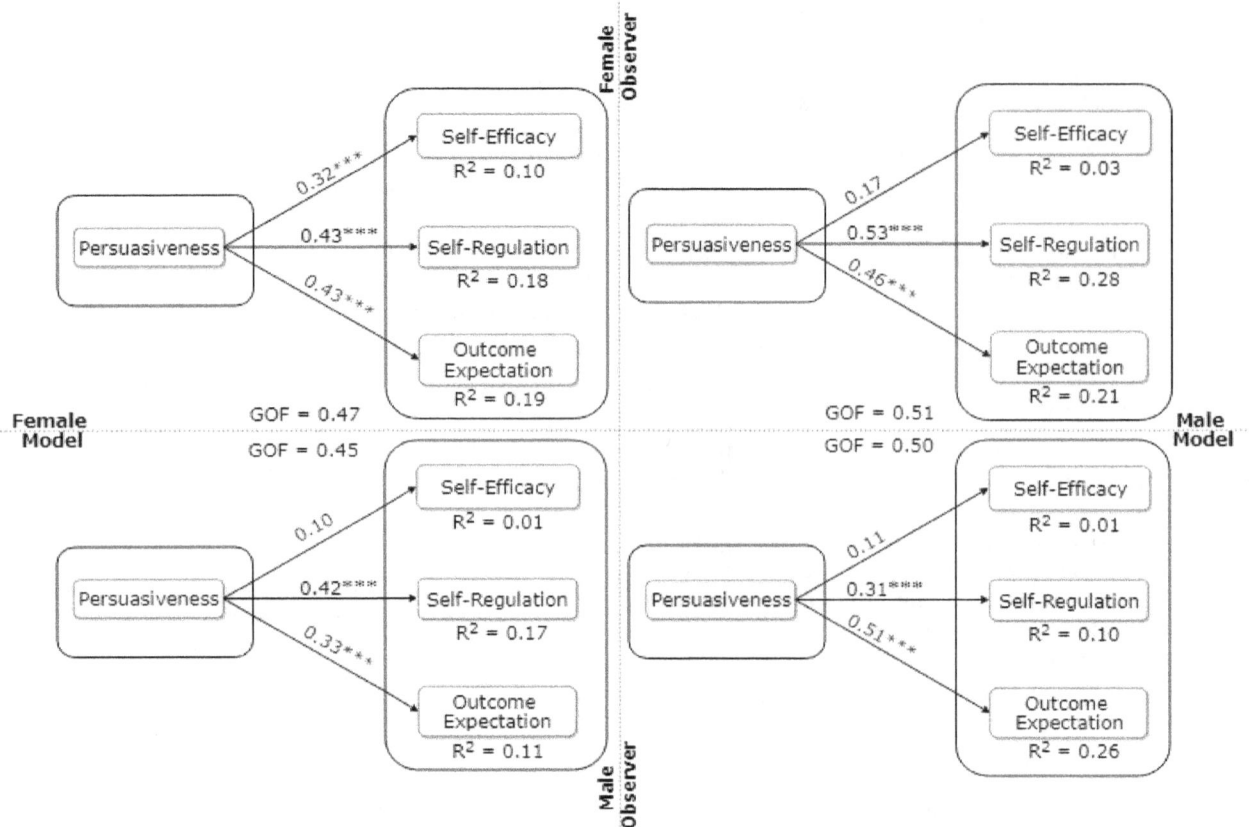

Figure 5: Subgroup models for different male and female groups observing males and females behavior models

Moreover, Table 4 shows the multigroup analysis (MGA) for the two pairs of submodels (MM vs. FM and FF vs. MF) shown in Figure 5. The results show that there is a significant difference (at $p < 0.05$) between the MM and FM subgroups in the relationship between *persuasiveness* and *self-regulation*. The relationship is stronger for the female group ($\beta = 0.53$, $p < 0.001$) than the male group ($\beta = 0.31$, $p < 0.001$) that observed the male behavior models. Finally, there is a near-significant difference (at $p = 0.05$) between the FF and MF subgroups in the relationship between *persuasiveness* and *self-efficacy*. The relationship is stronger for the female group ($\beta = 0.32$, $p < 0.001$) than the male group ($\beta = 0.11$, $p = $ n.s) that observed the female behavior models.

5 DISCUSSION

We have presented path models showing the potential effectiveness of behavior modeling as a persuasive strategy for motivating behavior change. Overall, our SEM analysis reveals that behavior modeling has a significant positive effect on users. Our findings are summarized in Table 5. Overall, the *perceived persuasiveness* of the behavior models has significant effects on all three SCT constructs, with the effect on *self-regulation* and *outcome expectation* being stronger than the effect on *self-efficacy*. However, the effect on females' *self-efficacy* is stronger when the behavior models are tailored to their gender.

Table 4: Multigroup analysis for personalized and non-personalized subgroups of observers of behavior models

Criterion	R^2-Value		β-Value		P-Value
MM vs. FM (ML = 352, FM = 317)					
	MM	FM	MM	FM	P-Value
PERS→SE	.01	.03	.11	.17	n.s
PERS→SR	.10	.28	.31	.53	**0.024**
PERS→OE	.26	.21	.51	.46	n.s
FF vs. MF (WM = 333, BM = 336)					
	FF	MF	FF	MF	P-Value
PERS→SE	.10	.01	.32	.10	**0.050**
PERS→SR	.18	.17	.43	.42	n.s
PERS→OE	.19	.11	.43	.33	n.s

PERS = Persuasiveness, SE = Self-Efficacy, SR = Self-Regulation, OE = Outcome Expectation; MM = Males observing male behavior models, MF = Males observing female behavior models, FF = Females observing female behavior models, FM = Females observing male behavior models

5.1 Persuasive Effect of Behavior Model

In the following subsections, in the light of our hypotheses, we discuss the persuasive and personalization effects of the behavior model design on the SCT determinants of behavior change.

5.1.1 Persuasive Effect of Behavior Model on Self-Efficacy. Our first hypothesis (H1) states that the *persuasiveness* of the behavior model design will have a significant effect on the *self-efficacy* of users. Self-efficacy is the strongest (proximal) determinant of behavior change in the SCT model. Overall, there is evidence that behavior model has the potential of influencing the self-efficacy beliefs of users. In the global model, we saw that the relationship between *persuasiveness* and *self-efficacy* is significant, though it is not as strong as the other relationships. Some of participants' comments confirm this finding; they include the following:

1. *"Having this app do exercise with you makes me feel more inclined to exercise" [P657, Push-Up].*
2. *"Watching this gives me the impression to do this" [P574, Push-Up].*
3. *"It seems like a friendly design that will not intimidate people by awing them, but make them feel capable of working with it" [P05, Squat].*

Table 5: Summary of the validation of study's hypotheses

H	Hypothesis	All	M	F
1	The *persuasiveness* of behavior model design will significantly influence the *self-efficacy* belief of the user.	✓	×	✓
2	The *persuasiveness* of behavior model design will significantly influence the *self-regulation* belief of the user.	✓	✓	✓
3	The *persuasiveness* of behavior model design will significantly influence the *outcome expectation* of the user.	✓	✓	✓
4	The influence of *persuasiveness* on *self-efficacy* will be stronger when the genders of the behavior model and the observer are the same than when they are different.	NA	×	✓
5	The influence of *persuasiveness* on *self-regulation* will be stronger when the genders of the behavior model and the observer are the same than when they are different.	NA	×*	×*
6	The influence of *persuasiveness* on *outcome expectation* will be stronger when the genders of the behavior model and the observer are the same than when they are different.	NA	✓*	×

NA = Not Applicable; ✓ = True; × = False, gender does not matter;
✓* = True but difference not significant at p<0.05; M = Male, F = Female;
×* = False, the reverse is the case, but difference not significant at p<0.05.

Moreover, in the submodels in Figure 5, there is evidence that behavior modeling will be more effective if they are tailored, in our case, to the gender of the user. In particular, for the females, we see that the persuasive effect of the behavior models on *self-efficacy* is stronger when females observe female behavior models ($\beta = 0.32$, $p < 0.001$) than when they observe male behavior models ($\beta = 0.17$, p = n.s). Similarly, the persuasive effect of the behavior models on *self-efficacy* is stronger when females observe female behavior models ($\beta = 0.32$, $p < 0.001$) than when males observe female behavior models ($\beta = 0.10$, p = n.s). In particular, the MGA for FF vs. MF shows that the difference between both groups is marginally significant ($p = 0.05$). Though not completely significant, the marginal p-value is an indication that **behavior models will be more effective if they are personalized to the user based on gender, especially for the females.** Specifically, in the personalized submodel (FF), we see that *persuasiveness* is able to account for 10% of the variance of *self-efficacy* beliefs. However, in the non-personalized submodels (FM and MF), the effect of *persuasiveness* on *self-efficacy* is not significant, with *persuasiveness* only being able to account for 3% and 1%, respectively, of the variance of *self-efficacy*. Therefore, we can conclude that our fourth hypothesis (H4), with respect to females observing female behavior models, is supported. This means that, **for females, the higher the perceived persuasiveness of a personalized behavior model design, the higher they believe in their ability to engage in the target exercise behavior.** This finding underscores **the need to tailor behavior models, especially to suit the gender of female users, to increase their self-efficacy to perform the target behavior.** However, for male observers, the submodels show that neither the *persuasiveness* nor *personalization* of the behavior models significantly affects males' *self-efficacy*. This suggests that, for the male observers, there are other factors (e.g., race, exercise-type, etc.), which we did not captured in the model, that may account for the variance of *self-efficacy*.

5.1.2 Perceived Persuasive Effect of Behavior Model on Self-Regulation. Our second hypothesis (H2) states that the *persuasiveness* of the behavior model design will have a significant effect on the *self-regulation* of users. In the submodels in Figure 5, the influence of *persuasiveness* on *self-regulation* seems to be stronger when each gender subgroup observes a behavior model of the opposite gender. For females, the effect is stronger when they observe male behavior models ($\beta = 0.53$, $p < 0.001$) than when they observe female behavior models ($\beta = 0.43$, $p < 0.001$). Similarly, for males, the effect is stronger when they observe female behavior models ($\beta = 0.42$, $p < 0.001$) than when they observe male behavior models ($\beta = 0.31$, $p < 0.001$). However, our MGA (not shown in Table 4) reveals that these differences between the MM and MF subgroups and between the FF and FM groups are not statistically significant at $p < 0.05$. This means that our fifth hypothesis shown in Table 5 is not validated. Therefore, we can conclude that, irrespective of the gender of the behavior model each gender subgroup of observers evaluated, the *persuasiveness* of the behavior model design has a significant effect on users' *self-regulation* beliefs. This means that **the higher the perceived persuasiveness of a behavior model design, the higher users believe in their ability to regulate themselves to engage in the target exercise behavior.** However, there may be a need for further investigation of the possibility of a stronger persuasive effect on *self-regulation* beliefs when a behavior model is observed by the opposite gender. We say this because our SEM results hint at this possibility, as shown in the submodels in Figure 5 and confirmed by the MGA in Table 4. In particular, the relationship between *persuasiveness* and *self-regulation* (β = 0.53, p < 0.001) in the FM submodel is significantly stronger (p < 0.05) than that in the MM submodel (β = 0.31, p < 0.001). Meanwhile, an example of participants' comments that indicate a behavior-modeling app has the potential of influencing users' *self-regulation* is "*I am motivated to set and achieve a goal. I want to look better and feel good about myself*" [P8, Squat].

5.1.3 Perceived Persuasive Effect of Behavior Model on Outcome Expectation. Our third hypothesis (H3) states that the persuasiveness of the behavior model design will have a significant effect on the *outcome expectation* of users. In the submodels in Figure 5, the influence of *persuasiveness* on *outcome expectation* is stronger when the male behavior models (β = 0.51, p < 0.001) are evaluated by male observers than when evaluated by female observers (β = 0.46, p < 0.001). However, the MGA shows that this difference between both gender groups of observers (MM and FM) with respect to the relationship between *persuasiveness* and *outcome expectation* is not statistically significant at p < 0.05. This means that our sixth hypothesis shown in Table 5 is not supported. Therefore, we can conclude that, irrespective of the gender of the behavior model, each gender group of observers evaluated, the *perceived persuasiveness* of the behavior model design has a significant effect on users' *outcome expectations*. This means that **the higher the perceived persuasiveness of a behavior model design, the higher the (positive) outcome expectations of users with respect to their engagement in the target exercise behavior.** An example of participants' comments to this effect is, "*Well, I think this type of exercise has got to improve my overall fitness and health level. It get the blood flowing, helps the joints and bones and muscles*" [P398, Squat]. However, **it is more likely that males will have higher outcome expectations of their workouts when behavior models of the same gender serve as their role model or virtual coach.** Specifically, we found that the relationship between *persuasiveness* and *outcome expectation* is stronger when males observed male behavior models (β = 0.51, p < 0.001) than when they observe female behavior models (β = 0.33, p < 0.001). However, this needs further investigation in future work as, currently, we found no significant difference between the male group that evaluated the male behavior models and the male group that evaluated the female behavior models.

5.2 Summary and Future Work

Regarding our research questions, we found that, overall, the persuasive effect of behavior modeling on the three SCT factors we investigated is significant. However, the *persuasiveness* of the behavior models seems to influence females and males differently. For example, the effect of the *persuasiveness* of the behavior model design appears to be stronger on males' *outcome expectation*, especially when the behavior model is personalized. However, this finding requires further investigation as there is no significant difference between the two male groups that evaluated the behavior models of opposite genders. With respect to the effect of *persuasiveness* on *self-efficacy*, one of the strongest proximal determinants of behavior, it seems that personalization with respect to the gender of the behavior model amplifies this effect, but only for

females, by increasing their *self-efficacy*. On the other hand, male personalization of the behavior models makes no difference on their persuasive effect on males' *self-efficacy*. This suggests that there may be a need to leverage other persuasive strategies to increase the *self-efficacy* of males and enhance that of females even further. We make this recommendation because, of all the SCT determinants of exercise behavior, *self-efficacy* is the least affected by the *persuasiveness* of the behavior models, especially in the global model and with respect to male observers. Thus, there may be a need to leverage other persuasive strategies than behavior models to enhance the *self-efficacy* of males.

One possible strategy to increase the *self-efficacy* of users in general other than vicarious modeling is *social support*—an environmental factor captured in the SCT triad of reciprocal determinism presented in Figure 2. Prior research [2, 17] on SCT has shown that *social support* is a significant determinant of *self-efficacy* in the context of exercise behavior. Thus, we look forward to augmenting our model with *social support* as a persuasive strategy to investigate whether it can enhance the *self-efficacy* of users. Other sources of *self-efficacy* put forward by Bandura [4], which we may not necessarily fall into the realm of persuasive technology strategies, include mastery experience, verbal persuasion and emotional/physiological states. Mastery experience is regarded as the primary source of *self-efficacy*. Theory holds that people who have mastered a behavior by successfully performing it in the past tend to have a stronger belief in their ability to perform it in the future. Verbal persuasion is related to *social support* and *suggestion* strategies in persuasive technology domain [16]. It entails words of encouragement and suggestions from influential people in one's life such as coaches, personal trainer, family members, etc. This could have a positive influence on the individuals' belief in their ability to engage in the target behavior. Finally, emotional/physiological state has to do with the mental state of individuals, which includes their health condition. This can either enhance or weaken the belief in their ability to engage in a given behavior such as exercise.

In closing, we opine that, in a persuasive application, there might be a need to combine various persuasive strategies targeted at increasing different determinants of behavior, with each strategy optimized to strongly influence a particular SCT determinant. For example, in this paper, we show that, irrespective of personalization, a persuasive application featuring behavior models has the potential to increase the *outcome expectation* and *self-regulation* of users more than it will increase *self-efficacy*. Thus, we recommend that persuasive systems designed to promote exercise behavior change should support multiple persuasive strategies, including those aimed at enhancing *self-efficacy* in particular (e.g., *social support*). Hence, in future work, we intend to investigate the inclusion of *social support* in our SEM model. Specifically, we hope to investigate the relative strength of influence of *social support* (friends and family) and *system support* (behavior models) on the three SCT factors we examined in this paper. It will be interesting to know which of these persuasive strategies has a stronger effect on the three SCT factors, especially *self-efficacy*, which is the least influenced by the behavior model design.

5.3 Contributions

In this paper, we presented a path model of the perceived effectiveness of behavior modeling as a persuasive strategy. We also investigated the overall effect of personalization based on gender. Our main contribution to knowledge, in the context of behavior modeling in the physical activity domain, is that we show that behavior modeling in fitness apps: (1) can be effective in motivating behavior change; and (2) will be more effective if personalized to suit the female gender. Our work, in the context of behavior modeling, is one of the first to show how the *persuasiveness* of behavior model design significantly influences SCT factors such as *outcome expectation* and *self-regulation* of both genders and the *self-efficacy* of females, in particular, if personalized.

5.4 Limitations

The main limitation of our study is that our findings are based on self-report questionnaire and prototyped behavior models. Thus, our findings may not generalize to an actual fitness app featuring behavior models. Therefore, in future research efforts, we intend to verify our findings in an actual system. A second limitation of our study is that most subjects are from North America. This may threaten the generalizability of our findings to other populations. Similarly, we intend to verify the generalizability of our findings with other demographics in our future work.

6 CONCLUSION

We have presented a path model showing the perceived persuasive effect of behavior model design on SCT determinants of behavior change in the exercise domain. Overall, our SEM analysis shows that the *perceived persuasiveness* of behavior model design influences the three SCT factors we investigated. However, the influence of *perceived persuasiveness* is stronger on *self-regulation* and *outcome expectation* than on *self-efficacy*. With respect to personalization, our subgroup models reveal that the influence of the behavior models on females' *self-efficacy* is stronger when they observed female behavior models than when they observed male behavior models. Similarly, the influence of the behavior models on males' *outcome expectation* is stronger when they observed male behavior models than when they observed female behavior models. However, the difference between both male groups is not significant. In future work, we hope to investigate the effect of other persuasive strategies on the three SCT factors. It will be interesting to see how the influence of such strategies (e.g., *social support*) on the three SCT factors (e.g., *self-efficacy*) compares with the influence of behavior models in the SEM model.

REFERENCES

[1]   Abraham, C. and Michie, S. 2008. A taxonomy of behavior change techniques used in interventions. *Health psychology: official journal of the Division of Health Psychology, American Psychological Association.* 27, 3 (2008), 379–87.

[2]   Anderson-Bill, E.S. et al. 2011. Social cognitive determinants of nutrition and physical activity among web-health users enrolling in an online intervention: the influence of social support, self-efficacy, outcome expectations, and self-regulation.

Journal of medical Internet research. 13, 1 (2011).

[3]   Bandura, A. 1997. *Self-efficacy: the exercise of control.* New York: W H. Freeman.

[4]   Bandura, A. 1977. Self-efficacy: Toward a unifying theory of behavioral change. *Psychological Review.* 84, 191–215 (1977).

[5]   Bandura, A. 1986. *Social foundations of thought and action: A social cognitive theory.* Prentice-Hall, Inc.

[6]   Bandura, A. 1971. Social learning theory. *Stanford University.* (1971), 1–46.

[7]   Bandura, A. 1978. The self system in reciprocal determinism. *American Psychologist.* 33, 4 (1978), 344–358.

[8]   Carillo, K.D. 2010. Social Cognitive Theory in IS Research – Literature Review, Criticism, and Research Agenda. *Information Systems, Technology and Management* (2010), 20–31.

[9]   Chin, W.W. 1998. Issues and Opinion on Structural Equation Modeling. *MIS Quarterly.* 22, March (1998), vii–xvi.

[10] Conroy, D.E. et al. 2014. Behavior change techniques in top-ranked mobile apps for physical activity. *American Journal of Preventive Medicine.* 46, 6 (2014), 649–652.

[11] Drozd, F. et al. 2012. Exploring perceived persuasiveness of a behavior change support system: A structural model. *Lecture Notes in Computer Science (including subseries Lecture Notes in Artificial Intelligence and Lecture Notes in Bioinformatics).* 7284 LNCS, (2012), 157–168.

[12] Fogg, B.J. 2003. *Persuasive Technology: Using Computers to Change What We Think and Do.* Morgan Kaufmann.

[13] Hair, J.F. et al. 2014. *A Primer on Partial Least Squares Structural Equation Modeling (PLS-SEM).* Sage Publications, Inc, Washington DC.

[14] Keller, C. et al. 1999. Predictive ability of social cognitive theory in exercise research: an integrated literature review. *The Online Journal of Knowledge Synthesis for Nursing.* 6, (1999), 2.

[15] Locke, E. a and Latham, G.P. 2002. Building a practically useful theory of goal setting and task motivation: A 35-year odyssey. *The American Psychologist.* 57, 9 (2002), 705–717.

[16] Oinas-kukkonen, H. and Harjumaa, M. 2009. Persuasive Systems Design Key Issues, Process Model, and System Features. *Communications of the Association for Information Systems.* 24, 28 (2009), 485–500.

[17] Oyibo, K. 2016. Designing Culture-based Persuasive Technology to Promote Physical Activity among University Students. *24th Conference on User Modeling, Adaptation and Personalization (UMAP 2016)* (Halifax, Canada, 2016), 321–324.

[18] Oyibo, K. et al. 2017. Investigation of the Persuasiveness of Social Influence in Persuasive Technology and the Effect of Age and Gender. *International Workshop on Persuasive Technology* (Amsterdam, 2017).

[19] Oyibo, K. et al. 2017. Investigation of the Social Predictors of Competitive Behavior and the Moderating Effect of Culture. *Workshop on User Modeling, Adaptation and Personalization (UMAP 2017)* (2017).

[20] Oyibo, K. et al. 2017. The influence of culture in the effect of age and gender on social influence in persuasive technology. *UMAP 2017 - Adjunct Publication of the 25th Conference on User Modeling, Adaptation and Personalization* (2017).

[21] Oyibo, K. and Vassileva, J. 2017. Investigation of social predictors of competitive behavior in persuasive technology. *International Conference on Persuasive Technology* (Amsterdam, 2017), 279–291.

[22] Rovniak, L. et al. 2002. Social cognitive determinants of physical activity in young adults: a prospective structural equation analysis. *Ann Behav Med.* 24, 2 (2002), 149–156.

[23] Sanchez, G. 2013. PLS Path Modeling with R. *Berkley: Trowchez Editions.* (2013).

[24] Schwarzer, R. and Luszczynska, A. 2007. Perceived Self-Efficacy. *Health Behavior Constructs: Theory, Measurement, and Research.* (2007), 1–33.

[25] Sheeshka, J.D. et al. 1993. Social cognitive theory as a framework to explain intentions to practice healthy eating behaviors.

Journal of Applied Social Psychology. 23, (1993), 1547–1573.

[26]   Social Cognitive Theory: *https://www.ruralhealthinfo.org/community-health/health-promotion/2/theories-and-models/social-cognitive.* Accessed: 2018-02-14.

[27]   Thompson, W.R. 2015. Worldwide survey of fitness trends for 2016. *ACSM s Health & Fitness Journal.* 19, 6 (2015), 9–18.

[28]   Thompson, W.R. 2016. Worldwide survey of fitness trends for 2017. *ACSM's Health and Fitness Journal.* 20, 6 (2016), 8–17.

[29]   Wójcicki, T.R. et al. 2009. Assessing outcome expectations in older adults: the multidimensional outcome expectations for exercise scale. *J of Gerontol. Ser B, Psychol Sci & Soc Sci.* 64, 1 (2009), 33–40.

[30]   Yoganathan, D. and Kajanan, S. 2015. Designing Fitness Apps Using Persuasive Technology: A Text Mining Approach. *PACIS* (2015), 40.

[31]   Young, Myles; Plotnikoff, Ronald; Collins, Clare; Callister, Robin; Morgan, P. 2014. Social Cognitive Theory and Physical Activity: A Systematic Review and Meta-analysis. *Obesity Reviews.* (2014), 1–40.

Susceptibility to Persuasive Strategies:
A Comparative Analysis of Nigerians vs. Canadians

Kiemute Oyibo
University of Saskatchewan
S7N 5C9, Saskatoon, Canada
kiemute.oyibo@usask.ca

Ifeoma Adaji
University of Saskatchewan
S7N 5C9, Saskatoon, Canada
Ifeoma.adaji@usask.ca

Rita Orji
Dalhousie University
B3H 4R2, Halifax, Canada
rita.orji@dal.ca

Babatunde Olabenjo
University of Saskatchewan
S7N 5C9, Saskatoon, Canada
b.olabenjo@usask.ca

Julita Vassileva
University of Saskatchewan
S7N 5C9, Saskatoon, Canada
jiv@cs.usask.ca

ABSTRACT

Personalizing persuasive technologies (PTs) is one of the hall-marks of a successful PT intervention. However, there is a lack of understanding of how Africans and North Americans differ or are similar in the susceptibility to persuasive strategies. To bridge this gap, we conducted a cross-cultural study among 284 subjects to investigate the moderating effect of culture on the susceptibility of users to Cialdini's principles of persuasion. Specifically, using Nigeria and Canada as a case study, we investigated how both groups vary in their levels of susceptibility to Authority, Commitment, Consensus, Liking, Reciprocity and Scarcity. The results of our analysis show that Nigerians are more susceptible to Authority and Scarcity than Canadians, while Canadians are more susceptible to Reciprocity, Liking and Consensus than Nigerians. However, both groups do not differ with respect to Commitment (the most persuasive strategy). Finally, we discussed our findings and mapped the most persuasive Cialdini's principles in each group to implementable persuasive strategies in the PT domain.

KEYWORDS

Persuasive Strategies; Cialdini; Personalization; Susceptibility; Cultural Difference; Individualist; Collectivist; Nigeria; Canada

ACM Reference format:
K. Oyibo, I. Adaji, R. Orji, B. Olabenjo, and J. Vassileva. 2018. Susceptibility to Persuasive Strategies: A Comparative Analysis of Nigerians vs. Canadians. In *Proceedings of ACM UMAP conference, Singapore, July 2018 (UMAP'18), 10 pages.* DOI: 10.1145/3209219.3209239

1 INTRODUCTION

Persuasive technologies (PTs) are interactive systems that are intentionally designed to bring about behavior change through system-based and/or social influence [9]. In recent years, the use of PTs have gained traction in many fields of human endeavors, including health, commerce, energy conservation, etc. Moreover, research [21] has shown that persuasive applications aimed at behavior change will be more effective if they are personalized to user characteristics. However, in PT research, there are limited studies that have investigated the influence of culture on the susceptibility of individuals to various persuasive strategies [15]. More specifically, the African continent has been practically left behind [24] in PT research despite the fact that it is faced with some of the world's most pressing social problems (e.g., physical inactivity [17], obesity [20], alcohol misuse [3], unsafe sex [3], etc.), which require PTs to motivate behavior change (e.g., [26]). So far, most of the prior studies in PT research have been conducted among Western and Asian populations. For example, in a systematic review of health PTs, among the 85 papers reviewed by Orji and Moffatt [24], 38% of the actual studies were conducted in the United States, 19% in the Netherlands, 6% in Taiwan, and 5% each in Finland and Japan. The rest of the reviewed studies were conducted in non-African countries. Moreover, studies comparing the Western and African populations in terms of their responsiveness to Cialdini's principles of persuasion are scarce.

To bridge this gap, we carried out a cross-cultural study among Nigerians (n = 88) and Canadians (n = 196) to investigate the differences and similarities in their responsiveness to Cialdini's six persuasive strategies: Authority, Commitment, Consensus, Liking, Reciprocity and Scarcity. These persuasive strategies are currently being applied in adaptive PTs [13] to motivate behavior change. Knowing the differences between both cultural groups will help designers of PTs to tailor behavior change applications to users from the respective countries and cultures. We based our investigation on three measures: rating of persuasive constructs, ranking of proxy items and participants' comments.

The results of our analysis show that both cultures are equally responsive to Commitment (the most persuasive strategy). However, they differ in their responsiveness to the other strategies. On one hand, Canadians are more responsive to Reciprocity, Liking and Consensus than Nigerians. On the other hand,

Nigerians are more responsive to Authority and Scarcity[1] than Canadians. Finally, we provided a number of design guidelines to enable designers to tailor persuasive systems to the respective cultures.

The rest of this paper is organized as follows. Section 2 focuses on background and related work. Section 3 dwells on the methodology. Section 4 focuses on the result. Section 5 focuses on the discussion. Finally, Section 6 focuses on the conclusion.

2 BACKGROUND AND RELATED WORK
This section provides a background and a review of related work on Cialdini's principles of persuasion and culture.

2.1 Cialdini's Persuasive Strategies
Cialdini's [4, 5] principles of persuasion are recognized as universal principles, traditionally employed in the domain of marketing and advertising [6]. We provide an overview of all six principles.

2.1.1 Authority. The Authority principle states that people are more likely to obey those in positions of authority than those who are not. In other words, people are more likely to be persuaded by authority figures, even though their authority position is not real.

2.1.2 Commitment. The Commitment principle states that people are more likely to do something if they commit to it, e.g., by giving their word verbally or in a written form. Specifically, it holds that people tend to keep their commitment and promise in order to maintain and preserve their self-image, even when the original motivation for keeping to their commitment is removed.

2.1.3 Consensus. The Consensus principle states that people tend to look up to other people around them, especially when they are uncertain about a given behavior, before taking a certain course of action.

2.1.4 Liking. The Liking principle states that people are more likely inclined to grant the request of those they like than those they do not like. In other words, people are more likely to perform a behavior if the request to do so comes from someone or a persuasive system they like (i.e., find attractive).

2.1.5 Reciprocity. The Reciprocity principle states that people are naturally bound to return favors done to them with another. In other words, the chances of people engaging in a certain behavior requested by another are higher when that other first does them a favor before making his/her own request.

2.1.6 Scarcity. The Scarcity principles states that people are more likely to value things they consider scarce or rare. In other words, the higher people perceive a certain commodity, product or service to be uncommon, the more they want or demand it.

2.2 Culture
Culture refers to a collective way of life (thinking, feeling, acting, etc.) upon which the beliefs, language, food, dressing, etc., of a group of people are based. Thus, it is defined as "*the collective programming of the mind distinguishing the members of one group or category of people from others*" (p. 6) [11]. In PT research (e.g., [23, 26, 29]), the framework of *individualism vs. collectivism*, which accounts "*for most of the variance in global differences*" (p. 74) [15], is one of the most commonly used cultural dimensions.

2.2.1 Individualist Culture. An individualist culture is one in which people focus on their personal interests and goals than those of their in-group. Thus, they care more about themselves (and their immediate family at the very most) than the larger in-group. Examples of individualist cultures include Western countries such as Britain, United States, Germany, etc. [12]. In our study, the Canadian group falls under the individualist culture.

2.2.2 Collectivist Culture. A collectivist culture is one in which people are more concerned about the interests and goals of the in-group they belong to than their personal interests and goals. Thus, they care about the welfare of the larger in-group than that of their individual selves. Examples of collectivist cultures include African, Asian and South American countries such as Ghana, China, Brazil, respectively [12]. In our study, the Nigerian group falls under the collectivist culture.

2.2 Related Work
In PT research, fewer studies have investigated the influence of culture on the effectiveness of Cialdini's principles of persuasion. Orji [23] conducted a study on the differences between individualist and collectivist cultures with respect to their susceptibility to Cialdini's persuasive strategies. They found that both cultures are most susceptible to Commitment and Reciprocity. However, they found that the collectivist culture is more responsive to all of the six persuasive strategies (except Scarcity) than the individualist culture. However, the investigated populations were North America and Asians only. Selassie et al. [33] also conducted a study on the responsiveness of workers to Cialdini's persuasive principles. They found that Applied Behavior Analysis (ABA) frontline employees in Canada are more susceptible to Commitment and Reciprocity and least susceptible to Consensus and Scarcity. However, their focus was on subjects from Canada only. Similarly, Oyibo et al. [31] examined the responsiveness of Nigerians to Cialdini's persuasive strategies. They found that they were most responsive to Commitment. However, the study was based on quantitative analysis only. Moreover, Oyibo et al. [27] as well as Alkış, and Temizel [2] carried out a similar study on the effect of Big-Five personality traits on Cialdini's six persuasive strategies. Both groups of authors found that the more conscientious people are, the more susceptible they are to Commitment and Reciprocity. However, the investigated populations by Oyibo et al. [27] and Alkış, and Temizel [2] comprised only individuals from Canada and Turkey, respectively. Finally, Abdullahi et al. [1] investigated the influence of cognitive ability on the susceptibility to persuasive strategies. However, the persuasive strategies they investigated were not Cialdini's, except for Consensus, which, in their study, was regarded as Social Learning.

---

[1] The significant difference between Nigerians and Canadians with respect to Scarcity was based on the ranking measure only, unlike the other strategies that were based on the rating measure only, or the rating and ranking measures.

Overall, our review reveals that, in the context of PTs, limited studies have been conducted with respect to the susceptibility of individuals to Cialdini's universal principles of persuasion. Specifically, there is little or no research on how individuals from Western countries compare with individuals from African countries. To bridge this gap in the literature, we compared Nigeria and Canada (as a case study) in terms of their susceptibility to Cialdini's six principles of persuasion. Specifically, we compared how both countries from collectivist and individualist cultures, respectively, differ and are similar and mapped the most persuasive strategies to implementable strategies in the PT domain.

3 METHOD
This section covers our research objective, measurement instruments and participants' demographics.

3.1 Research Objective
The aim of study is to answer the following research questions on Cialdini's persuasion profile for the two different cultural groups:

1. *What is the persuasion profile of Nigerians with respect to Cialdini's persuasive strategies?*
2. *What is the persuasion profile of Canadians with respect to Cialdini's persuasive strategies?*
3. *How are the Nigerian persuasion profile similar to or different from the Canadian persuasion profile?*
4. *Can the persuasion profile of the Nigerians based on the rating of the six persuasive strategies be replicated by using the ranking of a set of proxy items from the respective persuasive strategies' constructs?*
5. *Can the persuasion profile of the Canadians based on the rating of the six persuasive strategies be replicated by using the ranking of a set of proxy items from the respective persuasive strategies' constructs?*

By persuasion profile, we mean a collection of estimates of each group's levels of susceptibility to the six Cialdini's persuasive strategies [13]. Moreover, we aim to investigate whether the respective profiles can be uncovered by rating the constructs separately and replicated by ranking proxy items comparatively.

3.2 Measurement Instruments
To address our research questions, we adopted a three-pronged approach, which includes rating of six Cialdini's persuasive strategies; ranking of proxy items; and the eliciting of qualitative comments on the persuasive strategy, which participants ranked best and worst described them. In so doing, we hoped to gather insightful data that could inform a more effective PT tailoring to the different cultural groups. Thus, we designed an online survey based on the Susceptibility to Persuasive Strategies (STPS) scale developed by Kaptein et al. [14]. First, we asked participants to rate all of the items in the STPS (see Table 1), presented in a random fashion. Each item was measured using a Likert scale ranging from "*Completely Disagree (1)*" to "*Completely Agree (7)*." The overarching question that preceded the survey items is: "*Please kindly read questions and answer the following as honestly as possible.*" Second, as shown in Table 1, we asked participants

to rank a set of six proxy items from "*described me best (1)*" to "*described me worst (6)*." Each item was selected from each sub-scale (construct) in the STPS and assumed to represent the construct well enough. Finally, we asked participants to provide the reason for ranking a particular item as "*described me best (1)*" or "*described me worst (6)*." Note that the numbering was reversed during data analysis. Moreover, the bracketed constructs, e.g., "[Authority]," were not part of the original questions presented to participants.

Table 1: Rating and Ranking Measures based on STPS [14]

Measure	Example Items and Questions
Authority [7 items]	(1) I am very inclined to listen to authority figures. (2) I always obey directions from my superiors. (3) I am more inclined to listen to an authority figure than a peer.
Commitment [5 items]	(1) Once I have committed to do something I will surely do it. (2) Whenever I commit to an appointment I always follow through. (3) I try to do everything I have promised to do.
Consensus [3 items]	(1) When I am in a new situation I look at others to see what I should do. (2) I often rely on other people to know what I should do. (3) It is important to me to fit in.
Liking [3 items]	(1) I will do a favor for people that I like. (2) If I am unsure, I will usually side with someone I like. (3) The opinions of friends are more important than the opinions of others.
Reciprocity [6 items]	(1) I always pay back a favor. (2) When I receive a gift, I feel obliged to return a gift. (3) When someone helps me with my work, I try to pay them back.
Scarcity [5 items]	(1) I believe rare products (scarce) are more valuable than mass products. (2) Products that are hard to get represent a special value. (3) I would feel good if I was the last person to be able to buy something.
Ranking [3 questions]	(1) Please rank the following statements in order of which describes you best. a. *I am very inclined to listen to authority figures* [Authority]. b. *Once I have committed to do something, I will surely do it* [Commitment]. c. *I often rely on other people to know what I should do* [Consensus]. d. *I will do a favor for people that I like* [Liking]. e. *If someone does something for me, I try to do something of similar value to repay the favor* [Reciprocity]. f. *I believe rare products (scarce) are more valuable than mass products* [Scarcity]. (2) What is your reason for ranking the statement that "Describes me best"? (3) What is your reason for ranking the statement that "Describes me worst"?

3.3 Participants

Our research questionnaire was submitted to and approved by the behavioral ethics board of the first author's university. Thereafter, the survey was posted on the first author's university website and Amazon Mechanical Turk (AMT) to recruit participants. AMT is a crowdsourcing platform based in the United States. Other participants were recruited on social media (e.g., Facebook) and via email. Participants on AMT were compensated with $0.8, while those on other media were given the chance to enter for a draw to win C$50. A total of about 350 people took part in the study. However, after filtering out participants whose country of origin was neither Nigeria nor Canada, we were left with 284 participants for our data analysis. Table 2 shows their demographic information. As shown in Table 2, 69.0% of the participants (196) were from Canada, while the other 31.0% (88) were from Nigeria.

Table 2: demographics of participants (n = 284)

Criterion	(Canada, Nigeria) = (196, 88)
Age	18-24 (90, 17); 25-34 (69, 62); 35-34 (20, 8); 45-54 (12, 0); 54+ (5, 1)
Gender	Male (60, 60); Female (132, 28); Others (4, 0)
Education	Technical/Trade School (21, 4); High School (71, 6); Bachelors (78, 46); Masters (13, 29); Doctorate (8, 2); Others (5, 1)
Continent of Origin	North America (196, 0); Africa (0, 88)

4 RESULT

This section covers the results of our data analysis: measurement instruments' reliability analysis, main and interaction effects, and within- and between-group analyses.

4.1 Reliability Analysis

To ensure that the six STPS constructs, representing Cialdini's persuasive strategies, were reliably measured, we conducted McDonald's omega (ω) reliability test [32] due to our non-normal dataset. The McDonald's omega reliability test is the non-parametric equivalent of Cronbach's alpha (ρ) reliability test [25]. Our results show that half of our data met the high reliability requirement ($\omega >= 0.7$), except for Consensus ($\omega = 0.53$), Liking ($\omega = 0.68$) and Scarcity ($\omega = 0.67$), which are moderately reliable [10].

4.2 Mean Rating and Ranking of Persuasive Strategies' Measures

To determine the level of susceptibility of participants to the six persuasive strategies, we computed their overall mean rating and ranking of the strategies at the global level (see Fig. 1) and the subgroup level (see Fig. 2). Overall, participants are susceptible to all six strategies, as the overall average rating is greater than the neutral score of 3.5. Specifically, at the global level, as shown in Fig. 1, participants rated and ranked Commitment (5.61, 4.60) as the most persuasive, followed by Reciprocity (5.40, 3.97). On the other hand, they rated and ranked Consensus (4.40, 2.46), followed by Scarcity (4.43, 2.65), as the least persuasive.

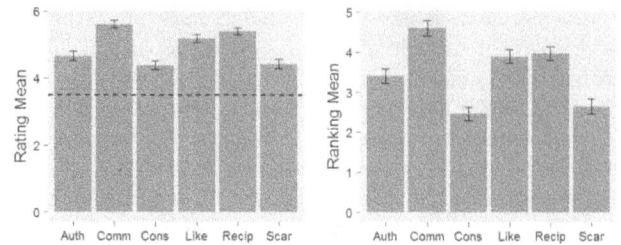

Fig. 1. Global persuasion profile based on the mean rating and ranking of the persuasive strategies (Auth = Authority, Comm = Commitment, Cons = Consensus, Like = Liking, Recip = Reciprocity, Scar = Scarcity)

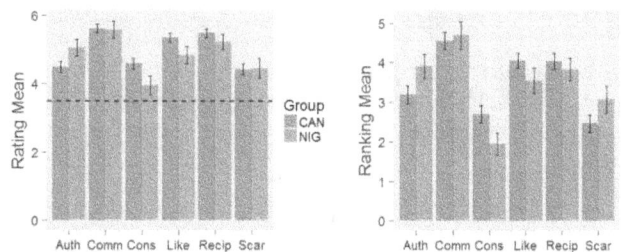

Fig. 2. Nigerian and Canadian Persuasion profiles based on the mean rating and ranking of the persuasive strategies (NIG = Nigeria, CAN = Canada)

4.3 Main and Interaction Effect

The non-parametric aligned rank interaction test [19] for repeated measures shows that there is neither main effect of strategy nor culture. However, there is an interaction between strategy and culture ($F_{4,16} = 1.30$, $p < 0.05$).

4.3.1 Within-Group Comparison. Table 3 shows the within-group analysis at the global and subgroup levels. For the global population, based on the rating measure, eleven pairwise comparisons are significantly different at $p < 0.05$, e.g., Comm-Auth, Like-Auth, etc. The other four (in bold) are not, e.g., Cons-Auth, Recip-Comm, etc. Moreover, all of the eleven significant pairwise differences and two of the four non-significant pairwise differences based on the rating measure are replicated by the ranking measure. Altogether, thirteen out of the fifteen (87%) pairwise-comparison findings based on the rating measure are replicated by the ranking measure. This is an indication that a given population's persuasion profile can be determined using the ranking measure based on proxy items (see Table 5). Furthermore, for the Canadian group, overall, based on the rating measure, nine pairwise comparisons are significantly different at $p < 0.0000$, e.g., Comm-Auth, Like-Auth, etc. The other six (in bold) are not, e.g., Cons-Auth, Scar-Auth, etc. All of the nine significant pairwise differences and five of the six non-significant pairwise differences based on the rating measure are replicated by the ranking measure. Altogether, fourteen out of the fifteen (93%) pairwise-comparison findings based on the rating measure are replicated by the ranking measure. This is another indication (at the subgroup level) that a population's persuasion profile can be determined using the ranking measure based on proxy items.

Table 3. Pairwise comparison of strategies using Friedman/Post-Hoc test (p-values shown)

Strategy	GLOBAL		CANADA		NIGERIA	
	Rating	Ranking	Rating	Ranking	Rating	Ranking
Comm - Auth	0.0000	0.0000	0.0000	0.0000	*0.0061*	***0.0609***
Cons - Auth	***0.1180***	*0.0000*	**0.9645**	**0.0926**	0.0000	0.0000
Like - Auth	0.0000	0.0259	0.0000	0.0001	**0.5153**	**0.7911**
Recip - Auth	0.0000	0.0053	0.0000	0.0001	**0.9263**	**0.9998**
Scar - Auth	0.0470	0.0000	***0.9285***	*0.0014*	0.0028	0.0384
Cons - Comm	0.0000	0.0000	0.0000	0.0000	0.0000	0.0000
Like - Comm	0.0000	0.0001	**0.2961**	**0.0866**	0.0000	0.0007
Recip - Comm	***0.1533***	*0.0009*	**0.8380**	**0.0651**	***0.1138***	*0.0267*
Scar - Comm	0.0000	0.0000	0.0000	0.0000	0.0000	0.0000
Like - Cons	0.0000	0.0000	0.0000	0.0000	0.0008	0.0000
Recip - Cons	0.0000	0.0000	0.0000	0.0000	0.0000	0.0000
Scar - Cons	**0.9993**	**0.8425**	**0.4764**	**0.8021**	***0.3257***	*0.0008*
Recip - Like	**0.2201**	**0.9971**	**0.9502**	**1.0000**	0.0753	0.9157
Scar - Like	0.0000	0.0000	0.0000	0.0000	0.3488	0.5639
Scar - Recip	0.0000	0.0000	0.0000	0.0000	*0.0000*	***0.0835***

Note: Bolded p-values indicate there is no significant difference between each pair of strategies.
Italicized values indicate pairwise comparison based on rating and that based on ranking do not match.

Table 4. Between-group comparisons using Kruskal-Wallis rank sum test

STRAT	Rating-Based				Ranking-Based			
	GLO	CAN	NIG	P-Value	GLO	CAN	NIG	P-Value
Auth	4.67	4.49	5.07	0.0001	3.42	3.19	3.91	0.0003
Comm	5.61	**5.62**	**5.58**	**0.6134**	4.60	**4.56**	**4.69**	**0.2762**
Cons	4.40	4.59	3.95	0.0001	2.46	2.70	1.94	0.0000
Like	5.19	5.35	4.84	0.0005	3.90	4.06	3.55	0.0059
Recip	5.40	*5.48*	*5.22*	*0.0361*	3.97	***4.04***	***3.83***	***0.2473***
Scar	4.43	***4.42***	***4.46***	***0.8449***	2.65	*2.46*	*3.08*	*0.0010*

Note: GLO = Global population, CAN = Canadian group, NIG = Nigerian group
Bolded strategy values indicate no significant difference between both groups.
Italicized values indicate between-group comparison based on rating and that based on ranking do not match.

Finally, for the Nigerian group, overall, based on the rating measure, nine pairwise comparisons are significantly different at $p < 0.01$, e.g., Comm-Auth, Like-Auth, etc. The other six (in bold) are not, e.g., Like-Auth, Recip-Auth, etc. Moreover, seven of the nine significant pairwise differences and four of the six non-significant pairwise differences based on the rating measure are replicated by the ranking measure. Altogether, eleven out of the fifteen (73%) pairwise-comparison findings based on the rating measure are replicated by the ranking measure. Again, at the subgroup level, this is an indication that a population's persuasion profile, to a large extent, can be uncovered by simply using the ranking measure based on proxy items (as shown in Table 5).

One possible explanation for the lower percentage of the replication of the rating-based findings in the Nigerian group (73%) than in the global population (87%) and in the Canadian group (93%) is sample size. The Nigerian group (n = 88) has the smallest sample size compared to the sample size of the global population (n = 284) and the Canadian group (n = 196). This indicates the higher the sample size, the more likely the rating-based findings will be replicated by the ranking-based method. Another factor that may be account for a higher percentage of ranking-based replication of the rating-based findings is homogeneity of the investigated population. For example, we see that the percentage of replication is higher for the Canadian group (93%) than the global group (87%) despite the fact the global population sample size (more heterogeneous) is greater than the Canadian sample size (more homogeneous).

4.3.2 Between-Group Comparison. Table 4 shows the Kruskal-Wallis rank sum tests for the differences that exist between both cultural groups. Based on the rating measure, the two groups significantly differ in the level of susceptibility to four strategies (Authority, Reciprocity, Liking and Consensus). Three of these four significant differences (Authority, Consensus and Liking) and one of the two non-significant differences (Commitment) based on the rating measure are replicated by the ranking measure. Altogether, four out of the six (66.7%) between-group comparison findings based on the rating measure are replicated by the ranking method. This suggests that group differences, to some extent, can be uncovered by simply using the ranking method. As shown in Table 4, based on both measures, the Nigerian group (5.07 and 3.91)[2] is more susceptible to Authority than

---

[2] Rating measure is on the left, while ranking measure is on the right.

the Canadian group (4.49 and 3.19). However, based on the ranking measure only, the Nigerian group (3.08) is more susceptible to Scarcity than the Canadian group (2.46). On the other hand, based on both measures, the Canadian group (4.59 and 2.70) is more susceptible to Consensus than the Nigerian group (3.95 and 1.94). Similarly, based on both measures, the Canadian group (5.35 and 4.06) is more susceptible to Liking than the Nigerian group (4.84 and 3.55). However, based on the rating measure only, the Canadian group (5.48) is more susceptible to Reciprocity than the Nigerian group (5.22).

4.4 Persuasion Profile for the Global Population and Cultural Subgroups

Table 5 shows the persuasion profiles for the general population and the subgroups. The profiles (based on the rating and the ranking measures) range from the most persuasive to the least persuasive strategies. Overall, irrespective of the measure of profiling, Commitment (5.61 and 4.60), Reciprocity (5.40 and 3.97) and Liking (5.19 and 3.90) are the most persuasive strategies, while Consensus (4.40 and 2.46), Scarcity (4.43 and 2.65) and Authority (4.67 and 3.42) are the least persuasive strategies. For the Canadian group, the persuasion profile is similar to that of the general population, especially if Consensus is excluded from both profiles. While Consensus is in the fourth position in the Canadian profile, it is in the last position in the global profile mainly due to its very low rating/ranking by the Nigerian group, earning it the last position in the Nigerian profile. Moreover, the Nigerian persuasion profile is similar to the global profile as well, with Authority and Liking switching positions in the Nigerian profile. One of the main differences between the profiles is that, while Reciprocity and Liking are significantly higher than Authority in the global profile (as well as in the Canadian profile), each pair of these three strategies do not significantly differ in the Nigerian profile. Thus, in the Nigerian profile, Commitment, Reciprocity, Authority and Liking are the most persuasive strategies, while Consensus and Scarcity are the least persuasive.

Furthermore, for the most part, the ranking-based persuasion profile replicates the rating-based persuasion profile. This is most evident in the global population, where the persuasion profile based on the ranking measure completely matches the persuasion profile based on the rating measure (see Table 5). Moreover, the persuasion profile of the subgroups based on the ranking measure is similar to that based on the rating measure. The reason for this claim is that, as shown in Table 5, the posi-

tions of the consecutive superscripted pair of strategies (e.g., 2 and 3, or 4 and 5) with respect to the ranking measure are switchable given that there is no significant difference (at $p < 0.05$) between the pair of strategies in question. Thus, in each subgroup, owing to the switch, the order of the persuasive strategies based on the rating measure aligns with the order of the strategies based on the ranking measure.

5 DISCUSSION

We have presented the persuasion profiles of two different demographics (Nigeria and Canada) with respect to their susceptibility to Cialdini's principles of persuasion. Specifically, we show that the persuasion profiles of both groups are similar as well as differ as evident in the interaction between strategy and culture (see Section 4.3). Table 5 shows the respective persuasion profiles. At the global level, Commitment, Reciprocity and Liking are the most persuasive strategies, while Consensus, Scarcity and Authority are the least persuasive strategies. Similarly, for the Canadian group, Commitment, Reciprocity and Liking are the most persuasive strategies, while Scarcity, Authority and Consensus are the least persuasive strategies. However, for the Nigerian group, Commitment, Reciprocity, Authority and Liking[3] are the most persuasive strategies, while Consensus and Scarcity are the least persuasive strategies.

5.1 Answering of Our Research Questions

In this section, we discuss the answering of our five research questions. With respect to our first research question, the Nigerians persuasion profile, from the most persuasive strategy to the least persuasive strategy, is Commitment, Reciprocity, Authority, Liking, Scarcity, and Consensus. Similarly, with respect to our second research questions, the Canadian persuasion profile is Commitment, Reciprocity, Liking, Consensus, Authority and Scarcity. The major similarity between both groups, with respect to our third research question, is that they are most susceptible to Commitment and Reciprocity. On the other hand, one of the main differences between the two groups is that, for the Canadian group, Reciprocity and Liking are more persuasive than Authority, while, for the Nigerian group, there is no significant difference between each pair of the three strategies. Moreover, the Canadian group is more susceptible to Reciprocity, Liking and Consensus than the Nigerian group. On the other hand, the Nigerian group is more susceptible to Authority and Scarcity than the Canadian group.

Finally, with respect to our fourth and fifth research ques-

Table 5. Persuasion profile based on rating and ranking for the global population and subgroups

Sample	Measure	Relative Order of the Persuasiveness of Strategies
GLOBAL	Rating	Commitment, Reciprocity, Liking, Authority, Scarcity, Consensus
	Ranking	Commitment, Reciprocity, Liking, Authority, Scarcity, Consensus
CANADA	Rating	Commitment, Reciprocity, Liking, Consensus, Authority, Scarcity
	Ranking	Commitment, Reciprocity[3], Liking[2], Consensus[5], Authority[4], Scarcity
NIGERIA	Rating	Commitment, Reciprocity, Authority, Liking, Scarcity, Consensus
	Ranking	Commitment, Reciprocity[3], Authority[2], Liking, Scarcity, Consensus

Note: No significant difference between two consecutive superscripted strategies, so their positions were intentionally switched to align with the rating's order.

tions, we have shown that using ranking-based method for determining the persuasion profile of a given population could be as effective as using the rating-based method. For example, in the global population, as well as in the subgroups (see Table 5), we find that the ordering of the six persuasive strategies based on the rating measure and that based on the ranking measure are the same. Specifically, for the subgroups, we say that the orders of the persuasive strategies based on both methods are the same because there is no significant difference between the consecutive superscripted pairs of strategies (e.g., 2 and 3, or 4 and 5). As such, the positions of the consecutive superscripted pair of strategies based on the ranking method can be switched in order to align with the positions based on the rating method. Therefore, we conclude that, to a large extent, the ranking method (based on proxy items) of determining persuasion profiles can be as reliable as the rating method in the investigation of the relative persuasiveness of Cialdini's principles of persuasion. Thus, for the purpose of tailoring PTs, the ranking-based method could be used to determine which strategies among a given set of persuasive strategies a given population is more susceptible to. Specifically, the ranking-based method helps to prevent participant fatigue that may characterize the rating-based method. For example, in a survey where participants may have to rate a long list of reflective items (a subset of which defines a persuasive strategy's construct) in order for a researcher to determine their persuasion profile, the ranking method can be used as a substitute. Nevertheless, using the ranking method has to be done with caution as its reliability may depend on how well the selected proxy items reflect or represent the actual multi-item constructs.

5.2 Comparison of Our with Previous Findings

We compared our findings with those of a prior study by Orji [23]. We made a comparison between both studies because they both used the same measurement instrument (the STPS) and investigated two different but similar cultures: collectivist and individualist. However, while our study's individualist and collectivist groups are Canada and Nigeria, respectively, Orji's are North America and Asia, respectively.

Table 6 shows our study's persuasion profiles compared with Orji's [23]. Both studies' persuasion profiles differ in some respects and are similar in some other respects. Overall, at the

global and subgroup levels, both studies found that Commitment and Reciprocity are among the three most persuasive strategies, and Scarcity and Consensus are among the three least persuasive strategies. The fact that the two most persuasive strategies (Commitment and Reciprocity) are similar in both studies may not be surprising given that, generally, people tend to be most susceptible to these two strategies among Cialdini's six strategies (e.g., [33]). Second, for the individualist group, both studies found Liking as the third most persuasive strategy at the global level. The fact that, in both studies, the three most persuasive strategies for the individualist group are similar may not be surprising given that both studies used the same instrument and profiled the same continent: North America. Third, both studies found that the individualist group is less susceptible to Authority than the collectivist group. This suggests that, in the context of PTs, users in collectivist cultures are more likely to defer to authority figures (e.g., health domain experts) than users in individualist cultures.

On the other hand, one of the main differences in both studies is that the least persuasive strategy in the Nigerian collectivist group is Consensus, while, in the Asian collectivist group, it is Scarcity. This is an indication of continental differences between the collectivist groups. Moreover, in Orji's study, the Asian collectivist group is significantly more susceptible to Reciprocity, Liking and Consensus than the North American individualist group. However, in our study, the Nigerian collectivist group is significantly less susceptible to these three strategies than the Canadian individualist group—a role reversal between the collectivist group and individualist group in both studies. One possible explanation for this mixed finding is that some other factors (e.g., age, gender, education, etc.) may be at play, which both studies did not consider in their analyses. Thus, further research is needed in this area to ground the findings.

5.3 Design Guidelines

Based on our main findings (see Table 5), we provide some design guidelines for tailoring PTs to the two different cultural groups. The guidelines are based on the three most persuasive strategies in the persuasion profile of each cultural group.

Table 6. Comparison of Orji's [23] study's persuasion profiles and Our study's persuasion profiles.

Culture	Sample	Study	Relative Order of Persuasiveness of Cialdini's Strategies
GLO	General Population	Orji's	Commitment, Reciprocity, Liking, Consensus, Authority, Scarcity
		Ours	Commitment, Reciprocity, Liking, Authority, Scarcity, Consensus
IND	North America	Orji's	Commitment, Reciprocity, Liking, Scarcity, Consensus, Authority
	Canada	Ours	Commitment, **Reciprocity**, **Liking**, **Consensus**, Authority, Scarcity
COL	Asia	Orji's	Commitment, **Reciprocity**, **Liking**, **Consensus**, **Authority**, Scarcity
	Nigeria	Ours	Commitment, Reciprocity, **Authority**, Liking, **Scarcity**, Consensus

Note: GLO = Global, IND = Individualist culture (Canada), COL = Collectivist culture (Nigeria)
Bolded persuasive strategies indicate they are significantly more persuasive for the group in
question than for its counterpart group, with North America vs. Asia, and Canada vs. Nigeria.

5.3.1 Guideline #1. To tailor persuasive systems to both groups using Cialdini's principles of persuasion, the Commitment strategy should be favored the most compared to the other persuasive strategies. Based on our findings, we recommend that, irrespective of the culture of users, designers of persuasive apps should employ Commitment as much as possible to motivate users to perform a target behavior they are trying to encourage. The equivalent strategy for Commitment in PT design is Goal-Setting. Goal-Setting allows users to set goals and plan to achieve them. It also helps users to track their progress over time through self-monitoring and feedback. By setting goals, the user is indirectly making a commitment to the persuasive system. As a result, the likelihood of the user performing the target behavior is higher than when no goal is set. According to the theory of goal-setting, the goals people set influence their performance of the target behavior by directing their attention and effort towards achieving them [16].

In PT research [8, 18], Goal-Setting has been found to be an effective persuasive strategy for motivating behavior change. There are a number of ways to make the Goal-Setting strategy more effective. One way is to ensure that the set goals are "SMART." In other words, the set goals should be specific, measurable, attainable, relevant and timely [2]. Another way to make Goal-Setting more effective is by allowing a third party other than the persuasive system to be involved in the goal-setting process, e.g., allowing users to share their goals with peers, friends and family in a collaborative setting or on social media [18]. Yet another way to make Goal-Setting more effective is to accompany it with Reward [18]. Prior research [7] has shown that rewarding users for achieving set goals can reinforce the performance of the target behavior. Moreover, users can visualize the short-term benefit of their behavior [28]. Prior research [30] has shown that both Nigerian and Canadians are susceptible to Reward.

Table 7: Examples of participants' comments on why they ranked Commitment strategy as best described them

Nigeria	Canada
"In order to uphold my integrity, I must do what I say I will" [P233]	"I like to have a solid reputation among peers for being someone who can be relied on" [P03]
"I wouldn't commit myself to something I won't like to do in the first place" [P220]	"I follow through with plans once I have decided to do something. I don't like to turn away from something I have definitely decided to do" [P75]
"Because I always set tasks that are feasible and I follow through with it" [P285]	"If I set a goal and say I will do something, then I will do everything in my power to make sure I accomplish it" [P144].
"I am obedient and a great believer of Karma" [P254]	"Once I commit to something, I will finish it. I'm a man of my word and don't like to let people down" [P192]

Table 7 shows examples of participant's comments indicating the potential of Commitment as an effective strategy in a persuasive system and social context. The presented comments capture the main reasons why most participants ranked Commitment as the persuasive strategy that described them best. The main reasons range from personal principles (commitment to one's promises due to moral principles, e.g., P220, P75, etc.) to interpersonal relationships (commitment to one's promises to maintain one's reputations and relationships with peers, e.g., P03, P192, etc.).

5.3.2 Guideline #2. Apart from Commitment, Reciprocity should be used as the second most likely effective strategy in PT design for both groups as the persuasion profiles in Table 5 shows. One way of implementing Reciprocity in a persuasive system is having the system reward the user first, even before actually performing the target behavior [22]. However, Reciprocity may be more effective if implemented in a social context. Thus, persuasive apps should support collaboration by allowing, for example, a current user of the app, to invite other users (e.g., friends and family) as well. In a cooperative context, an invited user may be motivated to reciprocate the "kind gesture" of the inviter by attempting to meet his own part of a shared goal. P123's comment, "*I feel social pressure AND gratefulness,*" points to the potential effectiveness of Reciprocity in a collaborative context.

Table 8: Examples of participants' comments on why they ranked Reciprocity strategy as best described them

Nigeria	Canada
"When I repay favours, I get more favours" [P238]	"I feel social pressure AND gratefulness" [P123].
"I feel that what goes round comes around hence I try to repay favours" [P252].	"I feel that if someone does something for me I must return the favour because it is morally right" [P121].
"I believe in rewarding good for good" [P225].	"I do not like being in debt to others" [P157].
"Because I apprec[i]ate it when someone does som[e]thing for me" [P201].	"I believe in karma so I like to repay favors done for me" [P. 197].

5.3.3 Guideline #3. Apart from Commitment and Reciprocity, Authority and Liking should be used as the third most likely effective strategy in PT design for the Nigerian and Canadian groups, respectively. One way of implementing Liking and Authority is through the use of an attractive role model [21, 25] and a domain expert, respectively, e.g., exercise virtual coach. Moreover, to make the Liking and Authority strategies more effective, personalizing the visual design (e.g., gender of the virtual coach) and content (e.g., the language and message of the domain expert), respectively, could be leveraged. Research [21] has shown that personalized systems are more likely to be persuasive than non-personalized systems. In our case, a personalized attractive role model (for the Canadians) and a personalized domain expert (for the Nigerians) are more likely to be effective in changing behaviors. Table 9 shows a snippet of participants' comments in support of the potential effectiveness of Authority (for Nigerians) and Liking (for Canadians) in PT design aimed at behavior change. Nigerians are likely to be persuaded by Authority because they trust authority figures and because obedience to authority helps in defining who they are. On the other hand, Canadians are likely to be persuaded by the Liking principle because of the sense of commitment to and care for the people they like.

Table 9: Examples of participants' comments on why they ranked Authority/Liking strategy as best described them

Nigeria (Authority)	Canada (Liking)
"I like to obey authority" [P275].	*"I am very loyal and committed to the people I like"* [P30].
"I trust authority figures" [204].	*"I do favours of anyone who asks, but am more likely to do it for someone I like because it's easier"* [P171].
"I feel it tells me good of my personality" [218].	*"I would do anything to help out a family member or friend"* [P47].
"It fits my personality" [P248].	*"Because if I like someone then I care more and want to help them more"* [P121].

5.4 Summary and Contribution

In this paper, we have shown that, among the Cialdini's universal principles of persuasion, Commitment and Reciprocity are the most persuasive and Scarcity and Consensus are the least persuasive at the global level. Moreover, we showed that Canadians are more susceptible to Reciprocity, Liking and Consensus than Nigerians, while Nigerians are more susceptible to Authority and Scarcity than Canadians. Our main contribution to knowledge is that we showed how the Canadian and Nigerian populations differ and are similar in the susceptibility to Cialdini's principles of persuasion. Another contribution is that we showed that, in determining the persuasion profile of a given population, having participants rank proxy items holds potential as a substitute for the rating of multi-item constructs, especially when the target population is homogenous and the sample is relatively large. However, given that the ranking-based findings do not completely match the rating-based findings, we recommend that the replication be further investigated using a larger sample size of a homogeneous population. Finally, we provide a number of design guidelines by mapping the most persuasive Cialdini's principles to implementable persuasive strategies in PT domain.

5.5 Limitation

The main limitation of our study is that our persuasion profiles are based on users' perceived persuasiveness of the investigated strategies (i.e., self-report). As, such, we cannot guarantee our findings will generalize to an actual use context. Another limitation is that we considered only Canada, on one hand, and Nigeria, on the other hand, as a case study. This may threaten the generalization of our respective findings to the broader North American and African continents. However, the fact that we are able to replicate prior findings in similar cultures (individualist and collectivist) is indicative of the level of significance of our findings.

6 CONCLUSION AND FUTURE WORK

In this paper, we examined the susceptibility of Nigerians and Canadians to Cialdini's six persuasive strategies to determine and compare the persuasion profiles of both national/cultural groups. The results of our analysis show that, for the global population, Commitment and Reciprocity are the most persuasive strategies, while Consensus and Scarcity are the least persuasive strategies. Specifically, for the Canadian group, Reciprocity and Liking are more persuasive than Authority, while, for the Nigerian group, there is no significant difference between each pair. On the other hand, for the Nigerian group, Authority and Scarcity are more persuasive than Consensus, while, for the Canadian group, there is no significant difference between each of the former and latter. Thus, the Canadian group is more susceptible to Reciprocity, Liking and Consensus than the Nigerian group, while the Nigerian group is more susceptible to Authority and Scarcity than the Canadian group. In future work, we intend to investigate how other demographic factors such as age, gender, education, etc., moderate the respective persuasion profiles.

REFERENCES

[1] Abdullahi, A.M. et al. 2018. The Influence of Cognitive Ability on the Susceptibility to Persuasive Strategies. *International Workshop on Personalizing in Persuasive Technologies* (Waterloo, Canada, 2018), 22–33.
[2] Alkış, N. and Temizel, T.T. 2015. The impact of individual differences on influence strategies. *Personality and Individual Differences*. 87, (2015), 147–152.
[3] Bello, B. et al. 2017. Alcohol use and sexual risk behaviour among men and women in inner-city Johannesburg, South Africa. *BMC Public Health*. 17, (2017).
[4] Cialdini, R.B. 2001. Influence: Science and practice (4th ed.). *New York: HarperCollins*. 253.
[5] Cialdini, R.B. 2006. *Influence: The Psychology of Persuasion*. HarperCollins.
[6] Cialdini, R.B. and Rhoads, K.V.L. 2001. Human behavior and the marketplace. *Marketing Research*. 13, 3 (2001), 8–13.
[7] Consolvo, S. et al. 2006. Design requirements for technologies that encourage physical activity. *Proceedings of the SIGCHI conference on Human Factors in computing systems - CHI '06*. (2006), 457.
[8] Consolvo, S. et al. 2009. Goal-setting considerations for persuasive technologies that encourage physical activity. *Proceedings of the 4th International Conference on Persuasive Technology - Persuasive '09* (2009).
[9] Fogg, B.J. 2003. *Persuasive Technology: Using Computers to Change What We Think and Do*. Morgan Kaufmann.
[10] Hinton, P.R. et al. 2014. *SPSS Explained*. Routledge.
[11] Hofstede, G. et al. 2010. *Cultures and Organizations: Software of the Mind*. McGraw Hill.
[12] Hofstede, G. 2011. Dimensionalizing Cultures: The Hofstede Model in Context. *Online Readings in Psychology and Culture*. 2, 1 (2011), 1–26.
[13] Kang, Y. and Tan, A.-H. 2015. MAP: A computational model for adaptive persuasion. *Proceedings of the International Joint Conference on Autonomous Agents and Multiagent Systems, AAMAS*. 3, (2015), 1871–1872.
[14] Kaptein, M. et al. 2012. Adaptive Persuasive Systems: A Study of Tailored Persuasive Text Messages to Reduce Snacking. *ACM Transactions on Interactive Intelligent Systems*. 2, 2 (2012), 1–25.
[15] Khaled, R. et al. 2006. Our place or mine? Exploration into collectivism-focused persuasive technology design. *International Conference on Persuasive Technology* (Berlin, Heidelberg, 2006), 72–83.
[16] Locke, E. a and Latham, G.P. 2002. Building a practically useful theory of goal setting and task motivation: A 35-year odyssey. *The American Psychologist*. 57, 9 (2002), 705–717.
[17] McVeigh, J. and Meiring, R. 2014. Physical activity and sedentary behavior in an ethnically diverse group of South african school children. *Journal of Sports, Science and Medicine*. 13, 2 (2014), 371–378.
[18] Munson, S. and Consolvo, S. 2012. Exploring Goal-setting, Rewards, Self-monitoring, and Sharing to Motivate Physical Activity. *Proceedings of the 6th International Conference on Pervasive Computing Technologies for Healthcare*. (2012), 25–32.
[19] npIntFactRep: Nonparametric Interaction Tests for Factorial Designs with Repeated Measures: 2015. *https://cran.r-project.org/web/packages/npIntFactRep*. Accessed: 2017-11-11.

[20] Obesity: Africa's new crisis: 2014. http://www.theguardian.com/society/2014/sep/21/obesity-africas-new-crisis. Accessed: 2015-11-25.

[21] Oinas-kukkonen, H. and Harjumaa, M. 2009. Persuasive Systems Design Key Issues, Process Model, and System Features. *Communications of the Association for Information Systems.* 24, 28 (2009), 485–500.

[22] Orji, R. et al. 2015. Gender, age, and responsiveness to Cialdini's persuasion strategies. *International Conference on Persuasive Technology* (2015), 147–159.

[23] Orji, R. 2016. Persuasion and Culture: Individualism–Collectivism and Susceptibility to Influence Strategies. *Workshop on Personalization in Persuasive Technology (PPT'16).* (2016).

[24] Orji, R. and Moffatt, K. 2016. Persuasive technology for health and wellness: State-of-the-art and emerging trends. *Health Informatics Journal.* (2016), 1–26.

[25] Oyibo, K. et al. 2016. An empirical analysis of the perception of mobile website interfaces and the influence of culture. *CEUR Workshop Proceedings* (2016), 44–56.

[26] Oyibo, K. 2016. Designing culture-based persuasive technology to promote physical activity among university students. *UMAP 2016 - Proceedings of the 2016 Conference on User Modeling Adaptation and Personalization* (2016).

[27] Oyibo, K. et al. 2017. Investigation of the Influence of Personality Traits on Cialdini's Persuasive Strategies. *International Workshop on Personalizing in Persuasive Technologies (PPT'17)* (2017).

[28] Oyibo, K. et al. 2017. Investigation of the Persuasiveness of Social Influence in Persuasive Technology and the Effect of Age and Gender. *International Workshop on Persuasive Technology* (Amsterdam, 2017).

[29] Oyibo, K. et al. 2017. Investigation of the Social Predictors of Competitive Behavior and the Moderating Effect of Culture. *Workshop on User Modeling, Adaptation and Personalization (UMAP 2017)* (2017).

[30] Oyibo, K. et al. 2017. The Influence of Culture in the Effect of Age and Gender on Social Influence in Persuasive Technology. *Adjunct Proceedings of User Modeling, Adaptation and Personalization (UMAP 2017)* (2017).

[31] Oyibo, K. et al. 2018. The Susceptibility of Africans to Persuasive Strategies: A Case Study of Nigeria. *International Workshop on Personalizing in Persuasive Technologies* (Waterloo, Canada, 2018), 8–21.

[32] Peters G 2015. userfriendlyscience: Quantitative analysis made accessible. *R Package Version 0.3-0.* (2015).

[33] Selassie, H.H. et al. 2017. Responsiveness to persuasive strategies at the workplace: A case study. *Seventh International Multidisciplinary Conference on e-Technologies* (Ottawa, 2017), 273–284.

Investigating Serial Position Effects
in Sequential Group Decision Making

Thi Ngoc Trang Tran
Graz University of Technology
Graz, Austria
ttrang@ist.tugraz.at

Müslüm Atas
Graz University of Technology
Graz, Austria
muesluem.atas@ist.tugraz.at

Alexander Felfernig
Graz University of Technology
Graz, Austria
alexander.felfernig@ist.tugraz.at

Ralph Samer
Graz University of Technology
Graz, Austria
rsamer@ist.tugraz.at

Martin Stettinger
Graz University of Technology
Graz, Austria
martin.stettinger@ist.tugraz.at

ABSTRACT

Group decision making is performed in real life for the purpose of selecting an optimal solution for the whole group. Decision making behavior of group members could be impacted by item domains and the chronological order in which decision tasks are presented to groups. In this paper, we analyze situations where group members could apply different decision strategies depending on the chronological order of decision tasks. The data analysis results confirm that item domains and the order of decision tasks have an impact on group decision strategies. This is especially the case if preferences of a minority of group members are significantly different from the other group members and when decision tasks related to high-involvement item domains are arranged before decision tasks related to low-involvement item domains. In addition, we also figured out that group members invest different amounts of time in making a decision task depending on its position in a sequence of decision tasks.

CCS CONCEPTS

• **Information systems** → **Information systems applications**; **Decision support systems**; **Recommender systems**;

KEYWORDS

Group Recommender Systems; Group Decision Making; Group Aggregation Strategies; Serial Position Effects

ACM Reference Format:
Thi Ngoc Trang Tran, Müslüm Atas, Alexander Felfernig, Ralph Samer, and Martin Stettinger. 2018. Investigating Serial Position Effects in Sequential Group Decision Making. In *UMAP '18: 26th Conference on User Modeling, Adaptation and Personalization, July 8–11, 2018, Singapore, Singapore.* ACM, New York, NY, USA, 5 pages. https://doi.org/10.1145/3209219.3209255

1 INTRODUCTION

Group recommender systems can be regarded as tools that support group decision making processes ([7], [9], [11]). Group decision making behavior of group members could be influenced by different factors, such as *decision-making environments* [2], *decision tasks* [10], *decision makers' characteristics* [6], and the *item type* [4]. In the context of repeated group decision making, to some extent it is still unclear whether there exists any influence of the order of decision tasks (in a sequence of decision tasks) on the chosen group aggregation strategy. In other words, it needs to be clarified whether there exist *serial position effects* [5] that could unconsciously lead group members to different behaviors when making a sequence of group decisions. A realistic scenario could be defined as follows: a group of friends has to make different decisions which are arranged in a sequence of decisions corresponding to different domains. At the beginning, if the group is confronted with a decision on items with *low decision making effort* (e.g., selecting a list of *songs* to be played in the fitness center in the next hours), the item that satisfies the preferences of the *majority* of group members could be chosen by the group, i.e., the preferences of a *minority* of group members could be ignored. However, if this decision is performed after making a decision on items with *high decision making effort* (e.g., selecting an *apartment* to be shared for the next two years), then the decision making behavior of group members in the *song* domain could be unintentionally influenced by the behavior that the group already applied in the *shared-apartment* domain. That means, the decision of which songs to choose could be based on the preferences of *all* individual group members (i.e., nobody is ignored) since a similar behavior was most probably applied by the group in the *shared-apartment* domain.

To the best of our knowledge, in-depth analyses of group decision making behavior depending on the order of decision tasks (in a sequence of tasks) do not exist. A related work presented in [7] analyzes the influence of viewing an item on giving the ratings for other items. However, this work solely focuses on items in a certain domain (e.g., television programs). In this paper, we go one step further by investigating *serial position effects* in a sequence of decision tasks with many different domains. We analyze *group aggregation strategies* ([3], [8]) in order to figure out which strategy is applied by user study participants in which sequence of decision tasks. The in-depth knowledge of serial position effects in sequential group decision making is the premise of *improving the prediction quality* of group recommender systems. In addition, we also examine the influence of the decision task order on the time invested in group decision making. This is achieved by measuring and analyzing time duration that participants need to solve decision tasks in a given sequence.

The remainder of the paper is organized as follows. In *Section 2*, we briefly introduce the main idea of group aggregation strategies that are used to analyze the decision behavior of group members. In *Section 3*, we define the research questions in the form of hypotheses and present our user study. The data analysis results as well as discussions regarding the proposed hypotheses are presented in *Section 4*. In the last section, we conclude the paper and discuss issues for future work.

2 GROUP AGGREGATION STRATEGIES

Within the scope of our user study, we analyze the decision making behavior of group members by comparing it with various *group aggregation strategies* ([3], [8]). These strategies are applied to aggregate preferences of individual group members into a group model that represents the inferred preferences of the whole group.

A short description of applied aggregation strategies is the following. *Average (AVG)* recommends the item with the maximum average of individual ratings. *Multiplicative (MUL)* recommends the item with the maximum product of individual ratings. *Least Misery (LMS)* recommends the item with the highest of all lowest individual ratings. *Most Pleasure (MPL)* recommends the item with the highest of all individual ratings. *Minimal Group Distance (MGD)* recommends the item which has the minimum distance to all individual ratings. *Majority (MAJ)* recommends the item with the highest number of all ratings representing the majority of item-specific ratings. *Ensemble voting (ENS)* determines the majority of the results of all individual voting strategies.

A more detailed discussion of computation functions of the mentioned aggregation strategies is given in ([3], [4]). An example of the application of these strategies is shown in Table 2.

3 RESEARCH QUESTIONS AND USER STUDY

3.1 Research Questions

The main goal of our study is to answer the following research question: *"Do serial position effects occur in the context of group decisions which are performed in different domain sequences?"*. In this context, we defined the following two hypotheses (H_1 and H_2):

- H_1: *"User study participants are assumed to apply different group aggregation strategies for the same decision task depending on its position in the given sequence of different item domains"*. The motivation of H_1 is to figure out the tendency to reuse previously applied strategies when making sequential group decision tasks.

- H_2: *"In the context of repeated group decision making in a sequence of different decision tasks corresponding to different item domains, user study participants are assumed to invest different amounts of time for the same task depending on its position in a sequence of decision tasks"*. The motivation of H_2 is to show that different sequences of decision tasks require different time efforts. In addition, this hypothesis helps to better compare the difference between

Table 1: An example decision task where group members rated holiday destinations using a 5-star rating scale.

	holiday 1	holiday 2	holiday 3
user 1	3	1	5
user 2	3	4	2
user 3	3	4	2
user 4	3	4	2

Table 2: Based on the group members' ratings for the holiday destinations (see *Table* 1), group aggregation strategies can be used to recommend a corresponding holiday to the group.

strategies	holiday 1	holiday 2	holiday 3	recommendation
AVG	3	**3.25**	2.75	holiday 2
LMS	**3**	1	2	holiday 1
MPL	3	4	**5**	holiday 3
MGD	3	**4**	2	holiday 2
MAJ	3	**4**	2	holiday 2
ENS	3	**4**	2	holiday 2
MUL	**81**	64	30	holiday 1

decision task sequences with regard to the total time needed to complete all the tasks in a given sequence.

3.2 User study

Our user study was performed in the following three steps:

Step 1 - Define evaluation settings: We assumed a situation in which *four imaginary group members* already rated *three items* using a 5-star rating scale. The ratings of the four group members about an item were represented as *a setting with four ratings*. In this user study, we chose *five settings* to describe different situations of group members' preferences. *Average support (3,3,3,3)* represents a situation where all group members provides an average rating about the item. *Disagreement (1,2,3,4)* describes a situation where group members do not show a clear opinion about the item and their ratings range from negative to positive. *Majority positive (1,4,4,4)* represents a situation where a majority of group members likes the item, only a minority of group members does not like the item. *Majority negative (5,2,2,2)* represents a situation where a majority of group members doesn't like the item, only a minority of group members likes the item. *Polarization (4,4,1,1)* describes a situation where there exist two contrary opinion flows on the item (one half of the group members supports the item, other half does not support the item).

Step 2 - Construct decision tasks from evaluation settings: We defined *ten different decision tasks (Task 1, Task 2, ..., Task 10)* in which each task was tailored by combining *three out of the five* mentioned settings ($\binom{5}{3} = 10$ *tasks*). An example decision task is shown in Table 1. This task was constructed by combining three evaluation settings: *(3,3,3,3), (1,4,4,4),* and *(5,2,2,2)* corresponding to *holiday 1, holiday 2,* and *holiday 3* respectively. Within each task, settings were shown to user study participants in a randomized fashion. Each participant was asked to select an item from the set of three items for which the group ratings were provided.

Step 3 - Build sequences of decision tasks with regard to different domains and deliver to user study participants: Each sequence consisted of *four decision tasks* related to *four item domains*. Different participants received different sequences. Within sequences, decision tasks corresponding to different item domains were shown to participants in random orders. We chose four item domains: *very-low-involvement, low-involvement, high-involvement, and very-high-involvement*. A *(very)-low-involvement* item domain includes items with *(very)-low decision making effort* in terms of price, risk factor and decision making effort. In contrary, a *(very)-high-involvement* item domain includes items with *(very)-high decision making effort*. As a very-low-involvement item domain, we chose the *music genre* domain where a collection of songs from the chosen music genre will be played in a fitness center for next two hours. As a low-involvement item domain, we chose the *restaurant* domain where a group of users has to decide on a restaurant for the upcoming dinner. As a high-involvement item domain, we chose the *holiday* domain where a group of friends has to select a destination for the next summer vacation. As a very-high-involvement item domain, we chose the *shared-apartment* domain where a group of students has to decide on an apartment to be shared in the next couple of years.

We conducted our study with students from three Austrian universities.[1] In total, there are $N = 305$ participants (Male: 193, Female: 112) who had to individually select items in the mentioned domains. We want to emphasize that user study participants were not group members involved in decision tasks pre-defined in *Step 2*. They played the role of consultants who analyzed a given decision task and selected an item which was assumed to be optimal for the group. We used the resulting dataset (i.e., recommendations of group decisions given by participants) to evaluate the *prediction quality* (i.e., *precision*) of different group aggregation strategies. The precision of an aggregation strategy was measured in terms of *the ratio between the number of correctly predicted group decisions and the overall number of predictions*.

4 DATA ANALYSIS RESULTS AND DISCUSSIONS

In our user study, the chosen domains and decision tasks were arranged into sequences with different orders and categorized into two types. HIGH → LOW: (very)-high-involvement item domains were presented to participants before (very)-low-involvement item domains. LOW → HIGH: (very)-low-involvement item domains were shown to participants before (very)-high-involvement item domains. Possible sequences of each type are shown in Table 3.

Discussion of hypothesis H_1: In order to test this hypothesis, first we collected all possible sequences which belong to a sequence type (i.e., HIGH → LOW or LOW → HIGH). After that, within each item domain, recommendations of participants related to decision tasks that have been assigned to the domain were collected. The recommendation of a participant for a decision task is an item chosen from three items in the given decision task. This item was considered by the participant as the best solution for the group. A dataset of participants' recommendations in ten different tasks

[1]Graz University of Technology (www.tugraz.at), Karl-Franzens University of Graz (www.uni-graz.at), and University of Klagenfurt (www.aau.at)

Table 3: Possible sequences of four chosen domains. For instance, H-A-M-R denotes a sequence with the following order: *1st*: H (holiday), *2nd*: A (shared-apartment), *3rd*: M (music genre), and *4th*: R (restaurant).

sequence types	possible domain sequences
HIGH → LOW	H-A-M-R, H-A-R-M, A-H-M-R, A-H-R-M
	H-M-A-R, H-R-A-M, A-R-H-M, A-M-H-R
LOW → HIGH	M-R-H-A, M-R-A-H, R-M-H-A, R-M-A-H
	M-H-R-A, M-A-R-H, R-H-M-A, R-A-M-H

Table 4: The distribution of the average time consumption of participants on *Task 4* in different domains.

domain	average time consumption (seconds)
holiday	106.1
shared-apartment	65.9
music genre	41.1
restaurant	48.9

was analyzed for the purpose of investigating tasks where serial position effects really exist. In each task, the precision of aggregation strategies was calculated. The data analysis results show that serial position effects occurred in *Task 4* which were constructed from three evaluation settings (*(3,3,3,3)*, *(1,4,4,4)*, and *(5,2,2,2)*). Task 4 represents a scenario *where, for most items, preferences of one group member are different from preferences of other group members*. We recognize that there exists a significant change of the group decision making behavior of user study participants on this task. Serial position effects observed on this task are the following:

HIGH→LOW sequences: In such sequences, participants invested more time for making a decision on *Task 4* if it was delivered to the participants in *high-involvement item domains* (see Table 4). In addition, participants tended to apply *MUL* and *LMS* strategies in order to generate group recommendations (i.e., MUL and LMS strategies achieved the highest precision both in the *holiday* and *shared-apartment* domains) (see the upper part of Table 5). The precisions of the two strategies are the same since both of them recommend the same item to groups. Such group decision making behaviors could be explained as follows: *MUL* is recognized to perform best in the context of group decision making on a sequence of items [8] and this could be also the case for a sequence of domains. In addition, *LMS* makes sense in the context of high-involvement item domains because it considers the preferences of the least satisfied group member (i.e., the group member who gave the lowest rating about the item) and this helps to minimize misery within the group. In addition, spending more time on decision tasks related to high-involvement item domains could make participants stick with these decisions and tend to use the same strategies for the follow-up decision tasks in low-involvement item domains. The results in the upper part of Table 5 show that participants used the same strategies (i.e., *LMS* and *MUL*) to make group decisions for the *music genre* and *restaurant* domains. In other words, in situations where low-involvement items follow high-involvement items, there is a tendency to *keep the decision strategy* used for high-involvement

Table 5: An analysis of the precision of group aggregation strategies in two types of domain sequences for *Task 4*.

domain	AVG	LMS	MPL	MGD	MAJ	ENS	MUL
\multicolumn{8}{c}{HIGH → LOW}							
holiday	25%	75%	0%	25%	25%	25%	75%
shared-apartment	50%	50%	0%	50%	50%	50%	50%
music genre	25%	75%	0%	25%	25%	25%	75%
restaurant	12.5%	87.5%	0%	12.5%	12.5%	12.5%	87.5%
\multicolumn{8}{c}{LOW → HIGH}							
music genre	37.5%	62.5%	0%	37.5%	37.5%	37.5%	62.5%
restaurant	31.25%	62.5%	6.25%	31.25%	31.25%	31.25%	62.5%
holiday	62.5%	37.5%	0%	62.5%	62.5%	62.5%	37.5%
shared-apartment	50%	25%	25%	50%	50%	50%	25%

items. Moreover, we also figure out that reusing decision strategies applied in high-involvement item domains for the follow-up decision tasks in low-involvement item domains could help to improve the prediction quality of group recommender systems (e.g., the precision of *LMS* and *MUL* strategies significantly improved in the *restaurant* domain).

LOW→HIGH sequences: In such sequences, the group decision making behavior of participants in high-involvement item domains is not influenced by behaviors performed in low-involvement item domains. In other words, high-involvement items seem to *trigger a switch* in the decision strategy. This fact is confirmed by the data analysis results depicted in the lower part of Table 5. Participants applied *LMS* and *MUL* strategies for items in low-involvement domains, whereas *AVG, MGD, MAJ,* and *ENS* strategies were used for in high-involvement item domains. Moreover, the prediction quality of *AVG, MGD, MAJ,* and *ENS* in the *holiday* and *shared-apartment* domains is improved significantly whenever group decisions in these domains are performed after group decisions in (very)-low-involvement item domains have been made.

To conclude, the hypothesis H_1 can be partly confirmed for HIGH→LOW sequences consisting the task in which the preferences of a minority of group members about most items significantly differ from the preferences of other group members.

Discussion of hypothesis H_2: In order to confirm the hypothesis H_2, we measured the time that participants invested for all decision tasks in the four chosen domains. For each domain, time durations invested for decision tasks in HIGH→LOW and LOW→HIGH sequences were collected into different sets. Time duration values in these sets were normalized using Formula 1 (based on the Feature Scaling Normalization method [1]). After that, we used the *independent t-test* (*significant level* $\alpha = 0.05$) to determine whether there exists a statistically significant difference between the population means from two different sets of time duration.

$$norm\text{-}duration = \frac{duration - duration_{min}}{duration_{max} - duration_{min}} \quad (1)$$

The t-test analysis results on different sets of time duration obviously show that: Compared to LOW→HIGH sequences, in HIGH→LOW sequences, decision tasks related to *high-involvement item domains* (*holiday* and *share-apartment*) take longer ($P_{holiday}$ *one tail* = 0.00624 < α and $P_{shared-apartment}$ *one tail* = 0.033 < α). The opposite tendency is confirmed in decision tasks related to *low-involvement item domains*. That means, compared to the HIGH→LOW

sequences, in LOW→HIGH sequences, participants tend to spend more time for decision tasks in *low-involvement item domains* (P_{song} *one tail* = 3.75E − 08 < α and $P_{restaurant}$ *one tail* = 4.6E − 05 < α).

To conclude, in the context of repeated group decision making, the hypothesis H_2 is supported. In other words, with the same decision task, the duration for making a decision could differ depending on which position it appears in a sequence of different item domains. In addition, the confirmation of the hypothesis H_2 helps to figure out that participants tend to invest more time for the tasks arranged in the first positions of the sequence of decision tasks and less time for the tasks which appear at the end of the sequence.

5 CONCLUSIONS AND FUTURE WORK

In this paper, we focused on analyzing the existence of serial position effects in sequential group decision making. The results of our study confirm that the behavior of participants changes significantly when high-involvement item domains are shown before low-involvement item domains. This fact is also confirmed whenever participants are confronted with a decision task where preferences of a group member about most items significantly differ from preferences of other group members. In such decision tasks, participants tend to reuse the strategies already applied to make decisions in high-involvement item domains for the follow-up decisions in low-involvement item domains. The reusing tendency helps to improve the prediction quality of group recommender systems. Additionally, we figured out that there exist serial position effects on the group decision making duration of group members. In repeated group decision making scenarios, group members invest different amounts of time for the same decision task depending on its position in a given sequence of decision tasks. Within the scope of our future work, we will focus on the analysis of group decision strategies by comparing their item domain-specific sensitivity. For example, we will analyze the impact of integrating different aspects of risk-awareness into the design of group aggregation strategies. This helps to figure out which group aggregation strategy is optimal in terms of minimizing risk or misery within group members. In addition, we will repeat this user study by creating real groups (instead of artificial groups) and investigate the influence of different aspects that could occur in the group decision making process (e.g, *age, gender, cultural background, social influence, dominant players, etc.*).

REFERENCES

[1] Selim Aksoy and Robert M. Haralick. 2001. Feature normalization and likelihood-based similarity measures for image retrieval. *Pattern Recognition Letters* 22, 5 (2001), 563–582. http://dblp.uni-trier.de/db/journals/prl/prl22.html#AksoyH01

[2] In K. Chung and Carl R. Adams. 1997. A Study on the Characteristics of Group Decision Making Behavior: Cultural Difference Perspective of Korea vs. U.S. *J. Glob. Inf. Manage.* 5, 3 (July 1997), 18–29. http://dl.acm.org/citation.cfm?id= 264850.264852

[3] Alexander Felfernig, Müslüm Atas, Denis Helic, Trang T.N Tran, Martin Stettinger, and Ralph Samer. 2018. *Handbook on Group Recommender Systems.* Springer, Chapter Algorithms for Group Recommendation, 27–58.

[4] Alexander. Felfernig, Müslüm Atas, Trang T.N. Tran, Martin Stettinger, Seda P. Erdeniz, and Gerhard Leitner. 2017. An Analysis of Group Recommendation Heuristics for High- and Low-Involvement Items. In *IEA/AIE (1) (Lecture Notes in Computer Science)*, Vol. 10350. Springer, 335–344.

[5] A. Felfernig, G. Friedrich, B. Gula, M. Hitz, T. Kruggel, R. Melcher, D. Riepan, S. Strauss, E. Teppan, and O. Vitouch. 2007. Persuasive Recommendation: Serial Position Effects in Knowledge-based Recommender Systems. In *In 2nd International Conference of Persuasive Technology (Persuasive 2007)*, Vol. 4744. Springer, 283–294.

[6] Rawan T. Khasawneh and Emad A. Abu-Shanab. 2013. Factors Influencing Group Decision Making Performance in a GSS Enabled Environment. *Computer Science and Information Technology* 1 (2013), 145–152.

[7] Judith Masthoff. 2004. Group Modeling: Selecting a Sequence of Television Items to Suit a Group of Viewers. *User Modeling and User-Adapted Interaction* 14, 1 (01 Feb 2004), 37–85. https://doi.org/10.1023/B:USER.0000010138.79319.fd

[8] Judith Masthoff. 2011. Group Recommender Systems: Combining Individual Models. In *Recommender Systems Handbook*, F. Ricci, L. Rokach, B. Shapira, and P.B. Kantor (Eds.). Springer, 677–702.

[9] Kevin McCarthy, Maria Salamó, Lorcan Coyle, Lorraine McGinty, Barry Smyth, and Paddy Nixon. 2006. Group recommender systems: a critiquing based approach. In *IUI '06: Proceedings of the 11th international conference on Intelligent user interfaces.* ACM, New York, NY, USA, 267–269. https://doi.org/10.1145/1111449.1111506

[10] H. J. Reitz. 1977. *Behavior in Organizations.* Richard D. Irwin, Inc., Homewood, IL.

[11] Martin Stettinger, Alexander Felfernig, Gerhard Leitner, and Stefan Reiterer. 2015. Counteracting Anchoring Effects in Group Decision Making.. In *In the 23rd Conference on User Modeling, Adaptation, and Personalization (UMAP'15), Dublin, Ireland, (Lecture Notes in Computer Science)*, F. Ricci, K. Bontcheva, O. Conlan, and S. Lawless (Eds.), Vol. 9146. Springer, 118–130.

On Cultural-centered Graphical Passwords: Leveraging on Users' Cultural Experiences for Improving Password Memorability

Argyris Constantinides

Department of Computer Science,
University of Cyprus, 1678 Nicosia, Cyprus &
CiTARD Services Ltd., 2064 Nicosia, Cyprus
aconst12@cs.ucy.ac.cy

Marios Belk

Cognitive UX GmbH, 69253 Heidelberg, Germany &
Department of Computer Science,
University of Cyprus, 1678 Nicosia, Cyprus
belk@cognitiveux.de

Christos Fidas

Department of Cultural Heritage Management and New
Technologies, University of Patras, 26504 Rio, Greece
fidas@upatras.gr

George Samaras

Department of Computer Science
University of Cyprus, 1678 Nicosia, Cyprus
cssamara@cs.ucy.ac.cy

ABSTRACT

Adaptive user authentication policies are moving in the center of attention lately aiming to assist users in creating memorable and secure passwords. Focusing on graphical user authentication, state-of-the-art research has provided evidence that image-related attributes affect password memorability and security. Nonetheless, the effects of users' contemporary cultural-related memories towards password memorability and security have not been investigated so far, although it is known that user authentication is a cross-cultural task. Aiming to shed light on whether such effects exist, we conducted a study in which users created a graphical password with a contemporary culture-intensive *vs.* a culture-neutral image. Results indicate that image content related to one's cultural-related memories affects the interaction behavior during password composition, and consequently password memorability. Findings point towards a promising new direction for considering human contemporary cultural memories in the design of adaptive password policies to increase memorability and preserve security.

CCS CONCEPTS

• **Human-centered computing** → Human computer interaction → HCI theory, concepts and models; Empirical studies in HCI

UMAP '18, July 8–11, 2018, Singapore, Singapore
© 2018 Association for Computing Machinery.
ACM ISBN 978-1-4503-5589-6/18/07...$15.00
https://doi.org/10.1145/3209219.3209254

KEYWORDS

Cultural-centered Graphical Passwords; Memorability; Security.

ACM Reference format:

A. Constantinides, M. Belk, C. Fidas, G. Samaras. 2018. On Cultural-centered Graphical Passwords: Leveraging on Users' Cultural Experiences for Improving Password Memorability. In *Proceedings of ACM User Modeling, Adaptation and Personalization conference, Singapore, July 2018 (UMAP'18)*, 5 pages. https://doi.org/10.1145/3209219.3209254

1 INTRODUCTION

User authentication tasks are becoming important from a cultural-centered point of view since these tasks are performed daily by millions of users across diverse cultures which share distinct characteristics and behaviors. Evidence has shown that users across various cultures exhibit different behaviors in security systems [1-7], underpinning the added value of *cultural-centered adaptive security systems*.

Graphical user authentication (GUA) schemes, which ask users to complete an image-based task to login, are increasingly being adopted by researchers and practitioners as they leverage on new interaction design capabilities and adapt to nowadays mobile and immersive user interaction realms [8-10]. Many GUA schemes have been proposed (see [11] for a review) which either require users to sketch a secret pattern on the screen [12], select various positions on a background picture [13], or select pictures on a grid [14, 15].

Two important quality dimensions of an effective GUA scheme are related to its *security* and *usability* aspects. The security level of a graphical password determines its strength against adversary attacks, whereas usability levels are commonly determined by *memorability of selected passwords* [11]. A cornerstone factor that influences both the security and usability of graphical passwords is the background image(s) used [16].

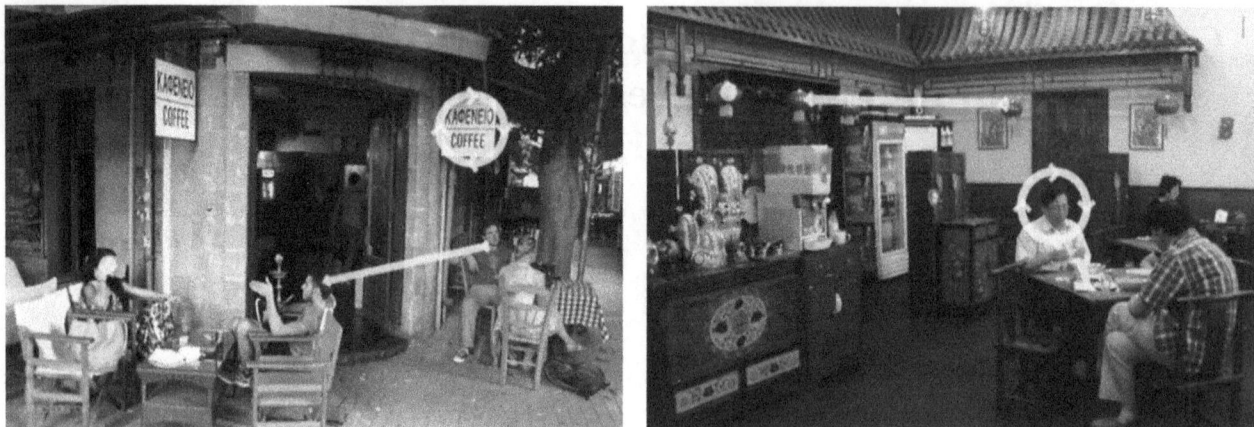

Figure 1: Contemporary culture-intensive image (left) illustrating people in a Greek coffee shop/restaurant *vs.* **culture-neutral image (right)** illustrating people in a Chinese restaurant[1]. We recruited participants that had spent the last 5 years in Greek societies; assuming that they would have had more experience with regional Greek coffee shops' and restaurants' culture, traditions, etc.

From the *security perspective*, studies have shown that the selection of images can be predictable since studies have shown that users prefer clear *vs.* incoherent images [16], and choose images that illustrate people [17, 18], sceneries [17], comics [17]. Furthermore, user choices are influenced by human attributes in an image (*e.g.*, race, age, gender [19]), image colors and type [20]. From the *usability perspective*, studies have shown that the background image attributes of a graphical password have an effect on memorability such as image type (*e.g.*, faces *vs.* abstract images) [15], image properties (*e.g.*, color, shape) [20], image distortion [21, 22], and interference [23]. Finally, the complexity of a background image (*i.e.*, how many attention points it entails) affects password strength and memorability [24-26]. A recent work in [27, 28] revealed that users with different human cognitive attributes follow different patterns of visual behavior and make different selections on images which affect the strength and memorability of graphical passwords.

Research Motivation. The aforementioned research works have provided evidence that several image-related attributes affect memorability and security of selected passwords. However, despite the fact that GUA is a globalized and a cross-cultural task in nearly every interactive system world-wide, *cultural-centered* studies and design issues have not been incorporated in state-of-the-art GUA policies for the benefits of the end-users. In this context, our work focuses on whether, how and why certain images related to the contemporary cultural-related memories of users (*e.g.*, societal habits like going to a coffee shop, going to concerts, etc.) will positively affect the time spent to create a password and subsequently memorability. Doing so, can assist service providers to deliver "best-fit" pictures in GUA schemes by considering intrinsic relationships among users' inter- and intra-cultural differences towards memorability, aiming to drive the *design of cultural-centered adaptive user authentication policies*.

2 METHOD OF STUDY

2.1 Null Hypotheses

H_{01}. There is no significant difference in *graphical password creation time* among users that utilize contemporary culture-intensive images *vs.* culture-neutral images[1];

H_{02}. There is no significant difference in *memorability* of the user-selected graphical password between users that utilize contemporary culture-intensive images *vs.* culture-neutral images;

H_{03}. There is no correlation between the time to create a graphical password and memorability for users that utilize contemporary culture-intensive images *vs.* culture-neutral images;

H_{04}. There is no significant difference in *graphical password strength* between users that utilize contemporary culture-intensive images *vs.* culture-neutral images.

2.2 Procedure

We developed a Web-based GUA scheme, similar to Windows™ Picture Gesture Authentication (PGA) [29] in which users draw three gestures (taps, lines and circles) on a background image to create a graphical password. To increase ecological validity, we applied the GUA task within an existing real-life service. To keep the authentication task as a secondary task, users were asked to comment on a blog that first required them to login.

The study was split in two phases. In *Phase A (Day 1)*, participants were introduced to the GUA scheme, completed a questionnaire on demographics and then created and confirmed their graphical password. Users were required to create three gestures on the image which was used as their secret graphical password. Half of the participants received a contemporary

---

[1] We refer to *culture-intensive images* as images that are relevant to the study participants' own culture (*i.e.*, Greek), and to *culture-neutral images* as images that are not relevant to the study participants' own culture (*i.e.*, China).

culture-intensive image, and the other half a culture-neutral image (Figure 1). We intentionally chose images with a scenery and people since research revealed that users tend to select images illustrating people [17, 25] and scenery [25, 30]. The *culture-intensive image* illustrated a common societal habit of people falling into the age category of our participants and within their cultural context (region they live in). In contrast, the *culture-neutral image* was related to the same societal habit, however in a different socio-cultural context.

Furthermore, given that image complexity affects password strength [26] and gesture combinations [17, 31, 32, 33], we intentionally chose two images of similar complexity (in terms of number of attention points), and examine whether image type during password composition affects the time spent to create the password, and eventually memorability. To control image complexity, we calculated the saliency map and the entropy of several images which is a common measure of image complexity [34], and accordingly used the images depicted in Figure 1.

Following the method in [35], in *Phase B* (performed in *Day 7, 10 and 14*), we sent out emails asking users to access blog posts which required them to login through the GUA scheme.

2.3 Study Variables

Password Creation Time: password creation time was measured from page load (after training) until the user successfully created the graphical password, for attempts that were completed at first trial;

Memorability: we used two metrics as a measure of memorability (following the approach in [35]): *i)* memory time which is the greatest length of time between a password creation and a successful password login using the same graphical password; and *ii)* number of password resets;

Password Strength: we adopted password guessability, a widely used metric for measuring password strength [18, 30]. Following existing approaches in [27, 36, 18, 30], we performed a brute-force attack starting from the segments covering the attention points, then checked the neighboring segments, and finally checked the rest of the segments. The final number of guesses represents the graphical password strength.

2.4 Participants

A total of 61 individuals (18 females) were recruited, ranging in age from 20 to 23 (m=21.13; sd=1.43). Participants are Greek Cypriots living in Nicosia, Cyprus. Participants were split evenly in two groups. The image type (contemporary culture-intensive *vs.* culture-neutral) was randomly varied across all users. To increase internal validity, we recruited individuals with no prior experience with PGA, and participants that had spent the last 5 years in Greek societies; hence we assumed that they would have had experience with Greek regional coffee shops' culture.

2.5 Analysis of Results

In the analyses that follow, data are mean ± standard deviation, unless otherwise stated. There were no significant outliers in the data. Figure 2 depicts a summary of all results.

Password Creation Time Differences. To investigate H_{01}, we ran a Welch t-test since the assumption of homogeneity of variances was violated, as assessed by Levene's test for equality of variances (p=.009). The analysis determined if there were differences in the total time spent to create a graphical password between users that utilized the contemporary culture-intensive image *vs.* those that utilized the culture-neutral image. Creation times for each level of image type were normally distributed, as assessed by Shapiro-Wilk's test (p>.05). Users with the culture-intensive image spent more time to create their graphical password (50.1 ± 23.79) than users with the culture-neutral image (38.06 ± 9.05), a statistically significant difference of 12.03 (95% CI, 955.67 to 23.12), t(29.882)=2.219, p=.034.

Memorability Differences. The maximum memory time that someone could achieve was approximately 336 hours (14 days x 24 hours). To investigate H_{02}, we ran an independent-samples t-test to determine if there were differences in memory time between users that utilized the contemporary culture-intensive image *vs.* those that utilized the culture-neutral image. Memory time for each level of user group was not normally distributed, as assessed by Shapiro-Wilk's test (p<.05). Since the sample sizes in each group are equal, the independent-samples t-test is considered robust under these circumstances. The assumption of homogeneity of variances was violated, as assessed by Levene's test for equality of variances (p<.05). Memory time was significantly longer for culture-intensive users (292.08 ± 27.4) than culture-neutral users (265.4 ± 40.96), a statistically significant difference of 26.68 (95% CI, 8.7 to 44.66), t(50.42)=2.98, p=.004.

As an additional measure of memorability, we recorded the number of password resets per participant. The median number of resets for the culture-intensive group was 0, since most participants did not reset their password, while for the culture-neutral group, the median was 1. A Mann-Whitney U test revealed that the number of resets for the culture-intensive group (6 resets; *mean rank*=36.27) was significantly less than the culture-neutral group (16 resets; *mean rank*=25.9), U=307, z=-2.740, p=.006.

To investigate H_{03}, we ran a Spearman's rank-order correlation to assess the relationship between the time spent to create a graphical password and memorability for both user groups. The analysis showed that there was a positive correlation between time spent to create the password and memorability, rs(61)=.536, p<.001.

Password Strength Differences. To investigate H_{04}, we ran an independent-samples t-test, with the user group (culture-intensive *vs.* culture-neutral) as the independent variable, and the number of guesses needed to crack the password as the dependent variable. The analysis revealed that password strength between the two user groups was not significantly different (t(55.66)=-.266, p=.791); images of the culture-intensive group required 315.08 ± 12.2 million guesses to crack, while images of the culture-neutral group required 324.53 ± 15.2 million guesses to crack.

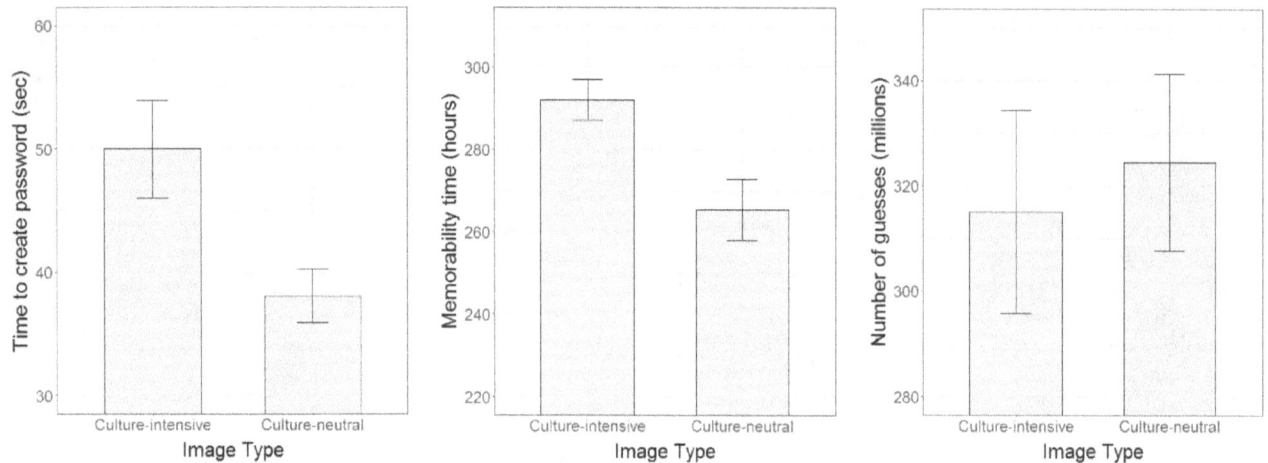

Figure 2: Summary of results; creation time (left), memorability (middle), security (right). Results indicate an increase of time to create the password in the culture-intensive group, which is correlated with memorability, while security was similar across groups.

3 DISCUSSION AND IMPLICATIONS

The results of the study suggest interdependencies between contemporary socio-cultural user memories, the time to create the password and memorability. Hence, it is possible to encourage users towards creating more memorable passwords by providing "best-fit" background images in the graphical password to better process the visual information, and thus trigger deeper information processing and recall. Correlation analyses further indicate that time spent to create the password was positively correlated with memorability, while security analyses showed no significant differences between the groups.

Considering that cultural characteristics (*e.g.*, societal habits, popular culture, etc.) can be assessed easily through explicit user data collection methods (*e.g.*, during user enrolment), studies like the reported one could drive the design of *cultural-centered adaptive and personalized GUA policies and schemes*. Building on our current work [27, 37, 39, 40], which addresses an optimization problem of assigning "best-fit" user authentication mechanisms based on security and usability attributes, the main results of this work could be transformed into specific context-based recommendation rules and be further applied in a procedure for recommending a specific GUA background image type by considering the users' cultural background.

Like structure-based adaptive policies [38], cultural-based adaptive policies could be considered for helping users who share common cultural characteristics to create more memorable graphical passwords. Simple rule-based mechanisms could be elaborated to serve images related to one's cultural attributes aiming to increase memorability. More sophisticated adaptive policies that would automatically evolve over time by taking advantage of the common behavioral patterns of users sharing a common cultural background (*e.g.*, societal habits, nationality) could be based on collaborative filtering mechanisms. These would suggest images that have been successfully used by existing users (in terms of memorability and security) that share common cultural attributes.

4 CONCLUSIONS AND FUTURE WORK

This paper reports results of a two-week user study that aimed to investigate whether memorability of graphical passwords can be increased through the delivery of contemporary culture-intensive images during password composition. Findings provide evidence about the value of considering image context at the intersection of the user's contemporary culture as an important personalization factor which indicates that improves memorability, while it simultaneously preserves security.

Limitations of the study relate to the selection of two specific background images. Although users tend to choose certain images [26], we have selected two representative images of the most widely used image categories (people [17, 25], scenery [25, 30]). Another limitation relates to the fact that participants belonged to the same culture. Nonetheless, to increase internal validity we recruited participants with the same age, contemporary culture, experiences, etc. to investigate how they interact with a contemporary culture-intensive *vs.* a culture-neutral image in relation to their own culture.

Future work entails conducting inter-cultural studies (*e.g.*, Eastern *vs.* Western cultures), studying the interdependency between users' collective past memories and popular culture, and investigating the influence of other cultural differences on GUA memorability and security, such as cognitive differences (holistic *vs.* analytic) [41, 42], visual behavior [43], etc. Given the global and multi-cultural character of user authentication today, we are optimistic that building cultural-centered adaptive GUA policies and schemes could provide a promising new perspective in GUA research to increase memorability and preserve security.

ACKNOWLEDGMENTS

This paper was partially supported by the project ADVisE, in the frame of the University of Cyprus' internal funded research projects, and the project SUCCESS, funded by the EU Active and Assisted Living Programme (AAL-2016-089).

REFERENCES

[1] Wang, Y., Xia, H., & Huang, Y. (2016). Examining American and Chinese Internet Users' Contextual Privacy Preferences of Behavioral Advertising. In *Proceedings of the 19th ACM Conference on Computer-Supported Cooperative Work & Social Computing* (pp. 539-552). ACM

[2] Lin, J., Benisch, M., Sadeh, N., Niu, J., Hong, J., Lu, B., & Guo, S. (2013). A comparative study of location-sharing privacy preferences in the United States and China. *Personal and ubiquitous computing, 17*(4), 697-711

[3] Wang, Y., Norice, G., & Cranor, L. F. (2011). Who is concerned about what? A study of American, Chinese and Indian users' privacy concerns on social network sites. In *International Conference on Trust and Trustworthy Computing* (pp. 146-153). Springer, Berlin, Heidelberg

[4] Zhao, C., Hinds, P., & Gao, G. (2012). How and to whom people share: the role of culture in self-disclosure in online communities. In *Proceedings of the ACM 2012 conference on Computer Supported Cooperative Work* (pp. 67-76). ACM

[5] Chaudhary, S., Zhao, Y., Berki, E., Valtanen, J., Li, L., Helenius, M., & Mystakidis, S. (2015). A cross-cultural and gender-based perspective for online security: Exploring knowledge, skills and attitudes of higher education students. *IADIS International Journal on WWW/Internet, 13*(1)

[6] Harbach, M., De Luca, A., Malkin, N., & Egelman, S. (2016). Keep on Lockin'in the Free World: A Multi-National Comparison of Smartphone Locking. In *Proceedings of the 2016 CHI Conference on Human Factors in Computing Systems* (pp. 4823-4827). ACM

[7] Sawaya, Y., Sharif, M., Christin, N., Kubota, A., Nakarai, A., & Yamada, A. (2017). Self-Confidence Trumps Knowledge: A Cross-Cultural Study of Security Behavior. In *Proceedings of the 2017 CHI Conference on Human Factors in Computing Systems* (pp. 2202-2214). ACM

[8] Chiang, H. Y., & Chiasson, S. (2013). Improving user authentication on mobile devices. In *Proceedings of the 15th international conference on Human-computer interaction with mobile devices and services* (pp. 251-260). ACM

[9] Dunphy, P., Heiner, A. P., & Asokan, N. (2010). A closer look at recognition-based graphical passwords on mobile devices. In *Proceedings of the Sixth Symposium on Usable Privacy and Security* (p. 3). ACM

[10] Von Zezschwitz, E., Dunphy, P., & De Luca, A. (2013). Patterns in the wild: a field study of the usability of pattern and pin-based authentication on mobile devices. In *Proceedings of the 15th international conference on Human-computer interaction with mobile devices and services* (pp. 261-270). ACM

[11] Biddle, R., Chiasson, S., & van Oorschot, P. C. (2012). Graphical passwords: Learning from the first twelve years. *ACM Computing Surveys, 44*(4), 19

[12] Jermyn, I. H., Mayer, A., Monrose, F., Reiter, M. K., & Rubin, A. D. (1999). The design and analysis of graphical passwords. In *Proceedings of the 8th USENIX Security Symposium* (Security '99), USENIX Association

[13] Wiedenbeck, S., Waters, J., Birget, J.C., Brodskiy, A., & Memon, N. (2005). PassPoints: Design and longitudinal evaluation of a graphical password system. *International Journal of Human-Computer Studies, 63*(1-2), 102-127

[14] Real User Corporation (2004). The Science Behind Passfaces. Technical report.

[15] Mihajlov, M., & Jerman-Blazic, B. (2011). On designing usable and secure recognition-based graphical authentication mechanisms. *Interacting with Computers, 23*(6), 582-593

[16] Aydın, Ü. A., Acartürk, C., & Çağıltay, K. (2013). The Role of Visual Coherence in Graphical Passwords. In *Proceedings of the Annual Meeting of the Cognitive Science Society*

[17] Alt, F., Schneegass, S., Shirazi, A. S., Hassib, M., & Bulling, A. (2015). Graphical passwords in the wild: Understanding how users choose pictures and passwords in image-based authentication schemes. In *Proceedings of the 17th International Conference on Human-Computer Interaction with Mobile Devices and Services* (pp. 316-322). ACM

[18] Zhao, Z., Ahn, G. J., Seo, J. J., & Hu, H. (2013). On the Security of Picture Gesture Authentication. In *USENIX Security Symposium* (pp. 383-398)

[19] Davis, D., Monrose, F., & Reiter, M. K. (2004). On User Choice in Graphical Password Schemes. In *USENIX Security Symposium* (Vol. 13, pp. 11-11)

[20] Mihajlov, M., Jerman-Blažič, B., & Shuleska, C. A. (2016). Why that picture? discovering password properties in recognition-based graphical authentication. *International Journal of Human–Computer Interaction, 32*(12), 975-988

[21] Hayashi, E., Dhamija, R., Christin, N., & Perrig, A. (2008). Use your illusion: secure authentication usable anywhere. In *Proceedings of the 4th symposium on Usable privacy and security* (pp. 35-45). ACM

[22] Hayashi, E., Hong, J., & Christin, N. (2011). Security through a different kind of obscurity: Evaluating distortion in graphical authentication schemes.

In *Proceedings of the SIGCHI Conference on Human Factors in Computing Systems* (pp. 2055-2064). ACM

[23] Everitt, K. M., Bragin, T., Fogarty, J., & Kohno, T. (2009). A comprehensive study of frequency, interference, and training of multiple graphical passwords. In Proceedings of the SIGCHI Conference on Human Factors in Computing Systems (pp. 889-898). ACM

[24] Chiasson, S., Biddle, R., & van Oorschot, P. C. (2007). A second look at the usability of click-based graphical passwords. In *Proceedings of the 3rd symposium on Usable privacy and security* (pp. 1-12). ACM

[25] Dunphy, P., & Yan, J. (2007). Do background images improve draw a secret graphical passwords?. In *Proceedings of the 14th ACM conference on Computer and communications security* (pp. 36-47). ACM

[26] Wiedenbeck, S., Waters, J., Birget, J. C., Brodskiy, A., & Memon, N. (2005). Authentication using graphical passwords: Effects of tolerance and image choice. In *Proceedings of the 2005 symposium on Usable privacy and security* (pp. 1-12). ACM

[27] Katsini, C., Fidas, C., Raptis, G. E., Belk, M., Samaras, G., & Avouris, N. (2018). Influences of Human Cognition and Visual Behavior on Password Strength during Picture Password Composition. In *Proceedings of the 2018 CHI Conference on Human Factors in Computing Systems* (p. 87). ACM

[28] Raptis, G. E., Katsini, C., Belk, M., Fidas, C., Samaras, G., & Avouris, N. (2017). Using eye gaze data and visual activities to infer human cognitive styles: method and feasibility studies. In *Proceedings of the 25th Conference on User Modeling, Adaptation and Personalization* (pp. 164-173). ACM

[29] Jeffrey Jay Johnson, Steve Seixeiro, Zachary Pace, Giles van der Bogert, Sean Gilmour, Levi Siebens, and Kenneth Tubbs. 2014. Picture Gesture Authentication. Retrieved from https://www.google.com/patents/US8910253

[30] Zhao, Z., Ahn, G. J., & Hu, H. (2015). Picture gesture authentication: Empirical analysis, automated attacks, and scheme evaluation. *ACM Transactions on Information and System Security (TISSEC), 17*(4), 14

[31] van Oorschot, P. C., & Thorpe, J. (2011). Exploiting predictability in click-based graphical passwords. *Journal of Computer Security, 19*(4), 669-702

[32] Zachary Pace (2011). Signing in with a picture password. Retrieved from https://blogs.msdn.microsoft.com/b8/2011/12/16/signing-in-with-a-picture-password

[33] Thorpe, J., & van Oorschot, P. C. (2007). Human-Seeded Attacks and Exploiting Hot-Spots in Graphical Passwords. In *USENIX Security Symposium* (Vol. 8, pp. 1-8)

[34] Perazzi, F., Krähenbühl, P., Pritch, Y., & Hornung, A. (2012). Saliency filters: Contrast based filtering for salient region detection. In *Computer Vision and Pattern Recognition (CVPR), 2012 IEEE Conference on* (pp. 733-740). IEEE

[35] Stobert, E., & Biddle, R. (2013). Memory retrieval and graphical passwords. In *Proceedings of the symposium on usable privacy and security* (p. 15). ACM

[36] Sadovnik, A., & Chen, T. (2013). A visual dictionary attack on Picture Passwords. In *Image Processing (ICIP), 2013 20th IEEE International Conference on* (pp. 4447-4451). IEEE

[37] Belk, M., Fidas, C., Germanakos, P., & Samaras, G. (2017). The interplay between humans, technology and user authentication: A cognitive processing perspective. *Computers in Human Behavior, 76*, 184-200

[38] Segreti, S.M., Melicher, W., Komanduri, S., Melicher, D., Shay, R., Ur, B., Bauer, L., Christin, N., Cranor, L.F. and Mazurek, M.L. (2017). Diversify to Survive: Making Passwords Stronger with Adaptive Policies. In *Symposium on Usable Privacy and Security (SOUPS)*

[39] Fidas, C., Hussmann, H., Belk, M., & Samaras, G. (2015). iHIP: Towards a user centric individual human interaction proof framework. In *Proceedings of the 33rd Annual ACM Conference Extended Abstracts on Human Factors in Computing Systems* (pp. 2235-2240). ACM

[40] Belk, M., Germanakos, P., Fidas, C., & Samaras, G. (2014). A personalization method based on human factors for improving usability of user authentication tasks. In *Proceedings of the International Conference on User Modeling, Adaptation, and Personalization* (pp. 13-24). Springer

[41] Varnum, M. E., Grossmann, I., Kitayama, S., & Nisbett, R. E. (2010). The origin of cultural differences in cognition: *The social orientation hypothesis. Current directions in psychological science, 19*(1), 9-13

[42] Engelbrecht, P., & Natzel, S. G. (1997). Cultural variations in cognitive style: Field dependence vs field independence. *School Psychology International, 18*(2), 155-164

[43] Nisbett, R. E., & Masuda, T. (2003). Culture and point of view. *Proceedings of the National Academy of Sciences, 100*(19), 11163-11170

The Effect of Gender and Age on the Factors that Influence Healthy Shopping Habits in E-Commerce

Ifeoma Adaji
University of Saskatchewan
Saskatoon, Saskatchewan
Canada
ifeoma.adaji@usask.ca

Kiemute Oyibo
University of Saskatchewan
Saskatoon, Saskatchewan
Canada
kiemute.oyibo@usask.ca

Julita Vassileva
University of Saskatchewan
Saskatoon, Saskatchewan
Canada
jiv@cs.usask.ca

ABSTRACT

People typically eat what they shop for; if consumers shop for healthy foods, they will likely eat healthy foods. In order to influence healthier eating habits among consumers, it is important to identify the factors that influence them to shop for healthy foods. To contribute to ongoing research in this area, we explore the influence of commonly used e-commerce strategies: *personality, persuasive strategies, social support, relative price*, and *perceived product quality* on healthy shopping habits among e-commerce shoppers. Research has shown that personalizing these strategies makes them more effective in achieving the desired behavior change among users. Age and gender have been identified as factors that can be used for group-based personalization. We thus investigate the moderating effect of age and gender on the factors that influence healthy shopping habits in e-commerce shoppers. To achieve this, we carried out an online study of 244 e-commerce shoppers. Using partial least squares structural equation modeling (PLS-SEM), we developed a path model using the commonly used e-commerce factors: *personality, persuasive strategies, social support, relative price, and perceived product quality*. The result of our analysis suggests that *social support, relative price* and *perceived product quality* significantly influence healthy shopping habits in e-commerce shoppers. In addition, females are more influenced by *social support* to adopt healthy shopping habits compared to male e-shoppers. Furthermore, older shoppers are more influenced by *social support* to adopt healthy shopping habits, while the younger shoppers are more influenced by the *relative price* of products.

KEYWORDS

Personality; persuasion; social support; e-commerce

ACM Reference format:

I. Adaji, K. Oyibo, and J. Vassileva. 2018. The Effect of Gender and Age on the Factors that Influence Healthy Shopping Habits in E-commerce. In *UMAP'18: 26th Conference on User Modeling, Adaptation and Personalization, July 8-11, 2018, Singapore*, ACM, NY, NY, USA, 5 pages. https://doi.org/10.1145/3209219.3209253

1 INTRODUCTION

The past decade has seen an increase in the number of people with obesity and obesity related diseases [3]. Healthy eating habits and non-sedentary lifestyles have been identified as two major ways to combat obesity and improve healthy living [3]. While a lot of research focuses on influencing people to live healthy live-styles such as [15], more can be done to influence healthy eating habits. With the increase in the number of e-commerce businesses, many products are now available online including groceries. While this is an opportunity for companies to increase revenue, this could also be a means to promote healthy eating habits. Since people will likely cook and eat what they shop for, we propose that promoting healthy shopping habits online (that is shopping for healthier foods), could influence healthier eating in consumers; if they buy healthy foods, they will likely eat healthy foods. Since many people are currently adopting online grocery shopping[1], implementing the right influence strategies in e-commerce, could persuade individuals to shop for and thus eat healthier foods.

To contribute to ongoing research in this area, we set out to answer the question **what factors significantly influence healthy shopping habits in e-commerce shoppers?** To do this, we explore the influence of various factors on e-consumers' intention to shop for healthy foods. These factors have been used successfully in e-commerce to influence behavior change in consumers. They include *personality, persuasive strategies, social support, relative price* and *perceived product quality*. Because these factors have been shown to influence e-commerce shoppers' intention [12], [1],[19], we set out to determine if this influence is similar with regards to shopping for healthy foods online. Research has shown that personalizing these factors based on demographics such as gender and age make them more effective [13], thus we further determine if there are any differences in the effect of these strategies based on age and gender.

To do this, we carried out a study of 244 online shoppers using an online questionnaire. We developed and tested a research model using partial least-squares structural equation modelling (PLS-SEM). The result of our analysis shows that of the factors investigated *(personality, persuasive strategies, social*

---

[1] https://www.cnbc.com/2017/01/30/online-grocery-sales-set-surge-grabbing-20-percent-of-market-by-2025.html

support, relative price and *perceived product quality*), only *social support, relative price* and *product quality* significantly influence healthy shopping habits in e-commerce shoppers and they predict almost 20% of e-consumers' healthy shopping habits. The result of a multi-group analysis between males and females suggest that females are more influenced by *social support* to adopt healthy shopping habits compared to male e-shoppers. Comparing older shoppers to younger ones, our results suggest that while the former group of e-shoppers are more influenced by *social support* to adopt healthy shopping habits, the latter group is more influenced by the *relative price* of products.

These results suggest possible design guidelines in developing and implementing personalized strategies that could influence healthier shopping habits in e-commerce.

2 RELATED WORK

2.1 Personality

One's personality includes the characteristics or qualities that form their individual distinctive character and they are known to determine significant outcomes in life such as success in one's occupation, quality of one's relationship, and adaptation to life changes among others [12]. In the current study, we adopted the Big Five Model [7] to classify shoppers according to their personality. We used the Big Five model because it has been used extensively in the past in e-commerce [9]. The Big Five Model describes a person's personality using five factors: *openness to experience, conscientiousness, extraversion, agreeableness* and *neuroticism* [7].

Huang and Yang [9] investigated the relationship between personality traits and online shopping motivations using the Big Five model. They mapped the Big Five model to online shopping motivations: *adventure, idea, sociality, lack of sociality* and *convenience*. Their results suggest that the e-shoppers that are *open to experience* shop online for the adventure and the possible ideas they get from their shopping experience. On the other hand, the *conscientious* e-shoppers patronize online vendors because of the convenience of online shopping, while the *extraverted* consumers are motivated to shop online due to social factors.

2.2 Persuasive Strategies

Persuasive technology (PT) is the use of interactive technology to change people's attitude and behavior without coercion or deception [6]. A key element in persuasive technology is persuasion. There are various persuasive strategies that influence behavior change in people. Cialdini [5] posits that these strategies can be grouped within six basic categories: *reciprocation, commitment and consistency, social proof, liking, authority* and *scarcity*. Cialdini further argues that each category targets human behavior and is based on basic psychological principles. These persuasive strategies were developed in the context of marketing, to get people to buy things, and are being used widely by e-commerce companies. For example, Amazon.com implements scarcity by using phrases such as *"Only 2 left in stock. Order soon".*

Cialdini's six principles of persuasion [10] are commonly used in online shopping [4], [11]. We thus included these strategies in our study.

2.3 Social Support

Social support has been shown to influence the online purchasing decisions of e-consumers [1]. In this study, we measure social support as the support one receives from their friends, family and significant other as suggested by Zimet et al. [20].

2.4 Relative price and perceived product quality

Relative price and product quality have also been shown to be great indicators of one's purchase intention in e-commerce. Valvi et al. [18] explored the factors that influence e-commerce shopping intention and concluded that price significantly influences online shopping intention in consumers. Similarly, Tsiotsou [17] investigated the role of product quality on purchase intention and concluded that product quality has a significant influence on purchase intention.

Because relative price and product quality significantly influence shopping intention [17]-[18], we adopted them in this study.

3 RESEARCH DESIGN AND METHODOLOGY

We developed a hypothetical path model using the six constructs *personality, persuasive strategies, social support, relative price, perceived product quality* and *healthy shopping habits.* Our research model is described in figure 1.

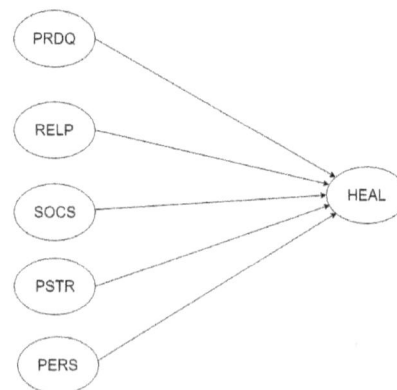

Figure 1: Research model. PRDQ – Perceived product quality, RELP –Relative price, SOCS – Social support, PSTR – Persuasive strategies, PERS – Personality, HEAL – Healthy shopping habits

All constructs were developed from preciously validated scales. Perceived product quality and relative price were measured using four and five items respectively using the scale of Zeithaml et al. [19]. Social support was measured with twelve items using the scale of Zimet et al. [20]. Persuasive strategies were measured using the scale of Kaptein et al. [10], while personality was measured using the scale of Gosling et al. [8]. We adopted the scale of Romani et al. [16] in measuring healthy shopping habits. All items were measured on a seven-point Likert scale (1=strongly disagree, 7=strongly agree).

3.1 Participants

Our test subjects were e-commerce shoppers. A total of 244 participants took part through an online survey. Participants were recruited through Amazon's Mechanical Turk, various social media platforms and news boards. Participation was voluntary, and the study was approved by the ethics board of the University of Saskatchewan. Table 1 shows some of the demographics of the participants.

Table 1: Demographics of participants

	Value	(%)
Age	Less than 30 years	63
	Between 30 and 50 years	30
	Over 50 years	7
Gender	Female	66
	Male	34
House hold size	1 to 3 persons	65
	More than 4 persons	35

4 DATA ANALYSES

Our data was analyzed using Partial Least Squares Structural Equation Modelling (PLS-SEM) with the SmartPLS tool. After establishing the reliability and validity of the constructs in our model, we examined the structural model. We computed the path coefficient (β value), coefficients of determination (R^2 values) and the level and significance of the path coefficients. Figure 2 shows the path coefficients between constructs. The number of asteriks represents the significance of each direct effect. The number of asteriks ranges from 1 to 4 which corresponds with the p-value of <0.05, <0.01, <0.001 and <0.0001 respectively.

5 RESULTS

The result of our analysis in figure 2 shows that of the five categories of strategies explored (*perceived product quality, relative price, social support, persuasive strategies* and *personality*), only *product quality, relative price* and *social support* significantly influence healthy shopping habits among the e-commerce participants. While *social support* had the highest significance (β = 0.205**), *persuasive strategies* and *personality* had no influence on healthy shopping habits. It was surprising to discover that *persuasive strategies* had no influence on healthy shopping habits in e-commerce. We attributed this to the type of persuasive strategies we used in the study; Cialdini's six influence strategies [5]. For example, while a persuasive strategy such as *scarcity*

could have significant influence on one's shopping habits for products such as books, it might not work when influencing healthy shopping habits. Research suggests that the use of gamification elements such as a points based system (where shoppers can earn points when they buy healthy products) or a leaderboard could result in the desired behavior change [14]. In the future, we intend to repeat the study using gamification elements.

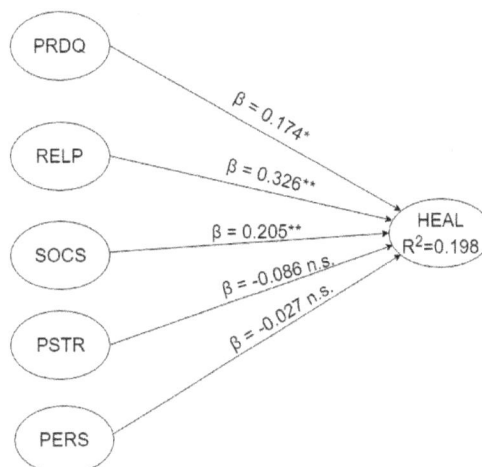

Figure 2. Structural model with results of PLS-SEM analysis. PRDQ = Perceived product quality, RELP =Relative price, SOCS = Social support, PSTR = Persuasive strategies, PERS = Personality, HEAL = Healthy shopping habits

To investigate any differences based on the gender and age of the participants, we carried our multi-group analysis between males and females and between older and younger participants. The result is presented in the following section.

5.1 Moderating Effect of Gender

The result of the multi-group analysis between females and males, as shown in figure 3, shows significant difference on the influence of *social support* on healthy shopping habits in e-commerce. While females are significantly influenced by *social support*, males are not. This suggests that **while considering healthy shopping options in e-commerce, females are influenced by their family, friends and significant other.** This is in line with Antonucci et al. [2] who suggest that women are more likely influenced by *social support* because they have larger networks and receive support from multiple sources. The significance of the other factors (*product quality, relative price, persuasive strategies* and *personality*) was similar for both genders.

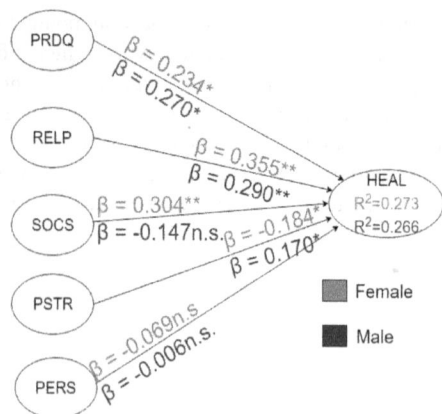

Figure 3. Path coefficient for females (red) and males (blue). PRDQ = Perceived product quality, RELP =Relative price, SOCS = Social support, PSTR = Persuasive strategies, PERS = Personality, HEAL = Healthy shopping habits. n.s. = Not significant

5.2 Moderating Effect of Age

We also compared the results between younger and older participants as shown in figure 4. The younger participants include those 30 years old or less while the older participants were those more than 30 years old. The result of our analysis shows significant differences between both age groups. *Social influence* significantly influences healthy shopping habits in the older participants, while *relative price* significantly influences healthy shopping habits in younger participants. This result suggests that **while the younger e-commerce shoppers were more influenced by the cost of products, the older adults were more influenced by their social circles to adopt healthy shopping habits.** The significance of the other factors (*product quality, persuasive strategies* and *personality*) were similar for both age groups.

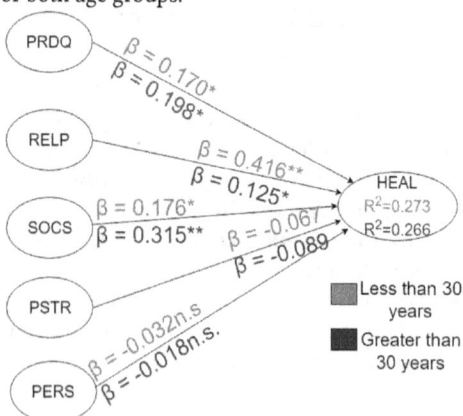

Figure 4. Path coefficient for Participants less than 30 years old inclusive (red) and those older than 30 years old (blue).

The moderating effect of gender and age suggest possible design guidelines in developing and implementing personalized strategies that could influence healthier shopping habits in e-commerce. For example, while presenting healthy food suggestions to females and older shoppers, using strategies that encourage support from their social circles could bring about the desired behavior change in these shoppers. Fitbit[2] is a typical example of how people can be influenced by social support. Fitbit users can take part in activities with people in their social circles while being influenced by them. E-commerce vendors could implement similar strategies that would influence females and older consumers to shop heathy by being influenced by their social circles. On the other hand, while presenting healthy options to younger shoppers, the emphasis should be on the price of the product since younger shoppers are influenced to shop for healthy foods by the relative price. E-commerce vendors could adopt the strategy of sites such as Amazon.com that include the suggested retail price and their own price (which is usually lower than the suggested retail price) for most products. Vendors could also display how much a buyer will potentially save by purchasing a particular product to emphasize the price.

6 CONCLUSION

To contribute to ongoing research in motivating e-consumers to adopt healthier shopping behavior, we explored the factors that influence healthy shopping habits online by conducting a study of 244 e-commerce shoppers. Using partial least squares structural equation modeling (PLS-SEM), we developed a path model using six commonly used e-commerce constructs namely: *personality, persuasive strategies, social support, relative price, perceived product quality* and *healthy shopping habits.* Because these strategies are more effective when personalized, we further explored the moderating effects of age and gender on these factors. The result of our analysis suggests that *social support, relative price* and *perceived product quality* significantly influence healthy shopping habits in e-commerce shoppers. Our analysis further suggests that females are more influenced by *social support* to adopt healthy shopping habits compared to male e-shoppers. In addition, while the older shoppers are more influenced by *social support* to adopt healthy shopping habits, the younger shoppers are more influenced by the *relative price* of products. These results suggest possible design guidelines in developing and implementing personalized strategies that could influence healthier shopping habits in e-commerce. In the future, we plan to explore other persuasive strategies and other demographics data such as household size.

Our study has a few limitations. We have unequal number of female and male participants. Similarly, the ratio of younger participants to older participants is not the same. We are still collecting data; we plan to repeat the study in the future when we have similar number of participants based on age and gender. Another limitation is that the study was self-reported and not based on observing the participants. While there is a possibility

---

[2] https://www.fitbit.com/

of participants providing wrong information, self-reported studies are common practice in the research industry.

REFERENCES

[1] Adaji, I. and Vassileva, J. 2017. Perceived Effectiveness, Credibility and Continuance Intention in E-commerce. A Study of Amazon. *Proceedings of 12th International Conference on Persuasive Technology* (Amsterdam, 2017).

[2] Antonucci, T.C. and Akiyama, H. 1987. An examination of sex differences in social support among older men and women. *Sex roles.* 17, 11 (1987), 737–749.

[3] Bischoff, S., Boirie, Y., ... T.C.-C. and 2017, undefined Towards a multidisciplinary approach to understand and manage obesity and related diseases. *clinicalnutritionjournal.com.*

[4] Bolton, R. and Kannan, P. 2000. Implications of loyalty program membership and service experiences for customer retention and value. *Journal of the academy of.* (2000).

[5] Cialdini, R.B. 2009. *Influence: Science and practice.* Pearson Education Boston.

[6] Fogg, B.J. 2002. Persuasive technology: using computers to change what we think and do. *Ubiquity.* 2002, December (2002), 5.

[7] Goldberg, L.R. 1990. An alternative description of personality: the big-five factor structure. *Journal of personality and social psychology.* 59, 6 (1990), 1216.

[8] Gosling, S.D., Rentfrow, P.J. and Swann, W.B. 2003. A very brief measure of the Big-Five personality domains. *Journal of Research in Personality.* 37, 6 (2003), 504–528. DOI:https://doi.org/10.1016/S0092-6566(03)00046-1.

[9] Huang, J. and Yang, Y. 2010. The relationship between personality traits and online shopping motivations. *Social Behavior and Personality: an.* (2010).

[10] Kaptein, M. 2011. Adaptive persuasive messages in an e-commerce setting: the use of persuasion profiles. *ECIS.* (2011).

[11] Kaptein, M. and Eckles, D. 2012. Heterogeneity in the Effects of Online Persuasion. *Journal of Interactive Marketing.* 26, 3 (2012), 176–188.

DOI:https://doi.org/10.1016/j.intmar.2012.02.002.

[12] Lumsden, J. and MacKay, L. 2006. How does personality affect trust in B2C e-commerce? *Proceedings of the 8th International Conference on Electronic Commerce (ICEC'2006)* (2006).

[13] Orji, R. 2016. The Impact of Cultural Differences on the Persuasiveness of Influence Strategies. *Adjunt proceedings of the 11th iternational conference on Persuasive Technology.* (2016), 38–41.

[14] Orji, R., Mandryk, R.L., Vassileva, J. and Gerling, K.M. 2013. Tailoring persuasive health games to gamer type. *Proceedings of the SIGCHI Conference on Human Factors in Computing Systems - CHI '13* (New York, New York, USA, 2013), 2467.

[15] Orji, R., Vassileva, J. and Mandryk, R.L. 2014. Modeling the efficacy of persuasive strategies for different gamer types in serious games for health. *User Modeling and User-Adapted Interaction.* 24, 5 (Dec. 2014), 453–498. DOI:https://doi.org/10.1007/s11257-014-9149-8.

[16] Romani, S., Grappi, S., Bagozzi, R.P. and Barone, A.M. 2018. Domestic food practices: A study of food management behaviors and the role of food preparation planning in reducing waste. *Appetite.* 121, (Feb. 2018), 215–227. DOI:https://doi.org/10.1016/J.APPET.2017.11.093.

[17] Tsiotsou, R. 2006. The role of perceived product quality and overall satisfaction on purchase intentions. *International Journal of Consumer Studies.* 30, 2 (Mar. 2006), 207–217. DOI:https://doi.org/10.1111/j.1470-6431.2005.00477.x.

[18] Valvi, A., Research, D.W.-J. of E.C. and 2013, undefined E-loyalty is not all about trust, price also matters: extending expectation-confirmation theory in bookselling websites. *search.proquest.com.*

[19] Zeithaml, V.A. 1988. Consumer perceptions of price, quality, and value: a means-end model and synthesis of evidence. *The Journal of marketing.* (1988), 2–22.

[20] Zimet, G., Dahlem, N. and Zimet, S. 1988. The multidimensional scale of perceived social support. *Journal of personality.* (1988).

Data-Driven Destination Recommender Systems

Linus W. Dietz
Technical University of Munich
Garching, Germany
linus.dietz@tum.de

ABSTRACT

Given vast number of possible global travel destinations, choosing a destination has become challenging. We argue that traditional media are insufficient to make informed travel decisions, due to a lack of objectivity, a lack of comparability and because information becomes out of date quickly. Thus, travel planning is an interesting field for data-driven recommender systems that support users to master information explosion. We present unresolved research questions with working packages for a doctoral project that combines the fields of recommender systems and user modeling with data mining. The core contributions will be a framework that integrates heterogeneous data sources from the travel domain, novel user modeling techniques and constraint-based recommender algorithms to master the complexities of global travel planning.

CCS CONCEPTS

• **Information systems** → **Data mining**; **Recommender systems**; • **Human-centered computing**;

KEYWORDS

recommender systems, data mining, user modeling, tourism

ACM Reference Format:
Linus W. Dietz. 2018. Data-Driven Destination Recommender Systems. In *UMAP '18: 26th Conference on User Modeling, Adaptation and Personalization, July 8–11, 2018, Singapore, Singapore.* ACM, New York, NY, USA, 4 pages. https://doi.org/10.1145/3209219.3213591

1 INTRODUCTION AND MOTIVATION

Global travel is booming. Airlines offer connections to all continents except Antarctica, and most destinations can be reached within a day. Affordable mobility has increased travel options, and it has become easier to explore the world and learn about foreign cultures. Given endless opportunities, how can the discretionary traveler make informed decisions about possible destinations?

Typically, tourists use websites, blogs, printed travel guides or travel agencies to make their travel plans. These sources are subjective, of uncertain quality, and can become outdated quickly [27].

UMAP '18, July 8–11, 2018, Singapore, Singapore
© 2018 Association for Computing Machinery.
ACM ISBN 978-1-4503-5589-6/18/07...$15.00
https://doi.org/10.1145/3209219.3213591

Moreover, information about destinations that have not yet exploited for tourism is often too limited to form an opinion about their attractiveness.

In this doctoral project, we want to investigate solutions for a variant of the Tourist Trip Design Problem (TTDP) [27] at a regional granularity. Mining and aggregating domain-related data will enable prospective travelers to independently choose their destinations through informed and independent travel recommendations. We assume that it is not obvious to have accurate expectations from far distant regions. Finally, attractions of specific ethno-cultural destinations are often not tangible but have to be experienced [25].

1.1 Scenario

We envision a user planning a multi-week travel comprising of several destinations within a larger query area. This query region could span across continents, or be a set of specific user-selected areas. Based on user preferences, query area, and boundary conditions (e.g., budget, travel season, and duration), the recommender system should compile a set of regions within the query area that considers the user's temporal and monetary constraints.

1.2 Problem Statement and Research Areas

Based on a query region and user preferences, we want to recommend a personalized travel plan comprising a set of destinations with respective durations of stay. Note that the problem space of such a travel recommender is inherently complex, and we have identified three major research topics related to the target problem.

- **Data-driven recommender system framework** (section 3) Destination information, such as attractiveness relative to preferences and costs, must be mined continuously from online sources. The data must be stored and made available in aggregated form for the other components of the system.

- **User modeling** (section 4) Relevant domain features must be identified and the user's preferences must be elicited effectively without requiring much effort. The interplay of automated solutions and different user interface concepts are to be evaluated.

- **Constraint-based recommendation algorithms** (section 5) Travel is constrained by multiple factors, such as time, costs, season, and visa regulations. In addition, the recommendation algorithm should consider diversity and balance the costs and benefits for visiting another region rather than staying at one location for a longer period.

Throughout this doctorate project, we plan to focus on selected aspects within these research topics. The foundation is a modular framework for destination recommender systems that can handle various subsystems, i.e., domain and user modeling, data warehousing, the recommendation algorithms, and the front-end.

2 RELATED WORK

Research into tourist recommender systems has been conducted for more than 15 years [22]. However, due to the complexities of global travel, existing approaches rather focus on urban trips or recommend fixed travel packages.

2.1 Tourist Trip Recommender Systems

Trip recommendations can be performed at different granularities. The least complex are recommendations for single venues and travel packages. Liu et al. [11] proposed the Tourist-Area-Season Topic (TAST) Model to identify traveler interests and the seasonal suitability of travel regions. In a follow-up paper [10], they evaluated their proposed model and augmented it with relationship information to recommend travel packages to groups. A similar approach introduced by Tan et al. [23] focused on feature selection to identify latent user interests. Using a framework of feature-value pairs to represent users and travel packages to calculate distance metrics, their approach employs collaborative filtering methods without any user ratings. Other approaches [7, 29] attempt to solve variants of the TTDP [27] to recommend a series of points of interest (POIs), typically limited to urban areas. The underlying problem for the TTDP is the Orienteering Problem [26]. Most recently, [6] proposed a fast algorithm for multi-day tourist trips.

Herzog and Wörndl [8] developed a region recommender for personalized continental travel. The user is asked to specify her interests, e.g., *nature & wildlife*, *beaches*, or *winter sports*, as well as potential travel regions and monetary and temporal constraints. Respecting these constraints, a recommendation comprises a set of regions that maximizes the user's preference score, while taking the travel season and diversity of the regions into account. Determining the duration of stay per region is done simultaneously, however, the algorithm applies a static reduction of 5–10% to the preference score per week; thus, it is quite coarse-grained. The destination information comes from several online and offline information sources, which must be incorporated and updated manually.

As opposed to these approaches, we propose to replace expert knowledge with automated data mining techniques, because manual maintenance of global travel data is infeasible.

2.2 Mining Traveler Mobility Patterns

A vast amount of spatial-temporal data is collected from GPS modules in mobile phones. Users can choose to publish such data in location-based social networks (LBSNs) whose general adoption has given opportunity for researchers to analyze human mobility combined with social activities. Since the user's locations and social graph reveal significant information about individual preferences such data has been analyzed to improve recommender systems [3], For example, spatial co-occurrences can be used to identify similar users and generate implicit ratings for collaborative filtering algorithms [30]. In a more elaborate approach [2], travelers in a foreign city are matched to local experts based on their respective home behavior when recommending Foursquare venues. Hsieh et al. [9] used past LBSN data to recommend travel routes along urban POIs. They present an approach to derive the popularity, best time to visit, transit time between venues, and the best order to visit POIs. By analyzing past trips, we aim to improve both user modeling side

by assessing how certain users prefer to travel, and also improve trip recommendations by determining a destination's typical time and duration of visit.

Working Package 1: Conduct a comprehensive literature survey.

3 A FRAMEWORK FOR DATA-DRIVEN RECOMMENDER SYSTEMS

We aim to create a modularized architecture to establish a destination recommender prototype. We want to compare different approaches for one component; therefore, we propose to establish a microservice architecture with strong encapsulation and standardized message passing protocols. This will enable a dynamic interchange of components, e.g., to conduct A/B experiments with different recommendation algorithms and front-ends.

3.1 Data Warehouse

Providing high-quality recommendations requires rich knowledge about the target domain. Currently, information for tourism purposes can be obtained from various online sources. Nonetheless, obtaining relevant features from heterogeneous sources is a data mining challenge [1]. We propose a data warehouse for data-driven recommendations to store and continuously update information about the items to be recommended, i.e., travel destinations. Having historical data enables the detection of trends and improves recommendations, e.g., by determining seasonal fluctuations.

3.2 Region Model

Recommending destinations requires a set of destinations. In an initial approach [8], regions were structured by hand into a region tree where the Earth was the root node followed by continents, sub-continental regions, countries, and states. The size of the query region determines the granularity of the model, resulting in some countries being combined to larger regions, e.g., the Baltic countries or islands in the Caribbean. The advantage of such a model is that, based on the query region, the depth of the region tree can be adapted dynamically to return destinations of a comprehensible size. An ideal solution would realize a trade-off between the features of GeoTree[1], a strict hierarchical data structure of political and administrative regions and the WikiTravel hierarchy[2], which has relaxed consistency for capturing travel-specific features of regions.

3.3 Region Characterization

With a fine-grained region tree, the regions must be enriched with information about relevant factors, such as costs per day, suitability for certain types of traveler, main attractions and potential activities. Our idea is to calculate these metrics based on the presence of venues in the given areas.

Personal Fit. We are currently investigating how collaborative sites, such as Wikipedia and Wikitravel, and online services, such as Google Places[3] and Foursquare, can be used to gather the features of regions. This information must be analyzed, aggregated, and normalized to obtain useful assessments of the individual suitability

---

[1] http://geotree.geonames.org
[2] https://wikitravel.org/en/Wikitravel:Geographical_hierarchy
[3] https://developers.google.com/places

of a given region relative to specific user preferences. Here, the basic assumption is that the density of certain venues can be used to derive a good measure of personal suitability.

Budget. The daily costs for a typical tourist usually consist of accommodation, food, and activity costs. Curated lists, such as the Price of Travel[4], which offers a *backpacker index*, are of limited help, because their data are sparse and we require up-to-date, and machine-readable information to estimate a budget. However, such sparse lists can be used as ground truth to validate novel approaches. To determine hotel prices, we calculate the median price of a representative set of hotels obtained via the Google Hotel Prices API[5]. Food prices are more difficult to estimate. A relatively accurate source of information could be Numbeo[6], which provides detailed information (e.g., a meal in a restaurant, cappuccino or transportation costs) about the cost of living in 511 cities in 86 countries around the world. The service offers a paid API; however, this API cannot be used to determine food prices for the other 160 countries.

Duration of Stay. In a previous paper [5], we investigated typical tourist travel patterns with a focus on the duration of stay. Although this initial step lacked generality due to sparse data, it revealed where travelers did or did not spend time. We plan to extend this research with more data and refined granularity.

Transportation Costs. Traveling between regions incurs costs. Although these costs are sometimes negligible, e.g., when driving between two neighboring regions, they can be significant depending on the mode of transportation and the distance between regions. The flight costs between regions can be queried using different APIs, such as Skyscanner[7]; the Google Transit API[8] provides information about public transportation.

WP 2: Create a framework for data-driven recommender systems with a data warehouse that aggregates heterogeneous data sources to be used in other parts of the recommender system.

4 USER MODELING

For personalized, content-based recommendations a good item characterization and detailed understanding of user preferences are fundamental. These are commonly elicited and refined through interaction with a user interface. We also plan to investigate how preferences can be extracted from information provided by the user.

In the original approach [8], users manually provided preferences with binary indications about their interest in certain predefined activities. We plan to improve this to continuous intensities per category whose values are derived automatically based on social media [4]. Here, the idea is that a history of travel destinations or information from posts, images, and other interactions in LBSNs, can be used to obtain a detailed profile of the user's personality [28]. This can be complemented with explicit question-answering about the intended type of travel, such as the seven traveler profiles described by Neidhardt et al. [18].

Travel planning is a process; thus, the user should be able to alter the original recommendations. Therefore, a conversational approach [20] with elements of active learning [19] appears to be quite promising. The possibility of critiquing [15] can help fine-tune algorithms such that the system can *"[...] automatically improve with experience [17, p. xv]"*, which is a key part of Mitchell's definition of machine learning. To understand the benefits of different user modeling techniques, we plan to conduct controlled lab experiments using human-centered research methods. The important dependent variables are the effort for users to provide their preferences and the level of detail of the user model.

WP 3: Develop efficient and effective strategies for eliciting user preferences using available data and user interface concepts.

5 CONSTRAINT-BASED RECOMMENDATION

The core of a recommender system is the recommendation engine that ranks items based on a query. However, in the TTDP, the challenge is not just returning the top n items but also to selecting a good combination of such items. Framing the initial ranking as a matrix factorization problem would result in extremely sparse data. We propose to obtain rankings based on weighted features of the items; thus, we plan to employ the content-based recommender systems paradigm [12].

Having computed a ranked list of destinations, the actual set of recommended items must be derived in consideration of various factors, such as temporal and monetary constraints, as well as item diversity. If the user preferences are rather specific and the destination model is fine-grained, the top-ranked items may be very similar. In such situations, the algorithm should skip some destinations in favor of improving the variety in the travel knapsack.

Messaoud et al. [16] proposed a variety-seeking model using semantic hierarchical clustering to establish diversity in a set of recommended activities. Similarly, Savir et al. [21] introduced an additional diversity constraints based on attraction types to ensure that the trip's diversity level is above a threshold. Another idea is to adjust item diversity based on the user's personality profile. For example, Wu et al. [28], assessed the user satisfaction based on the diversity level of the recommendations. That study and other approaches [18, 24], use the Five Factor Model of personality [14] to improve recommendations. Tailoring trip diversity to user preferences appears to be a promising avenue to improve the quality of recommendations.

Finally, given a set of regions that fulfills the basic constraints, we propose to fine-tune recommendations by determining how long each of the destinations should be visited, which depends on the typical time required to visit a specific region and of the type of traveler. Lu et al. [13] presented an approach to find an optimal trip in a city within temporal constraints. However, their data model does now allow adaptation of the duration of stay for each attraction. Thus, it is an interesting challenge to determine how aggregated mobility patterns [5] can improve personalized recommendations relative to the duration of stay.

Having implemented the system, we propose to evaluate it online to maximize the number of test subjects. The framework will support A/B testing of independent variables (i.e., novel algorithms

---

[4]https://www.priceoftravel.com
[5]https://developers.google.com/hotels/hotel-prices/api-reference
[6]https://www.numbeo.com
[7]https://partners.skyscanner.net/affiliates/travel-apis
[8]https://developers.google.com/transit

and baselines) and will collect the dependent variables derived from explicit and implicit feedback.

WP4: Develop content-based recommender algorithms that solve the TTDP without violating user-defined constraints.

6 CONCLUSIONS

In this exposé we have drafted a collection of open research problems whose solutions comprise a global destination recommender system for independent travelers. The main contributions have been organized into four working packages. First, literature in the corresponding fields must be collected, categorized and written up to form a basis for our own contributions. Then, a framework for data-driven recommender systems will be designed to enable continuous data acquisition for item characterization and domain modeling. User preferences will be elicited using novel data-driven user modeling methods, which are to be compared with traditional approaches. Finally, constraint-based recommender algorithms for multi-destination tourist trips will be designed.

These problems will be approached using adequate user-centered research methods, and by developing a research prototype, which will be evaluated in user studies and presented to the scientific community via peer-reviewed publications. We are confident that the data-driven contributions of this thesis can be generalized from the tourism domain and transferred to other complex domains where *Assistive AI* struggles to establish itself.

REFERENCES

[1] Xavier Amatriain and Josep M. Pujol. 2011. Data Mining Methods for Recommender Systems. In *Recommender Systems Handbook*, Francesco Ricci, Lior Rokach, Bracha Shapira, and Paul B. Kantor (Eds.). Springer US, Boston, MA, USA, 227–261. https://doi.org/10.1007/978-0-387-85820-3_2

[2] Jie Bao, Yu Zheng, and Mohamed F. Mokbel. 2012. Location-based and preference-aware recommendation using sparse geo-social networking data. In *Proceedings of the 20th International Conference on Advances in Geographic Information Systems (SIGSPATIAL '12)*. ACM, New York, NY, USA, 199–208. https://doi.org/10.1145/2424321.2424348

[3] Jie Bao, Yu Zheng, David Wilkie, and Mohamed Mokbel. 2015. Recommendations in location-based social networks: a survey. *GeoInformatica* 19, 3 (Feb. 2015), 525–565. https://doi.org/10.1007/s10707-014-0220-8 arXiv:1502.07526

[4] Philip Bonhard and M. Angela Sasse. 2006. 'Knowing me, knowing you' — Using profiles and social networking to improve recommender systems. *BT Technology Journal* 24, 3 (July 2006), 84–98. https://doi.org/10.1007/s10550-006-0080-3

[5] Linus W. Dietz, Daniel Herzog, and Wolfgang Wörndl. 2018. Deriving Tourist Mobility Patterns from Check-in Data. In *Proceedings of the WSDM 2018 Workshop on Learning from User Interactions*. Los Angeles, CA, USA.

[6] Zachary Friggstad, Sreenivas Gollapudi, Kostas Kollias, Tamas Sarlos, Chaitanya Swamy, and Andrew Tomkins. 2018. Orienteering Algorithms for Generating Travel Itineraries. In *Proceedings of the Eleventh ACM International Conference on Web Search and Data Mining (WSDM '18)*. ACM, New York, NY, USA, 180–188. https://doi.org/10.1145/3159652.3159697

[7] Damianos Gavalas, Charalampos Konstantopoulos, Konstantinos Mastakas, and Grammati Pantziou. 2014. A survey on algorithmic approaches for solving tourist trip design problems. *Journal of Heuristics* 20, 3 (June 2014), 291–328. https://doi.org/10.1007/s10732-014-9242-5

[8] Daniel Herzog and Wolfgang Wörndl. 2014. A Travel Recommender System for Combining Multiple Travel Regions to a Composite Trip. In *CBRecSys@RecSys (CEUR Workshop Proceedings)*, Vol. 1245. CEUR-WS.org, Foster City, Silicon Valley, California, USA, 42–48.

[9] Hsun-Ping Hsieh, Cheng-Te Li, and Shou-De Lin. 2012. Exploiting Large-scale Check-in Data to Recommend Time-sensitive Routes. In *Proceedings of the ACM SIGKDD International Workshop on Urban Computing (UrbComp '12)*. ACM, New York, NY, USA, 55–62. https://doi.org/10.1145/2346496.2346506

[10] Qi Liu, Enhong Chen, Hui Xiong, Yong Ge, Zhongmou Li, and Xiang Wu. 2014. A Cocktail Approach for Travel Package Recommendation. *IEEE Transactions on Knowledge and Data Engineering* 26, 2 (Feb. 2014), 278–293. https://doi.org/10.1109/tkde.2012.233

[11] Qi Liu, Yong Ge, Zhongmou Li, Enhong Chen, and Hui Xiong. 2011. Personalized Travel Package Recommendation. In *Proceedings of the IEEE 11th International Conference on Data Mining (ICDM '11)*. IEEE, Vancouver, BC, Canada, 407–416. https://doi.org/10.1109/icdm.2011.118

[12] Pasquale Lops, Marco de Gemmis, and Giovanni Semeraro. 2011. Recommender Systems Handbook. In *Recommender Systems Handbook*, Francesco Ricci, Lior Rokach, Bracha Shapira, and Paul B. Kantor (Eds.). Springer US, Boston, MA, USA, Chapter Content-based Recommender Systems: State of the Art and Trends, 73–105. https://doi.org/10.1007/978-0-387-85820-3_3

[13] Eric Hsueh-Chan Lu, Chih-Yuan Lin, and Vincent S. Tseng. 2011. Trip-Mine: An Efficient Trip Planning Approach with Travel Time Constraints. In *2011 IEEE 12th International Conference on Mobile Data Management*, Vol. 1. IEEE, Lulea, Sweden, 152–161. https://doi.org/10.1109/mdm.2011.13

[14] Robert R. McCrae and Oliver P. John. 1992. An Introduction to the Five-Factor Model and Its Applications. *Journal of Personality* 60, 2 (June 1992), 175–215. Issue 2. https://doi.org/10.1111/j.1467-6494.1992.tb00970.x

[15] Lorraine McGinty and James Reilly. 2011. On the Evolution of Critiquing Recommenders. In *Recommender Systems Handbook*, Francesco Ricci, Lior Rokach, Bracha Shapira, and Paul B. Kantor (Eds.). Springer US, Boston, MA, USA, 419–453. https://doi.org/10.1007/978-0-387-85820-3_13

[16] Montassar Ben Messaoud, Ilyes Jenhani, Eya Garci, and Toon De Pessemier. 2017. SemCoTrip: A Variety-Seeking Model for Recommending Travel Activities in a Composite Trip. In *Advances in Artificial Intelligence: From Theory to Practice*. Springer International Publishing, Arras, France, 345–355. https://doi.org/10.1007/978-3-319-60042-0_40

[17] Thomas M. Mitchell. 1997. *Machine Learning* (1 ed.). McGraw-Hill, Inc., New York, NY, USA. https://doi.org/10.1002/0470018860.ss0036

[18] Julia Neidhardt, Leonhard Seyfang, Rainer Schuster, and Hannes Werthner. 2015. A picture-based approach to recommender systems. *Information Technology & Tourism* 15, 1 (March 2015), 49–69. https://doi.org/10.1007/s40558-014-0017-5

[19] Neil Rubens, Dain Kaplan, and Masashi Sugiyama. 2015. Active Learning in Recommender Systems. In *Recommender Systems Handbook*, Francesco Ricci, Lior Rokach, and Bracha Shapira (Eds.). Springer US, Boston, MA, USA, 809–846. https://doi.org/10.1007/978-1-4899-7637-6_24

[20] Maria Salamó, James Reilly, Lorraine McGinty, and Barry Smyth. 2005. Knowledge Discovery from User Preferences in Conversational Recommendation. In *Knowledge Discovery in Databases*. Springer Berlin Heidelberg, Berlin, Heidelberg, 228–239. https://doi.org/10.1007/11564126_25

[21] Amihai Savir, Ronen Brafman, and Guy Shani. 2013. Recommending Improved Configurations for Complex Objects with an Application in Travel Planning. In *Proceedings of the 7th ACM Conference on Recommender Systems (RecSys '13)*. ACM, New York, NY, USA, 391–394. https://doi.org/10.1145/2507157.2507196

[22] Steffen Stabb, Hannes Werther, Francesco. Ricci, Alexander Zipf, Ulrike Gretzel, Daniel R. Fesenmaier, Cécile Paris, and Craig Knoblock. 2002. Intelligent Systems for Tourism. *IEEE Intelligent Systems* 17 (Nov. 2002), 53–64. https://doi.org/10.1109/mis.2002.1134362

[23] Chang Tan, Qi Liu, Enhong Chen, Hui Xiong, and Xiang Wu. 2014. Object-Oriented Travel Package Recommendation. *ACM Transactions on Intelligent Systems and Technology* 5, 3 (Sept. 2014), 1–26. https://doi.org/10.1145/2542665

[24] Marko Tkalcic, Matevž Kunaver, Jurij Tasic, and Andrej Kosir. 2009. Personality Based User Similarity Measure for a Collaborative Recommender System. In *5th Workshop on Emotion in Human-Computer Interaction-Real World Challenges*, Christian Peter, Elizabeth Crane, Lesley Axelrod, Harry Agius, Shazia Afzal, and Madeline Balaam (Eds.). Fraunhofer, 30–37.

[25] UNESCO. 2003. Convention for the Safeguarding of the Intangible Cultural Heritage. https://ich.unesco.org/en/convention. (Oct. 2003).

[26] Pieter Vansteenwegen, Wouter Souffriau, and Dirk Van Oudheusden. 2011. The orienteering problem: A survey. *European Journal of Operational Research* 209, 1 (Feb. 2011), 1–10. https://doi.org/10.1016/j.ejor.2010.03.045

[27] Pieter Vansteenwegen and Dirk Van Oudheusden. 2007. The Mobile Tourist Guide: An OR Opportunity. *OR Insight* 20, 3 (July 2007), 21–27. https://doi.org/10.1057/ori.2007.17

[28] Wen Wu, Li Chen, and Liang He. 2013. Using Personality to Adjust Diversity in Recommender Systems. In *Proceedings of the 24th ACM Conference on Hypertext and Social Media (HT '13)*. ACM, New York, NY, USA, 225–229. https://doi.org/10.1145/2481492.2481521

[29] Wolfgang Wörndl, Alexander Hefele, and Daniel Herzog. 2017. Recommending a sequence of interesting places for tourist trips. *Information Technology & Tourism* 17, 1 (Feb. 2017), 31–54. https://doi.org/10.1007/s40558-017-0076-5

[30] Yu Zheng and Xing Xie. 2011. Learning travel recommendations from user-generated GPS traces. *ACM Transactions on Intelligent Systems and Technology* 2, 1, Article 2 (Jan. 2011), 29 pages. https://doi.org/10.1145/1889681.1889683

Recommendation of Activity Sequences during Distributed Events

Diana Nurbakova*
LIRIS, INSA Lyon
Villeurbanne, France
diana.nurbakova@insa-lyon.fr

ABSTRACT

Leisure activities constitute an important part of our life. Nowadays, the offer of activities to undertake is constantly growing. This can be easily seen not only by the increasing number of social events created and promoted on Facebook, Couchsurfing, etc., but also by the appearance of specialised online services and event-based social networks, such as Meetup, Eventbrite, etc. Moreover, multi-day events (*e.g.* conventions, festivals, cruise trips, exhibitions), to which we refer to as distributed events, attract thousands of participants. Their attendees are often overwhelmed with the amount of available options. Recommender systems appear as a common solution in such a context. In this project, we formulate the problem of recommendation of activity sequences and aim at providing an integrated support for users to create a personalised itinerary of activities in order to facilitate their decision making process which events to join. Such assistance is expected to bring a positive impact on well-being and satisfaction with life of individuals.

CCS CONCEPTS

• **Information systems → Personalization**;

KEYWORDS

Recommender systems; event recommendation; itinerary recommendation; personalisation; users psychological profiles

ACM Reference Format:
Diana Nurbakova. 2018. Recommendation of Activity Sequences during Distributed Events. In *UMAP '18: 26th Conference on User Modeling, Adaptation and Personalization, July 8–11, 2018, Singapore, Singapore*. ACM, New York, NY, USA, 4 pages. https://doi.org/10.1145/3209219.3213592

1 INTRODUCTION

The selection of leisure activities is not always a trivial task. The process becomes even more complicated when it comes to organising one's time and creating a custom schedule of events at a festival, cruise, or any other big event that gathers multiple smaller events. We refer to the latter as *distributed events* [13]. The problem of

*D. Nurbakova was mainly supported by Région Auvergne-Rhône-Alpes. Additional support was received from the Franco-German University.

selection of the 'best' items faced by the attendees is of interest of Recommender systems. Let us consider two following scenarios.

Scenario 1. Didi is planning her weekend of 2-4 December 2016 (see Fig. 1). She has preselected 8 activities that she fancies to do but she struggles with the selection. When considered and rated individually, all these activities represent high interest to her (see the five-star rating given next to activity names on Fig. 1). Suppose, Didi's final choice is to go to Forró Wochenende 2016. The independent interest judgement of this selection is $\hat{s}(a_1) = 5$. An alternative option could be to chain other activities, *e.g.* $\xi = a_3 \rightarrow a_6 \rightarrow a_7 \rightarrow a_8$. If we consider that the total interest score of such a chaining equals the sum of its parts, then $\hat{s}(\xi) = 20$. Even though $\hat{s}(\xi) > \hat{s}(a_1)$, the final selection is made in favour to a_1, which indicates that not only independent judgements are considered. One can also note that the activities are overlapping in terms of time (*e.g.* $< a_3 \ vs. \ a_4 >$, or $< a_1 \ vs. \ others >$). This implies that they cannot be performed all, which amplifies the need for selection. Thus, while recommending a sequence of activities, their time availability should be considered.

Scenario 2. Didi is going to Comic-Con International: San Diego. It is one of the biggest multi-day conventions primarily focused on comic books and related culture. Each year, it offers about 1,900 events of the average duration of 108 minutes. To estimate the density of Comic-Con events (see Fig. 2), we divide a day into 15-minute timeslots and calculate the number of events occurring at each of them. We can see that the number of competitive events is 37 in average, with the maximum of 112. This makes it hard for attendees to select events and organise their time to be sure to perform the maximum of the activities they would enjoy. Recommender systems are powerful assistance tools in such a decision-making process.

We identified the following challenging research questions:

RQ1 ► What constitutes the problem of recommendation of spatio-temporal **a**ctivity **s**equences (STAS)?
  • How to define the STAS problem?
  • What makes it different from other recommendation problems, in particular, Event Recommendation and Trip recommendation? And what are the similarities?

RQ2 ► What drives the selection of activities by individuals?
  • What makes an individual to select one activity in a given time interval and not the other?
  • What are the types of influence on user's interest one can consider when dealing with leisure activities?

RQ3 ► Do psychological profiles of an individual define his/her preferences for leisure activities?
  • How to implicitly acquire the user's psychological profiles from their past engagement in leisure activities?
  • To which extent do psychological profiles of an individual define his/her preferences for leisure activities?

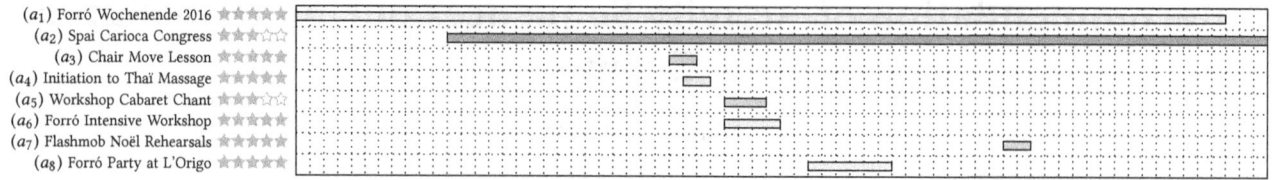

Figure 1: A choice of activities for a weekend during the time frame 1 December 21:00 - 5 December 01:00 (time windows of their availability). The bar colours indicate categories of activities: yellow - <Dance →Forró>, orange - <Dance →Samba de Gafieira>, pink - <Dance →Chair Dance>, green - <Well Being →Massage →Thaï>.

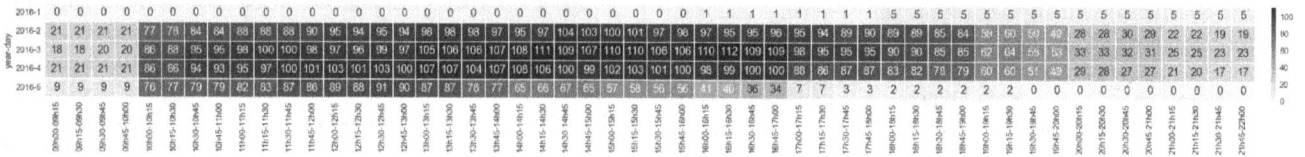

Figure 2: Heatmap of the overlapping events at Comic-Con 2016 with respect to 15 min long timeslots from 6am to 10pm.

RQ4 ▶ How to provide a user with the best support during a distributed event via personalised recommendation?

- How to take into account a set of constraints (time availability, travel time, etc.) in order to return to a user a sequence of activities he/she will be able to perform?
- How to acquire the relevant preference of an activity?

The main goal of this project is to provide *an integrated support* for users to create *a personalised itinerary of activities* and *a list of events to join*, in order to facilitate their selection process.

On our way to achieve this goal, the following **contributions** are expected. In the list below, we use the marker symbols to indicate the current state of an achievement: a checked box ☑ for accomplished work, an empty box □ for work in progress. The clock symbol ⊕ indicates a work which is currently under review.

☑ **C1** Definition of **STAS**, overview of related recommendation problems and their solutions, classification of types of influence used for estimation of user's interest scores. ⊕

☑ **C2** Design and implementation of **a n**ew approach for short-term **a**ctivity sequences and **i**tineraries recommendation during distributed events, **ANASTASIA** [7].

□ **C3** Design and implementation of a psychologically-driven approach for recommendation of events.

□ **C4** Design a new model for **p**ersonalised **r**ecommendation of **i**tineraries during **d**istributed **e**vents that takes into account users' psychological profiles, **PRIDE: C2 + C3.**

□ **C5** Design and building of **test collections**, namely:

   ☑ **C5-1 ANASTASIA-D**: a dataset for itinerary recommendation on board of a cruise [6]

   ☑ **C5-2 REvIt**: a dataset for recommendation of events and itineraries at Comic-Con International: San Diego ⊕

   ☑ **C5-3** a dataset of psychological profiles and selection of leisure activities [8]

   □ **C5-4 REvIt++**: a dataset of psychological profiles and selection of activities at Comic-Con International: San Diego for recommendation of events and itineraries

2 PROBLEM STATEMENT (C1)

In this project, we define the problem of recommendation of spatio-temporal activity sequences (STAS) and related notions. Here, we present the definitions briefly.

STAS problem: Let U be the set of users, $A = \{a_1, a_2, ..., a_N\}$ be the set of all available *activities*, N be the total number of activities. For a given user $u \in U$, we aim to provide a feasible *itinerary* ξ that maximises the user's overall *satisfaction* with all performed activities: Max $\sigma(\xi, u)$, subject to the set of *constraints*. The concepts of **activities**, **itineraries** and **satisfaction** are defined as follows.

An **activity** a is a unique action taking place at some geographical location during a particular time window, and, therefore, can be represented as a tuple $a = (id, n, l, t_s, t_e, \delta, c, d)$, where id is its identifier, n is its name, l is the location where it takes place, t_s and t_e are the start and the end time (time window) of its availability respectively, δ is its duration, $c = (c_1, ..., c_m)$ is a vector of categories associated with the activity, and d is its description.

An **itinerary** (or **activity sequence**) $\xi(u) = a_i \rightarrow a_j \rightarrow ... \rightarrow a_k$ is a chronologically ordered series of activities of the user $u \in U$.

The *feasibility* of a sequence is defined based on the satisfaction of the set of constraints, among which: (1) *Activity availability*: an activity can be performed only within the time window of its availability. (2) *Activity completion*: a user may join an activity if there is enough time to perform it. (3) *Time budget*: the total time needed to perform all the activities within a sequence should not exceed the time budget.

The **satisfaction** $\hat{s}(a, u)$ of a user u w.r.t. an activity a is a quantitative measure of the matching between an activity a and a user u, subject to several influences. In the most simple case, **the satisfaction w.r.t. an activity sequence** can be defined as the sum of satisfaction scores of individual activities forming the sequence, i.e. $\sigma(\xi, u) = \sum_{a \in \xi} \hat{s}(a, u)$.

3 BACKGROUND (C1)

This research is mainly dealing with the problem of recommendation of activity sequences (STAS). The latter brings our project

Table 1: Comparison of related recommendation problems

Characteristic	Event Rec	Trip Rec	STAS
Limited Availability	✓	✓	✓
Travel Time	X	✓	✓
Unique Unit	✓	X	✓
Unique Visit	✓	✓	✓
Future oriented	✓	X	✓

Table 2: Interconnection between contributions and the data used for evaluation. Colours correspond to project phases.

	C5-1 [6]	C5-2	C5-3 [8]	C5-4	External
C1	NA	NA	NA	NA	NA
C2 [7]					
C3					Meetup [1]
C4					

close to two related recommendation problems, namely: Event Recommendation and Trip Recommendation.

Event Recommendation. The event recommendation problem is usually defined as a top-k recommendation problem that seeks to provide a user with a ranked list of events that might be interesting for him/her. Thus, it is always formulated as a list-wise [1, 11] or a pairwise [5] ranking problem. Various influences can be taken into account in order to estimate the preference of an event for a given user, *e.g.* users' temporal and geographical preferences, set of groups to join, event content [1]. It has to be noted that event recommendation is known to be intrinsically cold-start and it differs from the 'traditional' recommendation domains (movies, books, etc.) in terms of the peculiarities of items, as events have limited life time and happen in future, which results in the lack of collaborative data such as ratings provided by other users [1].

STAS has many points in common with event recommendation. In our project, we get inspired by the works in this field, but the problem we treat goes beyond the state-of-the-art of event recommendation by searching for the most desirable sequence of activities for a user, particularly in the context of a distributed event.

Trip Recommendation. The trip recommendation problem can be perceived as en extension of the Point-of-Interest (POI) recommendation problem which has become very popular in tourism domain. Given a user, his/her starting and ending points, a starting time, and a time budget, the trip recommendation aims at finding an optimal trip route limited by a time budget, that maximises the user's happiness and satisfies the POI availability constraints [17]. Trip recommendation is usually treated in two steps, namely (1) the estimation of user's interest in POIs and (2) the itinerary construction [13, 17]. Another strategy consists in estimating the transition probabilities between POIs. Thus, Sang *et al.* [12] formulate the problem as a ranking problem w.r.t. the visiting probability of a sequence of POIs, estimated using POI transition probability under the given user context. The problem is addressed on two levels, namely POI category sequences and POI sequences, which constitutes the hierarchical structure of the proposed solution.

If we place STAS within the context of the two aforementioned problems (see Tab. 1), one can note that (1) what distinguishes STAS from Event Recommendation is its sequential nature, while (2) the uniqueness of activities and their occurrence in future differ STAS from Trip Recommendation, adding more challenges.

4 METHODOLOGY AND PROPOSALS

This project undergoes four phases. Table 2 depicts the data used at each of the phases and visualises the interconnection between contributions that this projects aims to achieve.

4.1 STAS: the problem of recommendation of Spatio-Temporal Activity Sequences (C1)

The **first phase** of this research was to explore the field of recommendation of sequences of spatial items in order to *identify* the peculiarities of leisure activities as recommendation items, *define* the STAS problem aiming for a *better understanding* and *providing more insight* into the process of selection of leisure activities by individuals. We have investigated different types of influence from the state-of-the-art solutions that may impact the user's interest in an item, and proposed their classification. Moreover, we have provided an overview of available datasets and have discussed their use for STAS. We summarised this work in the form of a survey paper that is currently under review. **C1**

4.2 ANASTASIA: A Novel Approach for Short-Term Activity Sequence and Itinerary recommendAtion (C2, C5-1)

In the **second phase**, we have proposed a novel approach for the recommendation of planning of activities that we call ANASTASIA presented in [7]. It makes use of users behavioural patterns to construct the planning of events that best suit users constraints and preferences. It is a hybrid approach that integrates categorical, temporal and textual scores of user's interest in an activity. Based on the estimated scores of activities and the extracted behavioural patterns a personalised itinerary is constructed. Our solution has shown the 9.7% improvement over the state-of-the-art [16] in terms of precision. For more details refer to [7]. **C2**

The evaluation has been performed on a dataset of a cruise attendance, issued from a user study based on a 7-night Disney Fantasy cruise. The main aim of the study was to simulate cruise attendance and create a dataset that could be used for personalised itinerary construction. Participants were recruited via a link to the online questionnaire sent by email to several research mailing lists. Some of the results of this study were reported in [6]. **C5-1**

4.3 Introducing Users' Psychological Profiles to Event Recommendation (C3, C5-2)

The selection of leisure activities is a complex process subject to various features of an activity and multiple layers of user's individuality. The **third phase** of this project is focused on investigating the impact of psychological profiles of individuals on the selection of leisure activities. We decompose this aim into three parts: (1) implicit acquisition of users' psychological profiles from their selection of leisure activities, (2) estimation of user's interest scores based on his/her psychological profile, (3) incorporation of these scores into a hybrid event recommendation model. It has been shown [15] that the use of personality is beneficial to address a number of challenges faced by recommender systems (e.g. cold-start, group recommendation). We aim at extending psychological profiles by focusing on the following dimensions: (1) Orientations to Happiness (OTH) [9]; (2) Big5 Personality traits (Big5) [4]; and (3) Fear of Missing Out (FoMO) [10]. Our objective is to study the use of psychological profiles in order to alleviate the cold-start problem and improve the recommendation quality in terms of precision and beyon-precision metrics (*i.e.* serendipity and diversity). As the initial step of this work, we have conducted a user study, some of the results of which we have reported in [8]. C5-3

This study will allow us to estimate the desirability of events for a user on a category level. We further incorporate this psychological profile based scores into a learning to rank model for personalised recommendation of events together with social, textual, geographical, temporal scores [1]. The evaluation will be performed on a large-scale dataset crawled from Meetup.com [1]. C3

4.4 PRIDE: Personalised Recommendation of Itineraries during Distributed Events (C4), REvIt (C5-2) and REvIt++ (C5-4)

The **fourth phase** aims at finding a new solution for STAS that exploits various types of influence, *i.e.* textual, categorical, temporal, social, psychological, sequential, in order to estimate the desirability of events and event sequence for a user (**PRIDE**). C4

In [6], we have identified the characteristics of the data treated by activity sequence recommendation. Among the list of 14 characteristics, we distinguish 5 core ones: (1) time windows (start and end time of activity), (2) coordinates (geographical location of an activity), (3) service time (duration of an activity), (4) categories, and (5) users historical data. We use these characteristics as the basis in the process of dataset creation. To obtain a dataset that can be used as is, we have crawled the website of the comic convention (www.comic-con.org). We call it **REvIt** (**R**ecommendation of **Ev**ents and **It**ineraries). It contains the event programs 2013-2017 and the pre-selection of the events made by participants, more precisely the following entities: events, locations, categories, tags, event-user, user-user, event-categories, event-tags. C5-2

We are further planning to extend REvIt by enriching it in terms of user profiles. Thus, we will launch a crowdsourcing campaign that will allow us to align the selection of events and psychological profiles of users. The study will consist of four parts. The first three parts are similar to [8], *i.e.*: demographic profile, psychological profiles (Big5, OTH, FoMO), and selection of categories of leisure activities. In the fourth part, the participants will be provided with the event program of the convention in 2017 and their task will be to simulate their attendance of Comic-Con by creating their schedules for each day of the convention. This user study aims at providing more insight into the process of event selection during a distributed event and users' time management. Moreover, it will allow us to investigate if the impact of psychological profiles of users on their selection and scheduling behaviour. The study will result in a new publicly available dataset **REvIt++**. C5-4

5 FURTHER RESEARCH

We foresee the following long-term perspectives of this project.

FR1 – Recommendation of activity sequences meets aggregation operators [2]: A collaboration project between LIRIS / INSA Lyon and the University of Milano-Bicocca, supported by grant of IDEXLYON as part of the program "Doctoral Students' International Mobility" has been set up.

FR2 – Satisfaction w.r.t. a sequence of activities: An interesting direction of future work consists in exploring the interdependence of activities within a sequence in terms of satisfaction a user gets (*e.g.* [3]).

FR3 – Leisure activities and Well-being: Another direction to explore is to conduct a long-term study of the affect of recommended activities on the individual well-being.

FR4 – STAS and recurrent events: A more practical direction of the further research will be considering multiple time windows of activity availability [14], multiple locations, etc. in order to better deal with the recurrent events.

REFERENCES

[1] Augusto Q. Macedo, Leandro B. Marinho, and Rodrygo L.T. Santos. 2015. Context-Aware Event Recommendation in Event-based Social Networks. In *RecSys '15*. 123–130.

[2] Stefania Marrara, Gabriella Pasi, and Marco Viviani. 2017. Aggregation operators in Information Retrieval. *Fuzzy Sets and Systems* 324 (2017), 3–19.

[3] Judith Masthoff and Albert Gatt. 2006. In Pursuit of Satisfaction and the Prevention of Embarrassment: Affective State in Group Recommender Systems. *User Modeling and User-Adapted Interaction* 16, 3-4 (Sept. 2006), 281–319.

[4] Robert R. McCrae and Oliver P. John. 1992. An Introduction to the Five-Factor Model and Its Applications. *Journal of Personality* 60, 2 (1992).

[5] Einat Minkov, Ben Charrow, Jonathan Ledlie, Seth Teller, and Tommi Jaakkola. 2010. Collaborative Future Event Recommendation. In *CIKM '10*. 819–828.

[6] Diana Nurbakova, Léa Laporte, Sylvie Calabretto, and Jérôme Gensel. 2017. Itinerary Recommendation for Cruises: User Study. In *Proceedings of the 2nd Workshop on Recommenders in Tourism co-located with 11th ACM Conference on Recommender Systems (RecSys 2017), Como, Italy, August 27, 2017*. 31–34.

[7] Diana Nurbakova, Léa Laporte, Sylvie Calabretto, and Jérôme Gensel. 2017. Recommendation of Short-Term Activity Sequences During Distributed Events. *Procedia Computer Science* 108, ICCS'17, Supplement C (2017), 2069 – 2078.

[8] Diana Nurbakova, Léa Laporte, Sylvie Calabretto, and Jérôme Gensel. 2017. Users psychological profiles for leisure activity recommendation: user study. In *Cit-Rec@RecSys*. ACM, 3:1–3:4.

[9] Christopher Peterson, Nansook Park, and Martin E. P. Seligman. 2005. Orientations to happiness and life satisfaction: the full life versus the empty life. *Journal of Happiness Studies* 6, 1 (2005), 25–41.

[10] Andrew K. Przybylski, Kou Murayama, Cody R. DeHaan, and Valerie Gladwell. 2013. Motivational, emotional, and behavioral correlates of fear of missing out. *Computers in Human Behavior* 29, 4 (2013), 1841 – 1848.

[11] Zhi Qiao, Peng Zhang, Yanan Cao, Chuan Zhou, Li Guo, and Binxing Fang. 2014. Combining Heterogenous Social and Geographical Information for Event Recommendation. In *Proc. of the 28th AAAI Conference on Artificial Intelligence*. 145–151.

[12] Jitao Sang, Tao Mei, and Changsheng Xu. 2015. Activity Sensor: Check-In Usage Mining for Local Recommendation. *ACM Trans. Intell. Syst. Technol.* 6, 3, Article 41 (April 2015), 24 pages.

[13] Richard Schaller, Morgan Harvey, and David Elsweiler. 2013. RecSys for Distributed Events: Investigating the Influence of Recommendations on Visitor Plans. In *SIGIR'13*. 953–956.

[14] Wouter Souffriau, Pieter Vansteenwegen, Greet Vanden Berghe, and Dirk Van Oudheusden. 2013. The Multiconstraint Team Orienteering Problem with Multiple Time Windows. *Transportation Science* 47, 1 (Feb. 2013), 53–63.

[15] Marko Tkalcic and Li Chen. 2015. *Personality and Recommender Systems*. Springer US, Boston, MA, 715–739. https://doi.org/10.1007/978-1-4899-7637-6_21

[16] Pieter Vansteenwegen, Wouter Souffriau, Greet Vanden Berghe, and Dirk Van Oudheusden. 2009. Iterated Local Search for the Team Orienteering Problem with Time Windows. *Comput. Oper. Res.* 36, 12 (Dec. 2009), 3281–3290.

[17] Chenyi Zhang, Hongwei Liang, Ke Wang, and Jianling Sun. 2015. Personalized Trip Recommendation with POI Availability and Uncertain Traveling Time. In *Proceedings of the 24th ACM International on Conference on Information and Knowledge Management (CIKM '15)*. 911–920.

Integrating Item Based Stereotypes in Recommender Systems

Nourah A. ALRossais
University of York
nar537@york.ac.uk

ABSTRACT

With the growing popularity of e-commerce, recommender systems play a critical role to enhance the user experience and increase sales revenue and profitability for a company. However, the accuracy of recommender systems is often suffering from data sparsity and the new user/item problems. A promising approach in solving the new user problem is stereotype based modeling. The proposed PhD research will go one step further and develop an item based recommender system employing the stereotype approach for item modeling. For the evaluation of our stereotype-based recommender system, the study will employ the MovieLens and IMDb datasets. These two datasets are integrated using the iSynchronizer tool that was developed by the researchers for tasks such as this. Early evaluation results demonstrate promising prediction accuracy with user-based stereotypes, especially for users with a small number of existing ratings.

KEYWORDS

Recommender Systems; Stereotypes; New Item; User-Item Modeling; Performance Evaluation

ACM Reference Format:
Nourah A. ALRossais. 2018. Integrating Item Based Stereotypes in Recommender Systems. In *UMAP '18: 26th Conference on User Modeling, Adaptation and Personalization, July 8–11, 2018, Singapore, Singapore.* ACM, New York, NY, USA, 4 pages. https://doi.org/10.1145/3209219.3213593

1 INTRODUCTION

Recommender systems are employed by e-commerce websites to recommend products to their customers and play the role of automating personalization on the Internet [11]. Every business which strives to grow needs to attract new customers. Hence, a considerable amount of money is spent for marketing campaigns to attract and direct new customers to their e-commerce sites. Once such new customers have been attracted to the e-commerce sites, there is a need to maximize the chances of them purchasing items. Thus, the sites want to present products that are of most interest to the customers early on. However, providing recommendations to a new customer whose history of transactions does not exist yet, is challenging.

One of the key concepts for resolving this new user problem and providing better recommendations even when user information is

UMAP '18, July 8–11, 2018, Singapore, Singapore
© 2018 Association for Computing Machinery.
ACM ISBN 978-1-4503-5589-6/18/07...$15.00
https://doi.org/10.1145/3209219.3213593

sparse, is the classic idea of stereotyping. In the stereotype approach, users are grouped instead of each being treated individually. This approach has an advantage of larger sets of training data available for a group of users in comparison to a single user. In e-commerce, for example, for a single user without a history of transactions, we will not be able to construct any model (the new user problem). However, if we can determine that the user shares some meaningful features with one of the predefined groups - we can use a model assigned to this group to generate recommendations. Rich [10] was the first to propose the utilization of stereotypes in user modeling and recommender systems, applying it to a book recommendation system.

In addition to a user model, which is a function that maps items to a preference value, we also consider item models in our work. The item models represent the "preference" of an item for a user, i.e. a mapping of users to preference values. In other words, we are inversing the concept of a user model, in the expectation that this will provide additional useful information for the recommender system. For such item models, it is also possible to design stereotypes analogously to user stereotypes, which will alleviate the new item problem. Finally, it is possible to combine user and item models, in the expectation that this will improve the accuracy of recommendations.

To the best of our knowledge, our work is the first to investigate item stereotypes for recommender systems. Initially, the stereotypes will be constructed manually by an expert but later on automatically.

The generated item-based stereotype models are models of the target-market for a given group of items, i.e. denoting how much an item "likes" a user (rather than the other way round as is done in user modeling).

1.1 Research Objectives

The research will look for answers to the following research questions.

(1) How do stereotype-based item models compare to other state of the art recommender systems models in terms of predictive performance?
(2) How can item based stereotypes be constructed automatically to improve recommendations?
(3) Since stereotype-based user modeling is an effective way for recommender systems, does integrating it with item based stereotype modeling (hybrid approach) result better recommendations?

For evaluation, the study will use an integrated dataset combining MovieLens and IMDb information. Movies are stereotypical and easy to define stereotypes from which will assist in evaluation and testing.

2 RELATED WORK

Rich [10] was the first to propose the utilization of stereotypes in user modeling and recommender systems. In that study, stereotyping was used as a method to tackle the new user problem. Stereotypes were also found to have the additional benefit of space-efficiency, since model characteristics that are applicable to a group of users are required to be stored only once and can be applied to all members belonging to a stereotype.

A stereotype has two indispensable parts: **(a)** the designation of the stereotype in terms of the characteristics similar to members or the features of typical users, and **(b)** the pre-conditions which must be fulfilled to allocate the stereotype to a user[7, 10].

Rich[10], in her pioneering work on stereotype-based recommender systems, developed GRUNDY which represented a good example of the manual construction of stereotypes.

GERMANE [7] is an instance of a stereotype-based user modeling system where stereotypes are automatically built from relevance feedback provided by users. Moreover, stereotype weights in GERMANE are based on stereotype performance during training instead of the extent to which a user is perceived to belong to a stereotype[7].

DOPPELGANGER [9] is a generalized tool for collecting, processing and presenting user information in which information flows in a bottom-up manner. In DOPPELGANGER, the existing sensors decide which inferences could be made, and consequently how users would be modeled effectively and the applications which are viable.

Krulwich[5] introduced Lifestyle Finder, in which large scale data are employed for the generalization of user-specified data in accordance to the patterns that are common to the population, covering areas not specified in the original data of users.

The PPG (Personal Program Guide) by Ardissono et al.[1] is grounded on a multi-agent architecture that integrates different user modeling techniques for recommending TV programs.

UM-TOOL by Brajnik et al.[2] provides a dynamic way to build stereotypes where such models are created and updated depending on the user activity. Shapira et al.[13] evaluated the approaches to building stereotypes and proposed a novel model for information filtering systems to resolves the issues related to those approaches. The above review of the literature on stereotyping shows that stereotypes have been applied to user modeling, but not to item modeling. Hence, to fill this gap in recommender system research, our study will endeavor to develop an item-based recommender system for e-commerce domain employing the stereotype approach for item modeling.

3 PLAN FOR THE RESEARCH STUDY

The objective towards answering our first research question will be to manually create item-based stereotypes for Movies in the integrated MovieLens and IMDb dataset. Our recommender system will provide recommendations to the user based on stereotyping of movies liked by the user and recommending similar movies. A preliminary design of the prediction algorithm is presented in Section 4. This includes building of a manual stereotype-based item model offline to predict rating.

Initial promising results are presented in Section 5. The proposed manual user stereotyping model provides good accuracy especially for users who rated fewer movies. Work is still in progress for the manual item stereotype model. However, following a manual approach and selecting a limited number of stereotypes for items (e.g. size, price, sold count, etc.) might not be efficient and effective for a recommender algorithm. Instead, stereotypes could be automatically selected from the pool of features. In other words, while price, similarity, and feedback are used for grouping products in one case, features such as popularity, click-through-rate, and sold count could be utilized in another case. The model should focus on user requirements to increase revenue by identifying the items which users are more interested in. Item-based stereotypes would be a model of a target-market for a given group of items. Hence, in the second phase of the project, we intend to develop an automatic item-based recommender system to overcome the shortcomings of manually designed stereotypes.

Lastly, we plan to integrate user-based stereotyping with the automatic stereotype-based item models and design a hybrid model, and compare the results of both. More details of the approach are provided in the next section.

4 STEREOTYPE BASED RECOMMENDATION ALGORITHM

In order to answer our first research question, we propose an algorithm that assigns users and items to stereotypes through our user and item preference model (i.e. P_u, P_i) as well as clustering technique and not based on similarity matrices such as Person correlation in which two movies will have high correlation if users felt the same way about them. Precisely, in user-based stereotype algorithm, we interpreted users average rating per genre as the membership function of user u to User Stereotype (US).

The stereotypes in this study are of a 'double stereotype' nature which implies that the information that the item choosing a target user is also influencing the allocation of items to stereotype. Double Stereotypes were suggested by Chin [3] in user based stereotypes for information filtering where the information that a user chooses to view is also examined as a way to allocate users to stereotypes. We apply a similar concept for item based stereotypes. Sub sections 4.1 through 4.3 explain our proposed algorithm in more detail.

4.1 User based Stereotype Recommendation Algorithm

Let $P_u(i)$ be the preference function of user $u \in U$ in item $i \in I$ and $P_{US}(i)$ the preference function of User Stereotype (US) in which user u is a member, in item $i \in I$ then:

$$P_u(i) = P_{US}(i) \qquad \forall i \in I$$

Having user u can belong to multiple User Stereotypes (USs), the recommendation setting is the sum of weighted preferences functions of User Stereotype (USs) to that item i, given by

$$P_u(i) = \sum_{S \in US(u)} w_S . P_{US}(i) \qquad (1)$$

Where US(u) is the set of users stereotypes for which user u is a member, w_S is weight of preferences functions as defined by an expert in the field and

$$\sum_{S \in US(u)} w_S = 1, w_S \in [0, 1] \qquad \forall S \in US(u)$$

4.2 Item Based Stereotype Recommendation Algorithm

Let $P_i(u)$ the preference function of item $i \in$ I in user $u \in$ U and $P_{IS}(u)$ the preference function of Item Stereotype (IS) in which item i is a member, in user $u \in$ U then:

$$P_i(u) = P_{IS}(u) \qquad \forall u \in U$$

Having item i can belong to multiple Item Stereotypes (ISs), the recommendation setting is the sum of weighted preferences functions of Item Stereotype (ISs) to that user u, given by

$$P_i(u) = \sum_{S \in IS(i)} w_S . P_{IS}(u) \qquad (2)$$

Where IS(i) is the set of item stereotypes for which item i is a member, w_S is weight of preferences functions as defined by an expert in the field and

$$\sum_{S \in IS(i)} w_S = 1, w_S \in [0, 1] \qquad \forall S \in IS(i)$$

4.3 Incorporation of Item based Stereotype in Recommender System

Output of User Stereotype recommender algorithm for user $u \in$ U is given in Equation (1). Output of Item Stereotype recommender algorithm for an item $i \in$ I is given in Equation (2) Combining (1) and (2) will produce a new user preference function as indicated in Equation (3)

$$P_u^c(i) = W_u . P_u(i) + W_i . P_i(u) \qquad (3)$$

For all user $u \in$ U, W_u and W_i are weights of preferences functions of user stereotypes and item stereotypes respectively as defined by an expert in the field, W_u and $W_i \in [0,1]$ and $W_u + W_i = 1$

5 EXPERIMENTAL EVALUATION

5.1 Dataset

In a previous work, we integrated MovieLens 20M data and IMDb data and generated dataset from integrated data. This dataset included a feature vector that represent useful information about users and movies that is not explicitly contained in the raw data. More specifically, our dataset contains information about user interest in movie genres, actors, etc. The dataset is different from other data in that the interest of users in movies features are calculated implicitly from his overall ratings rather that explicitly asking users his preferences. Figure 1 illustrates the generated matrix that is a combination of Item Profile and User Utility Matrix. A total of 20M ratings applied to 27,242 movies by 138,000 users. In our experiment, we applied our algorithm to 150,567 Ratings applied to 9734 Movies by 1000 users. Each person rates at least 20 movies. A

'0' cell in movie feature implies that movie is not a member of that feature while a NULL cell in User Utility Matrix implies that user did not watch/rate that movie.

5.2 Evaluation Procedure

As the efficiency of the utilization of user-based stereotypes has been proven in other systems [10], it is assumed that we can also effectively prove the efficiency of item-based stereotype in recommendation system by employing experimental means. Experiment must be carried out to compare the results with and without the utilization of item-based stereotype. We compare user preferences measured in Equation (1) and (3) in an offline experiment by considering two different predictive accuracy measures: Mean Absolute Error (MAE) and Root Mean Square Error (RMSE). To achieve this, we first choose an optimal combination of movie features and Users utility matrix. We clustered users into 28 user stereotypes based on genres of movies. We interpreted users average rating per genre as the membership function of user u to User Stereotype (US). For instance, a user u who rated an action, and horror movie but never rate a drama movie will belong to action and horror User Stereotypes (USs), i.e., {US$_{genre:action}$, US$_{genre:horror}$}.

As for item-based stereotype, we clustered items into 28 clusters representing 28 genres only. We interpret boolean attributes of Item features as the membership function of item i to Item Stereotype (IS) based on genre. For instance, an item i (movie) which is a war and drama genres will belong to war and drama Item Stereotypes (ISs),i.e., {IS$_{genre:war}$, IS$_{genre:drama}$}.

Genre is a well-known content attribute of movies and is the most important factor that effect user decision when watching a movie according to [6, 8, 12]. In our experiment, we used uniform stereotype weights as we assume all genres are equally important. Our main task is to impute users rating on a movie he rated previously. In concrete terms, we ask "given a user u has seen movie i, how likely is he to rate it?" Our prior knowledge that the person has seen i means we have his preferences observation and our goal is to guess the best rating, i.e., maximize $P_{US}(i)$ and $P_{IS}(u)$ in Equation (1) and Equation (2) respectively.

Model degree of specialization is one of the five dimensions which define user model as suggested by Kass and Finin [4]. Modeling user by means of stereotype is close to "generic end" of the scale as opposed to "individual model" which individually defines each user. Our experiment prove that as the prediction accuracy getting better as we remove users who rate specific amount of movies (mature users). More details in Sub section 5.4.

5.3 Baseline Methods for Evaluation

Our baseline method is pure user oriented collaborative filtering. The collaborative approach is possibly the most widely utilized and established, as verified by its deployment on e-commerce websites like Amazon.com. The collaborative filtering technique can be classified into (a) user-based and (b) item-based collaborative filtering techniques. In user-based collaborative filtering, recommendations for users are made grounded on items which are preferred by other comparable users.

User		Duration	Publish Year	Genres: War	Drama	...	Actor: A1	...	Director: D1	...	Writer: W1	...	Genres' Rating: War	Drama	...	Actor's Rating: A1	...	Direr's Rating: D1	...	Writer's Rating: W1	...	Rating TimeStamp	user's rating
U1	M1	94	1922	O	O	O	O	1	O	O	O	1	3.67	3.786	NULL	4	3.75	4.5	NULL	NULL	4.2	1094786056	3.5
U1	M2	85	1990	1	O	O	1	O	1	O	O	1	3.67	3.786	NULL	4	3.75	4.5	NULL	NULL	4.2	1112484994	4
U1	M3	70	1931	O	1	O	O	O	O	O	O	O	3.67	3.786	NULL	4	3.75	4.5	NULL	NULL	4.2	1094786017	3
...	....	64	1932	O	1	1	O	O	O	O	O	O	3.67	3.786	NULL	4	3.75	4.5	NULL	NULL	4.2	1094786027	5
U2	M1	94	1922	O	O	O	O	1	O	O	O	1	4.67	4.12	3.43	NULL	4.3	NULL	NULL	NULL	4.5	1094786172	3
U2	M6	102	1939	O	O	O	O	O	O	O	O	O	4.67	4.12	3.43	NULL	4.3	NULL	NULL	NULL	4.5	1094785621	3.5
....	....	110	1945	O	1	O	O	O	O	O	O	O	4.67	4.12	3.43	NULL	4.3	NULL	NULL	NULL	4.5	1112485781	3.5
U3	M2	85	1990	1	O	O	1	O	1	O	O	1	3.9	NULL	NULL	4.2	NULL	4	NULL	NULL	3.55	1094786148	3.5
U3	M10	88	1958	O	O	O	O	O	O	O	O	O	3.9	NULL	NULL	4.2	NULL	4	NULL	NULL	3.55	1112485816	4
....	....	109	1960	O	O	O	O	O	O	O	O	O	3.9	NULL	NULL	4.2	NULL	4	NULL	NULL	3.55	1094785994	4

Figure 1: Item's Profile and User's Utility Matrix

5.4 Initial Evaluation Result

Although stereotyping model help recommender system in alleviating cold start problem, such model is used to produce generic recommendations that match the preferences of the group members with high probability. Initial implementation of user based stereotype recommendation algorithm result MAE (0.866139). The behavior of MAE and RMSE improved extensively by excluding users who had provided enough rating. Moreover, we divided users within stereotype into three fine stereotypes based on their ratings values. Users with strong interest (3.5 < Avg rating <=5), Users with medium interest (2 < Avg rating <= 3.5) and users with low interest (0.5 <= Avg rating <=2).

Table 1: User-based stereotype model

Mature Users removed	MAE	RMSE
20	**0.7089**	**0.9136**
30	0.7154	0.9207
50	0.7243	0.9299
150	0.7559	0.9606
400	0.7879	0.9912

Table 2: User-based Collaborative Filtering

k nearest users	MAE	RMSE
20	0.7194	0.9156
50	0.6425	0.8268
100	**0.568**	**0.7294**
500	0.5849	0.747
750	0.5871	0.7498

Table 1 shows MAE and RMSE obtained as a function of the number of rated movies per user. The algorithm perform better for users with less rating as compared to mature users who rate a lot of movies. This imply that our stereotype approach is promising in solving new user problem. The best result achieved with users with 20 ratings only.

As for CF, Table 2 indicated the best result corresponds to k=100, as we increase k to 500 (half of total population), the performance reduces as we are considering users with very small similarity and this may introduce noise and thus fall in performance is observed.

At this stage, it is not clear weather item-based stereotype would be a better approach rather than user-based stereotype. More experiments will be conducted to incorporate item-based stereotype model and its ability to solve new item problem.

6 CONCLUSION AND FUTURE WORK

In this work, we show that user-based stereotype predict new users preferences and unnecessary permanence of users within stereotype might produce undesirable results. We evaluated the performance of our algorithm in an offline experiments according to various measures. We found that our simple algorithm do surprisingly well and promising. More experiments are necessary to prove the ability of stereotyping model in solving new user/item problem. As a future step, we will cluster items and predict ratings using Machine Learning approaches. This will enable us to compare the performance of our current approach with the ML approach.

REFERENCES

[1] Liliana Ardissono, Alfred Kobsa, and Mark T Maybury. 2004. *Personalized digital television: targeting programs to individual viewers.* Vol. 6. Springer Science & Business Media.
[2] Giorgio Brajnik, Giovanni Guida, and Carlo Tasso. 1990. User modeling in expert man-machine interfaces: A case study in intelligent information retrieval. *IEEE Transactions on Systems, Man, and Cybernetics* 20, 1 (1990), 166–185.
[3] David N Chin. 1989. KNOME: Modeling what the user knows in UC. In *User models in dialog systems.* Springer, 74–107.
[4] Robert Kass and Tim Finin. 1989. The role of user models in cooperative interactive systems. *International Journal of Intelligent Systems* 4, 1 (1989), 81–112.
[5] Bruce Krulwich. 1997. Lifestyle finder: Intelligent user profiling using large-scale demographic data. *AI magazine* 18, 2 (1997), 37.
[6] Bo Li, Yibin Liao, and Zheng Qin. 2014. Precomputed clustering for movie recommendation system in real time. *Journal of Applied Mathematics* 2014 (2014).
[7] Zoe Lock. 2005. *Performance and Flexibility of Stereotype-based User Models.* Ph.D. Dissertation. University of York.
[8] Mona Nasery, Matthias Braunhofer, and Francesco Ricci. 2016. Recommendations with optimal combination of feature-based and item-based preferences. In *Proceedings of the 2016 Conference on User Modeling Adaptation and Personalization.* ACM, 269–273.
[9] Jon Orwant. 1994. Heterogeneous learning in the Doppelgänger user modeling system. *User Modeling and User-Adapted Interaction* 4, 2 (1994), 107–130.
[10] Elaine Rich. 1979. User modeling via stereotypes. *Cognitive science* 3, 4 (1979), 329–354.
[11] J Ben Schafer, Joseph Konstan, and John Riedl. 1999. Recommender systems in e-commerce. In *Proceedings of the 1st ACM conference on Electronic commerce.* ACM, 158–166.
[12] Qusai Shambour, Mou'ath Hourani, and Salam Fraihat. 2016. An item-based multi-criteria collaborative filtering algorithm for personalized recommender systems. *International Journal of Advanced Computer Science and Applications* 7, 8 (2016), 275–279.
[13] Bracha Shapira, Peretz Shoval, and Uri Hanani. 1997. Stereotypes in information filtering systems. *Information Processing & Management* 33, 3 (1997), 273–287.

Towards Practical Link Prediction Approaches in Signed Social Networks

Xiaoming Li
School of Computer Science and Engineering
Nanyang Technological University
Singapore, Singapore
lixiaoming@ntu.edu.sg

ABSTRACT

The purpose of this research is to design practical link prediction models in signed social networks. Current works focus on the sign prediction, based on the assumption that it is already known whether there is a link between any two users. In other words, the no-relation status is ignored. Meanwhile, the strength of existing links are assumed to be equal, which is also not realistic. In this study, we will redefine the link prediction problem in signed networks and take a deep investigation on no-relation status. Then, we aim to propose a personalized ranking model from the individual's perspective. This research explores link prediction models in a more realistic scenario, and it will contribute to ongoing research in development of link prediction and recommendations in signed networks. Furthermore, our research will provide a better understanding on the link formation mechanism behind signed network evolution.

KEYWORDS

Signed social networks, Link prediction, Personalized ranking

ACM Reference Format:
Xiaoming Li. 2018. Towards Practical Link Prediction Approaches in Signed Social Networks. In *UMAP '18: 26th Conference on User Modeling, Adaptation and Personalization, July 8–11, 2018, Singapore, Singapore.* ACM, New York, NY, USA, 4 pages. https://doi.org/10.1145/3209219.3213595

1 INTRODUCTION

Signed social networks become more and more popular nowadays, in which exist both positive and negative relationships among online users. A substantial number of online systems, such as Slashdot (friend or foe, www.slashdot.org), Epinions (trust or distrust, www.epinions.com) and WikiVote (agree or disagree), have adopted the signed network structure. Compared with traditional unsigned networks, it can better reflect real-life social relation [25]. The increasing interests in signed social networks have brought great impacts on many traditional research topics, one of which is link prediction. Link prediction, which aims to infer the formation of a possible link in the near future, is well studied in the last few

years [16]. However, the link prediction in signed networks is dramatically different from that in unsigned scenarios.

Link prediction in unsigned networks aims to predict the future connection status between two nodes, either linked or not. On the contrary, connection status of two nodes in signed networks could be three cases, i.e., positive, negative, and no-relation, which greatly enlarges the difficulty of the original link prediction problem. However, current link prediction models in signed networks focus on predicting signs of existing links [4, 9, 12, 23, 28]. In other words, they are based on an unrealistic assumption that it is already known whether there is a link between any two users.

In reality, given any two nodes, it is very likely that they will still keep no-relation in the future. Therefore, we argue that a more realistic setting should consider no-relation as a future status. Furthermore, it's more practical and meaningful to rank based on the link formation probability among users other than only predict the certain status. Based on the ranking list, applications like recommender systems [7] can be greatly facilitated.

To summarize, given a series of network snapshots with different timestamps, our research questions can be stated as:

(1) **RQ1**: given any node pair (i, j) (i.e. dyad) which currently have no relation between i and j, to predict the connection status of (i, j) in the near future, which can be positive link, negative link, or keep no-relation.
(2) **RQ2**: given any two node pairs (i, j) and (i, k) which both have no relation, to predict which one is more likely to form a positive (or negative) link.

To answer these questions, we aim to address following challenges: 1) a better understanding on no-relation. The features proposed for link prediction in the unsigned structure are likely to be inappropriate for that in the signed structure due to the introduction of negative links. Meanwhile, no-relation status is also ignored in current studies in signed scenarios. Therefore, we need to conduct a feature engineering to check whether there exists features can distinguish three social statuses; and 2) ranking user pairs requires us to measure link strength between users. Current studies treats all links as the same, however in reality, link strength (trustworthiness) is different between users. One idea is that we can leverage the proposed features to represent the link strength. However, it is still difficult to learn the weight for each feature due to the lack of ground truth of link strengths.

In summary, in this research, we aim to design link prediction models, which are more realistic and can be applied in real world scenarios. Our research will also provide a better understanding on the link formation mechanism behind signed network evolution.

UMAP '18, July 8–11, 2018, Singapore, Singapore
© 2018 Association for Computing Machinery.
ACM ISBN 978-1-4503-5589-6/18/07...$15.00
https://doi.org/10.1145/3209219.3213595

2 RELATED WORK

Link prediction techniques in unsigned network have been well studies during past few years. Related works on designing features for distinguishing two link statuses (i.e. linked or not) can be mainly divided into two parts: neighbor-based and path-based methods. Neighbor-based methods describe neighborhoods of users, and popular neighbor-based methods include: the number of common neighbors [1], Adamic/Adar Index [1], Jaccard Coefficient [20], Resource Allocation Index [29] and hierarchically cluster [22]. Meanwhile, path-based techniques characterize paths connecting users in a social network, which include: Katz [16], Vertex Collocation Profile [17] and ProfFlow [18]. However, the aforementioned methods (i.e. these feature frameworks) can not be directly applied in signed scenarios because of the existence of negative links.

Current studies on link prediction in signed networks mainly focus on the sign inference, i.e., predict either positive or negative on the assumption of the link existence. Feature-based approaches are dominant, which design topological features and feed them into a regression model [4, 12, 14]. Regression results can be used to distinguish positive and negative links. Another type of approach is low rank model. Hsieh et al. [9] propose a matrix factorization model to infer the link sign. Those works are based on an unrealistic assumption where it is already known whether there is a link between users.

With regard to the personalized ranking models, there are only a few attempts in signed networks. Symeonidis et al. [24] propose a similarity metric based on user's out/in degree of positive and negative links respectively. A higher similarity score between two users indicates a higher chance to establish a positive link, while a lower score indicates a negative link. Zhu et al. [30] use the number of common friends minus the number of common enemies as the similarity metric. However, these studies adopt heuristic settings on the similarity, and cannot gain a good prediction performance. [23] learn users' latent vectors by adopting matrix factorization technique, and represent the ranking score as the inner product between the corresponding two user vectors. However, it ignores the social connections between two users, which may lead to misprediction. Shahriari et al. [21] split the signed graph into a positive and a negative graph respectively, and apply random walk with restart on each graph. Then they combine the results from two random walks to generate the ranking list. In [27], signed graph is converted to a positive weighted graph, and thus get the global score based on the random walk. [11] proposes a model named SRWR, which introduces a sign into a random surfer so that negative links can be considered, by changing the sign of walking. In [15], Li et al. combine both explicit features and implicit features to represent the link formation probability. However, these methods treat all the link as the same, which ignore the fact that link strength between users are different in reality.

3 METHODOLOGICAL APPROACH

In this study, we will use techniques from social theory analysis (balance theory, status theory, centrality, .etc), machine learning (matrix factorization, supervised random walk), and statistics (significance test). Specifically, we investigate the research problems by three phases.

3.1 Phase 1: Feature engineering

Since we redefine the link prediction problem in signed social networks by also considering "no-relation" , the first step is to thoroughly explore potential features for the newly identified problem. We will try to create features based on social theories, like "balance theory" and "status theory". We aim to extend no-relation status to those theories since they don't take no-relation into consideration. For example, balance theory mainly means "a friend of my friend is my friend" and "an enemy of my enemy is my friend". Then what will happen if two users have largely the same number of 'friends' and 'enemies? Theoretically, either a positive or negative link will make the network more imbalanced. We will statistically check the mean values of each feature for each class (i.e. positive, negative or no-relation), and conduct One-Way ANOVA test. Meanwhile, we will adopt multinomial logistic regression model to check the classification performance over the three classes based on the features.

3.2 Phase 2: Ranking on two-hop neighbors

In this phase we will simplify the research problem that we only focus on ranking the user pairs with many common neighbors. Specifically, given a user i, we only rank the users who have at least N numbers of common neighbors with user i ($N = 10$ in this work, followed the same setting as [12]). This setting has two benefits: 1) based on social homophily theory, these candidate users are more likely to form links with user i than others; and 2) it will greatly reduce the computation.

We use designed features to describe the link strength between two nodes, i.e., link strength is represented as the linear combination of those features. The main idea is, two users who have the same best friends will more likely become friends. As the network evolves by introducing new links, these "new links" should have a large link strength than other user pairs without relation, we can thus learn the feature weighting by matching the ranking order. Therefore, we can adopt a ranking-oriented loss function to learn the weights of the features. Specifically, we plan to adopt SVM-ranking model [10] in this phase.

3.3 Phase 3: Personalized ranking model

In this phase we shall explore whether random walk can work well in signed network since random walk method is the most influential method for personalized ranking in unsigned networks [3, 8, 19]. Even though there are some attempts on this issue [11, 21, 27], those works are unsupervised and all the links are treated as the same (same link strength).

The main idea is to adopt supervised random walk to learn the link strength. Specifically, we will try to manipulate the transition matrix to influence the random walk results, to make the random walk visit those new connected nodes more often than the other unconnected node pairs. Second, we attempt to learn user's bias on negative links (e.g. distrust) by minimizing the differences between the generated ranking list and the ground-truth.

4 EVALUATION SETTING

Dataset. In this project, four publicly available datasets will be used in this study which are all based on signed network structure. They are Epinions[1], Slahsdot[2], Wikipedia RFA[3] , and Bitcoin network[4]. Details of the dataset are shown in Table 1.

Table 1: Dataset statistics.

	Epinions	Slashdot	Wikipedia	Bitcoin
Users	131, 828	82, 140	9, 654	3, 783
Positive links (P)	717, 667	425, 072	87, 766	22, 650
Negative links (N)	123, 705	124, 130	16, 788	1, 536
No-relation (U)	$1.73*10^{10}$	$6.7*10^9$	$9.3*10^7$	$1.4*10^7$

Evaluation Metrics. As aforementioned, we will use ranking metrics rather than the accuracy metric. Since traditional metric AUC is only applicable for two classes, in this project, we will use Generalized AUC [23] as a metric which can measure the ranking performance for three classes. A score of 1.0 indicates a perfect classifier while 0.5 represents a random classifier. This metric is insensitive to the imbalanced data. Besides, we will also check the recommendation performance, via evaluations metrics such as Precision of positive and negative top-K etc.

One thing to note is that we only generate ONE ranking list for each user, with positive links be ranked higher at the top, and negative links lower in the bottom of the list. In other words, the ranking order comes as positive, no-relation, negative ones.

5 PROGRESS TO DATE

To date, we have finished the feature design and developed a simplified personalized ranking model.

RQ1. We derived 41 features from social theories and observations including: Balance theory [2], Status theory [5], Reciprocity [6], Rich-get-richer [26], Clustering [16], and Frequent Subgraph [12]. Take balance theory as an example, we check the fraction of the common 'positive' neighbors (friends) between two users, denoted by **pp_ratio**. Based on balance theory, a large **pp_ratio** represents a high chance for a positive link establishment. In this research, balance theory is extended such that the no-relation status can make the graph more balanced. We statistically check whether these features can distinguish three classes (i.e. positive, negative or no-relation), in all 4 datasets. To do it, we conduct One-Way ANOVA test on the mean of each feature, and results show that all these features can distinguish three social statuses with p-value <0.001. Figure 1 is the distribution of the feature **pp_ratio** in Epinions dataset, which shows totally different distributions for different link statuses. [13] describes more details on the feature study.

RQ2. We have developed a simplified personalized model to rank user pairs. The preliminary results demonstrate the superior of our approach, which inspires us to further explore a more comprehensive model in Phase 3.

Specifically, let r_{ij} be the final ranking score of node j, and let a_{ij} be the link strength of (i, j), which will be 0 if there is no direct link from node i to j. x_{ij} is the feature vector. **w** is the vector we aim to learn, which can be treated as the feature weights. In this study,

---

[1] www.trustlet.org/epinions.html
[2] snap.stanford.edu/data/soc-Slashdot0902.html
[3] snap.stanford.edu/data/wiki-RfA.html
[4] cs.umd.edu/~srijan/wsn

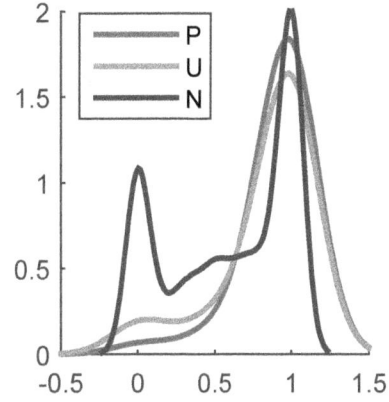

Figure 1: Kernel smoothed density distribution of the feature. P, U and N in legends represent positive, no-relation and negative link respectively.

we adopt a linear function to represent link strength, specifically, we have

$$a'_{ij} = \begin{cases} f_w(x_{ij}) & \exists(i, j) \\ 0 & \text{otherwise} \end{cases} \tag{1}$$

We aim to find the optimal parameter set **w**, which can enlarge positive links' ranking scores, meanwhile diminish no-relation and negative links' ranking scores. Since the candidate set only contains i's two-hop neighbors, therefore, based on the homophily theory, we further approximate r_{ik} as

$$r_{ik} \propto \sum_j a_{ij}a_{jk} \tag{2}$$

Generally, if two links (i, j) and (j, k) both have a strong link strength, the ranking score of node pair (i, k) will be large, which indicate a higher chance to form a positive link. However, as there exists both positive and negative links, we need to figure out how to handle negative links. Based on balance theory, which means "a friend's enemy is an enemy" and "an enemy's enemy is a friend", we calculate the ranking score into two parts: positive influence r^+ and negative influence r^-, which are:

$$r^+_{ik} \propto \sum a^+_{ij}a^+_{jk} + a^-_{ij}a^-_{jk}$$
$$r^-_{ik} \propto \sum a^+_{ij}a^-_{jk} + a^-_{ij}a^+_{jk} \tag{3}$$

Then we use the differences between r^+_{ik} and r^-_{ik} as the final ranking score:

$$r_{ik} = r^+_{ik} - \delta r^-_{ik} \tag{4}$$

where δ is user i's bias towards negative links (e.g. distrust). A positive ranking score indicates the positive influence among neighborhood is dominant, which implies a higher chance to establish a positive link. If the ranking score is close to 0, user i keep no-relation with user k since positive and negative influences are nearly the same.

Then we learn the weight set w by observing the network evolution. For any $m, n \in$ the candidate set, if there is new positive link generated from i to m at time $t + 1$, then $r_{im} \geq r_{in}$. In summary, we aim to optimize the following function:

$$\underset{w, \delta}{\text{minimize}} \quad F(w, \delta) = ||w||^2 + (\delta - 1)^2 + \frac{1}{mn} \sum s_{mn} \qquad (5)$$
$$\text{subject to} \quad r_{in} - r_{im} + s_{mn} \geq 1$$

Here we can also expand $\sum s_{mn}$ by adding a weight coefficient to each type of ranking error:

$$\alpha \sum_{m \in N, n \in P} s_{mn} + \beta \sum_{m \in U, n \in P} s_{mn} + \gamma \sum_{m \in N, n \in U} s_{mn}$$

This quadratic programming problem can be efficiently solved by solving its dual problem. Through this optimization, we can find the corresponding **w**.

6 FUTURE WORK

In the remainder of this project, we will: 1) conduct more experiments on the ranking model proposed in RQ2, especially to check its robustness on different datasets; and 2) design a more comprehensive model based on supervised random walk, which is also the ultimate goal of this research.

REFERENCES

[1] Lada A Adamic and Eytan Adar. 2003. Friends and neighbors on the web. *Social networks* 25, 3 (2003), 211–230.
[2] Tibor Antal, Paul L Krapivsky, and Sidney Redner. 2006. Social balance on networks: The dynamics of friendship and enmity. *Physica D: Nonlinear Phenomena* 224, 1 (2006), 130–136.
[3] Lars Backstrom and Jure Leskovec. 2011. Supervised random walks: predicting and recommending links in social networks. In *Proceedings of the fourth ACM international conference on Web search and data mining*. ACM, 635–644.
[4] Kai-Yang Chiang, Nagarajan Natarajan, Ambuj Tewari, and Inderjit S Dhillon. 2011. Exploiting longer cycles for link prediction in signed networks. In *CIKM*. ACM, 1157–1162.
[5] James A Davis and Samuel Leinhardt. 1967. The structure of positive interpersonal relations in small groups. (1967).
[6] Armin Falk and Urs Fischbacher. 2006. A theory of reciprocity. *Games and economic behavior* 54, 2 (2006), 293–315.
[7] Hui Fang, Guibing Guo, and Jie Zhang. 2015. Multi-faceted trust and distrust prediction for recommender systems. *Decision Support Systems* 71 (2015), 37–47.
[8] Marco Gori, Augusto Pucci, V Roma, and I Siena. 2007. ItemRank: A Random-Walk Based Scoring Algorithm for Recommender Engines.. In *IJCAI*, Vol. 7. 2766–2771.
[9] Cho-Jui Hsieh, Kai-Yang Chiang, and Inderjit S Dhillon. 2012. Low rank modeling of signed networks. In *SIGKDD*. ACM, 507–515.
[10] Thorsten Joachims. 2002. Optimizing search engines using clickthrough data. In *Proceedings of the eighth ACM SIGKDD international conference on Knowledge discovery and data mining*. ACM, 133–142.
[11] Jinhong Jung, Woojeong Jin, Lee Sael, and U Kang. 2016. Personalized ranking in signed networks using signed random walk with restart. In *Data Mining (ICDM), 2016 IEEE 16th International Conference on*. IEEE, 973–978.
[12] Jure Leskovec, Daniel Huttenlocher, and Jon Kleinberg. 2010. Predicting positive and negative links in online social networks. In *WWW*. ACM, 641–650.
[13] Xiaoming Li, Hui Fang, and Jie Zhang. 2017. A Feature-Based Approach for the Redefined Link Prediction Problem in Signed Networks. In *International Conference on Advanced Data Mining and Applications*. Springer, 165–179.
[14] Xiaoming Li, Hui Fang, and Jie Zhang. 2017. Rethinking the Link Prediction Problem in Signed Networks.. In *The Thirty-First AAAI Conference on Artificial Intelligence*. 4955–4956.
[15] Xiaoming Li, Hui Fang, and Jie Zhang. 2018. FILE: A Novel Framework for Predicting Social Status in Signed Networks.. In *The Thirty-Second AAAI Conference on Artificial Intelligence*.
[16] David Liben-Nowell and Jon Kleinberg. 2007. The link-prediction problem for social networks. *Journal of the American society for information science and technology* 58, 7 (2007), 1019–1031.
[17] Ryan N Lichtenwalter and Nitesh V Chawla. 2012. Vertex collocation profiles: subgraph counting for link analysis and prediction. In *WWW*. ACM, 1019–1028.
[18] Ryan N Lichtenwalter, Jake T Lussier, and Nitesh V Chawla. 2010. New perspectives and methods in link prediction. In *SIGKDD*. ACM, 243–252.
[19] Linyuan Lü and Tao Zhou. 2011. Link prediction in complex networks: A survey. *Physica A: Statistical Mechanics and its Applications* 390, 6 (2011), 1150–1170.
[20] Mark EJ Newman. 2001. Clustering and preferential attachment in growing networks. *Physical review E* 64, 2 (2001), 025102.
[21] Moshen Shahriari and Mahdi Jalili. 2014. Ranking nodes in signed social networks. *Social Network Analysis and Mining* 4, 1 (2014), 172.
[22] Donghyuk Shin, Si Si, and Inderjit S Dhillon. 2012. Multi-scale link prediction. In *CIKM*. ACM, 215–224.
[23] Dongjin Song and David A Meyer. 2015. Recommending Positive Links in Signed Social Networks by Optimizing a Generalized AUC.. In *AAAI*. 290–296.
[24] Panagiotis Symeonidis and Eleftherios Tiakas. 2014. Transitive node similarity: predicting and recommending links in signed social networks. *World Wide Web* 17, 4 (2014), 743–776.
[25] Jiliang Tang, Yi Chang, Charu Aggarwal, and Huan Liu. 2016. A survey of signed network mining in social media. *ACM Computing Surveys (CSUR)* 49, 3 (2016), 42.
[26] Zeynep Tufekci. 2010. Who Acquires Friends Through Social Media and Why?" Rich Get Richer" Versus" Seek and Ye Shall Find".. In *ICWSM*.
[27] Zhaoming Wu, Charu C Aggarwal, and Jimeng Sun. 2016. The troll-trust model for ranking in signed networks. In *Proceedings of the Ninth ACM International Conference on Web Search and Data Mining*. ACM, 447–456.
[28] Jihang Ye, Hong Cheng, Zhe Zhu, and Minghua Chen. 2013. Predicting positive and negative links in signed social networks by transfer learning. In *WWW*. ACM, 1477–1488.
[29] Tao Zhou, Linyuan Lü, and Yi-Cheng Zhang. 2009. Predicting missing links via local information. *The European Physical Journal B-Condensed Matter and Complex Systems* 71, 4 (2009), 623–630.
[30] Tianchen Zhu, Zhaohui Peng, Xinghua Wang, and Xiaoguang Hong. 2017. Measuring the Similarity of Nodes in Signed Social Networks with Positive and Negative Links. In *Asia-Pacific Web (APWeb) and Web-Age Information Management (WAIM) Joint Conference on Web and Big Data*. Springer, 399–407.

WikiRec: A Personalized Content Recommendation Framework to Support Informal Learning in Wikis

Heba Ismail
Department of Computer Science and Software Engineering
UAE Univerity, UAE
201590003@uaeu.ac.ae

ABSTRACT

Wikis are attracting lots of attention for informal learning. The nature of wikis enables learners to freely navigate the learning environment and independently construct knowledge without being forced to follow a predefined learning path in accordance with the constructivist learning theory. Recommendation systems (RS) can provide useful content recommendations in different contexts. To our best knowledge, no effective personalized content recommendation approach has yet been defined to support informal learning in wikis. Therefore, we propose a personalized content recommendation framework to extrapolate topical navigation graphs from learners' free navigation and integrate them with fuzzy thesauri for automatic and adaptive personalized content recommendations to support informal learning in wikis.

ACM Reference Format

Heba Ismail. 2018. WikiRec: A Personalized Content Recommendation Framework to Support Informal Learning in Wikis. In *Proceedings of the 26th Conference on User Modeling, Adaptation and Personalization (UMAP'18), July 8–11, 2018, Singapore.* ACM, New York, NY. 4 pages. https://doi.org/10.1145/3209219.3213594

1 INTRODUCTION

Personalization in learning contexts has proved to provide better learning outcomes [1], [2]. Several personalization approaches have long been adopted to support formal learning in various learning environments such as game-based learning [3], e-learning [4], [5], [6], [7], and mobile learning [8]. Personalized formal learning systems attempt to model formal education normally delivered at schools or colleges by defining specific learning content aligned with a curriculum, learning outcomes, and assessments. However, learning personalization is not only desirable in formal learning settings, it is also needed in informal learning which is self-directed, does not follow a specified curriculum, and does not lead to a formal qualification [9]. Studies of informal learning reveal that up to 90% of adults are engaged in hundreds of hours of informal learning [10]. It has also been estimated that up to 70% of learning in the workplace is informal [11]. Many research works recently investigated how online text issuing platforms such as wikis and blogs can contribute to informal learning [12], [13], [14]. Wikis, among other platforms, gained most of the attention [15], [16], [17], [18], [19]. Wikis are interlinked web pages based on the hypertext system of storing and modifying information.

Each page can store information and is easily viewed, edited, and commented on by other people using a web browser [16]. This nature of wikis enables learners to freely navigate the learning environment and independently construct knowledge without being forced to follow a predefined learning path in accordance with the constructivist learning theory [20]. Wiki repositories are considered one of the greatest sources of learning, in particular the Wikipedia site which is targeted in this study. In addition, statistics had shown that 82% of students in higher education turn to Wikipedia to give their research a jump start [21]. One method to navigate articles in Wikipedia is using keyword-based search. In many cases users may fail to choose representative keywords. Another method to navigate articles is following hyperlinks. This method is powerful, but, may drive the user away from the main topic of interest. Recommendation systems (RS) can provide useful content recommendations in different contexts. However, to our best knowledge, no effective personalized content recommendation approach has yet been defined to support informal learning in wikis. Therefore, our research objective is *to develop an effective personalized content recommendation framework to support informal learning in wikis.*

In view of this objective, there are two main challenges that need to be addressed to ensure effectiveness of the personalization approach. **First**, wikis primarily deliver learning content in the form of unstructured free text. This makes it challenging to process and analyze for personalization purposes, especially when context and semantics are concerned. **Second**, on a typical wiki environment, learners' interests are diverse. Furthermore, learning interests of individual learners are more likely to change over learning sessions, or sometimes within a single learning session.

RSs are used successfully to provide content recommendations in different learning contexts [22]. Most of the existing RSs approaches require either sufficient historical data of learners' interactions, collaborative filtering (CF), or identification of learning content attributes, content-based (CB). CF approaches are less effective in recommending content to new learners with no or minimum interaction data. In addition, CF approaches are less effective when learning interests are frequently changing. That is because, a learner may not maintain a consistent pattern of interests. CB approaches are less effective with unstructured text, especially that converting unstructured text into bag-of-words representation eliminates essential semantic relationships in the text.

Consequently, to overcome these limitations and address the research challenges, we propose a personalized content recommendation framework to extrapolate topical navigation graphs from learners' free navigation and integrate them with

UMAP'18, July 8–11, 2018, Singapore.
© 2018 ACM. ISBN 978-1-4503-5589-6/18/07...$15.00.
DOI: https://doi.org/10.1145/3209219.3213594

fuzzy thesauri for automatic and adaptive personalized content recommendations to support informal learning in wikis.

2 BACKGROUND AND RELATED WORK

Modeling Learners' Interests for personalized recommendations. User modeling is the process of inferring information about learners by analyzing users' characteristics, choices, or behavior [23]. Therefore, to build a user model, suitable profiling data needs to be collected for the user model. In our personalization framework we need to model the changing learning interests of individual learners.

The two most commonly used educational recommendation approaches are CF and CB [22]. CF approaches assume that a learner follows a consistent pattern of interests. Hence, learners with similar patterns of interests are more likely to like to same items in the future. This might not always apply to learning interests in heterogenous information networks such as wiki environments. In addition, this approach requires sufficient historical data for individual learners which makes it ineffective for new learners. On the other hand, CB approaches rely on items' attributes. Unstructured text can be converted to bag-of-word feature vectors representation. However, converting unstructured text into bag-of-words representation eliminates essential semantic relationships in the text which are vital for effective content recommendations.

To overcome these limitations, Beal et. al. [24] utilized mind maps generated by researchers on Docear's research paper system to provide content-based research papers recommendations. However, in his approach researchers need to create their mind maps which is time and effort consuming.

On the other hand, Gauch et. al. [25] reported some approaches for automatic interest modeling that rely on extracting weighted vectors of keywords or weighted vectors of concepts. These approaches provide less effective personalization for our research problem since keywords' weights are calculated based on corpus statistics, e.g. TF-IDF, rather than individual user's perception of importance and relevance.

Therefore, we intend to model the changing learning interests in a wiki through extrapolating interesting topics from learners' free navigation behavior and weight them based on structural analysis of users' navigation graphs.

Using Topical Graphs' Structure to Model Learners' Interests. In our research we intend to use topical graphs' content and structure. In the literature, there exist some research efforts in different domains focusing on utilizing topical graphs' structure for eliciting important knowledge about specific users [26], [27]. Zualkernan et. al. [26], proposed that the closer two concepts in the user's topic map the closer their semantic relationship will be and hence the more similar their search results should be. Ismail [27], utilized topological analysis of concept maps to personalize RSS feeds with high degree of accuracy. In addition, Leak et. al. [28], [29], studied further concept map's structural influences, proposed three models for graph structural analysis, and validated through user studies that different concept maps topologies reflected different users' perceptions of concepts' importance. These studies provided evidence on the effectiveness of topical graph's structures in inferring learners' perceived importance of different topics. However, in these studies static topical graphs are explicitly

constructed by learners. In our research we intend to automatically extrapolate topical graphs from learners' free navigation, and dynamically adapt the topical graphs to learners' changing behavior.

Fuzzy Set Information Retrieval Model. Unstructured texts suffer from several complications. Unlike structured data, there are no predefined features and attributes with well-defined values. Approaches of semantic analysis of unstructured text relying on external semantic knowledgebases such as ontologies and semantic networks are domain dependent and expensive to build. An alternative to conceptual approaches is contextual approaches that rely on statistical analysis of the relationships between terms in the text. These approaches tend to be more flexible given the possibility of automation. A fuzzy set IR model is one of the most effective approaches of contextual semantic analysis that has been successfully applied in various contexts [30], [31]. A fuzzy set IR model is based on the fuzzy set theory [32]. The fuzzy set theory relies on two main principles: sets are not crisp, and elements belong to the fuzzy set at different levels of membership. Language sentences and documents are typical examples of fuzzy sets. Hence, we intend to adopt a fuzzy set IR model to associate learning content to interesting topics defined in the learner model.

3 PROPOSED PERSONALIZED CONTENT RECOMMENDATION FRAMEWORK - WikiRec

The proposed framework is composed of 4 main modules, namely, session tracking, TNG analyzer, personalization, and semantic analysis modules. Figure 1 illustrates our conceptualization of the proposed framework. The semantic analysis module is designed to be used offline to build and process custom corpora and generate inverted indices of topics which are used online by the personalization module to generate personalized content recommendations based on the learner models generated by the TNG Analyzer module. We briefly describe each module in the following sections.

Semantic Analysis Module. The ultimate objective of this module is to generate inverted indices of detailed topics corresponding to distinct pages in the wiki. These indices associate each topic with a set of semantically relevant learning documents. ***First***, custom corpora are extracted from Wikipedia for each *main topic* category[1] using a web crawler. ***Second***, natural language processing of the custom corpora is performed to generate inverted indices of unique terms. ***Third***, the inverted indices of terms are used to generate custom fuzzy thesauri that define the semantic similarity, Cf, between every two distinct terms in each custom corpus as explained in [30], [31]. ***Finally***, custom fuzzy thesauri are used to calculate the semantic similarity between detailed distinct topics, indicated by articles' titles[2], and all documents in each custom corpus. That is, every term, T_i, in every topic, Topic, is compared with every word, W_j, in a document, d, to retrieve the corresponding semantic similarity factor, Cf_{ij}, from the custom fuzzy thesaurus which indicates the word-word semantic similarity. Once a term, T_i, is compared to each word, W_j, in a given document, d, the semantic

---

[1] https://en.wikipedia.org/wiki/Category:Main_topic_classifications
[2] https://en.wikipedia.org/wiki/Wikipedia:Article_titles

similarity between the term and the whole document is calculated as follows:

$$\mu_{T,d} = 1 - \Pi \left(1 - Cf_{ij}\right) \qquad (1)$$

which indicates the Term-Document semantic similarity. The average of all μ-values for a given topic, Topic, and a given document, d, is calculated to yield the overall similarity between the topic and the document as follows:

$$Sim\ (Topic, d) = \frac{\mu_{T1,d} + \mu_{T2,d} + \cdots + \mu_{Ti,d}}{i} \qquad (2)$$

Session Tracking Module. Session tracking module first captures raw learning interests for every individual learner in a topical navigation graph (TNG) by tracking individual learning sessions. A learning session starts when the learner first accesses the wiki and ends when the learner leaves the wiki domain. We will model the learner navigation as a directed graph, TNG (V, E). Every vertex (V) in TNG corresponds to a learning topic in the wiki environment. A learning topic corresponds to the overall subject of the article as indicated by the article title. Pages that don't have learning content are filtered out and not captured in the graph. Every edge (E) in TNG corresponds to a navigation action performed by the user to access an article or to move from one article to another. Navigation actions occur through clicking on hyperlinks within the page, browsing back and forward, or clicking on topics' indices provided in the wiki. The process of capturing navigation into TNG is dynamic and continuous throughout the learning session.

TNG Analyzer Module. The two topological models CRD, and HARD adapted from Leak et. al. [28], [29] are used to calculate topics' structural weights relevant to individual learners' navigation behavior. The analysis of the structural weights goes through two steps. *First*, the structural characteristics of each topical node in TNG need to be defined as per the selected model. For CRD model, each topical node, V, needs to be characterized for its connectivity, outgoing connections, o(V), and incoming connections, i(V), and direct steps from the first topical node, d(V). For HARD model, each topical node, V, needs to be characterized as being a hub, h(V), with mostly outgoing connections, authority, a(V), with mostly incoming connections, or upper node, u(V), that is closer to the starting node in TNG. *Second*, using the structural characteristics the relative node's weight is calculated as follows:

For CRD Model:

$$W(V) = \left(\alpha \cdot o(V) + \beta \cdot i(V)\right) \cdot \left(\frac{1}{d(V)+1}\right)^{\frac{1}{\delta}} \qquad (3)$$

For HARD model:

$$W(V) = \alpha \cdot h(V) + \beta \cdot a(V) + \gamma \cdot u(V) \qquad (4)$$

Personalization Module. Based on the structural weights calculated earlier, a weighted or ranked topical navigation graph can be used as a learner model to associate personalized learning articles from topics' inverted indices generated by the semantic analysis module such that:

$$W(V)^* Sim\ (Topic, d) = W(V) * \left[\frac{\mu_{T1,d} + \mu_{T2,d} + \cdots + \mu_{Ti,d}}{i}\right] \qquad (5)$$

Therefore, learning documents with higher semantic similarities to topics that have higher structural weights in the learner model are retrieved and recommended to the learner. Adaptation is accomplished through continues update of TNG and, accordingly, the structural weights and the recommendations.

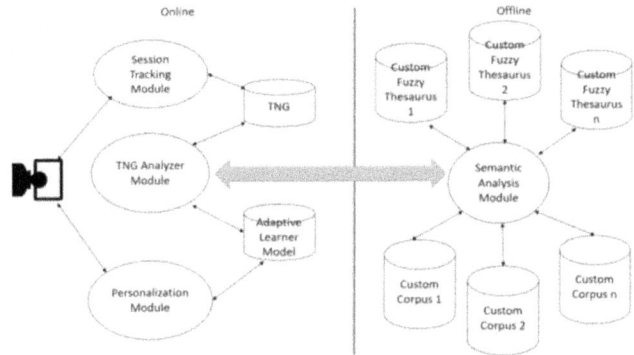

Figure 1 Illustration of the proposed approach

4 EVALUATION

User Studies. To validate the proposed approach, we will run user studies using an online compressed version of Wikipedia equipped with the personalized content recommendation framework proposed in section 3. Different experimental conditions and test scenarios will be evaluated. The compressed version of Wikipedia is used from the 2007 Wikipedia DVD Selection[3] which is a free, hand-checked, and non-commercial selection from Wikipedia, targeted around the UK National Curriculum. It is about the size of a fifteen-volume encyclopedia including all topics in Wikipedia rated "Good" or higher by Wikipedia itself at date of production. Experiments will be carried out at a local private schools teaching the UK National Curriculum. All year 6 and year 5 students will be invited to participate in the experiments.

Performance Measures. User-centric metrics as well as objective statistical measures will be used. For the user-centric metrics, we will use questionnaires to collect users' feedback. For the objective measures, we will collect some browsing and navigation related data from the user's navigation session which will be used to calculate the click rates, accuracy, and precision.

5 FUTURE RESEARCH

The remainder of this project will revolve around 1) running the user studies in various informal learning contexts to test the generalizability of the proposed approach; and 2) looking into the best parameters and settings of the proposed approach.

---

[3] https://en.wikipedia.org/wiki/Wikipedia:Wikipedia_CD_Selection

REFERENCES

[1] Khrib, M. K., Jemn, M., & Nasraoui, O, "Automatic recommendations for e-learning personalization based on web usage mining techniques and information retrieval," in *Eighth IEEE International Conference on Advanced Learning Technologies, ICALT08*, 2008.

[2] Bray, B., & McClaskey, K, "A STEP-BY-STEP Guide to Personalize Learning," 2013.

[3] Mills, C., & Dalgarno, B., "A conceptual model for game-based intelligent tutoring systems.," in *Proceedings of the 2007 Australasian Society for Computers in Learning in Tertiary Education*, 2007.

[4] Schiaffino, S., Garcia, P., & Amandi, A., "eTeacher: Providing personalized assistance to e-learning students.," *Computers & Education*, vol. 51, no. 4, pp. 1744-1754, 2008.

[5] Hong, C. M., Chen, C. M., Chang, M. H., & Chen, S. C., "Intelligent web-based tutoring system with personalized learning path guidance.," in *Seventh IEEE International Conference on Advanced Learning Technologies*, 2007.

[6] Verdú, E., Regueras, L. M., Gal, E., de Castro, J. P., Verdú, M. J., & Kohen-Vacs, D. , "Integration of an intelligent tutoring system in a course of computer network design.," *Educational Technology Research and Development*, vol. 65, no. 3, pp. 653-677, 2017.

[7] Zhang, B., & Jia, J., "Evaluating an Intelligent Tutoring System for Personalized Math Teaching," in *2017 International Symposium on Educational Technology (ISET)*, 2017.

[8] Motiwalla, L. F., "Mobile learning: A framework and evaluation.," *Computers & education*, vol. 49, no. 3, pp. 581-596, 2007.

[9] Misko, J., Combining Formal, Non-Formal and Informal Learning for Workforce Skill Development, Adelaide, Australia: National Centre for Vocational Education Research Ltd, 2008.

[10] Merriam, S. B., Caffarella, R. S., & Baumgartner, L. M. , Learning in adulthood: A comprehensive guide, John Wiley & Sons, 2012.

[11] Streumer, J. N., & Kho, M., "The world of work-related learning," *Work-related learning*, pp. 3-49, 2006.

[12] Selwyn, N., "Web 2.0 applications as alternative environments for informal learning-a critical review," in *International Expert Meeting on ICT and Educational Performance*, 2007.

[13] García-Peñalvo, F. J., Colomo-Palacios, R., & Lytras, M. D. , "Informal learning in work environments: training with the Social Web in the workplace," *Behaviour & Information Technology*, vol. 31, no. 8, pp. 753-755, 2012.

[14] Coll, S. D., & Treagust, D. , "Blended learning environment: an approach to enhance students's learning experiences outside school," *MIER Journal of Educational Studies, Trends and Practices*, vol. 7, no. 2, 2018.

[15] Zheng, B., Niiya, M., & Warschauer, M., "Wikis and collaborative learning in higher education.," *Technology, Pedagogy and Education*, vol. 24, no. 3, pp. 357-374, 2015.

[16] Neumann, D. L., & Hood, M., "The effects of using a wiki on student engagement and learning of report writing skills in a university statistics course.," *Australasian Journal of Educational Technology*, vol. 25, no. 3, 2009.

[17] Kimmerle, J., Moskaliuk, J., & Cress, U., "Using wikis for learning and knowledge building: Results of an experimental study.," *Journal of Educational Technology & Society*, vol. 14, no. 4, p. 138, 2011.

[18] Chu, S. K. W., Zhang, Y., Chen, K., Chan, C. K., Lee, C. W. Y., Zou, E., & Lau, W., "The effectiveness of wikis for project-based learning in different disciplines in higher education.," *The internet and higher education*, vol. 33, no. 1, pp. 49-60, 2017.

[19] Sharp, L. A., & Whaley, B., "Wikis as Online Collaborative Learning Experiences:"A Different Kind of Brainstorming"," *Adult Learning*, 2018.

[20] Piaget, J., Language and Thought of the Child: Selected Works, vol. 5, Routledge, 2005.

[21] Head, A. J., & Eisenberg, M. B., "How today's college students use Wikipedia for course-related research," *Peer Reviewed Journal of The Internet*, vol. 15, no. 3, 2010.

[22] Manouselis, N., Drachsler, H., Vuorikari, R., Hummel, H., & Koper, R., "Recommender systems in technology enhanced learning," *Recommender systems handbook*, pp. 387-415, 2011.

[23] Zukerman, I., & Albrecht, D. W., "Predictive statistical models for user modeling.," *User Modeling and User-Adapted Interaction*, vol. 11, no. 1-2, pp. 5-18, 2001.

[24] Beel, J., Langer, S., Genzmehr, M., & Nürnberger, A., "Introducing Docear's research paper recommender system.," in *In Proceedings of the 13th ACM/IEEE-CS joint conference on Digital libraries*, 2013.

[25] Gauch, S., Speretta, M., Chandramouli, A., & Micarelli, A., "User profiles for personalized information access," *The adaptive web*, pp. 54-89, 2007.

[26] Zualkernan, I. A., AbuJayyab, M. A., & Ghanam, Y. A. , "An alignment equation for using mind maps to filter learning queries from Google.," in *Sixth IEEE International Conference on Advanced Learning Technologies*, 2006.

[27] Ismail, H. M. , "Using Concept Maps and Fuzzy Set Information Retrieval Model To Dynamically Personalize RSS Feeds.," *IJCSNS*, vol. 14, no. 2, p. 10, 2014.

[28] Leake, D. B., & Maguitman, A., "Combining concept mapping with CBR: towards experience-based support for knowledge modeling.," in *fourteenth international florida artificial intelligence research society conference*, Florida, 2011.

[29] Leake, D., Maguitman, A., & Reichherzer, T., "Understanding knowledge models: Modeling assessment of concept importance in concept maps.," in *twenty-sixth annual conference of the cognitive science society*, 2004.

[30] Ogawa, Y., Morita, T., & Kobayashi, K., "A Fuzzy Document Retrieval System Using The Keyword Connection Matrix and a Learning Method," *Fuzzy Sets and Systems*, vol. 39, no. 2, pp. 163-179, 1991.

[31] Yerra, R., & Ng, Y. K., "Detecting Similar HTML Documents Using a Fuzzy Set Information Retrieval Approach," in *Granular Computing IEEE International Conference*, 2005.

[32] Zadeh, "Fuzzy Sets," *Information and Control*, vol. 8, pp. 338-353, 1965.

Interpreting User Input Intention in Natural Human Computer Interaction

Yuanchun Shi

Tsinghua University, China

shiyc@tsinghua.edu.cn

ABSTRACT

Human Computer Interaction (HCI)[1] is about information exchange between human and computers. Interaction between users and computers occurs at the User Interface (UI). Now, computers become pervasive, they are embedded in everyday things and UIs are the main value-added competitive advantages. UIs should be more natural for users. NUI (natural user interface) expands forms beyond formal input devices like the mouse and keyboard to more and more natural forms of interaction such as touch, speech, gestures, handwriting, and vision. Unlike speech, handwriting and vision, which have been researched for decades and put into practical use recently, touch and gestures are interaction tasks related, and yet lack of study. This talk will introduce methods of modelling user input action based on data with the random noise for fast touch input and natural gestures.

CCS Concepts

Human-centered computing ~ Interactive systems and tools

KEYWORDS

Natural user interface; user intention

1 CONTENTS

Human-computer interaction has already entered the post-pc era. The state-of-the-art research focuses more on mobile, wearable, and VR/AR devices rather than traditional mouse and keyboards. These new devices provide unique input and output capabilities that can enable richer tasks and activities. In this background, the value of usability is further emphasized. If we review the current development trend, we can see that human-computer interface is gradually moving closer to human: The form of interaction data is shifting from being discrete and accurate to being continuous and imprecise. The objective of this trend is to make interaction more natural to human, that is, easier to learn and easier to perform.

The ubiquity of interaction raises a number of challenges to the sensing and data processing of interaction. The core difficulty is how to identify users' input intention from the continuous and random data, which is usually weakly correlated with the input intention. Note that such interaction occurs without having users to explicitly confirm the input, like clicking a mouse button. In addition, whether or not the interaction design satisfies users' expectation is also an essential factor that affects the naturalness of the interaction. This is related to the psychological aspect of interaction design. In this talk, I will focus on the former issue, that is, data processing.

In recent years, my research group is all around the topic of interpreting user's input intention through the behaviour data of users' natural input. Our main approach is the Bayesian method. Through Bayesian theorem, we transform the posterior probability of interaction intention into the product of the prior probability of interaction intention and the conditional probability of users' input behaviour. Both components have clear physical meaning and can be computationally modelled. The prior probability of interaction intention corresponds to what we usually call interaction tasks, while the conditional probability of users' input behaviour corresponds to human behaviour models. An advantage of this approach is that it does not suffer from the problem of insufficient labelling data or sparse data, which embodies the idea of intelligent data processing driven by knowledge, rather by data.

In particular, I will share with you a set of smart text entry techniques on natural user interfaces, including ten-finger air typing [3], accurate typing on small touchscreens [4], touch-typing on glass screens [1, 2], and on constrained user interfaces on google glass [5] and using pressure sensors [6]. These works instantiate the Bayesian method to interpret users' input intention on natural user interface, and demonstrate the state-of-the-art performance in these areas.

ACM ISBN 978-1-4503-5589-6/18/07.

DOI: https://doi.org/10.1145/3209219.3209267

REFERENCES

[1] Yiqin Lu, Chun Yu, Xin Yi, Yuanchun Shi, Shengdong Zhao: BlindType: Eyes-Free Text Entry on Handheld Touchpad by Leveraging Thumb's Muscle Memory. IMWUT 1(2): 18:1-18:24 (2017)

[2] Weinan Shi, Chun Yu, Xin Yi, Zhen Li, Yuanchun Shi: TOAST: Ten-Finger Eyes-Free Typing on Touchable Surfaces. IMWUT 2(1): 33:1-33:23 (2018)

[3] Xin Yi, Chun Yu, Mingrui Zhang, Sida Gao, Ke Sun, Yuanchun Shi: ATK: Enabling Ten-Finger Freehand Typing in Air Based on 3D Hand Tracking Data. UIST 2015: 539-548

[4] Xin Yi, Chun Yu, Weinan Shi, Yuanchun Shi: Is it too small?: Investigating the performances and preferences of users when typing on tiny QWERTY keyboards. Int. J. Hum.-Comput. Stud. 106: 44-62 (2017)

[5] Chun Yu, Ke Sun, Mingyuan Zhong, Xincheng Li, Peijun Zhao, Yuanchun Shi: One-Dimensional Handwriting: Inputting Letters and Words on Smart Glasses. CHI 2016: 71-82

[6] Mingyuan Zhong, Chun Yu, Qian Wang, Xuhai Xu, Yuanchun Shi: ForceBoard: Subtle Text Entry Leveraging Pressure. CHI 2018: 528

SHORT BIO

Yuanchun Shi is a Changjiang distinguished professor of the Department of Computer Science, the director of HCI & Media Integration Institute. Her research interests include pervasive computing, human computer interaction, distributed multimedia processing and e-learning. Prof..Shi has publications in IEEE Pervasive Computing, IJHCS, TPDS, TKDE, ACM CHI, MM, UIST, etc. She has won 2 National Science and Technology Advancement Awards and many best paper awards. Prof. Shi received all her PhD, MS and BS in Computer Science from Tsinghua University.

Investigating the Decision-Making Behavior of Maximizers and Satisficers in the Presence of Recommendations

Michael Jugovac
TU Dortmund
Dortmund, Germany
michael.jugovac@tu-dortmund.de

Ingrid Nunes
Universidade Federal do Rio Grande
do Sul (UFRGS)
Porto Alegre, Brazil
ingridnunes@inf.ufrgs.br

Dietmar Jannach
Alpen-Adria-Universität
Klagenfurt, Austria
dietmar.jannach@aau.at

ABSTRACT

Psychological theory distinguishes between maximizing and satisficing decision-making styles. Maximizers tend to explore more or all alternatives when making a choice, while satisficers evaluate options until they find one that is good enough. There is limited research that examines how the existence of a recommender influences the choice process and decisions of different types of decision-makers. We report the results of a controlled study, in which we monitored the choice process of participants when provided with automated recommendations and different types of additional information regarding available options.

Our analyses show that *none* of the differences that were expected based on the literature manifested itself in the experiment. Maximizers neither inspected more items, nor invested more time to study them. Instead, like satisficers, they mostly picked one of the top-ranked items recommended by the system, which emphasizes the value of recommenders in particular for maximizers, who would otherwise face a more challenging decision problem. The analysis of the preferences of participants over different types of additional information revealed that highlighting key pros and cons was perceived as particularly helpful for the maximizers, an insight that can be used for the design of explanation approaches for recommenders.

CCS CONCEPTS

• **Information systems** → **Recommender systems**; *Decision support systems*; • **Human-centered computing** → **User studies**;

KEYWORDS

Explanations; decision making policies; maximizer; satisficer

ACM Reference Format:
Michael Jugovac, Ingrid Nunes, and Dietmar Jannach. 2018. Investigating the Decision-Making Behavior of Maximizers and Satisficers in the Presence of Recommendations. In *UMAP '18: 26th Conference on User Modeling, Adaptation and Personalization, July 8–11, 2018, Singapore, Singapore*. ACM, New York, NY, USA, 5 pages. https://doi.org/10.1145/3209219.3209252

1 INTRODUCTION

Psychological theory suggests that people adopt different decision-making styles [14]. At one extreme, there are *maximizers*, who have a tendency to explore many or all available options before making a decision, whereas *satisficers* usually only scan the options until they find a satisfactory one [5, 24]. Interestingly, even though maximizers, as a result, tend to invest more time, they are often less happy with their final decisions [10].

Helping users in the decision process is one of the major goals of recommender systems (RS) [11, 13, 22], and a large amount of evidence exists on the impact of these systems on decisions made by their users [12, 15, 27]. While the recommendations of such systems are in many cases personalized according to the assumed preferences or personality of users, recommenders usually do not take possible differences in the users' decision making styles into account. There are only a few approaches in this context [6, 18]. They investigate, for example, the value of providing different user interfaces for different types of consumers or user interfaces that adapt themselves, e.g., according to the consumers' assumed expertise.

The long-term goal of our research is to customize recommenders to better support users with different decision-making styles. Examples of possible customizations are the presentation of larger choice sets for maximizers or the provision of certain types of complementary information to support users in the decision-making process according to their decision-making style. In this paper, we make a step towards achieving this goal and investigate foundational aspects by means of a user study. A first main question addressed in our study is to what extent the observations regarding the choice behavior of maximizers and satisficers manifest themselves in the context of a recommendation scenario. Differently from studies in the field of psychology, the decision process in our application scenario is supported by a recommender system and the choice set is presented to the study participants in a certain order determined by the system. Furthermore, to investigate if maximizers and satisficers have different information needs, we provided participants with different types of explanations [20] and measured their acceptance and perceived value for the different user groups. Differently from typical user studies on explanations, instead of only asking participants about their subjective experience regarding, e.g., the choice difficulty, we also rely on objective measures such as the time needed to make a decision, the number of inspected items, or the position of the selected item in the recommendation list.

The rest of the paper is organized as follows. After discussing previous work and our expectations in Section 2, we report the design of our user study in Section 3. The results of our analysis and our conclusions are discussed in Sections 4 and 5.

2 BACKGROUND AND EXPECTATIONS

As mentioned, a number of psychology studies have shown that maximizers generally spend more time on making decisions, yet ultimately experience more regret and less satisfaction with their choices than satisficers [5, 24]. For example, in a study about job seeking behavior [10], in which maximizers secured higher-paying jobs on average, they felt more negative affect during the decision process and lower satisfaction with their (objectively better) choices. In contrast to our study, in which we collected objective measurements about the participants decision behavior, such as time taken, many of the influential studies on this topic rely on self-reported experiences or thought experiments.

In the field of recommender systems, there is only limited research that takes the user's decision making style into account. For example, the users' decision making styles were considered in a study about diversification for recommender systems [26]. Based on the applied Structural Equation Model, the conclusion was that the maximization tendency of the participants did not affect any of the other measured variables, such as choice difficulty, recommendation attractiveness, or perceived diversity. Similarly, in a study about an energy-saving recommender system [18], maximizers and satisficers also showed no differences in terms of perceived control, interface satisfaction, recommender system effectiveness, etc. However, in contrast to the psychology literature, maximizers were actually *more* satisfied with their decisions.[1]

One hypothesis that could explain the above-mentioned observations is that the presence of a recommender system, which preranks the available options, influences the decision making behavior of users. In fact, changes in decision making policies have been previously observed, for example by Schnabel et al. [23], in which more users behaved like maximizers when they had access to a *shortlist* user interface element. In contrast, based on previous studies from the recommender systems literature, we expect that the presence of a recommender system can make more users behave like satisficers, i.e., engage less in search and comparison as would be expected for maximizers. Differently from previous studies, we also test this hypothesis based on *objective* measures, such as the decision time or the number of inspected items, which has not been done so far in recommender systems studies [18, 26].

Psychology literature, furthermore, suggests that maximizers and satisficers differ in their information needs. Maximizers, for example, tend to rely more on relative rather than absolute comparisons and consult external influences more frequently, such as expert opinions or social comparisons [24, 25]. Thus, in addition to examining the overall user decision behavior, we also investigate the effect of *additional explanatory information* provided during the decision making process. We compare three different explanation styles to find out whether they can be useful in the decision making process of maximizers or satisficers in different ways.

3 EXPERIMENTAL SETUP

In this section, we provide details about the study design and the recruited participants.

[1] In another recommender systems study, the maximization tendency was measured, but in the final model the construct did not converge and was excluded [17].

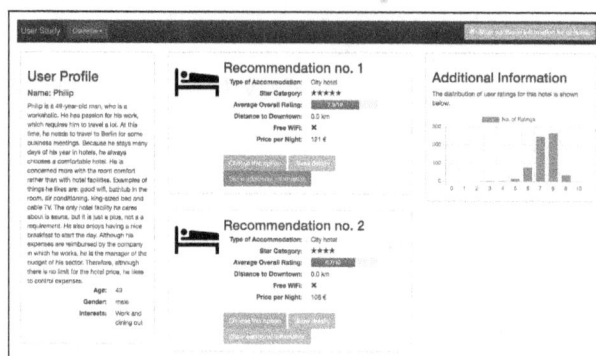

Figure 1: User interface of the recommender system.

Study Tasks. Based on empirical evidence that maximizing and satisficing behavior also transfers to decisions that are made on behalf of others [4], we implemented a web-based system (Figure 1) through which participants were asked to choose a hotel for someone else. The fictitious profile of the target user was displayed along with a set of recommendations, which were computed using a user-based nearest neighbor algorithm on a historical dataset of hotel rating data. At the start of the experiment, an initial set of 10 recommendations was displayed, and users could request more (up to 40) recommendations, which allowed us to roughly track how many options users inspected before they made a decision.

To investigate if the different user groups have different information needs, participants could request "additional information" for each item. During the experiment, participants were asked to make decisions for three different profiles for three different cities. In each round, a different type of information (explanation) was presented (initially hidden), which could be used as a further basis for their decisions. The explanations (see Figure 2) were based on three fundamentally different knowledge sources: the quality perception of other consumers in the form of the rating distribution (Style A) [9], a pros-and-cons comparison with other hotels with respect to certain features (Style B) [16, 19, 21], and information about the recommendation process itself in terms of selected neighbor ratings (Style C) [1, 2, 8]. Before each of the three tasks, participants received a detailed interactive tutorial on the user interface, decision task, and additional information shown in the respective trial. The order of the profiles, cities, and types of additional information were randomized in a round-robin fashion during the trials.

After participants had made their three choices, they provided demographic data, after which they were shown three four-item questionnaires (using 7-point Likert scales) regarding the provided additional information types, namely, if they found the explanations transparent, useful, trustworthy, and if the information made them more confident in their choice. Finally, the participants answered the 13-item questionnaire proposed by Schwartz et al. [24], which we used to classify the participants into maximizers and satisficers. As usual in the field [10, 24], we used the median maximization scores to distinguish between maximizers and satisficers.

Study Variables. Overall, the *independent* variables are (i) the participants' decision making style (maximizer or satisficer) and (b) the investigated explanation styles, a *within-subjects* variable with three possible values.

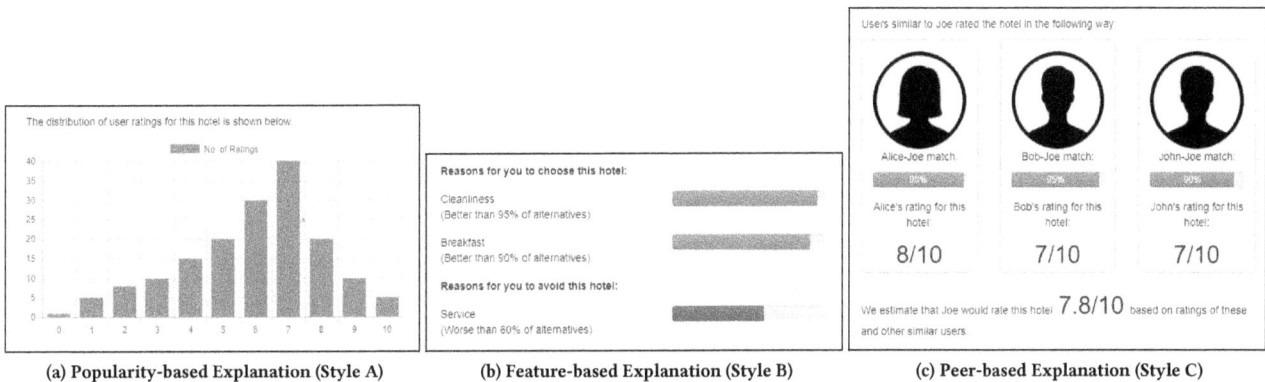

(a) Popularity-based Explanation (Style A)   (b) Feature-based Explanation (Style B)   (c) Peer-based Explanation (Style C)

Figure 2: Examples of the three types of additional explanatory information evaluated in the user study.

As *dependent* variables, we used the following *objective* measures to assess differences in the decision-making behavior of the participants.

- The time needed to complete the decision-making task.
- The number of times the participant requested to see a page with detailed item information (detail requests).
- The number of requested recommendations. For this, we recorded how many of the four recommendation pages were loaded by the participant (recommendation requests).
- The number of times the participants requested to see additional explanatory information (explanation requests).
- The list position of the hotel chosen by the participants (choice index).[2]

As *subjective* measures, we analyzed the participants' responses to the four questionnaire items mentioned above regarding the value of the additionally displayed information.

Participants. We recruited participants via email lists and social networks. Between October and December 2017, 243 subjects from 5 different countries participated, and 109 completed the study. The majority of the participants were in their twenties. Most of them were from Brazil and Germany and had a computer science or information technology background. We excluded 19 subjects from the study, because they completed the process in an unreasonable short or long time. We used a threshold of 60 seconds for task completion, which we determined as the minimum time to read the target user profile and make a decision. Additionally, we excluded participants who took longer than 90 minutes for one of the tasks, assuming they likely focused on something else during the study.

4 OBSERVATIONS

Decision-Making Behavior of Maximizers and Satisficers. Table 1 shows the outcomes of our objective measurements. The results are provided in accumulated form as well as separated based on the participants' decision making styles and the provided explanation styles. To test if any of the observed differences across the different conditions were significant, we applied an ANOVA test or, in case its assumptions were not fulfilled, a Kruskal-Wallis test. The analyses showed that none of the differences were significant at a significance level of $p = 0.05$. In other words, independently of the

explanation style, maximizers and satisficers did not differ significantly in their decision-making behavior in terms of the observed objective measures.

Thus, against our expectations and the existing research literature, maximizers did *not* take more time to make the decision, they did *not* look at more pages showing further alternatives, they did *not* inspect more item details or explanations, and they did *not* choose items further down the list than satisficers. In fact, from all participants, about 25% selected the first recommended hotel as their final choice, indicating that the recommendations were generally adopted well. The provision of different types of explanations also had no significant influence on their behavior. While we could not measure (e.g., through eye-tracking) how many alternatives the participants were looking at and for how long, the combination of measures (needed time, request for item details) suggest that there is no strong difference in the given sample.

As a result, our research leads to the hypothesis that the differences between maximizers and satisficers diminish or even disappear in the presence of recommendations, as was indicated in previous studies in the field of recommenders [18, 26]. One of the underlying reasons could be that maximizers (like satisficers) trust the recommendations and assume that there will be no better choices in the lower-ranked options. The recommendations in our study were, in fact, ordered by their assumed relevance for the given profiles, but there was no "objectively-best" ordering where one option strictly dominates another. Generally, the observed behavior might also be influenced by our everyday experiences, e.g., when using search engines, where users rarely inspect more than the first few pages [3]. Overall, to the best of our knowledge, no previous work in the field of psychology has examined the maximizer-satisficer theory for situations where the alternatives are pre-ordered according to some expected utility.

The Effect of Different Types of Additional Information. Table 2 shows the results obtained for the *subjective* measures regarding the different explanation styles. Combined with the objective results from Table 1, we can make the following observations.

Generally, we can observe that explanation style B (using pros and cons) received the highest absolute scores in all subgroups and all dimensions except trust. Considering the participants without distinguishing them based on their decision-making styles, the overall preference was for style B over styles A and C in terms

---

[2]The hotels in each city were presented in the same order for all participants.

Table 1: Mean (M), standard deviation (SD) and Median (Med) of scores obtained for objective variables. Choice=choice index, Detail=detail requests, Reco=recommendation requests, Expl=explanation requests. Results are shown separately by explanation style and combined in the last row of each group. Time is given in minutes.

Meas./ Expl.	Satisficer M±SD	Med	Maximizer M±SD	Med	All M±SD	Med
Time A	4.69± 3.50	3.55	4.69± 3.88	3.06	4.69± 3.67	3.18
B	6.18± 9.29	4.12	5.08± 4.83	3.40	5.63± 7.38	3.87
C	5.84± 6.29	3.79	4.85± 4.42	3.61	5.34± 5.43	3.64
All	5.57± 6.77	3.84	4.87± 4.36	3.18	5.22± 5.69	3.58
Choice A	5.47± 7.29	4	6.58± 6.31	6	6.02± 6.80	4
B	7.87± 8.21	4	5.64± 5.78	4	6.76± 7.15	4
C	5.60± 5.01	6	5.82± 8.37	2	5.71± 6.86	4
All	6.31± 7.00	4	6.01± 6.87	4	6.16± 6.93	4
Detail A	8.73±11.66	4	6.42± 6.00	5	7.58± 9.29	5
B	7.04± 7.27	5	5.76± 7.53	3	6.40± 7.39	4
C	6.73± 6.52	4	6.20± 7.81	4	6.47± 7.16	4
All	7.50± 8.76	5	6.13± 7.11	4	6.81± 7.99	4
Reco. A	0.76± 1.07	0	1.13± 1.32	1	0.9± 1.21	0.5
B	0.89± 1.05	1	1.00± 1.43	0	0.94± 1.25	0
C	0.69± 1.02	0	1.04± 1.45	0	0.87± 1.26	0
All	0.78± 1.04	0	1.06± 1.39	0	0.92± 1.23	0
Expl. A	7.82±10.39	3	9.56±12.87	4	8.69±11.66	3
B	9.09± 9.49	6	10.56±10.91	10	9.82±10.19	7
C	8.87±10.37	4	11.42±10.88	10	10.14±10.65	10
All	8.59±10.03	4	10.51±11.53	8	9.55±10.83	5

Table 2: Mean (M), standard deviation (SD) and median (Med) scores obtained for each measurement across difference groups (explanation style and decision making policy).

Meas./ Expl.	Satisficer M±SD	Med	Maximizer M±SD	Med	All M±SD	Med
Transp. A	4.93±1.70	5	4.89±1.67	5	4.91±1.67	5
B	5.56±1.14	6	5.73±1.07	6	5.64±1.10	6
C	5.09±1.68	6	4.67±1.58	5	4.88±1.63	5
Useful. A	4.80±1.60	5	5.11±1.35	5	4.96±1.48	5
B	5.67±1.09	6	5.64±1.19	6	5.66±1.13	6
C	5.13±1.34	5	5.00±1.12	5	5.11±1.23	5
Trust A	4.93±1.44	5	5.07±1.36	5	5.00±1.39	5
B	4.69±1.31	5	5.18±1.21	5	4.93±1.28	5
C	4.22±1.43	4	4.22±1.28	4	4.22±1.35	4
Confid. A	4.33±1.55	5	4.71±1.44	5	4.52±1.50	5
B	5.11±1.27	5	5.33±1.24	5	5.22±1.25	5
C	4.58±1.36	5	4.62±1.42	5	4.60±1.38	5

of transparency, usability, and confidence, with statistically significant differences (based on the corresponding statistical tests). Because style B is the only one that focuses on item features, this observation corroborates previous findings [7], in which different explanation styles were compared and "content-based" explanations were favored over, e.g., rating-based ones, in different dimensions. In contrast to this work, which used a slightly different visual representation, our pros-and-cons approach did not lead to a loss in decision efficiency, i.e., participants did not take more time when confronted with this type of explanations.

Nonetheless, even though the participants preferred explanations of style B (for example, in terms of usefulness), this did not lead to an increased actual use of the explanations. As mentioned earlier, the analysis of the results shown in Table 1 shows that users did not inspect significantly more explanations of style B than other explanation styles, leading to a gap between the participants' reported utility and their objectively observed behavior.

An interesting side-observation is that the "social" explanation style C received the lowest scores in terms of transparency, even though this style reveals the internal reasoning of the underlying recommender algorithm. This indicates that the participants had troubles understanding the meaning of what is presented in explanations of style C.

The differences between maximizers and satisficers in terms of their assessment of the different types of explanations were mostly small and not statistically significant. Statistical tests revealed only a significant preference of maximizers for style B over style C in terms of transparency. One reason for the maximizers' preference towards the feature-based comparison of the hotels could be their tendency to rely more on *relative* than absolute information, as previously observed [25]. Overall, except for this special case, in which maximizers seem to find feature-based explanations more transparent than peer-based information, maximizers and satisficers did not exhibit different information needs in the given scenario.

5 CONCLUSIONS AND IMPLICATIONS

In the presence of the recommender system that we employed in our user study, maximizers and satisficers did not exhibit significant differences in their observable decision-making behavior. This is in sharp contrast to existing psychology literature, but supports results of previous studies of this phenomenon in the context of recommender systems, which also observed no significant differences in terms of subjective measures. If these observations were generalizable, recommender systems could become a valuable assistive tool to mitigate the problems maximizers regularly face in decision-making tasks, such as negative affect and regret. However, further research is necessary to fully understand the effect that recommendations can have on users with different decision making styles, specifically in scenarios with different complexities, assortment sizes, and product domains.

Furthermore, the fact that participants from all groups preferred a pros-and-cons explanation style, which did not affect decision efficiency, could be a starting point for further detailed studies about the practical benefits of such explanations.

Finally, peer-based explanations received low scores overall, which is surprising, because maximizers are specifically known for engaging more in social comparison. Future work could focus on identifying the reason why maximizers did not prefer this social explanation type and which alternations should be made to better satisfy their information needs.

REFERENCES

[1] Svetlin Bostandjiev, John O'Donovan, and Tobias Höllerer. 2012. TasteWeights: A Visual Interactive Hybrid Recommender System. In *Proceedings of the Sixth ACM Conference on Recommender Systems (RecSys '12)*. 35–42.

[2] Yu-Chih Chen, Yu-Shi Lin, Yu-Chun Shen, and Shou-De Lin. 2013. A Modified Random Walk Framework for Handling Negative Ratings and Generating Explanations. *Transactions on Intelligent Systems and Technology* 4, 1 (2013), 12:1–12:21.

[3] Chitika, Inc. 2013. The Value of Google Result Positioning. https://chitika.com/2013/06/07/the-value-of-google-result-positioning-2/. (2013). Retrieved February 20, 2018.

[4] Tilottama G. Chowdhury, S. Ratneshwar, and Praggyan Mohanty. 2009. The time-harried shopper: Exploring the differences between maximizers and satisficers. *Marketing Letters* 20, 2 (2009), 155–167.

[5] Ilan Dar-Nimrod, Catherine D. Rawn, Darrin R. Lehman, and Barry Schwartz. 2009. The Maximization Paradox: The costs of seeking alternatives. *Personality and Individual Differences* 46, 5 (2009), 631–635.

[6] Alexander Felfernig, Gerhard Friedrich, Dietmar Jannach, and Markus Zanker. 2006. An Integrated Environment for the Development of Knowledge-Based Recommender Applications. *International Journal of Electronic Commerce* 11, 2 (2006), 11–34.

[7] Fatih Gedikli, Dietmar Jannach, and Mouzhi Ge. 2014. How Should I Explain? A Comparison of Different Explanation Types for Recommender Systems. *International Journal of Human-Computer Studies* 72, 4 (2014), 367–382.

[8] Brynjar Gretarsson, John O'Donovan, Svetlin Bostandjiev, Christopher Hall, and Tobias Hollerer. 2010. SmallWorlds: Visualizing Social Recommendations. *Computer Graphics Forum* 29, 3 (2010), 833–842.

[9] Jonathan L. Herlocker, Joseph A. Konstan, and John Riedl. 2000. Explaining Collaborative Filtering Recommendations. In *Proceedings of the 2000 ACM Conference on Computer Supported Cooperative Work (CSCW '00)*. 241–250.

[10] Sheena S. Iyengar, Rachael E. Wells, and Barry Schwartz. 2006. Doing Better but Feeling Worse: Looking for the "Best" Job Undermines Satisfaction. *Psychological Science* 17, 2 (2006), 143–150.

[11] Dietmar Jannach and Gediminas Adomavicius. 2016. Recommendations with a Purpose. In *Proceedings of the 10th ACM Conference on Recommender Systems (RecSys '16)*. 7–10.

[12] Dietmar Jannach and Kolja Hegelich. 2009. A Case Study on the Effectiveness of Recommendations in the Mobile Internet. In *Proceedings of the Third ACM Conference on Recommender Systems (RecSys '09)*. 205–208.

[13] Michael Jugovac and Dietmar Jannach. 2017. Interacting with Recommenders— Overview and Research Directions. *Transactions on Interactive Intelligent Systems* 7, 3 (2017), 10:1–10:46.

[14] Sahar Karimi, K. Nadia Papamichail, and Christopher P. Holland. 2015. The effect of prior knowledge and decision-making style on the online purchase decision-making process: A typology of consumer shopping behaviour. *Decision Support Systems* 77 (2015), 137 – 147.

[15] Evan Kirshenbaum, George Forman, and Michael Dugan. 2012. A Live Comparison of Methods for Personalized Article Recommendation at Forbes.com. In *Proceedings of the 2012 European Conference on Machine Learning and Knowledge Discovery in Databases (ECML-PKDD '12)*. 51–66.

[16] David A. Klein and Edward H. Shortliffe. 1994. A Framework for Explaining Decision-theoretic Advice. *Artificial Intelligence* 67, 2 (1994), 201–243.

[17] Bart P. Knijnenburg, Svetlin Bostandjiev, John O'Donovan, and Alfred Kobsa. 2012. Inspectability and Control in Social Recommenders. In *Proceedings of the Sixth ACM Conference on Recommender Systems (RecSys '12)*. 43–50.

[18] Bart P. Knijnenburg, Niels J.M. Reijmer, and Martijn C. Willemsen. 2011. Each to His Own: How Different Users Call for Different Interaction Methods in Recommender Systems. In *Proceedings of the Fifth ACM Conference on Recommender Systems (RecSys '11)*. 141–148.

[19] Khalil Muhammad, Aonghus Lawlor, Rachael Rafter, and Barry Smyth. 2015. Great Explanations: Opinionated Explanations for Recommendations. In *Proceedings of the 23rd International Conference on Case-Based Reasoning Research and Development (ICCBR '15)*. 244–258.

[20] Ingrid Nunes and Dietmar Jannach. 2017. A systematic review and taxonomy of explanations in decision support and recommender systems. *User Modeling and User-Adapted Interaction* 27, 3 (2017), 393–444.

[21] Ingrid Nunes, Simon Miles, Michael Luck, Simone Barbosa, and Carlos Lucena. 2014. Pattern-based Explanation for Automated Decisions. In *Proceedings of the 21st European Conference on Artificial Intelligence (ECAI '14)*. 669–674.

[22] Francesco Ricci, Lior Rokach, and Bracha Shapira. 2011. Introduction to Recommender Systems Handbook. In *Recommender Systems Handbook*, Francesco Ricci, Lior Rokach, Bracha Shapira, and Paul B. Kantor (Eds.). Springer, Boston, MA, USA.

[23] Tobias Schnabel, Paul N. Bennett, Susan T. Dumais, and Thorsten Joachims. 2006. Using Shortlists to Support Decision Making and Improve Recommender System Performance. In *Proceedings of the 25th International Conference on World Wide Web (WWW '16)*. 987–997.

[24] Barry Schwartz, Andrew Ward, John Monterosso, Sonja Lyubomirsky, Katherine White, and Darrin R. Lehman. 2002. Maximizing versus satisficing: Happiness is a matter of choice. *Journal of Personality and Social Psychology* 83, 5 (2002), 1178–1197.

[25] Kimberlee Weaver, Kim Daniloski, Norbert Schwarz, and Keenan Cottone. 2015. The role of social comparison for maximizers and satisficers: Wanting the best or wanting to be the best? *Journal of Consumer Psychology* 25, 3 (2015), 372–388.

[26] Martijn C. Willemsen, Mark P. Graus, and Bart P. Knijnenburg. 2016. Understanding the role of latent feature diversification on choice difficulty and satisfaction. *User Modeling and User-Adapted Interaction* 26, 4 (2016), 347–389.

[27] Markus Zanker, Marcel Bricman, Sergiu Gordea, Dietmar Jannach, and Markus Jessenitschnig. 2006. Persuasive Online-Selling in Quality and Taste Domains. In *Proceedings of the Seventh International Conference on E-Commerce and Web Technologies (EC-Web '06)*. 51–60.

A Cross-Cultural Analysis of Trust in Recommender Systems

Shlomo Berkovsky
Ronnie Taib
CSIRO Australia
Eveleigh, NSW, Australia
first.last@csiro.au

Yoshinori Hijikata
Kwansei Gakuin University
Osaka, Japan
contact@soc-research.org

Pavel Braslavski
Ural Federal University
Yekaterinburg, Russia
pbras@yandex.ru

Bart Knijnenburg
Clemson University
Clemson, SC, USA
bartk@clemson.edu

ABSTRACT

User system trust is critical to the uptake of recommendations, and several factors of trust have been identified and compared. In this paper we present a cross-cultural, crowdsourced study examining user perceptions of nine factors of trust and link the observed differences to trust development processes and cultural dimensions. While some factors consistently instil trust, others are preferred only in certain countries. Our findings and the discovered links are important for design of trusted recommender systems.

CCS CONCEPTS

• **Information systems** → **Recommender systems**; • **Social and professional topics** → *Cultural characteristics*;

KEYWORDS

Recommender systems; user-system trust; presentation of recommendations; cross-cultural comparison; user study.

ACM Reference Format:
Shlomo Berkovsky, Ronnie Taib, Yoshinori Hijikata, Pavel Braslavski, and Bart Knijnenburg. 2018. A Cross-Cultural Analysis of Trust in Recommender Systems. In *UMAP '18: 26th Conference on User Modeling, Adaptation and Personalization, July 8–11, 2018, Singapore, Singapore*. ACM, New York, NY, USA, 5 pages. https://doi.org/10.1145/3209219.3209251

1 INTRODUCTION

The success of practical recommender systems largely depends on the uptake of their recommendations. A multitude of factors, associated with the system performance, accuracy, and clarity alike, can potentially affect this uptake. Although some have been studied in depth, factors related to *user-system trust* have received less attention [2, 19, 27]. We argue that the degree of trust a user puts in the recommender plays an important role in the decision making processes related to following the system's recommendations [12].

Many factors and constructs of trust are not specific to recommenders and can be traced to earlier works on user-system trust. Specifically, trust perceptions can be decomposed into the *dispositional* (cultural and demographic), *situational* (context- and task-related), and *learned* (experiential and interaction) factors [10]. Prior work on user trust in recommenders [24, 26] outlines three dimensions of recommendations that affect trust: *presentation* –

ACM acknowledges that this contribution was authored or co-authored by an employee, contractor or affiliate of a national government. As such, the Government retains a nonexclusive, royalty-free right to publish or reproduce this article, or to allow others to do so, for Government purposes only.
UMAP '18, July 8–11, 2018, Singapore, Singapore
© 2018 Association for Computing Machinery.
ACM ISBN 978-1-4503-5589-6/18/07...$15.00
https://doi.org/10.1145/3209219.3209251

how the recommendation list is presented to users; *explanation* – what text accompanies the recommended items; and *priority* – what properties of the recommended items are deemed important by the system. Nine distinct, although partially interconnected, factors of trust instantiating these dimensions were synthesised and experimentally compared in [3].

In this work, we set out to investigate the links between the users' cultural group and their preferences towards various constructs of trust. To this end, we conduct a crowdsourced experiment across four different countries, involving in the study more than 460 subjects from France, Japan, Russia, and USA. Measuring six constructs of trust, we analyse the preferences of the subjects for nine interface factors spanning the above three dimensions. While some dominant factors are found to consistently instil user trust across the countries, other factors are preferred and trusted only in certain countries. We attribute the observed preferences to Hofstede's cultural dimensions [11] and overarching trust development processes [8]. Note that our work is independent of the recommendation task and the deployed algorithm, focussing primarily on the recommendation interfaces and human-recommender trust.

Hence, our contributions are two-fold. First, we identify the features of recommendation interfaces that are trusted by users in various countries. Second, we uncover differences across the countries and link them to established cultural dimensions. Our findings are important for practical recommenders, allowing to strengthen user trust and increase the uptake of recommendations.

2 RELATED WORK

The research in human-machine trust has produced various definitions of trust, with one of the most accepted being "the attitude that an agent will help achieve a goal in a situation characterised by uncertainty and vulnerability" [17]. This definition encapsulates the primary sources of variance (user and system) and identifies uncertainty and vulnerability as the pre-conditions of trust.

Three layers of variability in human-machine trust were identified: dispositional, situational, and learned [10]. The first reflects the user's tendency to trust machines due to demographic and personal factors. The second refers to system- and task-specific factors, e.g., the complexity of machine, user's workload, and perceived risks. Finally, the learned trust encapsulates experiential aspects directly related to the system itself. Both [17] and [10] claimed that the former two are likely to be overcome by the latter when the machine exhibits a steady behaviour.

The success of a recommender system largely depends on the uptake of the recommendations, highlighting the importance of trust in recommenders [19]. Several trust factors were taxonomised and compared in [3]. The factors considered were the *presentation* of recommendations, i.e., information that accompanies the items [21, 22, 25], *explanations*, aiming to persuade users follow the recommendations [7, 9, 24], and *prioritisation* of the recommendations, i.e., items included in the recommendation list [1, 15, 20]. It was found that quality-based prioritisation of the recommendations and their grouping by a domain feature were trusted most by the users. However, trust perceptions varied across user personalities, which resonates with the individual differences discussed in [10, 17].

In this work, we turn to another factor of the dispositional layer, *cultural differences*. To this end, we conduct the study reported in [3] again, but this time in four different countries. To the best of our knowledge, not much research looked at cross-cultural differences in recommender systems. Namely, only differences in the evaluation of recommendation interfaces [4], preferences for certain items [23], and attitudes towards mobile recommenders [5] have been studied.

3 EXPERIMENTAL METHODOLOGY

We present the factors of trust and dimensions in the context of movie recommendations and outline the design of the user study.

3.1 Dimensions and Factors

Various considerations related to the recommendation lists and their presentation may influence user trust in a recommender. We group them into three dimensions, each including three instantiations referred to as *factors* (more details can be found in [3]).

The *presentation* dimension (see Figure 1) considers three ways to present the recommendations. These are: item grouping according to a certain domain feature (here, by the genre of the recommended movies), use of a humanoid agent to present the recommendations (an image of a person and first-person text), and numeric score communicating the quality of the items (star-rating of the movies). The *explanation* dimension (Figure 2) refers to the text that accompanies the recommendations. The variations of this dimension include persuasive explanations highlighting the advantages of the items (awards or box office figures), personalised explanations listing the reasons for recommendations (list of similar movies liked by the user), and factual explanation (score and number of votes on IMDb). Lastly, the *priority* dimension (Figure 3) deals with the properties of the recommendation list that the system deems important. These are quality (top-scoring IMDb movies), diversity (movies covering many genres), and familiarity (recent movies).

3.2 Study Design and Participants

We conducted a crowdsourced user study comparing these dimensions and factors. The study was divided into two stages. First, the subjects' demographic data was collected and they selected movies they had already watched and liked, to be used for personalised explanations. Second, the subjects were shown nine pages with three lists of movies generated by recommenders denoted A, B, and C. Each page covered a single dimension with its three factors embodied by the recommenders. Sample pages for the three dimension (and three factors each) are shown in Figures 1-3.

The subjects went through nine pages, i.e., three iterations for each dimension. To counter-balance potential order effects, the order of the dimensions and factors on each page was randomised, implementing the factorial design [6]. On each page, the subjects

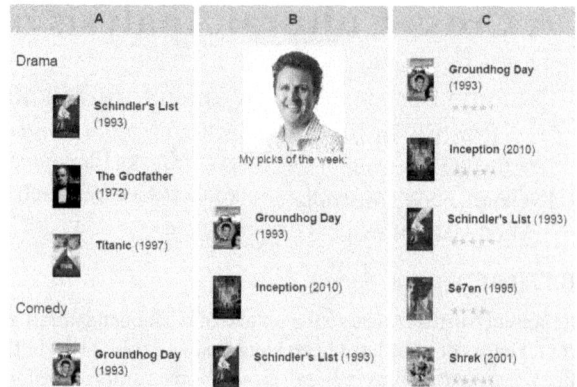

Fig. 1: *Presentation*: genre (A), human (B), star (C).

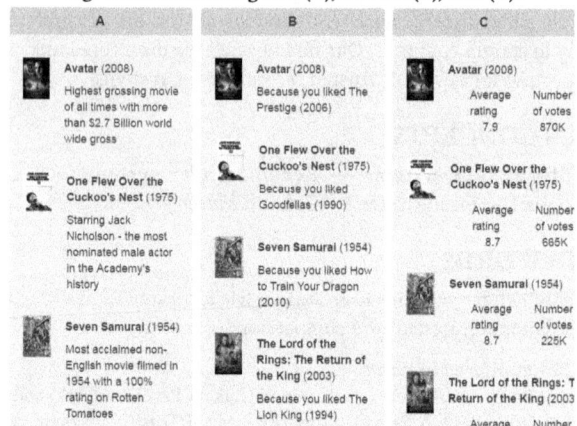

Fig. 2: *Explanation*: persuasive (A), personalised (B), IMDb (C).

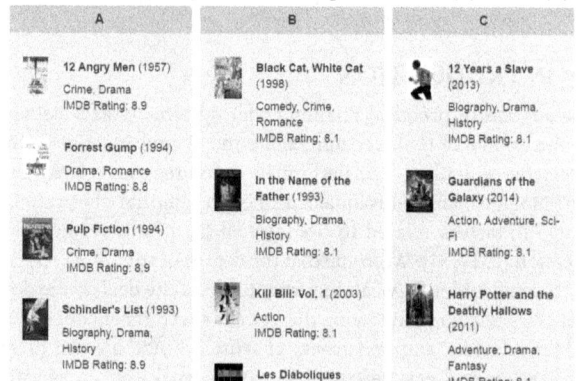

Fig. 3: *Priority*: quality (A), diversity (B), familiarity (C).

were asked to select to indicate their preferred list – A, B, or C – with respect to each of the six constructs of trust: *competence* ("recommender most knowledgeable about movies"), *benevolence* ("recommender best reflecting my interests"), *integrity* ("recommender providing most unbiased suggestions"), *transparency* ("I understand the best the reasons for the recommendations"), *intention to re-use* ("for selecting my next movie to watch, I would use"), and *overall trust* ("out of these, the most trustworthy recommender"). The constructs were phrased in a simple language shown in brackets, inspired by the operationalisation of [2].

We instructed the subjects to select their preferred list relying solely on the presentation of the recommendations and disregard the content of the lists, which may naturally contain more or less liked movies. Also, some of the factors listed in Section 3.1 may be dependent, e.g., high-scoring movies may cover multiple genres, boosting quality and diversity. As the lists were pre-compiled, we controlled for this. For example, movies listed in list A in Figure 3 have a higher IMDb rating than movies in lists B and C, while the number of genres and the year of release are comparable [3].

The study was conducted using the CrowdFlower platform. Crowdsourcing increases the risk of collecting spurious data; hence, strict quality assurance policies were implemented [18]. Specifically, responses were rejected on the basis of short completion times (under 5 minutes, half of those in [3]), repeating answers (AA.. or ABAB..), and inconsistent answers (AA.. and then BB.. for the same question).

We conducted the study in four countries, each with the content translated and fully adapted: France (FR, 112 subjects), Japan (JP, 110), Russia (RU, 123), and USA (US, 117). The reported sample sizes represent the data retained after the quality assurance. For the recruitment, we used the location and language of the subjects as inclusion criteria and a coarse-grain proxies of cultural homogeneity. Although some of these countries are multi-cultural on their own, we consider the subjects from each country as the relevant cultural group. Across the countries, we observed a comparable distribution of subjects in terms of gender, age, and IT literacy.

4 RESULTS

We present the results and analyse the differences observed across the countries. The results are summarised in Table 1. Note that we aggregate the results using the "majority voting" of every subject. As mentioned, every dimension was iterated thrice, which is treated as three votes. In the analysis, we consider only the users who preferred one of the factors twice or more. Users, who preferred every factor exactly once, are discarded. For example, out of the 112 subjects in the FR group, 60 subjects preferred twice or more the genre grouping, 5 subjects – human presentation, and 37 subjects – star presentation. Hence, we are left with 102 subjects.

4.1 Preference towards Constructs of Trust

Presentation. The presentation factors are dominated by the genre grouping presentation. In the FR, RU, and US groups, genre grouping achieves the majority of votes for all the constructs. In the JP group, it achieves the majority for five constructs, being inferior only to the star presentation for transparency. Hence, the grouping of movies according to their genres is clearly seen by the subjects as the most trusted presentation of recommendations.

Explanation. On the contrary, few trust votes converge for the explanation dimension. The results agree across the four groups only for the competence construct, where persuasive explanations are preferred. For integrity, two factors dominate: IMDb-based explanations are preferred by the FR, RU, and US subjects, while persuasive explanations are preferred by the JP subjects. Likewise, the JP and RU subjects prefer overall persuasive explanations, while

	Compet.	Benev.	Integr.	Transp.	Re-use	Overall
FR subjects (N=112)						
Genre	**60**	**57**	**51**	**55**	**51**	**51**
Human	5	1	7	10	5	3
Star	37	49	43	39	49	49
Persuasive	**88**	32	32	34	34	34
Personalised	4	27	11	28	23	13
IMDb	15	**48**	**63**	**41**	**49**	**55**
Quality	54	55	53	52	52	51
Diversity	13	10	12	7	9	11
Familiarity	18	23	24	23	20	16
JP subjects (N=110)						
Genre	**48**	**55**	**54**	39	**54**	**53**
Human	29	10	12	18	9	11
Star	27	33	38	**47**	44	49
Persuasive	**84**	33	**43**	28	**49**	**61**
Personalised	11	**59**	16	**57**	32	19
IMDb	14	11	44	15	24	24
Quality	54	46	41	49	50	49
Diversity	16	11	19	9	18	18
Familiarity	19	30	25	24	24	24
RU subjects (N=123)						
Genre	**80**	**67**	**55**	**62**	**64**	**65**
Human	5	11	6	11	7	6
Star	31	33	54	43	47	49
Persuasive	**77**	**50**	52	**52**	**53**	**54**
Personalised	14	31	14	28	24	13
IMDb	31	37	**56**	36	43	51
Quality	**72**	**72**	**73**	**73**	**71**	**70**
Diversity	9	8	9	8	9	9
Familiarity	27	22	25	23	28	29
US subjects (N=117)						
Genre	**57**	**60**	**58**	**54**	**62**	**55**
Human	17	16	15	16	12	13
Star	30	28	31	38	34	37
Persuasive	**59**	**40**	36	34	35	37
Personalised	16	38	21	**35**	**35**	29
IMDb	27	24	**53**	31	30	**38**
Quality	**55**	**42**	49	**51**	**38**	**42**
Diversity	13	11	14	18	15	17
Familiarity	25	30	27	21	37	24

Table 1: User preferences for trust constructs (dominant in bold).

the FR and US subjects prefer IMDb-based explanations. For the remaining constructs of benevolence, transparency, and intention to re-use, no clear trends are observed, with each of the three explanations being preferred in at least one group. In summary, the type of explanation used by a recommender depends on the target construct and on the target population. For example, we posit that persuasive explanations sustain competence, personalised explanations are linked to benevolence and transparency, while IMDb-based explanations promote integrity. Independently of this, persuasive explanations are trusted by the JP and RU subjects, while IMDB-based explanations are preferred by the FR subjects.

Priority. In the priority dimension, like in the presentation dimension, we observe a steady dominance of one factor – quality-based prioritisation of the recommendation lists is preferred over the diversity and familiarity prioritisations. This result is observed across the four groups and with respect to all the six constructs of trust. This indicates that the IMDb scores are perceived by the users to be the most trusted criterion for recommending movies.

4.2 Differences across Countries

We tested whether the subjects' preference within the three dimensions differed across the four countries. The differences were tested for significance using a series of chi-square tests. Where significant differences were found, specific deviations were tested by interpreting the standardised residuals. Given the exploratory nature of our analysis, only significant effects with $p < 0.01$ are reported.

Presentation. Although the genre grouping presentation is generally the most preferred, there are significant differences in the least preferred human presentation factor across the countries. The differences are observed for the competence ($\chi^2(6) = 37.7, p < 0.001$) and integrity ($\chi^2(6) = 19.6, p = 0.003$) constructs. Specifically, JP subjects are more likely ($p < 0.001$) and RU subjects are less likely ($p = 0.009$) to prefer the human presentation for competence. FR subjects are less likely to prefer the human presentation method for integrity ($p = 0.005$).

Explanation. There are also significant differences in the preferred explanations. These refer to the competence ($\chi^2(6) = 22.3, p = 0.001$), intention to re-use ($\chi^2(6) = 19.3, p = 0.004$), integrity ($\chi^2(6) = 45.9, p < 0.001$), transparency ($\chi^2(6) = 35.1, p < 0.001$), and overall trust ($\chi^2(6) = 33.5, p < 0.001$) constructs. Here, the differences refer to IMDb-based and personalised explanations. Specifically, JP subjects are more likely to prefer personalised explanations for the integrity ($p < 0.001$) and transparency ($p < 0.001$) constructs, but less likely to prefer IMDb-based explanations for integrity ($p < 0.001$), transparency ($p = 0.008$), and overall trust ($p = 0.008$). FR subjects are more likely to prefer IMDb-based explanations for integrity ($p < 0.001$), while US subjects are more likely to prefer personalised explanations for overall trust ($p = 0.010$).

Priority. In the priority dimension, significant differences are observed across the countries only for intention to re-use ($\chi^2(6) = 16.9, p = 0.010$). Subjects in the four countries prefer quality prioritisation, but US subjects are relatively more likely to prefer familiarity prioritisation, although not at the $p < 0.01$ level ($p = 0.040$).

5 DISCUSSION AND CONCLUSIONS

This work compared the perceptions of nine factors of trust in recommender systems across four countries. Some findings were consistent across the countries, e.g., in the presentation and prioritisation dimensions. However, in the explanation dimension the results varied substantially. We will discuss the observed trends and posit potential reasons underpinning the differences.

Presentation. Subjects in all the four countries were most likely to prefer the genre grouping presentation, for all trust factors. However, significant differences were observed in the share of users preferring the human presentation. Specifically, very few FR and

RU subjects, and unexpectedly many JP subjects preferred this presentation for competence. Why did we find such differences for competence? National culture may have played a role. According to Hofstede's cultural dimensions [11], Japan scores high on Masculinity (95), while Russia (36) and France (43) score low[1]. People in cultures scoring high on Masculinity are inclined to derive trust from inferred capabilities [8], such that recommender system users may overestimate the capability of a system represented by a humanoid agent [14]. This may potentially make JP subjects more likely, and RU and FR subjects less likely, to trust human presentation. We found that the cultures' Masculinity scores were strongly correlated with the subjects' preference for human presentation for the competence construct ($r = 0.989, t(2) = 9.583, p = 0.011$), indicating that human presentation of recommendations seems to be trusted most in Masculine cultures.

Explanation. Although in all the countries the subjects were likely to prefer persuasive explanations for competence, preferences varied for the other constructs. In particular, the FR subjects preferred IMDb-based explanations for the other criteria, RU subjects mainly preferred persuasive explanations, JP subjects preferred personalised explanations for integrity and transparency, while US subjects were split among these options. Again, we posit that cultural mechanisms may underpin these preferences. People in cultures scoring high on Masculinity are inclined to derive trust based on a calculative, self-serving process [8]. Hence, personalised explanations may instil more trust in people from Masculine cultures like Japan. Indeed, Masculinity scores of the countries strongly correlated with the subjects' preference for personalised explanations for integrity ($r = 0.969, t(2) = 5.475, p = 0.031$) and transparency ($r = 0.979, t(2) = 6.824, p = 0.021$), indicating that personalised explanations appear to be trusted most in Masculine cultures. In contrast, subjects in cultures scoring low on Masculinity are inclined to derive trust based on a transference process [8]. Hence, IMDb-based explanations that present the rating and number of votes by many others, may potentially instil trust in people from Feminine cultures like France and Russia. We found that Masculinity scores of the four countries were strongly negatively correlated with the subjects' preference for IMDb-based explanations for the overall trust ($r = -0.968, t(2) = -5.462, p = 0.032$), indicating that such rating-based explanations may potentially be trusted most in Feminine cultures.

Priority. Subjects in all the four countries are by far most likely to prefer quality prioritisation for all the trust constructs. Hence, there are no significant differences between the countries, except for the intention to re-use construct.

Implications for Recommenders. These findings are valuable for designers of recommender systems and recommendation interfaces. It is well-known that recommendations should be personalised to their users. This work resonates with previous works that demonstrated that the recommendation interface should also be tailored [13, 16, 21]. We establish that such tailoring should not only be attributed to individual and personality differences [3], but also consider the users' cultural characteristics. Our analysis raises the multi-dimensional nature of trust in recommender systems [27],

---

[1]The most pronounced correlations referred to Hofstede's dimension of Masculinity. Due to space limitations, the discussion focuses on this dimension only.

which may be interpreted in the context of the desired effect of the recommendations. For example, a thought-through application of presentation, explanation, and priority factors may strengthen the targeted construct of trust, e.g., factual explanations will increase competence and personalised explanations – benevolence. We show how to apply these factors to instil trust and highlight how trust perceptions vary across different groups of users. It is important to note that our work does not fully bridge the gap between individual and cultural features, and this is yet to be addressed both in research and in the design of practical recommender systems.

REFERENCES

[1] Azin Ashkan, Branislav Kveton, Shlomo Berkovsky, and Zheng Wen. 2015. Optimal Greedy Diversity for Recommendation. In *Proceedings of the International Joint Conference on Artificial Intelligence, IJCAI*. 1742–1748.

[2] Izak Benbasat and Weiquan Wang. 2005. Trust In and Adoption of Online Recommendation Agents. *Journal of the Association for Information Systems* 6, 3 (2005).

[3] Shlomo Berkovsky, Ronnie Taib, and Dan Conway. 2017. How to Recommend?: User Trust Factors in Movie Recommender Systems. In *Proceedings of the International Conference on Intelligent User Interfaces, IUI*. 287–300.

[4] Li Chen and Pearl Pu. 2008. A cross-cultural user evaluation of product recommender interfaces. In *Proceedings of the ACM Conference on Recommender Systems, RecSys*. 75–82.

[5] Jaewon Choi, Hong Joo Lee, Farhana Sajjad, and Habin Lee. 2014. The influence of national culture on the attitude towards mobile recommender systems. *Technological Forecasting and Social Change* 86 (2014), 65 – 79.

[6] Linda M Collins, John J Dziak, and Runze Li. 2009. Design of experiments with multiple independent variables: a resource management perspective on complete and reduced factorial designs. *Psychological methods* 14, 3 (2009), 202.

[7] Henriette S. M. Cramer, Vanessa Evers, Satyan Ramlal, Maarten van Someren, Lloyd Rutledge, Natalia Stash, Lora Aroyo, and Bob J. Wielinga. 2008. The effects of transparency on trust in and acceptance of a content-based art recommender. *User Modeling and User-Adapted Interaction* 18, 5 (2008), 455–496.

[8] Patricia M Doney, Joseph P Cannon, and Michael R Mullen. 1998. Understanding the influence of national culture on the development of trust. *Academy of Management Review* 23, 3 (1998), 601–620.

[9] Alexander Felfernig and Bartosz Gula. 2006. An Empirical Study on Consumer Behavior in the Interaction with Knowledge-based Recommender Applications. In *Proceedings of the International Conference on E-Commerce Technology, CEC*. 37.

[10] Kevin Anthony Hoff and Masooda Bashir. 2015. Trust in Automation: Integrating Empirical Evidence on Factors That Influence Trust. *Human Factors* 57, 3 (2015), 407–434.

[11] Geert Hofstede. 2003. *Culture's consequences: Comparing values, behaviors, institutions and organizations across nations*. Sage Publications.

[12] Anthony Jameson, Martijn C. Willemsen, Alexander Felfernig, Marco de Gemmis, Pasquale Lops, Giovanni Semeraro, and Li Chen. 2015. Human Decision Making and Recommender Systems. In *Recommender Systems Handbook*. 611–648.

[13] Bart P. Knijnenburg, Niels J. M. Reijmer, and Martijn C. Willemsen. 2011. Each to his own: how different users call for different interaction methods in recommender systems. In *Proceedings of the ACM Conference on Recommender Systems, RecSys*. 141–148.

[14] Bart P. Knijnenburg and Martijn C. Willemsen. 2016. Inferring Capabilities of Intelligent Agents from Their External Traits. *ACM Transactions on Interactive Intelligent Systems* 6, 4 (2016), 28:1–28:25.

[15] Sherrie YX Komiak and Izak Benbasat. 2006. The effects of personalization and familiarity on trust and adoption of recommendation agents. *Management Information Systems Quarterly* (2006), 941–960.

[16] Branislav Kveton and Shlomo Berkovsky. 2016. Minimal Interaction Content Discovery in Recommender Systems. *ACM Transactions on Interactive Intelligent Systems* 6, 2 (2016), 15:1–15:25.

[17] John D. Lee and Katrina A. See. 2004. Trust in Automation: Designing for Appropriate Reliance. *Human Factors* 46, 1 (2004), 50–80.

[18] Stefanie Nowak and Stefan M. Rüger. 2010. How reliable are annotations via crowdsourcing: a study about inter-annotator agreement for multi-label image annotation. In *Proceedings of the International Conference on Multimedia Information Retrieval, MIR*. 557–566.

[19] John O'Donovan and Barry Smyth. 2005. Trust in recommender systems. In *Proceedings of the International Conference on Intelligent User Interfaces, IUI*. 167–174.

[20] Umberto Panniello, Michele Gorgoglione, and Alexander Tuzhilin. 2016. Research Note - In CARSs We Trust: How Context-Aware Recommendations Affect Customers' Trust and Other Business Performance Measures of Recommender Systems. *Information Systems Research* 27, 1 (2016), 182–196.

[21] Pearl Pu and Li Chen. 2006. Trust building with explanation interfaces. In *Proceedings of the International Conference on Intelligent User Interfaces, IUI*. 93–100.

[22] Guy Shani, Lior Rokach, Bracha Shapira, Sarit Hadash, and Moran Tangi. 2013. Investigating confidence displays for top-N recommendations. *Journal of the Association for Information Science and Technology* 64, 12 (2013), 2548–2563.

[23] T. Y. Tang, P. Winoto, and R. Z. Ye. 2011. Analysis of a multi-domain recommender system. In *Proceedings of the International Conference on Data Mining and Intelligent Information Technology Applications*. 280–285.

[24] Nava Tintarev and Judith Masthoff. 2015. Explaining Recommendations: Design and Evaluation. In *Recommender Systems Handbook*. 353–382.

[25] Ye Diana Wang and Henry H Emurian. 2005. An overview of online trust: Concepts, elements, and implications. *Computers in Human Behavior* 21, 1 (2005), 105–125.

[26] Kyung Hyan Yoo, Ulrike Gretzel, and Markus Zanker. 2015. Source Factors in Recommender System Credibility Evaluation. In *Recommender Systems Handbook*. 689–714.

[27] Kun Yu, Shlomo Berkovsky, Ronnie Taib, Dan Conway, Jianlong Zhou, and Fang Chen. 2017. User Trust Dynamics: An Investigation Driven by Differences in System Performance. In *Proceedings of the International Conference on Intelligent User Interfaces, IUI*. 307–317.

Effects of Individual Traits on Diversity-Aware Music Recommender User Interfaces

Yucheng Jin
Dept. Computer Science, KU Leuven
Leuven, Belgium
yucheng.jin@cs.kuleuven.be

Nava Tintarev
TU Delft
Delft, Netherlands
n.tintarev@tudelft.nl

Katrien Verbert
Dept. Computer Science, KU Leuven
Leuven, Belgium
katrien.verbert@cs.kuleuven.be

ABSTRACT

When recommendations become increasingly personalized, users are often presented with a narrower range of content. To mitigate this issue, diversity-enhanced user interfaces for recommender systems have in the past found to be effective in increasing overall user satisfaction with recommendations. However, users may have different requirements for diversity, and consequently different visualization requirements. In this paper, we evaluate two visual user interfaces, *SimBub* and *ComBub*, to present the diversity of a music recommender system from different perspectives. *SimBub* is a baseline bubble chart that shows music genres and popularity by color and size, respectively. In addition, *ComBub* visualizes selected audio features along the X and Y axis in a more advanced and complex visualization. Our goal is to investigate how individual traits such as *musical sophistication* (MS) and *visual memory* (VM) influence the satisfaction of the visualization for perceived music diversity, overall usability, and support to identify blind-spots. We hypothesize that music experts, or people with better visual memory, will perceive higher diversity in *ComBub* than *SimBub*. A within-subjects user study (N=83) is conducted to compare these two visualizations. Results of our study show that participants with high MS and VM tend to perceive significantly higher diversity from *ComBub* compared to *SimBub*. In contrast, participants with low MS perceived significantly higher diversity from *SimBub* than *ComBub*; however, no significant result is found for the participants with low VM. Our research findings show the necessity of considering individual traits while designing diversity-aware interfaces.

CCS CONCEPTS

• **Human-centered computing** → **Visualization design and evaluation methods**; **User models**; • **Information systems** → *Recommender systems*;

KEYWORDS

Individual traits; diversity; recommender user interfaces; visual memory; musical sophistication

UMAP '18, July 8–11, 2018, Singapore, Singapore
© 2018 Association for Computing Machinery.
ACM ISBN 978-1-4503-5589-6/18/07...$15.00
https://doi.org/10.1145/3209219.3209225

ACM Reference Format:
Yucheng Jin, Nava Tintarev, and Katrien Verbert. 2018. Effects of Individual Traits on Diversity-Aware Music Recommender User Interfaces. In *UMAP '18: 26th Conference on User Modeling, Adaptation and Personalization, July 8–11, 2018, Singapore, Singapore*. ACM, New York, NY, USA, 9 pages. https://doi.org/10.1145/3209219.3209225

1 INTRODUCTION

Recommender systems are increasingly used in various on-line application domains, such as e-commerce and technology-enhanced learning. They provide users with personalized items based on a variety of information, including preferences, on-line history, and demographics. Traditionally, most researchers focused on the accuracy of recommender systems by proposing various algorithms to increase precision and recall. However, recent studies have shown that the overall user experience of recommender systems is affected by many factors beyond accuracy [15] in some domains, such as diversity and serendipity for the music recommenders. Recommender systems aim at helping users explore new items of interest [18]. Diversity is important because users will not be satisfied with recommendations that are overly similar to what they have consumed previously [19]. Moreover, diversity enables comparison among recommendations, thereby increasing the confidence in making a choice [8, 25].

In fact, the increase of personalization may prevent users from consuming diverse content, which is called the "filter bubble". To mitigate the issue, many approaches propose a diversity-enhancing algorithm, e.g., topic diversification [45], and a hybrid way of using multiple sources [41]. Other work [20, 37, 42] empowers users to manipulate recommender systems through an interactive user interface to explore items in a different way. Although the ranked list interface is still one of the most common ways to present recommendation results, several limitations have been identified [11]. Users tend to for instance pay less attention to the items at the bottom of the list [7]. In addition, predicting the perception of the diversity of items in a list is difficult. Recently, some researchers have proposed diversity-aware interfaces that present recommendations in different kinds of visualizations, such as two-dimensional scatter plots [37]. When using such an interface, users tend to perceive a higher diversity of content than in a ranked list interface.

In this paper, we explore how individual traits influence the effectiveness of a diversity-enhanced user interface. The individual traits that we are researching are **musical sophistication (MS)**, that measures the ability to engage with music effectively [28], and **visual memory (VM)**, that is temporary storage and manipulation of the information over an extended period of time [5]. We employ a design-based approach to explore how MS and VM can influence the effectiveness of the user interface. We developed a

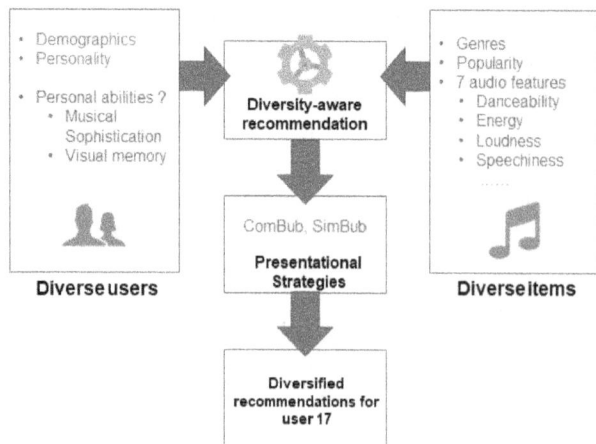

Figure 1: Diversity-aware recommendation model fitted to our research contexts.

music recommender based on Spotify API [1]. We designed and implemented two user interfaces: *SimBub* is the simplest visualization that clusters items by genres and shows popularity in a bubble chart. *ComBub* is more advanced and complex, and presents recommendations in a bubble chart with genres, popularity, and two selected audio features. In a music recommender, we hypothesize that *ComBub*, that presents additional audio features, may better support users with higher MS and VM to perceive diversity. On the contrary, the attributes of genres and popularity shown in *SimBub* may be sufficient to help users with low MS and VM to perceive diversity. In addition, we consider both item and user diversity for choosing a strategy to present recommendations by following a diversity-aware recommendation model (see Figure 1) [34]. More specifically, the user diversity is mainly measured by the user's *musical sophistication* and *visual memory*, and item diversity can be calculated by genres, popularity, and audio features.

To verify our assumption, we conduct a within-subjects user study, comparing the two interfaces, *SimBub* and *ComBub*, with an identical recommender algorithm and recommender sources. We employed *ResQue*, a user-centric evaluation framework for recommender system [32], to measure perceived diversity and other key aspects. Meanwhile, we are also interested in knowing if a specific interface encourages users to look for songs in under-explored genres (*blind-spots*), which has been researched in [36]. From this study, we attempt to answer the following three research questions:

- **RQ1**: In general, does visualizing the audio features of music increase perceived diversity of recommended songs?
- **RQ2**: How will the individual traits of musical sophistication and visual memory capacity influence the perceived diversity of the support?
- **RQ3**: Does a particular interface encourage users to look for items in under-explored genres?

The contributions of this paper are three-fold.

---
[1]https://developer.spotify.com/web-api/get-recommendations/

(1) We designed a diversity-aware user interface *ComBub* where users are able to explore diverse items from different aspects. Comparing to the baseline user interface *SimBub*, *ComBub* shows a great potential to augment user perceived diversity for the users with high MS and high VM.

(2) By measuring user's MS and VM before the study, we investigated the effects of the two individual traits on the perceived diversity of the interfaces. The results reveal a strong positive correlation between individual traits and the perceived diversity of the interface(s).

(3) We also investigated to what extent each interface is able to encourage users to explore blind-spots, which might mitigate the issue of the "filter bubble".

The remainder of the paper is organized as follows: after providing an overview of related research work on user interfaces for recommender systems and also some diversity enhancing approaches, we describe the design of our system. Then we describe the study design, followed by the study results, limitations, and discussion. Finally, we present the conclusions and future work.

2 RELATED WORK

Our research refers to three important topics of recommender systems: 1) using visualization techniques to enhance the user experience of the recommender system, 2) techniques to enhance recommendation diversity, 3) effects of individual traits on perceived diversity. We will briefly review related work of these topics.

2.1 Visualizations for Recommender Systems

Visualizations for recommender systems have been increasingly researched to improve various aspects of recommender systems. By visualizing the user profiles and recommendation process, transparency and user control of the system can be improved significantly. Jin et al. [21] for instance demonstrate an interactive flowchart based visualization that explains how a selected ad is filtered for the targeted user profile. Verbert et al. [39] present a system that increases the effectiveness of making a choice by explaining the provenance of recommendations and offering control to users. Some systems show increased accuracy by enabling users to adjust the weight of algorithm parameters [6, 31]. In addition, several studies show the positive effects of visualization on *perceived diversity* [20, 33, 37, 42]. Our study focuses on similar diversity-aware visualizations. More specifically, we investigate the effects of *individual traits* on perceived diversity through different visualizations.

2.2 Individual Traits for Perceived Diversity

In fact, the desired level of diversity for a satisfying recommender differs among users [3], which may be attributed to different preferences for agreeable and challenging items [29]. Therefore, it is beneficial to adapt diversification strategies to individual traits.

Several research works [12, 13, 35] have shown that visual memory has a significant impact on visualization effectiveness. Moreover, in the framework for the user-centric evaluation of recommender systems [25], a significantly positive effect of *expertise* (personal characteristics) on *diversity* (subjective system aspects) has been found. Music experts may, for instance, perceive higher diversity than laymen from the same recommendation list. Moreover, personality is also an important factor to perceived diversity. In our study, we measure a user's domain knowledge using musical sophistication index (MSI).

In the literature, we find two individual traits that may have an impact on the effectiveness of diversity-aware interfaces: musical sophistication (MS) and visual memory (VM). In this paper, we hypothesize that individual traits such as musical sophistication and visual memory tend to influence the perceived diversity through visual interfaces, which to the best of our knowledge has not been investigated yet.

2.3 Diversity-enhancing Approaches

The definition of diversity may vary in different application domains [9]. In this paper, diversity refers to the diversity of a recommended list measured by an intra-list similarity metric [45]. The adaptation of content to individual preference is normally associated with lower diversity of content [30]. To address this problem, researchers have proposed to enhance diversity, either with novel algorithms or user interfaces.

2.3.1 Diversity-aware Algorithms. Re-ranking is a widely used technique to enhance diversity by aggregating diversity and accuracy in the process of recommendations [1, 2, 38, 44]. Furthermore, Zhang et al. [43] present an optimization method to improve both diversity and accuracy for the top-N prediction problem. Ziegler et al. [45] propose an approach to diversifying content based on topics. Similarly, Giannopoulos et al. [16] present an algorithm that diversifies news according to opinion similarities. Several studies [10, 26] propose various methods to generate critiques for increasing diversity in a critiquing-based recommender system. To remedy the limitation of imposing diversity on an existing system, McGint et al. [27] demonstrate an adaptive diversity-enhancing algorithm in a conversational recommender system. Most of these algorithms improve diversity for a ranked list. However, from the perspective of the user, the increased diversity in a ranked list is difficult to predict due to the position bias of the list as explained earlier.

2.3.2 Diversity-aware User Interfaces. Comparing to algorithmic approaches, fewer works are found to enhance perceived diversity through the user interface. Graells-Garrido et al. [17] present the distance of latent topics in a visualization, which supports active exploration of diverse content by users. Schafer et al. [33] present a user interface with personalized control that allows the user to find more diverse content generated from multiple information sources. Faridani et al. [14] present a map-based interface that enables users to explore diverse on-line comments. Hu et al. [20] propose an organization based interface to increase users' perceived diversity of recommendations. Wong et al. [42] present a system named Diversity Donut that allows users to indicate the level of diversity for the recommended items. Tsai et al. [37] present a diversity-enhanced interface that presents recommendations with multiple attributes in a two-dimensional scatter plot inspiring our approach.

These previous interfaces are designed without considering *individual* requirements for diversity. In our work, we design two diversity-aware user interfaces that show different item attributes.

As a result, the study results show the necessity of tailoring the interface design to individual traits.

3 SYSTEM DESIGN

In this section, we first explain a seed-based recommendation algorithm implemented for a music recommender, and then we describe two interfaces designed for enhancing recommendation diversity.

3.1 Algorithm

The recommendation algorithm was implemented by leveraging the Spotify Web API. First, we get the **seeds** (a top artist and a top track of a user), by calculating the user's expected preference to a particular track or artist according to his/her listening history [2]. Due to ongoing interaction, the data is only updated once per day, thus two interfaces present the same seeds for the evaluation. Then, we take **seeds** as an input to call a recommendation service [3] (**RS**) that generates a play-list containing 20 songs matching similar artists and tracks. Each recommended song has a *popularity score*, *genres*, and *audio features*.

3.2 User interfaces

Figure 2 illustrates the design of the diversity-aware user interface which consists of two sections: *section a)* a visualization view shows an interactive visualization which allows users to explore songs by visualized attributes; *section b)* a list view shows all items in a list, and each of them is associated with a particular circle in visualization view. When the user clicks on a circle, the corresponding item in the list will be highlighted (red border) and vice versa. Each item in the list has a play icon and a thumb rating widget.

We hypothesize that visualizing additional meta-data of music such as audio features may result in higher diversity perceived by users with high MS and VM. Therefore, we designed the interfaces with two requirements. First, the visualizations should present multiple data dimensions effectively: in our case, we show two common attributes *genres and popularity*, and seven *additional audio features*. Second, the visualization should represent coverage by a particular attribute to reflect diversity, e.g., how the items are distributed by genres. Based on the above considerations, the bubble chart is selected as our primary visualization due to its good ability to present multidimensional data [23]. Moreover, to test our assumption, we also need to compare this relatively complex bubble chart (*ComBub*) with a baseline visualization. We consider a simple bubble chart (*SimBub*) as a good candidate since it meets the first requirement and uses almost the same visual presentation as *ComBub*. The visualizations were implemented with the D3.js library [4].

3.2.1 ComBub. Section a) of Figure 1 shows the design of *ComBub* that encodes the recommendations results in three ways. First, it uses a circle to represent each recommended song: the X and Y-axis are used to present two specified audio features. Second, the circle is color-coded for music genres, which allows users to distinguish song genres by their color. Third, the circle size (radius) is determined by the popularity score (from 1 to 100) which has

---

[2]https://api.spotify.com/v1/me/top
[3]https://api.spotify.com/v1/recommendations
[4]https://d3js.org/

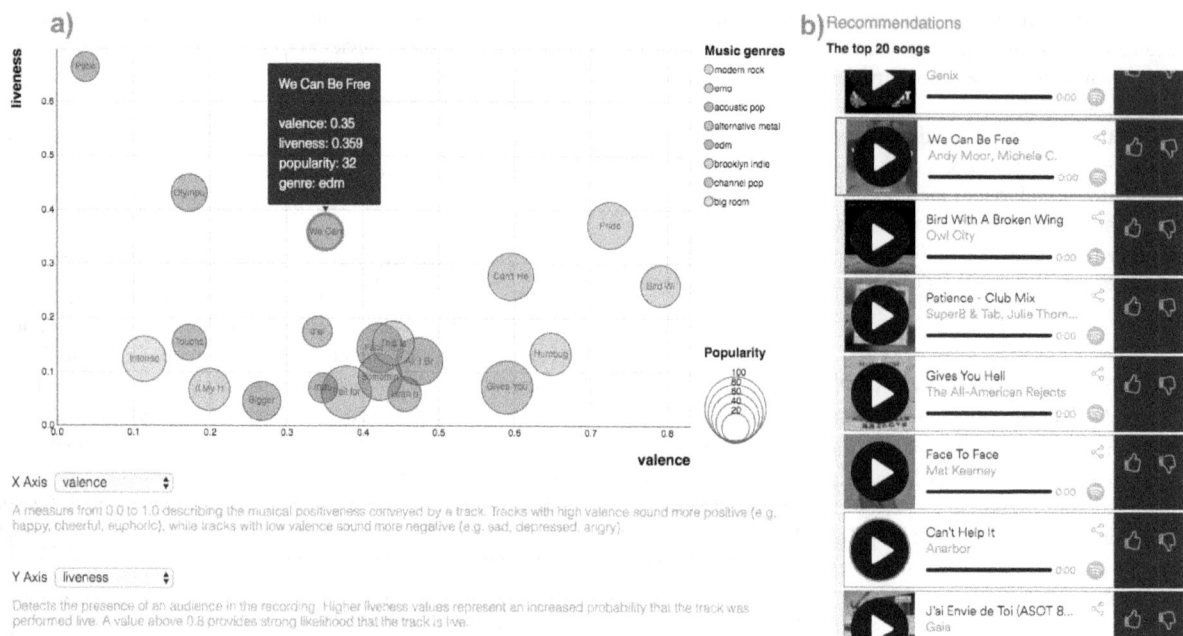

Figure 2: Design of the user interface for a music recommender, section a) a visualization view of the diversity of recommendations (ComBub); section b) a list view of recommendations.

been transformed by a visual square-root function. The function is defined as:

$$R(p) = 6 * \sqrt{\frac{p}{\pi}} \quad (1)$$

where p is an item's popularity score.

This encoding allows the user to inspect multiple dimension of the song simultaneously. The interface can be used to support advanced exploration for users such as popular pop songs with high danceability and high valence (happy, cheerful).

Most common interactions such as zooming and panning are supported. The details of a particular item will appear in a tooltip window when the mouse hovers over it. By clicking a circle, its associated item will be highlighted in the list synchronously. Below the plot, two drop-down menus are used to select audio features to visualize songs on the bubble chart. The scale of all audio features ranges from 0.0 to 1.0.

In summary, ComBub allows users to specify two audio features to plot recommendations in two dimensions and inspect the details and distribution of genres and popularity as they wish. As explained above, the visualization is able to explain the diversity of recommendations from various aspects.

3.2.2 SimBub. Figure 3 illustrates the design of *SimBub*. To save space, the figure omits the recommendation list associated to the visualization that is identical to the one in section b) of Figure 2. We designed the simplest form of a bubble chart as a baseline for two reasons. First, this bubble chart represents items by labeled circles, which is a popular visualization among 13 common visualizations evaluated for visualizations at Internet scale [40]. Second, it can be seen as a variation of ComBub without presenting

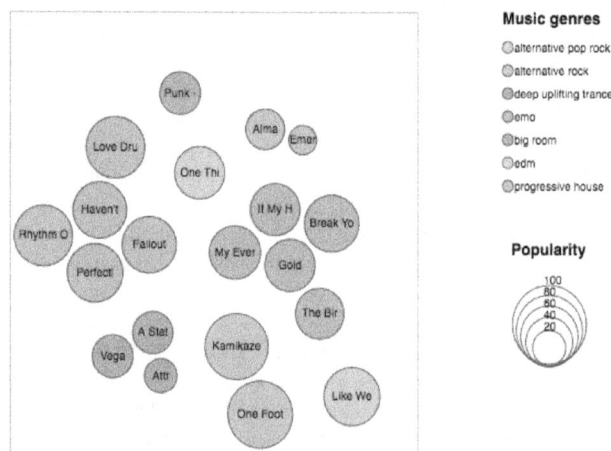

Figure 3: Design of the baseline SimBub visualization for enhancing perceived diversity of recommendations.

audio features. Thus, it is easier for us to investigate the effects of the additional visualized audio features in *ComBub*. Compared to *ComBub*, this chart may be easier and sufficient for casual users to interpret and perceive diversity. In this sense, our study answers the question whether showing the additional audio features can lead to added value in terms of diversity and other investigated metrics of recommendations.

4 EVALUATION

To address our research questions, we conducted a user study to evaluate two visualizations in terms of diversity and other key metrics of recommender systems such as overall usability and user preferences.

4.1 Platform and Measurements

We chose Spotify as our experimental platform because it has become one of largest on-line music service providers. Spotify provides access to more than 30 million songs and had more than 140 million monthly active users in June 2017 [5]. By leveraging the provided API, we generate recommendations according to real user data. In this study, we employ the native Spotify recommendation service to generate 20 songs based on a top artist and a top track of the user. Then, we implemented two visualizations on top of this recommender. In addition, the original list view interface and player widget were adopted to make playing music the same as in Spotify (See Figure 2).

We measure musical expertise by the Goldsmiths Musical Sophistication Index (Gold-MSI) [6], consisting of ten questions on a 7-point Likert scale. The visual memory capacity is measured by the "Corsi block-tapping test" [7] for short-term memory tasks. We also wrote a script to record user actions in a log file, which includes a timestamp, the times of checking song's details (mouse hover), the times of exploring songs from the visualization (mouse click), and the rating of each song.

Moreover, to separate the effects of algorithm, we also control the actual diversity of recommendations to stay at a compared and moderate level. The actual diversity was measured by intra-list similarity (ILS) [45] on music genres. We measure the similarity $C_o(b_k, b_e)$ between items b_k, b_e based on the Jaccard similarity coefficient. Intra-list similarity for a_i's list P_{w_i} is defined as follows:

$$ILS(P_{w_i}) = \frac{\sum_{b_k \in \Im P_{w_i}} \sum_{b_e \in \Im P_{w_i}, b_k \neq b_e} C_o(b_k, b_e)}{2} \quad (2)$$

The Jaccard similarity is the number of common features for two sets A and B divided by the total number of features in the two sets.

$$J(A, B) = \frac{|A \cap B|}{|A \cup B|} \quad (3)$$

For all participants, recommendations shown in the two visualizations have a similar actual diversity calculated by ILS score (ComBub: Mean=22.46, SD=1.75, SimBub: Mean=22.07, SD=1.71). Lower scores obtained denote higher diversity.

4.2 Participants

We recruited 83 participants (Age: mean=28.3, SD = 6.7; Gender: 45.6% female) whose task approval rate is above 90% on Amazon MTurk. Four users were discarded because of self-contradictory responses found in reversal questions. All participant were compensated by 1.5 USD, and average completion time is 43 minutes. The majority of participants (69%) stated that they listened to on-line music every day. The remainder of the participants listened to on-line music at least once per week.

[5] https://en.wikipedia.org/wiki/Spotify
[6] http://www.gold.ac.uk/music-mind-brain/gold-msi/
[7] http://www.psytoolkit.org/experiment-library/corsi.html

4.3 Evaluation Methods

We conducted a within-subjects study where participants evaluated two user interfaces (ComBub vs. SimBub). To minimize the learning effects, half of the participants evaluated two interfaces in a reverse order. The **independent variable** of the study is the type of visualization.

According to our research questions, there are three **dependent variables** in our study, *perceived diversity*, *usability*, and *support to identify blind-spots*. We modified the user-centric recommender evaluation questionnaire with thirteen statements (S) (*ResQue*) [32] to measure perceived diversity and interface usability. In particular, to measure *categorical diversity*, the following question was included "S1: The items recommended to me are of various kinds.". The second question refers to *item-to-item diversity* by asking whether "S2: The items recommended to me are similar to each other." Moreover, we measured *novelty* and *serendipity* by asking whether "S3: The recommender system helps me discover new songs." and "S4: I haven't heard of some songs in the list before." respectively. Additionally, we also measured three other key aspects, usefulness (S5-S7), user's attitude (S8-S10), and behavioral intention (S11-S13). The measured aspects by each statement are shown in Figure 4. All questions were measured by a 7-point Likert scale from "strongly disagree" (1) to "strongly agree" (7).

4.4 Hypotheses

Based on our research questions, we propose five hypotheses in our study.

H1: In general, *ComBub* supports the participants to gain higher percieved diversity than *SimBub*.

H2: *ComBub* supports the participants with high MS to gain higher perceived diversity than *SimBub*.

H3: *ComBub* supports the participants with high VM to gain higher perceived diversity than *SimBub*.

H4: *ComBub* is superior to *SimBub* in terms of overall usability.

H5: Both *ComBub* and *SimBub* are able to encourage the participants to identify the songs of under-explored genres.

4.5 Evaluation Procedure

First, we asked users to read a brief description of the study task and to watch a one minute video that shows all the functions and interactions supported by each visualization. After finishing the tutorial, the participants were required to sign in to our system with their Spotty accounts. Before showing the interface, they needed to fill out a pre-study questionnaire including demographic and background questions, and questions for testing musical sophistication and a link for measuring visual memory (Corsi test). To avoid cheating, participants needed to upload a screen-shot of the Corsi test score.

Participants were given the same **task** while testing the two visualizations: each participant needs to listen and rate all songs in the list with the possibility to explore recommendations through the interface. We required participants to spend at least ten minutes on testing each interface by disabling the questionnaire link. Despite the same algorithm and input seeds, the recommendations generated by Spotify vary between different requests. Thus, the potential influence of users' familiarity with recommendation data

MS levels	ComBub	SimBub
High MS	5.94 (0.46)	5.26 (0.93)
Low MS	4.84 (0.67)	5.21 (0.78)

Table 1: Mean (SD) of diversity perceived by two groups of MS.

VM levels	ComBub	SimBub
High VM	5.91 (0.52)	5.08 (1.01)
Low VM	5.21 (0.80)	5.32 (0.78)

Table 2: Mean (SD) of diversity perceived by two groups of VM.

is avoided. After using each visualization, the user was asked to fill out a post-study questionnaire. In the end, we asked all participants to indicate their preference for the two interfaces in terms of general preference, informativeness, usefulness, quality, and perceived diversity.

5   RESULTS

We present the results according to each dependent variable.

5.1   Perceived Diversity

We measured perceived diversity by aggregating the user ratings for four statements (S1-S4). Of note, we invert the rating of S2 because S2 is a reversal question. We performed a non-parametric Mann-Whitney test to analyze the significance of two visualizations on perceived diversity regardless of the variance of MS and VM. The results do not show a significance difference between the two visualizations, ComBub (Mean=5.45, SD=0.79) and SimBub (Mean=5.24, SD=0.86), on diversity (U = 2614.00, p = .08), thus **H1** is **not** accepted. To verify hypotheses **H2** and **H3**, we analyze the results of diversity by low and high levels of MS and VM separately.

5.1.1   Results Musical Sophistication. The average MS of all participants is 5.16 (SD=0.90). We quantified user's MS based on their ratings of ten 7-point Likert scale questions. We categorized participants with an average rating of less than 5 as low MS group (n=35), whereas participants with an average rating of 5 or more are categorized as high MS group (n=44). Table 1 shows diversity for each visualization perceived by different user groups. In the group of high MS, a Mann-Whitney test shows that ComBub significantly outperforms SimBub (U = 500.50, p < .001), whereas for the group with low MS, SimBub is significantly better than ComBub (U = 429.00, p < .05). In addition, we performed a correlation analysis between perceived diversity and MS for the two visualizations. For ComBub, the results show a significantly positive correlation between MS and diversity (r=0.53, p<.01), while no significant correlation was found for SimBub (r=-0.009, p=.60). We can accept hypothesis **H2**.

5.1.2   Results Visual Memory Capacity. Healthy adults have an average block span of 6.2 blocks (SD=1.3) in the Corsi test [22], and in our study the average score is 6.08 (SD=1.38). Similarly, we categorized users into two groups, high VM (>6 blocks, n=27)

index	ComBub	SimBub
Num. of explored genres	2.29 (2.75)	2.41 (2.80)
Num. of available genres	6.84 (0.58)	7.19 (0.67)

Table 3: Mean number (SD) of explored genres and available genres.

and low VM (<=6 blocks, n=52) according to their scores. Table 2 shows the mean diversity for two groups. In the group of high VM, ComBub led to significantly higher perceived diversity than SimBub (U = 171.50, p < .01), while no significant result was found for the group of low VM (U = 1268.00, p = .58). The result of correlation analysis between VM and diversity shows a significantly positive correlation for ComBub (r=0.44, p<.01), and no significance was found for SimBub (r=-0.007, p=.50). Hypothesis **H3** can be accepted.

5.2   Overall Usability

We compare the overall usability of the two visualizations by performing Mann-Whitney tests for the responses to the post-study questionnaire. Figure 4 shows the average rating to each statement. In total, we found that for three statements, item-to-item diversity (S2), satisfaction (S8), and intention to reuse (S11), ComBub was rated significantly higher than SimBub. For the rest of the statements except facilitation (S5), despite no significance, ComBub still received higher ratings than SimBub. Thus, we can accept hypothesis **H4**.

Moreover, after evaluating the interfaces, participants were asked to show their preferences for the two visualizations in terms of five aspects. Figure 5 shows the distribution of preferences. In general, participants prefer ComBub (42%) over SimBub (29%), and 23% like both of them. Over half of the participants (54%) thought ComBub was more informative than SimBub. In terms of usefulness and quality, they showed an almost equal preference (35% vs 34%, 39% vs 34%) to ComBub and SimBub. 42% of users liked both visualizations in terms of perceived diversity.

5.3   Support to Identify Blind-spots

We recorded user actions with the two visualizations. When a user clicked a circle (song) we judged if the genre of this song had been visited. Then, we counted how many genres the participant had visited. The number of available genres is equal to the sum of the number of explored genres and under-explored genres. Of note, users were not required to click the circles to listen to a song. Table 3 shows the average number of explored genres. The Mann-Whitney test does not show significance between the two visualizations (U = 3031.50, p = .74). Also compared to the average number of available genres in recommendations, we do not see a beneficial support for visiting the songs in (for the user) under-explored genres. Therefore, the hypothesis **H5** can **not** be accepted.

5.4   User Actions

Table 4 shows the results of user actions with the two visualizations. The number of "hover" interactions indicates the counts of hovering the cursor to check the song information; and the number of "click" interactions is calculated by counting the number of clicks to

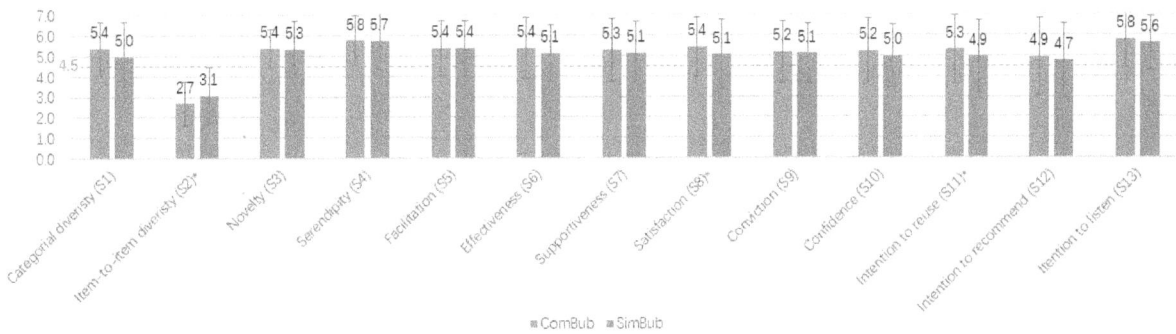

Figure 4: Results of the *ResQue* questionnaire. A cut-off value was set at 4.5 on the 7 point scale. The (*) sign means significant differences at the 5% level (p<.05) between visualizations. Of note, S2 is a reversal question.

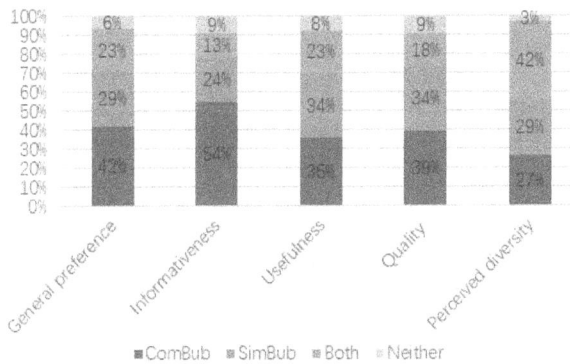

Figure 5: Preference results.

index	ComBub	SimBub
Num. of hover	58.28 (52.67)	8.18 (10.36)
Num. of click	6.51 (7.49)	3.85 (7.02)
Ratings	12.76 (3.82)	12.99 (3.96)

Table 4: Mean number (SD) of each user action.

highlight the associated item in the list. It is interesting to find that *ComBub* leads to significantly more user interactions ("hover": U = 900.50, p < .01; "click": U = 2197.00, p < .01) with songs than *SimBub*. The user's ratings of recommendations are calculated by the total number of liked songs. However, there is no significant difference between the ratings of the resulting recommendations in the two visualizations (U = 3031.00, p = .76). Unsurprisingly, *ComBub* results in more user actions as there are more possibilities for clicking, as different song feature variations are visualized on the axes.

6 DISCUSSION

To frame our work, we discuss the results with respect to the ability of two visualizations to support users with different levels of MS

and VM in two main aspects: 1) the perception of diversity, and 2) the exploration of blind spots.

Visualizing the audio features of music has a limited impact on perceived diversity. The results suggest that these two visualizations are generally appropriate to support users in the perception of recommendation diversity. However, compared to *SimBub*, additional audio features of songs visualized in *ComBub* do not have significant added value for increasing perceived diversity if we disregard the effect of the individual traits MS and VM. Thus, we do **not** accept hypothesis **H1** and answer the research question **RQ1**. We think that the understandability of what the features refer to could be a problem that hindered many people from profiting from the visualization of audio features. However, we do see a significant effect of audio features on item-to-item diversity (S2), which means *ComBub* was prone to help users to perceive the difference among items. We speculate that the visualization is good at helping users find how items are different in terms of their audio features.

Consider individual traits for designing diversity-aware recommendation interface. Overall, no significant difference was found between the two visualizations in terms of users' perception of diversity. Instead, we find the most appropriate diversity-aware user interface depends on the two investigated individual traits: MS and VM.

We aimed to investigate the effects of two individual traits on user's perception of diversity. We categorized the participants into two groups according to their MS and VM scores. The results indicate that for both users with high MS and users with high VM, their perceptions of diversity for recommendations in *ComBub* are significantly higher than the perceived diversity in *SimBub*, notwithstanding that the actual diversity of recommendations in *ComBub* is consistent with that in *SimBub*. Therefore, we could confirm the hypotheses **H2, H3** and answer the research question **RQ2** by finding the positive effects of MS and VM on perceived diversity. Of note, for those who have low MS, *ComBub* led to a significantly lower perception of diversity than *SimBub*. Thus, the additional audio features shown in *ComBub* do not seem to supply real benefits for users with low MS in terms of perception of diversity. Even the additional features in a visualization may result in higher cognitive load and a negative impact on user experience [4]. A similarly reversed result was not found for users with low VM.

The correlation analysis results show a significantly positive correlation between individual traits (MS, VM) and the perceived diversity in visualization *ComBub*; however, no such a significant correlation was found for *SimBub*. This result implies that an advanced visualization interface like *ComBub* allows experts to leverage their attribute knowledge to perceive higher diversity. In contrast, novices seem to prefer a simple interface that does not require intimate attribute knowledge such as the meaning of each audio features introduced in *ComBub*.

With this, we conclude that it is essential to consider the individual traits of users like MS and VM while presenting additional information like meta-data in a diversity-aware recommendation interface.

Limited support in the exploration of blind-spots. The subjective responses to the statements S3 and S4 (see Figure 4) show that participants were more likely to find songs which they had not yet listened to. Whereas the results of the user action log suggest that the visited songs through the visualizations only refer to a small portion (1/3) of all genres of recommendations. This may be explained by a relatively small number of clicks (see Table 4). It is interesting to find that the number of "hover" interactions is much higher than the number of "click" interactions. We surmise that most participants used the visualization as a tool of inspecting the details of items, or as a tooltip, rather than as an exploration tool. Despite the benefits of visualizations, users may still have checked the songs from the list directly, because interactions with visualization require extra click efforts. Thus, this addresses research question **RQ3**, we do **not** have evidence to support hypothesis **H5**.

7 LIMITATIONS

First, although we tried our best to minimize the potential harms to evaluation such as filtering workers and avoiding acquiescence bias by introducing contradictory statements, we cannot ignore the potential limitations [24] of using a crowd-scouring platform like Amazon Mechanical Turk to evaluate a system with relatively complex tasks.

Second, the classification of genres used in our study contains 126 genres, which are defined by Spotify, However, we find some genres are quite similar, such as, "Punk" vs "Punk-Rock". Therefore, the actual diversity should be lower than what we calculated.

Third, to ensure enough user engagement in testing two visualizations, we required users to spend at least ten minutes for each visualization and listen and rate all recommended songs. Thus, the recorded actions may not reflect the real user intention for clicking items on visualizations.

Despite these limitations, we are confident to argue that the music diversity perceived through user interfaces significantly depends on individual traits MS and VM, and considering these traits in the design of visualizations can lead to better support in enhancing diversity.

8 CONCLUSIONS AND FUTURE WORK

In addition to the approach that improves actual diversity by algorithms, increased attention has been paid to enhance user's perception of diversity through user interfaces. A diversity-aware recommendation model (see Figure 1) suggests that the design of diversity-aware user interfaces should consider both *user diversity* and *item diversity*. Therefore, we hypothesize that users' individual traits such as *musical sophistication* and *visual memory* may have a significant effect on the diversity perceived through user interfaces. In particular, our study investigates such an effect with a music recommender user interface having two different visualizations for recommendations, *ComBub* and *SimBub*. Moreover, we are also interested in knowing if such a user interface is able to encourage users to explore blind-spots.

We presented an in-depth study to assess the value of showing additional item attributes (seven audio features) in the visualization, *ComBub*, for the purpose of increasing users' perception of diversity. The results suggest that *ComBub* is particularly effective for enhancing the perceived diversity for users having high MS and high VM. In contrast, the baseline *SimBub* visualization (that shows fewer item attributes) is prone to increase the perception of diversity for the users having low MS. Furthermore, a strong positive correlation between individual traits and users' perception of diversity was found in the *ComBub* visualization.

For our future work, we plan to validate our findings in other application domains. Moreover, we plan to improve the design of *ComBub* to see if it is able to encourage users to explore blind-spots in an exploration-oriented task.

9 ACKNOWLEDGEMENTS

Part of this research has been supported by the KU Leuven Research Council (grant agreement C24/16/017).

REFERENCES

[1] Gediminas Adomavicius and YoungOk Kwon. 2009. Toward more diverse recommendations: Item re-ranking methods for recommender systems. In *Workshop on Information Technologies and Systems*. Citeseer.

[2] Gediminas Adomavicius and YoungOk Kwon. 2012. Improving aggregate recommendation diversity using ranking-based techniques. *IEEE Tran. on KDE* 24, 5 (2012), 896–911.

[3] Jisun An, Daniele Quercia, and Jon Crowcroft. 2013. Why individuals seek diverse opinions (or why they don't). In *Proc. of Web Science '13*. ACM, 15–18.

[4] Ivana Andjelkovic, Denis Parra, and John O'Donovan. 2016. Moodplay: Interactive Mood-based Music Discovery and Recommendation. In *Proc. of UMAP '16*. ACM, 275–279.

[5] Alan Baddeley. 1992. Working memory. *Science* 255, 5044 (1992), 556–559.

[6] Svetlin Bostandjiev, John O'Donovan, and Tobias Höllerer. 2012. TasteWeights: a visual interactive hybrid recommender system. In *Proc. of RecSys '12*. ACM, 35–42.

[7] John S Breese, David Heckerman, and Carl Kadie. 1998. Empirical analysis of predictive algorithms for collaborative filtering. In *Proc. of UAI '98*. Morgan Kaufmann Publishers Inc., 43–52.

[8] Sylvain Castagnos, Nicolas Jones, and Pearl Pu. 2010. Eye-tracking product recommenders' usage. In *Proc. of RecSys '10*. ACM, 29–36.

[9] Pablo Castells, Neil J Hurley, and Saul Vargas. 2015. Novelty and diversity in recommender systems. In *Recommender Systems Handbook*. Springer, 881–918.

[10] Li Chen and Pearl Pu. 2007. Preference-based organization interfaces: aiding user critiques in recommender systems. *Proc. of UM '07* (2007), 77–86.

[11] Li Chen and Pearl Pu. 2010. Eye-tracking study of user behavior in recommender interfaces. *Proc. of UMAP '10* (2010), 375–380.

[12] Cristina Conati, Giuseppe Carenini, Enamul Hoque, Ben Steichen, and Dereck Toker. 2014. Evaluating the impact of user characteristics and different layouts on an interactive visualization for decision making. In *Computer Graphics Forum*, Vol. 33. Wiley Online Library, 371–380.

[13] Cristina Conati, Giuseppe Carenini, Dereck Toker, and Sébastien Lallé. 2015. Towards user-adaptive information visualization. In *Proc. of AAAI '15*. AAAI Press, 4100–4106.

[14] Siamak Faridani, Ephrat Bitton, Kimiko Ryokai, and Ken Goldberg. 2010. Opinion space: a scalable tool for browsing online comments. In *Proc. CHI '10*. ACM, 1175–1184.

[15] Mouzhi Ge, Carla Delgado-Battenfeld, and Dietmar Jannach. 2010. Beyond accuracy: evaluating recommender systems by coverage and serendipity. In *Proc. of RecSys '10*. ACM, 257–260.

[16] Giorgos Giannopoulos, Ingmar Weber, Alejandro Jaimes, and Timos Sellis. 2012. Diversifying user comments on news articles. In *Proc. of WISE '12*. Springer, 100–113.

[17] Eduardo Graells-Garrido, Mounia Lalmas, and Ricardo Baeza-Yates. 2016. Data portraits and intermediary topics: Encouraging exploration of politically diverse profiles. In *Proc. of IUI '16*. ACM, 228–240.

[18] Jonathan L Herlocker, Joseph A Konstan, Loren G Terveen, and John T Riedl. 2004. Evaluating collaborative filtering recommender systems. *ACM TOIS* 22, 1 (2004), 5–53.

[19] Yoshinori Hijikata, Takuya Shimizu, and Shogo Nishida. 2009. Discovery-oriented collaborative filtering for improving user satisfaction. In *Proc. of IUI '09*. ACM, 67–76.

[20] Rong Hu and Pearl Pu. 2011. Enhancing recommendation diversity with organization interfaces. In *Proc. of IUI '11*. ACM, 347–350.

[21] Yucheng Jin, Karsten Seipp, Erik Duval, and Katrien Verbert. 2016. Go with the flow: effects of transparency and user control on targeted advertising using flow charts. In *Proc. of AVI '16*. ACM, 68–75.

[22] Roy PC Kessels, Martine JE Van Zandvoort, Albert Postma, L Jaap Kappelle, and Edward HF De Haan. 2000. The Corsi block-tapping task: standardization and normative data. *Applied neuropsychology* 7, 4 (2000), 252–258.

[23] Hannah Kim, Jaegul Choo, Haesun Park, and Alex Endert. 2016. InterAxis: Steering scatterplot axes via observation-level interaction. *IEEE TVCG '16* 22, 1 (2016), 131–140.

[24] Aniket Kittur, Ed H Chi, and Bongwon Suh. 2008. Crowdsourcing user studies with Mechanical Turk. In *Proc. of CHI '08*. ACM, 453–456.

[25] Bart P Knijnenburg, Martijn C Willemsen, Zeno Gantner, Hakan Soncu, and Chris Newell. 2012. Explaining the user experience of recommender systems. *UMUAI* 22, 4-5 (2012), 441–504.

[26] Kevin Mccarthy, James Reilly, Barry Smyth, and Lorraine Mcginty. 2005. Generating diverse compound critiques. *Artificial Intelligence Review* 24, 3 (2005), 339–357.

[27] Lorraine McGinty and Barry Smyth. 2003. On the role of diversity in conversational recommender systems. In *International Conference on Case-Based Reasoning*. Springer, 276–290.

[28] Daniel Müllensiefen, Bruno Gingras, Jason Musil, and Lauren Stewart. 2014. The musicality of non-musicians: an index for assessing musical sophistication in the general population. *PloS one* 9, 2 (2014), e89642.

[29] Sean A Munson and Paul Resnick. 2010. Presenting diverse political opinions: how and how much. In *Proc. of CHI '10*. ACM, 1457–1466.

[30] Tien T Nguyen, Pik-Mai Hui, F Maxwell Harper, Loren Terveen, and Joseph A Konstan. 2014. Exploring the filter bubble: the effect of using recommender systems on content diversity. In *Proc. of WWW '14*. ACM, 677–686.

[31] John O'Donovan, Barry Smyth, Brynjar Gretarsson, Svetlin Bostandjiev, and Tobias Höllerer. 2008. PeerChooser: visual interactive recommendation. In *Proc. of CHI '08*. ACM, 1085–1088.

[32] Pearl Pu, Li Chen, and Rong Hu. 2011. A user-centric evaluation framework for recommender systems. In *Proc. of RecSys '11*. ACM, 157–164.

[33] J Ben Schafer, Joseph A Konstan, and John Riedl. 2002. Meta-recommendation systems: user-controlled integration of diverse recommendations. In *Proc. CIKM '02*. ACM, 43–51.

[34] Nava Tintarev. 2017. Presenting Diversity Aware Recommendations. In *Proc. of FATREC 17'*.

[35] Nava Tintarev and Judith Masthoff. 2016. Effects of Individual Differences in Working Memory on Plan Presentational Choices. *Frontiers in psychology* 7 (2016).

[36] Nava Tintarev, Shahin Rostami, and Barry Smyth. 2018. Knowing the Unknown: Visualising Consumption Blind-Spots in Recommender System. In *Proc. of SAC '18*. ACM.

[37] Chun-Hua Tsai and Peter Brusilovsky. 2017. Enhancing Recommendation Diversity Through a Dual Recommendation Interface. In *Proc. of RecSys IntRS '17*. 10.

[38] Saúl Vargas and Pablo Castells. 2011. Rank and relevance in novelty and diversity metrics for recommender systems. In *Proc. of RecSys '11*. ACM, 109–116.

[39] Katrien Verbert, Denis Parra, Peter Brusilovsky, and Erik Duval. 2013. Visualizing recommendations to support exploration, transparency and controllability. In *Proc. of IUI '13*. ACM, 351–362.

[40] Fernanda B Viegas, Martin Wattenberg, Frank Van Ham, Jesse Kriss, and Matt McKeon. 2007. Manyeyes: a site for visualization at internet scale. *IEEE TVCG '07* 13, 6 (2007).

[41] Jing Wang and Jian Yin. 2013. Combining user-based and item-based collaborative filtering techniques to improve recommendation diversity. In *Proc. BMEI '13*. IEEE, 661–665.

[42] David Wong, Siamak Faridani, Ephrat Bitton, Björn Hartmann, and Ken Goldberg. 2011. The diversity donut: enabling participant control over the diversity of recommended responses. In *Proc. of CHI EA '11*. ACM, 1471–1476.

[43] Mi Zhang and Neil Hurley. 2008. Avoiding monotony: improving the diversity of recommendation lists. In *Proc. of RecSys '08*. ACM, 123–130.

[44] Xiaojin Zhu, Andrew B Goldberg, Jurgen Van Gael, and David Andrzejewski. 2007. Improving Diversity in Ranking using Absorbing Random Walks.. In *HLT-NAACL*. 97–104.

[45] Cai-Nicolas Ziegler, Sean M McNee, Joseph A Konstan, and Georg Lausen. 2005. Improving recommendation lists through topic diversification. In *Proc. WWW '05*. ACM, 22–32.

Who is Your Best Friend?: Ranking Social Network Friends According to Trust Relationship

Xiaoming Li
School of Computer Science and Engineering
Nanyang Technological University
Singapore, Singapore
lixiaoming@ntu.edu.sg

Hui Fang
Research Institute for Interdisciplinary Sciences
School of Information Management and Engineering
Shanghai University of Finance and Economics
Shanghai, China
fang.hui@mail.shufe.edu.cn

Qing Yang
Department of Computer Science and Engineering
University of North Texas
Denton, Texas
qing.yang@unt.edu

Jie Zhang
School of Computer Science and Engineering
Nanyang Technological University
Singapore, Singapore
zhangj@ntu.edu.sg

ABSTRACT

In online social networks (OSNs), e.g. Facebook, the relationship between users is binary, i.e., either friend (trust) or stranger (distrust). However, in real-world life, people always have different trust relationships with others (e.g., best friend, acquaintance, frenemy). For various applications such as social recommendation and semantic web, it is more worthwhile to know the trust strength between users. In this work, via a unique dataset obtained from a Facebook app and a carefully designed user study, we map trust values with users' online interactions, and thus build personalized trust models. For each individual, we learn her trust model via optimization on a ranking-oriented loss function. Experimental results demonstrate the superior of the proposed approach over state-of-the-art method and the good generalization ability of the approach.

KEYWORDS

Trust, Social networks, Facebook, Personalized ranking

ACM Reference Format:
Xiaoming Li, Hui Fang, Qing Yang, and Jie Zhang. 2018. Who is Your Best Friend?: Ranking Social Network Friends According to Trust Relationship. In *UMAP '18: 26th Conference on User Modeling, Adaptation and Personalization, July 8–11, 2018, Singapore, Singapore.* ACM, New York, NY, USA, 9 pages. https://doi.org/10.1145/3209219.3209243

1 INTRODUCTION

Online social networking has become an essential part in modern life [5]. Popular online platforms such as Facebook, Twitter, Instagram allow users to communicate with each other by means of different types of interactions, including messaging text, providing

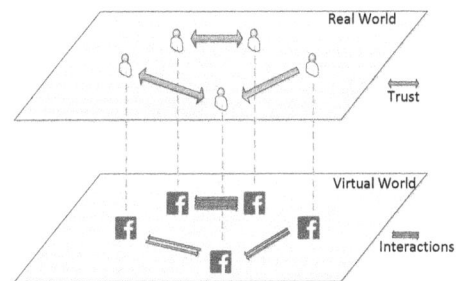

Figure 1: Mapping between the physical world and the virtual world: trust and social interactions.

comments and sharing photos. As reported in [6], there are over 2.13 billion Facebook active users in 2017. Online social networking can be treated as a mapping of social activities in real life, as demonstrated in Figure 1. Different with real life scenario, however, OSNs consider all users as the same. For example, in Facebook, friends of a user are treated similarly, even though trust (i.e. the strength of relationship) between the user and her friends can be varied, where she might trust some friends more (i.e. close friends) while trust others less (i.e. acquaintances).

In fact, the relationship that users have figured out with other users, i.e. their online social networks, has enormous applications in various scenarios. For example, to better facilitate users' online experience, online platforms can recommend news feeds or products to users based on their trust networks. Besides, online platforms can also improve their social recommendation algorithms by exploiting users' social networks and thus recommend better candidates to each user with whom each user might be more possibly to form an online relationship. Another example is in vehicular network, where online social networks can be applied to improve the vehicular communications and enhance the relationship among users and drivers [9, 26].

There is no formal definition of the trust strength, and different trust definitions addressing different trust aspects have been proposed in the literature [1, 8]. For example, in some studies, the

UMAP '18, July 8–11, 2018, Singapore, Singapore
© 2018 Association for Computing Machinery.
ACM ISBN 978-1-4503-5589-6/18/07...$15.00
https://doi.org/10.1145/3209219.3209243

trust between social friends is referred as interpersonal trust[16], or tie strength [7]. In the context of this paper, we adopt the idea of social intimacy [18] to represent trust strength between friends, where a higher trust value between two users indicates they have more intimate social relationship.

However, it is non-trivial to measure the strength of relationship (i.e. trust) between online users due to two reasons. First, the ground-truth of a trust value is quite difficult to obtain. Even though some users might be willing to share their trust values with others via means of surveys, they might be hard to quantify the exact trust value they have on each of their friends. Instead of indicating the concrete strength of their online relationships, it might be much more easily for them to rank the strength of their relationships. Second, trust is a personalized concept in the sense that different users have different propensity to trust others and distinguished standards to quantify trust values. For example, Alice might be more willing to form the trust relationship with others while Bob is more reluctant to identify others as friends. On the other hand, Alice might indicate the friends having trust value over "80" as close friends, while the threshold for Bob is "95". Third, the preferred types of interactions for each user is also varied [24]. For example, in Facebook, some users prefer to share photos with others while other users might be inclined to communicate with others via text messages. In this view, it is much more worthwhile to design a personalized model to measure the trust values towards others for each individual user instead of building a generalized trust model for everyone.

Several methods have been recently proposed to measure trust relationships between users in the social platforms. For example, [9] uses the frequency of email exchange between two users to represent the corresponding trust value which is far from convincing because email communications mainly reflect the business-related activities. Therefore, generally speaking, it is inappropriate for analyzing interpersonal trust. Podobnik et al. [21] collect 8 types of social activities, e.g. "list of friends who write on the Wall of Facebook", between every two users, and the corresponding trust value is computed as the weighted sum of the 8 types of activities. Similarly, Gilbert et al. [7] identify 7 groups of variables to predict tie strength in online social networks. However, these method merely focus on active users. In other words, all silent users (lurkers) will be inappropriately considered as untrustworthy because of their inactiveness [10]. Meanwhile, as demonstrated in our research, some of these variables, e.g. the number of mutual friends, are found to have insignificant correlation with the trust values.

Besides, the existing approaches are mainly built on the assumption that the strength of relationship between two users is stronger if they have more online interactions. We argue that in OSNs, the trust relationship is not only related to the number of online interactions, but also more importantly the corresponding user's activity level. In other words, for example, a user may interact more frequently with an active user (e.g., who have published lots of posts and photos in Facebook) than with an inactive user even though the user might have weaker relationship with the active user, as shown in Figure 2. Another problem of the existing approaches is that they generally focus on quantifying the trust values between users which is comparably meaningless as they ignore the personalized

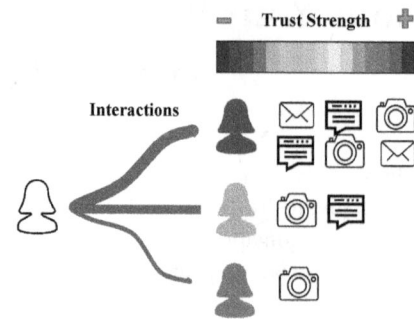

Figure 2: The number of interaction between two users is tightly related to users' activity levels. As illustrated, the user on the left has more interactions with the "Blue" user on the right which is mainly because the "Blue" user is much more active but not because the user trust the "Blue" user more.[It is better to view the figure in color.]

property of trust concept. Instead, a more reasonable and practical way is to rank the trust strength within each individual's friends.

In view of these issues, in our work, via a particularly designed Facebook app, we have collected 59 users' online social interactions in Facebook. Besides, via a user study, we also collected these users' trust values on their friends. Based on a thorough data analysis, we propose a novel approach to rank users' friends by their social interactions and corresponding personal trust values. Specifically, first, we analyze online users' interaction behavior and depict each user's character by their incoming interactions. We thus generate a feature set based on the normalized interaction data, with which we build personalized prediction model for each user, and learn the model via a well-designed ranking-oriented optimization function. Besides, we investigate whether the learned prediction model of a user can be generalized to other users having similar characters with the user. Experimental results demonstrate the superior of the proposed approach over state-of-the-art methods and the good generalization ability of the approach.

The contributions of this paper are summarized as follows:

- We rank a user's online friends in terms of the trust attitude towards her friends. Rather than quantify the strength of trust relationship, we adopt a personalized ranking model to learn users' preferences on social interactions, and thus rank their friends based on the obtained scores.
- The collected data in this work is quite unique and remarkable. Participants in the user study have specified the trust values towards their friends, and all the interactions data in Facebook have also been collected based on their privilege authorization.
- The prediction models can be generalized to other users outside the user study. We have demonstrated that the prediction model of a user in our studies can be generalized to other users having similar characters with the user.

The paper is organized as follows. First, we carry out a comprehensive literature study of measuring trust strength between users in Section 2. Second, we conduct a thorough data analysis about the collected social network, especially towards the correlation between trust and social interactions in Section 3. Third, we present our approach, including feature extraction, personalized ranking model and generalization method in Section 4. Finally, we conduct experiments over the collected dataset to demonstrate the effectiveness of our approaches in Section 5, followed by conclusions in Section 6.

2 RELATED WORK

Measuring trust values between users in online social media (i.e. abbreviated as trust measurement) has recently attracted many researchers. The common way of measuring trust is through reputation [12], which predicts user A's trust towards user B by using the former experience of other users with user B. Besides, lots of studies focus on trust propagation [8, 19, 22, 29], which heavily relies on the existing trust information. For example, if user A trusts user B, and user B trusts user C, user A's trust towards user C can be correspondingly inferred. Distrust is considered in [13–15], where relationship can be negative if two users are enemies. However, these models are built on indirect information and cannot guarantee the accuracy of the personalized trust between two users.

Therefore, there are also some recent studies which focus on users' direct evidence on social platforms. These studies try to select more representative features to imply trust relationship. For example, Huang et al. [9] try to measure trust based on the frequency of email exchange between users which is far from convincing because email communications mainly reflect the business-related activities but are inappropriate for measuring interpersonal trust between two users. [25] uses the frequency of phone calls and short messages (SMS) to indicate trust, but it might fail to distinguish strong and weak trust relationship, e.g. how to identify whether the phone calls or SMS is caused by business needs or personal communication. Tencent QQ, the most popular online social tool in China, provides a function called "intimacy measurement" [3], which calculates trust mainly based on common background and common activities. Both trust models in [27, 28] connect trust values between users with three variables: profile similarity, information reliability and social opinions in [28], and user similarity, familiarity and reputation in [27]. Those models eventually return a trust score by a weighted sum of these variables.

There are also some studies using users' activities in social media to infer trust values between users. For example, Podobnik et al. [21] firstly collect 8 types of social activities, e.g. "list of friends who write on the Wall of Facebook", and the trust between users are computed as the weighted sum of these 8 values, where the weights are manually and heuristically decided. Gilbert et al. [7] identify 7 variables to predict tie strength in online social networks, and apply regression model to obtain the weight for each variable and similarly the trust value is measured as the weighted sum of these variables. However, as shown in our work, some of these variables, e.g. the number of mutual friends, are found to have insignificant correlation with the trust. Besides, those studies only focus on active users, while recent trend inclines to address the issues of inactive users ranking and identification [10, 20, 23]. However, these new studies only rank within inactive users, but not all types of users together, which is different from our study.

In summary, most of the existing approaches try to identify different features and use simple linear model to infer trust, which fail to consider the personalized property of trust. Besides, they ignore that in most cases, users are more easily to rank their friends instead of quantifying the exact trust degrees with others. Moreover, some of the identified variables (or factors) cannot effectively imply trust. Therefore, in this work, to address these issues, we quantitatively check the correlation between trust and social interactions. Via a well-designed feature set from the social interactions, we adopt a prediction model to rank the strength of relationship between user pairs.

3 DATA ANALYSIS

In this work, we select Facebook as our study platform mainly because of two reasons. Firstly, Facebook is quite representative as it is the largest and most widely used social media in the world. Secondly, users can have multiple ways to interact with others such as sending messages and posting photos. These interactions provide rich information source for our study. As some of the social interactions data in Facebook are not available for public access, we particularly design an app based on Facebook API to crawl the data.

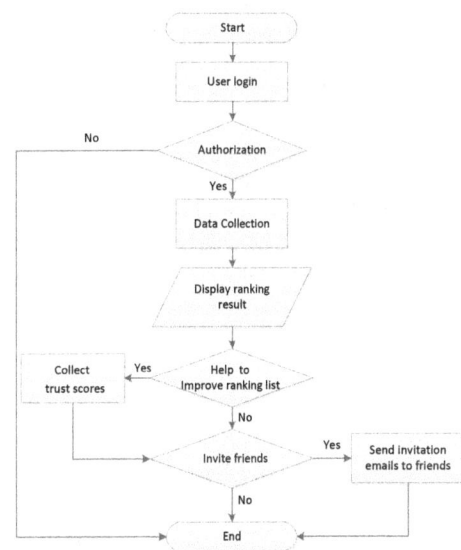

Figure 3: Flowchart of the data collection.

Figure 3 shows the flowchart of the data collection. After users' authorization with Facebook API, the app can collect a user's whole interaction data in Facebook. Then, the app conduct a user study with each participant who thus specify their trust values towards their online friends explicitly. Specifically, participants specify the trust values by dragging a sliding bar ranging from 0 to 100, and also be notified that correctly ranking friends is more important than the accurate values, considering that people are often uncertain how to translate their subjective feelings about trust strength into linear values. We hence obtain two kinds of data for each participant:

her social interactions and her weighted trust network with online friends.

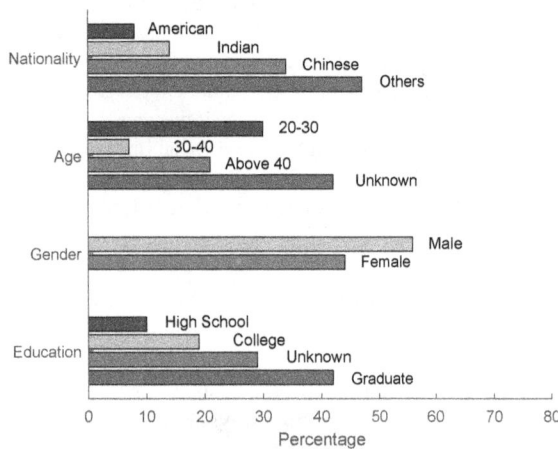

Figure 4: Statistics of the participants in our study.

Finally, there are totally 59 users who have participated in our study. The major statistics of these participants are shown in Figure 4. We can see that these users are diverse in gender, race, age and educational background. The topology of the network formed by all these participants is shown in Figure 5, from which we can see that all these users are connected, representing a small social network in Facebook. In the small social network, some users have a more centralized role while others have fewer friends. In this view, we argue that our data, although only contains 59 users, is representative. Besides, to the best of our knowledge, this is the only dataset containing both the comprehensive social interaction data and the trust values between users.

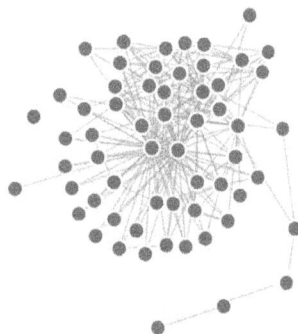

Figure 5: Network topology of all participants.

Moreover, for these users, the median number of friends is 230, which is quite consistent with the public release of Facebook which indicates that across all users the median number of friends is around 200 in Facebook [2]. Specifically, in our dataset, the maximum number of friends that a user has is 1, 081, while the minimum number is 6. In the following subsections, we carefully examine the two parts of our dataset: social interactions and the weighted trust networks.

3.1 Social interactions

As aforementioned, online users have different preferences on the usages of Facebook [24] which can be reflected by their varied use of social interactions. In Facebook, we collect totally 12 types of interactions between each user pair, as listed in Table 1.

The distribution and some statistics about the value of these features are listed in Table 2. We can see that they have different order of magnitude, but most features show a long tail pattern.

3.2 The relation between trust and social interactions

We further examine the correlations between trust and each of these types of social interactions. Besides the interaction data, there are some other factors used in previous research [7, 21], including the number of mutual friends, age differences or education differences. We analyze the correlations between these factors with trust on the basis of our data, and the results demonstrate that in generally the interaction data has more correlations with trust than other types of data, which supports the effectiveness of using interaction data to predict trust between users. For example, Figure 6 plots the relationship between the number of mutual friends and the trust values. It indicates no obviously positive correlation between these two factors (Pearson correlation coefficient = −0.0069 with p-value = 0.971799 which is far bigger than 0.05), which fails to support the underlying assumption in previous research. We further conduct a face-to-face interview with certain participants, and we find that a user might not be acquainted with some of her friends although she has a large number of mutual friends with these users.

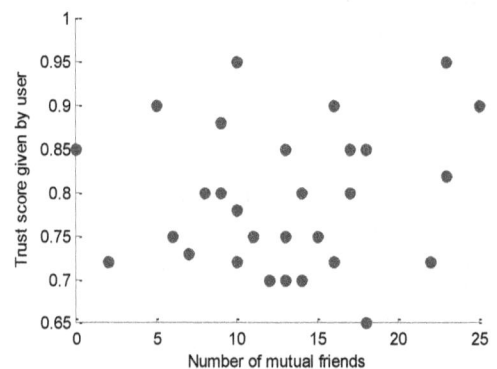

Figure 6: Relationship between number of mutual friends and trust.

Table 2 lists the Pearson correlation coefficients of each interaction with trust scores. All features show positive correlations with trust scores. We also conduct a statistical test on the correlation between the total number of interactions and trust, and the result shows that there are convincing evidences supporting the correlations (two-sided p-value < 0.0001 from f-stat= 294.1 on 1 and 442 d.f.). One unit increase in interaction times is associated with an estimated 0.62 units increase in the mean trust value, with an associated 95% Confidence Interval from 0.48 to 0.77 units. The result confirms the effectiveness of using the 12 types of interaction data to predict trust values between users in Facebook.

Table 1: Social interactions in Facebook

Symbol	Name	Description
IM_{ij}	Inbox Messages	The number of Inbox messages that user i received from user j
PC_{ij}	Photo Comments	The number of comments that j left on the photos of i
PL_{ij}	Photo Likes	The number of likes that j left on the photos of i
AC_{ij}	Album Comments	The number of comments that j left on the albums of i
AL_{ij}	Album Likes	The number of likes that j left on the albums of i
TP_{ij}	Tag Photos	The number of photos that j was tagged by in the photos of i
PT_{ij}	Photos Tagged	The number of photos that i was tagged in the photos of j
TC_{ij}	Tag Photo Comments	The number of comments that j left on the tag-photos of i
TL_{ij}	Tag Photo Likes	The number of likes that j left on the tag-photos of i
CT_{ij}	Co-tag	The number of photos that i and j were tagged together
SC_{ij}	Status Comments	The number of comments that j left on the status of i
SL_{ij}	Status Likes	The number of likes that j left on the status of i

Table 2: Distributions of social interactions & Pearson correlations with trust score

Feature	Distribution	Max	Correlation
IM_{ij}		47114	0.22
PC_{ij}		67	0.33
PL_{ij}		84	0.23
AC_{ij}		12	0.22
AL_{ij}		13	0.15
TP_{ij}		31	0.17
PT_{ij}		47	0.20
TC_{ij}		354	0.21
TL_{ij}		62	0.22
CT_{ij}		110	0.18
SC_{ij}		144	0.28
SL_{ij}		84	0.24

3.3 Types of online users

Another obstacle to predict trust is the diversity of user's behavior of online social activities. As aforementioned, interactions frequency is not only related to the trust strength, but also be influenced by users' attitude towards online social behavior (i.e. their activity levels in social platforms). We could classify Facebook users into four categories based on how active they are in online social activities [16]:

- Active users: who frequently publish contents (status updates, photos, etc.) and also frequently interact with other users.

- Actor users: who frequently publish contents, but infrequently interact with other users.
- Audience users: who infrequently publish contents, but frequently interact with other users.
- Inactive (or Silent) users: who infrequently publish contents and also infrequently interact with other users

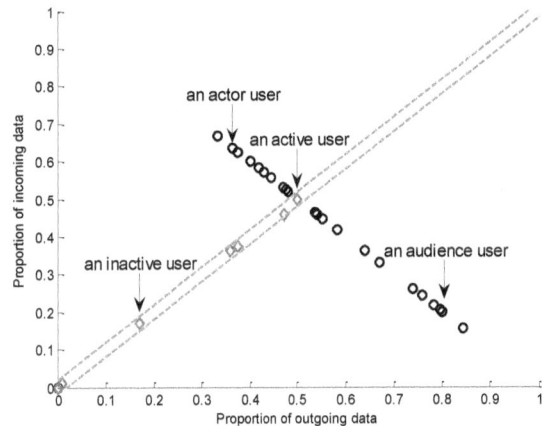

Figure 7: Different types of online users in our dataset.

From the perspective of a certain user like Alice, her online friends might be in different categories. Therefore, the number of interactions might not be truly reflect their trust relationships. For example, suppose Alice has two online friends Bob and David. Her close friend Bob is an inactive user in Facebook, while David is an active user but only an acquaintance to Alice. It thus is more likely that Alice will have more online interactions with David than that with Bob since there are limited opportunities for Alice and Bob to interact with each other in Facebook. As shown in Figure 7, we can easily identify actor and audience users by checking the proportions of incoming and outgoing data. An actor user tends to have more incoming data (e.g. receiving comments) but less outgoing data. On the other hand, an audience user would have less incoming data but more outgoing ones. Although both active and inactive users would have similar proportions of incoming and outgoing data, the total amount of interactions of active users should be much greater than that of inactive ones. As shown in Figure 7, there are various types of users in our dataset. Therefore, the number of interactions cannot be directly used as indications of trust strength due to the diversify of user types. In this case, we eliminate the effect by adopting a data normalization technique which has been validated to be effective in [16].

4 MODEL

On the basis of the data analysis in the previous section, we first extract the feature set based on the normalization of the social interaction data. With the obtained feature set, we then learn a ranking-based predictor for each user. Third, we present a generalization method to generalize the learned trust models to unknown users.

4.1 Feature Extraction

Given a user i and her online friend set F_i, for any $j \in F_i$:
r_{ij}^k is the number of type k interaction that user i receives from j; s_{ij}^k is the number of type k interaction that user i send to user j. Based on the definition, we have

$$r_{ij}^k = s_{ji}^k$$

The average number of type k interaction that j has received from all her friends is:

$$\bar{r}_j^k = \frac{\sum_{m \in F_j} r_{jm}^k}{|F_j|} \tag{1}$$

We use $\bar{r}_j^k$ to represent user j's activity level on type k interaction. A larger $\bar{r}_j^k$ indicates user j is more active in terms of the type k interaction. We thus normalize the outgoing interactions from i to j, by dividing the activity level of j. We use x_{ij} to represent the interaction vector (includes all types of interactions) from user i to j after normalization:

$$x_{ij} = \frac{s_{ij}}{\bar{r}_j} \tag{2}$$

The normalization vector x_{ij}, which has partially eliminate the interaction diversity caused by the user j's activity level, can better indicate the trust strength between user i and j than the original interaction vector.

4.2 Prediction Model

Given a user i and her social interactions, we aim to rank all her friends $j \in F_i$ by the trust strength, which is represented as a linear function:

$$a_{ij} = \begin{cases} w^T x_{ij} & j \in F_i \\ 0 & \text{otherwise} \end{cases} \tag{3}$$

where x_{ij} is the feature vector after interaction normalization from user i to her friend j. The advantages of adopting linear function are two folds: 1) we have normalized all the features, it is thus more reasonable to treat all the features in the same way (i.e. linearly); and 2) we can treat vector w as the weights of corresponding features,

which show a good explanatory power about the importance of different types of social interaction data in representing the trust strength.

As aforementioned, we consider that the ranking of trust relationship is much more valuable and practical than the concrete value, thus accordingly we aim to learn the best w which can minimize the occurrences of incorrect rankings through the rank-based optimization. Specifically, in our work, given a user i and her friends j and $k \in F_i$, we adopt the SVM-ranking [11] function:

$$\begin{aligned} \underset{w}{\text{minimize}} \quad & F(w) = C \sum \xi_{j,k} + \frac{1}{2}||w||^2 \\ \text{subject to} \quad & \forall (j > k) : w^T x_{ij} - w^T x_{ik} \geq 1 - \xi_{j,k} \\ & \xi_{j,k} \geq 0 \end{aligned} \tag{4}$$

where C is a constant. Because any two friends ($\in F_i$) of user i will constitute a user pair to be ranked, there will be $n(n-1)/2$ constraints for this optimization, where n is the number of i's friends.

Our problem can be further converted into the following non-constrained optimization problem:

$$\min_w \sum h \left[1 - y_{jk} \left(w^T (x_{ij} - x_{ik}) \right) \right] + \lambda ||w||^2 \tag{5}$$

where

$$y_{jk} = \begin{cases} +1 & w^T (x_{ij} - x_{ik}) > 0 \\ -1 & w^T (x_{ij} - x_{ik}) < 0 \end{cases} \tag{6}$$

and $h(\cdot)$ is the hinge loss function $\max(0, x)$, and $\lambda = \frac{1}{2C}$. This quadratic programming problem can be efficiently solved by solving its dual problem. Finally, we can obtain ranking-based trust predictors for each user to rank the friends in terms of trust strength.

4.3 Generalization Method

As our trust models are personalized ones, we can obtain at most 59 prediction models in our work. Therefore, it is naturally to consider that how to generalize the trust prediction models learned from the participants to other users, especially outside the user study? In this work, similar to most of the previous studies [4], to address the problem, our basic idea is that similar users will behave similarly in evaluating (or ranking) their friends. As discussed in Section 3.2, the trust value between two users are significantly correlated with the 12 types of interactions between them. In view of this, we argue that if two users have similar activity levels (measured by the interaction data) in terms of the interaction behavior, they are also probably to have similar ways of measuring trust in online social networks.

Particularly, we adopt the cosine coefficient of two users' activity levels (also referred as user character in the paper) to measure the similarity of these two users: given a new user i, we first calculate her character $\bar{r}_i$ based on the 12 types of interactions. Then, we search over the users with well-learned trust prediction models, and find the user having the highest cosine similarity with user i. We thus can generalize the trust prediction model of this user to user i.

5 EXPERIMENT

In this section, we conduct experiments to validate the effectiveness of the proposed model and the generalized method. Specifically, through the experiments, we aim to answer the following three questions:

(a) Can our proposed approach obtain a better performance than the benchmark approaches?

(b) Which type of the interaction behavior is more generally important for trust prediction?

(c) Is the generalization method effective in trust prediction for users with similar characters?

5.1 Experiment Setting

We use the standard 5-fold cross validation for training and testing. In our user study, some (of the 59 participants) indicate the trust values towards only a small set of their friends (not all friends), which might not be substantial for effective trust model learning. The cumulative distribution of users with different number of labeled friends are shown in Figure 8. In our experiments, to assure learning valid parameters for each trust model, we select 24 users who have labeled trust values of more than 8 friends, accounting for around 40% of all the participants.

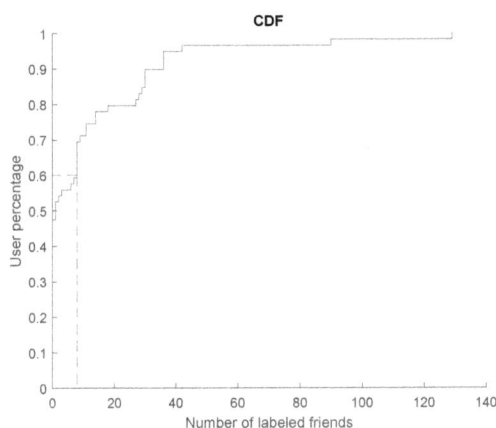

Figure 8: Cumulative distribution of users with labeled friends.

Besides, we use the ratio of correctly ranking pairs (i.e. r_c) as the metric to evaluate the performance of different approaches:

$$r_c = \frac{(\text{\# of correct ranking pairs})}{n(n-1)/2}$$

where n is the number of users in the testing set.

5.1.1 Benchmark Approaches. To evaluate the ranking performance of the proposed model, we compare it with the following approaches:

• Common Neighbors (CN) [17]: rank user pairs by the number of their common neighbors.

• Number of Interactions (IN): rank user pairs by the number of their interactions.

• Weighting [21]: manually assign weights for each interaction, and rank users based on the weighted sum of different interactions.

• Linear Model [7]: learn weights using the linear models and rank users based on the weighted sum of different variables.

• General Ranking: learn a global ranking prediction model for all users by the interactions and trust values, and the prediction model use the same optimization method in our model to learn the weights for different variables.

5.2 Results

In this section, we present the results in terms of the previous three questions respectively.

5.2.1 Performance Comparison. Table 3 shows the performance comparisons among different models regarding to the average ranking performance of all users.

Table 3: Performance comparison of our personalized ranking approach with benchmark approaches.

Feature	Performance	Improvement
Common Neighbors	0.567	22.57%
Interactions	0.585	18.80%
Weighting	0.593	17.20%
Linear Model	0.635	9.45%
General Ranking	0.616	12.82%
Personalized Ranking	**0.695**	––

As we can see, our personalized model performs much better than the other approaches. CN and IN do not perform well due to the weak correlation of the corresponding variable with trust, but IN gets a better performance than CN, indicating that the number of interactions is a better indicator for trust measurement than the number of common neighbors. Besides, Weighting performs better than CN and IN, which shows the effectiveness of jointly considering different types of interaction behavior, and the better performance of linear model over Weighting demonstrates the advantage of learning approach over ad-hoc models. Meanwhile, the outperforming of our personalized ranking over the general ranking approach further verifies the personalized property of trust measurement.

5.2.2 Feature Importance Analysis. As previously discussed, the learned weight vector w can represent the importance degrees of different types of interaction behavior. Generally speaking, a positive weight indicates that friends more frequently interacting in corresponding way should be ranked higher. And, for each individual user's trust prediction model, a larger positive weight value of a specific interaction type indicates a more importance position of this interaction behavior in ranking the individual's friends. In each trust prediction model for the 24 users, we order the 12 types of interaction behavior by the corresponding weight coefficients, and the number of each feature that has appeared in the top 1 and top 3 most important list respectively are shown Table 4.

As can be seen, photo related features, like "photo comments", "tag photos", and "co-tag" are more influential and important for personalized trust prediction. This is mainly because that it takes much efforts for users to involve these kinds of photos related interaction activities. The results also imply that in the future study,

Table 4: Top Feature statistics

Feature	Top1	Top3
Inbox Messages	1	3
Photo Comments	6	20
Photo Likes	1	3
Album Comments	2	5
Album Likes	1	2
Tag Photos	4	13
Photos Tagged	1	4
Tag Photo Comments	3	7
Tag Photo Likes	0	2
Co-tag	3	6
Status Comments	2	5
Status Likes	0	2

we can take the efforts that users have taken in different types of interaction behavior into consideration for effective personalized trust measurements.

5.2.3 Generalization Ability. We adopt leave-one-out strategy to test the performance of our generalization method. Specifically, as we have 24 personalized trust models for 24 users, given a user A and other 23 candidate users, we choose the prediction model of the user from the 23 users having the highest cosine similarity with user A with respect to their activity levels to rank friends of user A. In total, we have 24 trials, and Figure 9 shows the distribution of the generalization performance of these experiments.

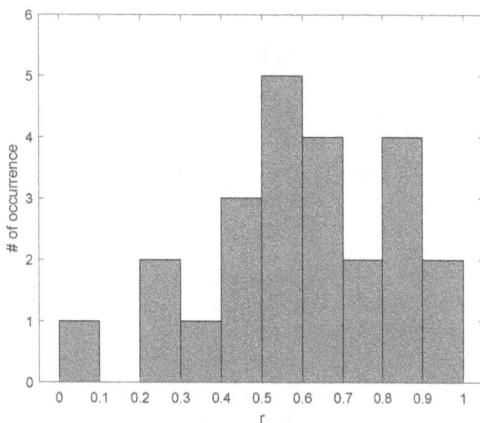

Figure 9: Generalization performance distribution.

We can see that the performance varies in a range of [0.08, 1], and the average performance of these 24 trials is 0.59, indicating the relative effectiveness of our generalization method. We further check the correlation between character similarity and the generalization performance, and the Pearson coefficient is 0.59, validating the soundness of the idea that similar users in terms of activity levels also behave similarly in measuring trust values. As shown in Figure 10, the average generalization performance steadily increases as the threshold of cosine similarity for choosing

effective prediction model in our experiments increase. Therefore, in practical applications, to build effective trust prediction model, a platform can firstly divide all users in the platform into a number of groups in terms of their activity levels, and then for each group of users, it can strive for building an effective trust model by only labeling a small number of data samples as the form of the dataset in this work.

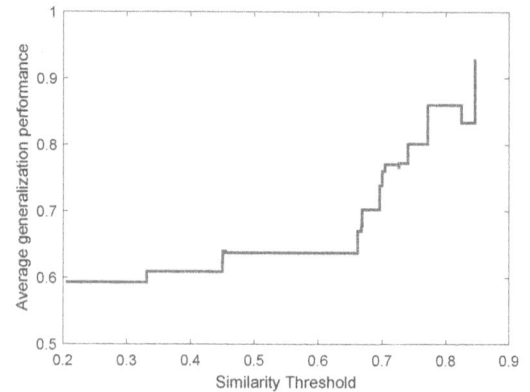

Figure 10: Average generalization performance with different similarity thresholds.

6 CONCLUSIONS AND FUTURE WORKS

In this paper, we proposed a personalized trust model for each individual user to rank her friends according to the trust strength of their social relationships. Specifically, we collect a unique dataset from Facebook, including a set of users' social interaction data and their trust towards their friends. Via a ranking-oriented optimization function, we learned each user's preferences on social interactions with respect to trust measurement on their friends. Besides, we also propose a generalization method to infer the trust network of new users other than the ones in our user study. Experiments show that our model outperforms the existing approaches on trust prediction, and also demonstrate the effectiveness of our generalization method, which has far-reaching implications for real-world applications.

For the future work, we will collect more social data to further verify the effectiveness of our approach. We will also explore our model in other types of OSNs like professional networks LinkedIn. Furthermore, we will consider to design a practical prediction framework for measuring trust strength for all user types (in terms of their activity levels) in online social networks.

7 ACKNOWLEDGMENTS

This work is supported by the MOE AcRF Tier 1 funding awarded to Dr. Jie Zhang (M4011261.020 and M4011894.020), and by the National Natural Science Foundations of China NSFC-71601104 and the Basic Academic Discipline Program for Shanghai University of Finance and Economics awarded to Dr. Hui Fang.

REFERENCES

[1] Beulah Alunkal, Ivana Veljkovic, Gregor Von Laszewski, and Kaizar Amin. 2003. Reputation-based grid resource selection. *Proceedings of AGridM* (2003), 432–438.
[2] bigthink.com. 2017. Do You Have Too Many Facebook Friends? http://bigthink.com/praxis/do-you-have-too-many-facebook-friends. (2017).
[3] Min Chen, Zhu Liang, Bo Zhang, Zhihao Zheng, Yong Yang, XIAO Keke, Yanqiang Zheng, Xiao Xu, GUO Runzeng, LIN Shuyang, et al. 2013. Method, system and server for managing friends' feed in network. (Jan. 3 2013). US Patent App. 13/611,180.
[4] Hui Fang, Guibing Guo, and Jie Zhang. 2015. Multi-faceted trust and distrust prediction for recommender systems. *Decision Support Systems* 71 (2015), 37–47.
[5] Adam D Farmer, CEM Bruckner Holt, MJ Cook, and SD Hearing. 2009. Social networking sites: a novel portal for communication. *Postgraduate medical journal* 85, 1007 (2009), 455–459.
[6] fb.com. 2018. Facebook Reports Fourth Quarter and Full Year 2017 Results. https://investor.fb.com/investor-news/press-release-details/2018/Facebook-Reports-Fourth-Quarter-and-Full-Year-2017-Results/default.aspx. (2018).
[7] Eric Gilbert and Karrie Karahalios. 2009. Predicting tie strength with social media. In *Proceedings of the SIGCHI conference on human factors in computing systems*. ACM, 211–220.
[8] Jennifer Golbeck and James Hendler. 2006. Inferring binary trust relationships in web-based social networks. *ACM Transactions on Internet Technology (TOIT)* 6, 4 (2006), 497–529.
[9] Dijiang Huang and Vetri Arasan. 2010. On measuring email-based social network trust. In *Global Telecommunications Conference (GLOBECOM 2010), 2010 IEEE*. IEEE, 1–5.
[10] Roberto Interdonato and Andrea Tagarelli. 2016. To trust or not to trust lurkers?: Evaluation of lurking and trustworthiness in ranking problems. In *International Conference and School on Network Science*. Springer, 43–56.
[11] Thorsten Joachims. 2002. Optimizing search engines using clickthrough data. In *Proceedings of the eighth ACM SIGKDD international conference on Knowledge discovery and data mining*. ACM, 133–142.
[12] Audun Jøsang, Roslan Ismail, and Colin Boyd. 2007. A survey of trust and reputation systems for online service provision. *Decision support systems* 43, 2 (2007), 618–644.
[13] Xiaoming Li, Hui Fang, and Jie Zhang. 2017. A Feature-based Approach for the Redefined Link Prediction Problem in Signed Networks. In *The 13th International Conference on Advanced Data Mining and Applications*.
[14] Xiaoming Li, Hui Fang, and Jie Zhang. 2017. Rethinking the Link Prediction Problem in Signed Social Networks. In *The Thirty-First AAAI Conference on Artificial Intelligence*. 4955–4956.
[15] Xiaoming Li, Hui Fang, and Jie Zhang. 2018. FILE: A Novel Framework for Predicting Social Status in Signed Networks. In *The Thirty-Second AAAI Conference on Artificial Intelligence*.
[16] Xiaoming Li, Qing Yang, Xiaodong Lin, Shaoen Wu, and Mike Wittie. 2016. Itrust: interpersonal trust measurements from social interactions. *IEEE Network* 30, 4 (2016), 54–58.
[17] David Liben-Nowell and Jon Kleinberg. 2007. The link-prediction problem for social networks. *journal of the Association for Information Science and Technology* 58, 7 (2007), 1019–1031.
[18] Guanfeng Liu, Yan Wang, Mehmet A Orgun, et al. 2010. Optimal Social Trust Path Selection in Complex Social Networks. In *AAAI*, Vol. 10. 1391–1398.
[19] Jan Overgoor, Ellery Wulczyn, and Christopher Potts. 2012. Trust Propagation with Mixed-Effects Models.. In *ICWSM*.
[20] Diego Perna and Andrea Tagarelli. 2017. An Evaluation of Learning-to-Rank Methods for Lurking Behavior Analysis. In *Proceedings of the 25th Conference on User Modeling, Adaptation and Personalization*. ACM, 381–382.
[21] Vedran Podobnik, Darko Striga, Ana Jandras, and Ignac Lovrek. 2012. How to calculate trust between social network users?. In *Software, Telecommunications and Computer Networks (SoftCOM), 2012 20th International Conference on*. IEEE, 1–6.
[22] Daniele Quercia, Stephen Hailes, and Licia Capra. 2007. Lightweight distributed trust propagation. In *Data Mining, 2007. ICDM 2007. Seventh IEEE International Conference on*. IEEE, 282–291.
[23] Andrea Tagarelli and Roberto Interdonato. 2014. Lurking in social networks: topology-based analysis and ranking methods. *Social Network Analysis and Mining* 4, 1 (2014), 230.
[24] Bimal Viswanath, Alan Mislove, Meeyoung Cha, and Krishna P Gummadi. 2009. On the evolution of user interaction in facebook. In *Proceedings of the 2nd ACM workshop on Online social networks*. ACM, 37–42.
[25] Jason Wiese, Jun-Ki Min, Jason I Hong, and John Zimmerman. 2015. You never call, you never write: Call and sms logs do not always indicate tie strength. In *Proceedings of the 18th ACM conference on computer supported cooperative work & social computing*. ACM, 765–774.
[26] Qing Yang and Honggang Wang. 2015. Toward trustworthy vehicular social networks. *IEEE Communications Magazine* 53, 8 (2015), 42–47.
[27] Guangyu Yin, Fan Jiang, Shaoyin Cheng, Xiang Li, and Xing He. 2012. Autrust: A practical trust measurement for adjacent users in social networks. In *Cloud and Green Computing (CGC), 2012 Second International Conference on*. IEEE, 360–367.
[28] Justin Zhan and Xing Fang. 2011. A novel trust computing system for social networks. In *Privacy, Security, Risk and Trust (PASSAT) and 2011 IEEE Third Inernational Conference on Social Computing (SocialCom), 2011 IEEE Third International Conference on*. IEEE, 1284–1289.
[29] Cai-Nicolas Ziegler. 2009. On propagating interpersonal trust in social networks. In *Computing with Social Trust*. Springer, 133–168.

Kindness is Contagious: Study into Exploring Engagement and Adapting Persuasive Games for Wellbeing

Ana Ciocarlan
University of Aberdeen
Aberdeen, UK
ana.ciocarlan@abdn.ac.uk

Judith Masthoff
University of Aberdeen
Aberdeen, UK
j.masthoff@abdn.ac.uk

Nir Oren
University of Aberdeen
Aberdeen, UK
n.oren@abdn.ac.uk

ABSTRACT

Intentional engagement in positive activities, such as practicing kindness, showing generosity or expressing gratitude, can help people increase their happiness levels and improve their wellbeing. In this paper we explore how a gamified digital behaviour change intervention can be adapted to encourage people of different personality types to engage in simple acts of kindness. Participants were assigned 5 daily activities for 7 days, and asked to complete as many as possible by the end of each day. Participants received different persuasive notifications every day to encourage them to complete a higher number of activities. We investigated how participation levels are influenced by different personality types, different persuasive message types and different categories of activities. Furthermore, we analysed the influence of the intervention on participant behaviour and the effect on behavioural intention, by comparing pre-intention and post-intention to perform different kinds of positive activities. The findings from this study have implications for future work on personalising persuasive interventions to improve wellbeing and prevent mental health problems.

CCS CONCEPTS

• **Human-centered computing** → User studies; • **Applied computing** → **Computer games**;

KEYWORDS

Persuasive Technology, Persuasive Games, Adaptation, Personality, Kindness, Wellbeing, Engagement

ACM Reference Format:
Ana Ciocarlan, Judith Masthoff, and Nir Oren. 2018. Kindness is Contagious: Study into Exploring Engagement and Adapting Persuasive Games for Wellbeing. In *UMAP '18: 26th Conference on User Modeling, Adaptation and Personalization, July 8–11, 2018, Singapore, Singapore.* ACM, New York, NY, USA, 9 pages. https://doi.org/10.1145/3209219.3209233

1 BACKGROUND

The number of students in UK Universities who require mental health care is increasing very rapidly and the problems they experience are becoming more and more complex [1]. Approximately 75% of students experience high levels of psychological distress, manifesting in the forms of intense stress, anxiety, depression and loneliness [1, 24]. This can lead to numerous health complications and have a major negative influence on student confidence and academic performance. It is therefore critical that students receive appropriate support tailored to their needs throughout their academic journey. However, mental health support services in Universities are struggling to meet the overwhelming rising demand for care provision [10]. As a result, preventive models that target the reduction of risk factors and enhancement of protective factors, as well as initiatives which focus on proactive responses, promoting general wellbeing, are highly desirable solutions [36].

Persuasive interventions help motivate, shape and reinforce beneficial behaviours, as well as support individuals in avoiding and reducing the negative impact of risk factors [8]. While digital behaviour change interventions can be delivered using various approaches, persuasive games have attracted attention in recent research work, due to their strong motivational pull [30]. Persuasive games are very interactive and require active engagement from participants, which can increase the emotional quality of the intervention [25] and act as an incentive to keep users engaged with the intervention [16]. An increasing number of persuasive games have been developed in recent years as novel solutions for motivating healthier behaviours, such as encouraging physical activity and balanced nutrition [2, 13, 14, 34].

Despite the growing interest in persuasive games, there remains a need for further research into their application in the wellbeing domain and design of games which promote happiness. Interventions which use gamification may facilitate the integration of preventive models and enhance current proactive strategies. Technology for wellbeing can promote initiative and self-care, empower individuals and improve self-management skills.

Approximately 54% of students who experience mental ill health feel nervous about receiving care and do not seek support from their institution or local practitioners [1]. Thus, a digital persuasive game would allow a larger number of individuals to access support remotely and would facilitate early detection of symptoms, reducing time costs and financial expenses for mental healthcare providers.

Our wider research project investigates the design of a persuasive intervention for preventing mental health problems and improving subjective wellbeing [4]. The intervention will use persuasion to encourage engagement in meaningful, achievable and enjoyable activities, that increase happiness and help individuals manage stressors effectively. Our work is inspired by positive psychology research, as described in [18], and focuses on adapting happiness-inducing activities, which suit user values and interests. Recent work shows that positive activities are effective in increasing happiness and reducing negative emotions [31]. A number of studies investigated how happiness is influenced by engaging in positive activities, such as writing letters to express gratitude [17], practicing optimism [15], or performing acts of kindness [7, 20]. Park et al. [28] used fMRI to investigate the neural link between generosity and happiness. In their experiments, participants in two groups received a weekly sum of money. The first group verbally committed to be generous and use the money for others, while the second group was instructed to be generous only towards themselves. Participants who behaved generously showed significantly more activity in brain areas associated with happiness and reward compared to the second group. Furthermore, the amount of generosity did not correlate directly with the level of happiness, and even small acts and intentions appear to have a positive impact.

In this paper we present the results of a study which investigates how a gamified persuasive intervention can encourage random acts of kindness and the effect of different personality traits and persuasive messages on participant engagement levels. The findings from our study will inform the design of our larger studies to investigate persuasive game-based interventions for subjective wellbeing.

2 STUDY DESIGN

We designed a digital persuasive intervention to encourage simple kind acts that increase happiness. The aim of this experiment was to investigate how participation levels are influenced by different personality types, different persuasive messages and different activities. We also wanted to explore how persuasive interventions affect behavioural intention to engage in different positive activities. This study builds on our previous findings in a small-scale offline pilot study [5] and related work in personalising persuasive messages and activities. For example, it has been found that adapting messages and strategies to personality may impact persuasiveness [12, 27, 32, 33], and we have done some initial qualitative research on how to adapt activity complexity to personality, stress level and attitude [6]. Moreover, this study investigates multiple persuasive messages, building for example on the work by Vargheese et al [35].

The study was conducted over a period of 7 days, with participants being assigned 5 activities each day. All daily activities involved performing simple acts of kindness and were centered around 5 key categories that inspire positivity and promote wellbeing: being positive, being generous, expressing gratitude, being friendly and self-kindness. A different persuasive message was shown to participants every day to encourage the completion of a higher number of activities. Therefore, activity category and message type were within-subject variables. A pre-questionnaire and post-questionnaire were also completed by the participants, as well as daily questionnaires in which participants rated the activities and described their experiences in more detail. Participants' pre-intention and post-intention to perform random acts of kindness pertaining to the key categories were also evaluated.

2.1 Research Questions

The study was designed to investigate the following research questions:

(1) How do different personality types influence participant engagement?
(2) How do different persuasive message types influence participant engagement?
(3) How do different activity categories influence participant engagement?
(4) What is the impact on behavioural intention?
(5) What is the impact on subjective wellbeing?

2.2 Participants

A total of 45 unique participants took part in the experiment (17 females and 28 males, age ranges between 20 and 63 years old). Participants' geographical territories of origin were Asia and Pacific (2 participants), Africa South of the Sahara (2 participants), The Middle East and North Africa (1 participant) and Europe (40 participants). Participants were recruited using social media platforms. Participants reported that they generally played phone or computer games a few times per year (7 participants), a few times per month (4 participants), once per week (5 participants), a few times per week (8 participants), every day (15 participants) and almost never (6 participants). Participants were not offered any monetary payment or reward to take part in this study.

Participants were assigned to 2 different groups and these groups received different persuasive messages during Day 4 and Day 5 of the experiment. Group A was shown messages which used the social comparison strategy and set out group goals. Group B was shown messages which used the self monitoring strategy and set out individual goals. Participants were not told which groups they were assigned to. Participants were assigned randomly generated usernames and took part in the study anonymously. However, given some participants shared offices and the public nature of some of the activities, participants may have become aware of the identity of other participants. This may have had some influence, which we tried to minimise by participants not knowing they have been distributed into groups. Additionally, some participants knowing the experiment leader, and hence the source of the persuasive messages, could have had an impact (see [23] on the impact of the source of persuasive messages). We ensured these participants were distributed evenly over the groups. Table 1 shows the demographics of the participants.

Table 1: Participants' demographics and division into groups

Group	Participants			Goal Type	Strategy
	Total	Males	Females		
A	22	13	9	Group Goal	Social Comparison
B	23	15	8	Individual Goal	Self-Monitoring

2.3 Materials

An online platform was developed to facilitate running this experiment. After creating their accounts, participants could login to view their daily activities and create microposts to communicate anonymously with other participants and complete activities. Figure 1 shows the design of the platform and how participants interacted. A total of 35 activities were created to be assigned to participants for the duration of the study. Table 2 shows the activities for each day of the experiment. Participants received 5 activities every day, representing the 5 different categories reflected in Table 4. Participants were rewarded with 10 points for each activity they completed.

A set of persuasive messages were developed to encourage participants to complete more activities. Numerous persuasive strategies have been identified to influence behavioural determinants, in order to promote behaviour change. For example, Fogg [8] has developed 7 persuasive approaches, Cialdini [3] has developed 6 principles of persuasion, and Oinas-Kukkonen [26] built upon this work to identify 28 persuasive system design principles. Furthermore, Michie et al. [22] have recognised 93 techniques for promoting behaviour change. The messages for this study were created based on the 6 principles of persuasion developed by Cialdini [3]. On Day 4 and Day 5 participants received different messages depending on which group they belonged to. Table 3 shows a list of the persuasive messages used in the study.

We used social comparison and self monitoring strategies on Day 4, as well as group goals and individual goals during Day 5. Social comparison is a strategy which allows participants to compare their performance with others and setting group goals allows participants to work towards a shared objective. This strategy was chosen as it has been increasingly used in interventions, as humans feel motivated to perform better if they are competing with their peers [8]. Self-monitoring provides the means for participants to track their progress and builds on self-understanding. This strategy was selected as Health Interventions that combine self-monitoring with other persuasive strategies (e.g. setting goals) have been shown to be more effective than other types of interventions [21].

2.4 Procedure

Participants were told that the purpose of this experiment is to investigate what influences engagement and intention in a gamified persuasive intervention that promotes simple acts of kindness. Consent forms and information sheets were provided and participants were informed that taking part in the study was voluntary and that they could withdraw at any time, for any reason. All materials produced by the participants were stored securely. Ethical consent for our experiments was obtained from the Physical Sciences and Engineering ethics board at the University of Aberdeen.

2.5 Pre-Questionnaire

After collecting demographic information, participants were asked to describe their happiness level on a scale from 1 (not very happy) to 7 (very happy) at the time of completion. The Subjective Happiness Scale [19] was used to measure the subjective wellbeing of the participants. We were interested to learn about the participants' pre-intentions for performing random acts of kindness. We asked questions about their intention for performing 10 different positive activities reflecting the selected 5 key categories (as described in Table 4). In the final section we assessed participants' level of gratitude, using the VIA scale [29], as well as level of altruism (sub-scale

of Agreeableness) and friendliness (sub-scale of Extraversion) using the NEO-PI-R inventory [11]. Participants completed the TIPI scale [9] to determine their personality.

2.6 Daily Questionnaires

The activities became available each day at 12:00 PM UK Time and were reset the next day. Some of the activities could only be completed by creating microposts on the online platform, while others could be completed in any other way participants found suitable. An email reminder was sent to participants early in the afternoon to prompt them to login to the online platform and complete activities. A different persuasive message was shown to participants. At the end of each day, participants filled in a short questionnaire describing their experiences. Participants rated their happiness levels at the time of completion. Each completed activity was rated by participants as detailed in Figure 2. If participants did not a complete a certain activity, they were asked to explain why.

2.7 Post-Questionnaire

In the post-questionnaire, participants were asked to describe their intentions to engage in positive activities and acts of kindness in the future. Participants were asked to comment on what influenced them to complete activities for the duration of the study. Finally, we measured participants' post behavioural intention to perform the 10 activities described in Table 4 in the upcoming 2 weeks.

3 RESULTS

A total of 1193 activities were completed during the experiment (187 activities on Day 1, 174 activities on Day 2, 166 activities on Day 3, 170 activities on Day 4, 169 activities on Day 5, 152 activities on Day 6 and 175 activities on Day 7). Participants engaged with the intervention and used the social feature to communicate with other participants. During the experiment participants created a total of 294 microposts to share their experiences and complete activities that were assigned to them.

3.1 Q1: Influence of personality types

To analyse the influence of different personality types we investigated the relationship between conscientiousness (how orderly, responsible, dependable one is), agreeableness (how good natured, cooperative, trustful one is) and extraversion (how talkative, energetic, assertive one is), and the total activities participants completed from the different categories[1]. We focused on the agreeableness and extraversion traits as some activities involved interaction with others and helping people. We found a strong correlation between conscientiousness and the total number of activities completed. Conscientiousness is moderately correlated to all the categories of activities. This suggests that participants high in this personality trait may not require as many reminders to complete activities as other people. We also identified a positive moderate correlation between agreeableness and activities completed from the friendliness category. Individuals with high levels of agreeableness tend to complete more activities that involve interactions and being friendly towards others. As a result, the intervention could be designed to

---

[1]Given participants had little variation in their scores for Gratitude, Altruism and Friendliness we did not use these results in our analysis.

Figure 1: Design of the Kindness is Contagious online social platform

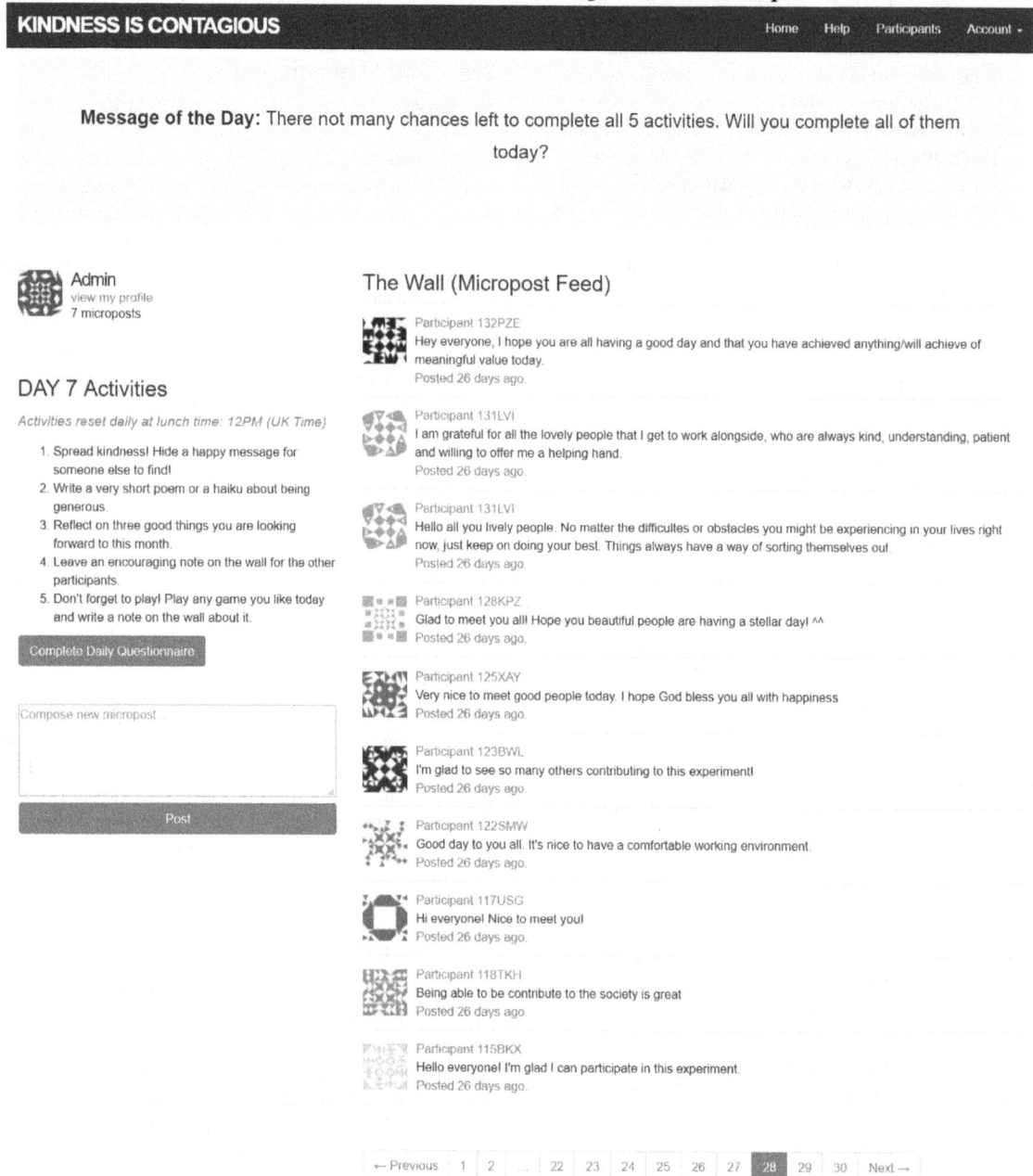

Figure 1: Design of the Kindness is Contagious online social platform

adapt to people high in agreeableness to assign more activities from the friendliness category and persuade them to complete activities from other categories as well. Additionally, we identified a weak negative correlation between extraversion and the number of activities completed. Participants with high extraversion complete less activities, especially if these belong to the self-kindness category. The results are shown in Table 5.

Our results indicate that the influence persuasive messages have differs based on the personality traits of an individual. People high in the conscientiousness trait are more persuaded by messages which use the authority principle, followed by messages using the scarcity principle. For those with high agreeableness, the most effective messages were the ones using the commitment and scarcity principles. However, people high in extraversion seem to be negatively influenced by persuasive messages which use the social proof or reciprocity principle. Table 6 shows the correlations between different personality traits and activities completed for each persuasive message.

Table 2: Activities

Day	Activity type				
	Positivity	Generosity	Gratitude	Friendliness	Self-Kindness
1	Write an uplifting note on the wall addressed to all the other participants.	Offer to make someone you know a hot drink.	Write a note on the wall about one thing you are grateful for in your work.	Ask someone how they are today.	Go on a 10 minute walk and observe the world around you.
2	Smile at 3 different people today.	Volunteer to help someone you know with a small task.	Say thank you to a friend who has been kind to you.	Talk to friend you have not talked to recently.	Write a note on the wall with a compliment for yourself. You deserve it!
3	Don't forget to laugh! Write a funny joke on the wall! (Remember to be respectful to all other participants.)	Share your favourite book with a friend. Write a note on the wall with its title and author.	Write a note on the wall about one thing you are grateful for today.	Give a hug to one of your friends.	Eat one of your favourite fruit today!
4	Collaborate with the other participants to write a positive story on the wall. You can contribute as many times as you wish, but you must contribute exactly 5 words each time.	Make a nice drawing and gift it to one of your friends.	Write a thank you card addressed to a teacher. You do not have to send it, but you can if you like!	Send an honest compliment to one of your friends!	Play your favourite song! Enjoy it, sing along, dance or simply listen to it with all your heart.
5	Notice the positive qualities of everyone you meet today.	Share a dessert with someone!	Send someone a message to let them know how much they mean to you.	Make a plan to meet up with your friends and do something fun!	Drink at least one glass of water!
6	Give as many sincere compliments as possible today! Write a note on the wall with the number of compliments you gave.	Learn something new and share it with others. It does not have to be complicated! For example, it can be something as simple as a few words in a different language.	Look around you and notice 5 things that are beautiful. Write a note on the wall to tell us what you observed.	Ask a friend about things they have enjoyed recently and actively listen.	Take a deep breath, stretch and think a happy thought!
7	Spread kindness! Hide a happy message for someone else to find!	Write a very short poem or a haiku about being generous.	Reflect on three good things you are looking forward to this month.	Leave an encouraging note on the wall for the other participants.	Don't forget to play! Play any game you like today and write a note on the wall about it.

We also investigated the relation between personality traits and improvements in behavioural intention, but found no significant correlations. A moderate correlation was found between agreeableness and the pre-intention to complete acts of kindness (r = .452, p<0.01), as well as a weak correlation for extraversion and pre-intention (r = .356, p<0.05). It is interesting to note that people with high extraversion report good intentions to perform acts of kindness, but actually complete fewer kind activities.

3.2 Q2: Influence of persuasive message types

We compared the number of activities completed in each day to investigate the effect of different message types. Table 7 summarizes the mean and standard deviation in changes of participation for the 7 days of the study. Overall, we observed a slow, gradual

decrease in participation over time, which could be explained by time constraints. A high number of activities was completed on the final day of the study, which could show the effect of the scarcity persuasive message used to encourage participants. When asked why they have not completed some of the activities on certain days, participants generally reported having other personal or work commitments: "I completely ran out of time" (P108EBT), "I had a very busy day at my job today and I forgot about it" (P102POY), "I was out all day, so I couldn't do it. (P101FTI)". Figure 3 shows the distribution of completed activities based on the different persuasive messages.

On Day 4 and Day 5 participants received different messages based on the group they were assigned to. Table 8 shows the means and standard deviations of activities completed by the two groups.

Table 3: Persuasive Messages (SOP = Social Proof; AUT = Authority; COM = Commitment; REC = Reciprocity; LIK = Liking; SCA = Scarcity)

Day	Message
1	Welcome to the Kindness is Contagious Study!
2 (SOP)	Congratulations! Most participants have completed all 5 activities on Day 1! How many will you complete today?
3 (AUT)	Did you know? Experts suggest taking part in at least 5 kind activities a day. Will you complete all 5 activities today?
4 (COM)	(Group A) You have already complete many activities until now and are in the Top 5 Leaderboard! Let's see if you can keep up or improve your performance and complete all 5 activities today! (Group B) You have already completed many activities until now! Yesterday you did very well! Let's see if you can keep up or improve your performance and complete all 5 activities today!
5 (REC)	(Group A) If all participants complete 150 activities today, everyone will receive 50 extra points! (Group B) If you complete all 5 activities today, you will receive 50 extra points!
6 (LIK)	You are amazing and are making great progress completing acts of kindness! This cute puppy asks you to complete all 5 activities today!
7 (SCA)	There not many chances left to complete all 5 activities. Will you complete all of them today?

Table 4: Target Behaviours promoting Kindness

Category	Behaviour
Positivity	I will try to cheer others up; I plan to encourage others;
Gratitude	I plan to express my thanks to those who have been kind to me; I intend to reflect on things I am grateful for in my life;
Generosity	I intend to volunteer to help someone with a small task; Made a spontaneous nice gesture for someone;
Friendliness	I intend to have meaningful conversations with someone; I will try to listen to someone share their emotions and experiences;
Self-Kindness	I intend to take time for myself to enjoy the things I love; I plan to be kind to myself by eating well and exercising.

While, the groups were influenced to complete more activities overall, there are no significant differences between the two. Further investigation is required to determine the effects of social comparison, self-monitoring, group goals and individual goals.

In the post-questionnaire participants wrote qualitative comments to describe what motivated them to complete more activities. Participants indicated that they enjoyed the activities and felt positive emotions completing them (P102POY: "It made me feel good!"; P148BIJ: "To make me feel happier and more confident."; P142JAE: "I thought it would be fun to try them out."; P101FTI: "The joy I see

Figure 2: Daily Questionnaire for Completed Activities

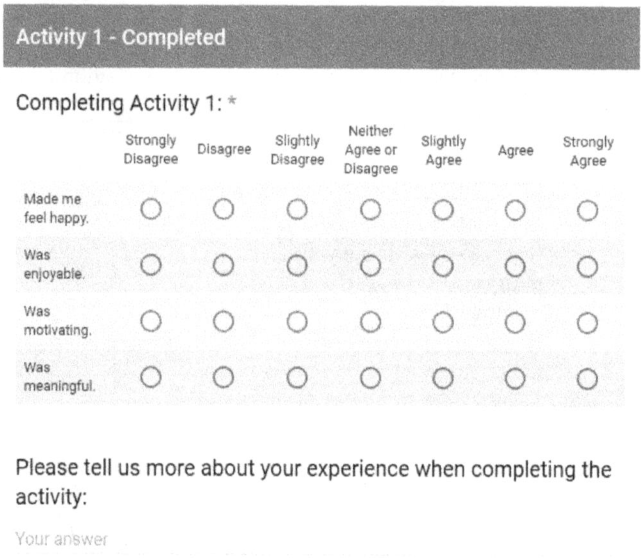

Figure 3: Distribution of Completed Activities

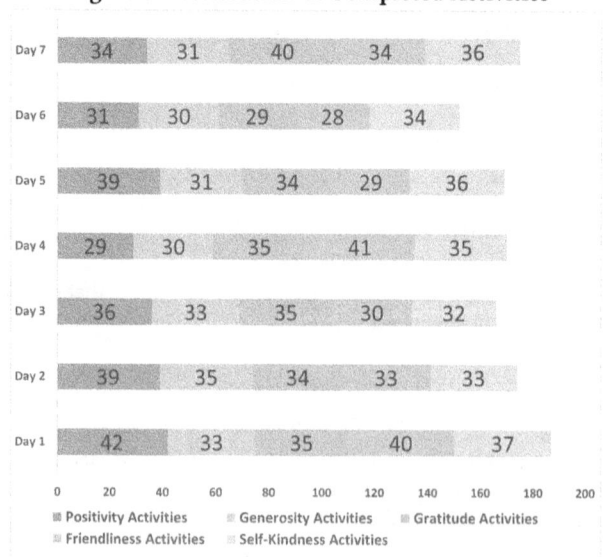

Table 5: Correlations between Personality and Activities Completed (* = p<0.05; ** = p<0.01; *** = p<0.001;)

	Total Activities	Positivity	Generosity	Gratitude	Friendliness	Self-Kindness
Conscientiousness	0.712***	0.641***	0.563***	0.586***	0.600***	0.525***
Agreeableness	0.462***	0.385**	0.432**	0.434**	0.595***	0.98
Extraversion	-.288*	-.122	-.229	-.199	-.218	-.362*

Table 6: The influence of different persuasive messages on different personality traits (* = p<0.05; ** = p<0.01; *** = p<0.001; SOP = Social Proof; AUT = Authority; COM = Commitment; REC = Reciprocity; LIK = Liking; SCA = Scarcity)

	Day 1	Day 2 (SOP)	Day 3 (AUT)	Day 4 (COM)	Day 5 (REC)	Day 6 (LIK)	Day 7 (SCA)
Conscientiousness	0.292*	0.530***	0.381**	0.421**	0.382**	0.389**	0.431**
Agreeableness	-0.060	0.375**	0.108	0.499***	0.277	0.210	0.430**
Extraversion	-0.291*	-0.316*	-0.169	-0.035	-0.295*	-0.067	-0.002

Table 7: Means and Standard Deviations for number of activities completed

	Mean (SD)	Total Activities
Day 1	4.16 (1.24)	187
Day 2 (SOC)	3.87 (1.53)	174
Day 3 (AUT)	3.69 (1.55)	166
Day 4 (COM)	3.78 (1.24)	170
Day 5 (REP)	3.76 (1.65)	169
Day 6 (LIK)	3.38 (1.99)	152
Day 7 (SCA)	3.89 (1.61)	175
Total	27 (6.17)	1193

Table 8: Group Comparison

	Mean (SD)	
	Group A	Group B
Activities Completed on Day 4	3.64 (1.43)	3.91 (1.04)
Activities Completed on Day 5	3.86 (1.73)	3.65 (1.61)

and how enjoyable, motivating and meaningful the activities were. We averaged the ratings provided to determine participants' appreciation for different categories of activities. A reliability analysis was carried out and Cronbach's alpha for the 4 items of appreciation showed high reliability, $\alpha = .90$. In general, participants highly appreciated the activities assigned to them and indicated that they provided them with a feeling of happiness and meaningfulness. Table 10 shows the relationship between the number of completed activities and the appreciation for each of the categories.

Table 9: Means and standard deviations for total activities completed from different categories

	Positivity	Generosity	Gratitude	Friendliness	Self-Kindness
Mean (SD)	5.56 (1.29)	4.96 (1.59)	5.38 (1.53)	5.22 (1.40)	5.40 (1.79)

Table 10: Correlations of number of activities completed and participant appreciation for different categories (* = p<0.05; ** = p<0.01; *** = p<0.001)

	Positivity	Generosity	Gratitude	Friendliness	Self-Kindness
Appreciation	0.483***	0.262	0.294*	0.339*	0.290*

in others and thinking how nice it would make me feel if someone did the same."). Some participants mentioned the game elements of the intervention influenced them to be more involved (P140NPA: "The points made me feel accomplished."; P128KPZ: "The score, and the fact that I am a completionist."; P131LVI: "In a weird way it felt like a game, and I already said how competitive I get with games. But also each activity I did complete was fun and at the end of the day I did feel more happy and had a more positive attitude.").

3.3 Q3: Influence of activity categories

Overall, participants completed similar numbers of activities belonging to different categories. The categories with the most completions recorded were positivity (250 activities), self-kindness (243 activities) and gratitude (242 activities). Table 9 shows the means and standard deviations for completed activities in each category. Participants rated the activities for how happy they made them feel

People also differ in which activities they prefer to do, as shown in the number of times they completed the activity and the appreciation they provided for the activities they completed. For example, participant P111FVK, did a total of 7 self-kindness activities, showed a high appreciation for this category, and only completed 3 generosity activities and showed a low appreciation for this type. Partially this may be personality related and partially this seems related to interests. Some participants indicated that they did not complete certain activities because they did not align with their perceived skills, what they like to do or what captivates them. This is also clear from participants' qualitative comments (P111FVK: "I DO NOT SMILE!", "Not enthused by drawing, actually hate drawing"; P134GMN: "Not really a book person and I have no favourite books in memory"; P145WKP: "I rarely hug friends"; P108EBT: "Not an artist"; P137VRU: "I cannot draw!"; P142JAE: "I'm horrible at drawing and it makes me stressed instead of happy to do it"). Participants also expressed their interests and values directly when creating microposts to complete activities, which may contribute to the development of user models.

3.4 Q4: Impact on behavioural intention

Overall, behavioural post-intention shows an increase from the baseline pre-intention, suggesting that a gamified persuasive intervention can encourage people to perform more acts of kindness. We used Paired Samples t-tests to compare the behavioural pre-intention and post-intention to perform the different categories of activities. Overall, there was a significant average difference between pre-intention and post-intention scores (t(44) = 5.568, p < 0.001). On average, post-intention scores were .906 points higher than pre-intention scores (95% CI [.578, 1.234]). Figure 4 shows the means of the pre-intention and the post-intention to perform acts of kindness pertaining to the activities categories.

In the post-questionnaire participants indicated that they intend to reflect on their experiences from the experiment and continue performing acts of kindness in the future (P102PY: "This experiment made me realise the beauty of the little things in everyday life. Thank you! I will try to be more kind every day."; P135FBM: "This study has reminded me of the importance of doing this - It's beneficial to both givers and receivers and I will aim to incorporate this more into my lifestyle"; P149MZQ: "I feel this makes the world a better place and so I will endeavor to follow up on my increased motivation to do kindness activities, having participated in this study.") Most participants expressed their intention to be more kind, generous and appreciative of others around them (P101FTI: "I intend to take more time for others and be more careful to recognise their merits"; P102POY: "I will be more attentive to those around me"; P108EBT: "It does make you feel good so even if it's just smiling at someone I am going to make a effort to be more kind in

the future"). A small number of participants said that due to time constraints they might not engage in as many acts of kindness in the near future as they might like to (P148BIJ: "I am unfortunately on a very busy schedule and I will not be able to dedicate time to do good things in general"; P131LVI: "I usually get so immersed in my work, that when I do have free time I feel very sluggish and tired, and then end up feeling bad because I didn't do something meaningful with my time. I realise though that I shouldn't let myself get consumed by my work and neglect doing meaningful things that make me happy, so I'm going to make en effort to do more enjoyable activities, regardless of how small they might be").

3.5 Q5: Impact on subjective wellbeing

At the end of the study participants showed an increase from the baseline level of wellbeing reported in the beginning. This suggests that a digital intervention to encourage acts of kindness can have a positive effect on people's levels of happiness and wellbeing. A Paired Samples t-test was used to evaluate the the the reported before and after wellbeing states of the participants. We found a significant average difference between the scores (t(44) = 4.673, p < 0.001). Participants reported wellbeing scores which were on average 0.522 higher than those reported in the beginning (95% CI [.297, .747]. Participants appreciated taking part in the study and being encouraged to perform more acts of kindness. This is reflected by qualitative comments left by participants in the post-questionnaire (P108EBT: "Thank you for making me smile more over the last 7 days."; P115BKX: "I think the activities in this project should become a lifestyle for everyone, for me, for sure. Thanks for reminding me about some of the values in life." P128FRZ: "Thank you for this great activity, which made me aware of opportunities of kindness."; P140TRI: "I liked this experiment, it was nice to see others are getting involved in acts of generosity and kindness.").

4 CONCLUSIONS AND FUTURE WORK

Our findings in this study help us conclude that different personality types influence engagement in positive activities and small acts of kindness. They also show that people may differ in their preferences for activity types and individual activities. The results regarding message type were less conclusive, and further investigations is necessary, independent of the day on which a message is shown. The findings provide us with an indication of how behavioural intention and level of wellbeing can be improved by engaging with the persuasive intervention. The novel design of our intervention allows us to conduct valid self assessment in support of objective behavioural outcomes to measure the effectiveness of different strategies and messages for different personality types. Based on our results, a behaviour change intervention could adapt the persuasive messages and activity categories to user personality and interests.

Future work could explore how behavioural intention changes over time, and the effect on actual participant behaviour after taking part in the intervention. Additionally, a new study could investigate whether the messages produced by the participants during the intervention can elicit positive emotions in a reader, thus contributing to the overall improvement in levels of subjective wellbeing. Finally, while the study showed that personality mattered for engagement and provided some evidence for the impact of user preferences,

Figure 4: Behavioural Pre-Intention and Post-Intention

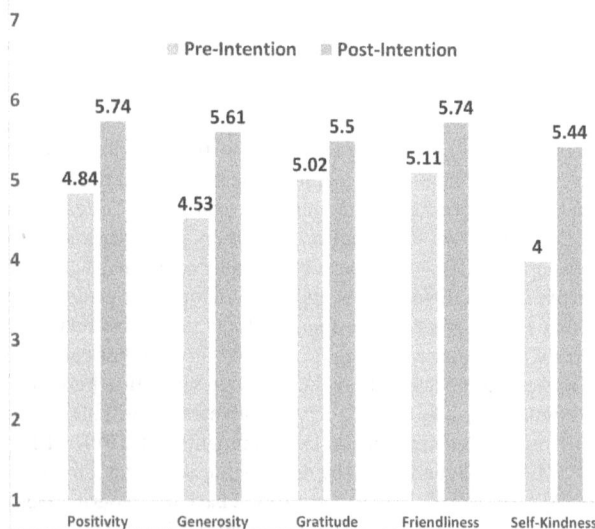

further work is needed to investigate the impact of any adaptations of the intervention to these aspects. Also, the most effective way of eliciting user preferences and personality types needs to be investigated.

ACKNOWLEDGMENTS

The authors would like to acknowledge and thank all the volunteers who participated in the experiment and provided helpful comments. The first author is funded by an EPSRC doctoral training grant.

REFERENCES

[1] All-Party Parliamentary Group (APPG) on Students. 2015. NUS Survey on Mental Health. *"Lost in transition? - provision of mental health support for 16-21 year olds moving to further and higher education"* (2015).
[2] Magnus Bang, Carin Torstensson, and Cecilia Katzeff. 2006. *The PowerHhouse: A Persuasive Computer Game Designed to Raise Awareness of Domestic Energy Consumption.* Springer Berlin Heidelberg, 123–132.
[3] Robert Cialdini. 1991. *The Psychology of Influence and Persuasion.* NY Quill, NY.
[4] Ana Ciocarlan. 2017. Adapting persuasive games for wellbeing. In *International Conference on Persuasive Technology Adjunct Proceedings.*
[5] Ana Ciocarlan, Judith Masthoff, and Nir Oren. 2017. Kindness is Contagious: Exploring Engagement in a Gamified Persuasive Intervention for Wellbeing. In *Proceedings of the Positive Gaming: Workshop on Gamification and Games for Wellbeing, ACM SIGCHI Annual Symposium on Computer-Human Interaction in Play (CHI PLAY 2017).*
[6] Ana Ciocarlan, Judith Masthoff, and Nir Oren. 2017. Qualitative Study into Adapting Persuasive Games for Mental Wellbeing to Personality, Stressors and Attitudes. In *Adjunct Publication of the 25th Conference on User Modeling, Adaptation and Personalization (UMAP '17).* ACM, New York, NY, USA, 402–407. https://doi.org/10.1145/3099023.3099111
[7] E.W. Dunn, L.B. Aknin, and M.I. Norton. 2008. Spending money on others promotes happiness. *Science* 319 (2008), 1687–1688.
[8] B. J. Fogg. 2003. *Persuasive Technology: Using computers to change what we think and do.* Morgan Kaufmann, San Francisco.
[9] S. D. Gosling, P. J. Rentfrow, and W. B. Jr. Swann. 2003. A Very Brief Measure of the Big Five Personality Domains. *Journal of Research in Personality* 37 (2003), 504–528.
[10] HEFCE. 2015. Understanding provision for students with mental health problems and intensive support needs. (2015).
[11] J. A. Johnson. 2014. Measuring thirty facets of the Five Factor Model with a 120-item public domain inventory: Development of the IPIP-NEO-120. *Journal of Research in Personality* 51 (2014), 78–89.
[12] Maurits Kaptein, Panos Markopoulos, Boris De Ruyter, and Emile Aarts. 2015. Personalizing persuasive technologies: Explicit and implicit personalization using persuasion profiles. *International Journal of Human-Computer Studies* 77 (2015), 38–51.
[13] Pamela M. Kato, Steve W. Cole, Andrew S. Bradlyn, and Brad H. Pollock. 2008. A video game improves behavioral outcomes in adolescents and young adults With cancer: a randomized trial. *Pediatrics* 122, 2 (2008), e305–e317.
[14] Rilla Khaled, Pippin Barr, James Noble, Ronald Fischer, and Robert Biddle. 2007. *Fine Tuning the Persuasion in Persuasive Games.* Springer Berlin, 36–47.
[15] Laura King. 2001. The Health Benefits of Writing about Life Goals. *Personality and Social Psychology Bulletin* 27 (2001), 798–807.

[16] Pal Kraft, Filip Drozd, and Elin Olsen. 2009. ePsychology: Designing Theory-Based Health Promotion Interventions. *Communications of the Association for Information Systems* 24, 24 (2009).
[17] Sonja Lyubomirsky, R. Dickerhoof, J.K. Boehm, and K.M. Sheldon. 2011. Becoming happier takes both a will and a proper way: an experimental longitudinal intervention to boost well-being. *Emotion* 11 (2011), 391–402.
[18] Sonja Lyubomirsky, Laura King, and Ed Diener. 2005. The Benefits of Frequent Positive Affect: Does Happiness Lead to Success? *Psychological Bulletin* 131, 6 (2005), 803–855.
[19] Sonja Lyubomirsky and H. Lepper. 1999. A measure of subjective happiness: Preliminary reliability and construct validation. *Social Indicators Research* 46 (1999), 137–155.
[20] Sonja Lyubomirsky, Kennon Sheldon, and David Schkade. 2005. Pursuing happiness: The architecture of sustainable change. *Review of General Psychology* 9, 2 (2005), 111–131.
[21] S. Michie, C. Abraham, C. Whittington, J. McAteer, and S. Gupta. 2009. Effective techniques in healthy eating and physical activity interventions: a meta-regression. *Health Psychology* 28, 6 (2009), 690–701.
[22] Susan Michie, Michelle Richardson, Marie Johnston, Charles Abraham, Jill Francis, Wendy Hardeman, Martin P. Eccles, James Cane, and Caroline E. Wood. 2013. The Behavior Change Technique Taxonomy (v1) of 93 Hierarchically Clustered Techniques: Building an International Consensus for the Reporting of Behavior Change Interventions. *Annals of Behavioral Medicine* 46, 1 (01 Aug 2013), 81–95.
[23] Hien Nguyen and Judith Masthoff. 2007. Is it me or is it what I say? Source image and persuasion. *Persuasive Technology* (2007), 231–242.
[24] Nightline Association. 2014. Psychological Distress in the UK Student Population: Prevalence, Timing and Accessing Support. (2014).
[25] Donald A. Norman. 2003. Emotional Design: Why We Love (Or Hate) Everyday Things. (2003).
[26] Harri Oinas-Kukkonen and Marja Harjumaa. 2008. A systematic framework for designing and evaluating persuasive systems. In *Persuasive Tech. Conf.* 164–176.
[27] Rita Orji, Regan L. Mandryk, and Julita Vassileva. 2017. Improving the Efficacy of Games for Change Using Personalization Models. *ACM Trans. Comput.-Hum. Interact.* 24, 5, Article 32 (Oct. 2017), 22 pages. https://doi.org/10.1145/3119929
[28] Soyoung Q. Park, Thorsten Kahnt, Azade Dogan, Sabrina Strang, Ernst Fehr, and Philippe N. Tobler. 2017. A neural link between generosity and happiness. *Nature Communications* 8, 15964 (2017).
[29] C. Peterson and M. E. P. Seligman. 2004. *Character strengths and virtues: A handbook and classification.* New York: Oxford University Press.
[30] Scott Rigby and Richard M. Ryan. 2011. *Glued to Games: How Video Games Draw Us in and Hold Us Spellbound.*
[31] N. L. Sin and Sonja Lyubomirsky. 2009. Enhancing well-being and alleviating depressive symptoms with positive psychology interventions: a practice-friendly meta-analysis. *Journal of Clinical Psychology* 65 (2009), 467–487.
[32] Kirsten A Smith, Matt Dennis, and Judith Masthoff. 2016. Personalizing reminders to personality for melanoma self-checking. In *Proceedings of the 2016 Conference on User Modeling Adaptation and Personalization.* ACM, 85–93.
[33] Rosemary Josekutty Thomas, Judith Masthoff, and Nir Oren. 2017. Adapting Healthy Eating Messages to Personality. In *International Conference on Persuasive Technology.* Springer, 119–132.
[34] Debbe Thompson, Tom Baranowski, Richard Buday, and et al. 2010. Serious Video Games for Health How Behavioral Science Guided the Development of a Serious Video Game. *Simulation & Gaming* 41, 4 (2010), 587–606.
[35] John Paul Vargheese, Somayajulu Sripada, Judith Masthoff, and Nir Oren. 2016. Persuasive Strategies for Encouraging Social Interaction for Older Adults. *International Journal of Human Computer Interaction* 32, 3 (2016), 190–214.
[36] World Health Organization. 2005. Prevention of Mental Health Disorders. (2005).

Modeling and Predicting News Consumption on Twitter

Claudia Orellana-Rodriguez
Insight Centre for Data Analytics
School of Computer Science
University College Dublin, Ireland
claudia.orellana@insight-centre.org

Mark T. Keane
Insight Centre for Data Analytics
School of Computer Science
University College Dublin, Ireland
mark.keane@ucd.ie

ABSTRACT

While much is known about how people tweet and interact on Twitter, surprisingly little is known about how the news items tweeted by journalists – *news tweets* – act as a distribution channel for the news that is spread by social media reading and sharing. This paper aims to fill this gap by analyzing the dynamics of news on Twitter, by revealing what drives users to consume news, and by developing a news consumption prediction model. We present the Twitter News Model (TNM), a computational data-driven approach to elucidate the dynamics of news consumption on Twitter. We apply the TNM to a dataset of interactions between users and journalists/newspapers to reveal *what* drives users' consumption of news on Twitter, and predictively relate users' news beliefs, motivations, and attitudes to their consumption of news. Our findings reveal that news motivations, followed by news attitudes and news beliefs, impact users' behavior of news consumption on Twitter.

CCS CONCEPTS

• **Human-centered computing** → **Web-based interaction**;

KEYWORDS

News consumption, digital journalism, social media, audience engagement, news, twitter

ACM Reference Format:
Claudia Orellana-Rodriguez and Mark T. Keane. 2018. Modeling and Predicting News Consumption on Twitter. In *UMAP '18: 26th Conference on User Modeling, Adaptation and Personalization, July 8–11, 2018, Singapore, Singapore.* ACM, New York, NY, USA, Article 4, 9 pages. https://doi.org/10.1145/3209219.3209245

1 INTRODUCTION

Daily newspaper reading and the viewing of national TV news, have been traditionally correlated with a civic obligation to stay informed about current events [21]. For older people, the daily habit of following the news and this civic sense seems to have persisted as news has moved online and onto social media. For younger people, news consumption has, perhaps, become a more personalized activity to gather information about events that directly affect them

or, more a matter of social interaction, as they use news items in online conversations with friends and colleagues [1].

For news providers, it is critically important to understand the dynamics of news consumption in this new social media context. They need to understand the beliefs, motivations and attitudes that drive news consumption in social media users. Such insights should allow news providers to better serve their audiences and motivate future news consumption [24]. Indeed, users who read the news on social media often play an important role in modern journalism, not only as direct consumers, but also as gatekeepers, with almost half the social media users sharing and reposting news stories, images, or videos, and discussing news issues or events online [4]. Also, journalists who post/share their news and interact with social media audiences, can use their knowledge of such factors to influence people's satisfaction [17], which may in turn, have a positive impact in news consumption.

Social media is a particular environment in which news consumption is not a passive activity, but rather one in which users interact with news providers, form communities, express their interests, ask questions, or request more information, via mechanisms such as shares, likes/dislikes, retweets, or mentions.

Figure 1 illustrates some of these dynamics of news consumption, as seen in the interactions of an Irish Twitter audience with 200 journalistic accounts. Each graph represents news audiences (nodes in gray), journalists (nodes in color), and their interactions (edges from news audiences to journalists nodes). The larger the node, the more interactions it has received. We have labeled the top-10 journalists/news outlets in each graph, according to the number of interactions received from the audience. In Figure 1a, the edges represent the news audience mentioning journalists in their tweets. Corporate accounts such as *@Independent_ie*, *@rtenews*, *@IrishTimes*, and *@thejournal_ie* receive most of the audience mentions; however, individual accounts including political journalist *@gavreilly* and sports journalist *@MiguelDelaney*, receive considerable attention as well. In terms of retweets (see Figure 1b), corporate accounts *@rtenews* and *@IrishTimes* receive the bulk of them, with political journalists *@gavreilly*, *@Oconnellhugh*, and *@colettebrowne* also being important targets of audience retweets.

Overall, Irish news audiences tend to interact (i.e., mentions+retweets) more with corporate and political journalists (see Figure 1c).

In this paper, we propose the *Twitter News Model (TNM)*, a computational data-driven approach to predict and explain people's consumption of news by analyzing their interactions with journalists and news-tweets. Our *Twitter News Model (TNM)* is based on the Motivational Consumption Model (MCM) [19] previously developed to better understand the consumption of "conventional" news. We apply the TNM to an empirical study of news consumption on Twitter, designed to (i) reveal *what* drives users to consume

UMAP '18, July 8–11, 2018, Singapore, Singapore
© 2018 Association for Computing Machinery.
ACM ISBN 978-1-4503-5589-6/18/07...$15.00
https://doi.org/10.1145/3209219.3209245

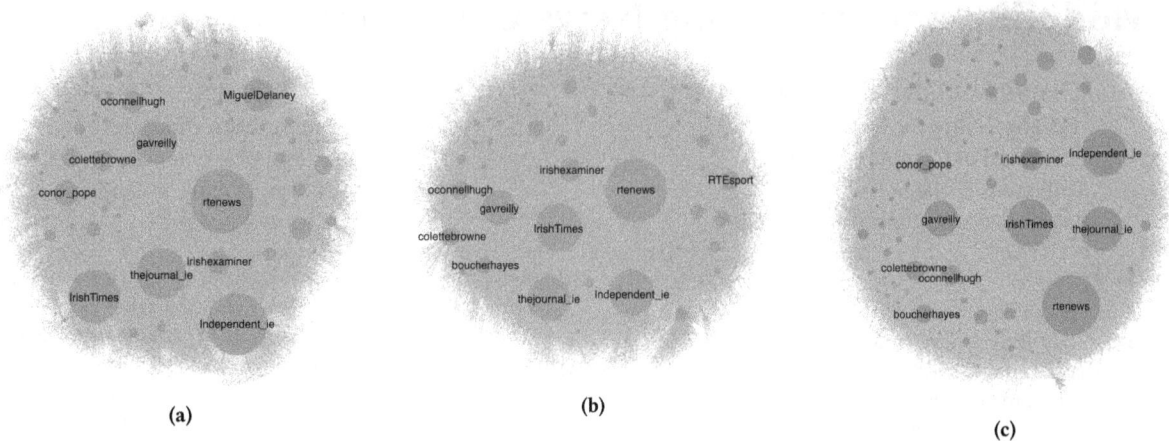

(a)   (b)

(c)

Figure 1: Dynamics of news audiences' interactions with journalists on Twitter. Gray nodes represent the audience and colored nodes represent journalists. Each edge represents a member of the audience (a) mentioning a journalist, (b) retweeting a journalist's tweet, and (c) overall interacting (mentioning + retweeting) with a journalist. The nodes' sizes are proportional to the number of (a) mentions, (b) retweets, and (c) overall interactions they received. On each figure, we have labeled the top-ten most popular Twitter accounts according to the corresponding metric.

news, and (ii) predictively relate users' news beliefs, motivations, and attitudes to their consumption of news.

In the next section we review related work (Section 2), before presenting the theoretical background (Section 3), instantiating our Twitter-specific model for news consumption (Section 4), and predicting news consumption on Twitter (Section 5). We conclude our work and discuss future directions in Section 6.

2 RELATED WORK

Previous work has analyzed the dynamics of news consumption in social media from different angles, be it by exploring the perception of news, by modeling users' engagement with news articles and trust in news providers, or by studying how news is shared.

Perception of news. Users' perception of news may affect their decision on whether or not to read or share news stories. In Reddit, news stories with titles that have been modified by users are more popular (i.e., receive more votes and more comments) than those with their original title [12]. In Twitter and Facebook, which have different demographics of readers, the same news headline may exhibit different patterns of shares [35]. This fact suggests a correlation between demographics and news perception [31]. In Twitter, political news stories that are negative, short, and with high emotional load, tend to receive more shares from the audience [6]. The perception of political news slant can also affect news consumption. Users belonging to a community (i.e. that are connected to each other), tend to consume similar news articles, and these articles have been found to exhibit political slants [18].

Users' engagement with news. The characteristics of a news item and the type of interaction between users and news providers that can signal audience engagement, have also been an ample subject of study. Wu and Chen [37] found that the frequency of interactions between Twitter users and news sources is an indicator of news being perceived as popular, and Keneshloo et. al [15, 16], using social, contextual, and temporal features of Twitter users

who share news stories, found that the freshness of a news story is one of the most important factors in predicting its page views. In our previous works [28, 29], we explored whether Twitter users engage with news differently depending on the news category (e.g., sports vs. politics), and found that what attracts people's attention differs considerable. For example, Irish audiences tend to share sports news-tweets when these contain mentions (i.e., *@user*), and the source is a well known journalist. While for business news, the timeliness of news-tweets has a higher impact on engagement.

Trust in news providers. When deciding on whether or not to consume a given news item, the trust that users have in other users, particularly in news providers, may be of great importance. In [5], Choi et al. explored how customers' trust in content is influenced by the content's source. The authors show that User Generated Content has a stronger effect on cognitive trust, than Marketeer Generated Content. De Meo et al. [22, 23] studied how trust relationships can be leveraged to identify those users producing the most helpful content for a community; and that trust is a crucial factor to keep stable levels of user engagement within a group.

News sharing. In online social media, news audiences are active participants of the news distribution cycle, as they can disseminate and spread news to their social networks. In [32], Reis et al. explored the relationship between demographics and news sharing in Twitter. Their findings reveal that male and white users tend to share more news, and that sharing rates vary according to the news category. For example, Asian female audiences are more inclined to share world and health news, while white male audiences focus more on science and technology news. Kalsnes and Larsson [14] analyze the sharing of news articles for four Norwegian news outlets in Facebook and Twitter. They found that people more frequently shared editorial comment pieces about soft news topics, but that depending on the news outlet, this can change, with sensational news and news involving celebrities becoming the center of attention. Bruns et al.'s [3] analysis of Australian news sharing in Twitter, reveals that for many users, the decision on sharing news is highly related to the popularity and credibility of the news source.

News consumption. An important body of research focuses not only on what news is shared or how users engage with news, but on *why* people consume news. Edgerly et al. [8] analyzed news consumption habits in young adults, and found that besides spending fewer total minutes consuming any news than any other age group, young adults nowadays consume less news than young adults 20 years ago. The authors also found that parents highly influence the news consumption habits of their children. Parents' news habits and reinforcement of news consumption can lead to children consuming more news themselves. For many users, news consumption is consequence of incidental finds [2], they get news on their mobile devices because they are constantly connected and not because they look for it. Following ideas from these previous works and, particularly, those introduced by Lee and Chyi in [19], we now present our approach to computationally modeling the psycho-behavioral factors of news consumption on Twitter.

3 MODELING NEWS CONSUMPTION

Our aim in this paper is to model news consumption on Twitter. Our starting point is the prior work that has modeled motivational aspects of human intention and specific models of news consumption in "conventional" news media. Hence, we explore a psychological theory (i.e., the Reasoned Action Model) that has been applied to the consumption of printed and digital news (i.e., Motivational Consumption Model). In this section, we review these previous models before discussing how they can be operationalized to the consumption of news on Twitter (see section 4).

3.1 Reasoned Action Model

Fishbein and Ajzen's Reasoned Action Model (RAM) [9] maintains that there are three main predictors of intention to engage in a behavior, namely attitude, social norms, and self-efficacy. *Attitude* deals with a person's orientation towards performing the behavior. *Social Norms* consider the normative pressure perceived by the person to perform a given behavior in context. *Self Efficacy* relates to the behavioral control the person perceives themselves to have over the target behavior. RAM has been used to understand specific situations where people have manifested intentions to act. For instance, in political science, the RAM has been used to model voters' attitudes towards candidates and political parties, and how these attitudes impact polls and subsequent voting behavior; in public health research, RAM has been used to understand the key beliefs that influence individuals' health care utilization [13].

3.2 Motivational Consumption Model

Lee and Chyi have adapted the RAM framework to understand news consumption in their Motivational Consumption Model (MCM) [19]. In the MCM, a variety of demographic factors are seen as influencing news consumption via the mediators of news beliefs, news motivations, and news attitudes.

This adapted model backgrounds the effects of RAM's social norms and self-efficacy. Social norms play less of a role in news consumption because of the broadly shared belief that it is one's responsibility to follow the news, to stay informed. Self-efficacy

also plays a lesser role as people can easily control their own news consumption given the ubiquitous access they have to news content via a variety of to-hand digital devices [19]. In their model, Lee and Chyi go on to describe and operationalize the three key mediators as follows:

– *News beliefs:* refer to the *value* that news has for people, that news can be conceived to be a means to empower and mobilize the public. These news beliefs were operationalized by 7-point Likert scale ratings of survey questions that asked participants (i) how important the news is to you, and (ii) whether being informed was empowering.

– *News motivations:* refer to the *reasons* driving people's consumption of news. For instance, some people consume news because it helps them keep up with current events that are topics of conversations in their social circle or it allows them to make informed decisions in their daily life; whereas others consume news as a source of entertainment. These news motivations were operationalized by combining ratings from five survey questions that asked participants whether they consumed news (i) to find out what is going on in the world, (ii) to keep up with the way your government functions, (iii) to make yourself an informed citizen, (iv) to gain important new information, and (v) to fulfill your need to know.

– *News attitudes:* reflect positive views of the news, that see news consumption as an enjoyable and advantageous behavior. These news attitudes were operationalized by survey questions that asked participants if they agreed with the following statements: (i) getting the news is enjoyable to you, and (ii) getting the news is advantageous to you.

In their survey, Lee and Chyi gathered data from a US-nationwide sample of 1.1K American adults that varied in several demographic features (e.g., gender, age, income, and race). The survey asked people about their news consumption – reading, watching, or listening – on several news sources, including *New York Times*, *CNN*, and *Google News*, in both traditional and digital formats. The responses were analyzed using a regression method. Based on the MCM, demographics such as age and education were found to positively influence news beliefs, and more positive news beliefs were found to lead to better news motivations and news attitudes, which in turn resulted in more frequent news consumption.

In the present paper, we adapt the Motivational Consumption Model to apply it to news consumption on Twitter, by developing new operationalizations of its mediators that were appropriate to this social media context.

4 NEWS CONSUMPTION ON TWITTER

Lee and Chyi applied their Motivational Consumption Model to the consumption of news found in newspapers (i.e., either printed or online), on news aggregators (e.g., *Google News*, *Yahoo News*), and on network Sunday talk shows [19]. The present paper aims to model news consumption on Twitter, which constitutes quite a different context. On Twitter, the dynamics of news consumption differ in that the users do not need to actively buy/access the news but rather browse their *timelines* at any time/place, and find news posts distributed (i.e., tweeted/retweeted) by Twitter accounts from followed journalists or newspapers, or that appear in the timeline because one or more of the other user's followees (e.g., family,

Mediator	Measure	Description
News Beliefs B	$B(u) = \begin{cases} 1, & \text{if } N_u \geq R_u \\ 0, & \text{otherwise} \end{cases}$	How valuable are news for user u?
News Motivations M	$\forall c \in C, M(u,c) = \frac{i_{uc}}{I_u}$	What motivates user u to consume news?
News Attitudes A	$A(u) = \frac{1}{N_u} \sum_{m_u} Polarity(m_u)$	What is user u's approach toward news?
News Consumption C	$C(u) = I_u$	How much does user u consume news in Twitter?

Table 1: New operationalizations for Twitter.

friends, or public figures) has tweeted or retweeted them. In this social media context, our conception of news beliefs, news motivations and news attitudes needs to be adapted with Twitter-specific instantiations of these notions. We will call our adapted model the Twitter News Model (TNM).

4.1 News Beliefs

News beliefs refer to the value that the news has for people (i.e., whether people find news to be important). In Twitter, users express the value that a news-tweet has for them by retweeting it, liking it, or mentioning the author of that tweet.

To quantify the value of news (B) to a Twitter user u, we use the proportion of retweets and mentions resulting from the interaction between the user and news-tweets, journalists, or newspapers. If a user u mentions journalists in her/his tweets more or as many times as she/he retweets news-tweets, then we can assume they value news on Twitter to a greater extent (see Equation 1).

$$B(u) = \begin{cases} 1, & \text{if } N_u \geq R_u \\ 0, & \text{otherwise} \end{cases} \tag{1}$$

where N_u is the total number of tweets in which user u has mentioned a journalist or a newspaper, and R_u is the total number of news-tweets that user u has retweeted, in the same period of time.

Mentions, in comparison to retweets, require more effort and time. Mentions help users create awareness of a tweet's author and even spread the author's tweets to new audiences, including non-followers, thus increasing diffusion. By mentioning a journalist or a newspaper, user u might help other users find more tweets from such accounts on a timely manner [36].

4.2 News Motivations

News motivations refer to the reasons that drive people to consume news (e.g., to become an informed citizen). In Twitter, these motivations can be operationalized by tracking how a user interacts with different news categories (e.g., a user who only interacts with tweets about sports may be mainly motivated by entertainment).

To quantify news motivations (M) for news consumption on Twitter, the observed interaction behavior of each user u with tweets/journalists for different news categories is computed as follows:

$$\forall c \in C, M(u,c) = \frac{i_{uc}}{I_u} \tag{2}$$

where C = {sci & tech, sports, politics, business, breaking news, lifestyle, corporate} represents the main content categories found

for news[1], i_{uc} is the total number of interactions (i.e., retweeting of a news-tweet and/or mentioning a journalist or newspaper) by user u in a particular news category c, and I_u is the total number of interactions (i.e., retweets and mentions) by user u across all news categories. $M(u,c)$ falls in the range of $[0,1]$ where 0 means user u did not interact with category c and 1 means that all interactions of user u were with category c.

It should be noted that using news categories to identify motivations is quite a coarse-grained approach, as precise motivations within a category may vary [19]. A user only interacting with lifestyle news might be motivated by reasons of entertainment or social interaction. A user interacting mostly with business or political news, may be looking to make specific business decisions or just to track broad societal changes. So, while using news categories gives us broad partitions of motivations, a more fine-grained analysis of these motives remains to be discovered. Finally, it should also be noted that the way users interact with the news, is known to vary by news category. For example, Irish Twitter users consuming sports news engage more with news-tweets that contain mentions, while those who engage with science and technology news are influenced more by the temporal arrival of the tweets [29].

4.3 News Attitudes

News attitudes refer to people's overall orientation to the consumption of the news (e.g., whether it is viewed as an enjoyable behavior). In Twitter, these attitudes can be operationalized by tracking the polarity of users' tweets. To quantify the news attitudes (A) of a user u to news consumption on Twitter, the following is computed:

$$A(u) = \frac{1}{N_u} \sum_{m_u} Polarity(m_u) \tag{3}$$

where $Polarity(m_u)$ is the polarity score (i.e., positive or negative) of each tweet in which user u mentions a journalist or newspaper, and N_u is the total number of tweets with mentions – of a journalist or a newspaper – posted by user u.

In our operationalization of news attitudes, we do not consider retweets, only the users' original tweets in which they mention journalists or newspapers. We make this distinction because news attitudes represent a person's tendency to react favorably towards the news [19]. Retweeting a news-tweet may signal users' interests; however, news-tweets are not tailored by the users themselves but rather by the source of the tweet (i.e., a journalist or a newspaper).

---

[1] A more detailed explanation on how we classify tweets into these categories can be found in Section 5.

Through mentions, a person can express themselves, in their own words, thus giving a better indication of their news attitudes.

4.4 News consumption

News consumption is generally measured by the frequency with which people read/watch/listen to news. In Twitter, we measure a user u's news consumption (C) by the number of interactions between the user and news-tweets, journalists and newspapers, which are defined as follows:

$$C(u) = I_u \qquad (4)$$

$$I_u = N_u + R_u \qquad (5)$$

where I_u is the number of interactions of user u, N_u is the total number of tweets in which user u mentions a journalist or newspaper, and R_u is the total number of news-tweets that user u retweeted.

We consider that both retweets and mentions give us an indication of the users' overall tendency to consume news. For example, by retweeting a news-tweet, a person may indicate interest in a topic or a specific news article, while by mentioning a journalist or a newspaper, a person may express an interest in the work of the journalist or the coverage of the newspaper. Therefore, we use these interactions as a proxy for news consumption.

In conclusion, Table 1 summarizes the components of the Twitter News Model (TNM) with its news beliefs, motivations and attitudes as they are characterized in the context of Twitter, along with a Twitter-specific definition of news consumption. In the next section, we describe how the TNM can be leveraged to predict and explain news consumption.

5 REALIZING THE TWITTER NEWS MODEL

In this section, we apply the proposed Twitter News Model (TNM) to a dataset of interactions between users and journalists/newspapers to elucidate the dynamics of news consumption on Twitter. Specifically, this empirical study is designed to (i) reveal *what* drives users' consumption of news on Twitter, and (ii) predictively relate users' news beliefs, motivations, and attitudes to their consumption of news on Twitter. We characterize the various components of the model – news beliefs, motivations and attitudes – and relate them to the computation of consumption.

Dataset. We collected all tweets posted by 200 manually curated Irish media sources and journalists accounts covering 79 different news outlets.[2] The accounts were selected to cover all major national and regional media outlets for Ireland, in addition to individual journalists writing for these outlets. From these 200 accounts, 117 are individual journalists' (31 female and 86 male) and 83 are corporate accounts. In addition, we collected all the retweets and mentions received by these 200 Twitter accounts. Previous work has shown that the use of Twitter for news in Ireland is broadly similar to that found in other western countries (e.g., the UK and France [28]). The data collection spans a period of four months from August 10th to December 10th, 2017. This period covers a series of news events including Hurricane Harvey, the North Korea's launch of missiles, and the Las Vegas shooting. In total, 16.6K users retweeted and/or mentioned one or more of the 200 journalists and

# News media accounts	200 (117 individual and 83 corporate)
# Interactions	352,500 (tweets with mentions and retweets)
# Users	16,683 unique users
Time period	from August 10th to December 10th, 2017

Table 2: Dataset statistics.

newspapers under study, producing a total of 352,500 ($\mu = 22$, $\sigma = 48$) interactions.

As our aim is to understand what makes audiences interact with news-tweets, journalists, and newspapers in Twitter, we focus on the 352.5K interactions (retweets and tweets with mentions) posted by the 16.6K users. We do not analyze the tweets posted, nor the interactions started by our 200 journalistic accounts.[3] Table 2 summarizes the main statistics of our Twitter corpus.

News Beliefs. News beliefs are defined in terms of user mentions of journalists and newspapers, more than merely retweeting their news-tweets (see Equation 1). In our corpus, we found a total of 52% (8.7K) of users who post at least as many tweets with mentions as they do retweets (i.e., $B(u) = 1$). Of these, 4.3% (713) of users post retweets and mentions in a 50/50 ratio.

Users mention journalists or newspapers for different reasons, including discussing topics of interest (e.g., *@IrishTimes Each year the housing prices rise. How do we rebuild at a rate of such increase? We can't. Stop housing...*), expressing opinions and concerns (e.g., *@gavreilly 2017 results at home terrible. Two draws and defeat from Wales, Austria and Serbia cost great chance to top the group*), or simply to establish conversations (e.g., *@MiguelDelaney Really great piece Miguel, fair play. I think the FAI need to import some bright minds from Germany...*). Users who mention news providers more often, spend time and put effort into tailoring their tweets, which could indicate that news (and its discussion), is valuable to them. The remaining 48% (7945) of users in our corpus, retweet more than they mention (i.e., $B(u) = 0$); and 54% (4330) of them do so with a retweets-mentions ratio of at least 80/20.

These findings indicate that for the majority of users in our dataset, news is important to the extent in which they feel the urge to not only spread tweets from journalistic sources, but to express their own opinions, post their own tweets, and become active participants in the discussion of news.

News Motivations. News motivations are what drive people to consume news. In order to better understand the reasons behind the news consumption for each user in our corpus, we separated her/his interactions (i.e., retweets + mentions) by news category.

Our model proposes that the proportion of interactions a user has with a given news category, indicates their motivation for consuming news. For example, if a user only retweets sports news-tweets and/or mentions sports journalists, then this indicates they are largely consuming news for entertainment purposes, in contrast to the motivations of a user that only interacts with news-tweets/journalists in the business category.

To identify the news category of the tweets posted by the users in our corpus, we followed the process described in [29]. We first

---

[2]We use Twitter streaming API. Every 30 minutes, the crawler collected the new tweets posted and received by these accounts of interest.

[3]Note, that our data collection only includes the interactions between users and journalistic accounts, during the time-period under study; these users' interactions with other users (i.e., non-journalists), were not collected.

News Category	Accounts
Business	13 (11%)
Lifestyle	15 (13%)
Breaking News	30 (26%)
Politics	25 (21%)
Science and Technology	6 (5%)
Sports	28 (24%)
Total	117

Table 3: News categories and corresponding number of individual journalists' accounts.

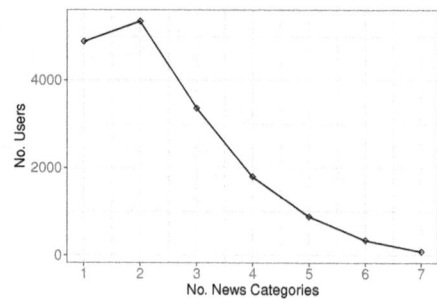

Figure 2: Audience vs. number of different news categories they interact with.

separated the 200 Twitter accounts into individual and corporate. Corporate accounts (e.g., *@Independent_ie*) post tweets that span all news categories, while individual accounts (e.g., *@conor_pope*) tend to focus on a specific area, such as sports or business. Three annotators judged the news category of each individual account based on (i) a random sample of 50 tweets sent by the individual journalist, and (ii) a list of the top-100 terms used by the journalist in her/his tweets during the period of interest. The news categories considered are business, lifestyle, science and technology, breaking news, politics, and sports.[4] We follow this human annotation approach, so we could obtain high quality labels that can be used as ground truth in related future tasks. The distribution of accounts across the six news categories is shown in Table 3. We group the remaining 83 Twitter accounts under a category that we will call *corporate*, as they cannot be classified under any specific news category. The Fleiss' Kappa inter-rater agreement over all news categories is $\kappa = 0.51$.

The interactions between a user and a news category were calculated as follows: if user u mentions a journalist or retweets a news-tweet from a journalist who belongs to news category c (e.g., sports), then we add 1 to user u's interactions with c. We follow the same procedure for all user u's tweets. We then normalize the total number of user u's interactions per category (i_{uc}) by the total number of user u's interactions over all news categories (I_u). We repeat this procedure for all users (U) in our corpus.

Using this analysis a number of interesting regularities can be found in the way users interact with news categories. Figure 2 shows the number of users in our corpus who interact with one or more news categories. Out of the 16.6K users, 4887 (29.3%) interact (i.e., retweet and mention journalists) solely with one news category. The three most popular categories among these users are corporate (3383 users only interact with corporate accounts), sports (1134 users), and politics (220 users). A further third of this audience (5350 or 32%) interacts exclusively with two news categories. The most popular pairs of news categories are corporate-sports (1882 users only interact with corporate and sports accounts, with 717 users interacting more with sports than with corporate accounts, and 1165 doing the opposite), corporate-politics (1847 users), and corporate-breaking news (843).

Of the remainder, 3358 (20.1%) of users interact with three different news categories. The most popular triplet for these users

is politics-corporate-breaking news (1074 users only interact with these three news categories). From four to seven news categories, we observe a sharp decrease in the number of users. Only, 1796 (10.8%) users interact with four news categories, 877 (5.3%) with five, 338 (2%) with six, and 79 (0.5%) with all the seven news categories.

These findings show that, for this user cohort, the majority of people who follow news on Twitter tend to interact with 1-3 news categories. Corporate accounts (e.g., *@Independent_ie*) seem to be a major focus of user attention and interactions, independently of the other specific news categories that a user follows. One possible reason for this behavior, may be that audiences in Twitter are consuming news as a source of general knowledge, and/or to keep up with events of public interest. Sport and politics are the two other news categories that receive considerable attention. This result evidences more niche interests, in which users have a news category of choice, that presumably fulfills more fine-grained motives such as entertainment (e.g., sports news), or keeping an up-to-date knowledge on government-related affairs (e.g., political news).

News Attitudes. News attitudes reflect users overall orientation to the consumption of news and, in our model is measured by extracting the polarity of the users' mentions (i.e., tweets in which users mention journalists or newspapers). This means that for a given user, we first need to determine the polarity of her individual tweets and then average the polarities of all her tweets. These aims were achieved in three steps: (i) all the tweets of concern were transformed into vector representations using a word-embedding technique, (ii) a polarity classifier was trained on a corpus of tweets with known polarities, (iii) this classifier was used to find the polarity score for each tweet of a given user and then these scores were averaged over all the user's tweets. Each of these three steps is detailed further as follows.

(i) Transforming tweets into word vectors. Several word-embedding techniques have been proposed to transform words into vector representations (e.g., *Word2Vec* [25], and *GloVe* [30]). The tweets of concern here were processed using GloVe, an unsupervised learning algorithm that provides a collection of word vectors pre-trained on 2B tweets/27B tokens [30]. These vectors are available in different dimensionalities: 25, 50, 100, and 200 dimensions.[5] Using the 200-dimension vectors, we found the GloVe for each word in a

---

[4]Note that the same news categories can have different names depending on the news provider, we show here particularly representative ones.

[5]https://nlp.stanford.edu/projects/glove/

tweet,[6] and averaged all these word vectors to obtain the overall tweet vector.

(ii) Training a polarity classifier. To train a tweet polarity classifier[7], we used the word vectors (i.e. GloVe) representation of the SemEval-2017[8] dataset [33] consisting of 19.9K tweets. These tweets were posted between 2013 and 2016 and had identified polarities: 8157 positive, 8101 negative, and 3079 neutral tweets. In training the classifier, only positive and negative tweets were used; we used upsampling on the negative tweets to ensure a balanced dataset (i.e., 8157 positive and 8157 negative tweets). The classifier was trained to predict the probability that a given tweet belonged to the positive class (i.e., the closer to 1 the more probable the tweet was positive, the closer to 0, otherwise). Using 5-fold cross validation, the final classifier had an average F1 measure of $F1 = 0.78$. The SemEval datasets are widely used for sentiment analysis tasks [7, 20, 34]. An interesting extension to polarity classification, would be to analyze the presence of other emotions known to be expressed in tweets, such as anger, joy, surprise, or sadness, as done in [26, 27].

(iii) Aggregating the polarity of a user's tweets. For each user u in our corpus, we extract the polarity for each individual tweet in which user u mentioned a journalist or a newspaper. As a final step, we average the polarity scores of all user u's tweets (i.e., tweets with mentions) and assign that average as the overall user's polarity.

Out of the 16.6K users in our corpus, 13,097 (78.5%) show a positive attitude ($A(u) \geq 0.5$) toward journalists and newspapers; of these users, 190 had a strongly positive polarity average ($A(u) > 0.8$). The remaining 3,578 (21.5%) users show an average attitude that is more inclined toward a negative polarity ($A(u) < 0.5$); of these users, 62 had a strongly negative polarity average ($A(u) < 0.2$). Although we find some news consumers to be more negative than positive, the majority of people show a positive attitude toward news and news providers.

News Consumption. News consumption is captured by the total number of interactions (i.e., retweets + mentions) that user u has with news-tweets, journalists, and newspapers. Here, we found that on average, each of our 16.6K users interacts 21.3 times ($\sigma = 48$) with news-tweets/news providers. Of these users, 508 (3%) interact 100 times or more, 9,303 (56%) users interact 10 times or less, and the remaining 6,874 (41%) of users interact between 11 and 99 times in the four-month period spanned by our data collection. These results show that 41% of the Twitter users in our dataset, turn to news on a regular basis. Some of these users tend to do so approximately once a day. A small group (3%), interacts with news tweets and/or news providers on average 4 times a day, with some users retweeting and mentioning as much as 13 times a day, on average. For more than half of our news consumers (56%), interacting with news-tweets and news providers seems to be more of an sporadic activity.

5.1 Predict & Explain News Consumption

Having captured the behavior of our news consumers using the Twitter News Model, we turn our attention to building a predictive

model to better understand the drivers of news consumption. We cast the news consumption prediction as a regression task in which our goal is to predict, based on users' features, their corresponding news consumption. Our aim is to train a machine learning regressor to predict the news consumption, which in our model corresponds to the *number of interactions (i.e., retweets + mentions)* between each user and news-tweets/news providers (cf. Section 4). We use the z-score of the users' interactions as our target variable.

User representation. Each user in our data collection is characterized using a feature vector. Users' features are extracted using three methods described as follows:

- *Twitter News Model (TNM).* We construct users' vectors using the TNM mediators; these are 9-dimensional vectors with one dimension for news beliefs (i.e., whether the user tends to mention more than retweet), seven for news motivations (i.e., one per each news category and one for corporate accounts), and one for news attitudes (i.e., the polarity score for the user).

- *Word-Embeddings (WE).* Using the same procedure described in Section 5, we construct feature vectors based on the content of the users' interactions. For each user, we averaged the GloVe word-embeddings [30] of her/his retweets and mentions to obtain a 200-dimensional vector that is fully based on the content of the user's tweets.[9]

- *Twitter News Model+Word-Embeddings (TNM+WE).* Vectors combining the Twitter News Model and the word-embeddings representations of the tweets. This results in vectors of 209 dimensions: 9 from the TNM and 200 from the word-embedding representations.

Experimental setup. We split our data into training and test sets using an 80%/20% ratio. We explore three different regression models, namely Random Forest (RF) [11], Gradient Boosting Trees (GBT) [11], and Extremely Randomized Trees (ET) [10] and grid-search their best hyperparameters using 10% of the training set for validation. We conduct 25 rounds of experiments and measure the prediction quality of our models using the *Mean Squared Error (MSE)* metric. The results reported are the average MSE on the test set over the 25 rounds. Based on this exploration, the model that exhibits the best predictive performance for all three user representations is Extremely Randomized Trees (ET),[10] and therefore, the one chosen for our task. ET fits a number of randomized decision trees on various sub-samples of the dataset and uses averaging to improve the predictive accuracy and control over-fitting. The best hyperparameters found for our task are 1000 estimators (n_estimators=1000) and a minimum of 3 samples required to be at a leaf node (min_samples_leaf=3).

We train three separate ET regression models, one per each set of features extracted, namely TNM, WE, and TNM+WE. Figure 3 shows each model's average MSE, whose values correspond to 0.587 for TNM, 0.439 for WE, and 0.433 for TNM+WE.

Interpretability vs. predictive power. As we observe from Figure 3, the model trained using the TNM features has the highest error. In terms of predictive power, the Word-embeddings and TNM+Word-embeddings models are better. However, the model based on the Twitter News Model has one overriding benefit; namely, that it is fully interpretable, in that we know the semantics of the

---

[6]If the word does not have a GloVe representation, we set to 0 all the 200 dimensions of the corresponding vector

[7]scikit-learn.org/stable/modules/generated/sklearn.ensemble.RandomForestClassifier.html

[8]SemEval (Semantic Evaluation) is an ongoing series of evaluations of computational semantic analysis systems, organized under the umbrella of SIGLEX, the Special Interest Group on the Lexicon of the Association for Computational Linguistics.

[9]Unlike in the calculation of News Attitudes (Section 5), these vectors also take into account users' retweets, not just their original tweets with mentions.

[10]scikit-learn.org/stable/modules/generated/sklearn.ensemble.ExtraTreesClassifier.html

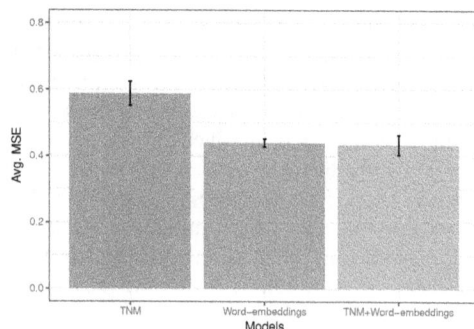

Figure 3: Average MSE values for the different models in predicting news consumption, showing 95% confidence intervals (as these are error values, the lower the better).

corresponding TNM feature. Notably, the hybrid TNM+WE model, combines WE's predictive power with TNM's interpretability, allowing us to produce predictions of comparable quality (to those produced by the WE model alone), while identifying the meaningful features that explain these predictions. We cannot obtain the same interpretability from the WE model on its own given its nature, i.e., lack of semantics of the word embeddings.

From our hybrid model (TNM+WE), we extracted the features that were most important (to the ET regressors) in the prediction of news consumption. Interestingly, the top-2 features are TNM's news motivations, specifically, users' interaction with the news categories business and breaking news. In rank 3, we find a content feature (i.e., from the word-embeddings representation), followed by two other features of news motivations in ranks 4 and 5, the interaction with corporate accounts and the politics news category. The remaining features in the top-20 are content features, with the exception of the interaction with lifestyle news in position 13. For our hybrid model, the TNM's features considered less important for prediction were news attitudes (i.e., the polarity of users' interactions), users' interactions with the news categories of science and technology and sports (remaining features of news motivations), and news beliefs (i.e., whether the users tend to mention more than to retweet).

5.2 Discussion

By applying the Twitter News Model to our dataset, we were able to extract interesting insights into Twitter users' news consumption. We found that the most telling features in the prediction of users' news consumption are *news motivations*, or the reasons that drive them to consume news. This finding is consistent with the findings of the Motivational Consumption Model, in which the authors explain that news motivations influence both news attitudes and news consumption. While we are now able to indicate that users' interactions with certain news categories (e.g., business and politics) are useful in predicting their news consumption, further analyses are necessary in order to explain whether this means they consume more or less news than if they interacted with other news categories.

Although most of the observed effects can be attributed to news motivations, *news attitudes* also play a role. We found that the cohort in our sample tends to approach journalists with a positive

attitude, as reflected in the polarity of the tweets in which they mention journalistic accounts.

The features reflecting *news beliefs* appeared to have the least importance in the prediction of news consumption. This finding is in line with the MCM, in which *news beliefs* are seen as having a direct effect on news motivations and news attitudes, and only through these, showing an effect on news consumption itself. This result might suggest that users who are active participants in the news conversation in Twitter, implicitly convey the value that news has for them, by virtue of such interactions (which explicitly reflect their news motivations and attitudes).

Using the TNM features alone to learn and predict users' news consumption, did not result in the best model; as the predictions had the highest error. Other approaches, including those using content-based features, for example word-embeddings, have higher predictive power. However, the TNM models help make results more interpretable. This characteristic is essential, particularly in environments where beyond predicting news consumption, is the knowledge obtained in the process that matters, for example, if journalists learn what makes Twitter users consume news, they can apply the knowledge to future interactions and thus, keep their audience and/or possibly attract more readers. For tasks such as news recommendation and personalization, journalists can use these results to segment their audience by creating *personas* based on the news consumption behavior. News can then be tailored and targeted to each persona, highlighting the aspects that will make it more likely to be consumed.

6 CONCLUSION

We have presented our Twitter News Model (TNM), a computational approach to modeling the news consumption behavior of Twitter users. Our approach is based on the Motivational Consumption Model (MCM), developed to model the consumption of news in conventional media such as newspapers, news aggregators, and TV. To the best of our knowledge, this is the first time that MCM has been adapted to this social media context. We started by discussing the theoretical background on which the MCM was based, described how we used the theory to instantiate our Twitter-specific model for news consumption (TNM), showed the usefulness of our model by applying it to a real-world scenario in which we learn the dynamics of news consumption in Twitter, and used this knowledge in a news consumption prediction task. Our findings reveal that news motivations, followed by news attitudes, and news beliefs, impact users' behavior of news consumption in Twitter. In future work, we aim to apply our findings to tasks such as user segmentation, and to inform strategies that journalists might use to promote their news on Twitter, so that they can better understand the dynamics of news consumption on social media. In addition, we aim to explore other interpretable user representations that can be used in prediction tasks related to the one addressed in this paper.

ACKNOWLEDGMENTS

The authors would like to thank *The Irish Times* for their funding and help on this project. This work is supported by Science Foundation Ireland through the Insight Centre for Data Analytics under grant number SFI/12/RC/2289.

REFERENCES

[1] 2015. *Reuters Institute Digital News Report.* Technical Report. http://www.digitalnewsreport.org/

[2] Pablo Boczkowski, Eugenia Mitchelstein, and Mora Matassi. 2017. Incidental News: How Young People Consume News on Social Media.. In *HICSS.* AIS Electronic Library (AISeL).

[3] Alex Bruns, Brenda Moon Moon, Felix Münch, Jan-Hinrik Schmidt, Lisa Merten, Hallvard Moe, and Sander Schwartz. 2016. NEWS SHARING ON TWITTER: A NATIONALLY COMPARATIVE STUDY. *Selected Papers of AoIR 2016: The 17th Annual Conference of the Association of Internet Researchers* 0, 0 (2016).

[4] Pew Research Center. 2014. How social media is reshaping news. http://www.pewresearch.org/fact-tank/2014/09/24/how-social-media-is-reshaping-news/

[5] Boreum Choi and Inseong Lee. 2017. Trust in open versus closed social media: The relative influence of user- and marketer-generated content in social network services on customer trust. *Telematics and Informatics* 34, 5 (2017), 550–559.

[6] Sophie Chou and Deb Roy. 2017. Nasty, Brutish, and Short: What Makes Election News Popular on Twitter?. In *ICWSM.* AAAI Press, 492–495.

[7] Mathieu Cliche. 2017. BB_twtr at SemEval-2017 Task 4: Twitter Sentiment Analysis with CNNs and LSTMs. *arXiv preprint arXiv:1704.06125* (2017).

[8] Stephanie Edgerly, Kjerstin Thorson, Esther Thorson, Emily K Vraga, and Leticia Bode. 0. Do parents still model news consumption? Socializing news use among adolescents in a multi-device world. *New Media & Society* 0, 0 (0), 1461444816688451. https://doi.org/10.1177/1461444816688451 arXiv:https://doi.org/10.1177/1461444816688451

[9] Martin Fishbein and Icek Ajzen. 2010. *Predicting and Changing Behavior.* Psychology Press.

[10] Pierre Geurts, Damien Ernst, and Louis Wehenkel. 2006. Extremely Randomized Trees. *Mach. Learn.* 63, 1 (April 2006), 3–42. https://doi.org/10.1007/s10994-006-6226-1

[11] Trevor Hastie, Robert Tibshirani, and Jerome Friedman. 2001. *The Elements of Statistical Learning.* Springer New York Inc., New York, NY, USA.

[12] Benjamin D. Horne and Sibel Adali. 2017. The Impact of Crowds on News Engagement: A Reddit Case Study. *CoRR* abs/1703.10570 (2017). arXiv:1703.10570 http://arxiv.org/abs/1703.10570

[13] JAMES JACCARD. 2012. The Reasoned Action Model: Directions for Future Research. *The Annals of the American Academy of Political and Social Science* (2012), 58–80.

[14] Bente Kalsnes and Anders Olof Larsson. 2017. Understanding News Sharing Across Social Media. *Journalism Studies* 0, 0 (2017), 1–20. https://doi.org/10.1080/1461670X.2017.1297686 arXiv:https://doi.org/10.1080/1461670X.2017.1297686

[15] Yaser Keneshloo, Shuguang Wang, Eui-Hong Sam Han, and Naren Ramakrishnan. 2016. Predicting the Popularity of News Articles.. In *SDM,* Sanjay Chawla Venkatasubramanian and Wagner Meira Jr. (Eds.). SIAM, 441–449.

[16] Yaser Keneshloo, Shuguang Wang, Eui-Hong Sam Han, and Naren Ramakrishnan. 2016. Predicting the shape and peak time of news article views.. In *BigData,* James Joshi, George Karypis, Ling Liu, Xiaohua Hu, Ronay Ak, Yinglong Xia, Weijia Xu, Aki-Hiro Sato, Sudarsan Rachuri, Lyle H. Ungar, Philip S. Yu, Rama Govindaraju, and Toyotaro Suzumura (Eds.). IEEE, 2400–2409.

[17] Yonghwan Kim, Youngju Kim, Yuan Wang, and Na Yeon Lee. 2016. Uses and Gratifications, Journalists' Twitter Use, and Relational Satisfaction with the Public. *Journal of Broadcasting & Electronic Media* 60, 3 (2016), 503–526. https://doi.org/10.1080/08838151.2016.1164171 arXiv:https://doi.org/10.1080/08838151.2016.1164171

[18] Huyen T. Le, Zubair Shafiq, and Padmini Srinivasan. 2017. Scalable News Slant Measurement Using Twitter.. In *ICWSM.* AAAI Press, 584–587.

[19] Angela M Lee and Hsiang Iris Chyi. 2014. Motivational consumption model: Exploring the psychological structure of news use. *Journalism & Mass Communication Quarterly* 91, 4 (2014), 706–724.

[20] Quanzhi Li, Sameena Shah, Armineh Nourbakhsh, Rui Fang, and Xiaomo Liu. 2017. funSentiment at SemEval-2017 Task 5: Fine-Grained Sentiment Analysis on Financial Microblogs Using Word Vectors Built from StockTwits and Twitter. In *Proceedings of the 11th International Workshop on Semantic Evaluation (SemEval-2017).* 852–856.

[21] Maxwell McCombs and Paula Poindexter. 1983. The Duty to Keep Informed: News Exposure and Civic Obligation. *Journal of Communication* 33, 2 (1983), 88–96. https://doi.org/10.1111/j.1460-2466.1983.tb02391.x

[22] Pasquale De Meo, Fabrizio Messina, Domenico Rosaci, and Giuseppe M. L. SarnÃÍ. 2017. Forming time-stable homogeneous groups into Online Social Networks. *Inf. Sci.* 414 (2017), 117–132.

[23] Pasquale De Meo, Katarzyna Musial-Gabrys, Domenico Rosaci, Giuseppe M. L. SarnÃÍ, and Lora Aroyo. 2017. Using Centrality Measures to Predict Helpfulness-Based Reputation in Trust Networks. *ACM Trans. Internet Techn.* 17, 1 (2017), 8:1–8:20.

[24] Siakalli Michailina, Andreas Masouras, and Christos Papademetriou. 2015. Uses and Gratifications in Online News: Comparing Social Media and News Media Use by Users. (05 2015).

[25] Tomas Mikolov, Ilya Sutskever, Kai Chen, Gregory S. Corrado, and Jeffrey Dean. 2013. Distributed Representations of Words and Phrases and their Compositionality.. In *NIPS,* Christopher J. C. Burges, LÃÍon Bottou, Zoubin Ghahramani, and Kilian Q. Weinberger (Eds.). 3111–3119.

[26] Claudia Orellana-Rodriguez, Ernesto Diaz-Aviles, and Wolfgang Nejdl. 2013. Mining emotions in short films: user comments or crowdsourcing?. In *Proceedings of the 22nd International Conference on World Wide Web.* ACM, 69–70.

[27] Claudia Orellana-Rodriguez, Ernesto Diaz-Aviles, and Wolfgang Nejdl. 2015. Mining affective context in short films for emotion-aware recommendation. In *Proceedings of the 26th ACM Conference on Hypertext & Social Media.* ACM, 185–194.

[28] Claudia Orellana-Rodriguez, Derek Greene, and Mark T. Keane. 2016. Spreading the News: How Can Journalists Gain More Engagement for Their Tweets?. In *Proceedings of the 8th ACM Conference on Web Science (WebSci '16).* ACM, New York, NY, USA, 107–116. http://doi.acm.org/10.1145/2908131.2908154

[29] Claudia Orellana-Rodriguez, Derek Greene, and Mark T. Keane. 2017. Spreading One's Tweets: How Can Journalists Gain Attention for their Tweeted News? *J. Web Science* 3, 2 (2017), 16–31.

[30] Jeffrey Pennington, Richard Socher, and Christopher D Manning. 2014. Glove: Global Vectors for Word Representation.. In *EMNLP,* Vol. 14. 1532–1543.

[31] Alicja Piotrkowicz, Vania Dimitrova, Jahna Otterbacher, and Katja Markert. 2017. Headlines Matter: Using Headlines to Predict the Popularity of News Articles on Twitter and Facebook.. In *ICWSM.* AAAI Press, 656–659.

[32] Julio C. S. Reis, Haewoon Kwak, Jisun An, Johnnatan Messias, and FabrÃncio Benevenuto. 2017. Demographics of News Sharing in the U.S. Twittersphere.. In *HT.* ACM, 195–204.

[33] Sara Rosenthal, Noura Farra, and Preslav Nakov. 2017. SemEval-2017 Task 4: Sentiment Analysis in Twitter. In *Proceedings of the 11th International Workshop on Semantic Evaluation (SemEval '17).* Association for Computational Linguistics, Vancouver, Canada.

[34] Alon Rozental and Daniel Fleischer. 2017. Amobee at SemEval-2017 Task 4: Deep Learning System for Sentiment Detection on Twitter. *CoRR* abs/1705.01306 (2017). arXiv:1705.01306 http://arxiv.org/abs/1705.01306

[35] Terrence Szymanski, Claudia Orellana-Rodriguez, and Mark T Keane. 2017. Helping News Editors Write Better Headlines: A Recommender to Improve the Keyword Contents & Shareability of News Headlines. *arXiv preprint arXiv:1705.09656* (2017).

[36] Beidou Wang, Can Wang, Jiajun Bu, Chun Chen, Wei Vivian Zhang, Deng Cai, and Xiaofei He. 2013. Whom to Mention: Expand the Diffusion of Tweets by @ Recommendation on Micro-blogging Systems. In *Proceedings of the 22Nd International Conference on World Wide Web (WWW '13).* ACM, New York, NY, USA, 1331–1340. https://doi.org/10.1145/2488388.2488505

[37] Bo Wu and Haiying Shen. 2015. Analyzing and predicting news popularity on Twitter. *Int J. Information Management* 35, 6 (2015), 702–711.

Predict Demographic Information Using Word2vec on Spatial Trajectories

Adir Solomon, Ariel Bar, Chen Yanai, Bracha Shapira, Lior Rokach
Department of Software and Information Systems Engineering
Telekom Innovation Laboratories at BGU
Ben-Gurion University of the Negev, P.O. Box 84105, Beer-Sheva, Israel
{adirsolo, arielba, chenyan}@post.bgu.ac.il, {bshapira, liorrk}@bgu.ac.il

ABSTRACT

Inferring socio-demographic attributes of users is an important and challenging task that could help with personalization, recommendation, advertising, etc. Sensor data collected from mobile devices can be utilized for inferring such attributes. Previous works have focused on combining different types of sensors, such as applications, accelerometer, GPS, battery, and many others, to achieve this task. In this study, we were able to infer attributes, such as gender, age, marital status, and whether the user has children, using solely the GPS sensor. We suggest a novel inference technique, which learns an embedding representation of preprocessed spatial GPS trajectories using an adaption of the Word2vec approach. Based on the embedding representation, we later train multiple classification models to achieve the inference goals. Our empirical results indicate that the suggested embedding approach outperforms a classification approach which does not take into consideration the embedding patterns. Experiments on real datasets collected from Android devices show that the proposed method achieves over 80% accuracy for various demographic prediction tasks.

KEYWORDS

Trajectories; Word2vec; Embedding; Deep Learning

ACM Reference Format:
Adir Solomon, Ariel Bar, Chen Yanai, Bracha Shapira, and Lior Rokach. 2018. Predict Demographic Information Using Word2vec on Spatial Trajectories. In UMAP '18: 26th Conference on User Modeling, Adaptation and Personalization, July 8–11, 2018, Singapore, Singapore. ACM, New York, NY, USA, 9 pages. https://doi.org/10.1145/3209219.3209249

1 INTRODUCTION

The ability to predict demographic attributes of users based on just a single mobile sensor is a very challenging task. This is even the case with the GPS which can provide a significant amount of information about users based on their location. However, the data collected from the GPS sensor is not always accurate and may contain noise and misleading samples. Additionally, not all records are equally important, as some of the records represent transitions between places which may not contain any significant information. In order to address this challenge, we suggest a preprocessing stage that utilizes density based clustering along with additional filtering conditions on the frequencies of the clusters and the time users stayed at a location; we to refer the outputs of the preprocessing stage as stay points (e.g., the user's home, workplace, etc.). Our novel approach accurately predicts important user demographics by transforming the stay points to embeddings using the Word2vec model.

Our motivation comes from the traditional Word2vec approach, in which similar words appear in similar contexts. We believe that stay points can be modeled in the same way and may be represented by the embedded vectors.

There are two main contributions of our approach: the first is its ability to predict users' demographic attributes using the data from just a single sensor. We manage to provide useful information, including the user's age range, whether the user has children, and the user's marital status and gender. Furthermore, for users who are students, we also managed to predict the students' academic faculty. The second contribution of our method is the use of Word2vec embeddings for locations instead of employing any feature engineering. We transform a large space of GPS coordinates to a fixed number of dimensions in the embedding space; by doing so, we manage to discover patterns that can provide demographic information about the users.

Our comprehensive evaluation includes an analysis of our method's ability to predict demographic attributes based on the trajectories all of the users. We also analyze the results for predicting demographic attributes based only on the daily trajectories of new users that have not yet been observed in the training set. All of our results are based on two different datasets; the first dataset was obtained by sampling the mobile phones of 45 users every minute for a six month period. The second dataset is based on data that was obtained by sampling the mobile phones of 81 users (all of whom were students) every 30 minutes for one month.

Our method outperformed baselines, all of which were based on statistical and embedded representation, for the demographic prediction tasks assessed.

The paper is organized as follows: Section 2 reviews related work. Our proposed method is presented in Section 3. The algorithm results and evaluation, comparing our model to baseline models, are described in Section 4. Finally, Section 5 provides concluding remarks and discusses future work.

2 RELATED WORK

In this section we introduce prior work related to our research, focusing first on research that identifies stay points (locations that the users stayed at for a period of time, such as work or home) based on spatial trajectories. Trajectories generated from the GPS sensor usually contain a set of samples that are in the form of longitude, latitude, and timestamp. We aim to convert the samples to stay points. Then, we mention work that shows the relationship between demographic attributes and spatial trajectories. Finally, we present research that uses embedded representation for locations and their contexts.

2.1 Stay Point Detection

This section presents research in the area of stay point detection from the GPS.

Li et al. [13] suggest a stay point detection algorithm. The algorithm checks two conditions, one for the distance and the other for the time span, i.e., if the user stayed within a specified area (a distance threshold) for more than a specified amount of time (a time threshold), the area is detected as a stay point.

Instead of applying conditions of time and distance, clustering techniques can be used in order to detect stay points. Ashbrook et al. [1] propose an algorithm that utilizes a k-means algorithm, however previous research [10] shows that the use of popular clustering algorithms, such as k-means and the Gaussian mixture model (GMM), has some limitations. One of them is the need to select the number of clusters as a parameter in order to run the algorithm; this parameter actually represents the number of stay points from the trajectory. Another problem with these algorithms is that they also consider the transition between the significant places a significant place (to the point that another cluster will be created for it) which does not accurately reflect reality.

Our preprocessing algorithm (described in Section 3.1) was developed based on the research mentioned above. Our model uses density clustering techniques by applying the mean shift algorithm [5], without the limitation of specifying the number of clusters. Like some of the research mentioned above, we also implement constraints on the time and distance in order to only detect stay points and remove outliers.

2.2 Demographic Attribute Prediction

Previous studies have dealt with the relationship between spatial trajectories and demographic characteristics of users, such as the difference between the trajectories of males and females, single

and married users, etc. Do et al. [7] suggest statistical analysis on the relation between demographic attributes and visiting patterns, focused on weekly visiting patterns of distinct and new places. They found that males and females had the same number of visits to distinct places per week. When it comes to the number of new places visited per week, men are likely to be more mobile than women (statistically significant). Marital status showed the strongest connection to mobility features; the visits to distinct places and new places are significantly different between two groups: 1) a group made up of people that are in a relationship, and 2) a group comprised of people that are single (or divorced) and people that are married (or living with a partner). Xie et al. [24] show that demographic attributes have an impact on the spatial trajectories and that the spatial trajectories are significantly different for each type of user (based on gender, age, occupation, and annual income). Their statistical model used the Kruskal-Wallis test. Lu et al. [14] focus on the difference between activity inside the home and outside the home, and their results suggest that people with different demographic attributes have different activity patterns. They also found that users' travel behavior was related to their socio-demographic attributes. For example, women tend to make more trips than men, and the more children the user has, the fewer trips the user takes. Biagioni et al. [3] found a few algorithms that can detect similarity between users' daily trajectories with high accuracy. They also examine the use of clustering algorithms, which showed how to separate the daily trajectories effectively. Based on the relationship of spatial trajectories and demographic attributes, some research has tried to predict the demographic attributes of users based on the locations visited.

Herder et al. [9] show how mobility patterns mined using trajectories based on the GPS can be modeled in order to predict the user's next place using just a simple Markov model.

Zhong et al. [31] use location check-ins in order to predict demographic attributes. The researchers consider different information about check-ins, such as spatiality, temporality, and knowledge about the locations. They were able to predict users' gender and educational background with high accuracy based on the F1 score. Other previous work [11] uses only mobile location sensors like GPS, Wi-Fi, and cell tower data in order to show that social and demographic characteristics can be learned from user locations. In this study, the researchers were able to predict the gender and age groups using various models (for example, HMM and PCA) and a decision tree classifier with the leave-one-out technique.

Ying et al. [28] predict the users' demographic attributes using data from 45 mobile features which are categorized as follows. Behavior features include movement in a location, application usage, and statistics about calls and texts. Environment features include statistics about Bluetooth and wireless devices, etc. In order to handle imbalanced data and the multi-class classification problem, the authors suggested a multi-level classification model. They split the original classification problems into smaller problems where each model deals with one problem at a time and combined all of the results for each model, in order to predict the user's marital status, gender, and age group.

Zhong et al. [30] show that by using the probabilities of activities based on their given context (similar to the bag of words algorithm), location visiting sequence, and mobile features, such as calendar, call log, contacts, etc., the gender, marital status, and exact age of the users could be predicted with high accuracy.

In contrast to the abovementioned articles on this subject, our research is based on data collected from just the GPS sensor.

2.3 Stay Points' Embedded Representation

Two recent papers suggest transforming locations to embedding representations. Zhou et al. [32] use vectors for different contextual features from check-in records. The records contain information about the user ID, location, category of the location, and timestamp of the check-in. They chose to focus on four contexts: user, trajectory, location, and temporal contexts. Based on all of those contexts, they create an average contextual vector as input for softmax classification in order to make recommendations for locations and predict the social link between the users.

Yang et al. [26] consider four factors in order to generate mobile trajectories: user visit preference, friends' influence, short-term sequences which represent the context of the last places that the user visited, and long-term sequences which represent the context of the first places that the user visited. They model the context of short and long term sequences with embedded representation using RNNs (recurrent neural networks) and GRUs (gated recurrent units) respectively. Similar to the research that introduced by Zhou et al. [32], the authors use their model in order to make a friend prediction and a recommendation for the next location. In our case, we aim to predict users' demographic attributes using Word2vec embedded representation, as opposed to RNN or GRU. RNNs and GRUs are deeper and more complex, consisting of more hidden layers, and a more comprehensive process for tuning the parameters is required compared to those needed in Word2vec. Unlike the other research conducted on this subject, our model does not consider friendship, user interest, or long or short-term context, which contributes to our model's simplicity. Additionally, our model is based solely on the GPS coordinates, as opposed to the check-in information which contains more information on the semantic meaning of the places.

By relying only on this data, we are able to minimize 1) the battery consumption when collecting the data, 2) the impact on the subjects' (users) privacy, based on the embedding of the stay points representing the different locations rather than the coordinates themselves, and 3) the number of device permeations; this is possible, because we only need to access one sensor.

Additionally, this is the first time that the Word2vec model has been used in order to transform stay points to embeddings in order to predict demographic attributes of the users. Using the embeddings from Word2vec enables us to achieve high accuracy for the prediction tasks (described in Section 4.4).

The use of embedded representations introduced in the Word2vec model was also shown to be very efficient with NLP tasks [17]. We believe that by applying this approach on the users' trajectories will enable us to discover patterns that can aid us in predicting users' demographic attributes.

3 METHOD

In order to predict the demographic attributes of users, we suggest the following process as presented in Fig. 1. The process begins with the data from the GPS sensor (described in Section 4.1); this data is then preprocessed in order to enable us to focus only on the stay points. Next, we apply the Word2vec model on the results of the previous stage, in order to transform the stay points into vectors that capture the context of each stay point from the user's trajectory. In order to represent the users, we calculated an average vector for each user based on all of his/her stay point vectors. In the final stage of our method we use the users' vectors as input features for various classifiers (decision tree, logistic regression, etc.), in order to predict users' demographic attributes.

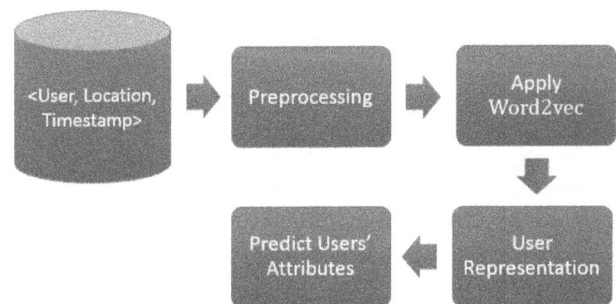

Figure 1: Overview of the methodology.

3.1 Preprocessing

All of the GPS records in our datasets were sampled from the mobile device with a time interval between samples, but not all of records are equally important. Some of them may represent GPS errors (in this case, the records may not be based on the actual places) or transitions between places (in this case, they may not contain any significant information). In order to exclude such records and obtain only the significant places that the user has stayed at for a while (such as the user's home, workplace, etc.), we implemented our preprocessing algorithm, which is presented in Fig. 2 and described below.

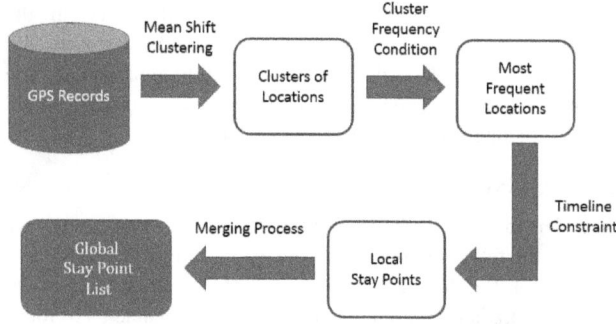

Figure 2: Scheme of the preprocessing algorithm.

The first stage of our algorithm is concerned with identifying the significant places by removing the records that were outliers and focusing only on the dense areas, based on the assumption derived from the research of [27] that clusters that represent stay points have more records than clusters that represent transitions between stay points or GPS sampling errors. Identification of the stay points was accomplished by using a clustering technique called the mean shift algorithm [5].

The purpose of the mean shift clustering algorithm is to create clusters based on the density of the data. This algorithm generates the number of clusters automatically and doesn't need any pre-defined parameters.

The algorithm updates candidates for centroids, which are represented by the mean of the records within a specific region, using this equation:

$$x_i^{t+1} = x_i^t + m(x_i^t) \tag{1}$$

where x_i is a candidate centroid, t is the iteration, and m is the mean shift vector which points towards the center of the mass for the region. m is computed for a given centroid, for all of the records that are within a given distance, which are represented by $N(x_i)$, using this equation:

$$m(x_i) = \frac{\sum_{x_i \in N(x_i)} K(x_j - x_i) x_j}{\sum_{x_i \in N(x_i)} K(x_j - x_i)} \tag{2}$$

where K is a flat kernel function:

$$K(x) = \begin{cases} 1, & if\ ||x|| \leq \lambda \\ 0, & if\ ||x|| > \lambda \end{cases} \tag{3}$$

The algorithm stops when the delta between the values of the candidates for each iteration is small enough. We applied the algorithm over all of the users' trajectories. The output of the mean shift algorithm is a list of clusters for each user.

In order to focus only on the clusters that represent stay points, in the second stage of our algorithm, we applied a frequent cluster condition regarding the frequencies of the clusters (the number of times each cluster appears in the user's routine). To do this, we sorted the clusters by their frequencies (in descending order), and then using a threshold of 90% of the user data, we selected all of the clusters that met this frequency threshold.

In the third stage we used a timeline constraint; based on this constraint we selected only the clusters in which the user stayed continuously for more than a specified time (a time threshold of 15 minutes in our case). We refer to those clusters as local stay points. The thresholds for the second and third phases were determined during a calibration process of the algorithm. Using the timeline constraint, we assume that the places that the user does not stay at for more than a certain amount time do not contain any relevant information for our analysis (unlike the user's home or workplace which may provide more relevant information); this is similar to the algorithm introduced by Yan et al. [25].

In the final preprocessing stage we merged all of the local stay points over all of the users in the dataset that are within a specified distance threshold using a geographic midpoint calculation. We performed this process in order to represent the same stay points for all of the users; for example, a restaurant is represented by its own unique ID in each of the users' trajectories, so we do not lose any information about the users' shared places.

In order to ensure this and achieve a more accurate location for the local stay points, we used the following steps:

- In the first step we sorted the local stay points by their weight, where weight is the number of GPS events. We moved the stay point with the highest weight to the empty merged stay point list, and we gave it a new ID.

- In the second step, we obtained an unmerged local stay point and searched for a merged stay point within the given distance threshold (in our case 100 meters, similar to previous research [7]) in the merged stay point list, starting with the stay point with the highest weight.

- In the third step, we checked if a stay point was found, we merged both stay points' coordinates using:

$$Latitude_{new} = \frac{Latitude_n \cdot w_n + Latitude_{total} \cdot w_{total}}{w_{total} + w_n} \tag{4}$$

$$Longitude_{new} = \frac{Longitude_n \cdot w_n + Longitude_{total} \cdot w_{total}}{w_{total} + w_n} \tag{5}$$

keeping the merged stay point ID and adding the new stay point's weight to the merged stay point's weight, where $Latitude_n, Longitude_n$ are the unmerged stay point's latitude and longitude coordinates, and w_n is the unmerged stay point's weight. $Latitude_{total}, Longitude_{total}$ are the merged stay point's latitude and longitude coordinates, and w_{total} is the merged stay points' weight.

The output of the final step of the preprocessing algorithm is a list of global stay point IDs. From now on, each of the user's trajectories will be represented by these stay points, and each stay point receives its own unique ID.

3.2 Applying Word2vec

We applied the Word2vec model by using the gensim [20] software framework. For each dataset we created a text file that contained a number of sentences which is equal to the number of users. The analogy that we made is that each word which has a unique ID represents a stay point, and each sentence represents a user trajectory. The user trajectory is composed from the first day to the last day in the data. All of the IDs were ordered chronological by their sequence. This text file was supplied as input to the Word2vec model. The output of this step is an embedding vector representation for each of the stay points.

Fig. 3 provides an example of an input file for the Word2vec model. In this example, user 1 spent all day at stay point 115 on 01.04.16 and 02.04.16. On 03.04.16 this user started the day at stay point 115, went to stay point 473, and ended the day back at stay point 115.

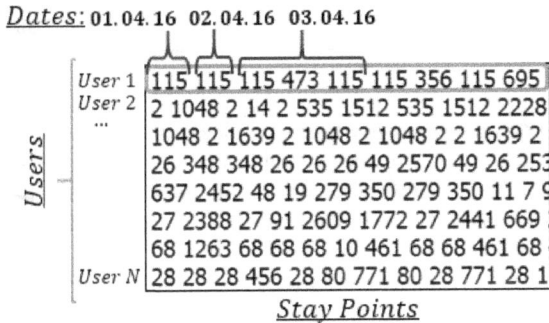

Figure 3: Example of an input file for the Word2vec model and the analogy of the sentences to users and the words to stay points.

We used the continuous bag of words (CBOW) [17] model which aims to predict the current stay point based on the context of the other stay points that are in the same window. Fig. 4 describes the CBOW architecture in our stay point domain.

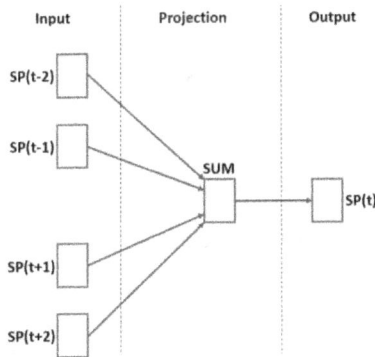

Figure 4: The CBOW architecture of the Word2vec model.

The output for the probability distribution on the vocabulary of the stay points W_{SP}, where C_{SP} represents the stay point's context, and α and β are parameters of the linear transformation using the softmax function:

$$\hat{y} = P(\cdot \,|C_{SP}; \alpha, \beta) = softmax_\beta \left(\sum_{W_{SP} \in C_{SP}} \alpha_{W_{SP}} \right) \qquad (6)$$

Using this model, we are able to capture important information about the relationship between each stay point and the stay points surrounding it. For example, the users' stay points representing their home location, along with the visited locations that before/after the stay points representing home, stay points representing their work locations, etc. This corresponds with the semantic analysis presented in Section 4.4.4. An advantage of this method is the dimensionality reduction and compact representation of the information it provides. We are able to transform millions of GPS records to thousands of stay points which ultimately result in a compact and fixed representation of the embeddings (as can be seen in Sections 4.1.1-4.1.2).

3.3 User Representation & Demographic Classification

Using the output from the previous stage, which consists of an embedding vector for each of the stay points, we were able to calculate the average vector for each of the different users' trajectories. For each user we totaled all of the stay point vectors and divided this by the length of the user trajectory.

We used each of the average vectors as features for different classifiers in order to predict users' demographic attributes. We used the logistic regression [22], naïve Bayes [16], decision tree [19], SVM [6], and random forest [4] classifiers.

4 EVALUATION

In this section, we provide a detailed description of the data collection process, statistics about the datasets, distributions for the users' demographic information, a semantic analysis of the stay points, and a summary of the accuracy results for each of the classifications that we performed and compared them to baseline algorithms. It is important to note that our method is generic, and it will work with any sequential data.

4.1 Datasets

This section describes the two datasets that were evaluated in our experiments: Sherlock [18] and CARS (Context-Aware Recommender Systems) [21].

4.1.1 Sherlock Dataset

This dataset comes from the Sherlock project [18]. In our research we focus on the location data generated from the GPS. The raw data contains the users' location data: longitude and latitude, with a timestamp for each sample. The data was sampled each minute. We used the data that was collected from April through September 2016 for 45 users: 21 males and 24 females. Twenty-one of the users do not have children, while 24 have at least one child. 30 users are married, and the rest are single. Twenty-three of the users are age 29 or under. The dataset contains a total of 6,219,330 GPS samples from all of the users; after using the mean shift algorithm, the number of clusters was 46,620. Applying the frequent cluster constraint reduces the number of clusters to 13,737, and the timeline

Table 1: Prediction accuracy results for the demographic tasks - complete trajectories

	Task	Accuracy (%)				
		Statistical Baseline	SVD	PCA	NMF	Model Using Word2vec
Sherlock	Gender Prediction	53.33	51.11	62.22	51.11	**86.67**
	Age Group Prediction	75.56	55.56	62.22	68.89	**80.00**
	Marital Status Prediction	66.67	73.33	66.67	60.00	**82.22**
	Has Children Prediction	71.11	68.89	51.11	55.56	**84.44**
CARS	Gender Prediction	64.19	64.19	64.19	60.49	**79.01**
	Age Group Prediction	72.83	71.60	71.60	69.13	**75.30**
	Academic Faculty Prediction	61.72	65.43	62.96	61.72	**74.07**

constraint reduces it further to 12,657. After the last stage of cluster merging, there were 2,896 global stay points. The dataset is available online and provided to academics and the research community with no charge[1].

4.1.2 CARS Dataset

This dataset comes from an Android application that captures the user's location in order to make a recommendation of nearby stay points that are in the user's area.

All of the users in this dataset were students, therefore with the labeled data we added another task: predicting the academic faculty of the user. The raw data contains GPS, accelerometer, Wi-Fi, battery, light, etc. We focus on the GPS sensor which was sampled by two triggers; the first trigger was sampled every 30 minutes, while the second was collected with certain actions made by the user (e.g., like for a recommendation). One should notice that most of the records belong to the first trigger (92.63% of the records). This low frequency rate increase the challenge of the prediction tasks, compared to the Sherlock dataset.

We used the data that was collected from April through May 2015 for 81 users: 47 males and 34 females. Thirty-eight of the users are age 26 or under. Twenty-seven of the users are students in the faculty of social sciences, and 33 students are in the faculty of engineering sciences. The rest were tagged as students of "Other". The dataset contains a total of 185,032 GPS samples from all of the users. All of the samples consist of the following fields: longitude, latitude, and timestamp. After using the mean shift algorithm, the number of the clusters was 13,632. Applying the frequent cluster constraint reduces the number of clusters to 7,759. The timeline constraint reduces it further to 5,550. After the last stage of cluster merging, there were 1,850 global stay points.

4.2 Experimental Setup

We define two main tasks; The first is to predict demographic attributes of the users based on their complete trajectories, which are trajectories that are based on all of the data for each

user (from the first day to the last day in the data). The second task is to predict the demographic attributes of the users based solely on the daily trajectories of the users. The second task is considered to be a challenging one, due to the fact that the classification of the demographic attributes is relying on only one day's worth of trajectories, for each of the days and users. All of the prediction tasks are considered to be binary classifications tasks, except for the academic faculty prediction which is multi-class task. For this multi-class problem, we used the one-vs-all classification approach. We used the continuous bag of words (CBOW) Word2vec model to generate the stay point vectors. We chose the best parameters for each of the prediction tasks from the following set of values: embedding vector size - 5 or 10, number of iterations - from 50 to 400 with steps of 50, learning rate - from 0.025 to 0.1 with steps of 0.025, and negative samples – from 3 to 9 with steps of 2. We also discuss how to determine the Word2vec embedding size in order to achieve the highest prediction accuracy, as well as the use of clustering on the embedding space for understanding the semantic meaning of the stay points.

4.3 Baselines

We compare our method with several baselines; the first baseline uses traditional statistical features of the different trajectories, and this required feature engineering.

Based on the observed trajectories of the user we extracted several features that focused on the diversity, distribution, and length of stay point trajectories. This feature set acts as a baseline for the proposed embedding approach, and we refer to it as the statistical baseline. In particular, we extracted the following features:

1) One feature for the length of the trajectory made by the user, which represents the sentence length in the Word2vec model.
2) One feature for the number of unique places the user visited, which represents the unique words per sentence.
3) Five features for the top five stay points' percentage from the user's trajectory.
4) Twenty binary features for the top 20 most frequent stay points over all of the users' data. One indicates that the user

---

[1] http://bigdata.ise.bgu.ac.il/sherlock/

Table 2: Prediction accuracy results for the demographic tasks - daily trajectories

	Task	Accuracy (%)				
		Statistical Baseline	SVD	PCA	NMF	Model Using Word2vec
Sherlock	Gender Prediction	51.85	51.85	51.85	55.55	**64.44**
	Age Group Prediction	62.22	57.77	62.22	60.00	**68.88**
	Marital Status Prediction	68.89	73.33	71.11	**75.56**	73.33
	Has Children Prediction	68.89	66.67	68.89	66.67	**71.11**
CARS	Gender Prediction	58.02	55.55	55.55	58.02	**65.43**
	Age Group Prediction	51.85	67.90	65.43	65.43	**67.90**
	Academic Faculty Prediction	51.85	54.32	51.85	54.32	**56.79**

has visited the stay point at least once in his/her trajectory, and 0 indicates otherwise.

We compared this baseline algorithm and our algorithm, which makes use of the embeddings that are generated by Word2vec as features for the classifiers.

Our method does a dimensionality reduction, such that we also compare our results to other baselines which also make use of dimensionality reduction:

- SVD [8] - We use the SVD algorithm, in which each stay point is considered as an item-ID. The algorithm also represents stay points with embeddings, but unlike the Word2vec model, this algorithm does not consider the sequential order of the stay points.

- PCA [23] - Using a binary matrix for each user for his/her visited stay points (1 indicates that the user has visited the stay point at least once in his/her trajectory, and 0 indicates otherwise), we perform a dimensionality reduction using the PCA algorithm.

- NMF [12] - We use a binary matrix for each user for his/her visited stay points, as was in the PCA baseline. We perform a dimensionality reduction using non-negative matrix factorization.

Unlike our method, these baselines don't consider the context of the stay point representation. Our assumption is that the context has important significance when performing dimensionality reduction.

4.4 Results

In this section we present all of the results on the various tasks that we defined in Section 4.2.

4.4.1 Analysis of Complete Trajectories

In this section we present the results of the classifiers for the tasks of predicting gender, age group, marital status, whether the user has children, and academic faculty. The prediction accuracy results are presented in Table 1. We used logistic regression, naïve Bayes, decision tree, SVM, and random forest classifiers. We chose the classifier with the highest accuracy result for each task based on leave-one-out cross-validation (LOOCV); using our

model, the best classifier for all of the tasks was the decision tree classifier. Comparisons of the different classifiers with additional measures such as accuracy, precision, recall, and F-measure, can be found in the flowing link[2]. The results obtained by combining our model with the decision tree classifier were consistent for all tasks, unlike the other baselines which obtained different results with different classifiers; the best results achieved by the baselines with the classifiers varied depending on the prediction task, e.g., using PCA and the CARS dataset, the highest accuracy for the gender prediction task was achieved by the decision tree classifier, and the highest accuracy for the age group prediction task was achieved by the naïve Bayes classifier. As can be seen in Table 1, our model outperformed the various baselines over all of the prediction tasks. Our model performed 28.22% better than the second best results with the Sherlock dataset, and performed 18.76% better than the second best results with the CARS dataset. The traditional dimensionality reduction baselines produce inconsistent results with the different prediction tasks. For example, in the task of marital status prediction, SVD reached to accuracy of 73.33%, while in the task of gender prediction it reached only to accuracy of 51.85%. However, our suggested model produced consistent results cross these different tasks.

The main difference between the accuracy results of the two datasets can be explained by the difference in the amount of time analyzed of all of the trajectories in each dataset (half a year for the Sherlock dataset and one month for the CARS dataset).

4.4.2 Analysis of Daily Trajectories

In this section we present the results of the classifiers for the tasks of predicting gender, age group, marital status, whether the user has children, and academic faculty based only on the trajectories of each user for each day. In fact, we are dealing with a challenging classification task which is based solely on the stay points for each day, for each user (which we have never seen before in the data), meaning that there is a cold start per user's day. In the Sherlock dataset the daily trajectories consist of only 2.717 stay points (on average), and in the CARS dataset the daily

---

[2] https://tinyurl.com/ybphbwbo

trajectories consist of only 2.867 stay points (on average). Focusing on daily trajectories results in more records. In the Sherlock dataset there are 6,157 records, and in the CARS dataset there are 2,354 records. We were able to accomplish this by calculating an average vector for each day for each user.

In order to evaluate the performance of our method, we use leave-one-out cross-validation for each user. We assess the accuracy for each of the days and users. Each user receives a score based on the average accuracy results for all of his/her days. The average accuracy results over all of the users are presented in Table 2. Similar to the evaluation performed on the complete trajectories, we present the highest results among the classifiers: logistic regression, naïve Bayes, decision tree, SVM, and random forest. Our model's best (highest) prediction results were achieved by the decision tree classifier.

Our model outperformed the baselines on all of the prediction tasks, except the marital status prediction task with the Sherlock dataset. Our model performed 13.80% better than the second best results with the Sherlock dataset, and performed 13.33% better than the second best results with the CARS dataset. Once again, we believe that the main difference between the accuracy results of the two datasets can be explained by difference in the amount of time analyzed in the datasets.

4.4.3 Choosing the Embedding Vector Size

We explored the connection between the embedding vector size and the accuracy results of the complete trajectories for each task. We evaluate it for the best classifier (decision tree) with the Sherlock dataset. As can be seen in Fig. 5, the best accuracy results were provided by an embedding vector size of 5 or 10, where in most cases adding more dimensions reduces the accuracy of the prediction.

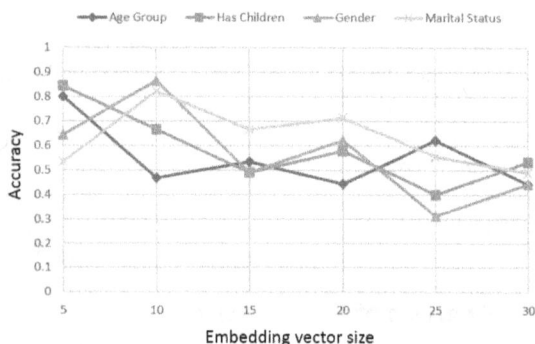

Figure 5: Accuracy as a function of embedding vector size.

4.4.4 Stay Point Semantics

We applied the k-means algorithm on the vector space base from the embedding vectors that we generated using Word2vec for the stay points for each user with the Sherlock dataset. In our experiments we test different amounts of centroids, ranging from three to seven, and chose to present the results for k=4 (for larger k values the improvement of the sum of squared error was minimal). We used t-SNE (t-distributed stochastic neighbor

embedding) [15] in order to reduce the dimensionality to two dimensions and visualize the vector space of the stay points. We believe that similar stay points' vectors will be clustered together by their semantic meaning (for example, most of the users' workplaces or the users' homes). The output graph from t-SNE is presented in Fig. 6. A different color is used for each cluster (cluster 1 - yellow, cluster 2 - red, cluster 3 - blue, and cluster 4 - green). We found that cluster 2 represents only 2% of the total number of stay points in the data, but the frequency of the stay points that belong to cluster 2 is relatively high, represent 45% of the data. Furthermore, we found that most of the users' home stay points are found in cluster 2 of the vector space; in fact, this was the case for 29 of the 45 users. In addition, we calculated Cosine similarity matrix between the embedding representation of the users' home stay points. The average value in the matrix was 0.782. This is also indicates that our algorithm was able to capture the semantic meaning of the different stay points.

The results presented in Fig. 6 correspond with the findings of other research aimed at determining the number of stay points that users have [29, 2]. Zhao et al. [29] showed that 80% of their users have between two and five stay points, while Bayir et al. [2] indicate that the users in their study spent approximately 85% of their time at three to five stay points.

Figure 6: tSNE graph of the vector space of the stay points.

5 CONCLUSIONS AND FUTURE WORK

In this study we presented a novel approach that uses embeddings to represent users' stay points and showed how it can be used to predict users' socio-demographic attributes with high accuracy, based on the data from just one sensor. In this paper we also demonstrated the efficiency of the Word2vec model in a new area, beyond the NLP domain.

Future research may explore the use of other embedding methods in order to predict demographic attributes, and on larger datasets. In particular, to investigate whether different patterns could be discovered by applying time series algorithms on the embedding space.

Moreover, it will be interesting to utilize the embeddings representations in other domains, such as recommender systems. More work should be done in order to create an algorithm that will determine the optimal embedding vector size for each of the prediction tasks.

REFERENCES

[1] Ashbrook, Daniel, and Thad Starner. "Using GPS to learn significant locations and predict movement across multiple users." Personal and Ubiquitous computing 7.5 (2003): 275-286.

[2] Bayir, Murat Ali, Murat Demirbas, and Nathan Eagle. "Discovering spatiotemporal mobility profiles of cellphone users." World of Wireless, Mobile and Multimedia Networks & Workshops, 2009. WoWMoM 2009. IEEE International Symposium on a. IEEE, 2009.

[3] Biagioni, J., & Krumm, J. (2013, June). Days of our lives: Assessing day similarity from location traces. In International Conference on User Modeling, Adaptation, and Personalization (pp. 89-101). Springer, Berlin, Heidelberg.

[4] Breiman, L. (2001). Random forests. Machine learning, 45(1), 5-32.

[5] Cheng, Yizong. "Mean shift, mode seeking, and clustering." IEEE transactions on pattern analysis and machine intelligence 17.8 (1995): 790-799.

[6] Cortes, C., & Vapnik, V. (1995). Support-vector networks. Machine learning, 20(3), 273-297.

[7] Do, Trinh Minh Tri, and Daniel Gatica-Perez. "The places of our lives: Visiting patterns and automatic labeling from longitudinal smartphone data." IEEE Transactions on Mobile Computing 13.3 (2014): 638-648.

[8] Golub, G. H., & Reinsch, C. (1970). Singular value decomposition and least squares solutions. Numerische mathematik, 14(5), 403-420.

[9] Herder, E., Siehndel, P., & Kawase, R. (2014, July). Predicting user locations and trajectories. In International Conference on User Modeling, Adaptation, and Personalization (pp. 86-97). Springer, Cham.

[10] Kang, J. H., Welbourne, W., Stewart, B., & Borriello, G. (2004, October). Extracting places from traces of locations. In Proceedings of the 2nd ACM international workshop on Wireless mobile applications and services on WLAN hotspots (pp. 110-118). ACM.

[11] Kelly, D., Smyth, B., & Caulfield, B. (2013). Uncovering measurements of social and demographic behavior from smartphone location data. IEEE Transactions on Human-Machine Systems, 43(2), 188-198.

[12] Lee, D. D., & Seung, H. S. (2001). Algorithms for non-negative matrix factorization. In Advances in neural information processing systems (pp. 556-562).

[13] Li, Q., Zheng, Y., Xie, X., Chen, Y., Liu, W., & Ma, W. Y. (2008, November). Mining user similarity based on location history. In Proceedings of the 16th ACM SIGSPATIAL international conference on Advances in geographic information systems (p. 34). ACM.

[14] Lu, Xuedong, and Eric I. Pas. "Socio-demographics, activity participation and travel behavior." Transportation Research Part A: Policy and Practice 33.1 (1999): 1-18.

[15] Maaten, Laurens van der, and Geoffrey Hinton. "Visualizing data using t-SNE." Journal of Machine Learning Research 9.Nov (2008): 2579-2605.

[16] McCallum, A., & Nigam, K. (1998, July). A comparison of event models for naive bayes text classification. In AAAI-98 workshop on learning for text categorization (Vol. 752, pp. 41-48).

[17] Mikolov, T., Chen, K., Corrado, G., & Dean, J. (2013). Efficient estimation of word representations in vector space. arXiv preprint arXiv:1301.3781.

[18] Mirsky, Y., Shabtai, A., Rokach, L., Shapira, B., & Elovici, Y. (2016, October). Sherlock vs moriarty: A smartphone dataset for cybersecurity research. In Proceedings of the 2016 ACM workshop on Artificial intelligence and security (pp. 1-12). ACM.

[19] Quinlan, J. R. (1993). C4. 5: programs for machine learning (Vol. 1). Morgan kaufmann.

[20] Rehurek, Radim, and Petr Sojka. "Software framework for topic modelling with large corpora." In Proceedings of the LREC 2010 Workshop on New Challenges for NLP Frameworks. 2010.

[21] Unger, M., Shapira, B., Rokach, L., & Bar, A. (2017, July). Inferring Contextual Preferences Using Deep Auto-Encoding. In Proceedings of the 25th Conference on User Modeling, Adaptation and Personalization (pp. 221-229). ACM.

[22] Werbos, P. (1974). Beyond regression: New tools for prediction and analysis in the behavioral sciences.

[23] Wold, S., Esbensen, K., & Geladi, P. (1987). Principal component analysis. Chemometrics and intelligent laboratory systems, 2(1-3), 37-52.

[24] Xie, Kaiqiang, Hui Xiong, and Chunyan Li. "The correlation between human mobility and socio-demographic in megacity." Smart Cities Conference (ISC2), 2016 IEEE International. IEEE, 2016.

[25] Yan, Z., Chakraborty, D., Parent, C., Spaccapietra, S., & Aberer, K. (2013). Semantic trajectories: Mobility data computation and annotation. ACM Transactions on Intelligent Systems and Technology (TIST), 4(3), 49.

[26] Yang, C., Sun, M., Zhao, W. X., Liu, Z., & Chang, E. Y. (2017). A Neural Network Approach to Jointly Modeling Social Networks and Mobile Trajectories. ACM Transactions on Information Systems (TOIS), 35(4), 36.

[27] Ye, Y., Zheng, Y., Chen, Y., Feng, J., & Xie, X. (2009, May). Mining individual life pattern based on location history. In Mobile Data Management: Systems, Services and Middleware, 2009. MDM'09. Tenth International Conference on (pp. 1-10). IEEE.

[28] Ying, J. J. C., Chang, Y. J., Huang, C. M., & Tseng, V. S. (2012). Demographic prediction based on users mobile behaviors. Mobile Data Challenge, 1-6.

[29] Zhao, X., Qiao, Y., Si, Z., Yang, J., & Lindgren, A. (2016, June). Prediction of user app usage behavior from geo-spatial data. In Proceedings of the Third International ACM SIGMOD Workshop on Managing and Mining Enriched Geo-Spatial Data (p. 7). ACM.

[30] Zhong, E., Tan, B., Mo, K., & Yang, Q. (2013). User demographics prediction based on mobile data. Pervasive and mobile computing, 9(6), 823-837.

[31] Zhong, Y., Yuan, N. J., Zhong, W., Zhang, F., & Xie, X. (2015, February). You are where you go: Inferring demographic attributes from location check-ins. In Proceedings of the eighth ACM international conference on web search and data mining (pp. 295-304). ACM.

[32] Zhou, N., Zhao, W. X., Zhang, X., Wen, J. R., & Wang, S. (2016). A general multi-context embedding model for mining human trajectory data. IEEE transactions on knowledge and data engineering, 28(8), 1945-1958.

Regulating Collaborative Learning in SQL-Tutor

Ashish Sharma
University of Canterbury
Christchurch, New Zealand
ashish.sharma@pg.canterbury.ac.nz

ABSTRACT

In recent years, there has been a surge in the use of intelligent computer-supported collaborative learning (CSCL) tools to improve student learning. The aim of this project is to provide adaptive support for student collaboration. My work will focus on designing effective interventions to enhance peer-to-peer collaboration in the context of an Intelligent Tutoring System (ITS), as well as to promote socially-shared regulation of learning (SSRL). In online collaborative learning environments, it can be challenging to engage students. A lack of genuine interaction, social identity, background of students and user empowerment may have negative effects on the learning process. This research will focus on virtualization of the online collaboration, such that the system would help students collaborate as well as support self-regulation and group regulation to achieve higher learning gains.

ACM Reference format:
Ashish Sharma. 2018. Regulating Collaborative Learning in SQL-Tutor. In *UMAP'18: ACM User Modeling, Adaptation and Personalization conference, July 8–11, 2018, Singapore.* ACM, NY, NY, USA, 4 pages. DOI: https://doi.org/10.1145/3209219.3213597

1. INTRODUCTION

Intelligent Tutoring Systems (ITS) imitate human tutors with the focus of establishing the relation with students as to what content to teach, method of teaching, when and what to advise in a certain metacognitive state [1, 2]. The effectiveness of human tutors lies in the tutor's ability to assess the student's knowledge and adapt interactions accordingly. On the similar lines, ITSs come a long way in replicating human tutors. ITSs promised the truly adaptive learning almost three decades ago and since then, some ITSs even excelled the human tutors in terms of learning gains achieved by students [3].

The field of Computer-Supported Collaborative Learning (CSCL) focuses on how students can learn together and enhance peer interaction using technology in a collaborative environment [4, 5]. CSCL researchers have shown that collaborative learning is beneficial for individuals as well as for group learning gains [6]. According to some researchers, the learning gain in collaborative set-up is more and time spent to solve problems is less than individual learning environments [7, 8]. Collaborative strategies mainly emphasize on i) Positive interdependence of task, goal, role, ii) Individual and group accountability (challenging and motivating every student), iii) Authentic interaction (planning, team building skills, social skills, brainstorming) [9]. It is common for groups to struggle from an unbalanced participation of students, which may lead to ineffective learning behavior [10, 11]. Thus, collaborative learning demands careful construction of environment, structure of various components and interaction interface that benefits individual and group.

2. PROPOSED RESEARCH

2.1 Motivation for the Proposed Research

Researchers in the field of ITS have focused more on the individual learning (one-on-one learning) than on collaborative learning [12]. In collaborative environments, it is not that easy to simply put students together and ask them to collaborate using an interactive interface. The encouraging effects of collaboration do not emerge spontaneously but require careful structuring of the collaboration so that particular interactions emerge [13]. One effective way of doing so is by scripting the collaboration, that is, by classifying roles and various activities for students to follow [14]. Traditionally, computer-supported collaboration provides the same script to all students (i.e., the same level of support to every student). This type of fixed support to all may hinder learning or collaborating for students who have good domain knowledge. The main focus of collaboration should be individual learning as well as the positive impact on the group performance. Solving problems together in collaborative environment does not only increase the learning gains but also higher order thinking skills such as planning, reflection, and metacognition [7]. Group discussions are seen to help students think about problems and thus revise their answers, so as to achieve the higher rate of problem solving. While collaborating, students share the domain knowledge with each other, which may contribute to learning. Strong self-regulated learning skills enable learners to plan, manage and control the learning process. They develop the ability to learn at faster pace and to perform better at an academic level. Self-regulated learning plays a vital role in online learning environments that provide timely guidance and support. For instance, through the system, learners can be trained and actively supported with prompts and some activities to engage in self-regulated learning. In this study, we will also use pedagogical agents to enhance self-regulated learning.

2.2 Description of the Proposed Research Work

The proposed research will be done in context of SQL-Tutor, the first constraint-based ITS for teaching SQL [15, 16]. SQL-Tutor is a complement to traditional lectures and assumes that students have prior knowledge gained in lectures and tutoring sessions. There are more than 200 problems defined on 13 databases in the system. In this project, I will create a collaborative extension of SQL-Tutor, which will empower students to collaborate, guide them to collaborate successfully using pedagogical agents, and engage them in self-regulated learning (SRL). First and foremost, the idea is to create a common problem area for a group and provide an interface to discuss and solve problems. The pilot study will be conducted on the usability of this environment.

This project will not only promote collaboration but would also use tools to support self-regulation and socially-shared regulation of learning. There have been successful studies that enhance cognitive performance, help in knowledge construction and provide interaction tools among group in CSCL. The self-regulated learning in CSCL is not only the regulation of individual learning but also as group and contextual process [17]. Self-regulated learning focuses on constructive learning by the student and how they monitor and control their cognition, motivation and learning behavior [18]. In most ITSs, students are required to set their own goals, pace and sequences. Self-regulated learning is important, because students need to set realistic goals [19] and regulate themselves, each other (co-regulated learning) and together (socially-shared regulation of learning) [20]. To succeed, individuals in groups need skills for regulating themselves, each other and together. Left on their own, some students lack skills to regulate themselves or group and thus struggle to work in collaborative environment [20]. For that reason, we will develop an approach for supporting collaborative learning which will provide domain knowledge as well as support for regulation so that groups collectively regulate to think, act and behave instead of individuals [21]. One way to do this would be through the visualization of participation. This may push students to contribute more in collaboration. Collaborative support can be provided via conversational agents, who will provide feedback, suggestions and comments on the overall session and after every activity. This is explained in Section 4.

2.3 Research Questions

The overall aim of my research is to develop an efficient approach to support collaboration and self-regulation, to study how students construct their conversation and solve problems while receiving interventions from the system. The project will address the following questions:

a) How would the collaborative environment impact learning in comparison to individual learning?
b) How would the visualization of participation affect collaboration, self-regulation and SSRL?
c) How do groups regulate challenges during collaboration?
d) Is there any difference in the progress of SSRL between low and high performing groups?
e) How and when to provide supportive interventions of the conversational agent? How do we measure the impact of animated conversational agent on learners' motivation and academic success?

3. PROGRESS TO DATE

The initial version of collaborative SQL-Tutor supports pairs of students learning together. Two tools have been implemented so far: the group planning tool and the emotion monitoring tool. The latter tool (Figure 1) is shown to the student when he/she logs in initially, and its goal is to capture mood of the user and eagerness to collaborate. This tool is an individual tool, that is each user will have to answer few questions as individual before they can join the group. The data collected from this tool would be used to corroborate the successful collaboration, as this tool will let us know the initial emotional stage of student, and thus interventions can be altered for each student of the basis on this data. As of now, this tool only provides the internal reflection to user regarding their emotions and how comfortable they are before the session. During this phase, the student can specify the alias he/she wants to be shown to the group, to maintain anonymity.

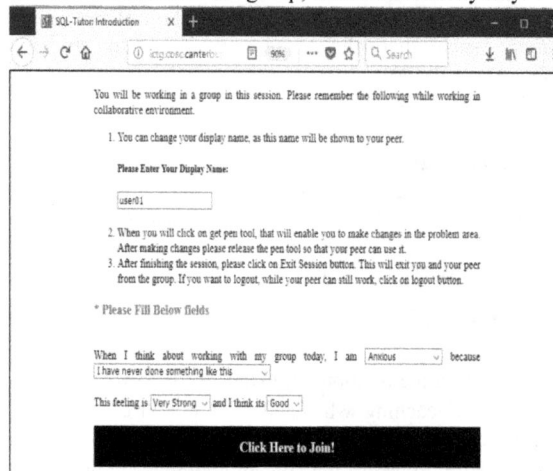

Figure 1: Emotion Monitoring tool

The second tool is the group planning tool (Figure 2); this tool allows both users to discuss and plan how they are going to collaborate. Our hypothesis is that the questions asked would help users to thoroughly analyze the explicit (*While Collaborating, the challenge would be*) and implicit (*What is the outcome you are looking to achieve in this session?*) session features, which will have a positive impact on collaboration. The questions regarding the collaboration would give them idea, when to help each other during the session. This tool would enable us to capture cognitive actions, planning, and monitoring strategies of a group. As of now, this tool lets student decide what and how they want to achieve in this session and when they should converse with each other. So, while planning the session, students can plan and control as a group that what, when and how session should be. Later, these responses would be used to provide adaptive interventions to group, to analyze and to help them achieve goals that they have set at the start of the session.

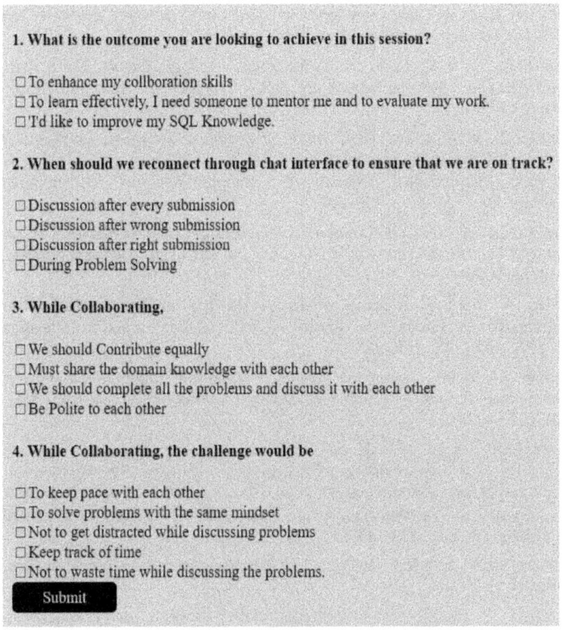

1. What is the outcome you are looking to achieve in this session?

☐ To enhance my collaboration skills
☐ To learn effectively, I need someone to mentor me and to evaluate my work.
☐ I'd like to improve my SQL Knowledge.

2. When should we reconnect through chat interface to ensure that we are on track?

☐ Discussion after every submission
☐ Discussion after wrong submission
☐ Discussion after right submission
☐ During Problem Solving

3. While Collaborating,

☐ We should Contribute equally
☐ Must share the domain knowledge with each other
☐ We should complete all the problems and discuss it with each other
☐ Be Polite to each other

4. While Collaborating, the challenge would be

☐ To keep pace with each other
☐ To solve problems with the same mindset
☐ Not to get distracted while discussing problems
☐ Keep track of time
☐ Not to waste time while discussing the problems.

Submit

Figure 2: Group Planning Tool

The group model works as the storehouse of information pertaining to the group's performance. The group model in SQL-Tutor represents the learning progress, it shows the correct understanding, incorrect understanding and the problems yet to be covered by the group. The system also maintains the session history, which contains the conversation of group while solving the problem, information for both users, feedback levels for each problem and successful and unsuccessful attempts of each problem along with violated or followed constraints.

Figure 3: Collaborative SQL-Tutor

In the current version of the collaborative SQL-Tutor, students are allocated to groups randomly, because the aim of the pilot study is to analyze the usability of newly added components. Students determine the nature of their collaboration in terms of when they communicate and will submit their answers as dyad.

This initial version of Collaborative SQL-Tutor (Figure 3) was used in the pilot study. In addition to evaluating the usability, we also wanted to investigate how students use the planning tool and to study the emotional aspects of user before and after collaboration. The participants in the pilot study were 18 postgraduate students enrolled in the course on Intelligent Tutoring Systems at the University of Canterbury. New components in Collaborative SQL-Tutor are the shared problem area, and the chat area for discussions. A pen-tool is also included

in this version. The Pen-tool enables the user to make changes in the problem area. At any time, only one student can grab the pen. The student who has the pen can add/modify the group solution, while the other student will be locked out from problem area until the first student releases the pen. The moment the first student releases the pen, the change made by that student in problem area will be visible to other student too and pen-tool will be available for both students to grab. All other components are enabled for both students for whole session.

During the pilot study, we found in that in eight groups only one student completed the group plan without consulting their partner. As this was not the expected behavior, the group planning tool will be modified: additional instructions will be provided to the students about making the plan together. There will also be checkpoint such that form can be submitted only when both students have edited it. The results of form can be showed to group in form of visualization, which would act as reminder for them as what exactly they want to achieve in session.

Another observation from the pilot study is that for the first problem, 23% of students who get the pen initially solved the problem on their own and did not interact with other student. In the next version of Collaborative SQL-Tutor we can make improvements so that both users start solving problem together. In almost all sessions, the chat interface was used by both users from the start, but after exchanging pleasantries, both users waited for the completion of first problem by either of them solely. After the submission of first problem, it was observed that both users started exchanging their views frequently for other problems.

4.   Plans for future research

In the next phase of the project, we will develop the components for self-regulation and group regulation will be added, and then conduct an evaluation study. Based on the observations from the pilot study, we will add adaptive visualization to the collaboration panel. Both users would be able to view the number of sentences exchanged in chat area, number of words typed by each student in problem area and their reactions in the form of emojis regarding collaboration experience and level of problem will be displayed to each other, so that they can have view of their own and partner's contribution in collaboration. To support collaboration and self-regulation, the system will promote equal sharing of ideas among collaborators. If one student has not shared for some time or a student is monopolizing the conversation, the agent will present appropriate feedback. This can be seen as a load-balancing task [10]. It would encourage group processing or group and self-assessment of performance by providing individual and group evaluation [10]. We would try to promote on-topic conversation among collaborators. Off-task behavior results in feedback encouraging focus and motivation. Text analysis using text synthesis tools would be used to promote it. Role-switching would also be included in system, as it promotes turn-taking behavior that contributes to social grounding [10, 22]. It includes activities such as asking questions, clarifying views, and commenting on peer work. The focus would be to develop an environment that can capture the social nature of regulation during the collaborative learning contexts. We will observe how students motivate each other and regulate the learning process. The hypothesis is that motivation and academic emotions have a positive influence on self-regulated learning strategies and increase students' academic motivation and the academic achievements. Furthermore, these interventions can be provided as interactive instruction support in the form of conversational agents. The role of conversational agent in this study would not be task-oriented but would be to guide, promote and sustain self-regulation. We would also investigate the learning gains resulted after the conversational agent interventions and whether there would be any impact on the SRL and SSRL after the agent's intervention. The hypothesis is that the inclusion of animated agent would improve motivation and learning gains.

5. CONCLUSIONS

To summarize, collaboration is a strategic competency, but as the evidence suggests too, to develop a collaborative system which not only supports domain level knowledge but also regulate the session and provide timely interventions is challenging to develop. This doctoral research focuses on facilitating the collaboration and self-regulation to regulate individual as well as social motivation and emotions by planning tasks and use affective strategies. The various scripting tools such as emotion monitoring tool and group planning tool along with tools responsible to regulate the sessions and conversational agents would improve the overall experience of users and would help in strategic planning, would keep check on students when they will deviate from the tasks and thus increase the overall learning gains.

REFERENCES

[1]   Vanlehn, K., *The behavior of tutoring systems*. International journal of artificial intelligence in education, 2006. 16(3): p. 227-265.

[2]   Woolf, B.P., *Building intelligent interactive tutors: Student-centered strategies for revolutionizing e-learning*. 2010: Morgan Kaufmann.

[3]   Sottilare, R.A., et al., *Design Recommendations for Intelligent Tutoring Systems: Volume 2-Instructional Management*. Vol. 2. 2014: US Army Research Laboratory.

[4]   Tchounikine, P., N. Rummel, and B.M. McLaren, *Computer supported collaborative learning and intelligent tutoring systems*, in *Advances in intelligent tutoring systems*. 2010, Springer. p. 447-463.

[5]   Magnisalis, I., S. Demetriadis, and A. Karakostas, *Adaptive and intelligent systems for collaborative learning support: A review of the field*. IEEE transactions on Learning Technologies, 2011. 4(1): p. 5-20.

[6]   Lehtinen, E., et al., *Computer supported collaborative learning: A review*. The JHGI Giesbers reports on education, 1999. 10: p. 1999.

[7]   Kaptelinin, V., B.A. Nardi, and C. Macaulay, *Methods & tools: The activity checklist: a tool for representing the "space" of context*. interactions, 1999. 6(4): p. 27-39.

[8]   Baghaei, N., A. Mitrovic, and W. Irwin, *Supporting collaborative learning and problem-solving in a constraint-based CSCL environment for UML class diagrams*. International Journal of Computer-Supported Collaborative Learning, 2007. 2(2-3): p. 159-190.

[9]   Floryan, M., et al. *Collaboration and content recognition features in an inquiry tutor*. in *International Conference on Intelligent Tutoring Systems*. 2010. Springer.

[10] Soller, A., *Supporting social interaction in an intelligent collaborative learning system*. International Journal of Artificial Intelligence in Education (IJAIED), 2001. 12: p. 40-62.

[11] Kobbe, L., et al., *Specifying computer-supported collaboration scripts*. International Journal of Computer-Supported Collaborative Learning, 2007. 2(2): p. 211-224.

[12] Olsen, J.K., et al., *Using an Intelligent Tutoring System to Support Collaborative as well as Individual Learning*, in *Intelligent Tutoring Systems: 12th International Conference, ITS 2014, Honolulu, HI, USA, June 5-9, 2014. Proceedings*, S. Trausan-Matu, et al., Editors. 2014, Springer International Publishing: Cham. p. 134-143.

[13] Johnson, D.W. and R.T. Johnson, *Cooperative learning and achievement*. 1990.

[14] Kollar, I., F. Fischer, and F.W. Hesse, *Collaboration scripts–a conceptual analysis*. Educational Psychology Review, 2006. 18(2): p. 159-185.

[15] Mitrovic, A. *Experiences in implementing constraint-based modeling in SQL-Tutor*. in *Intelligent Tutoring Systems*. 1998. Springer.

[16] Mitrovic, A. and S. Ohlsson, *Evaluation of a constraint-based tutor for a database language*. 1999.

[17] Hadwin, A.F., S. Järvelä, and M. Miller, *Self-regulated, co-regulated, and socially shared regulation of learning*. Handbook of self-regulation of learning and performance, 2011. 30: p. 65-84.

[18] Zimmerman, B.J., *Attaining self-regulation: A social cognitive perspective*, in *Handbook of self-regulation*. 2000, Elsevier. p. 13-39.

[19] Azevedo, R. and J.G. Cromley, *Does training on self-regulated learning facilitate students' learning with hypermedia?* Journal of educational psychology, 2004. 96(3): p. 523.

[20] Winne, P.H. and A.F. Hadwin, *nStudy: Tracing and supporting self-regulated learning in the Internet*, in *International handbook of metacognition and learning technologies*. 2013, Springer. p. 293-308.

[21] Miller, M. and A. Hadwin, *Scripting and awareness tools for regulating collaborative learning: Changing the landscape of support in CSCL*. Computers in Human Behavior, 2015. 52: p. 573-588.

[22] Inaba, A. and R. Mizoguchi. *Learners' roles and predictable educational benefits in collaborative learning*. in *International Conference on Intelligent Tutoring Systems*. 2004. Springer.

Modeling Learners' Interest with a Domain-Independent Ontology-Based Framework

DeKita G. Moon
University of Florida
Gainesville, FL
dekita@ufl.edu

ABSTRACT

Ontologies are recognized as a promising approach to support the reusability and interoperability of learners' preferences; which is useful for the optimization and flexibility of data and resources. However, little to no research on adaptive learning systems or semantic technologies explore personalized experiences based on the various out-of-school experiences and activities of the users. This research investigates the design, development, and evaluation of an ontology-based framework for students' interests in a math word problem generator that may be applied to various other learning systems and possibly other domains. The cohesiveness of the problems in addition to the usability, usefulness, and the short-term effectiveness of the derived technology will be investigated by comparing the generated questions to numerical and traditional Algebra I problems. We aim to better understand students' interests to identify the role that their interests can play in semantic technologies, further supporting the recent advances in ontology-based educational technologies and personalized math word problem generators.

KEYWORDS

human-centered computing; educational technologies; semantic technologies; domain ontologies, knowledge graphs

ACM Reference Format:
DeKita G. Moon . 2018. Modeling Learners' Interest with a Domain-Independent Ontology-Based Framework. In *UMAP '18: 26th Conference on User Modeling, Adaptation and Personalization, July 8–11, 2018, Singapore, Singapore*. ACM, New York, NY, USA, 4 pages. https://doi.org/10.1145/3209219.3213598

1 INTRODUCTION

Students' motivation and engagement is a national concern in K-12 math education. Research suggests that there are several factors which may contribute to students' academic disengagement and the decline in attitudes towards math. Students' disengagement is associated with unfamiliar and uninteresting math content in addition to the disconnect between students' individuality and the generic nature of their academic curriculum [11, 12, 16]. To counteract influences that may lead to students' disengagement

with math, personalized Math Word Problem (MWP) generators have been designed to incorporate students' interests and real-life experiences in connection with their learning activities.

Personalized MWP generators are systems that provide students with relevant questions pertaining to their individual interests, which can potentially improve students' situational interests, overall interest in math, and long-term learning achievements [4, 26]. Previous work has focused on both template-based and natural language generation methods. However, very few systems with linguistic capabilities have addressed the various interests and out-of-school activities that are specific to each individual student. Specifically, many of the systems use biographical questionnaires to capture the students' interests, which are then added to the slots within the template problems [1, 11, 18]. These systems lack linguistic capabilities that give meaning to students' interests, resulting in possible pronoun confusion [20] and preventing changes to the context of the problems [17]. Those that use linguistic and statistical methods mainly focuses on predetermined topics chosen by the researchers, including movie themes [20], literary themes [21], and other educational subjects from the students' curriculum [21]. As a result, other interests which may be more engaging to the students are excluded. Thus, the level of topic personalization is minimized. The topic personalization of problems demonstrates the contextual fluidity of the questions that students can take part in modifying based on their interests.

Many advances in MWP generation literature focuses on incorporating various natural language processing techniques using the stand-alone application approach. They cover the utilization of parts-of speech parsing tools [10], probabilistic models, [16], and linguistic theories [8, 16]. Despite the growth in this area, few researches adopt some of the recent approaches in the field of adaptive learning systems. One of the recent developments across educational technologies extend to the processing of interpretable data that support the interoperability between systems and the exchange of the shareable data across product lines and platforms, as expressed at the Artificial Intelligence in Education (AIED) Conference Workshop in 2009 [5]. The exploitation of student preferences in adaptive learning and intelligent tutoring systems are expressed by their learning styles, cognitive abilities, prior knowledge, task performance, and learning goals [7]. These preferences are usually presented in the form of domain ontologies among user models to provide relevant information that supports the personalization of instructional materials [13]. These tutoring systems can offer both meta-cognitive and effective support to improve learning gains among standardized tests, the students' engagement, and affect [2, 28]. However, in this space, very little attention has been given to the inclusion of the various out-of-school interests and activities of students to maximize the level of personalization of learning materials and further improve learning and motivation. Therefore, there is a technological need for enhancing educational systems using a semantic technology approach to incorporate students' interests. With this intent, we seek to understand the needs and address the potential benefits of this approach, specifically for generating personalized MWPs.

In this research, we intend to develop, design, and evaluate an interest domain-ontology for the personalization of MWPs. A framework will be created, using natural language processing methods, information extraction, and semantic and lexical relations to preserve the semantic and syntactic structure of traditional MWPs with the students' interests incorporated. In doing so, we seek to explore the design needs of the proposed technology using a learner-centered approach for personalized MWP generation. Furthermore, we look to develop a system that extracts and organizes relevant information about students' interests, which we plan to obtain from a student profile questionnaire. Lastly, the outcomes of students' cognition, engagement, and affect will be measured. The remainder of this paper is organized as follows. In Section 2, we present the relevant literature. In Section 3, we introduce the framework of this research, while Section 4 establishes the research challenges and the work plan. In Section 5 we conclude with the expected contributions.

2 RELATED WORK

There is limited research focused on the generation of Math Word Problems (MWPs). Many of them use templates to provide the system with a semantic and syntactic structure that outlines the produced questions. For example, Polozov et al. proposed a system that allows users to select the problem type, the characters, and the character roles in their choice of the three literary themes (Fantasy, Science Fiction, School of Wizardry). Their logic-based system uses an answer-set programming paradigm that synthesizes the narrative into a plot graph using natural language processing. The system's ontology consists of the roles and actions of the characters and the objects that play into the plot of each of the three literary themes [21].

Some of the systems require that the input of the sampled data for the derived questions are done manually. The Intelligent Math Tutor presented in [10] describes MWP generating as a way to include other instructional materials from various subjects, such as science. Sample MWPs are included in the system along with the required input of concepts or facts from a different subject topic. The concepts are extracted from both the sample problems and the learning materials which are mapped together using a natural language processing parser to generate new problems.

In [16], the domain concepts and thematics is retrieved from a textual corpus. Their work focuses on the development of a MWP generator based on three movie themes (Star Wars, Western, and Cartoon). Their system uses the semantic and syntactic structure of the original story to rewrite the problems based on the theme that is selected by the student.

Theune et al. proposed a similar approach to creating probability problems, allowing the user to choose a problem type and varying

narratives among the context repository. The semantic-based system also used natural language techniques linking the entities to the corresponding lemma (e.g. bikes are a specific color and have a specific price) to create sentence trees for any of the available problem types [25].

In [15], they developed a web-based intelligent tutor system called the Math Story Problem Tutor, which includes a Question Generation Module based on natural language generation. They manually created the semantic and linguistic descriptions of coin and die story problems to characterize the possible objects, events, and conditions which may occur within these problems and the linguistic patterns of each. With the detailed and interchangeable descriptions, this system is independent of templates, unlike most generating systems.

Among the limited research in the generation of MWPs, ontologies based on semantic web standards are seldom described. Williams focuses on a MWP generator using domain-independent ontologies written in Web Ontology Language (OWL). The system interprets the elements (axioms and integers) in the OWL statements to render English sentences that form the multiplicative compare MWPs [27].

The main drawbacks to the previous systems is that student preferences and the elements that are used to build the MWPs are limited to the system in which it is deployed and that there are limited to topics that are available. This research addresses these limitations and drawbacks by using a learner-centered approach to understand the user preferences with implications to provide machine-readable data.

3 INTEREST DOMAIN FRAMEWORK

We propose a framework, which focuses on extracting and organizing the underlying concepts among students' interests that can be applied to other learning platforms and possibly to various other domains. With the proposed system, we will collect Algebra I students' out-of-school activities and hobbies (i.e. pet's name, favorite hobbies, favorite sports, etc.) using a unique identification (Participant 1, Participant 2, etc.). The entities, concepts, relations, and other relevant information will be drawn from the resources that describes the acquired interests to create the ontology and the knowledge graph. The interest ontology will give meaning to the terms among their interests and enable its reuse while the knowledge graph will aid in the discovery of the semantic relations between the context of the traditional MWPs and the students' interests. As a result, the individual interests of students will be applied to a database of traditional Algebra I Math Word Problems (MWPs) using the annotated information that each problem possesses. The database of problems aligns with teachers' reuse of instructional materials and exercises [23].

Take for example the following problem, *"You are selling tickets for a high school play. Student tickets cost 4 dollars and general admission tickets cost 6 dollars. You sell 525 tickets and collect $2,876 dollars. How many student tickets and general admission tickets did you sell?"* The possible tagged word of the given, *play* could be annotated to elicit other content words related to an event involving students' favorite hobbies, interests, or activities. In turn, students who are interested in *football* may receive the question as, *"You are* *selling tickets for a high school football game..."* Students interested in *dancing* would receive the question possibly referring to a *dance competition* and so forth.

4 RESEARCH CHALLENGES AND WORK PLAN

To address the gaps in the literature and further personalizing users' experiences, the following key challenges will be examined:

(1) Elicit the user needs, including identifying the out-of-school interests and hobbies of Algebra I students
(2) Developing a framework encapsulating the syntactic and semantic trajectories and lexical relations of the content words for the ontology
(3) Discovering the lexical and semantic relationships between the content words of the traditional math word problems (MWPs) and users' interests to effectively rewrite problems that students perceived to be personalized

Based on these challenges, a learner-centered approach will be used to address the following research goals:

- Better understand and identify the needs, preferences, and concerns that students have with the context of traditional Algebra I MWPs
- Explore the development of the ontology-based framework for students' interests that improves the experiences of Algebra I students
- Evaluate the coherence, usefulness, usability, and short-term effectiveness of the problems from the derived technology compared to existing math problems

To achieve these goals, this research will be executed in the following phases: requirement analysis, participatory design, the developmental phase, and user evaluation. The phases are described in detail below.

4.1 Requirement Analysis

The first step in this research is to better conceptualize the interests and the design needs of participating students from urban, rural, and suburban schools. Focus groups will be conducted to gather empirical evidence through understanding the concerns, challenges, needs, and preferences of Algebra I students regarding the MWPs and their context. At the beginning of each session, students' interests will be gauged using a personalized questionnaire adopted from the works of Anand and Ross [1] and Bates and Wiest [3]. Shortly after, students will be asked a series of questions to obtain additional interests that were not collected with the questionnaire. Additionally, their likes and dislikes with MWPs will be discussed using a semi-structured interview. Traditional MWPs taken from their classroom text and teachers' instructional materials will be viewed to further extract information that will inform the design and specify the scope. The data and feedback from this phase will be video recorded, transcribed, and coded to discover reoccurring themes.

4.2 Participatory Design

The next phase focuses on identifying the content words and their annotations among the MWPs in the database. The aim of this phase is to observe the authoring of MWPs using a heuristic approach to understand how experienced students would rewrite the word problems. The identified content words and their annotations will be used to replace the context of the traditional problems with students' interests. The content words will be tagged, and the annotations will be gathered using experienced students who have taken Algebra and/or Calculus courses. These students will be given a predefined number of traditional MWPs from the database and will be asked to use these problems to create problems that are more personalized to them. For each problem, the general context that can be used to generate their rewritten problem will be solicited. Additional annotations and feedback will be retrieved, using a brief focus group to gather the students' thought processes used to create their personalized problems.

4.3 Developmental Phase

The developmental phase consists of building the database, the knowledge graph, the ontology, and the interface of the derived technology. First, the database is created to house the students' interests, the traditional MWPs, and the content words among the traditional MWPs. The terms among the student interests and the tagged content words obtained in the first two phases will aid in the identification of the initial core content. Similar to the approach in [29], the domain concepts will be obtained from the core ontology and the hypernyms, synonyms, and hyponyms for these concepts and terms will be obtained from the WordNet database. Altogether, the content words, their derived forms (draw, drawing, drawn), the inherited linguistics, and the natural language descriptions for each word will be obtained. Relevant content words will be extracted from Wikipedia to obtain relevant domain knowledge about the interests, which will be used to find additional relations among the data [16]. Terms from Wikipedia will be found using the tdf-idf score derived from [24]. The knowledge graph developed is essential to cross linking and finding the semantic similarities between the interests and the tagged content words in the traditional problems [22]. This includes the information that is extracted from the online resources, their parts of speech, and their inherited hypernyms. Similar to [16], the most semantic compatible interests of the students will be discovered and inputted into the problems using a probabilistic language model.

4.4 Evaluation

We will test the performance of the ontology in conjunction with the derived system. First, the usability of the proposed system will be observed, as measured by the System Usability Scale (SUS) [6] and obtaining qualitative feedback from the students. Students will be asked to complete several tasks based on the features of the proposed system prior to completing the SUS questionnaire and the interviews. The evaluation phase also focuses on the impact that the questions from the derived technology has on students' performance, perceived personalization, and perceived comprehensiveness compared to the corresponding Algebra I numerical and traditional MWPs. The students will complete a number of the three types of questions stated above using a within-subject design approach. The performance will be measured by examining the accuracy and the time to complete each question. Additionally, the perceived personalization 7-point scale survey adopted from [14] will be used. Students will be asked if they perceive each question to be design specifically for them and if the question targets them as a unique individual. The perceived comprehensiveness will also be measured using a subjective questionnaire, with students reporting how clear/unclear, easy/difficult, and logically structured/not logically structured is the text [19]. The cohesiveness of the personalized questions from the derived technology will also be compared to the corresponding traditional MWPs. This research will use the Coh-Metrix Tool to gauge the difficulty of the text. The text will be inputted into the tool to automatically examine the syntactic complexity, word concreteness, and the cohesion of the text [9].

5 CONCLUSIONS

The aim of this research is to better understand and investigate the design needs to inform the design and the development of a novel ontology-based framework using students' out-of-school interests in math word problems in a way that could possibly be integrated and reused in other learning technologies and for other domains. The following are the expected contributions in the fields of HCI, Semantic Technologies, and Education:

- HCI: A system with reusable and shareable data for the novel interest domain-ontology to further support students' personalized learning experiences
- Semantic Technologies: Providing a novel framework for user interests that can be used in learning systems and within other domains
- Education: Impact personalized and adaptive learning systems so that further considerations are made during the development systems for students of diverse backgrounds and experiences

Our current work focuses on the initial phases of this research, which includes exploring the design needs through the exploratory studies with the students. Further considerations will also be given to the ontology generation techniques and information extraction methodologies that are the most appropriate at reflecting the best practices for ontology development.

ACKNOWLEDGMENTS

Special thanks to my advisor, Dr. Juan E. Gilber and my committee, Dr. Lisa Anthony, Dr. Katie Indarawis, and Dr. Bonnie Dorr for their support and feedback on this research. I would also like to extend gratitude to the reviewers for their valuable comments and to the Human-Experience Research Lab at the University of Florida.

REFERENCES

[1] Padma G Anand and Steven M Ross. 1987. Using computer-assisted instruction to personalize arithmetic materials for elementary school children. *Journal of educational psychology* 79, 1 (1987), 72.
[2] Ivon Arroyo, Beverly Park Woolf, Winslow Burelson, Kasia Muldner, Dovan Rai, and Minghui Tai. 2014. A multimedia adaptive tutoring system for mathematics that addresses cognition, metacognition and affect. *International Journal of Artificial Intelligence in Education* 24, 4 (2014), 387–426.
[3] Eric T Bates and Lynda R Wiest. 2004. Impact of Personalization of Mathematical Word Problems on Student Performance. *Mathematics Educator* 14, 2 (2004), 17–26.
[4] Matthew L Bernacki and Candace Walkington. 2014. The Impact of a Personalization Intervention for Mathematics on Learning and Non-Cognitive Factors.. In *EDM (Workshops)*.
[5] Jacqueline Bourdeau and Monique Grandbastien. 2010. Modeling tutoring knowledge. In *Advances in intelligent tutoring systems*. Springer, 123–143.
[6] John Brooke et al. 1996. SUS-A quick and dirty usability scale. *Usability evaluation in industry* 189, 194 (1996), 4–7.
[7] Konstantina Chrysafiadi and Maria Virvou. 2013. Student modeling approaches: A literature review for the last decade. *Expert Systems with Applications* 40, 11 (2013), 4715–4729.
[8] Paul Deane and Kathleen Sheehan. 2003. Automatic Item Generation via Frame Semantics: Natural Language Generation of Math Word Problems. (2003).
[9] Arthur C Graesser, Danielle S McNamara, Max M Louwerse, and Zhiqiang Cai. 2004. Coh-Metrix: Analysis of text on cohesion and language. *Behavior research methods, instruments, & computers* 36, 2 (2004), 193–202.
[10] Monika Gupta, Neelamadhav Gantayat, and Renuka Sindhgatta. 2017. Intelligent Math Tutor: Problem-Based Approach to Create Cognizance. In *Proceedings of the Fourth (2017) ACM Conference on Learning@ Scale*. ACM, 241–244.
[11] Sigve Høgheim and Rolf Reber. 2017. Eliciting mathematics interest: New directions for context personalization and example choice. *The Journal of Experimental Education* 85, 4 (2017), 597–613.
[12] Ensign Jacque. 1996. Linking Life Experiences To Classroom Math. (1996).
[13] Jelena Jovanović, Dragan Gašević, Colin Knight, and Griff Richards. 2007. Ontologies for effective use of context in e-learning settings. *Journal of Educational Technology & Society* 10, 3 (2007).
[14] Sriram Kalyanaraman and S Shyam Sundar. 2006. The psychological appeal of personalized content in web portals: Does customization affect attitudes and behavior? *Journal of Communication* 56, 1 (2006), 110–132.
[15] Nabila Khodeir, Nayer Wanas, Hanan Elazhary, and Nadia Hegazy. 2017. Addressing student misinterpretations of story problems in MAST. In *Advanced Control Circuits Systems (ACCS) Systems & 2017 Intl Conf on New Paradigms in Electronics & Information Technology (PEIT), 2017 Intl Conf on*. IEEE, 204–211.
[16] Rik Koncel-Kedziorski, Ioannis Konstas, Luke Zettlemoyer, and Hannaneh Hajishirzi. 2016. A Theme-Rewriting Approach for Generating Algebra Word Problems. *arXiv preprint arXiv:1610.06210* (2016).
[17] Audra Eileen Kosh. 2016. *The effects on mathematics performance of personalizing word problems to students' interests*. Ph.D. Dissertation. The University of North Carolina at Chapel Hill.
[18] Heng-Yu Ku, Christi A Harter, Pei-Lin Liu, Ling Thompson, and Yi-Chia Cheng. 2007. The effects of individually personalized computer-based instructional program on solving mathematics problems. *Computers in human behavior* 23, 3 (2007), 1195–1210.
[19] F van Meurs, HPLM Korzilius, and JJ Hermans. 2004. The influence of the use of English in Dutch job advertisements: An experimental study into the effects on text evaluation, on attitudes towards the organisation and the job, and on comprehension. (2004).
[20] Kumaresh Nandhini and Sadhu Ramakrishnan Balasundaram. 2011. Math word Question Generation for Training the students with learning difficulties. In *Proceedings of the International Conference & Workshop on Emerging Trends in Technology*. ACM, 206–211.
[21] Oleksandr Polozov, Eleanor O'Rourke, Adam M Smith, Luke Zettlemoyer, Sumit Gulwani, and Zoran Popovic. 2015. Personalized Mathematical Word Problem Generation.. In *IJCAI*. 381–388.
[22] Ankita Prasad, Archana Praveen Kumar, and Ashalata Nayak. 2015. Construction and evaluation of metaontology using databases. In *India Conference (INDICON), 2015 Annual IEEE*. IEEE, 1–6.
[23] Jean-Marc Robert and Gracia Gingras. 2005. Experimental study on the reuse of learning objects and teaching practices. In *Proc. Intâ€Žl Conf. on Education and Technology, Calgary, Canada*.
[24] Gerard Salton and Christopher Buckley. 1988. Term-weighting approaches in automatic text retrieval. *Information processing & management* 24, 5 (1988), 513–523.
[25] Mariët Theune, Roan Boer Rookhuiszen, Hanneke Geerlings, et al. 2011. Generating varied narrative probability exercises. In *Proceedings of the 6th Workshop on Innovative Use of NLP for Building Educational Applications*. Association for Computational Linguistics, 20–29.
[26] Candace Walkington and Matthew L Bernacki. 2014. Motivating students by â€œpersonalizingâ€ learning around individual interests: A consideration of theory, design, and implementation issues. In *Motivational Interventions*. Emerald Group Publishing Limited, 139–176.
[27] Sandra Williams. 2011. Generating Mathematical Word Problems. In *AAAI Fall Symposium: Question Generation*.
[28] Beverly Park Woolf, Ivon Arroyo, David Cooper, Winslow Burleson, and Kasia Muldner. 2010. Affective tutors: Automatic detection of and response to student emotion. In *Advances in Intelligent Tutoring Systems*. Springer, 207–227.
[29] G. Zhou, J. Lu, C.-Y. Wan, M. D. Yarvis, and J. A. Stankovic. 2008. *Body Sensor Networks*. MIT Press, Cambridge, MA.

"why" questions. Such questions compel the human tutor to explain (1) the reason for selecting a particular problem to solve, (2) the reason for an incorrect suggestion, and (3) the reason for the student's demonstration.

In this study, a modified version of the ITS to provide adaptive assistance on how to teach or proceed with the tutoring task was used. When the tutor requests assistance (e.g. *"What should I do now?"*), Mr. Williams, an embedded metatutor agent, provides one of the four types of help: (a) *quiz assistance* to suggest when students should take the quiz and why, (b) *problem selection assistance* to suggest what problem students should pose next and why, (c) *resource assistance* to suggest when students should review a particular resource and why, and (d) *impasse recovery assistance* to suggest a problem restart or give a new problem when students are stuck for a predetermined amount of time.

Aside from the adaptive scaffold the system provides, APLUS is embedded with resources to support activation of self-regulatory processes. These features aid tutors in setting up their goals by learning what the task is all about, planning strategies by understanding the subject domain, teaching their tutee, and assessing their own understanding and performance.

The ITS logs all interactions with the system capturing students' behavior, agents and system responses and all other related information for more or less 120 minutes. The interaction events include actions prior to, during and after the tutoring tasks. The log files record information such as attempt identifier (e.g. UserID, sessionID), timestamp, the specific action taken (e.g., new problem attempted, hint requested, hint explained, new step started, problem submitted, and problem abandoned), action evaluation (e.g., correct action, error action, and hint followed), and problem/task category (i.e., oneStep, twoStep, bothSides). Linear equation problems having variables on both sides or problem category bothSides are the considered the challenge tasks in this context.

4 PROPOSED METHODS AND CURRENT PROGRESS

This research work will utilize data acquired from the students use of an ITS as well as machine learning methodologies to build the models of persistence. To be able to derive the models, the following steps will be carried out: review of works on persistence to identify possible features associated with the construct to be modeled, derive ground truth data, and develop and evaluate models.

Several theories have been studied to explore student persistence. From literature, Tinto's *student integration theory* [28] and Astin's *student involvement theory* [29] are arguably two of the most well-known frameworks on students' persistence. This work is grounded upon postulates that associate persistence with student's compatibility with the academic demands (i.e. prior skills and experiences) and his patterns of interaction within the learning environment.

As most studies on persistence utilized traditional measures (e.g., self-reports and observer's reports), this work will attempt to utilized behavioral measures of persistence, patterned after previous studies mentioned in Section 2 and distilled from students' domain knowledge assessments and their interaction logs.

As supervised and semi-supervised machine learning tasks necessitates ground truth for training, the researcher is currently focused on deriving ground truth data set for the target construct to be used in model derivation. A tool to visualize students' action sequences was developed and will be utilized by human coders to label student action sequences (e.g., as positive persistence, negative persistence, or non-persistence) based on some labeling criteria. Considering the cost of manual labeling, active learning [30] for ground truth will be explored for this work.

Lastly, this work presents an opportunity to explore the use of more advanced techniques, like deep learning, in investigating educational data sets. Deep learning is an emerging class of machine learning that explores many layers of non-linear information processing for supervised or unsupervised feature extraction and transformation, and for pattern analysis and classification [31]. Typically using artificial neural networks, deep learning automatically learns feature representations from large volume of unlabelled data by learning complex function mappings of the input to the output directly from data, without depending completely on human-crafted features. Deep learning has been shown to successfully learn layers of feature representation for static datasets which can be stacked to create deep networks that is more capable of modeling complex structures in the data. Hence, this work will attempt to use such methodology to determine whether meaningful features of the construct being studied can be automatically learned from the raw logs of an ITS and to verify if these features can detect student task persistence better than the features derived using traditional machine learning techniques.

5 POTENTIAL CONTRIBUTIONS

It is a fact how computer based learning systems revolutionized educational landscape. While students benefit from these learning systems, learner diversity poses a challenge to the "one size fits all" learning models in these environments. As shown in a recent work, [32] students tend to customize their virtual peer's avatar in their own ethnicity implying that learner profiles (e.g., prior knowledge, preferences, interests and behaviors) vary, hence students cannot be treated homogeneously.   This gives importance to learning platforms that personalize user interactions and experiences that is only achievable by adapting to student profiles. Hence, the importance of models to represent students' attributes and patterns of thoughts and behavior in designing personalized learning system. Student models could provide educational technology designers a guide in designing personalized learning environments catering to individual needs and abilities, and in developing interventions to improve not only students' cognitive abilities but their non-cognitive skills as well. Specifically, the models that may be derived from this work, will provide additional insights on student persistence, which can serve as basis for guideline formulation on the design of educational systems to encourage persistence among students and incorporation of appropriate interventions that induces the learner to persist in difficult tasks.

6 ADVICE SOUGHT

The research is still at the early stage and I hope to gain experts' opinion on how to improve and best approach this research. Particularly, I am seeking advices and insights related to:

- Features of students' persistence: What students' actions can be most effectively tied with persistence?
- Methodology: What methods should be used to most effectively model student persistence? Is deep learning a practical option for this line of research?

ACKNOWLEDGMENTS

The author would like to thank her adviser Dr. Ma. Mercedes T. Rodrigo of the Ateneo de Manila University. Acknowledgment is likewise extended to the Department of Science and Technology-Engineering Research and Development for Technology (DOST-ERDT) for their support, Dr. Noboru Matsuda of Texas A & M University for allowing the use of SimStudent in the Philippines, and Ateneo de Davao University, Krus Na Ligas High School, and University of the Cordilleras for letting the author to do her fieldwork in their institutions.

REFERENCES

[1] A.A. Valencia. 1994. The Attributes of Academically Successful Mexican-American University Male and Female Students. *Journal of multicultural counseling and development.* 22, 4 (1994), 227–238.

[2] D. Clarke, J. Cheeseman, A. Roche, & S. van der Schans. 2014. Teaching Strategies for Building Student Persistence on Challenging Tasks: Insights Emerging from Two Approaches to Teacher Professional Learning. *Mathematics Teacher Education and Development.* 16, 2 (2014), 46–70.

[3] V. Aleven, B. Mclaren, I. Roll, & K. Koedinger. 2006. Toward meta-cognitive tutoring: A model of help seeking with a Cognitive Tutor. *International Journal of Artificial Intelligence in Education.* 16, 2 (2006), 101–128.

[4] A.F. Cabrera, A. Nora, & M.B. Castaneda. 1993. College Persistence: Structural Equations Modeling Test of an Integrated Model of Student Retention. *The Journal of Higher Education.* 64, 2 (Mar. 1993), 123. DOI:https://doi.org/10.2307/2960026.

[5] K. E. DiCerbo. (2014). Game-based assessment of persistence. *Journal of Educational Technology & Society,* 17(1).

[6] Farrington, C.A. et al. 2012. *Teaching Adolescents to Become Learners: The Role of Noncognitive Factors in Shaping School Performance--A Critical Literature Review.* Consortium on Chicago School Research.

[7] T. Kautz, J.J. Heckman, R. Diris, B. Ter Weel and L. Borghans. 2014. *Fostering and measuring skills: Improving cognitive and non-cognitive skills to promote lifetime success* (No. w20749). National Bureau of Economic Research.

[8] N. Shechtman, A. deBarger, C. Dornsife, S. Rosier, & L. Yarnall. 2013. Promoting grit, tenacity, and perseverance: Critical factors for success in the 21st century. *Washington, DC: US Department of Education, Department of Educational Technology.* (2013), 1–107.

[9] Duckworth, A. L., Peterson, C., Matthews, M. D., & Kelly, D. R. (2007). Grit: perseverance and passion for long-term goals. Journal of personality and social psychology, 92(6), 1087.

[10] American Management Association. 2012 Critical Skills Survey. *Executive Summary.* Retrieved from www.amanet.org

[11] S. Conceicao, and R. Lehman. 2013. Persistence Model for Online Student Retention. (Jun. 2013), 1913–1922.

[12] H.R. Glazer, and J.A. Murphy. 2015. Optimizing Success: A Model for Persistence in Online Education. *American Journal of Distance Education.* 29, 2 (Apr. 2015), 135–144. DOI:https://doi.org/10.1080/08923647.2015.1023093.

[13] Y. Fang, Y.J. Xu, B. Nye, A. Graesser, P. Pavlik, and X. Hu. 2017. Online Learning Persistence and Academic Achievement.

[14] J. Mostow, J.E. Beck, J. E. and J. Valeri, J. 2003. Can automated emotional scaffolding affect student persistence? A Baseline Experiment. In *Proceedings of the Workshop on" Assessing and Adapting to User Attitudes and Affect: Why, When and How?" at the 9th International Conference on User Modeling (UM'03)* (pp. 61-64).

[15] J. Xie, A. Essa, S. Mojarad, R.S. Baker, K. Shubeck and X. Hu. 2017, Student Learning Strategies and Behaviors to Predict Success in an Online Adaptive Mathematics Tutoring System. *transfer, 15*(16), p.17

[16] B.W. Roberts, O.S. Chernyshenko, S. Stark and L.R. Goldberg. 2005. The structure of conscientiousness: An empirical investigation based on seven major personality questionnaires. *Personnel Psychology, 58*(1), pp.103-139.

[17] T. F. Field, B.J. McCroskey, R. Sherman, and D.T. James. 1975. Modeling and persistence levels of university students and prison inmates. *The Journal of Experimental Education, 43*(3), 22-24.

[18] T. Bouffard-Bouchard. 1990. Influence of Self-Efficacy on Performance in a Cognitive Task. *The Journal of Social Psychology.* 130, 3 (Jun. 1990), 353–363. DOI:https://doi.org/10.1080/00224545.1990.9924591.

[19] E. E. Boe, H. May, and R. F. Boruch. 2002. Student Task Persistence in the Third International Mathematics and Science Study: A Major Source of Achievement Differences at the National, Classroom, and Student Levels.

[20] M. Ventura and V. Shute. 2013. *The validity of a game-based assessment of persistence.*

[21] T. del Solato and B. Du Boulay. 1995. Implementation of motivational tactics in tutoring systems. *Journal of Interactive Learning Research, 6*(4), 337.

[22] Shimin Kai, Ma. Victoria Almeda, Ryan S. Baker, Cristina Heffernan and Neil Heffernan. 2017. Modeling Wheel-spinning and Productive Persistence in Skill Builders. *Journal of Educational Data Mining.* (in press) (2017).

[23] G. Biswas, J.R. Segedy and K. Bunchongchit. 2015. From Design to Implementation to Practice a Learning by Teaching System: Betty's Brain. *International Journal of Artificial Intelligence in Education.* (2016), 26(1), 350-364.

[24] W. Schneider. 2008. The Development of Metacognitive Knowledge in Children and Adolescents: Major Trends and Implications for Education. *Mind, Brain, and Education.* 2, 3 (Sep. 2008), 114–121. DOI:https://doi.org/10.1111/j.1751-228X.2008.00041.x.

[25] C. Kirkegaard, A. Gulz, A. Silvervarg. 2014. Introducing a challenging teachable agent. *Learning and Collaboration Technologies. Designing and Developing Novel Learning Experiences.* Springer, Cham.. 53–62.

[26] J. Werfel. 2013. Embodied teachable agents: Learning by teaching robots. *Intelligent Autonomous Systems, The 13th International Conference on* (2013).

[27] N. Matsuda, N. Barbalios, Z. Zhao, A. Ramamurthy, G.J. Stylianides and K.R. Koedinger. 2016, June. Tell me how to teach, I'll learn how to solve problems. In *International Conference on Intelligent Tutoring Systems* (pp. 111-121). Springer, Cham.

[28] V. Tinto. 2006. Research and practice of student retention: What next?. *Journal of College Student Retention: Research, Theory & Practice, 8*(1), 1-19.

[29] A. W. Astin. 1984. Student involvement: A developmental theory for higher education. *Journal of college student personnel, 25*(4), 297-308.

[30] A. Fathi, M.F. Balcan, X. Ren, and J.M. Rehg. (2011). *Combining Self Training and Active Learning for Video Segmentation.* Georgia Institute of Technology.

[31] L. Deng and D. Yu. 2014. Deep Learning: Methods and Applications. *Foundations and Trends® in Signal Processing.* 7, 3–4 (Jun. 2014), 197–387. DOI:https://doi.org/10.1561/2000000039.

[32] E. Yarzebinski, C. Dumdumaya, M.M.T. Rodrigo, N. Matsuda, and A. Ogan. 2017, June. Regional Cultural Differences in How Students Customize Their Avatars in Technology-Enhanced Learning. In *International Conference on Artificial Intelligence in Education* (pp. 598-601). Springer, Cham.

Exploring Users' Perception of Rating Summary Statistics

Extended Abstract

Ludovik Coba
Free University of Bozen
Bolzano, Italy
lucoba@unibz.it

Markus Zanker
Free University of Bozen
Bolzano, Italy
mzanker@unibz.it

Laurens Rook
TU Delft
Delft, The Netherlands
L.Rook@tudelft.nl

Panagiotis Symeonidis
Free University of Bozen
Bolzano, Italy
psymeonidis@unibz.it

ABSTRACT

Collaborative filtering systems heavily depend on user feedback expressed in product ratings to select and rank items to recommend. These summary statistics of rating values carry two important descriptors about the assessed items, namely the total number of ratings and the mean rating value. In this study we explore how these two signals influence the decisions of online users based on choice-based conjoint experiments. Results show that users are more inclined to follow the mean indicator as opposed to the total number of ratings. Empirical results can serve as an input to developing algorithms that foster items with a, consequently, higher probability of choice based on their rating summarizations or their *explainability* due to these ratings when ranking recommendations.

KEYWORDS

Recommender systems, User studies, Explanation styles

ACM Reference Format:
Ludovik Coba, Markus Zanker, Laurens Rook, and Panagiotis Symeonidis. 2018. Exploring Users' Perception of Rating Summary Statistics: Extended Abstract. In *UMAP '18: 26th Conference on User Modeling, Adaptation and Personalization, July 8–11, 2018, Singapore, Singapore*. ACM, New York, NY, USA, 2 pages. https://doi.org/10.1145/3209219.3209256

1 INTRODUCTION

User ratings are one of the key ingredient to collaborative filtering algorithms to automatically assess how likely items might match users' tastes. Although, recently, implicit signals on users' actual behavior have turned out to possess even more predictive power for practical systems [4, 6], ratings still play a dominant role in constructing the value and quality perception of an item in the eyes of online consumers [2]. Collaborative explanations [3] provide justifications for recommendations by displaying information about the rating behavior of a users' neighbourhood, as has been already identified by Herlocker et al. [5]. Also, e-commerce sites usually provide at least rating summary statistics along with the products in their catalogs.

This extended abstract therefore discusses a study that explores how the two dominant characteristics of a rating summarization, namely the number of ratings and their mean value, impact the choice behavior of users. Results show that - all things being equal -

users are clearly biased towards selecting items with higher means as opposed to larger numbers of ratings, which provides clear indications about the degree of *persuasiveness* [12] of collaborative explanations for different products and different user neighborhoods. Note, that a full-length paper including a full description of the methodology and all results can be accessed in [1].

2 RELATED WORK

Explanations for recommendations have received considerable research attention over the past years [3, 11]. There are different ways of explaining recommendations based on collaborative filtering mechanisms as presented in Herlocker et al. [5]. They explored 21 different interfaces and demonstrated that specifically the "user" style improves the acceptance of recommendations. The "user" style of explanation provides information about the neighborhood, which is determined based on a generic notion of similarity between users when analyzing their observed behavior or expressed opinions (i.e., buys, clicks, ratings etc.).

In this work we are interested in shedding light on users' trade-off between rating numbers and their mean values when they have to make a choice.

Conjoint analysis is a market technique suitable for revealing user preferences and trade-offs in the decision making process[9]. Conjoint analysis has successfully been employed in a wide range of areas, such as education, health, tourism, and human computer interaction.In the field of recommender systems and online decision support, Zanker and Schoberegger [13] employed a ranking-based conjoint experiment to understand the persuasive power of different explanation styles over the users' preferences.

To the best of our knowledge, the persuasive effect of the characteristics in rating summarizations has not yet been studied. The conjoint methodology as employed in market research for decades represents a best practice in order to quantify the perceived utility of the characteristics of different rating summarizations.

3 METHODOLOGY AND DESIGN

We perform an experimental user-study in order to understand the trade-off mechanisms between confrontation with different configurations of rating summarizations. We base our analysis on the Choice-Based Conjoint (CBC) methodology, which is also denoted as Discrete Choice Experiments by several authors [8]. In conjoint designs, products (a.k.a., *profiles*) are modeled by sets of categorical or quantitative *attributes*, which can have different *levels*. In CBC experiments, participants have to repeatedly select one profile from different *sets of choices*, which nicely matches real-world settings when users are confronted with recommendation lists.

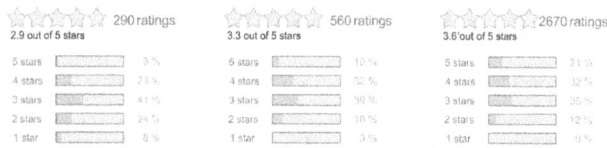

Figure 1: An example snapshot of a choice set, with three different rating summary profiles based on different attribute levels.

Table 1: Probability of choice over profiles in decreasing order.

	# of Ratings	Mean Rating	Pr. of choice	Utility
1	Large	High	35.47 %	3.31
2	Medium	High	23.73 %	2.90
3	Small	High	20.80 %	2.77
4	Large	Average	6.65 %	1.63
5	Medium	Average	4.45 %	1.23
6	Low	Average	3.90 %	1.10
7	Large	Low	2.22 %	0.53
8	Medium	Low	1.48 %	0.13
9	Small	Low	1.30 %	0.00

We used a 3 x 3 choice experiment, where 3 different levels of mean values and of number of ratings have been defined in order to build 9 different summary statistics. Formally, a rating summary statistic is a frequency distribution on the class of discrete rating values. We choose the movie domain for our study and employed the Netflix dataset[4] to identify representative real-world levels for characterizing rating frequency distributions. In addition, variance and skewness of the rating frequency distributions is controlled for, by fixing them with the median values from the respective Netflix rank distributions, which are 1 for variance and -0.5 for skewness.

Our CBC design consisted of $N = 6$ choice sets with $m = 3$ alternatives (see Figure 1). The design was generated and evaluated using SAS MktEx macros [7]. The SAS code for replicating and evaluating the survey is accessible for download[1].

Between January and February 2018 a group of *54 people* were invited to participate in our choice experiments. The participants were presented with the following hypothetical situation:

"Assume that you find yourself in the situation that you need to make a choice between three movies to watch on a movie platform. These three movies are equally preferable to you with respect to all other movie information you have access to (title, plot, actors etc.). Other users' ratings are aggregated and summarized by their number of ratings, the mean rating value and their distribution. Therefore, we would like to know your choice, by solely considering these ratings summary statistics."

4 RESULTS

Detailed results and an extensive discussion is provided in [1]. There was a clear and statistically significant preference relation over the three levels for mean rating values. However, in terms of the total number of ratings, users did not seem to care that much.

From the different levels of preference weights (partial utilities) for our two signals (i.e. levels of the profile attributes) we can also

derive the perceived overall utility (see Table 1). The probability of selecting any of the 9 profiles was computed and ordered by decreasing values in Table 1. Changes in mean value were well and strongly perceived, while the number of ratings had far less impact on users' choice - i.e., an increase in the mean rating value by one level increased the probability of choice by a factor of three to four, when everything else was kept constant.

5 DISCUSSION

Rating summarizations provide important clues to users in online choice situations. Marketing research has shown that consumers are strongly guided by online reviews, and that the mean rating value is interpreted as an indicator for the quality of a product [2]. Also in our study, participants seem to have been following this quality hypothesis.

The total number of ratings, on the other hand, is typically regarded as an indicator for the popularity of a product or an item in general. Given that with larger sample sizes, all things being equal, the mean rating value becomes more informative, it is also very reasonable that, in case of a large number of ratings, users would be more likely to follow this choice. This work is in line with prior research on the effects of potential decision biases such as position, decoy or framing effects, on the choice behavior of users [10] and it can be purposefully exploited to develop more persuasive systems [12].

REFERENCES

[1] Ludovik Coba, Markus Zanker, Laurens Rook, and Panagiotis Symeonidis. 2018. Exploring Users' Perception of Collaborative Explanation Styles. (5 2018). http://arxiv.org/abs/1805.00977
[2] Wenjing Duan, Bin Gu, and Andrew B Whinston. 2008. Do online reviews matter?-An empirical investigation of panel data. *Decision support systems* 45, 4 (2008), 1007–1016.
[3] Gerhard Friedrich and Markus Zanker. 2011. A Taxonomy for Generating Explanations in Recommender Systems. *AI Magazine* 32, 3 (2011), 90. https://doi.org/10.1609/aimag.v32i3.2365
[4] Carlos A Gomez-Uribe and Neil Hunt. 2016. The netflix recommender system: Algorithms, business value, and innovation. *ACM Transactions on Management Information Systems (TMIS)* 6, 4 (2016), 13.
[5] Jonathan L Herlocker, Joseph A Konstan, and John Riedl. 2000. Explaining collaborative filtering recommendations. In *Proceedings of the 2000 ACM conference on Computer supported cooperative work - CSCW '00.* 241–250. https://doi.org/10.1145/358916.358995
[6] Dietmar Jannach, Lukas Lerche, and Markus Zanker. 2018. *Recommending Based on Implicit Feedback.* Springer International Publishing, Cham, 510–569. https://doi.org/10.1007/978-3-319-90092-6_14
[7] Warren Kuhfeld. 2005. Experimental design, efficiency, coding, and choice designs. *Marketing research methods in sas: Experimental design, choice, conjoint, and graphical techniques* (2005), 47–97. https://support.sas.com/techsup/technote/mr2010c.pdf
[8] Jordan J Louviere, Terry N Flynn, and Richard T Carson. 2010. Discrete choice experiments are not conjoint analysis. *Journal of Choice Modelling* 3, 3 (2010), 57–72.
[9] Vithala R Rao. 2014. Choice Based Conjoint Studies: Design and Analysis. In *Applied Conjoint Analysis.* 127–183. https://doi.org/10.1007/978-3-540-87753-0{_}4
[10] Erich Christian Teppan and Markus Zanker. 2015. Decision Biases in Recommender Systems. *Journal of Internet Commerce* 14, 2 (2015), 255–275.
[11] Nava Tintarev and Judith Masthof. 2015. Explaining recommendations: design and evaluation. In *Recommender Systems Handbook.* Springer US, Boston, MA, 217–253. https://doi.org/10.1007/978-1-4899-7637-6
[12] Kyung-Hyan Yoo, Ulrike Gretzel, and Markus Zanker. 2012. *Persuasive recommender systems: conceptual background and implications.* Springer Science & Business Media.
[13] Markus Zanker and Martin Schoberegger. 2014. An empirical study on the persuasiveness of fact-based explanations for recommender systems. In *CEUR Workshop Proceedings,* Vol. 1253. 33–36. http://ceur-ws.org/Vol-1253/paper6.pdf

[1]SAS code: https://github.com/ludovikcoba/CBC;

Lea's Box' Persuadable Open Learner Model: A Case Study in the Field of Speed Reading Training

Extended Abstract[†]

Michael D. Kickmeier-Rust
Institute for Educational Assessment
University of Teacher Education St. Gallen
Switzerland
michael.kickmeier@phsg.ch

Blandine Ginon
School of Engineering
University of Birmingham
United Kingdom
bginon@gmail.com

Matthew D. Johnson
School of Engineering
University of Birmingham
United Kingdom
m.d.johnson@bham.ac.uk

Ali Türker
SEBIT
Education and Information Technologies
Turkey
ali.turker@sebit.com.tr

ACM Reference format:

Michael D. Kickmeier-Rust, Blandine Ginon, Matthew D. Johnson, and Ali Türker. 2018. Lea's Box' Persuadable Open Learner Model: A Case Study in the Field of Speed Reading. In *UMAP'18: ACM User Modeling, Adaptation and Personalization conference, July 8-11, 2018, Singapore,* ACM, NY, NY, USA, 2pages. DOI: https://doi.org/10.1145/3209219.3209257

1 INTRODUCTION

Much of education has been moving towards a competency-based approach. This introduces a new series of potentially large and complex competency frameworks to which educational interactions map. Many online systems, of differing maturity, generate educationally relevant data, but not all contain competency-based analytics. Overall, learners leave a large digital footprint and bringing this together in a common place is not without its challenges. To support formative assessment and learning, technologies such as *Open Learner Models* (OLMs) may have a key role. OLMs are models of learners that are presented in a form that is understandable to their users [1]. Amongst other benefits, they are designed to support metacognition, self-monitoring and planning, promote learner reflection and autonomy [2], and have been shown to increase self-assessment accuracy [3]. OLMs can be linked to educational tools to combine data from external sources to build the model with a competency-based approach, and in some instances using multiple sources [3]. There is, however, potential for some of the information's context to be lost, in addition to technical challenges such as differing design approaches prior to connecting APIs. Inaccuracy may also arise from missing information, such as actions completed away from the

educational tool. To help address issues of accuracy, and to promote learner reflection, some learner models allow interactive maintenance and to amend the model where there is disagreement [3]. Lea's Box (www.leas-box.eu) targets at typical classroom scenarios, which are most often characterized by a technology-lean environment, a scattered used of digital tools, and by a poor overall data basis for conducting analytics. Lea's Box focuses on developing a flexible interface (based on *xAPI,* experienceapi.com) and a central set of core functions to aggregate and homogenize multi-source, multi-modal data. One part of this system is Lea's OLM; it provides learners and teachers with seven visualizations. On the one hand, simple one-dimensional visualizations such as skill meters, table, radar plot and network, on the other hand, more complex multi-dimensional visualizations such as heat maps, across time and level of activity charts. The skill meter and table visualizations are very simple structured visualizations. The radar plot and the network visualizations are unstructured, the radar plot uses a continuous value and the network visualization uses a discrete value with a 5 points scale. The heat map visualization makes possible to see the link between two kinds of element of the model (competencies, activities, data sources...).

2 LEA'S BOX PERSUASION FUNCTION

The persuasion facility, shown in Figure 1, allows learners (i) to access the system evidences, (ii) to see parts of the learner model calculation, (iii) to add justifications and additional evidences, and (iv) to access the self-assessment function. This provides the learner with the system's reasoning and information through which they are prompted to further consider the accuracy of their OLM. In the example of Figure 1, the student proposed a change from 61 to 90 after viewing evidence, and stated that extra reading has been completed and challenging the most recent piece of evidence with value 44. A compromise of 76 is *UMAP '18, July 8–11, 2018, Singapore.*

offered by the system. If the student agrees, the model will be updated with this value. However, the student can also de-cline the persuasion, or try to continue to persuade the system by providing additional justifications and eventually by offering a compromise between his/her initial self-assessment of 90 and the compromise offered by the system of 76. As the current implementation is a persuasion feature rather than a negotiation, we can observe two main differences between the moves available to the learner and the system. First, only the learner can try to persuade the system to change a value in the learner model – the system does not have the facility to request that the learners revise their own learner model value. Secondly, the discussion can only be initiated by the learner, and only they have the option to challenge the evidence used by the system to calculate the value in the model – i.e. the system cannot make a corresponding challenge. The statement, only available for the system, is not exactly a move but a step between two moves to sum up the current state of the discussion, such as reminding of the student's current level, their self-assessment and any justification that they have already provided to try to persuade the system to change their model. When a discussion of a given competency is initiated by the student, the system displays the student's current level for this competency as a statement. Then, the student can either request evidence or self-assess. The move "request evidence" is available for the student during all the discussion. The evidence explains how the current level of a student is calculated for the competency being discussed. It takes into account all pieces of evidence directly associated with this competency and the student's current level in its sub-competencies. A direct piece of evidence can be a score in a quiz, a teacher assessment, or the result of a past discussion of this competency. Each piece of evidence has a weight: the more recent a piece of evidence, the higher its weight. A student's self-assessment is followed by a statement by the sys-tem that reminds the student of their current level and their self-assessment. Then, the system requires justifications in order to increase or decrease the student's level to fit the student's self-assessment. In or-der to either accept or decline the student's self-assessment, the system uses the discussion parameters defined by the teacher. These parameters can take into account the student's justifications, current level and self-assessment. The system can propose a compromise between the student self-assessment and their currently represented level. In the case that either accepts a self-assessment or a compromise, the discussion is considered as resolved and the model is updated with a level that both the student and the system agreed. This leads to the generation of a new piece of evidence in the model. All evidence that is older will no longer contribute to the modelling process for the persuaded competency, but it will remain in the system in case the student or system wishes to access it later. If new evidence is added after a successful persuasion, the outcome is treated the same as any other piece of evidence in the modelling process. If a self-assessment or a compromise is declined, the discussion ends but the model is not updated as the system, parameterised by teacher, ultimately

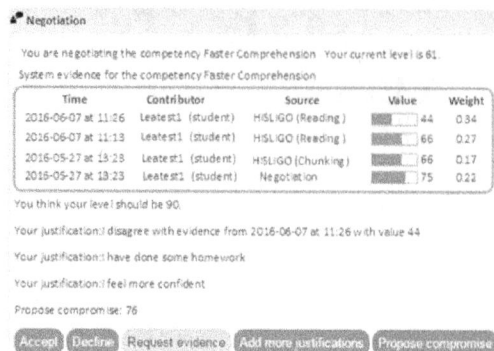

Figure 1: Persuasion example for the competency "Faster comprehension".

retains the control (as in other persuadable models [4]). In both cases, the discussion is recorded. The discussion parameters are defined in the teacher's preferences page. Thus, the teacher can define a minimum time between two discussions. The teacher can also define a minimum number of pieces of evidence with a source other than discussion be-tween two discussions, such as evidence from a teacher assessment or the result of a pedagogical activity. The teacher can also define a maximum threshold to increase and a maximum threshold to decrease the level. For instance, with a maximum increase of 10 out of 100, if a student has a level of 65 and self-assesses with more than 75, then the system will offer a compromise between 65 and 75. Finally, the teacher can define the justifications that the student can provide during the discussion, each associated with a maximum weight. When a student self-assesses with a level higher than their current level, they will be able to provide the sys-tem with one or more justifications, which are assigned a positive weight. In this case, if the student's self-assessment is higher than their current level plus the sum of their justification weights, then the system will offer a compromise between the student's current level and their current level plus the sum of their justification weights. Likewise, when a student self-assesses with a level below their current one, they will be able to provide the system with justifications, and these will be assigned a negative weight.

REFERENCES

[1] Kay, J., Reimann, P., Diebold, E. & Kummerfeld, B. (2013). MOOCs: So Many Learners, So Much Potential, IEEE Intelligent Systems 28(3), 70-77.
[2] Bull, S., Kay, J. (2013). Open Learner Models as Drivers for Metacognitive Processes. In International Handbook of Metacognition and Learning Technologies, Springer New York, 349-365. DOI: 10.1007/978-1-4419-5546-3_23.
[3] Bull, S., Ginon, B., Boscolo, C., Johnson, M.D. (2016). Introduction of Learning Visualisations and Metacognitive Support in a Persuadable Open Learner Model, Proceedings of Learning Analytics and Knowledge.
[4] Bull, S., Mabbott, A. & Abu-Issa, A. (2007). UMPTEEN: Named and Anonymous Learner Model Access for Instructors and Peers, Int. Journal of Artificial Intelligence in Education 17(3), 227-253.

Culture-Aware Music Recommendation

Eva Zangerle
Department of Computer Science,
University of Innsbruck, Austria
eva.zangerle@uibk.ac.at

Martin Pichl
Department of Computer Science,
University of Innsbruck, Austria
martin.pichl@uibk.ac.at

Markus Schedl
Department of Computational
Perception, Johannes Kepler
University Linz, Austria
markus.schedl@jku.at

ABSTRACT

Integrating information about the listener's cultural background when building music recommender systems has recently been identified as a means to improve recommendation quality. In this paper, we therefore propose a novel approach to jointly model users by the user's *musical preferences* and his/her *cultural background*. We describe the musical preferences of users by relying on the acoustic features of the songs the users have been listening to and characterize the cultural background of users by cultural and socio-economic features that we infer from the user's country. To evaluate the impact of the proposed user model on recommendation quality, we integrate the model into a culture-aware music recommender system. We show that incorporating both acoustic information of the tracks a user has listened to as well as the cultural background of users in the form of a *music-cultural user model* contributes to improved recommendation performance.

CCS CONCEPTS

• **Information systems** → **Recommender systems**; *Clustering and classification*; *Music retrieval*;

KEYWORDS

recommender systems, music information retrieval, user modeling

ACM Reference Format:
Eva Zangerle, Martin Pichl, and Markus Schedl. 2018. Culture-Aware Music Recommendation. In *UMAP '18: 26th Conference on User Modeling, Adaptation and Personalization, July 8–11, 2018, Singapore, Singapore.* ACM, New York, NY, USA, 2 pages. https://doi.org/10.1145/3209219.3209258

1 INTRODUCTION

Recent advances in recommender systems and music information retrieval have shown that contextual information is vital for highly personalized recommendations. To this end, the geographic location of a user is often exploited as one notion of context. However, location alone does not necessarily serve as a good indicator for the cultural background of a user as geographically close users might have a very different cultural background and cultural aspects may not coincide with political borders [5]. Notably, for recommender systems, the cultural background of a user was found to play a vital role in how recommended items are judged [7]. We hence argue

that modeling users based on musical properties of the songs they listen to on the one hand and the user's cultural background on the other hand contribute to capturing music-cultural listening patterns. These patterns particularly describe the complex interrelation between users, their cultural background, and the characteristics of the music they listen to. In this paper, we propose a novel music-cultural user modeling approach to exploit such listening patterns for recommender systems by integrating information about (i) the acoustic qualities of the music users have listened to and (ii) culture-specific information derived from the users' location.

2 MUSIC-CULTURAL USER MODEL

For the proposed music-cultural model, we incorporate a user's musical preferences as well as his/her cultural background.

As for modeling individual *musical preferences*, we gather content-based audio features for each of the tracks in the used LFM-1b dataset [6] by querying the Spotify API[1] (following the lines of [4]). These content features are extracted and aggregated from the audio signal and comprise: danceability (suitability of a track for dancing), energy (perceptual measure of intensity and activity), speechiness (presence of spoken words), acousticness (probability whether a track is acoustic), instrumentalness (signifies whether a track contain vocals), tempo (beats per minute), valence (musical positiveness conveyed) and liveness (presence of audience in the recording).

As for *cultural aspects*, we propose to model these on a country level and integrate two different data sources. First, we use Hofstede's widely accepted model of cultural dimensions [3]. This framework describes a nation's culture and values by the following six dimensions: power distance, individualism, masculinity, uncertainty avoidance, long-term orientation and indulgence. Second, we complement Hofstede's cultural dimensions with socio-economic characteristics of countries. We capture these by figures extracted from the World Happiness Report (WHR) [2]. The WHR provides the following set of measures capturing the perceived happiness of countries: GDP, freedom, healthy life expectancy, generosity, social support, trust, and happiness.

As for the proposed user model, we characterize a user's individual musical preferences along with his/her cultural background in a single feature vector. To capture a user's *individual musical preferences* based on his/her listened tracks, we consider the Spotify audio features. For each of the features, we compute a user's arithmetic mean and standard deviation across all tracks in his/her listening history and add these mean and standard deviation (SD) values to the user's feature vector. We chose to add the standard deviations to mitigate the effects of averaging a large number of features that potentially differ substantially. For the approximation of the *cultural background* of users (or rather, the country they live

---

[1]https://developer.spotify.com/web-api/get-several-audio-features/.

in) by socio-economic aspects, we rely on the variables of Hofstede's cultural dimensions and the WHR and extract these based on the user's country information. We add these variables to the user's feature vector to find *cultural* listening patterns that presumably reflect cultural similarity better than sole geographic distance. For each of these variables, we perform a linear min-max scaling such that all elements of the vectors are within [0, 1]. This eventually yields an 21-dimensional feature vector per user.

EXPERIMENTS AND RESULTS

For the evaluation of the proposed music-cultural user model for music recommendation, we rely on the LFM-1b dataset [6], which provides the full listening histories of 120,322 Last.fm users. Each listening event contains information about the track, artist, album, and user. Since we aim to model musical preferences jointly by individual musical preference and the cultural background of users, we require the data to contain information about the location of the user. For 45.87% of all users within the LFM-1b dataset, country information about the user is available. Therefore, we restrain the dataset to those users (and their tracks). This provides us with a dataset comprising 55,191 users, who have listened to a total of 26,022,625 distinct tracks, which are captured by a total of 807,890,921 listening events. Besides the information contained within the LFM-1b dataset, we also require information about the tracks the users listened to in order to retrieve descriptive content features. For all listening events of users for whom we can obtain country information, we therefore search for the <track, artist, album>-triples extracted from the LFM-1b dataset using the Spotify search API[2] to gather the Spotify URI, which we subsequently use to collect the set of audio features for each track using the audio features API.[3] This results in a dataset of 55,149 users, 394,944,868 listening events and 3,478,399 distinct tracks. The average number of listening events per user is 7,161.

We model the computation of context-aware music recommendations based on the proposed user model as a classification task. Particularly, we utilize the popular XGBoost classifier [1], a scalable end-to-end tree boosting approach. Using XGBoost, we set the learning objective to logistic regression for binary classification. Furthermore, we set the training objective to be the binary classification error rate. For the classification task carried out, we require a rating for each track that allows us to define whether a given track was listened to (and thus considered relevant) for a given user. Hence, we add a binary factor rating to the dataset, that is set to 1 if the user has listened to a track. As our dataset does not contain any implicit feedback of users, we assume tracks the user has not listened to as negative examples. For training the classifier, we split each user's listening history into five folds and use four folds for training an XGBoost model and use the withheld fold as the test set. To evaluate the performance of the proposed contextual user model with respect to recommendation quality, we perform a per-user evaluation. Therefore, we use each user's listening history and perform a *leave-k-out* evaluation per user.

We evaluate the music-cultural model (*Music + Culture*) and also individually evaluate the performance of a model solely relying

Model	RMSE
Music + Culture	0.30
Music	0.33
Culture	0.42
Music + Country	0.43

Table 1: Evaluation results of investigated models

on musical preferences of users captured by content-based audio features (*Music* model), and analogously a model that describes users and tracks by their cultural background only (*Culture* model). Furthermore, we evaluate an approach that uses each user's listening history and utilizes the country code of each user (e.g., US for users from the United States) as sole contextual information. Here, we aim to evaluate whether the country code may act as a proxy for cultural factors of users (Music + Country).

The results of this evaluation are depicted in Table 1, where we list the Root Mean Squared Error (RMSE) for each of the evaluated models. As can be seen, our proposed music-cultural model (Music + Culture) outperforms a model that solely describes the musical preferences of a user. Similarly, relying solely on cultural user features also results in a higher RMSE. Notably, the model relying only on the musical preferences of users and their country code achieves the highest RMSE. This shows that the country of a user can not be used as a proxy to accurately describe cultural aspects.

3 CONCLUSIONS AND FUTURE WORK

We have proposed a user model that incorporates a user's musical preferences and his/her cultural background to improve music recommendation systems. Our experiments have shown that such a music-cultural model indeed contributes to improved recommendation quality. Future work includes an analysis of the influence of each of the individual cultural and musical features. Also, we are interested in the differences between countries to obtain a deeper understanding of country-specific listening patterns.

REFERENCES

[1] Tianqi Chen and Carlos Guestrin. 2016. XGBoost: A Scalable Tree Boosting System. In *Proc. of the 22Nd ACM SIGKDD International Conference on Knowledge Discovery and Data Mining (KDD '16)*. ACM, New York, NY, USA, 785–794. https://doi.org/10.1145/2939672.2939785
[2] John F Helliwell, Richard Layard, and Jeffrey Sachs. 2016. *World Happiness Report*. Sustainable Development Solutions Network.
[3] Geert Hofstede, Gert Jan Hofstede, and Michael Minkov. 1991. *Cultures and organizations: Software of the mind*. Vol. 2. McGraw-Hill.
[4] Martin Pichl, Eva Zangerle, and Günther Specht. 2016. Understanding Playlist Creation on Music Streaming Platforms. In *2016 IEEE International Symposium on Multimedia (ISM)*. IEEE, 475–480.
[5] Martin Pichl, Eva Zangerle, Günther Specht, and Markus Schedl. [n. d.]. Mining Culture-Specific Music Listening Behavior from Social Media Data.
[6] Markus Schedl. 2016. The LFM-1b Dataset for Music Retrieval and Recommendation. In *Proc. of the ACM International Conference on Multimedia Retrieval (ICMR)*. ACM, New York, NY, USA, 103–110.
[7] Markus Schedl and Dominik Schnitzer. 2014. Location-Aware Music Artist Recommendation. In *Proc. of the 20th International Conference on MultiMedia Modeling (MMM 2014)*. Springer Berlin Heidelberg, 205–213.

---

[2]https://developer.spotify.com/web-api/search-item/
[3]https://developer.spotify.com/web-api/get-several-audio-features/

Enhancing Session-Based Recommendations through Sequential Modeling

Stéphane Martin
EPFL, LIA
Lausanne, Switzerland
stephane.martin@epfl.ch

Boi Faltings
EPFL, LIA
Lausanne, Switzerland
boi.faltings@epfl.ch

Vincent Schickel
Prediggo SA
Lausanne, Switzerland
schickel@prediggo.com

ABSTRACT

Recommender systems typically determine the items they should recommend by learning models of user-preferences. Most often, those preferences are modeled as static and independent of context. In real life however, users consider items in sequence: TV series are watched episode by episode and accessories are chosen after the main appliance. Unfortunately, since sequences are more complex to model, they are often not taken into account.

We developed an efficient sequence-modeling approach based on *Bayesian Variable-order Markov Models* and combined it with an existing content-based system, the *Ontology Filtering*. We tested this approach through live evaluations on two e-commerce sites. It dramatically increased performance, more than doubling the CTR and strongly increasing recommendation-mediated sales. These tests also confirm that the technique works efficiently and reliably in a production setting.

CCS CONCEPTS

• **Information systems → Online shopping; Recommender systems**;

KEYWORDS

Recommender Systems, Sequence-modeling, E-commerce, Context-tree, Variable-order Markov Model

ACM Reference Format:
Stéphane Martin, Boi Faltings, and Vincent Schickel. 2018. Enhancing Session-Based Recommendations through Sequential Modeling. In *UMAP '18: 26th Conference on User Modeling, Adaptation and Personalization, July 8–11, 2018, Singapore, Singapore*. ACM, New York, NY, USA, 2 pages. https://doi.org/10.1145/3209219.3209259

1 ONTOLOGY FILTERING AND BAYESIAN VARIABLE-ORDER MARKOV MODELS

Ontology Filtering (OF, [5]) is a fast recommendation technique that has been used commercially for years with great success by Prediggo SA[1]. On the other hand, the *Bayesian Variable-order*

[1]Prediggo SA − http://www.prediggo.com/ − is a Swiss-based start-up specializing in recommendation and search solutions for e-commerce. The OF technology is protected by a pending US patent and is available commercially through Prediggo SA.

Markov Models (BVMM, [2]) have already proven quite effective for news recommendation [3] but can be slower. Our implementation combines them by first generating a candidate set of M items with OF. The final set of $N < M$ recommendations is then selected from the candidate set according to a model of sequential page-views embodied in the BVMM.

OF proceeds by organizing a catalogue of products as a hierarchical ontology in order to infer ratings. As most businesses lack a predefined ontology for their products, the ontology is constructed automatically out of the attributes of the products and their descriptions in natural language. Ratings are then inferred based on the user's behaviour. The method has been shown to provide excellent results [6], especially on long-tail items, and has been exploited commercially for years by Prediggo SA. It has proven to work well with large numbers of users and items (more than 1,000,000 products).

A BVMM is a variant of Markov-chain models in which the probability of the next item in a sequence is computed by averaging the probabilities predicted by a series of *experts* associated with subsequences of varying length. In its applications to online recommendation [3], the sequences model the succession of page-views by the visitors of a website. In each step, the aim is then to predict the N pages with the highest probability of being visited next.

The algorithm organizes those sequences into a context tree [1], i.e. a suffix-tree in which the page most recently visited is a direct child of the root. Each path from the root to a node n_s matches a sequence s, observed at least once, called the *context* of the node. Each node is associated with a weight w_s and an *expert* object e_s, that keeps statistics on the items visited immediately after the node's sequence. The function of e_s is to estimate the probability for each item to be visited next by a user having just gone though s.

A user currently browsing the last item of a sequence s has also traversed all the suffixes of s. The probabilities emitted by the experts of all those suffixes, including the root, are thus aggregated into a weighted average that forms the predicted probability of the next item. The computation of this weighted probability can be done in time linear to the height D of the tree [2]. The weights are also adjusted in $O(D)$ in accordance with the observations, following a Bayesian approach − this is the peculiarity of the BVMM.

Although the BVMM computes the probability of each item in $O(D)$, it has to do so over the whole set of candidates to determine the best ones. When the size K of the catalogue becomes too big, this approach in $O(KD)$ does not scale well. We thus use the learned product-ontology to preselect a subset of $M \ll K$ candidates by extracting from the ontology the M products closest to the user's current product. Besides lowering the computational complexity to $O(MD)$, this policy of *ontological preselection* ensures the semantic relevance of the candidates by adding a content-based aspect to the collaborative filtering nature of the BVMM.

2 LIVE-USER EXPERIMENTS

We tested this method by organizing live experiments on the websites of two of Prediggo's clients. The first one, a retailer of furniture, home appliances and electronic equipment, operates a high-traffic e-commerce website in Switzerland. The second one manages a medium-sized e-boutique specializing in youth fashion. The tests were run from the 21st of November to the 30th of December 2017, on the same servers where Prediggo's engine operates normally.

In both experiments, the traffic was divided into two buckets each covering 50% of all sessions. Sessions in the first bucket received recommendations selected as usual by the OF, while the sessions of the second were assigned to the BVMM with ontological preselection. The trees were built at intervals of 30 minutes out of the 500,000 most recent page-views and were allowed to grow until a limit of 100,000 nodes. The purchases of the visitors and their clicks on the recommendations were logged for analysis.

During the first experiment (E1), the system received $\approx 5,700,000$ calls for recommendations to be chosen among 10,951 products. Tab. 1 (top) shows the number of requests for recommendations, the number of clicks performed by the users, the CTR (clicks / requests ratio), the mean time to generate one recommendation and the values of sales following a recommendation within 24 hours[2]. There is little doubt that the BVMM is more effective at triggering the interest of the users. Taking the equivalence of the recommenders as the 0-hypothesis, Fisher's exact test yields a p-value over the clicks so small that our statistical library rounded it to zero.

Table 1: CTR, time for 1 reco. (ms), post-recom. revenue.

	Clicks	Total Calls	CTR	Time	Revenue
E1, OF	18,148	2,782,676	0.652%	1.912	100 %
E1, BVMM	66,631	2,886,756	2.308%	3.487	298 %
E2, OF	1371	129,431	1.059%	1.523	100 %
E2, BVMM	2827	133,804	2.113%	0.755	124 %

The second experiment (E2) covered $\approx 263,000$ calls for recommendations for 2219 products. Its results confirm the conclusions of the first one, although the differences were not as striking (Tab. 1, bottom). This can be because a smaller site lacks sufficient traffic to train the sequence model. The BVMM achieves a CTR clearly higher than OF, 1.059% against 2.113%. The p-value on clicks, also computed with Fisher's exact test, is just as tiny as it was in the first experiment (≈ 0). The difference between the post-recommendation revenues is also in favour of the BVMM, although the volume of purchase was smaller. The improvements in accuracy do not entail a significant increase in computational complexity. Both methods can run on a standard server.

---

[2]For reasons of confidentiality, the amounts are shown here in percent of OF.

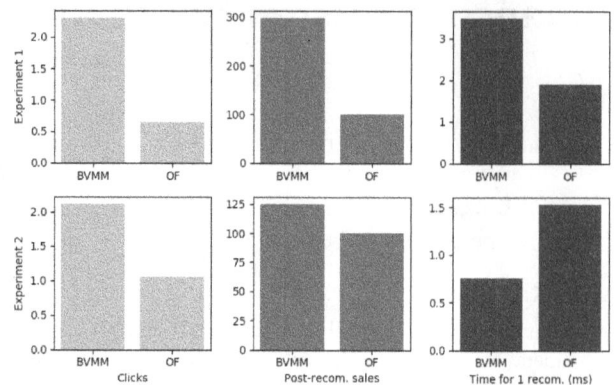

Figure 1: CTR, post-recom. revenue and time.

3 CONCLUSIONS

Our experiments confirm that taking into account the *sequence* of preferences strongly enhances the predictive power of user-behaviour modeling [4]. Markov-chain models such as the BVMM are well suited to model the sequential nature of user-preferences, and they can be efficiently implemented using context-trees.

Our implementation relies on an initial step of candidate preselection. Since the time taken to collect the candidates does not depend on the total number of items, and since the ontologies are created automatically through an offline procedure, the efficiency of the method does not depend on the size of the catalogue.

Our evaluations were carried out through live A/B tests on operational e-commerce sites. They are thus free of the biases that often distort the results obtained using static datasets. Moreover, they were realized with the normal settings and infrastructure that Prediggo, or similar-sized companies, would normally use to serve their customers. The results presented above can hence be taken as representative of the normal operation of an online business, and demonstrate that BVMM models are suitable to be applied in practical recommendation systems.

ACKNOWLEDGMENTS

This work was supported by a grant from the Swiss Commission for Technology and Innovation CTI/KTI under contract 18384.1 PFES-ES.

REFERENCES

[1] Ron Begleiter, Ran El-Yaniv, and Golan Yona. 2004. On Prediction Using Variable Order Markov Models. *J. Artif. Int. Res.* 22, 1 (Dec. 2004), 385–421. http://dl.acm.org/citation.cfm?id=1622487.1622499
[2] Christos Dimitrakakis. 2010. Bayesian variable order Markov models. In *JMLR*.
[3] Florent Garcin, Christos Dimitrakakis, and Boi Faltings. 2013. Personalized News Recommendation with Context Trees. In *Proceedings of the 7th ACM Conference on Recommender Systems (RecSys '13)*. ACM, New York, NY, USA, 105–112. https://doi.org/10.1145/2507157.2507166
[4] Massimo Quadrana, Paolo Cremonesi, and Dietmar Jannach. 2018. Sequence-Aware Recommender Systems. *CoRR* abs/1802.08452 (2018). arXiv:1802.08452 http://arxiv.org/abs/1802.08452
[5] Vincent Schickel-Zuber. 2007. *Ontology Filtering*. PhD. Thesis No 3934. Swiss Federal Institute of Technology (EPFL), Lausanne (Switzerland).
[6] Vincent Schickel-Zuber and Boi Faltings. 2006. Inferring User's Preferences using Ontologies. In *Proceedings of the Twenty-first National Conference on Artificial Intelligence (AAAI-06)*. AAAI press, 1413–1416.

Multi-view Visual Bayesian Personalized Ranking from Implicit Feedback

Haihua Luo, Xiaoyan Zhang
College of Computer Science & Software Engineering
Shenzhen University, China
lloh@foxmail.com,xyzhang15@szu.edu.cn

Bowei Chen, Guibing Guo
Software College
Northeastern University, China
boweichen_public@outlook.com,guogb@swc.neu.edu.cn

ABSTRACT

In this paper, we propose a new factorization model that combines multi-view visual feature information with the implicit feedback data for prediction and ranking. The visual information is integrated into a collaborative filtering framework. The visual features of images are extracted by using a deep neural network. In order to conduct personalized recommendation better, the multi-view visual features are fused through user related weights. The user related weights reflect the personalized visual preference for items. They are different and independent between users. Experimental results show that our model with multi-view visual information achieves the better performance than models without or with only single-view visual information.

CCS CONCEPTS

• **Information systems** → **Recommender systems**; Personalization; Probabilistic retrieval models; Top-k retrieval in databases;

KEYWORDS

Recommendation System; Bayesian Personalized Ranking; Implicit Feedbacks; Multi-View Visual Feature; Restaurant Recommendation

ACM Reference Format:
Haihua Luo, Xiaoyan Zhang and Bowei Chen, Guibing Guo. 2018. Multiview Visual Bayesian Personalized Ranking from Implicit Feedback. In *UMAP '18: 26th Conference on User Modeling, Adaptation and Personalization, July 8–11, 2018, Singapore, Singapore*. ACM, New York, NY, USA, 2 pages. https://doi.org/10.1145/3209219.3209260

1 INTRODUCTION

The current recommendation systems use quantitative explicit feedback implicit feedback (such as users' click history, viewing history, etc.) which is larger and denser than explicit feedback dataset to explore user's preferences. Matrix Factorization (MF) based on Bayesian formulation is proposed to uncover the latent factors in implicit feedback data, such as BPR-MF[4]. Some methods based on multi-type auxiliary implicit feedback[1] or heterogeneous implicit feedback[3] are also proposed for integrating data from multiple sources.

The visual features extracted by DNN (Deep neural network) model, are often considered as additional information to add to the recommendation system, such as VBPR. VBPR model is a visual-aware MF method based on BPR-MF introduced by He et al.[2]. It used only single-view features extracted from DNN as added visual information. In this paper, we focus on combining the DNN extracted visual features and implicit feedback data for personalized restaurant recommendation. We proposed a multi-view visual bayesian personalized ranking from implicit feedback method (MVBPR) to account the food, drink, inside and outside visual features (multi-view visual information) of the restaurant together to make personalized restaurant recommendation and ranking.

2 OUR MODEL

In this section, we will introduce our MVBPR model. We downloaded an open dataset that contains records of the user visiting the restaurant. We use U to represent the user, and I to represent the restaurant. A user-restaurant pair, which means that the user has visited the restaurant, is seen as a positive example of implicit feedback. All the positive restaurant for user u are represented by I_u^+. The training set D_s is composed of triples of the form (u,i,j):

$$D_s = \left\{ (u, i, j) | u \in U \wedge i \in I_u^+ \wedge j \in I \setminus I_u^+ \right\} \quad (1)$$

where u denotes the user, i is the index of the restaurant that the user u has visited (observed item), and j is a non-observed item (the user has not visited the restaurant).

Our multi-view personalized ranking model is defined as:

$$\widehat{x_{u,i}} = \alpha + \beta_u + \beta_i + \gamma_u^T \gamma_i + \theta_u^T (EF_i w_u) + \beta'^T F_i AW \quad (2)$$

Here, user preferences (user u to restaurant i) are represented by a specific, formal value $\widehat{x_{u,i}}$, and α is global offset, β_u and β_i are user/restaurant bias terms, γ_u^T and γ_i represent the latent vectors of the user and the restaurant respectively. θ_u are user's visual preferences. E is an embedding matrix. We use the matrix F_i (f × 4, 4 categories) to represent the visual features of restaurant i. For each image under each category, the visual features are extracted by DNN, and the visual features of all images under each category are aggregated into a visual vector by average pooling. Parameter w_u is a four-by-one vector to represent user u's preferences for different categories of visual features. In the final, A is a overall bias weight of multi-view visual features. W is the category visual preference matrix for all users. The product of A and W models users' overall preference toward the multi-view visual appearance of a given restaurant. β' is visual bias vector.

For pair-wise ranking, the predicted values are expressed in terms of $\widehat{x_{uij}}$:

$$\widehat{x_{uij}} = \widehat{x_{u,i}} - \widehat{x_{u,j}} \quad (3)$$

Our model is optimized by BPR-MF[4] and the parameters is learned by stochastic gradient ascent.

The optimization criterion C is followed:

$$C = \sum_{(u,i,j)\in D_s} ln\sigma\left(\widehat{x}_{uij}\right) - \lambda_\Theta \left\|\Theta\right\|^2 \qquad (4)$$

where σ is the logisitc (sigmoid) function and λ_Θ is a regularization hyperparameter which is tuned by the experimental results. Θ is the parameter that need to be learned.

3 EXPERIMENTAL RESULTS

The dataset we use is from Yelp. We processed the raw dataset and obtained a subset for the experiment. This subset consistsed of 17,644 users with 327586 reviews for 1,327 restaurants, including 29,664 pictures of food, 3235 drink, 12,350 inside view and 4,538 outside view. The images have been classified by the Yelp. The visual features were extracted by VGGNet19[5]. We used AUC, Precision@k, Recall@k as evaluation metrics and all experiments were done under the same python module and physical environment.

Table 1: Prediction performance on Yelp dataset. The numbers in boldface are the best performance. The plus sign '+' represents a percentage increase to the highest evaluation.

Model	Pre@10	Rec@10	AUC
BPR-MF	$0.0093_{+105.4\%}$	$0.0715_{+61.96\%}$	$0.8001_{+11.16\%}$
VBPR-food	$0.0168_{+13.69\%}$	$0.1020_{+13.53\%}$	$0.8693_{+2.31\%}$
VBPR-drink	$0.0123_{+55.28\%}$	$0.0746_{+55.23\%}$	$0.8348_{+6.54\%}$
VBPR-inside	$0.0172_{+11.05\%}$	$0.1044_{+10.92\%}$	$0.8759_{+1.54\%}$
VBPR-outside	$0.0162_{+17.9\%}$	$0.0984_{+17.68\%}$	$0.8731_{+1.87\%}$
MVBPR	**0.0191**	**0.1158**	**0.8894**

Table 1 shows the experiment results of MVBPR and baselines. Here, the VBPR model is tested by using each of the four categories of images, and named as VBPR-food, VBPR-drink, VBPR-inside, VBPR-outside, respectively. Model MVBPR is the multi-view visual feature model with four categories of images proposed in this paper. Through the experimental results shown in Table 1, we can summarize the following information:

1. Our MVBPR model has a higher performance than BPR-MF and VBPR in the three evaluation metrics of AUC, Precision, Recall. The BPR-MF model, which does not use the visual information in the recommendation system, has the lowest AUC, Precision and Recall values. This proves that the visual information places an important role in the restaurant preference. The multi-view visual features provide more information for the bayesian model than the single-view visual features and get better ranking results.

2. The VBPR-food and VBPR-inside have relatively higher performance in the restaurant recommendation than the VBPR-outside and VBPR-drink models. The performance of VBPR-drink is the worst among the four VBPR models. This indicates that the food and the environment of a restaurant place more important roles in rating a restaurant than the drink. The inside environment also affects more than outside environment in rating a restaurant. The above findings are reasonable and coherent with common customs.

Table 2: The weight vector w_u for the four visual aspects (food, drink, inside and outside). We use F, D, I, O to represent food, drink, inside, outside, respectively (MVBPR-DIO means a combination of drink, inside and outside visual information).

	w_u-food	w_u-drink	w_u-inside	w_u-outside
MVBPR-DIO	-	0.2385	0.4070	0.3544
MVBPR-FIO	0.3872	-	0.3158	0.2969
MVBPR-FDO	0.4253	0.2222	-	0.3524
MVBPR-FDI	0.4070	0.2124	0.3804	-
MVBPR	0.2870	0.1936	0.2651	0.2541

The weight vector w_u reflects the user preference for the four visual aspects (food, drink, inside and outside). Table 2 shows the experimental results for user's mean category visual preference ('w_u-food', 'w_u-drink', 'w_u-inside', 'w_u-outside') in multiple combinations. The food visual feature information has the highest weight value. This proves that the visual feature information of food is the most important visual information in restaurant recommendation. The user's preference for the visual information of inside and outside is gradually reduced, and the drink's has the lowest preference.

4 CONCLUSIONS

We propose a new factorization model, which combines multi-view visual feature information and implicit feedback data for prediction and ranking. The user specific preference on multi-view visual information is considered by setting a user related visual features fusion factor. Through the experiments, we have verified that the multi-view visual feature information can describe the characteristics of objects more sufficiently than the single-view visual feature information on the Yelp dataset.

ACKNOWLEDGMENTS

This work was supported in part by: (i) the National Natural Science Foundation of China (Grant No. 61602313, 61702084); (ii) Shenzhen Commission of Scientific Research & Innovations under the Grant No. JCYJ20170302153632883; (iii) Tencent "Rhinoceros Birds" - Scientific Research Foundation for Young Teachers of Shenzhen University; (iv) Startup Foundation for Advanced Talents, Shenzhen.

REFERENCES

[1] Guibing Guo, Huihuai Qiu, Zhenhua Tan, Yuan Liu, Jing Ma, and Xingwei Wang. 2017. Resolving data sparsity by multi-type auxiliary implicit feedback for recommender systems. *Knowledge-Based Systems* 138 (2017), 202 – 207. https://doi.org/10.1016/j.knosys.2017.10.005
[2] Ruining He and Julian McAuley. 2016. VBPR: Visual Bayesian Personalized Ranking from Implicit Feedback.. In *AAAI*. 144–150.
[3] Huihuai Qiu, Yun Liu, Guibing Guo, Zhu Sun, Jie Zhang, and Hai Thanh Nguyen. 2018. BPRH: Bayesian personalized ranking for heterogeneous implicit feedback. *Information Sciences* 453 (2018), 80 – 98. https://doi.org/10.1016/j.ins.2018.04.027
[4] Steffen Rendle, Christoph Freudenthaler, Zeno Gantner, and Lars Schmidt-Thieme. 2009. BPR: Bayesian personalized ranking from implicit feedback. In *Proceedings of the twenty-fifth conference on uncertainty in artificial intelligence*. AUAI Press, 452–461.
[5] Karen Simonyan and Andrew Zisserman. 2014. Very Deep Convolutional Networks for Large-Scale Image Recognition. *CoRR* abs/1409.1556 (2014). arXiv:1409.1556 http://arxiv.org/abs/1409.1556

A Bayesian Point Process Model for User Return Time Prediction in Recommendation Systems

Sherin Thomas
Indian Institute of Technology
Hyderabad, India
sarasherinthomas@gmail.com

P. K. Srijith
Indian Institute of Technology
Hyderabad, India
srijith@iith.ac.in

Michal Lukasik*
University of Sheffield
m.lukasik@sheffield.ac.uk

ABSTRACT

In order to sustain the user-base for a web service, it is important to know the return time of a user to the service. We propose a Bayesian point process, log Gaussian Cox process (LGCP), to model and predict return time of users. It allows encoding the prior domain knowledge and non-parametric estimation of latent intensity functions capturing user behaviour. We capture the similarities among the users in their return time by using a multi-task learning approach. We show the effectiveness of the proposed approaches on predicting the return time of users to *last.fm* music service.

CCS CONCEPTS

• **Information systems** → **Information systems applications**;
• **Computing methodologies** → **Machine learning**;

KEYWORDS

Return time, log-Gaussian Cox Process, recommendation systems

ACM Reference Format:
Sherin Thomas, P. K. Srijith, and Michal Lukasik. 2018. A Bayesian Point Process Model for User Return Time Prediction in Recommendation Systems. In *UMAP '18: 26th Conference on User Modeling, Adaptation and Personalization, July 8–11, 2018, Singapore, Singapore.* ACM, New York, NY, USA, 2 pages. https://doi.org/10.1145/3209219.3209261

1 INTRODUCTION

Web services such as recommendation systems benefit a lot from learning the temporal dynamics of users. Modeling the return time of users is of great interest to these web services. It allows them to understand user engagement and provides an early feedback on user experience with the service. It helps the web service to devise measures to retain the customer base such as targeted marketing to those users who may not return soon.

In this work, we address the problem of modeling the temporal dynamics of music listening patterns of users, specifically their return times to the *last.fm* web service. Recently, this was modeled using recurrent neural networks with survival loss function in [3]. A hazard based approach based on Cox proportional Hazard model [4] considered features such as active weeks and visit number, while

---

*Michal Lukasik is now at Google.

recurrent activities of users were captured using self exciting point process in [2].

We propose to use a Bayesian point process model which could encode prior knowledge on user behaviour such as periodicity in return times. Specifically, we use log Gaussian Cox Process (LGCP) [6], which models user behaviour through a stochastic intensity function. It is genrally difficult to represent the latent intensity function modeling the user's complex temporal behaviour in point processes. LGCP learns the intensity function non-parametrically from the data by modeling it using a Gaussian Processes (GP) [8] prior. We also capture the similarities across the users using a multi-task learning approach based on GPs [1]. We compare the performance of the proposed approaches with various GP Kernels against several baselines and demonstrate their usefulness on the data from the *last.fm* music web service. We find that the RBF kernel which is often used in temporal applications is outperformed by alternatives[5].

Notations: We assume there are M users with each user associated with a set of sessions. Let $\mathbf{t}_m = \{t_n^m\}_{n=1}^{N_m}$ denote the sessions associated with a user m where t_n^m denotes the start time of the nth session and N_m the number of sessions. The task is to predict the next return time of a user given the previous session start times.

2 MODEL

User interest to start a new session and its duration changes over time. This can be captured using a point process with an intensity function $\lambda(t)$. Users exhibit complex temporal behavior and it is difficult to come up with an appropriate intensity function capturing their temporal behavior. This motivates us to use log Gaussian Cox Process (LGCP), where the logarithm of the time varying intensity function is assumed to come from a Gaussian Process prior [6]. This allows us to learn the intensity function non-parametrically from the data in addition to specifying the domain knowledge through the GP kernel. The intensity function for a user m at a session starting time t_n^m is defined as $\lambda^m(t_n^m) = exp(f^m(t_n^m))$, where $f^m(t) \sim \mathcal{GP}(\mu^m(t), cov^m(t, t'))$, $\mu^m(\cdot)$ is the mean function, and $cov^m(\cdot, \cdot)$ is the covariance function of a GP for a user m. The covariance function is specified through a positive semi-definite kernel $k^m(t, t')$, which determines the properties of the intensity function such as periodicity and smoothness.

We capture the similarities existing across different users in order to learn better intensity functions for a user. This is achieved using a multi-task LGCP model which learns the user similarities from their temporal activities through a user covariance matrix B [1, 5]. The multi-task learning kernel is defined jointly over users and times as

$$k_{MTL}((m, t), (m', t')) = B_{m,m'} \cdot k(t, t') \tag{1}$$

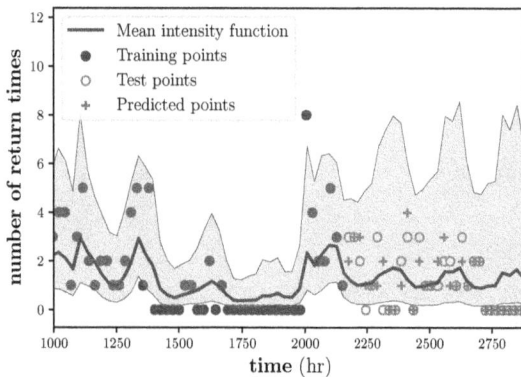

Figure 1: Intensity function learnt for a user using LGCP-MULTITASK model with *RQ + Periodic* kernel on *last.fm* data. The x axis denotes the time and the y axis denotes the number of user returns within a 24*h* interval. The dark line denotes the predictive mean and the shaded region denotes the predictive variance. Note that we sample the predictions rather than using the predictive mean.

The various model hyper-parameters such as the kernel parameters and the covariance matrix *B* are learnt by maximizing the marginal likelihood and a predictive distribution is obtained over the intensity function [5]. The return times of users are predicted using a mean intensity function and using the Ogata's thinning algorithm [7].

3 EXPERIMENTAL EVALUATION

Experimental setup We consider publicly available *last.fm* data which comprises of the music listening log of 992 unique users, with a total of 19,150,868 listening time stamps spanning from 2004 to 2009. For each user, the listening time stamps are split into different sessions if two consecutive time stamps differ by a gap of 1 hour or more [3]. The pre-processed session data is split into training and testing set by taking 3 consecutive months of data for training and 1 month data for testing purpose. Users with less than 100 listening events in training set and 50 events in test test are considered inactive and hence removed. This results in 394 active users with 243 sessions on an average per user. We consider various kernels in the LGCP model including the rational quadratic (RQ), periodic, and radial basis function (RBF) [8]. The RBF kernel models smooth functions, RQ models more complex functions with multiple length-scales and periodic kernels model the periodicity in the latent function. We also use LGCP with multitask learning kernel which captures similarities across users.

Evaluation Metrics In order to evaluate the model, we use mean absolute error (MAE) and root mean square error (RMSE) between the actual and the predicted times for each user in hours. [5] Since the data varies in size for each user, we take the micro average of the errors to obtain the final result.

Baselines The proposed models are compared against homogeneous Poisson process (HPP), linear regression, GP regression (RBF kernel), and recurrent neural networks (RNN) with one hidden layer and 50 neurons.

Method	Kernel	MAE	RMSE
LGCP	Periodic	9.37	19.45
	Rat Quad	8.68	18.74
	Periodic + Rat Quad	9.22	20.48
	RBF	15.89	22.44
LGCP-Multitask	Periodic	8.89	19.25
	Rat Quad	8.69	18.76
	Periodic + Rat Quad	8.90	19.07
	RBF	15.87	22.41
HPP		9.41	22.02
Linear Regression		10.25	22.56
GP Regression	RBF	10.30	22.98
RNN		11.05	20.46

Table 1: Mean Absolute Error (MAE) and Root Mean Squared Error (RMSE) between the actual and predicted user return time for proposed methods and baselines on *last.fm* data.

Results In Table 1 we compare the predictive performance of LGCP and LGCP-Multitask approaches against various baselines. We find that the standard kernel used in GP models, the RBF kernel, performs poorly due to the complex temporal patterns exhibited by users in their session start times. The RBF kernel typically models smoothly varying functions and is not suitable to model this situation. The RQ kernel could model such complicated behaviour patterns better than RBF by considering multiple length scales. This is evident from the experimental results where it outperforms other kernels and baselines. The periodic kernel could model the periodicity in the data (for instance, users tend to be more active on weekends) and are found to perform better than RBF but fails to capture other complex behavioral patterns captured by RQ. This is overcome by combining RQ with Periodic which improved the performance. The LGCP models with these kernels (except RBF) outperformed the baseline approaches such as HPP, linear regression, GP regression, and RNN. LGCP-Multitask brought significant improvements in performance with RBF, periodic and *RQ + Periodic* kernels, while it retained the performance with RQ kernel. Figure 1 plots the intensity function of a user, learnt using LGCP-Multitask with *RQ + Periodic* kernel. We found that considering other users temporal activity pattern through LGCP-Multitask could improve the predictive performance for a user.

REFERENCES

[1] Mauricio A. Álvarez, Lorenzo Rosasco, and Neil D. Lawrence. 2012. Kernels for Vector-Valued Functions: A Review. *Found. Trends Mach. Learn.* 4, 3 (2012).
[2] Nan Du, Yichen Wang, Niao He, and Le Song. 2015. Time-sensitive Recommendation from Recurrent User Activities. In *NIPS.* 3492–3500.
[3] How Jing and Alexander J. Smola. 2017. Neural Survival Recommender. In *WSDM.* 515–524.
[4] Komal Kapoor, Mingxuan Sun, Jaideep Srivastava, and Tao Ye. 2014. A Hazard Based Approach to User Return Time Prediction. In *KDD.* 1719–1728.
[5] Michal Lukasik, P. K. Srijith, Trevor Cohn, and Kalina Bontcheva. 2015. Modeling Tweet Arrival Times using Log-Gaussian Cox Processes. In *EMNLP.* 250–255.
[6] Jesper Møller, Anne R. Syversveen, and Rasmus P. Waagepetersen. 1998. Log Gaussian Cox Processes. *Scandinavian Journal of Statistics* 25, 3 (1998), 451–482.
[7] Yosihiko Ogata. 1981. On Lewis' simulation method for point processes. *IEEE Transactions on Information Theory* 27, 1 (1981), 23–30.
[8] Carl E. Rasmussen and Christopher K. I. Williams. 2005. *Gaussian Processes for Machine Learning (Adaptive Computation and Machine Learning).* The MIT Press.

Using the Explicit User Profile to Predict User Engagement in Active Video Watching

Alicja Piotrkowicz
University of Leeds, UK
A.Piotrkowicz@leeds.ac.uk

Vania Dimitrova
University of Leeds, UK
V.G.Dimitrova@leeds.ac.uk

Antonija Mitrovic
University of Canterbury, NZ
Tanja.Mitrovic@canterbury.ac.nz

Lydia Lau
University of Leeds, UK
L.M.S.Lau@leeds.ac.uk

ABSTRACT

In this paper we leverage the explicit user profile (relating to experience, knowledge, and self-regulation) to predict user engagement in active video watching. Data from two user studies for informal learning of presentation skills in a Higher Education context is used to develop and validate the prediction models. Our results show that these user characteristics can reasonably predict the overall engagement (inactive, passive and constructive learners). Our approach can be used to inform adaptive interventions that prevent disengagement and enhance the learning experience.

CCS CONCEPTS

• **Applied computing** → **Interactive learning environments**;
• **Information systems** → *Personalization*;

ACM Reference Format:
Alicja Piotrkowicz, Vania Dimitrova, Antonija Mitrovic, and Lydia Lau. 2018. Using the Explicit User Profile to Predict User Engagement in Active Video Watching. In *UMAP '18: 26th Conference on User Modeling, Adaptation and Personalization, July 8–11, 2018, Singapore, Singapore.* ACM, New York, NY, USA, 2 pages. https://doi.org/10.1145/3209219.3209262

1 INTRODUCTION

There is a growing area of adaptive learning systems that model learner engagement [1, 4, 5, 7, 11]. We address the engagement detection challenge in a new context: *using videos for informal learning of soft skills*. Videos enable independent self-regulated learning where students familiarise themselves with, or revisit key concepts in their own time [10]. We have developed an active video watching platform (AVW-Space) [6, 8], which taps into students' experiences with social video-sharing platforms (e.g. YouTube) and integrates interactive note-taking during video watching. Our focus is on the early prediction of user engagement in AVW-Space by using the explicit user profile relating to users' experience, knowledge, and self-regulation. We address the following research question: *Can we predict overall video engagement using only the user profile?*

Table 1: Feature values comparison (significant differences at $p < 0.01$ in bold; calculated using the Mann-Whitney test).

Feature	Range	Study A (463)	Study B (204)
Training	[1-5]	1.67	1.74
Experience	[1-5]	2.19	2.29
YouTube	[1-5]	4.11	4.01
YouTube for Learning	[1-5]	**3.15**	**2.66**
Conceptual Knowledge	[0-n]	12.49	11.79
MSLQ-I	[1-5]	3.68	3.61
MSLQ-E	[1-5]	4.07	4.01
MSLQ-TV	[1-5]	3.89	3.87
MSLQ-C	[1-5]	4.11	4.17
MSLQ-SE	[1-5]	3.59	3.63
MSLQ-MSR	[1-5]	3.22	3.28
MSLQ-R	[1-5]	**3.08**	**3.51**
MSLQ-E	[1-5]	3.59	3.64
MSLQ-O	[1-5]	**3.11**	**3.36**
MSLQ-ER	[1-5]	3.45	3.44

2 FEATURES AND METHODS

We conducted two studies (referred to as Studies A and B) within two first-year UG courses at the University of Canterbury in 2017. AVW-Space was provided as an online training resource on presentation skills. **Study A** was conducted in a mandatory course for Engineering students. The participation in the study was worth 1% of the final grade. Of the 904 students enrolled in the course, 463 completed the user profile survey. There were 150 constructive, 153 passive, and 160 inactive students (categorised according to the ICAP framework [2]). **Study B** was conducted with Business students in their second semester of study. Of 400 students enrolled in the course, 204 completed the user profile. There were 62 constructive, 26 inactive, and 116 passive students.

The user profile survey yielded 15 features. Four features capture previous **Training** on giving presentations, **Experience** in giving presentations, frequency in using **YouTube**, and the extent to which they use **YouTube for learning**. The total number of concepts relating to presentation the student could name is used as a proxy for the student's **Conceptual Knowledge**.

The remaining ten features are aggregations of scores on the MSLQ questions [9]: intrinsic motivation (**MSLQ-I**), representing

Table 2: Classification results using user profile data. Metrics include: accuracy (Acc.), precision (Prec.), recall (Rec.).

		Study A				Study B		
Three class	Acc.	0.41			Acc.	0.63		
		In.	Pass.	Con.		In.	Pass.	Con.
	Prec.	0.5	0.55	0.53	Prec.	0.88	0.87	0.81
	Rec.	0.71	0.29	0.55	Rec.	0.98	0.69	0.88
Binary		In.	Pass.	Con.		In.	Pass.	Con.
	Acc.	0.66	0.62	0.62	Acc.	0.86	0.46	0.7
	Prec.	0.77	0.77	0.77	Prec.	0.93	0.71	0.85
	Rec.	0.79	0.82	0.79	Rec.	0.93	0.66	0.82

the degree to which the student participates in academic tasks for reasons linked to challenge, curiosity and mastery; extrinsic motivation (**MSLQ-E**), the degree to which the student participates in academic tasks for reasons such as grades and rewards; Task Value (**MSLQ-TV**), which refers to the student's perceptions of academic studies in terms of interest, importance and utility; Control (**MSLQ-C**) indicating whether the learner feels in control of his/her own performance; Self Efficacy (**MSLQ-SE**), the student's confidence in having skills to perform academic tasks; Metacognitive Self-Regulation (**MSLQ-MSR**); and several learning strategies: Rehearsal (**MSLQ-R**), Elaboration (**MSLQ-E**), Organisation (**MSLQ-O**) and Effort Regulation (**MSLQ-ER**). In Table 1 we present an overview of values for the profile features and compare them across studies. Only three features had statistically significant differences between Study A and Study B: YouTube for Learning is higher for Study A, both MSLQ-Rehearsal and MSLQ-Organisation are higher for Study B.

Prediction models. Our task is to predict the overall engagement using just the explicit user profile. We consider two task settings. (1) Simply predict whether the student would be inactive, passive, or constructive. (2) Use binary classification, whereby for each category we build a binary classifier of the format One-class-vs-Others (e.g. Inactive vs. Passive + Constructive). We use all the explicit user profile features as predictors, and the categorisation relevant for each task setting as the target variable. The features are first preprocessed by removing near-zero variance predictors, and scaling the remaining ones between 0 and 1. We use upsampling to balance out the class distributions and prevent the classifier from always predicting the majority class. The classifiers are trained separately for each study. We use a Leave-One-Out cross-validation (LOOCV). From a range of classifiers we found support vector machines (SVM) with RBF kernel to yield best results.

Results. We evaluate using accuracy averaged over the LOOCV iterations, and precision and recall, calculated using the predictions from the final model. We report results in Table 2. In the three-class prediction setting, the results were noticeably higher for Study B (Acc.=.63), compared to Study A (Acc.=.41). That was also the case when looking at the precision and recall for each of the categories. Although better than a random choice (which would have an accuracy of approx. 33%), the results of the three-category prediction for Study A are not reliable enough to predict user engagement. The results for the binary classifiers are overall higher. The only

binary classifier that suffers a drop in performance compared to the three-class prediction is the Passive classifier for Study B. In particular, the results for Study A show an improvement. Overall, the fairly high (at least 0.7) precision and recall values mean that the prediction model can be reliably used to predict user engagement.

3 DISCUSSION AND CONCLUSIONS

Key findings. We found that by using the explicit user profile we can predict whether a given user will be Inactive, Passive, or Constructive with a fair degree of accuracy, in particular when conducting binary classification. Our work gives supporting evidence that self-regulation abilities are important user characteristics to consider in adaptive video learning. Hence, surveys like MSLQ offer valuable insights for personalisation and adaptation. **Applications of the prediction models.** The models can be applied in several personalisation and adaptation contexts, such as planning interventions, e.g. implementing nudges is one of the primary goals for the AVW project [3]. The presented prediction models can help identify *whom* to target soon after the users start watching videos.

Conclusions. We leveraged the user profile to predict user engagement with the view of implementing early interventions to support beneficial video engagement. We found that experience, knowledge, and self-regulation can be used for early prediction of user engagement with a reasonable degree of accuracy.

Acknowledgements. Support by EU-FP7-ICT-257184 ImREAL, Ako Aotearoa and University of Canterbury teaching development grants. We thank Amali Weerasinghe for her work on the experiment design, as well as the study participants.

REFERENCES

[1] Robert Bixler and Sidney D'Mello. 2016. Automatic Gaze-based User-independent Detection of Mind Wandering During Computerized Reading. *User Modeling and User-Adapted Interaction* 26, 1 (March 2016), 33–68.
[2] Michelene TH Chi and Ruth Wylie. 2014. The ICAP Framework: Linking Cognitive Engagement to Active Learning Outcomes. *Educational Psychologist* 49, 4 (2014), 219–243.
[3] Vania Dimitrova, Antonija Mitrovic, Alicja Piotrkowicz, Lydia Lau, and Amali Weerasinghe. 2017. Using Learning Analytics to Devise Interactive Personalised Nudges for Active Video Watching. In *Proceedings of 25th Conference on User Modeling, Adaptation and Personalization.* ACM.
[4] Joanna Drummond and Diane Litman. 2010. In the Zone: Towards Detecting Student Zoning Out Using Supervised Machine Learning. In *International Conference on Intelligent Tutoring Systems.* Springer, 306–308.
[5] Jin Kwang Hong, Antonija Mitrovic, and Kourosh Neshatian. 2015. Predicting Quitting Behaviour in SQL-Tutor. In *ICCE 2015 Proceedings.* Asia-Pacific Society for Computers in Education, 37–45.
[6] Lydia Lau, Antonija Mitrovic, Amali Weerasinghe, and Vania Dimitrova. 2016. Usability of an Active Video Watching System for Soft Skills Training. In *Proceedings of the 1st International Workshop on Intelligent Mentoring Systems (ITS).*
[7] Caitlin Mills, Nigel Bosch, Art Graesser, and Sidney D'Mello. 2014. To Quit or not to Quit: Predicting Future Behavioral Disengagement from Reading Patterns. In *International Conference on Intelligent Tutoring Systems.* Springer, 19–28.
[8] Antonija Mitrovic, Vania Dimitrova, Amali Weerasinghe, and Lydia Lau. [n. d.]. Reflective Experiential Learning: Using Active Video Watching for Soft Skills Training. In ICCE 2016, W Chen (Ed.). *Proceedings of the 24th International Conference on Computers in Education*, 192–201.
[9] Paul R Pintrich et al. 1991. A Manual for the Use of the Motivated Strategies for Learning Questionnaire (MSLQ). (1991).
[10] Daniel L. Schacter and Karl K. Szpunar. [n. d.]. Enhancing Attention and Memory During Video-recorded Lectures. *Scholarship of Teaching and Learning in Psychology* 1, 1 ([n. d.]), 60–71.
[11] Yue Zhao, Dan Davis, Guanliang Chen, Christoph Lofi, Claudia Hauff, and Geert-Jan Houben. 2017. Certificate Achievement Unlocked: How Does MOOC Learners' Behaviour Change?. In *Adjunct Publication of the 25th Conference on User Modeling, Adaptation and Personalization (UMAP '17).* ACM, New York, NY, USA, 83–88.

A Dataset for Inferring Contextual Preferences of Users Watching TV

Miklas S. Kristoffersen
Bang & Olufsen A/S & Aalborg Univ.
Struer, Denmark
mko@bang-olufsen.dk

Sven E. Shepstone
Bang & Olufsen A/S
Struer, Denmark
ssh@bang-olufsen.dk

Zheng-Hua Tan
Aalborg University
Aalborg, Denmark
zt@es.aau.dk

ABSTRACT

Studies have shown that contextual settings play an important role in users' decision processes of what to consume, but data supporting the investigation of context-aware recommender systems are scarce. In this paper we present a TV consumption dataset enriched with contextual information of viewing situations. The dataset is designed for studying the intrinsic complexity of TV watching activities, and hence we also evaluate the performance of predicting chosen genres given contextual settings, and compare the results to contextless predictions. The results suggest a significant improvement by including contextual features in the prediction.

CCS CONCEPTS

• **Information systems** → **Recommender systems**; • **Human-centered computing** → **User studies**;

KEYWORDS

Context-Awareness; Recommender Systems; Machine Learning; Experience Sampling; Dataset; Television.

ACM Reference Format:
Miklas S. Kristoffersen, Sven E. Shepstone, and Zheng-Hua Tan. 2018. A Dataset for Inferring Contextual Preferences of Users Watching TV. In *UMAP '18: 26th Conference on User Modeling, Adaptation and Personalization, July 8–11, 2018, Singapore, Singapore.* ACM, New York, NY, USA, 2 pages. https://doi.org/10.1145/3209219.3209263

1 INTRODUCTION

The concept of context-aware recommendations has been studied in several academic and commercial projects [2, 9], but there is still a need for publicly available datasets since only a limited number of such datasets exist, e.g. [1, 6, 10]. Also, temporal context has constituted a significant part of development and evaluation within context-aware recommender systems (CARS), since timestamps are often logged together with events, e.g. ratings, which allows for a simple way to reformulate challenges designed for traditional recommender systems into the CARS domain by using timestamps as temporal context. However, previous studies of users' TV watching behavior in given contexts have shown that the TV is mostly a social platform and consumption takes place in a wide variety of

situations [8]. Furthermore, it has been shown that both temporal and social settings are key contextual indicators of what content is consumed [5, 11]. It is, however, challenging to collect TV consumption data that includes contextual information beyond timestamps, such as social settings. People meters, for instance, are challenged, [3], by non-compliance (participants neglect to push a button), and secondly, since meters log the opportunity to consume some content, there is no information of the actual exposure, i.e. the TV could be showing some content that the user does not watch.

In this work, we collect and analyze self-reported TV consumption data using the Experience-Sampling Method (ESM) [4]. We structure the data to accommodate quantitative analyses, e.g. in the CARS community. Lastly, using well-established Machine Learning methods we show performance in predicting consumed content given contextual settings, and compare this with contextless prediction.

2 CONTEXTUAL TV WATCHING DATASET

To obtain data from participants we developed a web page, and asked participants to answer questions five times every day at 8, 12, 17, 20, and 22 (or when going to bed) for a five week period. These intervals were chosen to accommodate work and study schedules, while still providing ample opportunity to participate over a full day period. Participants were allowed to answer more frequently (and at other times) than the five pre-specified intervals. To remind participants when to answer, we used a public calendar with alerts for iOS devices and web push notifications for all other types of devices.

Table 1: Questions and selection options in the dataset.

Questions		Options
Q1:	Have you watched TV within the last four hours?	Yes, no
Q2:	Who were you watching it with?	*Multiple-option:* Alone, partner, child (0-12), child (12+), sibling, parent, friend, other (text)
Q3:	How many people (including yourself) watched TV?	1, 2, 3, 4, 5+
Q4:	What did you watch?	*Multiple-option:* News, sport, movie, series, music, documentary, entertainment, children's, user-generated, other (text)
Q5:	Which service(s) did you use?	*Multiple-option:* Traditional TV, DRTV, TV2 Play, Viaplay, Netflix, HBO Nordic, YouTube, other (text)
Q6:	How much attention did you pay to the TV?	None-full (5 steps)

We collect the following background information the first time a participant login: gender, age group, language, device type, household size, additional household members, frequency of TV watching, and favorite TV genres. On subsequent logins, participants are asked the questions listed in Table 1. The general flow is that Q2-Q6 are asked only if the selection for Q1 is *yes*. Also, Q3 is skipped if *alone* is selected for Q2. For Q5 all except *Traditional TV* (and possibly *other*) are streaming services, some specific to Denmark/Scandinavia. The multiple-option questions allow more than one selection, e.g. *partner* and *friend*. Participants are instructed to split answers with different contextual settings, e.g. watching news alone and children's TV with a child. Answers are logged with the following format: Answer ID, User ID, timestamp, Q1, Q2, Q3, Q4, Q5, Q6. For further information see the publicly available dataset consisting of 118 participants and more than 6000 answers.[1]

3 EXPERIMENT

The goal of the experiment is to predict what genre a user is going to watch (Q4) in the reported context. The task is defined as a multi-class classification problem with the users' selections for Q4 as target. The selections for the remaining questions are used as contextual features. All features are categorical and represented using one-hot encoding. The optional text input for *other* in Q2, Q4, and Q5 are not included in this study.

The experiment includes two methods based on contextless (CL) and context-aware (CA) predictions, respectively. CL only takes the user ID of the respondent into account, while CA includes all the collected contextual features. A scikit-learn [7] implementation of logistic regression (LR) is used. We fit the LR weights using stochastic average gradient descent with L2 regularization, and set the multi-class parameter to "multinomial" for 10-way softmax regression. We also include two baseline methods for comparison, namely random and toppop. The random predictor randomly ranks the genres for each prediction. For toppop, genres are ranked by their popularity judged by the number of observations in the training set.

The methods are evaluated using nested cross-validation with five outer folds and three inner folds. That is, the training data for each outer fold are divided into three inner folds for optimization of hyperparameters. We report the average performance across the outer folds and the standard deviation. Performance is measured in terms of accuracy at K predictions (A@K)[2], F1 (macro), and mean reciprocal rank (MRR).

The results are shown in Table 2. Note that toppop outperforms random in terms of A@1, A@3, and MRR, but random performs better than toppop for F1 (macro), due to the diversity in predicted genres. The LR-based methods achieve considerably higher scores than both baseline methods, and furthermore CA-LR outperforms CL-LR. The MRR of CA-LR indicates that on average the true genre is ranked among the first and second (as indicated by 1/MRR≈1.5) of the 10 possible genres. The corresponding number for CL-LR

Table 2: Results for the genre predictions (standard deviation in parentheses).

Method	A@1	A@3	F1 (macro)	MRR
random	0.093 (0.010)	0.296 (0.005)	0.083 (0.011)	0.289 (0.008)
toppop	0.245 (0.009)	0.560 (0.014)	0.039 (0.001)	0.460 (0.008)
CL-LR	0.368 (0.026)	0.761 (0.008)	0.244 (0.023)	0.586 (0.016)
CA-LR	0.487 (0.005)	0.849 (0.005)	0.446 (0.025)	0.679 (0.005)

is 1.7. McNemar's test[3] shows statistical significant improvement ($\chi^2(1)$=146.92, p<0.001, V=0.22) between the two methods.

4 CONCLUDING REMARKS

In this paper, an extensive field study over a period of five weeks with a group of more than 100 participants is used to evaluate to which degree contextual knowledge influences the performance of predicting what content will be consumed. The experimental results show that inclusion of contextual information significantly improves accuracy compared to contextless predictions.

In future work, we will apply state-of-the-art CARS methods to the dataset, and investigate the contribution of each contextual dimension.

ACKNOWLEDGMENTS

This work is supported by Bang and Olufsen A/S and the Innovation Fund Denmark (IFD) under File No. 5189-00009B.

REFERENCES

[1] G. Adomavicius, R. Sankaranarayanan, S. Sen, and A. Tuzhilin. 2005. Incorporating Contextual Information in Recommender Systems Using a Multidimensional Approach. *ACM Trans. Inf. Syst.* 23, 1 (2005), 103–145.
[2] G. Adomavicius and A. Tuzhilin. 2015. Context-Aware Recommender Systems. In *Recommender Systems Handbook.* Springer, 191–226.
[3] B. Jardine, J. Romaniuk, J. G. Dawes, and V. Beal. 2016. Retaining the primetime television audience. *European Journal of Marketing* 50, 7/8 (2016), 1290–1307.
[4] R. Larson and M. Csikszentmihalyi. 1983. The experience sampling method. *New Directions for Methodology of Social & Behavioral Science* (1983).
[5] K. Mercer, A. May, and V. Mitchel. 2014. Designing for video: Investigating the contextual cues within viewing situations. *Personal and Ubiquitous Computing* 18, 3 (01 Mar 2014), 723–735.
[6] C. Ono, Y. Takishima, Y. Motomura, and H. Asoh. 2009. Context-Aware Preference Model Based on a Study of Difference between Real and Supposed Situation Data. In *Proceedings of the 17th International Conference on User Modeling, Adaptation, and Personalization (UMAP '09).* Springer Berlin Heidelberg, 102–113.
[7] F. Pedregosa, G. Varoquaux, A. Gramfort, V. Michel, B. Thirion, O. Grisel, M. Blondel, P. Prettenhofer, R. Weiss, V. Dubourg, J. Vanderplas, A. Passos, D. Cournapeau, M. Brucher, M. Perrot, and E. Duchesnay. 2011. Scikit-learn: Machine Learning in Python. *Journal of Machine Learning Research* 12 (2011), 2825–2830.
[8] D. Saxbe, A. Graesch, and M. Alvik. 2011. Television as a Social or Solo Activity: Understanding Families' Everyday Television Viewing Patterns. *Communication Research Reports* 28, 2 (2011), 180–189.
[9] Y. Shi, M. Larson, and A. Hanjalic. 2014. Collaborative Filtering Beyond the User-Item Matrix: A Survey of the State of the Art and Future Challenges. *ACM Comput. Surv.* 47, 1, Article 3 (May 2014), 3:1–3:45 pages.
[10] R. Turrin, A. Condorelli, P. Cremonesi, and R. Pagano. 2014. Time-based TV programs prediction. In *1st Workshop on Recommender Systems for Television and Online Video at ACM RecSys (RecSys '14).*
[11] J. Vanattenhoven and D. Geerts. 2015. Contextual aspects of typical viewing situations: a new perspective for recommending television and video content. *Personal and Ubiquitous Computing* 19, 5 (2015), 761–779.

---

[1]Available at http://kom.aau.dk/~zt/online/ContextualTVDataset.

[2]At K larger than one, multiple guesses are allowed for each test sample. It is calculated using: A@K = $\frac{1}{N}\sum_{n=1}^{N}\sum_{k=1}^{K}\mathbf{1}(\hat{y}_{n,k} = y_n)$, where N is the number of tests. $\mathbf{1}$ is the indicator function, which is one if the prediction, $\hat{y}_{n,k}$, is equal to the actual target, y_n, and zero otherwise.

---

[3]A matrix, $A_{2\times2}$, is formed with $a_{1,1}$ being the number of tests where both methods are correct, $a_{1,2}$ and $a_{2,1}$ are the tests where one of the methods fail, and $a_{2,2}$ is when both are incorrect. McNemar's χ^2 test statistic and Cramér's V are then computed as:

$$\chi^2 = (a_{1,2} - a_{2,1})^2 / (a_{1,2} + a_{2,1}), V = \sqrt{\chi^2 / \sum_{i,j} a_{i,j}}.$$

Predicting Emotions From Multimodal Users 'Data

Ange Tato
Université du Québec à Montréal
Montréal, Québec, Canada
nyamen_tato.ange_adrienne@
courrier.uqam.ca

Roger Nkambou
Université du Québec à Montréal
Montréal, Québec, Canada
nkambou.roger@uqam.ca

Claude Frasson
Université de Montréal
Montréal, Québec, Canada
claude.frasson@umontreal.ca

ABSTRACT

Prediction of emotions is important for understanding human behavior and modeling users in learning environments. In this paper, we present a deep multi-modal architecture for emotions prediction, which takes advantage of deep learning, user multimodal data and the hierarchy of human memory. The architecture consists of the combination of Long Short-Term memory (LSTMs). One of the novelty of our approach is that, we enhance the LSTM with an explicit memory since in brain studies, the memory is often divided into two further main types: explicit (or declarative) memory and implicit (or procedural) memory, the last one being the main purpose of LSTMs architectures. The resulting model has been tested on a public multi-modal dataset.

KEYWORDS

Affective forecasts, Emotions prediction, Multi-modal deep learning, Long Term Memory, User modeling

ACM Reference Format:
Ange Tato, Roger Nkambou, and Claude Frasson. 2018. Predicting Emotions From Multimodal Users 'Data. In *UMAP '18: 26th Conference on User Modeling, Adaptation and Personalization, July 8–11, 2018, Singapore, Singapore*. ACM, New York, NY, USA, 2 pages. https://doi.org/10.1145/3209219.3209264

1 INTRODUCTION

Multimodal learning involves relating information from multiple sources [3]. We propose a multimodal neural network model inspired by human long-term memory for the prediction of emotions. The proposed model is intended to extend a user model with the ability of automatically predicting the affective state of a learner/player at a given time in the future. The model is grounded on the theory of human hierarchical memory by Atkinson-Shiffrin [1] and implemented from the LSTM architecture.

This paper presents, to the best of our knowledge, the first approach in the literature that: 1) Actually automatically "predicts" emotions feels at time $t + n$ ($n \in \mathbf{N}$) based on information at time t; 2) Fuses emotions from FaceReader and EEG data in a multimodal setting for continuous prediction of emotions; 3) proposes a deep learning architecture taking advantage of multimodal data plus an integration of the LSTM architecture with an explicit memory

for affective forecasting. The model is trained (from facial expression data) to predict the 6 basics emotions according to Ekman's theory[2], plus the neutral emotion.

2 DEEP MULTIMODAL LONG TERM MEMORY (DM-LTM): ARCHITECTURE

The Deep Multimodal Long Term Memory (DM-LTM) we are proposing includes the two types of long term memory according to human memory theory [1] which are the implicit memory (correspomding to the standard LSTM) and the explicit memory. DM-LTM has 4 branches (expandable depending on the number of modalities). As shown in (Figure 1), the 3 first branches (for emotions, Workload and engagemet) are composed of LSTM, and the last branch is a simple Feed forward network representing the explicit memory. The explicit memory produce a vector of size 7 (representing the number of classes to predict) based on a vector of size $7*(n-1)$ where n is the window size (ranging from 3 to 15 seconds and specify by hand) and 7 is the emotions vector length. The proposed model is able to predict both the emotion which has the maximum numerical value associated with, and the whole vector (representing the well known 7 basic emotions) after a time t (specify by hand) from multimodal data of users. For this first experiment, the rule define in the explicit memory is as follows: the future emotions is likely to be the maximal basic emotion feels by the user during time t to $t + (n-1)$. Each branch specializes in extraction of the latent characteristics of one modality.

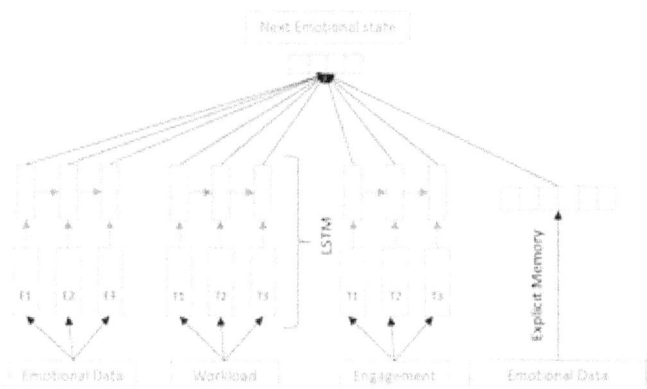

Figure 1: Deep Multimodal Long Term memory enhanced with an explicit memory for emotions prediction

3 EXPERIMENTS AND RESULTS

3.1 Experiments setting

Dataset : Seempad[1] is a public multimodal dataset of natural language arguments labelled with emotions (from Noldus FaceReader) and EEG data. 4 persons participated in 10 different debates where everyone had to give their opinion on the topics. For this experiment, we did not consider the arguments since we did not obtain good results. For each participant, we have their emotional state (the 6 basic emotions + Neutral), and their electrical brain activity EEG data (Workload and engagement). There is 38764 lines in the dataset. Each line corresponding to information (the 7 emotions + Workload + Engagement) captured at each second.

Parameters : We fixed the size of the hidden state of the 3 LSTMs to 200 units. The window size vary between 3 and 15 (arbitrary values). For regularization we employ dropout on each LSTM. The dropout rate was set to .75, the mini-batch size is a size of 1000 and the epoch was set to 40 first then 100. Training is done through stochastic gradient descent with AdamOptimizer over randomly shuffled mini-batches. We trained the model on 90% and 70% of the data. Our model was ran on Google Colaboratory[2] under python using Tenrsorflow library.

3.2 Results and Discussion

We compared our model to the standard LSTM. Results of our model against the LSTM on 90% and 70 % of data for training, are showed in (Figure 2). At first glance we can already see that the DM-LTM outperformed LSTM on all settings. We obtained a maximum of 69% of accuracy on the test set compared to 67.2% for the LSTM. One interesting thing we noticed during our experiments is that, decision-level fusion (the current version of the proposed solution) leads to better performance than a feature-level fusion. Therefore, considering each modality alone is prone to give best results in emotions prediction than fuse them at the beginning. The automatic emotion prediction not only depends on multimodal user data but also on the architecture used. Our solution is however a little slower in the training process compared to standard LSTM. This is mainly due to the complexity of the model architecture which means more parameters to train. The problem can be solved by fixing the amount of new data or the time after which the training process will be renewed. This study shows that, simply adding an explicit memory (in the form of a neural network) to a standard LSTM architecture clearly improves the prediction task of the LSTM. Indeed, we gained +0.7% of accuracy when using DM-LTM in lieu of standard LSTM. This suggests that, one should sometimes think about adding an explicit memory to the standard LSTM to improve its behavior. The proposed solution can be extended to any neural network architecture, thereby opening the door to new generation of neural networks with explicit memory.

4 INTEGRATING DM-LTM IN VARIOUS APPLICATIONS

We have shown that DM-LTM is able to predict emotional state of users in a multimodal setting. As far as it uses user data, DM-LTM

[1] https://project.inria.fr/seempad/datasets/
[2] https://colab.research.google.com/

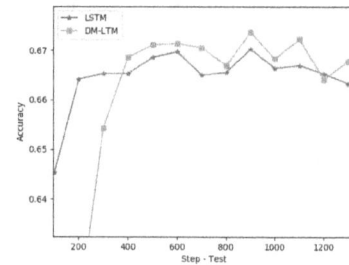

Figure 2: Accuracy of LSTM and the proposed model (DM-LTM) on 90% of data for training.

is suitable for subject-sensitive tasks. For instance, we plan to integrate it into two learning environments. The first is a learning environment for doctors (a virtual operating room) for predicting bad actions against the good ones made by learners so as to provide them with adequate help. The second is a first-person serious game called "LesDilemmes" [4] which aims to assess and improve the social reasoning skills of the player. The goal being the development of the next generation of intelligent and emotional sensitive learning environments (or serious games).

5 CONCLUSION

In this paper, we presented DM-LTM, a deep multimodal neural network Long Term Memory that aims at : 1) enrich a deep learning architecture with an explicit memory and 2) predict user emotional state at a given time t + n, based on sequential multimodal user data at time $t, t + 1, ... t + (n - 1)$. The proposed model is intended to be plug as a facet of a learner model in platforms whose adaptation is a key issue (eg. Intelligent Tutoring Systems, Serious Games). The proposed model outperformed state-of-the-art architecture on a similar task. This suggests that, the multimodal setting and the explicit memory we added can capture latent features of the evolution of the user emotional state and use them to predict the future emotions. The next steps of this research include: the assessment of the DM-LTM in our learning environments and the improvement of the architecture to increase its prediction ability by considering other interesting modality such as text (e.g. the arguments provided by the users).

ACKNOWLEDGMENTS

The work is supported by the Natural Sciences and Engineering Research Council of Canada Discovery Grant Program.

REFERENCES

[1] Richard C Atkinson and Richard M Shiffrin. 1968. Human memory: A proposed system and its control processes1. In *Psychology of learning and motivation*. Vol. 2. Elsevier, 89–195.
[2] Paul Ekman, Wallace V Friesen, and Phoebe Ellsworth. 2013. *Emotion in the human face: Guidelines for research and an integration of findings*. Elsevier.
[3] Jiquan Ngiam, Aditya Khosla, Mingyu Kim, Juhan Nam, Honglak Lee, and Andrew Y Ng. 2011. Multimodal deep learning. In *Proceedings of the 28th international conference on machine learning (ICML-11)*. 689–696.
[4] Ange Tato, Roger Nkambou, Aude Dufresne, and Miriam H Beauchamp. 2017. Convolutional Neural Network for Automatic Detection of Sociomoral Reasoning Level. In *Proceedings of the 10th International Conference on Educational Data Mining (EDM)*. 284–289.

IDEA: Instant Detection of Eating Action using Wrist-Worn Sensors in Absence of User-Specific Model*

Junghyo Lee, Prajwal Paudyal, Ayan Banerjee, Sandeep K.S. Gupta
iMPACT Lab (http://impact.asu.edu), CIDSE, Arizona State University
{jlee375,ppaudyal,abanerj3,sandeep.gupta}@asu.edu

ABSTRACT

Eating activity monitoring using wearable sensors can potentially enable interventions based on eating speed for critical healthcare problems such as obesity or diabetes. We propose a novel methodology, IDEA that performs accurate eating action identification and provides feedback on eating speed. IDEA uses a single wristband with IMU sensors and functions without any manual intervention from the user. The F1 score for eating action identification was 0.92.

CCS CONCEPTS

• **Human-centered computing** → **Ubiquitous and mobile computing**;

KEYWORDS

Wearable; Gesture; User Adaptive Modeling; Diet Monitoring

ACM Reference Format:
Junghyo Lee, Prajwal Paudyal, Ayan Banerjee, Sandeep K.S. Gupta. 2018. IDEA: Instant Detection of Eating Action using Wrist-Worn Sensors in Absence of User-Specific Model. In *UMAP'18: 26th Conference on User Modeling, Adaptation and Personalization, July 8-11, 2018, Singapore.* ACM, New York, NY, USA, 2 pages. https://doi.org/10.1145/3209219.3209265

1 INTRODUCTION

Eating action monitoring is important for administering and facilitating eating speed based dietary interventions. In the paper, we propose *IDEA*, Instant Detection of Eating Action that can operate with any wristband based IMU sensors (accelerometers, orientation, and gyroscope) to instantly identify eating action without any manual input from user.

Challenge: An eating action is a sequential arrangement of three distinct components interspersed with gestures that may be unrelated to the eating action. This makes it extremely challenging to accurately identify eating actions. The primary reason for the lack of acceptance of state-of-art eating action monitoring techniques [3] includes: i) the need to install wearable sensors that are cumbersome to wear or limit mobility of the user, ii) the need for manual user input, and iii) poor accuracy in absence of adequate user input.

The core hypothesis of *IDEA* is that despite variations in arm movements, locations of the mouth and food plate, type of food,

*Partly funded by NIH NIBIB (Grant #EB019202) and NSF IIS (Grant #1116385).

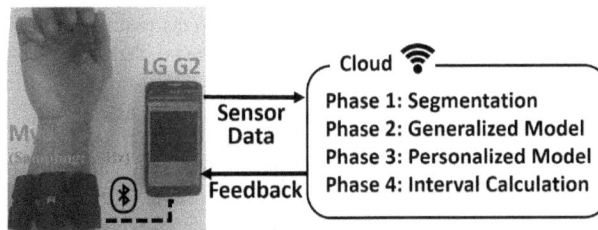

Figure 1: IDEA architecture and overview.

and utensils used, an eating action is universal and is expected to have commonalities amongst individuals. For example, if a person is using an utensil to pick up food from a plate on a table, the arm action to lift the food up from the table to mouth is assumed to be common across all individuals. Once such common actions are identified, other information such as picking action, putting food in mouth, twisting of wrist to orient spoon or fork towards the mouth can then be added to the common action to identify whether that common action is a part of an eating action. To exploit such commonalities, *IDEA* uses a two-step process, **i) Generalized Model** and **ii) Personalized Model**. Also, *IDEA* uses a small set of users, **donors**, from which the training data is collected to derive a set of eating action candidates. A practical deployment of *IDEA* does not need any data from a given user and identifies eating actions in a plug-n-play manner. *IDEA* in effect provides automated labeling.

2 METHODOLOGY

The *IDEA* methodology consists of four phases as seen Fig. 1: segmentation, generalized model, personalized model, and interval calculation. For segmentation, we utilize an extrema based segmentation method. From our observation of dataset, we conclude that when the user starts and finishes any eating action component, their hand pauses momentarily or there is a sharp change in the orientation of their wrist. Based on this observation, we utilized the extrema to segment the continuous movement of hand gesture into two types of segments: a) "Eat" and b) "No Eat". The extrema based segmentation method generates irregular size segments so we used the interpolation to obtain uniform size segments. The aim of generalized model, where data from an individual A is compared with the data of other users in a set S, is to detect strong and weak candidates for eating action of A. This is done using a Deep Neural Networks (DNN), four hidden layers with nodes starting from 512 and exponentially reducing to 64. The activation function is ReLU, the output layer is sigmoid for binary classification. The output of this phase is two folds: i) two sets including the set of actions that are confirmed eating actions, and unconfirmed ones, and ii) a set of users in the set S that are "similar" to the given user. In the personalized model phase, the eating actions obtained from the set of "similar" users given by generalized model are used as training set to classify the unconfirmed actions set as true eating actions or not. The interval calculation provides the eating speed feedback. In this phase, we obtain eating intervals by simply calculating the time-stamp difference between previous 'Eat' and current 'Eat'.

3 RELATED WORK

Nearly all eating behavior monitoring systems require an initial training phase, where the user must provide labeled data related to an eating action as in Sen et al. [6]. This initiation task is time consuming and often annoying. Moreover, such training must be redone if the food item, plate, and utensil changes. *IDEA* is plug-n-play and automates the training process by first using a general model to detect few eating actions and using them as training data.

A distracted eating pattern is when a user is involved in other activities like talking, swallowing saliva, shifting in their seats, and multiple picking before eating. Liu et al. [4] could not account for distracted eating situations. However, since *IDEA* identifies the three actions separately, it can detect such distracted situations.

4 EXPERIMENTAL RESULT

Setup: Fig. 1 displays *IDEA* architecture. The user wears a Myo wristband [1] which collects accelerometer, orientation, gyroscope, Electromyogram (EMG) data at a frequency of 50Hz. LG G2 (smartphone) is connected to the Myo through Bluetooth to receive Myo data. For each user, we also recorded video simultaneously using LG G2 camera. The video data is used to build the ground truth. Myo provides 18 data streams from four sensors including 3 accelerometer data streams, 4 orientation data streams, 3 gyroscope data streams, and 8 EMG data streams.

Data Acquisition: We recruited thirty-six subjects following IRB approvals. Each subject participated as a volunteer for an eating episode that lasted for at least 15 mins with an average of 30 eating actions. Subjects were asked to sit facing a smartphone camera during the eating episode and wore the Myo. Subjects ate food either obtained from a restaurant or cooked at home in different types of containers. The subjects brought their own containers and used two types of utensils: a fork and spoon. They were free to eat whatever they want. Hence, the collected data has user-dependent eating factors resulting in variations on eating directions, speed, relative distance between the food plate and the mouth, etc. In the collected data, each subject has at least 20 eating actions, which are distributed across different areas in the food plate. Also, there are a total of 1246 eating actions and 8400 non-eating gestures.

Labeling: It is important to develop the ground truth. After synchronization between the video and Myo data, we annotated the meal video manually through visual inspection. To reduce human error the annotations were performed by four independent human observers and were cross validated against each other. Each annotated video is labeled as one of the following: (1) picking, (2) carrying, and (3) putting in mouth. A cycle of these three annotated eating components is considered as one eating action. Then, the sensor data streams are labeled based on the annotated videos.

Result: With a training set of eight donors and a test set of 28, the precision of eating action identification was 0.93 while the recall was 0.89. For the worst case users, on an average, *IDEA* improves

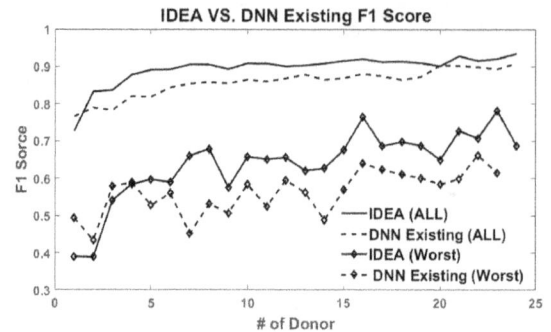

Figure 2: F1 Score Comparison between IDEA and Existing DNN. (ALL) is for all users and (Worst) is for worst users.

precision by 0.11 and recall by 0.15 with respect to other deep learning strategies without getting any training data or any manual user interventions. *IDEA* can also be used for automated labeling of eating action. The mislabeling rate for *IDEA* is 11 out of nearly 10,000 eating or non-eating actions and that for human eye is 18 as observed in our study. Fig. 2 shows that on an average *IDEA* improves the F1 score by 0.05 for 8 donors with respect to the DNN based approaches. *IDEA* has an F1 score of more than 0.9 if at least 7 users are included in the training set. The figure also shows the performance for the worst case user set. On an average *IDEA* improves F1 score by 0.15 for the worst case users with respect to traditional DNN based approach.

5 CONCLUSIONS

In this paper, we have proposed *IDEA*, a novel methodology for detecting eating actions using only a wristband sensor without the need for collecting training data from the user. The proposed methodology is plug-n-play and does not need any initialization from the user, hence working in an user-independent manner. *IDEA* can also be used to automatically annotate eating actions for future use in a personalized model. When combined with image based food type identification projects such as MT-Diet [2], *IDEA* can be applied to build a nutritional retrieval system. Also, the *IDEA* methodology will be useful for wristband based sign language recognition projects such as DyFAV [5]. Plug-n-play recognition of such complex gestures can result in fast and accurate sign language translation systems and will be explored as a crucial future work.

REFERENCES

[1] Myo Armband. https://www.myo.com Accessed: 2015-07-10.
[2] Junghyo Lee, Ayan Banerjee, and Sandeep KS Gupta. 2016. MT-diet: Automated smartphone based diet assessment with infrared images. In *PerCom*. IEEE, 1–6.
[3] Junghyo Lee, Prajwal Paudyal, Ayan Banerjee, and Sandeep KS Gupta. 2017. FIT-EVE&ADAM: Estimation of Velocity & Energy for Automated Diet Activity Monitoring. In *Machine Learning and Applications (ICMLA), 2017 16th IEEE International Conference on*. IEEE, 1071–1074.
[4] Jing Liu, Edward Johns, Louis Atallah, Claire Pettitt, Benny Lo, Gary Frost, and Guang-Zhong Yang. 2012. An intelligent food-intake monitoring system using wearable sensors. In *Wearable and Implantable Body Sensor Networks (BSN), 2012 Ninth International Conference on*. IEEE, 154–160.
[5] Prajwal Paudyal, Junghyo Lee, Ayan Banerjee, and Sandeep KS Gupta. 2017. DyFAV: Dynamic Feature Selection and Voting for real-time recognition of fingerspelled alphabet using wearables. In *Proceedings of the 22nd International Conference on Intelligent User Interfaces*. ACM, 457–467.
[6] Sougata Sen, Vigneshwaran Subbaraju, Archan Misra, Rajesh Krishna Balan, and Youngki Lee. 2015. The case for smartwatch-based diet monitoring. In *Pervasive Computing and Communication Workshops (PerCom Workshops)*. IEEE, 585–590.

Tutorial: Sequence-aware Recommender Systems

Massimo Quadrana
Pandora Media
Milan, Italy
max.square@gmail.com

Paolo Cremonesi
Politecnico di Milano
Milan, Italy
paolo.cremonesi@polimi.it

Dietmar Jannach
Alpen-Adria-Universität
Klagenfurt, Austria
dietmar.jannach@aau.at

ABSTRACT

The majority of research works in the field of collaborative filtering recommender systems is based on the assumption that the input to the recommendation algorithms is a matrix containing user-item interactions. In reality, however, the input often is a sequence of various types of user-item interactions that are recorded over time and where we can have multiple data points per user-item pair. These sequential logs contain a variety of useful information that can be leveraged in the recommendation process, e.g., to predict the immediate next action of a user or to detect short-term trends in the community.

In this tutorial we review what we call *sequence-aware* recommenders, i.e., approaches that aim to exploit the information in sequential interaction logs for a variety of different purposes. We in particular focus on sequential and session-based recommendation techniques and discuss algorithmic proposals as well as evaluation challenges.

CCS CONCEPTS

• **Information systems** → **Recommender systems**; **Collaborative filtering**;

KEYWORDS

Recommender Systems, Sequence-Awareness, Session-based Recommendation

ACM Reference Format:

Massimo Quadrana, Paolo Cremonesi, and Dietmar Jannach. 2018. Tutorial: Sequence-aware Recommender Systems. In *UMAP '18: 26th Conference on User Modeling, Adaptation and Personalization, July 8–11, 2018, Singapore, Singapore.* ACM, New York, NY, USA, 2 pages. https://doi.org/10.1145/3209219.3209270

1 INTRODUCTION

Research in the field of recommender systems is often based on the following simplifying problem abstraction: Given a sparse matrix of logged user-item interactions, predict the missing entries of the matrix. In such a problem formulation, typically only one explicit or implicit user-item interaction pair is considered in the recommendation process. In real-world systems, however, much more information is usually available to providers of a recommendation service. On an e-commerce site, for example, one can track the

users' browsing behavior (e.g., item views, purchases, navigation actions, search behavior) over longer periods of time and use this rich information to derive their long-term preferences and their short-term shopping intents. Similarly, a recommender system for a music streaming service can profit from taking the user's long-term listening preferences into account when selecting tracks to play in a given situation.

In such scenarios, we usually can observe multiple interactions of a single user with a recommendable item over time, e.g., when a user repeatedly listens to the same track or repeatedly inspects the details of a shopping item before a purchase on an e-commerce site. These types of temporal and sequential information can, however, not be easily represented in the typical matrix-completion problem formulation, in particular as the recorded interactions can also have different types (e.g., view events vs. purchase events). As a result, certain types of research questions regarding, e.g., the repeated recommendation of an item to the same user, cannot be reasonably addressed when only one user-item interaction is recorded.

2 APPLICATION AREAS

In this tutorial, we review the existing literature on what we call *sequence-aware* recommender systems [8]. These types of recommenders take a sequentially ordered log of user interactions as an input, and base their recommendations, at least partially, on the sequential patterns that they extract from the data. An overview of sequence-aware recommender systems is shown in Figure 1.

The output of a sequence-aware recommender, as usual, is a ranked list of item suggestions. However, sequence-aware recommenders are typically designed to support certain types of goals and recommendation purposes [2], among them the following:

- Context adaptation
- Trend detection
- Repeated recommendation
- Consideration of Order Constraints and Sequential Patterns

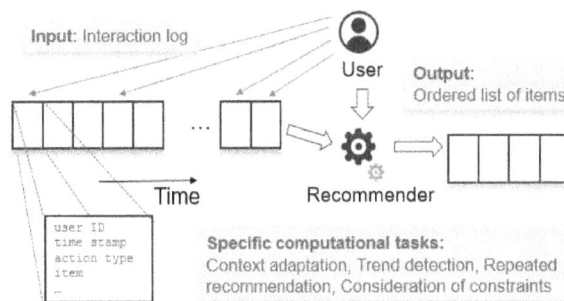

Figure 1: Overview of the Sequence-Aware Recommendation Problem, adapted from [8].

Context adaptation is the most widely explored problem setting for sequence-aware recommenders. The goal in this problem setting is to tailor the recommendations to the user's assumed contextual situation and current interests. The central input here are the most recent recorded interactions of the users and typical problem settings are to make recommendations to (i) anonymous or first-time users (*session-based* recommendation) or (ii) to returning ones (*session-aware* recommendation) [9].

Trend detection refers to the capability of a sequence-aware recommender to take the short-term *community trends* into account in the recommendation process. An approach to consider short-term sales trends and the recent popularity of individual items in the e-commerce domain was for example discussed in [4].

The repeated recommendation of items is not uncommon in practice, but barely explored in the recommender systems literature. Recent research however shows that recommendations as *reminders* are not only possibly helpful navigation aids for users, but also can lead to higher prediction accuracy and increased business value [4, 5, 10].

Order constraints and sequential patterns *within the recommendations* finally also represent a little-explored area in the research field. A typical are where there exists strong order constraints is that of course recommendation in the e-learning domain [7]. The consideration of sequential patterns representing *weak* ordering constraints can, for example, be relevant in the music domain, where the ordering of the recommended tracks can be considered to obtain smooth track transitions.

3   ALGORITHMS AND APPLICATIONS

Various types of algorithmic approaches were presented in the literature to deal with the problem settings described above. Most of them fall into the category of *sequence learning*. This approaches can be further categorized into approaches based on (i) frequent pattern mining, (ii) sequence modeling (e.g., using Markov models or Recurrent Neural Networks [1, 11]), and (iii) distributed item embeddings. A few alternative approaches were proposed as well, including in particular hybrids that combine matrix factorization with sequence modeling or sequence-agnostic nearest-neighbor techniques for session-based recommendation.

The application areas for these types of algorithms include, for example, the recommendation of shopping items in the e-commerce domain, music recommendation, the recommendation of the next point-of-interest (POI), or the prediction of the user's next action on a mobile app or web site.

4   EVALUATION ASPECTS

Differently from the matrix completion setup, no commonly accepted standards for the evaluation of sequence-aware recommender systems exist today. For certain problem settings like the prediction of the next user action, e.g., on an e-commerce site, standard metrics from the information retrieval (IR) literature like precision and recall can be applied. For other problem settings, however, like the repeated recommendation of items, it is not fully clear yet how algorithmic proposals in that area can be evaluated in a realistic way through offline experiments.

But even when standard IR metrics are used, different evaluation protocols are nowadays applied in the literature, which makes the comparison of new algorithmic approaches challenging. Typically, given the sequential nature of the input data, standard cross-validation procedures cannot be directly applied. As a result, researchers have to rely on other techniques like repeated random subsampling, with the problem that no established standard exists in that context.

Finally, for several problem settings, in particular for that of session-based recommendations, it is not fully clear yet against which baselines one should benchmark new algorithmic proposals. The work in [3] for example indicated that a recent deep learning approach was in many cases outperformed by a much simpler nearest-neighbors technique. A later analysis in [6] for a variety of datasets then revealed that the relative performance of various session-based algorithms strongly depends on the characteristics of the underlying data and the problem domain.

5   SUMMARY

The tutorial covers all of the above-mentioned topics from the problem characterization, over algorithmic approaches, to open questions regarding the evaluation of sequence-aware recommenders. A specific focus will be on the problem of session-based recommendation scenarios, which have received increasing interest in the past few years, and where we still see much room for improvement with respect to the development of more sophisticated machine learning models.

REFERENCES

[1] Balázs Hidasi, Alexandros Karatzoglou, Linas Baltrunas, and Domonkos Tikk. 2016. Session-based recommendations with recurrent neural networks. In *International Conference on Learning Representations (ICLR '16)*.
[2] Dietmar Jannach and Gedas Adomavicius. 2016. Recommendations with a Purpose. In *Proceedings of the 10th ACM Conference on Recommender Systems (RecSys 2016)*. 7–10.
[3] Dietmar Jannach and Malte Ludewig. 2017. When Recurrent Neural Networks meet the Neighborhood for Session-Based Recommendation. In *Proceedings of the 11th ACM Conference on Recommender Systems (RecSys 2017)*. Como, Italy.
[4] Dietmar Jannach, Malte Ludewig, and Lukas Lerche. 2017. Session-based Item Recommendation in E-Commerce: On Short-Term Intents, Reminders, Trends, and Discounts. *User-Modeling and User-Adapted Interaction* 27, 3–5 (2017), 351–392.
[5] Komal Kapoor, Vikas Kumar, Loren Terveen, Joseph A. Konstan, and Paul Schrater. 2015. "I Like to Explore Sometimes": Adapting to Dynamic User Novelty Preferences. In *Proceedings of the Ninth ACM Conference on Recommender Systems (RecSys '15)*. 19–26.
[6] Malte Ludewig and Dietmar Jannach. 2018. Evaluation of Session-Based Recommenation Algorithms. (2018). arXiv:1803.09587 [cs.IR] https://arxiv.org/abs/1803.09587
[7] Aditya Parameswaran, Petros Venetis, and Hector Garcia-Molina. 2011. Recommendation Systems with Complex Constraints: A Course Recommendation Perspective. *ACM Trans. Inf. Syst.* 29, 4 (2011), 20:1–20:33.
[8] Massimo Quadrana, Paolo Cremonesi, and Dietmar Jannach. 2018. Sequence-Aware Recommender Systems. *Comput. Surveys* (2018). https://mquad.github.io/static/papers/2018-seqrec_survey.pdf
[9] Massimo Quadrana, Alexandros Karatzoglou, Balázs Hidasi, and Paolo Cremonesi. 2017. Personalizing Session-based Recommendations with Hierarchical Recurrent Neural Networks. In *Proceedings of the Eleventh ACM Conference on Recommender Systems (RecSys '17)*. 130–137.
[10] Tobias Schnabel, Paul N. Bennett, Susan T. Dumais, and Thorsten Joachims. Using Shortlists to Support Decision Making and Improve Recommender System Performance. In *Proceedings of the 25th International Conference on World Wide Web (WWW '16)*. 987–997.
[11] Guy Shani, David Heckerman, and Ronen I. Brafman. 2005. An MDP-Based Recommender System. *J. Mach. Learn. Res.* 6 (2005), 1265–1295.

Personalisation and Privacy Issues in the Age of Exposure

Esma Aïmeur

Department of Computer Science and Operations Research

University of Montreal, Canada

aimeur@iro.umontreal.ca

ABSTRACT

We live in an age in which the dependency on technological tools is inescapable. At the same time, privacy-related issues are emerging in a way that we are at the breakpoint of losing control over our data. Information sharing by social-network, users can result in violations of privacy and security. For example, when a user is asking for a personalised service, he may find his contact details revealed, and may become the subject of harassment (cyber-bullying) or a potential victim of online deception or identity theft. Moreover, as Tim Berners-Lee stated, "The major players are making profit from our data. Therefore we lose out on the benefits we could realise if we had direct control over this data and choose when and with whom to share it". Today, more than ever, users need to keep control over their personal data when they ask for a personalised service. This tutorial, addresses how to reach this delicate balance between privacy and personalization.

KEYWORDS

Personalization; data disclosure; economics of privacy; ethics; best practices

ACM Reference format:

E. Aïmeur. 2018. Personalisation and Privacy issues in the age of exposure. In *UMAP '18: 26th Conference on User Modeling, Adaptation and Personalization, July 8–11, 2018, Singapore.* ACM, New York, NY, USA, 2 pages. https://doi.org/10.1145/3209219.3209271

1 MOTIVATION

Personalization is well known in online stores and web-based information systems, and is used in a wide range of applications and services including digital libraries, e-commerce, e-learning, search engines as well as for personalized recommendations of movies, music, books and news.

Recommender Systems enable merchants to assist customers in finding products that best satisfy their needs. Unfortunately, current recommender systems suffer from various privacy-protection vulnerabilities [5; 9-12]. Too often, people give up the

UMAP'18, July 8–11, 2018, Singapore.
ACM ISBN 978-1-4503-5589-6/18/07.
https://doi.org/10.1145/3209219.3209271

privacy of their personal data, sharing their buying preferences and their locations in order to obtain better recommendations. *Privacy Protection* is concerned with the misuse of information that has been entrusted to someone, in order to receive goods or services [3]. The most obvious example occurs when your own service provider sells your personal data to another service provider with whom you had never intended to do business.

The ultimate goal of this tutorial is to allow everyone to benefit from personalization in their daily activities without having to fear that their privacy is constantly being invaded.

2 INFORMATION DISCLOSURE

The tutorial analyses *Risk perception, privacy attitudes and concerns* [14] as well as willingness to self-disclose in order to get a better service on the Internet. According to Harvard Business Review, "The major sources of cyber threats aren't technological. They're found in the human brain, in the form of curiosity, ignorance, apathy, and hubris. These human forms of malware can be present in any organization and are every bit as dangerous as threats delivered through malicious code."

A well-known obstacle to the widespread deployment of privacy mechanisms is known as the *Privacy Paradox* [8], which occurs because most users who claim to be concerned about their privacy will nevertheless give away their private information for insignificant rewards. It is therefore essential to study people's use of online activities, especially when users are non-specialists in security and privacy, to reduce such violations [4].

3 PRIVACY PRESERVING MECHANISMS

The tutorial introduces Privacy-preserving mechanisms that include algorithms based on *pseudonyms or user anonymization, algorithms* involving user *data perturbation* (also called obfuscation), *differentially private* algorithms, and *cryptography-based* algorithms. The application of *Data perturbation* (or obfuscation) techniques to recommender systems, was inspired by earlier works from outside the field of recommender systems. The basic idea underpinning this body of work is that modifying a certain number of data points in the user profiles, e.g., by adding noise to the real data, will have a limited effect on the recommendation accuracy. In the context of recommender systems, this solution is of limited interest because the data is often binary, in which case perturbation is meaningless. *Differential privacy* [6] is a privacy model based on the principle that the output of a computation should not allow inference about any individual record in the input. This is achieved by requiring that the probability distribution over the possible outcomes does not change significantly when any particular record is added to or removed from the input. *Cryptographic Solutions* mitigate privacy risks triggered by the exposure of user data, such as intentional misuse (e.g., sharing data with third parties or inferring sensitive information), as well as unintentional disclosure (e.g., data theft). In principle, secure multiparty computation protocols make it possible to accurately compute recommendations, while keeping user input confidential [2].

4 PRIVACY AND ECONOMY

The tutorial focuses on Privacy and economy [6; 13]. Two concepts closely linked because disclosing or protecting personal information has significant economic benefits for both users and Online Services (OSs). Among them are monetary benefits for users and marketing spending reduction for OS. Indeed, personal data is viewed as a new asset because of its potential to create added value for companies and consumers. Furthermore, users are increasingly aware of the value of their personal information, and would like to earn from their use by OSs. To answer the relevant question "What is privacy worth?", it was found that the value depends on whether users are asked to consider how much money they would *request* in order to disclose otherwise private information or how much they would *pay* to protect otherwise public information [1].

5 ETHICS

The tutorial addresses an important topic namely *ethics of privacy* because users are typically not aware of their responsibilities towards other users. Many additional ethical issues need to be considered, therefore numerous examples will be provided and some legislation issues will be presented

6. HANDS-ON SESSIONS

An exercise session

To begin with, the participants in this tutorial are provided with a collection of real life cases, where privacy invasion, trust issues and reputation damages occurred online. . Second, a discussion is initiated with them to examine how these cases could have been avoided.

Moreover, they will be exposed to the problem of balancing personalization and privacy. Actual commercial websites are taken as an example, and the participants are shown, when they want to get a product or a service, what information is sufficient to get accurate personalized content and what information should not be disclosed.

Finally, to study the ethics of privacy, (different) quizzes will be administered to users in which they shall see how they would react to simulated ethically sensitive situations.

A game session

In this session, the participants are divided into 2 different groups. Two games are provided (one for each group) in which there are respectively privacy, and trust issues in personalized services [7]. Participants are to take decisions and justify them. Participants from the privacy group will move to the trust group while trust people will move to the privacy group. The idea is to have each participant experience different situations.

7 OBJECTIVES

By the end of this tutorial, participants should better understand:

- Personal information disclosure issues such as attitudes, meanings, perceptions, measurement, responsibilities, etc.
- Ethical issues and the economics of privacy in terms of: privacy policies, personal data value and risk perception.
- Best practices for a safe online user behaviour to reach a balance between privacy and personalization

8 REFERENCES

[1] ACQUISTI, A., TAYLOR, C., and WAGMAN, L., 2016. The economics of privacy. *Journal of Economic Literature 54*, 2, 442-492.

[2] AÏMEUR, E., BRASSARD, G., FERNANDEZ, J.M., and ONANA, F.S.M., 2008. A lambic: a privacy-preserving recommender system for electronic commerce. *International Journal of Information Security 7*, 5, 307-334.

[3] AÏMEUR, E., BRASSARD, G., and RIOUX, J., 2013. Data Privacy: An End-User Perspective. *International Journal of Computer Networks and Communications Security 1*, 6, 237-250.

[4] AÏMEUR, E., LAWANI, O., and DALKIR, K., 2016. When changing the look of privacy policies affects user trust: An experimental study. *Computers in Human Behavior 58*, 368-379.

[5] BASU, A., VAIDYA, J., KIKUCHI, H., and DIMITRAKOS, T., 2013. Privacy-preserving collaborative filtering on the cloud and practical implementation experiences. In *Cloud Computing (CLOUD), 2013 IEEE Sixth International Conference on* IEEE, 406-413.

[6] DWORK, C., 2008. Differential privacy: A survey of results. In *International Conference on Theory and Applications of Models of Computation* Springer, 1-19.

[7] EL-HADDAD, G., AÏMEUR, E., and HAGE, H., 2018. Understanding Trust, Privacy and Financial Fears in Online Payment In *IEEE TrustCom/BigDataSE 2018 (to appear)*.

[8] GARG, V., BENTON, K., and CAMP, L., 2014. The privacy paradox: a Facebook case study.

[9] JECKMANS, A., TANG, Q., and HARTEL, P., 2012. Privacy-preserving collaborative filtering based on horizontally partitioned dataset. In *Collaboration Technologies and Systems (CTS), 2012 International Conference on* IEEE, 439-446.

[10] KAY, J. and KUMMERFELD, B., 2006. Scrutability, user control and privacy for distributed personalization. In *Proceedings of the CHI2006 Workshop on Privacy-Enhanced Personalization*, 21-22.

[11] KOBSA, A., 2007. Privacy-enhanced web personalization. In *The adaptive web* Springer-Verlag, 628-670.

[12] MOBASHER, B., BURKE, R., BHAUMIK, R., and WILLIAMS, C., 2007. Toward trustworthy recommender systems: An analysis of attack models and algorithm robustness. *ACM Transactions on Internet Technology (TOIT) 7*, 4, 23.

[13] SPIEKERMANN, S., ACQUISTI, A., BÖHME, R., and HUI, K.-L., 2015. The challenges of personal data markets and privacy. *Electronic Markets 25*, 2, 161-167.

[14] VAN SCHAIK, P., JANSEN, J., ONIBOKUN, J., CAMP, J., and KUSEV, P., 2018. Security and privacy in online social networking: Risk perceptions and precautionary behaviour. *Computers in Human Behavior 78*, 283-297.

Group Recommender Systems

Amra Delic
TU Wien
Research Division of E-Commerce
Vienna, Austria
amra.delic@tuwien.ac.at

Judith Masthoff
University of Aberdeen
Department of Computing Science
Aberdeen, Scotland, U.K.
j.masthoff@abdn.ac.uk

ABSTRACT

Recommender systems for groups are becoming increasingly popular since many information needs originate from group and social activities, such as listening to music, watching movies, traveling, etc. There has been substantial progress on systems which recommend items to groups of users. However, many challenges remain. The goal of this tutorial is to introduce group recommendation and group modeling to the UMAP audience. First we will introduce the problem of making recommendations to groups and adapting to groups, and give an overview of the state-of-the art approaches to group recommendation. Next, we will also analyze more challenging topics, such as including different behavioral aspects into group modeling, and evaluation of group recommendations. Throughout, hands-on activities will be included. The tutorial will conclude with a summary of challenges and open issues.

CCS CONCEPTS

• **Information systems** → **Recommender systems**; • **Human-centered computing** → **User models**; **User studies**;

KEYWORDS

Group recommender systems; Group modeling; User studies

ACM Reference Format:
Amra Delic and Judith Masthoff. 2018. Group Recommender Systems. In *UMAP '18: 26th Conference on User Modeling, Adaptation and Personalization, July 8–11, 2018, Singapore, Singapore.* ACM, New York, NY, USA, 2 pages. https://doi.org/10.1145/3209219.3209272

1 INTRODUCTION

Recommender systems (RS) help their users to deal with choice overload on the web by supporting them to find items of interest among many options. They are applied in various domains, e.g., for recommending books, music, movies, restaurants, events, travel destinations, etc. [19]. Many types of items that are being recommended to individual users are actually experienced by groups of people. Consequently, the research in the area of RSs further broadened to group recommendations. In recent years, group recommender systems (GRSs) have received a considerable amount of attention, with an increasing number of papers being published on the topic[14].

As UMAP deals with user modeling, we strongly believe that we should also address the issue of modeling groups of people more thoroughly. In this tutorial, we want to raise awareness of the different behavioural aspects that group recommendations and group models should incorporate, which go beyond explicit preference aggregation techniques.

2 TUTORIAL OUTLINE

The tutorial will be structured in four sections:

(1) **Introduction to group recommendations** [14]
   (a) *Problem statement and definition*
   (b) *Application domains* - Group recommender systems are applied in various domains, e.g., movies, music, restaurants, traveling, etc. Different domains have their specific challenges. Hereby we introduce those domain-dependent challenges.
   (c) *Examples of GRSs* Numerous implementations of GRSs in different application domains exist. In this section we introduce the basic aspects of those implementations [11, 12, 16, 17, 20, 22].
   (d) *Classification of GRSs* - Several dimensions are identified in order to classify GRSs, i.e., type of user preferences, type of item being recommended, and type of the group.
   (e) *Aggregation strategies* - The focus of GRSs research is how to combine individual preferences into a group preference model. Various methods, i.e., aggregation strategies were developed, mostly inspired by Social Choice Theory [1, 3, 10, 13, 14].

(2) **Behavioral aspects for group modeling**
   (a) *Affective state in groups* - Obviously, there are situations when group recommendation will not satisfy all group members equally. However, when delivering group recommendations, it is of great importance to make sure that none of the group members gets too dissatisfied. Due to the emotional contagion phenomenon, such dissatisfaction can spread within the group. Conformity is yet another effect to be considered when designing a group preference model [15].
   (b) *Personality, social identity and satisfaction* - Continuing with the importance of satisfaction in GRSs, personality, as one of the basic models to explain individuals' behavioral patterns, plays a significant role when modeling group satisfaction [7, 8]. Social identity is related to the sentiment of belonging to a particular social environment, and therefor affects one's satisfaction when in a group [5].
   (c) *Social relationships* - Group dynamics, and therefore group behavior is strongly determined by the social relationships

within a group [9, 15]. Including social relationships in a group preference model and understanding its effect on members' satisfaction is another task of GRSs [2, 4, 18].

(d) *Group decision making process* - Understanding how groups reach their decisions in real world situations can help us design more effective GRSs [6].

(3) Evaluation

(a) *Offline evaluation* - Group recommendations, as any other recommendation, clearly require evaluation. One of the greatest challenges of GRSs is the lack of real world data sets. To this end, different methods are used to generate synthetic data sets, or to perform simulations.

(b) *User studies* - Another approach to evaluate GRSs are user studies. A user study can be conducted in order to evaluate an existing GRS, or to collect data to explore and evaluate different GRSs approaches. For instance, an observational user study in the travel and tourism domain is introduced in [6]. As a result, the authors obtained a data set, containing various dimensions, with real groups and participants making travel related decisions, which can be used to evaluate different group recommendation approaches.

(4) Open challenges and issues

(a) *Explaining group recommendations* - Providing explanations of recommendations can increase users' trust towards the system, improve transparency, effectiveness, efficacy, etc. of recommendations [21]. However, explanations still missing in the area of GRSs.

(b) *Affective state* - Even though the affective state in groups has been shown to be of great importance, especially when recommending sequences, only a small fraction of RSs research is dealing with it.

(c) *Privacy issues* - Both group recommendations and explanations of such recommendations can impact group members' privacy.

3 PRESENTERS

Amra Delic is a final year PhD student at the Faculty of Informatics in Vienna. Her PhD research deals with group recommender systems in the travel and tourism domain. Specifically, her research covers a variety of human behavior aspects, such as personality traits, travel behavioral patterns, intra-group social relationships, social identity theory, choice satisfaction, etc., providing a more in-depth, and comprehensive overview of group modeling for group recommender systems.

Professor Judith Masthoff is a chair in Computing Science at the University of Aberdeen and from June 2018 also at Utrecht University. Her research is in personalization and intelligent user interfaces. She has authored many papers on recommender systems, particularly on group recommender systems and explaining recommendations, with over 1500 citations to this work. She is Editor in Chief of the User Modeling and User-Adapted Interaction journal, and a director of User Modeling Inc., the professional association of user modeling researchers. Judith has co-organized

tutorials at UMAP before on the "Design and Evaluation of Adaptive Systems" and "Personalization for Behaviour Change". She has also co-organized many UMAP workshops, including one on group recommender systems, and has been programme chair of UMAP.

REFERENCES

[1] I. Ali and S. W. Kim. 2015. Group recommendations: approaches and evaluation. In *Proceedings of the 9th International Conference on Ubiquitous Information Management and Communication*. ACM, 105.

[2] I. Alina Christensen and S. Schiaffino. 2014. Social influence in group recommender systems. *Online Information Review* 38, 4 (2014), 524–542.

[3] L. Baltrunas, T. Makcinskas, and F. Ricci. 2010. Group recommendations with rank aggregation and collaborative filtering. In *Proceedings of the fourth ACM conference on Recommender systems, RecSys'10*. Barcelona, Spain, 119–126.

[4] A. Delic, J. Masthoff, J. Neidhardt, and H. Werthner. 2018. How to Use Social Relationships in Group Recommenders: Empirical Evidence. In *Proceedings of the 26rd international conference on User Modeling, Adaptation and Personalization, UMAP 2018*. Singapore, Singapore.

[5] A. Delic and J. Neidhardt. 2017. A Comprehensive Approach to Group Recommendations in the Travel and Tourism Domain. In *Adjunct Publication of the 25th Conference on User Modeling, Adaptation and Personalization*. ACM, 11–16.

[6] A. Delic, J. Neidhardt, T. N. Nguyen, and F. Ricci. 2018. An observational user study for group recommender systems in the tourism domain. *Information Technology & Tourism* (19 Feb 2018).

[7] A. Delic, J. Neidhardt, T. N. Nguyen, F. Ricci, L. Rook, H. Werthner, and M. Zanker. 2016. Observing Group Decision Making Processes. In *Proceedings of the tenth ACM conference on Recommender systems, RecSys'16*.

[8] A. Delic, J. Neidhardt, L. Rook, H. Werthner, and M. Zanker. 2017. Researching Individual Satisfaction with Group Decisions in Tourism: Experimental Evidence. In *Information and Communication Technologies in Tourism 2017*. Springer, 73–85.

[9] D.R. Forsyth. 2014. *Group Dynamics* (6th ed.). Wadsworth Cengage Learning.

[10] M. Gartrell, X. Xing, Q. Lv, A. Beach, R. Han, S. Mishra, and K. Seada. 2010. Enhancing group recommendation by incorporating social relationship interactions. In *Proceedings of the 16th ACM international conference on Supporting group work*. ACM, 97–106.

[11] F. Guzzi, F. Ricci, and R. Burke. 2011. Interactive multi-party critiquing for group recommendation. In *Proceedings of the 5th ACM Conference on Recommender systems*. 265–268.

[12] A. Jameson. 2004. More than the sum of its members: challenges for group recommender systems. In *Proceedings of the working conference on Advanced visual interfaces*. 48–54.

[13] Judith Masthoff. 2004. Group Modeling: Selecting a Sequence of Television Items to Suit a Group of Viewers. *User Modeling and User-Adapted Interaction* 14, 1 (2004), 37–85.

[14] J. Masthoff. 2015. Group recommender systems: aggregation, satisfaction and group attributes. In *Recommender Systems Handbook* (2nd ed.), F. Ricci, L. Rokach, and B. Shapira (Eds.). Springer, 743–776.

[15] J. Masthoff and A. Gatt. 2006. In pursuit of satisfaction and the prevention of embarrassment: affective state in group recommender systems. In *User Modeling and User-Adapted Interaction*, Vol. 16. Springer, 281–319.

[16] K. McCarthy, L. McGinty, B. Smyth, and M. Salamo. 2006. The needs of the many: a case-based group recommender system. *Advances in Case-Based Reasoning* (2006), 196–210.

[17] T. N. Nguyen and F. Ricci. 2017. A chat-based group recommender system for tourism. In *Information and Communication Technologies in Tourism 2017*. Springer, 17–30.

[18] L. Quijano-Sanchez, J. A. Recio-Garcia, B. Diaz-Agudo, and G. Jimenez-Diaz. 2013. Social factors in group recommender systems. *ACM Transactions on Intelligent Systems and Technology (TIST)* 4, 1 (2013), 8.

[19] F. Ricci, L. Rokach, and B. Shapira. 2015. *Recommender Systems Handbook* (2nd ed.). Springer US, Boston, MA, Chapter Recommender Systems: Introduction and Challenges, 1–34. https://doi.org/10.1007/978-1-4899-7637-6

[20] M. Stettinger, A. Felfernig, G. Leitner, and S. Reiterer. 2015. Counteracting anchoring effects in group decision making. In *Proceedings of the 23rd international conference on User Modeling, Adaptation and Personalization, UMAP 2015*. Dublin, Ireland, 118–130.

[21] N. Tintarev and J. Masthoff. 2015. Explaining recommendations: Design and evaluation. In *Recommender Systems Handbook*. Springer, 353–382.

[22] A. Venturini and F. Ricci. 2006. Aplying Trip@dvice Recommendation Technology to www.visiteurope.com. In *ECAI 2006, 17th European Conference on Artificial Intelligence, August 29 - September 1, 2006, Riva del Garda, Italy, Including Prestigious Applications of Intelligent Systems (PAIS 2006), Proceedings*. 607–611.

Author Index

www.ingramcontent.com/pod-product-compliance
Lightning Source LLC
Chambersburg PA
CBHW080704220326
41598CB00033B/5306